Ideas, Concepts, Doctrine

Ideas, Concepts, Doctrine

Basic Thinking in the United States Air Force

1907-1960

Volume 1

By

Robert Frank Futrell

GOVERNMENT REPRINTS PRESS
Washington, D.C.

© Ross & Perry, Inc. 2002 All rights reserved.

No claim to U.S. government work contained throughout this book.

Printed in The United States of America

Ross & Perry, Inc. Publishers
216 G St., N.E.
Washington, D.C. 20002
Telephone (202) 675-8300
Facsimile (202) 675-8400
info@RossPerry.com

SAN 253-8555

Library of Congress Control Number: 2001094276
http://www.GPOreprints.com

ISBN 1-931641-78-1

Cover *Escort to Berlin* © 1980 Keith Ferris - keithferrisart.com

♾ The paper used in this publication meets the requirements for permanence established by the American National Standard for Information Sciences "Permanence of Paper for Printed Library Materials" (ANSI Z39.48-1984).

All rights reserved. No copyrighted part of this publication may be reproduced, stored in a retrieval system, or transmitted, in any form or by any means, electronic, photocopying, recording, or otherwise, without the prior written permission of the publisher.

**Originally Published by Air University Press with the following
Library of Congress Cataloging–in–Publication Data**

Futrell, Robert Frank.
 Ideas, concepts, doctrine; vol. I

  Originally published: Maxwell Air Force Base, Ala. : Air University, 1971.
  Bibliography: p.
  Includes index.
  1. United States. Air Force — History. 2. United States — Military policy. 3. Military art and science — United States — History — 20th century. 4. Aeronautics, Military — Study and teaching — United Sates. I. Title.
  UG633.F84 1989   358.4'00973   89–165

To the memory of

Brig Gen Kenneth N. Walker
1898-1943

who taught the credo

A well-organized, well-planned, and well-flown air force attack will constitute an offensive that cannot be stopped.

CONTENTS

Chapter		Page
	DISCLAIMER	ii
	FOREWORD	xi
	ABOUT THE AUTHOR	xv
	ACKNOWLEDGMENTS	xvii
1	EMERGING PATTERNS OF AIR FORCE THOUGHT	1
	Notes	12
2	EARLY DAYS THROUGH WORLD WAR I, 1907–26	15
	The Beginning of Army Aviation	16
	European Adversaries Speed Aviation Development	17
	US Military Preparations	19
	The American Air Service in World War I	19
	Thoughts on Strategic Bombing	24
	America's Wartime Aviation Accomplishments	26
	The Mitchell Era: From Air Service to Air Corps	27
	Mitchell's Early Thinking on Air Power	31
	Aviation Is Integrated into Army and Navy	34
	General Patrick and the Air Service	39
	Establishment of the Army Air Corps	44
	The Mitchell Era Reexamined	51
	Notes	53
3	GROWTH OF THE AIR FORCE IDEA, 1926–41	61
	The Air Corps Wins a Foothold	62
	Beginnings of the GHQ Air Force	66
	Toward a Long-Range Bombardment Mission	68
	Baker Board Influences Air Organization	70
	Organization of the General Headquarters Air Force	73

Chapter		Page
	Development of Doctrine in the Air Corps and GHQ Air Force	75
	Beliefs in Bomber Invincibility...	78
	Thoughts on Air Support Aviation..	83
	War Department General Staff Reorients Air Programs	84
	Efforts to Describe Air Doctrine	88
	Aviation in Support of the Monroe Doctrine	89
	Mobilization for Western Hemisphere Defense.......................	90
	An Air Power Mission for the Air Corps	92
	Battle Experience from Europe	96
	Mobilizing the Army Air Forces for War	101
	Organization of the Army Air Forces	102
	Early AAF Organization for Basic Thinking	105
	AWPD-1: Air Planning for War	108
	Notes	114
4	AIR FORCE THINKING AND WORLD WAR II	127
	Planning and Analysis in the Army Air Forces.........................	127
	Many Procedures for Developing Air Doctrine	132
	New Conceptions of Tactical Air Power...................................	135
	Wartime Work of the AAF Board	138
	Official Evaluations of Air Operations.....................................	142
	Wartime Air Doctrine Development Phases Down	146
	Examination of the Strategic Air War......................................	147
	Thoughts on Air Organization for War.....................................	149
	Battling for Air Superiority	151
	Effect of Flak and Fighters...	155
	Problems of Strategic Air Targets	156
	Early Strategic Bombing in the Pacific-Far East	158
	Strategic Air against Japan	162
	Atomic Attack at Hiroshima and Nagasaki	165
	Thoughts on Air Power and Air Force	167
	Lessons on Air Superiority...	171
	Development of Tactical Air Power	173
	Importance of Airlift..	178
	General Arnold's Final Word	180
	Notes	180
5	THE AIR FORCE IN NATIONAL DEFENSE: ORGANIZATION AND STRATEGY, 1944–49	191

Chapter	Page
Armed Service Unification and the Air Force	191
Key West Agreements on Roles and Missions	196
Unified and Specified Commands	200
Building the Air Force's Internal Structure	201
Postwar Air Organization Plans	203
Recognition of Research and Development	205
General Spaatz's Air Force Reorganization	206
Continuing Thinking about Research and Development	208
Organization of USAF Headquarters	212
The Air Force in the Developing Cold War Strategy	214
Problems of Aircraft Procurement	216
First Policies on Missiles and Rockets	219
Emerging Soviet Threats	221
The Finletter Commission	224
Air Power and the Berlin Airlift	231
Strategic Bombing and the B-36 Controversy	237
Fiscal Limits Affected the Military	240
A Collective Defense and Air Power Strategy	245
Investigations of the B-36 and Defense Unification	251
Notes	259
6 RESPONSES TO SOVIET NUCLEAR WEAPONS AND LIMITED WAR, 1949–53	273
Evolving Patterns of Defense Organization	273
Toward the Air Research and Development Command	275
Military Support for Foreign Policy	278
Soviet Nuclear Weapons and Technological Challenge	282
Developments in Nuclear Weapons	282
Thoughts on Nuclear Air Power	285
NSC-68: Call for US Rearmament	288
Strategic Implications of Limited War in Korea	291
Bases of American Action in Korea	294
Tactical Air Operations	296
General Vandenberg on Air Power	298
Air Power Stalemates the Communists	302
Rebuilding the Worldwide Air Force	304
Establishment of the Air Force Council	305
Army-Air Force Accommodations on Air-Ground Doctrine	306
Air Force Organization Act of 1951	314
Air Buildup: 95-Wing Program	316

		Page
	Added Requirements for Air Power	320
	Air Objectives Expand to 143 Wings	323
	Tactical Air and Air Defense Studies	327
	Secretary Finletter's Assessments	334
	Global Air Power and the Korean Armistice	335
	Air Power and Armistice Negotiations	336
	Air Pressure as a Strategy	340
	Evaluations of Air Power's Effects in Korea	345
	Notes	352
7	THE AIR FORCE WRITES ITS DOCTRINE, 1947–55	365
	Early Efforts to Identify Air Force Doctrine	365
	Air Force Activities in the Field of Joint Doctrine	373
	The Air University as a Doctrinal Center	379
	Successful Preparation of Air Doctrine Manuals	384
	Continuing Air Doctrinal Activity	396
	Failing Efforts to Produce Interservice Doctrine	401
	Interservice Disagreements on Doctrine	406
	Notes	408
8	STRATEGIC IMPLICATIONS OF THE NEW LOOK, 1953–57	419
	Statements of Defense Policy: The New Look and Massive Retaliation	419
	Department of Defense Reorganization	423
	New Look Military Force Objectives	424
	Massive Retaliation as a Strategy	428
	Air Force Views on Massive Retaliation	432
	Air Force Thinking on Counterforce and Air Power	433
	Efforts to Define Air Power	437
	Air Force Positions on Nuclear Stalemate and Limited War	443
	Air Thinking on Nuclear Stalemate	445
	Limited Wars Are a Problem	447
	Emergence of Flexible Response as a Strategy	452
	A "New" New Look Strategy	458
	Nuclear Weapons and Limited Wars	461
	Increased Acceptance of Flexible Response	465
	Notes	467

Chapter		Page
9	MISSILE TECHNOLOGY AND THE AIR FORCE, 1945–60	477
	Guided Missiles: The Research and Development Phase	477
	Starts and Stops in Early Missile Programs	477
	Technological Breakthrough in Ballistic Missiles	485
	Soviet Threats Speed Missile Development	493
	Decisions for Production and Deployment	496
	Interservice Disputes about Antimissile Defense	500
	Integrating Missiles into the Air Force	504
	Integrating Missiles into the Strategic Air Command	506
	Missiles for Air Defense and Air-Ground Support	520
	Aircraft and Missile Projection in Tactical Air Command	523
	Development in Continental Air Defense	528
	Origins of Aerospace Doctrine in the Air Force	541
	Visualizations of Satellites and Space Stations	545
	A Concept of Space Superiority	549
	Notes	555
10	IMPACT OF MISSILES AND SPACE ON NATIONAL ORGANIZATION AND STRATEGY	573
	The Defense Reorganization Act of 1958	573
	Drives for Closer Defense Unification	574
	Air Force Demands for a Single Service	584
	New Authority for United Commands	586
	Organization of Military and National Space Programs	589
	Establishment of the National Aeronautics and Space Administration	594
	Strategic Dialogue: Minimum Deterrence or Counterforce	606
	Meeting Crises in Lebanon and the Taiwan Straits	610
	Minimum Deterrence or Counterforce?	618
	Notes	629
	INDEX	639

FOREWORD

This history seeks to discover and record the mainstream of thought within the United States Air Force (and its predecessors) concerning the role to be played by air and aerospace power in a deadly struggle for national survival. It seeks to trace the development of a theme of institutional thought, describe the organizational framework in which the thinking took place, and identify individual thinkers and their ideas. In great measure this chronology is the story of dedicated professional men who were attempting to discover the capabilities and limitations of new forms of air and aerospace power and to relate these new characteristics of military power to the defense of the United States and its national interests. The story begins with the first heavier-than-air flight in 1903 and closes at the end of 1984. This ending date permits a coverage of Air Force thinking about counterinsurgency warfare and the military operations in Southeast Asia.

The existing state of professional historical art does not provide much guidance as to the way a history of military ideas ought to be approached. Edward Mead Earle's *Makers of Modern Strategy, Military Thought from Machiavelli to Hitler* is a monumental study of military thinking that is worthy of emulation, but Earle's volume is a series of case studies of the ideas of the Great Captains drawn from their formal writings. The authors in Earle's book focus attention upon a relatively few individuals and assess their specific contributions to the art and science of warfare. A study of Air Force thought, on the other hand, involves a consideration of the views of a substantially large number of men, most of whom did little formal writing. Although air officers have not been prolific writers, they have expressed their beliefs freely, especially before congressional committees and commissions. In fact, one may almost say that the Air Force has developed an oral rather than a written tradition. Speeches, lectures, and testimony of Air Force leaders have provided the richest source of data for this study of the ideas, concepts, and doctrine of the Air Force. Since such lectures are considered privileged, quotations from or citations to a National War College, Army War College, or Air War College lecture have been cleared with the lecturer, even though they may have been unclassified as to military security. To a man these lecturers have been generous and enthusiastic in granting approval to quote or cite their work.

A constant concern in developing the narrative has been the problem of how to present the matters under consideration in the most meaningful manner. Since ideas and concepts are frequently interpretations of facts and not facts themselves, a thinker may predict meanings before events transpire or, even more likely, continue over a period of years to draw interpretative meanings from the factual happenings of the past. Fundamentally, ideas often lack a temporal quality, hence a history of ideas lacks the neatness of a history of past events. It is possible that this history of ideas, concepts, and doctrine of air power should have been presented as an anthology of pertinent discourse with accompanying commentary. This technique, however, would have obscured a proper recognition of the circumstance wherein the developing Air Force was itself an excellent manifestation of air ideas. The notion of an anthology was, nevertheless, so persuasive that the author, as often as possible, has allowed the thinkers to speak for themselves and to work their dialogue into the narrative. This practice frequently makes for tedious progress when citations are lengthy, and short quotations run the danger of lifting thoughts out of context. Still, summarization of a man's words in contemporary language can easily distort original meanings. The record will show, for example, that air superiority had different meanings to different thinkers during the course of Air Force history. As a matter of practice, the author has sought to present the story of the way things were and what men were thinking in a developing time frame, without attempting a high-gloss interpretation of either the events or the thoughts.

In the course of the unfolding story, the reader will perceive that Air Force thinkers have seldom addressed themselves to purely theoretical matters but usually have tended to respond to specific situations. Since the United States has always been a defense-minded nation, the nature of the hostile threat has been the greatest stimulant to military thinking. Air Force thinking also has been reactive to the activities and ideas of other defense services. Thus, it is frequently necessary that Departments of Defense, Army, and Navy positions and actions be noted in order that readers may better understand Air Force thinking. The focus of the narrative on the Air Force dictated that the views of others be presented, but in shorter compass. Since this procedure inevitably oversimplified the views of the Office of Secretary of Defense (OSD) and the other services, an informed reader ought to consult the works of such military thinkers as Generals Matthew B. Ridgway, Maxwell D. Taylor, and James M. Gavin, and, certainly, Robert S. McNamara's *The Essence of Security, Reflections in Office*.

This revised two-volume history is an extended version of *Ideas, Concepts, Doctrine: A History of Basic Thinking in the United States Air Force, 1907–1964*, which the author completed during 1961–64. This original book was first published in 1971 by the Aerospace Studies Institute, Air University, in a two-volume format; it was reprinted in 1974 as a single volume in the numbered-text series of the Air University as AU-19. In view of a continuing demand for the book, the author was brought back from retirement at the end of September 1982 with a two-year contract calling for revision of the original book as necessary to bring it up to date, as of 1984.

DENNIS M. DREW, Colonel, USAF
Director, Airpower Research Institute
Center for Aerospace Doctrine,
Research, and Education

ABOUT THE AUTHOR

Dr Robert Frank Futrell

Robert Frank Futrell was a senior historian at the Albert F. Simpson Historical Research Center. He holds bachelor of arts and master of arts degrees from the University of Mississippi and a PhD from Vanderbilt University (1950). During World War II, he served as historical officer of the AAF Tactical Center, Orlando, Florida, and assistant historical officer of Headquarters Far East Air Forces in the Philippines.

After World War II, Doctor Futrell joined the new Army Air Forces/United States Air Force Historical Office, which was moved from Washington, D.C., to the Air University, Maxwell AFB, Alabama, in 1949. At the Air University he was professor of military history and became emeritus professor at his retirement from the US Civil Service in 1974. He also retired as a lieutenant colonel from the Air Force Reserve.

Doctor Futrell is author of *The United States Air Force in the Korean War, 1950-1953; The United States Air Force in Southeast Asia, The Advisory Years to 1965;* and has authored and coauthored many other air history books and articles. Recently under contract with the Airpower Research Institute, he revised and updated one of his former works—*Ideas, Concepts, Doctrine: A History of Basic Thinking in the United States Air Force*. Volume I covers the period through 1960; volume II picks up with 1961 and goes through 1984.

ACKNOWLEDGMENTS

This project was first recommended by Robert B. Lane, director, Air University Library, and was accepted by Lt Gen Charles G. Cleveland, then Air University commander, as one of the initiatives in his Project FLAME (Fresh Look at Military Education). The author extends his thanks to Col Dennis Drew for his support of this project and to the many people in the Air University Press who helped turn the manuscript into a polished book.

Although many persons have provided information and assistance toward the writing of this history, the author assumes the responsibility for the errors of fact or interpretation that doubtless have escaped into print.

CHAPTER 1

EMERGING PATTERNS OF AIR FORCE THOUGHT

"A very knowledgeable reporter stated recently that in the early 1950s he felt he knew what the Air Force stood for, but today he doesn't. His statement puzzled me. It also alarmed me because understanding our doctrine and concepts is basic and important to our very existence."[1] In these words on 21 September 1961, Gen Curtis E. LeMay, chief of staff, US Air Force, called attention to a matter that had concerned Air Force officers for many years. In December 1957 Gen Thomas D. White, who was then Air Force chief of staff, had stated: "The Air Force has so recently achieved its full stature as to be something of a doctrinal mystery in comparison with the older, more familiar services."[2]

Unlike the US Navy, which appeared to operate in accordance with a seemingly complete set of sea power principles recorded by Adm Alfred Thayer Mahan, or the United States Army, which drew its principles from generations of American and foreign military scholars, an Air Force officer speaking in 1955 could only conclude that "the Air Force as a service does not have a set of ideas against which it is operating, at least not a complete set of ideas."[3] Moreover, according to a 1948 Air University staff study, "the Air Force has never maintained a complete and current compilation of those concepts, principles, policies, tactics, techniques, practices, and procedures which are essential to efficiency in organizing, training, equipping, and employing its tactical and service units."[4] Provoked by an Army officer's magazine article entitled, "Air Power Needs Its Mahan," Maj Gen John DeForest Barker, deputy commander of the Air University, observed in 1953: "We definitely need a body of air principles backed by the historical evidence of air employment."[5]

Such testimony clearly indicated that these and other Air Force authorities believed that the Air Force required a recording of its fundamental beliefs. In the midst of World War II, an Army Air Forces staff officer had pointed out:

> In any field of endeavor, private or public, the first essential is a body of working principles and the next is a clear concept of the manner of following those principles with the means at hand. Without such principles and concepts being clearly expressed, at least in the minds of the users, it is not at all possible to attain coordination and efficiency, and it is not reasonable to expect, as is desirable, that all workers to the common end will have in mind the same possibilities and objectives. In military matters, especially those of the magnitude of the operations of the present was, where mistakes and inconsistencies cost thousands of lives and millions of man-hours, it is all the more important that there be clearly expressed guiding principles which are clearly

understood by all planners, as well as by all who are charged with the handling of forces in the field.[6]

Moreover, a study conducted by an Air War College seminar in 1951 concluded that the US Air Force had a vital requirement for a codification of its doctrine. "Without a well-established doctrine," the seminar concluded, "the efforts of all but a few key personnel, who can remain sensitive to the changes as they occur, are to a very considerable extent negated."[7]

Prior to World War II virtually all of the senior Air Corps officers and many of the lesser ranking officers had been able to pass through the Office of the Chief of Air Corps, exchange views with the division heads, and draw from their conversations "the essence of air doctrine." During and after World War II, however, the Army Air Forces (AAF) and the US Air Force had grown into a large and very complicated organization, with many thousands of officers. But if an officer in the field were to point his efforts along constructive lines, he had to know "the overall policies and objectives of the Air Force."[8]

The reasons why the Air Force has been hesitant to engross its fundamental beliefs demand some explanation. "Air activities have most often attracted men of active rather than literary leanings.... The Air Force has never boasted a high percentage of scholars," as Col Noel F. Parrish observed in 1947.[9] In fact this spate of writings by senior commanders led W. Barton Leach to describe the Air Force as "the Silent Service."[10] But this line of endeavor has not always received a sympathetic hearing in the air arm. "As you know," wrote General Barker in reference to the provocative article regarding the Air Force's need to develop a Mahan, "the scholarly life is not particularly respected in the profession of arms." And he continued,

> I don't believe, however, that we can ever detail an officer to do a work of this sort. Mahan, as with all great thinkers, was inspired. Of course he had to spring from an environment which allowed him to study long and deeply the problems of sea power. His many years on shipboard were devoted to these exhaustive studies—but he would have been playing poker... and reading fiction if he hadn't been inspired to learn all he could of naval history and give it pattern and meaning.[11]

Other factors worked against the expression of fundamental Air Force beliefs. Prior to World War II the subordinate position of the Air Force to the Army is said to have hampered air publications, as did the fact that the Army's system of field manuals was unsuited to the need of the Air Force. Moreover, some Air Force leaders felt that because of the lessons learned in World War II, the Air Force should not try to develop a doctrine based just on air power. Maj Gen Follett Bradley opined that

> we do not need a Mahan of air power so much as an oracle of combined operations—triphibious, if you like. The true expositor of military things to come must... know thoroughly the changes in sea power as taught by Mahan, and in land warfare as taught by Clausewitz, which have been wrought not only by new weapons but by air power itself. He must evaluate correctly the effect of air power in combination with land and sea

power on a battle, a campaign and a war, and he must know something of the technique by which that effect is produced.[12]

Still further, an Air University study in 1948 stated that the major "obstacle to writing air force doctrine in the past was the rapidity of the development of air power ... from a limited supporting role to its present position of pre-eminence in warfare."[13] A 1951 Air War College study observed that, in some cases, senior Air Force officers were said to have discouraged the preparation of air doctrine because they felt that air doctrines were too short-lived to warrant publication. Word of mouth generally sufficed to keep senior air commanders well abreast of Air Force policy, and it was much easier "to scrap the worn out doctrine that remains unpublished than it is to drop a doctrine that has been published." But the basic shortcoming of "verbal doctrine" was that it remained vague. "It is this reluctance to publish as official anything imperfect that restrains our commanders from the dissemination of current doctrine. Until we accept the fact that all doctrine is imperfect ... and that it is highly changeable we cannot hope for the issuance of doctrine." The same Air War College study noted that, as of 1951, "the air leaders of today are not so old that they can easily forget the punishment meted out to the doctrinaires of the past."[14]

Air Force thinkers not only have found it difficult to face the task of codifying the Air Force's fundamental beliefs, but, as the foregoing quotations reveal, they also have employed a diversity of discourse to categorize these fundamental beliefs. Indeed, the above mentioned Air War College study concluded that "there appears to be a fine line of demarcation between concepts and doctrine on the one hand, and doctrines and principles on the other hand." They added: "It is difficult to differentiate between concepts which existed in the minds of some farsighted individuals in the Air Force and the doctrine which was accepted as official by the War Department. Also doctrine is easily confused with strategy."[15] Adding additional complexity to any attempt to analyze basic Air Force thought patterns is the fact that the terms used to categorize fundamental Air Force beliefs apparently varied with the persons using them and certainly varied with the time period in which the terms were employed. It is not too hard to imagine why early Air Force thinkers began to refer to their fundamental ideas as doctrines. The term *doctrine* had an old meaning in military establishments as a teaching, or, in a collective sense, a body of teachings.

In teaching the art of war, however, Marshal Ferdinand Foch laid great emphasis upon doctrine: The writings of this hero of the Marne and Yser strongly influenced the post-World War I US Army. Where commanders in the past had preferred to remain mysterious (to handle armies like pawns on a chess board) Foch had taught at the École de Guerre that commanders should instead make their intentions known to their subordinates. "We have, then, a doctrine," he explained. "All the brains have been limbered up and regard all questions from an identical point of view. The fundamental idea of the problem being known, each one will solve the problem in his own fashion, and these thousand fashions, we may be very sure, will act to direct all their efforts to a common objective."[16] In his introduction in *The Principles of War*, Foch promised: "In the course of the practical applications our strategical studies will lead us to, you will also arrive at what we call the *doctrine* or *mental discipline*, which consists first in a common way of objectively approaching the subject; second, in a common way of handling it, by adapting without reserve the means to the goal aimed at, to the object." Teachings derived from history, Foch emphasized, would come "out in the shape of a *theory* of war which can be taught . . . and in the shape of a *doctrine*, which you will be taught to practice."[17]

In spite of the newness of aviation and its subsequent lack of history on which to base doctrine, Brig Gen William Mitchell referred to "our doctrine of aviation."[18] Moreover, in the draft of what could well be called the Air Force's first doctrinal manual, which was prepared for instructional purposes at the Air Service Field Officers School in 1921, Maj William C. Sherman wrote: "In deriving the doctrine that must underlie all principles of employment of the air force, we must not be guided by conditions surrounding the use of ground troops, but must seek out our doctrine . . . in the element in which the air force operates."[19] Although the Air Service and Air Corps were unable to make much of an impact upon the War Department's official field service and training regulations, the chief of the Army's air arm, in common with the chiefs of other Army arms and services, enjoyed certain liberties in issuing the doctrinal literature for the Air Service and its successor, the Air Corps. The War Department General Staff emphasized, however, that doctrine should be formulated only by the chief of an Army arm or service.[20] "Doctrinal literature," said an Army Air Forces staff officer in 1944, "originates with the highest authority and states in general the overall policy to be followed."[21]

Given agreement on the proposition that air doctrine derived from the highest authority, there was less agreement as to its precise nature. In 1938 the Air Corps Board stated:

> Principles change not at all, or but slightly, over considerable periods. Doctrines generally change slowly, but will change as different applications of principles bring forth different beliefs and teachings. Methods are influenced both by doctrine and technical improvement and will change more rapidly than doctrines. The most satisfactory Field Service regulation would be one dealing only with principles and expressed in terms that would never change. However, air warfare is relatively new and there is much difference of opinion as regards principles of employment.[22]

In 1943 an AAF staff officer defined doctrine as

> a body of fundamental principles expressing the logical possibilities and objectives of air warfare, as well as its general limitations. Like any other doctrine, especially one for a weapon so new as the air arm still is, it is only natural that the AAF doctrine should include speculative as well as proven truths, but they are all necessary to provide a basis for initial decisions in the design of airplanes and in the training of personnel to accomplish the desired end.

This same officer defined policies as "derivatives of doctrine and the expressions of decisions based upon doctrine."[23]

By 1948 the growth of the Army Air Forces during World War II and the achievement of a separate status by the United States Air Force led Air University thinkers to suggest that the time was opportune to undertake that part of their mission which charged the institution to prepare, review, and revise all Air Force publications pertaining to basic doctrine.[24] As this work progressed, the Air University acknowledged the definition of doctrine provided by the Joint Chiefs of Staff:

> A compilation of principles and policies, applicable to a subject, which have been developed through experience or by theory, that represent the best available thought, and indicate and guide but do not bind in practice. Its purpose is to provide that understanding within a force which generates mutual confidence between the commander and his subordinates in order that timely and effective action will be taken by all concerned in the absence of instruction.[25]

Looking backward at Air Force experience, these Air University students of doctrine noted that there had been an implication that doctrine represented an official view and that once stated some general efforts had been made to follow it. These students recognized, however, that the Air Corps and Army Air Forces had not always been guided by the "prevailing existing doctrines," which had been influenced by the War Department General Staff. The students accordingly undertook to find Air Force doctrine through "a logical analysis of historical fact" rather than through official statements, organizational designs, or other apparent factors that might appear to contradict the actual doctrine that was practiced.[26]

The vigorous efforts of the Air University to define basic Air Force doctrine in the early 1950s did much to clarify the semantic thought patterns of the Air Force. "In this attempt to strike out on our own," said Col William W. Momyer, Air War College deputy commandant for evaluation, "we have encountered many obstacles that were certainly anticipated, and others that could not be foreseen. Of course, we have encountered . . . prejudice in respect to what constitutes doctrine."[27] In the foreword to the final product, published on 1 April 1953 as Air Force Manual (AFM) 1-2, *United States Air Force Basic Doctrine*, Gen Hoyt S. Vandenberg, Air Force chief of staff, noted: "Basic air doctrine evolves from experience gained in war and from analysis of the continuing impact of new weapons systems on warfare." The purpose of the basic doctrine manual was to provide and impart to all Air Force personnel a basis for understanding the use of air forces in peace and in war and to serve as a background for the preparation of succeeding operational doctrine manuals that would cover the tactics and techniques of employing air forces.[28] In preparing the contents of the basic doctrinal manual, Air University evaluators found that they had to relate doctrine to the hoary principles of war, to the roles and missions of the US armed forces, to tactics and strategy, and to a relatively new Air Force term called *concepts*.

As a part of its Army heritage, the Air Force received the age-old principles of war that were derived from the writings of Napoleon, Clausewitz, and Jomini and which had been best summarized in modern times by Great Britain's Maj Gen J. F. C. Fuller. The American version of the principles of war had first appeared in War Department Training Regulation 10-5 in 1921. When Maj William C. Sherman published his personal opinions on aviation in a book entitled *Air Warfare* in 1926, he included a chapter that applied the principles of war to air warfare. These principles also were discussed in the Air Corps Tactical School text, *Air Warfare*, dated 1 March 1936. In September 1943 Col Ralph F. Stearley wrote a paper on the applicability of the principles of war to air power; it was published as AAF Memorandam 200-7, October 1943. Colonel Stearley stated that the nine fundamental principles of war (which applied to all forms of military power) were: cooperation, objective, offensive, mass, movement, economy of force, surprise, security, and simplicity. Colonel Stearley also stated that the application of principles of war to the preparation for war and the direction of war constituted strategy, whereas their application to specific operations comprised tactics. In an article entitled "Air Power and Principles of War," published in 1948, Col Frederick E. Calhoun of the Air University suggested that air power had strengthened the validity of the first eight principles, but he argued that air warfare could not be simple and the ninth principle should be replaced by the term *capacity* or *constant combat readiness*.[29]

In the early 1950s these principles of war were accepted and taught by both the Army and the Air Force. The Navy's attitude, however, was that these principles were permissible as maxims, precepts, factors, guides, or even basic considerations, but it questioned whether they were to be accepted as principles. The Navy did not list these principles in its US fleet publications, but the basic thoughts of the principles were taken cognizance of in these doctrinal publications.[30] The Royal Air Force (RAF) distinguished between the principles of war, which it considered not to be principles but guides or aides-mémoire, and the doctrines that were derived from them.[31] Like the Navy and the RAF, the Air University did not include a specific discussion of the principles of war in its proposed manual, "Air Force Basic Doctrine."[32] In Washington, however, an Air Force committee revised the draft manual and inserted a section, Air Forces and the Principles of War; it then published the revised draft as AFM 1-2, *United States Air Force Basic Doctrine*, on 1 April 1953.[33] An Air War College officer protested that the consideration of the principles of war was a "dissertation" that was hardly doctrinal, while Gen Otto P. Weyland, the commander of the Far East Air Forces, stated that this section was too brief and ought to be developed and elaborated.[34] Still, even though later editions of AFM 1-2 prepared at the Air University did not include specific discussions of the principles of war, there was a continuing recognition that these principles applied to air power as well as to the other forms of military power.[35]

In drawing up the statement of Air Force basic doctrine, the Air University preferred to relate the role of the Air Force to the national objectives and policies of the United States rather than to what was thought to be a possibly transitory statement of armed forces organization, roles, and missions that was included in the National Security Act of 1947. Lt Gen Idwal H. Edwards, the commander of Air University, insisted in June 1952 that "current decisions on matters of organization and roles and missions . . . are not basic doctrine."[36] Meanwhile, the Air University included a list of national objectives and policies that was much too precise to be acceptable to the Air Staff in Washington. Accordingly, the basic air doctrine manual, published on 1 April 1953, accepted the broad proposition that the Air Force supported the nation's objectives and policies, but without attempting to say what they were.[37] As a matter of fact the Air University believed that the nature of modern war and the national objectives and policies worked closely together to determine the correct use of military aviation.[38] In a speech on 4 December 1957, however, Gen Thomas D. White strongly asserted a contrary view, when he said: "Air Force doctrine is not a thing apart nor a code sufficient unto itself. The Air Force is a national instrument and evolves no doctrine, makes no preparation other than those clearly and unmistakably called for or anticipated by the national policy."[39] The requirement that Air Force doctrine must support national objectives and policies necessarily marked it as distinct from pure air power doctrine, which would enunciate through theory and logic immutable principles that characterize air power as different from land power and sea power.[40]

A 1951 Air War College study noted that doctrine was easily confused with strategy on the one hand and with tactics and techniques on the other hand. Air University found little difficulty in distinguishing doctrine from tactics and technique: the latter depended quite manifestly upon specific equipment and special situations and were designed to implement specific actions within the broad framework of basic doctrine. Strategy also was judged to be concerned with specific situations, although on a tremendously broader scale than tactics. Brig Gen Alfred R. Maxwell, an Air Force author on the subject, stated that the tools of strategy were a sound plan, adequate forces, appropriate execution, and guidance by proper principles. "Strategy," wrote Maxwell, "is the act of infusing into a plan and/or applying a central idea, design, or timing which will give the greatest possible advantage in a campaign or situation. The strategy is the specific design used."[41]

Prior to World War II, the Air Corps Tactical School's teachings frequently had gone beyond the somewhat narrow confines of officially approved doctrine.[42] But, probably because it held that the principal characteristics of doctrine that would be reasonable and progressive, the Air Corps Tactical School did not differentiate between the doctrinal and the nondoctrinal in its teachings.[43] As early as March 1943, however, AAF officers were referring to ideas that did not have the proven validity of doctrine as concepts. "No concept, particularly one pertaining to a new weapon," wrote Col Charles G. Williamson on 3 March 1943, "can reasonably be stated as a fixed and permanently inviolable rule, but must be accepted as a guide until actualities justify, in the mind of the proper authority, a change in concept."[44] Writing in the winter of 1948, Maj Gen Robert W. Harper, deputy commander of

Air University, described Gen Billy Mitchell as being among the "visionaries and missionaries" of the Air Force. "For atomic warfare," Harper wrote, "new concepts of Air Power will have to be formulated."[45] Early in 1951 Air Force regulations charged Air University with the responsibility for developing doctrine. But in its charge to the Air War College, Air University specified that the Air War College's mission consisted not of developing doctrine but of "the conduct of special studies and evaluation which will provide sound air power concepts" and "the preparation ... of doctrinal manuals." The first objective of the Air War College Evaluation Division was "to develop doctrines and concepts for the employment of air power."[46] In September 1951, General Edwards stated that the Air War College had the mission of "promoting sound concepts on the broad aspects of air power in order to assure the most effective development and employment of the air arm."[47]

By the autumn of 1951, Air Force usage already suggested that the term *concept* was more visionary, more dynamic, and more comprehensive than the term *doctrine*. An Air War College study of Air Force ideas proposed to establish concept at an orderly position in Air Force thought. "In the field of ideas," according to this study, "there is evidently a degree of general acceptance ranging from the first nebulous ideas of an individual, up successively through concepts, doctrines, and principles. The point at which an idea becomes a concept, a concept a doctrine, and a doctrine a principle is not always clear. Thus at any one time our Air Force doctrine may be said to be partly concept, partly doctrine, and partly principle."[48] In his pioneering book *US Military Doctrine*, Brig Gen Dale O. Smith, who had worked with the Air War College students in the preparation of their study, accepted the proposition that Air Force thought progressed from ideas to concepts to doctrines, the last having gained enough official support to be taught at service schools or to be accepted at the highest military staff levels. General Smith additionally proposed that a service doctrine which was accepted by the president, the Congress, or the people of the United States became an executive, a legislative, or a national "policy."[49]

General usage thus accepted the proposition that a concept was a hypothesis that had not received the acceptance required by doctrine, but there was less agreement as to whether doctrine was confined to the service level of the armed forces.[50] In 1957, for example, Col Wendell E. Carter contemplated a national doctrine that would grow out of the deliberations of the Joint Chiefs of Staff and would dictate how wars would be fought.[51] In this same year, Prof Henry A. Kissinger visualized that strategic doctrine enabled society "to act purposefully as a unit ... by reducing most problems to a standard of average performance which enables the other members of the group to take certain actions accordingly." "By explaining the significance of events *in advance* of their occurrence," Kissinger asserted that strategic doctrine "enables society to deal with most problems as a matter of routine and reserves *creative* thought for unusual or unexpected situations."[52] Kissinger thought that this strategic doctrine should desirably issue from the Joint Chiefs of Staff and the National Security Council.[53] Apparently willing to broaden the definition of doctrine, an Air War College study completed in 1958 identified a need for a US military doctrine that would represent "some substantial consensus of the whole body politic, and particularly among all military personnel, as to objects of military enterprise."[54]

Early in the 1950s Air University had maintained the proposition that "USAF doctrine, developed within the parameters of the more valid concepts of air power, is intended for practical purposes to be used as a guide for organization, development, equipment, and employment of the United States Air Force."[55] Some Air Force officers, however, were more skeptical of the role of doctrine in Air Force development. "The Air Force," Gen Nathan F. Twining, acting Air Force chief of staff, had stated in 1952, "is not bound to any fixed doctrine or concept. It grew out of scientific achievement."[56] When he approved AFM 1-2 on 1 April 1953, General Vandenberg thought it necessary to warn that "the dynamic and constant changes in new weapons make periodic review of this doctrine necessary."[57] Looking backward at past events, Gen Laurence S. Kuter admitted that he could not suggest that doctrine had ever been the controlling factor in setting the rate of development of air power. Instead, he recognized a "mutual interdependence of doctrinal technological, political, and other elements."[58] Even though there was general agreement that Air Force doctrine ought to be forward-looking, Maj Gen Lloyd P. Hopwood, a former commandant of the Air Command and Staff College, expressed dismay at the idea that doctrine could not be anything more than descriptive of an existing state of the military art. "We try to make our doctrine and strategy conform to glamorous hardware," Hopwood wrote, "instead of studying modern conflict to find acceptable solutions from which to establish the hardware requirements we need."[59]

Arguments about the parameters of doctrine did not slack up after the "perfection" of AFM 1-2 in mid-1955. In retrospect this manual reflected strategic air lessons drawn from World War II. The main emphasis stressed offensive air actions as providing the ultimate prospect of victory by reducing an enemy's will to fight, chiefly through selective destruction of population centers. There was some acknowledgment of a need for defense against hostile air attack, but the subject of defense was less emphasized than that of offense. The manual noted that air power should support national objectives, but said nothing authoritative on the subject, perhaps because the authors were vague about what our national objectives might be.[60]

After the issuance of a revised AFM 1-2 in April 1955, there did not appear to be an immediate need for more considerations of the subject of air doctrine — this despite changes in national policies and the maturity of intercontinental ballistic missiles.[61] Since the Air University was charged to maintain currency of the basic air doctrine manual, a suggested revision of AFM 1-2 was prepared and forwarded to the Pentagon in 1958. The Air Staff refused to accept the revision, expressing a general satisfaction with the currently approved statement of doctrine. Another reason behind the Air Staff's action was a fatalistic assumption that technology was developing so fast that it was useless to try to capture doctrine in printed pamphlets that became out of date overnight. Some argued that after the reorganization of the Department of Defense in 1958 a new unified doctrine would flow downward from the Joint Chiefs of Staff and energize the activities of the armed services. Finally there was some divergence of opinion in high places as to whether the manual on basic doctrine should be limited to historical doctrine or whether it could attempt to project doctrine into the future.[62] About this same time, an Air Force research and development community study urged that doctrine should be replaced by a new field that could be called "militology." Doctrine it was said had never adequately guided research and development. Militology, on the other hand, would examine the basic tenets of military success and would weld together the bits and pieces of military thought that had been described up until then as objectives, principles, strategy, tactics and techniques, long-range plans, general operational requirements, doctrines, and concepts. This intensive study would produce models or theoretical projections of military concepts and principles of military influence.[63]

As a part of the reorganization of US Air Force headquarters necessitated by the Defense Reorganization Act of 1958, the Air Force thought it necessary to transfer the responsibility of preparing basic air doctrine to the Air Staff. In July 1958 an Air Doctrine Branch was established under the Air Policy Division of the Directorate of Plans. This branch was to advise the Air Force chief of staff on possible doctrinal inputs that might be required by the Joint Chiefs of Staff, which was now vested with responsibility for making joint doctrine. For several months the Air Doctrine Branch served in this advisory role. But on 6 March 1959 responsibility for preparing basic air doctrine and for monitoring the preparation of operational doctrine manuals was transferred back to Headquarters USAF and to the Air Doctrine Branch from the Joint Staff.[64] At this time Air Staff told Air University to revitalize its research activities and to fulfill its function as a doctrinal center for developing sound concepts concerning elements of military influence and aerospace power.[65]

When the responsibilities for developing Air Force doctrine were transferred to Washington, it was expected that air doctrines could be kept more current. But Lt Gen W. E. Todd, commander, Air University, protested that AFM 1-2 was "so far out of date that it has practically become archaic"; the existing manual failed to recognize the impact of missiles and space technology. General Todd's protest apparently sparked action. The Air Staff coordinated the revision and on 1 December 1959 General White signed a new printing of AFM 1-2. The new printing substituted the term *aerospace* in each instance where the word *air* had appeared in the earlier editions, but made virtually no other changes in the old manual. Aerospace was defined as an "operationally indivisible medium consisting of the total expanse beyond the earth's surface."[66] In explaining why the new manual was issued, General White wrote: "The predominant characteristics of air forces (now aerospace forces) have changed only in degree. Range, mobility, flexibility, speed, penetration capability and firepower delivery—the characteristics that continue to make aerospace forces unique among military forces—must be developed to the maximum to guarantee national security."[67] General LeMay, White's successor as chief of staff, also appeared to be happy with the old presentation of air doctrine. In an address on 21 September 1959, he told his audience that Air Force concepts and doctrine had not changed through the years, at least since the establishment of General Headquarters Air Force in 1935. "The purpose of aerospace power," LeMay said, "is to deter attack against us and, if we are attacked, to destroy the enemy's means to wage war."[68] Since there seemed to be some misunderstanding about what the Air Force stood for, General LeMay called for more attention to air concepts and doctrine. New means were soon mobilized to spread Air Force thinking. The Aerospace Policy Division provided "positions" on subjects of defense interest, many of which began to appear as speeches and statements of air leaders. The Secretary of Air Force, Office of Information, already published the *Air Force Information Policy Letter for Commanders* and the monthly *Supplement to the Information Policy Letter for Commanders*. In September 1961, the secretary specified that the Air Force *Policy Letter* would "provide concepts, doctrine, facts, references, and suggestions for all Air Force commanders and their staffs in meeting their responsibility to advance understanding inside and outside the Air Force."[69] At this juncture, Maj Gen Dale O. Smith observed that printed doctrinal manuals apparently could not keep pace with technological advances. For this reason he suggested that true Air Force doctrine—definable as military thought on how to conduct war—might well be the unspoken and sometimes unconscious beliefs that truly guided Air Force actions. "Actions, not pronouncements," he said, "are the real indicators of doctrine."[70]

By 1960 the Air Force had laboriously assembled a body of thinking that was described as doctrine. It was essentially simplistic—concerned with the employment of air power in a World War II-type scenario. The feeling in high places in the Air Force was that these principles of air power were enduring. This first volume traces the development of Air Force rationale from the first thoughts of the employment of military aviation in 1904 to the year 1960. It records the emergence of the Air Force as a manifestation of Air Force thought, and will, insofar as possible, record the way in which the Air Force attempted to manage the exploration of ideas about what air power could and should do.

After 1960, however, the administration of President John F. Kennedy changed the military strategy of the United States from a primary reliance on an air strategy to one of flexible response to a broad spectrum of hostile threats. Thus, it soon became evident from policy trends that aerospace doctrine would be subject to reasoned change caused by shifting circumstances arising from analyses of: (1) the principles and aims of US society and government; (2) the threats to the American system and way of life, both internally and externally; (3) the advances in technology and weaponry; (4) the impact of many levels of leadership, both friendly and enemy; (5) assessments of proper courses for the United States to pursue; and (6) the place of aerospace power in these systems of values and predictions.[71] The second volume tells how these factors have influenced the emergence of the Air Force as a manifestation of Air Force thought and how the Air Force has tried to manage the discussion of ideas about what air power can or should do during the period of 1960 to 1984.

NOTES

1. Gen Curtis E. LeMay, chief of staff, US Air Force, address to Air Force Association Convention, Philadelphia, Pa., 21 September 1961.
2. Gen Thomas D. White, "USAF Doctrine and National Policy," *Air Force Magazine*, January 1958, 47–51.
3. Col W. J. Cain, "An Air Force Concept for the Attack," lecture, Air War College, Maxwell AFB, Ala., 18 February 1955.
4. Evaluation Division, Air University, "To Analyze the USAF Publications System for Producing Manuals," staff study, 13 July 1948.
5. Maj Gen John DeF. Barker, deputy commanding general, Air University, to Lt Gen Howard A. Craig, commandant, National War College, letter, 8 April 1953. The article was written by Col George C. Reinhardt, US Army, "Air Power Needs Its Mahan," United States Naval Institute, *Proceedings*, April 1952, 363–87.
6. Col Charles G. Williamson, chief, Status of Operations Division, Directorate of Bombardment, Headquarters Army Air Forces, Status of Operations Report, 3 March 1943, tab B: Discussion of Army Air Forces Policies and Doctrine.
7. Air War College, "Command and Employment of Air Forces, World War II and Korea," consolidation of extracts of student seminar solutions, study no. 5, Air War College Class of 1952, 43–44.
8. Ibid.
9. Col Noel F. Parrish, "New Responsibilities of Air Force Officers," *Air University Quarterly Review* 1, no. 1 (Spring 1947): 29–42.
10. W. Barton Leach, "Obstacles to the Development of American Air Power," *The Annals of the American Academy of Political and Social Science*, May 1955, 67–75.
11. Barker to Craig, 8 April 1953.
12. Maj Gen Follett Bradley to editor, *New York Times*, 9 April 1944.
13. Evaluation Division, Air University, staff study, "To Analyze the USAF Publications System for Producing Manuals," 13 July 1948.
14. Air War College, "Command and Employment of Air Forces, World War II and Korea," 43–44.
15. Ibid.; Maj Gen John DeF. Barker, deputy commanding general, Air University, to Maj Gen William F. McKee, assistant vice chief of staff, US Air Force, letter, 22 May 1950.
16. Comdt A. Grasset, *Preceptes et Judgements du Marechal Foch* (Nancy, France: Berger-Levrault, 1919), x.
17. Marshal Foch, *The Principles of War*, trans. Hilaire Belloc (London: Chapman & Hall, Ltd., 1918), 7, 18–19.
18. Brig Gen William Mitchell, *Our Air Force, The Keystone of National Defense* (New York: E. P. Dutton & Co., 1921), 15.
19. Maj William C. Sherman, "Air Tactics," sec. 2, Langley AFB, Va., 1921, 7.
20. Brig Gen Carl A. Spaatz, chief, Plans Division, Office of the Chief of the Air Corps, to chief, Training and Operations Division, Office of the Chief of the Air Corps, record and routing (R&R) sheet, 28 May 1941.
21. Brig Gen Mervin E. Gross, chief, Requirements Division, Aviation Section, Signal Corps, Office of the Chief of Research, Army Air Forces, R&R sheet, subject: Centralization of Certain Literature Producing Functions at Orlando, 27 November 1944.
22. Report of Air Corps Board, "Revision of Field Service Regulations," study no. 46, 15 November 1983, 2.

23. Williamson, Status of Operations Report, 3 March 1943, tab B.
24. "The USAF Publications System."
25. Quoted in "Command and Employment of Air Forces, World War II and Korea," 4.
26. Ibid., 3.
27. Memorandum by Col William W. Momyer, deputy commandant for evaluation, Air War College, to Maj Gen John DeF. Barker, deputy commanding general, Air University, subject: Progress of the Manual Program, 17 September 1952.
28. AFM 1-2, *United States Air Force Basic Doctrine*, 1 April 1953, i.
29. Maj William C. Sherman, *Air Warfare* (New York: Ronald Press, 1926), 15–37; Col Ralph F. Stearley, commanding general, I Tactical Air Division, to Lt Col Orin H. Moore, Headquarters Army Air Forces, letter, 9 September 1943; Col Frederick E. Calhoun, "Air Power and Principles of War," *Air University Quarterly Review* 2, no. 2 (Fall 1948): 37–47.
30. Vice Adm R. L. Conolly, "The Principles of War," lecture, Air War College, Maxwell AFB, Ala., 28 August 1951.
31. Sir Robert Saundby, "British Air Doctrine," lecture, Air War College, Maxwell AFB, Ala., 10 November 1953.
32. Air University Manual 1 (draft), "United States Air Force Basic Doctrine," Maxwell AFB, Ala., 1951.
33. AFM 1-2, 1 April 1953, 7–10.
34. Memorandum by Col Charles M. McCorkle, academic director, Air War College, to Maj Gen John DeF. Barker, deputy commanding general, Air University, subject: Basic Doctrine Manuals, 25 May 1953; memorandum by Col William W. Momyer, deputy commandant for evaluation, Air War College, to Maj Gen Roscoe C. Wilson, commandant, Air War College, subject: Revision of AFM 1-2, 15 June 1953.
35. Col Richard C. Weller, "The Principles of War Will Get You if You Don't Watch Out," *Air University Quarterly Review* 7, no. 1 (Spring 1954): 63–65.
36. Lt Gen Idwal H. Edwards, commanding general, Air University, to chief of staff, US Air Force, letter, subject: Manual, Basic Air Power Doctrine, 25 June 1952.
37. Lt Gen Howard A. Craig, Inspector General, US Air Force, to Maj Gen John DeF. Barker, deputy commanding general, Air University, letter, 12 December 1951; AFM 1-2, 1 April 1953, 1–2.
38. AUM 1 (draft), 1951, 1–4.
39. White, "USAF Doctrine and National Policy," 47.
40. Maj Gen Robert F. Tate, "USAF Doctrine and Its Influence on Military Strategy," lecture, Air War College, Maxwell AFB, Ala., 12 December 1957.
41. Air War College, "Command and Employment of Air Forces, World War II and Korea," 1; Lt Gen Idwal H. Edwards, commanding general, Air University, to Gen Nathan F. Twining, vice chief of staff, US Air Force, letter, 2 September 1951; Brig Gen Alfred R. Maxwell, "The Word Strategy," *Air University Quarterly Review* 7, no. 1 (Spring 1954): 66–74.
42. Robert T. Finney, *History of the Air Corps Tactical School, 1920–1940*, USAF historical study 100 (Maxwell AFB, Ala.: Research Studies Institute, 1955), 35–36.
43. Air Corps Tactical School, "A Study of Proposed Air Corps Doctrine Based Upon Information Furnished by the War Plans Division," 31 January 1935.
44. Williamson, Status of Operations Report, 3 March 1943.
45. Maj Gen Robert W. Harper, editorial in *Air University Quarterly Review* 2, no. 3 (Winter 1948): 76.
46. AFR 23-3, *Organization: Air University*, 8 May 1950; AFR 23-2, *Organization: Air University*, 3 August 1951.
47. Air University, *Air War College Manual*, 18 June 1951, 19.
48. Air War College, "Command and Employment of Air Forces, World War II and Korea," 2.
49. Brig Gen Dale O. Smith, *U.S. Military Doctrine, A Study and Appraisal* (New York: Duell, Sloan, and Pearce, 1955), 4–6.

IDEAS, CONCEPTS, DOCTRINE

50. Woodford A. Heflin, ed., *The United States Air Force Dictionary* (Maxwell AFB, Ala.: Air University Press, 1956), 173.

51. Col Wendell E. Carter, "Pursestrings and Pressures," *Air University Quarterly Review* 9, no. 1 (Winter 1956–1957): 47.

52. Henry A. Kissinger, *Nuclear Weapons and Foreign Policy* (New York: Harper & Bros., 1957), 403–4.

53. "Strategy and Organization for the Nuclear Age," *Air Force Magazine*, May 1957, 49.

54. Evaluation Staff, Air War College, "Service Roles and Missions in the Future," project no. AU-3-58-ESAWC, May 1958, 24.

55. Maj Gen Robert F. Tate, "USAF Doctrine and Its Influence on Military Strategy," 12 December 1957.

56. Senate, *Department of Defense Appropriations for 1953: Hearings before the Subcommittee of the Committee on Appropriations*, 82d Cong., 2d sess., 1952, 672.

57. AFM 1-2, 1 April 1953, i.

58. Lt Gen Laurence S. Kuter, "An Air Perspective in the Jetomic Age," *Air University Quarterly Review* 8, no. 2 (Spring 1956): 109.

59. Maj Gen Lloyd P. Hopwood, deputy chief of staff for personnel, Directorate of Personnel Procurement and Training, Headquarters USAF, to Lt Gen W. E. Todd, commander, Air University, letter, 23 December 1958.

60. AFM 1-2, 1 April 1955.

61. Maj Gen Dale O. Smith, special assistant for arms control, Joint Chiefs of Staff, "Development of Air Force Doctrine," 15 April 1963.

62. Ibid.

63. USAF Directorate of Development Planning, Development Planning Note 58-DAP-2, "A Program for Coherent Research and Development of Military Science," 17 February 1958.

64. History, Deputy Chief of Staff for Plans and Programs, Directorate of Plans, Headquarters USAF, July–December 1958, 114, 163–64; Lt Gen W. E. Todd, commander, Air University, to Lt Gen John K. Gerhart, deputy chief of staff for plans and programs, Headquarters USAF, letter, 27 October 1959; Maj Gen Lloyd P. Hopwood, deputy chief of staff for personnel, Directorate of Personnel Procurement and Training, Headquarters USAF, to Lt Gen W. E. Todd, letter, 23 December 1958; Lt Gen John K. Gerhart, deputy chief of staff for plans and programs, Headquarters USAF, to Lt Gen W. E. Todd, letter, 4 March 1959; History, Air University, January–June 1959, 1:33–34; History, Research Studies Institute, July–December 1959, 1.

65. Gerhart to Todd, 4 March 1959.

66. Todd to Gerhart, 27 October 1959; AFM 1-2, 1 December 1959.

67. *Air Force Information Policy Letter for Commanders*, 1 February 1960, 1.

68. LeMay, address to Air Force Association Convention, 21 September 1961.

69. AFR 190-18, *Information Activities: Air Force Internal Information Program*, 8 September 1961.

70. Maj Gen Dale O. Smith, "Air Force Doctrine," lecture, Air Command and Staff College, Maxwell AFB, Ala., 1 February 1961.

71. Smith, "Development of Air Force Doctrine," 15 April 1963.

CHAPTER 2

EARLY DAYS THROUGH WORLD WAR I
1907-26

Without military expenditures for its development, it is quite likely that the airplane would not have become a safe and usable vehicle. "Had it not been for the support of the military for military purposes," Dr Clifford C. Furnas, chancellor of the University of Buffalo and a knowledgeable scientist, would conclude in April 1958, "we would even now I am sure not have safe commercial aviation."[1] In 1898, while the Spanish-American War was in progress and well before the Wright brothers made their first flight, the War Department's Board of Ordnance and Fortification secretly had allocated $50,000 to Dr Samuel P. Langley, who subsequently was unable to produce a promised flying machine. When this information became generally known, both Congress and the press had been extremely critical of this so-called wastage of public funds.[2] In reminiscences about their epic controlled- power flight at Kitty Hawk, North Carolina, on 17 December 1903, Orville and Wilbur Wright always contended that they meant the airplane to be a contribution to international communications, trade, and goodwill. When they made their first efforts to sell a plane, however, the Wright brothers looked to the US War Department. "The series of aeronautical experiments upon which we have been engaged for the past five years," Orville Wright wrote on 18 January 1905, "have ended in the production of a flying machine of a type fitted for practical use. ... The numerous flights ... have made it quite certain that flying has been brought to a point where it can be made of great practical use in various ways, one of which is that of scouting and carrying messages in time of war."[3]

Writing directly to the secretary of war on 9 October 1905, Orville Wright renewed this earlier informal offer "to furnish to the War Department practical flying machines suitable for scouting purposes."[4] Still again, on 15 June 1907, he wrote: "We believe that the principal use of a flyer at present is for military purposes; that the demand in commerce will not be great for some time."[5] Possibly as a result of the experience with Langley, the Board of Ordnance and Fortification declined to enter into negotiations with the Wrights in October 1905 "until a machine is produced which by actual operation is shown to be able to produce horizontal flight and to carry an operator."[6]

The Beginning of Army Aviation

Because of interest expressed by President Theodore Roosevelt, aviation matters received added emphasis in the War Department in 1907. On 1 August Brig Gen James Allen, the Army's chief signal officer, established an Aeronautical Division within the Signal Corps, and the Board of Ordnance and Fortification reopened negotiations with the Wright brothers. In a letter to the board on 10 October, Allen was skeptical of the value of the Wright plane. "The military uses of a flying machine of any type," he thought, "will be only for purposes of observation and reconnaissance, or, as an offensive weapon, to drop explosives on the enemy." For either purpose, he believed that the airplane would be less efficient than the dirigible balloons that were already being used by France, Germany, and England. "For the purpose of dropping explosives on an enemy," he asserted, "a high speed aeroplane is hardly suitable.... In passing over the enemy's works a flying machine should travel at least 4,000 feet above the earth.... Traveling at the rate of thirty miles an hour at this altitude, even after considerable practice, it is not thought a projectile could be dropped nearer than half a mile from the target."[7] Even though the airplane lacked range, load-carrying capability, and came out second best in an effectiveness comparison with the dirigible, the Board of Ordnance and Fortification nevertheless instructed General Allen on 5 December 1907 to solicit bids for the delivery of a heavier-than-air flying machine designed to carry two persons and sufficient fuel for a flight of 125 miles and capable of a speed of at least 40 miles an hour.[8]

The Signal Corps specifications for its first airplane did not include an operational requirement that it would be expected to satisfy. Hence, when the first Wright plane was eventually accepted on 2 August 1909, the Army had a new item of experimental equipment that was in need of a mission. Several minds went to work to bridge this gap. In his student thesis at the Army Service School, Fort Leavenworth, Kansas, in 1907, Lt Benjamin D. Foulois had predicted that large fleets in the air would operate well in advance of ground troops and that these opposing air fleets would be the first military forces to engage at the outbreak of a war.[9] In 1911 Lt Thomas DeWitt Milling tested an experimental aircraft bombsight, and in the following year Milling and Capt Charles DeForest Chandler first fired a Lewis machine gun from an airplane. Even these early aviation enthusiasts, however, recognized that "the very limited flight performance of aircraft in 1912 had not demonstrated any military value other than reconnaissance."[10] US Army field service regulations of 1910 merely noted that for purposes of reconnaissance: "The dirigible balloon or flying machine is used as the commander directs."[11]

During hearings in the spring of 1913 held by the House Military Affairs Committee on a bill to create a separate air corps as one of the line components of the Army, Assistant Secretary of War Henry S. Breckinridge explained the War Department position that military aviation was "merely an added means of communication, observation and reconnaissance" that "ought to be coordinated with and subordinated to the general service of information and not erected into an independent and uncoordinated service." Significantly enough, Lieutenant Foulois agreed that it was too early for a separate air corps; Lt Henry H. Arnold was sure that the Signal Corps was doing all it could to advance aviation; Lieutenant Milling considered the proposed change premature. "The offensive value of this thing has yet to be proved," argued Capt William Mitchell. "It is being experimented with—bomb dropping and machines carrying guns... but there is nothing to it so far except in an experimental way."[12] Nevertheless, during a period of strained relations with Mexico, Army aviators were ordered to Texas City, Texas, in February 1913 to work with the 2d Division. Early in March, this detachment was provisionally organized as the 1st Aero Squadron.[13]

A new edition of US Army field service regulations, issued on 19 March 1914, addressed the subject of the use of combined arms and of aviation. These regulations, which would continue to be in effect when the United States entered World War I, assigned the predominant combat role to the infantry: "The infantry is the principal and most important arm, which is charged with the main work on the field of battle and decides the final issue of combat. The role of the infantry, whether offensive or defensive, is the role of the entire force, and the utilization of that arm gives the entire battle its character. The success of the infantry is essential to the success of the combined arms." Aircraft—captive balloons, dirigible balloons, and aeroplanes—served to provide information. For strategical reconnaissance, the dirigible had the greatest practical value, but aeroplanes were said to be more dependable for field service with a mobile army since dirigibles required substantial shelter from winds while they were on the ground. "In forces of the strength of a division, or larger," the regulations stated, "the aero squadron will operate in advance of the independent cavalry in order to locate the enemy and to keep track of his movements."[14]

European Adversaries Speed Aviation Development

Feeling the threat of hostile neighbors, European nations accelerated the development of aeronautics during the 1900s. At the Hague Conference in 1899 the European nations had been willing to accept a US proposal and impose a five-year prohibition against "the discharge of projectiles or explosives from balloons or by other new methods of similar nature." The US delegate had rationalized: "The balloon ... can carry but little; it is capable of hurling ... indecisive quantities of explosives, which would fall, like useless hailstones, on both combatants and noncombatants alike."[15] But in 1907, when the Second Hague Conference declaration extended this moratorium on aerial bombing, no major powers except the United States and Great Britain proved willing to ratify it. There were ominous predictions that a future war would begin with air bombardments of belligerent capitals. For the most part, the opposing powers hurriedly developed aviation as an added means of reconnaissance.

As the war approached, however, a new strategic concept began to take hold: military commanders in Germany, France, and Russia began to discount the prospect that any means of reconnaissance could dispel the fog of war in an all-out modern conflict. First Germany and then France and Russia accepted the strategic concept of *offense à l'outrance* – a headlong offensive that would attain victory before an enemy could maneuver or react and before battlefield reconnaissance would be worthwhile.[16]

Reflecting popular fears of aerial bombing, the first days of World War I were marked by many false alarms of hostile air raids. The Germans in their declaration of war handed to France on 3 August 1914, apparently were sincere in alleging that French aircraft had bombed the railroad near the German city of Nuremberg on the day before. As hostilities began on the Western Front, the air orders of battle were fairly evenly matched: each side had about 180 airplanes, the Germans had 12 Zeppelins, and France and Britain together had 13 dirigibles. The much feared Zeppelin did not perform well in early fighting; the Germans lost one Zeppelin when it was attempting to bomb the forts at Liège on 6 August and two others were shot down on 21 August when they attempted to reconnoiter under low clouds in the Belfort area. In the confusion of the active field campaign, neither the attacking German armies nor the Anglo-French defense forces made effective use of reconnaissance aircraft.[17]

The employment of reconnaissance aircraft became more effective as the German attack continued. When the exhausted opposing armies entrenched late in 1914, aerial vehicles became virtually the sole source of intelligence. In some measure, aircraft reconnaissance added to the stalemate of trench warfare since neither opposing army could make large local buildups of munitions and reserves without being detected and countered. Both the Allies and the Central Powers exploited fixed balloons for frontline observation and aircraft for deeper-in reconnaissance. Success of local campaigns depended on blinding the opposing intelligence service; thus, both sides developed fighter aircraft and employed them over active sectors in barrage patrols designed to sweep enemy aircraft from the skies. The appearance of a technologically superior Fokker fighter aircraft over the front lines in June 1915 gave a working air superiority to the Central Powers and demanded extreme efforts on the part of the Allies to develop higher performance pursuit aircraft and better tactics. By 1917 the Germans also developed an armed Junkers strafing aircraft that was especially designed for attacks against troops and equipment. As the ground war stalemated, German Zeppelins began bombing attacks against England in January 1915 to weaken the British psychologically. On the Allied side in 1916, the Italian aircraft manufacturer, Gianni Caproni Count di Taliedo, prepared a memorandum for Allied headquarters that proposed to destroy German and Austrian naval vessels by bomber attack against fleet bases. In January 1917, Caproni argued that his large triplane bombers, if built in sufficient numbers, could destroy Austria's factories, thus ending the war with Italy's main opponent.[18]

US Military Preparations

Recognizing that the United States was lagging in aeronautics, Congress approved a measure on 3 March 1915 that established the National Advisory Committee for Aeronautics (NACA) as an independent agency for the "scientific study of the problems of flight with a view to their practical solution." This action was hardly taken, however, before the new evidence emerged to show the low state of readiness of Army aviation. On the Mexican border in March and April 1916, the 1st Aero Squadron valiantly attempted to support Brig Gen John J. Pershing's punitive expedition against the Mexican outlaw Pancho Villa. However, a combination of poor flying machines and severe operational weather made it impossible for the squadron to provide desired observation to the ground forces.[19]

As the United States reluctantly began to arm itself, the National Defense Act of June 1916 included a modest expansion of personnel in the Signal Corps, Aviation Section; large appropriations for Army aviation were included in the fiscal year 1917 appropriation. Looking toward industrial mobilization, Congress authorized establishment of the Council of National Defense on 29 August 1916. One of the groups comprising the council was the nucleus for the creation of the Aircraft Production Board on 16 May 1917. The Aircraft Production Board worked in conjunction with the Joint Army-Navy Technical Board in the selection and procurement of the aircraft chosen for large-scale production.[20]

The American Air Service in World War I

When the United States entered World War I on 6 April 1917, the US Army did not possess a single modern combat aircraft; but the beginnings of an industrial mobilization had been made. As a nonbelligerent, the United States had not shared Allied war secrets and badly needed information on which to base its war plans. In the first place, the hard-pressed Allies wanted rapid support from US industry. In a cable to President Woodrow Wilson on 26 May, Premier Alexandre Ribot of France asked that an American flying corps of 4,500 planes, 5,000 pilots, and 50,000 mechanics be sent to France during 1918 to "enable the Allies to win the supremacy of the air." If it were to meet this requirement, the United States would have to produce 16,000 planes and 30,000 engines by 1 July 1918. Congress immediately appropriated funds for the requisite production, but, for some reason, Ribot had not specified what type planes ought to be produced.[21]

To determine specific US aircraft requirements and to coordinate Allied patent problems, Secretary of War Newton D. Baker sent an aeronautical commission, headed by newly commissioned Maj Raynal C. Bolling, a leader in civil aeronautics, to Europe in June 1917. Earlier in 1917, Bolling had worked closely with Foulois, now a major, to justify the $640-million congressional appropriation for the production of aircraft and expansion of the Air Service. Secretary Baker apparently believed that Bolling's background in business would enable him to deal with Allied war producers.[22] The report filed by Bolling on 15 August 1917 provided the doctrinal and technical bases for building the Air Service, American Expeditionary Forces (AEF). Bolling reported general agreement that the United States would immediately require aircraft for use in training, aircraft for use strictly in connection with the operation of US ground forces in the field, and after these immediate requirements were met, fighting airplanes and bombers that would be "in excess of the tactical requirements of its Army in France." Since he did not know how large the US Army field force would be, Bolling was unable to suggest the extent of the air force component of the field force, but he recommended that an air force which could be used "independently of United States military forces" should be about 37.5 percent fighting airplanes, about 25 percent day bombers, and about 37.5 percent night bombers. The composition of the bomber force would actually vary according to the number of fast fighting machines that the enemy operated on a given portion of the front at a given time. In an extended discussion of the bomber force he desired to put into action in 1918, Bolling explained that day bombardment required faster aircraft, which desirably would be employed freely "if it should be possible to drive from the air practically all the enemy fighting machines." By bombing at night, however, large and slow airplanes could carry large numbers of bombs. In response to the question, "Could night bombing be conducted on a sufficiently great scale and kept up continuously for a sufficient time?" Bolling replied, "there seems good reason to believe that it might determine the whole outcome of military operations. Up until the present time, the trouble seems to have been that all bombing has been carried on intermittently and sporadically because of a lack of attention to the subject and provision for large enough numbers of the right kinds of airplanes."[23]

Even though American aviation pioneers had thought of aviation as a combat arm, the idea of a massive independent bombing force, which was so readily accepted by the aeronautical commission, was relatively new, even in Europe. Shortly after arriving in Europe, Bolling had conversations with Gen Sir David Henderson of the British air board, who divided aviation into three categories: service aviation allocated to ground forces, fighter aviation in requisite quantities (preferably a three-to-one numerical superiority) to drive the enemy out of the air, and bomber aviation in the greatest amounts that a country was able to produce "to use against the enemy in bombarding him out of his position and cutting off his communications and destroying his sources of supply."[24] As a result of a visit to Italy, the Bolling commission was evidently favorably impressed with Italian bombing raids against Austria, and the commission recommended that the United States should purchase Caproni biplanes and the license to manufacture Caproni triplanes.[25] The strongest influence on the Bolling commission, however, was undoubtedly Lt Col William Mitchell. While on the War Department General Staff in 1915, Mitchell made a directed survey of US aviation needs. In 1916, Mitchell, now a member of the Signal Corps, Aviation Section, took flight instruction at his own expense and became an aviation enthusiast. Sent to Europe as an observer, Mitchell arrived in Paris four days after the United States entered the war. In May 1917, Mitchell spent several days visiting the headquarters of Maj Gen Hugh

Trenchard, the Royal Air Force (RAF) commander in France. Mitchell learned that Trenchard's policy was to unify all aviation under one commander, to place the minimum number of airplanes necessary for the use of ground troops in action with each army, and to concentrate the bulk of bombardment and pursuit so that he could "hurl a mass of aviation at any one locality needing attack." When Gen John J. Pershing arrived in Paris to take command of the American Expeditionary Forces on 13 June, Mitchell assumed the duty of chief of air service, American Expeditionary Forces. In this position, Mitchell worked intimately with the Bolling commission while it was preparing its recommendations to Washington.[26]

Back in Washington, the Joint Army-Navy Technical Board accepted the Bolling commission recommendations as being essentially sound; and the idea of conducting an air war against the Germans apparently caught the fancy of the American people. However, fanciful statements made by Secretary Baker and other people in authority as to the tremendous numbers of American planes that would deluge the Western Front caused the Germans to redouble their air production effort in what they called their *Amerikaprogramm,* but these statements did very little to mobilize the American productive effort.[27] According to the War Department organization, the Signal Corps, Aviation Section (which was variously redesignated as the Aeronautical Division, the Airplane Division, the Air Division, and the Air Service Division), was responsible for the recruitment and training of aviators and aviation personnel.

Separately responsible to the secretary of war, the Aircraft Production Board, which was enlarged and redesignated as the Aircraft Board by congressional authority in October 1917, was in charge of aircraft requirements and the placing of contracts for aircraft and air materiel production. The Joint Army-Navy Technical Board was responsible for making final decisions as to the types of aircraft to be procured. But, in August 1917, General Pershing demanded and received final authority to determine aircraft types. After this decision, the role of the Joint Army-Navy Technical Board speedily deteriorated.[28] When it was evident early in 1918 that extravagant fighting-plane programs could not be met, the Aircraft Production Board and the Aviation Section of the Signal Corps became the targets of bitter public criticism and congressional investigation. After preliminary War Department steps had been taken during April, President Wilson on 21 May 1918 transferred aviation matters from the Signal Corps to the Division of Military Aeronautics, which was to be headed by Brig Gen William L. Kenly, and to the Bureau of Aircraft Production, headed by John D. Ryan, who continued to be chairman of the Aircraft Production Board.[29]

In Europe much of the same confusion as was occurring in Washington marked the organization of the Air Service, American Expeditionary Forces. Promoted to colonel, Mitchell served as air officer, AEF, until 3 September 1917, when Pershing installed General Kenly as chief of air service, AEF, and made Mitchell air service commander, Zone of Advance. On 27 November, General Foulois, accompanied by a headquarters staff, arrived in Paris with orders to relieve General Kenly, who returned to the United States. Mitchell had respected General Kenly, but he referred to the Foulois staff as "carpetbaggers." General Pershing described the officers who came to France with Foulois as "good men running around in circles." In an effort to restore order, Pershing, on 29 May 1918, finally installed an engineer officer and West Point classmate, Brig Gen Mason M. Patrick, as chief of air service, AEF. At this time, Foulois was appointed chief of air service, First Army, but he instead asked to serve as assistant to Patrick and recommended Mitchell for the combat position, to which Mitchell was assigned on 27 July 1918. Thereafter, new combat air posts were formed as new Army organizations reached France. In October 1918, Col Frank P. Lahm became chief of air service, Second Army. Relieved by Col Thomas D. Milling at First Army in October, Mitchell was promoted to brigadier general and appointed chief of air service, Army Group.[30]

The priority task of the Air Service, AEF, was to provide the trained air units that were assigned to US divisions, corps, and armies as they arrived in France. As an integral combat arm of the ground forces, the air units assigned to the front were commanded, in the full sense of the word, by the commanding generals of the armies, corps, and divisions to which they were assigned. "The Air Service," stated General Patrick, "originates and suggests employment for its units but the final decision is vested in the commanding general of the larger units, of which the Air Service forms a part." In most instances, however, Patrick acknowledged that ground commanders lacked experience with aviation and depended heavily on their Air Service officers.[31] To guide the air effort in the autumn of 1917, Colonel Mitchell drew up what was probably the Air Service's first formal statement of doctrine in a paper entitled "General Principles Underlying the Use of the Air Service in the Zone of Advance A.E.F." In the preface, Mitchell stated that the outcome of war depended primarily on the destruction of an enemy's military forces in the field; no one of the Army's offensive arms alone could bring about complete victory. Hence the mission of the Air Service was to help other arms in their appointed missions.

Mitchell divided aviation into two general classes: tactical aviation, which operated in the immediate vicinity of troops of all arms, and strategical aviation, which acted far in advance of troops of other arms and had an independent mission. According to Mitchell, tactical aviation consisted of observation, pursuit, and tactical bombardment. Observation squadrons performed visual and photographic reconnaissance, adjusted artillery fire, and provided liaison services. Pursuit aviation attained mastery of the air in air battles and, when necessary, created diversions by attacking enemy personnel on the ground. Tactical bombardment operated within 25,000 yards of the front lines. Its objectives were to assist in the destruction of enemy materiel, to undermine the morale of enemy personnel, and to force hostile aircraft to arise and accept combat by attacking enemy airdromes. Mitchell considered that strategical aviation included pursuit, day-bombardment, and night-bombardment squadrons. The radius of actions of strategical aviation units was usually more than 25,000 yards in advance of friendly troops. The object of strategical aviation was "to destroy the means of supply of an enemy army, thereby preventing it from employing all of its means in combat." Such would be accomplished, Mitchell stated, by destroying enemy aircraft, air depots, and defensive air organization, as well as enemy depots, factories, lines of communications, and personnel.[32]

The issuance of Mitchell's "General Principles" apparently coincided both with his assumption of duty as air service commander, Zone of Advance, and with the first arrivals of US Air Service squadrons in France. The 1st Aero Squadron arrived overseas on 3 September 1917, where it was equipped with Salmson aircraft and trained as a corps observation squadron before it was assigned to the front on 8 April 1918. By the Armistice on 11 November 1918, the US Air Service in France would comprise 45 squadrons, including six army observation, 12 corps observation, 20 pursuit, one night-bombardment and six day-bombardment squadrons. Twelve of these squadrons were ultimately equipped with American-built DH-4 aircraft; the other squadrons flew Salmson, Spad, Breguet, or Sopwith Camel planes purchased from the French and British. After training in the inactive Toul sector of the Western Front, US Air Service units were employed in support of the US I Corps at the Marne and Vesel rivers in July and August 1918. The greatest American air action, however, came in support of the US First Army in the Saint-Mihiel and Argonne-Meuse offensives beginning in September 1918. For the Saint-Mihiel offensive, Mitchell had the services of British and French as well as US squadrons; altogether he had the use of 701 pursuit, 323 day-bomber, 91 night-bomber, and 366 observation aircraft — a total of 1,481 planes of which about one-third were American.

The air action in these battles illustrated the value of concentrated air forces, but the employment of aviation continued to be planned in terms of the ground mission. Although Air Service officers spoke of the desirability of attaining aerial supremacy, they considered that this was possible only in certain selected sectors for limited periods of time. The major mission of pursuit aviation was described as being "to keep clear of enemy airplanes an area about 10,000 yards deep in front of the line of battle." This zone was the area in which corps and division observation aircraft flew and, thus, the objective of pursuit aviation was defined as "the destruction of the enemy air service and the protection of our own observation aircraft." The primary object of day-bombing attacks was said to be "the destruction of the enemy's morale, materiel and personnel." In this effort, "the ratio of the effect of lowering the enemy's morale over that of destruction was estimated as about 20 to 1." Bombing and strafing of ground targets proved advisable only when air supremacy was attained, a lesson learned by hard experience. According to Colonel Milling, the US Air Service's day-bombing force sustained about 60 percent losses during the Battle of Saint-Mihiel when it was closely escorted by pursuit aircraft. Being tied to the bombardment planes, the pursuit aircraft always had to fight on the defensive. The solution, which cut losses to 8 percent, was a double offensive wherein the bombardment planes carried out their attacks against ground targets and the pursuit aircraft aimed their attacks against the enemy fighters that always arose to meet the bombardment planes. Even bombardment missions were thought of in terms of the high-priority observation function, since these missions "invariably drew enemy pursuit from the rest of the front, rendering it safe for our corps observation."[33]

In the battles of France the employment of tactical aviation by the Air Service officers was generally in accordance with the plan of the ground battle. At the end of World War I, General Patrick believed that experience had "clearly demonstrated the fact that the work of the observer and observation pilot is the most important and far-reaching which an Air Service operating with an Army is called upon to perform."[34] Colonel Lahm agreed that "the main function of aviation is observation and that all hinges on that Program." And Colonel Milling emphasized that "the Air Service is of value to the military establishment only insofar as it is correlated to the other arms."[35]

Thoughts on Strategic Bombing

In the summer of 1917, the members of the Bolling aeronautical commission had enthusiastically supported a plan whereby US strategical bombers and fighters would be employed against Germany. When the Bolling commission broke up on 15 August 1917, Bolling was promoted to the rank of colonel and given the title of assistant chief of air service, line of communication. Maj Edgar S. Gorrell, a young aeronautical engineer who had come to France with Bolling, was detailed in charge of the Air Service, Technical Section, in Paris. Gorrell was in charge of initiating purchases of air materiel in Europe. His studies led him to believe that the United States should purchase or build a sufficiently large number of night bombers to carry out a systematic bombardment of Germany. Gorrell believed that a force of from 3,000 to 6,000 bombers would be adequate for this purpose. What the influence of Caproni had been on the original Bolling commission report may only be speculative, but in October 1917 both Bolling and Gorrell were in active correspondence with the Italian aircraft manufacturer. Sometime during October, Caproni collaborated with his friend Capt Giulio Douhet in the preparation of a "Memorandum on the 'Air War' for the US Air Service," which urged that mass attacks made at night by long-range Allied bombers against industrial targets deep within Germany and Austria definitely could overwhelm the enemy by substantially reducing his war production at the same time that Allied production was increasing. That same month, Caproni gave Gorrell a little book signed by Nino Salveneschi and entitled *Let Us Kill the War; Let Us Aim at the Heart of the Enemy*. Evidently written by a journalist to represent Caproni's views, this small, English-text book was a further exposition of the concept of strategic bombardment. In November 1917 Bolling personally advised Howard Coffin, the chairman of the Aircraft Production Board in Washington, that the United States ought to give a higher priority to the production and procurement of bomber aircraft than to observation and fighter aircraft.[36]

When General Foulois arrived in Paris in November 1917, he divided the Air Service, Zone of Advance, into Tactical Aviation and Strategical Aviation and placed Colonel Gorrell in charge of the latter organization, which was to be a planning staff pending the arrival of bombardment squadrons. For staff support, Gorrell obtained Majors Harold Fowler and Millard F. Harmon and borrowed Wing Comdr Spencer Gray, a British Royal Navy Air Service officer. These men drew up a proposal for a bombing campaign, which they submitted to Foulois on 28 November 1917. This paper pointed out that the Germans were reported to be building great numbers of large Gotha bombers in preparation for a bombing campaign. The Gorrell plan, therefore, stated that it was "of paramount importance that we adopt at once a bombing project ... at the quickest possible moment, in order that we may not only wreck Germany's manufacturing centers but wreck them more completely than she will wreck ours next year." The plan proposed that the bombing attacks would be mounted by day and night from airfields in the Toul-Verdun area against industrial plants around Düsseldorf, Cologne, Mannheim, and in the Saar Valley. Up to 100 squadrons should be directed against each of these targets in turn, the idea being to keep a given target under a sustained bombardment up to five hours at a time. Such an assault would overwhelm target defenses, wreck manufacturing works, and shatter the morale of workmen.[37]

In Great Britain popular dissatisfaction with the ability of the the air defenses to deal with Zeppelin and Gotha attacks against London forced a reorganization of aviation affairs. On the advice of a board headed by Lt Gen Jan Christian Smuts (with strong support from Winston Churchill), the British government set up a separate Air Ministry in December 1917. In the culmination of this reform in April 1918, the Royal Flying Corps and the Royal Naval Service were recombined into the Royal Air Force, but, as a more immediate action, General Trenchard was directed to concentrate a bomber force at Nancy and begin attacks against German industrial centers. Since the British were already operating from Nancy, the US Air Service agreed with Trenchard's suggestion in December 1917 that American bomber squadrons arriving in France initially operate with British units. Here matters stood on 5 February 1918 when Colonel Gorrell was transferred to the AEF General Staff. On 26 March Colonel Bolling was killed by German soldiers while reconnoitering the ground front.[38]

Although Gorrell's successor in Strategical Aviation busied himself making plans for the eventual reception of US bombardment squadrons, the establishment of the British Independent Air Force at Nancy under command of General Trenchard on 5 June 1918 forced a reconsideration of American planning. Since the British Independent Air Force received its orders from the Air Ministry rather than from the Allied commander in chief Marshal Ferdinand Foch, the American Expeditionary Forces ruled that US bomber squadrons could not operate integrally with it. General Pershing's chief of staff also notified General Patrick that all Air Service officers "must be warned against any idea of independence and ... that every force must be closely coalescent with those of the remainder of the Air Service and with those of the Grand Army." Believing that the use of the term *strategical aviation* had led persons to think that this activity was independent, General Patrick directed in June 1918 that the activity would be known as the General Headquarters Air Service Reserve.[39] Marshal Foch believed that the enemy's army was the enemy's strength; he maintained that bombers should attack the enemy's economy only as a secondary function. The military representatives of the Allied Supreme War Council on 3 August 1918 accordingly established an Inter-Allied Bombing Force that was to operate against the German economy only after requirements of the armies in the field had been met or in lulls between ground battles.[40]

Although the Allies moved toward acceptance of strategic bombing, the amount of effort that could be devoted to attacks against Germany's economy was not large. From 6 June 1918 to the Armistice, the British Independent Air Force consisted of only nine squadrons, some of which were equipped with planes that had been obsolete for several years. In these months, the Independent Air Force dropped some 550 tons of bombs on about 50 targets. Trenchard recognized that his effort was spread very thinly, but his major hope was to disrupt enemy morale.[41] Had the war continued, the US Air Service would have joined the strategic bombing effort. Back in the United States, however, indecision as to which bombers would be produced and then slowness in production denied the Air Service a bomber force. In line with the original Bolling recommendations, the United States initially undertook to manufacture Caproni bombers; it also decided to produce British-designed Handley-Page bombers. Since it would be difficult to ship the bombers across the ocean, Handley-Page parts would be manufactured in the United States and the planes would be assembled in Great Britain. On 28 June 1918 an Air Service, Night Bombardment Section, was opened in England to superintend the equipment and training of a night-bomber force, but none of the expected Handley-Page aircraft became available before the Armistice. A single US night-bomber squadron, equipped with improvised DH-4B and old Farman FE-2B aircraft, was committed to the front on 9 November 1918. Looking backward at the failure of the strategical aviation program, Colonel Gorrell observed that "entirely too much optimism was felt for the American Production Program" and that "the Air Service failed to secure the approval of the General Staff of its plans for the employment of this aviation and consequently suffered from the fact that its plans for the use of the Strategical Air Service were not synchronized properly . . . with the ideas of GHQ."[42]

America's Wartime Aviation Accomplishments

In view of the divided War Department authority for training and operations and for aircraft production, it was not remarkable that US air unit programs were subject to frequent revision during the course of World War I. In August 1917 the Aviation Section secured approval for a program including 345 combat squadrons, of which 263 were intended for use in Europe by June 1918. Because of lagging aircraft production early in 1918, however, the War Department approved a program of 120 combat squadrons to be at the Western Front by January 1919. In August 1918 the War Department and General Pershing finally agreed on a program calling for 202 squadrons to be at the front by July 1919. This force would have included 60 pursuit, 49 corps observation, 52 army observation, 14 day-bombing, and 27 night-bombing squadrons, plus 133 balloon observation companies. Since aircraft production was beginning to achieve success late in 1918, it appeared probable that this program objective could have been met had the war continued.[43] When hostilities ended on 11 November 1918, however, just 45 American air squadrons—with 740 airplanes, 767 pilots, 481 observers, and 23 aerial gunners—were actually assigned to the Air Service, AEF. On the Marne, at Saint-Mihiel, and in the Argonne, US pilots shot down 781 enemy aircraft and destroyed 73 enemy observation balloons. US losses in air battles included 289 airplanes and 48 balloons brought down by the enemy. The US squadrons participated in 150 bombing raids, during which they dropped more than 275,000 pounds of explosives.[44] During the war the United States manufactured 11,760 airplanes, and, as of 11 November 1918, the Air Service, AEF, had received 6,284 planes—4,791 from the French, 261 from the British, 19 from the Italians, and 1,213 from the United States.[45]

Viewed in themselves, the statistics of US Air Service activities in World War I were somewhat less than impressive. According to his memoirs, Gen William Mitchell was not entirely happy that the Armistice had come before aviation had proven itself. Mitchell would recall that by the spring of 1919 he had expected to see great bombardment attacks against Germany's economy and even a paratroop employment of the 1st Infantry Division behind German lines. "I was sure that if the war lasted," Mitchell recollected, "air power would decide it."[46]

The Mitchell Era: From Air Service to Air Corps

"It is important for the winning of the war," stated the report of Field Marshal Jan Christian Smuts's committee on air organization and home defense to the British prime minister on 17 August 1917, "that we should not only secure air predominance, but secure it on a very large scale; and having secured it in this war we should make every effort and sacrifice to maintain it for the future. Air supremacy may in the long run become as important a factor in the defense of the Empire as sea supremacy."[47] In the United Kingdom, the finding of the Smuts committee that the Royal Flying Corps and the Royal Navy Air Service had been bitterly struggling over limited supplies of planes, engines, and personnel available led to the establishment of the Air Ministry in December 1917 and the Royal Air Force in April 1918. Word of the British action reached the United States without delay and caused a renewed congressional and popular demand for a US Air Service altogether separate from the War and Navy departments.

Within the War Department, it was evident that the separation of responsibilities between the Division of Military Aeronautics and Bureau of Aircraft Production presented an inherent organizational defect. In a memorandum written on 6 June 1918, Col Henry H. "Hap" Arnold, assistant director of the Division of Military Aeronautics, stated that the division must control the design of the equipment with which it was to operate. Arnold did not care who handled supply, but he argued that the Division of Military Aeronautics could not properly be held accountable for operational and military efficiency as long as the Bureau of Aircraft Production was responsible for the quality, design, and production of military aircraft. To alleviate some of the criticism of military aeronautics organization, Secretary Baker on 28 August 1918 appointed John D. Ryan as second assistant secretary of war and director of air service. Since Ryan continued to head the Bureau of Aircraft Production, all Army aviation affairs were in theory under one civilian head. This reorganization, however, had hardly taken effect before the Armistice brought Ryan's resignation, leaving all the offices he had held vacant. In January 1919 Maj Gen Charles T. Menoher, a nonflying officer who had commanded the 42d (Rainbow) Division and the VI Army Corps in France, was appointed director of air service. On 19 March 1919 President Woodrow Wilson signed an executive order that dissolved the old Aircraft Production Board and placed the Bureau of Aircraft Production immediately under the director of air service. This executive action finally united all Army aviation functions in the Air Service, but President Wilson had acted under wartime reorganizational authority and the final status of the Air Service would have to be enacted into law by Congress.[48]

Desiring that the lessons of World War I should be recorded promptly by the leaders who had participated in field operations, General Pershing on 19 April 1919 convened a superior board in Paris under the presidency of Maj Gen Joseph T. Dickman to review the findings of boards of senior officers to be appointed from each branch of the American Expeditionary Forces, including the Air Service. The report of the Air Service Board headed by General Foulois was generally conservative and recommended that most of the Air Service should be assigned to armies, corps, and divisions. The report, nevertheless, proposed that a separate general headquarters (GHQ) reserve be created. This air reserve would be no smaller than an aerial division, comprised of a bombing brigade (a night-bombing wing and a day-bombing wing) and a pursuit brigade (two day wings) plus a 10-percent reserve of all units assigned to armies, corps, and divisions. But General Patrick took exception with the Foulois board's insisting that the prime function of the Air Service was to obtain and transmit information, that the prime function of pursuit was to prevent enemy observation and protect friendly observation planes, and that aircraft intended for bombing distant objectives or industrial centers were a "luxury." "It follows," Patrick wrote, "that when it is possible to place such a bombing force in the field, its size should be limited only by the nation's ability to provide it and by the number and importance of the enemy activities which are to be attacked."[49]

The Dickman board's report noted that the Air Service, AEF, had developed along four general lines: observation, distant reconnaissance and bombing operations, aerial combat, and combat against ground troops. The board stated that air combat against ground troops was not well developed and predicted that this type of aerial work could be made more effective and decisive than distant bombing operations. The Dickman board concluded,

> Nothing so far brought out in the war, shows that aerial activities can be carried on independently of ground troops, to such an extent as to materially affect the conduct of the war as a whole. It is possible, perhaps, that future wars may develop aerial forces of far greater extent than those provided in this war. It is safe to assume that Air Forces will not be developed for war purposes to such an extent as to largely supplant ground and water forces, until such a proportion of the people become airfaring people as are now known as seafaring people.

The board added that "so long as present conditions prevail . . . aviation must continue to be one of the auxiliaries of the principal arm, the Infantry."[50]

Other reports, manuals, and histories prepared at the Headquarters Air Service, AEF, in Paris and elsewhere in Europe during the immediate posthostilities period reflected the overriding importance of observation in the Air Service mission. Written in March 1919, but not published until later, General Patrick's *Final Report of the Chief of Air Service, AEF* stated that to regard air forces as separate and distinct from other component parts of the Army would be "to sacrifice the cohesion and unity of effort which alone distinguishes an army from a mob."[51] Two tentative manuals prepared under the direction of Colonel Gorrell — entitled "Notes on the Employment of the Air Service from the General Staff Viewpoints" (February 1919) and "Tentative Manual for the Employment of Air Service" (April 1919) — represented the belief "that in the future, as in the past, the final decision in war must be made by men on the ground, willing to come hand-to-hand with the enemy. When the Infantry loses the Army loses. It is therefore the role of the Air Service, as well as that of the other arms, to aid the chief combatant, the Infantry."[52] The latter manual also noted that "the greatest value of the Air Service to date has been in gathering information of the enemy and of our own troops." As a final basic consideration relative to air attack, the manual observed that "the morale effect on ground troops is out of all proportion to the material destruction wrought."[53] The manual of operations for Air Service units which General Mitchell issued at Koblenz as Air Service commander, US Third Army, on 23 December 1918 portrayed aviation as a supporting arm for the infantry rather than as a decisive force.[54]

Meanwhile back in Washington during 1919 and 1920, eight separate bills proposing the creation of a separate military aviation establishment were introduced in the US Congress. The leading measures were the New and Curry bills, each of which sought to create an executive department of aeronautics.[55] On 8 August 1919, the secretary of war appointed a board of general officers headed by General Menoher to report on these bills. After study, the Menoher board reported general agreement on several fundamental considerations: aeronautics would play an increasingly important role in a future war in proportion to the capacity of a nation to produce aircraft and train personnel for aircraft maintenance and operation; no nation could afford to maintain military air fleets required for war in time of peace; the nation that first mobilized a superior air fleet after a war began would have an undoubted advantage; and a nation desirably should have a full development of commercial aviation in order to provide military potential in time of war. The board stated that a single government agency ought to be established for research and development and for procurement of military, naval, and commercial aircraft. It recommended that the government also should develop and operate air route facilities and that it might provide direct subsidies to airline companies but that it should not undertake the production of aircraft. Whether or not a single separate governmental agency for research and development, procurement, and subsidization of the civil air fleet could be established, however, would depend on the magnitude of federal expenditures that Congress would be willing to vote for national aeronautics.[56]

The Menoher board revealed an understanding of the nation's requirement for a progressive development of aviation potential, but it could see no need for a separate Army-Navy aeronautical service. It stated: "An air force acting independently cannot win a war against a civilized nation, nor by itself, accomplish a decision against forces on the ground." On the other hand, military forces could not be efficiently trained nor could they operate effectively without air force support. With respect to an army, an air force was an essential combat branch, and it had to be an integral part of an army command "not only during battle but also during its entire period of its doctrinal training." The Menoher panel stated that the outstanding defect of the Air Service, AEF, had been its lack of cooperative training with the Army, and it quoted extensively from the Dickman board's findings to substantiate the air mission as being one of support for ground operations. The creation of the Royal Air Force in Great Britain was said to have been motivated "for political rather than military reasons." In regard to the exact organization of the air component of the Army, the Menoher board recommended that the military air force was an essential combat branch and ought to be placed on an equal footing with the infantry, cavalry, and artillery. "Whatever may be the decision as to a separate Aeronautical Department," the board concluded, "the military air force must remain under the complete control of the Army and form an integral part thereof both in peace and war."[57]

In the late spring of 1919 the case for a separate air force drew support from the report of a mission headed by Assistant Secretary of War Benedict Crowell. Including American industrialists as well as Army and Navy officers, the Crowell mission visited France, Italy, and England, and conferred with civil and military leaders. The report noted a general agreement in Europe that "any future war will inevitably open with great aerial activity far in advance of contact either upon land or sea, and that victory cannot but incline to that belligerent able to first achieve and later maintain its supremacy in the air." Italy and France were said to realize the military-naval and civil-commercial aspects of aircraft, and Great Britain was reported "to consider the dominance of the air as at least of equal importance with that of the seas, and is frankly and avowedly planning a definite policy of aerial development to that end." Presented to the secretary of war on 19 July 1919, the Crowell mission report recommended the establishment of a single department of air that would be coequal to the departments of War, Navy, and Commerce, and would have subdepartments including civil aeronautics, military aeronautics, naval aeronautics, and supply and research. Apparently because the Crowell report did not follow accepted viewpoints, Secretary Baker allegedly made efforts to suppress it. The general contents of the report were soon known to aviation enthusiasts; but Secretary Baker did not release it until December 1919, when he made the observation that the mission had "gone too far in suggesting a single centralized Air Service." Military pilots, Baker stated, had to be trained "to fight singly or in formation, and to operate in coordination with other branches of the military service."[58]

Mitchell's Early Thinking on Air Power

In his combat command in Europe, Gen Billy Mitchell had become America's hero and "prince of the air." While he would later rewrite and add explanatory notes to his "diary of war-time experiences" that would indicate his early support for the concept of strategic bombardment, Mitchell's wartime activities and writings indicated that he cooperated with the desires of his Army superiors with little real question.[59] In January 1919, however, Mitchell was ordered to return to the United States to become director of military aeronautics. He may well have recognized that he was returning to the United States at a time when the nation lacked an air policy. Instead of looking backward at World War I, he began to look ahead to logical projections of air power capabilities. One thing was clear, the Air Service needed a definite mission of a distinctive nature. In 1915, when he had been assigned to the War Department General Staff, Mitchell had prepared a survey of America's aviation needs in which he had theorized that Army aviation would be a valuable "second line of defense" if the Navy's "first line of defense" should fail to stop an invasion of the United States. He had made the point that aviation attached to harbor and coastal defenses would be useful both for reconnaissance and for preventing similar enemy activity. Aircraft could destroy an invader's airplanes, attack his submarines, and disrupt the operations of his minelayers.[60] Something of these earlier thoughts may have been in Mitchell's mind while he was returning to the United States; a naval officer with him aboard the westbound *Aquitania* duly reported that Mitchell was "fully prepared, with evidence, plans, data, propaganda, posters and articles, to break things wide open" for air power.[61]

When Mitchell assumed office as director of military aeronautics on 6 March 1919, the duties of this position had already been superseded in large measure by the appointment of General Menoher as director of air service. Menoher, however, assigned Mitchell as the chief of the Air Service's Training and Operations Group, the headquarters agency charged with the preparation of tactical manuals and war plans.[62] In the Training and Operations Group, Mitchell gathered a team of veteran airmen, including Colonel Milling and Lt Cols William C. Sherman, Leslie MacDill, and Lewis H. Brereton. Obviously stimulating each other's thinking, these men developed many of the ideas that eventually would be recognized as Air Force doctrine. The activities of the Training and Operations Group were so clearly contrary to the official positions of the War Department and of General Menoher that Lt Col Oscar Westover, who was Menoher's executive officer, recommended on 5 May 1919 that Menoher ought either to get a statement of loyalty from Mitchell or to relieve all of the division heads of the Training and Operations Group.[63]

As Mitchell and his associates assessed the situation confronting the Air Service, they recognized, first of all, that normalcy was wrecking the nation's armed forces and particularly its air forces. In the rapid demobilization, the number of Air Service officers dropped from 20,000 to a little more than a nucleus of 200 regular officers in 1919, and these regulars were only on detail from other branches of the Army. While Mitchell maintained his rank by occupying a statutory assignment, most Air Service officers returned to their regular ranks, mostly in company grades, when they reached the United States. General Foulois would later recall the sheer shock that he felt when he walked down the gangplank in New York as a wartime brigadier general and became a captain when he stepped on the dock; within a few months, however, he was promoted to major.[64] Even more important was the affect of the return to peace on the development of the airplane. "The airplane," Sherman wrote,

> is in its infancy. Many of its features today show the crudity characteristic of all early efforts. But as we compare the airplane of 1918 with that of 1914, it is apparent that progress during that period was unbelievably rapid. This was due, of course, to the urgent demand of war. Now the acceleration of war has been lost; nor does there appear to be any great stimulus to advancement in commercial demand. We may expect, therefore, that progress will be materially slowed down, either until development makes the airplane widely useful to commerce, or until we encounter again the insistent demand of war.[65]

In their assessment of the impact of the airplane on the art of war, the Mitchell group drew an important distinction between the effect of air action on land warfare and sea warfare. "On land," Sherman reasoned, "battle is determined by morale: The aim therefore is to destroy morale by methods that are based on unchanging human nature." Naval warfare, on the other hand, was a product of industrial and inventive genius and firepower. Aircraft, together with submarines, had the ability to destroy naval vessels, and it was obvious that the airplane had altered the means by which sea power was to be attained.[66] At a meeting of the Navy's General Board on 3 April 1919, Mitchell urged that aircraft could successfully attack naval warships, stated that the aerial defense of the nation's coasts should be assigned to land-based aircraft, and urged that the United States should organize a ministry of defense, combining army, navy, and air forces under one direction.[67] Mitchell was not again invited to appear before the Navy's General Board, but he presented a steady flow of aviation ideas to the congressional committees that sat almost continuously during 1919. He advocated a single department of aviation with military, naval, and civil divisions. "The principal mission of aviation is fighting hostile aviation," he said, "and it does not make any difference where it is found, whether over the water or over the land, the mission of aviation is to destroy that force." "We believe if we are allowed to expand," he continued, "we can put the navy under the water in a comparatively few years as an offensive force against us. We believe we can have a great effect on land operations, although not to the same extent that we can against a navy, because an army can hide itself too well."[68] "If we give up the air to a foreign power," Mitchell testified on 5 December 1919, "it has been proved during the war that they can cause incalculable damage with their air service alone by hitting our industrial and other centers of organization for war, and in all probability they could bring about a decision by their air service alone." Mitchell also emphasized a need for unity of air command:

> The principal mission . . . of aviation . . . is the destruction of the hostile aviation, in the same way that the principal mission of the navy is the destruction of the hostile navy, or the principal mission of an army is destruction of the hostile army. Therefore, in order to unite and bring your greatest effect to bear in any one place it is necessary to unite all the elements of your aviation at the place where the decision is called for, no matter whether it is war on the sea or war on land.[69]

In the same months that Mitchell was carrying on the fight for a separate department of aviation, he and other officers were also defining a role for an expanded Air Service within the Army. Major Foulois, who was assigned to the director of air service's office, bitterly attacked the shortsighted policies of Army General Staff officers in testimony before a congressional committee on 16 October 1919. These officers, Foulois said, were interested only in a "defensive use" of aircraft and had neglected "the fighting side of aircraft." Although Foulois presented an elaborate justification of the materiel and logistical advantages to be obtained from a Department of Aeronautics and although he was far more critical of the General Staff than was Mitchell at this early date, he was somewhat less positive about the relationship of aeronautics to the national defense. "The use of aircraft during the recent war," he said, "has fully demonstrated the fact that in future wars aircraft will play a part second only to the infantry." He added: "In time of war there is no question but that, in order to get the maximum efficiency of all elements of a military command, air service units as well as any other units, must come under the command of the supreme military commander in the field."[70]

In a paper entitled "Tactical Application of Military Aeronautics," apparently prepared in January 1920, Mitchell defined the principal mission and the secondary employment of aeronautics. "The principal mission of Aeronautics," he stated, "is to destroy the aeronautical force of the enemy, and, after this, to attack his formations, both tactical and strategical, on the ground or on the water. The secondary employment of Aeronautics pertains to their use as an auxiliary to troops on the ground for enhancing their effect against the hostile troops." In this paper, Mitchell divided combat aviation into four branches (which would be classic for many years): pursuit, bombardment, attack, and observation aviation. Pursuit aviation was "designed to take and hold the offensive in the air against all hostile aircraft" and it was to be the branch with which "air supremacy is sought and obtained." Bombardment aviation was "organized for the purpose of attacking enemy concentration points of all sorts at a distance from their front lines. Probably its greatest value is in hitting an enemy's great nerve centers at the very beginning of the war so as to paralyze them to the greatest extent possible." Attack aviation was a specialized branch that had only begun coming into being when the war ended in Europe. Attack planes would be heavily armed and armored "flying tanks" that would prosecute low-level attacks against hostile troops, tanks, artillery, motor vehicles, railway trains, or anything of that sort. Observation aviation was the branch "concerned more with the troops on the ground than any other." In the conduct of combat air operations, Mitchell envisioned that the superior command would outline the broad plan of operation and that the Air Service commander would prepare detailed air plans in conjunction with the Army G-3 operations and G-2 information branches. When approved by the superior commander, these plans would become orders.[71]

Aviation Is Integrated into Army and Navy

Despite the ardent pleadings of aviation enthusiasts, the War and Navy departments acted in unison during 1919 and 1920 to integrate aeronautics into the existing establishment. One of Mitchell's most telling arguments in favor of a separate air force had to do with its potential effectiveness for the coastal defenses of the United States. Allegedly to meet this line of argumentation, Secretary Baker in July 1919 sponsored a reconstitution of the Joint Army and Navy Board, which had been organized in 1903 but had ceased to function. Baker expressed confidence that the Joint Board would produce cooperation in developing the air services of the Army and Navy.[72] Late in December 1919 the Joint Board recommended a statement of Army-Navy functions in war that was immediately accepted by the secretaries of war and Navy. The policy statement directed that Army aircraft would operate from bases on shore as an arm of the mobile army; against enemy aircraft in defense of all shore establishments; or alone, in cooperation with other arms of the Army, or with the Navy against enemy vessels engaged in attacks on the coast, such as bombardment of the coast, operations preparatory to or during the landing of troops, and operations such as laying mines or attacks on shipping in the vicinity of defended ports. Navy aircraft would operate from mobile floating bases or from naval air stations on shore as an arm of the fleet; for overseas scouting; against enemy shore establishments when such operations were conducted in cooperation with other types of naval forces or when their mission was primarily naval; to protect coastal sea communications by reconnaissance and patrol of coastal sea areas, to defend convoy operations, and to attack enemy submarines, aircraft, or surface vessels through the sea area; and alone or in cooperation with other arms of the Navy or with the Army against enemy vessels engaged in attacks on the coast. Marine aircraft would perform the functions normally assigned to Army aircraft when the operations were in connection with an advance base in which operations of the Army were not represented. The name of the old Joint Army and Navy Board on Aeronautics was changed to the Aeronautical Board, and it was agreed that to prevent duplication and secure coordination of effort for new projects for the construction of aircraft, experimental stations, coastal air stations, and stations to be used jointly by the Army and Navy would be submitted to the Aeronautical Board for study and recommendations.[73]

When General Pershing returned from Europe in the autumn of 1919, Air Service partisans had great hope that he might support their stand for a separate aviation department. Pershing had organized the Air Service, AEF, as a separate component, and in an appearance before a joint meeting of the Senate and House Committees on Military Affairs he indicated a belief that cooperation and coordination between the different departments of the government that used airships would be essential to the development of aviation. In a letter to General Menoher on 12 January 1920, however, Pershing explained that his testimony had been misunderstood. He unequivocally asserted: "An air force, acting independently, can of its own account neither win a war at the present time nor, so far as we can tell, at any time in the future. An air force by itself cannot obtain a decision against forces on the ground." He stressed that a military air force was an essential combat branch and should form an integral part of the Army not only during battle but during the entire period in which troops received doctrinal training. He hoped that the Air Service would be established as a separate arm of the Army, coordinate in status with the Infantry, Cavalry, and Artillery.[74]

Despite indications of a considerable sentiment among its members for a separate department of aeronautics, Congress finally voted to preserve the status of organization already existing as a result of wartime changes. As a part of the Army Reorganization Act of 1920, which became law on 4 June 1920, the Air Service was made a part of the combat line of the Army and no changes were made in its existing relations with the War Department General Staff.[75] Still far from beaten by the course events were taking, General Mitchell urged the House Committee on Military Affairs to add a clause to the Army appropriation bill for fiscal year 1921 to provide that the Army Air Service should control all aerial operations from land bases and that the Navy should control all aerial operations attached to a fleet. This clause was opposed by the secretaries of war and Navy, but, as approved on 5 June 1920, the Army Appropriation Act provided: "That hereafter the Army Air Service shall control all aerial operations from land bases, and Naval Aviation shall have control of all aerial operations attached to a fleet, including shore stations whose maintenance is necessary for operation connected with the fleet, for construction and experimentation and for the training of personnel."[76]

Reportedly under pressure from the War Department General Staff to bring Mitchell into line, General Menoher made a number of changes within the Office of the Chief of Air Service following its legal establishment on 4 June 1920. Since the position of director of military aeronautics was abolished, Menoher named Mitchell as assistant chief of the Air Service and gave him no specific duties in the new position other than to advise upon Air Service matters.[77] Mitchell was also relieved as chief of the Training and Operations Group. Majors Milling and Sherman, having lost their wartime ranks, were transferred to the new Air Service Field Officers School, which the War Department had authorized at Langley Field, Virginia, on 25 March 1920. The Training and Operations Group continued to be responsible for prescribing tactical methods and enunciating tactical doctrine. But, hampered by a serious loss of personnel, the group tended to retrogress in its doctrinal thinking. Prepared by the old regime and printed in April 1920, the Air Service's *Aerial Bombardment Manual* looked to the future. "Bombardment from occupying a practically nonexistent and unimportant part in the war," it asserted, "has become a very important branch of the Air Service, and it is believed by many that if carried out in sufficient numbers it will win a war." But no such forward-looking thoughts appeared in the next edition of this same manual, which was issued in September 1920 after the reassignments and cutbacks of personnel. This latter edition of *Aerial Bombardment* was, in fact, little more than a reprint of the manual that had been prepared by the Air Service, AEF.[78]

Since he now lacked formal duties in the Air Service, Mitchell spent much of his time presenting the argument for a separate aeronautical department to the public and continuing the aircraft versus naval vessels controversy.[79] During the winter of 1920-21 he wrote *Our Air Force*, which summarized his views on aviation. He predicted that future wars would include the destruction of entire cities by airborne gas attacks. "As a prelude to any engagement of military or naval forces," he predicted, "a contest must take place for control of the air. The first battles of any future war will be air battles. The nation winning them is practically certain to win the whole war, because the victorious air service will be able to operate and increase without hindrances." He called for the development of a metal-skin aircraft, which would replace fabric-covered planes, and stated that the United States should possess about 5,000 modern airplanes, with twice that number in reserve. Fifteen hundred of the active aircraft should be assigned to the Army and Navy for observation and the remaining 3,500 planes should be held in an air striking force that would be about 60 percent pursuit, 20 percent bombardment, and 20 percent attack planes. He asserted that the Navy should possess 20 aircraft carriers, but no battleships, cruisers, or similar warships. Reductions in the Navy's surface fleet would sustain the added cost of aeronautical development.[80]

Seeking to secure some evidence with which to refute Mitchell's charges that capital ships were vulnerable to air attack, the Navy secretly exploded a 900-pound bomb on the deck of the obsolete battleship *Indiana* in October 1920. It subsequently announced that the tests demonstrated that aircraft could not sink a battleship, but publication of photographs of the battered vessel led Mitchell to comment that "neither coast defense guns nor a defending fleet of battleships need fire a gun in repelling the attack of a foreign fleet if we have a properly organized Air Force."[81] In testifying on the Army appropriation bill in January 1921, Mitchell pointedly challenged the Navy to permit a live bombing test. "Aviation," he said, "must be ready when the war starts, because that is when aviation will be called on.

That is when it will have its greatest effect, and we want to keep the organizations we have in service equipped with modern equipment and have enough in storage to last for two or three months of an ordinary war." As for the role of an air force in a land war, Mitchell saw its chief employment against hostile lines of communication. "I want it to be distinctly understood," he said, "that I do not consider that the air force is to be considered as in any sense supplanting the Army. You have always got to come to man power as the ultimate thing, but we do believe that the air force will control all the communications, and that it will have a very great effect on the land troops, and a decisive one against a navy."[82]

Spurred on by congressional demands, the Navy agreed to stage aerial-bombing tests against captured German warships off the Atlantic coast during the summer of 1921. Based at Langley Field, the 1st Provisional Air Brigade—with Mitchell in command and Milling as chief of staff—practiced bombing for several weeks, and on 18 and 21 July the brigade successfully attacked and sank the cruiser *Frankfort* and the battleship *Ostfriesland*.[83] In his report to General Menoher (which was leaked to the press when Menoher would not make it public), Mitchell claimed that "the problem of the destruction of seacraft by Air Forces had been solved and is finished." He concluded his statement by calling for the organization of a department of national defense, with a staff common to all services and with subsecretaries of army, navy, and air forces; only with such an organization would the United States be able to make correct decisions in choosing weapons for the future defense of the nation.[84] As early as June 1921, Menoher had asked that Mitchell be transferred away from Washington; and following the illicit publication of the bombing report, Menoher told Secretary of War John W. Weeks that either he or Mitchell had to go.

Allegedly because he had failed "to handle and discipline" Mitchell, Menoher was relieved as chief of the Air Service. Selected by Secretary Weeks because of his reputation for having straightened out "a tangled mess" in the Air Service, AEF, General Patrick was appointed chief of the Air Service and undertook the duty on 5 October 1921.[85] As a nonflyer, Patrick told Mitchell that he would consult him on major decisions including general Air Service doctrine and policies, but that he would be the chief in fact as well as in name and would make all final decisions. Patrick said that Mitchell talked of resignation from the Army, but that on a little reflection he saw fit to continue as assistant chief of the Air Service.[86]

In the winter of 1921-22, allegedly to get him off the scene while the delicate negotiations attending the Washington conference of the limitation of naval armaments were in progress, Patrick sent Mitchell, accompanied by Lt Clayton Bissell and aeronautical engineer Alfred Verville, on an inspection trip to France, Italy, Germany, Holland, and England. In each of these countries, Mitchell attempted to determine "the national policy of the country and the way in which it was applied from an aeronautical standpoint." Mitchell professed to have found a great emphasis upon aviation: "It is well known by all European nations," he reported, "that an air force can be ready to strike at least two weeks before any armies join battle. . . . If an air force is sufficiently well organized, equipped, and instructed, these armies probably never will come into contact as the air force will settle the matter itself." Applying what he had observed in Europe to the strategic problem of the United States—namely, "the ability to attack at a distance and the ability to attack possible debarkations, other troops on the ground, and to cover landings"—Mitchell advocated a unity of air command. The air force commander not only should control the air force and army observation planes (in the beginning of hostilities before ground combat was joined), but also all antiaircraft weapons, searchlights, and barrage balloons. Since aviation's primary mission was to destroy hostile air forces, Mitchell urged that bombardment wings should be formed out of two groups of high-speed, diving-type pursuit and one group of high-level bombardment aircraft. Attack wings should comprise two groups of fast-climbing, maneuverable pursuit and one group of armored attack aircraft. Mitchell specifically recommended that the minimum air force for the United States should be one brigade of 600 planes behind the East Coast, one division of 1,200 planes on the Pacific Coast. This force should be roughly one-fifth active air force and four-fifths reserve, which could be mobilized in two days. Mitchell ended his report by pointing out:

> The organization along our coasts is so complicated between the corps area, the coast artillery, the naval districts, the coast guard, the air forces, the meteorological service which is under the Department of Agriculture, and the radio service which is partly under the navy and partly under the army that we would be terribly handicapped and our hands almost tied in case we were attacked by a first-class power.[87]

In commenting upon his visit to Europe, Mitchell reported that he had met "more men of exceptional ability in Italy than . . . in any other country." Ten years would pass before Mitchell would mention that he had had "frequent conversations: with the Italian air strategist Giulio Douhet, whose career paralleled Mitchell's own in many ways. Douhet had begun to write about military aviation in 1909; he had been imprisoned for a year in 1916–17 for having criticized Italy's wartime military policy; the court-martial had been expunged in 1920. Promoted to general officer rank in 1921, Douhet completed his first serious treatise on military aviation—*Il Dominio dell' Aria* [the command of the air]—in October 1921. In this essay on the art of aerial warfare, Douhet demonstrated that two new instruments of war—the aerial arm and poison gases—had been introduced in World War I. For the future, he predicted: "Not only explosives, but also chemical and bacteriological poisons can be carried by the aerial arm to any point of the enemy's territory, scattering death and destruction over the entire country of the foe." Douhet argued that ground warfare would be progressively stalemated by improvements in guns but that aircraft were instruments of incomparable potentialities against which no effective defense except for the establishment of command of the air could be foreseen. "To prevent the enemy from harming us by means of his air forces," he wrote, "there is no other practical method than to destroy his air forces. . . . Command of the air means to be in a position to prevent the enemy from flying, while at the same time retaining this right for one's self."

Believing that "it is easier to destroy the potentiality of the enemy in the air by destroying the nests and eggs of the flyers rather than to seek the flyers in the air for the purpose of bringing them down," Douhet thought that an independent air force should be an air fleet of bombers and combat planes—the latter to be a bomber-type plane that would be equipped with many guns and used to convoy bombers and fight off hostile pursuit planes. Following establishment of command of the air, the independent air force would be able to destroy an enemy nation by attacking transportation lines and population centers. Conversely, if two opposing air fleets began operations simultaneously and command of the air could not be established, Douhet reasoned that it would be necessary "to resign one's self to suffer offensives which the enemy is capable of inflicting upon us, so that all the means we possess may be utilized for the purpose of inflicting on the enemy more powerful offensives."[88]

In his writings, Mitchell never attributed any special influence on his thought to Douhet—US air officers would not publicly cite Douhet for several years.[89] Even though Douhet's works would not be generally available in a published translation until 1942, a five-page extract of *The Command of the Air* was prepared by the War Department Military Intelligence Division on 23 March 1922 and found its way into the files of the Air Service Plans Division.[90] A typescript translation of the first 100 pages of the book (the substantive portion) was received by the Air Service Field Officers School on 3 May 1923.[91] Moreover, during 1922 Lt Col A. Guidoni, the Italian air attaché in Washington, sent a summary of the book to Air Service headquarters and to Lester Gardner, editor of *Aviation* magazine. Guidoni reported that Gardner had discussed the summary with Mitchell and had said that Mitchell was greatly impressed with Douhet's ideas.[92]

Air Service officers, thus, certainly knew of Douhet's ideas, but probably recognized that these concepts were politically unacceptable in the United States. As Secretary Baker had reported in November 1919,

> Air raids upon great unfortified cities like London and Paris brought into the war a new element and constituted an abandonment of the time-honored practice among civilized peoples of restricting bombardment to fortified places or to places from which the civil population had an opportunity to be removed.... The actual loss of life caused by these bombardments was relatively small and the destruction of property, while large, had no appreciable effect upon the war-making power of either nation. Indeed it may rather be said that the willingness of the enemy casually to slaughter women and children, and to destroy property of no military value or use, demonstrated to England and France the necessity of beating so brutal a foe, and it is most likely that history will record these manifestations of inhumanity as the most powerful aids to recruitment in the nations against which they were made.[93]

General Patrick and the Air Service

When he took charge of the Air Service in October 1921, General Patrick faced the challenge of bringing order to the Air Service. The Air Service as a whole, Patrick observed, "was in about as chaotic a condition as [what he] had found ...

when some three years before [he] had been placed in charge of it in France."[94] Much of the confusion grew out of the absence of a unified body of thought among Air Service officers. As Patrick believed, thinking about military aviation tended toward the extremes and he preferred a middle way. "There are, on the one hand," he stated, "enthusiasts who believe that the coming into being of aircraft have practically scrapped all other combat agencies; and, on the other hand, conservatives who consider aircraft as merely auxiliaries to previously existing combat branches. The truth, of course, lies somewhere between those two views."[95] As an able but conservative administrator, he favored evolutionary rather than revolutionary changes in the national military organization.[96] Unlike many of the Army-indoctrinated officers of his generation, Patrick had an open mind as to the future of aviation. After months of practice, he passed a normal test and was recognized as a qualified junior airplane pilot. While he had no hope of becoming a skillful pilot, Patrick believed that his ability to fly helped him win the confidence of many younger men whom he was trying to contact, direct, and guide "in an effort to make of the Air Service a united body of men all working toward one end."[97]

A part of the chaos also stemmed from the vast mass of material that had been issued in the Army during World War I for instructional purposes. In the autumn of 1920, the War Department had issued instructions to each of its branches that all training data would be prepared in a new training regulation series. Looking toward the accomplishment of this and other tasks, General Patrick, during the reorganization of the Office of Chief of Air Service on 1 December 1921, replaced the Training and Operations Group with a Training and War Plans Division, which was made responsible for conducting service tests of new equipment and for preparing training literature. In the other branches of the Army, general boards representing the chief of the service handled test and training literature projects, but the Air Service did not have an Air Service board. In the absence of such an agency, the Air Service Training and War Plans Division assigned training literature projects to the various schools and units best qualified for each particular project.[98]

Maj William Sherman attempted to deal with many of these issues during 1921 while writing a text on air tactics for the Air Service Field Officers School. In this text, Sherman accepted the prevailing belief that the success or the failure of the infantry determined the success or failure of an army, but he maintained that this had not always been true in the past and might not be true in the future. He also believed that the Army aviation was comprised of two portions: air-service aviation was an auxiliary of the ground forces, while air-force aviation (pursuit, bombardment, and attack aircraft) constituted a true arm. Sherman suggested that the air force portion of army aviation would support the infantry in the same manner that the Navy did—by seeking out its doctrine in the element in which it operated. The first duty of the air force was "to gain and hold control of the air, by seeking out and destroying the hostile air force, wherever it may be found." Although he did not believe that control of the air could ever be completed, Sherman believed that "the backbone of the air forces on which the whole plan of employment must be hung is pursuit." Having established control of the air, the mission of the air force was "to destroy the most important enemy forces on the surface of the land or sea."[99] During 1922 Sherman's manuscript on air tactics was revised into manual form; early in 1923 it was issued in preliminary form for use in the Air Service as Training Regulation No. 440-15, *Fundamental Principles for the Employment of the Air Service.*[100]

While the doctrinal project was in progress, General Patrick gave close attention to the pitiful plight of aircraft procurement and the poor state of health of the nation's aircraft manufacturers. While the development of experimental aircraft had made substantial progress since 1918, the quantity procurement of new aircraft and accessories had been penalized by the tremendous stock of equipment still on hand from World War I. Some new planes – such as the Martin MB-2, which could carry 2,000-pound bombs – had been procured, but the Air Service had been able to purchase only a few of the many prototype planes that it wished to see developed to meet specific requirements.[101] In his report for fiscal year 1922, Patrick pointed out: "No nation can afford to support, in times of peace, an air force capable of meeting the requirements of war, and because of the rapid deterioration of aeronautical equipment in storage the proposition to maintain a sufficient war reserve of aircraft is equally untenable." In effect, the Air Service had to plan to use viable aircraft manufacturing companies for the production of its mobilization requirements in a war emergency. Aircraft production in the United States, however, was at such a low ebb that it would not be able to meet the Army's plans to mobilize six armies for a war emergency. General Patrick recommended that a program for the production and purchase of modern aircraft be considered and that a definite amount of aircraft purchase funds should be provided by Congress from year to year. He also stated that a properly balanced Army aviation force ought to have about 20 percent of its strength in air service units and the remaining 80 percent in air force or combat aviation. Because of reductions in Air Service strength and the requirement to keep enough observation units to conduct training with ground forces, 38 percent of the Air Service strength was in air service units. Patrick called for a restoration of a proper balance by the organization of additional air force combat units.[102]

Attentive to General Patrick's criticisms, the secretary of war on 18 December 1922 directed the Air Service to present a study on necessary remedial actions. Patrick accepted the project but he maintained that the study could not be made until the War Department had accepted the concept that Army aviation should be divided into air service and air force units. In addition, he argued that all air service observation units should be withdrawn from divisions and consolidated under the command of corps and armies, and that an "adequate well-balanced Air Force" ought to be built to serve as the GHQ Reserve. "Very often," Patrick wrote, "there is as distinct and definite a mission for the Air Force independent of the ground troops as there is for the Army and Navy independent of each other." For this reason he opposed the assignment of air force units to field armies, and he urged that the Air Service should be authorized to maintain a minimum of six bombardment groups instead of the existing authorization for only one bombardment group.[103] Possibly to emphasize Patrick's point, General Mitchell wrote a long pamphlet in the winter of 1922-23 entitled "Notes on the Multi-Motored Bombardment Group, Day and Night." This elaborate treatise on the tactical employment of bombardment aviation was prefaced by the observation: "Offensive aviation is employed most effectively at the beginning of hostilities during the period of ground and water mobilization and concentration.... Against an enemy not in possession of an adequate air force, offensive aviation, if employed effectively, can force a decision before the ground troops or sea force could join in battle."[104]

The secretary of war appointed a board of General Staff officers, headed by Maj Gen William Lassiter, to hear Patrick's plan and make recommendations on it. When the Lassiter board convened in daily sessions beginning on 22 March 1923, General Patrick argued the Air Service plan that he had outlined earlier. He wished to reduce the auxiliary services of aviation (mainly observation) and increase the primary services needed to secure control of the air (pursuit) and destroy hostile targets behind enemy lines (bombardment). "The principle of concentration of air forces becomes a maxim," he said. And again he urged: "I am . . . convinced that the concentration of all air force under one GHQ Reserve Commander is the most effective way of assuring aerial supremacy." But Patrick ran headlong into the opposition of Brig Gen Hugh A. Drum, of the War Department General Staff. General Drum insisted that the board should first determine what aviation would be needed to support the ground armies and then decide how large the air force ought to be. Under this formula, the board proved unwilling to divest divisions of their observation squadrons and to concentrate all air force units in a GHQ Reserve. Instead, the Lassiter board recommended that the observation air service should be an integral part of divisions, corps, and armies; that an air force of attack and pursuit should be an integral part of each field army; and that an air force of bombardment and pursuit aircraft and airships should be directly under the General Headquarters Reserve for assignment to special and strategical missions, the accomplishment of which might be either in connection with the operation of ground troops or entirely independent of them. This force should be organized into large units to ensure great mobility and independence of action. The Lassiter group, nevertheless, agreed that the Air Service ought to be augmented mainly because it recognized that "for lack of business our aircraft industry is languishing and may disappear." In place of the single bombardment group in the GHQ Reserve, the board recommended that there should be two bombardment groups and four pursuit groups. It also recommended that Congress be asked to make annual appropriations of $25 million for the Air Service each year for 10 years and that approximately $15 million each year should be used for the purchase of aircraft.[105]

The secretary of war approved the Lassiter board report on 24 April 1923, but the recommendations for buying aircraft subsequently went unimplemented after the War Department's attempt to coordinate a planned purchasing program with the Navy through the agency of the Joint Army-Navy Board proved unsuccessful.[106] Nonetheless, the War Department accepted the Lassiter report as the basis for the internal conceptual organization of the Air Service. The official Army field service regulations, 1923, declared that "the coordinating principle which underlies the employment of the combined arms is that the mission of the infantry is the general mission of the entire force," but the manual now recognized that "no one arm wins battles." Since pursuit aviation created "the conditions which enable the other elements to operate with the greatest degree of effectiveness," the regulations considered pursuit to constitute "the most vital element of the air service." Although the assignment of aviation elements to particular commands was said to be flexible, the regulations followed the assignment recommended by the Lassiter board — observation units to divisions, corps, and armies; pursuit and attack units to armies; and bombardment units and airships to the GHQ Reserve.[107]

Appreciation of the fact that the Air Service was "a growing factor in national defense," together with the year and a half that had elapsed without positive action on the Lassiter recommendations, led General Patrick on 19 December 1924 to propose a reorganization of the air forces to the War Department. Patrick wrote,

> I am convinced that the ultimate solution of the air defense problem of this country is a united air force, that is the placing of all the component air units, and possibly all aeronautical development under one responsible and directing head.... The great mobility of the Air Service and the missions it is capable of performing have created a problem in command, the solution of which is still far from satisfactory.... Future emergencies will require at the very outset, before the ground armies can get under way, and in many cases before the Navy can make its power effective, the maximum use of air power on strategic missions.... We should gather our air forces together under one air commander and strike at the strategic points of our enemy — cripple him even before the ground forces can come in contact. Air power is coordinate with land and sea power and the air commander should sit in councils of war on an equal footing with the commanders of the land and sea forces.[108]

"I personally believe," Patrick told the Army War College on 21 February 1925, "that the results desired can be best brought about by a Minister of Defense, under whom would be the Land Force, the Sea Force, and the Air Force."[109]

While he conceived that a department of defense with army, navy, and air force branches would be the ultimate organizational solution to national defense problems, General Patrick was not in favor of hasty action to separate the Air Service from the War Department.[110] Instead, he called upon the War Department on 19 December 1924 to secure legislation that would give the Air Service a status within the War Department analogous to that of the Marine Corps within the Navy Department and that would authorize the Air Service expansion recommended by the Lassiter board. He also recommended that the Army Air Service should be positively charged with all air operations conducted from shore bases, thus ending the overlap of functions of the Army and Navy air forces. He asked that the chief of the Air Service be made responsible for procurement, storage, and issue of Air

Service equipment; for the transportation by air of personnel and supplies; for management of Air Service personnel policies; and "for the tactical training and efficiency of all Air Service units with a doctrine first of offensive action." He further recommended that war plans should establish "one air commander who, in at least the initial stages of an emergency, should control all operations of the air forces, both in the performance of distant strategic missions and in joint action with the land and sea forces."[111]

Establishment of the Army Air Corps

Finally, on 24 March 1924, the House of Representatives, sensitive to growing demands for a thorough review of national air policy, established a Select Committee of Inquiry into Operations of the United States Air Services headed by Representative Florian Lampert and directed it to make a sweeping investigation of the United States Army Air Service, the Naval Bureau of Aeronautics, the United States contract air mail service, and "any corporations, firms, or individuals or agencies having any transactions with or being in any manner associated with or controlled or regulated by the said air services." The Lampert committee began its hearings in October 1924 and examined more than 150 witnesses over an 11-month period.[112]

When they appeared before the Lampert committee during the winter of 1924-25, Air Service officers demonstrated a growing recognition of a phenomenon they began to refer to as air power. In his testimony on 17 December 1924, General Mitchell spoke of the military and civil potentialities of air power. In an article appearing in the *Saturday Evening Post* on 20 December, he defined air power as "the ability to do something in or through the air."[113] In an elaboration of his testimony, Mitchell stated that military air power, civil air power, and commercial aeronautics were the three elements of national air power.[114] Another Air Service officer Maj Raycroft Walsh defined air power "as being the power of a country to wage war through aerial forces."[115] Majs Delos C. Emmons and Carl Spaatz spoke of the general agreement among airmen that the next war would start in the air and that the United States lacked preparedness for such a war. Spaatz stated his opinion that the service doctrines laid down by the Army made it impossible to develop a well-defined policy of independent operation by an air force.[116] Major Milling asserted that the Air Service had to be constantly ready for combat, even more so than the Navy. He also argued that the principal doctrinal problem for the Air Service, and one that defied solution, was the overlapping jurisdiction between the Army and Navy for coastal defense.[117]

General Patrick stated a concept that a nucleus of aircraft manufacturers had to be kept in readiness to expand in time of emergency to meet the requirements of war. Emmons called the aircraft industry "a war reserve and a most important one."[118] General Patrick stated to the Lampert committee on 5 January 1925,

> I believe, that as time goes on the importance of aircraft in national defense will greatly increase. I try to look ahead and to visualize what would take place if we should be so unfortunate as to engage in another war. I am satisfied that one of the first warlike acts would be an effort on the part of the belligerents each to obtain air supremacy; to sweep the enemy out of the air, in order that he might be free to operate his fleets, his armies, and his own aircraft. It is quite possible that such a move would take place very soon after or almost immediately upon the declaration of war. It would be necessary for every nation to have in being an air force that could be used thus offensively, or if attacked by air that could be used in order to defend itself.[119]

As a step in the direction of forming an independent air service, Patrick recommended the creation of an Air Corps under the secretary of war; the new air component would be "charged specifically with the development and utilization of air power as an arm for national defense." This move, Patrick argued, would have the benefit of eliminating the duplication of effort wherein both the Army and the Navy, because of different interpretations of the Army Appropriations Act of 5 June 1920, were both apparently charged with the air defense of sea frontiers of the United States. He stated that "the assignment to the air corps of all air coast defense functions which can be performed from land bases (the limit to be taken at about 200 miles under the present state of aircraft development) will be one of the most important and immediate economies, and one of the greatest gains to efficient national defense which will result from the formation of the air corps."[120]

The general tenor of Air Service testimony before the Lampert committee reflected the evolutionary program desired by General Patrick. Only General Mitchell, in repeated appearances before the committee and in his series of articles that appeared at almost the same time in the *Saturday Evening Post*, deviated from the Air Service position. Mitchell asserted that the national organizational pattern that divided aviation among the Army and Navy, the air mail service of the Post Office Department, and the National Advisory Committee for Aeronautics was designed to protect vested interests rather than to foster a national air power doctrine. "Air power claims that it is an entirely different element than either sea power or land power," Mitchell said, "and that unless you allow air power to have a coordinate voice in the councils of the Nations with sea power and land power, that you cannot organize an adequate defense." Mitchell sponsored two different plans for organizing aviation. First, he visualized establishing a department of aeronautics coequal with the Army and the Navy and with a division of fabrications, a division for civil aviation, and a division for military aviation. Second, he advocated a department of national defense with subsecretaries to control the air, the water, and the land. Many of Mitchell's statements were hardly calculated to endear him to either the Army or the Navy. He said, for example, that the Air Service could get control of the air in two years if it could get half the cost of a battleship as an appropriation each year." It is a very serious question," he stated, "whether air power is auxiliary to the Army and the Navy, or whether armies and navies are not actually auxiliary to air power."[121] As late as December 1924, Patrick had considered that Mitchell had cooperated with Air Service policies and he had recommended that Mitchell be reappointed as assistant chief of the Air Service. Because of the controversy that he stirred up during January and February 1925, however, Secretary Weeks told Patrick to recommend another officer for Mitchell's position. Patrick chose Lt Col James E. Fechet, a veteran pilot and commander of the Advanced Flying School at Kelly Field, to replace Mitchell. On 26 April 1925, Mitchell accordingly reverted to his permanent rank of colonel and was transferred to San Antonio to serve as air officer of the VIII Corps Area.[122]

In the early autumn of 1925, before the Lampert committee was able to make its report, the secretary of war and the secretary of the Navy jointly requested that President Calvin Coolidge appoint a board to study the best means of developing and applying aircraft in national defense. Agreeing with the request, Coolidge appointed a board headed by Dwight W. Morrow, lawyer and banker, on 12 September 1925. In an appearance before the President's Aircraft Board, which would be better known as the Morrow board, Patrick, on the first day of its hearings, again emphasized the poor state of preparedness of the Air Service and again requested that an Air Corps be created. He spoke out against a department of aeronautics, stating that the United States would continue to require a Navy for sea operations beyond the range of land-based aircraft. Patrick conceded that the United States was not in immediate danger of hostile air attacks, but he maintained that without an adequate air force the nation would soon be jeopardized by the aircraft carrier forces that foreign powers were constructing.[123] Now the Air Service's chief engineer at McCook Field, Major MacDill agreed that a department of aeronautics would be no more logical than a department of automobiles or a department of shipping, and he predicted that within five years it would be technologically possible to build an airplane that could fly across the Atlantic and drop up to 4,000 pounds of bombs.[124] Nearly all of the Air Service officers who testified, including Colonel Foulois and Majors Arnold, Milling, and Horace M. Hickam, supported Patrick's plan to establish an air corps and eventually a department of defense. Milling additionally pointed out that the commander in chief of US armed forces in future wars would inevitably have to exercise his authority through subordinate army, navy, and air commanders.[125]

Once again the only Air Service officer who presented strongly divergent viewpoints was Col William Mitchell. On 5 September, Mitchell had made a public statement that the loss of the Navy dirigible *Shenandoah* in stormy weather over the Ohio River Valley was the direct result "of incompetency, criminal negligence and almost treasonable administration of the national defense by the war and navy departments."[126] Before the Morrow board, Mitchell asserted that the United States was strategically vulnerable to an aircraft carrier invasion force that could be mounted by Great Britain in the Atlantic and by Japan in the Pacific. The answer to this strategic problem was an army to hold the land, a navy with a good force of submarines to patrol the seas, and, above all, an air force to protect the seaboard and insular possessions of the United States. "There need to be little or no change in the organization of the Army or Navy," he said, "but beside them there should be the department of the air." After he had given this "constructive" testimony,

Mitchell recalled the long-standing opposition of Army and Navy officers to the development of aviation. He repeated many of these same grievances at his court-martial when he was brought to trial on 28 October on charges of conduct prejudicial to military discipline and of a nature to bring discredit upon the military service. Mitchell was convicted of these charges on 17 December 1925 and resigned from the Army on 1 February 1926.[127]

The hearings before the Lampert committee and the Morrow board found Army and Navy officials solidly arrayed in opposition to the Air Service position—even the moderate official position of General Patrick. "I regard the statement that the next war will be in the air as an absurdity, partaking of the Jules Verne type of literature," Secretary of the Navy Curtis D. Wilbur told the Lampert committee.[128] "Aviation as an independent force cannot operate across the sea," said Rear Adm William A. Moffett, chief of the Bureau of Aeronautics. "The thing to do is to put aviation on something," he continued, "and carry it to the enemy, and the only way to carry it is on board something that will float—on board a ship, in other words."[129] "I believe," testified Lt Ralph A. Ofstie of the Navy Bureau of Aeronautics, "that air power does not exist, absolutely; that it exists only in conjunction with other forces which can cooperate with it or which can transport it."[130] Leading the Navy witnesses before the Morrow board, Secretary Wilbur stated that the mission of the naval air force was to serve as an arm of the fleet. "Its mission is to aid the surface units in gaining and maintaining command of the sea. It may best carry out this mission by gaining and maintaining control of the air in the theater of naval operations."[131] Admiral Moffett saw no difficulty in maintaining coordination for coastal defense through the agency of the Joint Army and Navy Board and he regarded the "Joint Army and Navy Action in Coast Defense" agreement to be a clear definition of aerial responsibilities.[132] The Navy also held to the official position that the establishment of a central procurement agency for military aircraft was undesirable. "There is very little duplication of effort on the part of the services and such duplication as exists is not only justifiable but, I believe," noted Admiral Moffett, "decidedly necessary, in order that there may be competition, that there may be rivalry, that there may be initiative; otherwise there is bound to be stagnation."[133]

The high-ranking Army officials appearing before the Morrow board also opposed changes in the Air Service. Secretary of War Dwight F. Davis stated that the War Department was "convinced that a strong airplane industry is vital to the national defense." However, he asserted that the subordination of civil aviation to a military department would be an economically unsound and basically unwise practice. Davis admitted that the nation's aircraft industry had been starving and that the amount of equipment in the Air Service was inadequate, but these situations were caused by the scarcity of funds appropriated by Congress.[134] Maj Gen John L. Hines, who had succeeded Pershing as chief of staff on 14 September 1924, stated that the combat readiness of the Air Service should perhaps excel that of the other branches of the Army, but he could see no reason for a separate air service or a separate air corps within the Army. "I am of the opinion," he said, "that the Air Service, because of the limitations imposed by natural laws on the operation of aircraft as well as the necessity for unity of action, will always be an auxiliary arm or service. It can never by itself defeat an enemy."[135] The principal Air Service opponent before both the Lampert committee and the Morrow board was General Drum, now the assistant chief of staff for operations on the War Department General Staff. In the Lampert hearings, Drum argued that the United States had little to fear from hostile air attack because of the inherent range limitations on land-based aircraft and the tonnage restrictions that had been placed on the construction of aircraft carriers by the Washington treaty of 1922.[136] Both in his initial statement and in his rebuttal testimony before the Morrow board, Drum insisted that "the air power principle and its application as recently proposed by the Chief of Air Service ... is unsound from a national defense viewpoint, as well as from purely Army considerations. At the present and so far as the future of aviation can be foreseen, air power has no function independent of the Army and Navy." Possibly one of his most telling points—and Drum repeated it several times—was the opinion of the august General Pershing. "The Infantry," Pershing had said on the eve of his retirement, "still remains the backbone of the attack, and the role of the other arms is to help it reach the enemy.... The idea that principles of warfare have changed and that armed contests will be settled in any other way have nothing substantial in our experience to warrant serious consideration."[137]

What circumstances lay behind the Morrow board's speed in acting were never definitely known, but it presented its report on 30 November 1925, exactly two weeks before the Lampert committee could report. "We do not consider," stated the Morrow board, "that air power, as an arm of the national defense, has yet demonstrated its value—certainly not in a country situated as ours—for independent operations of such a character as to justify the organization of a separate department. We believe that such independent missions as it is capable of can be better carried out under the high command of the Army and Navy." The board concluded that the United States was in no danger from air attack, and it further stated that "the belief that new and deadlier weapons will shorten future wars and prevent vast expenditures of lives and resources is a dangerous one which, if accepted, might well lead to a readier acceptance of war as the solution of international difficulties." The board, nevertheless, recommended that the name of the Air Service be changed to that of the Air Corps, that an assistant secretary of war be established to give special attention to aviation matters, that aviation be given special representation in the General Staff sections, and that a five-year program of aircraft procurement be initiated with a lesser magnitude than had been recommended by the Lassiter board.[138] In its report on 14 December 1925 the Lampert committee stated that aircraft would be "the first resort of our country in case of a war emergency" and would comprise "one of the most essential arms of our military defense." The committee accordingly recommended the establishment of a department of national defense, representation of Army and Navy aviation on the General Staff of the Army and the General Board of the Navy, and that not less than $10 million should be appropriated and expended annually by both the Army and the Navy on the procurement of new flying equipment.[139]

Far from being daunted by what he called the "time-worn, threadbare, reactionary plea" of those who resisted change, General Patrick told Army War College students on 9 November 1925 that he considered it his duty, when done in a proper way, to suggest improvements in national defense. In this lecture, Patrick repeated many of the statements he had presented to the Lampert committee and the Morrow board, but he also revealed that he had "recently been quite impressed by a little book written by an Englishman, Capt Basil H. Liddell Hart." The book, published earlier that year, was *Paris: Or the Future of War*. Patrick was impressed with Liddell Hart's thesis that the main military objective in war should be the will of the enemy to fight rather than the defeat of his armed forces in the field. He agreed with Liddell Hart's conclusion that the German army still had had a lot of fight left in the fall of 1918 and that the war had ended because the will of the German people to fight had been shattered. While the use of gas was now prohibited by treaty, Patrick doubted that such a prohibition would hold in war. "Assume," he suggested, "that aircraft are able to fly at will over enemy territory, in other words, assume air supremacy. Imagine, in consequence, the enemy's industrial establishments, his munitions factories, his means of communication, destroyed; add to this drenching with gas, which even though not deadly, would cause great discomfort, and then estimate how long such a harassed enemy would fight." The waging of such "air pressure" against an enemy nation, Patrick said, "can best be done by an organization which is developed and directed by those who know thoroughly its achievements, its possibilities, and its limitations."[140]

During the winter of 1925–26, William Mitchell continued to wage a strong fight for an air power concept and the emotional responses engendered by his court-martial ensured him a wide audience. Published in August 1925 as a summarization of some of his articles, Mitchell's *Winged Defense* was extensively quoted during his trial. Before the House Committee on Military Affairs on 5 February 1926, Mitchell made a statement that represented the culmination of his thinking on the nature of war and of air power:

> There has never been anything that has come which has changed war the way the advent of air power has. The method of prosecuting a war in the old days always was to get at the vital centers of the country in order to paralyze the resistance. This meant the centers of production, the centers of population, the agricultural districts, the animal industry, communications — anything that tended to keep up war. Now, in order to keep the enemy out of that, armies were spread in front of those places and protected them by their flesh and blood. You had mass killings there, sometimes for years before these vital centers were reached. It led to the theory that the hostile army in the field was the main objective, which it was. Once having been conquered, the vital centers would be gotten at.... Now we can get today to these vital centers by air power.... So that, in the future, we will strike, in case of armed conflict, when all other means of settling disputes have failed, to go straight to the vital centers, the industrial centers, through the use of an air force and hit them. That is the modern theory of making war.[141]

Four years later in *Skyways*, the last of his three books, Mitchell would again emphasize this theory of war.

Although the Morrow board report dampened any general reorganization of the armed services, the War Department was prepared to grant some concessions, but not much independence, to the Air Service. On 26 January 1926 the War Department officially issued Training Regulation No. 440-15, *Fundamental Principles for the Employment of the Air Service* – the same pamphlet that had been drafted by Major Sherman in 1921 and that had been revised and accepted as a policy statement by the Office of Chief of Air Service. Subsequently, it had been reviewed by the Army's Command and General Staff School and War College, and the General Staff's G-3 division had stamped final approval on it. The pamphlet noted that the primary objective of the whole Army was to destroy hostile armed forces and that the mission of the Air Service was "to assist the ground forces to gain strategical and tactical successes by destroying enemy aviation, attacking enemy ground forces and other enemy objectives on land or sea, and in conjunction with other agencies to protect ground forces from hostile aerial observation and attack. In addition it furnishes aerial observation for information and for artillery fire, and also provides messenger service and transportation for special personnel." It stated further: "The organization and training of all air units is based on the fundamental doctrine that their mission is to aid the ground forces to gain decisive success." The regulation recognized the distinction between observation (which was an integral part of divisions, corps, and armies) and the GHQ air force (which was to be self-contained and capable of rapidly shifting its activities from one theater of operations to another). Obviously pleased with the training regulations, General Drum described it as "the most advanced thought in the world today on aviation."[142]

In September 1925, less than a week after Patrick testified before the Morrow board, the War Department directed him to submit within five days a complete plan to implement his Air Corps idea. The heads of the Army branches that would support the Air Service were given a similar brief period to comment on Patrick's plan. Each objected that the organization of the Air Service on the model of the Marine Corps would upset coordination between the branches of the Army. Secretary of War Dwight F. Davis, nevertheless, insisted that it was very important to pass an air bill through Congress in the spring of 1926 because it was necessary to increase the efficiency of the air force and because, in his opinion, the country demanded it. In the end, the War Department proved willing to accept the findings of the Morrow board and the Air Corps Act of 2 July 1926 constituted a legislative enactment of the Morrow recommendations. The name of the Air Service was changed to the Air Corps, the implication being that the Air Corps was capable of independent as well as auxiliary operations. An additional assistant secretary of war was authorized to perform duties delegated to him by the secretary, and air sections were authorized in the General Staff divisions. A five-year program for expansion of Air Corps personnel and aircraft was to be initiated. The Air Corps attained little autonomy within the War Department by these actions; and no decision was made to delineate the coast defense responsibilities of the Army and Navy, as air officers had desired. In hearings on the legislation, Patrick suggested that it would be economical and practical to combine Army and Navy flying training under one agency, but he noted that "naval officers . . . feared they would lose a certain measure of control over their air component, and . . . insisted also that all of the flyers with the Navy should be trained in naval tactic and should understand all of the tactics employed in naval battles." Thus Patrick's suggestion was not accepted.[143]

For the time being, the Air Corps Act of 1926 ended the struggle for an autonomous air force. General Patrick continued to insist that a department of defense with army, naval, and air components would be the ultimate solution to the defense problems of the United States, but he privately expressed the opinion that the best that the Air Corps could hope for in a span of years in which nations were reducing their armaments was some expansion and considerable modernization. Patrick accordingly hailed the Air Corps Act as "a long step in the right direction."[144] Viewed in retrospect, the Air Corps Act of 1926 was only one of several pieces of legislation that manifested a belief within Congress that the pioneering years of aviation were ending. On 24 June Congress had enacted the Morrow board recommendations relevant to the Navy: the appointment of an assistant secretary of the Navy to assist in furthering naval aeronautics and a five-year naval aviation expansion program. The Air Mail Act of February 1925 had already turned the Post Office Department's federal air mail system over to private contractors, and the Air Commerce Act of 21 May 1926 had created the post of assistant secretary of commerce for air and authorized the Department of Commerce to license pilots, map and operate airways, provide flight information, and develop new air navigation facilities.[145] In its infancy, aviation had been nurtured by military expenditures; now military aviation would begin to share the technological advances that would come from rapidly developing commercial aviation.

The Mitchell Era Reexamined

"The former isolation of the United States is a thing of the past," William Mitchell wrote in 1925. "The coming of aircraft has greatly modified this isolation on account of the great range and speed which these agents of communications are developing."[146] Believing that "changes in military systems come about only through the pressure of public opinion or disaster in war," Mitchell hoped that he could modify the military policy of the United States by laying "aeronautical facts" before Congress and the people.[147] Though he counted himself a close personal friend of Mitchell, General Arnold looked backward many years later and observed that Mitchell's agitation for air power had a considerable effect upon the development of naval aviation but that it had made Army officers "set their mouths together, draw more into their shell, and if anything, take even a narrower point of view of aviation as an offensive power in warfare." As Arnold remembered the early

1920s, the American people were fascinated with flying and loved Billy Mitchell, but no one was willing to think that the United States required a military policy—let alone an air power policy.[148]

It was General Arnold's theory that a growth of air power of a marked magnitude depended on a combination of a critical state of international relations and a favorable state of aviation technology. To his way of thinking, such a coincidence of national military requirements and air technology had been near at hand just before the Armistice in 1918 but would not again occur for more than a decade.[149] The successful conclusion of World War I and the Washington Disarmament Treaty of 1922 stunted the development of military aviation. Early in 1925, General Patrick predicted that the Locarno agreements, which marked a relaxation of tension in Europe, would lessen the amount that the American people would be willing to pay for national defense.[150]

The Baker board stated an unequivocal opinion that the United States was in no danger of air attack from any potential enemy of menacing strength. Even Army and Navy war planners—who made it their business to provide against all contingencies—found it difficult to determine which enemy or enemies might threaten the United States. Although the Washington Disarmament Treaty had terminated the Anglo-Japanese alliance, the logical opponents of the United States continued to be Great Britain (Red) and Japan (Orange). General Patrick thought in terms of the employment of a mobile GHQ air force in a war with Red and Orange forces in which the British would debark at Halifax and Japanese troops would land at Vancouver.[151] Mitchell visualized a requirement for defensive air forces to be stationed in Hawaii, Panama, and Alaska, but he opposed the establishment of a strong air force in the remote Philippine Islands lest it be easily destroyed. Patrick believed, however, that "our only salvation" in the Philippines "is to have an air force there that is competent and qualified to oppose an enemy air force."[152] Oddly enough, the more conservative Patrick believed that there was no question but that the time was coming when "we can bomb trans-sea countries."[153] Mitchell, on the other hand, visualized that strings of islands would be seized so that aircraft based on them might fly from one island to another. He pointed out on numerous occasions in 1924 and 1925 that there was no stretch of water in the northern hemisphere between the United States and Europe or Asia greater than the cruising range of the modern aircraft of the day.[154]

Despite their impatience with military conservatism, Air Corps officers of the Mitchell era frequently talked and thought in terms of the strategic situation of World War I. In 1924 these air officers formally introduced the concept that air power was different from land and sea power; but Patrick, Milling, and Mitchell all agreed that air power could be divided into air force and air service (auxiliary) aviation. By 1926, moreover, Mitchell stated that the air service of the Navy could "stay just the way it is ... for work on the high seas."[155] The Air Service accepted the doctrine that control of the air was necessary for effective air, ground, or naval operations, and Milling stated that "the main role—almost the only role, properly speaking—of Pursuit aviation is to seek out and destroy the hostile air force."[156]

Thinking in terms of World War I, however, Patrick described "control of the air" as the condition in which "we get the upper hand of our adversary, make life miserable for him every time he comes on our side of the lines, and even endeavor to meet him on his own side of the lines, and finally his morale is shaken to such an extent that he would rather stay at home. We then have control of the air."[157] Patrick thought of air supremacy as a condition wherein one adversary practically wiped out another's air force and thus went virtually unchallenged in the air.[158]

Air Service leaders agreed that an air force had to be an effective D-day force and that it had to be supported by a healthy domestic aircraft industry. In their thoughts on strategic air warfare, the air leaders did not seem to be entirely certain whether air bombardment could win a war without army and navy action. Patrick drew upon Liddell Hart's concept of a future war under conditions similar to the ground-siege situation of World War I and visualized aerial pressure as breaking the morale and capabilities of an enemy nation that was presumably first brought to bay by air and naval action.[159] Even Mitchell hesitated to say that air power could be decisive without ground and naval action. "I believe," he told congressmen on 5 February 1926, that "air power in the future will have a great influence in determining any conflict, so I believe if you figure your whole national defense as 100 percent, air power would make approximately 50 percent, the land forces 30 percent, and the sea forces 20 percent."[160]

Writing in 1948, an Air Force leader evaluated the significance of William Mitchell as being that of a "visionary and missionary."[161] Certainly Mitchell saw beyond his times but, because of the close-knit fellowship of air leaders in the early 1920s, one may wonder how many of the basic ideas attributed to Mitchell actually may have originated with his associates. Mitchell, Patrick, Milling, and other air officers did not differ markedly in their essential thinking except for the impetuousness manifested by Mitchell. It is significant that Mitchell's last book on aviation, *Skyways*, published in 1930 after the author had been out of touch with his fellow air officers for some four years, continued few thoughts that he had not presented before 1926.[162] In his early writings, however, Mitchell had publicized the ideas which would be continued, expanded, and refined to become the doctrine of the Air Force.

NOTES

1. House, *Astronautics and Space Exploration: Hearings before the Select Committee on Astronautics and Space Exploration*, 85th Cong., 2d sess., 1958, 733.
2. Samuel Pierpont Langley Memorial Meeting, *Miscellaneous Collections*, vol. 49 (Washington, D.C.: Smithsonian Institution, 1907), 33–34.
3. Wilbur and Orville Wright to Hon R. M. Nevin, US Congress, letter, 18 January 1905.
4. Wilbur and Orville Wright to secretary of war, letter, 9 October 1905.
5. Wright brothers to Board of Ordnance and Fortifications, War Department, letter, 15 June 1907.
6. Minutes of the War Department Board of Ordnance and Fortification, 24 October 1905, quoted in Jones Aviation Chronology, 1900–1906, 61.

7. Charles DeForest Chandler and Frank P. Lahm, *How Our Army Grew Wings* (New York: Ronald Press Co., 1943), 40–43; Brig Gen James Allen, chief signal officer of the Army to recorder, War Department Board of Ordnance and Fortification, 10 October 1907, in Jones Aviation Chronology, 1900–1906, 93–95.

8. Minutes of the War Department Board of Ordnance and Fortification, 5 December 1907; appendix no. 1, Signal Corps specification no. 486, 23 December 1907, in Jones Aviation Chronology, 1900–1906, 104, 109.

9. Senate, *Reorganization of the Army: Hearings before the Subcommittee of the Committee on Military Affairs*, 66th Cong., 1st sess., 1919, 1257.

10. Chandler and Lahm, *How Our Army Grew Wings*, 206, 222–24.

11. War Department, Office of the Chief of Staff, *Field Service Regulations, United States Army, 1910* (Washington, D.C.: Government Printing Office, 1910), 54.

12. R. Earl McClendon, *Autonomy of the Air Arm* (Maxwell AFB, Ala.: Documentary Research Division, Air University, 1954), 16–21; Isaac Don Levine, *Mitchell: Pioneer of Air Power* (New York: Duell, Sloan and Pearce, 1943), 83–84; Maj Alfred F. Hurley, *Billy Mitchell, Crusader for Air Power* (New York: Franklin Watts, 1964), 17.

13. Alfred Goldberg, ed., *A History of the United States Air Force, 1907–1957* (Princeton: D. Van Nostrand, 1957), 7.

14. War Department, Office of the Chief of Staff, *Field Service Regulations, United States Army, 1914*, corrected to 31 July 1918 (Washington, D.C.: Government Printing Office, 1918), 13, 20–21, 74.

15. Russell J. Parkinson, "Aeronautics at the Hague Conference of 1899," *The Air Power Historian* 7, no. 2 (April 1960): 106–11.

16. John R. Cuneo, *The Air Weapon, 1914–1916* (Harrisburg: Military Service Publishing Co., 1947), 1–7.

17. Ibid., 7–110; Col C. M. McCorkle, "The Air Weapon and Immediate Reaction to It," lecture, Air War College, Maxwell AFB, Ala., 19 January 1953.

18. Cuneo, *The Air Weapon, 1914–1916*, 12–288; "Some Papers of Count Caproni di Taliedo, Controversy in the Making?" ed. William G. Key, *The Pegasus*, a supplement, n.d., 7–11; J. L. Boone Atkinson, "Italian Influence on the Origins of the American Concept of Strategic Bombardment," *The Air Power Historian* 4, no. 3 (July 1957): 141–49.

19. McClendon, *Autonomy of the Air Arm*, 6–8; Juliette A. Hennesy, *The United States Army Air Arm, April 1861 to April 1917*, USAF historical study 98 (Maxwell AFB, Ala.: USAF Historical Division, 1958), 167–76.

20. McClendon, *Autonomy of the Air Arm*, 6–8.

21. Henry Greenleaf Pearson, *A Business Man in Uniform, Raynal Cawthrone Bolling* (New York: Duffield & Co., 1923), 107; Goldberg, *A History of the United States Air Force*, 14.

22. Pearson, *A Business Man in Uniform*, 109–18.

23. Maj Raynal C. Bolling to chief signal officer of the Army, letter, subject: Report of Aeronautical Commission, 15 August 1917.

24. I. B. Holley, Jr., *Ideas and Weapons* (New Haven: Yale University Press, 1953), 58.

25. Ibid., 56–57; Atkinson, "Italian Influence on the Origins of Strategic Bombardment," 141–94; extracts from diary of Gianni Caproni, 25 January and 3 February 1917; Pearson, *A Business Man in Uniform*, 122–23, 230–35.

26. Brig Gen William Mitchell, *Memoirs of World War I* (New York: Random House, 1960), 103–11, 133–37; Hurley, *Billy Mitchell, Crusader for Air Power*, 19–29.

27. Holley, *Ideas and Weapons*, 59; Henry H. Arnold, *Global Mission* (New York: Harper & Bros., 1949), 57–58.

28. Holley, *Ideas and Weapons*, 66–73; McClendon, *Autonomy of the Air Arm*, 8–9.

29. Chase C. Mooney and Martha E. Layman, *Organization of Military Aeronautics, 1907–1935*, USAF historical study 25 (Washington, D.C.: Office of Assistant Chief of Air Staff for Intelligence, Historical Division, 1944), 29–32; McClendon, *Autonomy of the Air Arm*, 8–9.

30. Mitchell, *Memoirs of World War I,* 135, 155–56, 165–66, 177–78, 205, 232–33; Mason M. Patrick, *The United States in the Air* (Garden City, N.Y.: Doubleday, Doran & Co., 1928), 3–28; Goldberg, *A History of the United States Air Force,* 22–23; Maj Gen Mason M. Patrick, *Final Report of the Chief of Air Service AEF* (Washington, D.C.: Government Printing Office, 1921), 23, 24, 28, 30.

31. Patrick, *Final Report of the Chief of Air Service AEF,* 4, 19, 37; Edgar S. Gorrell, *The Measure of America's World War Aeronautical Effort* (Burlington, Vt.: Lane Press, 1940), 30–32.

32. Lt Col William Mitchell, "General Principles Underlying the Use of the Air Service in the Zone of the Advance AEF," *Bulletin of the Information Section, Air Service AEF* 3, no. 132 (30 April 1918).

33. Patrick, *Final Report of the Chief of Air Service AEF,* 3–37; Gorrell, *The Measure of America's World War Aeronautical Effort,* 30–32; Lt Col Kenneth F. Gantz, "The Education of a Chief of Staff," *Air University Review* 15, no. 4 (May–June 1964): 97–112; "Notes on Recent Operations . . . Copied from a proposed manual prepared under the direction of Col Edgar S. Gorrell, Assistant Chief of Staff, A.S., AEF. . . ." *US Air Service Information Circular* 1, no. 76 (30 June 1920); "Notes on the Characteristics, Limitations, and Employment of the Air Service, a tentative manual prepared under the direction of Col Edgar S. Gorrell . . . evolved from 'Notes on the Employment of the Air Service from the General Staff Viewpoint' . . .," *Air Service Information Circular* 1, no. 72 (12 June 1920); House, *Inquiry into Operations of the United States Air Service: Hearings before the Select Committee of Inquiry into Operations of the United States Air Service,* 68th Cong., 2d sess., 1924, 2269–70.

34. Patrick, *Final Report of the Chief of Air Service AEF,* 49.

35. Quoted in Holley, *Ideas and Weapons,* 158.

36. Pearson, *A Business Man in Uniform,* 142–43; Col Edgar S. Gorrell, History of Strategical Section, Air Service, American Expeditionary Forces, 1 February 1919; Holley, *Ideas and Weapons,* 57–58, 135–36; Key, "Some Papers of Count Caproni di Taliedo," 16–20; Atkinson, "Italian Influence on the Origins of Strategic Bombardment," 145–46.

37. Gorrell, History of Strategical Section, 1 February 1919.

38. Ibid.; Lt Gen Ira C. Eaker, "The War in the Air," in *A Concise History of World War I,* ed. V. J. Esposito (New York: Frederick A. Praeger, 1964), 262–63; Pearson, *A Business Man in Uniform,* 199–201.

39. Gorrell, History of Strategical Section, 1 February 1919; Holley, *Ideas and Weapons,* 137–38.

40. Holley, *Ideas and Weapons,* 137–38.

41. Ibid., 138–39; Thomas H. Greer, *The Development of Air Doctrine in the Army Air Arm, 1917–1941,* USAF historical study 89 (Maxwell AFB, Ala.: USAF Historical Division, Air University, 1955), 9–10.

42. Holley, *Ideas and Weapons,* 141–45; Patrick, *Final Report of the Chief of Air Service AEF,* 51; Gorrell, *The Measure of America's World War Aeronautical Effort,* 29, 31; Gorrell, History of Strategical Section, 1 February 1919.

43. Goldberg, *A History of the United States Air Force,* 14; Patrick, *Final Report of the Chief of Air Service AEF,* 23–24, 28, 30.

44. Patrick, *Final Report of the Chief of Air Service AEF,* 3.

45. Gorrell, *The Measure of America's World War Aeronautical Effort,* 34–35.

46. Mitchell, *Memoirs of World War I,* 267–68; Levine, *Mitchell: Pioneer of Air Power,* 146–48.

47. "Air Organization, Second Report of the Prime Minister's Committee on Air Organization and Home Defense against Air Raids," 17 August 1917, reprinted in *The Air Power Historian* 3, no. 3 (July 1956): 153.

48. McClendon, *Autonomy of the Air Arm,* 12–13; Levine, *Mitchell: Pioneer of Air Power,* 167.

49. Proceedings of Board of Officers, Air Service, American Expeditionary Forces, 13 May 1919; Maj Gen Mason M. Patrick, chief, Air Service, American Expeditionary Forces, to commander in chief, American Expeditionary Forces, letter, subject: Air Service Organization, 19 May 1919.

50. General Headquarters, American Expeditionary Forces, Report of Superior Board on Organization and Tactics, ca. 1 July 1919, in House, *Department of Defense and Unification of Air Service: Hearings before the Committee on Military Affairs,* 69th Cong., 1st sess., 1926, 952–53.

51. Patrick, *Final Report of the Chief of Air Service AEF,* 19.

IDEAS, CONCEPTS, DOCTRINE

52. "Notes on the Characteristics, Limitations, and Employment of the Air Service," *Air Service Information Circular* 1, no. 72 (12 June 1920).

53. "Notes on Recent Operations," *Air Service Information Circular* 1, no. 76 (30 June 1920): 3.

54. Third Army, American Expeditionary Forces, Provisional Manual of Operations for Air Service Units, 23 December 1918.

55. Mooney and Layman, *Organization of Military Aeronautics, 1907–1935*, 41–43.

56. Report of a Board of Officers Convened to Report Upon the New (S.2693) and Curry (H.R. 7925) Bills...., ca. 27 October 1919.

57. Ibid.

58. Benedict Crowell et al., to secretary of war, letter, subject: Report of American Aviation Mission, 19 July 1919, and statement by Secretary of War Newton D. Baker in House, *United Air Service: Hearings before a Subcommittee of the Committee on Military Affairs*, 66th Cong., 2d sess., 1920, 16–31.

59. Hurley, *Billy Mitchell, Crusader for Air Power*, 168–69.

60. Ibid., 19–20.

61. Archibald D. Turnbull and Clifford L. Lord, *History of United States Naval Aviation* (New Haven: Yale University Press, 1949), 177.

62. Hurley, *Billy Mitchell, Crusader for Air Power*, 41; Outline of Organization and Functions of the Office of the Director of Air Service, 5 November 1919; House, *United Air Service*, 42.

63. Greer, *The Development of Air Doctrine in the Army Air Arm*, 23.

64. Hurley, *Billy Mitchell, Crusader for Air Power*, 41; American Heritage interview with Gen Benjamin D. Foulois, 20 January 1960.

65. Maj William C. Sherman, "Air Tactics," sec. 2, Langley AFB, Va., 1921, 1.

66. Ibid., 14–21.

67. Levine, *Mitchell: Pioneer of Air Power*, 168–72.

68. House, *Army Reorganization: Hearings before the Committee on Military Affairs*, 66th Cong., 1st sess., 1919, 907–8.

69. House, *United Air Service*, 44, 46.

70. Senate, *Reorganization of the Army*, 925–55, 1255–98.

71. William Mitchell, "Tactical Application of Military Aeronautics," in Air Service file: Notes on the Application of GO 132 to Air Service Units, 9 January 1920.

72. House, *United Air Service*, 31.

73. Air Service 4-352-AS, Notes on the Functions of the Army Air Service, ca. January 1920; General Order 4, War Department, 1920.

74. House, *Inquiry into Operations of the United States Air Service*, 1726–27; Levine, *Mitchell: Pioneer of Air Power*, 187–88.

75. McClendon, *Autonomy of the Air Arm*, 56–57; Mooney and Layman, *Organization of Military Aeronautics, 1907–1935*, 48–49.

76. Mooney and Layman, *Organization of Military Aeronautics, 1907–1935*, 48–49; Public Law 251, 66th Cong., 5 June 1920, 6–7.

77. Patrick, *The United States in the Air*, 74–76.

78. Report of Air Service Training and Operations Group, 1 July 1920 to 31 December 1920; *Aerial Bombardment Manual* in *Air Service Information Circular* 1, no. 54 (21 May 1920): 5; *Air Service Manual* in *Air Service Information Circular* 1, no. 84 (20 September 1920).

79. Patrick, *The United States in the Air*, 76.

80. William Mitchell, *Our Air Force, The Keystone of National Defense* (New York: E. P. Dutton & Co., 1919), xix, 200–1.

81. Mooney and Layman, *Organization of Military Aeronautics, 1907–1935*, 54–55, with quotation from *New York Tribune*, 21 December 1920.

82. Air Service Stencil 4-471, statement of Brig Gen William Mitchell, assistant chief of the Air Service, 4 January 1921.

83. Levine, *Mitchell: Pioneer of Air Power*, 218–59; Turnbull and Lord, *History of United States Naval Aviation*, 193–204.

84. Hurley, *Billy Mitchell, Crusader for Air Power*, 68–69.
85. Ibid., 69; Mooney and Layman, *Organization of Military Aeronautics, 1907–1935*, 58–59; Patrick, *The United States in the Air*, 81–85.
86. Patrick, *The United States in the Air*, 86–89.
87. Report of inspection trip to France, Italy, Germany, Holland, and England, made during the winter of 1921–22 by Brig Gen William Mitchell, 1st Lt Clayton Bissell, and Alfred Verville, 1922; Levine, *Mitchell: Pioneer of Air Power*, 274–77.
88. Hurley, *Billy Mitchell, Crusader for Air Power*, 75–76; Edward Warner, "Douhet, Mitchell, Seversky: Theories of Air Warfare," in *Makers of Modern Strategy*, ed. Edward Mead Earle (Princeton: Princeton University Press, 1944), 487–88; Air Service Field Officers School document: A translation of the first 100 pages of Giulio Douhet, *The Command of the Air, Being an Essay on the Art of Aerial Warfare, With an Appendix Containing Elementary Notions on Aeronautics* (Rome: Printing Office for the Use of the War Department, 1921).
89. Hurley, *Billy Mitchell, Crusader for Air Power*, 75.
90. Giulio Douhet, *The Command of the Air*, trans. Dino Ferrari (New York: Coward-McCann, 1942); extracts from *The Command of the Air* by G. Douhet, M.I.D., Italy #6271 3/23/2 (C70-73).
91. A translation of the first 100 pages of Douhet, *The Command of the Air*. Stamped received 3 May 1923, Field Officers School, Langley Field, Va.
92. Hurley, *Billy Mitchell, Crusader for Air Power*, 75.
93. *Annual Report of the Secretary of War*, 11 November 1919, quoted in Jones Aviation Chronology, July–December 1919.
94. Patrick, *The United States in the Air*, 89.
95. House, *Inquiry into Operations of the United States Air Service*, 519.
96. Ibid., 522.
97. Patrick, *The United States in the Air*, 112–13.
98. Annual Report, chief, Training and War Plans Division, Office of the Chief of Air Service, fiscal year ending 30 June 1922.
99. Sherman, "Air Tactics," 1921.
100. Office of the Chief of Air Service, Training Regulation 440-15, *Air Tactics*, 31 August 1922; draft of War Department Training Regulation 440-15, *Fundamental Conceptions of the Air Service*, 1923.
101. Engineering Division, Air Service, "Aircraft Development since the Armistice," *Air Service Information Circular 5*, no. 402 (15 January 1923).
102. Report of a Committee of Officers Appointed by the Secretary of War [Lassiter Board], 27 March 1923, appendix 2: General Statement of the Chief of Air Service.
103. H. H. Tebbetts, The Adjutant General, War Department, to chief of Air Service, letter, subject: Preparation of a Project for the Peace Establishment of the Air Service, 18 December 1922; 1st ind., Maj Gen Mason M. Patrick to The Adjutant General, 19 January 1923; 3d ind., Patrick to The Adjutant General, 7 February 1923.
104. Mitchell, "Notes on the Multi-Motored Bombardment Group, Day and Night," n.d.
105. Report of a Committee of Officers Appointed by the Secretary of War [Lassiter Board], 27 March 1923.
106. The Joint Planning Committee to the Joint Board, letter, subject: Joint Army and Navy Air Program, 28 January 1925.
107. War Department, *Field Service Regulations, United States Army, 1923* (Washington, D.C.: Government Printing Office, 1924), 11, 21–24.
108. Maj Gen Mason M. Patrick to The Adjutant General, War Department, letter, subject: Reorganization of Air Forces for National Defense, 19 December 1924.
109. Maj Gen Mason M. Patrick to Maj Gen H. E. Ely, commandant, Army War College, letter, 21 February 1925.
110. Patrick, *The United States in the Air*, 190.
111. Maj Gen Mason M. Patrick to The Adjutant General, letter, 19 December 1924.

112. House Report No. 1653, *Report of Inquiry into Operations of the United States Air Service*, 68th Cong., 2d sess., 1925, 1.
113. House, *Inquiry into Operations of the United States Air Service*, 291, 2032. Mitchell's articles in the *Saturday Evening Post* were incorporated into the committee hearings.
114. Ibid., 2758.
115. Ibid., 1699.
116. Ibid., 44, 2246.
117. Ibid., 2252–53, 2270–71, 2266, 2270, 2265–76.
118. Ibid., 130–31, 44.
119. Ibid., 519–20, 528.
120. Ibid., 522–23.
121. Ibid., 291–93, 296, 300, 1676–77, 1689–90, 1912, 1915, 2032–39, 2240, 2758–59.
122. Patrick, *The United States in the Air*, 179–80; Levine, *Mitchell: Pioneer of Air Power*, 318.
123. "Verbatim Report of Morrow Commission of Inquiry," in *Army and Navy Journal*, 26 September 1925, 8–10.
124. Ibid., 16.
125. Ibid., 4, 8–9, 17, 21–24.
126. Levine, *Mitchell: Pioneer of Air Power*, 327–29.
127. Ibid., 342–70; "Verbatim Report of Morrow Commission of Inquiry," 9–16.
128. House, *Inquiry into Operations of the United States Air Service*, 366.
129. Ibid., 380.
130. Ibid., 2177.
131. "Verbatim Report of Morrow Commission of Inquiry," 10.
132. Ibid., 15.
133. House, *Department of Defense and Unification of Air Service: Hearings before the Committee on Military Affairs*, 69th Cong., 1st sess., 1925, 719–21.
134. "Verbatim Report of Morrow Commission of Inquiry," 1–3.
135. Ibid., 3–4.
136. House, *Inquiry into Operations of the United States Air Service*, 1758.
137. Ibid., 1833; "Verbatim Report of Morrow Commission of Inquiry," 4–7, 15–19.
138. *Report of President's Aircraft Board* (Washington, D.C.: Government Printing Office, 1925), 7, 11, 14, 15–21.
139. House, Inquiry into Operations of the United States Air Service, 5–9.
140. Maj Gen Mason M. Patrick, "The Army Air Service," lecture, Army War College, Carlisle Barracks, Pa., 9 November 1925; Greer, *The Development of Air Doctrine in the Army Air Arm*, 19–20.
141. House, *Department of Defense and Unification of Air Service*, 397; Levine, *Mitchell: Pioneer of Air Power*, 322.
142. House, *Department of Defense and Unification of Air Service*, 638–50; War Department Training Regulation 440-15, *Fundamental Principles for the Employment of the Air Service*, 26 January 1926.
143. Senate, *The Army Air Service: Hearings before the Committee on Military Affairs*, 69th Cong., 1st sess., 1925, 44; Mooney and Layman, *Organization of Military Aeronautics, 1907–1935*, 73–80; Senate, *Reorganization of the Army Air Service: Hearings before the Committee on Military Affairs*, 69th Cong., 1st sess., 1926, 5–7.
144. Maj Gen Mason M. Patrick to W. Frank Jones, acting chairman, Military Affairs Committee, House of Representatives, 4 May 1926.
145. Hurley, *Billy Mitchell, Crusader for Air Power*, 106; Turnbull and Lord, *History of United States Naval Aviation*, 257–58.
146. William Mitchell, *Winged Defense: The Development and Possibilities of Modern Air Power—Economic and Military* (New York: Putnam's, 1925), xiii.
147. Ibid., xviii.
148. Arnold, *Global Mission*, 122, 158–59.

149. Ibid., 158.

150. Maj Gen Mason M. Patrick, "Future of the Air Service," lecture, Army War College, Carlisle Barracks, Pa., 17 February 1925; Patrick, "The Army Air Service," 9 November 1925.

151. Patrick, "Future of the Air Service," 17 February 1925.

152. Conference at the Army War College, following Patrick lecture, 9 November 1925; Mitchell, *Winged Defense*, 218–19.

153. Conference at the Army War College, Carlisle Barracks, Pa., 9 November 1925.

154. Mitchell, *Winged Defense*, 12.

155. House, *Department of Defense and Unification of Air Service*, 436.

156. Maj Thomas D. Milling, "Tactics of the Air Forces in War," lecture, Army War College, Carlisle Barracks, Pa., 27 November 1923.

157. Patrick, "Future of the Air Service," 17 February 1925.

158. Conference at the Army War College, Carlisle Barracks, Pa., 9 November 1925.

159. Patrick, "The Army Air Service," 9 November 1925.

160. House, *Department of Defense and Unification of Air Service*, 398.

161. Maj Gen Robert W. Harper, editorial in *Air University Quarterly Review* 2, no. 3 (Winter 1948): 76.

162. William Mitchell, *Skyways* (Philadelphia: Lippincott, 1930).

Orville Wright.

Wilbur Wright.

Gen John J. Pershing, Army chief of staff, 1921-24.

Col Frank P. Lahm, chief of Air Service, Second Army.

Maj Gen Benjamin O. Foulois, chief, Air Corps, 1931-35.

Brig Gen William Mitchell, assistant chief, Air Service, 1921-25.

Col William C. Sherman.

Maj Gen Mason Patrick, chief, Air Service and Air Corps, 1921-27.

CHAPTER 3

GROWTH OF THE AIR FORCE IDEA
1926–41

"Despite popular legend," reminisced Gen Henry H. Arnold, "we could not have had any real air power much sooner than we got it."[1] Arnold reasoned that in the early 1920s the state of the technological art of aeronautics was not far enough advanced to support air power doctrines. In the field of national aviation policy and military aviation technology, the early developmental period clearly ended in 1926. In that year the World War I stocks of such items as Liberty engines were used up or declared obsolete, as were many of the war stocks of aircraft. The ten aircraft production companies that had survived the stringent years of the early 1920s were getting on sound footing and were receiving some orders for commercial aircraft. Research and development in aeronautics was making headway in the National Advisory Committee for Aeronautics (NACA), at the Air Corps Materiel Division at Wright Field, Ohio, and in Guggenheim Foundation laboratories. The Air Corps Act of 1926 stated the policy that the government should encourage aircraft production companies to develop design and engineering staffs by following a rather liberal policy of placing experimental orders for prototype aircraft. It also provided that the government ought not to enter into competition with private industry by manufacturing aircraft in government arsenals.[2]

In the early years, the Air Service had considered it logical that the military services should bear the brunt of the burden of developing aeronautics until such time as the utility of air transportation could be established. In 1922 the Air Service had opened a model airway connecting New York, Norfolk, Washington, and Dayton; by 1925 the airway was extended to St. Louis, Kansas City, Dallas, and Fort Worth. Lighted beacons guided night flying, and radio-meterological stations were established along the routes. The Air Mail Act of 1925 and the Air Commerce Act of 1926 took the Post Office Department and the military services out of commercial aviation, and the acts served as legislative cornerstones for the development of commercial aviation in the United States. After competitive bidding, the Post Office Department negotiated 12 airmail contracts; these initial contracts provided the eventual base upon which the nation's great trunk airlines were built. The real breakthrough in aviation, however, occurred in 1927 when Charles A. Lindbergh's pioneer trans-Atlantic solo flight on 20–21 May galvanized the imagination of the people. After May 1927 the public suddenly wanted to fly. During 1927 the new airline companies carried only 8,679 passengers, but the number of passengers transported reached 48,312 in 1928, 161,933 in 1929, and 384,506 in 1930. In 1926 US aircraft production totaled 1,186 planes and in 1929 the total was 6,193 – 5,516 of which were civil aircraft.[3]

The Air Corps Wins a Foothold

Both Maj Gen Mason Patrick and Maj Gen James E. Fechet, who became chief of the Air Corps on 14 November 1927, considered the Air Corps Act of 1926 to have been farsighted legislation. F. Trubee Davison was appointed to the newly created position of assistant secretary of war for air on 16 July 1926 and Air Corps officers were assigned to the War Department general staff divisions. After a year's delay while studies were made, the Air Corps was authorized a five-year expansion program in which it was expected to attain a strength of 1,650 officers, 15,000 enlisted men, and 1,800 serviceable airplanes. The only difficulty with the Air Corps Act—according to Secretary Davison—was that it was never fully implemented. The legislation was never popular with other agencies of the War Department who lost funds and personnel spaces to the Air Corps expansion, and there was jealousy that the Air Corps was permitted special representation at the secretary and General Staff level. "Those in higher places . . . ," Davison noted, "were looking more for an alibi rather than a means of carrying out this program." Davison also noticed that Congress did not appropriate authorized funds in full amounts and the Bureau of the Budget impounded some of the Air Corps funds that were appropriated.[4]

As the Air Corps expansion got under way, the chief of the Air Corps continued to be responsible for the preparation and issuance, through the War Department General Staff, of training doctrine for all Air Corps organizations. Because of the small number of officers in his office, the chief of the Air Service had required the Air Service Field Officers' School to prepare basic drafts of doctrinal manuals. Subsequently redesignated as the Air Service Tactical School in 1922 and the Air Corps Tactical School in 1926, the institution at Langley proved to be the only common location of experienced Air Corps officers who had enough time for creative thinking. Following the practice of other arms and services, an Air Service Board was established at Langley in 1922 and was redesignated as the Air Corps Board in 1926. But the Air Corps did not have enough senior personnel to assign to this board; thus, the commandant of the Tactical School and several of its staff members doubled as members of the Air Corps Board.[5] The chief of the Air Corps also took advantage of the experienced men at Langley by referring problems originating in the War Department to the Air Corps Tactical School for study and comment.[6]

Early in the 1920s the manuals of the Air Corps Tactical School closely followed the ideas expressed in statements of air leaders in Washington. Published early in 1926 when Maj Oscar Westover was commandant, the instructional manual *Employment of Combined Air Force* envisioned the air arm as coordinate with land and sea forces and having as its aim the destruction of the enemy's morale and will to resist, preferably by means of attacks against targets in the enemy's interior. Pursuit aviation was designed to establish localized aerial supremacy; command of the air was held to be temporary and fleeting. Bombardment was said to cooperate with air and ground forces by giving direct support in tactical operations or by giving indirect support to them through strategical operations.[7] In the spring of 1928, the Air Corps Tactical School undertook a general revision of its texts; on 30 April Lt Col C. C. Culver, now the school's commandant, forwarded to Washington a paper entitled "The Doctrine of Air Force," which was proposed as a basis for all texts. This draft doctrine obviously followed the letter of the law set forth in War Department Training Regulation 440-15 and concluded: "In the final analysis, the army is the principal component of the nation's militia, both the air and the naval forces being used to further its interest. ... The Air component ... always supports the ground forces, no matter how decisive its ... operations may be, or how indirect its support."[8] When efforts to revise this statement were not accomplished to his satisfaction, General Fechet stated his own idea on 1 September:

> The objective of war is to overcome the enemy's will to resist, and the defeat of his army, his fleet or the occupation of his territory is merely a means to this end and none of them is the true objective. If the true objective can be reached without the necessity of defeating or brushing aside the enemy force on the ground or water and the proper means furnished to subdue the enemy's will and bring the war to a close, the object of war can be obtained with less destruction and lasting after effects than has heretofore been the case. At present the Air Force provides the only means for such an accomplishment.[9]

The procurement of aircraft under its expansion program was indicative of Air Corps ideas and concepts; and the performance of the new equipment had a substantial impact upon Air Corps doctrine. In 1924 the Air Service Tactical School had stated that a combat air force could not depend upon surface transportation but required air transport aircraft. The Air Corps began to buy such planes, although in very small numbers since civilian airliners would be available for military service in a war emergency.[10] In the first year of the expansion, the Air Corps gave emphasis to the purchase of new observation and pursuit aircraft. Because of alarming experiences with flutter in experimental monoplanes, the standard Air Corps pursuit aircraft of the 1920s were predominately biplanes. In the several years following initial purchases in 1925, the Air Corps bought a total of 150 Curtiss Hawks series planes. However, in 1928 the Air Corps began to buy Boeing P-12F biplanes—which had a top speed of 194 miles an hour—as the standard pursuit planes.[11]

Since observation planes had higher priority, the Air Corps was not permitted to purchase any new bombers in the first year of its augmentation. In May 1928 Maj Hugh J. Knerr, the commander of the 2d Bombardment Group (who was additionally named as chairman of a special Air Corps Bombardment Board), recommended the development of a light and fast day bomber and a heavier and longer range night bomber. This proposal was soon rejected when the War Department insisted that a twin-engine observation plane be developed and that provision be made for its modification as a bomber. In March 1930 the Air Corps Tactical School recommended that night bombing was inefficient and proposed that light and heavy bombers should be built solely for day operations. The school believed that speed and armament could protect a day bomber. As a result of circular design proposals in 1930, the Air Corps issued procurement orders for both Boeing B-9 and Martin B-10 aircraft. Built in 1931, the Boeing B-9 was a twin-engine monoplane that bore a superficial resemblance to the later B-17. However, the B-9 subsequently developed a fuselage vibration that made it unacceptable to buy in quantity. The Martin B-10, on the other hand, was to be the first of the modern bombers. First flown in early 1932, this all metal monoplane had front and rear machine-gun turrets, a top speed of 212 miles an hour, and a service ceiling of 21,000 feet.[12]

At the Air Corps Tactical School the increasing capabilities of military aircraft opened new vistas of air power that visionary instructors desired to exploit. After completing the school in 1928 and 1929, Capt Robert Olds and Lt Kenneth N. Walker remained on the faculty as instructors in bombardment aviation. Olds had assisted Mitchell in his appearances before the Morrow board; Walker was an experienced bombardment officer who had been a member of the Air Service Board in 1925. What these two men doubtlessly already believed was confirmed in May 1929 during the annual Air Corps maneuvers held in Ohio. Maj Walter H. Frank, assistant commandant of the Air Corps Tactical School, served as chief umpire. At the close of the maneuvers he reported: "There is considerable doubt among the umpires as to the ability of any air organization to stop a well organized, well flown air force attack.... The difficulty that pursuit had, not only in attacking, but in finding some of the missions that were sent into hostile territory during these maneuvers, would make it appear that a well planned air force attack is going to be successful most of the time." Major Frank obviously had studied Douhet's writings, since he observed: "Douhet, a well known Italian writer, says that 'now that aviation has entered the ranks as a means of carrying on war, more than ever war is going to be a question of give and take.' It emphasizes the fact that air force is principally an offensive weapon rather than a defensive one."[13]

Back in the classroom at Langley, Lieutenant Walker saw the major significance of the theorem that "a well organized, well planned, and well flown air force attack will constitute an offensive that cannot be stopped." In fact, his students subsequently would credit him with originating the whole idea.[14] The revised Air Corps Tactical School text *The Air Force*, issued in April 1930, boldly stated: "a defensive formation of bombardment airplanes properly flown, can accomplish its mission unsupported by friendly pursuit, when opposed by no more than twice its number of hostile pursuit" and that "defensive formations of attack can accomplish their missions, unsupported by friendly pursuit, when opposed by no more than their own number of hostile pursuit."[15] Bombers would rely upon superior speed and firepower for protection in deep penetrations into enemy territory; the only pursuit support they would require would be in cutting through the crust of enemy air opposition along the front lines.[16]

To Olds and Walker the supremacy of the bomber held important significance. Under the older air doctrines, air superiority, air supremacy, or control of the air had been considered to be fleeting and attainable only by the concentration of a predominant number of pursuit aircraft in a local area. And although the April 1930 version of *The Air Force* continued to mention the old doctrine, it marked a shift in air force thinking by suggesting that bomber attacks against enemy airdromes would be the best method of destroying enemy aircraft.[17] The next revision of *The Air Force* (February 1931) went even further, boldly predicting that control of the air, air superiority, or air supremacy (the terms were said to be synonymous) would be attainable throughout a combat theater by destroying the hostile air force in the air, on its airdromes, and in the enemy's depots and factories. "Victory is practically assured to the commander whose air force has gained and can maintain, control of the air," the text stated, "even if his ground forces are merely equal or somewhat inferior to those of his enemy."[18] "Pursuit alone," the text continued, "cannot ensure protection from air attack, but . . . bombardment and attack must participate to a degree undreamed of in the World War in the contest for control of the air, but attacks against the hostile air force on the ground."[19] What friendly control of the air would mean in the course of a war had already been suggested in the April 1930 text:

> An army with an air force strong in bombardment and attack should be able to defeat its opponent, as when its air force has reduced the bombardment and attack of enemy to a negligible quantity, its ground operations will progress without important hostile air interference, and its air force will then be able to assist these operations directly by attack on terrestrial objectives. An air force preponderately pursuit, cannot materially affect the ground situation except through the indirect method of destroying hostile aircraft.[20]

At the same time that the concept of the primacy of bombardment aviation was becoming firmly established at the Tactical School, the War Department also appeared to have gotten a clear mandate to develop aviation for the performance of its traditional mission of coast defense. Unwilling to accept General Patrick's demands for legislation defining the exact division of Army-Navy responsibilities for aerial operations at the nation's sea coasts, the War Department had preferred in 1926 to rely upon the Joint Army-Navy Board for such decisions. As a portion of the *Joint Board's Joint Action of the Army and the Navy*, approved in December 1926, the secretary of war and the secretary of the Navy had agreed that the Navy's peacetime purchases of land-based aircraft would be "limited to those primarily designed and ordinarily used for scouting and patrolling over the sea." In time of war, however, the Navy would be authorized to conduct "operations from shore bases for overseas scouting, and for the observation and patrol of sea communications and their defense against raids."[21]

Notwithstanding this agreement, both Patrick and Fechet continued to fear that the Navy intended to take over coastal air defense. The matter came to a head in August 1930 when Secretary of War Patrick J. Hurley received a copy of a Navy letter to President Herbert Hoover containing severe criticism of the Army program for coastal air defense. In an effort to clarify the apparent confusion, Army chief of staff General Douglas MacArthur and chief of naval operations Adm W. V. Pratt reached an agreement between themselves on 9 January 1931, which General MacArthur described in these terms:

> Under it the naval air forces will be based on the fleet and move with it as an important element in performing the essential missions of the fleet afloat. The Army air forces will be land based and employed as an element of the Army in carrying out its mission of defending the coasts, both in the homeland and in overseas possessions. Through this arrangement the fleet is assured absolute freedom of action with no responsibility for coast defense.

Admiral Pratt apparently entered into this agreement because he wished to develop the Navy's fleet as an offensive rather than a defensive force. The Navy's General Board, however, strongly disapproved of the agreement since it feared that the Air Corps might lay claim to the Navy's air stations ashore. After a detailed study had been made by the War Plans Division, General MacArthur issued an order on 3 January 1933 specifically requiring the Air Corps "to conduct the land-based air operations in defense of the United States and its overseas possessions."[22]

Beginnings of the GHQ Air Force

When Maj Gen Benjamin D. Foulois moved up from assistant chief to become chief of the Air Corps on 22 December 1931, he brought with him a long record of experience that went back to the earliest days of Army aviation and a new assessment of the international situation. From 1920 to 1924, Foulois had served as the assistant military observer with the American commission and as assistant military attaché at the American embassy in Berlin. He had had intimate talks with many of the German airmen who smarted from defeat: they had insisted that Germany would rise again and would use aviation to conquer Europe. "The first phase of the next war," Foulois reasoned, "is going to be the conquest of Europe, and the second phase is going to be the conquest of the United States. They're going to use short range aircraft to do the conquest of Europe job, but they'll need long range stuff to lick us." Anticipating that the United States could well be isolated in the Western Hemisphere, Foulois had returned home as an active advocate of long-range bombers.[23]

As the Air Corps five-year expansion program approached a delayed completion in 1933, the added War Department responsibilities for coastal defense and the increasing technological capabilities of bombardment aircraft led General Foulois to suggest that an air power strategy was appropriate for the United States.

At the completion of the five-year program, the Air Corps would possess 13 squadrons of observation, 12 squadrons of bombardment, 4 squadrons of attack, and 21 squadrons of pursuit aviation. Instead of the 1,800 aircraft authorized to it, however, the Air Corps had only 1,619 planes, of which 442 were either obsolescent or nonstandard.[24] The Air Corps based its new defense strategy on the assumption that the United States would be attacked by a coalition of two or more naval powers who would muster a superior force of carrier-based aviation and upon the fact that the War Department was responsible for coastal air defense. Based upon this appreciation of the situation, Brig Gen Oscar Westover, the assistant chief of the Air Corps, requested that the War Department on 15 March 1933 strengthen the air garrisons of the Panama Canal department, the Hawaiian Islands, and the Philippines, and that it authorize the organization of bombardment and coast defense patrol units in the six critical defense areas along the Atlantic and Pacific coasts of the United States. Noting that Air Corps operational doctrine varied according to the various Air Corps tactical commanders, General Westover asked authority to establish a center for tactical research at the Air Corps Tactical School, which had moved from Langley to Maxwell Field, Montgomery, Alabama, on 1 July 1931.[25]

The timing of the Air Corps plan was appropriate since General MacArthur was considering a reorganization of the Army into four continental armies, but the War Department General Staff viewed the Air Corps submission with skepticism. Like the rest of the world, the United States was in the throes of an economic depression. The five-year Air Corps expansion plan that was just concluding, moreover, had worked hardships upon the Army's ground arms, which had been compelled to give up personnel spaces to the Air Corps since ceilings on overall Army strength had been curtailed while Air Corps authorizations had increased.[26] On 3 June 1933 the War Department directed the chief of the Air Corps to submit a new plan, staying within his approved ceiling of 1,800 aircraft, that would recommend the manner in which a general headquarters air force would be employed under war plans Red, Red-Orange, and Green. War plan Red visualized conflict with Great Britain, Orange with Japan, and Green visualized certain operations against a hostile force in Mexico. The Air Corps submitted these plans on 13 July; on 11 August a special committee of the Army General Council chaired by Maj Gen Hugh A. Drum, who was now deputy chief of staff, was designated to review the Air Corps plan. General Foulois was a member of this special committee, usually known as the Drum board.[27]

When it reported in October 1933, the Drum board was concerned chiefly about the worst possible strategic alignment that could confront the United States: a two-front coalition attack by Great Britain and Japan, who would capitalize on the inferiority of US Navy forces and mount probable surface invasions of the northeastern and northwestern United States from beachheads established in the vicinity of Halifax and Vancouver. Such a war would also be accompanied by attacks against Alaska, Hawaii, the Philippines, and the Canal Zone. Because of the elaborate logistical requirements and the rather slow progress of the flight of

Italian bombers under Gen Italo Balbo to the opening of the Chicago World Fair, the Drum board did not fear attacks by land-based bombers against the United States; but it was apprehensive about carrier-based air that would support landings of British and Japanese forces in Canada. Both Army and Navy air forces would have to oppose this two-front operation, and the strategic problem posed a distinct requirement for the organization of a mobile GHQ air force that could be concentrated in the peripheral areas of the United States to oppose the landings of hostile forces and to support subsequent ground operations against the invaders. The Drum board recommended that the GHQ air force should be organized, and it stated that the Air Corps had a requirement for 2,320 aircraft to be organized into 27 bombardment, 17 pursuit, 11 attack, and 20 observation squadrons. The Drum board, however, was unwilling to recommend an immediate increase in Air Corps personnel or aircraft strength until other Army requirements needed to augment ground forces were met. Secretary of War George H. Dern approved the Drum board report on 11 October 1933.[28]

Toward a Long-Range Bombardment Mission

While the War Department was examining its strategic planning, additional information became available from the concentration of a GHQ Air Force (Provisional) on the Pacific coast for a maneuver defense against a simulated hostile fleet and accompanying aircraft. In his July 1933 report on this maneuver, General Westover called attention to the wide disparity between the speed of new bombers and of pursuit and observation planes. "The modern trend of thought," Westover wrote,

> is that high speed and otherwise high performing bombardment aircraft, together with observation aviation of superior speed and range and communications characteristics, will suffice for the adequate air defense of this country. The ability of bombardment aviation to fly in close formation and thus to insure greater defense against air attack . . . warrants the belief that no known agency can frustrate the accomplishment of a bombardment mission.

Lt Col Henry H. "Hap" Arnold, who served as Westover's chief of staff during the maneuver, called for the development of air task forces (including transport planes) built around the modern bombers. He also recommended that the time had come to establish an Air Corps board with experienced membership, which could study and recommend policy for the ultimate development of the air force.[29]

On 12 September, General Foulois, in an appearance before the Army War College, defined air power "as the strength of a nation in its ability to strike offensively in the air" and stated that the size of the air force should "be determined as that which can operate successfully against that amount of hostile aviation to which it may be opposed on our frontiers." He stated that "the real effective air defense will consist of our ability to attack and destroy the hostile aviation on the ground before it takes to the air." In response to a question put to him on this same occasion at the Army War College, General Westover explained: "Within the Army Air Corps, there has been a growing conviction that we have got to come down to practically two types of aircraft. One type designed in general for the patrol missions, and the other designed for the high-powered, bombing offensive missions with sufficient machine gun fire power to protect itself."[30]

Although it is impossible to assess the exact degree of influence the ideas of Giulio Douhet had upon the development of American air power doctrine, there is no doubt that Air Corps thinkers were familiar with Douhet's writings. Copies of Douhet's "The War of 19 . . . ," which appeared in *Revista Aeronautica* in March 1930 were in the Air Corps Tactical School library as early as November 1931.[31] In 1933 Capt George C. Kenney, who had been an instructor at the Air Corps Tactical School from 1927 to 1929 and was assigned as chief of the Air Corps Plans Division between 1933 and 1935, made a translation of an epitome of Douhet's ideas, which appeared in the French magazine *Les Ailes*. This translation seems to have provided the basis for an article published by retired Col Charles DeF. Chandler entitled "Air Warfare Doctrine of General Douhet" in *U.S. Air Services* in May 1933.[32] At the very least, Douhet's arguments for building "battle cruiser" aircraft that would not require fighter escort and in favor of the decisiveness of air attack as a means of winning a war, for establishing command of the air by air attacks against an enemy's airdromes, and for developing commercial air transport aviation as an adjunct to military aviation proved useful as a corroboration of Air Corps ideas. Thus, on 9 May 1933 General Foulois sent 30 mimeographed copies of Chandler's article to the chairman of the House Committee on Military Affairs with the notation that the paper "presents an excellent exposition of certain principles of air warfare."[33]

Although the War Department was unwilling to permit any immediate Air Corps expansion, General MacArthur was sympathetic with Air Corps proposals for the development of experimental long-range bombers. Completed in July 1932, a study by the Air Corps Materiel Division indicated that a bomber with a speed of 200 miles per hour, a range of 5,000 miles, and a 2,000-pound bomb load was technically possible. In December 1933 the Air Corps suggested and the War Department approved the commitment of funds for Project A: the development of a long-range bomber that not only would be able to "reinforce either coast line . . . but would definitely enable . . . reinforcement of . . . Panama and Hawaii." The single XB-15 that the Boeing Company would deliver under this contract in 1937 would be too large for existing engines (someone once humorously remarked that if the engines on the XB-15 had ever looked back to see what they were pulling, all four of them would have quit simultaneously). But technology was catching up with requirements, and the Air Corps was learning to write military characteristics for planes that would be good yet attainable. In 1933 the Air Corps distributed proposals to manufacturers specifying a design competition for a multiengine bomber with a range of 2,000 miles and a speed of 250 miles per hour. In the design competition the following year, Douglas offered the DB-1 (an extrapolation from its DC-3 transport that would be the prototype for the twin-engine B-18); Martin proposed a modification of its already successful B-10; and Boeing offered a four-engine Model 299, which would be the prototype of the B-17 Flying Fortress.[34]

Baker Board Influences Air Organization

While making plans to implement the recommendations of the Drum board in the winter of 1933–34, the Air Corps was suddenly launched into a tragic undertaking that would center public attention and criticism upon it. Convinced that there was evidence of collusion and fraud in airmail contracts with commercial air transport companies, President Franklin D. Roosevelt ordered the Air Corps to start flying the airmail effective on 19 February 1934. Undertaking this mission without proper equipment, with inadequate ground organization, in the face of extremely bad winter flying weather, and with only ten days' preparation, the Air Corps experienced 57 accidents and suffered 12 fatalities while flying 1,590,155 miles with 777,389 pounds of mail. Alarmed by the loss of life, President Roosevelt, on 10 March, directed the Air Corps to operate only in favorable weather conditions. On 8 May new contracts with private companies went into effect and the Army Air Corps flew its last scheduled mail flight on 1 June 1934. General Foulois remembered the airmail episode as a dramatic illustration to the American people that the Air Corps had been neglected. "In the blaze of editorial and Congressional reaction to the deaths of Army flyers," Foulois recalled, "the President and the Congress were, in my opinion, forced to release funds for immediate use in Air Corps experimental and research work, for the immediate procurement of advanced types of aircraft and aircraft materiel and for the immediate advanced training of Army Air Corps personnel."[35]

Even before the Air Corps completed its airmail duty, the secretary of war on 17 April 1934 named Newton D. Baker to head a special committee of civilian and military members to make a constructive study and report of the adequacy and efficiency of the Army Air Corps for the performance of its missions in peace and war. In 25 days, the Baker board heard 105 witnesses, but, possibly because General Drum was its executive vice-chairman, the report released on 18 July 1934 accepted virtually all of the conclusions of the Drum board report (which had been approved the previous October). "Our national defense policy," stated the report of the Baker board, "contemplates aggressive action against no nation; it is based entirely upon the defense of our homeland and overseas possessions, including protection of our sea and air- borne commerce." The board found that the purpose of the Army was "to hold an invader while the citizen forces are being mobilized." Aviation was advantageous to the national defense, but the board stated: "The idea that aviation can replace any of the other elements of our armed forces is found, on analysis to be erroneous. . . . Since ground forces alone are capable of occupying territory, or with certainty, preventing occupation of our own territory, the Army with its own air forces remains the ultimate decisive factor in war." Citing the Drum board report as evidence that the United States was in no danger of land-based transoceanic air attack, the Baker board stated that "the ideas that aviation, acting alone, can control the sea lanes, or defend the coast, or produce decisive results in any other general mission contemplated under our policy are all visionary, as is the idea that a very large and independent air force is necessary to defend our country against air attack."[36]

As was to be expected from its concept of national military policy, the Baker board recommended that the existing Army and Navy organizations be continued, with air forces an integral part of each. The board found the only potential area of Army-Navy disagreement to be the use of aircraft in coastal defense and recommended that the Joint Board should continue to resolve any such controversy in accordance with the old formula expressed in the Army Appropriation Act of 5 June 1920. The board thought that the position of assistant secretary of war for air should be abolished and that the Air Corps should "become in all respects a homogenous part of the Army, under General Staff control, and be subject to military coordination, study, influence, and operation." Following and elaborating on the Drum board recommendations, the Baker board recommended that a headquarters air force be established outside of Washington to supervise the training and operations of combat air units, that an Air Corps board be created to formulate uniform tactical doctrines, and that a model Air Corps unit be created at the Air Corps Tactical School for employment in tactical testing and experimentation. The board recognized that the Air Corps had a requirement for 2,320 airplanes, but it proposed that any Air Corps expansion ought to be a part of a comprehensive Army augmentation plan.[37]

Of the several members of the Baker board—including General Foulois and Edgar S. Gorrell—only James H. Doolittle filed a minority report. "I believe," stated Doolittle, "that the future security of our Nation is dependent upon an adequate air force. This is true at the present time and will become increasingly important as the science of aviation advances and the airplane lends itself more and more to the Art of Warfare." Doolittle insisted that the air force could be most rapidly developed if it were separated from the Army. If this were impossible, the Air Corps should have a separate budget and promotion list and should be removed from the control of the General Staff.[38] There is no indication that these remarks by Doolittle, an experienced Army aviator who had resigned from the service to take an engineering job with the Shell Oil Company, were ever considered by the secretary of war. In fact, Secretary Dern, who was in Panama when the Baker board completed its report, immediately messaged Baker that he had "no hesitancy in approving in principle your conclusions."[39]

In June 1934 President Roosevelt created the Federal Aviation Commission under the chairmanship of newspaper editor Clark Howell to make recommendations concerning all phases of aviation. When the commission began its hearings, Secretary Dern informed it that the War Department endorsed the report of the Baker board. Brig Gen C. E. Kilbourne, assistant chief of staff, War Plans Division, moreover, instructed all officers summoned to testify to familiarize themselves with the approved policy and not to express personal opinions unless they were so identified.[40] William Mitchell seized the opportunity before the

Howell commission and denounced the Baker board report. The testimony of Air Corps officers was marked by restraint. Colonel Arnold stated his personal opinion that an independent air force would be desirable, but he evidently stated off the record that a GHQ air force ought to be organized and given a two-year trial. Other Air Corps officers favored no immediate change in defense organization until a GHQ air force had been tested.[41] In spite of a general reticence to talk, Maj Donald Wilson, Captains Harold Lee George and Robert Olds, and Lt Kenneth Walker freely expressed many of the ideas that were being taught at the Air Corps Tactical School.

When he appeared before the Howell commission, Captain George emphasized that "the object of war is now, and always has been, the overcoming of the hostile will to resist.... When that will is broken down, when that will disintegrates, then capitulation results." Reasoning that the strength of opposing air forces would never permit a nation to utilize its potential to build air power after a war began, George defined air power as "the immediate ability of a nation to engage effectively in air warfare." "Future wars," he predicted, "will be fought by the air forces which are in existence when the war breaks out and not by air forces which are created after the war commences." George argued that in a future war air forces would be in action for weeks or months before land forces got into action and that an air force, therefore, required independent organization.[42]

Emphasizing that he was expressing personal opinion, Maj Donald Wilson pointed out that world conditions were leading toward war, that the basic principles of war applied by an intelligent enemy portended that the principal hostile effort against the United States would be through the air, that the defense problem of the United States with planes of limited range was particularly disadvantageous, and that an air force organized, equipped, and trained to defend the United States was an essential element in providing the national defense.[43]

Lieutenant Walker prefaced his testimony by reading the statement of primacy of the ground force mission as it appeared in the field service regulations of 1923, and he charged that Army leaders refused "to consider that an Air Force is of real value, other than to cover the mobilization of the Army." "We insist," said Walker, "that the defeat of the enemy results from breaking his will to resist and that this is most quickly accomplished, in the scheme of modern war, by disruption, by direct action, of his means for prosecuting the war.... An Air Force is an arm which, without the necessity of defeating the armed forces of the enemy, can strike directly and destroy those industrial and communications facilities, without which no nations can wage modern war." Walker believed that the Army should control observation aviation and that the Navy should have aircraft carriers to protect its fleets, but he urged that a separate air force had to be created for the air defense of the United States—the air defense mission being defined as seeking out and destroying the enemy air force on its home bases. "Gentlemen," Walker concluded, "unless we create an adequate and separate Air Force, this next war 'will begin in the air and end in the mud'—in the mud and debris of the demolished industries that have brought us to our knees."[44]

At the outset of his testimony, Captain Olds expressed opposition to the creation of a unified air force that would amalgamate all of the aviation components of the Army and Navy, because he held that the Army mission required observation aviation and balloons while the Navy mission necessitated sea-based aircraft. Olds, nevertheless, pointed out that the waging of air warfare was of equal importance to the waging of ground and sea warfare. "We simply cannot predict a limit," he said, "nor is it safe to predict the definite role aircraft will fill in a future war. . . . A determined air armada loaded with modern agencies of destruction, in readiness within range of our great centers of population and industry, may eventually prove to be a more convincing argument against war than all the Hague and Geneva Conventions put together." Olds called for the establishment of a department of national defense, with subordinate departments of army, navy, air, and procurement and with a supreme general staff headed by a single chief. He urged that a national air force should be organized and should have subordinate air forces in the North Atlantic, South Atlantic, Gulf, and Pacific states and in Alaska. He proposed no changes for the defensive air garrisons assigned to the Army commands in Hawaii, the Panama Canal Zone, and in the Philippines.[45]

The members of the Federal Aviation Commission had a splendid opportunity to make a fresh approach to aviation problems. However, on 31 January 1935, the Howell commission reported to Congress that "the present degree of mutual understanding between the Army and Navy is less than might be desired, that the machinery for settling differences in matters of detail lacks something in effectiveness, and that the arrangements for keeping commanders in the field notified of their respective responsibilities in joint operations . . . are strikingly inadequate." Furthermore, the commission did not believe that it would be easier to coordinate three services than two. Since plans for the GHQ Air Force were already being issued, the Howell commission preferred to refrain from comment on the matter of an independent air force. "It must be noted, however," the report stated,

> that there is ample reason to believe that aircraft have now passed far beyond their former position as useful auxiliaries, and must in the future be considered and utilized as an important means of exerting directly the will of the Commander in Chief. An adequate striking force for use against objectives both near and remote is a necessity for a modern army, and the projected G.H.Q. Air Force must be judged with reference to its effectiveness in this respect.[46]

Organization of the General Headquarters Air Force

Both in his first conceptual thinking and later in more exact planning, General Foulois urged the War Department General Staff to observe the principle of unity of command when it organized the GHQ Air Force. In March 1933 Foulois stated his belief that the Army chief of staff, in a time of war, should go into the field as the supreme military commander and leave his second in command in the zone of interior. Following the same pattern, Foulois believed that the chief of the Air

Corps should accompany the supreme military commander into the field, and he accordingly made his assistant chief, General Westover, his executive officer so that Westover would be able to take over all incumbent zone of interior duties in time of war.[47] Actually, however, the younger Westover commanded the Provisional GHQ Air Force in the field maneuvers of 1933 and he headed the airmail operation. As a part of the planning for the organization of a GHQ air force under the Army's four-army plan, Foulois got War Department approval for a procedure whereby officers from the Office of Chief of Air Corps would additionally serve as the mobilization staff for a GHQ air force. Under this same type arrangement, Foulois intended that most of the officers of the Air Corps Plans Division would, in a war emergency, become the Aviation Section of the Army General Headquarters in the field.[48]

In this argument for unity of command within the Air Corps, Foulois expressed his conviction that it was wholly impracticable to divorce the authority for training and operations from the functions and responsibilities for research, experimentation, procurement, supply, and repair. In what was widely interpreted as a direct rebuff to Foulois for his advocacy of a separate air force, however,[49] the Baker board not only recommended increased General Staff supervision over the Air Corps, but it also insisted that the primary functions of the Air Corps were fighting and development, procurement, and supply of equipment and trained personnel. The first function should be assigned to the commanding general of a GHQ air force, who would be directly subordinate to the Army chief of staff. The second function should continue to be handled by the chief of the Air Corps as a staff officer of the War Department.[50]

The War Department required little time to effect the top-level change recommended by the Baker board. The position of assistant secretary of war for air had been left vacant when F. Trubee Davison resigned at the outset of the Roosevelt administration, and this post remained vacant.[51] On 24 August 1934 the War Department announced that four additional Air Corps officers were being detailed to General Staff divisions, bringing the number of Air Corps officers on the high staff level to nine, a proper quota in view of the relative size of the Air Corps.[52]

Because a GHQ air force represented a new concept, the War Department proceeded more cautiously with its organization. On 31 December 1934 the secretary directed that the GHQ Air Force be organized and begin operation at a headquarters at Langley Field on 1 March 1935. Headquarters of the Air Force's three wings would be at Langley Field, Virginia; March Field, California; and Barksdale Field, Louisiana. All Air Corps pursuit, bombardment, and attack groups were assigned to the GHQ Air Force.[53] Lt Col Frank M. Andrews, an experienced Air Corps officer who had been serving on the War Department General Staff, was announced as commanding general, GHQ Air Force, with a temporary rank of brigadier general. On 19 February 1935 the War Department provided Andrews with tables of organization for the new command, and he was directed to service test the new organization and make a final report on its effectiveness before 1 February 1936.[54]

Along with its other organizational changes, the Baker board had recommended the creation of an Air Corps board to formulate uniform tactical doctrine. As has been seen, such a board had existed on paper since 1922 and had been moved with the Air Corps Tactical School from Langley to Maxwell in 1931. For more than two years, General Foulois resisted suggestions from within his own office that the Air Corps Board ought to be revitalized, both because he had a scarcity of senior officers and because he preferred to rely on the Air Corps Plans Division for policy recommendations. Although the Baker board forced him to act, Foulois continued to plead that the Air Corps did not have the five to eight senior officers needed to man the Air Corps Board. He accordingly received permission to name the commandant and assistant commandant of the Tactical School to serve on the board as an additional duty. Two officers already at Maxwell, Maj William O. Ryan and Lt Gordon P. Saville, were assigned to the board on full-time duty. In a statement of mission, the Air Corps Board was directed to consider such subjects as might be referred to it by the chief of the Air Corps and to originate and submit to the chief of the Air Corps recommendations looking toward the improvement of the Air Corps.[55]

Development of Doctrine in the Air Corps and GHQ Air Force

Looking backward with regret at his failure to have convinced "those earnest and conscientious men" of the Baker board of the urgent national need to unify our military forces and to form an independent air force, James H. Doolittle observed in 1945 that the report of the Baker board should have borne the subtitle: Pearl Harbor, Here We Come. "Basically," reminisced Doolittle, "the trouble was that we had to talk about air power in terms of promise and prophecy instead of in terms of demonstration and experience."[56] When the GHQ Air Force was organized and began to receive modern aircraft, the Air Corps was able to begin basing its doctrine on a lengthening record of demonstrations and experience.

Because of fundamental changes in the Air Corps mission resulting from the MacArthur-Pratt agreement and the Drum board report, the War Department directed the Air Corps on 27 December 1933 to review and revise its training regulations and manuals to ensure that the new principles and doctrines were disseminated. The project was assigned to the Air Corps Training and Operations Division, but it made little progress because of continuing changes in the Air Corps mission.[57] What the War Department General Staff judged the role and mission of the GHQ Air Force to be was demonstrated in a directive for a GHQ command post exercise prepared in the War Plans Division in June 1934. That directive indicated that the bombardment plane was to be the most important element of the GHQ Air Force. The mission of the GHQ Air Force included bombardment of enemy establishments and installations beyond the range of artillery, pursuit action to counter enemy air operations, long-range reconnaissance, and attacks against critical targets in the battle area. In addition to furnishing air protection to bombardment, pursuit aviation was to assist in preventing hostile aviation from operating over friendly territory. The most important point in the directive was the manner in which the GHQ Air Force would receive its targets. The preferred method would designate objectives to the GHQ Air Force commander to "insure the cooperation of the Air Force with the ground units and that it will be directed against those objectives which will further the operations of the ground forces and the general plan of campaign."[58] In commenting on this directive, General Westover stated that because of its limited range, pursuit aviation rarely would be able to protect bombardment or long-range observation aircraft. Instead of the Army General Headquarters assigning air objectives, General Westover recommended that the GHQ Air Force commander be informed about the campaign and its objectives and that he be charged to prepare and present an air plan to support the campaign. This air plan could be modified by General Headquarters or by the GHQ Air Force as a result of mutual consultation that would take place as the campaign progressed.[59]

One of the reasons for establishing the GHQ Air Force was that the MacArthur-Pratt agreement had given the coastal air defense mission to the Army. This agreement apparently was not popular within the Navy and the Navy Department promptly reopened the matter in Joint Board discussions following Admiral Pratt's retirement in June 1933. In these discussions, Navy spokesmen insisted that the Navy had a primary mission for "air operations in support of local naval defense forces operating for the protection of lines of sea communications and coastal zones against attacks by hostile submarines and surface raiders." Although the Baker board report of July 1934 called for a resolution of this matter in accordance with the act of Congress of 5 June 1920, the Joint Board agreement of 26 September 1934, entitled "Doctrine for the Employment of the GHQ Air Force," stated that the Navy would have "a paramount interest" in operations at sea when the fleet was present and free to act. Moreover, the agreement authorized the Navy to maintain "shore stations at strategical centers, where scouting and patrolling seaplanes may be concentrated to meet naval situations."[60] Air Corps officers protested that the agreement gave the mission of coastal frontier air patrol to the Navy and permitted it to maintain as many shore bases and patrol planes as it deemed necessary in peacetime as well as wartime. The Navy apparently wanted to circumscribe the Army air mission still further. In a presentation to the Federal Aviation Commission in November 1934, the Navy urged that

> the Army should develop and build those types of airplanes required by the Army to fulfill its mission in land operations. The Navy should develop and build those types of airplanes required by the Navy in its operation over the sea or for operation from fleet air bases or naval stations. The Army should have paramount interest over the land and the Navy over the sea. Neither service should build or operate planes intended to duplicate the functions of the other.[61]

At an assemblage of naval officers at San Diego on 14 June 1935, Adm W. H. Standley, chief of naval operations, stated that the Navy was going to build up a striking force of 1,000 aircraft.[62]

General MacArthur, convinced by the Baker and Howell hearings that the Army ought to arrive at a united front on the subject of aviation, directed that a statement of facts, principles, and doctrines relating to the Army Air Corps should be prepared. In the past the Air Service and the Air Corps had been permitted to initiate such work, but now the initial task was undertaken by the War Department General Staff. As a "sighting shot" the War Plans Division (WPD) drew up a draft revision of War Department Training Regulation 440-15, *Employment of the Air Forces of the Army,* and General Kilbourne circulated the draft paper for criticism. As written the WPD draft asserted that the "land campaign and battle" was "the decisive factor in war." While it noted that air force action would be intensive at the beginning of a war, it stated that the advantages of alluring air missions at such a time should be weighed against the requirement to keep superior air forces in being to support operations that would take place after the ground armies made contact. The greatest part of the draft dealt with the employment of air forces in continental defense. In fact, the revised training regulation defined air defense as "the means whereby a nation exerts Air Power." During the period of strategical development before ground contact, the GHQ Air Force commander would work from "a broad general mission." However, once the battle began, he would receive specific assignments from General Headquarters.[63]

A copy of the War Plans Division's proposed doctrinal statement was transmitted to Maxwell Field, where Col John F. Curry served both as commandant, Air Corps Tactical School, and president, Air Corps Board. Since the Air Corps Board had only two full-time officers, the study and commentary on the WPD draft was made by the staff of the Air Corps Tactical School. In the introduction to its critique, completed on 31 January 1935, the Tactical School pointed out that any doctrine which would receive more than lip service had to appeal to reason and to be acceptable in principle. The Tactical School was critical of the fact that the WPD draft was predicated upon the geographic isolation of the United States and that the mission of countering enemy air forces was narrowly conceived in terms of continental defense. "The principal and all important missions of air power, when its equipment permits," stated the Tactical School critique, "is the attack of those vital objectives in a nation's economic structure which will tend to paralyze that nation's ability to wage war and thus contribute to the attainment of the ultimate objective of war, namely, the disintegration of the will to resist." When employed from bases in the United States, the GHQ Air Force would have such a limited range that the only positive way in which it could ensure the success of the Army would be to defeat the hostile air force. The possibility of simultaneously defeating the hostile air force and of attacking the enemy army in support of friendly ground forces was described as an alluring but false doctrine. Only if the hostile air force were defeated would occasions arise when the GHQ Air Force would be able to attack targets in direct support of the ground battle.[64]

IDEAS, CONCEPTS, DOCTRINE

Very little of the thought contained in the Air Corps Tactical School critique appeared in the final draft of the War Plans Division paper that was officially published as the revised War Department Training Regulation 440-15 on 15 October 1935. This regulation defined air power as "the power which a nation is capable of exerting by means of its air forces." But, it stated, "Air forces further the mission of the territorial or tactical commands to which they are assigned." It contemplated that a phase of air operations would probably precede the contact of the surface forces and that the outcome of this phase would exert a potent influence upon subsequent operations. The functions of the GHQ Air Force included air operations beyond the sphere of influence of the ground forces, in immediate support of the ground forces, or in coastal defense and other Army-Navy operations. The regulation stated that the effect which air forces were capable of producing and the extent to which they would influence warfare was still undetermined. Complete control of the air was considered to be an unlikely prospect. But attacks were to be made against hostile air forces prior to ground army contact and the interdiction of enemy reconnaissance and hostile attacking aircraft was to be a continuing function during ground battles. In effect the new edition of Training Regulation 440-15 was a middle-ground compromise between extreme viewpoints of both air and ground officers. There were enough loopholes to permit continued air force development. The regulation, for example, respected the unity of the GHQ Air Force and allowed leeway for independent air operations that were to be conducted before ground armies made contact. For the first time, Maj Gen Follett Bradley later remarked, the regulation spelled out an air doctrine "to which most Air Force officers could subscribe."[65]

Beliefs in Bomber Invincibility

Much of the reorientation of the Air Corps that was required when the GHQ Air Force was being established fell to General Westover. This reorientation had to do with organization, the procurement of new aircraft, and the promulgation of a uniform tactical doctrine for the employment of all branches of aviation. General Westover relied heavily upon the Air Corps Tactical School and the Air Corps Board to prepare basic studies in each of these areas. The latter was, in effect, an arm of the Office of Chief of the Air Corps on detached location at Maxwell Field. While he was acting chief of air corps in the absence of Foulois (who was nearing retirement), Westover directed the Air Corps Board on 11 March 1935 to devote its efforts to preparing a uniform tactical doctrine for all types of Air Corps units. But he indicated that the board's mission would be expanded when more personnel could be assigned to it.[66]

As an immediate solution to the task, the Air Corps Board surveyed the Air Corps Tactical School's textbooks and, following some changes in bombardment and pursuit pamphlets, obtained authorization to make these books available to field units as doctrine.[67] In June 1935 Lt Col Jacob H. Rudolph was assigned as director, Air Corps Board, and the Office of Chief of the Air Corps reopened the question of the board's mission. There was general agreement that the board should be responsible for developing doctrine, making recommendations on air force organization, and making tactical evaluations of equipment. The Air Corps Materiel Division demanded that it continue to be responsible for preparing the specifications for and conducting service tests on new equipment, but it suggested that the Air Corps Board ought to function as a planning agency that would look several years ahead and visualize developmental objectives for air force equipment. All of these ideas were incorporated in the expanded mission of the Air Corps Board.[68]

Even though air officers considered the establishment of the GHQ Air Force to be a major psychological victory, they recognized that control of the Army's air force had been undesirably compartmented. On 2 November 1935 General Andrews decried the arrangement whereby the GHQ Air Force was responsible for combat efficiency while the Office of Chief of the Air Corps selected equipment and personnel, prescribed tactics and methods of employing combat units, and controlled funds. General Andrews recommended the creation of an air division within the War Department General Staff, to be headed by an assistant chief of staff who would be responsible for military aviation. Alarmed by the rumored possibility that the Navy might try to take control of continental air defense and organize a large shore-based air force — said to be favored by Rear Adm Ernest J. King, chief of the Navy's Bureau of Aeronautics — the Air Corps Tactical School forwarded a study to Westover on 13 January 1936 that proposed to establish a United States air force as a part of the War Department under a chief of air staff. Under this plan, the chief of the Air Corps would become the deputy staff. Westover was unwilling to accept either General Andrews's suggestion or the Tactical School proposal. He instead urged on 17 January 1936 that the GHQ Air Force be placed under the chief of the Air Corps. During the next two years, both Andrews and Westover continued to urge that unity of command was required in the Air Corps. However, Gen Malin Craig, who became Army chief of staff on 2 October 1935, was quite opposed to according preferential treatment to the Air Corps.[69]

With the secretary of war's approval of the Drum board report, the Air Corps had an approved requirement for an expansion to 2,320 aircraft that were to be organized into 27 bombardment, 17 pursuit, 11 attack, and 20 observation squadrons. Several of these squadrons were committed to overseas air garrisons in the Philippines, Hawaii, and Panama; most of the observation squadrons were to be in the National Guard. The War Department did not indicate a time schedule for achieving the limited Air Corps expansion. As a matter of fact, it was going to authorize personnel increases in the Air Corps only in conjunction with an ordered expansion of the basic ground forces.

At its organization in March 1935, the GHQ Air Force consisted of four bombardment, three pursuit, two attack groups, and four reconnaissance squadrons, with a total of approximately 1,000 airplanes.[70] Since this force could not be greatly expanded, General Andrews desired a continued modernization of its aircraft. Because of the limited funds available to the Air Corps during the middle 1930s, however, much thought had to be given to the planned tactical usage and the state of the art of aviation technology before awarding contracts for aircraft purchase. Any arm or service or individual could propose military characteristics of a required type of equipment; the Air Corps, like other arms, submitted its requests, after approval by the Office of Chief of the Air Corps, to The Adjutant General for General Staff study. Approval of the military characteristics by the War Department constituted a requirement for the item. Thereafter an aircraft went through a design phase, the letting of contracts for an experimental model, the testing and evaluation of the experimental model, the procurement of a small quantity of aircraft for service testing, and finally the procurement and delivery of standardized aircraft in numbers. So much time was involved in this process that when standard aircraft were put in service they were already obsolescent in the sense that newer ideas for tactical employment and subsequent advances in aeronautical science had already created a demand for improved types of planes.[71]

During the early and middle 1930s, the state of aeronautical technology, the strategic requirements of the Red-Orange war plans, and the industrial fabric theory of war, which was being put together at the Tactical School, melded together to produce an emphasis on the development of long-range bombers. Using the latest model P-26 pursuit aircraft and B-12 bombers in tests flown at March Field, California, in 1934, Colonel Arnold—who would become assistant chief of the Air Corps in January 1936—concluded that the speeds of bombers and fighters were so evenly matched that "pursuit or fighter airplanes operating from front line airdromes will rarely intercept modern bombers except accidentally."[72] Arnold suggested that the Air Corps ought to develop a two-place, long-range pursuit aircraft that would be able to provide escort for bombers. During 1935 the Air Corps Materiel Division experimented with the design of such a pursuit plane, which basically turned out to be a heavily armed B-10 type. When the matter was referred to the Air Corps Board, the board reasoned that a large pursuit plane with pursuit safety factors, with at least 25 percent greater speed than bombers, with at least the range of bombers, with a higher ceiling capability than bombers, and with an extremely high rate of climb would probably not be technologically possible. The board recommended that experiments to develop such a plane should be continued, but every conceivable means of self-defense for bombardment aircraft should be exhausted before such long-range fighters were provided.[73]

The principal concern of the Air Corps continued to be developing long-range bombers. From data developed in the Project A bomber program, the Air Corps Materiel Division reported early in 1936 that an 8,000-mile range, 230-mile-per-hour bomber could be built. Ignoring some protest that such an intercontinental bomber would be a weapon of aggression not required for defense, the War Department authorized General Westover in April 1936 to secure a prototype plane from the Douglas Aircraft Company. Given the name Project D and, when it was completed in 1941, the XB-19, this intercontinental bomber would provide a great quantity of technological information needed for the development of long-range bombers. But, like the B-15, the XB-19 would be underpowered for its size and weight and would never be placed in quantity procurement.[74]

Already, as a result of design competitions announced in 1934, the Boeing Company offered a prototype XB-17 and the Douglas Company provided an XB-18. In its initial tests during 1935, the four-engine XB-17 flew nonstop at 232 miles per hour for a distance of 2,100 miles. The Air Corps was so favorably impressed that it wished to purchase 65 of these aircraft, but an unfortunate crash on 30 October 1935 destroyed the original XB-17 before it could be formally evaluated. As a result, the War Department awarded the 1935 bomber competition contract to Douglas for the purchase of 133 twin-engine B-18s. In February 1936 the Air Corps obtained permission to order 13 YB-17s for service testing. One justification used at this time was that a limited purchase order would assist Boeing in developing a commercial transport aircraft. Delivery of these 13 planes was completed in August 1937.[75]

During May 1937 GHQ Air Force tested the first seven of the B-17s delivered in an Army-Navy maneuver off the Pacific coast. Because it had greater range and speed than the B-10s that also participated, the B-17s showed important advantages both in sea search and in bombing operations against the battleship *Utah,* which was deployed for maneuver purposes under a fog bank 385 miles off the California coast. Using new Norden bombsights, the crews of the B-17s were able to score many hits with water-filled bombs with as little as five-second bomb runs over the battleship.[76] After nearly a year of service testing the B-17 in the 2d Bombardment Group, Lt Col Robert Olds recommended that the B-17 be classified as standard and that the GHQ Air Force's three bombardment groups be equipped with them. Col Hugh J. Knerr, chief of staff of the GHQ Air Force, positively stated that his headquarters was convinced that the B-17 airplane "is the best bombardment aircraft in existence; particularly for coastal defense purposes."[77]

At the Air Corps Tactical School, news of the superb performance of the YB-17 and the hope that the intercontinental XB-15 might prove practical strengthened proponents of strategic bombing. As demonstrated by its critique of the draft of Training Regulation 440-15, the Tactical School as early as January 1935 had rejected the idea that Air Corps doctrine be solely linked to continental defense and had argued that the mission of air power was to paralyze a hostile nation's will and ability to wage war. The Air Corps Tactical School text *The Air Force,* issued on 1 March 1936, stated that a hostile air force was a primary strategic air objective. But, it argued, the defeat of an enemy air force might entail difficult and time-consuming operations that might not prevent the enemy from quickly attaining his purpose by direct attack. "In selecting the hostile air forces as the objective," the text stated, "it is intended to remove the only force that can successfully oppose the attainment of the ultimate objectives and thus achieve a status that will permit unhampered application of pressure against the nation."[78] By 1938 the school was teaching:

> Air warfare may be waged against hostile land forces, sea forces, and air forces, or it
> may be waged directly against the enemy nation. The possibility for the application of
> military force against the vital structure of a nation directly and immediately upon the
> outbreak of hostilities is the most important and far reaching development of modern
> times.[79]

The concept of bombardment invincibility and of the defensive character of air battles was not implicitly accepted through the Air Corps. Even at Maxwell Field, in the five years that he served as an instructor and post officer prior to his retirement in 1937, Maj Claire L. Chennault argued that pursuit aviation was a weapon of opportunity that might be employed either offensively or defensively. To support his contention, Chennault devised and advocated a workable plan for aircraft warning and pursuit control services based upon visual aircraft observers and radio and telephone communications nets.[80] Lt Col Millard F. Harmon subscribed wholeheartedly to the requirement for the development of bombardment, but he was "irked [to] no end" at the lack of prestige accorded to pursuit. Named to head a board of GHQ Air Force officers at Barksdale Field to review the Air Force text in 1935, Harmon suggested that it was entirely possible that a hostile air force could be defeated by air combat and other activities. His board also argued that defense of the United States was the established national policy—not the destruction of vital elements within enemy nations.[81] Maj O. S. Ferson, a member of the board at Barksdale, argued that improved interplane radio communications would enable an air commander to control large airborne forces and thus to fight major coordinated air battles.[82] Lt Col A. H. Gilkeson, commander of the 8th Pursuit Group, stated bluntly that "this recent academic tendency to minimize, if not entirely dismiss, the consideration of the fighting force as a powerful and extremely necessary adjunct of the air force has led to the teaching of doctrines which have not been established as being true and might even be fatally dangerous to our aims in the event of armed conflict." Gilkeson urged that "a superior fighting force will always gain control of the air in at least a restricted sense."[83]

In an effort to develop facts on pursuit aviation, General Westover directed the Air Corps Board in 1935 to determine whether the Air Corps had a requirement for developing an interceptor. In February 1937 the board reported that the most efficient means of neutralizing an enemy air offensive was to attack operation against the bases that supported the offensive. The board recommended that friendly defenses against hostile aircraft would be necessary, and it recommended an immediate development of an interceptor that would have aircraft cannon and at least 20 percent greater speed than proposed bombardment planes. The board also recommended that immediate steps be taken to provide ground observer posts and aircraft reporting nets in the United States and its overseas possessions. Without having waited for the delayed Air Corps Board report, the Air Corps Technical Committee in November 1936 had already identified military characteristics for an interceptor aircraft. During fiscal year 1937 the Air Corps ordered an XP-37, which would be the progenitor of the P-40, and an XP-38, which would become standard as the P-38 Lightning. Like the XP-39, which was ordered in fiscal year 1938, the Lightning would be a short-range, cannon-equipped interceptor.[84]

Thoughts on Air Support Aviation

During the 1920s, possibly because of Mitchell's enthusiasm for such an aircraft, the Air Corps had been interested in developing and employing heavily armored attack planes that could seek out and destroy enemy personnel and materiel in low-level strikes. The Lassiter board of 1923 recommended that both observation squadrons and a force of attack and pursuit aviation should be an integral part of field armies. The assumption was that attack aircraft would be designed for strafing and fragmentation bombing. In the late 1920s, however, the Air Corps did not have a standard attack aircraft; thus, in Air Corps maneuvers pursuit squadrons frequently were employed to simulate attack missions. In 1932 tests of the all metal, low-wing Curtiss XA-8 aircraft led to the procurement the following year of 46 of these planes, which were redesigned with radial engines and designated A-12s. Following development from a commercial aircraft model, the Air Corps secured delivery of 110 Northrop A-17s in 1936. These two-place monoplanes carried five .30-caliber machine guns and stowed fragmentation and demolition bombs internally.[85]

When the Army began looking toward a reorganization of its basic ground forces, the Air Corps initiated serious studies of ground support aviation. In a report on the modernization of the Army completed on 9 January 1936, the Air Corps Board recommended that there should be no change in the existing assignment of an observation group and a balloon observation group as organic parts of each corps and an observation group as an organic part of each field army. The board, however, displayed misgivings about the proposed assignment of attack aviation as an organic part of an army. It noted that attack aviation would appear to be "an ideal weapon in the hands of an Army commander." But, the board argued, because of its expense, relative scarcity, and capability to penetrate, attack aviation ought to be assigned to the GHQ Air Force, in order that it could be used anywhere in a theater of operations as directed by General Headquarters. "A weapon capable of giving direct support to more than one subordinate unit," the board reasoned, "should be assigned to a superior headquarters." The board also indicated that one of the principal missions of attack aviation would be to disrupt the railways that supported an enemy's front; highways were thought to be much less vulnerable to air attack.[86]

At a 13 April 1936 meeting of the General Staff committee that was studying the reorganization of the Army, General Westover reported his approval of the Air Corps Board report. In some cases, Westover said he would be willing to attach aviation to armies or corps, but he emphasized that aviation supporting an army normally ought to operate under the control of the GHQ Air Force. Westover further stated that because of the relative invulnerability of dispersed ground troops, aviation should not be used against frontline troops except in vital situations.[87] In commenting on one of the Army reorganization planning papers sent to him, General Andrews took strong exceptions to the term *air-ground military team*. He could understand how observation aviation could be a part of the air-ground team, but he argued that pursuit, attack, and bombardment received no assistance from the ground forces in their combat operations. The War Department General Staff did not agree with these independent ideas. It insisted that "even independent air operations are carried out as part of the general plan of the Commander-in-Chief . . . and must be designed to support the general strategic purpose which he desires to attain."[88]

War Department General Staff Reorients Air Programs

Early in the 1930s the War Department had been willing to permit the development of experimental long-range bombers, apparently because General MacArthur held a permissive attitude toward such an endeavor. The attitude of the War Department General Staff switched abruptly after October 1935 when General Craig became Army chief of staff. Beginning in 1936 General Craig and his deputy chief of staff, Maj Gen Stanley D. Embick, pressed the entire Army to reduce expenditures for research and development.[89] In June 1936 the War Department turned down Westover's request for authority to buy a test quantity of XB-15s and enough B-17s to equip at least two groups. At a General Staff conference on bombardment held on 28 August, both Westover and Andrews argued that the four-engine bomber would be the most effective weapon that the Air Corps could procure, but the General Staff held that the "bulk of bombardment aviation operating with a mobile Army should be the size and capacity of the standard B-18 medium bomber." Alleging that no action could be taken until the YB-17s were thoroughly service tested, the War Department cut B-17 procurement out of the Air Corps budget requests for fiscal years 1937 and 1938 and added twin-engine bombers. Because of the successful service tests of the YB-17s in the summer of 1937, however, the War Department later authorized the Air Corps to procure 26 B-17Bs from fiscal year 1938 carryover funds and 13 B-17Bs from current funds in fiscal year 1939.[90]

Although the Air Corps was not obtaining the type of aircraft that it felt necessary for its missions, the War Department procurement actions of the middle 1930s pushed the Air Corps toward its authorized strength of 2,320 aircraft, which would be attained with fiscal year 1939 purchases. Looking toward stabilizing and modernizing Air Corps strength at this figure by the annual purchase of newer replacement aircraft, Secretary of War Harry H. Woodring directed the General Staff to provide him with a five-year aircraft replacement program that would take effect beginning in fiscal year 1940.[91] After it had been drawn up in conferences between Westover and Andrews and had been modified by the General Staff, Secretary Woodring on 18 March 1938 approved the Balanced Air Force Program (better known as the Woodring program), which authorized the Air Corps to maintain a combat strength of 144 four-engine bombers, 266 twin-engine bombers, 259 attack aircraft, and 425 pursuit aircraft. Although the Air Corps had also asked to purchase a modest number of transport planes, Woodring instead directed that obsolete bombers would be used for transport purposes. The Air Corps was specifically authorized to purchase 67 four-engine bombers in fiscal year 1940 and 48 in fiscal year 1941.[92]

Although the Woodring program was said to manifest "an excellent spirit of cooperation with the ultimate objective of the Army," events were brewing that would cause the War Department to suspend heavy bomber procurement. In April 1937, the chairman of the House Appropriations Subcommittee that handled War Department estimates recorded his protest against the unwise tendency to build larger and more expensive bombers such as the B-17. On 23 September, however, Andrews forwarded an elaborate defense of the planned four-engine bomber procurement under the Woodring program. He argued that: (1) the heavy-load, long-endurance multiengine bomber was a powerful instrument of defense and, in view of the nation's fortunate strategic position and defensive policy, such an airplane as the basic element of the GHQ Air Force was essential to accomplishing the GHQ Air Force mission; (2) such an airplane, with bomb and fuel loads interchangeable to a high degree, offered the most economical and efficient means of performing the functions of reconnaissance and bombardment (though not on the same mission); (3) based on per ton load of bombs carried or per square mile of area reconnoitered, a multiengine aircraft was actually cheaper to operate than medium bombers such as the B-10 or the B-18; and (4) in view of these factors the process of experimental aircraft and engine development had to continue so that bombers of longer range and superior performance could be made available.[93] On 9 October 1937 Andrews told an audience at the Army War College that "from some sources comes the statement that the modern development of large bombers is for the purpose of aggressive action on the part of the United States. Often we hear of our large bombers spoken of as 'Weapons of Offense,' 'Superbombers,' and similar appellations. These terms are unfortunate and misleading."[94]

At the same time that General Andrews was pleading the cause of the multiengine bomber, Army officers were drawing different lessons as a result of reports received from the Italian campaign in Ethiopia and the Spanish Civil War. An Army War College course conducted during September 1937 taught that air power had limited value when employed independently and was chiefly useful as a support for surface operations. The course text *Air Forces and War* cited military attaché reports received from Spain, which said that high-altitude bombing was ineffectual, that the Flying Fortress concept had "died in Spain," and that small bombers and fighters, which could operate from cow-pasture facilities, were of the utmost utility.[95] What made the text seem more authoritative was the fact that Col B. Q. Jones, a long-time Air Corps officer who had served as a sector commander in the airmail episode and was now an instructor at the Army War College, completely endorsed it in a summary lecture. Colonel Jones, who would transfer to the cavalry in 1939, stated that the Spanish Civil War had demonstrated that the capabilities of air power had not progressed markedly from those displayed in World War I. He advocated using bombardment aviation as long-range artillery, attaching attack and bombardment aircraft to lower echelons of the Army for use in the same manner as artillery, and employing GHQ aviation in close support of ground forces. Seeking to counteract the influence of the Jones lecture in War Department General Staff, Lt Cols Ralph H. Wooten and Walter F. Kraus, the Air Corps officers assigned to the G-3 division, drew up a paper which pointed out that Jones was inconsistent with approved Army doctrine incorporated in Training Regulation 440-15. General Embick, however, refused to accept this finding. "Aviation," he wrote on 23 October 1937, "is a new arm. Our present War Department doctrine has had to be based necessarily on theory and assumption rather than on factual evidence. Now we are getting evidence of that character. No doctrine is sacro-sanct, and of all military doctrines that of our Air Corps should be the last to be so regarded."[96]

Even though the Woodring program authorized the procurement of four-engine bombers for the Air Corps, the War Department General Staff apparently had approved the program with severe misgivings. The whole matter was thrust back into controversy in May 1938, when General Westover, mindful of the fact that the B-17s were already four years old, requested the War Department to authorize the Air Corps to undertake the development of a new high-altitude, 4,000-mile-range bomber, that could carry two tons of bombs. General Embick exploded into action. "Our national policy," he wrote on 9 May, "contemplates preparation for defense, not aggression. Defense of sea areas, other than within the coastal zone, is a function of the Navy. The military superiority of a plane the size of even the B-17 over the two or three smaller ships that can be procured with the same funds, remains to be established, in view of the vulnerability, air base limitations, and complexity, of the former type. . . . If the equipment to be provided for the Army Air Corps be that best adapted to carry out the specific functions appropriately assigned it under Joint Action as an integral part of the national defense team, there would appear to be no need for a plane larger than the B-17, and only the relatively small number of the latter desirable as potential reinforcing units for Oahu or Panama."[97]

At General Embick's instigation, the War Department referred Westover's request for the development of a high-altitude, long-range bomber to the Joint Army-Navy Board for review. On 29 June the Joint Board reported that it visualized no likelihood that the Army Air Corps would be called upon in time of war to perform missions requiring the use of bombers with greater capabilities than those of the B-17. It believed that the Air Corps would be called upon to perform many missions with less expensive medium bombers. It recommended, therefore, that the largest proportion of Army bombardment and reconnaissance planes ought to be aircraft smaller than the B-17.[98] The assistant chief of staff G-4 estimated that the funds required to buy 67 B-17s in the first year of the Woodring program could otherwise be used to purchase nearly 300 attack bombers. He recommended that such a change in procurement should be made. General Craig approved the recommended change, noting: "This is O.K. and solves the problem of 17-Bs vs. medium bombers." On 29 July the War Department informed Westover that the approval given to the Woodring program was withdrawn and that estimates for bombardment planes to be procured in fiscal year 1940 would be restricted to light, medium, and attack types.[99] On 6 August Westover was additionally informed that the developmental expenditures for fiscal years 1939 and 1940 would be "restricted to that class of aviation designed for the close support of ground troops and the protection of that type of aircraft."[100]

In the same season, General Craig gave indications that he wished to transfer Army responsibilities for coastal defense to the Navy. As a part of the Navy expansion program submitted to Congress in January 1938 by President Franklin D. Roosevelt, the Navy not only requested funds to purchase a large number of patrol aircraft, but also asked relief from the proviso that had been incorporated in all naval appropriation bills since 1920, which limited it to not more than six air bases on the coasts of the United States.[101] In the opening phase of the GHQ Air Force war games in the northeastern United States, however, General Andrews employed B-17 and B-18 bombers in sea search and simulated attack missions against vessels bound toward the United States. In one mission, on 12 May, three B-17s successfully located and simulated attacks against the ocean liner *Rex* at a distance of 725 miles out of New York.[102] To the Air Corps, the interception of the *Rex* proved the value of the B-17 for coastal defense, but the demonstration of effectiveness apparently displeased either the Navy or the War Department General Staff.

What happened next has never been exactly documented. General Arnold later suggested that the Navy protested the flight of the B-17s so far out to sea and that the War Department agreed to limit Air Corps patrol activities. Ira C. Eaker, who was then a major, recalled that he was in General Andrews's office when General Craig telephoned and verbally instructed him to limit Army flights to a 100-mile zone off the nation's coasts. According to Arnold, the War Department would not put this order in writing; nonetheless, it was binding and evidently represented a coordinated Army-Navy policy.[103] Indicating that old policies had somehow changed, a revision of the manual *Joint Action of the Army and the Navy,* issued on 8 August 1938, authorized shore-based naval aircraft "to operate effectively over the sea to the maximum distance within the capacity of aircraft development."[104] Army aircraft, on the other hand, had to operate at a reduced range. As the report on the annual tactical inspection of the GHQ Air Force made on 28 July 1939 protested, "navigation training in the GHQ Air Force has suffered because of the 100-mile restriction, except by special permission, placed by the War Department on the distance to which airplanes may fly to sea."[105]

Westover protested that disapproval of the Woodring program had set the development of the Air Corps back by at least five years and would restore hit-or-miss procurement. He formally requested that the original Woodring program be reestablished and that the Air Corps be authorized to develop a successor aircraft to the B-17.[106] The War Department General Staff deliberated Westover's reclamé at great length. In the end the G-4 Division provided General Craig with what he described as "a very able study," which was used as the basis for the carefully weighed War Department decision rendered on 5 October 1938. In this decision the War Department professed to recognize the increased potential of aircraft, but it still proclaimed that "none of this progress . . . has changed the conception that the Infantry Division continues to be the basic combat element by which battles are won, the enemy field forces destroyed and captured territory held." Moreover, the War Department held to the position that all combat arms ought to be brought up to nearly equal preparedness status and that the Air Corps could not be maintained "in a higher state of immediate war readiness than the other arms." It enjoined the Air Corps "to obtain and develop aircraft suitable for the close support of ground troops to the same extent that now pertains with respect to types suitable for strategic and more distant missions." Only one concession was made. In order to provide a replacement for the B-17 at some future date the restriction previously imposed on the development of four-engine bombing planes was rescinded.[107]

Efforts to Describe Air Doctrine

At least in theory the chief of air corps was responsible for preparing Air Corps doctrine. In June 1935 General Westover had first directed the Air Corps Board to formulate a uniform tactical doctrine for the Air Corps. But with never more than five full-time members, the Air Corps Board had found it difficult to complete the doctrinal manuals project. At the top level in Washington — as Colonel Kraus pointed out — the War Department General Staff exerted "an important influence on the tactical doctrine" of the Air Corps since "such doctrines obviously must be governed to a large extent by the characteristics of the weapons made available."[108] Located as it was at Maxwell Field, the Air Corps Tactical School was far from sympathetic toward official Army doctrine. As a matter of fact, the Tactical School frankly questioned and invited academic disagreement with all doctrine. "Battles have been won too often," stated Capt Laurence S. Kuter, in a lecture on 2 March 1938, "by the judicious violation of doctrine. . . . Disagree with doctrine in the conference room — be familiar enough with it to violate it in the conference room — but know it well enough to know what it is and why you are violating it."[109] The school was able to think and teach about absolutes in war that were not necessarily related to current war plans. "Even though air warfare may be waged simultaneously against both the enemy armed forces and the enemy national structure," the school argued in 1938, "the main purpose of the air offensive will be to nullify the former so as to permit breaking down or conclusively threatening the latter."[110]

While the Air Corps Board was mindful of the mandate requiring it to provide a uniform tactical doctrine for the Air Corps, work on this project could not get under way prior to the final publication of War Department Training Regulation

440-15 in October 1935. Even when this regulation appeared, Colonel Rudolph, the Air Corps Board's director, pointed out that it did not contain the fundamental principles that were needed to guide Air Corps development. For one thing, the Army was not definitely committed to provide aviation for coastal defense. Rudolph pointed out these facts to General Westover in May 1936. Consequently, Westover instructed the board to prepare a study on the functions of the Army air force. This study recommended that the War Department commit itself to develop air forces for continental defense, immediate support of ground combat, and conduct of strategic offensive operations. In April 1937 Brig Gen Henry C. Pratt, commandant of the Tactical School and ex officio as president of the Air Corps Board, requested that the War Department approve these functions as a guide for both the board and the school. The War Department refused to do so, noting that such strategic questions had no place in an Air Corps field manual.[111]

In response the Air Corps Board reduced the scope of its field manuals project to two volumes: the first to deal with tactics, technique, and training, and the second to deal with maintenance, base functions, logistics, and staff data. Giving priority to the first volume, the board forwarded a complete draft to the Office of the Chief of the Air Corps on 11 March 1938. General Pratt pointed out that the manual represented "an enormous amount of work, thought, and study ... and constitutes the best available thought on the use of a D-day air force."[112] After making some suggested changes in wording, the Office of the Chief of the Air Corps submitted the draft manual to the War Department on 14 September 1938. The General Staff reviewed the draft and returned it to the chief of the Air Corps on 29 March 1939. Maj Gen R. M. Beck, assistant chief of staff G-3, suggested an outline for its revision. Beck stated that the manual ought not to make any mention of independent air operations or of air attacks that were designed to destroy the morale of the enemy's population. He also said that discussion of air action against naval forces should be avoided since this was within the province of Joint Board papers. Beck provided a statement of basic Air Corps doctrine that had been drawn up in his division and which he directed would become the first chapter of the Air Corps manual. The basic tenor of this G-3 doctrinal statement, which was not to be changed without coordination with G-3, left little doubt that it was the intention of the War Department General Staff to develop and employ aviation in support of ground operations. "The mission of the air component of the Army," the statement read, "is to perform effectively the air operations devolving upon the Army in its assigned functions in the National Defense. . . . Air operations beyond the sphere of action of the surface forces are undertaken in furtherance of the strategical plan of the commander of the field force."[113]

Aviation in Support of the Monroe Doctrine

Meanwhile, General Arnold, the assistant chief of the Air Corps, expressed doubts that the roles and missions of the Air Corps could be justified on an abstract basis. Early in June, Arnold expressed concern that the forces of aggression building up in Europe could well threaten the Western Hemisphere. He, therefore, saw the need to study the employment of the Air Corps in support of national policy as represented by the Monroe Doctrine. He thought it best that the study remain unknown to the War Department until the Air Corps had "crystallized its own thought." Among its other undertakings, the Air Corps Board was already working on a study to determine the most effective methods of using aircraft in defense of the continental United States. Arnold accordingly assigned the secret Monroe Doctrine project to the Air Corps Board on 6 June. When General Pratt protested that neither the Tactical School nor the Air Corps Board was equipped for making war plans, General Westover told him that the board would undertake the study with such assistance as it could get from the Tactical School faculty.[114]

But because of a shortage of personnel during the summer vacation season at Maxwell Field, the Air Corps Board made little progress on the Monroe Doctrine until August 1938, when Col J. H. Pirie and Maj Orvil A. Anderson reported as the board's director and recorder. As Anderson later recalled, the Air Corps Board had never before addressed a specific situation that so clearly demanded long-range bombers and quasi-independent air actions as did the requirement for air defense of the hemisphere under the Monroe Doctrine. After an analysis of the potential military requirements for support of the Monroe Doctrine, Anderson, who drew up the logistical requirements for the study, was able to demonstrate the inherent efficiency of long-range aircraft in terms of planes, personnel, and bases required to defend the North American continent and the South American continent down to the 36th parallel against seaborne threat or invasion. The study was not developed in full detail because Arnold, who became chief of the Air Corps on 22 September 1938 following Westover's death in an air accident, demanded that it be put in his hands not later than 18 October. Nevertheless, the study recommended in some detail the development and procurement of bombardment and reconnaissance aircraft with a radius of action of at least 1,500 miles, a surface ceiling of 35,000 feet or more, and the highest speed consistent with its range and altitude.[115] General Arnold immediately approved the Air Corps Board report. And believing that the appeasement manifested at Munich at the end of September portended an almost certainty that Germany would regain her former African colonies and use them as a springboard to establish points of strength in South America, Arnold argued that the Air Corps needed seven heavy bombardment groups and an equal number of heavy reconnaissance squadrons for stationing in the United States, Alaska, Panama, and Hawaii to close the aerial doors to the United States.[116]

Mobilization for Western Hemisphere Defense

Despite Adolf Hitler's ability to gain concessions in Europe partly because of the Luftwaffe's superiority, the US War Department continued to advocate a phased augmentation of all of its basic forces, including the Air Corps. In October and early November, General Arnold submitted several proposals to the War

Department looking toward an increase in Air Corps strength and an immediate expansion of aircraft production industries, but General Craig could not see how these actions could be taken without upsetting the orderly balance of Army forces.[117] Whether any of the Air Corps proposals got through the General Staff to the White House appears in doubt.

But President Roosevelt had his own sources of information and he was going to make decisions independently of the recommendations of the War Department. For instance, in a confidential letter dated 11 July 1938, Ambassador Hugh Wilson in Berlin was emphatic in his discussion of the German air potential either for war or political blackmail. Likewise, in a long conversation with Roosevelt on 13 October, William C. Bullitt, the ambassador to France, brought out the belief of the French military chiefs that Hitler's power rested upon an already large air force that could be expanded rapidly. Both the British and French wanted the United States to increase aircraft production drastically in order that they could buy planes to build up aerial fleets that would either overawe Hitler or, if war came, could help to defeat the Axis without American armed intervention.[118]

At a meeting of civilian and military leaders at his White House office on 14 November 1938, President Roosevelt issued instructions that General Arnold later described as the Magna Carta of the Air Force. Roosevelt announced that airplanes — not ground forces — were the implements of war that would influence Hitler's actions. In view of the air orders of battle of the Axis nations, he continued, the United States had to prepare itself to resist assault on the Western Hemisphere "from the North to the South Pole." Roosevelt's desired objective was an Army air force of 20,000 planes and an annual productive capacity of 24,000 aircraft, but he did not think that Congress would approve more than 10,000 planes—2,500 trainers, 3,750 combat line, and 3,750 combat reserve—and this became the objective. Roosevelt's plan also called for the construction of seven government-financed aircraft plants, two of which would be put into operation, the remainder to be temporarily in reserve.[119] President Roosevelt's announcement that he would present an Air Corps expansion program to Congress in his State of the Union message early in January 1939 left little time for planning. The Office of the Chief of the Air Corps had no staff agency that was able to state immediately what the complexion of the Air Corps ought to be. Arnold quickly began to transfer into his office a roster of experienced Air Corps officers. This group included Lt Cols Carl Spaatz, Joseph T. McNarney, Ira C. Eaker, and Maj Muir S. Fairchild. When Captain Kuter stopped on a flight to Bolling Field to refuel, he found orders to report to the basement of the Munitions Building where Major Fairchild and Captain Kenney were attempting to determine how big an air force was needed and for what it was needed. Many of the answers came from an Air Corps Tactical School map problem that had focused on the defense of the Western Hemisphere against an Axis air threat from the direction of Dakar and Natal. Largely on the basis of this strategic concept, the Air Corps stated requirements for a 5,500 airplane program that promised to fall within the cost figure of $500 million that Roosevelt had said he would request for airplanes. When the plan went to the War

Department General Staff for review, however, the War Plans Division insisted that an augmentation of ground combat strength would have to accompany the Air Corps buildup to combat Axis intrigue in South America. When Roosevelt was briefed on the final plan, he complained that the War Department offered him everything except the airplanes he wanted. On 12 January 1939 he asked Congress for $300 million—instead of $500 million—for the Air Corps. In three months Congress passed the emergency Army air defense bill substantially as requested: the Air Corps was authorized a total strength of 5,500 aircraft and given authority to procure 3,251 new planes.[120]

As finally enacted, President Roosevelt's somewhat hastily managed Army air defense program promised a larger expansion of American aviation production facilities than it did an increase in the size of the active Army Air Corps. The War Department, however, inclined a more sympathetic ear to the Air Corps in part because of the personal influence of Brig Gen George C. Marshall, who replaced General Embick as deputy chief of staff. Employing arguments long used by Air Corps officers, General Marshall, on 29 November 1938, cited to General Craig numerous reasons why it was essential for the Air Corps to purchase maximum quantities of B-17B aircraft.[121] Yielding to Arnold's argument that unity of purpose and planning were necessary to attain the Air Corps mission, the War Department on 1 March 1939 placed the GHQ Air Force under the immediate responsibility of the chief of the Air Corps rather than the chief of staff.[122]

In view of General Craig's impending retirement on 1 September 1939, General Marshall was made acting chief of staff on 1 July. That same day he assembled 10 new Air Corps officers who were joining the General Staff and told them that they had a war assignment. On 4 August, Marshall also brought General Andrews to the General Staff as assistant chief of staff, G-3. Andrews immediately organized an Air Section in the G-3 Division, thereby causing lifted eyebrows all over the Munitions Building.[123] On 24 August the War Department's old restriction against Air Corps flights of more than 100 miles out to sea finally was rescinded by the issuance of an Air Corps circular that permitted air operations over the sea to the maximum range of multiengine aircraft.[124]

An Air Power Mission for the Air Corps

President Roosevelt's decision to emphasize air power touched off an expansion of the Army Air Corps, but it did not end the controversy as to what the mission of the Air Corps should be. Looking toward this end, Secretary of War Woodring appointed an Air Board on 23 March 1939 to consider and recommend the fundamental policies that would govern the tactical and strategical employment of the Army's air force under current national policies, including hemispheric defense. Woodring designated Arnold as president of the Air Board and named as members Generals Andrews and Beck and Brig Gen George V. Strong, the assistant chief of staff, War Plans Division.[125] Colonel Spaatz privately stated to General Arnold that the Air Board could not perform its tasks until it first determined the Air Corps' mission, the doctrines for its employment, and the characteristics of the forces it would require.[126] At its first meeting on 31 March, the Air Board agreed to study each of these matters.[127]

To provide an input to the War Department Air Board, the Air Corps Board at Maxwell Field was required to expedite the preparation of its study "Employment of Aircraft in Defense of the Continental United States." To hasten the work, the Air Corps Board found ideas in studies made at the Tactical School and in the answers to a questionnaire it sent out to the GHQ Air Force and its unit commanders. Completed on 7 May 1939, the Air Corps Board study visualized the primary purpose of the national defense as being to hold US territory inviolate, to discourage an enemy from attempting an invasion, and to defeat an invasion if it were attempted. The Air Corps Board assumed that an enemy nation would employ combined air, ground, and naval forces in a series of expeditionary operations designed to establish bases progressively closer to vital areas of the United States. It defined air power as "a measure of a nation's capacity to wage air warfare" and stated that air power would be effective only if it could strike an enemy decisively and simultaneously preserve its own integrity. Under this definition, the range of bombardment aircraft both increased the ability of a plane to apply pressure against the enemy and increased the security of the bombardment bases against enemy attack. Since air forces were said to lack the ability to control the air to a degree that would positively deny hostile air operations, an air force could be defeated only by attacks against its bases. The report asserted that the mission of air power was the offensive, and it accordingly argued that primary emphasis should be given to the development of a striking force (bombardment and attack aircraft) with secondary emphasis to security force aviation (pursuit aircraft and fighters) and to information aviation (reconnaissance and observation aircraft). Although it would be desirable to have fighter escort for bombardment missions, such was believed to be impractical. The Air Corps Board recommended that the main aircraft production capacity should be devoted to the production of the bombardment planes, which would be of greatest value in the initial phases of an attack against the United States. Although it was apparently valuable only for local air defense, pursuit aviation would be required and ought to be assisted by an aircraft warning service.[128]

The GHQ Air Force replies to the Air Corps Board questionnaire differed from the board's report in a few respects, principally in the characteristics of the aircraft desired for development. Where the board wished to standardize the air fleet chiefly upon bombers with a 1,500-mile range to meet the needs of hemisphere defense, GHQ Air Force wanted a family of bombers that included a heavy bomber with a 5,000-mile radius which could make reprisal attacks against an enemy's homeland, a medium-range bomber with a 2,500-mile radius for hemisphere defense, a short-range bomber with a 1,500-mile radius to attack hostile naval forces, and an attack bomber with a 500- to 750-mile radius to support ground forces. GHQ also wanted reconnaissance aircraft with ranges equal to bombers, a speedy 350-mile range interceptor, and a 1,500-mile range fighter. Like the Air

Corps Board, the GHQ Air Force assumed that bombers would not require fighter escort; but the 8th Pursuit Group in a subjoined statement said that the Air Corps had a requirement for a fighter aircraft that could accompany bombers over enemy territory and render support in the vicinity of defended objectives. The 1st Pursuit Group, on the other hand, did not think that bombardment aviation would require pursuit protection unless a situation demanded prolonged bomber operations against a single objective or several objectives in a specific, limited area.[129]

As formally undertaken on 12 June 1939, the Aviation Expansion Program authorized an approximate threefold expansion of the combat strength of the Air Corps, and the construction of hemisphere defense bases in the northeastern and southeastern United States, Alaska, Puerto Rico, and Panama.[130] The Air Corps planned to attain within two years an overall strength of 24 groups — including five heavy bombardment, six medium bombardment, two light bombardment (formerly attack), seven pursuit interceptor, two pursuit fighter, one composite (for the Philippines), and one demonstration (for Maxwell Field). The program also included nine corps and division observation squadrons. Each of the heavy (four-engine) groups and medium (twin-engine) bombardment groups would have a reconnaissance squadron of the same basic type aircraft.[131] Of the 5,498 aircraft in the expansion program, 2,084 combat aircraft were to be assigned to tactical units, 1,341 combat aircraft were to be maintained in a rotating reserve, and 2,073 training aircraft were to be in service or in reserve. The purchase of aircraft for the rotating reserve apparently was authorized in order to expand US aircraft production capacity. But the Air Corps believed that these planes would permit units to maintain themselves at full strength and replace any combat losses incurred between M-day and the time that aircraft facilities could meet wartime demands.[132]

New aircraft for the Air Corps not already on order were quickly placed on order. In fiscal year 1939, even though heavy bomber purchases had not been authorized, the Air Corps issued procurement orders for 206 Douglas A-20 attack bombers and for 200 Curtiss P-40 pursuit interceptors. In fiscal year 1940 it ordered 70 B-17s and, in order to have a second source of production for four-engine bombers, it procured a test quantity of 16 new Consolidated B-24 aircraft. As replacements for the twin-engine B-18s, the Air Corps ordered 183 North American B-25s and 201 Martin B-26s; ordered as pursuit fighter planes were 66 Lockheed P-38s and as pursuit interceptors, 95 Bell P-39s. As a potential additional pursuit fighter aircraft, the Air Corps ordered a single experimental XP-47 from Republic Aircraft. Early in 1939 the Air Corps Materiel Division examined what had been learned from the design of the XB-15 and XB-19. In May 1940 the Air Corps circulated a request for bids for the production of prototype bombers that would have a tactical operating radius of 2,000 miles, a cruising speed of 200 miles per hour, and a normal bomb load of 2,000 pounds. In the autumn of 1940 the air arm ordered an XB-29 from Boeing and an XB-32 from Consolidated Aircraft.[133]

After deliberating through a summer of sweeping changes, the War Department Air Board completed a report that was approved by General Marshall with a few changes on 1 September and by Secretary Woodring on 15 September 1939. The report declared: "Air Power is indispensable to our national defense, especially in the early stages of war. . . . Our aviation in peacetime, both its organization and its equipment, must be designed primarily for the application of Air Power in the early days of war. The basis of Air Power is the bombardment plane." Assuming that "a well led and determined air attack once launched may be interfered with, but it can rarely, if ever, be entirely stopped by local defense," the report stated that "the only reasonable hope of avoiding air attack is in the possession of such power of retaliation as to deter an enemy from initiating air warfare." Because of the vital relationship of air bases to air power, the report stated that such bases would be primary air objectives. For the defense of the United States and its possessions, aircraft with superior range were vital. The board recommended a heavy bomber with a range of 2,000 miles and a medium bomber with a 1,000-mile range; it judged that a pursuit fighter with a range of 500 miles would satisfactorily perform such support as bombers might require. The report functionally divided air power into Army aviation (to include training and special purpose aviation, observation and liaison, and overseas garrison aviation) and GHQ aviation (which included striking and defense forces). The major function of the GHQ aviation striking force was to attack and destroy enemy aviation at its bases, whether on land or sea; the GHQ aviation defense forces were intended only to provide reasonable protection to the most vulnerable and important areas. GHQ aviation was also to include a nucleus of aviation properly trained to support ground troops and capable of expanding to meet war requirements. In General Marshall's words, the Air Board report established "for the first time a specific mission to the Air Corps, and provides for its organization on functional lines."[134]

Given the approval of the Air Board report, Lt Col Carl Spaatz, chief of the Air Corps Plans Section, called for an early completion of the Air Corps basic doctrinal manual that had been held up for so many years. Early in October 1939 Spaatz called Col D. B. Netherwood, who was now the director of the Air Corps Board, to Washington. In conferences with the new G-3 Air Section, Netherwood not only received permission to junk the old statement of basic doctrine that had been prepared by the G-3, but also secured authority to prepare a small basic doctrinal manual that could be elaborated by several more detailed field manuals. A draft of the basic manual was put together while Netherwood was in Washington, and the completed project was published as Field Manual 1-5, *Employment of the Aviation of the Army*, on 15 April 1940.[135]

In approving the Air Corps basic field manual, which superseded Training Regulation 440-15, General Andrews remarked that the manual did not endorse radical theories of air employment. As a matter of fact, the portions of the manual dealing with mission, characteristics, and purposes of aviation were lifted bodily from the Air Board report. The manual continued to respect the old relationships between air and ground warfare: portions of GHQ aviation could be attached to armies or corps for the accomplishment of specific missions, but they were to revert to GHQ control as soon as the necessity for the attachment ended. Reconnaissance, observation, and liaison squadrons were to be assigned or attached to armies, corps, and divisions. Strategic air operations were to be undertaken by bombardment aviation "to nullify the enemy's war effort or to defeat important elements of the hostile military forces." Pursuit aviation was to be designed for the defense of important areas, installations, and forces and for the protection of other aircraft in flight. Since pursuit aircraft would have a shorter range than bombers, they would need to be based well forward of the aircraft they might be called upon to escort.[136]

Battle Experience from Europe

The report of the War Department Air Board and War Department Field Manual 1-5, *Employment of the Aviation of the Army*, were based upon theoretical air warfare. However, with the German invasion of Poland and the beginning of World War II on 1 September 1939, air warfare was no longer theoretical but had become an actuality. The announced policy of the War Department continued to be one of planning and building an adequate defense of the Western Hemisphere rather than preparing expeditionary forces. The War Department, nevertheless, anticipated that the war in Europe would indicate the desirability of many changes, particularly in reference to air forces, since this was the first time in history that powerful air forces had been available for use in a war between major powers.[137]

Although the initial Luftwaffe operations in Poland were mainly in support of German ground forces, American air officers generally agreed that their theoretical doctrines were being substantiated in combat. At the Air Corps Tactical School, Lt Col Donald Wilson wrote in September that Hitler's air force had "voluntarily undertaken the job of demonstrating our theories." The Luftwaffe had established control of the air by destroying the Polish air force on its airfields; it had conducted strong attacks against Poland's lines of communications; and then it had supported the invading ground armies in a blitzkrieg attack.[138] Operating under conditions of almost complete air superiority, the Ju-87 Stuka dive-bomber proved to be very effective for delivering firepower and inflicting terror. Air Corps officers, however, were quick to note that the Stuka was operating only against sparse, small caliber antiaircraft fire. They predicted that it would not be able to defend itself against determined opposition in the air.[139]

As he looked at the German campaign in Poland, however, General Arnold was far from happy. On 14 November 1939 Arnold stated that the doctrine so widely propounded in Air Corps circles for so many years to the effect that fighter aircraft could not shoot down large bombardment aircraft flying in defensive formations had been "proven wholly untenable." Arnold blamed the problem on the teachings of the Air Corps Tactical School and the fact that older and higher ranking Air Corps officers had sought to avoid strenuous service in pursuit units. He called on Maj Gen Delos C. Emmons, commander of the GHQ Air Force, to submit a study looking toward the development of pursuit tactics, planes, and equipment. In the GHQ Air Force, Maj Harold L. George, commander of the 96th Bombardment Squadron, advised Emmons: "There is no question in my mind but that American bombardment units could not today defend themselves against American pursuit units." Pilots in the 8th Pursuit Group, as reported by Lt Col William E. Kepner, unanimously agreed that existing types of bombers would probably suffer a 50-percent loss from attacks by existing fighters unless the bombers operated at night. On the basis of these opinions, the GHQ Air Force stated: "Aerial operations of the present European conflict confirm the results of the World War; that is that the present bombardment airplane cannot defend itself adequately against pursuit attack."[140]

In the winter of 1939–40 the Air Corps considered the matter of pursuit and bombardment to be grave, but no one found any definite answers. Even though prevailing testimony indicated that existing pursuit aircraft were already superior to existing bombers, the GHQ Air Force recommended improving both pursuit aircraft and the caliber of pursuit personnel. Antedating what would later be called the weapon system concept, the GHQ Air Force suggested that a pursuit plane should be built around a previously determined armament rather than being built as an airframe and fitted with whatever armament possible.[141] Working through the Christmas holidays, the Air Corps Board completed its report on 3 January 1940. This report, "Fire Power of Bombardment Formations," noted that the firepower of American bombers was decidedly greater than that of European bombers. It recommended increased numbers of guns as practicable, better sighting systems, and increased gunnery training. It also recommended that consideration be given to developing a long-range fighter, a means whereby bombers could refuel accompanying fighters in flight, or a means by which bombers could carry, release, and recover high-performance pursuit aircraft. Despite the demonstrations of the vulnerability of bombardment aircraft, the Air Corps Board recommended that no thought should be given to reducing the importance attached to bombardment aviation in Air Corps doctrine. While pursuit escort was highly desirable for bomber penetrations into heavily defended areas in order to minimize losses of bombardment aircraft, the absence of such pursuit protection should not justify the abandoning of important missions.[142]

Even though he remained committed to heavy bombardment, General Arnold continued to be troubled about the ability of bombers to operate in the face of strong hostile fighter operation. Accordingly, on 2 March 1940, he instructed the Air Corps Board to obtain a consensus at Maxwell Field on the types of pursuit and fighter aircraft required and the steps that could be taken to develop them from existing aircraft types. Taking into consideration the existing defensive mission of the Air Corps, the board after seven days of study recommended that highest priorities be given to the development of a fighter-interceptor for local air defense. The only possible solution that the board could see for developing bomber escort aircraft was to adapt some bombers to defensive purposes. While the board was not entirely certain that such would be necessary if the bomber defenses were strengthened by additional machine guns, it suggested that some bombardment planes might be very heavily armed with extra guns and gun turrets. Three of these special aircraft could be employed as the rear element of a nine-plane bombardment flight to defend the vulnerable rear area of the formation from attacks by hostile fighters.[143] This solution apparently caught the attention of General Marshall, who asked Arnold on 13 June to consider the practicability of developing an air cruiser that would perform both air combat and bombardment missions. At this juncture, however, Arnold argued that the Air Corps had to emphasize production of existing equipment instead of research and development on an entirely new aircraft.[144]

During the spring of 1940 a steady steam of reports from France and England kept the War Department informed of the doctrinal lessons of the war in Europe. These reports noted that the Luftwaffe preserved the integrity of its air fleets and air corps, employing them as unified and flexible striking forces in support of the blitzkrieg. On 11 and 12 May, for example, two air fleets supported the German northern army group in Belgium and Holland, but on 13 and 14 May the whole air mass shifted southward to place a tremendous concentration of fire on French defenses at Sedan in support of a few armored divisions. In contrast, the British initially attached a Royal Air Force component to the British Expeditionary Force in France and maintained an independent advanced air striking force on the continent. On 15 January 1940, however, the British Air Ministry put all this aviation under the commander, British air forces in France, who was directed to use the whole force to the best possible effect in support of the allied armies as a whole. From Paris, Colonel Kenney reported that captive observation balloons were completely impracticable, as were slow and vulnerable observation planes.[145]

As time passed, the German victories over British and French forces in Holland, Belgium, and northern France caused American air leaders to increase rather than to diminish their requirements for heavy bombers. On 12 June 1940 General Emmons advised Arnold that Great Britain had made a serious mistake in building a defensive air force consisting largely of interceptor fighters and light reconnaissance bombers. Emmons suggested that if the Royal Air Force had a stronger bomber force it could have effected heavy destruction on the German troop and supply columns which had jammed the roadways leading toward Dunkirk. He recommended that the United States must materially increase its long-range bomber force.[146] On 4 June 1940 Brig Gen J. E. Chaney, commander of the new Air Defense Command at Mitchel Field, in a letter to General Marshall, argued that the United States must develop a long-range bomber force that could carry destruction to Germany. Chaney believed that a huge force of bombers, capable of taking the war to Berlin, would prove to be the only effective deterrent to German aggression and would permit operations against the Luftwaffe and any attempt Hitler might make to establish bases in or near the Western Hemisphere. Chaney's letter was endorsed by both Andrews and Arnold.[147]

These Air Corps assessments had hardly been put on paper before the Luftwaffe launched the Battle of Britain and began a phase of air combat that fostered still more thinking. As a special observer in London from May to September 1940, Colonel Spaatz had a firsthand view of some of the heaviest fighting of the Luftwaffe blitz. As shown by his diary and his reports, Spaatz quickly reached a conclusion that the Germans had developed "a mass of air geared to the Army" which was not going to be able to prevail against the "real air power" developed by the British. German bombers were inadequately armed and lacked capabilities for heavy bombing attacks. Held to close support of bombers, German pursuit forces were unable to gain a general control of the air. Spaatz noted that British airmen discredited the American concept that a hostile air force was easiest destroyed on the ground. They found a well-dispersed air force to be an exceptionally difficult bombing target, and they believed that it was more efficient to destroy hostile aircraft in the air by fighter attack. When enemy planes were shot down, both planes and crews were destroyed. "General opinion," Spaatz noted in his diary, "is that German fighters will not attack a well-closed-in day-bombing formation."[148] Visiting Great Britain in August and September 1940, Emmons reached much the same conclusion. He attributed the severe losses taken by the Luftwaffe to the large volume of fire that could be delivered by British fighters, the poor rear-hemisphere gun defenses of German bombers, the Germans' use of vulnerable dive-bombing tactics and large inflexible formations, and the Germans' poor air discipline. Emmons also reported that the British believed that six-plane formations of bombers with sufficient guns and armor could conduct daylight attacks without sustaining serious losses.[149] Early in 1941 Spaatz urged that every effort be made to expand American production of four-engine bombers. The British, he said, had committed themselves to short-range planes only to find that they urgently needed long-range bombers.[150]

In August and September General Emmons and Colonel Spaatz also learned the well-kept secret that the British had developed a system of electronic early warning and fighter control without which the RAF Fighter Command probably could not have defeated the Luftwaffe during the Battle of Britain.[151] Actually, the basic principle that very short radio waves produced echoes when reflected from targets had become known quite early by scientists in all nations of the world. In 1925 scientists of the Carnegie Institution and Naval Research Laboratory had devised and used radio pulse ranging to explore the ionosphere. Using these same principles, the Naval Research Laboratory and Army Signal Corps scientists had developed prototype radio ranging and detection equipment, which would later be called radar. On 18 and 19 May 1937 the experimental Signal Corps radar equipment and also an infrared aircraft detector were demonstrated to the secretary of war and a group of high-ranking Army officers, including General Arnold. On 21 March 1938 the *New York Herald Tribune* printed a very accurate and comprehensive description of radar. The Army had begun to develop a radar set to direct antiaircraft artillery guns and searchlights, and the Air Corps had stated a requirement for the development of an early warning radar that would have a range of 120 miles.[152] Electronic development in Germany had produced a prototype radar in 1938, but neither the Wehrmacht nor the Luftwaffe considered

IDEAS, CONCEPTS, DOCTRINE

the production of radar equipment sufficiently important to divert available facilities to it. In 1939, however, Hermann Goering, the Luftwaffe commander, preempted some 100 warning radar sets that had been ordered by the German navy and sited them along Germany's coast and borders.[153]

But only the British had fully developed the potential of radar. Recognizing the vulnerability of the British Isles to German air attack, the British Air Ministry had established a special Committee for the Scientific Survey of Air Defense under the chairmanship of Henry T. Tizard in 1934. In a highly secret program, Robert Watson-Watt and other scientists had devised radio direction finding (RDF) equipment. A chain of these RDF stations was sited to guard Britain in a hurried program following Munich. As a result of expedited research, the British developed air-to-surface vessel (ASV) search radar by September 1938 and experimental airborne-intercept (AI) radar by June 1939. The demonstration of a working model of a new type of microwave radar tube in February 1940 portended an additional important breakthrough in the whole field of radar.[154] "Unless British science had proven superior to German," Winston S. Churchill subsequently wrote of the Battle of Britain, "and unless its strange sinister resources had been effectively brought to bear on the struggle for survival, we might well have been defeated, and being defeated, destroyed."[155]

In the United States during the 1930s the existence of radar was a heavy secret and the air warfare theorists at the Air Corps Tactical School were uninformed about its potential. As long as aircraft warning services depended upon visual reports of ground observers (who could not be stationed within enemy territory), the problem of massing fighter defense against a bombing attack was practically insurmountable, considering the great advantages the bomber force had in selecting the time, altitude, density, and place of attack. In 1938 Air Corps maneuvers, pursuit units had been unable to locate inward-bound bombers except on the occasions when the bomber crews intentionally revealed their positions by radio transmissions, thus allowing the pursuit pilots to get some intercept training. In short, the theorem that "a well planned and coordinated bombardment attack, once launched, cannot be stopped" was heavily based on the belief that pursuit aircraft would have great difficulty locating bombardment formations.[156] Looking backward at the air doctrine of the 1930s, Maj Gen Haywood S. Hansell later commented that the Air Corps Tactical School correctly had assumed that modern bombers could penetrate to their targets within enemy nations, but the edge of the offense over the defense had been much narrower than anyone had believed. As Hansell later remarked:

> Our ignorance of radar development was probably a fortunate ignorance. Had this development been well known it is probable that theorists would also have reasoned that, through the aid of radar, defensive forces would be massed against incoming bomber attacks in a degree that would have been too expensive for the offensive. As it ultimately developed the School's basic concept that the offensive enjoyed a peculiar advantage in air warfare did later turn out to be substantially correct.[157]

In the winter of 1940–41, however, General Arnold was not inclined to be very philosophical. In view of reports from the Battle of Britain, he stated in September 1940 that the Air Corps might well have to conduct the bulk of its bombardment operations at night.[158] Based upon already completed development, the War Department placed production orders for SCR-268 antiaircraft artillery radars and for a new SCR-270 early-warning radar. Early in September 1940 Sir Henry Tizard brought the secret of the improved microwave radar to Washington.[159] In February 1941 Arnold complained that air defense was getting "nowhere fast." Asked whether the United States should produce existing early warning radars or delay production in the expectation of getting improved microwave equipment, he stated that the Air Corps "was badly in need of detector equipment for tactical use" and required equipment without delay for training purposes, even if it was not the ultimate type that would be produced.[160] Arnold may well have been thinking about the new capabilities of electronic-directed pursuit when he wrote: "During daylight in good weather, when pursuit aviation is present in strength in an area, it can pretty nearly bar the air to the bomber."[161]

Mobilizing the Army Air Forces for War

To President Roosevelt the German victories in Europe in the spring of 1940 presaged increased aerial threats to the Western Hemisphere. Apparently selecting a good round number that would jolt the nation's thinking, Roosevelt asked Congress on 16 May to provide 50,000 planes for American defense and a productive capacity for at least that many more planes each year. In addition to building up the Army and Navy, Roosevelt had in mind an even-Stephen division of new bombers with the British.[162] Shortly after he took office, the new Secretary of War Henry L. Stimson declared on 9 August: "Air power has decided the fate of nations; Germany, with her powerful air armadas, has vanquished one people after another. On the ground, large armies had been mobilized to resist her, but each time it was additional power in the air that decided the fate of each individual nation."[163]

Despite the president's willingness to talk about large numbers of planes and an increasing awareness that the United States might be required to fight overseas, the expansion of the Army Air Corps was related to the defensive Rainbow War Plans, which originated in the General Staff's War Plans Division and were put into final shape by the Joint Army-Navy Board. With the approval of Secretary Stimson on 12 July 1940, the Air Corps was authorized to expand to 54 combat groups and six transport groups. Under this program—called the Army's First Aviation Objective—the Air Corps was authorized 4,006 combat aircraft, including 498 heavy, 453 medium, and 438 light bombardment aircraft; 1,540 pursuit interceptors and 220 pursuit fighters; 539 observation, liaison, and photographic-reconnaissance planes; 252 transports; and 66 amphibian aircraft. The group strength included 14 heavy, seven medium, and seven light bombardment groups; five fighter and 18 interceptor pursuit groups; and three composite groups. The large increase in pursuit units over the number under the old 24-group program apparently required little justification, but both Congress and the National Defense Advisory Commission asked questions about the heavy bombers. Arnold defended the requirement for the heavy bombers by citing the strategic mobility they afforded.[164] Assistant Secretary of War Robert P. Patterson explained to the National Defense Advisory Commission that the range of four-engine aircraft was mandatory for the distances involved in hemispheric defense, and that, in the event of military operations in the Far East, long-range bombers would be the only weapons that could exert immediate pressure.[165]

Hardly before the First Aviation Objective was under way, General Marshall discussed the national need to expedite aircraft production in government-owned plants with representatives of the Air Corps Plans Division. On 24 October 1940 Marshall asked whether the Air Corps ought not to visualize expansion beyond the 54-group program. As a result of this conversation, the Air Corps planned a Second Aviation Objective, which was not so much designed to increase the number of air groups as to provide an internal augmentation of existing units. As far as possible, the Air Corps handled an additional number of aircraft by increasing the unit equipment of bombardment and transport groups, and by the addition of two squadrons (one designed to be a training squadron) in each interceptor and fighter pursuit group. In addition to these augmentations, the Air Corps expanded its overall force objective to 84 groups, including 24 heavy, 12 medium, and 13 light bombardment; five fighter and 18 interceptor pursuit; one photographic; and 11 observation groups. Not included in the 84-group strength were seven transport groups. Because General Marshall announced that he wanted to see significant numbers of Ju-87 Stuka-type aircraft in the program before he would approve it (and positively overruled the objection of air officers that dive-bombers would be very vulnerable), the 84-group program included 12 groups of dive-bombers in the light-bombardment category. On the basis of this planning, the War Department approved the plans for the Army's Second Aviation Objective on 14 March 1941, thus authorizing a combat strength of 7,799 planes — including 1,520 heavy bombers; 1,059 medium bombers; 770 light and dive-bombers; 2,500 pursuit interceptors; 525 pursuit fighters; 806 observation, liaison, and photo; 469 transport; and 150 amphibian aircraft.[166] The Second Aviation Objective was designed and justified as being necessary for hemispheric defense.

Organization of the Army Air Forces

Early in 1940 General Arnold opposed a suggested congressional reorganization of the armed forces that would provide air autonomy because he felt that the main requirement was to get on with the expansion of the Air Corps. With the expansion of the Army, however, General Marshall found it more and more difficult to get decisions through the War Department General Staff. In a move to decentralize the War Department, Marshall established General Headquarters US Army, under Brig Gen Leslie J. McNair at the Army War

College on 26 July 1940. According to the plan, the decentralized GHQ field headquarters received command over the GHQ Air Force. The War Plans Division assured General Arnold that this development would cause no substantial change in the relationship between the chief of the Air Corps and the GHQ Air Force.[167] But neither this disclaimer nor the explanation that establishing the General Headquarters meant no more than an effort to take training out of the G-3 Division of the General Staff satisfied Arnold, who ordered his Plans Division to prepare a study showing why the GHQ Air Force should remain under the chief of the Air Corps. In lieu of the General Headquarters plan, Arnold formally proposed that three Army deputy chiefs of staff, one each for ground, air, and service forces, should be established and that each should have broad authority under the chief of staff to control the field activities of their respective forces. The War Department General Staff disapproved the plan, observing: "The Air Corps believes that its primary purpose is to defeat the enemy air force and execute independent missions against ground targets. Actually, its primary purpose is to assist the ground forces in reaching their objective." As an immediate compromise, however, Marshall appointed Arnold as acting deputy chief of staff for air on 30 October 1940; Maj Gen George H. Brett became acting chief of the Air Corps. On 19 November 1940 the GHQ Air Force was removed from the control of the Office of the Chief of the Air Corps and placed under General Headquarters.[168] In December 1940, General Brett further recommended that there ought to be three assistant secretaries of war to correspond to the three deputy chiefs of staff. Late in December, Secretary Stimson named Robert A. Lovett as his special assistant for all air matters; in April 1941 Lovett was named assistant secretary of war for air, a post which had been vacant since 1933.[169]

The Army's First Aviation Objective necessitated an expanded subordinate command organization within the GHQ Air Force. On 26 February 1940 the GHQ Air Force had established an Air Defense Command at Mitchel Field and planned to establish a bombing command, which, like the Air Defense Command, would be directly subordinate to the GHQ Air Force commander. Instead of moving in this functional direction, the First Aviation Objective outlined a geographical distribution of air units into the northeast, northwest, southeast, and southwest air districts, which were thought of as being defensive air theaters of operations within the United States. In the event of the establishment of theaters of operations outside the United States, Arnold suggested that the GHQ Air Force commander detail one of the air district commanders to command the air component of the theater. These districts were activated on 18 December 1940, with headquarters at Mitchel Field in New York, McChord Field in Washington State, MacDill Field in Florida, and March Field in California. The Air Defense Command at Mitchel Field was superseded and absorbed by the Northeast Air District.[170]

Meanwhile, Brig Gen Carl Spaatz added his voice in support of the need to reorganize the Army's air arm. "A numerically inferior air force has been phenomenally successful in stopping the unbroken chain of victories of the world's strongest air power," wrote Spaatz on 29 February 1941 in reporting his observations of the British victory over the Luftwaffe. "A great part of this British success has, undoubtedly," he continued, "been due to the realization for the necessity of a unified command which centralizes control of all military air matters under an air high command concerned solely with air matters." Having been promoted to higher rank and made chief of the Air Corps Plans Division, Spaatz recommended that a staff study be initiated at once "with a view to adopting the better features of the British Air Organization and providing an air organization and an air high command for the efficient control of the military aviation of the United States."[171]

Although the Air Corps had gained increased autonomy, General Brett continued to protest that too much vital time was lost in getting air matters cleared through the General Staff. After conferring with Brett and Arnold on 26 and 27 March 1941, Marshall issued orders that the chief of the Air Corps would prepare, for final action, all papers pertaining to purely Air Corps matters, except those pertaining to war plans and intelligence, and that the deputy chief of staff for air would be responsible for coordination in air matters. Secretary Stimson, moreover, directed that still further steps would be taken to place the air arm under one responsible head. By May 1941 the Air Corps Plans Division had prepared a reorganization that was put into effect by the publication of a new Army Regulation 95-5 on 20 June 1941. This regulation created the Army Air Forces, headed by Arnold, who continued to be Marshall's deputy chief of staff for air. The Army Air Forces was given authority to coordinate the Office of the Chief of the Air Corps, the Air Force Combat Command (the GHQ Air Force was so redesignated), and all other Army air elements. Direct responsibility for Army aviation matters was given to the chief of the Army Air Forces, who was to be assisted by the Air Staff. Arnold formed the Air Staff by removing most of the Plans Division from the Office of the Chief of the Air Corps and designating its sections as A-1 (Personnel), A-2 (Intelligence), A-3 (Operations and Training), A-4 (Supply and Maintenance), and Air War Plans. The Air War Plans Division was charged to prepare "over-all plans for the control of the activities of the Army Air Forces."[172]

Within the Air Force Combat Command, the beginning of the Army's Second Aviation Objective demanded further internal expansion. At its establishment, the Air Force Combat Command took command over the First, Second, Third, and Fourth Air Forces, as the former air districts had been redesignated on 17 March 1941. Placed under command of the similarly numbered air forces, the I, II, III, and IV Bomber Commands were constituted on 4 September 1941 and were quickly activated.[173] With the implementation of the Second Aviation Objective, the War Department also resolved to reform the organization of the corps and army observation squadrons, which had always been assigned to ground force commands. As a result of fiscal year 1938 expansions, 11 corps and army observation squadrons had been included in the Air Corps strength and 21 National Guard observation squadrons had been inducted into federal service during fiscal year 1941. Based upon the lesson that Luftwaffe fighters easily destroyed slow-flying Allied observation planes and captive observation balloons, the War Department decided in the autumn of 1940 to abandon observation balloons and develop two types of observation planes: a short-range, slow-flying liaison type and a long-range, relatively high-performance observation aircraft. However, in the Army's spring maneuvers of 1941, General McNair concluded that observation equipment and tactics had not progressed since 1918. In Washington there was a growing appreciation of the fact that the observation squadrons were orphans that had been cut off for too long from the advancing air force. On 3 July 1941, General Emmons and General McNair accordingly agreed to establishing the Air Force Combat Command and to the plan that all observation squadrons would be gathered into groups and assigned to five air support commands under the Air Force Combat Command. The War Department directive for the reorganization was issued on 25 July; on 30 August the Air Force Combat Command issued orders establishing the 1st (Mitchel Field), 2d (Will Rogers Field, Oklahoma), 3d (Savannah, Georgia), 4th (Hamilton Field, California), and 5th (Bowman Field, Kentucky) air support commands. These commands were to support the four continental armies and the armored force. They were immediately charged to organize parent groups for all observation squadrons. While the groups would continue to be assigned to armies, corps, and armored forces, they would be detached from the ground forces for a considerable portion of each year in order that the air support commands might superintend their basic air training.[174]

Early AAF Organization for Basic Thinking

With the expansion of the Air Corps after 1939, the capabilities and functions of the Air Corps Board were progressively reduced and eventually dissipated. Following the successful completion of Field Manual 10-5, *Employment of the Aviation of the Army*, in the winter of 1939-40, the War Department and the Office of the Chief of the Air Corps charged the board to produce manuals on tactics and techniques concerned with air attack, air fighting, air reconnaissance and observation, air navigation, aerial photography, combat intelligence, and signal communications – the whole task to be completed not later than 1 June 1940. Since preparing of the manuals was only a part of the small Air Corps Board's mission of tactical testing and developing, it had depended heavily upon the Air Corps Tactical School for much of its pick-and-shovel work. During the school year 1939-40, however, the Tactical School ran four accelerated courses, each for 100 officers, and had little time to assist the board. In the winter of 1939-40, moreover, several officers of the board completed their tours at Maxwell and other experienced officers preferred command assignments to the often discouraging work on the board. Recognizing that Lt Col Edgar P. Sorenson, who took over as Air Corps Board director in January 1940, faced personnel difficulties, the Air Corps directed him to use Air Corps Tactical School people where possible and to call in experts from other air commands to perform needed research. Using temporary duty personnel, the board completed drafts of each of the required tactics and techniques manuals and forwarded them to Washington early in May 1940, where they were subsequently published with little or no revision.[175]

As a part of the Army's First Aviation Objective and in view of the establishment of the 23d Composite Group at Maxwell Field for test and demonstration purposes, Col Walter R. Weaver, commandant of the Air Corps Tactical School, proposed on 17 January 1940 that an Air Corps tactical center be established at Maxwell with academic, research, and test departments. Weaver also recommended that the Air Corps Board be reorganized to comprise the commander of the tactical center and three departmental directors. General Arnold was willing to commend the proposal, but he was unwilling to act on it. He specifically feared that the Air Corps Board might become a rubber stamp agency for academicians at Maxwell.[176]

Because nearly all regular air officers had completed the Tactical School as a result of the accelerated courses and because the Air Corps needed Maxwell as the site for a new southeast training center, effective 30 June 1940, the Tactical School was accordingly suspended and its faculty was reduced to seven caretaker officers. Looking at the new state of affairs in September 1940, Arnold asked his Plans Division why the Air Corps Board should not be brought to Washington and put to work evaluating information received from Europe. The Plans Division agreed that the board ought to evaluate these lessons but it considered that it was "vital that the Air Corps Board continue its present work at its present location and away from the turmoil of this office."[177]

In view of the many changes that were sweeping the War Department in 1941, it was remarkable that any doctrinal lessons were committed to paper that year. In the spring of 1941 Colonel Sorenson, who was now both the commandant of the inactive Tactical School and the director of the Air Corps Board, used available personnel to complete a revision of Field Manual 1-5 — to include matter on the aerial support for armored forces — and to prepare a new manual on weather. Pointing out that the responsibility of the Air Corps Board for preparing training literature was causing undesirable delay in its accomplishment of more important test and evaluation studies, Colonel Sorenson recommended that he be permitted to organize a small training literature unit with at least four qualified officers and five professional civilians and put it under the Tactical School. With approval from the Army Air Forces, this action was taken on 1 July 1941.[178] This decision was no sooner made when General Brett pointed out that Army Regulation 95-5 charged the Air Force Combat Command with "the development of doctrines of air tactics and technique of Air Force." Brig Gen Muir S. Fairchild, the executive of the Office of the Chief of the Air Corps, protested that the arrangement would be too awkward to work, but General Spaatz, now chief of air staff of the Army Air Forces, ruled that the Air Force Combat Command would develop doctrines and forward drafts of such literature to the chief of the Army Air Forces. The chief of the Air Corps would receive the drafts, prepare them for publication, and, following final approval of the Army Air Forces, submit them to the War Department adjutant general for publication.[179]

In July 1941 Colonel Sorenson was summoned to Washington to serve as assistant chief of air staff, intelligence. Several acting directors now headed the Air Corps Board, which was physically transferred from Maxwell to the new Air Corps Proving Ground at Eglin Field, Florida, on 10 September 1941. During the summer of 1941, the Air Corps Tactical School with its Training Literature Unit was physically transferred to Washington, where it was made responsible to the Air Corps Training and Operations Division. Here the Training Literature Unit was greatly expanded by the assignment of reserve officers from colleges and universities, but its major work was the editorial production of technical manuals and extension courses. At Eglin Field the remnant of the Air Corps Board became moribund. According to the recollection of Col H. G. Montgomery, who was assigned to the board in the autumn of 1941, the board continued to do good work, but many of its reports were promptly filed and forgotten by Air Staff divisions that disagreed with the conclusions and recommendations. In a final effort to save the board, its director wrote personally to Arnold recommending that a whole new group of officers would be assigned to the board if the ones serving were not to be believed. This action went without result.[180]

As General Fairchild had protested, the divided responsibility for formulating and promulgating doctrine was indeed awkward and the contemplated cooperation was not going to materialize. Under the Air Force Combat Command, test and experimentation in air defense was centered at I Interceptor Command at Mitchel Field. Major Saville, now the executive officer of I Interceptor Command, visited Great Britain early in 1941. In the autumn of that same year following the nation's first large-scale air defense maneuvers, Saville prepared the draft of an air defense doctrine that integrated pursuit interceptors, antiaircraft artillery, barrage balloons, and signal air warning units into a coordinated air defense establishment. This draft manual distinguished, for the first time, between air defense (which was a direct defense against enemy air operations) and operations against enemy air forces (which were said not to be properly within the scope of air defense).[181] The draft of the manual provided a basis for air defense training and organization, but it would not be officially approved and published. Based upon the agreement between Emmons and McNair, the air support section of their respective commands was made responsible for the supervision of cooperative air-ground training and for the development of air support doctrine. With the passing of time, the air support section would produce a doctrine manual. However, during 1941 no one knew how an air support command was to support an army or what its composition would be. The only War Department letter touching on the subject on 7 October 1941 merely stated: "Air Support Command may be attached to army or armored force upon entry into Theater of Operations or as directed by the Theater Commander."[182]

With the Air Corps Board in a moribund state, the Army Air Forces turned to other devices for basic thinking. On 11 October 1941 the assistant chief of air staff for operations assembled a special board of knowledgeable officers headed by Col Earl L. Naiden to study and make recommendations on the future development of pursuit aviation. This ad hoc board assembled, studied the problem, and recommended on 27 October that the Army Air Forces should develop high- and low-altitude interceptors, night fighters, and long-range multiplace fighter escorts—with the lowest priority to be given to the escort fighters. Although it arrived at a decision, Naiden's ad hoc pursuit board protested that no group of men ought to be expected to plunge into the middle of a complex problem, assimilate background material, and formulate definitive answers. The pursuit board accordingly recommended that the Army Air Forces should establish an operational requirements agency that could maintain a current familiarity with developmental problems and recommend guidance to General Arnold.[183]

AWPD-1: Air Planning for War

Although War Department planning remained committed to the defense of the United States and its possessions, President Roosevelt grew increasingly aware that America's security required the defeat of the Axis powers. In May 1938 the Joint Army-Navy Board and its adjunct Joint Planning Committee addressed themselves to the preparation of a new series of Rainbow strategic war plans, of which Rainbow 5 visualized hemispheric defense coupled with concerted action between the United States, Great Britain, and France to effect the decisive defeat of either Germany or Italy, or both. The collapse of France and the adherence of Japan to the Axis on 27 September 1940 required that the scope of Rainbow 5 be expanded.[184]

In recognition of the growing peril that the Axis presented to the free world, Anglo-American military staff conferences began in Washington on 29 January 1941 with the purpose of laying down principles of cooperation "should the United States be compelled to resort to war." The three aviation experts at the conference were Air Vice-Marshal John C. Slessor of the Royal Air Force, Col J. T. McNarney (an Air Corps officer assigned to the War Plans Division), and Capt DeWitt C. Ramsey of the Navy. On 27 March the military experts formally approved a document subsequently cited as American-British Conversations-1 (more usually ABC-1), which visualized a basic Anglo-American war plan and a summary of strategic policies. Since Germany was the most powerful Axis partner, the main Allied effort would be conducted in the European theater. The United States was to depend largely upon its Pacific Fleet to maintain a defensive against Japan in the Far East. The Allied offensive in Europe was to include economic pressure through blockade, a sustained air offensive against German military power, early defeat of Italy, and the buildup of forces for an eventual land offensive against Germany. As rapidly as possible, the Allies were to achieve "superiority of air strength over that of the enemy, particularly in long-range striking forces." On the basis of ABC-1, the Joint Planning Committee rapidly completed war plan Rainbow 5, and the secretary of war and the secretary of the Navy approved both ABC-1 and Rainbow 5 and sent them to President Roosevelt on 2 June 1941. The president indicated his satisfaction with the plans, which he said should be returned for his formal approval in case of war.[185]

To provide some realistic guidance to the Office of Production Management (which had superseded the National Defense Advisory Commission), President Roosevelt requested the secretary of war and the secretary of the Navy on 9 July 1941 to explore "the over-all production requirements required to defeat our potential enemies."[186] In the War Department, the War Plans Division broadened the scope of the problem by undertaking to base the production program on a prior determination of strategic concepts. After some delay the Army Air Forces Air War Plans Division, headed by Lt Col Harold L. George, was brought into the problem. At this time the only other officers assigned to the Air War Plans Division were Lt Cols Orvil Anderson and Kenneth Walker and Maj Haywood S. Hansell; but George secured the temporary services of several other officers including Lt Cols Max F. Schneider (A-4) and Arthur W. Vanaman (A-2) and Majs Hoyt S. Vandenberg (A-3), Laurence S. Kuter (G-3), and Samuel E. Anderson (Combat Command). The War Plans Division had only asked to know the maximum number of air squadrons that the Army Air Forces might ultimately require to garrison a great number of geographic sites and to hold as "reserves of opportunity." But George and his associates, most of whom had been faculty members at the Air Corps Tactical School, undertook to prepare a comprehensive air plan for the defeat of the Axis. Beginning on 4 August, teams of two or three officers worked up separate subjects and supporting documents, and Air War Plans Division-1 (AWPD-1), "Munitions Requirements of the Army Air Force," was completed on 12 August 1941.[187] The completion of the first major strategic air war plan by the newly formed Army Air Forces staff in only nine days was a notable achievement, which marked both the apex of prewar air force doctrinal thought and a blueprint for the air war that would follow.

As conceived in AWPD-1 the military mission of the United States was the defeat of the nation's potential enemies – Germany and her allies. The air mission outlined followed ABC-1 in that it required a sustained air offensive against German military power, supplemented by air offensives against other regions under enemy control which contributed to that power. The air mission also required the air force "to support a final offensive, if it becomes necessary to invade the continent" and "to conduct effective air operations in connection with Hemisphere Defense and a strategic defensive in the Far East." The air planners thought it improbable that a land invasion could be mounted against Germany for at least three years. Moreover, they posited, if the air offensive were successful, a land offensive might not be necessary. Three lines of US air action were possible against a German economy and society that was already strained by the military campaign in Russia. The first line of air action – which would accomplish the air mission in Europe – required disruption of Germany's electric power system and transportation system, destruction of Germany's oil and petroleum resources, and undermining of Germany's morale by air attack against civilian concentrations. The second line of air action – representing intermediate objectives that might be essential to the principal effort—required neutralization of German air forces by attacks against their bases, aircraft factories, and aluminum and magnesium factories. A third line of action—to safeguard operating air bases—included attacks against submarine bases, surface seacraft, and invasion ports. The planners advocated a concentration of daylight, precision bombing attacks against the principal objectives. They did not favor attacks against cities unless the enemy people were known to be low in morale either because of sustained suffering and deprivation or because of a recognition that their armed forces could not win a favorable decision. The planners believed that heavy bombers—relying on speed, massed formations, high altitude, defensive firepower and armor, and simultaneous penetrations at many places—could make deep penetrations of German defenses in daylight hours. They, nevertheless, felt that it would be used to develop a large, heavily armed escort fighter that would have the range and speed slightly superior to the bombers it would escort.

Simultaneously with the strategic air campaign against Germany, other Army Air Forces units would be dispersed in Alaska, Hawaii, Iceland, and South America to maintain hemispheric defense. To maintain a strategic defensive in Asia, the planners visualized a buildup of bomber forces in the Philippines and shuttling B-29 and B-32 aircraft from Alaska and the Philippines to a refueling and staging area in Siberia. This concept was so persuasive in fact that the planners urged immediate efforts be made to deploy four groups of B-17s or B-24s to the Philippines to deter the Japanese from moving toward the Netherlands East Indies. It was assumed that the hemisphere and Asian defensive forces would provide the aircraft needed to control adjacent seas against the operation of hostile seacraft.

In establishing requirements for pursuit aircraft, the planners reasoned that the principal role of pursuit was defensive—the protection of bases and vital areas—and that air superiority would be won by bombers. Because of an anticipated shortage of air bases, especially in England, the air planners urged that pursuit complements should be kept at a minimum level consistent with safety so that the strength of the bombardment strike force would not be reduced. Much the same line of reasoning was applied to air support aviation. Ground operations were not to be mounted until strategic air campaigns had already attained a preponderant air superiority; in appropriate situations, available combat aviation would support theater operations of ground armies. Both for training with ground forces and for eventual overseas employment in air support forces, however, the air force required pursuit aircraft, light bombers, dive-bombers, observation aircraft, photomapping planes, and transports and gliders. In addition to the transport aircraft required for employment of airborne forces, the air planners placed a requirement for long- and medium-range transport aircraft that would provide quick delivery of essential aircraft and engine spares from air depots to worldwide operating units.

However, because they did not have any available valid production data based on historical experience, air planners could not project a definite schedule for fielding the air units visualized. The planners expected that by 1943 or 1944 the

Army Air Forces would include 203 groups and 108 observation squadrons and a grand total of 59,727 airplanes. Of this force, 10 groups of B-25s and B-26s, 20 groups of B-17s and B-24s, 24 groups of B-29s, and 21 groups of pursuit would be committed to the air offensive against Germany. The smaller bombers would be used only because they were available. The planners specified that an ideal force from a standpoint of economy would consist entirely of B-29s. The major difficulty in mustering the air attacks against Germany appeared to be the scarcity of airfields in England and in the Middle East, the latter area being tentatively designated as the operating location for long-range B-29s. Based on intelligence estimates of 154 strategic targets in Germany, expected bombing accuracy, and a desire to complete the air campaign in a six-month period, the planners computed that 98 bombing groups would be required, of which only 54 could be based in England and the Middle East. For this reason, the planning staff stated an urgent requirement for developing 44 groups (3,740 aircraft) of bombers, which would have a 4,000-mile tactical operating radius. These planes would be able to operate against Germany from bases in Newfoundland, Greenland, Africa, India, or the northeastern United States. The use of these 4,000-mile-range bombers would permit some reductions in other types of units, with the result that the ultimate force—which could not be ready before 1945—would consist of 239 groups and 108 observation squadrons, for a grand total of 63,467 planes.

AWPD-1 was signed by General Arnold and its findings were immediately the subject of almost daily briefings to Air Corps and War Department officers. Comments were generally favorable, although Lt Col Clayton Bissell, an Air Corps officer in the War Plans Division, argued that the need for an escort fighter was just as great as the need for a 4,000-mile-range bomber. He thought it peculiar that the plan called for only 13 experimental escort fighters but called for 3,740 of the 4,000-mile-range bombers, when the latter would be just as much a developmental problem as the former.[188] Nevertheless, Secretary Lovett tacitly approved the study and General Marshall marked it "Okay, G. C. M." on 1 September. On the afternoon of 11 September and the morning of 12 September, George, Walker, and Kuter presented AWPD-1 to Secretary Stimson and Assistant Secretary John J. McCloy. Stimson apparently accepted the study as a matter-of-fact statement of the air forces required to defeat the Axis, but he mentioned that the expansion of aviation manufacturing facilities and Air Corps training establishments proposed in the plan depended entirely upon the nation being in a war spirit or at war. McCloy expressed pleasure that AWPD-1 was offensive instead of defensive in nature because, he said, ground and air plans were being stifled by the out-of-date conception of hemispheric defense. McCloy felt that both the ground and air forces had made a major error in failing to press for an early seizure of African air bases.[189] While the briefings were in progress, AWPD-1 also went forward to the War Plans Division and from there to the Joint Army-Navy Board. There was some reason for optimism that the plan might be acceptable to the Joint Board, since, in view of the increased importance being accorded to air operations, General Arnold and the chief of the Navy Bureau of Aeronautics had won seats on the Joint

Board on 2 July 1941. On the board, however, General Arnold had found that he was not a full-fledged member. "When air problems came up," he would recall, "I sat as a member of the Board; at other times I could sit in as a 'listener' but not as a member."[190]

When the Joint Board issued its report "Estimate of United States Over-All Production Requirements" on 11 September 1941, it accepted AWPD-1 as a statement of Army Air Forces requirements and incorporated its tabulations in the joint estimate. Like AWPD-1 the Joint Board estimate proposed that hemispheric defense was an insufficient national policy. The major national objectives of the United States, which were related to military policy, were believed to be preserving the territorial, economic, and ideological integrity of the United States and the Western Hemisphere; preventing the disruption of the British Empire; preventing further expansion of Japanese territorial dominion; eventually establishing in Europe and Asia balances of power that would most clearly ensure the political stability in those regions and the future security of the United States; and, as far as practicable, establishing regimes favorable to economic freedom and individual liberty. The fundamental military policy of the United States was hemispheric defense, but attaining the complete list of national policies could be effected "only through military victories outside this hemisphere, either by the armed forces of the United States, by the armed forces of friendly powers, or by both."[191]

Based upon its assessment of the strategic objectives of Germany and Japan, the Joint Board stated that "the principal strategic method employed in the immediate future should be the material support of present military operations against Germany, and their reinforcement by active participation in the war by the United States, while holding Japan in check pending future developments." In view of the impossibility of mounting an early land offensive against Germany, the board recommended continuing the economic blockade, conducting land offensives in distant regions where German troops were weak, prosecuting economic and industrial resources, and supporting subversive activities in conquered territories. The board warned: "Naval and air power may prevent wars from being lost, and by weakening enemy strength may greatly contribute to victory. By themselves, however, naval and air forces seldom, if ever, win important wars. It should be recognized as an almost invariable rule that only land armies can finally win wars."

The Joint Board's statement that "only land armies can finally win wars" indicated a polite disbelief of the contention in AWPD-1 that a strategic air offensive against Germany might preclude the need for a land campaign. In its annex to the Joint Board report, the Army insisted that the United States should have forces in being for a land offensive against Germany by 1 July 1943 and that prior to the undertaking of a land campaign against the continent of Europe, sea and air forces should have accomplished overwhelming air superiority, rendered the economic and industrial life of Germany ineffective, weakened the combat effectiveness of German air and ground units, and reduced the popular support of the German people for the continuation of the war.

Although a summary with verbatim extracts of the Joint Board estimate was published in the *Chicago Daily Tribune* on 4 December 1941 as an exposure of Roosevelt's secret war plan, neither the Joint Board estimate nor AWPD-1 was a war plan. They were, rather, efforts to provide the Office of Production Management with a good feel for what America's wartime military requirements might be. As a matter of fact, the visualization in AWPD-1 to the effect that the Army Air Forces would require an ultimate force of 239 air groups and 108 observation squadrons turned out to be an estimate that was remarkably similar to the 269 tactical groups that the Army Air Forces would possess at its maximum strength during World War II.[192] Much of the strategic thought expressed in the two studies would turn up in one form or another during World War II. The studies produced at least two immediate actions. On 11 April 1941 the Air Corps initiated a design competition for a high-altitude, 10,000-mile-range intercontinental bomber. On 19 August General Arnold indicated that the project must be pushed. Both Douglas and Northrop submitted preliminary designs and on 15 December 1941 a contract for developing two experimental XB-36 aircraft was awarded to the Douglas Aircraft Company.[193] AWPD-1 also provided new hope that Japanese aggression could be deterred and that the Philippines could be defended.

In November 1938, when he had stated that only long-range bomber aircraft could affect Hitler's mad course toward war, President Roosevelt had appeared to grasp the close relationship between effective military force and the national foreign policy objectives. On 26 July 1941, President Roosevelt issued an executive order freezing Japanese assets in the United States and halting all trade with the aggressor nation. Both General Marshall and Adm Harold R. Stark recommended against this action, reasoning that an embargo on Japan's oil supplies would force Japan either to surrender its long-range aggressive aims or, much more likely, to strike for oil in the Netherlands Indies at the cost of war with the United States. Only belatedly, after the diplomatic move had been made, was attention given to strengthening the defense of the Philippines. To maintain the strategic defensive in the Far East, AWPD-1 recommended, and the Joint Board estimate accepted, an immediate need for the movement of additional air units — principally four heavy bombardment groups — to the Philippines. On 18 August, Secretary Stimson approved a Philippine reinforcement plan including moving one B-17 group there without delay and sending three other groups there by February 1942. Whether or not the reinforcement could have been effected as scheduled — the Air Force Combat Command had difficulties getting together 35 B-17s for the first group and there was doubt that air facilities could have been readied by February — would remain academic, for the Japanese found themselves becoming weaker as a result of the economic embargo at the same time that the United States was strengthening its Pacific garrisons. On 6 September 1941 Japan made the fateful decision to preempt with military force if diplomatic negotiations could not end the embargo. When negotiations deadlocked, the Japanese began the war with an attack on Pearl Harbor on 7 December 1941, coinciding with a simultaneous assault on the

IDEAS, CONCEPTS, DOCTRINE

Philippines.[194] Military ideas, concepts, and doctrine would now be tested in global warfare.

NOTES

1. Henry H. Arnold, *Global Mission* (New York: Harper & Bros., 1949), 157.
2. Senate, *Reorganization of the Army Air Service: Hearings before the Committee on Military Affairs*, 69th Cong., 1st sess., 1926, 20, 22–28.
3. Leslie B. Tribolet, "A Decade of American Air Policies, 1922–1932," *Air Law Review*, January 1938, 181–95; Samuel T. Moore, "Pony Express with Wings," *Air Force Magazine*, January 1956, 12–119; Robert F. Futrell, "Background and Growth of Military Civic Actions: The Role of Military Civic Action in the Development of the United States" (Maxwell AFB, Ala.: Aerospace Studies Institute, 1964), 9–10.
4. House, *Air Corps Progress Under Five-Year Program: Hearings before the Committee on Military Affairs*, 69th Cong., 2d sess., 1927, 8–9; statement of Brig Gen Oscar Westover, assistant chief, Air Corps, to US Chamber of Commerce, 27 April 1935; statement of F. Trubee Davison in "U.S. President's Air Policy Commission," unclassified testimony before the President's Air Policy Commission (Washington, D.C.: n.p., 1 December 1947, mimeographed), 6:2644–49.
5. Robert T. Finney, *History of the Air Corps Tactical School, 1920–1940*, USAF historical study 100 (Maxwell AFB, Ala.: Research Studies Institute, 1955), 7–9.
6. Maj W. G. Kilner, executive, Office of Chief of Air Service, to commandant, Air Service Tactical School, letter, subject: Proposed Revision of the Policy of the Army and Navy Relating to Aircraft, 12 April 1925.
7. Air Corps Tactical School, *Employment of Combined Air Force*, 1926, 1, 9–10.
8. Lt Col C. C. Culver, commandant, Air Corps Tactical School, to chief, Air Corps, letter, subject: "The Doctrine of Air Force," prepared at Air Corps Tactical School, 30 April 1928.
9. Lt Col C. C. Culver to chief, Air Corps, letter, subject: Doctrine of Employing an Aerial Force, 9 June 1928; 1st ind., Maj L. W. McIntosh, executive, Office of the Chief of the Air Corps, to commandant, Air Corps Tactical School, 1 September 1928.
10. Genevieve Brown, "Development of Transport Airplanes and Air Transport Equipment" (Wright Field, Ohio: Air Technical Service, Command Historical Division, 1946), 22–23.
11. Davis A. Canham, "Development and Production of Fighter Aircraft for the United States Air Force" (Wright-Patterson AFB, Ohio: Air Materiel Command Historical Office, 1949), 30–34.
12. Edward O. Purtee, *The Development of Light and Medium Bombers* (Wright Field, Ohio: Air Materiel Command Historical Section, 1946), 75–77, 87–93; Jean H. DuBuque, *The Development of the Heavy Bomber, 1918–1944*, USAF historical study 6 (Maxwell AFB, Ala.: USAF Historical Division, 1951), 7–10.
13. Finney, *History of the Air Corps Tactical School*, 27, 55; Maj Walter H. Frank, assistant commandant, Air Corps Tactical School, to Brig Gen Benjamin D. Foulois, director, Air Corps, Ohio Maneuvers, report, subject: Report on Maneuvers, 30 August 1929, with critique, Air Ground Maneuvers Fifth Corps Area, May 1929; Maj Walter H. Frank, Air Corps, address at Wright Field, Ohio, 26 May 1929.
14. Air Corps Tactical School, *The Air Force*, February 1931, 56; Maj Gen Haywood S. Hansell, "Pre-World War II Evaluation of the Air Weapon," lecture, Air War College, Maxwell AFB, Ala., 16 November 1953.
15. Air Corps Tactical School, *The Air Force*, April 1930, 88–89.
16. Ibid., February 1931, 49–50.
17. Ibid., April 1930, 72–74.
18. Ibid., February 1931, 49–50.
19. Ibid., 56.

20. Ibid., 74.
21. The Joint Board, *Joint Action of the Army and the Navy* (Washington, D.C.: Government Printing Office, 1927), 7–9.
22. DuBuque, *The Development of the Heavy Bomber, 1918–1944*, 133–35; Annual Report of Chief of Staff Army in *Report of the Secretary of War to the President, 1931* (Washington, D.C.: Government Printing Office, 1931), 38; chief of staff, US Army, to commanding generals, armies, corps, and departments, letter, subject: Employment of Army Aviation in Coast Defense, 3 January 1933.
23. Interview with Maj Gen Benjamin D. Foulois, *American Heritage*, 20 January 1960.
24. Maj Gen Benjamin D. Foulois, chief, Air Corps, "The Present Status of Military Aviation and Its Trend of Development," lecture, Army War College, Carlisle Barracks, Pa., 12 September 1933.
25. Brig Gen Oscar Westover, acting chief, Air Corps, to The Adjutant General, letter, subject: Air Corps Peacetime Requirements to Meet the Defense Needs of the United States, 15 March 1933; Finney, *History of the Air Corps Tactical School*, 14–15.
26. Mark S. Watson, *Chief of Staff: Prewar Plans and Preparations, US Army in World War II* (Washington, D.C.: Office of the Chief of Military History, Department of the Army, 1950), 23–26.
27. Report of Special Committee, General Council on Employment of Army Air Corps under Certain Strategic Plans, ca. 11 October 1933.
28. Ibid.; Maj Gen Benjamin D. Foulois, "Developments in Organization, Armament and Equipment of the Air Corps," lecture, Army War College, Carlisle Barracks, Pa., 22 October 1934.
29. Report of the General Headquarters Air Force (Provisional) 1933, ca. 20 July 1933.
30. Foulois, "The Present Status of Military Aviation."
31. Gen Giulio Douhet, "The War of 19. . . ," manuscript in files of Air Corps Tactical School Library, Maxwell Field, Ala.
32. Capt George C. Kenney, "The Proper Composition of the Air Force" (thesis, Army War College, Carlisle Barracks, Pa., 29 April 1933); Col Charles DeForest Chandler, "Air Warfare Doctrine of General Douhet," *U.S. Air Services*, May 1933.
33. Maj Gen Benjamin D. Foulois to John J. McSwain, chairman, Committee on Military Affairs, House of Representatives, letter, 9 May 1933.
34. Wesley F. Craven and James L. Cate, eds., *The Army Air Forces in World War II*, 7 vols., *Plans and Early Operations*, vol. 1 (Chicago: University of Chicago Press, 1948), 65–66; D. W. Finlay, Boeing Aircraft Co., "B-17 History," lecture, Air War College, Maxwell AFB, Ala., 20 February 1951; Brig Gen John B. Montgomery, "The Development of US Strategic Air Doctrine in the Pacific," lecture, Air War College, Maxwell AFB, Ala., 21 September 1951.
35. Lt Col Eldon W. Downs, "Army and the Airmail—1934," *The Air Power Historian* 9, no. 1 (January 1962): 35–51; Paul Tillett, *The Army Flies the Mails* (University of Alabama: The Inter-University Case Program, 1955); comments on "The Army Flies the Mails" by Maj Gen Benjamin D. Foulois, USAF, Retired, 25 March 1954.
36. *Final Report of War Department Special Committee on Army Air Corps*, 18 July 1934 (Washington, D.C.: Government Printing Office, 1934), 1–15.
37. Ibid., 14–75.
38. Ibid., 75.
39. Secretary of War George H. Dern to Newton D. Baker, letter, 16 July 1934.
40. *Report of the Federal Aviation Commission, January 1935*, 74th Cong., 1st sess., 1935, 1; George H. Dern to chairman, Federal Aviation Commission, letter, 31 August 1934; memorandum by Brig Gen Charles E. Kilbourne, assistant chief of staff, War Plans Division, to chiefs, General Staff Division et al., 11 September 1934.
41. Chase C. Mooney and Martha E. Layman, *Organization of Military Aeronautics, 1907–1935*, USAF historical study 25 (Washington, D.C.: Office of Assistant Chief of Air Staff for Intelligence, Historical Division, 1944), 96–97.
42. A brief of testimony presented by Capt Harold Lee George to the Federal Aviation Commission.
43. Testimony of Maj Donald Wilson before the Federal Aviation Commission.

IDEAS, CONCEPTS, DOCTRINE

44. Testimony of 1Lt Kenneth N. Walker before the Federal Aviation Commission.
45. Testimony of Capt Robert Olds, Air Corps, before the Federal Aviation Commission.
46. *Report of the Federal Aviation Commission, January 1935*, 119–20, 123.
47. Memorandum by Maj Gen Benjamin D. Foulois to Brig Gen Charles Kilbourne, 13 March 1933.
48. Robert L. Collins, The Adjutant General Office, War Department, to chief, Air Corps, letter, subject: Organization of Headquarters, General Headquarters Air Force, under Four Army Organizations, 24 November 1933; memorandum by Maj Gen Benjamin D. Foulois to Army chief of staff, War Plans Division, subject: Assignment of Regular Officers for Mobilization of General Headquarters, 1 May 1934.
49. Mooney and Layman, *Organization of Military Aeronautics, 1907–1935*, 95.
50. *Final Report of the War Department Special Committee on Army Air Corps*, 66–67, 72.
51. "U.S. President's Air Policy Commission," 6:2644.
52. War Department Immediate Release, War Department Takes First Action on Report of War Department Special Committee on Army Air Corps, 24 August 1934.
53. The Adjutant General to commanding generals, all corps areas et al., letter, subject: General Headquarters Air Force, 31 December 1934.
54. Robert L. Collins, The Adjutant General Office, War Department, to Lt Col Frank M. Andrews, letter, subject: Tentative Organization, General Headquarters Air Force and Service Test Thereof, 10 January 1935; Maj Gen James F. McKinley, The Adjutant General, to commanding generals, all corps areas et al., letter, subject: General Headquarters Air Force, 19 February 1935.
55. Memorandum by Maj W. W. Weaver, chief, Plans Division, Office of the Chief of the Air Corps, to assistant chief, Air Corps, 23 February 1932; memorandum by Brig Gen Oscar Westover to Lt Col James E. Chaney, chief, Plans Division, Office of the Chief of the Air Corps, 13 February 1933; memorandum by Lt Col James E. Chaney to assistant chief, Air Corps, subject: Air Corps Board, 28 March 1933; War Department Release, War Department to Change Status of Air Corps Board, 25 September 1934; memorandum by Col A. G. Fisher, chief, Plans Division, Office of the Chief of the Air Corps, to chief, Air Corps, subject: The Air Corps Board, 24 August 1934; Joe N. Dalton, Adjutant General Office, War Department, to chief, Air Corps, letter, subject: Recommendations of the Baker Board Relative to the Air Corps Board, 28 September 1934; 1st ind., Maj R. M. Jones, acting executive, Office of the Chief of the Air Corps, to The Adjutant General, 15 November 1934; Army Regulation 95–20, 9 November 1934.
56. Senate, *Department of Armed Forces, Department of Military Security: Hearings before the Committee on Military Affairs*, 79th Cong., 1st sess., 1945, 283–84.
57. Robert L. Collins, The Adjutant General Office, War Department, to chief, Air Corps, letter, subject: Development of Army Air Corps, 27 December 1933; memorandum by the executive, Office of the Chief of the Air Corps, to chief, Training and Operations Division, Office of the Chief of the Air Corps, 2 January 1934.
58. Memorandum by Brig Gen Charles E. Kilbourne to chief of staff, Army, subject: GHQ Command Post Exercise, with draft memorandum, subject: Control of the GHQ Air Force in the GHQ Post Exercise, 12 June 1934.
59. Memorandum by Brig Gen Oscar Westover, assistant chief, Air Corps, to assistant chief of staff, War Plans Division, subject: Control of the GHQ Air Force in the GHQ Command Post Exercise, 26 June 1934.
60. Memorandum by Brig Gen Charles E. Kilbourne, assistant chief of staff, War Plans Division, to chief of staff, Army, subject: Air Corps Programs, 5 October 1934; Gen Douglas MacArthur, senior member present, the Joint Board, to secretary of war, letter, subject: Doctrine for the Employment of the GHQ Air Force, 26 September 1934.
61. Memorandum by Brig Gen James E. Chaney, Office of the Chief of the Air Corps, to Maj Gen Benjamin D. Foulois, 23 October 1934; Navy doctrine as submitted to the Federal Aviation Commission, November 1934.
62. Herbert A. Dargue to Brig Gen Oscar Westover, letter, 13 January 1936.

GROWTH OF THE AF IDEA

63. Memorandum by Brig Gen Charles E. Kilbourne, assistant chief of staff, War Plans Division, to assistant chief of staff G-1 et al., subject: Doctrine of the Air Corps, 21 December 1934.

64. Air Corps Tactical School, "A Study of Proposed Air Corps Doctrine," based on a memorandum dated 21 December 1934, furnished by the War Plans Division, General Staff, 31 January 1935.

65. War Department Training Regulation 440-15, *Employment of the Air Forces of the Army*, 15 October 1935; Maj Gen Follett Bradley, "Pre-World War II Military Air Doctrines," lecture, Air War College, Maxwell AFB, Ala., 12 February 1951.

66. Lt Col John F. Curry, commandant, Air Corps Tactical School, to chief, Air Corps, letters, 5 February 1935 and n.d.; 1st ind., Brig Gen Oscar Westover to president, Air Corps Board, 13 March 1935.

67. William F. Pearson, Adjutant General Office, War Department, to chief, Air Corps, letter, subject: Directive for the Air Corps Board, 28 May 1935; 2d wrapper ind., Curry to chief, Air Corps, 3 June 1935.

68. Memorandum by Col A. G. Fisher, chief, Plans Division, Office of the Chief of the Air Corps, to chief, Air Corps, subject: The Air Corps Board, 14 May 1935; memorandum by Brig Gen A. W. Robin, chief, Materiel Division, Office of the Chief of the Air Corps, to chief, Air Corps, 7 June 1935; memorandum by Maj W. E. Lynd, chief, Plans Division, Office of the Chief of the Air Corps, to chief, Air Corps, subject: Comments on Letter of General Robins, 16 July 1935.

69. R. Earl McClendon, *Autonomy of the Air Arm*, Air Documentary Research Study (Maxwell AFB, Ala.: 1954), 101–4; Drague to Westover, letter, 13 January 1936.

70. Maj Gen Frank M. Andrews, commanding general, General Headquarters Air Force, "The General Headquarters Air Force," lecture, Army War College, Carlisle Barracks, Pa., 9 October 1937.

71. Maj Robert C. Candee, "The Air Corps," lecture, Army Engineering School, 18 April 1935.

72. Lt Col Henry H. Arnold, commander, March Field, Calif., to chief, Air Corps, letter, subject: Employment of Tactical Units Equipped with Modern Pursuit and Bombardment Airplanes, 26 November 1934.

73. Capt Harry A. Johnson, Command and General Staff School, to chief, Air Corps, letter, subject: Multiengine Fighter Aircraft, 18 January 1935; 2d ind., Lt Col H. A. Pratt, chief, Air Corps, Materiel Division, to chief, Air Corps, 16 February 1935; 3d ind., Col A. G. Fisher, president, Air Corps Board, to chief, Air Corps, 15 July 1945.

74. Craven and Cate, *Plans and Early Operations*, 69.

75. DuBuque, *The Development of the Heavy Bomber, 1918–1944*, 16–17; Maj Gen Orvil A. Anderson, "Development of US Strategic Air Doctrine, ETO World War II," lecture, Air War College, Maxwell AFB, Ala., 20 September 1951.

76. Andrews, "The GHQ Air Force."

77. Lt Col Robert Olds, commanding, 2d Bombardment Group, to commanding general, 2d Wing, letter, n.d.; 2d ind., Col Hugh H. Knerr, chief of staff, General Headquarters Air Force, to chief, Air Corps, 31 July 1937.

78. Hansell, "Pre-World War II Evaluation of the Air Weapon"; Air Corps Tactical School, *Air Force*, pt. 1, *Air Warfare*, 1 March 1936, 14.

79. Air Corps Tactical School, *Air Force*, pt. 1, *Air Warfare*, 1 February 1938, 1.

80. Thomas H. Greer, *The Development of Air Doctrine in the Army Air Arm, 1917–1944*, USAF historical study 89 (Maxwell AFB, Ala.: Research Studies Institute, 1955), 60–66.

81. Lt Col Millard F. Harmon, comments on Air Corps Tactical School document, n.d.; report of Board of Officers, 3d Wing, General Headquarters Air Force, Barksdale Field, La., ca. 21 April 1936; Col Millard F. Harmon, assistant commandant, Air Corps Tactical School, to Brig Gen B. K. Yount, Office of the Chief of the Air Corps, letter, 25 November 1939.

82. Maj O. S. Ferson, comments on tentative text *Air Force* published by Air Corps Tactical School, ca. April 1936.

83. Letter, General Headquarters Air Force to commanding general, 2d Wing, subject: Criticism of Air Corps Tactical School text *Air Force*, 14 March 1936; 2d wrapper ind., Lt Col A. H. Gilkeson, commanding officer, 8th Pursuit Group, to commanding general, 2d Wing, 28 March 1936.

IDEAS, CONCEPTS, DOCTRINE

84. Report of Air Corps Board, "Development of an 'Interceptor Type' Airplane," study 11, February 1937; Canham, "Development and Production of Fighter Aircraft for the United States Air Force," 43–57.

85. Greer, *The Development of Air Doctrine in the Army Air Arm*, 66–67, 87–88; Purtee, *The Development of Light and Medium Bombers*, 25–30.

86. Report of Air Corps Board, "Modernization of the Organization of the Army," study 21, 9 January 1936.

87. Memorandum by Maj William E. Lynd, Office of the Chief of the Air Corps, subject: Summary of Talk Given by General Westover before the Committee of General Hughes on the Subject of "Reorganization of the Army," 13 April 1936.

88. AG 320.2, Modernization of the Organization of the Army, letter, 6 December 1935; 2d ind., The Adjutant General to commanding general, General Headquarters Air Force, 25 March 1936.

89. Watson, *Chief of Staff: Prewar Plans and Preparations*, 42–44.

90. Robert W. Krauskopf, "The Army and the Strategic Bomber, 1930–1939," *Military Affairs* 22, no. 4 (Winter 1958–1959): 208–11.

91. Memorandum by Lt Col H. R. Bull, assistant secretary, General Staff, to The Adjutant General, 23 October 1937.

92. Memorandum by Brig Gen G. R. Spaulding, assistant chief of staff G-4, to chief of staff, Army, subject: Five-Year Program for the Air Corps, 3 March 1938; 1st ind., The Adjutant General, War Department, to chief, Air Corps, 18 March 1938; Office of the Chief of the Air Corps Chart $24,000,000 Aircraft Program, 14 February 1938.

93. Maj Gen Frank M. Andrews to The Adjutant General, letter, 23 September 1937, summarized in DuBuque, *The Development of the Heavy Bomber, 1918–1944*, 23.

94. Andrews, "The GHQ Air Force."

95. Army War College, "Air Forces and War," Preliminary Command Course, 1–25 September 1937.

96. Col B. Q. Jones, "GHQ and Army Air Forces," lecture, Army War College, Carlisle Barracks, Pa., 9 September 1937; memorandum by Lt Col R. S. Wooten to Brig Gen G. P. Tyner, assistant chief of staff G-3, subject: Lecture by Col B. Q. Jones, 18 October 1937; Lt Col Walter K. Kraus, comments on extracts from lecture by Col B. Q. Jones, 18 October 1937; memorandum by Maj Gen Stanley D. Embick, deputy chief of staff, Army, to Gen G. P. Tyner, 23 October 1937.

97. Memorandum by Maj Gen Stanley D. Embick to assistant chief of staff G-4, 9 May 1938, as quoted in Watson, *Chief of Staff: Prewar Plans and Preparations*, 35–36, and in Krauskopf, "The Army and the Strategic Bomber, 1930–1939," 210.

98. Krauskopf, "The Army and the Strategic Bomber, 1930–1939," 210, citing J. B. no. 349 (serial 629), subject: Limitation of Development of Army Bombardment and Reconnaissance Aviation, 29 June 1938.

99. Ibid., 212; The Adjutant General, War Department, to chief, Air Corps, letter, subject: Aircraft Program, 29 July 1938.

100. Quoted in letter from Brig Gen Oscar Westover to The Adjutant General, subject: Air Corps Program and Directive, 31 August 1938.

101. Archibald D. Turnbull and Clifford L. Lord, *History of United States Naval Aviation* (New Haven: Yale University Press, 1949), 300–1.

102. Air Corps press release, Long-Range Reconnaissance Mission of Flying Fortresses as GHQ Maneuvers Open, 12 May 1938.

103. Arnold, *Global Mission*, 176–77; Greer, *The Development of Air Doctrine in the Army Air Arm*, 91–92.

104. Draft memorandum by chief, Air Corps, to chief of staff, Army, subject: Additional Naval Air Bases, 28 March 1938; memorandum by Gen Malin Craig, chief of staff, Army, 8 August 1938.

105. Maj Gen Delos C. Emmons, commanding general, General Headquarters Air Force, to The Adjutant General, letter, subject: Report of Annual Tactical Inspection, GHQ Air Force, 1939, 28 July 1939.

106. Brig Gen Oscar Westover to The Adjutant General, letter, subject: Air Corps Program and Directive, 31 August 1938.

107. Westover to The Adjutant General, letter, 31 August 1938; 1st ind., E. R. Householder, War Department, Adjutant General Office, to chief, Air Corps, 5 October 1938.

108. The Adjutant General to chief, Air Corps, letter, 28 May 1935; 2d wrapper ind., Lt Col John F. Curry to chief, Air Corps, 3 June 1935; Col Jacob H. Rudolph, director of Air Corps Board, to Col R. B. Lincoln, Office of the Chief of the Air Corps, letter, subject: Preparation of Air Force Manual, 20 October 1936; Lt Col Walter F. Kraus, comments on extracts from lecture by Col B. Q. Jones, 18 October 1937.

109. Capt Laurence S. Kuter, "Operations against Naval Objectives," lecture, Air Corps Tactical School, Maxwell Field, Ala., 2 March 1938.

110. Air Corps Tactical School, *Air Force*, 1 February 1938, pt. 1:47.

111. Lt Col R. M. Jones, executive, Office of the Chief of the Air Corps, to president, Air Corps Board, letter, subject: Joint Action of the Army and the Navy, 9 June 1936; Air Corps Board Report 31, "The Functions of the Army Air Forces," 20 October 1936; Brig Gen Henry C. Pratt, commandant, Air Corps Tactical School, to chief, Air Corps, letter, subject: Statement of War Department Policy, 24 April 1937; Col Jacob H. Rudolph to chief, Air Corps, letter, subject: Air Corps Field Manual, 17 February 1937; 1st ind., Office of the Chief of the Air Corps to The Adjutant General, 4 March 1937; 2d ind., C. W. Christenberry, The Adjutant General Office, War Department, to chief, Air Corps, 16 March 1937.

112. Brig Gen Henry C. Pratt to chief, Air Corps, letter, subject: Air Corps Board Study 3 – "Air Corps Field Manual," 11 March 1938.

113. Brig Gen Oscar Westover to Henry C. Pratt, letter, 13 June 1938; Pratt to chief, Air Corps, letter, 11 March 1938; 1st ind., Office of Chief of Air Corps to president, Air Corps Board, 16 June 1938; 2d ind., Col. A. C. Sneed, president, Air Corps Board, to chief, Air Corps, 6 September 1938; 3d ind., Office of the Chief of the Air Corps to The Adjutant General, 14 September 1938; memorandum by Maj Gen R. M. Beck, Jr., assistant chief of staff G-3, War Department General Staff, chief, Air Corps, subject: Air Corps Field Manual, 29 March 1939.

114. Lt Col M. F. Davis, executive, Office of the Chief of the Air Corps, to president, Air Corps Board, letter, subject: Air Corps Mission under the Monroe Doctrine, 6 June 1938; Brig Gen Henry C. Pratt to Brig Gen Oscar Westover, letter, 8 June 1938; Col R. B. Lincoln, chief, Plans Section, to Office of the Chief of the Air Corps, to chief, Air Corps, R&R sheet, subject: Comments on Letters from General Pratt dated 8 and 10 June 1938; Westover to Pratt, letter, 13 June 1938.

115. Col J. H. Pirie, director, Air Corps Board, report, subject: Status of Studies of the Air Corps Board, 31 August 1938; Anderson, "Development of US Strategic Air Doctrine, ETO World War II"; Air Corps Board, "Report on Air Corps Mission under the Monroe Doctrine," study 44, 17 October 1938.

116. Maj Gen Henry H. Arnold, chief, Air Corps, on Air Corps Board Study 44; 1st ind., 4 November 1938; Office of the Chief of the Air Corps to The Adjutant General, draft letter, subject: Air Corps Board Study 44, 5 November 1938.

117. Watson, *Chief of Staff: Prewar Plans and Preparations*, 135–46.

118. Ibid., 132.

119. Ibid., 136–39; Arnold, *Global Mission*, 177–80. General Arnold erroneously cites this meeting as having taken place on 28 September 1938. See John McVickar Haight, Jr., *American Aid to France, 1938–1940* (New York: Atheneum, 1970), 56n.

120. Watson, *Chief of Staff: Prewar Plans and Preparations*, 140–44; Craven and Cate, *Plans and Early Operation*, 104; Maj Gen Laurence S. Kuter, "Organization of Top Echelons in World War II," lecture, Air War College, Maxwell AFB, Ala., 28 February 1949.

121. Memorandum by Brig Gen George C. Marshall, deputy chief of staff, Army, to chief of staff, Army, 29 November 1938.

122. Chase C. Mooney, *Organization of the Army Air Arm, 1935–1945*, historical study 10 (Maxwell AFB, Ala.: USAF Historical Division, 1956), 4–5; The Adjutant General, War Department, to

IDEAS, CONCEPTS, DOCTRINE

commanding generals of all corps areas et al., letter, subject: Organization of the Air Corps, 1 March 1939.

123. Kuter, "Organization of Top Echelons in World War II."

124. Maj Gen Delos C. Emmons to The Adjutant General, report, subject: Report of Annual Tactical Inspection, GHQ Air Force, 1939, 28 July 1939; 1st ind., Office of the Chief of the Air Corps to The Adjutant General, 8 September 1939; Office of the Chief of the Air Corps, circular 60-1, subject: Flying: Flights to Sea, 24 August 1939.

125. The Adjutant General, War Department, to chief, Air Corps, letter, subject: Aviation in National Defense, 23 March 1939.

126. Memorandum by Lt Col Carl A. Spaatz, chief, Plans Section, Office of the Chief of the Air Corps, 28 March 1939.

127. Office of the Chief of the Air Corps to commanding general, General Headquarters Air Force, letter, subject: Aviation in National Defense, 31 March 1939.

128. See Air Corps Tactical School Student Research Committee, "A Study of the Air Defense of the Western Hemisphere," 12 May 1939; 2d Wing, General Headquarters Air Force, discussion of Air Corps Board questionnaire, 30 January 1939; Air Corps Board Report Study 35, "Employment of Aircraft in Defense of the Continental United States," 7 May 1939.

129. 2d Wing, General Headquarters Air Force, discussion of Air Corps Board, questionnaire, 30 January 1939.

130. Maj Gen E. A. Adams, The Adjutant General, War Department, to chiefs of all arms and services, letter, subject: Air Corps Augmentation Program, 12 June 1939.

131. Memorandum by Office of the Chief of the Air Corps, to assistant chief of staff G-3, War Department General Staff, subject: Air Corps Expansion Program, 24 November 1939.

132. Office of the Chief of the Air Corps to David D. Terry, House of Representatives, letter, 20 December 1939.

133. DuBuque, *The Development of the Heavy Bomber, 1918–1944*, 38–41; James C. Fahey, *US Army Aircraft, 1908–1946* (New York: Ships and Aircraft, 1946), 20–24.

134. Watson, *Chief of Staff: Prewar Plans and Preparations*, 100–101; The Adjutant General, War Department, to chiefs of all arms and services et al., report, subject: Air Board Report, 15 September 1939.

135. Office of the Chief of the Air Corps to director, Air Corps Board, letter, subject: Final Revision of Field Manual 1-5, 20 November 1939; War Department Field Manual 1-5, *Employment of Aviation of the Army*, 1940.

136. Greer, *The Development of Air Doctrine in the Army Air Arm*, 113; War Department Field Manual 1-5, *Employment of Aviation of the Army*.

137. The Adjutant General, War Department, to Thomas E. Morgan, House of Representatives, letter, 31 October 1939.

138. Memorandum by Lt Col Donald Wilson, Air Corps Tactical School, to Lt Col L. F. Stone, Command and General Staff School, 23 September 1939.

139. Maj Gen Orvil A. Anderson, "Weapon Systems and Their Influence on Strategy," lecture, Air War College, Maxwell AFB, Ala., 30 August 1951.

140. Maj Gen Henry H. Arnold to commanding general, General Headquarters Air Force, letter, subject: Pursuit Training and Pursuit Plane Tactical Development, 14 November 1939; 1st ind., Col C. W. Russell, chief of staff, General Headquarters Air Force, to chief, Air Corps, 11 January 1940; Greer, *The Development of Air Doctrine in the Army Air Arm*, 116–17.

141. Arnold to commanding general, General Headquarters Air Force, letter, 14 November 1939; 1st ind., Col C. W. Russell to chief, Air Corps, 11 January 1940.

142. Air Corps Board Report 53, "Fire Power of Bombardment Formations," 3 January 1940.

143. Air Corps Board, Study of Pursuit and Fighter Aircraft, ca. 10 March 1940.

144. Memorandum by Brig Gen George C. Marshall to chief, Air Corps, 13 June 1940; memorandum by Maj Gen Henry H. Arnold to executive, Office of the Chief of the Air Corps, 14 June 1940.

145. Robert F. Futrell, *Command of Observation Aviation: A Study in Control of Tactical Air Power*, USAF historical study 24 (Maxwell AFB, Ala.: USAF Historial Division, 1956), 6–8.

146. Memorandum by Maj Gen Delos C. Emmons to chief, Air Corps, 12 June 1940.

147. Brig Gen James E. Chaney, commanding general, Air Defense Command, to Brig Gen George C. Marshall, letter, 4 June 1940; memorandum by Maj Gen Frank M. Andrews to secretary, General Staff, subject: Experimental Development of B-17, B-15, B-19 Types of Airplanes, 25 June 1940; memorandum by Maj Gen Henry H. Arnold to chief of staff, Army, 23 July 1940.

148. Gen Carl A. Spaatz, USAF, Retired, "Leaves from My Battle-of-Britain Diary," *The Air Power Historian* 4, no. 2 (April 1957): 66–75.

149. Memorandum by Maj Gen Delos C. Emmons to chief of staff, Army, subject: Observations in England, 25 September 1940.

150. Memorandum by Brig Gen Carl A. Spaatz, chief, Plans Division, Office of the Chief of the Air Corps, to Maj Gen George H. Brett, chief, Air Corps, 3 February 1941, quoted in DuBuque, *The Development of the Heavy Bomber, 1918–1944*, 47.

151. Memorandum by Maj Gen Delos C. Emmons to chief of staff, Army, 25 September 1940; Col Carl A. Spaatz and Col Frank O'D. Hunter to Military Intelligence Division, War Department General Staff, letter, subject: Organization Headquarters Fighter Group, 21 August 1940.

152. Dulaney Terrett, *The Signal Corps: The Emergency, US Army in World War II* (Washington, D.C.: Office of the Chief of Military History, Department of the Army, 1956), 35–48; Col F. R. Dent, "Technological Improvements in Airplanes from 1920 to 1939 and Their Influences on German Strategy," lecture, Army Air Forces of Technology, 15 November 1946; Col H. G. Montgomery, "Military Apparatus and Technology," lecture, Air War College, Maxwell AFB, Ala., 24 November 1947; Army Air Forces School of Applied Tactics, "Some Facts in the History of Radar," n.d.

153. Dent, "Technological Improvements in Airplanes."

154. Army Air Forces School of Applied Tactics, "Some Facts in the History of Radar."

155. Winston S. Churchill, *The Second World War*, vol. 2, *Their Finest Hour* (Boston: Houghton-Mifflin Co., 1949), 381–82.

156. Maj Gen Haywood S. Hansell, "Pre-World War II Evaluation of the Air Weapon"; Maj Gen Muir S. Fairchild, commanding general, Air University, to Dr Bruce Hooper, letter, 27 September 1946.

157. Hansell, "Pre-World War II Evaluation of the Air Weapon."

158. Maj Gen Henry H. Arnold to chief, Ordnance, letter, subject: Urgency of Bombing Flare Development, 7 September 1940.

159. Terrett, *The Signal Corps: The Emergency*, 128–29, 191–202; notes on meetings of the British Commission, 12–13 September 1940.

160. Quoted in Terrett, *The Signal Corps: The Emergency*, 255–57.

161. Henry H. Arnold and Ira C. Eaker, *Winged Warfare* (New York: Harper, 1941), 176.

162. Irving B. Holley, Jr., *Buying Aircraft: Material Procurement for the Army Air Forces, US Army in World War II* (Washington, D.C.: Office of the Chief of Military History, Department of the Army, 1964), 226–28; Watson, *Chief of Staff: Prewar Plans and Preparations*, 306.

163. Quoted in Arnold, *Global Mission*, 199.

164. Memorandum by Maj Gen Henry H. Arnold to deputy chief of staff, Army, subject: Activation of Additional Air Corps Units Under Army's First Aviation Objective, 24 July 1940; Greer, *The Development of Air Doctrine in the Army Air Arm*, 108; The Adjutant General, War Department, to commanding general, General Headquarters Air Force, and chief, Air Corps, letter, subject: Army's Second Aviation Objective, 14 March 1941.

165. Robert P. Patterson, assistant secretary of war, to [William S.] Knudsen, subject: Four Engine Bombers, 17 October 1940.

166. Memorandum by Col George E. Stratemeyer, acting chief, Plans Division, Office of the Chief of the Air Corps, to chief, Air Corps, subject: Plans Division Conference with General Marshall, 24 October 1940; memorandum by Lt Col Muir S. Fairchild, secretary of Air Staff, to chief, Air Corps, subject: Estimates for Second Aviation Objective, 2 August 1941; Maj Gen Orvil A. Anderson,

IDEAS, CONCEPTS, DOCTRINE

"Weapon Systems and Their Influence on Strategy"; Edwin H. Spengler, "Estimating Requirements for Army Air Forces Equipment, Supplies, and Spare Parts, 1930–1945," pt. 1 (Wright Field, Ohio: Air Technical Service Command Historical Office, ca. 1945), 17.

167. Maj Gen E. A. Adams, The Adjutant General, War Department, to commanding generals, all corps areas et al., letter, subject: General Headquarters, 26 July 1940; memorandum by Col B. K. Yount, chief, Plans Division, Office of the Chief of the Air Corps, to chief, Air Corps, subject: General Headquarters, 1 August 1940.

168. Watson, *Chief of Staff: Prewar Plans and Preparations*, 286–90; Mooney, *Organization of the Army Air Arm, 1935–1945*, 5.

169. Watson, *Chief of Staff: Prewar Plans and Preparations*, 290.

170. R. E. Fraile, The Adjutant General Office, War Department, to chief, Air Corps, letter, subject: Station List, Air Corps Organizations, 20 August 1940; 1st ind., Maj Gen Henry H. Arnold to The Adjutant General, 28 September 1940; memorandum by Maj Gen Frank M. Andrews to chief of staff, Army, subject: Organization of Air Districts, 11 October 1940; memorandum by Maj Gen Henry H. Arnold to chief of staff, Army, subject: Duties of Air District Commanders for Operations Outside the United States, 28 October 1940; Mooney, *Organization of the Army Air Arm, 1935–1954*, 5.

171. Memorandum by Lt Col Carl A. Spaatz to assistant chief of staff G-2, War Department General Staff, subject: Submission of Final Report, 28 February 1941.

172. Watson, *Chief of Staff: Prewar Plans and Preparations*, 292–95; Mooney, *Organization of the Army Air Arm, 1935–1945*, 5–7, 25.

173. Mooney, *Organization of the Army Air Arm, 1935–1945*, 5.

174. Futrell, *Command of Observation Aviation*, 1–11.

175. Office of the Chief of the Air Corps to director, Air Corps Board, letter, subject: Final Revision of Field Manual 1-5, 25 October 1939; Col Walter R. Weaver, commandant, Air Corps Tactical School, to Lt Col Carl A. Spaatz, letter, 3 January 1940; Office of the Chief of the Air Corps to director, Air Corps Board, subject: Air Corps Field Manuals, 9 February 1940; 2d ind., Lt Col Edgar P. Sorenson, director, Air Corps Board, to chief, Air Corps, 26 February 1940; Status of Studies of the Air Corps Board, 31 May 1940.

176. Col Walter A. Weaver to chief, Air Corps, letter, subject: Air Corps Tactical Center, 17 January 1940; 1st ind., Brig Gen B. K. Yount, assistant chief, Air Corps, to commandant, Air Corps Tactical School, 18 April 1940.

177. Memorandum by Col George E. Stratemeyer to chief, Air Corps, subject: Operation of the Air Corps Board and the Evaluation of War Information, 23 October 1940.

178. Col Edgar P. Sorenson, commandant, Air Corps Tactical School, to Office of the Chief of the Air Corps, letter, 30 December 1940; Office of the Chief of the Air Corps to commandant, Air Corps Tactical School, letter, subject: Training Literature Unit, Air Corps Tactical School, Maxwell Field, Ala., 22 June 1941; Lt Col W. W. Dick, air adjutant general, Army Air Forces, to director, Air Corps Board, letter, subject: Preparation of Training Literature, 1 July 1941.

179. Maj Gen George H. Brett to chief, Army Air Forces, R&R sheet, subject: Preparation of Training Literature, 18 July 1941; comment 3, Brig Gen Muir S. Fairchild, executive, Office of the Chief of the Air Corps, to chief, Air Staff, Army Air Forces, 11 August 1941; comment 4, Lt Col Carl A. Spaatz to chief, Air Corps, 28 August 1941.

180. Lt Col John A. Greene, acting commandant, Air Corps Tactical School, to The Adjutant General, letter, subject: Annual Report of the Air Corps Tactical School for School Year 1941–1942, 30 June 1942; History, Army Air Forces Board, 1:15–16; Col H. G. Montgomery, "Weapons Evolution and Air Power," lecture, Air War College, Maxwell AFB, Ala., October 1953.

181. History, I Interceptor Command, 2 June 1941–25 May 1942, 1–39, 188–227; Air Defense Doctrine, prepared by Maj Gordon P. Saville, Air Corps, 27 October 1941.

182. Futrell, *Command of Observation Aviation*, 12–18; The Adjutant General, War Department, to chief of staff, General Headquarters et al., letter, subject: Type Organization of Air Forces in a Theater of Operations, 7 October 1941.

183. Report of a Board of Officers Appointed to Make Recommendations with Respect to the Future Development of Pursuit Aircraft, Its Accessory Equipment and Operational Employment to the Chief of the Army Air Forces, 17 October 1941.

184. Ray S. Cline, *Washington Command Post: The Operations Division, US Army in World War II* (Washington, D.C.: Office of the Chief of Military History, 1951), 55–57.

185. Ibid., 57–59; Craven and Cate, *Plans and Early Operations*, 136–41; Watson, *Chief of Staff: Prewar Plans and Preparations*, 374–84.

186. Franklin D. Roosevelt to secretary of war, letter, 9 July 1941.

187. Memorandum by Lt Col G. W. Bundy, War Plans Division, War Department General Staff, to Lt Col Clayton L. Bissell, subject: Ultimate Air Force Requirements, 18 July 1941; Air War Plans Division, diary notes, 29–31 July 1941; memorandum by Air War Plans Division (AWPD), subject: Outlines of Basic Requirements and Coordinating Instructions Relative to AWPD-1, 4 August 1941; AWPD-1, "Munitions Requirements of the Army Air Forces," 12 August 1941.

188. Bissell, comments in AWPD-1 scrapbook, tab. 35.

189. Memorandum by Lt Col Harold L. George to chief, Air Staff, subject: Information References AWPD-1, 15 September 1941.

190. Arnold, *Global Mission*, 209.

191. Joint Board, J. B. no. 355 (serial 707), Joint Board Estimate of United States Over-All Production Requirements, 11 September 1941.

192. Craven and Cate, *Plans and Early Operations*, 150.

193. History, B-36 Procurement, presented to House Armed Services Committee, 1949, sec. 1, by Maj Gen Frederic H. Smith, Jr.

194. Maurice Matloff and Edwin M. Snell, *Strategic Planning for Coalition Warfare, 1941–1942, US Army in World War II* (Washington, D.C.: Office of the Chief of Military History, Department of the Army, 1953), 64–65, 67–73; Brig Gen L. T. Gerow, acting assistant chief of staff, Army, to chief, Army Air Forces, subject: Reinforcement of the Philippines, 18 August 1941; Robert F. Futrell, "Air Hostilities in the Philippines, 8 December 1941," *Air University Review* 16, no. 2 (January–February 1965): 33–45.

B-24.

B-17 Flying Fortress.

Norden bombsight.

B-25.

B-29.

B-26.

B-32.

Lt Gen George H. Brett, chief of Air Corps, 1941.

B-36.

Maj Gen Delos C. Emmons, commanding general, Air Force Combat Command, 1939–41.

P-40 Warhawk pursuit aircraft.

P-38 pursuit interceptors.

P-12F pursuit aircraft.

Maj Gen James E. Fechet, chief of Air Corps, 1927-31.

Maj Gen Oscar Westover, chief, Air Corps, 1935-39.

Lt Gen Frank M. Andrews, commanding general, General Headquarters Air Force, 1935-39; assistant chief of staff, Operations and Training, General Staff, 1939-40.

P-47 Thunderbolt.

P-51 Mustang long-range fighter escort.

P-39 pursuit aircraft.

B-17 Flying Fortress.

CHAPTER 4

AIR FORCE THINKING AND WORLD WAR II

"In the nineteen-thirties, when air power was the unseen guest at those grim conferences which marked the Nazi march to power," observed Gen Henry H. Arnold on 4 January 1944, "the Army Air Corps, which preceded the Army Air Forces, had drawn its blue-prints for war." The Air Corps Tactical School, Arnold noted, had developed the "strategic and tactical doctrines that would later guide our air campaigns in World War II."[1]

Planning and Analysis in the Army Air Forces

One week after the Japanese attack at Pearl Harbor, the Air War Plans Division (AWPD) sought to commit the United States and Great Britain to an air strategy against the Axis. AWPD-4, Air Estimate of the Situation and Recommendations for the Conduct of the War, which appeared on 15 December 1941, advocated that the United States give first concern to protecting the Western Hemisphere and Great Britain and to sustaining America's fighting men in the Philippines, and then bend every effort toward implementing an air offensive against the Axis powers in Europe. Since a successful air offensive would have to precede the launching of any land or sea offensive and inasmuch as a powerful air offensive might be decisive in itself, the air plans study recommended that first priorities in war production should be given to the Army Air Forces and that sea and ground force priorities should be allocated "in the light of their contribution to the Air Force mission"[2] AWPD-4 represented the thought of Harold George, Haywood Hansell, Kenneth Walker,* and Orvil Anderson.

---

* This document was the last contribution of the 44-year-old Walker to Air Force doctrinal thought. Having been promoted to the rank of brigadier general, Walker was transferred to the Southwest Pacific in June 1942 where he assumed command of the V Bomber Command. He was killed in action on 15 January 1943 while on a B-17 mission over Rabaul. In 1943 he was posthumously awarded the Medal of Honor, and in 1948 Roswell Air Force Base, New Mexico, was renamed Walker Air Force Base in his honor.

The plan of action recommended by AWPD-4 included three phases of activity and three sets of subordinate tasks, many of which would be undertaken concurrently. The first phase was to safeguard the United States and Great Britain by defending existing possessions and extending those defenses to Natal, the Cape Verde Islands, and Dakar. The second phase was to wage a decisive air offensive against the Axis powers in Europe, to engage in a defensive effort in the Far East, and to conduct a land invasion of Europe "when and if it becomes necessary." After defeating the European enemies, the third phase was to be sustained air offensives against Japanese military and civil strength, the use of land forces when and if necessary, and the maintenance of sufficient flexibility to exploit opportune openings for decisive action against Japan. The plan recommended an air force of 90,000 airplanes, a production rate of 3,000 airplanes a month, and an Army of 3,000,000 men and women. The recommended air order of battle included a force of 13 medium bomber, 64 heavy bomber, 32 B-29 or B-32 bomber, 59 long-range (4,000-mile) bomber, 35 light and dive-bomber, 72 pursuit, and 82 transport groups, plus 159 observation and photographic reconnaissance squadrons. The plan posed a requirement for naval strength "capable of safe-guarding our essential sea lanes of communication" and for ground forces sufficient to maintain the security of Allied base areas and eventually to undertake a final surface invasion of Germany and then Japan, if such became necessary.[3]

In reply to a request for information, the Air War Plans Division on 9 January 1942 also sought a high degree of autonomy for the Air Force. On 24 October 1941 Brig Gen Carl A. Spaatz already had formally proposed that GHQ Air Force be eliminated, that overall command be returned to the Army chief of staff, that the General Staff be limited to considering broad policy, and that broad responsibilities be delegated to the chiefs of ground, service, and air forces (the last already in existence). The Air War Plans Division proposed that coordinate ground, air, and naval services be created, with unity of command to be secured by a common head of all armed services who would report directly to the president and would have a small staff of ground, air, naval, production and supply, and political and economic warfare representatives. The Air War Plans Division urged that such an organization would provide each service with a desired freedom of action and at the same time ensure unity of command.[4]

Although the Air War Plans Division had forcefully asserted prevalent air doctrines, the United States was not going to adopt an undiluted air strategy nor would the air force attain full-fledged autonomy. Meeting in Washington between 22 December 1941 and 14 January 1942, the Anglo-American Combined Chiefs of Staff Arcadia conference did not favor such an overriding priority as AWPD-4 would have accorded to aircraft production but instead favored a victory program, calling for increases of air, land, and naval forces and for the allocation of resources for the manufacture of munitions in a sequence of limited schedules geared to successively approved operations. The combined staff planners accordingly accepted AWPD-1 with some modifications rather than AWPD-4. As a result of agreements with the British, Secretary of Defense Henry L. Stimson on 19 January

1942 authorized the Army Air Forces to expand during 1942 to a total of 115 groups, including 34 heavy bomber, 12 medium bomber, 10 light bomber, 31 pursuit, 12 transport, and 16 observation groups.[5]

The Arcadia conference also established the mechanism for directing the Anglo-American war effort and a precedent looking toward unified command of combined forces in theaters of operations. From his experience in World War I in France, General George C. Marshall held a conviction that "there must be one man in command of the entire theater — air, ground, and ships." Despite a lack of enthusiasm among the other military chiefs, Marshall convinced President Roosevelt and Prime Minister Winston Churchill of the need to establish a unified American-British-Dutch-Australian Command (ABDACOM) in the Western Pacific-East Indies. From this time on the US War Department believed that the Allies were committed to a supreme commander in combined operations. As a matter of fact, ABDACOM was disestablished on 23 February 1942 and future Allied theater commanders would not be given "supreme" authority. The question of the manner in which an Allied theater commander would receive his directives was solved at Arcadia by the establishment of the Combined Chiefs of Staff, a composite organization of the British army, navy, and air force chiefs of staff and their American counterparts. The use of the British chiefs of staff committee as a model for the Combined Chiefs of Staff raised an awkward complexity in that the Army Air Forces was part of the US Army, whereas the Royal Air Force was a separate service. Arnold, nevertheless, was recognized as a member of both the Combined Chiefs of Staff and the Joint Chiefs of Staff. The Joint Chiefs of Staff, which replaced the Joint Army-Navy Board, informally came into being at Arcadia and held its first formal meeting on 9 February 1942.[6]

Sweeping changes in the organization of the War Department and the Army Air Forces (AAF) closely followed the Arcadia agreements. Effective on 9 March 1942, the War Department was consolidated into three coordinate forces each under a commanding general: the Army Air Forces, the Army Ground Forces, and the Services of Supply (later the Army Service Forces). General Headquarters, the Office of Chief of Air Corps, and the Air Force Combat Command were abolished. The War Department General Staff was shaken up; approximately 50 percent of its personnel was to be from the air arm. The War Plans Division, soon renamed the Operations Division (OPD), became a general command post and had planning authority for the War Department. Under the reorganization, the mission of the Army Air Forces, as specified, was "to produce and maintain equipment peculiar to the Army Air Forces, and to provide air force units properly organized, trained, and equipped for combat operations." Headquarters Army Air Forces thus became a supply and training agency, not primarily concerned with actual combat operations or strategic planning.[7]

As part of the changes in the War Department, Headquarters Army Air Forces was restructured effective on 9 March 1942 to include two levels of staff activity — policy and operating staff. At the policy level, the functions of planning and establishing policies were lodged in A-1 (Personnel), A-2 (Intelligence), A-3

(Training), A-4 (Supply), and Plans. The Plans Division was viewed as a coordinating agency for the other four divisions since, in theory, it was not to be concerned with war planning. Three major directorates—Military Requirements, Technical Services, and Management Control—were the principal components of the operating staff. At this level, Maj Gen Muir S. Fairchild's Directorate of Military Requirements was described as a group of functional specialists whose research was to be the media through which combat lessons were to be reflected in training and procurement programs. General Fairchild had under him Air Defense, Bombardment, Ground Support, War Organization and Movement, Base Services, and Individual Training divisions. The directors of air defense, bombardment, and ground support, which were usually called "type" directorates because they were concerned with types of aviation, were to be experts in their respective classes of aviation and were charged with development of tactics and techniques for their specialties. The director of individual training was charged with directing, supervising, and giving final approval to Army Air Forces training literature.[8] Since so much experience was now concentrated in the Directorate of Military Requirements, the Air Corps Board at Eglin Field was inactivated when the Army regulation that authorized it was rescinded on 20 May 1942. The Air Corps Tactical School was suspended as an active unit on 24 June 1942, and the people in its Training Literature Unit were integrated into the Training Aids Section of the Individual Training Division.[9]

Although the War Department reorganization removed responsibility for operational planning from the Army Air Forces, President Franklin D. Roosevelt asked General Arnold on 24 August 1942 to submit his judgment as to which combat aircraft should be produced in 1943 in order to gain complete air ascendancy over the enemy. Such a judgment could not be divorced from operational planning, although it had to follow approved strategy and, thus, define the air mission in terms of cooperation with surface campaigns. Brig Gen Laurence S. Kuter, now deputy chief of air staff, Brig Gen Orvil A. Anderson, chief of air plans, and Brig Gen Haywood S. Hansell, who had been named deputy commander of the Eighth Air Force, undertook the study, which, when completed on 9 September 1942, was entitled AWPD-42, Requirements for Air Ascendancy.[10] Requirements were based on air operations visualized for 1943 and early 1944 to include: an air offensive against Europe to deplete the Luftwaffe, destroy the sources of German submarine construction, and undermine the German war-making capacity; air support for a land offensive in northwest Africa; air support for land operations to retain the Middle East; air support for surface operations in the Pacific and Far East to regain base areas for a final offensive against Japan proper; and hemispheric defense, including antisubmarine patrol. To meet such a schedule of operations, the planners calculated that the Army Air Forces would require 281 combat groups by 1 January 1944—including 76 heavy bomber, 43 medium bomber, 26 light and dive-bomber, 70 fighter, 20 observation, 12 photographic reconnaissance, and 34 troop carrier groups. The study proposed that 130,906 aircraft should be produced in 1943 — 75,416 for the Army, 33,050 for the Navy, and 22,440 for the Allies.

While it was prepared by several of the same officers who had written AWPD-1, AWPD-42 revealed something of the change in doctrinal thinking that was taking place in 1942. The former study had posed large requirements for B-29 and B-36 aircraft, but AWPD-42 expected few B-29s and no B-36s to come from production in 1943. It was also evident that it would be possible to base more bombers in Great Britain than had been thought earlier. The strategic philosophy of the two studies was virtually the same, but a new study of Germany's target system was included in AWPD-42. The priority targets were stated to be airplane assembly and aircraft engine plants, submarine yards, transportation and power centers and networks, and oil, aluminum, and rubber manufacturing facilities. The air campaign, thus, was to prepare the way for surface attack. While the changed target priorities reflected a growing demand for establishing air superiority over Germany, AWPD-42 confidently predicted that "our current type bombers can penetrate German defenses to the limit of their radius of operation without excessive losses."

Both AWPD-1 and AWPD-42 visualized that a land invasion of Europe would probably follow the strategic bombing campaign, but the timing of the air offensive had been changed. AWPD-1 had projected six months of intensified bombing to begin in mid-1942, however, AWPD-42 necessarily postponed it until late 1944 because of the failure to receive the overriding priorities for aircraft production as recommended in AWPD-42, plus the diversion of heavy and medium bombers to the US Navy for patrol and antisubmarine warfare. Moreover, to conserve strategic bomber resources, AWPD-42 urged that no allocations of heavy or medium bombers be made to the Navy from 1943 production.[11] This provision, together with the competition that the proposed aircraft production program posed to the building of ships, aircraft carriers, and naval aircraft, caused the Navy to reject AWPD-42 out of hand. In a compromise on 26 November 1942, President Roosevelt finally approved a program of building 107,000 aircraft and substantial portions of the Navy shipbuilding program.[12]

The decisions made in the winter of 1942–43 as to the final force objectives of the United States marked great changes in the internal composition of the Army. In the summer of 1940 the US victory program had called for a ground army of 215 divisions and an air force of 84 groups, but in the winter of 1942–43 the US Army changed its force plans to include 89 divisions and 273 air force groups, the 273 groups being considered to be the saturation point in the development of Army air power. Toward that end the Army Air Forces activated a total of 269 combat groups by December 1943. Some of these groups were paper units, and not a few of them were pledged to hemispheric defense. An agreement between the Army and Navy on 10 June 1943 led the Navy to take charge of antisubmarine defense, thus reducing Army requirements for air groups for hemispheric defense. As air planners had earlier predicted, moreover, the acquisition of more efficient B-29 Superfortress bombers permitted reductions in the number of bomber units needed. In a readjustment of the Army Air Forces program, most of the paper units among the 269 combat groups were inactivated in the spring of 1944. Thereafter the Army Air Forces built upward toward the maximum combat strength of 243 groups it would attain in February 1945. This maximum combat strength included 25 very heavy bombardment, 27 heavy bombardment, 20 medium bombardment, 8 light bombardment, 71 fighter, 13 reconnaissance, 29 troop carrier, and 5 composite groups.[13] Neither the peak strength of 269 groups nor the maximum combat strength of 243 groups equaled the 281 combat groups that AWPD-42 had predicted would be required for air supremacy over the Axis. Reduced requirements for hemispheric defense and the arrival of the B-29 very heavy bombers in the combat inventory permitted reductions in total group requirements.

Many Procedures for Developing Air Doctrine

During the frantic months in which the Army Air Forces was mobilizing for war, General Arnold obviously considered it appropriate that the largest concentration of experienced air officers should be situated in Headquarters Army Air Forces. The organization of the headquarters also reflected Arnold's notions about how a staff should work. Arnold often remarked that laborious staff review procedures tended to emasculate bold air concepts and decisions: "termites" in a staff could eat up good ideas before they could get through to the top. Arnold accordingly saw nothing wrong in dividing his headquarters into a policy and operating staff wherein 31 individuals had direct access to him and authority to sign action papers by his authority.[14] Air Force field commanders, however, complained of conflicts in orders and directives. The same thing was true of doctrinal and policy statements. The director of military requirements was chiefly concerned with formulating doctrine and employment policies, but his status was essentially advisory. At the same time other directorates were issuing instructions in various forms. As a result of this decentralization, many miscellaneous publications, each containing specialized fragments of air force ideas, were sent out to field commanders. These collections were too voluminous for any commander to study and the whole collection did not form a consistent and complete statement of air doctrines and employment policies. Col Charles G. Williamson, chief of the bombardment division, pointed out these facts in a discussion of air policies and doctrines written on 3 March 1943. "In military matters, especially those of the magnitude of the operations of the present war, where mistakes and inconsistencies cost thousands of lives and millions of man-hours," he warned, "it is all the more important that there be clearly expressed guiding principles which are clearly understood by all planners, as well as by all who are charged with the handling of the forces in the field."[15]

Heavily concerned with day-to-day operations that allowed little time for reflective thought, the Air Defense, Bombardment, and Group Support divisions within the Directorate of Military Requirements began to employ different means for the evaluation and preparation of the doctrine that they were expected to provide. In the March 1942 reorganization of the Army Air Forces, the Ground Support Division, headed by Col David M. Schlatter, had superseded the Army Air Support Staff Section that had been jointly manned by the Army General Headquarters and the Air Force Combat Command. Colonel Schlatter inherited a virtually complete draft manual that had been drawn up on the basis of experience with the new air support commands in the Louisiana and Carolina maneuvers of 1941. It was published as War Department Field Manual 31-35, *Aviation in Support of Ground Forces*, on 9 April 1942. This manual was heavily concerned with organization and had little to say about operations. It provided that the air support commander would function under the Army commander: it stated that an air support command, as one of several air force commands in a theater of operations, was "habitually attached to or supports an army in the theater." Aviation units, moreover, could be "specifically allocated to the support of subordinate ground units." The commander of a supported unit was given the authority to make the final decision as to target priorities: "the most important target at a particular time," the manual stated, "will usually be that target which constitutes the most serious threat to the operations of the supported ground force." At best the air support command would provide a centralized control for observation groups, transport groups, or other combat air units assigned or attached to it. Both Colonel Schlatter and Col William E. Lynd, who had shared in drawing up the manual, considered FM 31-35 to be highly tentative and subject to change.[16] As a matter of fact, ground force officers did not like the centralized control of support aviation inherent in the air support command, for they frankly favored the attachment or assignment of air units directly to the ground units they would support. Beginning on 7 December 1942 a special Air Support Board with ground and air members met in Washington to revise the manual. Even though this board proposed no radical changes in the manual, the revised manuscript was not approved by either the Army Air Forces or the Army Ground Forces.[17]

Recognizing that the Army Air Forces had much to learn about air defense and directing fighter interceptor forces by radar and radio, the Air Force Combat Command (shortly before its demise) laid plans for the establishment of a special school to deal with these matters. On 26 March 1942 the Third Air Force accordingly established an Air Defense Operational Training Unit at Orlando, Florida. When the reorganization of the Army Air Forces was completed, the Orlando activity was designated as the Fighter Command School and placed directly under Headquarters Army Air Forces. In its mission statement, Col Gordon P. Saville, director of air defense, charged the school to train air defense personnel to develop doctrines, tactics, and techniques of air defense; to test air defense equipment and operational procedures; and to recommend the organization of air defense for the United States and overseas theaters. A pursuit group, an aircraft warning regiment, a searchlight battalion, and other necessary troops were assigned to the school. To accomplish its research missions the Fighter Command School established an Operational Requirements Department, a Tactics and Technique Development Department, and an Air Defense Board, with the directors of the school's academic and research departments serving as members. As a first project the Air Defense Board revised the draft air defense manual that Saville had prepared in the winter of 1941-42. It was published as War Department Field Manual 1-25, *Air Defense,* on 24 December 1942. By this time the Air Defense Board had either completed or had under test 74 other air defense projects.[18]

In the spring 1942 the Air Staff in Washington began to recognize that the closing of the Air Corps Tactical School—although doubtlessly necessary—had been essentially shortsighted. In June 1942 Col Don Z. Zimmerman, the director of weather, called attention to the great lack of tactical experience among new Air Force officers and recommended that the Army Air Forces reopen the Tactical School, using returned combat veterans as an instructional staff. General Fairchild enthusiastically received the proposal, and the Training Aids Division was charged to lay the groundwork for the new school. The decision was soon made to re-create an expanded tactical school at Orlando and to use the Fighter Command School as one of the departments of the new school.[19]

After a summer of planning, the Army Air Forces School of Applied Tactics was established at Orlando on 27 October 1942 and charged both to "train selected officers under simulated combat conditions" and to "develop, prepare, and standardize training literature and ... other training material."[20] On 12 November the Army Air Forces established the Army Air Forces Board and the directorates of Academic Training, Tactical Development, Operations and Facilities, and Training Aids within the School of Applied Tactics. The Directorate of Academic Training consisted of the departments of Air Defense, Bombardment, Air Support, and Air Service. The AAF Board was to be comprised of a chairman, an executive, and additional members to be appointed by General Arnold as well as the commandants of each of the school's department. The board was charged to "determine major questions of policy and doctrine for all activities of the school and such other matters as may be assigned to it by competent authority." The director of tactical development was responsible for conducting test operations of aircraft and equipment and for improving the strategy, tactics, and techniques of air warfare. The Army Air Forces undertook to exercise control over the School of Applied Tactics through the director of military requirements; the directors of air defense, bombardment, air support, and base services were to approve the doctrines, tactics, and techniques taught in the department of the school.[21]

The terse language of Army Air Forces regulations gave the impression that the AAF Board was to be a school activity, but on 16 November 1942 General Fairchild instructed Brig Gen Hume Peabody, the commandant of the AAF School of Applied Tactics, that the board ought to be developed as an Army Air Forces activity. "The purpose of the Army Air Forces Board," Fairchild wrote, "is to study the over-all picture of Air Force matters with a view to making recommendations to the Commanding General, Army Air Forces, on such matters as Air Force strategy, technique, organization, equipment, training, etc., of all units making up an Air Force and of the Air Forces as a whole."[22] Since the Air Defense Board was agencies. In addition, Fairchild directed Peabody to form an equipment board. This board received directives for testing from the AAF Materiel Command and usually reassigned its projects to one of the other subboards, depending on the type of equipment to be tested.[23] When General Peabody assumed the duty as chairman of the AAF Board, he planned that it would function in a supervisory capacity. The AAF Board held its first recorded meeting on 2 February 1943, and it was soon meeting at regular intervals to review completed projects and to forward them, after approval, to Headquarters Army Air Forces.[24]

New Conceptions of Tactical Air Power

The organization of the Headquarters Army Air Forces, adopted in March 1942, had been designed to build quickly the world's most powerful air force. An operating echelon had been established to perform typical functions found in an air task force, and the directors of the operating echelon had been authorized to act with broad discretion on behalf of General Arnold. By the winter of 1942-43, however, the expansion program was firmly in hand. Upon his return home from the meeting of the Combined Chiefs of Staff in Casablanca in January 1943, General Arnold stated that AAF headquarters "must stop operating" and spend its time thinking "in order that we can correctly tell our commanders what to do and maybe sometimes when to do it" but not how to do it. As a result of continuing study, Headquarters Army Air Forces was greatly consolidated on 29 March 1943. Most staff functions were concentrated in six assistant chiefs of air staff: personnel; intelligence; training; materiel, maintenance, and distribution (MM&D); operations, commitments, and requirements (OC&R); and plans. The old subdirectorates were abolished. The functions of the air defense, bombardment, and air support divisions were split between OC&R and training and individual training was transferred to training. Among the responsibilities assigned to OC&R were determining proper tactics and techniques of aerial warfare, maintaining observers in theaters of operations, and supervising the AAF School of Applied Tactics and the AAF Proving Ground Command. Within OC&R, the Requirements Division was made responsible for tactical development; the division was comprised of Air Defense, Bombardment, Air Support, and Tactical Service branches.[25]

Even though he stated that the Army Air Forces ought not to tell subordinate commands how to perform their jobs, General Arnold was sensitive to the charge that the air force had no compact body of doctrine to guide the thinking of its thousands of newly commissioned officers. Indeed, as Colonel Williamson had noted in his March 1943 staff study for the bombardment division, "the most important single adverse factor, the condition which is the greatest cause of general failure of the Air Forces to attain proper results, is the lack of an authoritative and concise statement of AAF doctrine and employment policies. A ready guide is not available, and each combat zone is improvising its own doctrine or interpreting older doctrines that have not been kept up to date." General Arnold, in early March, recognized that his "seasoned and experienced officers are spread far and wide" and that the AAF needed a "tool of instruction whereby every officer may acquaint himself with both an over-all and particularized view of Air Force structure and objectives." Consequently, Arnold charged Brig Gen Byron E. Gates, chief of AAF management control, to direct the preparation and publication of a volume that would "present . . . a comprehensive picture of the objectives of Air Forces in Theaters of Operations and of the organization available to attain those objectives." The completed volume was published on 1 June 1943 under the title *The Air Force in Theaters of Operations: Organization and Functions.* It included six booklets with a total of 27 chapters that completely described the organization and missions of the Air Force as they existed in the spring of 1943. "The volume," Arnold stated, "represents Air Force doctrine. It is not rigid doctrine. It is subject to change when change is indicated. It points out what can be done with the means at our disposal, but it must not prevent us from utilizing those means fully in other ways and for other purposes."[26]

In many ways *The Air Force in Theaters of Operations* was the most ambitious and comprehensive doctrinal publication ever issued by the Air Force, and it was conveniently organized as a series of looseleaf pamphlets that could, in theory, be revised and kept up to date. However, the publication appeared at the very moment when air organization and doctrine were changing profoundly and most of it was almost immediately out of date. Despite a statement in the introductory chapter, "Air Force Mission and Organization," that some air forces could be considered strategic and others tactical, the principal pamphlet of the book described an operational air force as comprising the traditional air defense, bombardment, air support, and air service commands. (This pamphlet was the product of the AAF Board and the four departments of the School of Applied Tactics in Orlando.) The chapter "The Air Support Command" was forward-looking in its implications. It noted, for example, that the new North American A-36 (P-51) aircraft would be a substantial advancement over dive-bombers since it could both deliver bombs and serve as either a fighter bomber or a fighter escort plane. Nonetheless, the chapter was completely conservative in its wording and conformed to the approved air-ground doctrine established in FM 31-35. Although one booklet that described the functions of squadrons in an air force was kept in print and another pamphlet that described the functions of air force groups was published, few AAF officers apparently ever knew that *The Air Force in Theaters of Operation* had been issued.[27]

While it was seeking a headquarters organization suitable to its mission and attempting to prepare a comprehensive doctrinal manual, the Army Air Forces began to take a searching look at the results of combat operations in North Africa—the first major American air-ground offensive of World War II. Organized into standard air defense, bombardment, air support, and air service commands, the Twelfth Air Force enjoyed very little flexibility in its operations in Northwest Africa. In February 1943 the XII Air Support Command failed to give good results when it was attached to the US II Corps for the support of its operations in Tunisia. While the Americans sought new ideas, Gen Bernard L. Montgomery, commander of the British Eighth Army, in January 1943, issued a small pamphlet entitled "Some Notes on High Command in War," which described his experience in war. As a result of his experience of cooperating with the British Western Desert Air Force, Montgomery emphasized that the greatest asset of air power was its flexibility. He maintained that this flexibility could be realized only when air power was controlled centrally by an air officer who maintained a close association with the ground commander. "Nothing could be more fatal to successful results," Montgomery wrote, "than to dissipate the air resources into small packets placed under command of army formation commanders, with each packet working on its own plan."[28] In February 1943 in North Africa, Maj Gen Carl Spaatz organized the Northwest Africa Allied Air Force and gave it command over a strategic, a coastal, and a tactical air force. In a letter to Arnold dated 7 March 1943, Spaatz emphasized that "the air battle must be won first. . . . Air units must be centralized and cannot be divided into small packets among several armies or corps. . . . When the battle situation requires it, all units, including medium and heavy bombardment must support ground operations."[29]

In the United States, General Marshall and other influential Army officers accepted General Montgomery's basic principles relative to the control of air power.[30] Air Force leaders liked Montgomery's basic thinking, but there was some feeling that the air striking force ought not to be divided into a strategic and a tactical air force. As assistant chief of air staff for plans, Brig Gen Orvil Anderson urged that offensive air power ought not to be divided, and he maintained that the same air weapon system which fought through the decisive phase of a war ought to be available for subsequent exploitating operations, including all-out support of land operations. Since General Arnold, on the other hand, wished to ensure a freedom of action for the strategic air force, he was willing to provide the tactical air force in order to free the strategic air force from a routine requirement to support ground forces.[31] Brig Gen Laurence Kuter, who returned from a tour of duty as deputy commander, Northwest African Tactical Air Force, and became assistant chief of air staff for plans on 15 May 1943, actively supported the concept of a tactical air force. "It is the pattern of the future," Kuter wrote, "the way in which air power in collaboration with armies in the field will beat the enemy and win the war."[32]

In response to an air force request, the War Department, on 9 June 1943, named Col Morton H. McKinnon (commandant of the Air Support Department of the School of Applied Tactics), Col Ralph F. Stearley (commander of the I Air Support Command), and Lt Col Orin H. Moore (armored force liaison officer at AAF Headquarters) as a board to revise official doctrine in the light of theater-proven operations. Working intimately with the General Staff G-3 Division, this board of officers produced, in three weeks' time, War Department Field Manual 100-20,

Command and Employment of Air Power, which was published on 21 July 1943. The new manual advocated centralized control of air power. "The inherent flexibility of air power," stated the manual,

> is its greatest asset. This flexibility makes it possible to employ the whole weight of the available air power against selected areas in turn; such concentrated use of the air striking force is a battle-winning factor of the first importance. Control of available air power must be centralized and command must be exercised through the Air Force commander if this inherent flexibility and ability to deliver a decisive blow are to be fully exploited. Therefore, the command of air and ground forces in a theater of operations will be vested in the superior commander charged with the actual conduct of operations in the theater, who will exercise command of air forces through the air force commander and command of ground forces through the ground force commander.

The manual also stated that land power and air power were coequal and that the gaining of air superiority was the first requirement for the success of any major land operation. It described the mission and composition of a strategic air force, a tactical air force, an air defense command, and an air service command.[33]

As soon as FM 100-20 was published, General Arnold directed that a copy of it should be distributed to every Air Corps officer. In a letter to each AAF commander, he emphasized that "the interrelated role of air power must be constantly impressed upon all airmen through the medium of command."[34] But the Army Ground Forces viewed the manual with dismay and described it as the "Army Air Forces' 'Declaration of Independence.'"[35] Within the Air Force, moreover, Gen Orvil Anderson continued to deplore the division of air power represented by the tactical air force. At least one other old-line Air Corps officer, Brig Gen Robert C. Candee, suggested that the Air Force had "swallowed the RAF solution of a local situation in Africa hook, line and sinker, without stopping to analyze it or report it in 'Americanese' instead of British speech." Candee agreed that air power should not have been divided into tactical and strategic forces.[36]

Wartime Work of the AAF Board

The reorganization of Headquarters Army Air Forces and the publication of Field Manual 100-20 caused substantial changes at the AAF Board, AAF School of Applied Tactics, and the AAF Proving Ground Command. The assistant chief of air staff for training took control over the Training Aids Division, which, in May 1943, was moved from Orlando to New York City, where it was closer to commercial publishing and motion picture resources.[37] On 17 April, Brig Gen Gordon P. Saville, who had been director of air defense, was assigned as director of tactical development at Orlando. With characteristic energy, Saville began reorganizing the AAF Board. His efforts led to the issuance of an AAF regulation on the subject on 2 July 1943. The assistant chief of air staff, OC&R, was named president of the board and the director of tactical development was made ex officio executive; the commandant of the School of Applied Tactics and the commander of the Proving Ground Command were named as members of the board; the board was expected to coordinate the activities of the school, the proving ground, and the director of tactical development; and the director of tactical development was made specifically responsible for preparing programs, reviewing standards, and recommending appropriate actions to the board. In its essentials, the new regulation made the AAF Board a review agency and held the directorate of tactical development responsible for much of the planning that had been formerly done in Washington by the directorate of military requirements. But in late July 1943, just as General Saville was beginning to secure personnel for the directorate of tactical development, he was ordered to North Africa to take command of the XII Fighter Command.[38]

The new strategic and tactical concept of the Army Air Forces made the four departments of the School of Applied Tactics obsolete. General Peabody, the school commandant, and Brig Gen Eugene L. Eubank, who reported to Orlando as director of tactical development in September 1943, faced this fact and began to reorganize the school and the AAF Board. Peabody's announced object was to achieve an organization that would accomplish deep thinking.[39] Earlier in the year, Dr Robert L. Stearns, the educational adviser at the School of Applied Tactics, had pointed out that the research (or tactical development) function ought to be separated from the academic function since both were full-time tasks.[40] The reorganization, which was authorized in revised AAF regulations dated 8 October 1943 and effected three weeks later, incorporated this principle. The AAF Tactical Center was established under the command of General Peabody as the superior headquarters over a consolidated School of Applied Tactics and a Demonstration Air Force, whose tactical units and field installations were organized into model strategic and tactical air forces and a model air defense wing.[41]

The reorganization of the AAF Board was the work of General Eubank, who had earlier served as AAF director of bombardment. Under a revised AAF regulation published on 8 October 1943, the AAF Board was declared to be an agency of Headquarters Army Air Forces and was empowered to develop tactics, techniques, and doctrines and to determine all military requirements for the Army Air Forces. The assistant chief of air staff, OC&R, the commander of the AAF Tactical Center, the commander of the AAF Proving Ground Command, and the executive director of the board (Eubank's new position following the discontinuation of the director of tactical development) were members of the AAF Board. Since the AAF Board was domiciled away from Washington, an AAF Board Control Office was established within the OC&R. With the elimination of the departmental structure of the School of Applied Tactics and the old subboards, General Eubank was authorized to secure sufficient qualified personnel to discharge the AAF Board's responsibilities.[42]

On 13 December 1943 Col William F. McKee, deputy assistant chief of air staff for OC&R, announced that the reorganized board would do much of the work of the OC&R Requirements Division. "If there is any question as to whether a project should be carried out here or at the Board," he stated, "the issue should be resolved in favor of sending it to the Board."[43] For his own part, General Eubank, who became president of the AAF Board on 26 April 1944, wanted it to grow in stature from what was in effect a projects board for OC&R into an agency that would serve as an advisory body to General Arnold on all general policies.[44] Enjoying high priorities for experienced officers rotated home from overseas, the board built up to a strength of 98 officers, 65 enlisted men, and 53 civilians in September 1944 and kept this approximate strength during the remainder of the war. Five liaison officers were assigned to the air forces in the major combat theaters; these men proved to be an important source of information for the *Air Operations Briefs*, which were published, beginning 30 November 1944, to disseminate combat lessons throughout the Air Force.

The revamped board made many successful contributions to the use of air power in the war. Over Europe in the autumn of 1943, bomber formations devised by the AAF Board helped cut down Eighth Air Force combat losses. Another study, "Development of Tactics and Techniques for the Destruction of the German Air Force," was a guiding doctrine in establishing American air superiority over Europe. General Spaatz stated that board reports and lectures by its liaison officer, Lt Col Robert C. Richardson III, were of great assistance in overcoming the menace of German jet fighters. The massed B-29 fire raids over Japan, which were begun in March 1945, were initiated in accordance with a plan visualized in an AAF Board project entitled "Incendiary Attack on Japanese Cities."[45]

Although it was active in testing aircraft and equipment and in developing and disseminating tactics and techniques for employing air power, the AAF Board made slower progress in revising and preparing new doctrinal publications. Only after completing a higher priority study entitled "Initial Post-War Air Force" did the AAF Board approve and forward to Washington, on 4 May 1944, a draft titled "The Tactical Air Force: Organization and Employment," which it considered to be an adequate revision of the obsolete FM 31-35. Upon completing another study, "Combat Fighter Formations," the board felt that it had adequately revised FM 1-15, *Tactics and Techniques of Air Fighting*, and it believed that it had accomplished all outstanding manual projects. This optimism was premature. The board's responsibilities were soon to be expanded.

While the board was working on the tactical air force study, Colonel Stearley had been assigned to the Office of the Assistant Chief of Air Staff for Training in Washington. In March 1944 he had assembled a committee that prepared a draft paper on air-ground cooperation. The Army Air Forces submitted this paper and the study on the tactical air force to the War Department G-3 for approval and publication as War Department training circulars. But G-3 refused to approve the tactical air force study until the air-ground cooperation paper was coordinated with the Army Ground Forces. Moreover, on 22 June Brig Gen Mervin E. Gross, chief of the requirements division of OC&R, called attention to the fact that "all field service regulations and field manuals dealing with air force subjects, with the exception of FM 100-20, are abominably obsolete and confusing." Gross proposed to make the AAF Board responsible for preparing all AAF publications on doctrine. He also proposed to augment its strength to permit it to handle the complete task of reviewing, writing, and compiling manuals that would be approved and published by the Army Air Forces. However, General Gates, the director of management control, offered a counterproposal that the AAF Board be responsible for the substance of operational manuals, Management Control for administrative manuals, and Materiel and Services for supply and maintenance manuals, with the Training Aids Division preparing all manuscripts for final publication. General Gates's recommendations were accepted in June at a meeting of representatives from the interested agencies, and the AAF Board was accordingly directed to ensure the continuing of a project to prepare, review, and revise all field service regulations, field manuals, and publications which established AAF operational and training doctrine.[46]

To meet the added responsibilities for preparing the doctrinal publications and the new *Air Operations Briefs*, General Eubank organized an Evaluation Division within the AAF Board. The Policy Branch of this division received the task of reviewing and determining requirements for doctrinal manuals. Having determined the need for a manual, the Policy Branch was expected to establish committees made up of qualified personnel from the AAF Board, the School of Applied Tactics, the Proving Ground Command, and any other interested command to prepare a draft of the manual. Even though the Policy Branch outlined a comprehensive series of air manuals that should be written, it was not notably successful in producing manuals. The Policy Branch had difficulty committing qualified personnel to its project committees and preparing a draft manual required the examining of a mass of pertinent reports and the soliciting and evaluating of suggestions from many different headquarters. The Policy Branch also ran into problems in trying to coordinate its work with the Army Ground Forces. Headquarters Army Ground Forces, for example, refused to approve the draft training circular entitled "Air-Ground Cooperation," which was forwarded to it in April 1944; it complained that the draft was theoretical and contained far too much of the thinking incorporated in FM 100-20. As the debate continued, Headquarters Army Ground Forces broadened the discussion to include attacks on FM 100-20. In January 1945, for example, this headquarters challenged both the statement that gaining air superiority should be the first requirement for the success of any major land operation and the proposition that in the absence of air supremacy the initiative passed to the enemy by citing the success of the German army in launching its Ardennes offensive without possessing air superiority. As a result of the debate, the several theaters of operations were compelled to adopt their own techniques for air-ground cooperation. More than a year had passed before the War Department G-3 succeeded in patching together compromises that enabled it to issue definitions of doctrine required in preparation for the invasion of Japan. On 20 April 1945 the War Department published Training Circular 17, *Air-Ground Liaison*, and on 19 June 1945 it released Training Circular 30, *Tactical Air Command: Organization and Employment*. In yet another project, the AAF Board required a long period to coordinate the effort with interested parties. On

11 February 1944, the board began a manual entitled "Tactical Doctrine of Troop Carrier Aviation" but did not complete the text in final form until 21 August 1945.[47]

Official Evaluations of Air Operations

Under the leadership of General Eubank, the Army Air Forces Board became a respected and valuable agency for making evaluations and devising solutions to far-reaching problems encountered in the theaters of operations. But the board never attained the authority to recommend air policy to General Arnold to the same degree that the Navy General Board could influence the chief of naval operations. As World War II progressed, moreover, other agencies began to undertake a large part of the work that might have fallen within the province of a more powerful AAF Board.

A new level of bureaucracy slowly emerged in the United States to perform the functions of operations analysis, a development which paralleled the British experience. Having recognized the close relationship between scientific development and warfare during the 1930s, the Royal Air Force (RAF) had gotten good results from using civilians who possessed unusual scientific or analytic talents for operations analysis—a function which was described as the study of operations within a command for the purpose of improving tactics, equipment, methods of training, or methods of supply. In 1940 President Roosevelt named Dr Vannevar Bush, who was then chairman of the National Advisory Committee on Aeronautics, to chair the National Defense Research Committee. Its purpose was "to coordinate, supervise, and conduct scientific research on the problems underlying the development, production, and use of mechanisms and devices of warfare, except scientific research on the problem of flight." In May 1941 Roosevelt expanded the committee into the Office of Scientific Research and Development. As early as April 1942 a group of about 20 civilian analysts began to work with the Navy and the Army Air Forces in search of solutions to the problem of antisubmarine warfare. Dr Edward L. Bowles, the head of the group, ultimately devised the system of radar and related techniques that effectively checked the Nazi submarine menace during the latter half of 1943. At the request of General Spaatz, eight civilian operations analysts joined the Eighth Air Force in the United Kingdom on 15 October 1942. A few days later, on 24 October, General Arnold authorized the establishment of operations analysis sections throughout the Army Air Forces.[48]

The genesis for this committee came, when in the course of a conversation on the afternoon of 3 December 1942 with General Gates, chief of AAF management control, General Fairchild recalled some of the perplexities that had confronted him as a member of the Joint Strategic Survey Committee of the Joint Chiefs of Staff. The Joint Intelligence Committee had made many criticisms of the air target list included in AWPD-42; some of the criticisms appeared fully justified. When Gates's executive, Col Guido R. Perara, joined in the conversation, Fairchild suggested that he (Perara) might like to find the answer to the fundamental matter in question: "How can Germany be so damaged by air attack that an invasion of the continent may be possible within a relatively short period, say one year?" After thinking about the matter overnight, General Gates addressed a memorandum to Fairchild pointing out that nowhere in the War Department was there a group of analysts or research workers who were capable of assembling raw data and drawing conclusions from it. In search of a solution to the problem, Colonel Perara and Maj W. Barton Leach, who had been recruiting operations analysts for air force commands, proposed that a high-level committee of operations analysts should be formed to study Germany and to recommend target systems to General Arnold. The idea won Arnold's prompt approval and General Gates assembled a small group of distinguished scholars and industrialists in a first meeting of the Committee of Operations Analysts on 10 December 1942. In early spring 1943 the committee made its first report on German target systems to Arnold. After completing this effort, the committee addressed itself to determining the strategic vulnerabilities of Japan to air assault.[49]

The operations analysis function continued to slip further out of the domain of the AAF Board. Leach, who was promoted to colonel and served both as a member of the committee and as chief of the AAF Operations Analysis Division, provided general guidance to the buildup of some 17 operations analysis sections throughout the Air Force. By the end of the war more than 400 civilian and military analysts were serving in the Air Force. These operations analysts, most of whom were civilian specialists, followed "a considered policy of keeping very quiet — not asking for recognition, not claiming credit for accomplishments, not getting publicity." The operations analysis sections lent their peculiar skills to such command problems as bomb and fuze selection, bombing accuracy, battle damage and loss, and general mission analysis. The memorandum reports of each operations analysis section were forwarded to Washington and were circulated to interested commands. At the IX Bomber Command in Europe, for example, three operations analysts prepared a basic aerial gunnery manual, called "Get That Fighter," that was eventually adopted for use in the Army Air Forces, the Navy, and the Chinese air force. The operations analysts dealt with many of the same problems that the AAF Board was charged to consider, but the principal difference was that the operations analysis sections were prepared to solve problems on the spot in combat theaters. On some occasions the findings of the operations analysis section disagreed with those of the AAF Board. On 18 October 1944, for example, the AAF Board issued what it considered to be a definitive doctrine on weapons selection entitled "Selection of Bombs and Fuzes for Destruction of Bombardment Targets." But air force commanders preferred to follow the recommendations of their own operations analysis sections, which were in serious conflict with the board recommendations.[50]

In its initial report on the strategic vulnerability of Germany to air attack, the Committee of Operations Analysts recommended, on 8 March 1943, making a continuing analysis of the successes and failures of air operations. The Army Air Forces did not act on this recommendation until the spring of 1944, when it took two steps toward solving the problem of evaluating air operations. The first came on 29 June 1944 when, in response to a request for such authority, the War Department directed General Arnold to establish AAF evaluation boards in the several combat theaters and charge them to make "a critical evaluation of the effectiveness of air attack." "It is essential," the War Department stated, "that we determine now the merits of our past use of air power so that we may, with economy, direct and employ air power to the attainment of maximum results during the war and in the future." Each of the boards would be expected to forward evaluations with supporting data to the Army Air Forces at 30-day intervals, and the reports were to be screened by the OC&R and plans directorate and sent to the AAF Board for thorough analysis. Within a few weeks the evaluation boards departed for the combat theaters, each headed by an experienced air officer — Maj Gen Jacob E. Fickel for the European theater of operations, Maj Gen John F. Curry for the Mediterranean theater of operations, Maj Gen William E. Lynd for the Southwest Pacific area, Brig Gen Shepler W. Fitzgerald for the China-Burma-India theater, and Brig Gen Martin F. Scanlon for the Pacific Ocean areas. The boards were given a list of suggested topics for investigation, but they had complete freedom in selecting the exact subjects they investigated—the only criteria being that the subject was to be of sufficient importance "to permit intelligent redirection of policy and effort in attaining maximum economy of forces in the employment of air."[51] In the theaters, the AAF evaluation boards generally undertook to prepare evaluations of air actions by campaigns rather than by months. As a result their often voluminous reports would provide an important source of documentation about air operations in World War II but were not as valuable as they might have been for a current evaluation of the war effort. At the end of hostilities, the European theater and Southwest Pacific AAF evaluation boards had not completed all of their reports, so after September 1945 some personnel from these two boards were returned to Orlando to finish their tasks.

The second step toward solving evaluation problems emerged from discussions in the Air Staff in March 1944. General Fairchild suggested that a separate analysis should be made of strategic bombing, and he recommended that General Spaatz have US Strategic Air Forces in Europe submit a plan for a comprehensive evaluation. In a letter to Arnold on 5 April, Spaatz endorsed the proposal for a survey of the American strategic bombing effort and suggested that the survey be headed by a civilian of higher caliber and reputation. Although the British wanted to make a joint bombing survey, Spaatz argued against this approach because he wanted to get plain facts from a committee headed by an impartial chairman; he feared that the Soviets might be offended at being excluded from a combined undertaking; and he wanted a quick survey that would be concluded in time to be of use in planning for the strategic air campaign against Japan. The arrival of General Fickel's evaluation board threatened some duplication of effort, but Fickel agreed to confine his studies to the tactical air warfare effort.[52]

When the necessary groundwork had been laid, President Roosevelt directed Secretary Stimson on 9 September 1944 to form a qualified and impartial group to study the effect of strategic aerial attacks against Germany. On 3 November, Stimson asked Franklin D'Olier, president of the Prudential Insurance Company, to serve as chairman of the United States Strategic Bombing Survey. Various civilian experts were selected as directors of proposed divisions. The research activities of the survey were divided into three large units: military, economic, and civilian studies—each broken down into divisions. At the end of hostilities in Europe, Maj Gen Orvil Anderson came to the survey as chief of the Military Analysis Division and chairman of a panel of military advisers that included Gen Omar N. Bradley and Vice Adm Robert L. Ghormley. As finally constituted, the United States Strategic Bombing Survey in Europe consisted of some 300 civilian experts, analysts, technicians, and production men assisted by 350 officers and 574 enlisted men. Beginning in November 1944, teams of investigators followed Allied military forces into Germany and compiled enough basic information to fill up 208 published reports. The investigators gathered their data from inspections and examinations of target areas, captured records of the German government and industrial corporations, and interviews and interrogations of thousands of Germans, including practically all of the surviving German political and military leaders.[53]

As the United States Strategic Bombing Survey was completing its field work in the European theater, President Harry S Truman asked D'Olier to head a group that would conduct a joint Army-Navy analysis of the air war against Japan. Truman directed that the Japanese survey would be given help by the secretary of the Navy, thus making it a joint function, although still to be controlled by the civilian chairman and his associates. Paul Nitze, who had directed the equipment and utilities division of the survey, became acting vice-chairman under D'Olier. Many of the same civilian directors agreed to serve in the Pacific; the military advisers included General Anderson, Rear Adm Ralph A. Ofstie, Maj Gen Leslie R. Groves, and Brig Gen Grandison Gardner. Some 485 individuals were on the roster of the Pacific survey. By 3 October 1945 the survey and its detachments were located in Tokyo and in other places throughout Japan.[54]

In analyzing the Pacific war, the United States Strategic Bombing Survey depended heavily upon interrogations of more than 700 Japanese government, military, and civilian leaders. And, while many records had been destroyed, the survey was able to secure reasonably accurate statistics on Japan's economy and war production. After a hard-hitting, fast-moving field investigation, D'Olier and Nitze returned to Washington on 5 December. The key survey personnel assembled there early in January 1946 to complete the 108 volumes of evaluation on the Pacific war that would be published. In view of the great public interest in atomic warfare, Truman decided to receive and to release the Pacific survey's principal reports personally and directed that the three principal reports be coordinated with the State Department. During July 1946 Truman released the Pacific survey's three main reports: *Summary Report (Pacific War), Japan's Struggle to End the War*, and *The Effects of Atomic Bombs on Hiroshima and Nagasaki*.[55]

Wartime Air Doctrine Development Phases Down

During the rapid growth of the Army Air Forces, both the number of Headquarters Army Air Forces functions and the number of Army Air Forces field commands had tended to multiply. When the Army Air Forces reached its maximum strength, General Arnold thought that many of the details of operations that had burdened the Air Staff should be handled at appropriate field commands. This decentralization and consolidation began on 31 August 1944 with the combination of the Air Materiel Command and the Air Service Command into the Air Technical Service Command, which would administer operating programs in the fields of materiel and supply. On 1 April 1945 the Continental Air Forces was organized to assume jurisdiction over the four domestic air forces and the I Troop Carrier Command. In another move to clear up lines of authority, the AAF Center was established on 1 June 1945 to exercise command over the AAF School (the former AAF School of Applied Tactics) and the AAF Proving Ground Command. The Army Air Forces Board—whose members would be the board president, the commander of the AAF Center, and the commanding general of the AAF Proving Ground Command—was authorized to report directly to General Arnold rather than to the assistant chief of air staff for OC&R. The board would continue to be responsible for the development of tactics, techniques, doctrines, and other military requirements of the Army Air Forces.[56]

For a few months it appeared that the AAF Board might achieve a status similar to that of the Navy General Board, but the end of World War II brought a sudden decrease in the AAF Board's work. It ceased publication of the *Air Operations Briefs* and the board's activities fell from a wartime high of 514 active projects, reached on 15 March 1945, to only 230 projects in work, as of 15 September 1945, most of which were operational suitability tests on new items of equipment that were in the production pipelines at the war's end.[57] In the hope that it would be possible to record operational experience while it was still fresh, the Army Air Forces on 7 September 1945 directed the AAF Board to prepare a field service regulation that would incorporate all of the proven air-ground doctrine of World War II. On 8 October the Army Air Forces further directed the board to revise FMs 100-5 and 100-20 and then to bring all air force field manuals in the 1- series into conformity with these two basic manuals. The board completed a draft of a combined air-ground operations manual on 14 March 1946. Representing the best thought to come out of World War II, the manual was coordinated through the War Department G-3 and the Army Ground Forces and was published as War Department Field Manual 31-35, *Air-Ground Operations*, on 13 August 1946.[58] Since General Eubank was unable to obtain experienced personnel, the revision of other manuals had to await the readjustment that followed the establishment of the postwar air force.

Thus, World War II was doubtlessly the best reported and most thoroughly documented conflict of all time. Because of this sheer volume of documentation, however, few persons—military or civilian—would have the time or the incentive to master it. One natural result, according to the civilian scholar Bernard Brodie, was "the divorcement of doctrine from any military experience other than that which has been intensely personal with its proponents."[59] Under such circumstances, the operational experience of World War II could be cited to prove almost any preconception. In 1946, for example, reports by ranking Army officers such as Gen Omar N. Bradley, Gen George S. Patton, and Lt Gen Lucian K. Truscott were offered as a justification of a continuing requirement for horse cavalry in the postwar Army.[60] "If you will only let experience be your teacher," warned Maj Gen Orvil Anderson, "you can have any damn lesson you want." Anderson believed that the lessons of the past had to be interpreted in terms of the potentialities of the future. "Progress in the development of military science and strategy," he said, "is vitally dependent upon the soundness of the evaluations of past battle experience and upon the boldness, inspiration and depth of the projected thinking which creates the solution for the future."[61]

Examination of the Strategic Air War

"Because the last war saw the weapons of all services employed in profusion," wrote General Spaatz, who had commanded the US Strategic Air Forces (USSTAF) in Europe and the US Army Strategic Air Forces in the Pacific, "one may argue the exact degree of contribution made by strategic bombing to the final decision." According to Spaatz, "the war against Germany was fundamentally an infantry war supported by air power, much as the war against Japan was fundamentally a naval war supported by air."[62] Writing in 1948 an Air University instructor noted that the "Douhet Theory did not receive a thorough test in World War II." The same officer also noted that the "Douhet Theory was somewhat less than an unqualified success in World War II due to the inability of the equipment of the times to fulfill Douhet's expectations."[63] Bernard Brodie, on the other hand, considered World War II to have been a fair test of Douhet's ideas. "If we disregard the over-all vision and consider only specific assertions," Brodie wrote, "it is clear that in World War II Douhet was proved wrong on almost every important point he made. . . . But it is also true that he was able to create a framework of strategic thought which is considered by many responsible airmen to fit the atomic age astonishingly well."[64]

"No useful purpose would be served now," Spaatz wrote in 1948, "by refighting these wars [against Germany and Japan] as the airman might have wished to fight them."[65] Nevertheless, other air force officers, in their effort to establish a conceptual basis for forward thinking, sought to draw what lessons they could from World War II. To Lt Gen George C. Kenney, who had commanded the Allied Air Forces, Southwest Pacific Area, and the US Far East Air Forces, one of the major lessons of the war against Japan was the value of air power for keeping the peace. In November 1945 he said: "I believe that air power is this Nation's first line of defense and that only in air power can we find a weapon formidable enough to maintain the peace." In a lecture several years later, Kenney developed the same theme:

> If the value of air power in the defense had been recognized a few years earlier our national policy would not have accepted the inevitability of losing the Philippines at the outbreak of a war with Japan. Fairly strong bomber and fighter forces in the Philippines and in Hawaii, with the warning services available at that time, could have prevented the disasters at Pearl Harbor, Bataan and Corregidor. It is extremely doubtful that Japan would even have challenged us at all.[66]

In a Senate hearing in October 1945, General Arnold emphasized that responsibility for the defense of the United States rested upon the air force. "The defense," he said, "has got to be an offensive mission against the source [of enemy power].... But, better still, the actual existence of these weapons of our own in sufficient quantities and so located that a potential aggressor knows we can use them effectively against him, will have a very deterring effect, particularly if the aggressor does not know the whole story and only knows part of the story."[67] General Marshall agreed that "the future peace of the world will largely depend not only on the international policies of the United States but even more on our practical ability to endow those policies with the strength to command international respect." He insisted, however, that "national security is measured by the sum, or rather the combination of the three great arms, the land, air, and naval forces."[68]

The Anglo-American military strategy for the defeat of the Axis that emerged in 1941-42 contemplated early initiation of sustained air offensives against Germany and later against Japan but did not accord overriding production priorities to the air forces for undertaking these offensives. Instead, the strategic planners posed requirements for the development of land, sea, and air forces to accomplish a series of surface campaigns designed eventually to culminate in invasions of the German and Japanese homelands. According to Brig Gen George A. Lincoln, chief of the War Department General Staff Plans and Policy Group, the Anglo-American political objectives required for the guidance of military planning were available in the form of the Atlantic Charter—the master US lend-lease agreement, which pledged recipients to encourage freer postwar trade—and in the United Nations declaration of 1 January 1942, which pledged that the Allies would work for a postwar world political organization. But General Lincoln noted that these political objectives were stated in such broad language that they give little precise guidance to military strategy.[69] Lt Gen Albert C. Wedemeyer recalled that as a military planner he was "vague about the national aims of our own country."[70] One result of the broad political guidance was General Hansell's recollection that American military planners eventually tended to ignore the fact that the war should be fought "from the standpoint of continuing international relations to which the war was an unhappy interlude." As Hansell recalled, "My military bosses and my associates and I were consumed with one overpowering purpose: How to win the war with assurance and fewest American casualties. We had little concern for what happened afterward."[71]

In the early months of 1942 the Allies were on the defensive, but at Casablanca in January 1943 the Anglo-American heads of state and combined military staffs undertook to define their war aims and to visualize offensive operations against Germany. On 7 January, prior to leaving Washington for the conference, President Roosevelt met with the Joint Chiefs and told them that he intended to secure an agreement that the Allies would not end the war until they had attained the unconditional surrender of the Axis nations. No military staff work had been done on unconditional surrender and Roosevelt did not invite military discussion of the matter. To Roosevelt the statement of unconditional surrender as the Allies' war aim simplified the political complexities of the alliance's diplomacy. "We have the British, de Gaulle, the Russians, and several other elements," he would explain in private, "all of whose war aims are totally divergent. If we, the United States, now state our war aims we will split asunder the allied war effort which will result in squabbling over the particular interests."[72]

The unconditional surrender formula was useful in rallying popular support and effecting cohesion in the Grand Alliance. Moreover, it could be attained by military operations. American military planners, nevertheless, viewed it as an unfortunate war aim that would make the people of Germany and Japan resist to the bitter end. At Casablanca as assistants to Generals Marshall and Arnold, Wedemeyer (then a brigadier general) and Col Jacob E. Smart insisted that the Allies should direct their war aims against the Axis governments and not their people. These objections not withstanding, the Allies announced the objective of unconditional surrender on 23 January 1943. Viewed after the fact, the objective of unconditional surrender not only prolonged the resistance of Germany and Japan, but, in the case of Germany, resulted in a complete military and political disintegration that opened central Europe to the entry of Soviet Russia; Japan, meanwhile, would refuse to surrender until the unconditional surrender formula had been relaxed.[73] "During World War II," General Lincoln observed in 1947, "we had driven home to us the accepted principle that military power and military policy are related to political policy, and that these two policies must be closely integrated. We realize very clearly what this inextricable relationship between political and military policies means, that our military policies and actions are based on international political policies and that these two policies must be closely integrated."[74]

Thoughts on Air Organization for War

"Had the revolutionary potentialities of the strategic air offensive been fully grasped," General Spaatz concluded, "some of the fateful political concessions made to hold the Russians in the European war and to draw them into the Japanese war might never have been made."[75] Because the Allied strategy was directed toward unconditional surrender, the Casablanca conferees logically laid out a strategic air campaign against Germany in terms of the eventual physical capture of that nation by surface forces. On 21 January 1943 the Casablanca combined bomber directive stated that the ultimate objective of the air campaign was to be "the progressive destruction and dislocation of the German military, industrial and economic system, and the undermining of the morale of the German people to a point where their capacity for armed resistance is fatally weakened." Addressed to "the appropriate British and United States Air Force commanders," the Casablanca directive established no definite command authority for the combined bomber offensive; the directive implied that the Army Air Forces would conduct daylight attacks and that the RAF Bomber Command would continue its night attacks against area targets. The function of the strategic bomber offensive would be to soften the enemy nation preparatory to surface invasion. "The air weapon system," General Kuter would later comment, "was assigned a supporting role to facilitate the implementation of this conventional surface strategy."[76]

Where General Arnold advocated establishing an overall air command for Europe and Africa in December 1942, the Casablanca conference charged Sir Charles Portal, chief of air staff, RAF, with the strategical direction of British and American bomber operations from the United Kingdom. This responsibility did not include decisions on matters of tactics or techniques. Instead, those two areas remained the provinces of Lt Gen Ira C. Eaker, commander of the US Eighth Air Force, and Sir Arthur Harris, commander of the RAF Bomber Command. And the command of Allied air power in the African and European theaters remained divided throughout the war. In view of the impending Overlord ground invasion of Europe, the Allied Expeditionary Air Force was established on 17 November 1943 under the command of Air Marshal Sir Trafford Leigh-Mallory. It was given operational control over the RAF Tactical Air Force, the Air Defence of Great Britain, and the US Ninth Air Force. But at this same time, the US Joint Chiefs of Staff proposed to establish a strategic air commander in the United Kingdom to control the operations of the Eighth and Fifteenth Air Forces, the latter being based in Italy. The British chiefs of staff did not favor the plan; nevertheless, it was effected on 1 January 1944 when General Spaatz assumed command of the US Strategic Air Forces (USSTAF) in Europe. Since the RAF Bomber Command remained outside this framework, Sir Charles Portal continued to be the coordinating agent of the Combined Chiefs of Staff for strategic bombing until 14 April 1944 when USSTAF passed to the control of Gen Dwight D. Eisenhower as commander, Allied Expeditionary Forces. Following completion of Overlord, the combined chiefs reassumed control of the strategic bomber forces on 14 September 1944.[77]

Maj Gen Orvil Anderson, who served as chairman, Combined Operational Planning Committee, England, from June 1943 to January 1944 and as assistant chief of staff for operations of the VIII Bomber Command from January to June 1944, was critical of the division of fighting air and exploitation air represented in the command arrangements for air power. Anderson thought that all air power should have been concentrated for coordinated attacks against Germany until the strategic air campaign had been successfully completed; after that point, he continued, all air power could have been used to support exploitative surface operations. The Eighth Air Force had 15 fighter groups and the Ninth Air Force 18 fighter groups by the time of the Overlord invasion. When the Ninth Air Force established itself in Great Britain on 16 October 1943, it took control of those fighter groups designated for it which had arrived in Great Britain. This was said to be necessary in order that the groups might receive fighter-bomber training, but the Eighth Air Force was actively in combat and retained the right to request fighter support from the Ninth Air Force. Anderson recollected that this decentralized command structure often made it difficult to coordinate requirements for fighter support. When he was asked about Anderson's statements on command arrangements, General Spaatz held a different viewpoint: "There was no difficulty in using Ninth Air Force fighters when we needed them," he said. "If we had a mission we could always get them."[78]

While the combined bomber offensive against Germany was designed to prepare the way for a surface invasion of the Continent, the buildup of Anglo-American bomber forces was relatively slow; in the end the major weight of the strategic bombing attack followed rather than preceded the invasion of Europe. Weak at the war's beginning, the RAF Bomber Command did not begin strategic bombing attacks against Germany until May 1940. After a slow buildup the US Eighth Air Force conducted its first daylight bombing mission from bases in the United Kingdom on 17 August 1942, but much of the strength of this small air force was soon drained away to support the Allied land campaign in North Africa. In January 1943 the Army Air Forces had only 12 heavy bombardment groups deployed in theaters against Germany. The maximum strength of 62 heavy bomber groups was not attained against Germany until May 1944, less than a month before the invasion of Normandy on 6 June 1944. The total of the first-line B-17s and B-24s deployed against Germany increased from 413 in January 1943 to a maximum of 5,072 in March 1945.[79] The RAF Bomber Command's strength increased from a miscellany of 515 light, medium, and heavy bombers in January 1943 to a total of 1,069 Halifax, Lancaster, and Mosquito bombers in April 1945.[80] Of the total 2,770,540 tons of bombs dropped by AAF and RAF aircraft against Germany, only 17 percent fell prior to 1 January 1944 and only 28 percent prior to 1 July 1944.[81] By mid-1944 the limited strategic air campaign had fatally weakened Germany's capacity to counter the Allied ground invasion, but the maximum military benefits did not accrue to the invading forces because the greatest weight of the strategic air attack had not yet been felt by the German people or the German military forces.[82]

Battling for Air Superiority

One of the basic premises of Army Air Forces doctrine was that its heavy bomber aircraft, flown in massed and self-defending formations, could successfully penetrate enemy defenses and perform precision-bombing attacks in daylight hours. In confidential talks with General Arnold in December 1941, moreover, Air

Marshal Portal had asserted that British bases were going to be saturated with aircraft. Hence the Army Air Forces ought to concentrate on moving bombers to Britain and delay the deployment of fighters there until they were needed to support a ground invasion of Europe.[83] Arnold and Portal decided to limit the deployment of US fighters to the United Kingdom to the few groups required for local air defense. AAF programs, nevertheless, gave a reasonable priority to activating and training the fighter groups that would be needed to provide a canopy for the invasion of Europe even though early Eighth Air Force bomber attacks, albeit relatively shallow, seemed to indicate that the bombers could defend themselves.[84]

The Casablanca directive nominated the German aircraft industry for destruction and directed the Eighth Air Force "to impose heavy losses on the German day fighter force and to contain German fighter strength away from the Russian and Mediterranean theaters of war," but it made no requirement for establishing air superiority over Germany.[85] During the first half of 1943, General Eaker used Eighth Air Force P-47s and RAF fighters to help the heavy bombers penetrate the German fighter belt inward from the channel coast. Nevertheless, he remained convinced that his main requirement was for larger bomber forces that would permit the planes to fly more effective defensive formations and additional deception missions. But opposition began to build against Eaker's position. As early as 23 March 1943, Eaker's own plans section argued that "our primary objective should be the German Fighter Force in the air, on the ground, and the industry which supports it. . . . A sufficient depletion of the German Fighter Force is the one essential preliminary to our imposing our will by the use of air power on any portion of the German war effort which may be subsequently selected, be it submarines, oil, transportation or morale." Back in the United States, following the old Air Corps Board's idea for the development of a "bomber-destroyer" aircraft, the AAF Board tested several YB-40s — heavily armed B-17s designed to provide tremendously augmented firepower to a bomber formation. A similar modification of the B-24, called the YB-41, also was tested at Eglin Field. These experiments indicated methods of increasing the armament on basic B-17s and B-24s. However, when the YB-40s were employed in combat in May 1943, they were too heavy to stay in formation with B-17s and the whole concept proved impracticable.[86]

Alarmed by the increasing success of Luftwaffe fighters (which were not armed with cannon and could outrange the bombers' defensive fire), the Combined Chiefs of Staff, in June 1943, directed that the "first priority in the operation of British and American bombers based in the United Kingdom shall be accorded to the attack of German fighter forces and the industry upon which they depend." On 28 June, Arnold gave the Army Air Forces six months to provide some escort aircraft that could accompany bombers to targets deep within Germany, but the heavy losses suffered by Eighth Air Force bombers on the long-range missions to Schweinfurt and Regensburg on 17 August and on the repeat attack on Schweinfurt on 14 October gave warning that escort planes would be required well before 1 January 1944. In Washington, Kuter pointed out to Arnold that the invasions of

Europe—Overlord on the Normandy coast and Anvil in southern France (tentatively set for May or June 1944)—might not be possible unless immediate efforts were made to establish air superiority.[87]

In the United Kingdom, General Eaker was under pressure to abandon daylight bombing and convert to night attacks. However, he believed that a climax was approaching in the air war, and he asked Arnold to send him every available fighter, thus abandoning the idea of unescorted bombers. Eaker also asked the AAF Board to study his problem and recommend solutions. In December 1943 the AAF Board recommended that immediate efforts be made to provide pressurized, droppable fuel tanks to extend the range of P-51 Mustang and P-38 Lightning aircraft. The North American Aviation Company had developed the P-51 on its own initiative. The British had purchased some Mustangs, while the Army Air Forces had bought some for use as A-36 dive-bombers. But even though other agencies had liked the P-51 before this, not until the AAF Board focused its attention on the Mustang, was it developed and procured in quantity as a high-performance, long-range fighter that would accompany bombers to any target in Germany.[88] Meanwhile, on 1 January 1944, General Spaatz was given command of both the Eighth Air Force and the Fifteenth Air Force. And between October 1943 and February 1944 the number of heavy bombardment groups operating against Germany increased from 26 to 48. Thus, the strategic air forces gained in numbers at the same time that they got P-47 and P-51 fighters for escort and the command structure became more open to fighter protection.

"It is a conceded fact," General Arnold told the commanders of the Eighth and Fifteenth Air Forces on 27 December 1943, "that Overlord and Anvil will not be possible unless the German Air Force is destroyed. Therefore, my personal message to you—this is a MUST—is to, *'Destroy the Enemy Air Force wherever you find them, in the air, on the ground and in the factories.'*" On 13 February 1944, the Combined Chiefs of Staff issued a new directive for the combined bomber offensive that ordered: "The progressive destruction and dislocation of the German military, industrial and economic systems, the disruption of vital elements of lines of communication and the material reduction of German air combat strength, by the successful prosecution of the combined bomber offensive from all convenient bases."[89]

Because, on given days, the vagaries of weather closed some strategic targets while leaving others open, both the US Strategic Air Forces (USSTAF), Europe, and the RAF Bomber Command found it difficult to give overriding priority to sustained attacks against any one category of targets. However, taking advantage of a short period of good flying weather beginning on 20 February 1944, USSTAF directed six extremely heavy bombardment attacks at German fighter aircraft production plants, and the RAF Bomber Comand flew night attacks against area targets related to aircraft production. Benefiting from fighter support flown by the Eighth, Ninth, and Fifteenth Air Forces and the RAF Fighter Command, the USSTAF bombers incurred a lower percentage of losses in daytime operations than did the RAF Bomber Command. The Big Week broke the back of the

IDEAS, CONCEPTS, DOCTRINE

Luftwaffe fighter force and in effect established Allied air superiority over Germany.

As a result of the experience, the usual interpretation was going to be that bombers required fighter escort to operate safely and effectively. Brig Gen Orvil Anderson, however, would point out that attaining Allied air superiority over Europe was in no small part attributable to mistakes made by Hermann Goering. For one thing, the German fighters never attempted significant morning attacks over Great Britain when the American bombers were taking off and laboriously forming up for missions and would have been most vulnerable. For another, the German fighters could have met the P-47s and P-51s near the channel coast and forced them to drop their wing tanks, thus making it impossible for the Americans to continue their missions. Instead, the German fighters preferred to meet the American formations deep within Germany, usually over the bomber target. In Anderson's opinion, Goering made his greatest mistake at the end of December 1943 when he ordered his fighter pilots to avoid Allied fighters and concentrate their attack on the bombers. This order ignored the basic fact of air fighting that when aircraft of roughly equal performance meet, the one that seeks to avoid combat is automatically at an almost certainly fatal disadvantage. After some argument, Anderson was able to persuade Maj Gen James H. Doolittle to issue orders on 4 January for the Eighth Air Force fighters to take the offensive—"to pursue the Hun until he was destroyed"—rather than to continue to provide position defense to friendly bombers. Goering's mistake and the Eighth Air Force's quick recognition of his error helped assure the attainment of Allied air superiority.[90]

A close reading of Air Force correspondence of the Schweinfurt-Regensburg time period reveals a confidence that although strategic bombers, employed in force, could perform their missions over Germany even without air superiority, most planners and commanders acknowledged that an early attainment of Allied control of the air was necessary if the surface invasions of Europe were to succeed. The United States Strategic Bombing Survey reached the opposite conclusion, however, stating that the establishment of Allied domination of the air over Europe had proven essential to the strategic bombing campaign. Without domination of the air, the bombing survey reported, "attacks on the basic economy of the enemy could not have been delivered in sufficient force and with sufficient freedom to bring effective and lasting results."[91] In describing the Schweinfurt-Regensburg losses, the official Air Force history of World War II likewise concluded: "The fact was that the Eighth Air Force had for the time being lost air superiority over Germany. And it was obvious that superiority could not be regained until sufficient long-range escort became available."[92] When questioned in October 1949 about the validity of this statement and about the history's general conclusion that the Eighth Air Force had sustained unacceptable losses late in 1943, Gen Hoyt S. Vandenberg pointed out that bombers had been able to get through to their targets in spite of strong enemy defenses. "No bombing mission set in motion by the Army Air Forces in World War II," Vandenberg pointed out, "was ever stopped short of its target by enemy opposition." He further explained that the question of acceptable or unacceptable losses to a bomber force depended upon "the destructive effect of bomber weapons and the value of the strategic target."[93]

Effect of Flak and Fighters

Army Air Force doctrine in the 1930s had displayed little concern for the effect that hostile antiaircraft artillery fire might have on strategic bomber missions. Ground fire had not been effective against aircraft in World War I or in the Spanish Civil War. When American heavy bombers began to make daylight strikes against enemy targets in France in the autumn of 1942, however, it suddenly appeared that hostile flak might be more of an obstacle to the bomber mission than enemy fighters. When Col Curtis E. LeMay was en route to England with the 305th Bombardment Group in October, he and his key officers happened to be in Prestwick at the same time as Col Frank A. Armstrong, Jr., who was heading back to Washington. Armstrong had led the first daylight bomber mission to Sotteville-Rouen on 17 August, had flown two additional missions, and was as much of an expert as the fledgling airmen had ever seen. Armstrong told LeMay and his staff that a heavy bomber crew would not be able to survive over a gun-defended target if it maintained a straight course for more than 10 seconds. "This," LeMay recalled, "was pretty discouraging information." Even good peacetime bombardiers could hardly hit a target precisely with such a short run. LeMay knew that his crews would need to fly a straight-in bomb run in order to get enough aiming time, but the question was whether they could survive with such tactics. Using an old ROTC manual on the French 75-millimeter field artillery gun, LeMay worked out a fire problem on the number of rounds that a gun crew would require to hit a target the size of a B-17, sitting still on a hillside at a distance of 25,000 feet. He computed that the gun crew would have to fire 372 rounds. These looked like good odds, and LeMay convinced his group that it would go straight in and make its attack without evasive action. Over Saint-Nazaire on 23 November 1942, with LeMay leading, the 305th encountered intense flak that damaged 6 of the 16 B-17s on the mission (including LeMay's lead plane), but no planes were lost and the target was well covered with bombs. "We never did take any evasive action from then on," LeMay recalled, "and within three weeks no one else was taking evasive action either."[94]

Operating over France and Germany, American heavy bombers and other aircraft met exceedingly strong antiaircraft artillery defenses. From the start of the war Germany had given flak equipment an equal production priority with aircraft, and in December 1944 she gave it an even higher priority. By the end of 1944, German flak defenses included 16,000 heavy guns, 50,000 light and mobile guns, 7,500 searchlights, and 1,500 barrage balloons; more than 1,000,000 men manned these defenses. Important targets were defended all around by emplacements of heavy guns—the principal gun being the 88-millimeter piece that could fire 20 rounds per minute. The great Ruhr defenses were capable of hurling 200 tons of metal and explosives into the air every minute; the Cologne defenses, 80 tons; and the Berlin defenses, 70 tons. The German flak defenses, firing for one minute, could have put 5,000 tons of shells into the sky.[95] Within the Ninth Air Force, flak evaluation intelligence and counterflak tactics helped tactical aircraft maintain the element of surprise that they needed to survive fire from very mobile and always moving light antiaircraft guns.[96] The Eighth and Fifteenth Air Forces also used flak intelligence in the planning of their missions. However, in view of the circumjacent defenses at most strategic targets, about the best that could be said was that a mission approaching a hypothetical target from the north might be expected to draw 372 rounds, while one from the east would receive 374. In the last months of the war, some bombs would be directed at flak emplacements for flak suppression purposes. But, for the most part, strategic bomber mission planners usually ignored flak and picked target approaches for some other tactical reason such as a course that would have a good initial point or that would keep the sun at the backs of the bombardiers. The best tactic against heavy flak was to get as many bombers over a strategic target as quickly as possible to saturate the defense.[97]

In the early years of the war in the European theater, hostile flak and fighters worked together effectively; many of the bombers shot down by the Luftwaffe were first crippled by flak and forced to straggle. When the back of the German air force was broken early in 1944, antiaircraft artillery became the major combat risk for the Allied bomber units. In the European theater from August 1942 through May 1945, the Army Air Forces lost 4,274 aircraft in air-to-air combat (2,452 heavy bombers, 131 medium and light bombers, and 1,691 fighters) and 5,380 aircraft to hostile antiaircraft fire (2,439 heavy bombers, 492 medium and light bombers, and 2,449 fighters). Figured in terms of total American combat sorties flown in the European theater (274,921 by heavy bombers, 96,523 by light and medium bombers, and 527,314 by fighters), the loss rate was less than 2 percent even against the most effective antiaircraft defenses. Despite this evidence to the contrary, Army wargamers, testing modern methods of wargaming shortly after the war ended, played the B-17s and B-24s against the German fighter and 88-millimeter gun defenses of World War II and concluded that the heavy bombers could not live in such an environment. When told of these conclusions, General LeMay responded: "Experience, I think, is more important than some of the assumptions you make."[98]

Problems of Strategic Air Targets

The Anglo-American strategic air campaign against Germany marked the first significant effort to do something drastic to an enemy other than to defeat his combat forces. In this pioneer effort, planners sought to describe air target systems whose destruction would accomplish desired objectives. One of the major problems facing these planners was a lack of basic information about German industry when the war began. As strategic bombing commenced, German industries were dispersed, adding to the complexity of identifying targets.

Moreover, since Hitler did not order full-scale German mobilization for war until 1942, the German economy had a cushion of capability that could be employed to expand production in 1943-44.[99]

Thinking in terms of a survey of the vulnerability of US industry to strategic air attack that had been made at the Air Corps Tactical School in the early 1930s, the air officers who drew up AWPD-1 recommended strategic air attacks against Germany's electric power, transportation, oil, and petroleum capacities as well as against civilian morale. AWPD-42 specified the order of priority of air targets as being: aircraft and aircraft engine factories, submarine building yards, transportation facilities, electric power plants, oil refineries, aluminum manufacturing plants, and rubber plants. The major difference between the two target lists was that AWPD-1 assumed that an air offensive might eliminate the necessity for a subsequent ground invasion, whereas AWPD-42 looked toward the establishment of an air ascendancy necessary to subsequent surface operations. The strategic targets suggested in AWPD-1 much more closely approximated the findings of the United States Strategic Bombing Survey as to what the optimum target system for the destruction of Germany's industrial life would have been than did either AWPD-42 or the attack program that, under orders from higher authority, was actually implemented.

Under directives from the Combined Chiefs of Staff, the Eighth Air Force was required to direct much of its effort against other targets. But these attacks generally failed to weaken the German war effort. Because of heavy Allied ship losses in the battle of the Atlantic, the Casablanca directive of January 1943 required the strategic bombers to give first priority to attacks against German submarine bases and construction yards. Although tons of bombs were dropped on the heavily fortified submarine pens, those bombing raids did little to diminish the German submarine offensive. The ultimate solution for the German submarine menace, after May 1943, proved to be their detection and destruction at sea.[100]

Lacking sufficient force to destroy decisive target systems, General Eaker attempted to discover a "long-chance objective" whose destruction would produce results greatly out of proportion to the effort involved. In Washington on 8 March 1943, General Arnold's Committee of Operations Analysts recommended that the destruction of three ball-bearing plants at Schweinfurt would eliminate 43 percent of a most essential ingredient to the Axis war effort. The committee concluded that "on the basis of American experience, as well as in the opinion of responsible authorities in the United Kingdom, ball bearings represent a potential bottleneck in German industry, particularly in the manufacture of war material."[101] Although about 12,000 tons of bombs were dropped on the ball-bearing plants in a series of attacks over several months beginning on 17 August 1943, the United States Strategic Bombing Survey later found that "the attacks on the ball-bearing industry had [no] measurable effect on essential war production."[102]

By the organization of USSTAF in January 1944, General Spaatz had a growing capability to destroy selected strategic targets in Germany. In the months that followed the Big Week, however, USSTAF strategic bombing capabilities were diverted to attacks against German V-weapon sites and to missions in direct or general support of Allied ground troops in Europe. Even though Spaatz was permitted to begin attacks against Germany's oil resources on 12 May 1944, a massive, sustained air campaign against strategic air targets in Germany did not begin until after D-day, when Allied ground troops were safely ashore on the Normandy coast. The intensive strategic air campaign undertaken in September 1944 against Germany's transportation was described by the United States Strategic Bombing Survey as "the decisive blow that completely disorganized the German economy." Contrary to the intention of early AAF planners, the German electric power system was never a principal target. "Had electric generating plants and substations been made primary targets . . .," the United States Strategic Bombing Survey stated, "the evidence indicates that their destruction would have had serious effects on Germany's war production." In addition, by December 1944, German reserves of fuel had become insufficient for sustaining effective military operations. Under the full force of strategic bomber attack and with war requirements multiplying more swiftly than production could handle, the economic life of Germany virtually collapsed as 1944 drew to a close. "The German experience," stated the United States Strategic Bombing Survey, "suggests that even a first-class military power — rugged and resilient as Germany was — cannot live long under full-scale and free exploitation of air weapons over the heart of its territory."[103]

Early Strategic Bombing in the Pacific-Far East

In the Pacific, the pattern of Allied operations and commitment of forces was different from that employed in Europe, but the strategy relative to the employment of air power was essentially the same. Because of Japanese expansion in the first year of the war, Air Force planners recognized that even the very long range B-29s would be unable to reach the Japanese homeland until the enemy's perimeter had been reduced. "Our armed forces in the Far Eastern Theater," stated AWPD-42, "are not within effective striking distance of the vital sources of Japanese military policy. . . . Hence from the standpoint of air requirements, the Far Eastern operations may be divided into two phases: (1) Air operations in support of our land and sea forces to regain bases within striking distance of Japan. . . . (2) Air operations against Japan proper to destroy her war making capacity." During 1942, defensive battles at the Coral Sea and Midway contained Japan's efforts to extend her perimeter, and limited American offensives in the Solomon Islands and eastern New Guinea added security to Allied bases. The Allied leadership was presented with competing strategies to bring Japan within reach. In Washington early in 1943, the Joint Strategic Survey Committee favored a drive supported by carrier-based aircraft across the Central Pacific to the China coast, where air bases could be established to permit an extended air campaign against Japan. Meanwhile, in the Southwest Pacific area, Gen Douglas MacArthur urged an advance along the New Guinea-Philippines axis to the China coast. At the

Quadrant conference in Quebec in August 1943, the Combined Chiefs of Staff authorized limited operations along both lines of advance. Between the Quadrant and the Sextant conference, which was held in Cairo in November-December 1943, the Joint Staff planners in Washington debated two controversial ideas at length and with some heat.[104]

Easiest to resolve of the two controversies was the concept of operations set forth in a Joint War Plans Committee overall plan for the defeat of Japan. The initial draft of the plan included a statement to the effect that the campaigns in Europe had demonstrated clearly that air forces by themselves were incapable of decisive action; hence, an invasion and conquest of the Japanese home island would be necessary to conclude the war. When he returned from Europe to become chief of the Combined and Joint Staff Division of AAF Plans in November 1943, General Hansell tried to get this basic thought in the concept paper eliminated but managed only to get it modified materially. The plans division under Hansell was willing to admit that air power in Europe had not demonstrated thus far that it could of itself bring a powerful modern nation to defeat. However, the circumstances in the island nation of Japan were quite different from those in Europe, and no one had proved that such an achievement could not be attained in the Japanese case. Whether or not Japan could be brought to surrender by air attack, Japanese resistance would have to be drastically reduced through a sustained bombing effort if an invasion of the Japanese homeland was to be feasible. Thus, a first priority would have to be given to the development and employment of air forces to conduct a sustained offensive against the Japanese homeland.[105]

The second part of the planning controversy had to do with the prospective employment of the new B-29 Superfortress bombers that had been bought from blueprints and would be service-tested in combat beginning in 1944. With General MacArthur's support, Lt Gen George C. Kenney wanted to station the B-29s at Darwin, Australia, and employ them against strategic targets in the Netherlands East Indies. But General Arnold was determined that the B-29 force would be used against targets in or adjacent to the Japanese home islands. In March 1943 AAF/ACS Plans had begun to study a project for using B-29s against Japan from bases in south-central China. Arnold also had asked the Committee of Operations Analysts to analyze potential strategic targets in Japan. The Sextant conference approved this planning in December 1943, agreeing that the Matterhorn project would include the construction of bases near Calcutta, India, and at Chengtu, China, for the USAAF XX Bomber Command and two wings of B-29s. The Committee of Operations Analysts recommended that merchant shipping, steel production, urban industrial areas, aircraft plants, the antifriction bearing industry, and the electronics industry as preferred targets for the B-29s. The committee believed that these B-29 missions could immobilize Japan's steel production by destroying a few coke plants in Manchuria and Japan. It also pointed out that Japan's urban industrial areas were few, concentrated, and very vulnerable to incendiary attack.[106]

Because of logistical problems the XX Bomber Command would be able to operate only a few B-29 groups from bases in isolated south-central China. From Chengtu, moreover, the B-29s would not have enough range to reach Tokyo and other industrial targets on Honshu. Hence, AAF planners favored the Mariana Islands as potential bases for B-29s but had no real information as to the number of bases that could be built in these islands, which were held by the Japanese. Bases were accordingly constructed in the Aleutians at Adak and Shemya to accommodate four B-29 groups; an existing airfield on Ceylon was enlarged to permit B-29 staging for attacks against the oil fields in the Netherlands East Indies; and consideration was given to eventually establishing a B-29 command in the Philippines. At the Sextant conference in Cairo, however, Arnold urged that B-29 operations ought to be begun from China in May 1944 and from the Marianas before the end of that year. Once again the Combined Chiefs of Staff authorized continued advances through the Central and Southwest Pacific without definitely accepting either line of attack as being better than the other. During February 1944 the Pacific strategy was more fully debated in Washington by representatives of General MacArthur and Adm Chester W. Nimitz, commander in chief of the Pacific Fleet and Pacific Ocean areas. General Hansell, siding with Nimitz's representative, presented the AAF concept of the Pacific war, which stressed the importance of the Marianas to the bomber offensive against Japan proper to the Joint Chiefs of Staff on 15 February. After hearing all parties, the Joint Chiefs on 12 March 1944 ordered Admiral Nimitz's Pacific forces to invade the Marianas beginning on 15 June 1944. Since a new XXI Bomber Command would be based in the Marianas, the Joint Chiefs limited the size of the XX Bomber Command to a single wing of four B-29 groups.[107]

Only after the European hostilities had ended, would British air forces be available for use in the Pacific. Moreover, in the Pacific, the B-29s would be based in several different theaters of operations. Arnold later recalled that a visit to the Pacific in autumn 1942 had made him realize that he would have to retain command of the very long range B-29s: "There was nothing else I could do," he remarked, "with no unity of command in the Pacific."[108] If the B-29 forces had been assigned to the European theater of operations, they doubtless would have been under the general direction of the Combined Chiefs of Staff and would have been organized in a strategic air force similar to that used to control the heavy bomber strategic forces. The conduct of a strategic air war against Japan, however, posed different command problems.

In the first thinking about Matterhorn, the AAF staff favored establishing a strategic air force headquarters in Washington similar in concept to the old GHQ Air Force, which would be directly responsible through Arnold to the Joint Chiefs of Staff. When the Joint Chiefs accepted this concept, the US Twentieth Air Force was activated on 4 April 1944. Arnold assumed personal command as the executive agent of the Joint Chiefs, Hansell was designated chief of staff, and members of the Air Staff did double duty as the staff of the Twentieth Air Force. Commands of the theaters in which the Twentieth Air Force's XX and XXI Bomber

Commands were based were directed to coordinate B-29 operations with other air operations in their theaters, to construct and defend B-29 bases, and to provide logistical support and common administrative control of the B-29 forces. Should strategic or tactical emergencies arise requiring the use of the B-29 forces for purposes other than the missions assigned to them by the Joint Chiefs, the theater commanders were authorized to use the B-29 forces upon immediately informing the Joint Chiefs of such action. As will be seen, the B-29 command organization would be revised again in 1945. Several years later an Air Force officer described the wartime creation of the Twentieth Air Force as "one of the most important events in United States Air Force history. If that had not occurred," he thought, "we might still be parcelling out our big punch in penny packets to numerous theater and lower commands."[109]

In spite of this improved command structure, the early operations of the Twentieth Air Force's XX Bomber Command were similar to the early indecisive results of the Eighth Air Force in Europe. What made these results even more disappointing was the fact that the Japanese army and navy air forces had already been reduced to low effectiveness by earlier theater air battles. Like the fledgling Eighth Air Force, the XX Bomber Command was a piecemeal commitment of too little capability to perform effective strategic air attacks. Once again, the available force was employed against long-chance objectives. Called upon to operate the new B-29 planes on very long range missions against priority iron and steel targets in Japan and Manchuria, the XX Bomber Command faced the additional problem of providing logistical support across the Himalayas to the forward operating bases at Chengtu. In final analysis, only about 14 percent of the command's capability could be employed against the enemy, the remaining 86 percent being absorbed by the use of B-29s as tankers to haul fuel from India into China. At the start of its operations on 15 June 1944 the XX Bomber Command sent 47 B-29s to attack the Yawata iron and steel works on Kyushu. By January 1945, the command had dropped about 800 tons of bombs on targets in the Japanese home islands, but the raids were of insufficient weight and accuracy to produce significant results. Several daylight precision attacks were flown against coke ovens in Anshan, Manchuria, but these attacks were later determined to have had little strategic significance since Japanese iron and steel production already had been severely curtailed because of a loss of shipping needed to transport raw materials.[110]

In an effort to get results from the XX Bomber Command, Arnold put General LeMay in command on 29 August 1944. In the months that followed, LeMay substantially improved the operating record of the B-29s. But there was little that he could do to increase the effectiveness of attacks against Japanese targets that were too far distant from the Chengtu bases. In the autumn of 1944, the XX Bomber Command was used to attack targets on Formosa, in Burma, at Singapore, and in the Netherlands East Indies. In January 1945, LeMay was transferred to the Marianas; in the following months the XX Bomber Command also moved to Pacific bases. Looking backward at the XX Bomber Command's experience, Brig Gen John B. Montgomery, who had been the deputy chief of staff for operations of the XXI Bomber Command, concluded that the piecemeal employment of the B-29s had proved a psychological boost for China's sagging morale, but from a military standpoint he suggested that the B-29 effort flown from China and India might just as well have been saved until facilities were ready to permit the B-29s to be marshaled and employed as an effective striking force. "Had we done that," Montgomery thought, "we would have saved airplanes and crews . . . and I think the war would have been over at about the same time."[111]

Strategic Air against Japan

Only three days after Admiral Nimitz's forces invaded the Marianas on 15 June 1944, construction of a B-29 base, named Isley Field, began on Saipan. When General Hansell, who had taken command of the XXI Bomber Command, landed the first B-29 at Isley on 12 October, however, he found that only a single unpaved airstrip had been built. In the Marianas, the B-29 command found it difficult to obtain adequate logistical support from a theater command that was primarily intent on building a fleet base and other facilities to support continuing surface operations.[112] Meanwhile, back in Washington, Twentieth Air Force target planners were making a new appreciation of the strategic vulnerability of Japan to air attacks that could be flown by the XXI Bomber Command. During the summer the target planners lost their enthusiasm for Japanese iron and steel targets in favor of attacks against Japan's aircraft plants. At Arnold's request, the Committee of Operations Analysts submitted a fresh estimate of Japan's strategic vulnerability based on the separate assumptions that Japan might either be defeated by an air and sea blockade or by those means plus a surface invasion.

On the first premise, the committee recommended a general air campaign against shipping including extensive aerial mining operations, an attack against the aircraft industry, and saturation bombing of six urban industrial areas. In the event of a surface invasion, the committee recommended priority attacks against the aircraft industry, with an effort also against industrial targets and intensification of the antishipping campaign. In the European theater, AAF commanders had not favored the area bombing attacks that were flown against cities by the RAF Bomber Command. In its earliest analyses of Japan, however, the Committee of Operations Analysts had brought out the fact that Japan's cities were highly flammable and that a substantial part of Japan's war production was done in small factories dispersed throughout urban areas. On 24 April 1944 General Kuter had called the Twentieth Air Force's attention to incendiary tests against simulated Japanese city targets that were being conducted at Eglin Field. The AAF Board soon completed two reports recommending the proper admixture of incendiaries and fragmentation bombs and the tactics and techniques of B-29 incendiary missions that might prove most effective against Japan's cities.[113]

Although it accepted the report of the Committee of Operations Analysts, the Joint Target Group of the Joint Chiefs of Staff discounted the possibility that the Japanese war might be ended by any means short of surface invasion; hence, the group recommended that an emphatic priority be given to the destruction of Japan's air power and that urban attacks and mining operations be delayed. Acting for the Joint Chiefs, the Twentieth Air Force accordingly directed the XXI Bomber Command to attack Japan's major aircraft plants. Following delays caused by weather, the XXI Bomber Command sent its first bombing mission on a high-level attack against Tokyo's Nakajima aircraft plant on 24 November 1944. Against the high-flying B-29s, Japanese fighter interceptors had little real effect. But, in the months that followed, the precision bombing effort appeared rather unsuccessful. Adverse winter weather scattered bomber formations, obscured targets, and reduced bombing accuracy. The long flights to Japan and the need to lift heavy bomb loads to more than 25,000-foot bombing altitudes strained engines and brought about substantial losses of aircraft at sea. Impatient with the performance of the XXI Bomber Command, General Arnold moved General LeMay to its command on 20 January 1945, but neither the new commander nor the commitment of another bomb wing to combat from North Field on Tinian on 4 February appeared to give better results.

Actually the B-29 attacks against the Japanese aircraft factories proved more effective than was realized. The United States Strategic Bombing Survey discovered that the damages caused by the B-29s were enough to convince the Japanese of a need to disperse their aircraft plants. The destruction inflicted, plus the confusion resulting from frantic dispersal efforts, reduced the preattack capacity of aircraft engine plants by 75 percent, of airframe plants by 60 percent, and of electronics and communications equipment plants by 70 percent.[114]

General Arnold, apprehensive about reports that the Japanese were building a new and heavily armed fighter interceptor that might inflict heavy losses upon the B-29s and mindful of the need for fighter escort in the European theater, had sent a memorandum to the Joint Plans Section in July 1944 recommending the seizure of the island of Iwo Jima midway between the Marianas and Japan to serve as a base for long-range escort fighters. The same month Arnold committed five long-range P-47N and P-51 fighter groups to the XXI Bomber Command. As it happened, Japanese air defenses were never a serious threat to the B-29s. Although the Japanese were able to stage a few heckling attacks through Iwo Jima against the airfields in the Marianas in November 1944 and even though in the early months of B-29 operations against aircraft factories, the Japanese were able to concentrate their fighters on occasion and to shoot down a few B-29s. Japan's air defenses actually were rapidly losing their effect and the heckling attacks had ceased before Nimitz's forces invaded Iwo Jima on 19 February 1945. After very severe ground fighting had cleared the island, the VII Fighter Command deployed three fighter groups to Iwo Jima in March. Long-range Mustangs escorted B-29s to Tokyo on 7 April. But the fighters were not often called upon for such support. Meanwhile the XXI Bomber Command had begun to operate mostly at night. After 5 June 1945, the Japanese made their last effective air opposition against day-flying B-29s. Thereafter, the Japanese yielded complete air supremacy, electing to hoard their remaining aircraft for suicide attacks against an expected surface invasion.[115]

Until 6 March 1945, General LeMay had considered that the XXI Bomber Command had not "really accomplished a hell of a lot of bombing results." The command, however, was gaining strength. A third bombardment wing began operations from North Field on Guam on 25 February. Anticipating the arrival of this third B-29 wing, Arnold had issued a new target directive on 19 February that continued to give first priority to precision attacks against aircraft engine factories but made incendiary attacks against urban industrial concentrations in Tokyo, Nagoya, Osaka, and Kawasaki a strong second priority. While the fire raids were desired by Washington, General LeMay kept his own counsel on the tactics that he would employ on the great Tokyo fire raid, which would be mounted on the night of 9-10 March 1945. He called for a stream of bombers from the three wings to come in low (4,900 to 9,200 feet) and to drop their incendiaries on fires started by pathfinder crews. Since gunners who would be unused to night attack might shoot at each other's planes in the dark, LeMay ordered both guns and gunners removed from the B-29s. The weight saved by the removal of armament and the low attack altitude would permit the B-29s to carry very heavy loads of firebombs. Many aircrewmen were certain that LeMay's radical tactics would do nothing but get them killed. Yet, even though over the target in a steady stream in the early morning hours of 10 March, the B-29s sustained only moderate losses as they kindled fires that destroyed about one-fourth of metropolitan Tokyo. LeMay had staked his professional career on the decision to operate the bombers at a low level. "This decision, combining technical acumen with boldness of execution," General Hansell said later, "was one of the classic air decisions of the war."[116]

With 385 B-29s available in his combat wings, General LeMay was able to order combat missions every fourth to sixth day, depending on the weather, which was the most serious obstacle affecting operations. Daylight precision-bombing attacks against industrial targets were conducted from medium levels, and fire raids continued against Tokyo, Kobe, Osaka, and Yokohama. On 27 March the XXI Bomber Command began to mine Japan's shipping channels and harbors. On the same day, other B-29s struck Japanese airfields on Kyushu. And, as he was authorized to do in an emergency, Nimitz directed that approximately 75 percent of the XXI Bomber Command's combat effort be flown against airfields on Kyushu and Shikoku in the period between 17 April and 11 May. Recognizing the gravity of the situation caused by Japanese suicide air attacks against the American forces at Okinawa, LeMay did not strongly resist this commitment of his forces even though he suggested that bomber attacks could not completely neutralize the hostile airfields. The Iwo-based long-range fighters of the VII Fighter Command also made sweeps over Japanese airfields on Honshu and Kyushu, but without scoring very good results. Hostile planes were widely dispersed and the enemy pilots did not come up and fight.[117]

Believing that an all-out air attack could force Japan to surrender prior to a surface invasion, LeMay was willing to commit his command to maximum operations, even at the risk of exhausting all available crews. In the waning weeks of May and the early days of June, the XXI Bomber Command returned to strategic air attacks and completed the conflagration of Japan's five principal urban industrial areas. The 58th Bombardment Wing, arriving from India, began missions from Tinian on 5 May. Another B-29 wing that had been especially equipped to make radar attacks against oil storage facilities rounded out the XXI Bomber Command's strength when it arrived on 26 June. By late spring 1945, Brig Gen Emmett O'Donnell, Jr., commander of the 73d Bombardment Wing, which had been first into action from the Marianas, noted a general conviction throughout the bomber command that the Japanese could not stand up under the terrific amount of damage that the B-29s were placing upon them. "I thought personally," recalled O'Donnell, "in a couple of weeks it would be all over." When Arnold visited Guam early in June, LeMay told him that 30 to 60 of Japan's cities and every industrial target in the home islands would be destroyed by 1 October. In the air, the B-29s were virtually unopposed. "The record will show," LeMay later commented, "that in the last two months of the war it was safer to fly a combat mission over Japan than it was to fly a B-29 training mission back in the United States."[118]

Atomic Attack at Hiroshima and Nagasaki

Meanwhile the Japanese government had begun to seriously consider ways to end the war. On 20 June 1945 Emperor Hirohito told his council that it would be necessary to have a plan to close the war at once. Early in July the Japanese government asked the Soviet Union to intercede with the United States to stop the war, but the Soviets refused to relay the proposal. These peace feelers faced much internal opportunities as Japan's militarists continued to play for time; they believed that if Japan could somehow survive the air attacks she might be able to inflict such a high rate of casualties on American surface invaders as to be able to get a negotiated peace. The reiteration of the unconditional surrender formula in the Potsdam Declaration on 26 July 1945 gave new strength to the Japanese militarists.[119] Top-level American officials in Washington knew of Japan's desire to end hostilities, but in September 1944 the Combined Chiefs of Staff had committed the United States and Great Britain to the seizure of "objectives in the industrial heart of Japan." This strategy was reaffirmed at Yalta in February 1945. To help ensure the success of this strategy, the Allies granted the Soviet Union territorial concessions in East Asia in return for its promises to join the war against Japan when hostilities were concluded in Europe.[120]

In the spring of 1945 the question was not so much whether Japan would be invaded but how the effort would be ordered and commanded. Arnold thought that a supreme commander should be appointed, with coequal status for ground, naval, and air force subordinates—an arrangement that would permit all AAF units in the Pacific to serve under one top air commander. Not willing to accept this proposal, the Joint Chiefs, on 3 April 1945, instead approved a directive that designated General MacArthur as commander in chief, Army forces in the Pacific, and named Admiral Nimitz as commander in chief, Pacific, with command over all naval forces. The Joint Chiefs agreed on 2 July to authorize the establishment of the United States Army Strategic Air Forces (USASTAF), Pacific, under the command of General Spaatz, with a headquarters on Guam. Under this plan, the Headquarters and Headquarters Squadron, XXI Bomber Command, was redesignated as the Headquarters Squadron, Twentieth Air Force, and the Eighth Air Force was to be redeployed from Europe to command new B-29 wings based on Okinawa. The Joint Chiefs of Staff would direct USASTAF operations; Arnold would act as Joint Chiefs' executive agent for USASTAF.[121]

Under the new command organization, the Twentieth Air Force had five wings and 21 B-29 groups plus the fighters based on Iwo Jima that previously had been assigned to the now inactivated XXI Bomber Command. Employing 923 B-29s the Twentieth operated virtually at will over Japan during July; after 4 July, General Kenney's Far East Air Forces began to strike targets on Kyushu from bases on Okinawa. During the Okinawa crisis, General LeMay had supported naval operations without demur. He had other thoughts, however, when Adm William F. Halsey requested on 14 July that the B-29s fly maximum effort strikes against airfields in the Tokyo area on 24-25 July and again on 1-2 August to support Third Fleet carrier air strikes into the Tokyo-Nagoya areas. LeMay protested that it was foolish to expend 6,500 tons of B-29 bombs to protect the carriers while their aircraft would be dropping 500 tons of bombs. He agreed, however, to use Iwo-based fighters in support of the Third Fleet strikes. Thinking differently, the Joint Chiefs ordered LeMay to employ the B-29s as Halsey requested. On 24 and 25 July, Iwo-based P-51s were sent out against airfields in the Tokyo area, but bad target weather somehow prevented B-29 attacks, which were diverted to their original strategic targets.[122]

General Spaatz, arriving on Guam on 29 July, began organizing the United States Army Strategic Air Forces – work which would not be completed before the war's end. If the organization had been fully accomplished, the Eighth and Twentieth Air Forces would have controlled a total of 49 B-29 groups. As it was, General Doolittle established the Eighth Air Force on Okinawa on 19 July, but its first B-29 wing was still getting into place when Japan surrendered.

Before reaching the theater, Spaatz had been briefed on the atomic bomb, which the 509th Composite Group on Tinian would drop on a target designated by Washington as soon as it could be delivered from laboratory production. Escorted only by photo planes, a 509th Group B-29 dropped the first atomic bomb against Hiroshima on 6 August. Three days later another of the group's B-29s dropped the second atomic bomb over Nagasaki. In haste, the Soviet Union declared war on Japan. On 10 August the Japanese government officially announced its decision to accept the Potsdam surrender terms, provided the surrender would not alter the institution of the emperor. Although Japan did not surrender unconditionally, the United States and its Allies accepted Japan's offer and terminated active hostilities on 12 August 1945.[123]

The revolutionary employment of nuclear air weapons and the entry of the Soviet Union into the war tended to obscure the contributions of the sustained conventional strategic air offensive to the defeat of Japan. Looking backward, Spaatz could not see how the entry of Russia into the war had any effect on Japan's decision to surrender. He believed that conventional bombing could have ended the war, but he thought that the employment of the atomic bomb had been justified as a means of ensuring, without doubt, that many Americans would not have to lose their lives in a tremendously costly surface invasion.[124] "Without attempting to minimize the appalling and far-reaching results of the atomic bombs," Arnold observed, "we have good reason to believe that its actual use provided a way out for the Japanese government. The fact is that the Japanese could not have held out long, because they lost control of their air. They could not offer effective opposition to our bombardment, and so could not prevent the destruction of their cities and industries."[125] Based upon a thorough investigation, the United States Strategic Bombing Survey stated its opinion that "certainly prior to 31 December 1945, and in all probability prior to 1 November 1945, Japan would even have surrendered even if the atomic bombs had not been dropped, even if Russia had not entered the war, and even if no invasion had been planned or contemplated."[126]

Thoughts on Air Power and Air Force

"The air power of a nation," the Air Corps Tactical School had taught as early as 1935, "is its capacity to conduct air operations; specifically, the power which a nation is capable of exerting by means of its air forces. Air power is actual and not potential. Air power is measured by the immediate ability of a nation to engage effectively in air warfare."[127] In the view of the Air Corps Tactical School, air power was synonymous with the military air striking force in being, but to many observers the experience of World War II indicated that this definition was much too restrictive.[128]

When he published his widely read *Victory through Air Power* in 1942, Alexander de Seversky drew upon his experience as a tsarist military pilot and as an inventor, airplane designer, and aircraft producer in the United States and boldly predicted that aircraft would be developed with global ranges, thus ending the isolation of the Western Hemisphere. "Range deficiency," de Seversky wrote, "has been the curse on Hitler's aviation." The United States would soon be open to air attack from every point of the compass. "It is sheer waste," he concluded, "to maintain advanced bases instead of hurling the full aerial potential directly against the adversary. The entire logic of aerial warfare makes it certain that ultimately war in the skies will be conducted from the home grounds, with everything in between turned into a no-man's land." De Seversky's concept of global air warfare paralleled the naval warfare ideas that he had obtained from studying Alfred Thayer Mahan. As he later admitted, de Seversky also followed Mahan in offering a wide conception of the nature of air power, which included a striking air force, a defensive air force, and cooperation [air support] air forces as well as the industries, the personnel, and the materials; or, in short, everything that produced the power to navigate in the air.[129]

When General Arnold made his official report to the secretary of war on 12 November 1945, he accepted the same extrapolation of Mahan's classic definition of naval power. "Air power," Arnold stated, "includes a nation's ability to deliver cargo, people, destructive missiles and war-making potential through the air to a desired destination to accomplish a desired purpose. Air power is not composed alone of the war-making components of aviation. It is the total aviation activity—civilian and military, commercial and private, potential as well as existing."[130] This definition was accepted by General Spaatz, when he became chief of staff of the US Air Force in 1947.[131] Moreover, the Congressional Aviation Policy Board stated in 1948 that: "Air power is the total ability of a nation to capitalize on the medium of flight. . . . National air power is an entity not fundamentally divisible as a weapon, or as a carrier. Materials, organization, and craftsmanship which go to make a great aviation industry are as readily turned to the combat plane as to the transport."[132]

Before World War II, Air Corps thinkers had visualized the air force as a striking arm quite separate and distinct from the auxiliary aviation that supported surface action, although the separate air striking arm could be used as necessary to support ground action. By 1945, however, General Arnold equated air force with military air power. Only a few years later Spaatz was emphasizing that Congress had assigned the nation's "primary air power role to the Air Force."[133] Moreover, in 1945, Arnold had described the air force as comprising a global striking force that would be employed from strategically located bases and that could meet and overpower an aggressor's air threat as near as possible to its source; a tactical air force which would work closely with the army, air transport and troop carrier aviation; and an up-to-date training establishment fully supplied with the latest aircraft and equipment.[134]

Addressing the first class in the new Air Command and Staff School in September 1946, an Army Air Forces instructor stated: "Air power is a force in itself capable of being used alone or in cooperation with other forces. The early prophets of air power, careless of their terminology, claimed that air power rendered obsolete all other weapons and armed forces. Though these men were led to false prophecy, their vociferous claims no doubt helped to hasten the development of air power."[135] Although this lecture was not authoritative, it manifested an apparently prevalent opinion springing from the highest levels of authority that World War II had been a composite victory of cooperative air, ground, and naval forces. "The elementary lessons which we have learned from the hard experience of World War II," stated Secretary of War Robert P. Patterson in October 1945, "is that there must be a single direction of the Nation's land, sea, and air forces . . . these arms must operate as a single team under single direction, which has final responsibility and final power of decision over all."[136] In January 1947, Secretary Patterson wrote: "Air power tipped the scales for victory in the war." But in November 1947 he stated: "World War II was not won in the air alone. It was won by the combined effort of ground forces, sea forces and air forces, working as members of a single team."[137]

The team concept of Allied victory in World War II was strongly supported by high-ranking Army officers. "The national security is measured by the sum, or rather the combination of the three great arms, the land, air, and naval forces," General Marshall stated in October 1945.[138] "In my opinion," said Gen Omar Bradley in November 1945, "no one service won this war or is going to win any future war of any magnitude. It takes all our services together, plus the industrial effort of our Nation to win any major war." To illustrate his point, Bradley granted that air attacks cut down the employment of German V-2 rockets against England, but he invited attention to the fact "that not until the Navy and the Army forces got together and went over and captured the launching sites did the V-2 attacks completely come to a stop."[139] As chief of the War Department Plans and Policy Group in February 1947, Brig Gen George A. Lincoln argued that World War II had demonstrated that air power was a dominant factor in war and peace but that it had also taught that a tremendous hidden Army and Navy effort was required "to make air power effective over the target." This effort included air-ground battles required to seize and hold air bases needed to put air power over its target.[140] "The war also illustrated," as Secretary of the Army Kenneth C. Royall stated in December 1947, "that final victory had to be won by tanks, guns and men, on the ground." Allied forces, Royall continued, "never stopped the launching of the V-bombs, and never engaged in any material damage to them or to the submarine pens, until the infantry did so from the ground, despite the enormous bombing and almost unopposed bombing of Europe for a considerable period of time, and in great volume."[141] "Although I am personally convinced that Air Power will again be the dominant factor," said Gen J. Lawton Collins in October 1948, "I'm equally convinced that Air Power alone cannot win the war. . . . It took, and it will again take, in my opinion, the combined operations of land, sea and air forces to reach a conclusion."[142]

Although the Navy appeared somewhat less enthusiastic about the "team" concept than did the Army, the theater commanders of the Pacific war — General MacArthur and Admiral Nimitz — saw the defeat of Japan as a victory of combined forces. "The victory was a triumph for the concept of the three dimensions of war — ground, sea and air," MacArthur stated in October 1945. He added: "By a thorough use of each arm in conjunction with the corresponding utilization of the other two, the enemy was reduced to a condition of helplessness. By largely avoiding methods involving the separate use of the services and by avoiding methods of frontal assault as far as possible, our combined power forced the surrender."[143] Admiral Nimitz thought in 1945 that without the atomic bombs the surrender of Japan "would have taken a longer time," but he thought that the victory resulted from

> the strangulation of her industry, her being cut off from all supplies, her lack of gasoline, her inability to get raw materials from China. . . . Such gasoline as they had was stored in places from which it could not be distributed, because the transportation systems had been destroyed by the air attacks; the very efficient destruction carried on by the B-29s.

> It was just a question of time before the Japanese would have been forced to this same surrender. The atomic bomb undoubtedly hastened that surrender.[144]

Army Air Forces leaders also accepted the point of view that World War II had been won by combined arms. Thus, in April 1944, Maj Gen Follett Bradley could argue that the "true expositor of military things to come must ... evaluate correctly the effect of air power in combination with land and sea power on a battle, a campaign and a war, and he must know something of the technique by which that effect is produced."[145] In October 1945, Arnold hailed the command decisions of February 1943 by which "the air had been consolidated under an air command, coordinated with similarly concentrated land and naval forces.... With this change it became possible to exploit fully the versatility and weight of air power and to exert fully the over-all commander's strategic will in the air."[146] In November 1945, he wrote that the doctrine of the air force comprehended the fact "that it is the team of the Army, Navy and Air Forces working in close cooperation that gives strength to our armed services in peace or war."[147] Speaking of the termination of hostilities in the Pacific, General Doolittle said in November 1945: "The Navy had the transport to make the invasion of Japan possible; the Ground Forces had the power to make it successful; and the B-29 made it unnecessary." In its broad aspects, however, he pointed out that "the recent war was won by teamwork.... No single service won the war. The Navy fought magnificently as did the Ground Army and the Air Army.... The smooth functioning of the team was the direct result of having unity of command — one supreme commander in each theater of war."[148]

The emphasis upon combined forces was accompanied by a subtle downgrading of the significance of the role of strategic bombardment in World War II. In Secretary Patterson's view, "the hammering that German industry and transportation took from the American and British air forces so seriously crippled the mobility of the German army that it was unable to withstand the combined assaults from the East and from the West."[149] Speaking of strategic bombing, Gen Jacob L. Devers, commander of the Army Ground Forces, said: "The Ground Forces recognize this strategic battle role of the air which must be successfully conducted before the Infantry and Artillery can close with the enemy."[150] General Bradley concluded that strategic bombing in Europe "was ultimately an effective deterrent to the success of the enemy on the battlefield.... It had a decisive effect on the ultimate ability of the Allies to defeat Germany in a shorter time, saving many, many lives and dollars."[151]

In the immediate aftermath of World War II, Air Force officers were inclined to agree that a second phase of ground conflict would characterize a future war. "Japan," General Spaatz said in March 1947, "was a peculiar situation, being an island empire.... But when you are up against a continental empire you have the problem of winning against great masses of people with great internal resources.... We had established almost complete air superiority over Germany at the time of the invasion, but it took a considerable amount of fighting to subdue

Germany after air superiority had been established." Speaking in August 1949 after he had become chief of staff of the Air Force, Gen Hoyt S. Vandenberg announced: "My opinion of the effectiveness of strategic bombing in both Europe and in the Pacific was that it contributed in large measure to the success in the conclusion of the war and saved a great many lives that otherwise would have been lost."[152] "We of the Air Force," Vandenberg stated in a speech in August 1952, "have never claimed that air power, in alliance with mass destruction weapons, could decide a war alone."[153]

Lessons on Air Superiority

In the 1930s, the Air Corps had regarded establishing control of the air to be essential only in support of surface operations. Based upon his observations of the Battle of Britain and other early World War II operations, however, de Seversky boldly asserted, *"We cannot and must not dream of conquering the enemy without first capturing dominance in the air—but once we have clear-cut dominance in the air, all else becomes a secondary subordinate, auxiliary operation."* And he stated the further rule: *"Only air power can defeat air power* [emphasis in original]."[154] In view of the experience of the Eighth Air Force over Germany, the Army Air Forces found it easy to abandon Douhet and to adopt a doctrine of "air superiority" or "control of the air," which—like the definition given to air power—was an extrapolation from Mahan. As the United States Strategic Bombing Survey's summary report of the European war stated, "the significance of full domination of the air over the enemy—both over its armed forces and over its sustaining economy—must be emphasized. That domination of the air was essential. Without it, attacks on the basic economy of the enemy could not have been delivered in sufficient force and with sufficient freedom to bring effective and lasting results."[155] Looking backward at World War II in October 1945, Arnold said: "The Air Force's primary mission the world over was to knock out enemy air power—to win the air war.... All types of aircraft shared in this task in many different roles."[156] Doolittle pointed out that the United States had to have control of the air over Japan before it could deliver the atomic bomb. "The first lesson," he said, "is that you can't lose a war if you have command of the air, and you can't win a war if you haven't."[157] "You know, at first hand," Spaatz told a convention of air veterans in November 1947, "the penalty paid by Germany and Japan for their failure to control the air over their own territories. You know the inevitable outcome of any failure to control the air over our own country."[158] Writing in 1950, Col Dale O. Smith and Maj Gen John DeForest Barker, noted: "It has long been held as Air Force doctrine that air superiority should be the primary mission of air power."[159]

The Air Force doctrine of air superiority or control of the air was quite acceptable to War Department and Army spokesmen. Robert P. Patterson stated: "World War II drove home the lesson that a nation lacking in air power has no chance of winning a war.... In every campaign fought out on the surface, success went to the side that had local command of the air.... Without command of the air, the launching of a military operation on land or sea was virtually unthinkable."[160] As Lt Gen Manton S. Eddy stated in March 1949, "There is no question in a soldier's mind that air power is as indispensable to the national security as bread and water are to life. Land forces cannot fight decisively unless the air is controlled by its sister services."[161] "In spite of the fact that air power can never be decisive in total war," General Bradley told an audience in November 1951, "the air battle must be won if a war is to be won."[162]

While the doctrine of control of the air was firmly implanted in Air Force thinking as a result of conventional air operations in Europe, some second thoughts about the influence of nuclear bombing capabilities indicated a trend back toward Douhet. Written largely by Maj Gen Orvil Anderson and published in 1947, the concluding report of the United States Strategic Bombing Survey, *Air Campaigns of the Pacific War*, observed that

> air superiority is not an end in itself. Air superiority was necessary in the past war in order that surface operations could be successfully undertaken and in order that decisive bombing of the enemy's vital components could be accomplished. If science and technology produce an air weapon which can, unaided, penetrate enemy defenses and accurately deposit its bombs, it may not be necessary to fight the conventional air battle and obtain conventional air superiority before the decisive attacks on an enemy's economy are mounted. Any force, having successfully made such attacks, however, probably would quickly inherit air domination for the exploitation phase of the war.[163]

In a lecture in June 1949, General Anderson warned that conventional ideas of air superiority would not always hold good: "You will reach the point in the distant future when you won't even think of opposing air in the air. It will be moving too fast.... You'll fight them at the launching site or you won't fight them."[164] "Future defense and future security," Col David A. Burchinal pointed out in the autumn of 1949, "would seem to stem from the basic premise that successful air defense must be capable of destroying an attacking force or an aggression potential before the attack can be launched or the potential realized."[165]

In his book *Air Power: Key to Survival*, published in 1950, de Seversky continued to attach great importance to air dominance. "We can undertake nothing through military force," de Seversky also told an Army War College audience in March 1952,

> unless first we have secured command of the air. To gain command of the air, we must win the air battle.... The idea that we can send a lot of bombers, either from bases abroad, or from bases at home or from aircraft carriers, and destroy everything in Russia without first winning command of the air is, in my estimation, sheer bunk.... Therefore, the battle for command of the air is just as much in the cards today as it was in the last war.... Just the same as it would have been impractical in the last century to control a part of the ocean—just a patch of the ocean.... So the air battle will be widespread, and will be fought for the command of the entire air space, clear around the globe.[166]

Development of Tactical Air Power

In a talk with one of his assistants on 22 August 1945, Maj Gen Lauris Norstad, who was then the chief of Army Air Forces plans, stated that the conception of the tactical air force was "one of the greatest developments" of World War II. However, he immediately added that the atomic bomb might have made a tactical air force "as old-fashioned as the Maginot line."[167] The Air Force would continue to debate the effect of nuclear weapons on air power at the same time that it was recording the doctrinal lessons of World War II applicable to tactical air power.

The experience of World War II left no doubt as to the impact of air power on land battles. "The Normandy invasion," Gen Dwight D. Eisenhower explained on 16 November 1945,

> was based on a deep-seated faith in the power of the air forces, in overwhelming numbers, to intervene in the land battle. That is, a faith that the air forces, by their action could have the effect on the ground of making it possible for a small force of land troops to invade a continent, a country strongly defended, in which there were 61 enemy divisions and where we could not possibly on the first day of the assault land more than 7 divisions. . . . Without that air force, without the aid of its power, entirely aside from its anticipated ability to sweep the enemy air forces out of the sky, without its power to intervene in the land battle, that invasion would have been fantastic. . . . Unless we had that faith in the air power to intervene and to make safe that landing, it would have been more than fantastic, it would have been criminal.[168]

One of the major ironies of World War II was that, when operating against a first-class adversary on a continental landmass, air units assigned or attached to ground forces proved incapable of providing effective support to the ground forces. As has been seen, such penny packets of air power were unable to accomplish missions of importance to the ground forces—which the Allied experience in North Africa demonstrated to be the attainment of air superiority, the interdiction of the movement of hostile troops and equipment to or within the battle area, and the close support of friendly ground troops by aerial attack of battlefield objectives which could not be handled by friendly artillery. Although War Department Field Manual 100-20, *Command and Employment of Air Power*, prescribed the tasks of a tactical air force as being air superiority, interdiction, and close support, it did not attempt to describe the exact organization to be used in combat theaters. In Italy the Fifth Army and the XII Tactical Air Command attained unity of purpose by maintaining adjacent headquarters and holding nightly planning conferences. Calls for close air support went back from frontline units to the army air section and were monitored by the corps air section. If the corps remained silent, it was assumed that the corps could not handle the mission by artillery or other means. The request was reported at once by the army air section to ground liaison officers at the airdromes, while G-3 and tactical air command officers determined whether the mission should be flown. About 50 percent of these requests were refused. Approximately 75 percent of the refused missions were disapproved by G-3 as not in conformity with army plans, while the remainder were rejected by the tactical air command on technical grounds. At the front lines, experienced pilots served tours of duty as forward air controllers to direct support aircraft to their targets. When necessary, especially in the mountainous terrain of Italy, a Rover Joe or Horsefly airborne tactical air controller flying a liaison plane would lead support aircraft to their targets.[169]

The organization for tactical air control adopted in the European theater was an expansion of the system employed in Italy. In the battles of France and Germany, the Ninth Air Force cooperated with the 12th Army Group while subordinate air commands developed very close relationships with various armies: the IX Tactical Air Command with the First Army, the XIX Tactical Air Command with the Third Army, and the XXIX Tactical Air Command with the Ninth Army. Each of these tactical air commands possessed microwave ground control interception radars, and their fighter-bomber groups were employed alternatively as required either for defense or for air support. With the demise of the dive-bomber, the US air forces modified the P-47 to serve as a tactical fighter-bomber, and the P-47 fighter, although originally designed as a high-altitude interceptor, proved to be superb in this new role. The radical air-cooled engine on this plane made it less vulnerable to hostile ground fire than was the P-51, which had an in-line liquid-cooled engine. To permit flexibility, medium bombers and tactical reconnaissance aircraft were retained under the direct command of the Ninth Air Force. The reconnaissance aircraft flew missions requested by army and air force units. They also proved invaluable in leading fighter-bombers directly to targets of opportunity. While many Army officers questioned the inherent wisdom of such a centralization of reconnaissance capabilities, Gens Courtney H. Hodges, George S. Patton, Jr., and W. H. Simpson, the commanders of the First, Third, and Ninth US Armies respectively, expressed their individual approval of the tactical air reconnaissance system.[170] By March 1945, Lt Gen Walter Bedell Smith, the chief of staff to General Eisenhower, noted that "the tactical coordination of air and ground forces has become an instrument of precision timing."[171]

In Europe all air force capabilities were available for the support of the surface campaign. Even though heavy bombardment was employed on occasion to augment tactical bomber forces (most notably on 25 July 1944 when 1,508 heavy bombers softened the German lines at Saint Lô preparatory to the First Army's breakthrough out of Normandy), the outstanding contribution of the heavy bombers to the overall ground campaign was the elimination of the Luftwaffe as an effective fighting force. Although the Ninth Air Force stood ready to maintain friendly air superiority, it was committed routinely to interdiction and close support operations, with roughly 15 percent of the tactical air effort going to close air support. But in static periods such as existed prior to the Saint Lô breakthrough and while the armies were building up before the Siegfried Line, the proportion of air effort allotted to targets along the front lines did not exceed 10 percent of the tactical air forces capability. The remaining tactical air effort was committed to armed reconnaissance and to attack against interdiction targets behind the enemy lines.[172] A flexible employment of tactical air groups on varied missions ensured that no one unit suffered debilitating losses. Fighter-bombers, for example, suffered their highest rate of loss to flak on the dive-bombing missions commonly required for bridge attacks and close air support; armed reconnaissance, area support, and fighter-sweep missions were only about two-thirds as dangerous as dive-bombing missions.[173] What could happen when a group was solely committed to the most hazardous mission was illustrated during the Ardennes offensive. Because it was based closest to the area, the 406th Fighter-Bomber Group provided the burden of the close air support to the 101st Airborne Division, which was besieged at Bastogne; from 23-28 December the group flew 529 close support sorties into this area. Of its 60 operational P-47s at the beginning of the period, the group lost 17 shot down and had more than 40 damaged by flak.[174] Although the evidence was not conclusive, such experience indicated that an air unit committed solely to close air support in the European theater would have encountered disproportionately high casualty rates that would have adversely effected its continuation in operations.

In the Pacific theaters of World War II, American forces accepted the same tasks of tactical air power as were recognized in Europe, but organizational patterns were different. In General MacArthur's Southwest Pacific theater, the entire Fifth Air Force cooperated intimately with the Sixth Army and, after June 1944, the Thirteenth Air Force usually worked with the Eighth Army. While General Kenney began to organize tactical air commands for the planned invasion of Japan, he elected to use standard bombardment and fighter wings to provide cooperation with individual ground task forces during the war.[175] In the early days in the Pacific Ocean areas, Marine Corps and Thirteenth Air Force aircraft were organized in the same naval task group to support ground fighting on Guadalcanal. Marine F7F Tigercats usually flew air patrols overhead while Air Force P-39 squadrons, which lacked the ability to intercept high-flying enemy aircraft, performed close support missions. In the island invasions of the Central Pacific, Navy and Marine carrier-based air units provided air superiority, interdiction, and air support as necessary. Some years later, after he had become commandant of the Marine Corps, Gen David M. Shoup would recall that "the finest close air support for ground troops that I experienced in World War II came from Navy squadrons at Saipan." In working from fast aircraft carriers, Marine airmen not only were virtually losing their service identity, but also a serious defect in fast-carrier support for ground operations came to light on 17 June 1944 when the Fifth Fleet suddenly had to withdraw from Saipan to fight the naval battle of the Philippine Sea. Lightly gunned Marine Corps infantry was left ashore without close air support. Rather than allow this to happen again, Lt Gen Holland M. Smith, the Marine Corps officer in command of Expeditionary Troops, recommended and the Navy accepted, the proposition that Marine Corps air groups would be designated as air support specialists and would be assigned to escort carriers, which would not be withdrawn from an invasion objective for a fleet engagement. According to the organization worked out and employed by the marines at Peleliu and Okinawa, a Marine Corps air wing became an integral part of a Marine Corps division. Since Marine ground commanders could normally expect only flat trajectory fire of naval guns during critical phases of ship-to-shore amphibious operations and since they would usually go ashore with limited amounts of organic artillery, Marine air wings would be organized, trained, and employed as a substitute for Marine artillery.[176]

In the winter of 1945-46, the War Department began to refine the air-ground lessons of World War II for the purpose of determining future organization. Army officers generally preferred the system which had been employed in the European theater of operations to that which had been devised by the Marine Corps in the Pacific. General Eisenhower, who became Army chief of staff on 19 November 1945, subsequently explained the reasons why he believed that the Army should not attempt to develop its own organic air support.

> The Army concept of the land, sea and air principle of organization of the armed forces is well-known; this Service accepts without reservation the concept of complementary roles — air, ground and sea — and consequent mutual dependence of the three components of the armed services. Under this three service concept it is axiomatic that no single service should acquire forces or equipment necessary to accomplish joint missions single-handed, if such forces or equipment unnecessarily duplicate those characteristics of and fundamental to either of the other two services. The experiences of this war have indicated that in many operations, if not in the majority, the task was of necessity accomplished by contributions from two or three services acting under the principle of unified command. Furthermore, the welding of the forces resulted in the greatest possible concentration of combat power at the decisive point while at the same time permitting the greatest economy of force on lesser tasks.
>
> Employment of tactical air in World War II is an outstanding illustration of the application of this concept to a specific problem. Battle experience proved that control of the air, the prerequisite to the conduct of ground operations in any given area, was gained most economically by the employment of air forces operating under a single command. This assured a maximum of flexibility, providing a command structure under which all forms of available air power could be concentrated on tactical support missions or on strategic missions, as the situation demanded — in other words, it permitted the maximum concentration of combat air power at the decisive point at the decisive time. Throughout the war, the Army depended on the necessary tactical air support from a practically autonomous Air Force. This type of close, accurate, and effective support of the frontline fighting units was provided and proved an essential element in the achievement of the Army objectives.
>
> The case for the concept that tactical air units belong under the Air Force rather than under the Army is supported by the abundant evidence of World War II, but does not rest on this evidence alone. Basically, the Army does not belong in the air — it belongs on the ground. Planes are but a facet of the over-all problem, which is basically much broader and includes responsibilities now involving approximately one-third of the Air Force. Control of the tactical Air Force means responsibility, not merely for the fighters and medium bombers themselves, but, as well, for the entire operating establishment required to support these planes. This includes the requisite basic air research and development program necessary to maintain a vital arm and the additional specialized service forces to support the arm; for example: air maintenance units, aircraft warning units (radar, DF stations), tactical air communications nets, etc. In short, assumption

of this task by the Army would duplicate in great measure the primary and continuing responsibilities of the Air Force and, in effect, would result in the creation of another air establishment.[177]

Some other factors also evidently bore on the Army's rejection of the Marine Corps air support system. The Marine Corps was designated, equipped, manned, and trained to engage in shock-type action that would be limited in time, magnitude, and scope. Army divisions, on the other hand, were intended to operate in sustained ground campaigns on broad theater fronts. While Marine Corps commanders would have to depend on air support as a substitute for artillery firepower, Army commanders preferred to rely upon the supporting fire of their own organic artillery within the first thousand yards beyond the front lines.[178]

As has been seen, Army and Army Air Forces officers were so generally satisfied with the tactical air system employed in Europe that it was in effect engrossed in War Department Field Manual 31-35, *Air-Ground Operations*, with little difficulty in August 1946. There were, however, evidences that at least some influential Army officers did not like the cooperative air support system. Writing in 1949 about his experiences as commander of the US Fifth Army in Italy, Gen Mark Wayne Clark was willing to admit that his forces had received "splendid air support of all kinds by both British and American planes." "Nevertheless," he continued, "the command setup was never satisfactory from my point of view and it still is not satisfactory.... I believed then, and my experiences in Italy did not change my view, that ground troops cannot be successful in battle unless adequately supported by combat aviation, and that such planes as are used for this purpose are necessarily auxiliary weapons, as is the artillery, and that they should come under the direct orders of the ground commander."[179] The Army's chief historian found that satisfaction with air-ground cooperation was greatest at the higher command levels and less pronounced at the lower levels. "The air and ground forces of the Army," he wrote, "... did not develop an effective air-ground battle team in World War II. The Marines did, in cooperation with naval aviation and their own."[180]

At the same time that some Army officers wished a closer command subordination of tactical air units to ground control, some Army Air Forces commanders visualized a much more decisive role for tactical air power. According to Gen Omar Bradley, Maj Gen Elwood R. "Pete" Quesada, commander of the IX Tactical Air Command (which was paired with the US First Army in Europe), "had come into the war as a young and imaginative man.... To Quesada the fighter was a little-known weapon with vast unexplored possibilities in the support of ground troops."[181] Late in 1944, Quesada made a suggestion that got back to Washington in a roundabout manner, that a concentration of available Allied fighter strength in Europe in low-level attacks against Germany could win the war during the winter of 1944-45. After World War II, Quesada was promoted to lieutenant general and given command of the Tactical Air Command. He was willing to accept the relationships of the air-surface force team as it existed at the cessation of hostilities only as a point of departure for future doctrine. Writing in

1948 he thought it axiomatic that the first prerequisite for a successful major campaign would be air supremacy or control of the air. He suggested, however, that World War II had only superficially indicated the "inherent ability of Tactical Air Power to be a decisive force in a strangulation campaign." In World War II, air doctrine had envisaged the isolation of a hostile force from its means of support, but it had not looked toward preventing an enemy force from engaging in battle. Quesada thought that by a vigorous interdiction campaign tactical air power could "paralyze the enemy's means of communication" and "sources of industrial support" and "prevent opposing armies from coming into contact." If such a concept of the employment of tactical air power was effectively pursued in a future conflict, direct support of ground troops in a zone of contact might well constitute only a small portion of the total tactical air effort. Only if tactical air power did not perform its primary functions in a convincing manner would friendly ground troops evidence a requirement for close air support.[182]

Importance of Airlift

A final aspect of doctrine emerging in the postwar period related to airlift. As Maj Gen Robert M. Webster, who had headed both tactical and transport commands in Europe in World War II, remarked in 1947, "I would say that we went into the last war with only two basic types of military aircraft, the bomber and the fighter. I feel that we have come out of that war with an additional type, the transport plane, and that we should think in terms of bomber-fighter-transport — since they are all equally important — and they must be properly balanced to each other if we are to be prepared to conduct successful war operations."[183] Back in the 1930s the Air Corps, prodded relentlessly by Maj Hugh J. Knerr who insisted that air striking forces could not depend upon ground lines of communications for logistical support, had established a requirement that both the GHQ Air Force and the Air Corps Materiel Division ought to possess transport aircraft. Both because of shortages of procurement funds and because of the Baker board's recommendation that civilian airliners could be requisitioned for a war emergency, the Army Air Forces had acquired only six air transport groups with 124 aircraft by hand in December 1941. Lacking any firm basis of experience with the air transport, the officers who drew up AWPD-1 estimated that the ascendant air force would require only 19 troop carrier groups with 1,520 planes for airborne troop employment and only 13 transport groups with 1,040 planes for air logistical support. Early in 1942 the Army Air Forces established the Air Transport Command and the I Troop Carrier Command, the former to provide worldwide air transport services and the latter to train troop carrier organizations for service in overseas theaters. At its maximum strength in February 1945, the Army Air Forces possessed 32 troop carrier groups and nine air transport divisions with a total of 10,138 aircraft.[184]

As events transpired, the Air Transport Command became responsible for the transportation, by air, of personnel, materiel, mail, strategic materials, and other cargoes for all War Department agencies (and other authorized government agencies) except those served by troop carrier units. The primary mission of troop carrier units was found to be: "To carry troops and auxiliary equipment to effective locations in combat zones from which to begin active combat operations." The control and employment of troop carrier organizations was hardly the same in any two theaters. In each theater, however, logistical services found continuing demands for the employment of troop carrier planes for intratheater movement of essential personnel and freight, but the combat employment of troop carrier planes and gliders for airborne operations always was given a higher priority. Resolution of the competing demands of the logisticians and the airborne commanders was never accomplished completely.[185]

Since there were never enough transport planes to permit them to be parceled out among using organizations, the Anglo-American organization of theater airlift forces accordingly placed central control of most such units under some form of theater troop carrier headquarters, which could employ the transport planes interchangeably for airlift or air assault operations. The organization in the European theater included the establishment of a combined air transport operations room (CATOR) in the Air Staff, Supreme Headquarters Allied Expeditionary Forces, the assignment of the IX Troop Carrier Command to the First Allied Airborne Army, and the activation of the 302d Transport Wing under the Air Service Command, USSTAF. Lt Gen Lewis H. Brereton, commander of the First Allied Airborne Army, subsequently complained that CATOR emphasized the logistical employment of his troop carrier crews to the detriment of their preparation for airborne operations. Other commanders, however, stated that the removal of aircraft from airlift operations for intensive air assault training and for the execution of airborne missions adversely deprived them of badly needed logistical support.[186]

"We have learned and must not forget," Arnold informed Secretary Stimson on 27 February 1945, "that from now on air transport is an essential of air power, in fact, of all national power.... We must have an air transport organization in being, capable of tremendous expansion."[187] In spite of this positive statement, the Army Air Forces was not too certain about the manner in which troop carrier and air transport aviation ought to be organized; there was a considerable sentiment that the two functions ought to be combined. At this time, Brig Gen William D. Old, commander of the I Troop Carrier Command, vigorously dissented from the proposals for combination and instead suggested that Army Airborne Forces should be established under the War Department on a parity with the Army Air Forces, Army Ground Forces, and Army Service Forces. Based in part upon studies conducted in OC&R and at the AAF Board, Arnold decided on 5 December 1945 that the Army Air Forces would retain the Air Transport Command to support the strategic air forces and would keep troop carrier aviation as a part of the tactical air forces.[188]

General Arnold's Final Word

In his final report to the secretary of war on 12 November 1945, General Arnold recalled the course of the successful air war that had been waged against the Axis. While he expressed satisfaction, he warned against complacency. "National safety," Arnold emphasized,

> would be endangered by an Air Force whose doctrines and techniques are tied solely to the equipment and processes of the moment. Present equipment is but a step in progress, and any Air Force which does not keep its doctrines ahead of its equipment, and its vision far into the future, can only delude the nation into a false sense of security.... The basic planning, development, organization and training of the Air Force must be well rounded, covering every modern means of waging air war, and the techniques of employing such means must be continuously developed and kept up to date. The Air Force doctrines likewise must be flexible at all times and entirely uninhibited by tradition.[189]

NOTES

1. Report of the commanding general of the Army Air Forces to the secretary of war, 4 January 1944, 2; Henry A. Arnold, *Global Mission* (New York: Harper & Bros., 1949), 149.

2. Air War Plans Division-4 (AWPD-4), Air Estimate of the Situation and Recommendations for the Conduct of the War, 15 December 1941.

3. Ibid.

4. Mark S. Watson, *Chief of Staff: Prewar Plans and Preparations, US Army in World War II* (Washington, D.C.: Office of the Chief of Military History, Department of the Army, 1950), 295–96; Chase C. Mooney, *Organization of the Army Air Arm, 1935–1945*, USAF historical study 10 (Maxwell AFB, Ala.: USAF Historical Division, 1956), 9.

5. Wesley F. Craven and James L. Cate, eds., *The Army Air Forces in World War II*, 7 vols., *Plans and Early Operations*, vol. 1 (Chicago: University of Chicago Press, 1948), 237–51.

6. Forrest C. Pogue, *George C. Marshall: Ordeal and Hope* (New York: Viking Press, 1965), 276–84; Ray S. Cline, *Washington Command Post: The Operations Division, U.S. Army in World War II* (Washington, D.C.: Office of the Chief of Military History, Department of the Army, 1951), 96–106; Maurice Matloff and Edwin M. Snell, *Strategic Planning for Coalition Warfare, 1941–1942, U.S. Army in World War II* (Washington, D.C.: Office of the Chief of Military History, Department of the Army, 1953), 135, 171.

7. Mooney, *Organization of the Army Air Arm, 1935–1945*, 9; Cline, *Washington Command Post*, 93–94.

8. Mooney, *Organization of the Army Air Arm, 1935–1945*, 29–31; Army Air Forces Regulation 20–21, *Organization: Army Air Forces*, 31 March 1942.

9. History, Army Air Forces Board, pt. 1:15–16; Gen Bernard L. Montgomery, "Weapons Evaluation and Air Power"; War Department Circular no. 204, 24 June 1942; Lt Col John A. Greene, acting commandant, Air Corps Tactical School, to The Adjutant General, War Department, letter, subject: Annual Report of the Air Corps Tactical School for the School Year 1941–1942, 30 June 1942.

10. Air War Plans Division-42, Requirements for Air Ascendancy, 9 September 1942.

11. Maj Gen Haywood S. Hansell, "A Case Study of Air Force Programming – Air Force Build-Up, 1941–1942," lecture, Air War College, Maxwell AFB, Ala., 1 December 1954.

12. Craven and Cate, *The Army Air Forces in World War II*, 7 vols., *Europe: Torch to Pointblank*, vol. 2 (Chicago: University of Chicago Press, 1949), 288–95.

13. Craven and Cate, *The Army Air Forces in World War II*, 7 vols., *Men and Planes*, vol. 6 (Chicago: University of Chicago Press, 1955), 424; Alfred Goldberg, ed., *A History of the United States Air Force, 1907–1957* (Princeton: D. Van Nostrand Co., 1957), 93–94.

14. Maj Gen Laurence S. Kuter, "Organization of Top Echelons in World War II," lecture, Air War College, Maxwell AFB, Ala., 28 February 1949.

15. Col Charles G. Williamson, chief, Status of Operations Division, Directorate of Bombardment, Headquarters Army Air Forces, to Directorate of Bombardment, Headquarters Army Air Forces, staff study, subject: Status of Operations Report, 3 March 1943.

16. Robert F. Futrell, *Command of Observation Aviation: A Study in Control of Tactical Air Power*, USAF historical study 24 (Maxwell AFB, Ala.: USAF Historical Division, 1956), 12–21; War Department Field Manual 31-35, *Aviation in Support of Ground Forces* (Washington, D.C.: Government Printing Office, 1942); see also Kent R. Greenfield, *Army Ground Forces and the Air-Ground Battle Team*, Army Ground Forces historical study 35 (n.p.: US Army Ground Forces Historical Section, 1948), 1–8.

17. Maj Orin H. Moore, Directorate of Ground Support, Army Air Forces, to Maj Gen Paul Newgarden, commanding general, 10th Armored Division, letter, 18 September 1942; Maj Orin H. Moore to Col W. G. Cronk, Headquarters 2d Tank Group, letter, 10 December 1942; schedule of Air Support Board, 7–8 December 1942; Brig Gen Orvil A. Anderson, assistant chief of Air Staff, Operational Plans, to director, Air Support, R&R sheet, subject: Revision of Field Manual 31-35, 25 February 1943.

18. History, Fighter Command School, 28 March 1942–5 November 1942, 15–34, 320–34; History, Army Air Forces Board, 1:16–21; War Department Field Manual 1-25, *Air Defense* (Washington, D.C.: Government Printing Office, 1942).

19. Memorandum by Col Don Z. Zimmerman, director, Weather, Army Air Forces, to Maj Gen George E. Stratemeyer, chief, Air Staff, subject: The Command and General Staff School and the Air Forces Tactical School, 27 June 1942; memorandum by Col Harvey H. Holland, acting commandant, to Maj Gen Muir S. Fairchild, subject: Reactivation of the Army Air Forces Tactical School, 1 September 1942; memorandum by Col L. S. Smith, director, Individual Training, Army Air Forces, to Maj Gen Muir S. Fairchild, subject: The Army Air Forces Tactical Schools and the Fighter Command School, 1 September 1942.

20. Army Air Forces Regulation 350-500, change 1, 9 October 1942; The Adjutant General Office, War Department, to commanding general, Army Air Forces, letter, subject: Establishment of an Army Air Forces School of Applied Tactics, 27 October 1942.

21. Army Air Forces Regulation 20-14, *Organization: Army Air Forces School of Applied Tactics*, 12 November 1942.

22. Maj Gen Muir S. Fairchild to commandant, Army Air Forces School of Applied Tactics, letter, subject: Directive, 16 November 1942.

23. Brig Gen Hume Peabody, commandant, Army Air Forces School of Applied Tactics, to assistant commandants, Air Defense, Air Service, Air Support, and Bombardment departments, Army Air Forces School of Applied Tactics, letters, subject: Training Directive, 9 December 1942; History, Army Air Forces Board, pt. 1:39–42.

24. History, Army Air Forces Board, pt. 1:26–29.

25. Mooney, *Organization of the Army Air Arm, 1935–1945*, 43–45; Army Air Forces, Organization and Functions Chart, 29 March 1943; memorandum by chief, Air Staff, to Maj Gen Oliver P. Echols et al., 25 March 1943.

26. Chief, management control, Army Air Forces, *The Air Forces in Theaters of Operations: Organization and Functions* (Washington, D.C.: Government Printing Office, 1943); Air War College,

special study 6, 1947–48; Preparation of USAF Manual "Commanders Guide," 16 March 1948, 12–15, 17.

27. History, Air Support Department, Army Air Forces School of Applied Tactics, 5 November 1942–29 October 1943, 1:502–5.

28. Gen Bernard L. Montgomery, commander in chief, Eighth Army, "Some Notes on High Command in War," Tripoli, January 1943; Albert F. Simpson, "Tactical Air Doctrine: Tunisia and Korea," *Air University Quarterly Review* 4, no. 4 (Summer 1951): 5–20; Robert T. Finney, "The Development of Tactical Air Doctrine in the U.S. Air Force, 1917–1951" (Maxwell AFB, Ala.: USAF Historical Division, 1952), 27.

29. Maj Gen Carl A. Spaatz to Gen Henry H. Arnold, letter, 7 March 1943.

30. Lt Gen Jacob L. Devers, commanding general, Armored Force, to Lt Col Orin H. Moore, letter, 3 May 1943; Greenfield, *Army Ground Forces and the Air-Ground Battle Team*, 47.

31. Maj Gen Orvil A. Anderson, "Development of US Strategic Air Doctrine, ETO, World War II," lecture, Air War College, Maxwell AFB, Ala., 20 September 1951.

32. Brig Gen Laurence S. Kuter, "Air-Ground Cooperation in North Africa," *Air Force Magazine*, July 1943, 5.

33. Memorandum by Brig Gen Ray E. Porter, Army chief of staff G-3, War Department General Staff, to Col Morton H. McKinnon, Col Ralph F. Stearley, and Lt Col Orin H. Moore, subject: Revision of Training Literature, 9 June 1943; Lt Col Orin H. Moore, evaluation of basic doctrine entitled "Command and Employment of Air Power," 8 May 1961; memorandum by Col Morton H. McKinnon to G-3, War Department General Staff, subject: Revision of Manuals, 18 June 1943; War Department Field Manual 100-20, *Command and Employment of Air Power*, 1943, 1–2; History, Air Support Department, Army Air Forces School of Applied Tactics, 5 November 1942–29 October 1943, 1:494–501.

34. Army Air Forces Training Aids Division, liaison bulletin no. 73, 26 October 1943, 1.

35. Greenfield, *Army Ground Forces and the Air-Ground Battle Team*, 47.

36. Anderson, "Development of US Strategic Air Doctrine, ETO, World War II"; Brig Gen Robert C. Candee, department commandant, Armed Forces Staff College, Norfolk, Va., to Gen George C. Kenney, commanding general, Air University, letter, 16 February 1951.

37. History, 4th Army Air Forces Base Unit, Training Aids Division, January 1939–December 1944.

38. History, Army Air Forces Board, pt. 1:47–51; Army Air Forces Regulation 20-20, *Organization: Army Air Forces Board*, 2 July 1943; Army Air Forces Regulation 20-21, *Organization: Office of the Director of Tactical Development*, 2 July 1943.

39. Brig Gen Hume Peabody to commanding general, Army Air Forces, letter, 16 August 1943.

40. Robert L. Stearns to Brig Gen Hume Peabody, letter, 24 May 1943.

41. History, Army Air Forces Tactical Center, 11–12; Army Air Forces Regulation 20-14, *Organization: Army Air Forces Tactical Center*, 8 October 1943.

42. History, Army Air Forces Board, pt. 1:54–57; Army Air Forces Regulation 20-20, *Organization: Army Air Forces Board*, 8 October 1943.

43. Col William F. McKee, deputy assistant chief of Air Staff, Operations, Commitments, and Requirements, office memo, subject: Authority and Operations of the Army Air Forces Board and Its Relationship to Headquarters Army Air Forces, 13 December 1943.

44. Army Air Forces Board Project (U) 3A, Staff Study of Initial Post-War Air Force, 29 April 1944; minutes of Army Air Forces Board, 2 January 1945.

45. History, Army Air Forces Board, pt. 1:84, 87–89, 95, pt. 2:56–60; Brig Gen Eugene L. Eubank to commanding general, Army Air Forces, Attn.: Army Air Forces Board control officer, letter, 1 July 1944; 1st ind., Maj Gen Howard A. Craig, assistant chief of Air Staff, Operations, Commitments, and Requirements, to president, Army Air Forces Board, 5 August 1944; Army Air Forces Board, *Air Operations Briefs* 1, no. 1 (30 November 1944).

46. Army Air Forces Board, Catalogue and Summaries of Army Air Forces Projects, 20 September 1945, vol. 2, item 2588B; minutes of the staff conference, Army Air Forces Board, 31 May 1944; daily diary, Operations, Commitments, and Requirements, Army Air Forces, 20 June 1944; Lt Col Orin H.

Moore to Lt Col W. D. Coleman, Office of Assistant Chief of Staff G-3, Armored Force, letter, 16 April 1943; Lt Col Orin H. Moore to Lt Gen Jacob L. Devers, North African theater of operations, US Army, letter, 28 March 1944; Lt Col Orin H. Moore to Col Robert M. Lee, Headquarters III, Tactical Air Command, letter, 23 May 1944; Greenfield, *Army Ground Forces and the Air-Ground Battle Team*, 116–17; memorandum by Brig Gen Mervin E. Gross, chief of requirements, assistant chief of Air Staff, Operations, Commitments, and Requirements, to Maj Gen Howard A. Craig, subject: RAF Doctrine, Tactics, and Techniques, 22 June 1944; memorandum by Brig Gen Byron E. Gates, chief, Management Control, Army Air Forces, to Maj Gen Howard A. Craig, subject: AAF Doctrine, Tactics, and Techniques, 1 July 1944; Col William F. McKee, acting assistant chief of Air Staff, Operations, Commitments, and Requirements, to president, Army Air Forces Board, letter, subject: Doctrine Publications, 8 July 1944; minutes of staff meeting, Army Air Forces Board, 17 August 1944; Army Air Forces Regulation 5-28, *Publications and Reproduction: Tactical Doctrinal Publications*, 7 February 1945.

47. Brig Gen Eugene L. Eubank to commanding general, Army Air Forces, Attn.: Army Air Forces Board Control Office, letter, subject: Activation of Field Manual Branch, Army Air Forces Board, 21 July 1944; 1st ind., Maj Gen Howard A. Craig to president, Army Air Forces Board, 2 September 1944; History, Army Air Forces Board, pt. 1:90–95; minutes, Army Air Forces Board, 27 June 1944, 28 September 1944, 26 October 1944; Army Air Forces Board, project no. 3189, *Manual on Tactics and Techniques of Troop Carrier Aviation*, 21 August 1945; Greenfield, *Army Ground Forces and the Air-Ground Battle Team*, 116–19, 131–33; War Department Training Circular 17, *Air-Ground Liaison*, 20 April 1945; War Department Training Circular 30, *Tactical Air Command: Organization and Employment*, 19 June 1945.

48. For the history of the Office of Scientific Research and Development, see Vannevar Bush, *Modern Arms and Free Men* (New York: Simon and Schuster, 1949) and James Phinney Baxter 3d, *Scientists against Time* (Boston: Little, Brown & Co., 1946); memorandum by Dr Edward L. Bowles to Secretary of War Robert P. Patterson, 5 May 1947; Col Fred C. Milner, Air Adjutant General, Army Air Forces, to commanding generals, all air forces, letter, subject: Operations Analysis, 24 October 1942.

49. History, Committee of Operations Analysts, 16 November 1942–29 September 1944, 1–15.

50. Col Fred C. Milner to commanding generals, all air forces, letter, subject: Operations Analysis, 24 October 1942; memorandum by Dr Edward L. Bowles, to Assistant Secretary of War Robert P. Patterson, 5 May 1947; Craven and Cate, *Plans and Early Operations*, 549; L. R. Brothers, chief of operations analysis, Army Air Forces, *Operations Analysis in World War II* (Philadelphia: Stephenson Bros., 1948), 1–2; Col W. B. Leach, chief, Operations Analysis Division, Army Air Forces, to Lt Col Philip Shepley, letter, subject: Post-War Plans – Operations Analysis, 8 February 1945.

51. The Adjutant General Office, War Department, to commanding generals, European theater of operations, Mediterranean theater of operations, China-Burma-India theater, Southwest Pacific area, and Pacific Ocean area, letters, subject: Establishment of Army Air Forces Evaluation Board, 29 June 1944; The Adjutant General Office, War Department, to commanding generals, European theater of operations, Mediterranean theater of operations, China-Burma-India theater, Southwest Pacific area, and Pacific Ocean area, letters, subject: Establishment of Army Air Forces Evaluation Board, 23 August 1944; Brig Gen Shepler W. Fitzgerald, president, Army Air Forces Evaluation Board, China-Burma-India theater, to commanding general, Army Air Forces, letter, subject: Army Air Forces Evaluation Board, India-Burma and China theaters, 25 January 1945; 4th ind., Brig Gen Patrick W. Timberlake, deputy chief of Air Staff, to Department of Army Air Forces Evaluation Board, India-Burma theater, 3 March 1945.

52. United States Strategic Bombing Survey (USSBS), *History (European)*, 1944–1945, 1–67.

53. Ibid., 68–400; Franklin D'Olier, report, subject: United States Strategic Bombing Survey, *European and Pacific War*, 22 May 1947.

54. USSBS, *History (Pacific)*, 1945–1946, 1–15.

55. Ibid., 16–226.

56. Mooney, *Organization of the Army Air Arm, 1935–1945*, 57–60.

IDEAS, CONCEPTS, DOCTRINE

57. History, Army Air Forces Board, pt. 1:95, 96C, 98–104.
58. Army Air Forces Board, Status and Summaries of Projects, 15 January 1946, projects Q4793 and Q4807; daily diary, Army Air Forces Board, 15 March 1946; War Department Field Manual 31-35, *Air Ground Operations*, 1946.
59. Bernard Brodie, "Douhet in Perspective," lecture, Air War College, Maxwell AFB, Ala., 6 November 1953.
60. House, *Military Establishment Appropriation Bill for 1947: Hearings before a Subcommittee of the Committee on Appropriations*, 79th Cong., 2d sess., 1946, 366–67.
61. Anderson, "Development of US Strategic Air Doctrine, ETO, World War II" and "Some Fundamentals of Strategic Thinking."
62. Gen Carl A. Spaatz, USAF, Retired, "If We Should Have to Fight Again," *Life*, 5 July 1948, 35.
63. Lt Col Joseph L. Dickman, "Douhet and the Future," *Air University Quarterly Review* 2, no. 1 (Summer 1948): 3–15.
64. Bernard Brodie, "The Heritage of Douhet," *Air University Quarterly Review* 6, no. 2 (Summer 1953): 126–27.
65. Spaatz, "If We Should Have to Fight Again," 35.
66. Senate, *Department of Armed Forces, Department of Military Security: Hearings before the Committee on Military Affairs*, 79th Cong., 1st sess., 1945, 233–34; Gen George C. Kenney, "Air Power and National Policy in the Past," lecture, Air War College, Maxwell AFB, Ala., 12 September 1957.
67. Senate, *Department of Armed Forces, Department of Military Security*, 77–78.
68. Ibid., 49–50.
69. Col George A. Lincoln, "Reaping the Fruits of Victory (Second Quebec, Yalta, Potsdam)," lecture, Air War College, Maxwell AFB, Ala., 30 January 1951; Col George A. Lincoln, "War Objectives and Their Impact on Military Objectives and Strategy," lecture, Air War College, Maxwell AFB, Ala., 14 April 1953.
70. Lt Gen Albert C. Wedemeyer, "Concept for Employment of Military Forces in Future War," lecture, Air War College, Maxwell AFB, Ala., 18 April 1952.
71. Maj Gen Haywood S. Hansell, USAF, Retired, "Muir S. Fairchild Memorial Lecture," Air War College, Maxwell AFB, Ala., 1 December 1964.
72. Cline, *Washington Command Post*, 215–18; notes on discussion with the Honorable Adolf A. Berle, 8 September 1953, in "History of Project Control, 1953–1954," doc. 24.
73. Wedemeyer, "Concept for Employment of Military Forces in Future War"; Maj Gen J. R. Deane, "International Conferences – Trident thru Cairo and Tehran," lecture, Air War College, Maxwell AFB, Ala., 10 September 1951; Col Cecil E. Combs, "The Relation of Strategic Air Offensive to Over-All Strategic Concepts," Air War College, Maxwell AFB, Ala., 18 February 1947.
74. House, *Military Establishment Appropriation Bill for 1948: Hearings before a Subcommittee of the Committee on Appropriations*, 80th Cong., 1st sess., 1947, 2–3.
75. Spaatz, "If We Should Have to Fight Again," 35.
76. Craven and Cate, *Torch to Pointblank*, 274–307; Sir Charles Webster and Noble Frankland, *The Strategic Air Offensive Against Germany, 1939–1945*, vol. 2, *Endeavour* (London: Her Majesty's Stationery Office, 1961), 10–21; Col David A. Burchinal, "Ideas are Weapons," *Air University Quarterly Review* 3, no. 2 (Fall 1949): 2–3; Lt Gen Laurence S. Kuter, "An Air Perspective in the Jetomic Age," *Air University Quarterly Review* 8, no. 2 (Spring 1956): 110–14.
77. Craven and Cate, *Torch to Pointblank*, 733–56, and *Argument to V-E Day*, 57, 319–22.
78. Anderson, "Development of US Strategic Air Doctrine, ETO, World War II"; interview with Gen Carl A. Spaatz by Brig Gen Noel F. Parrish and Dr Alfred Goldberg, 21 February 1962.
79. Army Air Forces Statistical Digest, World War II, 4–7, 154–56.
80. Webster and Frankland, *The Strategic Air Offensive Against Germany, 1939–1945*, 4:428.
81. *United States Strategic Bombing Survey: Over-All Report (European War)*, 10.
82. Kuter, "An Air Perspective in the Jetomic Age," 110–14; Col H. G. Montgomery, "Weapons Evolution and Air Power," lecture, Air War College, Maxwell AFB, Ala., October 1953; Col James F.

Whisenand, "Evaluation of Weapons Systems and Past Military Experience," lecture, Air War College, Maxwell AFB, Ala., 16 March 1950.

83. Anderson, "Development of US Strategic Air Doctrine, ETO, World War II"; Arnold, *Global Mission*, 277.

84. Anderson, "Development of US Strategic Air Doctrine, ETO, World War II."

85. Bernard Boylan, *Development of the Long-Range Escort Fighter*, USAF historical study 136 (Maxwell AFB, Ala.: Research Studies Institute, 1955), 58–72; Webster and Frankland, *The Strategic Air Offensive Against Germany, 1939–1945*, 4:153–54.

86. Boylan, *Development of the Long-Range Escort Fighter*, 73–102; Col R. D. Hughes, Office of Assistant Chief of Staff A-5, Eighth Air Force, to commanding general, Eighth Air Force, letter, subject: Relative Priority of the German Aircraft Industry as a Target, 23 March 1943.

87. Boylan, *Development of the Long-Range Escort Fighter*, 73–102; Webster and Frankland, *The Strategic Air Offensive Against Germany, 1939–1945*, 4:158–60.

88. Maj Gen Haywood S. Hansell, "Development of Bombing Operations," lecture, Air War College, Maxwell AFB, Ala., 16 February 1951; Boylan, *Development of the Long-Range Escort Fighter*, 104–61.

89. Craven and Cate, *The Army Air Forces in World War II*, 7 vols., *Europe: Argument to V-E Day*, vol. 3 (Chicago: University of Chicago Press, 1949), 8–29.

90. Ibid., 3:30–36; Anderson, "Development of US Strategic Air Doctrine, ETO, World War II"; Eighth Air Force, Tactical Development, August 1942–May 1945, 50–52.

91. *United States Strategic Bombing Survey: Summary Report (European War)*, 16.

92. Craven and Cate, *Torch to Pointblank*, 705.

93. House, *The National Defense Program—Unification and Strategy: Hearings before the Committee on Armed Services*, 81st Cong., 1st sess., 1949, 457, 464–65, 478, 511.

94. House, *Department of Defense Appropriations for 1964: Hearings before a Subcommittee of the Committee on Appropriations*, 88th Cong., 1st sess., 1963, pt. 2:521–22; House, *Department of Defense Appropriations for 1965: Hearings before a Subcommittee of the Committee on Appropriations*, 88th Cong., 2d sess., 1964, pt. 4:516–18; History, 305th Bombardment Group, March 1942–January 1944.

95. Flak Section, Headquarters Ninth Air Force (Adv.), Flak Facts, A Brief History of Flak and Flak Intelligence in the Ninth Air Force, 9 May 1945, 31–33.

96. Ibid., 1–30.

97. United States Strategic Air Force, Army chief of staff A-2, minutes of Flak Conference held in London, 1–11 June 1945; Eighth Air Force, Tactical Development, 87–89; House, *Hearings on Military Posture and H.R. 2440 before the Committee on Armed Services*, 88th Cong., 1st sess., 1963, 1185–86.

98. Army Air Forces Statistical Digest, World War II, 221, 255; Senate, *Fiscal Year 1964 Military Procurement Authorization: Hearings before the Committee on Armed Services*, 88th Cong., 1st sess., 1963, 948–49.

99. Air Marshal Sir Robert Saundby, Royal Air Force, "British Strategic Bombing," lecture, Air War College, Maxwell AFB, Ala., 19 February 1951; *United States Strategic Bombing Survey: Summary Report (European War)*, 2.

100. Col J. H. DuRussy, "Selection of Target Systems and Targets," lecture, Air War College, Maxwell AFB, Ala., 18 February 1947.

101. History, Committee of Operations Analysts, 16 November 1942–29 September 1944; Report of Committee of Operations Analysts, 8 March 1943; J. T. Lowe, "Strategic Vulnerability," lecture, Air War College, Maxwell AFB, Ala., 6 April 1950.

102. *United States Strategic Bombing Survey: Summary Report (European War)*, 5–6.

103. Ibid., 8–10, 12–16; *United States Strategic Bombing Survey, Over-All Report (European War)*, 39.

104. Craven and Cate, *The Army Air Forces in World War II*, 7 vols., *The Pacific: Guadalcanal to Saipan*, vol. 4 (Chicago: University of Chicago Press, 1950), 194–96.

105. Maj Gen Haywood S. Hansell, "Offensive Air Operations Against Japan," lecture, Air War College, Maxwell AFB, Ala., 27 January 1953.

106. Ibid.; Craven and Cate, *The Army Air Forces in World War II*, 7 vols., *The Pacific: Matterhorn to Nagasaki*, vol. 5 (Chicago: University of Chicago Press, 1953), 3–29; Report of the Committee of Operations Analysts, 11 November 1943.

107. Craven and Cate, *Guadalcanal to Saipan*, 550–55, and *Matterhorn to Nagasaki*, 28–32; Hansell, "Offensive Air Operations Against Japan."

108. Arnold, *Global Mission*, 347–48.

109. Craven and Cate, *Matterhorn to Nagasaki*, 33–41; Hansell, "Offensive Air Operations Against Japan"; Col J. A. Johnson, "The USAF Prepares for Strategic Air Operations," lecture, Royal Air Force Staff College, 1 June 1954.

110. Brig Gen John B. Montgomery, "The Development of US Strategic Air Doctrine in the Pacific," lecture, Air War College, Maxwell AFB, Ala., 21 September 1951; Hansell, "Offensive Air Operations Against Japan"; *United States Strategic Bombing Survey: Summary Report (Pacific War)*, 14–15.

111. Craven and Cate, *Matterhorn to Nagasaki*, 115–75; Montgomery, "The Development of US Strategic Air Doctrine in the Pacific."

112. Hansell, "Offensive Air Operations Against Japan"; Craven and Cate, *Matterhorn to Nagasaki*, 536–45.

113. Revised Report of Committee of Operations Analysts on Economic Targets in the Far East, 10 October 1944; Maj Gen Laurence S. Kuter, assistant chief of Air Staff, Plans, Army Air Forces, to commanding general, Twentieth Air Force, letter, subject: Incendiary Bombing of Simulated Japanese Dwellings, 24 April 1944; Army Air Forces Board, project no. 3241C, Test to Determine the Proper Ratio and Technique for Employment of Incendiary and H. E. Bombs Against Japanese Type Structures, 26 June 1944; Army Air Forces Board, project no. 3569A, Incendiary Attack on Japanese Cities, 3 October 1944.

114. Craven and Cate, *Matterhorn to Nagasaki*, 546–76; Hansell, "Offensive Air Operations Against Japan"; USSBS, *Japanese Aircraft Industry*, 31–36.

115. Craven and Cate, *Matterhorn to Nagasaki*, 577–98; *United States Strategic Bombing Survey, The Strategic Air Operations of Very Heavy Bombardment in the War against Japan (Twentieth Air Force)*, 19–20.

116. Craven and Cate, *Matterhorn to Nagasaki*, 608–18; House, *Investigation of the B-36 Bomber Program: Hearings before the Committee on Armed Services*, 81st Cong., 1st sess., 1949, 161; Hansell, "Offensive Air Operations Against Japan."

117. Craven and Cate, *Matterhorn to Nagasaki*, 627–35; USSBS, *The Strategic Air Operation of Very Heavy Bombardment in the War against Japan*, 12–15; House, *Military Establishment Appropriation Bill for 1947*, 79th Cong., 2d sess., 1946, 443–44.

118. USSBS, *The Strategic Air Operation of Very Heavy Bombardment in the War against Japan*, 7, 12–18; Senate, *Military Situation in the Far East: Hearings before the Committee on Armed Services and the Committee on Foreign Relations*, 82d Cong., 1st sess., 1951, 3111; Arnold, *Global Mission*, 564; House, *Investigation of the B-36 Bomber Program*, 151.

119. USSBS, *Japan's Struggle to End the War*, 5–9.

120. Craven and Cate, *Matterhorn to Nagasaki*, 676–89.

121. Ibid.

122. USSBS, *The Strategic Air Operation of Very Heavy Bombardment in the War against Japan*, 7; House, *Military Establishment Appropriation Bill for 1947*, 79th Cong., 2d sess., 1946, 443–44; Seventh Fighter Command Mission Reports, 24–25 July 1945.

123. Craven and Cate, *Matterhorn to Nagasaki*, 700–2, 704–35; interview with Spaatz by Parrish and Goldberg, 21 February 1962; USSBS, *Japan's Struggle to End the War*, 8–13.

124. Spaatz interview, 21 February 1962.

125. Gen Henry H. Arnold, *Third Report of the Commanding General of the Army Air Forces to the Secretary of War*, 12 November 1945, 36 (hereafter cited as *Third Report to the Secretary of War*).

126. USSBS, *Japan's Struggle to End the War*, 13.

127. Air Corps Tactical School, *Air Force*, pt. 1, *Character and Strategy of Air Power*, 1 December 1935, 1.
128. Col Sidney A. Ofsthun, "Air Power," lecture, Air Command and Staff School, Maxwell AFB, Ala., 11 September 1946.
129. Alexander P. de Seversky, *Victory through Air Power* (New York: Simon and Schuster, 1942), 7–8, 136, 139; de Seversky, "Evaluation of the Air Weapon," lecture, Air War College, Maxwell AFB, Ala., 19 November 1953.
130. Arnold, *Third Report to the Secretary of War*, 61.
131. Gen Carl A. Spaatz, "Faith in Air Power," *Air Force Magazine*, November 1947, 19.
132. *Report of the Congressional Aviation Policy Board, National Aviation Policy, 1 March 1948*, 86th Cong., 2d sess., 1960, 3–4.
133. Arnold, *Third Report to the Secretary of War*, 61; House, *The National Defense Program—Unification and Strategy*, 408.
134. Gen Henry H. Arnold, *Second Report of the Commanding General of the Army Air Forces to the Secretary of War*, 27 February 1945, 93–95 (hereafter cited as *Second Report to the Secretary of War*).
135. Ofsthun, "Air Power."
136. Senate, *Department of Armed Forces, Department of Military Security*, 11.
137. Robert P. Patterson, "Decision or Disaster," *Air Force Magazine*, January 1947, 64; "U.S. President's Air Policy Commission," unclassified testimony before the President's Air Policy Commission (Washington, D.C.: n.p., 1 December 1947), 6:2412.
138. Senate, *Department of Armed Forces, Department of Military Security*, 50.
139. Ibid., 345–55.
140. House, *Military Establishment Appropriation Bill for 1948*, 2.
141. "U.S. President's Air Policy Commission," 6:2730.
142. Lt Gen J. Lawton Collins, "The Role of the Army in Future Warfare," lecture, Air War College, Maxwell AFB, Ala., 5 October 1948.
143. Senate, *Department of Armed Forces, Department of Military Security*, 24–25.
144. Ibid., 396.
145. Maj Gen Follett Bradley to editor, *New York Times*, letter, 9 April 1944.
146. Senate, *Department of Armed Forces, Department of Military Security*, 73.
147. Arnold, *Third Report to the Secretary of War*, 62.
148. Senate, *Department of Armed Forces, Department of Military Security*, 290–94.
149. "U.S. President's Air Policy Commission," 6:2413.
150. Senate, *Department of Armed Forces, Department of Military Security*, 313.
151. House, *The National Defense Program—Unification and Strategy*, 522.
152. House, *Military Establishment Appropriation Bill for 1948*, 619; House, *Investigation of the B-36 Bomber Program*, 189.
153. Gen Hoyt S. Vandenberg, "Under the A-Bomb Shield," *Air Force Magazine*, October 1952, 39.
154. De Seversky, *Victory through Air Power*, 26, 130.
155. *United States Strategic Bombing Survey: Summary Report (European War)*, 16.
156. Senate, *Department of Armed Forces, Department of Military Security*, 71.
157. Ibid., 290–91.
158. Spaatz, "Faith in Air Power," 19.
159. Col Dale O. Smith and Maj Gen John DeF. Barker, "Air Power Indivisible," *Air University Quarterly Review* 4, no. 2 (Fall 1950): 9.
160. "U.S. President's Air Policy Commission," 6:2413.
161. Lt Gen Manton S. Eddy, "Relationship of Land Power to Air Power," lecture, Air War College, Maxwell AFB, Ala., 1 March 1949.
162. "General Bradley Says," *Air Force Magazine*, December 1951, 19.
163. USSBS, Air *Campaigns of the Pacific War*, 65–66.
164. Maj Gen Orvil A. Anderson, "Air Warfare," lecture, Air Command and Staff School, Maxwell AFB, Ala., 14 June 1949.

IDEAS, CONCEPTS, DOCTRINE

165. Col David A. Burchinal, "Ideas Are Weapons," *Air University Quarterly Review* 3, no. 2 (Fall 1949): 3–12.

166. Alexander P. de Seversky, "New Concepts of Air Power," lecture, Army War College, Carlisle Barracks, Pa., 18 March 1952.

167. Memorandum by Col Philip D. Cole to Col Reuben C. Moffat, chief, Postwar Plans Division, subject: A Realistic Conception of a Post-War Air Force, 22 August 1945.

168. Senate, *Department of Armed Forces, Department of Military Security*, 360.

169. Finney, "The Development of Tactical Air Doctrine in the U.S. Air Force, 1917–1951," 33–39; Greenfield, *Army Ground Forces and the Air-Ground Battle Team*, 80–81.

170. Finney, "The Development of Tactical Air Doctrine in the U.S. Air Force, 1917–1951"; Futrell, *Command of Observation Aviation*, 28.

171. Walter Bedell Smith, *Eisenhower's Six Great Decisions: Europe 1944–45* (New York: Longmans, Green and Co., 1956), 144.

172. Army Air Forces Evaluation Board, European theater of operations, "The Effectiveness of Third Phase Tactical Air Operations in The European Theater, 5 May 1944–8 May 1945," 1–2, 91–94, 175–91.

173. Flak Section, Headquarters Ninth Air Force (Adv.), Flak Facts, 108.

174. Minutes of Flak Conference, United States Strategic Air Forces, 1–11 June 1945.

175. Finney, "The Development of the Tactical Air Doctrine in the U.S. Air Force, 1917–1951," 53–62.

176. Ibid., 62–65; Historical Division, US Marine Corps, *Saipan: The Beginning of the End* (Washington, D.C.: Government Printing Office, 1950), 250; House, *Department of Defense Appropriations for 1964: Hearings before the Subcommittee of the Committee on Appropriations*, 88th Cong., 1st sess., 1963, pt. 2:383; House, *The National Defense Program—Unification and Strategy*, 193–200.

177. Memorandum by General of the Army Dwight D. Eisenhower, chief of staff, US Army, to secretary of defense, subject: Tactical Air Support, 3 November 1947.

178. House, *Sundry Legislation Affecting the Naval and Military Establishments: Hearings before the Committee on Armed Services*, 85th Cong., 1st sess., 1957, 1:537–41.

179. Gen Mark W. Clark, *Calculated Risk* (New York: Harper & Bros., 1950), 161.

180. Kent R. Greenfield, *The Historian and the Army* (New Brunswick, N.J.: Rutgers University Press, 1954), 84–85.

181. Gen Omar N. Bradley, *A Soldier's Story* (New York: Henry Holt and Co., 1951), 337.

182. Memorandum by Col S. F. Giffin, executive, Requirements Division, assistant chief of Air Staff, Operations, Commitments, and Requirements, subject: Future Trends in Air Fighting, 25 November 1944; Lt Gen Elwood R. Quesada, "Tactical Air Power," *Air University Quarterly Review* 1, no. 4 (Spring 1948): 44–45.

183. Maj Gen Robert M. Webster, "Planning War Use of Air Transportation," lecture, National War College, Washington, D.C., 10 February 1947.

184. Genevieve Brown, "Development of Transport Airplanes and Air Transport Equipment" (Wright Field, Ohio: Air Tactical Service Command, 1946), 34–283; Army Air Forces Statistical Digest, World War II, 3, 7, 135; AWPD-1, tabs. 12 and 13.

185. Memorandum by Lt Col George C. Richardson, acting assistant chief of Air Staff, Plans, Air Transport Command, to assistant chief of Air Staff, Army Air Forces, subject: Post-War Air Force, 6 February 1944.

186. Lt Col F. H. Colby, Army Air Forces liaison officer, to the air engineer, assistant chief of Air Staff (ACAS-4), letter, subject: Troop Carrier Operations in World War II, 5 May 1947; Lt Gen Lewis H. Brereton, "The Airborne Army," lecture, Air War College, Maxwell AFB, Ala., 19 February 1947.

187. Lt Col Lewis H. Brereton, "Airborne Operations, World War II," lecture, Air War College, Maxwell AFB, Ala., 10 October 1951; Lt Col F. H. Colby to air engineer, letter, 5 May 1947.

188. Arnold, *Second Report to the Secretary of War*, 94–95; Brig Gen William D. Old, commanding general, I Troop Carrier Command, to Maj Gen Laurence S. Kuter, assistant chief of Air Staff, Plans,

Army Air Forces, letter, 7 November 1944; memorandum by Col Robert O. Cork to Col Reuben C. Moffat, subject: Troop Carrier Aviation, 5 April 1945; Gen Henry H. Arnold to Lt Gen Harold L. George, commanding general, Air Transport Command, letter, 5 December 1945; Lt Gen Ira C. Eaker, deputy commanding general, Army Air Forces, to assistant chief of Air Staff, Operations, Commitments, and Requirements (ACAS-4) and assistant chief of Air Staff, Plans (ACAS-5), R&R sheet, subject: Future Plans for Air Transport Command, 10 December 1945.

189. Arnold, *Third Report to the Secretary of War*, 62, 63.

Maj Gen Harold George, chief, Army Air Forces Air War Plans Division.

Maj Gen Haywood Hansell.

Maj Gen Orvil A. Anderson, commandant, Air War College, 1946–50.

Gen Muir S. Fairchild, assistant chief, Air Corps, 1941–42, and commander, Air University, 1946–48.

Gen Carl Spaatz, commanding general, Eighth Air Force, 1942–44; commanding general, United States Strategic Air Forces, 1944–46; commanding general, US Air Force, 1947–48.

Lt Gen Ira Eaker, commanding general, Eighth Air Force during World War II.

Carl de Seversky, author of Victory through Air Power.

Lt Gen Elwood R. Quesada, commanding general, IX Tactical Air Command, 1944–45; deputy chief of staff, Intelligence, 1945–46.

CHAPTER 5

THE AIR FORCE IN NATIONAL DEFENSE: ORGANIZATION AND STRATEGY, 1944–49

"Those of us who have seen this war fought . . . realize that there is no place in modern war for a separate air force, for a separate army, or for a separate navy," Brig Gen Haywood S. Hansell told the House Select Committee on Post-War Military Policy in March 1944. "The Army Air Forces (AAF) advocate, and strongly recommend," he continued, "the integration of the nation's fighting forces into a single unified organization. Hence, our conviction demands unity rather than separation."[1] The Army's air arm had traditionally sought a separate air force, but the experience of World War II had caused its leaders to believe that the nation needed integrated rather than separate armed services. The War Department, long a traditional opponent of a separate air force, now became the main driving force for armed service unification. Only the Navy, whose top-ranking officers proposed to General Arnold that AAF strategic bombardment ought to be joined with naval air forces to provide a national striking force, was going to oppose a close unification of the armed services.[2]

Armed Service Unification and the Air Force

As a background policy for the beginning of postwar planning, Gen Henry H. Arnold approved a statement on 25 February 1944 that advocated establishing a single secretary of war with four assistant secretaries heading the ground forces, the air forces, the naval forces, and a combined bureau of war resources. The plan visualized a compact general staff, directed by a single chief of staff to the president and a supreme war council consisting of the military commanders of the four major services that would be presided over by the single chief. Arnold's plan assumed that the air force would be coequal with the other services and would possess its own air commander and air general staff. The air force would include "all military aviation except shipborne units operating with the Navy, and those artillery-control and 'liaison' units operating with the Army."[3] In regard to the assigning of organic aviation to the Army, the Army Air Forces policy, announced on 10 October 1944, favored such assignments only if the aircraft would be put to sustained use; only if the separation of such aircraft from the mass of airpower would not seriously reduce that power; only if the function to be performed would not duplicate functions already being performed by AAF units; and only if no need would arise for separate and extensive airdrome, maintenance, or training facilities.[4] On 1 October 1945 General Arnold officially informed his subordinate commanders that he favored a department of armed forces under a military commander "who will command the Army, the Navy, and the Air Force and any combined task forces in existence."[5]

"The greatest lesson of this war," Arnold stated in his last report to the secretary of war on 12 November 1945, "has been the extent to which air, land, and sea operations can and must be coordinated by joint planning and unified command." Arnold, therefore, called for the establishing of "one integrated, balanced United States military organization that will establish, develop, maintain, and direct at the minimum expense the forces ... required for peace enforcement and for national security with the capability for the rapid expansion in case of all-out war." Arnold wished to retain the Joint Chiefs of Staff, headed by a chief of staff reporting directly to the president. He also emphasized that a permanent national intelligence organization would be essential to the future conduct of strategic air warfare.[6] Gen Carl A. Spaatz, who would assume command of the Army Air Forces on 1 March 1946, told the Senate Committee on Military Affairs that "unity of direction" and "equality for the Air Force which will insure unification of our air potential" were "absolute imperatives which stem from the lessons of this last war."[7] On 24 October 1946 Spaatz informed his subordinate commanders that the Army Air Forces "supports without reservation" the War Department position on unification, which comprehended a single secretary heading a single department of national defense with three branches of equal standing — army, navy, and air.[8]

In the three years that defense unification was being studied and debated, the Navy posed different objections to plans that were offered and submitted counterproposals to each plan. As a matter of continuing policy, the Navy objected to the high degree of consolidation inherent in the War Department plan for a single chief of staff for the armed forces. The Navy also desired guarantees that would preserve naval aviation and the Marine Corps, together with its integral aviation. On a visit to the Pacific in the winter of 1944–45, a Joint Chiefs of Staff study committee headed by Adm James O. Richardson found senior naval officers not averse to unification. Rear Adm Forrest P. Sherman, who was Adm Chester W. Nimitz's chief planner, later explained, however, that a general change in feeling toward unification occurred in the spring of 1945. Admiral Sherman said that establishing the independent Twentieth Air Force and deciding to divide the command of American Army and Navy forces between Douglas MacArthur and Nimitz "disrupted unified command in the Pacific and disillusioned naval officers who had given support to theories of a single department." Sherman also recalled that Gen George C. Marshall had told him in September 1944 that he would not tolerate further command of Army troops by Marine officers.[9]

In its report on 11 April 1945 Admiral Richardson's special committee proposed the organization of a department of armed forces, a single commander of the armed forces, and a joint staff, all to be superimposed on coordinate army, navy, and air branches. It also proposed that the secretary of the armed forces was to serve as a member of the Joint Chiefs of Staff and that both the Army and Navy would retain their special aviation components. Rather than merely oppose unification, Secretary of the Navy James V. Forrestal asked Ferdinand Eberstadt in June 1945 to head a study on national defense organization. When completed in September 1945, the Eberstadt report recommended that three coequal departments of war, navy, and air be recognized and that coordination between them would be achieved by the statutory establishment of the Joint Chiefs of Staff, a national security resources board, and a military munitions board. It recommended the establishment of a national security council, which would correlate the military and foreign policy of the United States.[10]

First presented to the public in October by Lt Gen J. Lawton Collins, the War Department's reorganization plan provided for a department of armed forces, a chief of staff of the armed forces (who would provide guidance to coequal army, navy, and air force chiefs), and a director of common supply and hospitalization. The chief of staff of the armed forces and a chief of staff to the president together with the chiefs of the three coequal branches would comprise the Joint Chiefs of Staff. On 19 December 1945 President Harry S Truman proposed to Congress a defense reorganization that made some concessions to the Eberstadt report but drew most heavily on the proposals made by Admiral Richardson's special committee and the War Department's plan. Under the president's proposal, the Navy would retain its carrier- and water-based air and the Marine Corps. While Congress prepared for hearings, Truman established the National Intelligence Authority by executive order on 22 January 1946. In his judgment, all of the services had agreed that there was a need for the coordination of foreign intelligence activities.[11]

During 1946 lengthy hearings before congressional committees and numerous Army-Navy conferences enabled the services to develop their respective positions and determine what Congress was likely to approve in the way of armed service reorganization. Speaking with candor, Adm Richmond K. Turner stated the Navy's opposition to unification: "Because the Navy has had and should retain in the future its position as the first line of military security for the United States, I believe the Navy will never willingly agree to a consolidation of national military forces in any manner that will silence the Navy's voice in military affairs or materially restrict its present responsibilities." Gen Alexander A. Vandegrift, commandant of the Marine Corps, feared that "the single Secretary for Common Defense and the all-powerful National Chief of Staff are entirely free either to abolish the Marine Corps outright or to divest it of all its vital functions." Adm John H. Towers bluntly charged that the new air force meant to take over naval aviation, saying in part: "I fear — and I have good reason to fear — that the Army Air Force advocates of a separate air force have well established in mind the plan, upon realization of a separate service, to absorb naval aviation. . . . Approximately 40 percent of our postwar Navy is aviation. Its loss would be completely disastrous to the Navy." On

15 May 1946, Sen David I. Walsh and Rep Carl Vinson informed Secretary Forrestal that Congress was not likely to approve the creation of one department of defense under the administration of a single secretary, the appointment of a single supreme commander of the armed forces, a curtailment of the Marine Corps, a transfer of vital naval aviation functions to a separate air force, or the elimination of the responsibilities of the secretaries of war and Navy to initiate and support their budgets before Congress.[12]

Held during May 1946, a series of conferences between Forrestal and Secretary of War Robert P. Patterson developed fundamental points of disagreement between the Navy and Army. The War Department position on aviation had been suggested by Arnold's testimony before the Senate Committee on Military Affairs in October 1945. Arnold had said: "I think there is a definite place for the air arm of the fleet, to work in conjunction with the fleet. . . . I do not think that the flat-top planes have the power to deliver the blows that are necessary for our primary air force." In May 1946 the War Department thought that the separate air force should develop and operate all military air resources except for carrier- and water-based aircraft deemed essential for Navy and Marine Corps operations and for such land-type aircraft as were necessary for the internal administration of naval affairs, for training, or for air transportation over routes of sole interest to naval forces where such requirements could not be met by normal air transport facilities. The Army Air Forces was already performing long-range reconnaissance, and the War Department proposed that it could provide such reconnaissance to the Navy and also meet surveillance requirements for antisubmarine warfare. As for the Marine Corps, the War Department agreed on the requirement for a "balanced fleet marine force including its supporting air component," but it wished to limit the marines to service with the fleet in connection with the seizure of enemy positions not involving sustained land fighting and with phases of amphibious warfare relating to waterborne aspects of landing operations. In rebuttal to these positions, the Navy insisted that to perform fleet reconnaissance, conduct antisubmarine warfare, and protect ocean shipping its aviation needs included a certain number of land-based planes completely under naval control and manned by naval personnel trained in naval warfare. The Navy insisted that the fleet marine force should participate with the fleet without limitations in the seizure or defense of advanced naval bases, in the conduct of limited land operations, and in amphibious warfare.[13]

In a letter to Patterson and Forrestal on 15 June 1946, President Truman agreed to eliminate the single armed service chief of staff, but he insisted that there would be a single department of defense with coequal army, navy, and air force branches. The president stated that naval aviation should be given every "opportunity to develop its maximum usefulness." He believed, however, that land-based planes for long-range reconnaissance, antisubmarine warfare, and protection of shipping should be manned by air force personnel. Truman approved Forrestal's plan for the continued functioning of the Marine Corps. Finally, the president expressed a hope that unification legislation might be speedily enacted on the basis of the Army-Navy agreements as supplemented by his decisions on the controversial matters. Congress refused to be prodded and took no substantial action on the desired unification legislation during the remainder of 1946.[14] Acting again by executive order, Truman vested in the chairman of the Army and Navy Munitions Board the final authority over military procurement, and on 17 October he established the President's Scientific Research Board to supervise military research and development activities.[15]

At an informal conference in his home early in November 1946, Secretary Forrestal argued that the Army and Navy must make some new efforts to arrive at a mutually acceptable unification plan. According to agreement, Maj Gen Lauris Norstad, who was serving as the director of plans and operations on the War Department General Staff, and Vice Adm Forrest P. Sherman, now the deputy chief of naval operations, would work together to secure agreements. As a first effort Norstad and Sherman sought to draft a directive that would provide uniform instructions to unified theater commanders, who would be charged with operations of land, naval, and air forces. In 1941 and 1942 Army and Navy planners had debated procedures for the command of joint operations without reaching final conclusions. One proposal was that a theater commander should depend on his subordinate air, ground, and naval commanders for advice and could have a staff comprising men from his own service. A second concept was that a theater commander ought to have a joint staff of officers from all services, who, after collaboration with subordinate service commanders, would draw up plans that would secure unity of action while leaving a good degree of freedom to the subordinate commanders. Of all the theater commanders of World War II, only Admiral Nimitz organized and used a joint staff. General MacArthur's staff was entirely composed of Army officers. In Europe, although General Eisenhower's staff had officers from the several services, it was, nevertheless, dominated by Army and AAF officers. And, even though he organized theater air and naval commands, Eisenhower chose to command the theater ground forces personally and did not establish a theater ground command. Despite the fact that they recognized that they could not make rigid rules for the exercise of unified command in the theaters, Norstad and Sherman recommended that each theater commander employ a joint staff. The Joint Chiefs of Staff accepted this proposal and issued a directive on 14 December 1946 that required unified commanders to establish "a joint staff with appropriate members from the various components of the services under this command in key positions of responsibility."[16]

Following the agreement on unified theater command staffs, Norstad and Sherman resumed consideration of the higher level problems of armed service unification. They forwarded their agreements on these subjects to President Truman on 16 January 1947 and continued to work in the president's office where a draft of a proposed national security act was drawn up and submitted to Congress on 27 February. In the late spring, Senate and House committees held hearings

IDEAS, CONCEPTS, DOCTRINE

and made amendments to the bill, many of them designed to prevent any change in the status of the Marine Corps or naval aviation. President Truman signed the National Security Act on 26 July 1947.[17]

The National Security Act of 1947 created the National Military Establishment and made substantial changes in the nation's defense organization to include a separate Air Force, but the act represented federalization rather than unification of the armed services. To coordinate national security efforts, the act established the National Security Council, which would advise the president on the integration of domestic, foreign, and military policies. The Central Intelligence Agency, which superseded all national intelligence authority, would coordinate all governmental intelligence activities and report to the National Security Council. The National Security Resources Board was established to advise the president concerning the coordination of military, industrial, and civilian mobilization problems. Within the National Military Establishment, the secretary of defense was authorized to establish general policies and programs, exercise general direction, take steps to eliminate duplication, and to supervise and coordinate the budget estimates of the departments of Army, Navy, and Air Force. Each service secretary, however, was accorded direct access to the president and to the director of the budget. The law also provided that each department should be administered as an individual executive department. With its membership to comprise the chiefs of staff of the Army and the Air Force, the chief of naval operations, and the chief of staff to the president, the Joint Chiefs of Staff were provided a joint staff of not more than 100 officers and was charged principally "to prepare strategic plans and to provide for the strategic direction of the military forces." The act also provided for the organization of a Munitions Board and a Research and Development Board within the National Defense Establishment.[18]

On the same day that he signed the National Security Act of 1947, President Truman nominated James Forrestal as the first secretary of defense and issued an executive order prescribing the functions of the several armed forces. Guarantees for the unchanged status of the Marine Corps and for land-based naval aviation already had been added to the basic law. But Truman's executive order charged the United States Air Force to organize, train, and equip air forces for air operations including joint operations; to gain and maintain general air superiority; to establish local air superiority where and as required; to develop a strategic air force and conduct strategic air reconnaissance operations; to provide airlift and support for airborne operations; to furnish air support to land and naval forces including support of occupation forces; and to provide air transport for the armed forces except as provided by the Navy for its own use.[19]

Key West Agreements on Roles and Missions

Speaking on 26 July 1947, retired Lt Gen James H. Doolittle exclaimed: "This is the day Billy Mitchell dreamed of." Toward the end of a transition period provided in the law, James Forrestal assumed the duties of secretary of defense on 17 September 1947 and on 18 September 1947 W. Stuart Symington took the oath of office as the first secretary of the Department of the Air Force. Although it hailed the National Security Act of 1947 as a substantial achievement, *Air Force Magazine*, voicing the sentiments of the new Air Force Association, pointed out that important matters remained to be resolved:

> Still to be decided is the irritating question of where naval air authority ends and Air Force responsibility begins.... Still to come are the increased economies which can only be achieved through the avoidance of duplication, multiple use of equipment, and a combined training program — and the even greater economies which will be realized only when it is possible to draw on one air force for the requirements of all other services.[20]

It is difficult to determine from available records exactly what opinions Air Force leaders held on the matter of integrating all military aviation into the United States Air Force. Even though his opinion was not official, Alexander P. de Seversky had suggested in *Victory through Air Power* that naval aircraft carriers would become unnecessary in view of the fact that "ultimately war in the skies will be conducted from the home grounds, with everything in between turned into a no-man's land." He also had argued that for purely aerodynamic and engineering reasons, naval carrier-based aircraft, which had to be designed to operate from the restricted areas of carrier flight decks, would always be inferior in performance to land-based aircraft of similar types.[21] On the basis of wartime lessons that carrier aircraft should be jet powered and able to carry heavier bombs, the Navy had initiated design of a 65,000-ton aircraft carrier in 1945; construction of the supercarrier, to be known as the CVA-58 or the USS *United States*, was begun prior to unification. The Navy conceived that the prototype flush-deck CVA-58 would be employed in task group, along with a *Midway*-class (CVB) carrier, two *Essex*-class (CV) carriers, and supporting and screening ships. Launching while the task group was still some 500 to 600 miles at sea, the CVA-58's long-range aircraft would neutralize hostile air bases ashore, permitting the task group to run within 200 miles of an enemy coast and launch its strike aircraft to accomplish naval missions.[22]

Shortly after he took office as secretary of defense, Forrestal remarked that the Navy believed that the Air Force wanted to get control of all military aviation, while the Air Force believed that the Navy was trying to encroach upon the strategic air prerogatives of the Air Force.[23] On 1 March 1948 the Joint Congressional Aviation Policy Board reported that there were basic differences of opinion between the Air Force and the Navy as to the mission of naval aviation set forth in Truman's executive order and in the provisions of the National Security Act of 1947. "As an example," the board reported, "the Navy interprets the law to permit it to develop any type of weapon and to base its plans and requirements on the utilization of any weapon. The Navy contends that it is complying with the law in disregarding the executive order on this point because the law and executive order are in conflict."[24]

Secretary Forrestal told Gen Omar N. Bradley, shortly after the latter became Army chief of staff in February 1948, that the large aircraft carrier had already been approved and would be built.[25] Forrestal, nevertheless, concluded that the time had come to decide "who will do what with what." Hence, he assembled the Joint Chiefs of Staff at Key West, Florida, on 11 March 1948 to thrash out roles and missions. As basic guidance, Forrestal demanded that the three services each recognize the need for mutual support of each other's legal missions. According to Forrestal, the Joint Chiefs reached basic agreement that the Navy would proceed with the developments of weapons that it considered essential to its functions — including the 65,000-ton aircraft carrier and nuclear bombs that could be transported on naval aircraft — provided that the Navy would not develop a separate strategic air force. The Air Force recognized the right and need for the Navy to participate in an all-out air campaign and to attack inland enemy targets, for example, airfields from which hostile aircraft might be launched to attack a fleet. The formal agreements of the Joint Chiefs of Staff were subsequently approved by President Truman on 21 April 1948 and issued under the title of "Functions of the Armed Forces and the Joint Chiefs of Staff."[26]

Following historical patterns, the Key West agreement specified that the Army had primary interest in operations on land, the Navy in operations at sea, and the Air Force in operations in the air. Forces developed to meet the requirements of primary functions were to be employable in collateral functions that supported and supplemented the other services in carrying out their primary functions. The primary functions of the United States Air Force were: to defend the United States against air attack, to gain and maintain general air supremacy, to defeat enemy air forces, to control vital air areas, to establish local air superiority, to conduct strategic air warfare, to organize and equip air forces for joint amphibious and airborne operations, to furnish close combat and logistical air support to the Army, and to provide (with exceptions) air transport for the armed forces. In coordination with the other services, the Air Force was charged to develop doctrines and procedures for the defense of the United States from air attack, joint amphibious and airborne operations, and air defense from land areas. Specific collateral functions of the Air Force included a responsibility to interdict enemy sea power through air operations, to conduct antisubmarine warfare and protect shipping, and to conduct aerial minelaying operations. Among its primary functions, the Navy was to conduct air operations as necessary in a naval campaign; to establish local air superiority in an area of naval operations; and to perform naval reconnaissance, conduct antisubmarine warfare, protect shipping, and perform minelaying, including the air aspects of such tasks. The Navy's collateral functions required it to interdict enemy land, air power, and communications through operations at sea; to provide close air support for land operations; to furnish aerial photography for cartographic purposes; and to participate in the overall air efforts as directed by the Joint Chiefs of Staff.[27]

Speaking for the Navy, Vice Adm Arthur W. Radford subsequently described the Key West agreements as "one of the most remarkable documents that has ever been produced along those lines."[28] In a conversation with Forrestal on 16 March 1948, however, General Spaatz objected to a proposed press release to the effect that agreements in all major areas had been reached at Key West. Spaatz said that the question of whether there were to be two air forces or one air force had not been resolved.[29] Gen Hoyt S. Vandenberg, who succeeded Spaatz as Air Force chief of staff on 30 April 1948, assured Forrestal on 28 July that the Air Force was not trying to get control of all aviation but suggested that the nation could not continue to spend scarce funds on two duplicating programs — long-range bombers and supercarriers. "I said," Forrestal recorded in his diary in regard to the conversation with Vandenberg, "I was against the development of a new fleet of supercarriers by the Navy but I felt it was most important that one such ship, capable of carrying the weight of a long-range bombing plane, go forward."[30] In an article appearing in *Life* magazine on 16 August, Spaatz charged that the Navy's 65,000-ton carrier represented an attempt to create a second air force for industrial bombing when much still needed to be done to provide a truly balanced structure around the core of one air force.[31]

Noting on 9 August that the Key West agreements apparently had not provided a solution of disputes in the field of strategic air warfare, Forrestal asked General Spaatz and Admiral Towers to return from retirement for a few days and to set down their concepts of strategic air warfare as it might have to be waged in defense of the United States. In a memorandum on 18 August, Spaatz and Towers were said to have agreed that the Key West decisions were sound but in need of interpretation, that "no sharp line can be drawn between strategic bombing and tactical bombing," and that the Navy's ability to perform its primary missions would require it "to provide for the delivery of atomic bombs."[32] In an effort to clarify the Key West agreements further, Forrestal assembled the Joint Chiefs of Staff at the Naval War College in Newport, Rhode Island, on 20 August 1948. Here it was agreed that "each service, in the fields of its primary missions, must have exclusive responsibility for programming and planning, and the necessary authority," but that "in the execution of any mission of the armed services, all available resources must be used to the maximum overall effectiveness."[33] At a meeting of senior officers in the Pentagon on 24 August, Forrestal expressed optimism that problems of roles and missions finally had been resolved. "I am convinced that at the top command levels," he said, "there is a clear understanding of the exclusive role of the Air Force in the field of strategic air warfare and ... the intent of the Air Force not merely to permit but to seek all the help it can get from Naval Air in the use of air power, either strategically or tactically. Likewise, the Navy is assigned the exclusive role in the field of anti-submarine warfare; and ... the intent of the Navy is also to invite all the help it can get from the Air Force in carrying out this mission."[34]

Although progress was being made in determining the roles and missions of the armed forces, at least two retired Air Force officers continued to believe that all military aviation should be consolidated. In December 1948 General Doolittle criticized the National Security Act of 1947 as "an unfortunate compromise" that had failed to accept Army Air Forces recommendations that there be one separate autonomous Air Force, complete coordination of the three armed forces, a head to the Joint Chiefs of Staff, and roles and missions designated by executive order rather than by legislation. Doolittle wished to concentrate all military aviation in the US Air Force: "One specialized branch of the Air Force," he said, "would operate with the Navy just as a specialized branch, the Tactical Air Force, now cooperates with the Army."[35] In October 1949 General Spaatz wrote: "The Navy now spends more than half its total appropriation in support of naval aviation. The result is that the Nation is dissipating its wealth and wasting aviation talent in supporting two air forces." Specifically queried about the Spaatz article, Secretary Symington emphasized that the view that there should be one air force was not an official Air Force position. "I know of no officer in the Air Force," he said, "who agrees with the position that there should be one Air Force for the country."[36]

Unified and Specified Commands

Although roles and missions were in dispute, the secretary of defense and the Joint Chiefs of Staff successfully provided command and control arrangements for unified and specified commands. When the unified theater commands were officially formed in December 1946, the Joint Chiefs of Staff continued to exercise command over them but designated an individual chief of staff as the executive agent for a particular unified command. When the Strategic Air Command was established, the general understanding was that the new command would be centrally controlled and directed by orders of the Joint Chiefs of Staff; but Air Force mission statements provided that the Strategic Air Command would operate in accordance with directives and policies received from the commanding general, Army Air Forces, and later the chief of staff of the Air Force. The Strategic Air Command could not be handled as a unified command (which included Army, Navy, and Air Force forces) since it was composed only of Air Force forces. To solve this problem, the Key West agreements authorized the Joint Chiefs of Staff to designate one of their members as executive agent for unified commands and for certain operations, and specified commands. A specified command thus came to be a single-service command under the Joint Chiefs. Though the Joint Chiefs ultimately stated that the Strategic Air Command had been responsible to them since 14 December 1946, they did not officially assign the mission of conducting strategic air warfare operations to the Strategic Air Command until 13 April 1949. At this time they provided that the Strategic Air Command — functioning under the Joint Chiefs of Staff with the Air Force chief of staff serving as their executive agent — was authorized to direct the strategic air offensive; assign targets, weight of effort, and timing of air operations; and coordinate strategic strikes with theater air activities to prevent interference between forces and secure maximum tactical advantages.[37] As the first fruits of tangible unification, Secretary Forrestal issued, on 3 May 1948, a final directive uniting the Air Transport Command and the Naval Air Transport Service in a new command to be known as the Military Air Transport Service (MATS); the merger was effective on 1 June 1948. The new MATS was charged to provide air transport for the National Military Establishment under the command and direction of the Air Force chief of staff.[38]

Building the Air Force's Internal Structure

Definitive planning for the organization of the air force in the postwar structure of the armed forces had begun within the War Department in the autumn of 1943. Establishing the structure of the separate postwar air force necessarily involved assumptions as to the fundamental purposes of military forces, the basic missions of the air force in national defense, and the probable nature of future hostilities. Closely related to each of these matters was the question about the amount of financial support that could be expected in the years of peace that were expected to follow the ending of World War II.

"The primary function of the armed forces is, when called upon to do so, to support and, within the sphere of military effort, to enforce the national policy of the nation," stated Maj Gen Thomas T. Handy's War Department Operations Division planning paper that went forward to General Marshall on 28 October 1943. "There must," Handy continued, "be a complete correlation of national policy with military policy; of the political ends to be sought with the military means to achieve them. Such correlation must be flexible; adaptable to changing conditions and changing needs."[39] Although the expressed idea that military forces should support national policy was relatively new in the United States, Marshall readily approved Handy's basic statement. In his final war report, Marshall additionally defined his own conception of the relationship of force to diplomacy. "Our diplomacy must be wise and it must be strong," he warned. "If our diplomacy is not backed by a sound security policy, it is, in my opinion, forecast to failure."[40]

Since the purpose of military force was to support national policy, Handy proposed that a force in being, not a potential one, was required "for prompt attack in any part of the world in order to crush the very beginnings of lawless aggression, in cooperation with other peace-loving nations."[41] General Marshall, however, would not approve the concept of a large standing Army because its cost would be prohibitive, because the men needed to fill its ranks would not be obtained by recruitment in time of peace, and because it would be repugnant to the American people. Marshall wanted to develop a system and an organization that would endure for years rather than be organized against the expectation that war might begin at some arbitrary date. "We were trying to avoid war," he explained, "but at the same time we carefully had to avoid a financial effect on our economy which would be as disastrous as a war might well be." With these basic beliefs, Marshall placed his faith in combat-ready air power rather than a large ground army. He endorsed Handy's paper with a marginal notation: "I think maintenance of sizeable ground expeditionary force probably impracticable except on a basis of allotment of fillers after six months. Having air power will be the quickest remedy."[42]

When Maj Gen Barney M. Giles, chief of Air Staff of the Army Air Forces, laid the basic ground rules for planning the postwar air force on 11 December 1943, he specified that the air force would be autonomous and would maintain "an 'M' day force, instantly ready to repel attack or to quash any incipient threat to world peace." Giles assumed that the air force would consist of a GHQ, six air forces, and air units stationed on a chain of permanent bases from the Philippines eastward to the west coast of Africa.[43] Brig Gen Howard A. Craig, chief of operations, commitments, and resources (OC&R), immediately protested the plan because it appeared to parcel out the air striking force among six commands. "Forty very heavy bomber groups," Craig argued, "could be moved from Kansas to prepared bases anywhere in the world in a matter of hours. This precious striking force should be retained centrally available for concentration against the enemy, safe from sabotage, treachery, or the dangers native to piecemeal distribution."[44] Maj Gen Westside T. Larson, commander of the Third Air Force, agreed with Craig: "The powerful very heavy air arm..., like a fleet 'in being,' must not be strategically disposed of in the Pacific or Atlantic areas on fixed or permanent location but on the contrary should remain a compact force, free to move and be temporarily based in any of the numerous strategic areas—strategy being a continuing element dependent upon the vacillating policy of foreign countries." Larson also urged that the postwar plan "should incorporate the operation of the Air Force directly under the Commander US Air Forces and not as a part of any task force organization that may be set up in the various strategic theaters."[45]

Although creating the Twentieth Air Force on 4 April 1944 established the precedent for the unified command and employment of strategic air striking forces, the postwar status of tactical air forces continued to be a problem. In December 1944 Brig Gen Frederic H. Smith, Jr., deputy chief of the Air Staff, stated that a proposal to establish a postwar tactical air force to handle air-ground training was "fallacious in principle and dangerous in implication." Smith argued that only two overseas theaters had established tactical air forces and he urged: "Strategic Air Forces must when the situation demands be employed in tactical operations and vice versa."[46] As has been seen, General Norstad was initially sympathetic to the tactical air force, but nuclear weapons caused him to change his mind. Since tactical air units obviously could not be employed until the strategic air offensive had been completed, Norstad favored the maintenance of a nucleus for a tactical air force that could be expanded after M-day.[47]

In view of the impending Allied victory in World War II, the air defense of the United States apparently was not considered to be of pressing importance. In a study prepared on 30 May 1945, however, Maj Gen H. R. Oldfield, the AAF special assistant for antiaircraft, pointed out that fighter-interceptors, signal aircraft warning services, and antiaircraft artillery units were complementary members of an air defense team. "To divorce the antiaircraft artillery from this team and place it on a cooperative basis," Oldfield thought, "not only violates the principle of unity of effort and of economy of force but endangers the success of the air defense mission."[48] Maj Gen Donald Wilson, who had become chief of OC&R, proposed on 6 June 1945 that air defense commands ought to be organized in the United States and charged to give their full attention to defense work. Wilson was critical of the wartime arrangement wherein three continental air forces had been charged with air defense at the same time that they were principally concerned with training of air force units.[49] After studying air defense requirements, Arnold forwarded a study to the War Department Operations Division on 4 August 1945, which outlined the unitary problem of air defense and recommended that antiaircraft artillery should be transferred from the Army to the postwar air force.[50]

Few of the postwar organizational problems were as perplexing as the future of air transport and troop carrier aviation. The Air Transport Command wished to continue into the postwar period at a strength of approximately six squadrons, each with 10 four-engine transports. Brig Gen William D. Old and Lt Gen Lewis H. Brereton advocated establishing a postwar airborne army, which would combine airborne troops and troop carrier aircraft.[51] According to rumor, the War Department General Staff bounced the airborne army proposal from office to office, with no one liking it but everyone hesitating to disapprove it. In the end the War Department G-3 indicated that it preferred that the headquarters of a troop carrier command and of the airborne force be maintained separately but located in close proximity to permit intimate coordination without consolidation.[52] In assessing the potential impact of nuclear weapons on air force organization, however, Norstad offered the opinion that troop carrier aviation ought to be integrated into the Air Transport Command and that the air force ought to procure large transport planes that could provide mobility to a strategic bombing force or lift large numbers of ground troops.[53]

Postwar Air Organization Plans

When the Air Staff began to make plans for the postwar air force, it based its organizational conception on the War Department's plan to maintain a postwar Army of 1,700,000 men. On this basis, Arnold approved an initial air force objective on 25 February 1944 calling for 105 groups, divided into 40 very heavy bombardment, two heavy bombardment, four medium and light bombardment, 45 fighter, three reconnaissance, and 11 troop carrier groups. The size of this force was devised without consideration of cost, but the force would be capable of "striking quickly and forcibly" on M-day and Maj Gen Laurence S. Kuter defended it as being necessary to keep the peace in a troubled world. When the 1,700,000-man Army was brought to General Marshall's attention on 13 November 1944, however, he rejected it out of hand because the annual cost of supporting such an Army would be excessive.[54]

To justify a more economical postwar plan, the War Department adopted more optimistic assumptions that an enemy would launch an all-out attack against the United States without a declaration of war and that the United States would have no allies for at least 18 months. But the War Department further assumed that "the United States will have cognizance of the possibility of war for at least one year, and during this year preparatory measures will be inaugurated." Marshall approved these assumptions on 13 March 1945.[55] A few months later, the War Department G-4 questioned the realism of the assumption that the United States would have 12 months' warning time; but the air force wished to continue using this assumption as the basis of its planning because it would pose a strong requirement for the development of alert national intelligence.[56] Given a year in which to mobilize, the Army Air Forces adopted a plan on 21 May 1945 calling for the retention of 78 groups in the interim air force. Since aircraft could not be stockpiled for a future mobilization emergency, Arnold also asked Congress to retain a substantial portion of the government-owned aircraft plants and machine tools on a standby status.[57]

When the 78-group strength was rejected by the War Department as financially impracticable, Lt Gen Ira C. Eaker, deputy commander of the Army Air Forces, reached a decision on 29 August 1945 that 70 groups with approximately 400,000 personnel would be the bedrock minimum strength required by the postwar air force. This absolutely minimum strength would provide a force that could be operationally ready on D-day and still provide training for a million and a half men that the air force would mobilize for a planned five-year war; it was the smallest size force that would keep aircraft production in a sufficiently ready state to meet mobilization requirements; and it was the size force that could man the essential air bases that would be required in a combat and mobilization emergency. The Army Air Forces projected that the 70-group strength would include 21 very heavy bomber, five light bomber, 22 fighter, three all-weather fighter, nine strategic and tactical reconnaissance, and 10 troop carrier groups, plus 22 separate specialized squadrons. This regular strength would be backed up by 27 Air National Guard and 34 Air Force Reserve groups.[58]

The reduction of the Army Air Forces postwar strength from 105 to 70 groups caused revisions in organizational planning. "In the interest of economy," General Eaker stated on 21 May 1945, "air power which can be applied to the accomplishment of more than one of its missions must not be duplicated."[59] The Headquarters Continental Air Forces already had begun to operate at Bolling Field on 1 April 1945; on 8 September its chief of staff, Maj Gen Samuel E. Anderson, proposed that the Continental Air Forces should be charged to provide a global striking force, to provide tactical air force units for cooperative training with Army and Navy forces, to plan the air defense of the continental United States, and to train combat units and crews for overseas service.[60] Seeking a similar organization of air transport resources, the Air Staff prepared a joint staff study on 5 September 1945 that recommended the consolidation of troop carrier and air transport units into a single Air Transport Command, which would serve as the major headquarters over the Troop Carrier Command, a continental air transport division, and a foreign air transport division.[61] General Arnold never acted on the proposal to place all combat aviation under the single Continental Air Forces. Instead, on 5 December 1945 he directed that the Air Transport Command and troop carrier forces would remain a separate organizational status.[62]

Recognition of Research and Development

At the same time the Air Staff was considering the organization of the postwar air force, Arnold gave an increasing amount of his own thought to postwar research and development. In the war years, the Air Technical Service Command had been more concerned with production than with research and development.[63] Research and development responsibilities had been divided among the air communications officer on the Air Staff, the Air Materiel Command, the AAF Board, and the Air Proving Ground Command; the system had worked only because of the cooperation of the various commanders involved.[64] Convinced that American military research and development had often been inferior to that of its enemies, General Arnold asked Dr Theodore von Karman on 7 November 1944 to head and to organize an AAF scientific advisory group that would outline a research and development program to guide the air force for 10 to 20 years. Arnold informed von Karman that the "object of total war is to destroy the enemy's will to resist thereby, enabling us to force our will on him," and he asked that the scientific advisory group indicate the potential scientific lines of advance that the air force might take to accomplish a predominantly offensive mission.[65] After a year's study, the von Karman group would complete on 15 December 1945 a monumental report entitled *Toward New Horizons*.[66]

While the scientific study was progressing, Arnold continued to point out that the air force "must have enough money and enough people and enough facilities to carry on necessary experimental research and development work to keep the US Army Air Forces and US aviation in the No. 1 position which they now occupy."[67] In a talk to his staff on 12 January 1945, Arnold "drew a picture of the next war as starting without warning with thousands of pilotless 'things' suddenly raining destruction over Washington and other prime targets in the United States." As a defense in this scenario, he visualized "other 'things,' not only seeking out the enemy's weapons, but also counteroffensive weapons which would seek out and destroy the enemy's ability to manufacture the articles for waging war."[68] Appearing before a Senate committee on 18 October 1945, Arnold said:

> The first essential of air power necessary for peace and security is the preeminence in research.... We must remember at all times that the degree of national security rapidly declines when reliance is placed on the quantity of existing equipment instead of its quality.... We must count on scientific advances requiring us to replace about one-fifth of existing Air Forces equipment each year and we must be sure that these additions

are the most advanced in the whole world. To this end the best scientific talents of the country must be mobilized continuously and without delay.[69]

Air officers had a good appreciation of the importance of research and development, but they were much less sure as to how to organize for it. At this juncture, no one apparently suggested that research and development in air materiel should be divided from procurement and production. Based on a postulate that tactical research and proof testing ought to be separate from the development function, the AAF Board recommended on 29 April 1944 that the wartime relationship of the AAF Board, the AAF Tactical Center, the AAF Proving Ground Command, and the Air Materiel Command ought to continue unchanged in the postwar air force.[70] In September 1945 Brig Gen Eugene L. Eubank recommended that if the AAF Board were made directly responsible to the highest command level and augmented with highly qualified officers it would be "capable of solving problems of any magnitude related to Air Force development, tactics, and techniques."[71] Other authorities regarded the AAF Board as being only one of several important research and analysis agencies. Col Barton W. Leach, chief of the Operations Analysis Division, for example, suggested that the AAF Board, the Operations Analysis Division, the AAF evaluation boards, and the Scientific Advisory Group were so closely related in function that they ought to be placed under the unified direction of an Air Staff officer in charge of analysis, evaluation, and research.[72] Apparently without recognizing that he was circumscribing the province of the AAF Board, General Arnold established an All-Weather Air Forces Board at Lockbourne AFB, Ohio, on 16 June 1945 and charged it to evolve and implement a long-range research and development program for all-weather air operations. Without guidance from above, the Lockbourne center was soon reported to be more concerned with "gadgeteering" than with orderly investigation.[73] At Orlando, Florida, the AAF Board had enjoyed a close relationship with the educational facilities of the AAF School, but on 29 November 1945 the school was physically transferred to Maxwell Field, Alabama, where the Air University was being established.[74]

General Spaatz's Air Force Reorganization

In the period prior to November 1945, the Army Air Forces laboriously planned a postwar organization, but the final approval of all planning would be dependent on the wishes of Gen Dwight D. Eisenhower, who became Army chief of staff on 19 November 1945, and General Spaatz, who began to assume the duties of commanding general, Army Air Forces, when General Arnold requested retirement on 8 November. Although Arnold would not begin his terminal leave until 1 March 1946, he thought that his successor should have the responsibility for forming the policies that he would have to carry out. On 29 November, Eisenhower appointed a board of officers under Lt Gen William H. Simpson and charged it to prepare a definitive plan for the reorganization of the Army and the Army Air

Forces that could be effectuated by executive orders and that would permit the separation of the air force from the Army. On 15 November, Spaatz had noted that there was a "tendency to over-emphasize long-range bombardment, and to ignore the versatile application of air power." In January 1946, Eisenhower and Spaatz laid aside the concept that all combat air power might be concentrated in the Continental Air Forces and agreed between them that the major commands of the Army Air Forces should be the Strategic Air Command, the Air Defense Command, the Tactical Air Command, the Air Technical Service Command,* the Air Training Command, the Air University, the Army Air Forces Center, and the Air Transport Command.[75] Even though the organization of the Tactical Air Command appeared to represent a reversal of earlier expressed concepts that combat air power ought to be capable of both strategic and ground support missions, Spaatz later stated that he organized the Tactical Air Command at his own volition with no pressure from General Eisenhower.[76]

The command reorganization of the Army Air Forces outlined by Eisenhower and Spaatz was keyed to the establishment of the Strategic Air Command, which was visualized as a long-range striking force equipped with atomic-capable B-29s and possibly B-36s. The Strategic Air Command's planes would be based in the United States and would be deployed to forward bases if necessary. Effective on 21 March 1946, Headquarters Continental Air Forces was redesignated as Headquarters Strategic Air Command; on 21 October 1946 the new headquarters moved from Bolling Field to Andrews Field, Maryland. In its mission statement, the Strategic Air Command was charged to conduct long-range operations in any part of the world at any time; to perform maximum long-range reconnaissance over land or sea; and to provide combat operations in any part of the globe, employing the latest and most advanced weapons. The Eighth and Fifteenth Air Forces were assigned to the Strategic Air Command.[77]

"We feel," stated Spaatz, "that the air defense of the United States cannot be left to chance. . . . We must be properly organized so that there cannot possibly be an air surprise such as occurred at Pearl Harbor."[78] AAF leaders continued to urge that the air defense of the United States should be a centralized system that would control fighter aircraft, radar, and antiaircraft artillery; and they believed that antiaircraft artillery should be integrated into the Army Air Forces. According to rumor, antiaircraft artillery officers in the Army Ground Forces did not want to integrate with the Army Air Forces. The Simpson board recommended that antiaircraft artillery should not be transferred to the Army Air Forces but that antiaircraft artillery units should be trained and attached to Army Air Forces units from time to time.[79] The Air Defense Command was activated at Mitchel Field, New York, effective on 27 March 1946, and the First, Second, Fourth, Tenth, Eleventh, and Fourteenth Air Forces assigned to it. The Air Defense Command was charged to provide for the air defense of the United States, but it was obvious

---

* In March 1946 the Air Technical Service Command was redesignated as the Air Materiel Command.

very early that providing tactical units to it would be difficult. Despite statements to the contrary, the War Department and the Army Air Forces held a relaxed view that air defense would be a mobilization measure. In the event of a war emergency, the Joint Chiefs of Staff would organize defense commands and make Navy, Strategic Air Command, and Tactical Air Command fighters available to the control of the Air Defense Command. In such an event, Air National Guard and Air Force Reserve fighter units would be mobilized and the Air Defense Command accordingly would be charged to organize, administer, train, and maintain the Air National Guard and the Air Force Reserve.[80]

Since the tactical air forces and ground forces had worked closely together in Europe, Spaatz wished to retain a close relationship between the headquarters of the Tactical Air Command and that of the Army Ground Forces. As a result, Headquarters Tactical Air Command was activated at Tampa, Florida, on 21 March 1946 but was moved on 27 May to Langley Field, Virginia, where it was proximate to Headquarters Army Ground Forces (later Army Field Forces) at Fort Monroe, Virginia. The mission of the Tactical Air Command required it to cooperate with land and sea forces in ground and amphibious operations and to train and equip tactical air units for operations anywhere in the world. It also was charged to promote "progressive development of air-ground coordination techniques and doctrines." Assigned to the Tactical Air Command were the Third and Ninth Air Forces and the IX Troop Carrier Command, but the latter was soon disbanded and replaced by the Third Air Force (Troop Carrier).[81]

In view of earlier decisions to retain them without change, the Air Materiel Command, the Air Transport Command, and the Air Training Command continued in being when the War Department reorganization was announced on 14 May 1946.[82] Still seeking to distinguish between the air transport and the troop carrier mission, the Army Air Forces stated the policy that the Air Transport Command would be responsible for air transport service between the United States and the overseas theaters and among the overseas theaters. The troop carrier units had to be prepared for airborne assault and for airlanded operations and for the performance of intratheater airlift at the discretion of the theater commanders.[83]

Continuing Thinking about Research and Development

Unlike the organization of the combat functions, which progressed rapidly toward a functional alignment of responsibilities, the establishment of a framework for air research and development was marked by numerous changes in plans. In order to "shake down" for peacetime operations, Headquarters Army Air Forces was reorganized on 15 September 1945 with five assistant chiefs of Air Staff: ACAS-1 (Personnel), ACAS-2 (Intelligence), ACAS-3 (Training and Operations), ACAS-4 (Supply), and ACAS-5 (Plans). Research and development functions, which had been handled by Organization, Commitments, and

Requirements, passed to ACAS-3.[84] In the last weeks before he retired, General Arnold spent most of his time thinking about the future development of the Air Force. At the advice of Dr Edward L. Bowles, Arnold, on 5 December 1945, directed the establishment of a deputy chief of air staff, research and development. Headed by Maj Gen Curtis E. LeMay, the new Air Staff office was charged to prepare the overall research and development program for the Air Force and to concern itself with policy matters affecting the research and development program. The Air Materiel Command would continue as the field agency responsible for research and development programs.[85]

At the same time that he was centralizing responsibility for future research and development in the Air Staff, Arnold wanted to initiate new research projects before plentiful wartime funds dried up. In September 1945 Arnold took Bowles with him on a trip to the west coast where, late in the month, they met Donald Douglas and F. R. Collbohm in a luncheon conference at Hamilton Field, California. At this meeting, Arnold proposed to divert $10 million from the Air Force's fiscal year 1946 procurement budget and to commit it to a long-range project wherein the Douglas Aircraft Corporation would assemble a staff of civilian engineers and scientists to study the entire subject of intercontinental warfare and the best means of waging it. The staff would also be prepared to evaluate the military worth of competing systems of warfare, current and future, with the objective of providing air planners with the best possible guides as to the most economical and effective means of achieving the AAF mission. When Douglas agreed to undertake the project, the Air Materiel Command negotiated a $10-million, three-year contract beginning in May 1946 for a study of future warfare. This contract was the genesis of the nonprofit Research and Development (Rand) Corporation, which would be located at Santa Monica, California, and which would split away from Douglas in a mutually agreeable action in 1948.[86]

In the summer of 1944 the Air Staff had discussed and dismissed a proposition that an air council ought to be created to sit in Washington and provide high-level policy guidance. This proposal was apparently voted down because of the belief that the Air Staff could act as an air council when such was necessary.[87] In spite of the transfer of the AAF School to Maxwell Field, where it would be redesignated as the Air University on 12 March 1946, air planning continued to visualize that the AAF Center would comprise the AAF Board and the AAF Proving Ground Command. In January 1946, however, Spaatz directed on 12 February that the Air Board be established with Maj Gen Hugh J. Knerr as its secretary-general. As formally established on 5 March, the Air Board comprised the commanding general, the deputy commanding general, the secretary-general, the commanders of major AAF commands, and such other retired officers, civilians, and Air National Guard and Air Reserve officers as the commanding general of the Army Air Forces might care to appoint. The mission of the Air Board required it to study problems and policies and make recommendations to the AAF commander.[88]

Establishing the Air Board necessitated disbanding the AAF Board, since, as General Eaker observed, "there should not be two air boards." In his study of the matter, Norstad suggested that the Air Board already had assumed responsibility for advising the AAF commander on all general policies. He suggested that the AAF Board mission of reviewing and evaluating tests of materiel and new developments should be assigned to the AAF Proving Ground Command, thus allowing that command to review and evaluate its own tests. He recommended that the missions of the AAF Board, which required it to "determine lessons learned from current combat operations" and to "develop and recommend the doctrines and techniques to be used in the training employment of the Army Air Forces," should be assigned to the new Air University. Norstad pointed out that at the Air University "hundreds of instructors, spurred on by the sharp analysis and questions of thousands of highly-experienced students," would constantly evaluate combat doctrines. "They," said Norstad, "can probably do a better job, resolve a greater amount of sound air thinking into usable doctrine than any other group of men anywhere. And they will do it whether or not they are charged with it."[89]

The disposition of the AAF Board and the distribution of its missions closely followed Norstad's recommendations. On 8 March 1946 the AAF Center was redesignated as the AAF Proving Ground Command, and the center's personnel—together with that of the AAF Board—moved to Eglin Field, Florida, where the AAF Board was formally inactivated on 1 July 1946.[90] On the same day the Air Staff directed the Air University to develop basic doctrines and concepts for the employment of air power; to review, revise, and prepare basic AAF doctrines for publication; to maintain continuing research into the strategic, tactical, and defensive concepts of air power; to review and evaluate new tactics, techniques, and organization and make recommendations regarding them; to collect, analyze, and disseminate information on new methods and techniques of aerial warfare; to plan and supervise the development and testing of new and improved methods and techniques of aerial warfare; and to approve, activate, and designate test agencies and monitor all projects involving tactical unit testing.[91]

The redistribution of the missions and responsibilities of the AAF Board marked the completion of the postwar organization of the Army Air Forces. At Maxwell Field, Maj Gen Muir S. Fairchild immediately began to seek the resources that would permit the new Air University to accomplish its test and development mission. Tentative guidance led him to believe that the Air University would be assigned a fighter, a bomber, and a guided missile group, together with other units, which would serve as a test and development force. Hearing of the Air University's expectation, Maj Gen Elwood R. Quesada, commander of the Tactical Air Command, immediately protested that the organization of a test and development force would be an extravagant use of scarce tactical units, and he demanded that tactical experimentation and development be entrusted to the operational commands. On 13 May 1946 Spaatz agreed with Quesada and informed Fairchild that tactical groups would not be assigned to the Air University. He enjoined that the Air University would devote itself to individual training and leave equipment and tactical tests and demonstrations to the Air Materiel Command, the Air Proving Ground Command, and the combat commands. "The doctrines taught at the Air University," Spaatz ordered, "will be those current in the various commands, approved as necessary by this Headquarters."[92]

Despite this curtailment in its mission, the Air University assumed many of the responsibilities of the AAF Board. At a meeting on 6 June, Eubank urged Fairchild to organize a small section or committee directly responsible to the Air University commander to accomplish the missions being transferred. "By keeping a separate group working together on these functions," Eubank explained, "I believe it will assure that the functions do not get lost and I believe it will help avoid the impression of a too academic interest in the problems that will come up."[93] To allay the suspicions of the combat commands, Maj Gen David M. Schlatter, deputy commander of the Air University, announced that in accomplishing its research, evaluation, and doctrinal functions, the Air University would "act in the capacity of a monitoring agency or steering committee utilizing the expert knowledge available in all of the commands of the Air Force."[94] On 18 June 1946, following Eubank's recommendation, Fairchild established a Research Section within the Air University's Academic Staff Division with spaces for 16 officers, most of whom were transferred from Eglin Field to complete projects on which they were assigned when the AAF Board was discontinued. A reorganization of the Academic Staff on 1 October 1946 resulted in the establishment of a Research Division with several sections and 18 officers. Since the division was evaluating rather than conducting research, the Research Division was redesignated as the Evaluation Division, Academic Staff, on 29 August 1947.[95] Cognizant that it was responsible for stimulating thinking and discussion on air power projects and for disseminating as well as formulating doctrine, the Air University began to publish the *Air University Quarterly Review* in May 1947.[96]

In spite of a rapid turnover of experienced officers in its research and evaluation function, the Air University worked off the backlog of projects that it had inherited from the AAF Board and undertook some new projects. Since it had no assigned combat units, the Air University relied on other commands to conduct tests. Especially where the Tactical Air Command was concerned, the split responsibility proved troublesome. In September 1946, for example, the Air University protested that the Tactical Air Command was providing very poor support for several test projects—notably the tactical tests of P-80 aircraft at March Field, California. Hearing of the protest, one Tactical Air Command officer retorted that the Air University ought to discontinue its research section and transfer the people to the operating commands where research ought to be performed.[97] The way in which the new system of preparing doctrine would function was gradually worked out. In August 1947, for example, the assistant chief of Air Staff for training and operations held a meeting in Washington to discuss the preparation of a common air defense doctrine. It was agreed that two panels would be established to prepare the doctrine. The Air University would monitor the panel concerned with policy and doctrine, and the Air Defense Command would monitor the panel studying tactics and procedures.[98] This same pattern would be repeated in other doctrinal studies.

Organization of USAF Headquarters

Even though the postwar organization of the Army Air Forces had been designed to provide for a smooth transition into the autonomous United States Air Force, some changes were necessary when the National Military Establishment got under way in September 1947. General Spaatz became chief of staff, United States Air Force, and General Vandenberg, who had been deputy commanding general and chief of Air Staff in the Army Air Forces, became vice chief of staff, United States Air Force. Looking forward to the establishment of the United States Air Force and not all sure that the postwar organization of the Army Air Forces would be suitable to the autonomous service, Spaatz had suggested that the Air University should use some of its highly experienced students to examine the whole scope of air organization. Prepared as a seminar activity in the first class of the Air War College, problem no. 4, "Proposed Reorganization Army Air Forces," was completed on 6 January 1947. This study recommended that the Headquarters United States Air Force should be "a policy and planning staff with virtually all the operational activity of the Air Forces to begin at the major command level below this staff." Believing that "wars are waged with two weapons—men and materiel—and the combination of the two provide for operations," the Air War College study recommended that all headquarters staffs in the Air Force should be organized into three activities: personnel and administration, materiel and logistics, and plans and operations. Possibly reflecting the views of Maj Gen Orvil A. Anderson, who was a founding commandant of the Air War College, the study also recommended that the most effective utilization of air power in an overall strategy required the consolidation of air defense, strategic striking, and tactical support forces into a single command. The study accordingly proposed to eliminate the Strategic Air Command, the Tactical Air Command, and the Air Defense Command and to place all air power capabilities under a single Air Combat Command.[99]

Whether by design or coincidence, Spaatz accepted the three-deputy system recommended by the Air War College when he reorganized Headquarters United States Air Force on 10 October 1947. This reorganization divided Air Staff functions between the deputy chiefs of staff for personnel and administration, operations, and materiel, and the comptroller, who would later be recognized as a deputy chief of staff. Some of the functions that had been exercised by the deputy chief of staff for research and development necessarily passed upward to the new statutorily created Research and Development Board of the National Defense Establishment. The October reorganization of the Air Staff placed the remaining responsibilities of the office in the Directorate of Research and Development under the deputy chief of staff for materiel. The new director of research and development would serve as the military director of Doctor von Karman's Scientific Advisory Board but would otherwise be subordinated to the deputy chief of staff for materiel.[100]

During the negotiations over unification, the Air Board was said to have served Spaatz in a role similar to that of a "board of directors in a business organization."[101] With unification attained in the summer of 1947, however, General LeMay suggested to Spaatz and Vandenberg that it might be wise to establish a US Air Force aircraft and weapons board, consisting of all major air commanders. LeMay reasoned, "We should have more than just the staff experience in Washington participating in the discussions of new weapons." He thought that the new board would constantly survey the research and development program to ensure that proper weapons were emphasized, developed, and procured for the combat units.[102] When it was assembled for its first meeting on 19 August 1947, the newly created USAF Aircraft and Weapons Board was comprised of the Air Force deputy chiefs of staff and the major air commanders. Meeting on call during 1948, the Aircraft and Weapons Board examined, discussed, and offered formal recommendations on programs that were submitted to it by subcommittees of officers drawn from Air Force headquarters and from the major commands. As a vehicle for handling high-level problems, the Aircraft and Weapons Board rapidly eclipsed the Air Board, especially after January 1948 when General Knerr was transferred from the secretary-general position to assume other duties.[103]

Shortly after becoming chief of staff of the Air Force on 30 April 1948, General Vandenberg began to show dissatisfaction with the manner in which the Aircraft and Weapons Board (which he had had a large part in establishing) was functioning. With 15 senior members talking and voting there was much confusion, and it was difficult to prevent leaks of information out of such a large body. Vandenberg also believed: "In the final analysis, the top command of the Air Force is responsible for the weapons with which it will fight the war." Effective on 29 December 1948, Vandenberg accordingly established the USAF Board of Senior Officers, headed by General Fairchild, who had become vice chief of staff; the other members included the deputy chief of staff for operations, the deputy chief for materiel, and the commanding general, Air Materiel Command, as voting members. Both Secretary of the Air Force W. Stuart Symington and Vandenberg referred problems to this board, but neither attended its sessions nor sought to influence its deliberations, which commonly included a solicitation of opinions from the major air commanders. The establishment of the USAF Senior Officers Board foreshadowed the end of the Air Board, which finally became completely dormant in the autumn of 1949.[104]

The Air Force in the Developing Cold War Strategy

When the War Department began its planning for a postwar defense establishment in 1943, no one identified a likely adversary for the United States. The fact that the Soviet Union would become an enemy to the free world apparently became known to different leaders at different moments. Thinking back to the time that General Bradley and he had gone forward to meet with Soviet Marshal Georgi K. Zhukov in May 1945, General Vandenberg recalled a feeling of foreboding about Russia. The Soviet army was digging in, and Zhukov proudly displayed new jet aircraft and Stormovik fighters that had technical features that American designers had said were impossible for the Soviets to achieve. "I remember talking to General Bradley," Vandenberg recalled, "about my concern over the apparent feeling . . . that the Russians had . . . masses of manpower and no brains."[105] Putting his thoughts on paper, Spaatz wrote Arnold on 11 October 1945: "With the rapid weakening of our forces in Europe and Asia, the USSR is able to project moves on the continent of Europe and Asia which will be just as hard for us to accept and just as much an incentive to war as were those occasioned by the German policies. . . . I believe we should proceed rather slowly toward demobilizing our armed forces, particularly units of our Strategic Air Command."[106] Looking back at the events of 1945, General Marshall agreed that the "confused and tumultuous demobilization was very injurious" and that it had weakened the diplomatic initiative of the United States. Marshall maintained that the United States could not have established "a very large force" in the period of postwar exultation, but he felt even more strongly that "the failure to establish a very definite procedure for maintaining our defensive posture was a very serious error."[107]

In 1945 and 1946 both the foreign and the military policy of the United States assumed that the United Nations "would gain rapid and growing recognition as a central factor in the establishment and maintenance of world security."[108] Based on this assumption, General Eisenhower directed that Army and Air Force strength levels for the fiscal year beginning in July 1946 should be kept to the minimum. In May 1946, Spaatz was willing to hope that the United Nations would establish international arrangements for collective security, but he was unwilling to rely upon a hope. "In modern war," he pointed out, "any nation losing command of the air approaches to its vital areas is in serious peril. . . . The surest defense will be our ability to strike back quickly with a counteroffensive, to neutralize the hostile attack at its source, or to discourage its continuance by striking at the vitals of the aggressor."[109] When it published its first plan for training and employment on 25 July, the Strategic Air Command pointed out: "No major strategic threat or requirement now exists nor, in the opinion of our country's best strategists, will such a requirement exist for the next three to five years." Serving in ACAS-3, Brig Gen Thomas S. Power endorsed the letter back with the admonition: "While the probability of a major strategic threat or a major armed conflict involving this nation in the next three to five years may appear to be remote, the possibility of such an occurrence cannot be excluded."[110]

During 1946 General Spaatz strongly supported a 70-group strength for the Army Air Forces, but his greatest immediate problem was to salvage something from the explosive demobilization that would reduce the air arm to a strength in December 1946 of only 55 groups, of which two could be counted as combat ready. In the emergency, Spaatz viewed the Air Force mission as being: "(a) To provide a long-range striking force in instant readiness and with the power and capacity to destroy the storehouse of enemy weapons and thereafter to reduce the enemy's industrial capacity and war-making potential [and] (b) To provide in peacetime a minimum establishment for prompt and rapid expansion from peace to war." In the critical months of 1946, Spaatz gave first priority to "the backbone of our Air Force – the long-range bomber groups and their protective long-range fighter groups organized in our Strategic Air Force."[111]

When the Strategic Air Command was established, air strategists were said to have recognized that the adaptability of nuclear weapons to delivery by air at great distances "makes the airplane at present, and its descendants in the future, the greatest offensive weapon of all times."[112] The plans for the Strategic Air Command, however, were predicated on scientific reports that fissionable materials were very scarce and that a state of nuclear plenty was improbable. Arnold had stated that nuclear weapons would be scarce and very expensive.[113] As a result of this prediction, the Strategic Air Command planned to employ both high-explosive and nuclear weapons. To perform its mission, the command asked that it eventually be assigned 21 bombardment groups (very heavy), nine fighter groups (very long range), and three reconnaissance groups (very long range). When he was assigned to head the Strategic Air Command in 1946, Gen George C. Kenney immediately organized one wing with three B-29 groups as the atomic-capable strategic striking force.[114] The size of this force was described as sufficient "to fully exploit the expected availability and effectiveness of new bombardment weapons including the atomic bomb."[115]

Before World War II, air power had been unable to project across ocean barriers without the aid of surface craft, but the prospective development of 10,000-mile-range aircraft – including the Northrop XB-35 Flying Wing and the Consolidated XB-36 – promised to open a new air frontier over the frozen wastes of the Arctic. "We must visualize," said Spaatz, "the launching of heavy blows from any point on the globe against any other point."[116] In November 1945 a 6,553-mile flight of four B-29s led by Brig Gen Frank A. Armstrong from Hokkaido to Washington over the top of the world demonstrated that the Arctic was no barrier to air travel.[117] The Strategic Air Command's plan for training and employment issued on 25 July 1946 acknowledged the concept of transpolar air operations and divided the world into three sectors of potential operations: North Atlantic, North Pacific, and Far East. In a future war the Strategic Air Command thought it certain that "there will be but one Theater of Operations covering the entire globe or at

IDEAS, CONCEPTS, DOCTRINE

least the Northern Hemisphere." Moreover, the next war almost certainly would "be primarily an air war until air supremacy is obtained, since surface forces cannot successfully operate without that supremacy." The Strategic Air Command's concept of operational employment accordingly called for a centralized control of the global strategic bomber force and a periodic rotation of bomber, long-range fighter, and reconnaissance groups from home bases in the United States to forward bases in the North Atlantic, North Pacific, and Far East. In a war emergency the plan assumed that a relatively few atomic-capable B-29s would be employed, probably on the direction of the president, either as a part of larger B-29 formations or as individual aircraft that would strike at night or under cover of bad weather.[118]

"Destruction is just around the corner for any future aggressor against the United States. Quick retaliation will be our answer in the form of an aerial knock-out delivered by the Strategic Air Command." A public relations release thus explained the Strategic Air Command's concept of employment in August 1946.[119] As a matter of fact, however, the strategic striking force was very weak. The Strategic Air Command had the only two operational groups in the United States that were fully combat ready; SAC did not expect to have a total of four B-29 groups and two long-range fighter groups operational before February 1947.[120] Thus, the Army Air Forces was unable to measure up to its first postwar crisis, which occurred in August 1946, when two American C-47s were shot down by Communist pilots over Yugoslavia and the State Department proposed an immediate and aggressive use of air power against that country. Norstad had to point out that the Air Force was too weak to risk war. In place of the show of force over Yugoslavia, Assistant Secretary of War for Air W. Stuart Symington proposed an around-the-world B-29 flight, only to have this turned down by the State Department. In November, however, the Strategic Air Command was suddenly directed to send six B-29s to Europe. Led by Col James C. Selser, Jr., these planes left the 43d Bombardment Group's base at Davis-Monthan Field, Arizona, on 13 November 1946, made the trans-Atlantic crossing, and landed safely at Frankfurt, Germany, despite low ceilings and half-mile visibility. In a 12-day stay in Europe, the B-29s made flights along the borders of Soviet-occupied territory and surveyed airfields to determine their suitability for B-29 operations.[121]

Problems of Aircraft Procurement

Besides the explosive demobilization of its strength, the Army Air Forces found it impossible to procure new aircraft that were needed for modernization and to keep the aircraft producers of the United States in a solvent condition. Believing that national security required the maintenance of a healthy aircraft industry that could rapidly expand within a one-year period, Assistant Secretary of War Robert A. Lovett had sponsored the establishment of an Air Coordinating Committee with members from the War, Navy, and Commerce departments in December 1944.

After detailed study of mobilization requirements, the Air Coordinating Committee recommended on 22 October 1945 that the military services procure a minimum of 3,000 aircraft, or an airframe weight of 30,700,000 pounds, each year to keep the nation's aircraft industries in a condition that would permit rapid expansion. This recommendation was predicated on an assumption that there would be a civilian requirement of 325 commercial transports and 20,000 private airplanes each year.[122]

As it finally materialized, the Air Force 70-group and 22-squadron program called for a total of 6,869 aircraft, while the 27 Air National Guard and 34 Air Reserve groups would be authorized an additional 5,572 aircraft, making a grand total of 12,441 aircraft. To replace losses in a period of conflict in which the aviation industry was gearing up for war production, the Air Force wanted to maintain an additional reserve of 8,100 aircraft.[123] Based on estimates of attrition and a planned program of obsolescence that would transfer aircraft from primary to secondary missions, such as training, after a given number of years, the Air Force computed that the annual procurement requirements of the 70-group and 22-squadron program would be its proportionate share of the 3,000 planes which the Air Coordinating Committee indicated as being the figure that the military services needed to purchase annually. The Air Force would expect to maintain technical air supremacy.[124] "Quality of equipment is of major consequence," Spaatz explained. "Only technical air supremacy will permit an air defense capable of detecting and intercepting a possible surprise attack with the air weapons of the future; an air offense capable of destroying critical targets in enemy territory; and effective cooperation with the surface forces on land and sea."[125]

Despite their appreciation of the need for aircraft modernization, both Arnold and Spaatz found it difficult to justify aircraft purchases while the Army Air Forces was retrenching. During the last years of World War II, the Army Air Forces had placed heavy orders for modern aircraft. In fiscal year 1944 it had ordered 100 global-range B-36 bombers and 498 new P-80 jet fighters; in fiscal year 1945 it had ordered an additional 417 P-80 fighters and 100 P-84 jet fighters. With new planes on order from war appropriations, it was difficult to justify the purchase of more aircraft at the same time that tremendous holdings of war-surplus planes needed liquidation. Rather than incur criticism for purchasing new and improved transport aircraft at the same time that it was releasing planes to the civil airlines, for example, Arnold directed on 27 August 1945 that the AAF would reduce its procurement objectives for transports "to the absolute minimum for development purposes."[126] In fiscal year 1946, which began on 1 July 1945 and was the first postwar year, the Army Air Forces purchasing authorization was cut back to 622 aircraft—the principal models including 60 of the improved Superfortresses (designated B-50s), 250 twin-fuselage Mustang fighters (which had been adapted as an interim all-weather interceptor and designated as P-82s), and 141 P-84 jet fighters.[127]

As it was drawn up in the spring of 1946, the postwar aircraft procurement plan of the Army Air Forces reflected the fact that large stocks of World War II planes were still combat capable, that atomic bombs were scarce, and that new jet aircraft were very expensive. Brig Gen Alfred R. Maxwell, chief of the Requirements Division (ACAS-3), visualized the following future aircraft requirements. Aircraft like the B-36 with its global range would be important as special weapons for employment against extremely distant targets — possible A-bomb targets, but such planes would not be procured in large numbers. Aircraft of the B-50 type would be the workhorse bombers for the medium range and would be procured in large numbers. Penetration fighters would continue to be the most important fighter type, but all-weather and interceptor fighters would increase in importance as enemy nations threatened US air supremacy. To give fighter support for long-range bombers, the Air Force proposed to develop a parasite fighter that would be transported by a bomber to a target area and then rejoined to the bomber for the trip home. Strategic and tactical reconnaissance planes would continue to be modifications of standard bomber and fighter models. Troop carrier aircraft would include large helicopters, which would replace gliders, and large transport models capable of moving completely equipped infantry and armored divisions to any combat zone in the world. As a matter of priority, the Army Air Forces wanted to develop jet bombers, but, with current technology, jet aircraft used large amounts of fuel and did not have the range demanded of bombers.[128]

In its budget requests for fiscal year 1947 the Air Force sought to follow the program summarized by General Maxwell and begin procuring the aircraft required for a modernized 70-group program. In its review of the military requests, the Bureau of the Budget severely reduced all items of the budget, including funds requested for aircraft procurement. The Bureau of the Budget struck out requests for authority to procure new transport aircraft on the ground that contractors would not be able to accomplish the proposed schedule although the Air Force believed that they could. The budget office also reduced the overall program by 35 bombers and 42 fighters; after Congress had voted aircraft purchase funds for fiscal year 1947, the Bureau of the Budget subsequently impounded $30 million of aircraft procurement funds and transferred that amount to the pay and travel funds of the Army.[129] In fiscal year 1947 the Army Air Forces accordingly expended $302,684,000 for aircraft procurement and placed orders for a total of 769 aircraft, including 73 B-50s, 96 B-45s, 80 P-80s, 191 P-84s, and 33 P-86s. The B-45 was a new, light jet bomber that was designated as a replacement for the A-26 as a ground support aircraft; the P-86 Sabre was a new swept-wing jet interceptor.[130]

The AAF aircraft procurement program for fiscal year 1947 was less than half of the Army Air Forces' proportionate share of the amount recommended by the Air Coordinating Committee as necessary to maintain a solvent aircraft industry.[131] In the spring of 1947, when it was drawing up its budget requests for fiscal year 1948, the Army Air Forces put in for 1,844 planes, a figure based on a modernization of 55 groups and 15 skeleton groups. This number was not keyed directly to any plan to keep the aircraft industry healthy.[132] An economy-minded House of Representatives, plus rising costs of aircraft, cut the Air Force program far below the requested figure. Based on an authorized expenditure of $495,507,000, the Air Force issued procurement orders for 965 aircraft in fiscal year 1948. The purchase included 82 B-50s, 43 B-45s, 154 P-84s, 188 P-86s, and, for the first time since the war, 120 new troop carrier and transport aircraft.[133] The transports included 27 C-97s, a global transport version of the B-29; the troop carriers included 36 C-119 Flying Boxcars.[134]

First Policies on Missiles and Rockets

"The weapons of today are the museum pieces of tomorrow," General Arnold had warned when he was in the process of leaving office in November 1945.[135] Based on guidance provided in Doctor von Karman's *Toward New Horizons*, Arnold talked confidently about supersonic flight and intercontinental missiles. As drawn up in the winter of 1945-46 by the Air Materiel Command, a five-year Army Air Forces research and development program generally reflected the findings of von Karman's scientists and was designated to provide a continuity to air research and development efforts. The program sought to conserve scarce engineering and scientific resources of the nation, but it was predicated on the basic rule that the Air Force would not engage in in-house research and development unless private agencies were unwilling to do the work on a contract basis.[136] In explanation of the five-year program, General LeMay observed: "Time in this period of unprecedented scientific progress can be the decisive factor in the continued existence of the United States."[137] General Spaatz spoke of the requirement for maintaining a technical air supremacy; and, in a statement of general AAF policy in October 1946, he emphasized that "the Army Air Forces must maintain a position of preeminent leadership in research and development."[138]

After studying the results of captured German scientific data, von Karman's AAF Scientific Advisory Group had reported that the Germans appeared correct in their conclusion that a transoceanic rocket could be developed. Von Karman also suggested that rocket-driven airplanes would be necessary to maintain air superiority. Rocket barrages with atomic warheads, von Karman said, could well become the only effective air defense weapons.[139] Von Karman's findings were quite different from those of Dr Vannevar Bush when he offered his scientific advice to the Senate Committee on Atomic Energy in December 1945. "We have plenty enough to think about," Bush said,

> that is very definite and very realistic—enough so that we don't need to step out into some of these borderlines which seem to be, to me, more or less fantastic. Let me say this: There has been a great deal said about a 3,000-mile high-angle rocket. In my opinion, such a thing is impossible today and will be impossible for many years. The people who have been writing these things that annoy me ... have been talking about a 3,000-mile high-angle rocket, shot from one continent to another, carrying an atomic

bomb and so directed as to be a precise weapon which would land exactly on a certain target, such as a city. I say, technically, I don't think anybody in the world knows how to do such a thing, and I feel confident it will not be done for a very long period of time to come.... I think we can leave that out of our thinking. I wish the American people would leave that out of their thinking.[140]

In making up its five-year research and development program, the Army Air Forces chose to believe von Karman rather than Bush. "There is great danger that the Air Force," stated General Knerr, secretary-general of the Air Board, in February 1946, "may find itself in the position of the Coast Artillery and the Navy in the not too distant future thru failing to realize that the airplane can well join the battleship and antiaircraft artillery as ineffective weapons carriers. The aerial missile, by whatever means it may be delivered, is the weapon of the Air Force."[141] During 1946, the Air Force accordingly negotiated a contract for Project MX-774 with Consolidated-Vultee Aircraft for study and investigation of missile guidance and control, rocket engine swiveling, and lightweight missile structures — the whole project looking toward the eventual development of an intercontinental ballistic missile. Another contract was negotiated with North American Aviation for rocket propulsion and for research and development of a pilotless aircraft, which would become known as the Navaho. In yet another contract, the Rand Corporation was asked to investigate the feasibility of a minimum-orbital satellite that would provide photographic reconnaissance of inaccessible areas of the earth.[142]

Despite the fact that it attached great importance to its five-year research and development program, the Air Force was not notably successful in getting funds for it. For fiscal year 1947, Congress appropriated $186 million for AAF research and development.[143] General LeMay was certain that all of this money could have been obligated by the end of the fiscal year, though not at a uniform rate. The Bureau of the Budget, however, did not feel that all of the appropriation could be obligated. In January 1947 it notified the War Department that the fund would be cut by $100 million. After a réclame, the bureau released $25 million of the amount in question but continued to impound $75 million of the air research and development fund, which was transferred to pay and travel of the Army, where there were deficiencies.[144] Both President Truman and an economy-minded House of Representatives reduced requested Air Force appropriations for fiscal year 1948, with the result that Congress finally appropriated only $145,300,000 for air research and development for the fiscal year beginning on 1 July 1947. This figure would be the nadir of Air Force research and development appropriations after World War II.[145]

Writing on 11 April 1947, General LeMay emphasized that "the greatest need at this time is assurance of a stabilized annual appropriation for research and development."[146] Later on, Department of Defense experts would state that the curtailment of research and development in the immediate postwar years had been a major mistake.[147] The reduction of air research and development funding had an immediate effect upon Air Force work on guided missiles. Making his last appearance as deputy commanding general of the Army Air Forces before the

House Appropriations subcommittee in March 1947, General Eaker explained that with an all-out program (similar to that which had expedited the nuclear weapon), a 5,000-mile-range missile probably could be developed in five years. The Air Force, however, could not bear the expense of such a program and had to progress on the research and development effort at a more leisurely pace, which might produce an intercontinental missile in 10 to 15 years. "We cannot," Eaker said, ". . . abandon the development of the very long-range very heavy bomber as a primary weapon of our long-range striking force but we should, as a wise precaution, spend the necessary experimental funds to insure that we are the first in the field with a long-range guided missile which may be the primary weapon at some future date, but probably not within 15 years."[148] As it happened, however, the Air Force was compelled to give even more emphasis in spending its scarce research and development funds to the support of the Air Force in being than Eaker had thought would be necessary. These projects included range extension, long-range strategic aerial reconnaissance, new jet bombers, high-thrust aircraft propulsion systems, short-range airborne guided missiles, and high-speed fighters.[149] In 1947 the Air Force reevaluated its guided missile requirements and gave priorities to research and development projects that promised to increase the capabilities of the Air Force in being. The new order of priority for missiles included: (1) missiles to enhance strategic air bombardment with conventional aircraft, (2) air defense missiles, (3) surface-to-surface missiles, and (4) interim missiles to include guided bombs and drone aircraft. Under this criteria and because of shortages of funds, the missile project MX-774 was not renewed in 1948, but the Consolidated-Vultee Aircraft Corporation continued some studies in the intercontinental ballistic missile field with its own funds.[150]

Emerging Soviet Threats

In the winter of 1946–47 the United States began to recognize that its policy of cooperation with the Soviet Union was rapidly breaking down. The antics of the Soviet representatives in the United Nations, the Iranian crisis of 1946, the Greek civil war, and Soviet pressure on Turkey gave the United States a better appreciation of the bipolar nature of world power and of the challenge of Soviet expansionism. As W. Barton Leach wrote in February 1947, "if we have war it is going to be with Russia," but "if we have no war with Russia we shall have no war at all for at least two decades." Although Leach had returned to academic life at Harvard University from his wartime service in the Army Air Services, he remained a close friend of General Vandenberg's and he may well have expressed some degree of Air Force thinking.[151] In an appearance before the House Subcommittee on Appropriations also in February 1947, Brig Gen George A. Lincoln again demonstrated—with increasing urgency—the close relationship between military capabilities and foreign policy. "The War Department's broad policies . . . ," he stated, "must be based on those of our State Department. Conversely, the State

Department, in formulating its national policies must take into consideration the capabilities of the armed forces to maintain a respectable position in the world which makes our emissaries respected."[152] Revealing clearly for the first time that the United States recognized the menace of the Soviet Union, President Truman requested authority from Congress on 12 March 1947 to extend military and economic assistance to Greece and Turkey to enable them to combat internal Communist subversion and external Soviet pressure. In view of the deterioration of relations with the Soviet Union, General Spaatz began to speak openly of a war with "a continental empire" and the "problem of winning against great masses of people with great internal resources."[153]

With full support from the War Department, Spaatz submitted a budget for fiscal year 1948 that would have permitted the Army Air Forces to attain a minimum, permanent postwar strength of 70 groups and 22 separate squadrons. The Bureau of the Budget, however, reduced the air request to an amount sufficient to maintain a peacetime strength of only 55 groups and 17 separate squadrons. The Air Force, nevertheless, obtained authority to base its procurement and training objectives on a 70-group strength and to activate 15 groups and five squadrons that would not be manned or equipped.[154] In appearances before the House Subcommittee on Appropriations, Spaatz emphasized America's vulnerability to air attack from across the Arctic and urged that the only way to prevent bombs from falling on the United States "is to get them at the place they start from, and that is primarily our mission." Maj Gen Otto P. Weyland, chief of AAF plans, pointed out that America's air strategy was one of defense and retaliation. "It is conceivable," said Weyland, "that the United States will start an aggressive war. Hence, it is obvious that at the start of a war, we will be the recipient of an all-out surprise attack."[155]

In May 1947 Congress appropriated the $400 million that President Truman requested as aid for Greece and Turkey, thus indicating approval for the Truman doctrine's objective of containing Soviet expansion. The first session of the 80th Congress was reluctant to vote military appropriations in the amounts requested. The House made a 10-percent cut in the AAF budget; part of it was restored by the Senate but only after General Eisenhower made a personal plea to get the money.[156] Some of the reluctance to vote military preparedness funds may have sprung from the findings of the President's Advisory Commission on Universal Military Training, which reported on 29 May 1947. This distinguished panel endorsed military preparedness as the surest way of checking international aggression. It believed that World War III would begin with atomic sneak attacks against the United States, but it felt that such attacks were not imminent. "For a period estimated by responsible scientists at not less than 4 years and not more than 10 years," the commission reported, "we can expect immunity from such an attack because we alone will possess the atomic bomb." In a final summation, the president's commission noted that "we cannot safely assume that we will have sole possession of atomic explosives beyond 1951, although most scientists and engineers familiar with the production of the atomic bomb believe it will be 1955 at the earliest before an attack in quantity can be made against us."[157] As a matter of record, moreover, the Joint Chiefs of Staff, and specifically both Spaatz and Vandenberg, placed more emphasis on aid to threatened nations under the Truman doctrine and the Marshall economic recovery program than they did to attainment of the 70-group program. "The 70-group program," Spaatz testified, "should not be reached at the expense of arms aid to Europe." Vandenberg said, "that the 70-group program, as visualized by the Air Force, with Europe unprepared, would not be as efficient as a lesser number of groups with a sound economy of the United States and a western Europe that could resist aggression and give us time."[158]

Acting on the basis of this official line of thought and understanding that most of its units would be equipped with World War II aircraft, the Army Air Forces obtained authority in July 1947 to activate or organize all of the groups in the initial 55-group phase of the 70-group program and to have them in place with some degree of operational effectiveness by the end of the year. In the final allocation of strength, the 55 groups included 13 very heavy bombardment, three light bombardment, 24 fighter, seven reconnaissance, and eight troop carrier groups.[159] Each major command sustained a reduction of combat strength, but the new allocation indicated that the Army Air Forces was beginning to mobilize against a particularized strategic threat somewhat different from the generalized concepts in initial postwar planning.

"As the initial blow will come from the air and be delivered by air power," stated Gen George C. Kenney, who headed the Strategic Air Command, in September 1947, "the answer must be for us to maintain our air power strong enough to deter any possible enemy from attacking us."[160] Under the 55-group phase, 12 very heavy bombardment groups, five fighter groups, and one very long range reconnaissance group were assigned to the Strategic Air Command.[161] Even though the Strategic Air Command enjoyed priorities in manning and equipment, it did not obtain new equipment or a complete acceptance of its operational concept. Immediately after V-J Day, the Twentieth Air Force had been assigned to the Pacific theater; hence, one very heavy bombardment group and one very long range reconnaissance squadron continued to be assigned to the Far East Air Forces in the Pacific. The Strategic Air Command maintained that these two units should be placed under its command and that their functions should be performed by SAC groups which would stage to Pacific bases as necessary. But Gen Douglas MacArthur, commander in chief, US Far East Command, did not agree to give up those units.[162] Other than the fact that B-29s would be unable to reach many targets in the Sovet Union, the Strategic Air Command's most pressing aircraft problem in organizing to meet the growing Soviet threat concerned fighter escort. The Army Air Forces accepted the position that "the necessity of providing adequate fighter protection for very long range bombardment aircraft was conclusively demonstrated during World War II." To protect its bombers against hostile jet fighters, SAC would require jet fighter escorts. However, no American jet fighter had enough range to escort a B-29, and it was problematical whether jet aircraft could escort relatively slow conventional B-29s. Pending solution of the problem, the Strategic Air Command indicated that it would expect to operate its bombers over hostile territory only at night.[163]

In initial postwar planning, the Army Air Forces had considered air defense essentially a mobilization problem. When he was named to head the Air Defense Command, Lt Gen George E. Stratemeyer accordingly was instructed to give most of his attention to establishing an aircraft control and warning system and to managing the Air National Guard and Air Reserve, which would, upon mobilization, provide fighter units for air defense.[164] As thus laid out, the air defense mission appeared simple, but Stratemeyer found it complex. Thinking in terms of scarce military funds and the eventual need to detect and destroy supersonic jet aircraft and nuclear missiles, Stratemeyer thought that the first priority in the Air Force budget should be given to research and development, the second to the Strategic Air Command, and the third to the air defense system.[165] Stratemeyer believed that both the equipment and doctrine for air defense was obsolete and he urged that a minimum nucleus of regular Air Force interceptor groups ought to be assigned to the Air Defense Command.[166] While it held to the concept that all available fighter units would be assigned to air defense in an emergency, the Army Air Forces agreed that the Air Defense Command should have some regular groups of its own. Thus, a fighter group was activated at Dow Field, Maine, in November 1946, and two additional fighter groups (all-weather) were assigned to the command in May and June 1947 with stations at Mitchel Field, New York, and Hamilton Field, California.[167] The fighter groups assigned to air defense were withdrawn from the Tactical Air Command. Despite efforts to dramatize the tactical air mission, General Quesada found it hard to maintain a going organization. Shortly after its establishment, the Tactical Air Command organized its assigned groups into the Ninth Air Force and the Third Air Force (Troop Carrier), but, because of the reduction in its troop carrier units, the latter organization was inactivated on 1 November 1946.[168] Since most tactical air units were assigned to the Far East Air Forces, the United States Air Forces in Europe, the Alaskan Air Command, the Pacific Air Command, and the Caribbean Air Command, the Tactical Air Command had only one light bombardment, three fighter, three tactical reconnaissance, and three troop carrier groups as its share of the 55-group strength.[169]

The Finletter Commission

After he had become secretary of defense, Forrestal noted, "At the present time, we are keeping our military expenditures below the levels which our military leaders must in good conscience estimate as the minimum which would themselves ensure national security. By doing so we are able to increase our expenditures to assist in European recovery." Forrestal considered that the United States was taking a calculated risk that was justifiable. "As long as we can out-produce the world, can control the sea and can strike inland with the atomic bomb," he wrote, "we can assume certain risks otherwise unacceptable in an effort to restore world trade, to restore the balance of power — military power — and to eliminate some of the conditions which breed war."[170] Forrestal's reasoning held good only as long as the United States possessed an aircraft industry that could meet the mobilization requirements of the nation's armed forces. By the spring of 1947 it was evident that many of the postwar assumptions regarding this industry were in error. The widespread assumption that a rising demand for commercial aircraft would help tide a number of companies over readjustments failed to materialize; the aircraft industry remained from 80 to 90 percent dependent on government purchases of military aircraft. The Air Force and the Navy had been unable to purchase a quantity of aircraft required to keep industry solvent, and the changing year-to-year purchasing programs had caused higher pricing of aircraft, thus reducing the quantity that could be purchased. Jet aircraft, moreover, cost substantially more than conventional planes, thus further decreasing quantity procurement.[171]

Despite their pressing concern for European recovery, both President Truman and Congress showed increasing alarm about the state of preparedness of the American aircraft industry. At the recommendation of the Air Coordinating Committee, Truman appointed a committee on 18 July 1947 headed by Thomas K. Finletter and charged it to make an objective inquiry into national aviation policies and problems and to assist him in formulating an integrated national aviation policy. The President's Air Policy Commission assembled on 29 July, held formal hearings from 8 September to 3 December, and completed its report on 30 December 1947.[172] Meanwhile, Congress — where the Republican party held a majority — felt "a general concern over national security and the threatened bankruptcy of the aircraft industry and civil air carriers." Authorized on 22 July 1947, a temporary Joint Congressional Aviation Policy Board was formed with Sen Owen R. Brewster as chairman. This board organized an advisory council of civil aviation representatives and retired military leaders, including General Arnold. The congressional board held its first meeting on 15 September. Although it held frequent meetings of its advisory council and staff, after the first session the panel chose to use the elaborate testimony of the president's commission rather than call witnesses. The Joint Congressional Aviation Policy Board made its report to Congress on 1 March 1948.[173] Although the conclusions of the Finletter and Brewster investigations were quite similar, the Brewster board was more pronounced in its criticism of the defense establishment. From the outset of its investigation, moreover, the Brewster board believed that "the primary problem of national aviation policy was one of providing well-balanced military and naval air forces rather than one of finding means to maintain an aircraft industry. If the former were accomplished," the board believed, "the health of the latter would be assured."[174]

In November and December 1947 the testimony of influential witnesses before the President's Aviation Policy Commission manifested a growing awareness of the importance of US military strength but illustrated diverse opinions as to what its composition ought to be. "Insofar as our thinking about preparation, readiness for war, or national security . . . is concerned," said Secretary Forrestal,

> we are faced with the hard and solid fact that as a democracy we do not start wars and therefore can never be in a complete state of readiness. . . . This nation's experience has been a clear demonstration that peace will not be furthered by the neglect of military strength. . . . In the past, we have invited aggression by that neglect. The military policies of this nation stem from a single desire and obligation. That is to use our strength as a force for peace.

He emphasized the close relationship between the State Department and the National Defense Establishment. "One of our principal tasks," he said, "is to see to it that there is integration between our foreign policy and our military attitude. In other words, to see to it that the policy does not outstrip power."

Forrestal pointed out that America's concept of national security had changed. Before World War II, he said,

> our concepts of security were the integrity of our own domain, and the freedom from . . . attack or danger of invasion. . . . In my own view . . . our security is now far broader than that. Our security is . . . our ability to contribute to the reconstruction of the world, and . . . our military requirements have to be fitted into the pattern of what we do toward the other larger results, in other words, the reconstruction of society.

He also said: "It would not serve us to have the greatest military establishment in the world and concurrently be going down the road to continued and continuous inflation." He did not agree that the individual military services should present their requirements to Congress because "even in wartime, you could never meet the requirements of all the services . . . there has to be an accommodation of both . . . saying what we need and then someone saying what we shall get." As for air power, Forrestal believed that "the United States must have air forces sufficiently powerful to protect its own security and territory and sufficiently powerful and versatile to be capable of making swift and effective counterattacks in the event of war." He felt that air power should be developed over a period of years in an orderly manner, and he expected that the Joint Chiefs of Staff would provide a strategic plan for the military establishment which would give "an opportunity to bring into better balance the components of that establishment."[175]

Leading the Navy testimony before the President's Air Policy Commission, retired Adm Chester W. Nimitz provided a statement prefaced with a warning: "Unless we retain our ability to control the sea . . . we may eventually find ourselves exchanging long range air attacks which will be indecisive alike against ourselves and our enemies, but at the same time damaging to our own cities and vital installations." Nimitz emphasized that naval aviation was an integral part of the fleet. "I cannot . . . accept the idea," he said, "that naval aviation is a part of the Air

Force.... I regard the Navy, the Air Force, and the Army as you would the three legs of a stool... and I think each one of those forces must be strong enough to carry out the mission which is assigned to it." Secretary of the Navy John L. Sullivan argued that "any de-emphasis in Naval aviation spells the end of America's control of the sea." "During the war," he said,

> England learned that whenever a sufficient number of German bombers came over on a determined raid, enough of them got through to give a great deal of trouble.... Later on, when the bombs kept coming over it was most apparent that the only defense against determined air attack or guided missiles—and the same proves true in the atomic techniques—the only defense is to... put a very large number of men on ships, transport them overseas and capture the platforms from which those weapons were launched.[176]

"I believe in air power, without 'ifs,' 'buts,' or 'howevers'," stated former Secretary of War Robert P. Patterson. "I believe that our national defense should be centered on air power... to a far greater degree than is the case at present. It is my opinion... that we will not need the strongest Army in the world or the strongest standing Navy in the world, but we will need the strongest Air Force in the world."[177] Secretary of the Army Kenneth C. Royall described air power as "our first line of defense in the event of war," but, in view of the fact that World War II had had "to be won by tanks, guns and men, on the ground," he asked the commission "not to forget that the Navy and the Army, as well as the Air Forces, must be taken into account in cutting up shares of national defense."[178] Representing views of a scientist, Dr Carl T. Compton, president of the Massachusetts Institute of Technology, stated that the question of whether more powerful nuclear weapons could be developed was still in the realm of speculation. However, he felt that a surprise atomic attack against the United States even with current weapons would be a "very unpleasant... prospect." He recommended that for a mobile striking air force to be employed "as a strategic weapon against the most important of the enemy's sources of industrial and military warfare." "I believe," he concluded, "that the existence of a striking Air Force of that type, always ready as a threat of retaliation, would be the strongest single thing that we could do in this country, to act as a deterrent against aggression by any other nation."[179]

Appearing in behalf of the Air Force, Secretary Symington offered the view that the United States had been "forced into a position of world leadership and of responsibilities of a global extent" at the same time that it had "lost the cushion of time and distance." Spaatz described the major segments of the Air Force plan for national security as being the 70 combat groups, adequately manned and equipped civilian components, plans and installations for aerial defense of the United States, a research and development program second to none, vigorous and alert aircraft manufacturing and air transport industries, and an industrial mobilization plan. Both Spaatz and Vandenberg devoted most of their testimony to explaining the aircraft requirements of the 70-group program.[180] Maj Alexander P. de Seversky, however, discussed broader aspects of air warfare. "As long as we use piloted aircraft," he argued, "the destruction of the enemy cannot be accomplished without first assuming control of the air above his territory. . . . Penetration by piloted airplanes, even with jet and rocket propulsion, will be unthinkable without all-out air combat. Only with the advent of intercontinental rockets can there be any talk of penetration without combat." He pointed out that the 70-group Air Force would not necessarily represent air power in being in the full strategic sense. "A strategic military force is one which is self-sustained in its own medium, regardless of its base; capable of assuming control of its medium while denying it to the adversary. By thus assuming freedom of action in its own medium, it can bring about the end of hostilities through the direct application of force upon the enemy's means to wage war." In the past, armies had been strategic forces on land and navies on the high seas. "Today," he said, "when neither of them can maintain a battle under hostile skies, they have ceased to be strategic forces and become auxiliaries to Air Power." De Seversky conceived that an air force in being should have two main divisions: an intercontinental striking force large enough to paralyze an enemy's industrial establishment and a continental defense force of a size sufficient to defend the vital industries of the United States.[181]

"We believe," stated the President's Air Policy Commission on the basis of testimony presented to it, "that the United States will be secure in an absolute sense only if the institution of war itself is abolished under a regime of law." Since early attainment of this condition seemed doubtful, the commission found that "our security includes . . . winning any war we may get into . . . not losing the first campaign of war . . . not having our cities destroyed and our population decimated in the process of . . . winning the first campaign . . . not having our way of life . . . taken from us in preparing for war."[182] The Joint Congressional Aviation Policy Board reported that the only defense against modern war "will be [a] swift and more devastating retaliatory attack." The board also noted that

> the primary military objective of modern warfare is no longer the armed forces of the enemy. The primary objective is the war potential or . . . the industrial organization and the resources of the enemy. . . . The great contenders in a possible war of the future will engage in the political and then the industrial phases of that war. The political phase of the next war has been actively engaged in since V-E Day—and the industrial phase is clearly recognizable.[183]

With professed reluctance, the President's Air Policy Commission stated that "relative security is to be found only in a policy of arming the United States so strongly (1) that other nations will hesitate to attack us or our vital national interest because of the violence of the counterattack they would have to face, and (2) that if we are attacked we will be able to smash the assault at the earliest possible moment." The commission recommended that the United States should maintain "an adequate Navy and Ground Force" but that the military establishment "must be built around the air arm. . . . Our military security must be based on air power." In view of the violence of an enemy attack against the United States, the commission stated: "What we must have and can support is a reasonably strong defensive establishment to minimize the enemy's blow, but above all a counteroffensive air force in being which will be so powerful that if an aggressor does attack, we will be able to retaliate with the utmost violence and to seize and hold the advanced positions from which we can divert the destruction from our homeland to his."[184]

The President's Air Policy Commission sought to base its military aircraft procurement recommendations on a firm estimate of the date by which an enemy nation might be expected to possess nuclear weapons. The commission found that expert opinion on the subject varied from that of some highly qualified persons who said that other nations might already possess the weapons to that of other equally well-qualified persons who estimated that other nations would not possess atomic weapons in quantity for fifteen years. The commission thus set its own date of 1 January 1953 as A-day—the date when the US air arm should be able to deal with a possible attack against the United States. The commission stated that a future hostility might well be a localized conflict or a practice war such as the Spanish civil war had been, but it urged that the United States must assume that "if the enemy can do it he will make a direct air assault on the United States mainland regardless how or where the first shooting starts." The commission recommended that immediate steps be taken to build the Air Force to 70 groups (6,869 first-line aircraft) and the Air National Guard to 27 groups (3,212 first-line aircraft) and to equip the 34-group Air Force Reserve adequately. The Air Force was also judged to require an additional reserve of some 8,100 aircraft. It recommended that the 70 groups should be ready for service by 1 January 1950 and the complete Air Force program should be in being by the end of 1952. The commission found it more difficult to evaluate Navy requirements for aircraft. Although the Navy would not be required to oppose a hostile surface fleet in the future, it would be expected to keep supply lines open to forward air bases and to overseas sources of essential war materials. The aircraft carrier would be the major ship of the future Navy; to carry out its future responsibilities (one of the most important being protection against modern submarines) the Navy would require 5,793 first-line planes plus about 5,100 in support. The Navy had presented strong arguments for increasing its air strength to 8,000 first-line planes with 6,500 planes in support, but the president's commission believed that such an increase would constitute a naval expansion which should be deferred until the Joint Chiefs of Staff had completed a strategic plan that would demonstrate the need for a naval expansion. In addition to providing the minimum-level combat air arm that the United States would require on 1 January 1953, the President's Air Policy Commission believed that expanded aircraft procurement would enable the nation's aircraft industries to maintain the industrial base necessary for a national mobilization emergency.[185]

The Joint Congressional Aviation Policy Board was openly critical of the fact that the Joint Chiefs of Staff had not completed a unified plan of action for a future conflict that would have allowed it to make an exact computation of the aircraft requirements of the Navy and the Air Force. In view of the "inability of the Joint Chiefs of Staff to prepare a unified plan," the congressional board accepted the unilateral statements of requirements offered to it under two plans of action: Plan A to provide the air strength necessary to mount promptly an effective, continuing, and successful air offensive against a major enemy, and Plan B to prevent the loss of a war at the outset of hostilities through effective retaliation but not a sustained offensive action. Plan A included the Air Force's 70-group program with 20,541 aircraft plus the Navy program of 14,500 aircraft, or a total of 35,041 aircraft to be procured between 1949 and 1953, when procurement would begin to level off. Plan B was substantially the same program, but with less reserve aircraft. "We believe," stated the Joint Congressional Aviation Policy Board, "that when ... a unified plan has been determined, the total requirements of the armed services may be materially reduced below the totals of the estimates prepared unilaterally."[186] As an additional means of maintaining a desirable mobilization base, both the congressional board and the president's commission suggested that the armed services should give thought to contracting with civilian firms for part of the military's aircraft maintenance. Contract overhaul of military aircraft should result in monetary savings and would build up civil staffs trained in such work for use in a mobilization emergency.[187]

Some of the men who worked on the President's Air Policy Commission report expressed regret that the commission had not been more critical of the weakness of the overall defense plan for the United States.[188] De Seversky later suggested that the president's commission "strategically didn't make much sense" except to the aviation industry, because it recommended everything that flew—strategic aviation, tactical aviation, naval aviation, marine aviation, airlines, helicopters, and private flying. He described the division of the strategic problem into two phases, according to whether or not Russia had atomic weapons, as being unrealistic. "That, I thought," said de Seversky, "was a great fallacy because improved explosives don't necessarily change strategy; they may change tactics, but they do not change strategy. Whether you are carrying TNT or atomic bombs, you will have to win control over the medium through which you want to make a delivery. The means of delivery are more important than the explosives."[189] A board of Air Staff officers named by Secretary Symington to analyze the reports of the president's commission and the congressional board took more optimistic attitudes when it reported on 23 March 1948. These officers judged the four primary functions of the Air Force to be: defense against air attack, the capability to deliver an immediate retaliatory attack against an aggressor, tactical air support of ground forces, and gaining and maintaining air supremacy in order to carry out sustained air operations against vital enemy installations. Since both the commission and the board had recommended that the Air Force attain a 70-group strength, the board of officers recommended that the Air Force begin an immediate expansion toward that program.[190]

Air Power and the Berlin Airlift

In the summer of 1947, prior to the organization of the National Defense Establishment and the investigations by the president's commission and the congressional board, the Army, Navy, and Air Force had unilaterally prepared their budgets for fiscal year 1949. The budgets were based on the overall target of $10 billion that President Truman had indicated would be available for military defense. The service budgets supposedly were developed from Joint Chiefs of Staff plans, but the Joint Chiefs neither reviewed nor approved the detailed military budget. When Forrestal appeared before the president's commission, he let it be known that he would be very reluctant to disturb the structure of the fiscal year 1949 military budget, except on the urgent request of the Joint Chiefs of Staff.[191] The Air Force portion of the national defense budget for fiscal year 1949 allowed the operation of a maximum of 55 combat groups and 17 separate squadrons and provided $700 million for the continued modernization of the combat groups by replacement of their World War II aircraft.[192]

In visualizing the expenditure of the $700 million for new aircraft, Air Force planners committed enough funds in the 1949 budget for the purchase of enough additional jet fighters to equip a total of 13 of the Air Force's 24 fighter groups with these aircraft.[193] However, none of the available jet fighters could escort bombers to far distant targets. Still the Air Force accepted the doctrinal lesson of World War II that an attainment of a preliminary air superiority was necessary in order that surface operations could be undertaken successfully or that decisive bombing of an enemy's vitals could be accomplished. In July 1947, however, in the United States Strategic Bombing Survey report titled *Air Campaigns of the Pacific War*, Maj Gen Orvil A. Anderson questioned the air superiority doctrine. "Air superiority is not an end in itself," suggested Anderson. "Operations must be evaluated in terms of the decisiveness of the action and the cost to our own war potential. If the over-all damage inflicted on the enemy significantly outweighs the cost of the operation in terms of manpower, materiel, and production potential, the operation may be strategically sound."[194] During World War II, the Eighth Air Force had found that the best method for daylight penetrations of Germany was with large bomber formations. In the summer of 1947, however, interceptor tests flown by the 1st Fighter Group against B-29s indicated that P-80 pilots had difficulty intercepting a single B-29.[195] As the speed of both bombers and fighters increased, General Kenney reasoned that dogfighting between aircraft would be impossible and that intercepting fighters might be able to make no more than a single head-on pass against a bomber.[196]

Although Air Force thinkers had begun to express cautious optimism that the employment of nuclear bombers without fighter escort might be strategically feasible, the USAF Aircraft and Weapons Board, when it began to study the problem of attacking Soviet targets in the autumn of 1947, was uncertain about the kinds of bombers that ought to be procured for the Strategic Air Command. At this time it still appeared that the future supply of atomic bombs would be very limited and that the Strategic Air Command would have to plan to use a heavy proportion of conventional bombs in a strategic air campaign. The major problem, however, was to penetrate Soviet defenses and attack heavily defended targets with atomic bombs.[197] The only intercontinental bomber that the Air Force had in prospect was the giant, conventional B-36. An order for 100 of these planes had been placed on 23 July 1943, but to meet price rises and the costs of improved engines this wartime order had been cut to 95 aircraft. Since the war appropriation covering the contract would run out in June 1948, the Air force would need new appropriations to complete it. The B-36 was large and appeared to be relatively slow, but it was the only aircraft that could bomb Soviet targets from bases in the United States.[198] B-29s and improved B-50s were already in the Strategic Air Command inventory, but these planes lacked the range to strike deep in Soviet targets and return. The Air Force had two jet strategic bombers under contemplation. In 1944 in response to a requirement, the Boeing Company had developed the six-jet, medium-range B-47. In 1946 Boeing had won the design contest for an intercontinental jet bomber that would be designated as the B-52. But, with available power plants and a requirement for built-in intercontinental range in its design stage, the B-52 was threatening to become even larger than the B-36.[199] Recognizing that Air Force bombers lacked global range, Col Dale O. Smith suggested in an article published in the autumn of 1947 that the Air Force might prepare its crews to fly one-way atomic combat missions. Smith suggested that the crews would have a good chance to evade and survive. Such blitz tactics would rapidly expend the bomber force, but Smith thought that there "seems to be little doubt that the nation making the first atomic bomb strike in force will be the victor."[200]

In an effort to clear up indecision within the Air Force regarding the strategic bomber program, General Spaatz formed a Heavy Bombardment Committee on 9 September 1947 with representatives from the Air Staff, the Strategic Air Command, the Air University, and the Air Materiel Command, and charged it to study "methods of and instrumentalities for air delivery of individual and mass atomic attacks against any potential enemy from bases within the continental United States." In its discussions, the bombardment committee shared the current concern that the B-36 might not have as good a chance to penetrate as would faster medium bombers. Based on this belief, the committee sought means to extend the range of medium bombers. General Kenney had already urged the development of tracked landing gears that would enable his bombers to operate from hastily prepared airstrips, possibly on the polar ice caps. Another alternative, favored by both the Strategic Air Command and the Air Materiel Command, was to develop air-to-air refueling equipment and to employ tanker aircraft that could refuel strike aircraft en route to a target. Such aerial refueling had been used in 1929 when then Major Spaatz and Captain Eaker had broken the world's aircraft flight endurance record in the *Question Mark*. Thought had been given to the use of aerial refueling during World War II, but the technique was logistically infeasible for supporting massed bomber attacks that employed iron bombs. As a means of extending the range of fighter-escort aircraft, General Vandenberg had urged aerial refueling in 1945. Aerial refueling would be expensive, however, since two aircraft — a bomber and a tanker — would be required to accomplish a single sortie.

After studying all aspects of the bomber problem, the Heavy Bombardment Committee recognized that the most practical way to extend the range of existing medium bombers and to lighten the design weight of the proposed intercontinental B-52 jet bomber was to develop equipment and techniques for air-to-air refueling of bombers from specially equipped tanker aircraft. Aerial refueling also would permit the B-47 jet bomber, which was still in prototype awaiting a decision for production, to strike far distant targets. The committee, therefore, recommended that air-to-air refueling be developed as a matter of first priority. It, nevertheless, emphasized that the Air Force should not completely close the door on the development of aircraft with built-in range. Since much of the information about the B-36 was still speculative, the panel recommended that the Air Force ought to continue the funding of the 95 B-36s that were on order. The latter serial models of these B-36s could be equipped with improved engines, and it might be possible to convert some of the earlier serial B-36As into aerial tankers. At sessions held on 27-30 January 1948, the USAF Aircraft and Weapons Board accepted the Heavy Bombardment Committee's recommendations, and Spaatz formally approved them on 3 March 1948.[201]

In the winter of 1947-48, the Soviet Union began revealing its aggressive designs upon Western Europe. According to unofficial reports reaching the US State Department late in 1947, the Soviet general staff sought permission from the Soviet government to push troops straight into Western Europe, thus preempting the rebuilding of Western Europe with military force before Marshall Plan aid could become effective. As the story was told, however, the Politburo overruled the Red Army and issued orders for internal Communist strikes and revolts throughout Western Europe. The organization for revolution was activated in December 1947, but the essential structure of most European governments held up despite an agonizing week of strikes and disorders.[202] On 24 February 1948, however, a Communist coup d'état overthrew the government of Czechoslovakia, which had been a model of democratic rule in central Europe. Few Communist acts of aggression shook the Western nations as profoundly as the loss of this friendly republic to the forces of Soviet subversion.[203] In a top-secret message from Berlin on 5 March, Gen Lucius D. Clay, commander in chief, US European Command, reported that war might well be imminent. "For many months, based on logical analysis," Clay messaged, "I have felt and held that war was unlikely for at least ten years. Within the last few weeks, I have felt a subtle change in Soviet attitude which I cannot define but which now gives me a feeling that it may come with dramatic suddenness."[204]

When he appeared before the House Subcommittee on Military Appropriations on 16 March 1948, Secretary Forrestal conceded that the international position of the United States had deteriorated. "Wars," he said, "are usually caused by the assurance on the part of an aggressive power that it possesses sufficient superiority to overcome any possible obstacles to the success of its military efforts.... Since the United States is a democracy—a form of government which traditionally does not start a war of aggression—its national defense policy must be directed at preventing the development of that tempting imbalance of power." Forrestal admitted that the president's commission and the congressional board had shown that the nation's air strength was less than its strategic position required. "There is no question," he said, "but that our national security would be greatly enhanced by such a powerful Air Force." He argued, nonetheless, that the armed forces budgets had "to strike a balance between funds which are available and expenditures which might be considered strategically desirable or even essential." Thus, Forrestal supported the $10 billion military budget, which would maintain the Air Force at 55 combat groups and would keep the Army and Navy in an appropriate balance with this force. "While the Air Force and naval aviation alone may be the cutting edge," he concluded, "we must also have the logistical organization to back them up, the adequately equipped Ground Force to seize and hold the bases from which planes fly, the ships with which to supply and help protect such bases, and all of the other elements of balanced strength."[205]

Speaking to the same committee later in the same day, Secretary Symington emphasized that an Air Force in being provided two assets: "It serves as an active deterrent to any aggressor, and it is the force which envelops him in prompt and decisive retaliatory action if he risks war with the United States." In response to a direct question, both Symington and Spaatz, who accompanied the secretary, asserted that the minimum air power necessary for the security of the United States was the 70-group program. Symington agreed that the "maintenance of an adequate Army" was "essential to the effectiveness of the Air Force." Several hundred thousand Army troops would be necessary for "holding and servicing an airbase complex in a forward area." In subsequent testimony, Gen Omar N. Bradley, who had succeeded General Eisenhower as Army chief of staff, demonstrated the Army's importance by visualizing how a future war would be fought: "First, by repelling any attack made against us, and repairing the damage, and preparing the people to receive that shock without getting too discouraged. Next, we would immediately secure bases we do not now have from which he might attack us.... Next, we would try to launch a counterattack against him by air. The next phase would be trying to move those bases closer to the enemy."[206]

While congressional hearings on the defense establishment's fiscal year 1949 budget continued, the Soviet commander in Germany served notice on 1 April 1948 that his troops would begin to inspect Allied trains and trucks going to Berlin. The Soviet military blockade of Berlin was beginning although it would not be clamped down in earnest until June. When Forrestal appeared before the House Armed

Services Committee on 12 April, Representative Carl Vinson told him frankly that he intended to seek to secure an additional $992 million for aircraft procurement funds to provide a 70-group Air Force. Answering a question that Forrestal had put to them earlier, the Joint Chiefs stated on 14 April that, based solely on military considerations, they believed that the administration should advocate a balanced military establishment commensurate with the 70-group program for the Air Force. To support such a balanced force, more than $9 billion would need to be added to the fiscal year 1949 budget. Forrestal returned this report with an additional request that the Joint Chiefs gave him an estimate of the additional force which could be obtained with an additional $3 billion rather than $9 billion. Within the Air Force share of this increment, Spaatz figured that the Air Force could — by utilizing many mothballed planes rather than buying a complete complement of new aircraft — afford to activate all of the 70-group program except for two light bomber and two troop carrier groups, which could be delayed since they would be scheduled to support ground divisions that would not be active before 1950. Apparently accepting the Joint Chiefs' planning, President Truman forwarded a supplemental appropriation request to Congress on 13 May asking for $3,068,441,000.[207] Truman stated that every effort should be made to reassure the public that the increased appropriation was "not one of mobilization for war, but rather one of maintaining a firmer foundation of preparedness on which a more rapid mobilization could be based than would be possible without the increases." Truman enjoined Forrestal to proceed with great care in making commitments and to give the entire program a realistic review in September and December 1948. On 25 June, Truman further directed that the Air Force would not expand beyond a strength of 411,000 men and 9,240 active aircraft pending further review in the autumn of 1948.[208]

Shortly after he succeeded Spaatz as Air Force chief of staff on 30 April 1948, Gen Hoyt S. Vandenberg faced the immediate problem of mobilizing existing Air Force capabilities to resist Soviet aggression in Germany and the longer range problem of expanding the Air Force within the limits set forth by President Truman. In Germany, on 24 June, Soviet troops finally halted all rail and road movement from the west into beleaguered Berlin. Later on, Gen Maxwell D. Taylor would assert that people like General Clay and others felt that the United States "should have used force on the highway, at least to verify what the Russian intent was."[209] Contemporary evidence, however, indicates that from the start of the crisis Washington authorities proceeded on the assumption that Berlin would be supplied as long as possible by airlift. "After discussion with the military services... and ... throughout the National Security Council and finally with the President and the appropriate committees of Congress to whom I reported," said Under Secretary of State Robert A. Lovett, "we decided to stand firm in Berlin and not be thrown out, confident that we could do the job ultimately by the same techniques that we used in lifting approximately 70,000 tons in one month over the hump from India into China at very high altitudes."[210]

In Germany, where he had been assigned as commander of the United States Air Force in Europe, General LeMay started the Berlin Airlift with locally available planes on 26 June 1948. Back in Washington, Secretary of State George C. Marshall and Lovett emphasized that the United States could not afford to bluff. "We had to have something to back us up," Lovett maintained, "in case the Russians wanted to use this as an excuse for a war." At a meeting on 27 June, Forrestal, Lovett, and high-ranking officers discussed the advisability of deploying two additional B-29 squadrons to join the squadron of the 301st Bombardment Group, which was on a rotational tour of duty at Fürstenfeldbruck Air Base in Germany and of securing approval from Great Britain for the movement of two other B-29 groups to British bases. With Truman's approval, the State Department queried Britain on her willingness to accommodate the groups and received an affirmative reply.[211] On 27 June, Air Staff officers went to Andrews Field and verbally briefed the Strategic Air Command as to what was expected of it. Without delay, the Strategic Air Command ordered the two remaining squadrons of the 301st Group to move to Goose Bay, Labrador, the normal summer staging point for Europe. The 28th and 307th Groups were put on short alerts at their home airfields. Given orders to continue the deployment, the 301st Group was in place in Germany on 2 July. Some additional time was required to prepare bases in Great Britain, but the 307th arrived there on 17 July and the 28th had its planes in England on 18 July.[212] As soon as the B-29 deployment was completed, the Military Air Transport Service was able to put most of its capabilities into the Berlin Airlift. Maj Gen William H. Tunner took command of the augmented Airlift Task Force (Provisional) in Europe on 30 July. Ultimately employing US Air Force, Navy, and Royal Air Force transport aircraft, Tunner soon geared up Operation Vittles to its maximum capacity; the airlift carried a total of 2,325 million tons of food, fuel, and supplies into Berlin before the blockade was ended. One of the most important immediate lessons of the airlift, according to Tunner, was the inherent efficiency of large transport planes to accomplish important airlift missions.[213]

"For the first time in history," stated *Air Force Magazine* in September 1948,

> the United States is employing its Air Force as a diplomatic weapon.... Today, in keeping with its coming of age as the nation's first line of defense, the USAF has taken on two big assignments in international affairs.... One is what has been called "the return of the American Air Force to Europe," the arrival of two groups of Strategic Air Command B-29s in England.... The second is the Berlin Airlift.... The first chapters of the "role of air power in diplomacy" are being written here.[214]

Earlier in the summer, Forrestal had feared that the British might not be willing to accept forceful diplomacy that carried a risk of war; but, in October, Chancellor of the Exchequer Sir Stafford Cripps assured him that "Britain is placing its main reliance on the development of fighter aircraft to insure the security of Britain. Britain must be regarded as the main base for the deployment of American air power and the chief offensive against Russia must be by Air." When Forrestal visited Britain in November 1948, Winston Churchill told him that the United

States ought not to minimize the destructive power of atomic weapons lest the Russians receive dangerous encouragement. Speaking in person in Boston on 31 March 1949, Churchill advanced the same view even more positively. "It is certain," he said, "that Europe would have been communized like Czechoslovakia and London under bombardment some time ago but for the deterrent of the atomic bomb in the hands of the United States."[215]

Strategic Bombing and the B-36 Controversy

"I am firmly convinced," wrote Dr Edward Teller, the nuclear physicist who had done pioneer work on the A-bomb and who would father the H-bomb, "that in the early postwar years secrecy was a powerful barrier between military men who were clinging to the past and scientists who were turning away from what seemed a frightening future."[216] The whole matter of atomic weapons continued to be a very heavy secret that was not even shared among all top-level military officers. Writing in November 1948, Bernard Brodie reported there was "reason to believe that the amount of uranium and thorium available in the world for the manufacture of atomic bombs is much more limited than was being assumed two years ago, and the deposits available are much more accessible to the United States than to the Soviet Union."[217] Knowledge of the size of the US atomic weapons production effort and the stockpile was confined to a very small circle. As late as May 1951, Gen Douglas MacArthur testified that he did not know the number of atomic weapons in the US stockpile.[218] Although two years had passed since Hiroshima and Nagasaki had been destroyed by atomic weapons and additional tests of atomic bombs had been made at Bikini and Eniwetok in the summer of 1946, there was lingering uncertainty in the military services as to the potential effect of atomic weapons on the old techniques of war. One viewpoint was that an atomic bomb was merely another weapon. While his statement was soon retracted, the head of the Navy's Aviation Ordnance Branch told the House Committee on Armed Services in October 1949: "You could stand in the open at one end of the north-south runway at the Washington National Airport, with no more protection than the clothes you now have on, and have an atom bomb explode at the other end of the runway without serious injury to you."[219]

Although Air Force thinkers never underestimated the destructive capabilities of atomic weapons, they apparently required time in which to grasp the potential gamut of effects that these weapons held for air operations and the modifications of air doctrines that could be accepted when they were employed. One of the principal results of the clear identification of Soviet Russia as the major menace to world peace was a vigorous analysis within the National Military Establishment of the potential influence of atomic weapons on future American military strategy. The concept that atomic air power could "kill a nation" apparently emerged in the Air Force Directorate of Intelligence during the winter of 1947–48 when target planners were attempting to work up a list of industrial objectives in the Soviet

Union that had been requested by the Joint Chiefs of Staff. In the aftermath of World War II, the United States Strategic Bombing Survey depreciated the effectiveness of Royal Air Force attacks against German population centers, thus US Air Force target planners attempted to develop Soviet steel, oil, aluminum, aircraft engines, tank factories, and electric power plants as air targets. Since most of these specific targets were located within 70 Soviet cities, some target planners suggested that atomic attacks might be directed against the Soviet cities rather than the specific industries. The concept followed that the mission of atomic air attack might be to destroy governmental control and industrial mobilization and support potential instead of specific industrial targets. "I think," recalled Col Grover C. Brown, who had been assigned to the Directorate of Intelligence, "it was a sort of a shock to a lot of people when a few began to talk about bonus effects and industrial capital and particularly when some began to ask what was a city besides a collection of industry?"[220]

When members of the State Department's Policy Planning Staff were briefed concerning the concept of atomic bombardment of Soviet cities, they were reported to be completely opposed to it. "If you drop atomic bombs on Moscow, Leningrad, and the rest," George Kennan was said to have commented, "you will simply convince the Russians that you are barbarians trying to destroy their very society and they will rise up and wage an indeterminate guerrilla war against the West." Charles Bohlen was quoted as responding: "The negative psycho-social results of such an atomic attack might endanger postwar peace for 100 years."[221]

Although the concept of atomic air attacks specifically directed against Soviet urban targets was not accepted, the thinking did much to direct Air Force concepts of its strategic capabilities. In his final report as Air Force chief of staff, Spaatz wrote: "The primary role of military Air Power is to attack—not other aircraft but targets on the ground that comprise the source of an enemy's military strength." In an article published shortly after his retirement, Spaatz asserted: "It is theoretically possible to demonstrate on the basis of the war just finished that the precision bombing of a few hundred square miles of industrial area in a score of Russian cities would fatally cripple Russian industrial power." But at the same time that he argued for the decisiveness of strategic atomic air attack, Spaatz reasoned that Army and Navy forces would be needed to secure forward air bases. "Only from forward air bases can the mass of American air strength, including fighters," he wrote, "gain control of the enemy air space. And not until we have won this control could we be absolutely sure of the outcome of a war." Since air power could not gain and hold forward air bases, Spaatz considered that ground and sea forces would "remain indispensable supporting instruments in the struggle for a mastery of the air" until intercontinental air weapons were developed.[222]

Speaking out in a "gloves-off" talk in Los Angeles on 16 July, Secretary Symington for the first time publicly criticized the balanced force concept of American defense that had come out of World War II. According to a newspaper report, Symington assailed "ax-grinders dedicated to obsolete methods" of warfare who contended that large Air Force appropriations might unbalance the three armed services, and he declared that air power should not be put in balance with the Army and Navy but with the power of potential adversaries.[223] In a letter on 11 August 1948, General Kenney pointed out that atomic bombs and other modern developments had made profound changes in the concepts of war.

> When we consider that 100 atom bombs will release more foot pounds of energy than all the TNT released by all the belligerents of World War II combined ... and that the effort could be put down in a single attack, it is evident that the long drawn out war is out of date.... No nation, including our own, could survive such a blow. A war in which either or both opponents use atomic bombs will be over in a matter of days so that our target analysis system should change. Bombing of targets which will effect enemy production in a few months is meaningless. There is no time to try to destroy the enemy air force. The air force that is superior in its capability of destruction plays the dominant role and has the power of decision. The inferior air force has no role. Before it can be built up the war will be over. The advantage accruing to the aggressor who makes such a surprise attack has become so great that it can almost be considered decisive.[224]

In making a reevaluation of Douhet's principles in the light of atomic explosives in the summer of 1948, Lt Col Joseph L. Dickman found that the Douhet theory was "not only a pattern for the conduct of the war but also a guide for the preparation for one." He argued that the power of atomic bombs validated Douhet's principles on air power. Dickman suggested a corollary rule: "If, at any time, it appears that expenditures for tactical aviation will jeopardize development in strategic, the former will have to be sacrificed."[225] In a study prepared on 10 August 1948, Col William W. Momyer, director of plans for the Tactical Air Command, analyzed the whole Air Force mission. He pointed out that the Tactical Air Command would not become involved in hostilities unless the atomic offensive failed and the war degenerated into a conventional air-surface action, a contingency that he did not anticipate would occur at all and, in any event, not until approximately two years after the onset of a war. Momyer pointed out that Tactical Air Command's fighters would pass to the operational control of the Air Defense Command at the onset of hostilities and argued for a more effective cross-training of fighters to perform both air defense and tactical air missions. Finally, he questioned the planned use of jet fighters in an escort capacity as "an obsolete concept of the last war."[226]

Three articles in the autumn 1948 issue of the *Air University Quarterly Review* strongly advocated a strategic bombardment strategy. "We have come to the realization that if we are to have peace in our time it will have to be a Pax Americana," wrote Lt Col Frank R. Pancake. "There has been a further awakening to the fact that the instrument of Pax Americana must be Air Power, just as the instrument of Pax Britannica a century ago was sea power. . . . In the event of another war our first and perhaps only major offensive effort will be strategic air attacks."[227] Writing on the relationship of air power and foreign policy, Lt Col John P. Healey stated: "The historic discrepancy between our foreign policy aims and their means of military support is now ended. The 'quantum jump' taken by military technology in this country affords a measure of military power sufficient to support our present aim if such power is wisely used as a deterrent."[228]

Looking backward at World War II, Col Dale O. Smith noted that air siege or strategic bombardment was "generally considered to have been the most decisive factor" in the defeat of the Axis, but that the strategic bombing effort had required the support of surface combat. In the war against Germany, the strategic bombing effort had been frequently switched from one target system to another in the expectation that a "key" target system could be destroyed with decisive results. In the end, Smith said, "when German industry collapsed, no single target system was responsible but rather a widespread disintegration of all industry occurred." From this experience, Smith thought it plausible to conclude that "the most effective air siege will result by concurrently attacking every critical element of an enemy's economy *at the same* time.... If all the critical industrial systems could be destroyed at one blow, so that recuperation were impossible within any foreseeable time, there seems little question but that a nation would die just as surely as a man will die if a bullet pierces his heart and his circulating system is stopped." Smith visualized an atomic striking force of 300 B-29s directed against an enemy nation, and he thought there was little doubt that "an offensive bomber force, utilizing tactical surprise, will be able to penetrate to targets in the enemy heartland." Believing that the strategic air assault with atomic weapons would destroy a modern nation, Smith suggested that the Air Force should abandon "the old doctrine of 'sustained' operations." "The atomic bomb is real.... There need be no doubt about its combat worthiness," he wrote. "Why then must we revert to the old TNT bombs and forever hamstring our logistical and tactical plans with the requirement for sustained operations?"[229]

Fiscal Limits Affected the Military

Even though a bill that authorized a peacetime Air Force strength of 70 groups and an eventual level-off purchase of 5,200 aircraft a year was lost in the closing rush of the 80th Congress during the late summer of 1948, General Vandenberg considered that Congress—by providing the first increment of funds for such a purpose—had given the Air Force a clear mandate to expand to the 70-group objective. The Air Force, therefore, decided that the purchase of the 2,201 new aircraft that could be funded with the augmented fiscal year 1949 appropriations would be pointed toward accomplishment of the 70-group program. The Air Force, thus, contracted to purchase 190 B-45 aircraft to partially equip five light bombardment groups and three night tactical reconnaissance squadrons. In the spring of 1948 many Air Force officers had continued to be skeptical of the B-36. However, when the Air Force began to get deliveries of some of these planes, the test data from them was so much better than had previously been reported that Vandenberg elected on 24 June to continue the funding on the original contract for 95 aircraft. Contracts were also awarded for 10 B-47 jet bombers, 132 B-50Ds,

1,457 jet fighters, and 147 transport and troop carrier planes. Moreover, by stretching available personnel strength rather thinly, the Air Force was able to activate a total of 60 combat groups before the end of 1948.[230]

In the spring of 1948 when work was begun on fiscal year 1950 budget request, the Air Force assumed that appropriations would be enlarged to support expanded personnel strength and aircraft procurement necessary for the 70-group program. The Air Staff, therefore, first submitted a request for an $8 billion appropriation to the secretary of defense. Then, as Secretary Symington explained, "word got around that again the three services were going to ask for everything they could get on a unilateral basis and then we were all going to be cut proportionately because there was no agreed on strategic plan against which to buy." Symington, therefore, took personal responsibility for raising the Air Force budget request to more than $11 billion. As a result, the uncoordinated original estimates of the three military services received by Forrestal totaled more than $30 million.[231] The indications were that no such amount of money would be available. During fiscal year 1949 the Bureau of the Budget had expected that the treasury would have a $5 billion surplus, but, because of an economic recession, there would be a deficit of almost $2 billion. In the summer of 1948, acting on advice from the Bureau of the Budget and apparently without consulting the National Security Council or the Joint Chiefs of Staff, President Truman established a ceiling of $14.4 billion on the national defense budget for fiscal year 1950.[232] The wide difference between the military requirements submitted by the individual services and the presidential ceiling forced the secretary of defense to make decisions.

In an effort to return responsibilities for stating force requirements to the Joint Chiefs of Staff, Secretary Forrestal secured the appointment of a budget review board of three officers from the services headed by Gen Joseph T. McNarney, commander of the Air Materiel Command. As early as 10 July, Forrestal also submitted a formal request for budgetary guidelines to the National Security Council. When he received no response, he evidently sought bits and pieces of advice elsewhere. Walter B. Smith, US ambassador to Russia, told Forrestal that the Russians did not, in his opinion, have the industrial competence to develop the atomic bomb in quantity for "five or even ten years." General Vandenberg reassured Forrestal that the Air Force could drop the atomic bomb "where, how, and when it was wanted." Working in terms of requirements for balanced forces, the McNarney board reduced the service requests to $23.6 billion but could go no lower. The Joint Chiefs of Staff estimated that the $14.4-billion defense budget would limit US action against the Soviet Union to a strategic air offensive from Britain and suggested that for $16.9 billion the United States could maintain forces needed to control the Mediterranean as well as conduct the strategic air offensive. Forrestal presented these facts to Truman on 5 October, but President Truman held to the $14.4 billion budget and planned to take care of the Mediterranean with a supplemental appropriation if an emergency arose.[233] In a final conference with the president on 9 December, Forrestal and the service secretaries again advocated the $16.9 billion budget, but Truman would not budge from $14.4 billion. Faced with this ceiling, the Joint Chiefs of Staff agreed that the funds should be subdivided at $4.834 billion for the Army, $4.624 billion for the Navy, and $5.025 billion for the Air Force.[234]

Aware that it faced definite strategic requirements and would be unable to expand to 70 groups, the Air Force began to reorganize its forces in the winter of 1948-49. Under the $14.4-billion budget ceiling, the Air Force mission (as defined by the USAF Senior Officers Board) would be:

> (a) initially, to launch a powerful air offensive designed to exploit the destructive and psychological power of atomic weapons against the vital elements of the Soviet war-making capacity. (b) To provide on an austerity basis for the air defense of the United States and selected base areas. (c) To provide the air components necessary for the advancement, intensification, and/or diversification of our initial offensive until forces generated from inadequate mobilization bases have become available.[235]

Seeking to pool resources that could be used for more than one purpose, the Air Force on 1 December 1948 established the Continental Air Command at Mitchel Field as a superior headquarters to the Air Defense Command and the Tactical Air Command. The Continental Air Command received direct command over the six air forces formerly assigned to the Air Defense and Tactical Air Commands, both of which were reduced to the status of operational headquarters. The Continental Air Command also took over three of the Strategic Air Command's fighter groups.[236] Although the consolidation of commands was a product of austerity, Col William H. Wise, deputy chief of the Air University's Evaluation Division, hailed it as being fundamentally correct and called for further consolidation. "An Air Force Combat Command," he recommended,

> should be so organized and constituted as to make it readily feasible to employ maximum strength in the performance of the mission at hand, be it strategic, tactical, or defensive. . . . Since an Air Force properly organized and equipped to achieve success in the decisive phase will be capable also of performing the necessary tactical operations in the exploitation phase, the peacetime maintenance of a specialized air arm at the expense of the strength and effectiveness of the decisive air echelons is unwarranted. The soundness of this concept is already recognized in the Air Force, but how soon corrective action can or will be accomplished is a matter for conjecture.[237]

Since the budgetary limitations would force the Air Force to reduce its combat strength to 48 groups and 10 separate squadrons and to change its aircraft purchase programs, General Vandenberg assembled the USAF Senior Officers Board in Washington on 29 December 1948 for the first of seven-day-long sessions. Because General Fairchild was ill, General McNarney presided as acting chairman. The other two members of the board were Generals Norstad and Craig. Recognizing that the Joint Chiefs of Staff had for the first time provided a strategic concept of operations against Soviet Russia, the board determined that "the launching of an atomic offensive and the defense of the Western Hemisphere and the essential base areas from which to launch the atomic offensive must be considered as the primary mission of the Air Force and must be given the greatest consideration and priority." Because of the supreme importance of the strategic air mission, which was now being vested in the Air Force, the board decided that means must be found to deliver the atomic stockpile under the most adverse conditions foreseeable, which included loss of advanced bases in the United Kingdom and an unexpected failure of aerial refueling techniques.[238]

In determining requirements for strategic bombers, the USAF Senior Officers Board heard testimony from General LeMay, who had taken command of the Strategic Air Command on 16 October 1948. LeMay stated his basic conviction that "the fundamental goal of the Air Force should be the creation of a strategic atomic striking force capable of attacking any target in Eurasia from bases in the United States and returning to the points of take-off." To deliver the atomic stockpile, LeMay needed four groups of bombers and one group of strategic reconnaissance aircraft. LeMay liked the B-36. In its tests in 1948, the B-36B had proven to be a better aircraft than had been predicted. By attaching two twin-jet pods (actually B-47 engines) to the big conventional bomber, the B-36B would be able to operate on a target run at an altitude of 45,000 feet and a maximum speed of 378 knots. Assuming that the Soviets were not more advanced in aerial defense than was the United States, the board reckoned that the B-36B would be able to penetrate Soviet defenses. With its range, moreover, the B-36B could cover 97 percent of Soviet target complexes from bases in North America. The B-36 also could haul 43 tons of conventional bombs over medium ranges, which would permit a great intensification of a conventional air offensive if advanced bases were available. The Strategic Air Command was programmed already to get two groups of B-36s, and the senior officers concurred with LeMay's request that the command be authorized a total of four groups of B-36Bs and one group of RB-36Bs, all to be equipped with supplemental jet pods.[239]

Since the 48-group program would reduce the Strategic Air Command's strength to 14 bomber groups, the Senior Officers Board gave careful consideration to the composition of the 10 groups that would be equipped with medium bombers. These planes might be called on to deliver nuclear weapons, but they more probably would be dispatched with conventional bombs in the wake of a B-36 atomic attack against targets, such as Soviet oil, that were too small to warrant atomic bombs. The Senior Officers Board noted that sufficient B-50s had been delivered or were on order to equip and maintain five medium bomber groups and one reconnaissance group. They recommended that two other medium groups and one medium reconnaissance group should be equipped with speedy but limited range B-47s. The remaining three medium bomber groups would continue to be equipped with B-29s and RB-29s, but the board noted that the Air Force had issued procurement orders for 30 B-54A aircraft — an ultimate development of the B-50 — which would probably become the replacement for the B-29s and RB-29s.[240]

The Senior Officers Board made no recommendations as to the aircraft to be used for modernizing the two strategic weather reconnaissance groups and the one strategic mapping group that would be retained in the 48-group program. The five light bomber groups that had been put in the 70-group program to perform ground support missions were reduced to a single group. Tactical reconnaissance also was reduced to the equivalent of one group (two squadrons in the United States and one in the Far East). The board postponed consideration of the aircraft requirements for the four heavy troop carrier groups and two light troop carrier groups that would remain in the 48-group program, but it gave careful attention to the equipment and composition of the 20 fighter groups that would be kept in active service. In World War II the P-47 and P-51 had served as admirable all-purpose fighters, but the board reasoned that the advent of jet power probably prevented the development of a successful all-purpose jet fighter. The F-80s, F-84s, and F-86s would be no more than marginally effective against any bomber faster than a B-29. Accordingly, the board recommended that a pure interceptor fighter should be developed by 1953–54. Pending further developmental work in fighters, the board recommended that the F-84 and F-86 should perform both interceptor and penetration missions, but it stated that the 20 fighter groups should be divided into eight penetration groups, seven interceptor groups, and five all-weather fighter groups.[241]

The cutback of the Air Force from its planned objective of 70 groups to 48 groups necessarily reduced the weight and speed of the initial air offensive, seriously delayed the time at which the Air Force would be prepared to support exploitative surface operations, and reduced the fighter defenses that had been planned for advanced US bases in the United Kingdom. Recognizing these limitations, Vandenberg approved the report of the USAF Senior Officers Board; Secretary Symington also gave his approval when it was submitted to him on 13 January 1949. On 5 February the Joint Chiefs of Staff approved the Air Force deployment inherent in the 48-group program.[242] The sudden termination of the 70-group objective meant that the Air Force had ordered aircraft from fiscal year 1949 money that it would be unable to use. By canceling various orders including 51 B-45s no longer needed for light bombardment groups, 118 F-93s ordered as penetration fighters, and 30 C-125B assault transports that had been designed to replace gliders, the Air Force recaptured some $269,761,000 from fiscal year 1949 supplemental funds that could be applied to the purchase of B-36s. In a series of actions begun on 29 January 1949, the Air Force requested authority from Secretary Forrestal to purchase 32 B-36s and 7 RB-36s and to modify the B-36s already on hand or on order with jet pods. While this request was under study in the National Military Establishment Research and Development Board, LeMay requested still more B-36s on 2 February. LeMay told Vandenberg that he carefully compared the projected performance capabilities of the B-36s against those of the B-54s and that he had decided that the B-54 contract ought to be canceled and enough B-36s be bought to equip two additional groups. The Senior Officers Board reconvened on 21 February to hear about the proposed change, and it agreed that either B-36s or B-47s ought to be procured instead of B-54s. Both the board and General Vandenberg were willing to cancel the B-54 contract, but they were reluctant to convert two medium bombardment groups into heavy bombardment groups. At another meeting of the Senior Officers Board on 8 March, LeMay offered a compromise proposal whereby he would retain the existing group structure but would increase the aircraft complements of each B-36 and RB-36 group from 18 to 30 aircraft. This proposal was accepted, and the Air Force secured the cancellation of the B-54 contract and a recertification of funds to purchase 36 B-36s and five additional B-47s. Shortly before his resignation as secretary of defense on 28 March, Forrestal approved the basic decisions to procure additional B-36s. On 4 May 1949 President Truman formally released the funds for the several B-36 projects.[243]

In other meetings during the spring of 1949, the USAF Senior Officers Board took long looks at Air Force development in relation to the new strategic planning. The board recommended, in January, that the B-52 be designed to transport atomic weapons and that any accommodation made to permit it to carry iron bombs should not increase its basic weight. In March the board accepted the B-52 as the follow-on replacement to the B-36 and recommended that B-36 production facilities should be changed over to B-52 production as soon as enough B-36s had been obtained to outfit four heavy bomber and two heavy reconnaissance groups. Also in March the board recommended that B-47 production ought to be accelerated so that these medium jets eventually could replace the conventional B-29s and B-50s. In a meeting in May the board gave detailed consideration to Air Force fighters and transports. After study of all available fighters, the board agreed with the recommendation of Maj Gen Gordon P. Saville, head of the Air Defense Command, that the F-86 Sabre was the best interim air defense fighter that could be procured. The board earlier had recommended that the Air Force should purchase no more than service test quantities of light cargo aircraft, but in May it concluded that all transports procured ought to be designed to meet emergency and wartime military cargo airlift requirements of the Army and Air Force. The board recommended that the C-97 be continued in production until the Douglas C-124, which most closely met wartime cargo requirements and should become the standard heavy transport, could begin to reach units in May 1950. Although the board reduced most requirements for smaller troop carrier planes, it recommended continued production and procurement of C-119s, planes that were suited for airdrop and air-delivered transport functions.[244]

A Collective Defense and Air Power Strategy

While military planning emphasized that budget ceilings necessitated redirections in strategy, President Truman apparently had begun to think seriously about collective security as early as the summer of 1948. In March 1948 the Western

European nations concluded the Brussels Pact pledging themselves to collective self-defense. The following July, Truman instructed Under Secretary of State Lovett to begin exploratory discussions looking toward the participation of the United States in a broadened Atlantic alliance. Agreements were reached on the general nature of such a treaty in September and in December Secretary of State Dean Acheson began to negotiate the treaty in private. In his inaugural address on 20 January 1949, Truman spoke of a need for a collective defense on the North Atlantic area.[245]

When they appeared before congressional committees in support of the National Military Establishment budget for fiscal year 1950, the military leaders generally emphasized the force reductions that were impending. Appearing before the House Subcommittee on Appropriations on 31 January 1949, Forrestal justified the budget as one "designed to maintain a military posture for the preservation of peace." Forrestal continued to believe in balanced forces, but he admitted that "as air power expands its radius it may be that you will have a war in the future where you will rely on it alone." He favored the 70-group concept as an authorized force, but he believed that this should be an ultimate—rather than an immediate—goal.[246] Army officers did not question the new strategy. Secretary of the Army Kenneth C. Royall mentioned that for the first time in American history the defense budget had been correlated for the three services; Lt Gen Albert E. Wedemeyer, the Army's deputy chief of staff for plans and combat operations, observed that "for the first time in my knowledge since I have been in the Army the strategy has been correlated and integrated."[247]

At Air Force hearings early in February, Secretary Symington explained that the Joint Chiefs of Staff had accepted strategic bombing as the primary mission of the Air Force and had approved the establishment and maintenance of the 48 combat groups and 10 separate squadrons. The Air Force assistant for programming, Maj Gen Frederic H. Smith, Jr., frankly described the 48-group program as having "definite capabilities in the strategic air-offense field and . . . a respectable defensive power," but noted that it was "deficient in its means to exploit the offensive, because it is shy in the essential close support of the ground-force elements and in pursuing the tactical advantage with fighter bombers and light bombardment." Appearing on 7 February, Vandenberg did not question the president's decision to limit the military budget but gave his own purely personal, military viewpoint on the matter. "Not taking into consideration the other factors which I realize must be taken into consideration," he said, "but speaking purely from a military point of view, it is my opinion that the minimum defense forces, as far as the Air Force is concerned—and with world conditions as they are today—would consist of a 70-group Air Force."[248]

In speaking of the 1950 budget, Secretary of the Navy John L. Sullivan made oblique remarks about the "enthusiasm of single-weapon experts." However, the Navy supported the budget even though under it the numbers of its attack carriers would have to be reduced from 11 to nine, and there would be other substantial reductions in naval vessels afloat.[249]

While the leaders of the National Military Establishment supported the presidential budget, Congress apparently believed that it would be necessary to have a stronger Air Force if the nation was to follow an air strategy. On 28 March, Chairman Carl Vinson of the House Committee on Armed Services proposed that the Air Force receive an additional $800 million to enable it to maintain 57 effective combat groups. Two days later, Chairman George H. Mahon of the House Subcommittee on Armed Services Appropriations stated that Congress had already taken the initiative to provide a 70-group program, and he recommended that Congress increase the Air Force appropriation by about $1 billion so that the Air Force could maintain about 60 groups.[250] With such an amount of money, the Air Force proposed to add six strategic bomber groups, thus restoring the Strategic Air Command to its strength under the proposed 70-group structure, and to maintain three fighter, one light bomber, and one troop carrier group in order to support the Army.[251] After exhaustive debate, Congress finally added more than $726 million to the Air Force appropriation for fiscal year 1950.[252]

At the same time that the fiscal year 1950 budget was under consideration in Congress, the Department of Defense had already begun to make its estimates for the 1951 budget. On 21 January 1949 Forrestal brought General Eisenhower back to Washington on temporary duty to work with the Joint Chiefs of Staff in the preparation of a war plan that he hoped would be the basis of future budgets. In preparing for the 1951 budget, Forrestal directed each service chief to review his portion of the war plan and state the forces that would be required. These force levels then were costed for budgetary purposes. Following the same procedure used the year before, the Joint Chiefs established a budget advisory group and headed it with Vice Adm Robert B. Carney. Assisted by the plans staffs on the three services, the Carney group took longer than expected in its deliberations and was unable to provide unanimous recommendations to the Joint Chiefs. Increasingly fatigued by his duties, Forrestal arranged to resign. President Truman requested that he introduce Louis A. Johnson to the duties of secretary of defense. Accompanied by Johnson, Forrestal took the Joint Chiefs to Key West in February 1949 for several days of uninterrupted study of force levels. The Joint Chiefs were still unable to resolve all their problems within the $14.4 billion that they expected to be the budget ceiling for fiscal year 1951, but they agreed to accord priorities to forces on the basis of what would be necessary in order to avoid defeat, what next would be necessary, and what they would require if each service could have every type of weapon that it wanted.[253]

In December 1948, when they had considered the force structure to be attained under President Truman's budget ceiling, the Joint Chiefs of Staff had been able to agree on all items except the number of attack carriers that the Navy would continue to operate. The Air Force recommended four, the Army six, and the Navy nine. Unable to agree, the Joint Chiefs had passed the problem to Forrestal, who had decided that the Navy would retain eight attack carriers and attendant forces on active duty.[254] Apparently troubled after his return from Key West about the matter of the supercarrier *United States*, which the Navy was beginning to build, Forrestal asked secretary-designate Johnson to make a thorough study of the problem, saying that he had come to have doubts about it but that he did not feel he could do anything about it. Shortly after he became secretary of defense on 29 March 1949, Johnson asked the Joint Chiefs to state their opinions on the aircraft carrier. Adm Louis E. Denfield, chief of naval operations, favored the completion of the $188 million vessel, on which some $20 million had already been expended. General Bradley, on the other hand, reasoned that budgetary restrictions already seriously limited the maintenance of minimum levels of balanced forces, that the fundamental purpose for which the supercarrier was designed lay within a primary function of the Air Force, that the Soviet Union was not a naval power, and that the potential use of carrier air forces against land targets was limited. He, therefore, concluded that it was "militarily unsound to authorize at this time the construction of additional aircraft carriers or to continue expenditures on the USS *United States*." Vandenberg also expressed his opposition to the large carrier because he could "see no necessity for a ship with those capabilities in any strategic plan against the one possible enemy." He added that limited defense funds imposed a necessity "of never buying a second priority item when essential items are still unbought." When his opinion was asked, General Eisenhower agreed that construction of the large carrier should be canceled. After consulting with President Truman, Secretary Johnson issued orders on 23 April discontinuing the construction of the *United States*.[255]

Meanwhile, the text of the *North Atlantic Treaty* was released to the public on 18 March 1949, a little more than two weeks before it was signed on 4 April in Washington by representatives of Belgium, Canada, Denmark, France, Iceland, Italy, Luxembourg, the Netherlands, Norway, Portugal, the United Kingdom, and the United States.* By adhering to the treaty, the member nations agreed that an armed attack against one or more of them in Europe or North America should be considered to be an attack against all of them. Each of the members agreed to "assist the Party or Parties so attacked by taking action as it deems necessary, including the use of armed forces, to restore and maintain the security of the North Atlantic area." The overall Western Union command structure established by the Brussels Pact would become a part of the North Atlantic Treaty Organization (NATO).

When he forwarded the draft treaty to Truman on 7 April, Secretary Acheson pointed out that it did "not mean that the United States would automatically be at war if we or one of the other parties to the treaty were attacked." The United States would be obligated to take promptly the action which it deemed necessary, but the

---

*Greece and Turkey were invited to join NATO on 15 February 1952 and these two nations signed the treaty later that spring. The Federal Republic of Germany was admitted to NATO in 1955.

decision would have to be made in accordance with the constitutional process under which only Congress had the power to declare war. President Truman sent the treaty to the Senate on 12 April 1949. In spite of spirited debate by opponents of US involvement in European affairs, the Senate voted 82 to 13 to accept it on 21 July 1949.[256] While the North Atlantic treaty was under consideration in the Senate, the Soviets evidently realized that the Berlin Airlift had thwarted their efforts to starve West Berlin and that the Berlin blockade was leading to Western European military unification. First informally on 27 April and then formally on 12 May, the Soviets agreed to end the Berlin blockade. Continued for a while to build up supply stockpiles, the Berlin Airlift officially ended on 30 September 1949.[257]

The principle of collective security manifest in the Atlantic Pact permitted a formalization of the American military strategy that already had been necessitated by the presidential budgetary ceilings in fiscal year 1949. On 25 July, President Truman asked Congress to appropriate $1.4 billion for military aid to countries that were vital to the security of the United States. The major portion of the appropriation would be devoted to the needs of the Western European nations. Appearing as the representative of the Joint Chiefs of Staff in support of the Mutual Defense Assistance Act before the House Committee on Foreign Affairs on 29 July, General Bradley outlined the new collective strategy. "The essence of our overall strategy," he said, "is this: There is a formidable strength, and an obvious economy of effort, resources, and manpower in this collective strategy, when each nation is capable of its own defense, as a part of a collective strategic plan." In approving the Mutual Defense Assistance Act, the Joint Chiefs followed "the principle that the man in the best position, and with the capability, should do the job for which he is best suited." The Joint Chiefs also assumed that:

- First, the United States will be charged with the strategic bombing.
- We have repeatedly recognized in this country that the first priority of the joint defense is our ability to deliver the atomic bomb.
- Second, the United States Navy and the Western Union naval powers will conduct essential naval operations, including keeping the sea lanes clear. The Western Union and other nations will maintain their own harbor and coastal defense.
- Third, we recognize that the hard core of the ground power in being will come from Europe, aided by other nations as they can mobilize.
- Fourth, England, France, and the closer countries will have the bulk of the short-range attack bombardment, and air defense. We, of course, will maintain the tactical air force for our own ground and naval forces, the United States defense.
- Fifth, other nations, depending on their proximity or remoteness from the possible scene of conflict, will emphasize appropriate specific missions.

Bradley argued that the defensive capabilities of the United States would be improved if the military assistance program was put into effect.[258]

Most members of Congress apparently accepted the idea that military aid was needed, but many objected to the manner and timing of the request, to the amount, and especially to the proposal that the president have a free hand in allocating the money and arms. A new administration bill, sent to Congress on 5 August, proved more acceptable because it eliminated the blank-check authority for the president. On 28 September, Congress passed the Mutual Defense Assistance Act of 1949, authorizing an appropriation of $1,314,010,000 and on 6 October the president signed the bill. The act authorized $1 billion in arms assistance to the North Atlantic countries but provided that $900 million of it would not be available until the president had approved recommendations for an integrated command structure. The remaining funds were committed to the military aid of Greece and Turkey, Iran, the Philippines, the Republic of Korea, and the Republic of China.[259]

In the spring of 1949, when Congress added $726 million to the Air Force appropriation for fiscal year 1950, President Truman and Secretary Johnson were willing to hear Secretary Symington's plea for a 70-group Air Force, but Truman subsequently impounded the additional funds and kept the Air Force at the 48-group level. Not waiting for the beginning of fiscal year 1950 to initiate its downward readjustment in strength, the Air Force began to inactivate tactical organizations in March 1949. By the end of the year it would possess 47 groups and 13 separate squadrons. Generally following the recommendations of the USAF Senior Officers Board, the aircraft authorized for procurement in fiscal year 1950 included 34 B-36Fs and 13 RB-36Fs, 81 B-47s, 709 jet fighters, 14 C-97s, 51 C-119Cs, and 50 C-124s, plus miscellaneous aircraft for a total of 1,252 planes.[260]

Based partly on the impoundment of the funds that Congress had voted for Air Force expansion, the Joint Chiefs of Staff assumed that the budgetary ceiling of all military forces during fiscal year 1951 would be the same austere $14.4 billion that had been authorized in fiscal year 1950. In May 1949 Secretary Johnson took the Joint Chiefs to another conference in Key West, where they established the force levels that could be supported with $14.4 billion. Quite without warning in July, however, President Truman summoned Department of Defense officials and the Joint Chiefs of Staff to his office, where the director of the budget told them that the national defense expenditures for fiscal year 1951 must be reduced to $13 billion.[261] "I was sick about it," said Secretary Johnson, as he recalled his reaction to the news. Although he tried to get the figure raised, he was unsuccessful. "The climate on the Hill, the climate of the President's economists and all the rest of the economists, the climate of the world at that moment—the airlift having been successful—the climate was," Johnson recalled, "there was going to be peace."[262] In view of the reduction of the budget, each armed service would have to stand a further reduction in forces. While the connection was not mentioned, the reduction in the defense budget was the same amount that Truman had requested; the president may have intended that reductions in US forces would be compensated for by an increasing effectiveness of friendly allied forces.

Investigations of the B-36 and Defense Unification

In the winter of 1948-49 the US Navy accepted the new American military strategy based on a primacy of the strategic bomber offensive. According to Vice Adm Arthur W. Radford, however, the Navy Department had not known of the Air Force plans to purchase additional B-36s for strategic bombing until reports to this effect appeared in the newspapers.[263] At the first Key West conference, the secretary of defense had laid down the principle that each service should develop the weapons it required to perform its mission: the cancellation of the *United States* on the split advice of members of the Joint Chiefs appeared to negate this principle. Secretary Johnson had canceled the supercarrier without consulting either the chief of naval operations or Secretary of the Navy Sullivan; in protest, Sullivan resigned his office on 26 April. Sullivan explained that he expected the decision not to develop a powerful weapon also would "result in a renewed effort to abolish the Marine Corps and to transfer all naval and marine aviation elsewhere."[264] Within the Navy Department, a civilian public relations specialist drew up an anonymous document, widely circulated in April and May, which charged that the B-36 had been selected through corruption; that the Air Force was obsessed with a belief that "airplanes can reduce warfare to a clean, quick, inexpensive and, to our side, painless procedures"; that Air Force statements about the performance capabilities of the B-36 were "false," "silly," and contrary to "all common sense and all engineering knowledge"; and that in the effort to obtain the B-36 the Air Force had canceled purchases of other aircraft to the detriment of continental air defense and the air support of the Army.[265] The Navy also anticipated that in its 1951 budget it would have to reduce its attack carriers from eight to six, its escort carriers from 19 to eight, its carrier air groups from 14 to six, its patrol squadrons from 30 to 20, and its Marine Corps air squadrons from 23 to 12.[266] In response to a request for an opinion, the new Secretary of the Navy Francis P. Matthews informed Congressman Vinson on 20 July that the Air Force was "unbalanced in favor of strategic bombing to the detriment of its ability to provide tactical air support for ground forces and for other missions involving tactical aviation. Some reduction of the large bomber groups translated into tactical aircraft would produce better balance with the entire program, still being within the 48-group limitation."[267]

As it was directed to do by the House of Representatives, Congressman Vinson's Armed Services Committee began hearings in August in which all principal officials who had been concerned with B-36 procurement were questioned. Early in the hearings the author of the anonymous charges appeared and confessed the falsity of his allegations. After three weeks the committee unanimously resolved on 25 August that not one iota of evidence had been presented that would support charges that fraud or favoritism had played any part in the procurement of the B-36 but that the testimony had shown that the Air Force had selected and procured the bomber solely on the grounds that it was the best aircraft for its purpose. Even though it suspended the B-36 hearing early, the committee expressed itself as deeply disturbed "by reason of recent developments within the Department of Defense which might have resulted in the impairment of the proper functioning of one or all of the services and thus endanger the national defense."[268] Because of this belief, the committee opened a second phase of its hearings on 6 October and for 12 days heard testimony on the national defense program. In the course of often repetitious testimony in the two hearings, Navy, Air Force, and Army officers presented detailed but somewhat different analyses of their concepts of national military capabilities and strategy.

In his letter to Vinson at the outset of the hearings, Secretary Matthews demonstrated that the primary mission of the Navy was to command the seas and in order to carry out its primary mission the Navy had to have weapons which could "destroy enemy forces threatening that command." Taking a corporate view of the responsibility of the Joint Chiefs of Staff to ensure the defense of the United States, Matthews was willing to grant each service a responsibility to inquire into the expenditure of scarce defense funds by the other services, but he argued that a chief of any service was best informed as to the weapons his service needed to carry out its responsibilities. As for the B-36, Matthews charged that the plane sacrificed performance characteristics to obtain intercontinental range. As long as the Navy controlled the seas, Matthews submitted that advanced bases would be available to the Air Force, which should, therefore, develop and employ shorter range and higher performance bombers.[269]

Heading a long visit of distinguished Navy witnesses, Admiral Radford expressed his opposition to the B-36 because it had "become, in the minds of the American people, a symbol of a theory of warfare—the atomic blitz—which promises them a cheap and easy victory if war should come." He believed the B-36 to be an obsolete aircraft suited only for city bombing. "Are we as a nation," he asked, "to have 'bomber generals' fighting to preserve the obsolete heavy bomber—the battleship of the air?" He insisted that a proper air strategy ought to be built around short-range jet aircraft such as the B-47 and naval jets that would operate from advanced land bases and aircraft carriers to establish control of the air over hostile territory and then wage strategic air warfare campaigns.[270] Rear Adm R. A. Ofstie made a distinction between strategic air warfare, which was directed against an enemy's will and ability to wage war, and strategic bombing, which he and the Navy witnesses arbitrarily described as an indiscriminate blitz against urban areas. Ofstie supported strategic air warfare and accurate attacks on precise military targets, but he deplored the strategic bombing that had unwisely destroyed Germany and Japan. Ofstie thought that the concept of instant retaliation had produced an illusion of power and even a kind of bomb-rattling jingoism. The strategic bomber force, moreover, was an independent force that served none of the primary demands for national security—the defense of Western Europe, the protection of forward bases, the early reduction of enemy military potential, or command of the sea. "Must the Italian Douhet continue as our prophet," he asked, "because certain zealots grasped his false doctrines many years ago and refuse to relinquish this discredited theory in the face of vast, costly experience? Must we translate the historical mistake of World War II into a permanent concept merely to avoid clouding the prestige of those who led us down the wrong road in the past?"[271]

Appearing as the next principal witness for the Navy, Brig Gen Vernon E. Megee, assistant director of Marine Corps aviation, emphasized the Marine Corps belief in tactical air power. "The evidence appears conclusive," he stated, "that in both the Atlantic and Pacific battle areas, tactical aviation, not strategic bombing, was the decisive factor." He charged that the Air Force was neglecting the development of tactical air power, and further asserted that the Air Force's "traditional doctrinal insistence on coequal command status at all levels of contact with the ground forces ... deprives the Army commander of operational control over his supporting elements and requires that [the] ultimate decision must be made at the level of the highest echelon, in case of dispute between ground and air commanders."[272] Continuing the Navy testimony, Fleet Adm Ernest J. King pointed out: "Mass bombing is merely a specialized task and big bombers alone will not assure us command of the air. Without control of the air, the job of the soldier, the sailor, and even the job of the strategic airman becomes more difficult, perhaps impossible."[273] As an advocate of air power, Adm Louis E. Denfield, chief of naval operations, favored an initial air offensive by the nation's total military air power—Air Force, Navy, and Marine Corps—at the outset of a war. He believed that the airplane had materially altered the conduct of war, but that it had not changed the basic principles and objectives of war. "The defeat of the armed forces of the enemy," he said, "is still the primary objective of war. Air power is not an end in itself."[274]

Because of the nature of the charges under investigation, Air Force leaders devoted most of their time to a detailed history of B-36 procurement. However, on 12 August Vandenberg described the strategic situation and the objectives and the capabilities of the Air Force. Disdaining to talk in riddles, he identified the Soviet Union as the "one military threat to the security of the United States and to the peace of the world." The aggressive thrust of the Soviets could be contained only by the economic and military power of Western nations. "The only war a nation can really win," he said, "is the one that never starts." "When reason, good will, and the accommodation of competing national interests give assurance of keeping the peace," he thought, "the maintenance of deterrent forces will be unnecessary. Until that day comes, the striking power of atomic weapons in the hands of this country is a prerequisite of national and world security."[275]

As his statement continued, Vandenberg described the Air Force mission as being the defense of the United States against air attack, the maintenance of forces in being necessary to attack, immediately and effectively, the vital elements of an enemy's war-making capacity, and the preparation of air power that would work in conjunction with surface forces. Even though all of these missions were important, the Joint Chiefs had determined that the capacity for immediate retaliatory strategic attack was essential: this attack would blunt an enemy's initial operations and lay a foundation for subsequent operations by land, sea, and air forces. Although the Air Force had given first emphasis to its strategic air elements, Vandenberg pointed out that the distinction made between strategic air operations (attacks against an enemy's industrial strength) and tactical air operations (attacks against an enemy's military forces) was not completely valid. Such a distinction, he said, "denies the unity of air power, by failing to recognize that strategic and tactical air units are component parts of a whole and are complementary forces." As a matter of practicality, he demonstrated that it was more difficult and more expensive to destroy a deployed tank or plane than to destroy them in the process of manufacture, but the choice of air targets depended on the situation. "The ultimate objective of the strategic air campaign," he said,

> is to reduce an enemy's capacity to below the level at which he can support his war effort. However, there may well be interim or emergency objectives of overriding importance. For example, this would be the case if the enemy had a long-range air fleet and a stock of atomic bombs, and if this disposition of these weapons rendered them vulnerable to attack by a strategic force. Before attacking an enemy's economic strength, it might be mandatory, in the interest of survival, to take action to prevent these weapons of mass destruction being employed against us. Likewise, a hostile army poised on a European frontier might, under certain circumstances, provide the best target for a strategic air force.[276]

In justifying the employment of B-36s under conditions where air superiority would not have been attained, the Air Force appeared to be deviating from its findings that control of the air was necessary for a strategic air campaign. Vandenberg was reluctant to discuss the matter in open sessions, but he reiterated the historic fact: "No bombing mission set in motion by the Army Air Forces in World War II was ever stopped short of its target by enemy opposition." In response to another pointed question, he said: "We have new tactics, new techniques, new speeds, new altitudes, an entirely different type of explosive. Where at one time the losses might be unacceptable, in another war, in order to destroy a target, they might be very acceptable."[277] Pressed still further, Vandenberg made an appraisal that would plague him for the next several years. "In our defensive system or in that of Britain or of any other country with an air defense system," he said, "the ultimate that we can ever hope for from the point of view of destruction of forces launched against us is in the neighborhood of 25 percent. That is the ultimate, and it undoubtedly would be less than that."[278]

In their testimony before the hearings, both Symington and Vandenberg emphasized that the Joint Chiefs of Staff were in full agreement that "the capacity for an immediate retaliatory strategic bombing offensive is considered essential to the security plans of the United States." "Today," said Vandenberg, "our air potential is the most effective single deterrent to aggression; it is the strongest single force working for peace."[279] "In the first place," said Symington, "the Air

Force believes that the atomic bomb plus the air power necessary to deliver it represent the one most important visible deterrent to the start of any war. . . . Secondly, if war comes, we believe that the atomic bomb plus the air power to deliver it represent the one means of unloosing prompt crippling destruction upon the enemy, with absolute minimum combat exposure of American lives."[280] Both Symington and Vandenberg disavowed any belief that an atomic blitz could produce a "quick, easy, and painless war." "We can hope, but no one can promise," said Symington, "that if war comes the impact of our bombing offensive with atomic weapons can bring it about that no surface forces ever have to become engaged. Disregarding such an illusory hope, we do know that the engagement of surface forces will take place with much greater assurance of success and much fewer casualties to the United States and its Allies if an immediate, full-scale atomic offensive is launched against the heart of the enemy's war-making power."[281] Vandenberg also emphasized that "any possible future war can be won only by the highest degree of teamwork among the Army, Navy, and Air Force." He specifically denied that the Air Force sought to take over Navy or Marine aviation, and he stated a belief that any future war "will be concluded on the ground." Vandenberg, nevertheless, pointed out that balanced forces were those that were "balanced against the task to be performed." "Balance among military forces," he thought, "should be based on the time sequence of military tasks called for in the strategic timetable."[282] This concept had caused him to oppose the construction of the supercarrier. "I am in favor," he said, "of the greatest possible development of carrier aviation to whatever extent carriers and their aircraft are necessary for fulfillment of a strategic plan against the one possible enemy we have to face." Aircraft carriers had been of great importance in the island campaigns of the Pacific, but Vandenberg believed that a future war would resemble the war against Germany rather than that against Japan. Although he did not believe that a supercarrier would be of value in a continental war, he saw a great requirement for the employment of aircraft carriers in antisubmarine warfare. He said that he was "not only willing but insistent that the types of carriers which can help meet the threat of an enemy submarine fleet shall be developed fully and kept in instant readiness. The sea lanes must be kept open."[283]

Speaking as the newly appointed chairman of the Joint Chiefs of Staff, General Bradley deplored the fact that too many secrets were being spread on the record. Nevertheless, he felt forced to disclose the military plans and preparations of the United States. With reference to the corporate Joint Chiefs of Staff, Bradley said: "We all believe that the No. 1 priority for the Air Force must be strategic bombing ability." The Joint Chiefs "considered the fact that we were able to retaliate quickly as one of the big deterrents to war today." He identified Soviet Russia as the major adversary to the United States and saw Europe as "the first prize for any aggressor in the world today." His basic concept of US military operations in a future war included the defense of the United States and North America, early retaliation from combat ready bases, the seizure of forward bases to permit attacks against enemy targets from shorter ranges, and—the ultimate necessity—the ability "to carry the war back to the enemy by all means at our disposal" including "strategic bombardment and large-scale land operations." In a continental war, he believed there would be little requirement for island-hopping and predicted that "large-scale amphibious operations, such as those in Sicily and Normandy, will never occur again."[284]

In his discussion of strategy, Bradley defined strategic bombing as "violent airborne attacks on the war-making capacity or potential of an enemy nation." He justified strategic bombing: "From a military standpoint, any damage you can inflict on the war-making potential of a nation, and any great injury you can inflict upon the morale of that nation contributes to the victory." As for the charge that mass bombing was immoral, he pointed out that "war itself is immoral." "Strategic bombing," he said, "has a high priority in our military planning, because we cannot hope to keep forces in being of sufficient size to meet Russia in the early stages of war. This is particularly true since we are never going to start the war, and the Soviet Union because of their peculiar governmental organization can choose the date of starting it. Lacking such forces in being, our greatest strength lies in the threat of quick retaliation in the event we are attacked." The insinuation that the atomic bomb was relatively ineffective drew Bradley's strongest refutation. "The A-bomb," he said, "is the most powerful destructive weapon known today.... As a believer in humanity I deplore its use, and as a soldier I respect it. And as an American citizen, I believe that we should be prepared to use its full psychological and military effect toward preventing war, and if we are attacked, toward winning it."[285]

Both Bradley and Gen J. Lawton Collins, who had become the Army chief of staff, refuted the charge that the Air Force had neglected tactical aviation. Bradley pointed out that in the face of very strong enemy opposition in Europe the Ninth Air Force had allocated approximately one group for the support of each two Twelfth Army Group divisions. Using this comparison as a guide, he questioned whether the Marine Corps required the equivalent of seven groups for the support of only two Marine divisions.[286] Speaking of his experience in Europe during World War II, General Collins recalled that "the tactical air forces were able both to support the ground forces and to assist in the safe conduct of our strategic bombers in their missions of destruction and isolation of the battlefields." To prevent the costly duplication that would have ensued if the army had insisted on retaining its own organic close-support aviation, Collins said: "The Army ... willingly agreed to the transfer to a Department of the Air Force of tactical air along with air transports." He expressed dissatisfaction with the lack of progress being made in developing joint interservice doctrine, but he stated unequivocally that the Air Force was cooperating with the Army. Purely as a personal opinion, Collins predicted that airborne operations would be much more important in a future war with "the only potential enemy" than large-scale amphibious operations.[287]

During the course of the unification and strategy hearings, Chairman Vinson and several committee witnesses took note of the fact that the secretary of defense had organized a Weapon Systems Evaluation Group (WSEG) to provide the secretary and the Joint Chiefs of Staff with objective analyses of the effectiveness of competing weapon systems. At Newport in August 1948 the Joint Chiefs had agreed that the establishment of a weapons evaluation group was desirable and necessary. Secretary Forrestal promptly established the Weapon Systems Evaluation Group, headed by Dr Philip M. Morse, who had headed the Navy's Operational Evaluation Group during World War II; the group's membership included military officers and civilian operations analysts. At the request of President Truman, the WSEG made a detailed study of the Strategic Air Command between August and December 1949. Though the results of the study were never released, a source described as knowledgeable stated on 6 January 1950 that the B-36 could be expected to have a better than even chance of delivering its bombs to a target area. The study apparently reinforced the Air Force position that the B-36, while not perfect, was capable of going anywhere of importance in the world and dropping an atomic bomb.[288] Although the fact could not be presented in the public hearings, General LeMay later recalled that the Soviet air defenses in 1949 and for several years afterward were too weak to have effected unacceptable losses on a nuclear-laden strategic bombing force. "We didn't have to worry about winning an air power battle," he reminisced, "because the Russians had no threat against us.... We could ignore the rule book in winning the air power battle and go about destroying their resources."[289]

Both at the time that the hearings were in progress and afterward, the B-36 and unification and strategy investigations were seen to involve challenges that had been made to broad concepts of unification and strategy. "Despite protestations to the contrary," General Bradley observed, "I believe that the Navy has opposed unification from the beginning, and they have not in spirit as well as deed, accepted it completely to date." Bradley called for team play in national defense: "This is no time for 'fancy dans' who won't hit the line with all they have on every play, unless they can call the signals."[290] In the course of the hearings, Chairman Vinson openly deplored the fact that the national military budget was being prepared in terms of ceilings worked out by the Treasury and the Bureau of the Budget rather than in terms of the nation's risks and foreign policy requirements. "The first duty of our Government," he said, "is to provide for the national defense. I am less fearful of deficit financing than I am of the designs of the Russians." Vinson told Secretary Johnson that he felt that Congress and the American people believed that the nation required a 58-group Air Force.[291]

Although the House Committee on Armed Services favored an expansion of the Air Force, the committee's formal report on the unification and strategy investigation made on 1 March 1950 explicitly endorsed strategic pluralism in defense organization. Speaking of strategy, the committee concluded that "the basic reason for this continuing disagreement is a genuine inability for these services to agree, fundamentally and professionally, on the art of warfare.... Of course, with the views so sharply opposed, both services cannot be right; the committee suspects that both are right — and that both are wrong. The true answer probably lies somewhere in the gulf between the two." Especially in the early stages of unification before the esprit of a single armed forces had developed, the committee expressed "strong doubts that it is a service to the Nation's defense for the military leaders of the respective services to pass judgment jointly on the technical fitness of either new or old weapons each service wishes to develop to carry out its assigned missions." Holding that "military air power consists of Air Force, Navy, and Marine Corps air power, and of this, strategic bombing is but one phase," the committee expressed an intention to examine any proposals for reducing the size of Marine aviation very closely, deplored the manner in which the construction of the USS *United States* had been canceled, and announced that it would rely on the professional endorsement of Air Force leaders (subject to evaluation by the Weapon Systems Evaluation Group) as to the capabilities of the B-36 bomber. The committee thought that the Weapon Systems Evaluation Group was a proper forum for examining competing weapon systems, but it stated that the appropriate role of the group would be "to evaluate weapons after they have been developed, not to instruct the services what types of weapons they will or will not develop." Finally, the Armed Services Committee emphasized its belief that unification ought to involve a comprehensive and well-integrated program for national security based on three separately administered military departments.[292]

Coming in the autumn of 1949, when the Soviet Union staged its first atomic explosion and, thus, served notice that the United States no longer possessed a nuclear monopoly, the strategic bombing controversy stood as a benchmark in the movement toward armed service unification. The "revolt of the admirals" clearly embittered interservice relations. "I have been here for some years," said Secretary Symington, "and I think the hatchet job that is being done, and has been done on the B-36 is the best hatchet job that I have seen since I have been in town."[293] On the other hand, General Bradley's reference to "fancy dans" left a false impression that difficulties in armed service unification arose from personality rather than more fundamental issues that needed attention. After a retrospective analysis of the controversy, a civilian James C. Freund concluded that "the budget-first approach to national security emerged as the real culprit on the scene." But he also pointed out that the controversy conclusively demonstrated that unification had not solved all defense problems, that military problems were becoming increasingly dependent on technological judgments, that Congress was unprepared to formulate or pass judgment on strategic and technological issues of defense, and that the military leaders had proven unable to arrive at unanimous decisions on weapons and strategy.[294]

Speaking shortly after the interservice row of 1949 had taken place, Maj Gen John A. Samford, the Air Force director of intelligence, pointed out that the armed forces leaders had been unable to agree on the art of warfare. "Since it has been stated that military men are unable to reach any fundamental agreement on the art of war," he predicted, "it seems very probable that civilian thought will go to work to help them."[295] This prediction would prove to be correct. The strategic bombing controversy had two other important effects. For a number of years after 1949, the Joint Chiefs of Staff accepted a practice of stating quantitative requirements for military forces and of leaving qualitative requirements to the providing service. For example, the Joint Chiefs determined the number of aircraft carriers or heavy bombardment groups that would be required to implement strategic plans, but they would not determine the size or the types of carriers or the kinds of bombers that would be provided.[296] The hearings also demonstrated that the Air Force had not given enough realistic thought to the problem of targeting nuclear weapons. This matter would receive serious attention within the year that followed the investigations.

NOTES

1. Quoted in R. Earl McClendon, *Autonomy of the Air Arm* (Maxwell AFB, Ala.: Research Studies Institute, 1954), 133.

2. Gen Henry H. Arnold, *Global Mission* (New York: Harper & Bros., 1949), 537–38.

3. Assistant chief of Air Staff, Plans (ACAS-5), Army Air Forces, study, "Initial Post-War Air Force," 14 February 1944, marked approved by Gen Henry H. Arnold on 25 February 1944.

4. Brig Gen William F. McKee, acting assistant chief of Air Staff, Operations, Commitments, and Requirements (ACAS-3), to Management Control, Army Air Forces, routing and record (R&R) sheet, subject: Army Air Forces Policy Book, 26 February 1945.

5. Lt Gen Ira C. Eaker, deputy commanding general, Army Air Forces, to commanding generals, major commands, Army Air Forces, letter, subject: Policy Guide, US Army Air Forces, 1 October 1945.

6. Gen Henry H. Arnold, *Third Report of the Commanding General of the Army Air Forces to the Secretary of War*, 12 November 1945, 65, 67, 72.

7. Senate, *Department of Armed Forces, Department of Military Security: Hearings before the Committee on Military Affairs*, 79th Cong., 1st sess., 1945, 342.

8. Gen Carl A. Spaatz to commanding general, Strategic Air Command, letter, subject: Current AAF Plans and Programs, 24 October 1946.

9. Senate, *Department of Armed Forces, Department of Military Security*, 506–7.

10. R. Earl McClendon, *Unification of the Armed Forces: Administrative and Legislative Developments, 1945–1949* (Maxwell AFB, Ala.: Research Studies Institute, 1952), 5–6.

11. Ibid., 6–10.

12. Ibid., 11–21.

13. Senate, *Department of Armed Forces, Department of Military Security*, 88; McClendon, *Unification of the Armed Forces*, 21–22.

14. McClendon, *Unification of the Armed Forces*, 23–29.

15. Ibid., 30.

16. Ibid., 31; Adm Richmond K. Turner, "Problems of Unified Command in the Marianas, Okinawa, and Projected Kyushu Operations," lecture, Air War College, Maxwell AFB, Ala., 11 February 1947; Col Shannon Christian, "Air Ground Relations in Theater Operations," lecture, Air War College, Maxwell AFB, Ala., 9 March 1954; Robert F. Futrell, *The United States Air Force in Korea, 1950–1953* (New York: Duell, Sloan and Pearce, 1961), 43.

17. McClendon, *Unification of the Armed Forces*, 32–49.
18. Public Law 253, National Security Act of 1947, approved 26 July 1947, 80th Cong., 1st sess., 1947.
19. McClendon, *Unification of the Armed Forces*, 49; Executive Order No. 9877, Functions of the Armed Services, 26 July 1947.
20. "Life Begins at Forty," *Air Force Magazine*, September 1947, 12–13.
21. Alexander P. de Seversky, *Victory through Air Power* (New York: Simon and Schuster, 1942), 131–32.
22. House, *The National Defense Program—Unification and Strategy: Hearings before the Committee on Armed Services*, 81st Cong., 1st sess., 1949, 258–59.
23. Walter Millis, ed., *The Forrestal Diaries* (New York: Viking Press, 1951), 466.
24. Senate, *National Aviation Policy: Report of the Congressional Aviation Policy Board*, 80th Cong., 2d sess., S. Rept. 949, 1948, 6–7.
25. House, *The National Defense Program—Unification and Strategy*, 6, 529.
26. Millis, *The Forrestal Diaries*, 370, 390–94; McClendon, *Unification of the Armed Forces*, 72–73.
27. Departments of Army and Air Force, Joint Army and Air Force Bulletin 13, *Functions of the Armed Forces and the Joint Chiefs of Staff*, 13 May 1948.
28. House, *National Military Establishment Appropriation Bill for 1950: Hearings before the Subcommittee of the Committee on Appropriations*, 81st Cong., 1st sess., 1949, pt. 3:58.
29. Millis, *The Forrestal Diaries*, 395–96.
30. Ibid., 467.
31. Gen Carl A. Spaatz, "Atomic Warfare," *Life*, 16 August 1948, 94.
32. Memorandum by Gen Carl A. Spaatz and Vice Adm John H. Towers to Secretary of Defense James V. Forrestal, 18 August 1948, summarized in Millis, *The Forrestal Diaries*, 476.
33. Millis, *The Forrestal Diaries*, 476–78; Joint Army and Air Force Bulletin 36, *II. Functions of the Armed Forces and the Joint Chiefs of Staff*, 14 September 1948.
34. McClendon, *Unification of the Armed Forces*, 73–74.
35. "Jimmy Doolittle Scores: Wasted Defense Billions," *Air Force Magazine*, December 1948, 13–15.
36. House, *The National Defense Program—Unification and Strategy*, 408–9.
37. Gen Carl A. Spaatz to commanding general, Strategic Air Command, letter, subject: Interim Mission, 12 March 1946; Army Air Forces Regulation 20-20, *Organization: Strategic Air Command*, 10 October 1946; Air Force Regulation 20-20A, 19 December 1947; message, TST-587, Joint Chiefs of Staff, to commanding general, Strategic Air Command, 13 April 1949; Lt Gen Curtis E. LeMay, "The Missions and Organization of the Strategic Air Command," lecture, Air War College, Maxwell AFB, Ala., 4 March 1949.
38. Memorandum by Secretary of Defense James V. Forrestal to the secretary of the Army et al., subject: Organization and Mission of Military Air Transport Service (MATS), 3 May 1948; McClendon, *Unification of the Armed Forces*, 68–69.
39. Memorandum by Maj Gen Thomas T. Handy, assistant chief of staff, Operations Division (G-3), War Department General Staff, to chief of staff, Army, subject: Outline of Post-War Permanent Military Establishment, 28 October 1943.
40. Gen George C. Marshall, Biennial Report of the Chief of Staff of the United States Army, 1 July 1943 to 30 June 1945, in *The War Reports of General of the Army George C. Marshall, General of the Army H. H. Arnold (and) Fleet Admiral Ernest J. King* (Philadelphia: J. B. Lippincott Co., 1947), 152.
41. Memorandum by Maj Gen Thomas T. Handy to chief of staff, Army, 28 October 1943.
42. Senate, *Department of Armed Forces, Department of Military Security*, 49; House, *The National Defense Program—Unification and Strategy*, 601; marginal comments by George C. Marshall on memorandum for chief of staff from Maj Gen Thomas T. Handy, 28 October 1943.
43. Maj Gen Barney M. Giles, chief of Air Staff, Army Air Forces, to Distribution, letter, subject: Post-War Air Force, 11 December 1943.

44. Brig Gen Howard A. Craig, assistant chief of Air Staff, Operations, Commitments, and Requirements, Army Air Forces, to assistant chief of Air Staff, Plans, R&R sheet, subject: Post-War Air Force, 13 January 1944.

45. Maj Gen Westside T. Larson, commanding general, Third Air Force, to assistant chief of Air Staff, Plans, Army Air Forces, letter, subject: Initial Post-War Air Force, 2 May 1944.

46. Memorandum by Brig Gen Frederic H. Smith, Jr., deputy chief of Air Staff, to assistant chief of Air Staff, Training, Army Air Forces, subject: An Operational Air Force in the United States, 31 December 1944.

47. Memorandum by Col Phillip D. Cole to Col Reuben C. Moffat, commander, Post-War Plans Division, subject: A Realistic Conception of a Post-War Air Force, 22 August 1945.

48. Memorandum by Maj Gen H. R. Oldfield, special assistant for antiaircraft, Army Air Forces, to assistant chief of Air Staff, Plans, Post-War Plans Division, subject: Assignment of Antiaircraft Units to the Air Forces in the Defense of the Philippine Islands, 30 May 1945.

49. Maj Gen Donald Wilson, assistant chief of Air Staff, Operations, Commitments, and Requirements to chief, Management Control, letter, subject: Organization of Continental Air Defense Command, 6 June 1945.

50. Memorandum by Col Reuben C. Moffat to Col Charles P. Cabell, subject: Problems Requiring Immediate Attention of General Eisenhower, 4 December 1945.

51. Brig Gen William D. Old, CGI Troop Carrier Command, to Lt Gen Barney M. Giles, letter, 22 September 1944; Brig Gen Laurence S. Kuter to Brig Gen William D. Old, letter, 14 October 1944; Old to Kuter, letter, 7 November 1944.

52. Memorandum by Maj E. L. Daniels to Col Robert O. Cork, assistant chief of Air Staff, Plans, Post-War Plans Division, subject: General Old's Proposal Concerning an Airborne Army, 2 April 1945; memorandum by Col Robert O. Cork to Col Reuben C. Moffat, subject: Troop Carrier Aviation, 5 April 1945.

53. Memorandum by Col Phillip D. Cole to Col Reuben C. Moffat, 22 August 1945.

54. Assistant chief of Air Staff, Plans, Initial Post-War Air Force, 14 February 1944, approved by Gen Henry H. Arnold, 25 February 1944; memorandum by Brig Gen Laurence S. Kuter to Gen Henry H. Arnold, subject: Status of Plans for the Post-War Air Force, 17 January 1945.

55. War Department Basic Plan for the Post-War Military Establishment, approved by chief of staff, Army, 13 March 1945.

56. Memorandum by Maj Gen Ray E. Porter, director, Special Plans Division, War Department General Staff, to commanding general, Army Air Forces et al., subject: Proposed Change in "War Department Strategic Assumptions," 19 October 1945; Brig Gen William F. McKee, deputy assistant chief of Air Staff, Operations, Commitments, and Requirements (ACAS-3), to assistant chief of Air Staff, Plans (ACAS-5), R&R sheet, subject: Proposed Change in "War Department Strategic Assumptions," 29 October 1945.

57. Lt Gen Ira C. Eaker to Special Plans Division, War Department General Staff, R&R sheet, subject: The Interim Air Force, 31 May 1945; House, *Military Establishment Appropriation Bill for 1946: Hearings before the Subcommittee of the Committee on Appropriations*, 79th Cong., 1st sess., 1945, 182.

58. Memorandum for record by Col Jacob E. Smart, subject: Decisions Reached at Staff Meeting in General Eaker's Office, 29 August 1945; memorandum by Brig Gen Glen C. Jamison, deputy assistant chief of Air Staff, Plans, to chief, Post-War Plans Division, assistant chief of Air Staff, Plans, subject: Strength of Permanent Military Establishment, 22 October 1945; memorandum by Col Reuben C. Moffat to Col Charles P. Cabell, subject: Problems Requiring Immediate Attention of General Eisenhower, 4 December 1945; memorandum by Lt Col K. L. Garrett to Brig Gen Glen C. Jamison, subject: Material for Briefing of Generals Arnold and Eisenhower, 8 December 1945; Report of the Chief of Staff, US Air Force, Secretary of the Air Force, 30 June 1948, 51.

59. Lt Gen Ira C. Eaker to Special Plans Division, War Department General Staff, R&R sheet, 31 May 1945.

60. Chase C. Mooney, *Organization of the Army Air Arm, 1935–1945*, USAF historical study 10 (Maxwell AFB, Ala.: US Air Force Historical Division, 1956), 57–58; Maj Gen Samuel E. Anderson,

chief of staff, Continental Air Force, to commanding general, Army Air Forces, letter, subject: Interim Air Force, 8 September 1945.

61. Representatives of assistant chief of Air Staff, Operations, Commitments, and Requirements (ACAS-3), assistant chief of Air Staff, Materiel (ACAS-4), and assistant chief of Air Staff, Plans (ACAS-5), staff study, subject: Supply by Air, 5 September 1945.

62. Gen Henry H. Arnold to Brig Gen Harold L. George, letter, 5 December 1945; Lt Gen Ira C. Eaker to ACAS-3 and ACAS-5, R&R sheet, subject: Future Plans for Air Transport Command, 10 December 1945.

63. History, Air Research and Development Command, 23 January 1950 to 30 June 1951, 32.

64. Memorandum by Col S. F. Griffin to Brig Gen Howard A. Craig, subject: Meeting on Air Development, 28 July 1944.

65. Memorandum by Gen Henry H. Arnold to Dr Theodore von Karman, subject: Army Air Forces Long-Range Development Program, 7 November 1944.

66. Robert Cahn, "Dr Theodore von Karman, Gemutlicher Genius of Aeronautics," *Air Force Magazine*, October 1957, 41–48.

67. General Arnold's statement to Post-War Plans Division, Army Air Forces, 1 December 1944.

68. Memorandum for record by Lt Col A. E. Settle, Post-War Plans Division, Army Air Forces, subject: Talk by General Arnold, 12 January 1945.

69. Statement of General Arnold at Joint Hearings of Subcommittee on War Mobilization of Senate Military Affairs Committee and two subcommittees of Senate Commerce Committee, 18 October 1945.

70. Army Air Forces Board, "Initial Post-War Air Force," Project (U)3a, staff study, 29 April 1944.

71. Minutes of monthly meetings of Army Air Forces Board, 2 January 1945.

72. Col W. B. Leach, chief, Operations Analysis Division, Army Air Forces, to Lt Col Philip Shepley, letter, subject: Post War Plans—Operations Analysis, 8 February 1945.

73. Army Air Forces letter no. 20-96, subject: Establishment of an Experimental All Weather Facility, 16 June 1945; T. A. Murrell, expert consultant to the secretary of war, to Dr Edward L. Bowles, expert consultant to the secretary of war, letter, 16 January 1945.

74. Memorandum by Maj Gen Charles C. Chauncey, deputy chief of Air Staff, Army Air Forces, to Maj Gen David Schlatter, subject: Directive, Army Air Forces School, 8 November 1945; General Order 20, Army Air Forces Center, 29 November 1945.

75. Arnold, *Global Mission*, 608–9; "The Future of the Air Forces," *Air Force Magazine*, March–April 1964, 9; Senate, *Department of Armed Forces, Department of Military Security*, 341–43; memorandum by Brig Gen Henry I. Hodes, assistant deputy chief of staff, Army, to Lt Gen William H. Simpson et al., subject: Board of Officers to Study Organization of the War Department, 29 November 1945; Lt Gen Ira C. Eaker to assistant chief of Air Staff, Personnel (ACAS-1) et al., letter, subject: Organization—Army Air Forces, 29 January 1946.

76. Interview with Gen Carl A. Spaatz by Brig Gen Noel F. Parrish and Alfred Goldberg, 21 February 1962.

77. Report of the chief of staff, US Air Force, to the secretary of the Air Force, 30 June 1948, 21; memorandum by Lt Gen Hoyt S. Vandenberg, ACAS-3, to Lt Gen Ira C. Eaker, subject: Establishment of a Strategic Striking Force, 2 January 1946; Gen Carl A. Spaatz to commanding general, Strategic Air Command, letter, subject: Interim Mission, 12 March 1946; Maj Gen E. F. Witsell, The Adjutant General, War Department, letter, subject: Establishment of Air Defense, Strategic and Tactical Air Commands, 21 March 1946.

78. House, *Military Establishment Appropriation Bill for 1947: Hearings before the Subcommittee of the Committee on Appropriations*, 79th Cong., 2d sess., 1946, 414.

79. Maj Gen Earle E. Partridge, ACAS-3, to ACAS-5, R&R sheet, subject: Air Forces Policy as to the Organization of the Antiaircraft Artillery, 1 February 1946; daily activity report, ACAS-3, 12 February 1946; Report of the Board of Officers on Organization of the War Department (Simpson Board), 28 December 1945, 14.

80. War Department, The Adjutant General Office, letter, subject: Establishment of Air Defense, Strategic and Tactical Air Commands, 21 March 1946; memorandum by Col Reuben C. Moffat to chief, Permanent Establishment Branch, subject: Assignment of Regular Fighter Unit to Air Defense Command, 23 April 1946; Lt Gen Ira C. Eaker to commanding general, Air Defense Command, letter, subject: Investment of Command Responsibilities of the Land, Sea, and Air Forces in Event of an Air Invasion, 10 June 1946; War Department Circular 138, War Department Reorganization, 14 May 1946.

81. House, *Military Establishment Appropriation Bill for 1947*, 414; War Department, The Adjutant General Office, letter, subject: Establishment of Air Defense, Strategic and Tactical Air Commands . . ., 21 March 1946; Report of chief of staff, US Air Force, to secretary of the Air Force, 30 June 1948, 22, 24; War Department Circular 138, 14 May 1946.

82. War Department Circular 138, 14 May 1946.

83. 1st ind. (letter, Tactical Air Command, subject: Proposed Plan for Third Air Force, Troop Carrier, 7 May 1946), Brig Gen Reuben C. Hood, Jr., deputy chief of Air Staff, Army Air Forces, to commanding general, Tactical Air Command, 6 August 1946.

84. Mooney, *Organization of the Army Air Arm, 1935–1945*, 62–63.

85. Memorandum by Edward L. Bowles to Secretary of War Robert P. Patterson, 5 May 1947; memorandum by Maj Gen Curtis E. LeMay, deputy chief of staff, Research and Development, Army Air Forces, to assistant secretary of war for air, 10 December 1946.

86. Memorandum by Edward L. Bowles to Gen Henry H. Arnold, 26 November 1945; memorandum by Edward L. Bowles to secretary of war, 4 October 1945; Maj Gen Lawrence C. Craigie, chief, Engineering Division, Wright Field, to Aeronautical Board, US Navy, letter, subject: Project RAND, 11 October 1946; Maj Gen Curtis E. LeMay to Army Air Forces, Operations Analysis, R&R sheet, subject: Report of Evaluation of Military Worth Activities, 5 August 1947.

87. Memorandum by Maj Gen Howard A. Craig, assistant chief of Air Staff, Operations, Commitments, and Requirements, to chief of Air Staff, subject: Establishment of "The Air Council," 13 June 1944; memorandum, Kuter to Craig, 21 September 1944.

88. Lt Gen Ira C. Eaker to assistant chief of Air Staff, Plans, R&R sheet, subject: General Air Board, 28 January 1946; Maj Gen Charles C. Chauncey, deputy chief of Air Staff, Army Air Forces, to assistant chief of Air Staff, Personnel et al., R&R sheet, subject: General Air Board, 8 April 1946; *Annual Report of the Secretary of Air Force for FY 1958*, chief of staff section, 23.

89. Lt Gen Ira C. Eaker to assistant chief of Air Staff, Plans, R&R sheet, subject: General Air Board, 28 January 1946; Maj Gen Lauris Norstad, ACAS-5, to deputy commanding general, Army Air Forces, subject: General Air Board, n.d.

90. Memorandum by Col Harry E. Wilson, chief of staff, Army Air Forces Center, to Air Staff, Army Air Forces Center, subject: Organizational and Functional Charts, 5 March 1946; General Order 1, Air Proving Ground Command, 17 July 1946; Army Air Forces, letter no. 20-10, 3 June 1946; History, Air Proving Ground, 2 September 1945–30 June 1949, 1:43–49.

91. Army Air Forces Regulation 20-61, 3 June 1946; History, Air University, 29 November 1945–30 June 1947, 218–20; Maj Gen David M. Schlatter, "Air University," *Air Force Magazine*, July 1946, 9–11.

92. History, Tactical Air Command, March–December 1946, 1:56–58; Tactical Air Command Staff Conference Notes, vol. 1, no. 17 (3 May 1946); Maj Gen Elwood R. Quesada, commanding general, Tactical Air Command, to Lt Gen Ira C. Eaker, letter, 24 May 1946; Gen Carl A. Spaatz to commanding general, Air University, letter, subject: Amendment to Directive, 13 May 1946.

93. Brig Gen Eugene L. Eubank to Maj Gen Muir S. Fairchild, letter, 6 June 1946.

94. Schlatter, "Air University," 9–11.

95. WOJG Dalton G. Feagler, acting assistant adjutant general, Air University, to commanding general, Army Air Forces, Attn.: DCS R&D, letter, subject: Activation of the Research Section, Academic Staff Division, Air University, 16 July 1946; History, Air University, 29 November 1945–30 June 1947, 218–23; History, Air University, 1 July 1947–30 June 1948, 1:45–48.

96. History, Air University, 29 November 1945–30 June 1947, 17–18.

97. Maj F. E. Langston, assistant adjutant general, Air University, to commanding general, Army Air Forces, Attn.: Policy and Review Section, ACAS-3, letter, subject: Air University Research Project

IDEAS, CONCEPTS, DOCTRINE

Priorities, 19 September 1946; A-5 Section, Tactical Air Command, to A-1 Section, Tactical Air Command, R&R sheet, subject: Air University Project No. H4856, 25 October 1946.

98. 1st ind. (letter, Headquarters Army Air Forces, subject: Responsibilities for Air Defense, 24 June 1946), Brig Gen Robert M. Lee, chief of staff, Tactical Air Command, to commanding general, Army Air Forces, Attn.: ACAS-3, 13 August 1946; weekly report of ACAS-3 to assistant adjutant general, General Council meeting, 29 August 1947.

99. Air War College, problem no. 4, 1946–1947; "Proposed Reorganization Army Air Forces," 6 January 1947.

100. Report of chief of staff, US Air Force, to secretary of the Air Force, 30 June 1948, 42–49; Dr Ralph P. Johnson to Maj Gen Curtis E. LeMay, letter, 11 June 1947; McClendon, *Unification of the Armed Forces*, 59–60.

101. *Annual Report of the Secretary of the Air Force, Fiscal Year 1948*, chief of staff section, 23.

102. House, *Investigation of the B-36 Bomber Program: Hearings before the Committee on Armed Services*, 81st Cong., 1st sess., 1949, 140–42.

103. Col Leslie R. Peterson, acting secretary, USAF Aircraft and Weapons Board, to ACAS-1 et al., R&R sheet, subject: USAF Aircraft and Development Program, n.d.; History of B-36 Procurement, presented to House Armed Services Committee by Maj Gen Frederic H. Smith, Jr., 1949, sec. 10, 1–5; House, *Investigation of the B-36 Bomber Program*, 49.

104. House, *Investigation of the B-36 Bomber Program*, 83, 174–75; History, Headquarters USAF, 1 July 1949–30 June 1950, 4.

105. Senate, *Military Situation in the Far East: Hearings before the Committee on Armed Services and the Committee on Foreign Relations*, 82d Cong., 1st sess., 1951, 1486.

106. Memorandum, Spaatz to Arnold, quoted in *Air Force Magazine*, June 1952, 24.

107. Senate, *Military Situation in the Far East*, 626–27.

108. House, *Military Establishment Appropriation Bill for 1947*, 27.

109. Ibid., 400–4.

110. Maj Gen St. Clair Streett, deputy commanding general, Strategic Air Command, to commanding general, Army Air Forces, letter, subject: Operational Training and Strategic Employment of Units of the Strategic Air Command, 25 July 1946; 1st ind., Brig Gen Thomas S. Power, deputy assistant chief of Air Staff, Operations, Commitments, and Requirements, to commanding general, Strategic Air Command, 9 October 1946.

111. House, *Military Establishment Appropriation Bill for 1948: Hearings before the Subcommittee of the Committee on Appropriations*, 80th Cong., 1st sess., 1947, 600.

112. Maj Kenneth F. Gantz, "The Atomic Present," *Air Force Magazine*, March–April 1946, 4.

113. Interview with Spaatz by Parrish and Goldberg, 21 February 1962; Bernard Brodie, "A-Bombs and Air Strategy," *Air Force Magazine*, October 1948, 33; Arnold, *Third Report to the Secretary of War*, 68.

114. Maj Gen St. Clair Streett to the commanding general, Army Air Forces, subject: Operational Training and Strategic Employment of Units of the Strategic Air Command, letter, 25 July 1946.

115. Memorandum by Gen Hoyt S. Vandenberg to Lt Gen Ira C. Eaker, subject: Establishment of a Strategic Striking Force, 2 January 1946.

116. House, *Military Establishment Appropriation Bill for 1947*, 401–2.

117. Weekly Report for Army Air Forces General Council from ACAS-3, 8 November 1945.

118. Streett to commanding general, Army Air Forces, letter, 25 July 1946; memorandum, Vandenberg to Eaker, 2 January 1946.

119. Richard R. Dann, "Strategic Air Command," *Air Force Magazine*, August 1946, 35–36.

120. Maj Gen St. Clair Streett, "The Strategic Air Command," lecture, Air War College, Maxwell AFB, Ala., 22 October 1946.

121. Millis, *The Forrestal Diaries*, 316; Maj Gen James C. Selser, Jr., deputy commander, Eighth Air Force, "The Bomber's Role in Diplomacy," *Air Force Magazine*, April 1956, 52–56; Samuel P. Huntington, *The Soldier and the State* (Cambridge: Harvard University Press, 1957), 382.

122. Report of the Standing Subcommittee on Demobilization of the Aircraft Industry to the Air Coordinating Committee, approved by the Air Coordinating Committee, 22 October 1945, 10–11.

123. Statement of Secretary of the Air Force W. Stuart Symington in "U.S. President's Air Policy Commission," unclassified testimony before the President's Air Policy Commission (Washington, D.C.: n.p., 26 November 1947).

124. House, *Military Establishment Appropriation Bill for 1947*, 431–32, 438.

125. Ibid., 406.

126. *United States Air Force Statistical Digest, 1947*, 110–11; memorandum by Gen Henry H. Arnold to Lt Gen Ira C. Eaker, subject: Interim Problems of the Army Air Forces, 27 August 1945.

127. *United States Air Force Statistical Digest, 1947*, 110–11.

128. Memorandum by Brig Gen Alfred R. Maxwell, chief, Requirements Division, ACAS-3, to Maj Gen Curtis E. LeMay, subject: Williamsburg Conference of the Aircraft Industries Association, 23 July 1946; report of chief of staff, US Air Force, to secretary of Air Force, 30 June 1948, 74–79.

129. House, *Military Establishment Appropriation Bill for 1947*, 488; House, *Military Functions, National Military Establishment Appropriation Bill for 1949: Hearings before the Subcommittee of the Committee on Appropriations*, 80th Cong., 2d sess., 1948, 14–15.

130. *United States Air Force Statistical Digest, 1947*, 110–11, 250; report of chief of staff, US Air Force, to secretary of Air Force, 30 June 1948, 74–79.

131. House, *Military Establishment Appropriation Bill for 1947*, 431.

132. Senate, *Military Establishment Appropriation Bill for 1948: Hearings before the Subcommittee of the Committee on Appropriations*, 80th Cong., 1st sess., 1947, 264.

133. Ibid., 298–99; *United States Air Force Statistical Digest, 1947*, 250; ibid., 1948, 1:276; 2:12.

134. *United States Air Force Statistical Digest*, 1948, 1:276; 2:12.

135. Arnold, *Third Report to the Secretary of War*, 69–70.

136. House, *Military Establishment Appropriation Bill for 1948*, 649–51.

137. Ibid., 650–52.

138. House, *Military Establishment Appropriation Bill for 1947*, 406; Gen Carl A. Spaatz to commanding general, Strategic Air Command, Current Army Air Forces Plans and Programs, letter, 24 October 1946.

139. Theodore von Karman, *Science, The Key to Air Supremacy* (Wright Field, Ohio: Air Materiel Command Publications Branch, 1945), 59–60.

140. Quoted in Senate, *Inquiry into Satellite and Missile Programs: Hearings before the Preparedness Investigating Subcommittee of the Committee on Armed Services*, 85th Cong., 1st and 2d sess., 1957 and 1958, 822–23.

141. Memorandum by Maj Gen Hugh J. Knerr, secretary-general of Air Board, to Gen Carl A. Spaatz, subject: Armament Organization, 26 February 1946.

142. Maj Gen Bernard A. Schriever, "The USAF Ballistic Missile Program," in *The United States Air Force Report on the Ballistic Missile*, ed. Lt Col Kenneth F. Gantz (Garden City, N.Y.: Doubleday & Co., 1958), 25–26; Maj Gen Lawrence C. Craigie to US Navy Aeronautical Board, letter, 11 October 1946.

143. *United States Air Force Statistical Digest, January 1949–June 1950*, 289.

144. House, *Military Establishment Appropriation Bill for 1948*, 616, 618; Senate, *Military Establishment Appropriation Bill for 1948*, 268.

145. House, *Military Establishment Appropriation Bill for 1948*, 626–29; *United States Air Force Statistical Digest, January 1949–June 1950*, 289.

146. Memorandum by Maj Gen Curtis E. LeMay to deputy director, War Department, Research and Development, 11 April 1947.

147. House, *Department of Defense Appropriations for 1954: Hearings before a Subcommittee of the Committee on Appropriations*, 83d Cong., 1st sess., 1953, 170.

148. House, *Military Establishment Appropriation Bill for 1948*, 638–41.

149. Maj Gen Lawrence C. Craigie, director, research and development, Deputy Chief of Staff, Materiel, US Air Force, to commanding general, Air Materiel Command, letter, subject: The Air Force Master Plan for Research and Development, 4 March 1948.

150. Report of chief of staff, US Air Force, to secretary of the Air Force, 30 June 1948, 84; Brig Gen William L. Richardson, "USAF Guided Missile Program," lecture, Air War College, Maxwell AFB, Ala., 18 January 1949; Maj R. T. Franzel, "Presentation of USAF Project Atlas (MX-1593)," lecture, Air War College, Maxwell AFB, Ala., 26 May 1953.

151. W. Barton Leach, "The Bear Has Wings," *Air Force Magazine*, February 1947, 17–19, 64.

152. House, *Military Establishment Appropriation Bill for 1948*, 2–4.

153. Ibid., 601–2.

154. Ibid., 629.

155. Ibid., 601–2, 642–43.

156. Senate, *Military Establishment Appropriation Bill for 1948*, 292–93, 298–99.

157. *A Program for National Security, Report of the President's Advisory Commission on Universal Training* (Washington, D.C.: Government Printing Office, 1947), 7–8, 89–92.

158. House, *Investigation of the B-36 Bomber Program*, 193, 400.

159. Report of chief of staff, US Air Force, to secretary of the Air Force, 20 June 1948, 57; Operations Statistics Division, US Air Force Operational Efficiency of the 70 Groups and 22 Separate Squadrons Report, 15 June 1948, 6.

160. Lt Gen George C. Kenney, "World War II Is Out of Date," *Air Force Magazine*, November 1947, 30–31.

161. Operational Statistics Division, US Air Force, Operational Efficiency Report, 15 June 1948, 16–17.

162. Streett, "The Strategic Air Command," lecture, 22 October 1946.

163. Col K. P. Bergquist, deputy assistant chief of Air Staff, Operations, Commitments, and Requirements (ACAS-3), Army Air Forces, to commanding general, Strategic Air Command, letter, subject: Fighter Escort for VHB, n.d.; 1st ind., Capt H. E. Cassing, acting assistant adjutant general, Strategic Air Command, to commanding general, Army Air Forces, 1 August 1946; weekly report of ACAS-3 for General Council, Army Air Forces, 19 July 1946.

164. Lt Gen Ira C. Eaker to commanding general, Air Defense Command, letter, subject: Investment of Command Responsibilities of the Land, Sea, and Air Forces in Event of an Air Invasion, 10 June 1946; House, *Military Establishment Appropriation Bill for 1948*, 634–35.

165. Lt Gen George E. Stratemeyer, "Mission and Organization of the Air Defense Command," lecture, Air War College, Maxwell AFB, Ala., 14 January 1984.

166. "Air Defense Plan," lecture, Air War College, Maxwell AFB, Ala., 23 April 1947.

167. Stratemeyer to commanding general, Army Air Forces, letter, subject: Air Defense Pacific Coastal Frontier, 19 April 1946; weekly report of ACAS-3 for General Council, Army Air Forces, 6 September 1946; Operational Status Division, US Air Force, Operational Efficiency Report, 15 June 1948, 12.

168. Draft of US Air Force historical study 134, "Troop Carrier Aviation in the USAF, 1945–1955," 3–11.

169. Operational Status Division, US Air Force, Operational Efficiency Report, 15 June 1948, 19–20.

170. Quotations from letter by Secretary of Defense Forrestal to Chairman Chan Gurney, Senate Armed Services Committee, 8 December 1957, in Millis, *The Forrestal Diaries*, 350–51.

171. Col William D. Eckert, United Nations Military Staff Committee, to Lt Gen Hoyt S. Vandenberg, deputy commanding general, Army Air Forces, letter, 21 July 1947; *Survival in the Air Age: A Report by the President's Air Policy Commission* (Washington, D.C.: Government Printing Office, 1948), 46, 48, 49; statement of Gen Carl A. Spaatz in "U.S. President's Air Policy Commission," 6:2343–44.

172. *Survival in the Air Age*, 158–61; Carl Norcross, "The Report of the President's Air Policy Commission," *Air Force Magazine*, March 1948, 5–6, 8, 48.

173. Senate, *National Aviation Policy*, 1–2.
174. Ibid., 1.
175. "U.S. President's Air Policy Commission," 6:2761–90.
176. Ibid., 2278–85, 2693–2715.
177. Ibid., 2412–14.
178. Ibid., 2727–34.
179. Ibid., 2386–92.
180. Ibid., 2343–50, 2512–48.
181. Ibid., 2606–31.
182. *Survival in the Air Age*, 3–4.
183. Senate, *National Aviation Policy*, 3, 10.
184. *Survival in the Air Age*, 6, 8–9, 23.
185. Ibid., 13, 22, 24–36, 45–46.
186. Senate, *National Aviation Policy*, 7–8.
187. Ibid., 12; *Survival in the Air Age*, 68–69.
188. Norcross, "The Report of the President's Air Policy Commission," 5–6.
189. Alexander P. de Seversky, "New Concepts of Air Power," lecture, Army War College, Carlisle Barracks, Pa., 18 March 1952.
190. Report of a Board of Officers to chief of staff, US Air Force, Recommending General Policy and Air Force Action Regarding the President's Air Policy Commission Report and the Congressional Aviation Policy Board Report, 23 March 1948.
191. House, *Military Functions, National Military Establishment Appropriation Bill for 1949*, 96–97; "U.S. President's Air Policy Commission," 6:2783.
192. House, *Military Functions, National Military Establishment Appropriation Bill for 1949*, 55.
193. Ibid.
194. United States Strategic Bombing Survey, *Air Campaigns of the Pacific War*, July 1947, 65–66.
195. Col Bruce K. Holloway, "High Sub-Sonic Speeds for Air Warfare," *Air University Quarterly Review* 1, no. 2 (Fall 1947): 42–52.
196. Memorandum by Gen George C. Kenney, commanding general, Strategic Air Command, to Secretary of Defense James V. Forrestal, 7 January 1948.
197. House, *Investigation of the B-36 Bomber Program*, 49, 55.
198. Smith, "History of B-36 Procurement," sec. 21, 1–8.
199. House, *Investigation of the B-36 Bomber Program*, 55–56; Senate, *Department of Defense Appropriations for 1962: Hearings before the Subcommittee to the Committee on Appropriations*, 87th Cong., 1st sess., 1961, 862–64.
200. Col Dale O. Smith, "One-Way Combat," *Air University Quarterly Review* 1, no. 2 (Fall 1947): 3–8.
201. Smith, "History of B-36 Procurement," sec. 14, 1–4; Gen Carl A. Spaatz to commanding general, Strategic Air Command, message WARX-85971, 9 September 1947; Air Materiel Command Historical Office, "Case History of Air-to-Air Refueling," March 1949; Lt Gen George C. Kenney, "Mission and Organization of the Strategic Air Command," lecture, Air War College, Maxwell AFB, Ala., 13 January 1948.
202. A. Berle, "The Democracies Face the Post-War Problem," lecture, Air War College, Maxwell AFB, Ala., 8 October 1952.
203. Millis, *The Forrestal Diaries*, 382.
204. Ibid., 387.
205. House, *Military Functions, National Military Establishment Appropriation Bill for 1949*, pt. 1:2–3, 9–10.
206. Ibid., pt. 2:5–6; pt. 3:9.
207. Millis, *The Forrestal Diaries*, 409–19; House, *The Supplemental Appropriation Bill for 1951: Hearings before a Subcommittee of the Committee on Appropriations*, 81st Cong., 2d sess., 1950, 2–4.

IDEAS, CONCEPTS, DOCTRINE

208. Memorandum by President Harry Truman to secretary of defense, 13 May 1948; Air Materiel Command, History of the USAF Five-Year Aircraft Procurement Program, 1 January 1948–1 July 1949, 8–9.
209. Senate, *Major Defense Matters: Hearings before the Preparedness Investigating Subcommittee of the Committee on Armed Services*, 86th Cong., 1st sess., 1959, 6.
210. Millis, *The Forrestal Diaries*, 452–55; House, *Investigation of the B-36 Bomber Program*, 32.
211. Millis, *The Forrestal Diaries*, 452–58; House, *Investigation of the B-36 Bomber Program*, 32–33.
212. History, Strategic Air Command, 1948, 1:146–48.
213. Alfred Goldberg, ed., *A History of the United States Air Force, 1907–1957* (Princeton, N.J.: D. Van Nostrand Co., 1957), 235–41.
214. John G. Norris, "Airpower in the Cold War," *Air Force Magazine*, September 1948, 25–26.
215. Millis, *The Forrestal Diaries*, 489–91.
216. Edward Teller with Allen Brown, *The Legacy of Hiroshima* (Garden City, N.Y.: Doubleday & Co., 1962), 31–32.
217. Bernard Brodie, "A-Bombs and Air Strategy," pt. 3, *Air Force Magazine*, November 1948, 50, 52.
218. Senate, *Military Situation in the Far East*, 77.
219. House, *The National Defense Program—Unification and Strategy*, 170.
220. Col Grover C. Brown, "Strategic Air Warfare Concepts," lecture, Air War College, Maxwell AFB, Ala., 3 December 1951.
221. Col Ray S. Sleeper, "The Political-Psychological Aspects of Offensive Air," lecture, Air War College, Maxwell AFB, Ala., 4 February 1952.
222. Quoted in *Air University Quarterly Review* 2, no. 2 (Fall 1948): 14; Gen Carl A. Spaatz, USAF, Retired, "If We Should Have to Fight Again," *Life*, 5 July 1948, 39–40.
223. Millis, *The Forrestal Diaries*, 463–64.
224. Lt Gen George C. Kenney to Maj Gen Robert W. Harper, commanding general, Air University, letter, 11 August 1984.
225. Lt Col Joseph L. Dickman, "Douhet and the Future," *Air University Quarterly Review* 2, no. 1 (Summer 1948): 3–15.
226. History, Continental Air Command, 1 December 1948–31 December 1949, 7–9, quoting a study by Col William W. Momyer, director of plans, Tactical Air Command, subject: An Evaluation of the Exchange of the 31st Fighter Group for the 82d Fighter Group, 10 August 1948.
227. Lt Col Frank R. Pancake, "The Strategic Striking Force," *Air University Quarterly Review* 2, no. 2 (Fall 1948): 48–56.
228. Lt Col John P. Healy, "Air Power and Foreign Policy," *Air University Quarterly Review* 2, no. 2 (Fall 1948): 15–26.
229. Col Dale O. Smith, "Operational Concepts for Modern War," *Air University Quarterly Review* 2, no. 2 (Fall 1948): 3–14.
230. House, *National Military Establishment Appropriation Bill for 1950*, pt. 1:227.
231. Ibid., pt. 2:16–17; Senate, *Military Situation in the Far East*, 2597–98; Huntington, *The Soldier and the State*, 455.
232. William Schaub, "The US Security Policy from the Standpoint of the Bureau of the Budget," lecture, Air War College, Maxwell AFB, Ala., 1 November 1955; Huntington, *The Soldier and the State*, 445; House, *National Military Establishment Appropriation Bill for 1950*, pt. 1:12.
233. Millis, *The Forrestal Diaries*, 450, 492–98; Huntington, *The Soldier and the State*, 445–56.
234. Millis, *The Forrestal Diaries*, 502–6, 535–36; House, *National Military Establishment Appropriation Bill for 1950*, pt. 2:99.
235. Memorandum by Secretary of the Air Force W. Stuart Symington to Secretary of Defense James V. Forrestal, subject: The Air Force 48 Group Program, 25 February 1949.
236. History, Continental Air Command, 1 December 1949–31 December 1949, 1–12; Lt Gen George E. Stratemeyer, "Organization and Mission of the Continental Air Command," lecture, Air War College, Maxwell AFB, Ala., 2 March 1949.

237. Col William H. Wise, "Future of the Tactical Air Force," *Air University Quarterly Review* 2, no. 4 (Spring 1949): 33–39.

238. Memorandum by Brig Gen Joseph T. McNarney, acting chairman, USAF Senior Officers Board, to secretary of the Air Force, subject: Final Report of Board of Officers, 13 January 1949.

239. Ibid.; memorandum, Symington to Forrestal, 25 February 1949; House, *Investigation of the B-36 Bomber Program*, 154–55; House, *National Defense Program—Unification and Strategy*, 511.

240. Memorandum, McNarney to secretary of the Air Force, 13 January 1949; memorandum, Symington to Forrestal, 25 February 1949.

241. Memorandum, McNarney to secretary of the Air Force, 13 January 1949; memorandum, Symington to Forrestal, 25 February 1949.

242. Memorandum, Symington to Forrestal, 25 February 1949.

243. Smith, "History of B-36 Procurement," secs. 23–36; LeMay to Vandenberg, letter, 2 February 1949; Maj Gen Edward M. Powers, assistant deputy chief of staff, Materiel, US Air Force, to chief of staff, US Air Force, letter, subject: Brief of the Recommendations of the Board of Officers Concerning Changes in the Procurement Program and the Research and Development Program of the USAF, 30 March 1949.

244. Memorandum, McNarney to secretary of the Air Force, 13 January 1949; memorandum for record by Maj Gen Muir S. Fairchild, subject: Report of the Board of Senior Officers, Third Meeting on 16 and 17 May 1949, 6 June 1949.

245. Dean Acheson to the president, letter, 7 April 1949; Congress, *North Atlantic Treaty*, 81st Cong., 1st sess., 1949, S. Doc. 48, 6–8.

246. House, *National Military Establishment Appropriation Bill for 1950*, pt. 1:12, 15, 16–17, 21, 52–53.

247. Ibid., pt. 4:7–8, 18.

248. Ibid., pt. 2:4, 26, 36–37, 104, 151.

249. Ibid., pt. 3:19, 31.

250. Ibid., pt. 1:211, 227.

251. Ibid., pt. 1:228.

252. House, *Department of Defense Appropriations for 1951: Hearings before a Subcommittee of the Committee on Appropriations*, 81st Cong., 2d sess., 1950, pt. 3:1234, 1252–53.

253. Ibid., pt. 1:104–5; Senate, *Military Situation in the Far East*, 2597–98; House, *National Defense Program—Unification and Strategy*, 473–74.

254. House, *National Military Establishment Appropriation Bill for 1950*, pt. 2:99.

255. Senate, *Military Situation in the Far East*, 2636–37; House, *National Defense Program—Unification and Strategy*, 471–72, 529–30.

256. Congress, *North Atlantic Treaty*, S. Doc. 48, 6–13; Maurer Maurer, History of USAF Activities in Support of the Mutual Defense Assistance Program (Wright-Patterson AFB, Ohio: Historical Office, Air Materiel Command, 1951), 1–4.

257. Goldberg, *A History of the United States Air Force, 1907–1957*, 241.

258. House, *Mutual Defense Assistance Act of 1949: Hearings before the Committee on Foreign Affairs*, 81st Cong., 1st sess., 1949, 1–9, 69–72.

259. Maurer, History of USAF Activities in Support of the Mutual Defense Assistance Program, 4–6; Senate, *Military Assistance Program: Joint Hearings before the Committee on Foreign Relations and the Committee on Armed Services*, 81st Cong., 1st sess., 1949, 1–5.

260. *Semiannual Report of the Secretary of the Air Force, 1 July 1949 to 31 December 1949*, 197; *United States Air Force Statistical Digest, January 1949–June 1950*, 4, 170; House, *DOD Appropriations for 1951*, pt. 3:1234, 1252–53.

261. Senate, *Military Situation in the Far East*, 2597–98; House, *DOD Appropriations for 1951*, pt. 1:43–44, 104–5.

262. Senate, *Military Situation in the Far East*, 2597–98, 2607.

263. House, *National Defense Program—Unification and Strategy*, 47.

264. Ibid., 622–23.

265. Semiannual Report of the Secretary of the Air Force, 230.
266. House, *National Defense Program—Unification and Strategy*, 111.
267. Ibid., 6.
268. House, *Investigation of the B-36 Bomber Program, Report of the Committee on Armed Services*, 81st Cong., 2d sess., 1950, 33.
269. House, *National Defense Program—Unification and Strategy*, 6–7, 9–10.
270. Ibid., 40–41, 45–47, 50–51, 57, 64–65, 74–75, 83, 89.
271. Ibid., 183–89.
272. Ibid., 193–200.
273. Ibid., 251–53.
274. Ibid., 350–54.
275. House, *Investigation of the B-36 Bomber Program*, 165–66.
276. Ibid., 167–70.
277. House, *National Defense Program—Unification and Strategy*, 402, 457, 464–65, 478.
278. Ibid., 511.
279. House, *Investigation of the B-36 Bomber Program*, 173, 208.
280. House, *National Defense Program—Unification and Strategy*, 402.
281. Ibid., 402–3.
282. Ibid., 462, 467–68.
283. Ibid., 471–72.
284. Ibid., 518–20; House, *Investigation of the B-36 Bomber Program*, 509, 519.
285. House, *National Defense Program—Unification and Strategy*, 535–36, 521–23, 525–26.
286. Ibid., 527.
287. Ibid., 544–48.
288. Ibid., 56; Millis, *The Forrestal Diaries*, 477; House, *National Military Establishment Appropriation Bill for 1951*, 81st Cong., 1st sess., 1949, pt. 1:74–75, 159–60; T. F. Walkowicz, "The New Look—How New?" *Air Force Magazine*, January 1954, 27; Lt Gen Samuel E. Anderson with Dr C. A. Boyd, Jr., "Are We Making the Most of the Tools We Have?" *Air Force Magazine*, July 1956, 49–54; History, Strategic Air Command, 1949, 1:80–81.
289. Maj Gen Curtis E. LeMay, "Capabilities and Employment of the Strategic Air Command," lecture, Air War College, Maxwell AFB, Ala., 4 February 1957.
290. House, *National Defense Program—Unification and Strategy*, 535–36.
291. Ibid., 594–95, 615.
292. House, *Unification and Strategy, A Report of Investigation by the Committee on Armed Services*, 81st Cong., 2d sess., 1950, 33, 53–56.
293. Ibid., 5.
294. James C. Freund, "The 'Revolt of the Admirals'," pt. 2, in *Air Power Historian* 10, no. 2 (April 1963): 41–42.
295. Maj Gen John A. Samford, "Identification of Strategic Concepts," lecture, Air War College, Maxwell AFB, Ala., 21 May 1951.
296. House, *Department of Defense Appropriations for 1958: Hearings before a Subcommittee of the Committee on Appropriations*, 85th Cong., 1st sess., 1957, 933, 1107.

Gen J. Lawton Collins, Army chief of staff, 1949–53.

Gen Lauris Norstad, deputy chief of staff, Army Air Forces, 1944–45; deputy chief of staff, Operations, 1947–50; commander in chief, United States Air Forces in Europe, 1950–1952.

C-124 Globemaster.

F-86 Sabre.

Dr Theodore von Karman, chairman, Army Air Forces Scientific Advisory Group.

Maj Gen Hugh J. Knerr, commander, Air Technical Services Command, 1945–46; secretary general, Air Board, 1946–48.

W. Stuart Symington, first secretary of the Department of the US Air Force, 18 September 1947.

Lt Gen William Tunner, commander of Military Air Transport Services during Berlin Airlift.

Gen Hoyt S. Vandenberg, Air Force chief of staff, 1948–53.

F-84 Thunderjet.

F-80 Shooting Star.

C-119 Flying Boxcar.

C-97A Stratofreighter.

CHAPTER 6

RESPONSES TO SOVIET NUCLEAR WEAPONS AND LIMITED WAR, 1949-53

Established by statute in the spring of 1948 to examine governmental organization and operations, the Commission on Organization of the Executive Branch (better known by the name of its chairman, former President Herbert Hoover) divided its work among special task force committees. For more than six months, one such panel, the Committee on National Security Organization, headed by Ferdinand Eberstadt, heard testimony on the functioning of the National Military Establishment. On 16 December 1948, the Eberstadt task force released a lengthy report, which was summarized by a Hoover commission report issued on 28 February 1949. The Hoover report concluded that "the authority of the Secretary of Defense, and hence the control of the President, is weak and heavily qualified by the provisions of the act of 1947 which set up a rigid structure of federation rather than unification. . . . The National Military Establishment . . . is perilously close to the weakest type of department."[1] After a year of operating under the 1947 act, Secretary Forrestal also reported firsthand observation of certain weaknesses and inconsistencies in the act, which had not been foreseen at its passage.[2]

Evolving Patterns of Defense Organization

In a message to Congress on 5 March 1949, President Truman accepted many of the recommendations made by the Hoover commission and Secretary Forrestal in proposing changes to the National Security Act of 1947. He wished basically to convert the National Military Establishment into an executive department to be known as the Department of Defense and to provide the secretary of defense with appropriate responsibility and authority and with civilian and military assistance adequate to fulfill his enlarged responsibilities. Truman specifically recommended that the Departments of Army, Navy, and Air Force be designated as military departments, and that the secretary of defense should be the sole representative of the Department of Defense on the National Security Council (NSC). Where the Hoover commission recommended that the departmental secretaries become under secretaries of defense, Truman wished to retain them to administer their respective military departments under the authority, direction, and control of the secretary of defense. He also recommended that Congress authorize an under secretary of defense and three assistant secretaries of defense; place the statutory duties of the Munitions Board and the Research and Development Board under the secretary of defense; and provide for a chairman of the Joint Chiefs of Staff who would take precedence over all other military personnel, be the principal military adviser to the president and the secretary of defense, and perform such other duties as they might prescribe.[3]

At hearings on the proposed legislation held by the Senate Committee on Armed Services in March 1949, Secretary Forrestal candidly acknowledged that he originally had opposed a too great concentration of power in the secretary of defense but he had come to believe that there were sufficient checks and balances inherent in the governmental structure to prevent misuse of the broad authority he felt must now be vested in the position. As a part of an evolutionary development, Forrestal thought that the proposed amendments to the National Security Act would "convert the military establishment from a confederacy to a federation."[4] At another appearance before the same committee in April, Secretary Symington expressed strong Air Force support for increased defense centralization. "From the very beginnings of hearings on the proposal to unify the armed services," he pointed out, "the Air Force has favored centralization and clear definition of authority and responsibility for the positions of the Secretary of Defense and the head of the Joint Chiefs of Staff." He personally favored the Hoover recommendation to designate the departmental secretaries as under secretaries of defense. "I would say," he concluded, "that any diminishing of the power and prestige of the Air Force as a result of making the Air Force a military department instead of an executive department would be very much in the interest of the United States."[5]

With a few modifications, President Truman's recommended amendments to the National Security Act passed the Senate unanimously on 26 May 1949. But, in the House of Representatives, Chairman Vinson's Committee on Armed Services was openly skeptical of the bill. "What has been worrying me ...," Vinson told the new secretary of defense Louis Johnson as hearings began on 28 June, "is that the Congress is frozen out, kept at arms' length, from the problems of the three Departments, I cannot reconcile this with the constitutional responsibility of the Congress, and I think this bill should be amended to keep Congress a part of the team."[6] Vinson felt that the secretary of defense already possessed powers that were adequate for the purposes of unification. While the House Armed Services Committee was considering the legislation, Congress passed and President Truman signed into law on 20 June the Reorganization Act of 1949, which authorized the president to institute reorganization plans within the executive branch, unless a house of Congress should veto the proposal by a majority vote within 60 days. In accordance with this authority, Truman submitted Reorganization Plan No. 8 on the National Military Establishment to Congress on 18 July, which proposed to accomplish most of the earlier legislative recommendations by executive action. While Truman preferred that Congress would act on a matter by regular legislative process, he apparently used the reorganization plan procedure to emphasize the importance of his recommendations. Since the bill passed by the House differed markedly from that voted by the Senate, the legislation was rewritten in a conference committee in an acceptable form, and the compromise bill became law on 10 August.[7]

The National Security Act Amendments of 1949 established the Department of Defense as the successor to the National Military Establishment, thus reducing the Departments of the Army, Navy, and Air Force to military rather than executive departments. The secretary of defense was given direction, authority, and control over the department, but the services were to be separately administered. The secretary was prohibited from transferring or consolidating any combat function, and he was required to report to Congress any reassignment of noncombat functions. The services could no longer appeal directly to the president or the Bureau of the Budget, but any service secretary or chief of staff could, after notifying the secretary of defense, make recommendations to Congress on his own initiative. The act established the position of chairman of the Joint Chiefs of Staff, who was charged to preside at meetings of the Joint Chiefs, to prepare agenda for the meetings, and to inform the president or secretary of defense of issues upon which the Joint Chiefs had not been able to agree. The act provided that the chairman of the Joint Chiefs of Staff could not vote and that he would have no command authority. No changes were made in the existing status of the Munitions Board or in the Research and Development Board. The deputy secretary of defense was given precedence within the Defense Department immediately after the secretary; three assistant secretaries were authorized. The secretaries and under secretaries of the military departments and the chairman of the Munitions and Research and Development Boards were designated as nonpermanent members of the National Security Council.[8]

Toward the Air Research and Development Command

In its report on 16 December 1948, the Committee on National Security Organization, headed by Ferdinand Eberstadt, proposed that immediate steps should be taken to establish closer working relations between the Joint Chiefs of Staff and the Research and Development Board to assure that advances in weapons and weapon systems were considered adequately in the formulation of strategic plans.[9] This recommendation, which could be effected without changes in legislation, apparently reflected a growing appreciation of the basic closed-circle relationship between scientific development and military strategy. According to Karl F. Kellerman, the executive director of the Research and Development Board's Committee on Guided Missiles, however, the board found it very difficult to obtain long-range strategic guidance from the Joint Chiefs of Staff. "We ask them," Kellerman said, "what the war will be like so we can plan intelligently for new weapon development and they counter by asking us what new weapons will be available so they can plan intelligently for the future war."[10] In the limited defense budgets of the late 1940s, moreover, research and development funding had been reduced in favor of operating forces. "There are those in high positions in the Air Force today," charged Maj Gen Donald L. Putt, the director of Air Force Research and Development, "who hold that research and development must be kept under rigid control by 'requirements' and 'military characteristics' promulgated by operational personnel who can only look into the past and ask for bigger and better weapons of World War II vintage.... They have not yet established that partnership between the strategist and the scientist which is mandatory to insure that superior strategy and technology which is essential to future success against our potential enemies."[11]

In a letter to Secretary Symington on 15 January, Dr Theodore von Karman, chairman of the USAF Scientific Advisory Board, doubted that the Eberstadt criticisms applied directly to the Air Force, but he observed they probably held a meaning for all of the military services. Von Karman reminded Symington that the facilities of the Air Materiel Command at Wright Field were inadequate for research in an era of supersonic flight, and he noted the impression that the Air Force had made research and development too subservient to the procurement of materiel. "When research work becomes too closely allied with operational and procurement problems," he postulated, "one gets too little farlooking research work."[12] Writing to Vandenberg on the same day that he addressed Symington, von Karman urged that the Air Force should again establish the position of deputy chief of staff for research and development. "Air supremacy," von Karman noted, "will be an indispensable factor in the event of another war. In the air battle, technical surprise and general technical superiority will always be decisive . . . DECISIVE technical superiority IN TIME OF WAR will go to the side which most rapidly and exhaustively transforms new technical developments into pieces of battlespace equipment IN TIME OF PEACE." He was certain that necessary long-range planning and more effective utilization of specialized personnel, critical facilities, and limited funds could come only through more centralized Air Staff control over research and development activities.[13]

When Vandenberg asked for guidance on research and development from retired Gen James H. Doolittle, he got much the same opinion that he had received from Dr von Karman. "Everyone is for research and development," Doolittle shrewdly observed, "just as everyone is against sin. However, very few people will sacrifice it."[14] Believing that some constructive action was necessary, Vandenberg asked the Air University to make a study of the research and development structure of the Air Force. In a companion effort on 7 April, General Fairchild asked the USAF Scientific Advisory Board to give him advice on the same problem. Maj Gen Orvil Anderson headed the Air University study committee and von Karman named Dr Louis N. Ridenour to head the Scientific Advisory Board's special committee on research and development. The two groups worked closely together during the summer of 1949; the Ridenour committee submitted its report on 21 September and the Air University committee sent forward its recommendations, including a review of the Ridenour report, on 19 November.[15]

"Any war which we can now foresee," the Ridenour committee stated, "will be an inter-continental war, and we must presume that in such a conflict the Air Force would play a major role, since naval blockade would be ineffective and land invasion against an unweakened enemy would be hazardous in the extreme. . . . Even more important . . . is the deterrent effect of our air power upon the Russians. . . . To maintain this impressive role during the years of negotiation and diplomacy to come, the Air Force must retain its present qualitative superiority." Hence, the committee observed: "If war is not imminent, then the Air Force of the future is far more important than the force-in-being" and research and development should be funded as a necessary expense. More specifically, the Ridenour committee recommended that a position of deputy chief of staff for research and development be established both to head such activities within the Air Staff and to command a new research and development command, which should be divorced from the procurement and production functions of the Air Materiel Command. The single agency research and development organization should be made responsible for unified budgeting, thus making it possible to identify the total costs of research and development. However, strong efforts were needed to increase the number of Air Force officers and civilians with advanced technical skills on the active roles and to make full use of their capabilities. The committee recommended that the air research and development command should be provided with expanded field facilities and that such facilities ought to be operated by civilian contractors, thus allowing the Air Force to concentrate its limited technical manpower in the work of contract supervision and operational evaluation. Finally, the Ridenour group recommended that the technical talent and facilities of US universities and industries should be utilized much more fully, particularly through contracts for specific research and development projects. As an operating procedure, the committee recommended that the Air Force make a needed distinction between components and systems. A system was conceived to be an assemblage of interacting components brought together to deal with a particular problem such as strategic bombardment of air defense. "Within the Air Force," the committee recommended, "the role of systems engineering should be substantially strengthened, and systems projects should be attacked on a 'task force' basis by teams of systems and components specialists organized on a semi-permanent basis."[16]

After making its own study of Air Force research and development, the Air University committee stated: "We cannot hope to win a future war on the basis of manpower and resources. We will win it only through superior technology and superior strategy." The committee believed that Air Force leaders generally recognized the importance of research and development but the pressures of day-to-day operational, materiel, and political problems prevented the implementation of vigorous exploratory programs. The Air University's panel believed that a positive system to secure interactions between science and strategy had to be established as an absolute and automatic function rather than as a voluntary functioning of personalities. Since program stability was the pressing requirement in research and development, the Air University recommended that fluctuations in availability of personnel and funds should be absorbed in activities that were associated with the force in being and not with the Air Force of the future.

The Air University committee generally endorsed the recommendations of the Ridenour group; Gen George C. Kenney, now the commander of the Air University, added a strong personal approval to the report of the Air University committee. "As long as we remain ahead of any possible opponent technically," he wrote, "we could not lose a war; but if we once fall behind technically, it is difficult to see how we could win a war of the future."[17]

In Washington on 2 December 1949, a conference headed by Lt Gen K. B. Wolfe, deputy chief of staff, the Air Materiel Command—with representatives from the Air Staff, Air Materiel Command, and the Air University—reviewed the Ridenour and Air University reports on research and development and recommended that General Vandenberg implement the philosophy contained in them. The conference noted that Vandenberg had four deputies who were responsible for the Air Force of today and suggested that it would be logical to establish a fifth deputy chief of staff for development who would be responsible for the Air Force of the future. The conference also recommended that the Air Force accept reductions in its combat force in being as were necessary to support the establishment of a separate air research and development command. By implication, the Wolfe group did not accept the unorthodox Ridenour recommendation that the deputy chief of staff for development should also command the separate air research and development command. With approval from Vandenberg, the Office of Deputy Chief of Staff, Development was established on 23 January 1950; Maj Gen Gordon P. Saville assumed the position as deputy chief. The new office was provided with two directorates: Requirements, and Research and Development.[18]

With the understanding that its growth would be evolutionary through a gradual assumption of research and development functions and facilities from the Air Materiel Command, the Air Research and Development Command (ARDC) was established under Maj Gen David M. Schlatter in Washington on 23 January 1950. Many months elapsed before the new command began operating, but the Air Force had indicated its intention to devote new emphasis to the building of force capabilities for the future.[19] "Based on our present concept, that of retaliation," explained Maj Gen Donald L. Putt on 16 February 1950,

> we have given our enemy two very important advantages, initiation and time. We shall, of necessity, have to depend on outwitting him in strategy and outpacing him in technology.... It is apparent that in modern strategy and technology, developments in the one are largely predicted on or affected by developments in the other. We, therefore, arrive at the general position that national security will depend on our combining these two variables which we control, our strategy and our technology. This in a sense defines the magnitude and importance of technology to our military security.[20]

Military Support for Foreign Policy

According to the basic War Department outline for the postwar organization of the US military establishment, "the primary function of the armed forces is, when called upon to do so, to support and, within the sphere of military effort, to enforce the national policy of the nation. There must be a complete correlation of national policy with military policy; of the political ends to be sought with the military means to achieve them."[21] Under this concept the role of the armed forces was to give authority to the conduct of American diplomacy; the foreign policy of the United States assumed the nature of an absolute, which desirably would be supported as necessary by appropriately prepared military forces. Actually, however, from the start of the postwar period, American foreign, military, and economic policies bore a closed-circle relationship in which a weakness in any one of the policies made for a weakness in them all. Dismissing for the moment that argument as to whether it was good or bad for the military to participate in the making of foreign policy, Maj Gen Lauris Norstad observed in May 1947 that "military considerations do, in fact, play a large part in the determination of foreign policy and its implementation. This being so, it is doubly important that the military at all times remain subordinate to the political."[22]

In a discussion with Secretary Forrestal in early September 1947, General Norstad, who was still troubled about the prospects of military participation in diplomatic decisions, stated his view that the National Security Council might well become a forum in which military representatives could ensure that the State Department did not undertake far-reaching policies requiring a level of military support that exceeded available capabilities. Seeking a clarification at the first meeting of the National Security Council on 26 September 1947, Forrestal volunteered his conception that the council "would serve as an advisory body to the President, that he would take its advice in due consideration, but that determination of and decisions in the field of foreign policy would, of course, be his and the Secretary of State's."[23] Henceforth, the National Security Council met ordinarily on the first and third Thursdays of each month to consider aspects of foreign, military, and domestic policy and to provide single sets of recommendations on particular problems to President Truman. If the president approved the policy recommendations, the NSC papers became the administration's policy. The chief advantage of the National Security Council appeared to be that it gave an opportunity for a member whose activity would be affected by a given policy to express his views and have his views expressed to the president.[24] To provide a means for exchanging political and military advice, a standing interdepartmental group known as the State-War-Navy Coordinating Committee (SWNCC) had been established in December 1944; in October 1945 the secretaries of state, war, and Navy had designated the SWNCC as "the agency to reconcile and coordinate action to be taken by . . . the departments on matters of common interest . . . and establish policies on politico-military questions." In 1947 the SWNCC was redesignated as the State, Army, Navy, Air Force Coordinating Committee (SANACC) and, despite the establishment of the National Security Council, the intergovernmental agency continued to function at the working level during the administration of Secretary Forrestal.[25]

According to the prevailing concept of proper military-civil relations of the late 1940s, the State Department was expected to define foreign policy and the Defense Department was expected to implement it with force commitments when requested. When State Department planners began preparing an integrated statement of foreign policy, however, they immediately found that no one could define authoritatively the basic national objectives of the United States. The files of the State Department and National Security Council were filled with papers dealing with separate problems and areas, each of which included specific objectives, but there was no consolidated statement of basic American purposes. The Joint Chiefs of Staff encountered this same problem. In October 1949 General Bradley told congressional investigators that in the absence of any authoritative definition, the Joint Chiefs of Staff had assumed that

> the people of the United States have as their national objective a desire for peace and security without sacrifice of either the basic rights of the individual or the present sovereignty we cherish.... Secondly, we intend to maintain our political way of life and our form of government in our own country.... Our third objective is to maintain, and to raise, if possible, our American standard of living. And fourth, we Americans would like to have peace and security for the entire world, and all the good that these conditions can bring.

Bradley conceived that the national objectives did not "demand a similar political way of life or a similar form of government in other countries of the world" and that they included a hope for "the successful development of an effective world organization, based on the United Nations." In their approach to the problem, the State Department planners finally decided that the basic national purpose of the United States was best expressed in the preamble to the Constitution: "to form a more perfect Union, establish Justice, insure Domestic Tranquillity, provide for the common defense, promote the general Welfare, and secure the Blessings of Liberty to ourselves and our Posterity." In 1949 the House Committee on Armed Services was in agreement with these generalized objectives, but it suggested that the National Security Council ought to issue "a firm statement of principles upon which the Joint Chiefs of Staff may rely as an official expression of their civilian leaders."[26]

Seeking "the containment of communism and ... the defense of America," the United States lent military and economic assistance to counter Soviet aggression in Iran, Greece, and Turkey and in Trieste and Berlin.[27] On 7 May 1948, however, President Truman told Secretary Forrestal that annual military budgets must be kept relatively stable in order that they would not "cut too deeply into the civilian economy"; at this time the domestic economic policy of the United States began to prevail in no small part over both the foreign and military policy.[28] Although the United States hoped to restore a balance of power in both Europe and Asia, the successful civil war waged by the Chinese Communists affected American influence in East Asia.[29] In Korea the United States remained committed to the political objective of securing the unification and independence of the divided nation, but on 25 September 1947 the Joint Chiefs of Staff considered that the American occupation troops could better be used elsewhere and would be extremely vulnerable in the event of a general war. They accordingly informed President Truman: "From the standpoint of military security, the United States has little strategic interest in maintaining the present troops and bases in Korea." In response to an American request, the United Nations General Assembly entertained the Korean unification problem; on 10 May 1948 it sponsored elections that formed the legitimate government of the Republic of Korea. The United States undertook to train and equip Republic of Korea armed forces to make them strong enough to provide security "against any but an overt act of aggression by North Korean or other forces." The last of the American occupation forces were withdrawn from Korea on 29 June 1949.[30] In the summer of 1949, subsequent to the defeat of the Chinese Nationalist government on mainland China and its retreat to Formosa, State Department planners queried the Defense Department as to whether, if political and psychological reasons demanded, the United States could commit military forces to the defense of Formosa without improperly imbalancing the force deployment necessary for security against the contingency of general war with the Soviet Union. The Defense Department replied it could not under the limitations of the $13-billion military budget.[31] Operating with a relatively fixed annual budget despite the growing costs of modernization and the need to counter growing Soviet air offensive capabilities, the Air Force was compelled to curtail its oversea operations. "We have already closed out the Caribbean Air Command," Vandenberg pointed out in May 1950. "Perhaps," he added, "the nation should be willing to sacrifice some of its influence in Europe and Asia in order to strengthen its air defenses at home."[32]

In the postwar years members of the State Department Policy Planning Staff assumed the habit of conferring directly with members of the Joint Strategic Survey Committee of the Joint Chiefs of Staff in regard to military problems, and the SANACC provided an additional working-level agency for exchanging information and arriving at policies. In the autumn of 1949, however, Secretary of Defense Johnson ruled that State Department contacts with the Defense Department would be cleared through his office. Johnson later explained that he was seeking to ensure that basic decisions would be made by the top echelons rather than by subordinate offices. But some persons believed that the secretary was concerned lest pressures from the State Department to increase military forces would make it difficult for him to carry out his mandate to limit military spending.[33] Because he thought it was improper for the National Security Council to be called upon to discuss matters that had already been agreed to at lower levels, Johnson abolished SANACC.[34] Sensitive to charges that the Department of Defense was attempting to determine foreign policy, Johnson asserted: "The Defense Department is concerned with the military.... Neither the Secretary of Defense nor his assistants nor the Joint Chiefs of Staff nor the Chairman have ... tried to fix ... foreign policy. We have stayed out of that.... When foreign policy is determined, then our line is determined. Within that foreign policy it is our duty to work."[35] General Bradley and the Joint Chiefs also attempted to adhere to this distinction between foreign and military policy. "We are asked the military implications of certain policies, and we try to restrict ourselves to military implications of various phases of foreign policy," he said. "This is our job as adviser to the Government on military matters.... We have never, to my knowledge, advocated any action which is not in accordance with the foreign policy in effect at that time."[36]

Soviet Nuclear Weapons and Technological Challenge

Although the leaders of the United States had recognized that no nation could maintain a complete monopoly on nuclear weapons, responsible American scientists had not expected the Soviet Union to detonate an atomic weapon before 1952, at the soonest. Early in 1949, an Air Force long-range detection service had begun to fly missions to search the upper atmosphere for evidence of atomic explosions anywhere in the northern hemisphere, and on 3 September 1949 one of the search planes picked up a radioactive air sample over the North Pacific. After reviewing the evidence, a special committee of Atomic Energy Commission experts stated positively that an atomic explosion had occurred somewhere in Asia between 26 and 29 August 1949. "We have evidence," President Truman told the American people on 23 September, "that within recent weeks an atomic explosion occurred in the USSR."[37]

What was surprising was not that the Soviet Union had developed an A-bomb but that it had done so more rapidly than had been predicted. In a magazine article published during October 1949, General Bradley cautioned that the Soviet A-bomb

> is no occasion for hysteria.... For an industrially backward country, the making of an atomic bomb is not so difficult as the problem of turning it out in quantity and delivering it. As long as America retains (as it can) a tremendous advantage in A-bomb quantity, quality and deliverability, the deterrent effect of the bomb against an aggressor will continue. Sustained research and development can keep us far in the lead with methods for intercepting enemy bomb-carriers. No one can predict what the weapons of the future may be; in the long run our promise of security lies in the combined, unparalleled inventiveness and industrial skill of Western Europe and America.[38]

Developments in Nuclear Weapons

In spite of an official analysis that "the fission bomb was not a mortal threat to the United States," both because of its finite destructive power and the fact that the Soviets would require several years to stockpile such weapons, American officials were shaken by the knowledge that the Soviets had the A-bomb.[39] The immediate effect of the Soviet nuclear capability was to stimulate research and development in the field of nuclear weapons: the products of the effort would have important effects on national strategic planning.

"At the end of World War II," observed W. Sterling Cole, chairman of the congressional Joint Committee on Atomic Energy, "there was a general slowdown in our entire military program, including atomic weapon development. This relaxation was due in large measure to a general belief that a lasting peace had been accomplished, that we would enjoy atomic monopoly for some years, and that there would be international control of atomic weapons."[40] The two World War II atomic bombs that had been employed against Japan had been large and awkward "laboratory" models which could not have been transported by planes smaller than B-29s, and even these aircraft had to be especially modified for the purpose. As has been noted, there was a prevalent belief in scientific and military circles in the late 1940s that the world's supply of fissionable uranium was very scarce. Air Force leaders recognized the desirability of a family of atomic weapons that could be employed against an entire spectrum of targets; however, they believed, on good authority, that fissionable material would always be scarce and that small atomic bombs could not be designed or produced. Consequently, these Air Force leaders favored the developing and stockpiling of the larger and more efficient atomic weapons that would be employed in a strategic air offensive. The Military Liaison Committee made Army, Navy, and Air Force requirements known to the Atomic Energy Commission, but the Department of Defense was only one of the customers of this production agency. Since 1946 many scientists had been more interested in the employment of the atom for peace than for war.[41]

As early as April 1942, atomic scientists Edward Teller and Enrico Fermi discussed the possibility of developing a fusion or thermonuclear weapon that would yield infinitely more power than the fission-type atomic weapon. But the decision had been made to develop the atomic bomb. And, although a small research program on the thermonuclear energy was continued, the Atomic Energy Commission (AEC) gave no major consideration to the question of undertaking active development of a thermonuclear weapon, which would be better known as the H-bomb. Immediately after Truman's announcement in September 1949 that an atomic explosion had occurred in the Soviet Union, a staff paper was prepared in the Joint Committee on Atomic Energy advocating that an H-bomb be developed, to which the Atomic Energy Commission replied that it was doing all that it could in the thermonuclear field. On the Atomic Energy Commission, however, retired Adm Lewis L. Strauss reasoned that the United States could not afford merely to seek to maintain an arithmetic lead over the Russians in stockpiling A-bombs. Therefore, on 5 October he proposed to his colleagues that the time had come for a quantum jump in the form of an intensive effort to develop the thermonuclear weapon. The Atomic Energy Commission's General Advisory Committee of scientists and engineers opposed a crash program to develop an H-bomb on both technical and moral grounds, and the majority of the membership of the Atomic Energy Commission did not favor an all-out thermonuclear program. On 9 November, however, the entire problem was laid before President Truman. Writing to Truman on 25 November, Strauss recommended that the president direct the Atomic Energy Commission "to proceed with the development of the thermonuclear bomb, at highest priority subject only to the judgement of the Department of Defense as to its value as a weapon, and of the advice of the Department of State as to the diplomatic consequences of its unilateral renunciation of its possession."[42]

Early in November the H-bomb controversy blossomed in the American public press, with elaborate arguments being developed on both sides. Troubled by the divided opinion in the AEC report, President Truman on 10 November designated Secretary of State Dean Acheson, Secretary of Defense Johnson, and AEC chairman David E. Lilienthal as a special subcommittee of the National Security Council to make recommendations to him. In the following weeks, the departments of State and Defense moved into accord on the necessity of producing thermonuclear weapons, as did the joint congressional committee. The matter, nevertheless, continued under consideration until late January 1950, when Dr Klaus Fuchs, a former group leader at the Los Alamos atomic weapons laboratory, confessed that he had passed nuclear secrets to the Soviets, a situation that demanded immediate action. In a day-long meeting on 31 January, secretaries Acheson and Johnson agreed upon the need for immediate and full-scale development of the thermonuclear bomb. Lilienthal opposed that view, arguing that there was a considerable doubt as to the technical feasibility of thermonuclear weapons and advocating that a better course of action would be to create more flexible atomic weapons. At the conclusion of the discussion, the special committee recommended that President Truman direct the Atomic Energy Commission to take immediate steps to develop a thermonuclear weapon. Accepting the recommendation, Truman announced on 31 January that on the previous day he had directed the Atomic Energy Commission "to continue its work on all forms of atomic weapons, including the so-called hydrogen or superbomb."[43] In protest Lilienthal resigned as chairman of the Atomic Energy Commission on 15 February and was shortly thereafter replaced by Gordon Dean.

The decision of the United States to emphasize the weapon aspects of thermonuclear energy shortly provided the beginnings of a family of nuclear weapons. Late in February 1950 the Atomic Energy Commission announced that it would turn out A-bombs on a virtual production-line basis. Thus, the critical problem of atomic supply, long considered a question in military planning, had apparently been solved. As a matter of fact, uranium ores were never scarce. The military had based its requirements on an assumption that the availability of raw materials would rigidly limit production; meanwhile the Atomic Energy Commission did not step up its materials procurement program because the limited requirements could not be met without expanding existing sources. Higher prices offered for uranium ores following the decision in 1950 to expand production led to the discovery of large mineral reserves in the United States. Technological innovations in the thermonuclear program also permitted refinements in A-bomb technology. In May 1950 a military requirement for a small bomb that could be delivered by high-performance aircraft was forwarded to the Atomic Energy Commission, and in this same month the Sandia Corporation reported that it would be possible to proceed with the manufacture of an efficient A-bomb that could be transported and dropped by fighter-type aircraft.[44] Where nuclear weapons previously had been available only for strategic air warfare employments, they could now be developed for tactical air warfare applications.

Thoughts on Nuclear Air Power

Under the privilege of academic freedom and with the understanding that their views did not necessarily represent official viewpoints, the faculty and students of the Air University had begun to make analyses of the effect of nuclear weapons on warfare as early as 1947. An Air War College seminar studying the import of the atomic bomb on strategy and tactics concluded in April 1947 that "the initial blow suffered by any nation from an atomic attack can be decisive."[45] Based on a detailed analysis of the threat to the United States posed by the Soviet Union, Air War College students conjectured in June 1948 that "all measures short of direct military action to contain the threat of Communist domination are of doubtful effect in meeting other exacting requirements in preserving our national life. Military action using weapons of mass destruction, prior to the Soviet development of these weapons, in final essence appears to be the only ultimate means of attaining security of our nation and the world."[46] Speaking to the Air Command and Staff School in June 1949, Maj Gen Orvil Anderson sought to outline the new patterns of air warfare in an atomic age. He said:

> In World War II no fighter cap ever . . . gave adequate protection to any surface target. . . . The attackers always came through. . . . They always paid in attrition . . . but air came through, and the indications are strong that as technology advances the ability of air to come through at lesser and lesser costs is quite clear, quite apparent. You will reach the point in the distant future when you won't even think of opposing air in the air. . . . We'll go back to a counter-artillery work. We'll fight them at the launching site or we won't fight them.[47]

In an article published in October 1949, Lt Col Harry M. Pike of the Air Command and Staff College faculty frankly questioned whether the United States ought to attempt an air defense effort. "If our enemies send over great numbers of aircraft carrying enough atomic bomb-type weapons to attain a goodly part of their strategic objective's and if our air defense system is capable of destroying only about ten percent of their planes and probably a lesser percentage of their missiles," Pike asked, "is the expenditure of such an enormous sum of money—probably billions of dollars—for an air defense system feasible and acceptable? Are there perhaps other places for us to put our money in order that the probability of attack might be made more remote?" If military funds were of little or no consideration, Pike would have favored "a mighty defense effort aimed at making this country literally unpenetrable." But, under existing funds limitations, he argued that an air defense system could not "rate a high rung on the priority ladder."[48]

The notion that the United States might conduct a preventive war against Soviet nuclear capabilities was completely unacceptable to Thomas K. Finletter, who replaced Symington as secretary of the Air Force on 24 April 1950. Speaking to the Air War College on 23 May, Finletter stated bluntly:

> I believe that preventive war is not a possible policy for the United States government to carry out at this time.... Anybody who advocates a preventing war... is simply taking the easiest way and is not willing to face up to the tremendously difficult political and military things we have to do. I think that the American people want their military leaders and their political leaders to work themselves out of this mess in some way which is consistent with the spirit and the creed of the American people.[49]

On 7 June, General Saville told Air War College students that there were good military reasons why the Air Force could not reasonably think about preventive war. While scientists assumed that the nuclear explosion in August 1949 had been Russia's first test, it was possible that earlier tests had not been discovered and the Soviet Union might have a stockpile of weapons. In order to wage preventive war and simultaneously shield the United States from counterattack, the Strategic Air Command would have to destroy the Soviet Long-Range Air Force in the initial air assault. As of early 1950 the Air Force did not have the reconnaissance capabilities and available intelligence information to pinpoint the location of Soviet aircraft for an initial attack or keep account of their deployments once an attack was begun. Saville suggested that, at best, preventive war might well turn into a situation wherein "I'll beat your brains out and you beat my brains out."[50]

At the Massachusetts Institute of Technology, Dr George Valley, Jr., a professor of physics and a member of the USAF Scientific Advisory Board, apparently read Colonel Pike's article that degraded the potential of air defense. Professor Valley believed that an air defense system capable of blunting an enemy attack could be had with modern technology at a cost that would not unduly detract from the support of the strategic air striking arm, and he recommended that a scientific study be made of air defense. Generals Vandenberg and Fairchild immediately called in key members of the Scientific Advisory Board and requested that action be taken to execute Valley's proposal. In November 1949 Vandenberg established an Air Defense Systems Engineering Committee under Valley and charged it to determine "the operational development of equipment and techniques—on an air defense system basis—which would produce maximum effective air defense for a minimum dollar investment." The committee of eight scientists—most of whom were associated with the Massachusetts Institute of Technology—met on weekends at the Cambridge Research Laboratories. In March 1950 the Valley committee proposed that a new system of close-in radar nets, communications facilities, information-processing computers, fighter-interceptors, and unmanned interceptor missiles would increase the probable kill ratio of attacking aircraft from 10 to 30 percent. It estimated that the interior defense would require some eight to ten mechanized air defense systems and that each would cost about $1 billion.[51]

"The period which we all realized must some day come when intercontinental air warfare would be a possibility," General Fairchild stated on 7 February 1950, "is now at hand. . . . Air Force thought and action is oriented about the concept that our primary effort must be directed toward providing the means of surviving such an atomic phase, not only without disaster, but so that our relative strength would be such that we may mobilize and bring to bear any forces that may be required to assure victory." Fairchild believed that the Soviet atomic weapon had increased the importance of the American strategic striking force. "Indeed," he said,

> its continued effective, efficient existence is the greatest deterrent against the possibility of occurrence of another great conflict. If, through the grave miscalculation of others, such a conflict should nevertheless occur, it is our strategic striking force that we must put primary reliance upon for protection of our homeland by the destruction of the bases and remaining aircraft of the long-range forces directed against us and for so reducing enemy capacity to support his war effort that we may gain the time required for ultimate victory.

Even though the strategic striking force continued to be of first importance and first priority, Fairchild called for a new emphasis on air defense forces. "We must," he said, "provide the greatest degree of air defense attainable, within the means available to us." The Air Force could no longer expect to mobilize air defense units in a time of emergency. "Air-defensive forces," Fairchild ruled, "must be trained and equipped and in place and actually on 24-hour alert if they are to be committed to combat in defense against any sudden atomic attack—possibly one in great force." In view of the budgetary situation and the need to emphasize both the air striking and air defense forces, the Air Force had no choice but to further reduce the priority of the tactical air force. Although the Air Force continued to program some tactical air groups to permit peacetime training and development of tactics and doctrine, the tactical air force would not be adequate for the support of any large-scale surface operation immediately on the outbreak of hostilities. Such a force would have to be mobilized after a war's beginning.[52]

Speaking candidly of the importance of the strategic striking force on 10 May, Vandenberg visualized a future war:

> An alert enemy will strike us first. Further, our defense forces in being will kill some of the attackers but only a small percentage. To be really effective, we must have an air defense capable of killing enemy air power at its source. We ourselves must strike effectively before much else can be done by anybody. As was the case in the last war, it is up to the Air Force to carry the war to the enemy and to gain air superiority before surface operations in force can be successively undertaken.[53]

Asked to explain the Air Force philosophy of air defense on 7 June, General Saville emphasized the "relationship between Air Defense, the Air Offensive, and Time." "I believe it's obvious to us all," said Saville, that when we had exclusive ownership of the A-bomb we had a relative position in which we were going over the enemy and drop A-bombs on him and he was going to drop TNT on us. . . . And, at that time, it was perfectly proper completely to ignore the Air Defensive business, go into the air offensive and give complete preoccupation to the air offensive. But when the enemy starts A-bomb stockpiling, you get a different situation. You're back into the relative war again.

Saville thought that the time had come to go back to the "15-year old theory . . . that a well organized air attack once launched cannot be stopped. . . . I think you have to stop it before it is launched and you can do so by offensive means only." Thus, Saville believed that the time had come for the Strategic Air Command to take the counteratomic offensive as its number one mission. Although Saville suggested that no form of air defense could be more than 60 percent successful, he urged that the United States must build a centralized air defense system of a magnitude that could be calculated in terms of its monetary costs both to the United States and to the Soviet Union. In other words, would a dollar expended by the United States for air defense cost the Russians comparatively more to augment their offensive capabilities in order to sustain the casualties that the US air defenses would inflict on an attacking Soviet force? Saville's "guesstimate" was that the United States could afford to build an air defense system with "two-notch" radar — one set of radars at the interior defense line and another on offshore picket vessels — and 67 air defense squadrons, the whole system to be capable of inflicting about 30 percent casualties on an attacking force. Such a defense would not prevent the Soviets from dropping some A-bombs on the United States, but it would introduce imponderables and additional requirements into their offensive plans, which would give the United States some five years to gear its forces to fight an atomic war. Saville did not favor the construction of a much more expensive three-notch radar system, with a very extended early warning radar line, until it could be determined whether other intelligence efforts could not provide the "early, early warning" more cheaply. He summed up his remarks by mentioning what he jocularly called the Saville theory of air defense: that the United States ought to try to gain as much time as possible to prepare itself to fight in an air war in which both adversaries would possess nuclear capabilities.[54]

NSC-68: Call for US Rearmament

At the same time that he directed the Atomic Energy Commission to begin developing thermonuclear weapons on 30 January 1950, President Truman called upon the secretaries of state and defense to undertake a basic review of the national policies and military strategy of the United States in the light of the Soviet atomic explosion. The two secretaries in turn ordered that the work be undertaken by an ad hoc group from the State Department's Policy Planning Staff headed by Paul H. Nitze and from the Joint Strategic Survey Committee with Maj Gen Truman H. Landon as head of its team. At the start of the study, General Landon was said to have felt that he had to support the $13-billion military budget that had been accepted by both Johnson and Bradley, but Nitze wanted a broader scale study that would compute requirements without reference to arbitrary financial support. Accepting the central purpose of American policy as being the establishment and maintenance of conditions throughout the world under which the democratic experiment as laid down in the Constitution could survive and prosper within the United States, the ad hoc group viewed the principal threat to this objective as stemming from the Kremlin's design for world domination. The planners believed, however, that the Kremlin placed first importance on the maintenance of their regime in the Soviet Union; second importance on the preservation of their power base in Russia; and third importance upon the objective of eventual world domination. The planners did not believe that the Communist leaders would initiate a general war until they had developed their atomic stockpile to respectable proportions, which might take them to 1954. Although the Soviets could be expected to attempt to subvert, weaken, and discredit the coalition forces opposing them, the planners doubted that the Kremlin would attempt any overt aggression until it was better prepared for the contingency that local war might spread into general war.

When the State Department planners had outlined foreign policy objectives, the determination of the alternatives permitted by the US military posture concerned both the State and Defense members of the ad hoc study group. One alternative was to continue with limited military forces. This course had already proven unsatisfactory. In the summer of 1949, when the Policy Planning Staff had queried the Joint Strategic Survey as to whether it was necessary to attain air superiority prior to the mounting of a strategic air offensive, it had been told that air superiority was essential but simply could not be planned for within a $13-billion military budget. Another equally unsatisfactory course was to sacrifice foreign commitments and to withdraw US power to the Western Hemisphere. A third alternative was to take advantage of the available nuclear stockpile and initiate hostilities as soon as possible. The fourth alternative recommended by the group was to initiate an immediate large-scale buildup of American and allied military and general strength in order to develop an adequate power shield under which the United States could both resist local Soviet aggressions and deter general war, while concurrently developing means other than all-out war that would eventually achieve a modification in the nature of the Soviet regime. In mid-March the ad hoc group circulated its paper through the Pentagon, where it was endorsed by the three service secretaries and the members of the Joint Chiefs of Staff. On 12 April, President Truman tentatively approved it by referring it to the National Security Council, which would estimate the programs and costs necessary to implement the recommendations. Handling the paper as NSC-68, the National Security Council soon estimated that the expanded military program would cost about $50 billion a year for several years. While these defense expenditures appeared large, they appeared also to be within the economic potential of the United States.[55]

At the same time that the State-Defense ad hoc study group was preparing NSC-68, Congress had begun hearings on the Department of Defense budget for fiscal year 1951. Even though the budget estimates had been set up well before the atomic explosion in Russia, Secretary Johnson and General Bradley defended the $13-billion budget when they appeared before the House Military Appropriations Subcommittee on 12 January 1950. The $13-billion budget was divided as follows: $4.018 billion to go to the Army, $3.881 billion to the Navy, and $4.433 billion to the Air Force. Within this budget ceiling, the Army would maintain 10 combat divisions and 48 antiaircraft artillery battalions — 47 of these battalions having been added to the Army program for 1951 to counter the Soviet air threat. By making reductions in force (including limited status for the battleship *Missouri*), Adm Forrest P. Sherman, the new chief of naval operations, had obtained concurrence from the Joint Chiefs to operate seven large aircraft carriers. However, because of its reduced appropriations the Navy planned to reduce its attack-carrier air groups from 14 to nine, its antisubmarine squadrons from eight to seven, its patrol squadrons from 30 to 20, and its Marine air squadrons from 23 to 12. The Air Force would continue to possess a regular force to 48 groups and 13 separate squadrons, while another 27 groups would be manned by the Air National Guard and 25 by the Air Force Reserve. Although these 48 regular groups could not be equipped with modern aircraft, the $1.2 billion allocated for Air Force procurement would permit the Air Force to introduce additional jet fighter aircraft into its inventory and to complete the equipping of three of the four heavy bomber wings and the two strategic reconnaissance wings with B-36 aircraft. Even though the $13-billion budget ceiling had been set before the Soviet atomic explosion, Secretary Johnson asserted that the Joint Chiefs had long anticipated such an event and had tailored the forces to such an eventuality. Barring unforeseen changes in the international situation, Johnson volunteered the additional information that the Department of Defense would submit a budget request for another $13 billion in fiscal year 1952. "Frankly, considering the intelligence estimates that we have available, and realizing that the amount of money which our economy can stand for defense is a Presidential responsibility," General Bradley said, "I am in complete agreement with that ceiling."[56]

Throughout the spring of 1950, President Truman faced the issue of whether the nation should go to the $50-billion military budget that the foreign situation required or adhere to the $13-billion ceilings set in terms of the internal domestic economy. The United States was still in an economic recession. During fiscal year 1950, receipts from taxes continued to decline and there would be a deficit of some $3 billion. To triple the military budget, the government would have to increase taxes heavily and impose various kinds of economic controls.[57] Although Truman postponed a decision on NSC-68, Secretary Johnson appeared before a reconvened meeting of the House Military Appropriations Subcommittee on 26 April and requested an additional $350 million for fiscal year 1951. "We want always that our Air Force, and Navy Air, shall be equal to the demand of the world situation. As long as there is doubt on anybody's part, who ought to be competent to judge," Johnson explained, "we shall try to err on the side of safety." Johnson accordingly asked that the additional money should be subdivided with $200 million going to the Air Force for aircraft procurement, $100 million to the Navy for new planes, and $50 million to be expended in converting and operating Navy antisubmarine vessels. Johnson also stated that four squadrons of Marine Corps aircraft slated for inactivation would be continued without additional appropriation.[58] The additional $200 million would permit the Air Force to procure 77 production aircraft (medium bombers and medium and heavy transports), to rehabilitate 228 primary trainer aircraft, and to convert 71 B-29 medium bombers into aerial-refueling tankers.[59] But the Air Force received no mandate for the expansion. To General Vandenberg (who had allowed General Fairchild to justify the Air Force budget for 1951 and thus had escaped having to endorse limited military expenditures) the gap between Air Force requirements and Air Force capabilities was nothing short of tragic. "The simple and appalling fact," he told Air War College students in May 1950, "is that we will not be able to support even 48 groups out of the resources which have been proposed for us for Fiscal Year 1952." In an address in Detroit on 19 May, Vandenberg disagreed in public with Secretary Johnson's contention that US military forces were sufficient and warned that the United States could not expect to mobilize for a war after it had absorbed a large-scale air attack. In another public address on 16 June, Vandenberg again disagreed with the administration's policy of limiting and reducing the strength of the Air Force, while at the same time it placed more and more responsibility on it.[60] Even though Vandenberg got on the record in opposition to the limited defense posture prevailing in the spring of 1950, his warnings did not move the administration toward rearmament. In East Asia, however, the Soviets were about to unleash the forces of aggression that would compel the United States to make a complete reappraisal of its military requirements.

Strategic Implications of Limited War in Korea

In a statement of American policy toward China on 16 December 1945, President Truman had looked upon the establishment of a strong, united, and democratic China as being of the utmost importance to the success of the United Nations. However, he had emphasized that the United States would not employ "military intervention to influence the course of any Chinese internal strife."[61] President Truman was not willing to deviate from this policy, and thus it will never be known whether the employment of American military forces might have made it possible for Nationalist China to have withstood the Chinese Communist military victory. Some Rand scholars later argued that the critical problems faced by the Chinese Nationalists were inflation and corruption and a consequent loss of troop morale. The Rand researchers believed that a relatively small number of American officers and enlisted men could have straightened out the problems of logistics, technical services, and finance for the Chinese Nationalist army and that this assistance together with American air support and a moderate aid program for the Chinese economy might have prevented the Chinese Communist victory.[62] "The decision to withhold previously pledged American support," Gen Douglas MacArthur would write, "was one of the greatest mistakes ever made in our history."[63]

Following the withdrawal of American military forces from Korea in June 1949, the mission of General MacArthur's Far East Command was limited to the defense of the geographical region including Japan, the Ryukyus, the Marianas, and the Philippines. In an interview with a newspaper correspondent in Tokyo early in 1949, MacArthur did not include the Republic of Korea within America's defense responsibilities. "Now the Pacific has become an Anglo-Saxon lake," MacArthur was quoted as saying, "and our line of defense runs through the chain of islands fringing the coast of Asia. It starts from the Philippines and continues through the Ryukyu archipelago which includes its broad main bastion, Okinawa. Then it bends back through Japan and the Aleutian Island chain to Alaska." In an apparent effort to clarify a position relative to Formosa, Secretary of State Acheson in a speech before the National Press Club on 12 January 1950 stated that the defensive perimeter of the United States ran from the Aleutians to Japan, then to the Ryukyus, and then to the Philippines. Should an attack occur in some area outside this perimeter, Acheson stated that initial reliance for resistance to such an attack would be expected from the people subjected to the attack and "then upon the commitments of the entire civilized world under the charter of the United Nations which so far has not proved a weak reed to lean on by any people who are determined to protect their independence against outside aggression." In explaining this speech, Acheson later maintained that he had said exactly what he meant to say. "Now, I think I said what I tried to say very clearly," he stated,

> that the United States had certain points which were a defensive perimeter. At those points United States troops were stationed; there they would stay and there they would fight. In regard to other areas, I said nobody can guarantee that; but what we can say is that if people will stand up and fight for their own independence, their own country, the guaranties under the United Nations have never proved a weak reed before, and they won't in the future.[64]

Although the strategic estimates included in NSC-68 reasoned that the Soviets would not initiate hostilities — not even a small war that might flare into all-out war — until they could stockpile atomic weapons, the Kremlin determined to take advantage of what appeared to be a strategic opportunity in East Asia. The Soviets apparently believed that their puppet forces from North Korea could easily overrun the defenses of the Republic of Korea, without necessitating an overt employment of either Soviet or Chinese Communist forces. Soviet strategy seems to have discounted any serious military response by the United States to an invasion of South Korea, and it evidently did not believe that the United Nations Security Council could muster any effective opposition. The Soviets may have been relatively sure of the latter assessment, because since January 1950 Jacob Malik, the Soviet delegate who could have wielded his country's veto, had been boycotting the Security Council. This assessment of Soviet strategy was arrived at by Rand associate Allen S. Whiting, after a careful study of admittedly fragmentary evidence.[65] As early as February 1951, however, Alexander de Seversky suggested that Malik's failure to attend the Security Council meetings and to veto initial United Nations actions in Korea might not have been a mistake. "I do not agree," he said, "that the Soviets did not expect us to fight in Korea, or that Malik was away from the Security Council... by mistake. It was all done by design, to draw us from the other side of the world and use up as much as possible of our potential, and we just fell right into the trap." Somewhat later, Seversky would also suggest that the Soviets may have opened the hostilities in Korea as a part of a well-concealed plan to encourage orthodox military thinking in the United States and to lead it to prepare "to fight again decisive battles on the ground... on Russia's terms and under conditions... that favor Russia in every respect."[66]

Whatever the strategy of the Soviet Union may have been, the North Korean armed forces began a well-prepared invasion of the Republic of Korea in the early morning hours of 25 June 1950. Even though Soviet forces were not overtly present, General Bradley found it evident that "militant international communism inspired the northern invaders" and that, for the first time, "communism is willing to use arms to gain its ends."[67] The major lesson to the free world was that the Communists would use force to accomplish foreign policy objectives. "The communist aggression in Korea," stated Secretary of Defense George C. Marshall, who assumed direction of the nation's defense effort on 12 September 1950, "marked the beginning of a new military policy for the United States. It left no doubt that the Soviet government and its satellites were willing to risk a general war by multiple aggression all over the world, unless confronted by substantial military strength."[68] Calling Korea a very special situation, Secretary Finletter pointed out that the United States was compelled to participate in a peripheral war in Korea, which was not a part of its global strategy, to demonstrate its national will and determination to resist aggression. "The western world," he noted, "has a very large periphery which fronts on Soviet Russia. In my opinion, it cannot defend that whole periphery with armed force. The real basic might of the western world, of which the United States is the center, is the capacity and will, if absolutely driven to it, to make war on anybody who attacks."[69]

In the last week of June 1950, President Truman with advice from the National Security Council and the Joint Chiefs of Staff heeded the request of the United Nations Security Council that all member nations "furnish such assistance to the Republic of Korea as may be necessary to repel armed attack and restore international peace and security in the area." In instructions received in Tokyo on 27 June, General MacArthur was authorized to employ air and naval forces in the area south of the 38th parallel in the hope that this support would enable the Republic of Korea army to rally and withstand aggression. On 30 June the Far East Air Forces (FEAF) and the Naval Forces Far East were empowered to attack military targets in North Korea. Later that day MacArthur was authorized to move ground combat troops from Japan and employ them against the North Korean People's Army. In authorizing these responses to the aggression, the Washington authorities approved the requests for conventional actions as they were made by MacArthur. By a fortunate circumstance, moreover, the Communists had launched their local aggression in Korea, which was one of the few spots along the Soviet periphery that was at all close to any concentration of available American military forces. In fact, the presence of US forces in Japan probably had much to do with the nature of the reaction. "The reason why we got involved in this periphery war, which is not a part of our global strategy," Finletter stated, "is that the enemy came down right under our noses, where we had the greatest concentration of American military power outside the United States."[70]

Despite a complete knowledge that the Soviet Union and Communist China were aiding the North Korean armed aggression, President Truman was adamant that the conflict would be limited to Korea's borders. "Every decision I made in the Korean conflict," he wrote, "had this one aim in mind: to prevent a third world war and the terrible destruction it would bring to the civilized world. This meant that we should not do anything that would provide the excuse to the Soviets and plunge the free nations into full-scale all-out war."[71] In the early days of the Korean emergency, Truman directed the US Seventh Fleet to isolate Formosa from the Communist mainland, ordered that Far East Air Forces and Naval Forces Far East aircraft would stay well clear of the frontiers of Manchuria and the Soviet Union, and instructed Secretary Johnson to revise a directive to MacArthur so as to eliminate an implication that the United States might be planning to go to war against the Soviet Union.[72] Secretary Acheson also believed that the Korean hostilities must be limited. "The whole effort of our policy is to prevent war and not have it occur," he stated. "Our allies," he added, "believe this just as much as we believe it, and their immediate danger is much greater than ours because if general war broke out they would be in a most exposed and dangerous position."[73]

Bases of American Action in Korea

As far as can be determined, the Washington authorities, without making any real consideration of the employment of an alternate strategy, accepted the orthodox surface strategy for handling the local war in Korea that General MacArthur presented during the last week of June 1950. At a later date, Lt Gen Albert C. Wedeymer, Army chief of plans, seriously questioned the wisdom of these initial decisions. "I think we Americans are surface-minded," he said. "We think in terms of the Army and Navy, and not up in the air with the new weapons that science has given us. I think that punitive action should have been taken with the Navy and with the Air Force, instead of putting ground forces in Korea."[74] When he arrived in the Far East in July 1950 as the commander of FEAF Bomber Command, Maj Gen Emmett O'Donnell was confident that with five groups of B-29s and with incendiary munitions, he possessed a capability to destroy everything of value in North Korea within three months. "It was my intention and hope, not having any instructions," he later recollected,

> that we would be able to . . . cash in on our psychological advantage in having gotten into the theater and into the war so fast, by putting a very severe blow on the North Koreans, with an advanced warning . . . telling them that they had gone too far in what we all recognized as being a case of aggression. . . . Tell them to either stop the aggression and get back over to the thirty-eighth parallel or they had better have their wives and children and bedrolls to go down with them because there is not going to be anything left up in Korea to return to.

After hearing O'Donnell's proposal, Lt Gen George E. Stratemeyer, the Far East Air Forces commander, told O'Donnell that overriding political and diplomatic considerations prevented its acceptance.[75]

In late August and early September 1950, some within the Department of Defense appear to have been of the opinion that the United States could find a solution for the Korean War by adopting stronger policies toward the Soviet Union. Although the full details of the story were never told, Secretary Johnson was reported to have favored action toward Russia. In a public speech on 25 August, Secretary of the Navy Francis Matthews advocated "instituting a war to compel cooperation for peace. . . . We would become the first aggressors for peace." On the same day, General MacArthur sent a statement to a veteran's organization that mentioned misconceptions about the value of Formosa to America's strategic position in the Pacific and stressed that air bases on an unbroken island chain would allow the United States to "dominate with air power every Asiatic port from Vladivostok to Singapore." When he was questioned at the Air War College by a newspaper reporter early in September, General Anderson reportedly stated: "We're at war, damn it. I don't advocate the shedding of illusions. Give me the order to do it and I can break up Russia's five A-bomb nests in a week." Acting more discretely inside the administration where he headed the National Security Resources Board, Stuart Symington was said to have advocated immediate action to resolve difficulties with the Soviets, while the United States still possessed a military advantage in atomic air power.[76]

According to Gen J. Lawton Collins, the Army chief of staff, the Joint Chiefs of Staff were opposed to an air campaign against North Korea's cities both because the United States might have to rebuild them and because they did not wish to spread enmity among the North Korean people. "What we had in mind," he said, "was what actually transpired in the Ukraine. When the Germans went into the Ukraine, there is no question but what if they had used their heads, they might well have gotten a great deal of support from the Ukranian people in their fighting against the Russians."[77] President Truman flatly refused to accept the idea that the United Nations should charge the Soviet Union with full responsibility for the Korean conflict and demand that Moscow put an end to it. Acting on peremptory orders from Truman, General MacArthur attempted without success to recall his statement to the veterans organization. General Anderson was immediately suspended as commandant of the Air War College and subsequently requested retirement. Secretary Johnson resigned as head of the Department of Defense on 12 September. Secretary Matthews, however, remained in office after he explained to Truman that he had heard preventive war talked so much that he had used the phrase in his speech without realizing its full implications to the administration's policy. Symington's suggestion that stronger action be taken on the basis of America's preponderance in atomic air power apparently did not meet the approval of the Joint Chiefs of Staff, at least two of whom reportedly "did not feel that atomic advantage was a sufficient guarantee to deter the Soviets."[78]

Tactical Air Operations

In accordance with the terms of the United Nations Security Council resolution of 27 June 1950, the mission of the United Nations Command forces in Korea during the summer of 1950, as detailed by Secretary Johnson, was "to stabilize, to build up the necessary equipment to go forward, and . . . to go forward to the thirty-eighth parallel."[79] Although somewhat hampered at first by the fact that it was equipped and trained for the air defense of Japan rather than for offensive employment, the Far East Air Forces committed most of its Japan-based Fifth Air Force to the Korean conflict. Assisted by carrier-based aircraft from the US Seventh Fleet, the Fifth Air Force easily destroyed the small North Korean air force, thus establishing local air superiority over Korea in the opening weeks of the war. To permit outnumbered United Nations ground forces to trade space for time and to prevent the North Korean People's Army (NKPA) from overrunning all of South Korea, Fifth Air Force and Seventh Fleet fighter-bombers and FEAF Bomber Command B-29s devoted an exceptionally large proportion of their capabilities to the support of the friendly group troops. In the emergency, air bombardment had to compensate for deficiencies in Army artillery support fire. In these same weeks understrength US Army divisions from Japan were committed piecemeal to the battle front in what seemed at first to be a futile effort to halt the Communist ground offensive. Speaking on 28 July to the question of why tactical air power had not stopped the North Korean ground attack, Secretary Finletter explained: "Tactical air power must be in relationship to Ground Forces. Tactical air power alone cannot win a war – any more than Ground Forces alone could win a war.... A force of ground troops is a kind of composite power of ground elements and air elements which support them." If opposing ground armies have capabilities which "are at all even," Finletter postulated, "air superiority will decide the outcome, because the force which has air superiority will ultimately win. However, where there is such gross disproportion as there is and has been in Korea between the ground elements, tactical air superiority of its own cannot win the immediate battle."[80]

In late July 1950, when United Nations ground forces were building a defensive perimeter around the port of Pusan in southern Korea, General MacArthur authorized United Nations Command air units to begin a comprehensive interdiction campaign against the enemy's overextended supply routes. In a six-week effort begun early in August, the B-29 groups easily smashed such war supporting industries as were to be found in North Korea. By 15 September, United Nations forces had been built up to a strength that they were required to attack northward from the Pusan defense perimeter. On that same day, an amphibious landing of a two-division force behind the enemy lines at Inchon was coordinated with the northward drive. "At this time," wrote Maj Gen Otto P. Weyland, who had come to Tokyo in July as vice-commander of the Far East Air Forces, "it became readily apparent that the air force had done its job well. The NKPA around the Pusan perimeter was nothing more than a skeleton which had been depleted by direct destruction and starved by the interdiction program." In three months of operations under conditions of virtual air supremacy, FEAF airmen were credited conservatively with having killed some 39,000 enemy personnel and with destroying 452 tanks, more than 6,000 vehicles, more than 1,300 freight cars, and some 260 locomotives. The number of hostile troops killed by air attack was surprisingly large: the 39,000 figure amounted to about one-third of the ten North Korean divisions that had attacked in June 1950.[81]

In the summer of 1950 the United Nations Command-Far East Command was under instructions to drive forward to the 38th parallel, thus clearing the Republic of Korea of invasion forces. In view of the impending United Nations offensive at Inchon, however, the National Security Council recommended a broader interpretation of the United Nations Security Council resolution of 27 June. "We regarded," stated Secretary of Defense Marshall, "that there was no . . . legal prohibition against passing the 38th parallel." Believing that the safety of the Republic of Korea would remain in jeopardy as long as remnants of the North Korean People's Army survived in North Korea, the National Security Council recommended that, if there was no indication of threat of entry of Soviet or Chinese Communist elements into Korea in force during the United Nations offensive, MacArthur should be authorized to extend his operations north of the 38th parallel. President Truman approved this recommendation on 11 September, and, following the recommendations of the United States, the United Nations General Assembly adopted a resolution on 7 October requiring that "all necessary steps be taken to ensure conditions of stability throughout Korea."[82]

Except for a logistical airlift and an airborne operation at Sukchon and Sunchon designed to trap retreating North Koreans, the United Nations ground forces required little air support during October as they drove forward against shattered remnants of the North Korean People's Army. Interdiction and attrition air strikes became less and less effective as Fifth Air Force and Seventh Fleet aircraft sought targets in a progressively narrowing strip of territory between the advancing grouped troops and Korea's northern boundary at the Yalu River. Free to build up their forces in the sanctuary north of the Yalu, the Chinese Communists moved air units equipped with Soviet-built MiG-15 jet fighters to airfields in Manchuria and began to fly combat sorties south of the international border on 1 November. The next night Chinese Communist ground troops attacked and encircled the advanced elements of an American regiment near the Yalu. When the United Nations ground forces renewed their offensive on 26 November, the Chinese Communists launched a massive counterattack that shattered the United Nations forces and forced them to seek safety in a full-scale retreat from North Korea.[83] General Spaatz subsequently described what had happened: "When our Air and Navy . . . had sufficient area of operations, the force of the North Korean Army was finally stopped and we had the Pusan beachhead secure. Then we were able to launch a counterattack. As soon as we pushed forward to the Yalu River and closed up the area that our Navy and Air could operate in, our ground forces were in the impossible position of being met by an onslaught of Chinese Communists with our dominant air and naval power impotent. . . . If the air power could have gotten into play, and gone in to a depth of two or three of four hundred miles back along the line of communication, the condition at the Yalu River might not have obtained."[84]

General Vandenberg on Air Power

At a press conference in Washington on 30 November, President Truman stated that the United States would take whatever steps were necessary to meet the situation in Korea, including the use of "every weapon that we have." "Every weapon" included the atomic bomb. "I don't want to see it used," Truman added. "It is a terrible weapon, and it should not be used on innocent men, women and children who have nothing whatever to do with this military aggression." With conditions worsening, however, MacArthur informed the Joint Chiefs of Staff on 3 December that the United Nations Command was "facing the entire Chinese nation in an undeclared war." He called for "political decisions and strategic plans . . . adequate fully to meet the realities involved."[85] At the moment the only direction that President Truman and the Joint Chiefs could give to MacArthur was the terse message: "We consider that the preservation of your forces is now the primary consideration."[86]

General MacArthur was not satisfied with this directive. In a message to the Joint Chiefs and in conversations with General Collins in early December, he argued that the United Nations Command should be permitted to bomb military targets in Manchuria. At least one high-ranking air officer agreed with MacArthur. "I was all for the bombing of Manchuria," stated General O'Donnell, "and I wanted very badly to do it as soon as we recognized the Chinese Communist forces . . . as bona fide forces. . . . I think we could have gotten in and for a very small cost in casualties we could have really hit them hard and perhaps even stopped them." Explaining his ideas more fully to the Joint Chiefs in a long message on 30 December, MacArthur suggested that an active air and naval campaign be launched against Communist China. "Should a policy determination be reached by our government or through it by the United Nations to recognize the state of war which has been forced upon us by the Chinese authorities and to take retaliatory measures within our capabilities," MacArthur wrote, we could: (1) blockade the coast of China; (2) destroy through naval gunfire and air bombardment China's industrial capacity to wage war; (3) secure reinforcements from the Nationalist garrison on Formosa to strengthen our position in Korea if we decided to continue to fight for that peninsula; and (4) release existing restrictions upon the Formosan garrison for diversionary action, possibly leading to counter-invasion against vulnerable areas of the Chinese mainland.[87]

In a few critical weeks in the winter of 1950–51, the United States made some fundamental decisions regarding the employment of nuclear weapons and about MacArthur's proposal that the limited Korean War should be expanded into a general war in Asia. Several factors affected the decision on nuclear weapons. A belief that the use of atomic weapons in Korea would result in a beginning of World War III was apparently very strongly held in Europe. President Truman's intimation that the A-bomb might be used in Korea brought Britain's Prime Minister Clement Attlee to Washington for hurried consultations on 4 December. The communiqué that marked the conclusion of the Truman-Attlee talks noted: "The President stated that it was his hope that world conditions would never call for the use of the atomic bomb. The President told the Prime Minister that it was also his desire to keep the Prime Minister at all times informed of developments which might bring about a change in the situation."[88] In later years Gen Frank F. Everest, who had been the Air Force's assistant deputy chief of staff for operations in the winter of 1950–51, stated that the original North Korean aggression probably could have been halted by the threat of the employment of the atomic bomb but that "the United States at that time was unwilling to use such a threat and, therefore, possibly increase the dangers of world conflict." Late in 1950 atomic weapons were still configured for strategic rather than tactical applications. Unlike the Soviet Union, which had many targets vulnerable to atomic attack, Communist China appeared to offer few targets for an atomic bombing campaign. The great strength of Communist China was manpower; the People's Republic of China was relatively independent of complicated logistical support facilities and was getting most of her weapons from the Soviet Union. According to General Everest, one other factor bore on the situation. In his opinion, the United States had accepted the position that atomic weapons would be used only when the issues to be resolved were vital to the United States. Everest said that these vital interests were not defined, but he was certain that an attack against the North American continent or against the North Atlantic Treaty Organization (NATO) allies would have been vital and would have been met with atomic firepower.[89]

During their conversations in December 1950, Truman and Attlee agreed that the United Nations should avoid a general war with China, primarily because of the threat of a global war. Much of the thinking lying behind this decision became apparent during Senate hearings in May and June 1951. Secretary Acheson believed that air attacks against Communist bases in Manchuria would "increase — and materially increase — the risk of general war in the Far East and general war throughout the world." The Joint Chiefs of Staff opposed the extension of the war to China on military grounds. "It would be militarily foolhardy," they declared on 3 January, "to embark on a course that would require full-scale hostilities against great land armies controlled by the Peking regime, while the heart of aggressive Communist power remained untouched." At the Senate hearings, Bradley stated: "Red China is not the powerful nation seeking to dominate the world. Frankly, in the opinion of the Joint Chiefs of Staff, this strategy would involve us in the wrong war, at the wrong place, at the wrong time, and with the wrong enemy."[90]

Believing that the American people needed to know the facts about the nation's air power and the relationship of the Korean War to global Air Force responsibilities, General Vandenberg published an article entitled "The Truth About Our Air Power" on 17 February 1951. He further developed his thought in two days of testimony before the Senate committee investigating the military situation in the Far East. He wrote, as a basic principle, that air power was indivisible and could not properly be characterized as strategic, tactical, or defensive. "The overriding purpose of every plane, whether it is a bomber or a fighter," he declared, "is to win the air battle on which final victory on land or sea is predicated." In an atomic age the air battle had to be won by an air offensive since no amount of money, however great, could provide static air defense which could "keep out a determined enemy attacking in strength."[91] Looking backward at the nineteenth century, Vandenberg pointed out that the British navy had maintained a world balance of power and had given the world many years of peace. In the twentieth century, air power was the only force that could maintain a world balance of power. With this thought in mind, Vandenberg demonstrated that the Air Force had to be kept continuously balanced against the threat of the Soviet Union. "As the power of the Russian air force increases and their stockpile of atomic weapons increases," he said,

> the job of the United States Air Force becomes roughly doubled. Whereas today it is a deterrent to war, because of its ability to devastate the industrial potential of any great nation on the globe; tomorrow, if the Russian air force has the atomic bombs and the ability to deliver them, we have to have an Air Force that can take the attrition that would be necessary to destroy that air force, and destroy it promptly; and after that, have a sufficient Air Force left to destroy the manufacturing potential of Russia, and do what we call policing action after that, to insure that it was not rebuilt.

As he saw it, the Soviets were already reducing the margin of superiority of the Air Force to keep the world's peace. "Today," he said, "we have only one job that we would have to do if we got into a major war with Russia, and that is to lay waste the industrial potential of that country. Tomorrow when they developed their long-range air force and they have more atomic weapons, we have two jobs. We would have to put into first place the job of destroying the Russian air potential that could utilize atomic bombs, and lay waste the industrial potential."[92]

Turning more specifically to the situation in Korea, Vandenberg believed that the Air Force was the "one thing that has, up to date, kept the Russians from deciding to go to war." But, in view of its global responsibilities, the Air Force was "a shoestring air force." If the Air Force were called upon to bomb across the Yalu, it could "destroy or lay waste to all of Manchuria and the principal cities of China." In so doing, however, the Air Force would undergo an attrition that, "with our start from approximately 40 groups, would fix it so that, should we have to operate in any other area with the full power of the United States Air Force we would not be able to." Because of the low rate of military aircraft procurement in the postwar years, the American aviation industry would be "unable until almost 1953 to do much of a job toward supplying the airplanes that we would lose in the war against any major opposition." For these reasons, Vandenberg urged that the Air Force could not sacrifice its deterrent capabilities for the sake of "pecking at the periphery" of communist power in Manchuria and China.[93]

After outlining his reasons why the air war should not be expanded to Manchuria and China, Vandenberg laid out his view on the way in which an air war ought to be fought. "No successful operations on the surface," he said, "can be conducted until you get air superiority. And when you go against a hostile air force in order to gain that air superiority, you must first destroy the enemy air force at the place where he is most vulnerable, which is on the ground and in his nest.... If you don't do that, your attrition mounts in arithmetical progression." After air superiority was attained, Vandenberg declared:

> Air power ... should go to the heart of the industrial centers to become reasonably efficient.... In my opinion, the proper way to use air power is initially to stop the flow of supplies and ammunition, guns, equipment of all types, at its source. The next most efficient way is to knock it out along the road before it reaches the front line. The least efficient way is after it gets dug in at the front line. Nevertheless, there are requirements constantly where the utilization of air power in close support is necessary.

Because of peculiar circumstances in Korea, Vandenberg demonstrated that the Air Force could not adhere to its doctrine. The war materiel that came to the enemy within Korea originated in the Soviet Union, which could not be attacked. Consequently war materiel had to be destroyed somewhere south of the Yalu, and, as a rule, Vandenberg explained, the greater the length "of road and rail that you can get the enemy from his main source of supply, the more advantageous it is to the Air Force and, therefore, as you decrease it, it becomes less advantageous.... As the distance between the Yalu River and our troops decreases, the effectiveness of our tactical air forces decreases in direct proportion." For these reasons, Vandenberg favored a negotiated peace in Korea which would "reestablish the freedom of the South Koreans and ... push the aggressor back." "I believe," he said, "our objective is to kill as many Chinese Communists as is possible without enlarging the war at the present time in Korea. I believe that there are reasonable chances of success in achieving a negoiated peace without endangering that one potential ... which has kept the peace so far, which is the United States Air Force."[94]

Air Power Stalemates the Communists

Even though the Washington leaders sympathized with the apparently desperate condition of the United Nations Command force in Korea, they felt compelled to view Korea in terms of the global defensive situation. Believing that attempts to unify Korea by military means would be to incur an unacceptable risk of an Asiatic or general world war, the Joint Chiefs of Staff recommended that the United Nations should seek a cease-fire in Korea. At the request of the United States, the United Nations General Assembly adopted a resolution on 14 December proposing that immediate steps be taken to end the fighting in Korea and to settle existing issues there by peaceful means. On 9 January 1951 the Joint Chiefs of Staff informed MacArthur that, while the war would continue to be limited to Korea, he would inflict as much damage upon the enemy as possible, subject always to the safety of the forces under his command. "In the worst case it would be important that, if we must withdraw from Korea," Truman told MacArthur on 14 January, "it be told to the world that that course was forced upon us by military necessity and that we shall not accept the result politically or militarily until the aggression has been rectified."[95] Apparently unable to accept the limited objective, General MacArthur was openly critical of the administration policy at intervals during the spring of 1951. On 20 March, he concluded a message to Congressman Joseph W. Martin with a statement of his fundamental belief: "There is no substitute for victory." Convinced that MacArthur did not agree with United States policy in Korea, President Truman relieved him from command on 11 April 1951. Truman explained to the American people that the military objective in Korea was "to repel attack . . . to restore peace . . . to avoid the spread of the conflict."[96]

As seen from the viewpoint of General Weyland, who assumed command of the Far East Air Forces on 10 June 1951, the principal task of the United Nations air forces in the winter of 1950–51 was to prevent the Chinese armies from enveloping the retreating United Nations ground forces. Air interdiction strikes and concentrated close air support retarded the Communist advance, worked heavy destruction on enemy personnel and materiel, and enabled the friendly ground troops to withdraw to defense lines in South Korea. If the Chinese Communist air force had been able to enter combat over the ground battle area, the story might have been different. However, the Far East Air Forces maintained local air superiority by a combination of combat air patrols and the threat of potential striking power. Rushed into combat in Korea, the F-86 Sabre fighter proved able to overcome Soviet MiG-15 planes in air-to-air combat. "The F-86 saved us in Korea," Gen Nathan F. Twining stated later. "If we had not had the top day fighter, those MiGs would have come down and ruined us over there, but the day fighter licked them." While United Nations airmen were not permitted to violate the Manchurian sanctuary, Vandenberg secured acceptance of one important proviso to the restriction. In the spring of 1951, the United States delegation in the United Nations passed the word that if the Reds launched massed air attacks against

United Nations forces in Korea, American airmen would destroy the airfields from which such attacks originated. Rather than jeopardize their sanctuary, the Communists attempted to build airfields within North Korea. But each time one of these airfields neared operational status, B-29s successfully neutralized it. The Communist air commander, Weyland said, was forced to learn "the basic lesson that an air force cannot be reconstituted or developed in an area where his foe has won air supremacy."[97]

"In a long-term war," Weyland remarked on 28 December 1950, "tactical air power will contribute more to the success of the ground forces and to the over-all mission of a theater air commander through a well-planned interdiction campaign than by any other mission short of the attainment of air supremacy." In times of crisis, the Far East Air Forces provided friendly ground troops with an extraordinary large amount of close air support. The FEAF Bomber Command developed radar-directed night-bombing techniques that permitted its B-29s to rain down proximity-fuze bombs on Red troops as they prepared to assault friendly ground positions. In the intervals between ground battles, however, United Nations air power was directed against the middle miles of the Korean transportation system that supported the Red armies. Constant air attacks against the overextended supply lines drained the Chinese Communist armies of their combat effectiveness. The massive Chinese ground attacks mounted in January and April 1951 failed because of a lack of logistical support. Seeking to exact heavy casualties upon the enemy rather than to defend geographical objectives, United Nations ground troops preserved themselves through maneuver during the Chinese attacks and launched counteroffensives when the Red assaults collapsed. During the period between November 1950 and June 1951, continued air assault against the enemy forward areas and supporting supply routes brought death to an estimated 117,000 enemy troops, destroyed 1,315 gun positions, 196 tanks, and more than 80,000 buildings used as troop and supply centers. The enemy's transportation system was crippled by the loss of over 13,000 vehicles, 2,600 freight cars, and 250 locomotives to air attack.[98]

Following the collapse of the vaunted Chinese Communist spring ground offensive, United Nations Command forces drove forward on all fronts in May 1951 to clear the Republic of Korea of hostile invaders. With their forces badly beaten and on the run, the Communists decided to take advantage of the willingness of the United Nations to negotiate a Korean cease-fire. The armistice talks began in Korea on 10 July 1951. At this time the conflict entered a new phase that ultimately would be concluded by accomplishing new undertakings, some of them remote from the Korean battleground. At the Kaesong truce talks, Lt Gen Nam Il, the senior Red delegate, gave a frank appraisal of the reason why the numerically superior Communist ground armies had not prevailed in Korea. "Without the support of the indiscriminate bombing and bombardment by your air and naval forces," he said, "your ground forces would have long ago been driven out of the Korean peninsula by our powerful and battle-skilled ground forces." At the juncture when the all-out ground battles were ending, Weyland also looked backward and drew lessons. "There is a tendency among many," he said, "to regard all ... air operations against ground forces merely as support of the Army. ... Would it not be better to recall that land, sea, and air forces are committed in support of the over-all mission of the theater commander? ... If we take such a view, it should ... be less difficult to see that over-all strategy must be geared to the air situation and the capabilities of the friendly air forces as much as to ground forces concepts of maneuver and fire. ... If the objectives and situation are such that, in order to be successful, air power must be exploited to the fullest, then the ground forces must support the air forces."[99]

Rebuilding the Worldwide Air Force

Viewing his service as secretary of the Air Force in retrospect, Thomas K. Finletter remarked that Korea was the stimulus that broke the logjam of fixed military budgets in 1950, but he also observed that the Korean War "had the unfortunate effect of emphasizing the importance of the weapons and tactics of the past."[100] General Vandenberg, however, saw four principal events as being instrumental in the substantial expansion of the Air Force that took place after 1950. The first was the explosion of an atomic bomb by the Soviet Union in August 1949. The second was the North Korean invasion of South Korea in June 1950, followed by the entry of the Chinese Communist armies into Korea in November. Both actions signified the willingness of the Communists to employ armed might for the achievement of foreign policy objectives. The third was the commitment of United States forces to assist in the defense of Western Europe. And the fourth was the calculation of the Joint Chiefs of Staff that by mid-1954 the Soviet Union would possess a stockpile of atomic weapons sufficient in size to mount a devastating attack against United States military installations, industry, and population centers.[101] Recognizing that the Air Force was on trial in Korea, Vandenberg ordered that every effort be made to give the utmost support to the Far East Air Forces; nevertheless, the reorganization and buildup of the United States Air Force was pointed toward the major threat presented by the growing atomic capabilities of Soviet air power.

Even though it had gained a high level of experience in the global air battles of World War II, the United States Air Force was still a new military organization in June 1950. Thus, at the same time that Vandenberg faced the problem of mobilizing larger air striking forces, he also had to speed decision-making capabilities in the Air Staff and to build a comprehensive field organization for the growing Air Force. The headquarters organization, field establishment, and force composition had to be tailored to new strategic concepts, since the strategy of minimum deterrence followed up until 1950 had not prevented the outbreak of conflict in Korea. In the House of Representatives, Chairman Vinson was openly apprehensive about Air Force capabilities for air defense and tactical air warfare. In the Senate, Paul Douglas urged that the internal organization of the Air Force ought to be established by law, as had long been the case with the Army and Navy.[102]

SOVIET NUCLEAR WEAPONS

Although the Air Force began to reorganize its field commands in the autumn of 1950, it asked for more time to evaluate the global air situation—including Korea—before taking a stand on an Air Force organization act. At the request of General Stratemeyer, Vandenberg sent Col Ethelred Sykes, who had been serving as a special assistant to Secretary Finletter, to Tokyo early in August 1950 to analyze the air warfare lessons being learned there. Within the headquarters of the Fifth Air Force in Korea, Maj Gen Earle E. Partridge organized a tactical airpower evaluation (TAPE) section. On 6 October, General Norstad, the Air Force vice chief of staff, initiated an even larger evaluation project. "Regardless of ... limiting conditions," Norstad said, "we must utilize the Korean experiences for future planning purposes." He sent Maj Gen Glenn O. Barcus and a team of senior officers to Tokyo to make a broad evaluation of the effectiveness of the Air Force in Korea. Believing that there also would be a requirement for an investigation by an informed but impartial civilian, Secretary Finletter sent Dr Robert L. Stearns, president of the University of Colorado, to the Far East to gather information that would be useful in making policy decisions. Stearns went to the Far East on 19 November, spent about 30 days in observing and gathering data, and returned to Washington, where he completed a study entitled "Korean Evaluation Project: Report on Air Operations" on 16 January 1951. The Barcus group continued to work in the theater until 31 December; its final report was printed in seven volumes with numerous appendixes on 12 March 1951.[103] In February the deputy chief of staff for development was designated as the staff monitoring agent to ensure that Air Staff agencies and field commands took action to meet deficiencies noted in the Stearns and Barcus reports. Following disbandment of the Barcus group, a small Korea evaluation group, headed by Colonel Sykes, was established within the Office of the Secretary of the Air Force to serve as a central clearinghouse for air studies and evaluations of the war.[104] One of the major values of these evaluations was the identification of the special circumstances prevailing in the limited war that would doubtless not be typical of general hostilities.

Establishment of the Air Force Council

In the autumn of 1950, while the Air Force was expanding and establishing new field commands, Vandenberg faced the fact that he could not as an individual handle the total direction of an institution as large and complex as the Air Force was becoming, especially since he had to spend at least three days a week with the Joint Chiefs of Staff and devote additional time to the Department of Defense and Congress. For this reason, he believed that command decisions ought to be made by any one of the officers who served as chief of staff, vice chief of staff, or a deputy chief of staff. He wanted each deputy chief of staff, in the conduct of business within the field of authority, to act as if he were the chief of staff. Each deputy chief, however, had to coordinate his actions with the members of the top command to prevent confusion; during the Air Force buildup, the deputies were frequently so busy in their own offices that they had no means for coordination other than by passing papers through a time-consuming interoffice pipeline.[105]

In an effort to speed the process of making basic policies and decisions, Vandenberg established the Air Force Council on 26 April 1951. At first, only the five deputy chiefs of staff served on the council, with their senior member acting as chairman. In July 1951, however, Gen Nathan F. Twining, who had become vice chief of staff, began to serve as permanent chairman of the council, whose membership now consisted of the five deputy chiefs of staff and the inspector general. The council met each Thursday and acted on an agenda that the members prepared prior to meetings. Vandenberg insisted that the council members were "wearing the hat of the Chief of Staff" and that they had to "leave the interests of their own particular shops back at their shops."[106] "The Air Council," General LeMay explained later when he had become vice chief of staff, "is a tool of the Chief of the Air Force, used to make sure that all major decisions that he has to make have been looked at and all the recommendations that have come to him have been looked at by the senior members of his staff."[107]

At the same time that the Air Force Council was formed to expedite the work of the top command, four other Air Force boards were formed at the directorate level of the Air Staff. The Aircraft and Weapons Board was established on 9 July 1951 to consider the matters that had been handled formerly by the Senior Officers Board. Shortly thereafter, the Force Estimates Board, the Budget Advisory Board, and the Military Construction Board were established. These directorate-level boards studied problems within their framework of authority and made recommendations to the Air Force Council. Although these four directorate boards and the Air Force Council would continue to be the top deliberative and advisory bodies during the 1950s, the secretary of the Air Force and the chief of staff continued to make the decisions that guided the Air Force.[108] "It should be noted," LeMay pointed out, "that the Air Force Council is not a decision-making body, but it is merely an advisory group to the Chief of Staff."[109]

Army-Air Force Accommodations on Air-Ground Doctrine

Based upon analysis of the contributions that air power could make to the national defense, the Joint Chiefs of Staff had charged the Air Force with responsibility for strategic bombing, the air defense of the United States, and the tactical support of surface forces. "Although those three jobs seemed pegged to different objectives," Vandenberg wrote, "it is impossible to separate them in practice because—and this is a principle ignored too often—air power is indivisible."[110] During the summer and autumn of 1950, the doctrine of the indivisibility of air power was a very real factor as the Air Force reconsidered its responsibilities and reorganized its forces.

Until the summer of 1950 the limited capabilities of the Strategic Air Command (SAC) were committed to preparing to execute a strategic air campaign against targets in the Soviet Union. However, the Strategic Air Command recognized that its atomic capability was increasing, that it was important to find some new means of defense for Western Europe against Soviet attack, and that the Army and Navy were dissatisfied with the existing air war plan. For this reason, General LeMay submitted a revised war plan, which was additionally revised and approved at a higher level on 12 August 1950. Under a new plan the Strategic Air Command would seek to accomplish three specific tasks during a strategic air offensive: destroying vital elements of the Soviet war-making capability, blunting of the Soviet capability to deliver an atomic offensive, and retarding Soviet ground advances into Europe. At the time these tasks (subsequently referred to as the Delta, Bravo, and Romeo missions) were assigned, the Strategic Air Command possessed the nation's only significant nuclear capability; but provision was made in the approved plan for the eventual employment of Navy aircraft in the prosecution of the expanded air offensive.[111] Even though he accepted the mission to slow a Soviet land invasion of Western Europe, General LeMay was not entirely convinced that the Strategic Air Command should be charged to perform tactical air warfare missions. "If you have to employ strategic air power against tactical targets," he said, "you are not getting the full use of the weapon."[112]

Largely for economy, but also because existing fighter aircraft were sufficiently versatile to perform either air defenses or tactical air support, the Air Force had reduced the status of the Air Defense and Tactical Air Commands in December 1948 and had placed them under the Continental Air Command. The reduced status of tactical air was not popular with the Army; by June 1949 the Army Field Forces had informed the Tactical Air Command that it was no longer satisfied with the cooperative air-ground establishment visualized in Field Manual 31-35, *Air-Ground Operations*.[113] In an informal word of advice in May 1950, Representative Vinson told Maj Gen Thomas D. White, the Air Force director of legislation and liaison, that for its own protection the Air Force would have to meet the Army's requirements for air support. Vinson jokingly suggested that the air-support mission might have to be given to the Marine Corps if the Air Force did not pay more attention to it.[114] Representatives Vinson and Dewey Short, taking an unusual step that they said was meant to assist rather than criticize, wrote Vandenberg on 2 August that the House Committee on Armed Services was "definitely dissatisfied" with the lack of progress being made in the development of the nation's radar warning network and had "strong reservations about the efforts of the Air Force to deal with close air support for the Army."[115] In 1950 the Air Force realized that it would be very difficult to develop an all-purpose fighter which would have the supersonic capabilities needed to intercept and destroy future generations of hostile jet bombers and still have the relatively slow speed and long flight-endurance characteristics that the Army felt necessary for a close air support aircraft.[116]

Even without the significant technological developments that were impending, the mobilization of additional Army and Air Force units during the autumn of 1950 probably would have forced the Air Force to reestablish a major Tactical Air Command. Moving in this direction, the Continental Air Command, effective on

1 August 1950, assigned the Ninth Air Force (Tactical) together with available fighter-bomber, troop carrier, light bomber, and tactical reconnaissance units to the Tactical Air Command. On 15 November the Air Force specified that the Tactical Air Command would "provide for Air Force cooperation with land, naval, and/or amphibious forces"; on 1 December it made the Tactical Air Command a major command directly responsible to the United States Air Force.[117] Recognizing that the Tactical Air Command would need strong leadership, Vandenberg assigned Lt Gen John K. Cannon to head it effective on 25 January 1951. In World War II, Cannon had commanded the Twelfth Air Force and the Mediterranean Allied Tactical Air Force in Italy.[118]

The vague wording of the Tactical Air Command's mission statement reflected a general uncertainty of Army-Air Force relationships. In 1947, General Collins had agreed with General Eisenhower's concept that the Air Force should furnish tactical air support to the Army. In November 1950, Collins still maintained that the Army had "no intention of attempting to take over the Tactical Air Force," but he informed Vandenberg that the Army was dissatisfied with the coequal status of air and ground forces. He specifically recommended that the Army commanders, down to corps level in some instances, should exercise operational control of close air support. He also recommended that the Army ought to participate in determining the requirements for close-support aircraft, which, he said, "should be designed primarily for close air support roles, to include types of missions and targets, necessity for all weather operations, reasonable operational endurance, and ability to operate from advance strips in combat zones." Collins stated that tactical air units ought to be provided overseas on a basis of one fighter-bomber group per field army.[119] In an article published in December, Gen Mark W. Clark, chief of the Army Field Forces, emphasized that the Army wanted a plane specifically designed for the close support mission. If the plane required protection from hostile fighters, the support plane could be escorted by Air Force high-performance fighters.[120] At a conference of Army and Air Force representatives, held in Washington on 7 February 1951 to discuss the development of a light close-support aircraft, Army representatives reportedly made the point that multipurpose tactical fighters frequently were diverted away from close-support operations, whereas a light, support aircraft that could do nothing but this mission would always be available when it was needed for air support.[121]

The Army proposals to attach supporting air groups to army units and to develop special close-support aircraft struck at the heart of the Army-Air Force air-ground doctrine that had emerged from World War II. General Cannon thought it significant that the concept of specially committed air support units had originated in the Central Pacific and had been fostered in Korea under conditions in which the maintenance of air superiority was quite different than it had been in Europe. In the event of a war with the Soviet Union, Cannon urged that all available aircraft initially be committed to gaining and maintaining friendly air superiority; he accordingly objected to the development and procurement of light close-support aircraft that would be too vulnerable to participate in an air war. "It appears infinitely wiser to direct our efforts toward removing present obstacles to the accomplishment of the missions of tactical air by aircraft types which are inherently capable of such accomplishment," he said, "than to design aircraft of reduced utility and performance in order to accept basic inadequacies."[122] Cannon also insisted that the Army's proposal to allocate aircraft to the support of divisions was counter to the principles of concentration of force and centralization of control.[123] Brig Gen Homer L. Sanders, deputy chief of staff for operations of the Tactical Air Command, pointed out that more than 100 close-support groups would have been needed in Western Europe during 1944-45 to have supported Army divisions on a one-for-one basis. The cost of such a tactical air force would have been prohibitive, and, at any rate, this tremendous establishment had not been needed because the flexibility in control in the air support system had permitted a rapid concentration of any number of aircraft at a given point in accordance with the needs of local situations.[124] In an article published in an Army service journal in May 1951, Col Francis C. Gideon, Air Force member of the Joint Strategic Plans Group, summarized Air Force thinking on the command of tactical aviation. "If air power were nothing more than flying artillery or jet-propelled cavalry," he wrote, "it would properly be placed under the command of the ground forces. But air power, of which the forces designed for close combat support of ground operations are a part, is more than this. Air power is the sum of the means necessary to dominate the air. Viewed in this light, the reasons for establishing an integrated Air Force are logical and wise; its integrity must be guaranteed."[125]

From the beginning of the controversy, Secretary Finletter and General Vandenberg assumed that resolution of such a highly complex question as the command and control of tactical aviation ought to be handled by military men rather than by the Department of Defense or Congress. On 21 March 1951, General Collins, after evaluating the Air Force positions on the subject, sent Vandenberg a readjustment of his original position. He recognized that centralized control of tactical air units under a senior Air Force commander might be necessary in a war against an enemy nation that had a great superiority of air power, but Collins wanted this senior air commander to allocate air groups to the support of field armies if the tactical situation permitted. Once air groups were so allocated to the support of an army or an independent corps, their responsible Army commanders should be able to exercise operational control over them.[126] At this juncture, Secretary of the Army Frank Pace and General Collins agreed in a conversation with Finletter that the idea of a separate tactical close-support air force ought to be laid aside until such time as the Air Force could build up tactical air forces capable of performing the multiple functions of tactical air power.[127] Although the matter was postponed, General Clark had changed none of his thinking. Writing to Collins, Clark stated:

> I consider that the traditional Air Force doctrine, which provides for coequal command status between ground and air at all but theater levels, constitutes a fundamental defect in command relationship. This doctrine of command by mutual cooperation is unacceptable because it reserves to the supporting arm the authority to determine whether

or not a supporting task should be executed. The theory of divided command in the face of the enemy is foreign to the basic concept of warfare wherein the responsible commander exercises undisputed directive authority over all elements essential to the accomplishment of his missions.[128]

At the same time that the Air Force leaders were discussing air-ground relationships, they had to make decisions as to the relationship between the Tactical Air Command and the Strategic Air Command. Even though the Tactical Air Command formed a Special Weapons Branch in its headquarters as soon as it learned that the development of atomic weapons which could be delivered by tactical aircraft was feasible, the assignment for the retardation mission to the Strategic Air Command in August 1950 beclouded the prospects of an atomic mission for the Tactical Air Command. Purely for test and development purposes, the Air Force permitted the modification of nine B-45s and seven F-84Es for atomic delivery and assigned them to the Tactical Air Command's 84th Bombardment Squadron (Light).[129] Early in 1951 a buildup of Soviet tactical air forces in Europe lent urgency to the reinforcement of air units in that theater. On 21 January, the United States Air Forces in Europe (USAFE) was made a separate command under the Joint Chiefs of Staff; USAFE activated the Twelfth Air Force in Germany to serve as the tactical air arm for NATO ground forces and activated the Third Air Force to exercise area command in the United Kingdom. The Strategic Air Command activated the 5th Air Division to command SAC units that would be deployed to bases being built in French Morocco and activated the 7th Air Division to command strategic air units in Great Britain.[130] At about this same time the Joint Chiefs of Staff made an allocation of atomic weapons to the defense of Western Europe.

As soon as atomic weapons were allocated to the defense of Europe, General Cannon informed the Air Force that the tactical air force ought to be charged to employ them. "A tactical fighter-bomber unit capable of delivering atomic weapons," he wrote in February 1951, "promises to be one of the most devastating striking forces that will be available to the military establishment." His position soon became quite clear. "I personally consider it extremely important," he said, "to have the strategic air forces tend to their own knitting, keep their minds on their own jobs and not be diverted from their primary mission." Cannon thought that the mission of strategic air forces was to effect the progressive destruction and disintegration of an enemy nation's morale and war-making capacity. At the outset of hostilities with the Soviet Union, he expected that the strategic air forces would be needed to help the tactical air forces to gain air superiority and interdict the advance of Soviet ground troops, but he maintained that such diversions ought to be as moderate as possible.[131]

In the Air Staff, officers who were looking for a means of augmenting theater air power in Europe before the spring of 1952 apparently looked with some favor on Cannon's thinking. In the Office of Assistant for Atomic Energy, Col John D. Stevenson authored a plan looking toward the establishment of tactical air division in the United Kingdom that would be equipped with atomic-capable B-45 and F-84 aircraft. Given authorization from the Joint Chiefs of Staff, the Air Force in July 1951 directed the necessary modification of aircraft and ordered the Tactical Air Command to organize the atomic air division. Even though they decided that an atomic-capable tactical air division would be fielded, the Joint Chiefs of Staff did not relieve the Strategic Air Command of its retardation mission, and the Air Force did not commit itself to provide a follow-up tactical bomber replacement for the old B-45. "It is my considered opinion," Cannon continued to insist, "that any planning basis that relies in the main upon the diversion of strategic air effort to tactical targets is inappropriate. Strategic air power must be conserved for its primary mission and tactical air must possess integral forces appropriate and adequate to its needs."[132]

Also, during the winter of 1950-51, the Air Force gave a good amount of attention to proposals for reorganizing military air transport and troop carrier aviation. During maneuvers in April and May 1950 in North Carolina, called Exercise Swarmer, troop carrier and military air transport elements were combined together in a provisional air transport force that was able to drop paratroopers to seize an airhead, to expand the airhead by the landing of transports with reinforcements, and to maintain resupply of troops surrounded by hostile forces.[133] Sent to Japan to take charge of theater airlift in September 1950, Maj Gen William H. Tunner organized available troop carrier and military air transport units together in the FEAF Combat Cargo Command (Provisional). Citing good experience with this organization, which could handle airborne operations and air-delivered supplies, Tunner proposed on 26 December 1950 that in the interest of both economy and efficiency the Air Force ought to unify all of its air transport organizations.[134] In October 1950, the Army Field Forces were reported to oppose any move to remove troop carrier aviation from the tactical air forces and to place it in a consolidated air transport command.[135] General Cannon also strongly opposed such a move. "Troop carrier units," Cannon insisted, "are combat units. The aircraft used by these units are weapons of war, just as are fighter-bombers, submarines, and tanks; therefore, troop carrier aviation is tactical aviation, and tactical aviation only. Any proposal to merge troop carrier and all air transport units into one air transport organization is basically in error in that it combines combat functions with service functions."[136]

Although the Air Force seriously considered the prospects for consolidating air transport and troop carrier aviation, final decisions allowed troop carrier units to remain under the Tactical Air Command and military air transport under the Military Air Transport Service. Effective 28 March 1951, the Tactical Air Command organized the Eighteenth Air Force to take over the training of all troop carrier wings in the zone of interior.[137] Although no change was made in basic organization, the experience of the Korean hostilities was such as to cause both the Army and Air Force to accord great importance to transport aviation. General Collins seldom made a speech without referring to the importance of airborne operations and of making the Army as air transportable as possible.[138] General Vandenberg pointed out that the Air Force was forced to prestock critical supplies in overseas areas, a practice that not only was expensive but also committed the striking forces to operate from bases that might be denied to them at the outset of a war. "Airlift on the scale we visualize," Vandenberg said, "would make it possible to move logistic support with and as the bombers move. If the bombers are forced to divert to alternate bases, the logistic support would likewise be diverted. Without this type support the strategic bombing force is neither truly strategic nor potent. To have truly strategic striking forces, logistics must be as strategically mobile and flexible as the forces it supports."[139] And even after the Air Force decision had gone against him, General Tunner continued to insist that air transport capabilities should be consolidated into one operating command. "Air transport today," he wrote in the autumn of 1952,

> is scattered among many commands of the Air Force as well as the Navy and Marine Corps, all of whom do not have the same standards of utilization and priority urgency for their use. I feel the consolidation of these aircraft into a single command is the most efficient way to do this job. This single command would be charged with the responsibility for airlift according to the urgency of the requirements of all the armed services—in other words, the first needs of the nation.[140]

In its roles and missions, the Air Force was charged to provide an air defense of the United States, but such an air defense required the integration of the Army's antiaircraft artillery battalions and the Air Force's interceptor groups into one operational organization. In the course of a long dispute, the Army Ground Forces had proposed in 1946 that the air defense mission actually ought to be divided: the antiaircraft artillery to be responsible for the air defense of local areas and the fighters to provide air defense beyond the range of the ground weapons. In 1949 the Air Force stated the doctrinal position that antiaircraft artillery battalions should be placed under the operational control of the Air Defense Command.[141] Until the spring of 1950 these disputes remained academic, since the Army meant to mobilize antiaircraft battalions from the National Guard and the Air Force intended to mobilize fighter interceptor groups from the Air National Guard—both actions to take effect in some future emergency. Following the Soviet atomic explosion, the Air Force stated immediate requirements for the establishment of an operational air defense system in the United States and Alaska by 1952, and the Army, which now budgeted for 48 regular antiaircraft artillery battalions, established an antiaircraft command to assume responsibilities for field air defense matters including air defense planning. In a memorandum of agreement signed on 1 August 1950, Generals Vandenberg and Collins decided between themselves that targets to be defended would be decided upon jointly by the departments of Army and Air Force; that the location of local antiaircraft artillery defenses would be "prescribed geographically" by similar agreements; and that Air Force air defense commanders would exercise operational control over antiaircraft artillery "insofar as engagement and disengagement of fire is concerned."[142]

The agreement between Vandenberg and Collins cleared the way for the integration of antiaircraft artillery into the growing air defense system, but it did not provide an overall air defense organization. In the latter half of 1950, the Continental Air Command, even though it was hard pressed to handle its multitude of duties, remained responsible for air defense matters. Seeking relief from overwork, Lt Gen Ennis C. Whitehead, the commander of the Continental Air Command, urged the Air Force to create a separate air personnel command to handle the mobilization of Air National Guard and Air Reserve units into the federal service, thereby allowing the Continental Air Command to concentrate on tactical air and air defense. Instead of accepting this proposal, the Air Force created the separate Tactical Air Command. Inasmuch as common fighter units would no longer be available for both air defense and tactical air, the Air Force additionally decided on 10 November 1950 to separate the Air Defense Command from the Continental Air Command. At this time, the Continental Air Command remained responsible for Air Reserve and Air National Guard affairs. General Whitehead accordingly relinquished his old command and moved to Colorado Springs, Colorado, where he assumed direction of the Air Defense Command on 1 January 1951.[143]

As its reestablishment as a major command, the Air Defense Command was assigned the Eastern and Western Air Defense Forces, together with the eight fighter-interceptor wings that had been assigned to the Continental Air Command. To spread the heavy burden borne by the two air defense forces, the Air Defense Command established a Central Air Defense Force on 1 March 1951. Operating in cooperation with the Air Defense Command, the Army Antiaircraft Command established its headquarters in Colorado Springs and established Eastern, Western, and Central Army Antiaircraft Commands adjacent to the respective air defense forces. Antiaircraft artillery brigades, groups, battalions, and batteries moved into the air defense system to complement the air divisions, defense wings, groups, and squadrons of the Air Defense Command.[144] Rounding out the defense organization, the Air Defense Command negotiated agreements with the Tactical Air Command and the Strategic Air Command during April and May 1951 whereby the forces of these organizations might be used for emergency air defense missions.[145] Even though a command organization for continental air defense had been established, Vandenberg felt it necessary on 23 April 1951 to warn that 70 percent of the hostile aircraft that might attack the United States would probably get through to their targets. "There has never been in the history of air warfare," he said, "anyone who has been able to maintain as high a percentage as 30 percent destroyed. In other words, 30 percent has never yet been attained. In fact I think the greatest percentage – this is over a period of time – that has ever been attained is 8 percent."[146]

IDEAS, CONCEPTS, DOCTRINE

Air Force Organization Act of 1951

Because of the general language of the National Security Act of 1947, the Air Force was able to generate much of its own internal organization. Air Force leaders felt that this was advantageous for an essentially new service, but there was a disadvantage in that the Air Force had no specific authorization for its strength and was bound by old laws that provided that Army appropriations could not be carried over for longer than two years before being expended. In congressional hearings during 1949, Secretary Symington and General Vandenberg accordingly supported the Army and Air Force authorization legislation, which was designed to create a legal framework for the Army and the Air Force with regard to their military strength, their basic composition, and their appropriation authority. As enacted on 10 July 1950, the Army and Air Force Authorization Act established the strength of the Regular Air Force at 70 groups and 22 separate squadrons and allocated an additional 61 groups to the combined Air National Guard and Air Force Reserve. The act provided that funds appropriated to the Air Force for the procurement of technical military equipment and supplies, for the construction of public works, and for research and development should remain available until expended unless otherwise provided.[147]

Satisfied with the Army and Air Force Authorization Act, the Air Force leaders were in no hurry to see the enactment of more detailed organizational legislation. "My own view," explained Secretary Finletter on 10 January 1951, "was that it was better to let the Air Force evolve for a further period of time, and to establish its ways of doing things, especially during such a dynamic time as the present, and then to codify." In the House Military Affairs Committee, however, Chairman Vinson believed that "we should try to run an establishment by law, by statute as much as possible and not entirely by the whims and views of any one individual, because individuals come and go." When the Air Force did not offer proposed legislation, Rep Paul J. Kilday's subcommittee to the Committee on Armed Services drafted a bill designated as the Air Force Organization Act of 1951. This measure generally described the existing Air Force organization but provided that the chief of staff "shall have supervision of all members and organizations of the Air Force"; that the major commands would be the Continental Air Command, Strategic Air Command, Tactical Air Command, Air Materiel Command, and European Support Command; and that an air adjutant general, an inspector general, and a provost marshal general would be statutory positions. The bill provided that the Army's surgeon general and the Navy's Medical Department would serve the Air Force, and it charged that the Army's quartermaster general, chief of engineers, judge advocate general, and chief of chaplains with extending their functions and duties to meet the needs of the Department of the Air Force.[148]

When the House Committee on Armed Services began hearings regarding the Air Force Organization Act on 10 January 1951, Finletter stated that the Air Force ought to be permitted to attain more experience before its internal establishment was codified. However, out of deference to Vinson, he and Vandenberg would not oppose the legislation if it was amended to remove restrictive provisions. Both Finletter and Vandenberg insisted that, under the direction of the secretary of the Air Force, the chief of staff should command rather than supervise the Air Force. The National Security Act of 1947 had authorized the chief of staff to command the Air Force. Although Vandenberg was willing to supervise support activities of the Air Force, he maintained that it was essential that he retain command over the strategic and the air defense forces. "When we are dealing with things like the type of explosives we have today, and . . . because half an hour may make the difference between the destruction of something and the saving of it based on information that Washington may have . . .," he explained, "I want to have clear command." Finletter and Vandenberg also opposed the legislative creation of adjutant general, inspector general, and other specialized corps within the Air Force. "Rather than having badges and differentiations," Finletter said, "what we are trying to get in the Air Force is one unified command without distinctions." He was willing to accept a unified medical service but maintained that the Air Force could not depend upon other services to provide medical, quartermaster, engineer, judge advocate, and chaplain support. "The Air Force," Finletter announced, "will not support something which singles out the Air Force and makes it a second-grade establishment." Believing that the legislation should not be so specific as to restrict organizational development, Finletter suggested that it should establish the Air Defense Command, the Strategic Air Command, the Tactical Air Command, the Air Materiel Command, and one other overseas command as might be directed established by the president, each command to be headed by a commander in the grade of general.[149]

Despite frequent meetings Air Force leaders were not able to persuade the House Committee on Armed Services to accept the principle that the chief of staff should command the Air Force. The committee recognized that the chief of naval operations commanded the nation's operational fleets, but it preferred the Army system wherein "the Army has for forty-some-odd years felt the Chief of Staff should act more or less as a coordinator or director of the Army Staff." Vinson was more than a little distrusting of the wide latitude the secretary of the Air Force wanted in order to organize the Air Force. The committee ultimately agreed not to recommend the legislative establishment of special corps and offices within the Air Force, while the Air Force agreed to accept a stipulation that established an Air Staff comprised of the chief and five deputy chiefs of staff. The committee also agreed to establish the Air Defense Command, the Strategic Air Command, and the Tactical Air Command by law, leaving additional commands to be established by the secretary of the Air Force.[150]

The amended Air Force organization measure passed by the House of Representatives on 24 January 1951 was generally acceptable to the Air Force, except that it specified that the chief of staff would supervise rather than command. In an appearance on 23 April, Finletter asked a subcommittee of the Senate Committee on Armed Services to accept the command concept. He argued that the Air Force chief of staff could not act independently of the constitutional powers of the president or of the statutory authority of the secretary and that "the word 'command' is the more proper one to define the relationship of the chief of staff to the Air Force, especially to the fighting commands of the Air Force." Both Finletter and Vandenberg spoke of their desire to have a homogeneous family in the Air Force and accordingly opposed the legal establishment of a judge advocate general — the only special corps authorization that had not been removed from the House bill.[151]

In its version of the Air Force Organization Act (passed on 21 June 1951), the Senate accepted the concept that the chief of staff should command the Air Force. As a result, the legislation went to a conference committee, which prepared a measure that was enacted as the Air Force Organization Act of 1951 and was signed by President Truman on 19 September. This act specified that the Air Force chief of staff, under the direction of the secretary of the Air Force, should exercise command over the Air Defense Command, the Strategic Air Command, the Tactical Air Command, and such other major establishments as might be created in a war or national emergency to supersede one of the enumerated major commands. The chief of staff would supervise other portions of the Air Force. Apparently because of a high degree of importance attached to the military justice function, the act provided for the appointment of an Air Force judge advocate general by the president for a four-year term. Based upon a Senate amendment, the act also provided that the secretary of the Air Force would charge the under secretary or an assistant secretary to supervise all activities of the reserve components of the Air Force. The Air Force was generally satisfied with the Air Force Organization Act, but there were reports that some commands which had not been recognized as major commands did not like the implication that they must be minor commands. The Tactical Air Command viewed the act as a milestone in its struggle for status and recognition. Representative Vinson also commented that the organization act obviously would result in greater emphasis being placed on the tactical air mission within the Air Force.[152]

Air Buildup: 95-Wing Program

While the Air Force was reorganizing in 1950 and 1951 to meet worldwide commitments, Secretary Finletter and General Vandenberg confronted the problem of expanding its strength. Based on the requirements noted in NSC-68, the expansion of the Air Force was initially undertaken in context with the expansion of all of the military services. Early in July 1950 the Joint Chiefs of Staff approved the force compositions it thought were necessary to support the additional requirements of the Korean fighting and to commence a limited augmentation of American armed forces. On 24 July, President Truman offered a supplemental estimate of appropriations required for this purpose. As enacted on 27 September, the First Supplemental Appropriation Act of 1951 made $11.7 billion available to the Department of Defense in addition to the $13.3 billion carried in the Defense Appropriation Act of 1951. Finletter estimated that only about $4.5 billion of the supplemental appropriation was designed to cover the current costs of the Korean War and that the remainder was to provide for a basic buildup. For the Air Force, the supplemental appropriation included the costs of an expansion from 48 to 58 wings, or the addition of 10 tactical air wings that were mobilized from the Air National Guard and the Air Force Reserve during the summer of 1950. For the Navy the supplemental appropriation permitted the operation of three additional attack carrier groups, three antisubmarine carrier groups, seven patrol squadrons, and nine attack and ten escort aircraft carriers.[153]

In its postwar planning the Air Force had emphasized a requirement for a minimum peacetime strength of 70 groups and 22 separate, autonomous squadrons. This objective had been stated at a time when Russia did not have an atomic bomb and possessed very little air power. During July and August 1950, however, it was obvious to air planners that 58 wings or even 70 wings would be insufficient to the tasks then confronting the United States. Studies as to the requirements within the Air Force finally firmed up at a figure of 163 wings (138 combat and 25 troop carrier), but Air Force planners feared that a request for such an authorization would be rejected out of hand as the project of air power extremists. In August 1950 Vandenberg accordingly forwarded a requirement to the Joint Chiefs for the augmentation of the Air Force to a strength of 130 wings — 114 combat and 16 troop carrier. Acting at the time of the initial United Nations' reverses in Korea, the Joint Chiefs on 1 September 1950 approved a buildup of the Air Force to a strength of 95 wings — 80 combat and 15 troop carrier — by 30 June 1954. In the emergency created by the entry of the Chinese Communists into the Korean War, the National Security Council (NSC) on 14 December recommended that the Air Force attain a strength of 87 wings by 30 June 1951 and 95 wings by June 1952. The NSC also directed establishing an expanded military production capacity that would considerably reduce the time required for a full mobilization of military forces. To cover the additional costs of the Korean War and the expansion of military forces during the balance of fiscal year 1951, funds in the amount of $16.8 billion were approved in the Second Supplemental Appropriation Act of 1951, which became law on 6 January 1951. In the Fourth Supplemental Appropriation Act of 1951, which became law on 31 May 1951, Congress voted the Department of Defense an additional $6.4 billion to cover deficiencies in the pay and support of the increased forces. The appropriation brought the total amount appropriated to the Department of Defense for fiscal year 1951 to $48.2 billion.[154]

In the summer of 1950 both the Air Force and the Navy recognized that the aircraft industries of the United States were in a very critical position because of the limited orders for military aircraft that had been placed in the late 1940s. In August 1950 Adm Forrest P. Sherman, chief of naval operations, stated that the requirement for a greatly augmented production of military aircraft was even greater than it had been in early May 1940, when the United States had markedly increased aircraft production to meet the needs of an impending World War II.[155] Under Secretary of the Air Force John A. McCone also explained that the Air

Force wanted an immediate increase in aircraft production. "The Air Force policy," he said, "has been to build up to maximum acceleration irrespective of the fact that by so doing we could look forward to the time when, in the absence of a further appropriation, production would drop off very precipitately."[156] Quickly implementing the National Security Council's directive to establish a military production capacity that would considerably reduce the time required for full mobilization if a decision was made to do so later in 1951, Secretary of Defense Marshall issued orders on 18 December that the Department of Defense would follow an extraordinary broad-based procurement policy. Marshall specifically directed that contracts were to be spread across industry as widely as possible; additional contractors instead of extra-shift or overtime operations were to be used whenever time permitted; open industrial capacity would be used to the maximum before the expansion of facilities was authorized; and the prime contractors were to be encouraged and, if necessary, required to subcontract in order that the fullest use would be made of small business.[157]

Given the acceptance of this broad-based production concept, which would permit a potential doubling of production in an emergency, the Air Force could agree to the relatively low strength of 95 wings.[158] Nevertheless, Vandenberg warned that "an Air Force of 95 wings cannot be considered sufficient to win a major war by defeating superior strength both in the air and on the ground. A force of this size is intended primarily as a deterrent. It is hoped also that such a force might be able to stave off defeat if the enemy should decide to risk the consequences of all-out warfare."[159] Finletter also supported the 95-wing program, but only as a means of preventing disaster.[160] The 95-wing program called for establishing and modernizing 95 Air Force wings, 34 separate squadrons, 30 military air transport squadrons, 11 Air National Guard wings, plus a war reserve of 3,578 modern aircraft.[161] As finally programmed, the composition of the 95-wing force included four heavy bombardment, 22 medium bombardment, three fighter escort, three heavy strategic reconnaissance, and five medium strategic reconnaissance wings for the Strategic Air Command; 20 wings of fighter interceptors for the Air Defense Command and theater air forces; and four light bombardment, 15 fighter-bomber, four tactical reconnaissance, three heavy troop carrier, and 12 medium troop carrier wings for the Tactical Air Command and theater air forces. The initial thrust toward attainment of the 95-wing strength came from the mobilization of reserve units; by the end of May 1951 all Air Force Reserve wings—20 troop carrier and five light bombardment—had entered the federal service, as had 22 Air National Guard wings—17 fighter, three light bombardment, and two tactical reconnaissance wings. Many of the Air Reserve wings were short of personnel; only 13 of them could be retained as units—the other 12 had to be broken up for fillers and replacements. One of the 22 Air National Guard wings ordered into active service was converted into a light bombardment combat crew training school.[162] In his specific comment regarding the allocation of units under the 95-wing program, Vandenberg was most dissatisfied with the air defense allocations. "The fighters that we have now," he said, "are spread very thinly and there are many holes. In the 95-group program, the provision of defense will still be, in my opinion, inadequate."[163] To bulwark continental air defense, the 95-wing planning called for the rebuilding of 11 Air National Guard wings and their equipment with jet fighter-interceptors.[164]

In comparison with fiscal year 1950, when only 1,246 aircraft had been authorized for its procurement, the Air Force's expanded aircraft procurement funds of fiscal year 1951 permitted it to place orders for 8,578 planes. Included were 44 B-36Hs, 39 RB-36Hs, 532 B-47s, 52 RB-47s, 3,993 jet fighters, 130 RF-84F tactical reconnaissance planes, 22 SA-16A search and rescue amphibians, 231 KC-97 tankers, 656 cargo aircraft, 2,373 trainers, 182 helicopters, and 111 liaison aircraft.[165] Even though the procurement program was greatly expanded, the Air Force had not been able to lay down a single new basic aircraft design since 1947, and the fiscal year 1951 procurements did not represent any substantial increases in the state of the aeronautical art. The B-47 jet bombers — ordered in substantial quantities as successors to B-29s — could cruise at 500 miles an hour, but their limited combat range would force them to operate from overseas bases.

The fighter-interceptors that were procured in quantity — the F-89, F-86D, and the F-94 — were designed to counter a Soviet Tu-4 capability that probably would not be a major threat after 1954. The only long-range escort fighter that could be provided to the Strategic Air Command was the F-84F, which would have in-flight refueling capabilities. However, because of a pressing requirement for fighter-bombers in autumn of 1951, most of the Strategic Air Command's fighter-escort wings were reassigned to the Tactical Air Command.[166]

During fiscal year 1951 the Joint Chiefs of Staff were no longer limited by a dollar budgetary ceiling given to them in advance. Instead, as Finletter pointed out, "as the Air Force went from 48 wings to 95, the number of Army divisions and of Navy warships went up apace. The Division-by-Services method continued to rule."[167] In June 1950 the Army possessed 10 divisions, but during fiscal year 1951 it was authorized to expand to 18 divisions and separate combat elements equivalent to six additional divisions. The augmentation of the Army reflected war requirements in Korea, but on 9 September 1950 President Truman announced that the Army would send four divisions to Europe to bolster the two divisions that were already assigned to the North Atlantic Treaty Organization.[168] In fiscal year 1951 the Navy increased its operating force of large carriers from seven to 12 and its force of light and escort carriers from eight to 15. This immediate increase returned reserve fleet units to active service. But, recognizing that converted World War II carriers could not well accommodate the heavier aircraft that the Navy was developing, Congress authorized the construction of a 57,000-ton aircraft carrier that would serve as a prototype for future development. The Marine Corps also increased to a strength of two and one-third divisions and two air wings.[169]

Added Requirements for Air Power

In discussing the Department of Defense buildup, Secretary Finletter was convinced that "the time is past when we can any longer go on with the idea that if one service gets something the other services must get, roughly speaking, a like amount."[170] The Air Force accepted the 95-wing program only because it included a broadening of the nation's industrial base to support a future all-out mobilization. "We believe," Finletter explained, "that we cannot afford now to build up a standing military establishment which will be able to fight the war through. We believe that any such military establishment would run into fantastic sums of money which would be a drain on the economy which the country should not be asked to bear."[171] Although Finletter and Vandenberg believed that the Air Force's strength should be increased to something on the order of 138 to 140 wings, they agreed to accept a force objective of 95 wings during fiscal year 1952. The national defense budget submitted to Congress early in 1951 called for an expenditure of $20.8 billion for the Army, $15.1 billion for the Navy, and $19.8 billion for the Air Force, plus additional amounts for military construction.[172] While Finletter and Vandenberg were willing to agree with administration policy, they were subjected to heavy pressure from forces outside the Air Force to come out in favor of large increases in air capabilities.

Alarmed by President Truman's intention of committing six US divisions to the North Atlantic Treaty Organization and favoring a buildup of the Air Force for the defense of Europe rather than the employment of ground forces, Sen Kenneth S. Wherry introduced a resolution calling upon the Senate's Armed Services and Foreign Relations Committees to report whether the Senate ought to adopt a policy on the movement of ground troops to Europe. Joint hearings conducted by two committees during February 1951 turned into an examination of the nation's strategy and particularly the contributions that air power could make to the defense of NATO. In common with the other members of the Joint Chiefs, Vandenberg supported the administration's plan to augment the NATO surface forces. "If we do have a strong strategic air arm," he explained,

> we would be able to knock out the industrial potential of an enemy country. The effect of that would take some time. In other words, down on the front lines, where there have been stockpiles of ammunition, food, gasoline, transportation, in the short distance that we are viewing in Western Europe I am of the opinion that without a delaying force it would be possible [for the Soviet forces] to move to the coast in spite of the fact that we did or were able to knock out [their] industrial potential.... The greatest effect, in my opinion, from that strategic effort would be if we had a force in place that was adequate to insure that they used up their stockpile of equipment and held them so that Western Europe could be saved from being overrun.[173]

In an interview in January 1951, de Seversky favored giving all possible assistance to European nations to permit them to rearm, but he wished to ensure that European rearmament would be orderly. "Russia will not sit passively by and tolerate our building a European army that eventually will be able to challenge it," he said. He noted further that

> Russia will nip that undertaking in the bud, unless we find means of deterring Russia while the reconstruction of European strength is going on. Only American long-range air power which has the vitality to denude Russia of its sinews of war, operating directly from the United States and partially from Great Britain, from bases inaccessible to Russian armies, can deter Russia from interfering with the rearmament of Europe.... Our present Strategic Air Force is well conceived, well manned and well led, but it is only a token force. The Strategic Air Force will not be able to destroy the Russian industrial complex until it destroys the Russian Air Force and wins command of the air.[174]

Writing in April, General Spaatz called upon the United States to provide the minimum divisions required to give Western Europe the courage to build up its strength; but he decried the acceptance of the "wall of the flesh strategy," which he said was "the prevailing philosophy in Washington today." Spaatz stated that the Soviet Union had built up a 10-to-1 superiority in jet fighters over the United States. "While we pursue the wall of flesh philosophy," he said, "we are losing the first and crucial battle in any possible war with Russia—the battle for command of the air."[175]

Many Republican senators opposed the commitment of American ground forces to the defense of Europe. However, on 3 April 1951 Sen Henry Cabot Lodge, Jr., led a bipartisan effort that defeated a joint resolution that would have forbidden Truman from sending more than four divisions to Europe. Another resolution calling upon Truman to send no ground troops until the Joint Chiefs certified that "sufficient air strength will be available to control the air over western Europe to the degree necessary to assure the safety and effectiveness of US ground troops" was also defeated. On 4 April the Senate passed a resolution approving the commitment of the four additional divisions to Europe, but only if the Joint Chiefs of Staff certified that this was an essential step in strengthening the security of the United States.[176] Writing to Lodge on 6 April, Prof W. Barton Leach agreed that the additional divisions ought to be sent to Europe; however, he asked Lodge to consider that the placing of so many troops and their dependents in "a fight-to-the-death combat zone" would be "a very serious matter unless a counterpoise to Soviet air power in this area is provided."[177] In a speech in the Senate on 30 April, which he credited Leach with inspiring, Senator Lodge called attention to the fact that published reports set the strength of the Soviet tactical air force at between 16,000 and 20,000 planes, of which some 9,000 were available for an attack in Western Europe. Based on his appraisal that air defense and strategic air forces ought to be increased in size and that the NATO air forces ought to have a two-to-one numerical superiority over Soviet tactical air forces, Lodge stated his conviction that the United States Air Force ought, as soon as possible, to be increased from 95 to a minimum of 150 groups. "Some say," Lodge remarked, "that to be certain of our superiority and not leave our destiny to the fortunes of battle, we should have 175 groups. Certainly 150 groups will get us started off the present dead center of disastrous military inadequacy."[178]

According to Leach, Finletter and Vandenberg were embarrassed to learn of his correspondence with Senator Lodge. Finletter had taken a strong position within the Air Force against end runs to Congress, and both he and Vandenberg felt that they should not communicate with Lodge unless he requested it. According to Leach, they also feared that a buildup of tactical air power in Europe might result in a reduction of the proper emphasis on the Strategic Air Command. They doubted that production would be adequate to sustain the larger Air Force, and they feared that the cost of building tactical air bases in Europe would require an excessive expansion of Air Force infrastructure.[179] Appearing before the Senate Subcommittee on Military Appropriations on 13 July, Senator Lodge made an extensive statement favoring an Air Force of 150 combat wings. At this time Finletter agreed that the proper way to allocate defense funds was to identify the tasks to be performed and make recommendations to carry them out. Both Finletter and Vandenberg pointed out the limited capabilities of a 95-wing Air Force, but Finletter proposed that any action to expand further than this ought to await a Department of Defense review, which would take place in the autumn. Other than for answering specific questions, neither Air Force official committed himself to Lodge's proposals. However, Finletter remarked: "The existing power of the Russians is such that it would probably be impossible to hold them if it were not for one factor, and that is at the moment the United States has a great superiority in atomic weapons and in the ability to deliver them." And Vandenberg noted that "within the limits of the money given to us we should endeavor to free the Air Force as much as possible from the requirement for overseas bases in the hands of other powers." Vandenberg also explained his rule for measuring the proper size of the Air Force:

> There is only one valid measure of the adequacy of our own strength in the air, and that is the air strength of a potential enemy. If he decreases his air strength-in-readiness, our requirements may be reduced. But as he increases his ready air forces ours must be correspondingly increased if we are to guard against the swiftest kind of military disaster. Whatever our plan or policy we have no choice but to maintain superiority in the air.[180]

Taking his case for expanded air power to the American people, Senator Lodge published an article entitled "Let's Face It—We're in a Jam" in the *Saturday Evening Post* on 28 July 1951.[181]

The "great debate" over the dispatch of American ground divisions to Europe produced many reasons for the expansion of American air power, but both the Truman administration and Congress remained committed to the balanced forces included in the original fiscal year 1952 budget. When the appropriations for fiscal year were totaled, Congress appropriated $59.4 billion of the $60.7 billion requested and subsequently provided another $1 billion to meet additional costs arising from combat operations in Korea.[182] Granted a total obligational authority of $21.6 billion, the Army increased its force level from 18 to 20 combat divisions.

With $15.6 billion in new obligational authority, the Navy continued the construction of its large aircraft carrier, which was now named the USS *Forrestal*, and began its sister ship, which Secretary of the Navy Dan A. Kimball indicated would be the second of the fleet of 12 modern carriers that the Navy would require. In August 1951 the Navy awarded a contract for the construction of a prototype nuclear submarine to be named the *Nautilus*. The Marine Corps organized and started training the Third Marine Division and the Third Marine Aircraft Wing.[183] With $22.2 billion in new obligational authority for fiscal year 1952, the Air Force completed the activation of its 95 wings in June 1952 and placed orders for 6,944 aircraft during the year. Most of these planes were already familiar types. But for the first time in several years the Air Force instituted procurement of new types of improved aircraft, including three B-52As and 17 RB-52Bs; the latter could serve as intercontinental jet bombers when their reconnaissance pods were replaced with bomb racks. In response to the Tactical Air Command's requirements for a night intruder and night tactical reconnaissance aircraft to replace obsolete B-26 types, the Air Force issued purchase orders for 110 B-57s and 67 RB-57s, these planes to be an American version of the British Canberra jet. Designed to replace RB-45 aircraft, the Air Force ordered a test quantity of five RB-66A jet aircraft from Douglas. The principal jet fighters on order were F-84s, F-86s, F-89s, and F-94s, but the Air Force issued an order for two YF-100As and a production quantity of 23 F-100s — these aircraft being improved F-86s, which would be known as the Super Sabre. Marking realization of the decision made in 1950 to abandon the use of powerless gliders in future airborne operations, the Air Force ordered 244 C-123s, which would be used as assault transports and would be capable of landings and takeoffs from short and rough strips.[184]

Air Objectives Expand to 143 Wings

During his tenure of office, Secretary Marshall had sought to meet immediate military requirements and to broaden the nation's mobilization base. When Robert A. Lovett became secretary of defense, he called upon the Joint Chiefs of Staff to make decisions as to the force levels beginning in fiscal year 1953 that the United States would require for the next several years. "We must try to do first things first," stated Lovett, "and not everything at once."[185] When they surveyed national requirements and capabilities during October 1951, the Joint Chiefs of Staff evidently were impressed by the growth of Soviet air capabilities as compared with those of the United States. The notion that the United States could easily and cheaply achieve qualitative superiority over a technically inept enemy was dispelled by the appearance and performance of MiG-15 aircraft in the air over Korea.[186] Vandenberg pointed out that the Soviet Union had engaged in a forced-draft development and expansion of its air power, with the result that the Red air force not only was quantitatively larger than the US Air Force but also converting to modern jet equipment more rapidly.[187] Speaking "not in prophecy but from facts," General Twining stated that the commander of the Soviet long-range air force had several hundred Tu-4s at his disposal and that a new Soviet bomber of original design had been observed over Moscow in 1951. According to best estimates, the Soviet atomic stockpile would soon reach a level that could critically cripple the war-making capabilities of the United States. In 1950-51 the Soviets also rapidly expanded the radar-intercept and antiaircraft artillery defenses of their homeland. In addition to these augmentations, the Soviets increased the strength of their already powerful tactical air armies. As a result of a prodigious postwar effort plus aircraft remaining from World War II, the Soviet Union had about 20,000 aircraft in organized air units and an equal number in various forms of reserve.[188] Unless the size of the US Air Force and its rate of development were increased, Vandenberg predicted that the narrowing margin of air superiority it held "will shrink to nothing in another 6 years, and control of the air, with all that it implies, will then be within the grasp of the Soviet Union."[189]

After what General Bradley described as "a very long study," the Joint Chiefs of Staff concluded that the Air Force was "assuming more than its share of the calculated risk" and agreed that the United States must increase its combat air power.[190] More specifically, the Joint Chiefs recommended that the Air Force should maintain a force level at which, in the event of a general war, it could accomplish the following essential D-day tasks: (1) defend, by both offensive and defensive air operations, critical areas in the western hemisphere, with particular emphasis on defense against atomic air attack; (2) conduct a strategic air offensive designed to destroy the vital elements of the enemy's war-making capacity; (3) assist in the defense of the NATO area and critical areas in the Far East, including the maintenance and defense of essential base areas and lines of communication; and (4) provide such aid to the nation's allies as would be essential to the execution of their responsibilities. The Joint Chiefs recognized that the missions of air defense and strategic air warfare were essential D-day tasks. Vandenberg stated the corollary rule

> that the No. 1 priority task of the Strategic Air Command, in event of war, is to attack the enemy's atomic delivery capability at the outset of hostilities. We place such high priority on this task because we know that our continental air defense system, however good, could not stop all the bombers that might be sent against us. Hence our long-range atomic counterattack against enemy air forces must of necessity provide the principal means of our air defense of American cities and centers of production.[191]

"In spite of the fact that air power alone can never be decisive in total war," said General Bradley, "the air battle must be won if a war is to be won."[192] Reflecting the importance of air power and the principle of putting first things first, the Joint Chiefs unanimously recommended that the Army be stabilized at a force level of 20 divisions and the Navy at 409 major combat ships with three Marine divisions and three Marine air wings and that the Air Force be expanded to 143 wings, including 126 combat and 17 troop carrier wings. Although 1954 had previously been mentioned as the year of maximum danger, the Joint Chiefs now officially accepted that date as being the threshold year in which the Soviet Union would attain the capability to inflict critical and possibly fatal damage to the war-making capabilities of the United States. They also expected that the buildup of North Atlantic defenses after 1954 would be such that the Kremlin's chances of overrunning Europe would begin to decrease. The Joint Chiefs did not assume that a war would begin in 1954, but they believed that the year would be a very dangerous period. Based on projection of America's industrial capabilities, the Joint Chiefs stated that the increase of the Air Force to 143 wings could be accomplished by 1 July 1954 and, from a military point of view, recommended that the 143-wing program ought to be accomplished by that date.[193] The Joint Chiefs submitted these recommendations to Secretary Lovett in October 1951. After the recommendations had been studied by an ad hoc committee chaired by Prof James R. Killian of the Massachusetts Institute of Technology, Lovett approved them and successfully defended the program before the National Security Council. President Truman approved the military buildup at a meeting in the White House on 28 December 1951, but he directed Lovett to stretch out the program in order that the armed forces budget, including military assistance for fiscal year 1953, would be less than $60 billion.[194]

Since the Air Force had stated requirements for an expansion to 155 wings (138 combat and 17 troop carrier), the acceptance by the Joint Chiefs of only 143 wings committed the Air Force to a program that Finletter described as having no fat in it. Except for "a very small number of wings" to be left in the Far East at the end of the Korean War, Finletter stated that the 143-wing program contained "no wings capable of fighting anywhere else outside of the air defense of the United States, the strategic air operations against any aggressor, and the tactical air operations in Europe."[195] As established, the 143-wing objective placed emphasis upon the strategic air force and the air defense force, which Vandenberg stressed as being "complementary parts of the air weapon system and ... each ... essential to the air defense of the United States." The Strategic Air Command's share of the 143-wing strength included seven heavy bombardment, 30 medium bombardment, 10 strategic fighter, four heavy strategic reconnaissance, and six medium strategic reconnaissance wings. Representing a substantial increase, 29 fighter-interceptor wings were programmed, most of them to be assigned to the Air Defense Command. Designed "to operate where the Army operates," the tactical air units of the 143-wing program were computed in terms of training requirements in the United States, a heavy commitment to the NATO area, and a minimal establishment in the Far East. Tactical air units would include two tactical bomber, five light bombardment, six day fighter, 22 fighter-bomber, five tactical reconnaissance, four heavy troop carrier, and 13 medium troop carrier wings.[196]

Secretary Finletter hailed the 143-wing authorization as "a decision of great moment" that broke the division-by-services defense funds allocation pattern, but Truman's decision to hold military spending below $60 billion delayed the earliest date of readiness of the modernized Air Force to 30 June 1955.[197] Even with the delay of the readiness date, the 143-wing program could be achieved only by the most stringent manning standards and economies of allocation of first-line aircraft, including the elimination of any combat reserve, the cancellation of a planned modernization of the 11 Air National Guard wings, and the equipping of no more than half of the Air Reserve wings with first-line aircraft.[198] The decision to eliminate the hoary old requirements for a combat reserve of aircraft and aircrews was not made lightly. "We are doing it," Finletter explained, "because we are trying to concentrate the dollar on the striking power on D-day. It is an enormous saving. . . . It is possible that we have made a mistake, but I do not think so. I think the important thing is to concentrate on striking power on D-day, even though the forces may be attrited downward sharply thereafter."[199] General Twining noted that the deficiency in war reserves would be felt in five ways.

> First, our capacity to continue long-range atomic attack would be sharply reduced after the crucial initial phase. . . . Second, our capacity to make good the attrition of our air units in Europe would remain slight for some time after the outset of hostilities. Third, our capacity to make good the attrition among Allied air units using American equipment would be extremely limited. . . . Fourth, our capacity to augment our air strength in the Far East in the event of a general war would be severely limited. Fifth, in the light of these realities the force contemplated . . . is down to the "bare bones."[200]

In view of the prominence accorded to the Air Force in the defense budget for fiscal year 1953, Air Force leaders fully presented their concepts of air power to Congress early in 1952. Finletter related air power to deterrence. "What we are trying to do," he said, "is to create and maintain a military force sufficiently strong—with relationship to a possible enemy's capability—to be able to persuade him not to attack us—and then back off this protective shield of strength to work to achieve peace. Nothing must be held back in terms of money or national effort which would prevent us doing the very best we possibly can to prevent the happening of such a catastrophe."[201] In view of the wide interest in the subject, Vandenberg again explained the meaning of air superiority. "The most inefficient way to operate one's air force against another force," he said, "is to try to destroy it in the air. . . . The main defense of the United States lies in the strategic air arm's ability to destroy the bases. That is the only efficient way to knock a possible air force out of the air and get air superiority. In the meantime, however, you must utilize also as much as possible planes to cause them attrition in their attack; to blunt their attack against us." Referring to the situation over North Korea, where neither side had destroyed the other's air bases, Vandenberg showed that local air superiority fluctuated between the Communists and the United Nations air forces according to which side put forward the most effort at a particular time. Under these circumstances, Vandenberg continued: "Air superiority is a fleeting thing . . . until either the factories that produce the aircraft or the oil and/or the airfields and the airplanes are eliminated. Anyone with a small force can get local air superiority at times."[202] Later on General Bradley was asked to comment on Vandenberg's explanation of air superiority. "In my opinion," Bradley said, "air superiority should be talked about only in relation to certain areas. You gain it over one area, and lose it over another one. Apparently, he was talking about over-all superiority of aircraft."[203]

Despite a very thorough presentation of national defense requirements, the Department of Defense had trouble getting the total amount of the fiscal year 1953 budget approved by Congress. As recommended by its Committee on Appropriations, the House made a $4.2 billion cut in requested appropriations, including a $1.6-billion cut in funds requested for the Air Force. "Some way must be found," stated the House committee, "to shock the people in the Department of Defense from top to bottom into the full realization that the Congress and the American people will not tolerate flagrant waste in money and manpower." Strong arguments offered by Finletter, Vandenberg, and Bradley resulted in the Senate Committee on Appropriations and subsequently the Senate restoring most of the requested Air Force funds. Approved during July 1952, the Department of Defense Appropriation Act for 1953 and the Supplemental Appropriation Act of Defense for 1953 covering military construction made $46.9 billion of new obligational authority available for the Department of Defense, including $13.2 billion for the Army, $12.6 billion for the Navy, and $20.6 billion for the Air Force.[204]

Under the ground rules adopted within the Department of Defense, the Army and Navy maintained their existing force levels but continued force modernization during the year following 1 July 1952. For the Navy this force modernization included the continued construction of the second large aircraft carrier (the *Saratoga*) and the start of a second nuclear submarine.[205] After attaining its 95-wing strength in June 1952, the Air Force began to build toward the 143-wing objective. The controlling factors in the Air Force's augmentation were the availability of personnel, equipment, and facilities, especially in overseas areas where airfield construction did not go as rapidly as anticipated. At the end of fiscal year 1953, the Air Force possessed 106 activated wings and an authorized total strength of 1,019,000.[206] In placing orders for aircraft procurement from fiscal year 1953 funds, the Air Force was affected increasingly by growing inflation — which accounted for an increase in dollar costs of 15 to 20 percent over 1950 levels — and by the high cost of complex modern aircraft.[207] Upon meeting its requirement for large conventional strategic bombers, the Air Force ordered no additional B-36s, but placed 500 B-47Es, 65 RB-47s, and 43 RB-52Bs on order for the Strategic Air Command. The RB-52Bs ordered with fiscal 1952 and 1953 funds would later be redesignated as ZB-52Bs. The Air Force ordered 26 B-66Bs, 73 RB-66Bs, 191 B-57Bs, and 80 RF-84Fs for service in tactical air units. It also issued orders for 2,510 jet fighters, 262 KC-97G tankers, 418 cargo aircraft, 1,158 trainers, 193 helicopters, and 20 liaison aircraft.[208]

Tactical Air and Air Defense Studies

Following the beginning of hostilities in Korea, Secretary Finletter and other Air Force leaders continued to give first priority to the development of the

Strategic Air Command; even though military appropriations were much larger, Finletter ruefully remarked that with the public and within the Department of Defense "the fashion moved away from strategic air in favor of tactical air and air defense."[209] Given the fact of life that total Air Force appropriations would continue to be a finite quantity calculated in terms of the economic product of the United States, the subtle downgrading of the Strategic Air Command was evident both in the proportional force composition of the 143-wing program and in the elaborate interest in tactical air and air defense that was manifest in studies conducted within the Department of Defense during 1951–53.

Following the same research pattern that was being used to study national air defense requirements, the secretaries of the Army, Navy, and Air Force early in 1951 asked the California Institute of Technology to study some of the problems of ground and tactical air warfare, especially as they would relate to the defense of Western Europe, and to report suggestions as to how the military establishment might improve its weapons, techniques, and tactics. To accomplish this study, called Project Vista, California Institute's president Dr Lee A. DuBridge, who served as chairman of the project, and William A. Fowler, who acted as the project's scientific director, built a scientific and technical staff of 113 members, of whom 39 were from the institute's faculty. Several retired military officers, including Generals Wedemeyer and Quesada, participated in the nine-month study before it was completed and forwarded to the secretaries of the Army, Navy, and Air Force on 4 February 1952.[210]

According to the Vista report, "any battle of Western Europe will ultimately be won or lost on the ground." Believing that it would be possible to defend Western Europe successfully prior to 1954, Vista recommended an augmentation of Army capabilities there and the adoption of ground tactics to force attacking enemy forces into concentrations that would make attractive targets for massive air strikes with atomic or conventional explosives. Despite this emphasis on the ground mission, Vista recognized that "the successful defense of Western Europe may hinge mainly on the extent to which United States and Allied tactical air power is effectively employed." Taking consideration of the increasing size of the American atomic stockpile, Vista recommended a substantial increase in tactical nuclear weapons and the building of NATO tactical air units to a strength of approximately 10,000 aircraft, to include 1,500 air-superiority fighters, 3,500 all-weather interceptors, 3,000 fighter-bombers, 1,500 attack aircraft, and 500 tactical bombers. Vista also recommended that the United States Army ought to have two airborne units of corps strength by 1954 — one to be stationed in the United States and the other in Europe — and that 400 C-124 and 850 C-123 transport aircraft should be procured to transport and support this airborne force.[211]

In its description of the air power mission in Europe, Vista contemplated that the battle for air superiority would be of "overwhelming importance" during the period immediately following the outbreak of war — a period which might "last only a few days and will probably not exceed a few months." In a special study on air superiority included in the Vista report, Albert C. Reed advanced the proposition:

"Air superiority has two parts, freedom and denial, both of which must be accomplished.... It is important to note that we are not attempting to deny the USSR the use of the air; but rather, we are trying to prevent the damage that their operations might do to our war effort. In turn, we are not asking for freedom to fly, but rather for freedom to inflict damage upon the USSR." Reed proposed that the criteria for air superiority were the principles of concentration, surprise, and versatility; he argued that air superiority could not be attained by a concentration of tactical atomic aircraft against Soviet airfields at the outset of hostilities. He further proposed that antiaircraft artillery would be useful chiefly for defense of point objectives, that air-to-air fighting did not promise to be very effective, that NATO air and ground forces should emphasize passive air defense measures, and that bomber aircraft should depend upon high-speed and low-altitude attacks, weather, darkness, and countermeasures rather than fighter escort and defensive armament as protection against hostile interceptors. He noted that during World War II when strong fighter escort was employed, the 8-percent loss rate that US daylight strategic bomber forces otherwise sustained was cut roughly in half. However, he argued that some part of this reduction in losses was attributable to the heavy air attacks mounted against German airfields prior to Normandy and to a shift of sizable numbers of German day fighters to the Russian and Normandy fronts. "There is strong reason to believe," he said, "that the escort fighters might have been much more effective as fighter-bombers used against German fighter bases."[212]

Based largely on the analysis of air superiority requirements, Vista recommended that the United States should assume responsibility for developing a NATO tactical air force — including a tactical atomic air force — and that Great Britain should assume responsibility for the operation of a NATO air defense force, the latter to operate in the zone beginning 150 miles behind the front lines. Vista proposed to recognize air transport and air reconnaissance as missions of essentially equal importance for planning purposes to the classical tactical air power missions of air superiority, interdiction, and close air support. In the initial stage of war, the tactical air force would be concentrated against Soviet air facilities, with secondary importance to be given to attacks against enemy forward supply depots, petroleum-oil-and-lubricant dumps, and high command headquarters. After the air battle had reached a conclusion, Army support operations and interdiction would be of major importance. Since the close integration of air and ground weapon systems would be important, Vista recommended major changes in air-ground doctrine. Although it recommended that the joint operations center at the tactical air force-field army level be retained as an allocating agency, Vista proposed that detailed control functions should be exercised by tactical air direction centers at the corps levels. The project report also proposed that, at a time directed by the supreme commander, approximately one squadron from the tactical atomic air force should be allocated to the mission control of each field army commander to accomplish ground support atomic delivery and reconnaissance missions. This mission control authority was to include detailed target selection, attack timing, and "go" and "no-go" commands. Although the major contention of the report was that a sufficient tactical air force should be built to accomplish basic theater air missions, Vista recommended that the Supreme Headquarters Allied Powers Europe (SHAPE) should be authorized to coordinate Strategic Air Command and naval air operations in the NATO theater.[213] "We believe," Vista concluded, "that the United States, in collaboration with its allies in the North Atlantic Treaty Organization, can prevent the military conquest of Western Europe by the Soviet Union—and can do this in 1952 if necessary—if we try."[214]

According to an understanding between the Air Force and the Massachusetts Institute of Technology, the university had conducted an initial study, Project Charles, of the nation's air defense requirements, which were to be further explored at a new electronics laboratory. The Air Force put up the money for the building of physical facilities near Bedford, Massachusetts; the Army, Navy, and Air Force jointly agreed on a charter for the laboratory, designated as Lincoln Laboratory; and the university was to be responsible for the day-to-day supervision of the laboratory. Much of the work of Lincoln Laboratory lay in the development of electronic equipment and techniques; but, in the summer of 1952, the laboratory's steering committee invited a study panel, called the Summer Study Group, to take a look at air defense problems that might be encountered in the period 1960-70. The Summer Study Group included a number of scientists who had been on the staff of Project Vista. In its report, which was presented simultaneously to the National Security Resources Board and the Department of Defense in late August 1952, the Summer Study Group foresaw no effective defense against intercontinental missiles. However, it believed that the establishment of an air defense "of a kind and scale not hitherto required" could result in the interception and destruction of 85 to 95 percent of such hostile aircraft as might attempt to attack the United States. Such a defense required three to six hours of early warning of approaching jet aircraft, and the Summer Study Group called for the establishment of a northward defense in depth. Included would be a distant early warning line—or DEW line—of radars to be sited as far north as the 75th parallel. Behind this line would be the double perimeter warning and control network that already was being established. At first the Summer Study Group estimated that the DEW line would cost $370 million plus $106 million in annual maintenance costs, but it later placed a $20-billion price on a total project that would include computerized air direction centers. The group recommended an all-out program to make the expanded air defenses operational by the end of 1954.[215] During the summer of 1952, there was evidently some interchange of concepts between the Summer Study Group and the concurrently active Project East River, a civil-defense oriented study jointly sponsored by the National Security Resources Board and the Air Force. This latter study project was administered by Associated Universities, Incorporated, and was headed by Lloyd V. Berkner, a naval reserve captain who had been a member of the wartime Research and Development Board. Issued on 1 October 1952, the Project East

River report concluded that the critical factor in civil defense would be to get enough advanced warning of an enemy air attack to permit civilian evacuation measures. Specifically, an hour or more of early warning was required if a civil defense program was to be effective.[216]

The net effect of projects Vista and East River and of the Summer Study Group was to focus a substantial amount of attention upon the national defense strategy and inferentially upon the role to be played by the Strategic Air Command. The reports challenged the Strategic Air Command indirectly. "We raise the question whether," stated Vista,

> if the United States prepares to counter Soviet aggression *solely* through the use of strategic air power, we will not be weakening rather than strengthening the political and psychological positions of the free nations. The Western European nations surely fear that a strategic air attack on the USSR would result in a retaliatory attack on their cities—and would at the same time not stop the march of Soviet armies before they overran all of Europe.... On the other hand, if we plan also to use our air power (including strategic, tactical and naval units) to destroy the march of Russian armies, we can win the confidence of the NATO nations, stimulate their cooperative efforts on the political and economic fronts, increase their strength and thus discourage a Soviet attack.[217]

Neither the Summer Study Group nor Project East River had any occasion to be concerned with the Strategic Air Command, but Berkner was critical of the strategic striking force. "The crux of our present danger," he stated,

> is in our complete dependence upon the "Strategic Striking Force" as the principal element in our defense. This Maginot-Line type of thinking can be out-maneuvered by an intelligent enemy by any one of a number of ways. Opposed to the Maginot-Line concept of "putting all our eggs in one basket," is the balanced and flexible force. Because a balanced force cannot be achieved at tolerable cost through conventional means, we have ignored both the vital need for such a force and the possibility of achieving it through new and unconventional measures.[218]

The Department of Defense and the Air Force already had implemented many of the concepts contained in the Vista report several months before it was completed, but the report did require action by the Defense Department. Many of the ideas presented in Vista continued to show up from time to time. The findings of the Summer Study Group, on the other hand, received immediate and intensive attention at the highest levels. On 24 September 1952 chairman Jack Gorrie of the National Security Resources Board recommended that the National Security Council accept the requirement for the DEW line. Rather than acting immediately as Gorrie desired, the National Security Council remanded the problem to the Department of Defense and the Air Force for study. Asked for its opinion on the DEW line, the Rand Corporation pointed out that the air defense system visualized by the Summer Study Group probably would cost far more than $20 billion and that the costs of air defense would have to come out of some other part of the Air Force. The Air Staff did not oppose establishing the DEW line but questioned the cost estimates for it, and invited attention to the fact that the radar equipment which would be needed was not far enough developed to warrant a crash construction program. With the approval of the Department of Defense, the Air Force allocated $20 million to accelerate research and development of early warning radar equipment suited for employment in an arctic environment. Lovett and Finletter opposed Gorrie's repeated demands for a policy statement authorizing the DEW line. In view of the continuing disagreement, Lovett appointed a Citizens Advisory Committee early in December. He asked the committee, which was headed by Dr Mervin J. Kelly, president of the Bell Telephone Laboratories, to make an independent evaluation of the possibilities of an improved warning system, the relationship of the warning system to other major continental defense measures, and the overall policies and programs needed to achieve a more effective defense of North America against airborne attacks. Without awaiting the additional study, President Truman accepted the National Security Resources Board recommendations on 31 December 1952 and ruled that a continental defense system capable of withstanding any eventuality should be ready for service by the end of 1955. Following this declaration of presidential policy, Lovett informed all concerned in the Department of Defense that the early warning line would be built.[219]

After taking office on 20 January 1953, the new administration of President Dwight D. Eisenhower wished to make a full evaluation of air defense requirements. It accordingly authorized the continuation of the Kelly study and named two other study committees, one under retired Lt Gen Harold Bull and another headed by Lt Gen Idwal Edwards, Air Force deputy chief of staff for operations. While these high-level studies were progressing, Air Force thinkers gave close attention to the theoretical aspects of air defense. The chief question troubling the Air Force was attaining a proper relationship of money allocations between offense and defense within the resources envelope available to the Air Force. Gen Benjamin W. Chidlaw, commander of the Air Defense Command, asserted that "true air defense is not . . . confined solely to the erection of a fortress-type weapons system around a critical area. . . . The tremendous countering power represented by our strategic air arm is . . . a most powerful element of our national defensive structure and warrants continuing high priority consideration." Based on this assessment, Chidlaw reasoned:

> Atomic and hydrogen bombs plus a means of delivering them to a target add up to an overriding need for insuring national survival as to the first step in any nation's military strategy.... This being so, it seems to me that the number one task—chronologically—of each service is to make certain that after the initial attack there remains the means and the reason to accomplish its assigned missions. . . . We must, with accuracy and timeliness, make a true estimate of the threat facing us, then build sufficient defense to insure that our counter offensive can be launched with crushing impact.[220]

Speaking from retirement about his old air defense speciality, General Saville cautioned that a proper defense of the nation required a system designed to ensure the detection, identification, interception, and destruction of attacking air vehicles well before they reached a bomb-release line. "We dare not," Saville said, "concentrate our air defense on merely warning the population to take shelter to save their lives from direct attack." As he had done before, Saville continued to emphasize that air defense was, in the language of the poker player, "an ante-raising operation." "Only a fool would run into a hornet's nest of opposition," he went on to say, "with aircraft too slow or so poorly armed that they would be shot down before they reached their objective. . . . So the first and greatest dividend of air defense is its ability to keep a war from starting by making an attack a difficult and unattractive venture."[221] Unlike other Air Force thinkers who assumed that there was a diminishing utility in expenditures for air defense, Maj Gen Frederic H. Smith, now the Air Defense Command's vice commander, asserted: "There appears to be no leveling off of the curve of cost versus capability which would require the expenditure of enormous sums of money for a small increase in kill. The curve seems to be a relatively straight line, with air defense capability increasing proportionately as additional money is used." As an absolute minimum, Smith urged that sufficient funds should be allocated to provide "that defense necessary to ensure survival of our retaliatory air arm, our industrial potential, and our people's will to fight. . . . It will be fatal if we rationalize ourselves out of providing a defense which will assure survival of our offensive forces and the nation's will to fight."[222]

After five months of study in close association with Army, Navy, Air Force, and Weapons Systems Evaluation Group representatives, Doctor Kelly's Citizens Advisory Committee completed its report in May 1953 and proposed an orderly development of an integrated air defense system for the North American continent. The report emphasized that the principal element of the air defense of the United States, both as a deterrent to war and as a counter to Soviet long-range air power, was the Air Force strategic air arm. It held that an air defense system could best be created by steady technological development supported by a stable and sustained research and development program. It warned that the technical resources for a near perfect air defense were not yet at hand. "So far as can now be foreseen," the Kelly committee reported, "any such level of protection is unattainable and in any case is completely impractical, economically and technically." Even though no system could provide a complete air defense that would destroy all attacking aircraft, the committee found an urgent need for a system "much better than that which is assured under present programs." It specifically recommended that a distant early warning line should be built. Early warning of the approach of hostile aircraft was declared to be the "first essential of an effective active air defense and of a civil defense capable of avoiding a large loss of life." The estimated cost for the full implementation of the Kelly report recommendations ranged from $20 to $25 billion over six years. As a result of the Kelly committee's recommendations, the DEW line would be built, but not as a crash project. The electronic fence would be sited along the 70th parallel, not as far north as recommended by the Summer Group.[223]

Secretary Finletter's Assessments

Spurred on by the Soviet atomic explosion and the local war in Korea, the United States made progress in rebuilding a worldwide air force. But as Secretary Finletter went out of office in January 1953, he was uncertain whether the United States would face up to defense requirements that would exist in about 1955, when the Soviets would possess an "absolute air atomic capability." To counter this threat, he urged that "the first and cardinal job of military planning must be to create a strategic air arm capable of accepting a sneak and devastating attack by assault and sabotage and to have enough left over to go back and utterly devastate Russia." When he spoke of the strategic air arm, Finletter had in mind both the Strategic Air Command and the atomic air units of the Tactical Air Command. Following this concept, he would soon advocate the consolidation of the whole atomic air potential under a single command that he proposed to call the strategic-tactical air command (STAC). In place of the old counter-industry concept for strategic air power, he urged acceptance of a front-to-rear attack concept that would make all enemy targets — from the front lines through communications and supply lines, airfields, and storage back to the sources of production and government direction — the objective of atomic air strikes. In November 1953 Finletter tentatively suggested that Navy atomic aircraft might be included in the nation's strategic air arm. But by August 1954 he had decided that "the whole responsibility for the Atomic-Air mission should be placed on the Air Force's STAC." He reasoned that aircraft carriers would be an increasingly vulnerable and expensive weapon system in a time of plentiful hydrogen bombs. Finletter also opposed the assignment of any "super priority" to air defense, and, because it lacked "powerful deterrent value," he recommended that air defense be put in a second priority immediately after the strategic-tactical air command.[224]

In his valedictory thoughts, Finletter attached priority importance to strategic air and air defense but charged that "the truth of the matter is that ... both strategic air and air defense are being treated in the same fashion — namely they are both being neglected in favor of lower priority forces." While the requirements for air defense had been extensively studied, no similar attention had been focused on the future requirements of the Strategic Air Command. "My main point about the strategic air arm," he said, "is this: it is neglected." Looking to 1955, when the Soviets would have an absolute air atomic capability, the Strategic Air Command would need to be widely dispersed at many operational bases and would require a high-speed refueling capability superior to the conventional KC-97 tankers. Although the Air Force had awarded a development contract for the supersonic-dash B-58 Hustler jet bomber in 1952, Finletter felt that the nation was "failing to move as rapidly as we should into the successors of the B-52." There were indications that the Russians might be leapfrogging bomber development from subsonic aircraft equivalent to B-47s and B-52s to a force composed of bombers equivalent to B-58s. If this development were true, the United States would lose its quality advantage over the Soviets in bomber aircraft.[225] In summary, Finletter recommended that the number one and number two national priorities for defense funds should be assigned to strategic air and air defense. He proposed that the third priority should be given to Army, Navy, and Air Force units needed to provide a force in being in NATO and in the "gray areas," his definition for the Asiatic perimeter running from Turkey to the Aleutians. He recommended that the last priority should be given to other general purpose forces, which would not be needed for A-day tasks but would be useful during the course of a general war or a limited war.[226]

Global Air Power and the Korean Armistice

At the start of the Korean conflict in June 1950, General Vandenberg ordered that the Air Force do its best to meet the requirements of the Far East Air Forces, but he insisted that the Korean War be viewed as a part of a global problem rather than as an isolated situation. From the very beginning, the Korean War was fought under the shadow of the global atomic air capabilities of the Air Force, particularly those of the Strategic Air Command. In July 1950, before Military Air Transport Service planes were fully committed to the trans-Pacific airlift, two Strategic Air Command medium-bomber groups joined another already in England. Early in August, an atomic-capable B-29 group went to Guam and another group augmented by two aerial refueling squadrons deployed to Northeast Air Command bases in Labrador and Newfoundland. At Vandenberg's request, the Joint Chiefs of Staff authorized the temporary movement of four B-29 groups to the Far East to augment firepower in Korea in July and August 1950. In September and October, SAC fighter pilots delivered 180 F-84E aircraft to American air units in Germany.[227]

According to General LeMay, the dispatch of the four Strategic Air Command B-29 groups to participate in the Korean conflict represented a severe reduction in general war deterrent capabilities. LeMay explained Air Force decisions to invest in modern aircraft rather than supply stocks — particularly aircraft engines — had made the Strategic Air Command "a one shot outfit, incapable of sustained operations."[228] Following the strategic bombing campaign against North Korea, two of the SAC B-29 groups returned to the United States in October 1950, but the sudden appearance of Communist MiG-15 jet fighters demanded the hurried movement of a SAC F-84 jet fighter-escort wing and an Eastern Air Defense Force F-86 fighter-interceptor wing to Korea in November 1950. Once again this emergency deployment reduced SAC's global combat capability and badly depleted the air defense of the United States. Early in December 1950, when the Chinese Communists were attacking, General MacArthur asked the Joint Chiefs of Staff to return the two SAC B-29 groups to the Far East. However, the Joint Chiefs proved unwilling to risk the groups on forward airfields that might be exposed to an all-out Communist air attack.[229] As the war conditions darkened, the Strategic Air Command dispatched a fighter-escort group to England in December. On 15 January 1951 six new B-36s took off from Limestone Air Force

Base in Maine, bombed targets on a range on Helgoland Island in the North Sea, and then landed at a poststrike recovery base in England.[230]

The flexing of these global air capabilities did not escape the notice of the Soviet Union and the Chinese Communists. After an extended tour in North Korea and a trip to Moscow, a special aviation inspection group from Red China's general staff described the reasons why the Chinese Communist air force was unable to gain air superiority in the months between March and September 1951. "The US has repeatedly declared that any attempt by the Red Air Force to bomb the US troops," stated the inspection group, "would be retaliated with relentless bombing of the Northeastern Provinces by the USAF. For this reason, the Red Chinese air force has not dared to make such an attempt in the past and may not make it in the future. The conservative policy adopted by Red China has apparently ensued from the high-handed policy of threats of the enemy." In this same report, the inspection group was openly critical of the Soviet decision to equip the Chinese Communist air force with MiG-15 defensive fighters. It noted that this action was doubtless the result of the mistaken Soviet policy of giving first production priorities to fighter aircraft. "With regard to the air defense of the homeland," the group stated, "the strategy of using intercepting fighters has become a thing of the past. The homeland cannot be adequately defended without long-range attacking air power."[231] The Red Chinese assumed that the Soviets outfitted them with MiG-15s out of necessity, but the decision might well have been based upon Soviet desires to prevent the expansion of the Korean conflict. Speaking frankly at a later date, Soviet Foreign Minister Vyacheslav M. Molotov inferred that the Soviet Union had made determined efforts to prevent the Korean conflagration from spreading. "When all facts are known," Molotov said, "you will realize that we acted as a restraining influence."[232]

Air Power and Armistice Negotiations

"The beginning of the Korean truce negotiations between United Nations and Communist delegates at Kaesong in July 1951," General Weyland observed, "ushered in a new phase of the war.... Both the enemy and we had abandoned our identical political objectives of unifying all of Korea by force, and both had given up the military objectives of capture and control. The political and military objectives of each side became the same – the accomplishment of an armistice on favorable terms."[233] When he assumed command of the Far East Air Forces in June 1951, Weyland noted that his command, employing a "minimum force which, for the most part, has been equipped and manned below authorized levels" had already "clearly indicated that air operations have been one of the most decisive elements in stopping the enemy's offensives and reducing his capacity to wage ground warfare." Making another strategic estimate on 12 July, Weyland pointed out in a message to Vandenberg that the Communists might well take advantage of the armistice negotiations and attempt to seize control of the air. In this event, he argued that Vandenberg should provide the Far East Air Forces with "the capability to absorb initial Chinese Communist Air Force attacks and immediately launch effective counterattacks." "The Korean war," Weyland concluded, "has demonstrated that air superiority is essential and the key to the success of military operations regardless of the numerical strengths of opposing surface forces and that air power is the most efficient weapon" for destroying opposing ground forces.[234]

The Air Staff received Weyland's requirements for additional forces sympathetically but had to continue to spread limited Air Force capabilities across a global spectrum. The rapid buildup of Chinese Communist air force strength to 1,050 aircraft including 415 MiG-15s posed an admitted threat to United Nations air superiority, but this force appeared to be intended for defense rather than for offense.[235] On the other hand, the buildup of NATO forces was going to be in a crucial stage early in 1952; those forces would be getting large enough to threaten the Soviet Union without being large enough to defend the NATO allies against a Soviet attack. The only way the Air Force could provide Weyland with the four additional fighter wings he required would be to take them from the Air Defense Command, the Strategic Air Command, or projected deployments to the United States Air Forces in Europe. Weyland could not be given the additional B-26 light bombers that he needed to bring his two light bombardment groups to war strength without robbing the night tactical reconnaissance wing and the light bombardment wing that were being readied for deployment to Europe. After studying the competing requirements, the Air Staff decided that in order to augment NATO, the Tactical Air Command would have to have the 49th Air Division with its atomic-capable B-45 light bomber and F-84 fighter-bomber wings in place in Great Britain by April 1952. On 17 July, Twining informed Weyland that Japan's air defense would be augmented by the movement there of one F-84 wing that had been preparing to go to Europe. This action was all that the Air Force could do to meet Weyland's requirements. "The vital object under the present conditions," Twining wrote Weyland, "is to maintain air superiority over Korea."[236]

Unable to secure the additional air forces that he needed, and faced with the prospect of continuing to wage an air war during the ground stalemate, Weyland could see only two potential employments for United Nations air power. It could either be committed to close support strikes along the front lines where the enemy had dug in and was relatively invulnerable, or it could be concentrated against interdiction targets in the enemy's rear areas. Weyland favored the latter employment and obtained agreement from Gen Matthew B. Ridgway, the commander in chief, United Nations Command, who was apprehensive that the Communists might take advantage of the respite in ground fighting during the truce negotiations to build up frontline stocks of supplies to be used in launching and sustaining a renewed ground offensive. Lt Gen James A. Van Fleet agreed to the interdiction campaign, provided his Eighth Army received 96 close support air sorties each day. At their headquarters in Korea, the Fifth Air Force and the Eighth Army collaborated in planning a comprehensive air interdiction campaign against North Korea's railways. Now commanded by Lt Gen Frank F. Everest, the Fifth

Air Force undertook to neutralize the greatest portion of the rail lines supporting the Communist ground force. He asked that Naval Forces Far East employ its carrier aircraft against sections of Korea's east coast railways, while the FEAF Bomber Command maintained a continuing interdiction of four key railway bridges. Begun suddenly on 18 August 1951, the United Nations Command's comprehensive railway interdiction campaign evidently took the Reds completely by surprise and initially was very successful. Fighter-bombers destroyed railway track much faster than the Reds could repair it, and night-flying B-26 intruders took a respectable toll of the motor truck convoys that jammed the roads in a desperate effort to supply frontline Communist divisions.[237]

During the summer of 1951 the Communists had been busily expanding their Manchurian airfield complex around Antung: the Communist air forces were apparently galvanized into action by the initial success of the United Nations railway interdiction campaign. Displaying flying skill that left no doubt in Weyland's mind that they were Russians,[238] MiG flight leaders led their formations in determined assaults against F-86 Sabre barrier patrols south of the Yalu. Enjoying superior numbers, other MiG formations evaded the Sabres and penetrated well southward into Korea to pounce on rail-cutting fighter-bombers. On 15 September, Weyland warned Vandenberg that the Communist air forces were getting out of control. "If the present trend continues," he said, "there is a definite possibility that the enemy will be able to establish bases in Korea and threaten our supremacy over the front lines." Near the end of September, Fifth Air Force reconnaissance pilots discovered that the Communists had begun building three major jet airfields within North Korea. Supported by F-86 barrier patrols and escorted by F-84s, FEAF Bomber Command B-29s began a series of daylight strikes against these airfields on 22 October. Until this time the FEAF Bomber Command had lost only six B-29s in combat over Korea; but in late October, over the Communist airfields, the Reds destroyed five B-29s and inflicted major damage on eight others. At 20,000-foot altitudes, the straight-wing F-84 Thunderjets could not fend off attacking MiGs without losing flight control, and the MiGs appeared in too great numbers to be handled by the few available Sabres.[239]

"Almost overnight," Vandenberg stated after making a fast trip to the Far East, "Communist China has become one of the major air powers of the world." In terms of the damage that they could do with iron bombs, the old B-29s had taken prohibitive losses. But the pessimistic predictions that the old B-29s would not be able to operate any longer did not reckon with the operational versatility of the FEAF Bomber Command. The command already possessed a small shoran bombing capability and soon converted all of its aircraft to operate only at night with this electronics guidance. Safe from Communist interception, the night-flying B-29s successfully neutralized the Communist airfields during November. Earlier in the summer, Vandenberg had refused to convert one of the Fifth Air Force's fighter-bomber wings to F-86 fighter-interceptors on the grounds that the Air Defense Command ought not to be weakened and that the Air Force did not have enough supply support to maintain two F-86 wings in active combat in Korea. On

22 October, however, Vandenberg directed the Air Defense Command to send 75 F-86s to Korea; on 1 December the Fifth Air Force's second F-86 wing went into action. In mid-December the Communists abruptly abandoned their air-superiority campaign. The United Nations Command received reports that the Chinese Reds were moving their experienced air divisions from Antung and replacing them with new air divisions. The Reds had apparently decided to rotate new classes of MiG pilots through limited air operations over North Korea to give them training in active air combat.[240]

After two months of success the United Nations Command comprehensive railway interdiction campaign became less successful. The Reds emplaced a growing amount of automatic weapons along their rail lines and exacted an increasing rate of losses and damages on attacking aircraft. Forced to fly at night and to give their attention to the enemy airfields, the B-29s were unable to keep their bridge targets interdicted. The conversion of the F-80 fighter-bomber wing into an F-86 interceptor wing reduced attack capability. On the ground, Communist rail-repair crews impressed local workers and were soon able to repair damaged rail track virtually as fast as the fighter-bombers could cut it. On instructions from Washington, the United Nations truce negotiators agreed to a proposition whereby the existing battle line would become the line of demarcation in any armistice agreement signed within thirty days after 27 November. Not wishing to lose lives taking territory that would be given up, Ridgway directed the Eighth Army on 15 November to cease local offensives and begin an active defense. Confident that they had little to fear on the ground, the Reds withdrew troops to rearward positions where they could be supplied more easily, while along the inactive ground front they were able to regulate their supply requirements by varying their expenditures.[241]

By the end of December 1951 the Fifth Air Force recognized that the comprehensive railway interdiction program was reaching a point of diminishing returns. On 5 January 1952 Brig Gen James Ferguson, vice commander of the Fifth Air Force, requested authority to attack North Korea's extensive hydroelectric power generating plants — facilities that had gone virtually undamaged and which were providing power to factories in both Manchuria and North Korea. On 4 January, however, Ridgway had informed the Joint Chiefs that he did not want to discontinue or reduce the air interdiction activity, since in such an event the Reds would be able to accumulate sufficient frontline supply stocks to launch and sustain a major offensive. During this same month Brig Gen Jacob E. Smart came to Tokyo as deputy for operations of the Far East Air Forces. He soon agreed that air power ought to be employed in a manner that would maintain effective and positive pressure upon the Communists to compel them to accept armistice terms. Given the task of determining how to conduct a campaign of air pressure, Col Richard L. Randolph and Lt Col Ben I. Mayo proposed that the Far East Air Forces give first priority to maintaining air superiority and then use its remaining effort to accomplish "the maximum amount of selected destruction, thus making the Korean conflict as costly as possible to the enemy in terms of equipment, supplies, and

IDEAS, CONCEPTS, DOCTRINE

personnel." Weyland liked this concept of waging air pressure through selective destruction. As long as United Nations air power had been limited to strikes against the usual tactical targets in North Korea, the Reds had been willing to stall the truce negotiations. But, through selective attack against economic and military targets in North Korea, the Far East Air Forces possessed an opportunity to make the effect of a local air campaign felt as far away as the seats of power in Moscow and Peking. Whether such a vigorous air campaign could be authorized would depend upon the state of the armistice negotiations, the inclinations of General Ridgway, and an augmentation of the Far East Air Forces' capabilities, which had suffered unreplaced losses during the 10 months of comprehensive railway interdiction.[242]

Air Pressure as a Strategy

Beginning in the early summer of 1952, the United States possessed the worldwide air force that was needed to back up more forceful measures in Korea. Serving as forward deployment stations for Strategic Air Command medium bombers, Nouasseur and Sidi Slimane Air Bases in Morocco had become operational in July 1951, while Thule Air Base in northwestern Greenland—only about 900 miles from the North Pole—was considered operational in November 1952.[243] Following a schedule that allowed it to expand and modernize while simultaneously maintaining combat readiness, the Strategic Air Command possessed five heavy bomber, 18 medium bomber, three heavy reconnaissance, four medium reconnaissance, and three strategic fighter wings at the end of 1952. The three heavy reconnaissance and four of the heavy bomber wings were equipped with intercontinental B-36s; although they were not yet operational, two of the medium bomber wings were converting to B-47 jet bombers.[244] Although the NATO air forces had not reached levels specified as necessary by Gen Dwight D. Eisenhower as supreme allied commander, Europe, the arrival of the atomic-capable 49th Air Division in England on 5 June 1952 added realism to the SHAPE mission. "We now had," said Maj Gen Dean C. Strother, commander of the 4th Allied Tactical Air Force in Central Europe, "the beginnings of a real tactical offensive capability. Employed with SAC's growing potential in one indivisible air effort, sense could now be made of the tactical situation."[245] The successful detonation of a thermonuclear test device in Operation Ivy on 1 November 1952 promised an almost incalculable increase in strategic bombing power. "We need no longer to argue," pointed out Bernard Brodie, "whether the conduct of war is an art or a science—in the future it will be neither. The art or science will come only in finding out . . . what not to hit."[246]

On 28 April 1952 United Nations truce negotiators in Korea offered a proposal for resolving all disputed questions on the agenda, and, when the Communists refused the solutions, the truce negotiations were at a complete impasse. On this same day in Washington, President Truman announced the appointment of Gen Mark W. Clark as commander in chief, United Nations Command-Far East

Command, in place of General Ridgway who became supreme allied commander, Europe. When he reached Tokyo on 12 May 1952, Clark already believed that "only through forceful action could the Communists be made to agree to an armistice the United States considered honorable." With approval from Clark and from the Joint Chiefs, the Far East Air Forces and the Naval Forces Far East, in a four-day action beginning on 23 June, launched a campaign of applying pressure through the air that successfully neutralized North Korea's hydroelectric generating plants. Beginning in July 1952, the United Nations air pressure operations were related closely to the state of the truce negotiations at Panmunjom and, when these were suspended, to diplomatic soundings of Sino-Soviet relations. With Weyland serving as coordinating agent, Far East Air Forces and the Naval Forces Far East aircraft made a massive 1,254-sortie day-long attack against military targets in the North Korean capital city of Pyongyang on 11 July. For several months after this, Far East Air Forces planes attacked industrial plants that either had been overlooked or had been rebuilt since the strategic air attacks of 1950. In a change of tactics, the Fifth Air Force flew streams of B-26 night-bombers laden with incendiaries against Communist towns and villages that served as storage or transshipment points on the main Red supply routes. At the same time that Sino-Soviet talks were under way in Moscow in late August and early September, United Nations air units prosecuted a series of air attacks against targets near the Manchurian and Siberian borders; on 29 August, these units teamed up for another massive assault against military targets in Pyongyang. When the Moscow talks ended and produced no apparent change in Communist attitudes at Panmunjom, the United Nations delegates suspended further negotiations on 8 October. Seeking to increase military pressure as the truce talks recessed, Clark directed the United Nations Command to intensify air operations, to begin limited ground offensives, and to undertake simulated airborne and amphibious operations against the east coast of North Korea. Begun on 15 October the intensified United Nations operations failed to evoke a response from the Communists. And the Eighth Army's attacks against the limited objectives of Triangle Hill and Sniper Ridge touched off a bloody see-saw battle that saw this terrain change hands several times. As a result of these experiences, Clark judged that an amphibious operation against North Korea's eastern coast "would have been most difficult." "We should not unless absolutely necessary," he told General Van Fleet, "initiate another action which may be a repetition of the bloody battle of Triangle Hill and Sniper Ridge."[247]

"I concur in the concept," Clark informed the Joint Chiefs of Staff, "that maximum pressure, within the capability of my means and which can be justified by results, should be applied and maintained against the Communists. The capability for such pressure without unacceptable cost, lies in the air arm."[248] As commander of the Army Field Forces, Clark had insisted that an Army field commander should have operational control of the tactical air elements that were provided for the execution of a ground campaign. Looking toward such an organization on 1 July 1952, General Van Fleet proposed that three squadrons of Marine fighter-bombers should be placed under the operational control of the

Eighth Army and that these squadrons would be further controlled by the three corps commanders, each of whom would thus have an attached squadron to provide close air support.[249] Despite his earlier arguments, Clark turned down Van Fleet's proposal. "With a specific job to do," he explained, "I had to maintain an air-ground team working as efficiently as possible."[250] After a careful study, Clark made his views on air-ground operations in Korea known on 11 August 1952. He concluded that "the theater commander, rather than any single service, bears over-all responsibility for successfully prosecuting the Korean war. Each component contributes its own specialized capabilities to the attainment of the theater commander's overall mission and in so doing assists the other components; however, no single service exists solely or primarily for the support of another." Generally endorsing existing Army-Air Force doctrine, Clark did not wish to see any far-reaching or drastic changes made, based solely on the often unusual conditions prevailing in Korea.[251]

Although Weyland and Air Force evaluation boards had long argued that United Nations Command air power could not be effectively employed as a unitary strength in the absence of a proper joint headquarters staff in the United Nations Command-Far East Command (UNC-FEC), Generals MacArthur and Ridgway had preferred to depend upon a staff that was predominately Army. The UNC-FEC headquarters staff also doubled in duty as the theater Army headquarters. General Clark, however, held that his staff "should be a joint tri-service operation, rather than an Army project," and on 20 August 1952 he announced that he intended to organize a joint staff and establish a headquarters for Army forces in the Far East. According to plan, the Army Forces Far East was activated on 1 October 1952; the reorganized Headquarters UNC-FEC began to function on 1 January 1953. "A truly integrated staff of the three services, in which men were picked for their ability rather than the color of their uniforms," Clark later observed, "is the answer to combined operations."[252] As the theater air commander, Weyland also established a new means of integrating the capabilities of the Fifth Air Force and the FEAF Bomber Command. Comprised of representatives of the Far East Air Forces, the Fifth Air Force, and the FEAF Bomber Command, the FEAF Formal Target Committee began to meet biweekly in July 1952 to study target opportunities and to recommend operational employments. After Weyland approved them, the committee's recommendations were distributed within the Far East for information. Weyland would have liked a Navy representative on the Formal Target Committee, but felt that he had no authority to order it. Very late in the war, a Navy air officer was invited to attend the committee's meetings. Except for its lack of authority over naval air operations, the FEAF Formal Target Committee became the basic theater agency for target selection and the medium through which basic air tasks outlined by Clark and Weyland were translated into planned air campaigns.[253]

In terms of numerical capabilities, the Communist air forces in the Far East posed a continuing obstacle to the success of the United Nations air pressure strategy and to the safety of the United Nations Command. In June 1952 these forces reached their apparent authorized strength: the Communist Chinese possessed some 1,830 aircraft (including 1,000 jet fighters) — some 1,115 of the Chinese planes were based in Manchuria; the Soviet air units possessed approximately 5,360 aircraft; and the reconstituted North Korean air force had about 270 planes. This Communist air order of battle dwarfed the United Nations air force; the Reds also conducted a vigorous modernization program. By November 1952 the Red Chinese obtained 100 of the latest model Il-28 light jet bombers and based them in Manchuria. An extensive radar network fed information to a Red aircraft control center at Antung. In defending their fixed installations within North Korea, the Reds employed some 786 antiaircraft artillery guns, 1,672 automatic weapons, and 500 mobile search lights during the winter of 1952-53.[254] Several factors, nevertheless, continued to work in favor of the United Nations Command. The Fifteenth Air Force maintained an atomic-capable medium bomber squadron and tanker detachment on continuous alert at Andersen Air Base on Guam. In December 1952, following the arrival of the hostile Il-28s in Manchuria, one of the Fifth Air Force's most proficient fighter-bomber squadrons was pulled back to Japan to be equipped and trained for the delivery of tactical atomic weapons.[255] Early in 1953, moreover, the Fifth Air Force was able to reequip two of its fighter-bomber wings with F-86F fighter-bombers (which could double as fighter-interceptors if needed), thus doubling its air-to-air fighting potential.[256] In spite of their numerical superiority, the Red air forces operated under restrictions; although MiG flight leaders — many of whom were believed to be Russians — were frequently proficient, the majority of MiG pilots were poorly skilled in air combat. Only in the night skies over northwestern Korea during the winter months of 1952-53 did the Reds seriously challenge the operation of Far East Air Forces planes — once again the old B-29s. In November 1952 two Soviet night fighter squadrons operated over northwestern Korea; the FEAF Bomber Command lost five B-29s between 18 November 1952 and 30 January 1953. Vigorous mission study and analysis enabled the bomber command to keep operating. The Fifth Air Force also provided F-94C Starfire and F3D-2 Skynight all-weather fighters to fly cooperative barrier and overhead cover for the B-29s. Had the Reds seen fit to employ electronic-equipped all-weather fighters, they probably could have terminated B-29 operations. As it was, FEAF Bomber Command's countermeasures were effective and no more medium bombers were lost to hostile night defenses after 30 January 1953.[257]

When the truce negotiations indefinitely recessed in Korea on 8 October 1952, the arena of armistice discussion shifted to the United Nations General Assembly and to diplomatic discourse. In the autumn of 1952 Ambassador Chester Bowles warned India's foreign office that an extension of hostilities would be inevitable unless some satisfactory cease-fire was soon reached. The only substantial point that blocked the cease-fire was the Communist position that all prisoners of war should be repatriated forcibly at the armistice, which would mean that many Koreans and Chinese who wished freedom would be returned to bondage.[258] In his successful campaign for the presidency in the autumn of 1952, General

Eisenhower expressed his determination to seek an honorable end to the war in Korea. In his state of the union message on 2 February 1953, he indicated that the United States was ready to act more forcefully and specifically announced that American naval forces would no longer shield Red China from attacks that might be launched by Chinese Nationalist forces from Taiwan. During a visit to New Delhi in May 1953, Secretary of State John Foster Dulles told Prime Minister Jawaharlal Nehru that the United States wanted an honorable peace in Korea, but that the United States had decided to attack Communist bases in Manchuria if an agreement on a truce was not soon reached. Dulles hoped that this warning would reach Peking, and it doubtless did.[259]

Benefiting from new force capabilities, Lt Gen Glenn O. Barcus, who commanded the Fifth Air Force in the last year of the Korean hostilities, made efforts to provoke reluctant MiGs into air battles. Toward this end, General Clark offered a reward of $50,000 and political asylum on 26 April to any Communist pilot who would deliver his MiG to an airfield in South Korea. Possibly to avoid defections, the Soviets seem to have withdrawn their pilots from combat; the Chinese and Korean airmen who swarmed out of Manchuria proved pitifully incompetent. In May and June 1953 the Sabres shot down 133 MiGs at a cost of only one F-86.[260] Finding special targets in North Korea became more difficult as the air pressure operations continued. However, as a standard fare, the bomber command attacked and destroyed 30 to 40 Red supply centers each month. In April 1953, moreover, air targets planners discovered that impounded irrigation water was the key to North Korea's substantial rice production. On 13 and 16 May, United Nations fighter-bombers released swirling floodwaters as they cut irrigation dams at Toksan and Chasan. "The breaching of the Toksan dam," Clark informed the Joint Chiefs, "has been as effective as weeks of rail interdiction." The Communist forces also were subjected to attack, since Red personnel encampments and logistical dumps back of the front lines proved to be small but collectively profitable targets for air attack.[261]

At the same time that he was willing to entertain stronger actions to attain an honorable truce, Eisenhower also took steps to renew truce negotiations. Following the new administration policy, the Joint Chiefs instructed Clark on 19 February to propose an immediate exchange of all sick and wounded prisoners of war. While the Reds were considering this proposal, the whole Communist bloc was shaken by the death of Joseph Stalin. At Stalin's bier, Soviet premier Georgi Malenkov spoke of the need for peaceful coexistence between Communist and capitalist nations. On 28 March the Communists agreed to the repatriation of sick and wounded prisoners. But, when the Panmunjom talks began again on 26 April, the Reds were still determined to haggle, particularly over the length of time that prisoners would be held in custody by a neutral nation's repatriation commission. On 4 June, following presentation of final United Nations terms and the start of the attacks on the irrigation dams, the Reds capitulated and accepted the proposal that prisoners who did not willingly accept repatriation within 120 days would be released as civilians. All outstanding truce issues were now resolved, but the

Communists continued to stall for time. They mounted last-gasp ground offensives in mid-June and mid-July in order to lend credence to a claim that the truce was signed while the Reds were winning and to dampen the ardor of South Korea's President Syngman Rhee, who still wanted to get the unification of Korea by military force. Employed all out, United Nations air power contributed in full measure to the exceedingly high casualties inflicted on the attacking Red ground armies. After trading casualties for a few miles of worthless terrain, the Reds signed the armistice agreement on 27 July 1953, thus ending active hostilities in Korea.[262]

Evaluations of Air Power's Effects in Korea

In view of the importance of the Korean conflict to American military thought, it would have been helpful if the Communists had seen fit to disclose the factors that led to their capitulation. Members of President Eisenhower's administration took a global view of the matter. Secretary of State Dulles stated that hostilities ended in Korea "because the aggressor, already thrown back to and behind his place of beginning, was faced with the possibility that the fighting might, to his own great peril, soon spread beyond the limits and methods he had selected."[263] Secretary of Defense Charles E. Wilson held much the same view. "I will always think," he said, "we got an armistice because they thought if they did not really do something, after all of the talking for a couple of years, something was going to happen. In other words, the war was either going to toughen and we were going to dive in and win it, or there was going to be an armistice."[264] Writing in 1955, Col Ephraim M. Hampton, the Air War College's deputy for evaluation, argued that the global activities of American air power had had profound effects upon almost every aspect of the war in Korea. "It would be almost impossible," he wrote, "to pinpoint the precise degree to which our global air base system, with its substantial elements of our national air power in position in the NATO area and the Far East and with its facilities for swift and massive redeployment of our air power, had on the course of events in Korea. Certainly the Soviets had to weigh these factors, [which] . . . certainly . . . must have been the compelling consideration in their decision as to just how far and in what ways they dared support their junior partner in the Korean war."[265]

Other American military men attached greater significance to the local circumstances in Korea. Clark suggested that the Communists yielded "only because the military pressure on them was so great that they had to yield. . . . In the end we got the ceasefire only because the enemy had been hurt so badly on the field of battle."[266] Speaking in January 1954, Brig Gen Don Z. Zimmerman, deputy for intelligence of the Far East Air Forces said: "We established a pattern of destruction by air which was unacceptable to the enemy. The degree of destruction suffered by North Korea, in relation to its resources, was greater than that which the Japanese islands suffered in World War II. These pressures brought the enemy to terms."[267] Tersely summing up his views in February 1954, General Weyland stated: "We are pretty sure now that the Communists wanted peace, not because of a two-year stalemate on the ground, but to get air power off their back."[268] After a conversation with Molotov at Geneva in the spring of 1954, Under Secretary of State Walter Bedell Smith suggested that the Soviets eventually gave up in Korea because the hostilities there were forcing them to "send more materiel into China than they wanted to send" and because "there was too great a drain on the Soviet economy." "The terrain in Korea," Smith added, "was against them and it was the one place in Asia where we were able to fight at an advantage because we controlled the sea and most of the air. They wanted to stop there and they will probably want it to start elsewhere a little later on."[269]

In the autumn of 1950 General Stratemeyer had warned that the Korean conflict presented so many unusual aspects as to make it a very poor model for planning future operational requirements. Issued under Weyland's authority on 26 March 1954, the *FEAF Report on the Korean War* repeated Stratemeyer's earlier conclusion that lessons drawn from Korea had of necessity to comprehend many unusual factors.[270] In his personal writings, Weyland agreed that the Korean air war had been very complex; he considered that it had been "a laboratory study of limited military action in support of a very difficult political situation" and that it provided the Air Force with "an opportunity to develop concepts of employment beyond the World War II concepts of tactical and strategic operations."[271]

In writing on the major lessons that emerged from Korea, Weyland stated that:

> One thing that should be clear to everyone by now is that air power is indivisible. It can put at risk all important elements of a national structure. Attempts to classify it by types of aircraft, types of operations, or types of targets have led to confusion and misunderstandings. For that reason I have tried to think of it in terms of objectives, threats, and opportunities. The results desired, balanced against threats and opportunities, determine the weight, timing, and phasing of air attacks.[272]

In the *FEAF Report*, Weyland attributed most interservice problems affecting the employment of air power in Korea to the continuing lack of a properly established joint headquarters at the United Nations Command-Far East Command level.[273] On 9 April 1951, however, Weyland had been more critical of the lack of an overall theater control for available air power, and he had recommended that the final FEAF war report would carry the lesson that "all aircraft operating in a theater, except those performing Naval missions, be placed under the command of the air commander."[274] Although carrier-based air forces represented an important theater air force potential, Navy commanders in the Far East were slow to commit themselves positively to the collateral missions they believed might hinder their ability to maintain control of the seas. Thus, the agreement for air coordination in defense of the Far East theater signed on 26 March 1951 gave the Far East Air Forces air defense commander operational control over all shore-based Navy and Marine fighter aircraft in an air defense emergency. However, it provided that carrier-based fighter aircraft were an integral part of the fleet and normally could not be precommitted to any emergency operational control of the air defense commander. Marine Corps land-based aircraft were successfully integrated into the Fifth Air Force-Eighth Army air-ground system, but Seventh Fleet aircraft could not be positively committed to ground support as long as the Naval Forces Far East had a mission in the Taiwan Straits. When relieved of this mission, the Seventh Fleet established a naval member in the Joint Operations Center in Korea in June 1953 and thereafter participated integrally in the support of the ground forces in Korea.[275]

The same concern that organizational diffusion might lead to a loss in air power's inherent flexibility caused Air Force thinkers to question the division of the Air Force into strategic and tactical air arms and to reexamine the mission of tactical air forces. As engrossed in the *Joint Training Directive for Air-Ground Operations*, issued jointly by the Tactical Air Command and the Army Field Forces in September 1950, the mission of tactical air power was related to the strategy and maneuver of ground forces. Late in 1950, however, a study prepared by the Office of Assistant for Evaluation, Deputy Chief of Staff for Development, Headquarters USAF, suggested that tactical air power need not be related directly to the maneuver of friendly ground troops. Tactical air power might be employed directly against enemy forces in the field without any friendly ground forces being present. "In this new concept," stated the study,

> tactical air power will be entering into direct combat with enemy ground forces — not only supporting our ground forces in their fight against the enemy ground forces. . . . Clearly, it is not acceptable to relegate tactical air to only a supporting role. It is no longer sufficient even to declare that tactical air and ground forces cooperate equally. Rather, tactical air must now be conceived as having a role in the battle against enemy ground forces at times completely on its own.[276]

The Air Force officially accepted the concept on 29 June 1953 when it issued a revised regulation governing the organization of the Tactical Air Command. This regulation defined tactical air operations

> as the application of all air power, under the command or operational control of a theater or area commander, against an enemy's military potential and capabilities in being, normally only within the theater area of responsibility. Restricted only by limitations of equipment and capabilities of designated units, tactical air operations may encompass any task necessary in the furtherance of the theater mission.[277]

In explaining the change in tactical air doctrine Brigadier General Ferguson noted that tactical air power

> was considered a supporting arm until recently when new weapons were introduced which in themselves produce decisive results. . . . The formidable nature of this new source of firepower, in fact, reverses the orthodox relationships of air and ground forces. Specifically, it is quite reasonable to say that we should look for a modification in our tactics and in our concepts of war . . . which would point toward the exploitation of tactical air atomic attacks by highly mobile ground forces.[278]

Many Army officers who served in Korea insisted that the ground forces ought to possess their own organic close-support aviation, but the several joint evaluation boards that met in the Far East Command during and at the end of the Korean hostilities generally endorsed the organizational concepts of extant Army-Air Force doctrine. A Joint Eighth Army-Fifth Air Force air-ground operations board, which reported on March 1951, found that "the Joint Training Directive for Air-Ground Operations... is sound and adequate and is applicable to the Korean theater of operations."[279] In his study on air-ground operations issued in August 1952, General Clark held that any comparison between the Army-Air Force and Marine systems of close air support was faulty because the two systems were designed for completely different types of functions and had different allocations of forces.[280] A conference of Fifth Air Force, Eighth Army, Seventh Fleet, and 1st Marine Aircraft Wing representatives that met in August 1953 for the war's end review of air-ground operations stated: "Little attempt has been made . . . to reiterate previously published doctrines and techniques which have been found fundamentally sound and workable."[281] "I don't think we ought to be in tactical air support. I don't know anybody at the top of the Army who is pressing for it," stated Under Secretary of the Army Earl D. Johnson in October 1953.[282]

Although the Department of the Army did not seek to undertake its own close air support, it vastly expanded the Army's organic aviation. According to a joint readjustment agreement of 20 May 1949, Army aviation was categorized as fixed-wing aircraft not exceeding 2,500 pounds in weight and rotary-wing aircraft (helicopters) weighing no more than 4,000 pounds. Such organic aircraft were to be used to expedite and improve ground combat procedures in forward areas of the battlefield. In addition to these planes, the Air Force would continue to provide liaison squadrons to support Army units. Based upon experience in Korea, both the Army and the Air Force effected new plans and ordered helicopters in larger numbers. Most Army helicopters were committed as organic aviation, but the Army also planned to establish helicopter transport companies, each able to lift an infantry rifle company. Since it was responsible for air-assault airlift, the Air Force planned to organize assault transport wings, each to include one conventional troop carrier group and one rotary-wing aircraft group. When not employed in air assault work, the helicopter group would accomplish frontline air transport functions. Early in 1951 the Army wanted to secure larger aircraft and helicopters, but the Air Force believed that such planes would infringe upon the Air Force's air transport mission. Seeking to settle this controversy, secretaries Frank Pace of the Army and Finletter of the Air Force signed an agreement on 2 October 1951 that omitted references to the weight of Army aircraft and stated that the Army would possess organic aircraft required "as an integral part of its components for the purpose of expediting and improving ground combat and logistical procedures within the combat zone." The combat zone was understood to be an area from 60 to 75 miles deep behind the battle line.[283]

In view of the Pace-Finletter agreement as well as a demonstrated need for increased Army mobility in Korea, General Ridgway recommended in November 1951 that the Department of the Army should procure enough cargo helicopters to allocate 10 helicopter battalions, each with three companies, to a typical field army. The Department of the Army was favorable to Ridgway's proposal, but it approved a lesser allotment order by which four helicopter battalions, each with three companies, would be assigned to each field army. The Air Force, however, demurred, arguing that such an allotment of Army helicopters would duplicate the helicopter services that could be provided by the rotary-wing groups of assault transport wings. Gen John E. Hull, deputy chief of staff of the Army, pointed out on the other hand that the Army had never cited any requirement for support by Air Force rotary-wing aircraft within the combat zone against which the Air Force was justified in programming units.[284] This jurisdictional controversy remained deadlocked until 4 November 1952, when, after intervention by Secretary Lovett, a second memorandum of understanding was jointly approved by the Army and Air Force. This understanding fixed the maximum weight of Army fixed-wing aircraft at 5,000 pounds but prescribed no weight limit for helicopters. It specifically recognized that Army aviation would have the function of transporting Army supplies, equipment, personnel, and small units within the combat zone, an area precisely defined as extending 50 to 100 miles deep behind the front lines. The Air Force remained responsible for airlifting Army supplies, equipment, personnel, and units between points outside the combat zone to points within the combat zone and also for the air movement of Army troops, supplies, and equipment in the assault and subsequent phases of airborne operations.[285]

While the Korean hostilities provided new lessons looking toward a future employment of theater air forces, those battles also reemphasized old air power lessons, which, albeit, tended to be obscured by the peculiar circumstances prevailing in Korea. The Strategic Air Command demonstrated well the flexibility and versatility of its force by employing medium bomber wings as a tactical bomber force, by committing one of its escort fighter wings for a time to an air-ground attack role, and by rotating fighter wings to the theater for the air defense of Japan. But the local peculiarities of the limited war did not permit a full exploitation of the strategic bombing function. Because of the artificial boundaries of the conflict, most of the production facilities that the Communists used to support their war effort could not be attacked. In the early months of the war, the few war-supporting industries of North Korea were easily destroyed; after this, very few targets could be found that would warrant a medium bomber formation large enough in size to provide the old B-29s with mutual self-protection. Early in the war many Air Force officers chafed at the employment of so-called strategic bombers in tactical air roles and vexed themselves over the question as to whether strategic targets even existed in Korea. General Stratemeyer had occasion to remark that strategic bombers could be freely diverted to ground-support purposes because the B-29s were available and because the ground situation was threatening, but he warned that it should not be assumed that such diversions superseded the real purpose of strategic aircraft. This same admonition held true throughout the war.[286]

"There is little doubt in my mind," wrote General Weyland, "that the outcome of the conflict would have been vastly different had enemy domination of the air reversed the positions of the Communists and the United Nations Command."[287]

At least one Navy officer concluded that the Korean War "clearly demonstrated that land battles can continue to be waged successfully in the face of complete air control,"[288] but few authorities questioned the Air Force assertion that "the first and most important lesson" of the Korean conflict was that "control of the air is a prerequisite for any large-scale military operation."[289] Free from the danger of hostile air attack, outnumbered United Nations ground forces were able to maneuver at will during daylight hours, while the Communists were compelled to move and to fight at night. Although the Communist armies proved able to exist in a battle zone covered by conventionally armed United Nations air power, these forces were unable to use their superior strength to accomplish their military objectives. In the autumn of 1950, General Stratemeyer feared that the relative ease with which the Far East Air Forces gained air superiority might lead to an erroneous conclusion that such a feat could be duplicated at will in a future conflict. In the course of the war, a small band of Sabre pilots successfully shielded the United Nations Command against much larger numbers of Communist aircraft. In the course of their barrier patrols, the Sabres met and destroyed 810 enemy aircraft (including 792 MiGs) at a cost of a combat loss of 78 of their own number. But the fact that this smaller Sabre force was able to maintain air superiority had to take into consideration a recognition that the Communists were unable to use their superior air capabilities effectively.[290]

"At any time since possibly the middle of 1951," stated Col James B. Tipton, an experienced Fifth Air Force wing commander, "I have seen no cogent reason why the Red Air Force Commander did not wipe out the United Nations Air Forces opposing him."[291] Some part of the inability of the Communists to employ their superior numbers in all-out air battles was attributable to a lack of skilled aircrews, but the controlling circumstance of air superiority in Korea was better summed up by Colonel Hampton, when he concluded: "The Communists feared to use their local air forces decisively because the United States had warned that any extension of the Korean war might bring down upon the aggressor the awesome force of the US Global air-atomic power."[292] "The second lesson," General Ferguson said in a discussion of the employment of tactical air power in Korea,

> was the most profitable attacks were those made deep in enemy territory where supplies, materiel, and personnel are fairly well concentrated. As supplies and men are moved closer to the line of contact, dispersal greatly reduces the effectiveness of air attacks. Consequently, where it is operationally feasible, tactical air should place the major emphasis for its interdiction program against those lucrative and concentrated targets which necessarily lie deeper in enemy territory.[293]

Few of the United Nations air actions in Korea drew more criticism than the comprehensive railway interdiction attacks prosecuted between August 1951 and May 1952, the air campaign which was popularly described as Operation Strangle. Gen Lemuel C. Shepherd, commandant of the Marine Corps, stated that Operation Strangle was "recognized as a fizzle." And Vice Adm J. J. Clark, the Seventh Fleet's commander, observed: "The interdiction program was a failure. It did *not* interdict."[294] In retrospect, Weyland admitted that Strangle was a poorly conceived name because it gave critics who did not understand the real objective of the railway interdiction a vehicle for proclaiming its failure. He insisted, however, that the railway campaign "was an unqualified success in achieving its stated purpose, which was to deny the enemy the capability to launch and sustain an offensive."[295] "No one can be foolish enough," stated Colonel Tipton, "to claim 100 percent effectiveness for any interdiction effort; to freeze all movement within complex areas of thousands of square miles is impossible." He, nevertheless, observed, "We can conclude that the unique features of the Korean operation have not changed the concept of air operations in the interdiction task."[296]

With regard to close support by the Air Force of Army troops, Gen Maxwell D. Taylor stated, "I would first say that dissatisfaction would not apply to the attitude shown by the Air Force in Korea. I was never more loyally supported by anyone, even by my own people, than by the Fifth Air Force when I commanded the Eighth Army."[297] Recognizing that the outnumbered United Nations ground forces in Korea never possessed a proper amount of organic artillery, Weyland noted that "FEAF and Fifth Air Force leaned over backward to provide more than adequate close air support."[298] But the final report of the Far East Air Forces, nevertheless, warned: "Because FEAF provided UNC ground forces lavish close air support in Korea is no reason to assume this condition will exist in future wars." In a future conflict the fighter-bomber forces would be hard put to attain air superiority and attaining air superiority would be more vital to the success of the mission of all forces than close support would be.[299] Speaking of his experience in Korea, General Ferguson outlined the potential worth of close air support under various battle conditions. "In my opinion," he wrote,

> close air support is of little use unless the associated army is ... on the offensive. When the army is holding along a riverline, or waiting for a supply buildup, or for strategic or political decisions to be taken, close air support does little more than keep the state of the art alive. ... It should and must be used under such conditions as we faced in April and May 1951 when great hordes of Communist Chinese poured in against soft points in our lines. But, given relatively static conditions along a line of resistance, the most effective employment of tactical air is to range forward and seal off the projected battle zone, while maintaining control of the air and conducting long-range interdiction. ... When the day does come for the all-out attack by our troops, every airplane of every category would participate in breaking the initial line of resistance and getting the offensive underway. From then on close support, close-in interdiction, and airfield sweeps all combine to keep the enemy off balance and to make the offensive an ultimate success.[300]

IDEAS, CONCEPTS, DOCTRINE

NOTES

1. R. Earl McClendon, *Unification of the Armed Forces: Administrative and Legislative Developments,* 1945–1949 (Maxwell AFB, Ala.: Research Studies Institute, 1952), 94–97; House, Committee on Armed Services, *Full Committee Hearings on S. 1843,* 81st Cong., 1st sess., 1949, 2682.

2. US National Military Establishment, First Report of the Secretary of Defense, 3–4; Walter Millis, ed., *The Forrestal Diaries* (New York: Viking Press, 1951), 539–40.

3. Senate, *National Security Act Amendments of 1949: Hearings before the Committee on Armed Services,* 81st Cong., 1st sess., 1949, 39–40, 277–78.

4. Ibid., 6–10.

5. Ibid., 93, 97.

6. House, *Full Committee Hearings on S. 1843,* 2686.

7. McClendon, *Unification of the Armed Forces,* 109–13.

8. Public Law 271, National Security Act Amendments of 1949, 10 August 1949.

9. House, *Full Committee Hearings on S. 1843,* 2761.

10. Karl F. Kellerman, "The Role of Guided Missiles in Future War," lecture, Air War College, Maxwell AFB, Ala., 17 January 1949.

11. Maj Gen Donald L. Putt, "USAF Research and Development," lecture, Air War College, Maxwell AFB, Ala., 17 November 1949.

12. Theodore von Karman to W. Stuart Symington, letter, 15 January 1949.

13. Theodore von Karman to Hoyt S. Vandenberg, letter, 15 January 1949, tab A: Discussion in Support of the Need for a Deputy Chief of Staff for Research and Development in Headquarters USAF.

14. Memorandum by James H. Doolittle to Hoyt S. Vandenberg, subject: Report on the Present Status of Air Force Research and Development, 20 April 1951.

15. History, USAF Historical Liaison Office, Air University, 1 July 1949 to 30 June 1950, 25–26.

16. Theodore von Karman to Hoyt S. Vandenberg, letter, 21 September 1949, w/incl.: Report of a Special Committee of the Scientific Advisory Board to the Chief of Staff, US Air Force, Research and Development in the United States Air Force.

17. Gen George C. Kenney to Hoyt S. Vandenberg, letter, 19 November 1949, with tab A: Research and Development in the United States Air Force.

18. History, USAF Historical Liaison Office, Air University, 1 July 1949 to 30 June 1950, 28–29; Lt Gen Kenneth B. Wolfe, deputy chief of staff, Materiel, US Air Force, staff study, subject: Implementation of Ridenour and Air University Reports on Research and Development, 2 December 1949.

19. History, USAF Historical Liaison Office, Air University, 1 July 1949 to 30 June 1950, 28–29.

20. House, *Department of Defense Appropriations for 1951: Hearings before a Subcommittee of the Committee on Appropriations,* 81st Cong., 2d sess., 1950, pt. 3:1621.

21. Memorandum by Maj Gen Thomas T. Handy to chief of staff, War Department, subject: Outline of Post–War Permanent Military Establishment, 28 October 1943.

22. Maj Gen Lauris Norstad, "Role of the Armed Forces in Implementing National Policy," lecture, Air War College, Maxwell AFB, Ala., 19 May 1947.

23. Millis, *The Forrestal Diaries,* 315–16, 320.

24. House, *DOD Appropriations for 1951,* pt. 1:4–5.

25. Ray S. Cline, *Washington Command Post: The Operations Division, U.S. Army in World War II* (Washington, D.C.: Office of the Chief of Military History, Department of the Army, 1951), 326–27; Timothy W. Stanley, *American Defense and National Security* (Washington, D.C.: Public Affairs Press, 1956), 10–11.

26. Paul Nitze, "The Relationship of the Political End to the Military Objective," lecture, Air War College, Maxwell AFB, Ala., October 1954; House, *The National Defense Program—Unification and Strategy: Hearings before the Committee on Armed Services,* 81st Cong., 1st sess., 1949, 516–17; House,

The National Defense Program—Unification and Strategy: Hearings before the Committee on Armed Services, 81st Cong., 2d sess., 1950, 14–15.

27. House, *DOD Appropriations for 1951*, 66.
28. Millis, *The Forrestal Diaries*, 431–32.
29. Ibid., 341.
30. Robert F. Futrell, *The United States Air Force in Korea, 1950–1953* (New York: Duell, Sloan and Pearce, 1961), 14–18.
31. Nitze, "The Relationship of the Political End to the Military Objective."
32. Hoyt S. Vandenberg, "Air Force Policies and Planning," lecture, Air War College, Maxwell AFB, Ala., 10 May 1950.
33. Senate, *Military Situation in the Far East: Hearings before the Committee on Armed Services and the Committee on Foreign Relations*, 82d Cong., 1st sess., 1951, 2594–95, 2687–88, 2690.
34. Stanley, *American Defense and National Security*, 11.
35. House, *DOD Appropriations for 1951*, pt. 1:66.
36. Ibid.
37. Harry S Truman, *Years of Trial and Hope* (Garden City, N.Y.: Doubleday & Co., 1956), 306–7.
38. Gen Omar N. Bradley as told to Beverly Smith, "This Way Lies Peace," *Saturday Evening Post*, 13 October 1949.
39. Thomas K. Finletter, *Power and Policy: US Foreign Policy and Military Power in the Hydrogen Age* (New York: Harcourt, Brace and Co., 1954), 377.
40. *Congressional Record*, 83d Cong., 2d sess., 8 April 1954, 100:A2716.
41. Maj Harry C. McCool, "Military Application of Atomic Energy," lecture, Army Air Forces Special Staff School, 1946–47; James R. Shepley and Clay Blair, Jr., *The Hydrogen Bomb* (New York: David McKay Co., 1954), 137; Brig Gen Roscoe C. Wilson, "Organization, Functions, and Relationship of AEC, MLC, and AFSWP," lecture, Air War College, Maxwell AFB, Ala., 26 October 1949; US Atomic Energy Commission, *Fifth Semiannual Report of the Atomic Energy Commission*, January 1949 (Washington, D.C.: Government Printing Office, 1949), 5–6, 49–104.
42. Lewis L. Strauss, *Men and Decisions* (Garden City, N.Y.: Doubleday & Co., 1962), 216–22; Morgan Thomas, *Atomic Energy and Congress* (Ann Arbor: University of Michigan Press, 1956), 86–90.
43. Truman, *Years of Trial and Hope*, 308–9; Thomas, *Atomic Energy and Congress*, 90–92; Shepley and Blair, *The Hydrogen Bomb*, 80–89.
44. Thomas, *Atomic Energy and Congress*, 94, 105; USAF Historical Liaison Office, Air University, *A History of the Air Force Atomic Energy Program*, 1943–1953, 5:137; Col Homer L. Sanders, vice commander, Tactical Air Command, to Maj Gen Gordon P. Saville, deputy chief of staff for development, US Air Force, letter, 16 May 1950.
45. Air University, Air War College, Student Composite Solution, Problem No. 12, "The Import of the Atomic Bomb on Strategy and Tactics," 28 April 1947.
46. Air University, Air War College, Student Composite Solution, Problem No. 9, "Air War College War Plan," 28 June 1948.
47. Maj Gen Orville A. Anderson, "Air Warfare," lecture, Air Command and Staff School, Maxwell AFB, Ala., 14 June 1949.
48. Lt Col Harry M. Pike, "Limitations of an Air Defense System," *Air University Quarterly Review* 3, no. 2 (Fall 1949): 46–48.
49. Thomas K. Finletter, "The Air Force Task in Providing for National Security," lecture, Air War College, Maxwell AFB, Ala., 23 May 1950; Finletter, *Power and Policy*, 13–14.
50. Maj Gen Gordon C. Saville, "Philosophy of Air Defense," lecture, Air War College, Maxwell AFB, Ala., 7 June 1950.
51. "The Truth About Our Air Defense," *Air Force Magazine*, May 1953, 28–29; History, Air Research and Development Command, January–December 1953, 1:546–48; History, USAF Historical Liaison Office, Air University, 1 July 1949 to 30 June 1950, 32.
52. House, *DOD Appropriations for 1951*, pt. 3:1219–21.
53. Vandenberg, "Air Force Policies and Planning."

IDEAS, CONCEPTS, DOCTRINE

54. Saville, "Philosophy of Air Defense."
55. Nitze, "The Relationship of the Political End to the Military Objective"; Najeeb Hallaby, "Implications of the Continuing Conflict," lecture, Air War College, Maxwell AFB, Ala., 16 April 1956; Samuel P. Huntington, *The Soldier and the State* (Cambridge, Mass.: Harvard University Press, 1957), 384; Paul Y. Hammond, "NSC–68: Prologue to Rearmament," in Warner R. Schelling, Paul Y. Hammond, and Glenn H. Snyder, *Strategy, Politics, and Defense Budgets* (New York: Columbia University Press, 1962), 217–344.
56. House, *DOD Appropriations for 1951*, pt. 1:43–46, 80–81, 2635–36.
57. William Schaub, "The U.S. Security Policy from the Standpoint of the Bureau of the Budget," lecture, Air War College, Maxwell AFB, Ala., 1 November 1955; Samuel P. Huntington, *The Common Defense, Strategic Programs in National Politics* (New York: Columbia University Press, 1961), 53.
58. House, *Department of Defense Appropriations for 1951: Additional Supplemental Hearings before a Subcommittee of the Committee on Appropriations*, 81st Cong., 2d sess., 1950, 2–9.
59. Ibid., 29.
60. Vandenberg, "Air Force Policies and Planning"; Senate, *Military Situation in the Far East*, 1385.
61. Hilton P. Goss, *American Foreign Policy in Growth and Action* (Maxwell AFB, Ala.: Air University, Documentary Research Division, 1955), 181.
62. Herman Kahn, *On Thermonuclear War* (Princeton, N.J.: Princeton University Press, 1960), 571–72.
63. General of the Army Douglas MacArthur, *Reminiscences* (New York: McGraw-Hill Book Co., 1964), 320.
64. Nitze, "The Relationship of the Political End to the Military Objective"; Allen S. Whiting, *China Crosses the Yalu: The Decision to Enter the Korean War* (New York: Macmillan Co., 1960), 39; Senate, *Military Situation in the Far East*, 1740–41.
65. Whiting, *China Crosses the Yalu*, 34–36.
66. Senate, *Assignment of Ground Forces of the United States to Duty in the European Area: Hearings before the Committee on Foreign Relations and the Committee on Armed Services*, 82d Cong., 1st sess., 1951, 355; Alexander P. de Seversky, "Evaluation of the Air Weapon," lecture, Air War College, Maxwell AFB, Ala., 19 November 1953.
67. House, *The Supplemental Appropriation Bill for 1951: Hearings before a Subcommittee of the Committee on Appropriations*, 81st Cong., 2d sess., 1950, 20.
68. Department of Defense, *Semiannual Report of the Secretary of Defense and the Semiannual Reports of the Secretary of the Army, Secretary of the Navy, and Secretary of the Air Force, January 1 to June 30, 1951* (Washington, D.C.: Government Printing Office, 1951), 2.
69. House, *The Supplemental Appropriation Bill for 1951*, 230.
70. Ibid.; Futrell, *The United States Air Force in Korea*, 23–27.
71. Truman, *Years of Trial and Hope*, 345.
72. Ibid., 337, 341, 346–47; Senate, *Military Situation in the Far East*, 732, 945–46, 1764.
73. Senate, *Military Situation in the Far East*, 1764.
74. Ibid., 2438, 2443.
75. Ibid., 3063, 3067.
76. Whiting, *China Crosses the Yalu*, 98; Truman, *Years of Trial and Hope*, 383; *Time*, 4 September 1950, 12; *Time*, 11 September 1950, 22; Col John R. Maney, "The Support of Strategy," *Air University Quarterly Review* 6, no. 3 (Fall 1953): 45.
77. Senate, *Military Situation in the Far East*, 1362–63.
78. Truman, *Years of Trial and Hope*, 383; Maney, "The Support of Strategy," 45; "Orvil Anderson and Our Tradition," *Air Force Magazine*, October 1950, 5.
79. House, *The Supplemental Appropriation Bill for 1951*, 10.
80. Ibid., 230–31.
81. Gen Otto P. Weyland, "The Air Campaign in Korea," *Air University Quarterly Review* 6, no. 3 (Fall 1953): 5–10.
82. Futrell, *The United States Air Force in Korea*, 187–88.

83. Ibid., 193–225; Weyland, "The Air Campaign in Korea," 10–12.
84. Senate, *Assignment of Ground Forces of the United States to Duty in the European Area*, 447.
85. Truman, *Years of Trial and Hope*, 391–96; Futrell, *The United States Air Force in Korea*, 225–27.
86. Futrell, *The United States Air Force in Korea*, 225.
87. Senate, *Military Situation in the Far East*, 3072; MacArthur, *Reminiscences*, 378–80.
88. Truman, *Years of Trial and Hope*, 395–413.
89. Lt Gen Frank F. Everest, "Our Airborne Triple-Threat Force,"*Air Force Magazine*, December 1960, 52.
90. Senate, *Military Situation in the Far East*, 732, 945–46, 1764.
91. Gen Hoyt S. Vandenberg and Stanley Frank, "The Truth About Our Air Power," *Saturday Evening Post*, 17 February 1951, 20–21.
92. Senate, *Military Situation in the Far East*, 1379–80, 1383, 1416–17, 1424–25, 1478–79.
93. Ibid., 1378–79, 1393, 1500–1.
94. Ibid., 1502, 1500, 1378–79, 1382, 1385, 1417, 1492, 1505.
95. Truman, *Years of Trial and Hope*, 415–36; Futrell, *The United States Air Force in Korea*, 227–29.
96. Truman, *Years of Trial and Hope*, 432–50; Senate, *Military Situation in the Far East*, 39–148.
97. Weyland, "The Air Campaign in Korea," 11, 22; House, *Department of Defense Appropriations for 1956: Additional Hearings before a Subcommittee of the Committee on Appropriations*, 84th Cong., 1st sess., 1955, 53; Futrell, *The United States Air Force in Korea*, 265–84.
98. Weyland, "The Air Campaign in Korea," 11–13; Futrell, *The United States Air Force in Korea*, 285–345.
99. Futrell, *The United States Air Force in Korea*, 345; Weyland, "The Air Campaign in Korea," 17–18.
100. Finletter, *Power and Policy*, 247, 257.
101. Gen Hoyt S. Vandenberg, "Valedictory of the Chief,"*Air Force Magazine*, July 1953, 26.
102. Maj Gen William F. McKee, "Philosophy, Origin, and Functional Interrelationships of the Air Staff," lecture, Air War College, Maxwell AFB, Ala., 13 February 1952; memorandum by Maj Gen Thomas D. White, director of legislation and liaison, to secretary of the Air Force, 4 May 1950; Carl Vinson and Dewey Short, Committee on Armed Services, House of Representatives, to Hoyt S. Vandenberg, letter, 2 August 1950; memorandum by Col K. S. Axtater, deputy director of legislation and liaison, to Thomas K. Finletter, 30 October 1950.
103. Message, AFCVC-51413, US Air Force to commanding general, Far East Air Forces, 14 August 1950; message, AFCPR-51762, US Air Force to commanding general, Far East Air Forces, 18 August 1950; Lt Gen Lauris Norstad, vice chief of staff, US Air Force, to Maj Gen Glenn O. Barcus, letter, subject: Evaluation of USAF Operations in Korea, 6 October 1950; memorandum for record by Gen Nathan F. Twining, vice chief of staff, US Air Force, subject: Functions of Dr Stearns, General Barcus, and General White, 17 November 1950; Thomas K. Finletter to Dr Robert L. Stearns, letter, 16 December 1950; Finletter to Stearns, letter, 16 December 1950; Department of the Air Force, "Korean Evaluation Project: Report on Air Operations," 16 January 1951; USAF Evaluation Group, "An Evaluation of the Effectiveness of United States Air Force in Korea," 12 March 1951; memorandum by Gen Nathan F. Twining, vice chief of staff, US Air Force, to deputy chief of staff for operations et al., subject: Staff Action Monitoring Group, 26 February 1951; memorandum for distribution by Maj Gen William F. McKee, subject: Korea Evaluation Group, 8 February 1951.
104. Memorandum by Gen Nathan F. Twining to deputy chief of staff for operations et al., subject: Staff Action Monitoring Group, 26 February 1951.
105. Dr E. P. Learned, "Fundamentals of Organization," lecture, Air War College, Maxwell AFB, Ala., 27 October 1949; McKee, "Philosophy, Origin, and Functional Interrelationships of the Air Staff."
106. McKee, "Philosophy, Origin, and Functional Interrelationships of the Air Staff," *USAF Research and Development Quarterly Review*, 30 September 1951, 45.
107. Senate, *Study of Air Power: Hearings before the Subcommittee on the Air Force of the Committee on Armed Services*, 84th Cong., 2d sess., 1956, 195–96.

108. Claude Witze, "USAF Makes Up Its Mind," *Air Force Magazine*, November 1960, 65–70; *USAF Research and Development Quarterly Review*, 30 September 1951, 45.

109. Senate, *Study of Air Power*, 198.

110. Vandenberg and Frank, "The Truth About Our Air Power," 20.

111. History, Headquarters USAF, 1 July 1950 to 30 June 1951, 9; Col W. C. Garland, "Readiness vs Modernization and Expansion," lecture, Air War College, Maxwell AFB, Ala., 23 February 1954; Senate, *Study of Air Power*, 126–27.

112. Senate, *Assignment of Ground Forces of the United States to Duty in the European Area*, 335.

113. Tactical Air Operations presented to the USAF Review Board by the Tactical Air Command, 21 June 1949, 1–2.

114. Memorandum by Maj Gen Thomas D. White to secretary of the Air Force, 4 May 1950.

115. Vinson and Short to Vandenberg, letter, 2 August 1950.

116. Col William M. Gross, deputy chief of staff for operations, Tactical Air Command, R&R sheet, subject: Historical Report, 3 January 1951; Gen Otto P. Weyland, "Tactical Air Operations," lecture, Air War College, Maxwell AFB, Ala., 25 February 1955.

117. History, Tactical Air Command, 1 July to 30 November 1950, 1:1–12; Continental Air Command Regulation 26-1, *Organization—Tactical Air Command*, 11 August 1950.

118. History, Tactical Air Command, 1 December 1950 to 30 June 1951, 1:6.

119. Memorandum by Gen J. Lawton Collins, chief of staff, Army, to secretary of the Air Force, subject: Tactical Air Support, 9 March 1950; memorandum by General Collins to chief of staff, US Air Force, subject: Close Air Support of Ground Operations, 21 November 1950.

120. Gen Mark W. Clark, "What Kind of Air Support Does the Army Want?" *Air Force Magazine*, December 1950, 24–25, 52.

121. Brig Gen Homer L. Sanders, deputy chief of staff for operations, Tactical Air Command, R&R sheet, subject: Report on Conference on Light Aircraft for Close Air Support, 9 February 1951.

122. Lt Gen John K. Cannon, "The Employment of Air Forces in the Defense of Western Europe," lecture, Air War College, Maxwell AFB, Ala., 6 June 1951; General Cannon to chief of staff, US Air Force, letter, subject: Light Aircraft for Close Air Support, 19 February 1951.

123. Lt Gen John K. Cannon to chief of staff, US Air Force, letter, 19 February 1951.

124. Brig Gen Homer L. Sanders, "Tactical Air Operations in Retrospect and Prospect," *Air University Quarterly Review* 4, no. 3 (Spring 1951): 40; General Sanders to Col Alexander W. Cortner, letter, 12 May 1951.

125. Col Francis C. Gideon, "Command of the Tactical Air Force," *Military Review* 21, no. 2 (May 1951): 3–8.

126. Memorandum by Gen J. Lawton Collins to Hoyt S. Vandenberg, subject: Army Requirements for Close Support Aviation, 21 March 1951.

127. Memorandum by Thomas K. Finletter, 30 March 1951.

128. Gen Mark W. Clark to chief of staff, Army, subject: Tactical Air Support of Ground Forces, letter, 13 September 1951.

129. Col William M. Gross, R&R sheet, subject: Historical Report, 3 January 1951; Headquarters USAF, *A History of the Air Force Atomic Energy Program, 1943–1953*, vol. 5, *Atomic Weapon Delivery Systems*, 55–56, 139–40; Maj Gen Glenn O. Barcus to commanding general, Continental Air Command, letter, 6 October 1950.

130. History, Headquarters USAF, 1 July 1950 to 30 June 1951, 4.

131. Col James O. Guthrie, deputy director of requirements, US Air Force, to commanding general, Tactical Air Command, letter, subject: Requirements for Tanker Aircraft for Tactical Operations, 11 January 1951; 1st ind., Headquarters Tactical Air Command, to director of requirements, US Air Force, January 1951; Lt Gen John K. Cannon to deputy chief of staff for operations, US Air Force, letter, subject: Requirement for the McDonnell F–88 Aircraft, 17 February 1951; Cannon, "The Employment of Air Forces in the Defense of Western Europe," lecture, 6 June 1951.

132. Headquarters USAF, *A History of the Air Force Atomic Energy Program, 1943–1953*, 5:56–57, 142; Senate, *Study of Air Power*, 126–27; History, Tactical Air Command, January to June 1952, 5:14–16;

Lt Gen John K. Cannon to chief of staff, US Air Force, letter, subject: Tactical Bombardment Program, 12 February 1952.

133. Ralph D. Bald, *Air Force Participation in Joint Army-Air Force Training Exercise, 1947-1950*, USAF historical study 80 (Maxwell AFB, Ala.: Research Studies Institute, 1955), 16-31; "Exercise Swarmer The Thunder of a Concept," *Air Force Magazine*, July 1950, 19-22, 45, 48.

134. Maj Gen William H. Tunner, commanding general, Far East Air Forces, Combat Cargo Command (Provisional), to Maj Gen William F. McKee, assistant vice chief of staff, US Air Force, letter, 26 December 1950.

135. Memorandum by Maj Gen Gordon P. Saville, deputy chief of staff for development, US Air Force, to Gen Hoyt S. Vandenberg, subject: Air Force Support of the Army, 23 October 1950.

136. Lt Gen John K. Cannon to director of requirements, US Air Force, letter, subject: Troop Carrier Critique, 15 May 1961.

137. History, Headquarters USAF, 1 July 1950 to 30 June 1951, 4.

138. Maj Gen William M. Miley, "Capabilities and Current Tactics of Airborne Forces," lecture, Air War College, Maxwell AFB, Ala., 6 November 1951.

139. Gen Hoyt S. Vandenberg, "Concept and Employment of Air Power," lecture, Air War College, Maxwell AFB, Ala., 29 February 1952.

140. Maj Gen William H. Tunner, "Technology or Manpower," *Air University Quarterly Review* 5, no. 3 (Fall 1952): 20-21.

141. Director, Historical Services, Air Defense Command, historical study 4, *Army Antiaircraft in Air Defense, 1946 to 1954*, 3-17.

142. Ibid., 30-33, 34-38.

143. History, Continental Air Command, July to December 1950, 33, 46-48; director, Historical Services, Air Defense Command, *The Air Defense of the United States*, 129.

144. Director, Historical Services, Air Defense Command, *The Air Defense of the United States*, 129-30; historical study 4, *Army Antiaircraft in Air Defense, 1946-1954*, 39, 42-43.

145. C. L. Grant, *The Development of Continental Air Defense to 1 September 1954*, USAF Historical Study 126 (Maxwell AFB, Ala.: Research Studies Institute, 1957), 108.

146. Senate, *Air Force Organization Act of 1951: Hearings before a Subcommittee of the Committee Armed Services*, 82d Cong., 1st sess., 1951, 24.

147. House, *Sundry Legislation Affecting the Naval and Military Establishments, 1949: Hearings before the Committee on Armed Services*, 81st Cong., 1st sess., 1949, 91-316; Edwin L. Williams, Jr., *Legislative History of the AAF and USAF, 1941-1951*, USAF Historical Study 84 (Maxwell AFB, Ala.: Research Studies Institute, 1955), 65-66.

148. House, *Sundry Legislation Affecting the Naval and Military Establishments, 1951: Hearings before the Committee Armed Services*, 82d Cong., 1st sess., 1951, 15, 21-25, 51.

149. Ibid., 25-45.

150. Ibid., 11-19, 102, 106-7, 115.

151. Senate, *Air Force Organization Act of 1951*, 1-28.

152. Williams, *Legislative History of the AAF and USAF, 1941-1951*, 66-70; McKee, "Philosophy, Origin, and Functional Interrelationships of the Air Staff"; History, Tactical Air Command, July to December 1951, 1:1-2.

153. *Semiannual Report of the Secretary of Defense January to June 1951*, 30; House, *The Supplemental Appropriation Bill for 1951*, 7, 103, 231-32, 252-53, 389.

154. Memorandum by W. Barton Leach to chief of staff, US Air Force, subject: Documents Relating to Genesis of 143 Wing Air Force, 27 December 1953; History, Headquarters USAF, 1 July 1950 to 30 June 1951, 17-18; *Semiannual Report of the Secretary of Defense January to June 1951*, 30-31.

155. House, *The Supplemental Appropriation Bill for 1951*, 378.

156. Ibid., 238; Senate, *Department of Defense Appropriations for Fiscal Year 1952: Hearings before a Subcommittee of the Committee on Appropriations*, 82d Cong., 1st sess., 1951, 1262.

157. *Semiannual Report of the Secretary of Defense January to June 1951*, 31, 34.

158. Roger Lewis, "Department of the Air Force," *Air Force Magazine*, October 1953, 49.

159. Senate, *DOD Appropriations for 1952*, 1272.
160. Ibid., 321, 1253.
161. History, Air Materiel Command, January to June 1951, vol. 6, appendix E; History, Office of the Assistant for Programming, US Air Force, January to June 1951, 10.
162. History, Headquarters USAF, 1 July 1950 to 30 June 1951, 18–19; *Semiannual Report of the Secretary of Defense January to June 1951*, 200.
163. Senate, *DOD Appropriations for 1952*, 1274.
164. History, Air Materiel Command, January to June 1951, vol. 6, appendix E.
165. *United States Air Forces Statistical Digest FY 1952*, 163.
166. Maj Gen Thomas S. Power, deputy commander, Strategic Air Command, to director of requirements, US Air Force, letter, subject: Consolidation of Requirements for Penetration Fighters, 28 October 1949; Power to director of requirements, US Air Force, letter, 1 September 1950; Maj Gen Carl A. Brandt, director of requirements, US Air Force, to commanding general, Strategic Air Command, letter, subject: Penetration Fighter, 25 September 1950; Power to Brandt, letter, 18 October 1950; Lt Gen Curtis E. LeMay, commanding general, Strategic Air Command, to Maj Gen Gordon P. Saville, deputy chief of staff, US Air Force, letter, 30 January 1951; History, Air Research and Development Command, July 1951 to December 1952, 2:22; Gen Nathan F. Twining to commanding general, Strategic Air Command, letter, subject: Fighter-Bomber Requirements, 22 October 1951.
167. Finletter, *Power and Policy*, 267.
168. Senate, *Assignment of Ground Forces of the United States to Duty in the European Area*, 40.
169. *Semiannual Report of the Secretary of Defense January to June 1951*, 2, 147, 151.
170. Senate, *Department of Defense Appropriations for 1952*, 1253.
171. Ibid., 32.
172. Memorandum by W. Barton Leach to chief of staff, US Air Force, 27 December 1953.
173. Senate, *Assignment of Ground Forces of the United States to Duty in the European Area*, 37–38, 222.
174. "What Hope is There Left? An Exclusive AIR FORCE Interview with Alexander P. de Seversky," *Air Force Magazine*, January 1951, 34–35.
175. Gen Carl A. Spaatz, "The Airpower Odds Against the Free World," *Air Force Magazine*, April 1951, 23–26, 51–52, 59.
176. Memorandum by W. Barton Leach to chief of staff, US Air Force, 27 December 1953.
177. W. Barton Leach to Senator Henry Cabot Lodge, Jr., letters, 6 April 1951 and 26 April 1951.
178. Lodge to Leach, letters, 10 April 1951 and 28 April 1951; memorandum by Lodge to Leach, ca. 30 April 1951; Congressional Record, 30 April 1951, 4636–44.
179. Memorandum by Leach to chief of staff, US Air Force, 27 December 1953.
180. Senate, *DOD Appropriations for 1952*, 313–31, 1253–54, 1259–60, 1272–74, 1506–7.
181. Henry Cabot Lodge, "Let's Face It–We're in a Jam," *Saturday Evening Post*, 28 July 1951, 22–23.
182. Department of Defense, *Semiannual Report of the Secretary of Defense and the Semiannual Reports of the Secretary of the Army, Secretary of the Navy, and Secretary of the Air Force, January 1 to June 30, 1952* (Washington, D.C.: Government Printing Office, 1952), 4.
183. Ibid., 79, 140, 148, 152, 191–93, 196.
184. Ibid., 242; *United States Air Force Statistical Digest FY 1952*, 163; History, Headquarters USAF, 1 July 1950 to 30 June 1951, 75–78; History, Tactical Air Command, 1 July to 1 November 1950, 362; History, Tactical Air Command, January to June 1952, 5:14–16.
185. Senate, *Department of Defense Appropriations for Fiscal Year 1953: Hearings before a Subcommittee of the Committee on Appropriations*, 82d Cong., 2d sess., 1952, 5.
186. House, *Department of the Air Force Appropriations for 1953: Hearings before a Subcommittee of the Committee on Appropriations*, 82d Cong., 2d sess., 1952, 284.
187. Senate, *DOD Appropriations for 1953*, 384.
188. Ibid., 661–64.

189. Ibid., 384.
190. "General Bradley Says," *Air Force Magazine*, December 1951, 19; House, *DOD Appropriations for 1954: Hearings before a Subcommittee of the Committee on Appropriations*, 83d Cong., 1st sess., 1953, 474, 478.
191. House, *DOD Appropriations for 1953*, 10.
192. "General Bradley Says," 19.
193. Senate, *DOD Appropriations for 1953*, 245, 248, 333, 384–86; House, *DOD Appropriations for 1954*, 478–79.
194. Stanley, *American Defense and National Security*, 101; memorandum by Robert A. Lovett to secretary of the Air Force, 10 January 1952; Department of Defense, *Semiannual Report of the Secretary of Defense and the Semiannual Reports of the Secretary of the Army, Secretary of the Navy, and Secretary of the Air Force, July 1 to December 31, 1951* (Washington, D.C.: Government Printing Office, 1952), 35.
195. House, *DOD Appropriations for 1953*, 1028–29.
196. Ibid., 2-3, 10; Maj Gen O. S. Picher, "Air Force Programs," lecture, Air War College, Maxwell AFB, Ala., 2 December 1954.
197. Finletter, *Power and Policy*, 267–68; House, *Air Force Appropriations for 1953*, 4.
198. History, Assistance for Programming, US Air Force, January to June 1952, 5.
199. House, *Department of the Air Force Appropriations for 1953*, 186.
200. Senate, *DOD Appropriations for 1953*, 670.
201. Ibid., 247–48, 598.
202. House, *Department of the Air Force Appropriations for 1953*, 10, 42, 69.
203. Senate, *DOD Appropriations for 1953*, 403.
204. History, Air Materiel Command, January to June 1953, 1:7; History, Assistance for Programming, US Air Force, January to June 1952, 5–7; Department of Defense, *Semiannual Report of the Secretary of Defense and the Semiannual Reports of the Secretary of the Army, Secretary of the Navy, and Secretary of the Air Force, July 1 to December 31, 1952* (Washington, D.C.: Government Printing Office, 1953), 9.
205. Department of Defense, *Semiannual Report of the Secretary of Defense and the Semiannual Reports of the Secretary of the Army, Secretary of the Navy, and Secretary of the Air Force, January 1 to June 30, 1953* (Washington, D.C.: Government Printing Office, 1953), 208.
206. *United States Air Force Statistical Digest, FY 1953*, 122; History, Assistance for Programming, US Air Force, July to December 1952, 3–4.
207. *Semiannual Report of the Secretary of Defense January to June 1952*, 6–7.
208. *United States Air Force Statistical Digest FY 1953*, 190.
209. Thomas K. Finletter, "Official U.S. Postwar Evaluations of the Air Weapon," lecture, Air War College, Maxwell AFB, Ala., 17 November 1953.
210. California Institute of Technology, Final Report Project Vista, *A Study of Ground and Air Tactical Warfare with Especial Reference to the Defense of Western Europe*, series B, vol. A, ix–xii.
211. Ibid., xxi–xxviii.
212. Ibid., series B, vol. C, Tactical Air Operations, appendix IVB1.
213. Ibid., series B, vol. C, 93–142.
214. Ibid., series B, vol. A, vi.
215. Grant, *The Development of Continental Air Defense*, 62–64; History, Air Research Development Command, January to December 1953, 1:546–57; "The Truth About Our Air Defense," *Air Force Magazine*, May 1953, 29; "To Clarify the Air Defense Record," *Air Force Magazine*, September 1953, 24.
216. Grant, *The Development of Continental Air Defense*, 64; History, Air Research and Development Center, January to December 1953, 1:546–57; "The Truth About Our Air Defense," 29.
217. Final Report Project Vista, series B, vol. A, 3.
218. Lloyd V. Berkner, "Science and Strategy," lecture, National War College, Washington, D.C., 16 January 1953, 3.

219. Grant, *The Development of Continental Air Defense*, 64–65; Alfred Goldberg, ed., *A History of the United States Air Force, 1909–1957* (Princeton: D. Van Nostrand, 1957), 135.

220. Gen Benjamin W. Chidlaw, "Philosophy of Air Defense," lecture, Air War College, Maxwell AFB, Ala., 12 January 1953.

221. Maj Gen Gordon P. Saville, USAF, Retired, "The Air Defense Dilemma," *Air Force Magazine*, March 1953, 30.

222. Maj Gen Frederic H. Smith, Jr., "Current Practice in Air Defense: Part I, Principles and Problems," *Air University Quarterly Review* 6, no. 1 (Spring 1953): 3; Smith, "Current Practice in Air Defense: Part II, Impact of Modern Weapons," *Air University Quarterly Review* 6, no. 2 (Summer 1953): 31–32, 38–39.

223. History, Air Research and Development Command, January to December 1953, 1:546–57; "Air Defense: Kelly vs. 'Summer Study' Group," *Fortune*, July 1953, 40; "To Clarify the Air Defense Record," 24.

224. Finletter, "Official U.S. Postwar Evaluations of the Air Weapon"; Finletter, *Power and Policy*, 54–55, 202–5, 206–11.

225. Finletter, "Official U.S. Postwar Evaluations of the Air Weapon."

226. Finletter, *Power and Policy*, 242–45.

227. Col Ephraim M. Hampton, "Air Power, Global Force in a Global Struggle," *Air University Quarterly Review* 7, no. 4 (Spring 1955): 70; History, Headquarters USAF, 1 July 1950 to 30 June 1951, 26–27; History, Strategic Air Command, January to June 1951, 2:1–23.

228. Lt Gen Curtis E. LeMay, commanding general, Strategic Air Command, to Gen Hoyt S. Vandenberg, letter, 21 September 1950.

229. Futrell, *The United States Air Force in Korea*, 195, 232–33, 356.

230. History, Strategic Air Command, January to June 1951, 2:1–23.

231. Gen Walter B. Smith, "Assessment of Recent Soviet and Allied Policies," lecture, Air War College, Maxwell AFB, Ala., 18 April 1955; "Summary Report on Inspection of Chinese Communist Air Force," Far East Air Forces, Intelligence Roundup, no. 69, 22–28 December 1951, sec. 3, 1–27.

232. Smith, "Assessment of Recent Soviet and Allied Policies."

233. Weyland, "The Air Campaign in Korea," 18.

234. Lt Gen Otto P. Weyland, commanding general, Far East Forces, to chief of staff, US Air Force, letter, subject: Requirements for Increased Combat Effectiveness, 10 June 1951; message, V-0254-CG, commanding general, Far East Air Forces, to chief of staff, US Air Force, 12 July 1951.

235. Message, AFOIN-55358, US Air Force to Far East Air Forces, 10 July 1951; Weyland to chief of staff, US Air Force, letter, 10 June 1951, and 1st ind. from Gen Nathan F. Twining, vice chief of staff, US Air Force, to commanding general, Far East Air Forces, 17 July 1951.

236. Weyland to chief of staff, US Air Force, letter, 10 June 1951, and 1st ind. from Twining to commanding general, Far East Air Forces, 17 July 1951; memorandum by Maj Gen R. M. Ramey, director of operations, US Air Force, to John A. McCone, assistant secretary of the Air Force, 6 June 1951; message, V-0254-CG, commanding general, Far East Air Forces, to chief of staff, US Air Force, 12 July 1951; message, AFCCS-195, to commanding general, Far East Air Forces, 20 July 1951; A History of the Air Force Atomic Energy Program, 1943–1953, 5:142.

237. Weyland, "The Air Campaign in Korea," 21; Futrell, *The United States Air Force in Korea*, 400–8, 435–36.

238. House, *Department of Defense Appropriations for 1960: Hearings before a Subcommittee of the Committee on Appropriations*, 86th Cong., 1st sess., 1959, pt. 2:426.

239. Futrell, *The United States Air Force in Korea*, 374–80.

240. Ibid., 380–88.

241. Ibid., 408–14; Adm C. Turner Joy, *How Communists Negotiate* (New York: Macmillan Co., 1955), 125–29.

242. Futrell, *The United States Air Force in Korea*, 413–18, 439–46.

243. Goldberg, *A History of the United States Air Force*, 192.

244. Col C. E. Putnam, "Readiness vs Modernization and Expansion," lecture, Air War College, Maxwell AFB, Ala., 23 March 1953; *United States Air Force Statistical Digest, FY 1953*, 125, 130.

245. History, Third Air Force, July to December 1952, vii; Maj Gen Dean C. Strother, "Problems in Theater Air Operations — Western Europe," lecture, Air War College, Maxwell AFB, Ala., 19 March 1954.

246. Bernard Brodie, "Alternate National Strategies and Policies as Related to Current National Capabilities," lecture, Air War College, Maxwell AFB, Ala., 16 April 1953.

247. Futrell, *The United States Air Force in Korea*, 448–97.

248. Message, C-54277, commander in chief, Far East, to Joint Chiefs of Staff, 27 August 1952.

249. Far East Command-United Nations Command, Command Report, August 1952, 8–9.

250. Mark W. Clark, *From the Danube to the Yalu* (New York: Harper & Bros., 1954), 91–92.

251. Commander in chief, Far East, to commanding generals, Eighth Army, XVI Corps, Far East Air Forces, and commander, Naval Forces Far East, letter, subject: Air-Ground Operations, 11 August 1952.

252. Clark, *From the Danube to the Yalu*, 133–34; command reports of Far East Command and United Nations Command, August 1952, 2; January 1953, 2.

253. Futrell, *The United States Air Force in Korea*, 456–57.

254. Ibid., 471–73.

255. Memorandum by Gen Hoyt S. Vandenberg to Secretary of Defense, subject: The Military Effectiveness and Desirability of Employing Atomic Weapons Tactically in Korea, 14 August 1951; History, 49th Fighter-Bomber Wing, July to December 1952.

256. Futrell, *The United States Air Force in Korea*, 448–66.

257. Ibid., 474–80, 565–75.

258. Chester Bowles, *Ambassador's Report* (New York: Harper & Bros., 1954), 242–43; Leland M. Goodrich, *Korea, A Study of U.S. Policy in the United Nations* (New York: Council on Foreign Relations, 1956), 193.

259. Robert J. Donovon, *Eisenhower, The Inside Story* (New York: Harper & Bros., 1956), 28–30, 115, 118–19.

260. Futrell, *The United States Air Force in Korea*, 565–70, 608–23.

261. Ibid., 575–87, 623–29.

262. Ibid., 605–8, 628–40.

263. Richard P. Stebbins, *The United States in World Affairs, 1953* (New York: Harper & Bros., 1955), 211.

264. House, *Department of Defense Appropriations for 1957: Hearings before a Subcommittee of the Committee on Appropriations*, 84th Cong., 2d sess., 1956, 41.

265. Hampton, "Air Power, Global Force in a Global Struggle," 75.

266. Stebbins, *The United States in World Affairs, 1953*, 211.

267. Memorandum by Brig Gen Don Z. Zimmerman, Department for Intelligence, Far East Air Forces, subject: A Survey of Enemy Air Power and Capabilities in the Far East, 7 January 1954.

268. *Pacific Stars and Stripes*, 3 February 1954.

269. Smith, "Assessment of Recent Soviet and Allied Policies."

270. *FEAF Report on the Korean War*, 26 March 1954, 1:126.

271. Weyland, "The Air Campaign in Korea," 27–30.

272. Ibid., 28; *FEAF Report*, 1:133.

273. *FEAF Report*, 1:128–29.

274. Memorandum by Lt Gen Otto P. Weyland to Lt Gen George E. Stratemeyer, 9 April 1951, quoted in History, Far East Air Forces, July to December 1951, 14–18.

275. Memorandum of agreement, Lt Gen George E. Stratemeyer, commanding general, Far East Air Forces (FEAF), and Vice Adm C. Turner Joy, commander, Naval Forces Far East (NavFE), 26 March 1951; commander, Naval Forces Far East, Command and Historical Report, May-June 1953, sec. 1, 16; Report on Joint Air-Ground Operations Conference Held at Fifth Air Force, 8–22 August 1953; *FEAF Report*, 2:82.

276. Assistant for evaluation, deputy chief of staff for development, USAF, staff study, subject: "What Can and Should the USAF Do to Increase the Effectiveness of Air-Ground Operations?" ca. December 1950, 6–7.

277. History, Tactical Air Command, January-June 1953, 1:1–2; AFR 23-10, *Organization: Air Commands and Air Forces, Tactical Air Command*, 29 June 1953.

278. Brig Gen James E. Ferguson, "The Role of Tactical Air Forces," *Air University Quarterly Review* 7, no. 2 (Summer 1954): 37–38.

279. Brig Gen John J. Burns, US Army, President, Joint Eighth Army-Fifth Air Force Air-Ground Operations Board, to commanding generals, Eighth Army and Fifth Air Force, letter, subject: Analysis of the Air-Ground Operations System in Korea, 26 March 1951.

280. Commander in chief, Far East, to commanding generals, Eighth Army, XVI Corps, Far East Air Forces, and commander, Naval Forces Far East, letter, subject: Air-Ground Operations, 11 August 1952.

281. Report on Joint Air-Ground Operations Conference Held at Fifth Air Force, 8–22 August 1953.

282. Earl D. Johnson, "Department of the Army," *Air Force Magazine*, October 1953, 89.

283. R. Earl McClendon, *Army Aviation, 1947–1953* (Maxwell AFB, Ala.: Research Studies Institute, 1954), 6–9, 21–23; Memorandum of Understanding between Secretary of the Army and the Secretary of the Air Force, 2 October 1951.

284. Far East Command-United Nations Command, command report, November 1951, 88–89; History, Joint Air Transportation Board, 2 July 1951 to 3 March 1955, 30–31; McClendon, *Army Aviation 1947–1953*, 24–26.

285. McClendon, *Army Aviation, 1947–1953*, 25–28.

286. *FEAF Report*, 1:128; message, DPL-16295, Strategic Air Command to commanding general, FEAF Bomber Command, 21 October 1953.

287. *FEAF Report*, 1:iii.

288. Capt J. B. Burns, US Navy, "A Concept for Global War," lecture, Air War College, Maxwell AFB, Ala., 24 May 1955.

289. Ferguson, "The Role of Tactical Air Forces," 30.

290. *FEAF Report*, 1:128; 2:15–16.

291. Col James B. Tipton, "Employment of Air Forces in Korea," lecture, Air War College, Maxwell AFB, Ala., 26 March 1953.

292. Hampton, "Global Air Power," 72–73.

293. Ferguson, "The Role of Tactical Air Forces," 30.

294. *U.S. News and World Report*, 12 December 1952, 25; Malcolm W. Cagle and Frank A. Manson, *The Sea War in Korea* (Annapolis: United States Naval Institute, 1957), 270.

295. Weyland, "The Air Campaign in Korea," 21; "Tactical Air Command," *Air Force Magazine*, August 1954, 44.

296. Tipton, "Employment of Air Forces in Korea."

297. House, *DOD Appropriations for 1957*, 472.

298. Weyland, "The Air Campaign in Korea," 20.

299. *FEAF Report*, 1:126.

300. Ferguson, "The Role of Tactical Air Forces," 30–31.

Lt Gen O. P. Weyland, commander, Far East Air Forces, 1951–54.

Gen John K. Cannon, commander, Tactical Air Command, 1951–54.

Gen Nathan F. Twining, Air Force chief of staff, 1953–57.

MiG-15.

B-58 Hustler.

Charles E. Wilson, secretary of defense, 1953–57.

Thomas K. Finletter, secretary of the Department of the Air Force, 1950–53.

Maj Gen Gordon P. Saville, commander, Air Defense Command, 1948–49; deputy chief of staff, Development, 1950–51.

CHAPTER 7

THE AIR FORCE WRITES ITS DOCTRINE 1947–55

"Where in the Air Force," asked Maj Gen Lauris Norstad, the assistant chief of air staff for plans in 1946,

> will there be assembled more of what it takes to study, discuss, devise, develop, test and formulate than at the Air University? Here, in an atmosphere dedicated to instruction, thinking, study and discussion, there will of necessity be a constant evaluation of any current combat and an immediate application of its lessons to existing tactical doctrines. "Shall we change; is our doctrine sound?" will be daily questions in the minds of hundreds of instructors, spurred on by the sharp analysis and questions of thousands of highly-experienced students. Why not give these men the job of evaluating combat and formulating tactical doctrine for the entire Air Force? . . . They can probably do a better job, resolve a greater amount of sound thinking into useable doctrine than any group of men anywhere. And they will do it whether or not they are charged with it.[1]

Early Efforts to Identify Air Force Doctrine

As a result of Norstad's recommendations and the favorable reputation enjoyed by the old Air Corps Tactical School, the Air Force issued a June 1946 mission summary that read that the Air University:

> reviews, revises, and prepares publication of AAF basic doctrine. . . . Develops basic doctrines and concepts for the employment of air power. . . . Maintains continuing research into the strategic, tactical, and defensive concepts of air power, both manned and unmanned aircraft and guided missiles. . . . Maintains close liaison with the Headquarters of the Strategic Air Command, the Tactical Air Command and the Air Defense Command with regard to matters of policy and doctrine.[2]

During 1946 the Air University established the Air War College at Maxwell Field, Montgomery, Alabama; the Air Command and Staff School at Craig Field, Selma, Alabama; and the Air Tactical School at Tyndall Field, Panama City, Florida. Believing that the Air University ought to furnish officers with facts, skills, and technical information and also to guide the future thinking of the Air Force, the Air University's Faculty Board stated that the new educational institution would not be bound to accept official policies without question but would only present them for study. Regardless of existing policies, students could be told of the Air University's beliefs. The Faculty Board stated that all curricula would incorporate a basic school doctrine: "the ultimate objective of air power is to force the capitulation of an enemy nation by air action applied directly against the vital points of its national structure. This may not at any given time be primary in importance, but it is the ultimate objective."[3]

The Air University's broad responsibility for developing concepts and doctrines and for testing tactics rested upon an initial assumption that the institution would be assigned typical combat air units that could be employed for test purposes. As has been seen, Gen Carl A. Spaatz found it impossible to assign such units to the Air University and ordered that the Air University would depend on other commands to conduct tactical tests and developmental work. Spaatz also stated that the "doctrines taught at the Air University will be those current in the various commands, approved as necessary" by Air Force headquarters.[4] Seeking to bridge the conflict in orders, Maj Gen David M. Schlatter, the Air University's deputy commander, announced that in accomplishing its research, evaluation, and doctrinal functions the Air University would "act in the capacity of a monitoring agency or steering committee utilizing the expert knowledge available in all of the commands of the Air Force."[5] Recognizing that its mission was one of evaluation rather than research, the Air University redesignated its Research Division as the Evaluation Division on 29 August 1947.[6]

Except for announcing the basic doctrine that would govern its instructors, the Air University made little progress in preparing statements of basic Air Force doctrine. In Washington on 13 May 1946, Brig Gen Francis H. Griswold, deputy chief of air staff for operations, urged that the Air Force ought to begin to formulate its doctrine. "There is a requirement for a field manual," Griswold wrote,

> which will establish the place of air power in the armed forces and define our policies, doctrines, strategy and tactics. . . . The theory or strategy of air power, particularly strategic bombing, has never been adequately put on paper. . . . A strong and logical framework must be developed from which can be provided appropriate manuals for the provisional education of officers of all ranks in all of the armed forces, and policies to guide our public relations and dealings with Congress.

Although War Department Field Manual (FM) 100-20, *Command and Employment of Air Power*, had been "a declaration of independence of air power," Griswold noted that it was already "obsolete and entirely inadequate." As written in 1943, this manual had emphasized the coequality of air and ground power. "Land power and air power," Griswold thought, "are not always interdependent forces. There are times when air power at least may be an independent force." At the time of Griswold's recommendation, however, Maj Gen Muir S. Fairchild, the Air University commander, was reluctant to commit his personnel to a doctrinal problem until the new institution was firmly established. Maj Gen Charles C. Chauncey, deputy chief of the Air Staff, additionally feared that any revision of FM 100-20 might stir up a political controversy that could hinder the cause of armed service unification.[7] Unlike the Air Force, the Navy moved boldly to provide a basic doctrine to its forces. In the closing months of World War II, it assembled a full-time panel of officers whose duties had involved combat command or important staff work and directed them to prepare a series of US fleet (USF) publications. The key manual in this series — USF-1, *Principles and Instructions of Naval Warfare* — went through many drafts within the panel, was circulated for comments from naval commanders, and was published on 1 May 1947 with the notation that it represented "the best service opinion and best knowledge that obtains in 1946."[8]

With armed services unification assured by the National Security Act of 1947, Brig Gen Thomas S. Power, now deputy assistant chief of air staff for operations, directed the Air University to undertake its doctrinal responsibility without further delay. "There is a requirement for an Air Force publication of field manual scope," he wrote, "that will establish the doctrine and command of air power in the Armed Forces and define our policies and strategies. . . . It is visualized that this manual will be the top level Air Force document from which will be derived all other Air Force publications relative to air power and joint operations." Power directed the Air University to revise FM 100-20 and to provide recommendations for the type of Air Force publication that would be employed to disseminate doctrine.[9] Without awaiting action on this problem, the Air Force in August 1947 summoned representatives of the Air University, the Air Defense Command, the Tactical Air Command, and the Strategic Air Command to form two panels to provide guidance for an Air Force position in regard to air defense procedures, doctrine, and organization. Headed by Col Richard H. Carmichael, chief of the Air Power Employment Section of the Air University's Evaluation Division, the Air Defense Policy Panel held meetings during the winter of 1947-48 and made its final written report to the Air Force chief of staff on 2 February 1948. The report concluded: "The security of the nation from air attack rests primarily upon our strategic air offensive capabilities, but air defense is necessary and can achieve a degree of effectiveness which may mean the difference between victory and defeat." It recommended that a unified continental theater of operations comprised of Army, Navy, and Air Force forces operating under a single commander would provide the most effective and economical organization to ensure the security of the United States against air attack.[10]

When the Air University was directed to revise FM 100-20 and to recommend a system of doctrinal publications, General Schlatter took account of the fact that the Air University's Evaluation Division had only 18 officers and that not all of them could be assigned to a manuals project. He, therefore, directed that the Evaluation Division monitor and evaluate such projects, which would be carried out in the Air University's schools and colleges. He specifically directed the Air War College to revise the field manual and to recommend a system of doctrinal publications.[11] During his tenure as founding commandant of the Air War College, Maj Gen Orvil Anderson frequently had student seminars study and report on major air problems, and he used this procedure to handle the doctrinal projects.

On 16 September 1947 two Air War College seminars began working on the assigned problems. In its report on 19 December, a seminar headed by Col W. M. Garland recommended that the Air Force develop a single integrated publications system under the Office of the Vice Chief of Staff. The seminar suggested that the old Army system of disseminating doctrine in field manuals and technical manuals had been too rigid and had never provided a comprehensive coverage. The Navy's US fleet series appeared more acceptable as a model for the Air Force. The seminar, therefore, proposed that the Air Force ought to use a series of "air employment instructions" that would promulgate the concepts of the roles and objectives of air power in national security, the principles and doctrines of command and employment of the Air Force in peace and war, and the strategy, tactics, and techniques of Air Force operations. Published under the authority of the chief of staff, these air employment instructions would "constitute essential guides" and would "reflect the most logical current thought in the employment of air power," but they would not seek "to suppress initiative or to establish a set formula for air warfare." The air employment instructions should be divided into three general categories. Category 1 would comprise a basic book on air power. Category 2 would outline in general terms the application of fundamental principles and basic doctrines of employment to specific operational fields of Air Force endeavor — for example, strategic air operations. Category 3 would deal with the operations, tactics, and techniques of type units of the Air Force, such as the tactics and techniques of fighter escort. Immediate responsibility for stating requirements for air employment instructions and for ensuring that they were properly revised would rest with the Air Force deputy chief of staff for operations. The seminar recommended that the air employment instructions be issued in loose-leaf binders so that they might be revised easily.[12]

The Air University accepted the requirement for such series of doctrinal publications, but it was not willing to limit the series to purely operational matters since it believed that the Air Force would need to express doctrine in administrative, logistics, communications, intelligence, and related special staff fields. Accordingly, on 5 February 1948 the Air University recommended that the air employment instructions should include three somewhat different categories from those proposed by the Air War College. Category 1 would continue to be the basic volume entitled "Air Power." Category 2 would be called "The Commander's Guide," and its single volume of seven books would include statements of Air Force operations in general and in strategic applications, joint endeavors, air defense, air transport, air reconnaissance, and special activities. Category 3 would be "The Group and Squadron Commander's Handbook," and its single volume of six books would deal with the tactical group and squadron and the tactics and techniques of bombardment, fighters, reconnaissance, air transport, and special air units. The Air University noted that "the interested agency on the highest level should be responsible for the doctrine promulgated in a given field."[13]

Both the Air War College and Air University emphasized that the number and type of publications within the Air Force ought to be greatly reduced. The Air Staff also endorsed this objective on 5 March when it directed the Air University to proceed with the preparation of the recommended air employment and administrative instructions, which quite likely would be issued as a series of Air

Force manuals rather than as a separate publications series.[14] Although the Air Staff appeared to have approved the Air University's planning, an Air Force Publications Board, which assembled in Washington early in 1948, refused to accept the plan of action. The Air Force regulation issued on the subject of publications on 26 April described 10 types of publications, including manuals. Manuals would include the types of material that had been called field and technical manuals, training standards, guides, handbooks, pamphlets, textbooks, and workbooks. Any Air Force command would be authorized to issue local command manuals on subjects peculiar to the command. Air Force manuals would normally be prepared by responsible functional Air Staff agencies, but, in certain instances, Headquarters USAF would delegate the preparation of the texts of manuals to a subordinate command. In those cases, the Air Staff would review and approve the draft manual. The air adjutant general was charged to edit and authenticate all Air Force manuals.[15]

While Colonel Garland's seminar was surveying the Air Force publications system, another Air War College seminar headed by Col C. P. Lessig was assigned the task of revising FM 100-20. Because of Garland's recommendations, Lessig's seminar undertook to draft the "Air Power" volume of the air employment instructions series and completed this project in February 1948.[16] Meanwhile, another seminar—headed by Col R. A. Grussendorf and composed of Cols Noel F. Parrish, Arno Leuhman, E. L. Sykes, and G. P. Disosway—was tasked with the problem of determining how the Air University ought to proceed with producing "The Commander's Guide." In a study completed on 16 March, this seminar suggested that the Air Force had been "organized and operated as a result of ideas existing in the minds of a very few men" that had "never been well stated" and had "never been brought together and organized into a complete and logical form" nor "explained in suitable terms bearing the sanction of official approval." It recommended that a permanent group of qualified Air Force officers and civilian writers, working under direct authority of the vice chief of staff, should be assigned the task of writing and continuously revising the text of the air employment instructions. Grussendorf's seminar also recommended that the collection of source material for this permanent group should be as comprehensive as possible, that the sources should encompass the best thoughts of all available experts on air power employment, and that personal interviews should be used to the maximum. Since few air leaders had written clearly on the fundamentals of air warfare, the seminar suggested that any complete and official statement of the meaning of air power could "be derived from only one source, the minds of leading military airmen." While they were brief and incomplete, the statements of Air Force leaders during the investigations of the Air Policy Commission and the Joint Congressional Aviation Policy Board headed by Sen Owen R. Brewster were judged to represent Air Force principles and purposes better than anything to be found in official publications. The seminar concluded with a flourish: "The principles of Air Warfare stem from Mitchell, Arnold, and Knerr more notably than from Frederick or Napoleon, and Air Force thinking needs no Old Testament text for justification"; air power doctrine would come largely from living men.[17]

Having received authorization to proceed with the preparation of the air employment and administrative instructions, Air University officers assumed that the Air Force Publications Board would accept the planning that had been done in the Air War College originally. On 5 April 1948, the Air University accordingly established a board of officers from the Evaluation Division and the Air Command and Staff School to draft "The Commander's Guide"; and on 16 April the command directed the Air Tactical School to prepare "The Group and Squadron Commander's Handbook."[18] Expressing a desire that the publications should have a high quality of styling, illustrations, content, and format, the Air University asked the Air Force to make available to it personnel "with literary or artistic experience and talent."[19] While on a visit to Fort Monroe and Washington to survey Army and Navy publications activities early in May, Colonel Carmichael, who would shortly become chief of the Air University Evaluation Division, was startled to learn that the Air Force regulation on publications had "rejected the Air War College plan completely." He pointed out that the new Air Force regulation placed responsibility for doctrinal manuals with Air Staff agencies and thus conflicted with the assignment of doctrinal responsibilities to the Air University. Under the new regulation no single Air Force agency was empowered to pass judgment on the content of manuals or review the whole field to ensure that manuals provided a comprehensive coverage. At no point in the new system was there a stated requirement for professional editors, writers, or illustrators. "The quality of USAF publications, particularly manuals which will become the media for the enunciation of USAF employment and training doctrine," Carmichael noted, "is not assured of being superior or even excellent."[20]

Although the Air Force regulation of 26 April made Air Staff agencies responsible for manuals on doctrine, the Air Force, nevertheless, stated on 25 June 1948 that the Air University planning represented "an advance in simplification and condensation of Air Force manuals." Therefore, the Air Staff directed the Air University to continue preparation of the category 1, 2, and 3 instructions and suggested subjects for several specialized administrative manuals that the Air Force would require.[21] At this juncture Colonel Carmichael again asserted the need for a single Air Force agency, under the vice chief of staff or able to speak with the authority of the vice chief, to provide a central direction for the planning, preparation, and revision of Air Force manuals. "It is completely unrealistic," he thought, "to believe that Headquarters staff agencies will 'normally prepare' all manuals." He thought that the three principal deficiencies in the Air Force publications system — divided responsibility at the top, lack of a master plan, and insufficient professional assistance — sprang from a "lack of appreciation for the prodigious amount of thought and labor required to produce a good manual." "A manual," he said, must first express sound doctrine. This requires careful research and evaluation of everything that has been written or spoken about the subject. Once the ideas have been assembled they must be arranged in a logical and orderly manner. Then the writing phase of the process begins, the most laborious part of the task. When ideas are expressed in such a way that the reader can readily grasp their meaning, the manual is readable as well as intelligible. There is more to readability than merely making the meaning clear to the reader, it is measured also by the use of illustrative materials within the text.... A well written and illustrated manual is the result of the ideas and work of many people. This fact must first be recognized before any effective manual system can be established.

Carmichael also noted that "manual writing cannot be effectively and efficiently accomplished as a part time, 'in addition to other duties' measure" and urged that the Air University ought to establish a production unit that "will take the writing load off of the instructors in the schools and place it upon qualified civilians under the direction of competent officer personnel."[22]

Anticipating that it would become "the 'Bible' of the Air Force and the keystone from which all other Air Force doctrinal publications will stem," the Air University expedited the preparation of the category 1 volume now titled "Air Power and the US Air Force." The initial draft prepared by the Air War College seminar in February 1948 was reviewed and revised by the Evaluation Division in March and April and was circulated through the Air University's schools and staff during May. Believing that the principal purpose of a manual was to teach, the Air University sought to ensure that the air power manual was "written in sufficient detail and with such clarity so as to be intelligible and attractive to the average junior officer." Although it did not consider its draft to be a final product, the Air University submitted "Air Power and the US Air Force" to the Air Force director of training and requirements on 2 July 1948, with a request that the Air Staff review its "scope, tenor, and general form."[23]

When the Air Staff had completed its review of "Air Power and the US Air Force," Maj Gen Frank F. Everest, assistant deputy chief of staff for operations, informed the Air University on 21 September 1948 that the manual did not fulfill the purposes for which it was intended. The Air Staff found the draft manual to be discursive and defensive rather than positive, to be written in a narrative form rather than concisely worded for reference purposes, to be lengthy and cumbersome, to contain much inessential in detail such as references to World War II experiences, to include controversial statements that did not contribute to an enunciation of doctrine, and to have other bits and pieces of information that were much too obvious for a high-level publication. Still the Air Staff disagreed with the reasoning of the manual only in a few particulars. It criticized as unnecessarily controversial the manual's statement: "Because air forces can be used in so many ways in the attack and because of the difficulties of protecting against such air attacks, the requirements for air defense measures are so great as to approach the unacceptable." The Air Staff believed that the description of an air mobilization phase at a war's beginning weakened the Air Force's emphasis on an air force in being. The strong assertion in the manual that "strategic bombing operations are normally conducted independently of ground and naval forces" was said to be contrary to the more moderate Air Force position that Army and Navy forces were essential for the defense of overseas air bases required for a strategic air campaign. "In the preparation of this high level doctrinal publication," the Air Staff advised,

> it is necessary that it be as timeless and far thinking as possible.... This publication on air employment is of such importance, covering high level doctrine and the principles of aerial warfare, that it should not be burdened with detailed instructional and procedural methods which are constantly changing. On the other hand, this type publication should cover general over-plans for doctrine and strategy which would stimulate flexibility of thought and action at all levels of command.[24]

In the spring of 1948 the Air University assigned responsibility for preparing the category 2 "Commander's Guide" to the Air Command and Staff School at Craig Field and for drafting the category 3 "Commander's Handbook" to the Air Tactical School at Tyndall Field. Each of these institutions, in turn, assigned the responsibilities for drafting the various books in the volumes to specific instructors. These instructors were unable to begin any serious attempts to write before the summer vacation period, and even then they could do little more than to prepare some highly tentative drafts on their assigned contributions. On 22 December the Air Force director of training and requirements asked that the drafts of the category 2 and 3 manuals be delivered to him in order that he might use them to provide guidance to the Air Staff in negotiations that were getting under way with the Navy. Although the Air University was reluctant to allow imperfect work to go to Washington, it complied with the Air Force request with misgivings but with some expectation that it might also begin to get some comments on the work.[25] After surveying the manuscripts, however, the Training and Requirements Division returned them with the notation that it had not considered them ready to be submitted to the Air Staff.[26]

During the spring and summer of 1949, the Air University Evaluation Division worked on revising the category 2 and 3 volumes, giving priority to the category 2 "Commander's Guide," which it intended to publish first. In the autumn of 1949 the Air University forwarded printed copies of the five books of the "Commander's Guide" to the Air Staff and to the major Air Force commands, with a request that they be reviewed for content, style, format, and suitability for Air Force usage. As had been the case with the "Air Power" volume, Air Staff comments on the guide were highly critical. One reviewer stated: "I don't believe a Commander would read it more than once—he might even stop after the first page." Other comments indicated that the volume contained information that was out of date, was too elementary to meet the purpose for which it was intended, was incomplete in scope, and generally did not measure up to standards required of an Air Force publication. The Air Staff directed on 25 July 1950 that the volume should be rewritten, and it further suggested that the Air University seek assistance from the

Air Force's operating commands. "Only then," stated Col Dorr E. Newton of the Directorate of Requirements, "will we get the latest tactical doctrine, tactics, and techniques incorporated."[27]

"I guess I personally am responsible for having sent out some poor tentative manuals," admitted Maj Gen John DeForest Barker, who had become the Air University's deputy commander in August 1949. "I decided to let them go out 'as is' for comment, and then rewrite them in manual form, rather than to write them in manual form, send them out for comment, and then again rewrite them according to the comments. I think we saved time by this method, but we certainly didn't improve our standing in the community."[28] Barker was free to admit that the Air University's manuals had been couched in "Adjutant General's language" which was "stilted, expressionless, and to a considerable extent meaningless." "They are the kind of a book which a man reads because he has to," he said, "not because he wants to. I would like very much to have them written in such a style that people enjoy reading them and hence will get more out of them."[29] Highly motivated to complete the doctrinal manuals project, Barker proved able to exercise some economies within the Air University and to secure spaces for four military and three civilian editors for assignment to the Air University Publications Office. In June 1950 the Publications Office took over the responsibility for completing the "Air Power," "Commander's Guide," and "Commander's Handbook" manuals. The work of revising these books appeared to be going well, perhaps because of the fact that the Air University had secured many indications of the sort of material that was not believed to be appropriate in a doctrinal publication. On 26 September 1950, however, Barker received word that a project was under way in Washington to prepare and publish joint armed forces doctrinal publications. Since the joint-force doctrines might well supersede the air employment instructions, Barker reasoned that the Air University must suspend its doctrinal work pending the maturity of the higher level discussions on doctrine.[30]

Air Force Activities in the Field of Joint Doctrine

At the end of World War II senior Air Force officers expected that the Army and Navy Staff College—which would become the National War College in mid-1946—would be able to provide joint-force doctrine in much the same manner in which it was expected that the new Air University would prepare air doctrine.[31] Under a directive from the Joint Chiefs, a Joint Operations Review Board of approximately 50 Army and Navy officers convened at the Army and Navy Staff College early in 1946 to study the joint operations of World War II and to revise joint doctrine as necessary.[32] Meanwhile, under the guidance of the National War College, the Joint Operations Review Board submitted a draft manual entitled "Joint Overseas Operations" to the Joint Chiefs on 15 August 1946, which the Joint Chiefs promptly transmitted to the Army and Navy for comment.[33] Although General Spaatz acknowledged the need for a new publication to replace prewar Army-Navy agreements, he was unwilling to accept the draft "Joint Overseas

Operations" manual. The proposed text envisaged some unity of command with an integrated, triservice joint staff, but it failed to develop this doctrine in any precise detail. The text did not consider the possibility that a hostile nation might be defeated by air attack, and it was chiefly concerned with amphibious landings of ground troops at an overseas objective.[34]

Thinking that the armed services must have an agreement on future overseas operations but being unwilling to accept the jointly prepared manual, Maj Gen Otto P. Weyland, assistant chief of air staff for plans, proposed on 29 August 1946 that the Army Air Forces extend the same type of cooperative arrangements accepted in War Department Field Manual 31-35, *Air-Ground Operations*, to the field of amphibious operations. Following this line of reasoning, the assistant chief of air staff for operations, Maj Gen Earle E. Partridge, prepared a paper entitled "Joint Procedures for Tactical Control of Aircraft in Joint Amphibious Operations," which the Army Air Forces promptly submitted to the Joint Chiefs as its concept of the command and control of air power in joint operations. This paper stated, "The Joint Task Force is normally divided into air, ground, and naval components, each under its own commander. All components of the team are under the Joint Task Force commander who is responsible for the joint effort." In brief, the Air Force paper sought to secure a unity of air action by expanding the joint operations center already being used as the instrument of Army-Air Force cooperation to include a Navy operations section as well as the Army air-ground section and the Air Force combat operations section.[35]

The Army informally concurred with the Air Force position, but the Navy preferred to look upon amphibious operations as a two-phase endeavor in which a fleet commander would command forces afloat and would pass command to the landing force commander when troops were set ashore. The Navy had already published its views in USF-6, *Amphibious Warfare Instructions*, and it looked upon the Air Force paper as containing "information which is contrary in many points to standard Navy doctrine and to experience gained in World War II."[36] The Navy opposition made it evident that the paper could not be approved by the Joint Chiefs, but General Partridge, director of training and requirements of the Air Force, believed, nevertheless, that it could be issued as a revision of Field Manual 31-5, *Landing Operations on Hostile Shores*. Seeking comments and recommendations, Partridge submitted the Air Force position to the Air University and the Tactical Air Command. The Tactical Air Command responded with a vigorous demand that the Air Force not "compromise or appease" and suggested that the wording on command structure should be stated even more strongly.

> The Air Force should advocate and persist as a basic principle that there should be a unified command for an amphibious operation; that there will be appointed an overall commander who commands the operation from the time of inception until completion; that the overall commander will not concurrently command one of the major subordinate forces involved; that the overall commander will have a joint staff consisting of Air, Ground and Naval personnel; that the amphibious force will be composed of a

Naval Force responsible for the conduct of all ground action, and an Air Force responsible for the conduct of all air action.

The Air University concurred in the Tactical Air Command's recommendations. It assumed that the proposed statement on command would "certainly be violently opposed by the Navy," but it thought that the manual might be issued as Army-Air Force doctrine. On 28 October 1948, however, the Army agreed that "a Manual of this type would be desirable as an interim statement of doctrine," but it believed that such a manual ought to be processed through the Joint Chiefs and was unwilling to consider its issuance as an Army-Air Force publication.[37]

Still seeking to secure a means for developing joint doctrines and procedures that would replace unilateral service publications, the Joint Chiefs of Staff established an Ad Hoc Committee for Joint Policies and Procedures in the autumn of 1948 and assigned it the task of revising the 1935 edition of *Joint Action of the Army and Navy*. The deputies for operations of the Navy and Air Force and the deputy for administration of the Army served as the members of the ad hoc committee.[38] Since one of the sections in the proposed publication was to concern tactical air support, the committee requested the Tactical Air Command and the Army Field Forces to prepare a joint statement on the matter. To the surprise of the Tactical Air Command, which saw no reason why the organizational lessons tested during World War II and incorporated in Field Manual 31-35 should be so soon out of date, the Army Field Forces indicated that the manual was already obsolete and should be revised. With this and other matters in dispute, the Army member of the committee proposed that the Joint Chiefs of Staff should establish at least four joint centers (airborne, tactical air support, air defense, and amphibious), which would be charged with the development of joint doctrines, tactics and techniques, joint training, and joint testing of equipment. Some Marine Corps officers interpreted this proposal as an Army attempt to deprive the Marine Corps of its responsibilities in the amphibious field. The Air Force did not like the proposal since it believed that it would be as inappropriate for ground officers to evaluate air tactics, techniques, and equipment as for air officers to attempt to do the same for similar ground activities. In the end, the Navy and Air Force members voted against the joint center proposal because it involved the transfer of legally established primary service responsibilities to new agencies.[39]

General Norstad, the Air Force deputy chief of staff for operations, agreed with the proposal of Maj Gen Robert M. Lee, commander of the Tactical Air Command, that a board of the Air Force's most experienced tactical air commanders ought to review current doctrine, tactics, procedures, and equipment; draw conclusions as to their suitability in the light of new developments; and make appropriate recommendations. Gen Muir S. Fairchild established the USAF Board of Review for Tactical Air Operations on 10 June 1949; the membership included Lt Gen Elwood S. Quesada, Maj Gen Richard E. Nugent, General Schlatter, General Weyland, and Brig Gen David W. Hutchison. Appearing before the review board on 14 July, Gen J. Lawton Collins, US Army chief of staff, urged that Field Manuals 100-20 and 31-35 be rewritten. Field Manual 100-20, for example, stated that missions against hostile forces at the front lines were "most difficult to control, are most expensive, and are in general least effective." Collins did not believe that this statement was necessarily true. He argued that Field Manual 31-35 should be revised to define tactical air support of ground forces as being "the application of tactical air power in the furtherance of a ground campaign as required by the ground force commander to achieve his mission." He also proposed that a joint tactical air support center be established in the Fort Bragg-Pope AFB area. After holding six formal sessions, each of several days' duration, the board reported in October 1949. Its major finding was the Air Force concept of tactical air power needed positive reaffirmation and ought to embrace three major concepts: (1) tactical air operations in concert with a major surface campaign designed to exploit the strategic air offensive by engaging the military forces of an enemy nation in combat; (2) tactical air operations in concert with a limited surface campaign to defend or to expand certain important base areas; and (3) tactical air operations in concert with the strategic air offensive within the capabilities of tactical air power to attrite the enemy air force, to destroy the mobile transportation facilities of the enemy nation, and to isolate deployed enemy forces from their source of sustenance. The Board of Review agreed that Field Manuals 100-20 and 31-35 required revision, but it asserted that the Air Force must be its own judge of tactics, techniques, and equipment.[40]

As early as 1 July 1948 General Spaatz informally indicated that the broad mission of the Tactical Air Command required it to develop and test tactical doctrines and techniques.[41] In a headquarters reorganization in January 1949, the Tactical Air Command accordingly established a deputate for plans, headed first by Col William W. Momyer and later by Col Henry Viccellio, and included within it a directorate of doctrine that was charged to represent the Tactical Air Command on joint agencies, boards, and committees that might examine and evaluate doctrine, tactics, techniques, and procedures related to tactical air operations.[42] Beginning in February 1949 the Tactical Air Command's deputy for plans worked closely with representatives of the Army Field Forces in preparing a joint paper for the Ad Hoc Committee for Joint Policies and in defining procedures that delineated the areas of agreement and disagreement on the tactical air support of ground forces.[43] The planned reorganization of the Tactical Air Command also authorized the establishment of a Headquarters Tactical Air Force (Provisional). Effective on 16 July 1949 the Tactical Air Force (Provisional) was established at Pope AFB where it would work closely with Headquarters V Corps at nearby Fort Bragg in planning and conducting joint maneuvers and exercises.[44]

In the spring of 1949 the Tactical Air Command and the Army Field Forces had been unable to agree on a joint paper for submission to the ad hoc committee sitting in Washington, but another project looking toward the preparation of a joint training directive for the Tactical Air Force and V Corps went more smoothly when it was begun in early August 1949. Working from an agreed outline of proposed chapters, Tactical Air Command representatives prepared drafts that went to the Office of the Chief of Army Field Forces. With concurrence from the Army Field Forces, the draft chapters were sent to the Tactical Air Force-V Corps for field tests.[45] Army officers were enthusiastic about the Tactical Air Force-V Corps agreement. General Collins, speaking with a degree of hyperbole, described it as an organization that was able "to work full time not only in training but also in the development of tactical doctrine of airborne and close support operations, as well as in the development and testing of proper equipment."[46]

Before the end of March 1950, drafts of most of the chapters of a joint training directive had been forwarded to the Tactical Air Force-V Corps for consideration and testing. According to the plan, the organization and equipment specified in the draft training directive were to be tested in the course of regular joint maneuvers and field exercises; based on these field tests, the Tactical Air Command expected to prepare a publication that could replace Field Manual 31-35.[47] The beginning of the Korean War, however, forced the cancellation of most planned field exercises and maneuvers and also increased the need for revisions in joint air-ground doctrine. Because of the urgency of the matter, Brig Gen Homer L. Sanders, vice commander of the Tactical Air Command, and Brig Gen William S. Lawton, chief of staff of the Army Field Forces, went ahead with the publication of the *Joint Training Directive for Air-Ground Operations* on 1 September 1950. In a preface they described the directive's purpose as being to establish "the urgently needed amplifications and revision of the principles, means, and procedures" set forth in Field Manual 31-35. They noted that much of the organization and technique specified in the directive had not been adequately field-tested, but they conceived that the directive's provisions would be incorporated in a joint departmental level publication after adequate field testing.[48] In Washington, Lt Gen Idwal H. Edwards, Air Force deputy chief of staff for operations, expressed pleasure that the Tactical Air Command and Army Field Forces had prepared "an excellent working doctrine for units of the field armies and tactical air force." "In my opinion," Edwards wrote on 2 November 1950, "this is the best available document on air-ground operations and it is one which will provide proper guidance and training in a vital phase of joint operations."[49]

The expansion of the Tactical Air Command in the late summer of 1950, together with the establishment of the Ninth Air Force (Tactical) at Pope AFB on 1 August 1950, represented an Air Force effort to provide a proper parallel organization with the Army at a working level. According to Maj Gen Willard R. Wolfinbarger, who assumed command of the Ninth Air Force, this "lack of parallel organization for both the Air Force and Army at a common working level has been a serious handicap in the promulgation of Joint Doctrine and in the supervision of Joint Operations to insure adherence to Joint Doctrine." But Wolfinbarger did not think that the new organizational pattern established the Tactical Air Command in a coordinate status with the Army Field Forces. As the primary Army agency for the supervision of operations and training within the zone of interior, the Army Field Forces were able to present the *Joint Training Directive* to Army service schools and numbered armies as approved joint doctrine that would be taught and practiced. On the other hand, the Tactical Air Command could only present the *Joint Training Directive* as joint doctrine approved by the command with an expression of "hope that other activities will accept it as such until it can be properly coordinated and made official."[50]

According to all reports the association between the Tactical Air Force (Provisional) and the V Corps as field agencies of the Tactical Air Command and Army Field Forces was generally harmonious, and General Collins apparently hoped that the establishments in the Pope Air Force Base-Fort Bragg area might grow into a joint center. Obviously moving toward this end in the autumn of 1950, the Army established the Army Airborne Center and the Army Air Support Center at Fort Bragg. These centers were parts of the Office of the Chief of Army Field Forces; each was headed by an Army major general. Going along with the plan a part of the way, General Wolfinbarger, who was now temporarily commanding the Tactical Air Command, established a Tactical Air Command Airborne Liaison Office at the Army Airborne Center on 14 November. But when the Army Field Forces requested on 13 December that three other Tactical Air Command liaison officers be assigned to the Army Air Support Center, Wolfinbarger declined to comply. He recalled that the Headquarters Tactical Air Command had been located at Langley AFB so that its personnel would enjoy close daily liaison with the people in the Headquarters Army Field Forces at nearby Fort Monroe. He pointed out that the location of the Army centers at Fort Bragg had already lessened the desirable daily contact between staff officers. "I feel," he concluded, "that the assignment of liaison officers to the Army Air Support Center would decentralize and undermine to an unacceptable degree Tactical Air Command's responsibility for establishing and revising the doctrine, tactics, and techniques of tactical aviation which, obviously, must be accomplished at Army Field Forces-Tactical Air Command level."[51]

Given the differences in service viewpoints that had to be reconciled, the Ad Hoc Committee for Joint Policies and Procedures of the Joint Chiefs of Staff made slow progress in its efforts to define principles and procedures for the joint action of the armed forces. One of the main points of contention continued to be the Army's position that major areas on interservice responsibility ought to be made the province of joint centers constituted under the principle of unified command and operated under the immediate jurisdiction of the Joint Chiefs of Staff. Named by the Joint Chiefs, the commander of a joint center would have a joint staff and one of the chiefs of staff would be designated as the executive agent for each joint center. The Navy and the Air Force did not agree that such joint centers should be established.[52] By the spring of 1951 the ad hoc committee reached some successful compromises, on 26 April the Joint Chiefs of Staff approved the first two chapters of *Joint Action Armed Forces*. Entitled "Principles Governing the Functions of the Armed Forces" and "Functions of the Individual Services," these chapters discussed the principles, responsibilities, and functions of the armed services that had been set forth in the Key West agreement, which had been issued in 1948 as

"Functions of the Armed Forces and the Joint Chiefs of Staff." During the summer of 1951, the Joint Chiefs also reached agreement on the last two chapters, "Principles Governing Joint Operations of the Armed Forces" and "Principles and Doctrines Governing Joint Aspects of Special Operations of the Armed Forces." In September 1951 the *Joint Action Armed Forces* (JAAF) paper was published as Army Field Manual 110-5, Navy JAAF, and Air Force Manual 1-1.[53]

An Air Force critique of *Joint Action Armed Forces* pointed out that the three separate service identifications of the same document appeared to violate the principle of "maximum practicable integration of policies and procedures" that was the announced goal of the publication. The same critique found the JAAF to be filled with "semantic compromises" that left "gray areas" of meaning, the interpretations of which in times of crisis "could prove costly in delay and indecisiveness in military action."[54] Among its other provisions, the JAAF authorized the establishment of six joint service boards, each to be under the direction of the service that had a primary interest in the particular field of endeavor. These joint boards were to develop joint doctrine and procedures; evaluate joint tactics and techniques, the adequacy of equipment, and the adequacy of joint training; and review publications covering the conduct of joint training. When the boards were established early in August 1951, the Air Force chief of staff was made responsible for the Joint Air Defense Board at Ent AFB, Colorado, and for the Joint Tactical Air Support Board and the Joint Air Transportation Board, both at Pope AFB. The chief of staff of the Army was responsible for the Joint Airborne Troop Board at Fort Bragg; the commandant of the Marine Corps for the Joint Landing Force Board at Quantico, Virginia; and the chief of naval operations for the Joint Amphibious Board at Little Creek, Virginia. Each of the boards responsible to the Air Force would be headed by an Air Force major general who would be directly responsible to the Air Force chief of staff but would forward all reports on air defense, air support, or air transport matters through the commanders of the Air Defense Command or the Tactical Air Command as the case might be.[55] The responsible service was charged to provide logistical support to each of its boards, and the directors or chairmen of the boards were instructed to draft basic charters and to prepare their requirements for representatives from the three armed services.[56] The joint boards were empowered to draft joint doctrine within their spheres of authority that after approval by the Joint Chiefs of Staff would supersede service doctrines. As they began work, however, each of the service representatives on the joint boards found that he required formal statements of the individual positions and doctrines of his services.

The Air University as a Doctrinal Center

"Since I have been here," wrote General Barker in August 1949, "we've been in a constant struggle to get out to our people a valid and clear-cut statement of operational doctrine. It's needed badly; not only in our schools but in the various joint boards on which the Air Force is represented, and throughout the entire Air

Force." Barker was convinced that the Air University was the best-qualified agency in the Air Force to prepare and publish doctrinal manuals. "To begin with," he argued,

> we have more qualified senior officers than any one place in the Air Force except the Pentagon. Their everyday work involves the preparation of matter appropriate to operational manuals. Of greatest importance is that they can and do devote many long hours to this preparation, to the complete exclusion of all other matters. This cannot be done in the Pentagon. Secondly, our people are unbiased as far as loyalty to strategic, tactical, air defense, etc., are concerned. They are able to view operational doctrine from the viewpoint of the whole Air Force—no compartmentation. This, to my mind, is of the utmost importance if we are going to develop proper air power employment.[57]

While attending an Air Force Educational Conference chaired by General Fairchild in February 1950, General Barker proposed that the commander of the Air University be authorized to approve and publish operational Air Force manuals under an authority from the chief of staff. He explained that the Air University would coordinate the subject matter of all proposed manuals with appropriate Air Force commands and would refer points of difference to the Air Staff for decision. He demonstrated that the Air Materiel Command already possessed a similar authority to approve and publish technical orders and manuals. General Fairchild felt that Barker's proposal had some merit; nevertheless, he ruled that the doctrinal manuals would have to be approved by the Air Staff, with the deputy chief of staff for operations acting as the approving officer for all operational manuals.[58]

In the summer of 1950 the immediate impact of the Korean War and the subsequent expansion of the Air Force had important effects upon the Air University's organization for the production of doctrinal manuals. The Air Force at once suspended all of the Air University's schools but indicated that many of the instructors would continue to be available to the Air University. Some of the instructors might be used to complete the "Commander's Guide."[59] Within a few weeks the Air Force decided that the Air War College ought to conduct accelerated classes and that the Air Command and Staff College would be moved from Craig AFB to Maxwell AFB, where it would also conduct short school sessions. The Air Tactical School at Tyndall, however, would be inactivated. On 24 July, Barker proposed that the surplus instructors from this school ought to be brought to Maxwell and assigned to the Air University Evaluation Division. Under former planning, the Air University had intended that manuals should be drafted in its several schools. Now, however, Barker wished to concentrate the function in the Evaluation Division, which would become a separate entity in the Air War College. This proposal did not please the Air War College inasmuch as it considered the evaluation function to be germane to the college's educational function. However, an Air University study committee pointed out that the war college mission already required it "to promote sound concepts of the broad aspects of air power in order to assure the most effective development and employment of the air arm." Effective on 9 October 1950, the Evaluation Division was transferred from the Academic Staff to the Air War College where it was redesignated as the Evaluation Staff.[60] But, as has been noted, the Air Force directed on 26 September that the production of doctrinal manuals should be held up pending the completion of the JAAF publication.[61]

Even though the Air University had not completed a basic doctrinal manual on air power before it was directed to suspend work on the project, it had generated several ideas as to what the doctrine ought to be. In the summer of 1950, Gen Hoyt S. Vandenberg had stated: "Tactical and strategic air power is part of the same ball of wax." Finletter had said: "Tactical air and strategic air are merely handles which have been developed to identify different functions, each of which is indispensable and each of which fits into the overall integrated structure of air power." While attending the weapons orientation course at Sandia, New Mexico, Barker was distressed to hear an Air Force instructor present a concept that the Tactical Air Command had functions distinct from those of the rest of the Air Force. Barker observed that the Air Force had revolted at the idea of assigning aviation in small packages to corps and armies, but he wondered if the Air Force might not be violating this same principle "by tying up, within the Air Force, pieces of aviation, each designed for a particular job." In the autumn of 1950 Barker collaborated with Col Dale O. Smith in the publication of an article entitled "Air Power Indivisible." On 21 December, Barker asked General Edwards, Air Force deputy chief of staff for operations, to approve a memorandum on Air Force doctrine that emphasized the fact that all elements of the Air Force had to be prepared to perform any operational function of the Air Force. The paper asserted: "A clear-cut differentiation between strategic missions and tactical missions is neither desirable nor possible." By demonstrating that air power was indivisible, Barker hoped to "break down the feeling on the part of the Army that unless we have huge forces set up under the label 'Tactical Air Force' they are not getting tactical support."[62]

Much to the surprise of Barker and Gen George C. Kenney, the Air University commander, General Edwards was unwilling to approve the proposed Air University statement of air doctrine. Edwards concurred "wholeheartedly" with the principle of the flexibility of air power and with the conclusion that there was a lack of clear differentiation between strategic and tactical air missions, but he insisted that the Strategic Air Command ought not to be diverted from its primary missions to perform tasks of lesser importance. "In view of the capability of the long-range bomber," Edwards wrote, "I feel that from an organizational point of view the authority for the higher direction of the war should retain direct control over some units which they can employ in a sustained drive against the war-making capacity of an enemy nation or which they can divert, *if necessary*, to the more direct support of any theater in overwhelming need." To safeguard the integrity of the Strategic Air Command, the Air Staff drafted an insertion to be placed in the Air University statement of air doctrine, the key portion reading:

> Although the labels "Strategic" and "Tactical" have been applied to two of our major commands, those titles were arbitrarily chosen and are not intended to connote strict compartmentation of functions. The Strategic Air Command as it exists today merely represents the one segment of air power reserved to the specific control of the authority for the higher direction of the war; it is an organization which can be used either independently or in conjunction with one or more theater commands to achieve the result desired. It not only represents a potent offensive weapon capable of obtaining a decisive result through the progressive destruction of an enemy's warmaking capacity, but represents as well a mobile reserve of air power that can be turned by the authority for the higher direction of the war to the immediate support of any theater overwhelmingly in need of help. In this light its organizational integrity, of course, must be preserved; however, whether allocated to the Strategic Air Command as we know it or to some other Air Force unit, heavy and medium bombardment aircraft like all other combat aircraft are flexible. Their flexibility is a vital part of air power.

Accepting the Air Staff changes, General Kenney on 3 February 1951 forwarded copies of the "Air University Doctrine on the Employment of Air Force Combat Units" to the commandants of the Air University's schools and to Air Force instructors at non-Air Force schools, with the added notation that the doctrine had been approved by Air Force headquarters.[63]

When he received the "Air University Doctrine" at Norfolk, where he was deputy commandant of the Armed Forces Staff College, Brig Gen Robert C. Candee said that it was "like a shot of fresh air and sunshine after all the hearsay and 'hooey' that has hung like a pall over the subject."[64] In Washington in December 1950 a staff study on air-ground operations prepared within the Air Force Office of Deputy Chief of Staff for Development had already noted that the *Joint Training Directive for Air-Ground Operations* continued to relate tactical air operations to the maneuver of ground forces and thereby limit tactical air power to a narrow supporting role.[65] In the autumn of 1950 the chief of Army Field Forces directed the commandants of all Army schools to use the *Joint Training Directive* as the basis for all instruction on the subject, but on 19 January 1951 General Barker took advantage of the fact that all Air Force instructors in Army schools were assigned to the Air University's 3894th School Squadron (non-Air Force schools) and directed them to continue to base their lectures on the Air Force doctrine contained in Field Manual 31-35. "The manual, *Joint Training Directive for Air-Ground Operations*," Barker directed, "cannot be accepted at this time by the Air Force inasmuch as there are areas in which basic concepts and terminology depart from those expressed in FM 31-35."[66] This directive placed the Air University in opposition to the Tactical Air Command; on 2 February, Maj Gen Glenn O. Barcus, deputy commander of the Tactical Air Command, requested that the Air Force approve the *Joint Training Directive* as working doctrine and asked the Air University to offer constructive criticisms looking toward the revision of the joint directive.[67] Resolution of the controversy apparently gave the Air Staff some difficulty since it had previously approved the "Air University Doctrine." However, on 9 March 1951 the Air Force directed that the *Joint Training Directive* would be used in order to provide uniformity in all air-ground training and instruction throughout the Air Force. The Air University was instructed to provide constructive comments and recommendations that would be useful in the revision of this still tentative doctrinal directive.[68]

The work just completed on the "Air University Doctrine" had convinced Kenney and Barker that the Air Force ought to place emphasis on the "tactical employment of air force" rather than on "the employment of tactical air force."[69] The controversy over the *Joint Training Directive* required the Air University to intensify its thinking on the subject. The Air University's concept for the command and employment of air power was that air forces be grouped logically by objectives in various echelons of command. Some air forces were to be under the immediate direction of the Joint Chiefs of Staff in order that they might carry out objectives lying beyond the immediate interest of any one theater commander or supporting more than one theater. Some air forces would be assigned to a theater commander to conduct air operations required by the theater mission. Other air forces would be assigned to the air defense of the continental United States. All wars would consist of campaigns — some defensive in purpose and some offensive — each satisfying the national war objectives in whole or in part. Theater commanders would conduct local campaigns necessary to achieve objectives assigned by the Joint Chiefs of Staff. Air forces committed to a theater should be prepared (1) to conduct air campaigns to satisfy theater requirements for security against the enemy air force or deployment of enemy ground forces; (2) to participate in such sea and ground campaigns as were conducted by the theater; and (3) to participate according to opportunity in air or sea campaigns charged to forces from outside the theater. Army and Navy forces also were to be committed to theater ground and sea campaigns and to participate in the air campaigns. Any doctrine for command and control of the Air Force — especially the theater air force — had to recognize that the lower the echelon of assignment the more limited would be the objective, hence the more limited the flexibility and usefulness of the air unit to accomplish multiple obligations. Decentralization in the command and control of air power could cause hazards within a theater. "Objection to this decentralization," Barker urged, "should not be considered just a fetish of the Air Force."[70]

After stating the Air University's concept of the relationship of theater air forces to the whole Air Force — the Air University preferred theater air forces to tactical air forces because the latter term had incurred adverse connotations — Barker made specific objections to the *Joint Training Directive*. "Basically, our objection to the doctrinal implications of the joint training directive," he explained, "is that it over-simplifies the problem of theater air forces. It leaves the impression that support of ground campaigns is the only reason for being of theater air forces. It implies that the gaining of air superiority is general support to the ground campaign without revealing the thought that the enemy air force is a matter of theater concern regardless of surface campaigns being conducted or contemplated." Making specific reference to several allusions in the *Joint Training Directive* to the supporting attributes of the tactical air force, Barker observed: "We feel that the

IDEAS, CONCEPTS, DOCTRINE

narrowness of the doctrinal implications of the subject directive make it unacceptable for use as uniform air-ground doctrine." He requested that the Air University be authorized to present its concepts of air power in resident and nonresident instruction and to use the *Joint Training Directive* for presenting the operational methods of conducting close tactical air support.[71]

The Tactical Air Command, which apparently feared that the Air University emphasis on the lack of difference between strategic and tactical missions might lead to a decision that the only tactical air mission was the close support of ground troops, was initially quite skeptical about accepting the Air University's proposal to use the terms *theater aviation* or *theater air forces* to indicate those air forces that were assigned either permanently or temporarily to a theater commander to assist him in carrying out his mission. The Air Force also had some doubts about the new term.[72] At the Air University on 1 June 1951, Barker explained the theater air force concept to Secretary Finletter. Three weeks later, after making a trip to Korea, Finletter wrote Barker that what he had seen in the combat theater convinced him that the Air University's concept ought to be properly defined and understood within the Air Force.[73]

While the doctrinal differences between the Air University and the Tactical Air Command were under discussion, the Tactical Air Command and the Army Field Forces had begun to take steps to ensure that the tentative doctrine in the *Joint Training Directive* would be field-tested and revised as appropriate. Meeting initially on 29 March, a steering committee of representatives from the Tactical Air Command and the Army Field Forces undertook studies looking toward revising the directive. Before very long, however, the representatives of the Army Field Forces began to advance the proposition that a theater commander must be authorized to allocate some portion of tactical air power to the support of ground troops and that this air power should not be withdrawn from such support except with the approval of the ground commander. The two sides of the steering committee now began to write unilateral positions for submission to the Joint Tactical Air Support Board. Seeking to perfect a manual that would meet Air Force requirements, representatives of the Tactical Air Command and the Air University met together early in September 1951 and prepared a paper entitled "Tactical Air Operations." This paper was approved by Lt Gen John K. Cannon and forwarded to the Air Staff on 10 September. On 19 October another conference at Air Force headquarters recommended that the Tactical Air Command should continue to adhere to the details of the *Joint Training Directive for Air-Ground Operations* in its relationships with the Army Field Forces but that the Air University should prepare an Air Force manual on theater air operations that would fully develop the Air Force view of tactical air doctrine.[74]

Successful Preparation of Air Doctrine Manuals

Contrary to some expectations the concentration of the Air University's schools and colleges at Maxwell AFB during the spring of 1951 resulted in the development of closer coordination of effort and thinking; for several years hence the Air University served as the Air Force's doctrinal center. As the Air University commander, General Kenney had given strong support to doctrinal studies; both General Edwards, who became Air University commander on 1 August 1951, and Lt Gen Laurence S. Kuter, who took the position on 1 March 1953, continued this tradition. General Barker continued as Air University deputy commander until his retirement in August 1953. In October 1951 Maj Gen Roscoe C. Wilson became commandant of the Air War College, and Brig Gen Lloyd P. Hopwood brought a pervasive interest in doctrine into the Air Command and Staff College when he became its commandant on 18 June 1953. Marking the beginning of the augmentation of the Air War College Evaluation Staff, Colonel Momyer was named as its director on 16 June 1951.[75] Something of the new esprit of the Air University was manifest in a statement by Col James W. Chapman, the assistant chief of staff for plans and operations of the Air University on 22 June 1951. "I believe," Chapman recommended, "that the Air University should strive to become the brains of Headquarters USAF. It is the one place in the Air Force system in which unbiased, reflective thinking can be accomplished. The atmosphere which prevails in Headquarters USAF is not conducive to productivity which is based on realistic, honest evaluations and appraisals."[76]

Even though the long-awaited JAAF publication had not been issued, General Barker's appraisal of Air Force doctrinal requirements in the late spring of 1951 led him to believe that the Air University could not delay any longer in beginning to exercise its doctrinal mission. New thinking in the Air War College Evaluation Staff gave a fresh approach to the problem: the evaluation staff began preparing a basic doctrine brief and a series of other briefs on such subjects as tactical air operations and proposed that these documents be issued as Air University doctrine. On 14 July, Barker forwarded a proposed Air Force manual on basic doctrine to Washington and asked the Air Force Council to approve and distribute it at the earliest possible date.[77] In personal negotiations during July, Colonel Momyer worked out a procedure for the preparation of doctrinal manuals that seemed likely to speed the work. In meetings with Tactical Air Command (TAC) representatives, Momyer prepared an itemization of basic factors affecting theater air operations and got TAC's concurrence with them. In Washington, where he was serving as deputy chief of staff for operations, General Edwards promised that he would get a prompt decision on any specific points of difference that might arise between the Air University and a major air command. Based on indications of Air Force approval, the Air University on 31 August canceled its plans to produce Air University doctrine and established an Air Force manuals project that called for the preparation of a basic Air Force manual and a series of manuals on such subjects as theater air operations, strategic air operations, and counterair operations.[78]

Early in September 1951 the Air Force Council gave formal consideration to the Air University's plan for producing basic doctrine manuals and "expressed concern that we have no organization or group in the Air Force making a continuing effort toward development of concept or doctrine." "While individuals or staff agencies develop pieces of the problem," the Air Force Council noted, "no single agency has the overall job as its primary duty." The council believed that older Air Force officers had an understanding of Air Force doctrine and concepts; but the council felt that the great majority of the Air Force officer corps did not possess the "'base line' of doctrine and concept upon which to build judgment commensurate with the importance of the jobs to which they must be assigned." Since an additional 25,000 rated Air Force officers had come to active duty in the year preceding September 1951, the Air Force Council believed that it was particularly important that doctrine and concept should be clearly enunciated and widely distributed without delay.[79]

When he informed General Edwards, now the Air University's new commander, of the decisions of the Air Force Council, Gen Nathan F. Twining observed that the Air University was already charged with "developing doctrine in the fields of strategy and employment of air power," but that he believed that the Air Force Council felt a need for something "of a more comprehensive, fundamental nature, and basic to such treatment of strategy and employment." Twining remembered that the Air War College had previously proposed that it ought to be allowed to continue a small, highly selective group of students through two additional years of resident postgraduate study and that the principal objective of this group would be "the formulation, establishment, review, compilation, and distribution of dynamic doctrine and concept."[80]

Although General Twining did not elaborate on the matter, the Air Force Council apparently saw some difference between the old realm of doctrine and something newer — dynamic doctrine or concept. Since its establishment, the Air War College had been responsible for "promoting sound concepts on the broad aspects of air power in order to assure the most effective development and employment of the air arm." Air War College students, however, had often been confused by an almost synonymous usage of the words *concept, doctrine, strategy,* and *policy*. Because of this confusion an Air War College seminar group in January 1948 had established its own definitions: Military concept was defined as "a mental image of the application of military science to future wars"; strategy was considered to be "the science and art of employing the strength of a nation to secure its objectives, or the science and art of military command, exercised to meet the enemy in combat under advantageous conditions," and policy was believed to be "a settled course adopted and followed by a government, institution, body, or individual."[81] Air War College students subsequently accepted the definition of doctrine appearing in the *Dictionary of United States Military Terms for Joint Usage*, published by the Joint Chiefs in June 1948. This dictionary defined doctrine as

> a compilation of principles and policies, applicable to a subject, which have been developed through experience or by theory, that represent the best available thought, and indicate and guide but do not bind in practice. Its purpose is to provide that understanding within a force which generates mutual confidence between the

commander and his subordinates in order that timely and effective action will be taken by all concerned in the absence of instruction.[82]

Considering these same semantic problems in September and October 1951, however, another Air War College seminar observed:

> There appears to be a fine line of demarcation between concepts and doctrines on the one hand, and doctrines and principles on the other hand. It is difficult to differentiate between concepts which existed in the minds of some far-sighted individuals in the Air Force and the doctrine which was accepted as official by the War Department. ... In the field of ideas there is evidently a degree of general acceptance ranging from the first nebulous ideas of an individual, up successively through concepts, doctrines, and principles. The point at which an idea becomes a concept, a concept a doctrine, and a doctrine a principle, is not always clear. Thus at any one time our Air Force doctrine may be said to be partly concept, partly doctrine, and partly principle.[83]

Something of all of these thoughts went into the Air War College recommendations of the actions necessary to secure the results desired by the Air Force Council. General Edwards approved the study and sent it to Washington on 26 September 1951. Edwards recommended that a postgraduate study group be established in the Air War College "to provide a single Air Force agency whose principal objective is to formulate, establish, review, compile and distribute concept and doctrine and to develop officers highly qualified in the study of National Defense needs." The study of concept would "include future USAF positions in and responsibilities for national security and the determination of future USAF objectives." Edwards stated: "Operational doctrine . . . must derive from one common Air Force concept. . . . The work of producing and maintaining current Air Force operational doctrine must be kept in harmony with the concept developed and appropriately both tasks should be assigned to the same agency." He noted that the Air University's failure to produce and distribute operational doctrine in the form of manuals was "due to a failure to assign the responsibility of producing and distributing manuals to this one agency of the Air Force." "We do not look upon this as a task," he continued, "which is to be performed solely here at the Air University. Rather, our idea is that the Air War College, charged with the study of concept, will be designated by the chief of staff, US Air Force, as the Air Force agency responsible for production of doctrinal manuals; that the work will be carried out in close partnership with appropriate commands; and that controversial issues will be submitted to Headquarters USAF for decisions." Edwards requested that up to 25 officers of broad experience should be assigned to the Air War College postgraduate study group. Its success would hinge on two factors: "First, officers of the highest caliber must be detailed to this work with assurance that they will remain for the entire tour. Second this group must not be used as a 'catch-all' to which are sent the day to day problems which should be solved by regularly established staffs."[84]

Acting on earlier recommendations, the Air Force on 3 August 1951 issued a new regulation that charged the Air University to "function as an Air Force doctrinal, educational, and research center." Recognizing that the new Air Research and Development Command was becoming effective, the Air Force relieved the Air University on 4 September of its old responsibility for initiating and reviewing studies, for testing tactics, and for the tactical testing of organization and equipment. Marking a partial acceptance of the plan for the postgraduate study group, the Air Force on 18 October charged the Air University to:

A. conduct two-year postgraduate study to develop Air Force officers exceptionally well qualified to treat with and solve the military aspects of national security problem.

B. foster and encourage the development of doctrine and concept within the Air Force.

C. formulate, review, compile and recommend military air doctrine, to include: (1) USAF responsibilities for national security; (2) future USAF objectives, including weapon systems; (3) special studies bearing on the above as directed by Headquarters USAF.

While the Air Force broadened the scope of the Air University's authority to study and recommend, it was unwilling to charge the Air University with any sole responsibility to produce and promulgate Air Force concepts and doctrines. As a result of discussions of the Air University's recommendations within the Air Force Council, Twining informed Edwards "that the council noted that the development of doctrine and concept is a dynamic process involving all Air Force commands and activities."[85] When he became commandant of the Air War College in October 1951, General Wilson attempted to sell "the idea of a graduate study program to generate new thinking in the fields of concept and doctrine." In response to a letter asking for clarification of the exact intent of the Air Force Council in regard to the postgraduate study group, Twining informed Edwards on 18 December 1951: "The primary emphasis for the study group is one of training, i.e., development of a high degree of skill in sound problem solution. A portion of the vehicle for achieving the desired level of training shall be the development and maintenance of a sound philosophy—or concept—or air power and military air force. Solutions to specific problems confronting the Air Staff will be assigned to this group only in rare circumstances."[86]

Even though the Air Force Council expressed its desire that Air Force doctrine should be produced and disseminated promptly, the Air Staff—which alleged that "these manuals are of extreme importance and must receive every consideration"—moved very slowly. On 2 October 1951, the Air Staff approved the projected titles in a family of operational manuals proposed by the Air University, but on 25 October the Air Staff returned the Air University's draft of the basic Air Force manual without approval.[87] "Some of the statements in the draft," explained Maj Gen Robert W. Burns, acting deputy chief of staff for operations, "although self-evident truths in substance, are stated in a form which makes them generalizations and in a sequence which is lacking in continuity." To get on with the job, Burns directed that a committee of two officers from the Air Staff and three from the Air University would assemble at Maxwell AFB early in 1952 and redraft the text.[88] In the months that the draft manual had been under consideration in the Air Staff, the Air University had meanwhile prepared and printed in October a somewhat rearranged version of it as Air University Manual-1, *USAF Basic Doctrine*. In order to get comments for the consideration of the review committee, Barker now circulated this manual to major Air Force commands and to key Air Force officers.[89] "I believe," wrote Maj Gen James A. Samford, Air Force director of intelligence, to Barker, "your 'theater air force' instead of 'tactical air force' is one of the biggest strides yet made."[90] On the one hand, Lt Gen Howard A. Craig, the Air Force inspector general, thought that the pamphlet had "much merit and enunciates quite clearly basic doctrine for the use of US Air Force personnel and is needed." On the other, he questioned the Air University's statement of the national objectives, especially one which stated that the United States would "prevent any unacceptably dangerous increase in strength by a probable enemy." Craig pointed out that this objective, if it were true, would justify preventive war.[91] The Tactical Air Command's USAF Air-Ground Operations School found the manual to be "a Doctrinaire statement rather than Doctrine." The faculty of this new school suggested:

> Each of the three major combat commands presently operate under specific command doctrines, which guide all activities leading to Operational Readiness to fulfill their respective missions. These respective doctrines, which have evolved principally from battle experience, are comparable to basic religious tenets in each command. It is not believed any command would surrender its basic doctrine willingly, or shift from a major to a subordinate role, unless it is consulted beforehand and is prepared to accept as an emergency measure such overriding doctrine.[92]

When it assembled on 8 February 1952, the Air Staff-Air University committee included Cols William B. Keese and Robert Orr from the Air Force Directorate of Plans and Colonels Momyer, Smith, and Douglas Williams from the Air University. This committee took cognizance of all the recommendations made by the Air Staff and by the major commands and completed a draft manual on 7 March that Edwards described as "the best of all previous efforts over the past five years." Edwards, nevertheless, believed that the draft did not meet manual requirements: it was too long, included too much discussion rather than concise statements, and included current decisions on organization and roles of the military services, which Edwards did not consider to be basic doctrine. Accordingly, Edwards, Barker, and Wilson rewrote the draft manual; on 25 June 1952, Edwards submitted it to the Air Force. "I feel that nothing will be gained," he recommended, "by giving this current proposal any general distribution to obtain further remarks and recommendations. Any further refinement should be limited to the Air Staff and the final review of the Air Council."[93]

While the preparation of the basic air doctrinal manual was proceeding at higher levels, the Air War College Evaluation Staff had begun work on the plan to produce four manuals deriving from the basic manual (theater air operations, air defense operations, air transport operations, and strategic air operations) and five manuals expanding the theater air operations manual (counterair operations, close-air-support operations, air interdiction operations, theater airlift operations, and theater air reconnaissance operations). At the request of the senior Air Force representative on the Joint Amphibious Board, who found himself unable to obtain guidance concerning Air Force positions with respect to joint amphibious operations, the Air University agreed early in 1952 to prepare an additional manual on the subject of air operations in conjunction with amphibious operations.[94] This series of manuals was a much less ambitious undertaking than the old air employment instructions had been, but the Air University now planned that the Evaluation Staff would produce these operational manuals by working in coordination with the responsible Air Force commands.

After nearly a year's work on the operational manuals, Colonel Momyer reported some of the difficulties that the Evaluation Staff had encountered:

> We have found from this past year of research that the writing of manuals is perhaps one of the most difficult tasks in the field of military writing. It is creative and yet it must be exact. These requirements dictate thorough research and imagination on the part of the author in translating the research into a manuscript that is easily understood and yet is complete in context. Unfortunately, there are very few individuals who possess this particular talent.... For the most part our greatest difficulty has been a lack of precedent in this field of writing.... The manuals we are attempting to produce have little similarity to the stereotyped and somewhat stultified type manual produced by the Army. In this attempt to strike out on our own, we have encountered many obstacles that were certainly anticipated, and others that could not be foreseen. Of course, we have encountered the additional prejudice in respect to what constitutes doctrine, tactics, techniques, and procedures. Thus, we have been seeking for a level of writing that has no definition and is not always apparent when one thinks it has been obtained.... Our experience to date reveals general acceptance of the fundamentals presented but non-concurrence in the manner in which those fundamentals have been expressed; not only non-concurrence in the expression but in some measure the degree of detail subscribed to those expressions and fundamentals. The only method by which we can strike a balance as to detail and scope is by trial and error. I recognize this to be a long and laborious task but all short cuts to date have failed.... We find ourselves constantly in a dilemma as to whether too much detail has been presented or whether we have become so terse that the meaning is clouded and darkness descends upon the reader.[95]

In addition to the problem of delimiting the characteristics of the operational manuals, the Evaluation Staff had difficulties getting assistance from the Air Force operating commands and in procuring the assignment of officers needed to maintain its strength. As a working procedure, the Evaluation Staff undertook to prepare a draft of a manual, submit it to the operational command for review, and then form a committee including representatives from the operating command to revise the draft. The Strategic Air Command participated enthusiastically in the review of the manual on strategic air operations and sent officers to the Air University to work with a review committee. The Air Defense Command was willing to work in this same fashion. The Military Air Transport Service (MATS) found so little wrong with the draft on the global air transport manual that it did not want a review committee. In fact, MATS so readily concurred with the proposed draft that Momyer was not satisfied that it had been given "the detailed review necessary for expressing sound doctrinal matter." In view of the number of manuals projected in the theater air warfare field, Momyer regretted that the Tactical Air Command "has not been able to participate to the extent that I believe is necessary."[96] In his annual Air War College report filed on 1 July 1952, General Wilson pointed out that the Evaluation Staff had suffered not only from a lack of technically qualified personnel but from a shortage in its authorized strength. Authorized 20 officers—18 of whom were to be qualified in doctrinal areas—the Evaluation Staff had only 12 officers assigned in the doctrinal area in November 1952. As a result of this demonstration of deficiency, the Air Force brought the Evaluation Staff up to its assigned strength and desired experience capabilities early in 1953.[97] However, the Tactical Air Command still found it difficult to participate with the Air University in doctrinal endeavors. "As you probably know," General Cannon wrote Edwards on 29 December 1952, "my personal attitude toward the Air University is that it should confine its efforts to teaching, and leave such matters as the development of tactics and doctrine, and the preparation of Air Force manuals to appropriate field commands and Headquarters USAF."[98]

Both because of the unusual amount of interest in the field of tactical air warfare and because of lingering controversies with the Tactical Air Command, the Air University encountered exceptional difficulty in preparing and teaching a doctrine of theater air operations. The Air University's contention that the term *theater air forces* should replace *tactical air forces* continued to draw opposition. Barker insisted that the use of the term *tactical air operations* focused student attention erroneously on the command relationship at the tactical air force-field army level. In an extension of the meaning of the term *theater air forces*, Colonel Momyer asserted that theater air forces could include Air Force tactical air units as well as Marine and Navy air units that might be assigned to a theater. He saw theater air forces as a more inclusive term, and he believed that the commander of the theater air forces ought to have a centralized command authority over all air units assigned to a theater. The Air University emphasized that a numbered tactical air force associated with a field army not only provided close combat air support to that particular field army but also participated in the counter air force and large-scale air interdiction operations under orders from the theater air force commander.[99] Early in June 1952 Barker's explanation of the matter resulted in the withdrawal of an Air Force recommendation that the Air University return to the use of "tactical air force" instead of "theater air force."[100] In a conversation with Barker in February 1953, however, General Kuter, then Air Force deputy chief of staff for personnel, once again brought up the subject of theater air operations, which the Air University conceived would be conducted under the central command of an area or a theater commander. Kuter was concerned lest the term *area commander* might be construed to mean an infantry division, corps, or army commander; he

IDEAS, CONCEPTS, DOCTRINE

argued in favor of continuing the use of strategic, tactical, and air defense. Barker was willing to delete references to the area commander, but he insisted that "the use of the words 'strategic' and 'tactical' hereinafter referred to as 'them words' has tended to compartment our operations." He continued, "The basic difficulty is the impossibility of finely defining 'them words.' We try to stress the need for unity of effort, singleness of purpose of all air forces, and find it difficult to do so if we divide operations into classes which are designated by undefinable words."[101]

The Tactical Air Command did not like the term *theater air forces* and was skeptical of the Air University's emphasis on the unity of air power; nevertheless, Cannon and Barker were able to achieve a meeting of minds on some other basic concepts. As written in July 1948, the Air University's draft of the air employment instructions manual entitled "Air Power and the US Air Force" had defined air superiority as "that degree of capability of one force over another which permits the conduct of air operations by the former at a given time and place without prohibitive interference by the opposing air force. Air superiority is local and possibly temporary."[102] Early in 1952, however, Cannon and Barker drafted a paper that pointed out that local air superiority could no longer be accepted as a concept in an era in which the high speeds and long ranges of modern aircraft permitted an enemy to shift air forces quickly and over considerable distances to any target without necessarily changing bases. In view of modern capabilities, Cannon and Barker agreed: "Offensive operations designed to defeat the enemy air force and insure an adequate degree of security from hostile attack should not be limited to restricted areas, nor can they be planned or carried out profitably in an uncoordinated fashion by commanders having limited jurisdiction such as those at numbered air force-field army level."[103]

Although the *Dictionary of United States Military Terms for Joint Usage* specified that the joint operations center manned by the numbered tactical air force and field army was a joint establishment, General Barker vigorously resisted a Department of Army position taken in December 1952 that the joint operations center "would retain over-all control of aircraft for air superiority, deep interdiction, and air defense." He already had made the case that the tactical air force received a part of its mission from the theater air force commander, and he now questioned whether the joint operations center was a joint establishment. Brig Gen Reuben C. Hood, who was commandant of the Air Command and Staff School at the time, pointed out, for example, that the joint operations center had no responsibility for planning ground operations and was actually an Air Force operations center with Army personnel present in what amounted to a liaison capacity. "The view," said Hood, "that close support missions are jointly planned and ordered is not believed consistent with practice. Army participation in planning consists of designating targets and times plus providing information. The decision to order a strike is an Air Force rather than a joint decision, and the planning of the strike to include strength, armament, route, and method of attack is by the Air Force combat operations section."[104]

By the end of 1952 the Evaluation Staff had substantially completed the four principal operational manuals that were designed to elaborate the basic air doctrine manual. However, after nearly six months in coordination, the Air Staff was still reviewing the draft of the basic manual that General Edwards had sent to Washington on 25 June. Seeking to pry the manual loose, Edwards on 1 January 1953 reported that the lack of a basic doctrine manual was a major deficiency hampering the Air University's accomplishment of its mission. This report of deficiency apparently got results since the Air Force director of plans was directed to turn out the manual as a matter of priority; an ad hoc committee within the Plans Directorate composed of Cols Harvey T. Alness, William B. Keese, and S. L. Fisher was named to revise the manual for final consideration by the Air Force Council. When stationed at the Air University a few years earlier, Alness had worked on drafts of this same document; now he described his committee's work as being one of assembling parts of previous draft efforts into a new format. The committee, nevertheless, included a new section discussing air forces and the principles of war — subject matter that had been included in the Air University's earliest draft of the category 1 "Air Power" manual but which had been subsequently omitted in later drafts because of a feeling that these principles were not a part of basic air doctrine. On 9 March, Alness presented the new draft to the Air Force Council, which, except for a few minor changes, accepted the manual practically as it was written. Acting in General Vandenberg's absence, Twining approved the draft on 13 March. However, he directed that comments would be collected on the manual for six months to a year and that it would be revised if the comments so warranted. Upon returning to Washington, Vandenberg also approved the manual. As published on 1 April 1953, Air Force Manual (AFM) 1-2, *United States Air Force Basic Doctrine*, carried Vandenberg's comment: "Basic air doctrine evolves from experience gained in war and from analysis of the continuing impact of new weapon systems on warfare. The dynamic and constant changes in new weapons makes periodic substantive review of this doctrine necessary."[105]

"I am disappointed with it," General Barker stated on 23 March after he had received and studied an advance copy of AFM 1-2. Barker considered that the Air University draft manual submitted on 25 June 1951 had presented "more clearly and more distinctly the why and wherefores of our doctrine" than did the approved manual, and he thought in terms of whether the Air University ought not to publish its own version of basic doctrine for the guidance of its personnel. Barker's main complaint, however, was the amount of time that had been required to publish the basic doctrine manual. "It has taken the Air Force five tedious years," he pointed out to Lt Gen Thomas D. White, Air Force deputy chief of staff for operations, on 27 March, "to get an approved manual on basic air force doctrine." The many rewritings of the manual had resulted "in no change of importance in the doctrine. The changes were in what to include or exclude, how to express an idea, arrangement of subject matter." At such a rate of progress, Barker estimated that 15–20 years would be required to publish the remaining doctrinal manuals. He again recommended that the Air University commander be authorized to approve and publish Air Force manuals on operational doctrine.[106]

After giving serious thought to Barker's proposals and informally discussing them with members of the Air Force Council, General White replied on 22 April that there "can be no question about the compelling need within the Air Force for clear-cut and succinct statements of operational doctrine or the fact that the Air University is the best-qualified Air Force agency to prepare such manuals." White, nevertheless, insisted that Air Force headquarters was the only agency in the Air Force that was always conversant with Department of Defense policies and interservice negotiations. For this reason, headquarters would have to review all operational doctrine manuals. General White agreed that "far too much time was spent in seeking a document that would be palatable to all," and he promised that future Air Staff review of operational doctrine manuals would be limited to "substance only." Matters of arrangement, expression, and illustration would be left to the Air University.[107] On 22 May, General Twining directed that the Air University be charged with receiving comments from the major air commanders regarding AFM 1-2 and with revising the manual in light of these comments and in light of developing air weapon technology.[108]

On 12 March 1953, the same day that Barker had received word that the Air Force Council had approved AFM 1-2, the Air University sent forward four basic operations manuals that were designed to expand the basic doctrine manual in the direction of strategic air, air defense, theater air, and air transport operations. During this same period, the Air War College Evaluation Staff sponsored a conference of representatives from the Air Staff, the Joint Amphibious Board, and the Tactical Air Command. On 4 June this group completed the draft of an Air Force manual concerned with air operations in conjunction with amphibious operations. It appeared that Tactical Air Command proposals for language changes would delay Air Staff review of the theater air operations manual. But General Kuter, after assuming command of the Air University, negotiated the compromise that the manual should be printed as written and that it and other manuals would be kept under constant study and revised at one-year intervals.[109] On 1 September 1953, the Air Force released printed copies of AFM 1-3, *Theater Air Operations*; AFM 1-4, *Air Defense Operations*; and AFM 1-5, *Air Operations in Conjunction with Amphibious Operations*. Dispute over corollary tasks to be specified for the strategic air forces—which were ultimately specified as being aerial mining, antisubmarine warfare, and interdiction of enemy surface forces—delayed publication of AFM 1-8, *Strategic Air Operations*, until 1 May 1954.[110] The manual on air transport operations was never published.

In view of the dissension that had accompanied the preparation of the *Theater Air Operations* manual and the Air University's plan to expand the subject with additional manuals, the Air Force assembled a wide-ranging conference on theater air forces during September 1953. This meeting included Evaluation Staff project officers and representatives of the Tactical Air Command, the Far East Air Forces, US Air Forces in Europe, and the Air Staff. The Evaluation Staff had prepared draft manuals on counterair, interdiction, and close air support, but the conferees decided that a single manual would suffice. The group also reviewed the manuscripts and agreed on desired language changes. With all commands represented in one room, one of the participants in the conference later recalled that coordination of the subject matter for the manual was surprisingly easy to accomplish. Completed in draft on 28 February, this single manual was printed on 1 March 1954 as AFM 1-7, *Theater Air Forces in Counterair, Interdiction, and Close Air Support Operations*. The Air Force subsequently printed AFM 1-9, *Theater Airlift Operations*, on 1 July 1954, and AFM 1-11, *Theater Air Reconnaissance*, on 1 December 1954.[111]

Viewed as a series, AFMs 1-3 through 1-11 represented the greatly refined results of more than 30 years of intermittent research, study, analysis, and codification. Although it had served as a project agency for their preparation, the Evaluation Staff described the manuals as "products of the entire Air Force." They had not been written in an "ivory-tower" atmosphere but in close collaboration with representatives of the Air Staff and of the major commands. The manuals expressed basic operational doctrine in broad terms. It was expected that the major commands would prepare command manuals describing how things were to be done.[112] However, the Air Force Directorate of Operations was not entirely satisfied with the operational manuals. Various officers pointed out that the manuals contained "background material . . . superfluous for doctrinal purposes," as well as material pertaining to "procedures and tactics rather than strictly doctrine." The doctrine on the command and control authority incumbent upon a theater air commander was more rigid than the Directorate of Operations believed to be justified. Air Force Manual 1-5, for example, specified that all theater air forces (Air Force, Navy, Marine Corps, and Allied) would be under the operational control of the theater air commander. The Directorate of Operations believed that the theater air commander should have operational control of Navy, Marine Corps, Allied, and Army air forces only when they were conducting operations in furtherance of the theater air mission. Both Air Force Manuals 1-3 and 1-5 adamantly opposed the allocation of the control of aircraft to a surface commander. In the Far East in July 1952, however, Brig Gen Jacob E. Smart had proposed that the Fifth Air Force could allocate mission control over specific air units for a specific length of time to a surface commander (in this case an Army corps commander) who could exercise this control through an air operations officer. After returning from the Far East to become commander of the Tactical Air Command, General Weyland described this concept in a lecture during the summer of 1954. Weyland urged that this concept of last phase of control could give a surface commander the prerogative of designating tasks for specific air units for a specific time in furtherance of his surface campaign. The control of air power was not allocated piecemeal since the theater air commander would have allocated air units for such a purpose only after he had viewed all theater air requirements. The Air Force Directorate of Operations was willing to accept the concept of last-phase control. But even though the Directorate of Operations was not entirely satisfied with the operational doctrine manuals, it was reluctant to push for any immediate revision of these documents since they generally met Air Force requirements and had been so excruciatingly difficult to prepare and coordinate. The best solution appeared to be a long-term project that would result in the incorporation of all basic doctrinal material into a single AFM 1-2.[113]

Continuing Air Doctrinal Activity

"In jet-atomic warfare," wrote General Kuter, after taking command of the Air University, "there will be no room for gross errors of judgment. There will be no time, should hostilities start, to correct mistakes in the types of forces that we have provided, the manner in which they have been organized and trained, or the way we fight." In order that the United States would be prepared for a future war, Kuter submitted that it would have to have proper doctrine and the doctrine would have to be accepted. In this same article, Kuter also suggested that the Air Force's doctrine had always stressed war and had failed to stress "the capabilities of our air forces to influence the behavior of other nations by actions short of war in support of national policy."[114] In a statement of command policy, Kuter observed: "The Air University's mission of education has coupled with it the responsibility to function and to produce as the doctrinal and related research center of the Air Force." Since as many as 2,000 man-hours of Air Force service could be contained in one class of Air War College students, he expected to reap great dividends from the accumulated talents available "in our obligation to keep our Air Force doctrine current and valid and to provide as a by-product of our learning activities, policies, concepts and plans of importance to our Air Force today and in the future."[115]

Kuter began holding regular meetings with Generals Barker, Wilson, Hopwood, and Smith, the last being the Air University director of education, to review the activities of the Air War College Graduate Study Group. These meetings became more and more worthwhile and were soon "guiding, monitoring, and coordinating the Air Force talent available at Maxwell in the faculties and great student bodies of the schools." Kuter hoped that the Air University would be able to do "really productive long-range thinking and planning with regard to subjects such as the size, general nature and organization of the USAF in an era of pilotless airplanes and ballistic missiles." He suggested that with the passing of time the Air University general officers might justify their designation "as a General Board of the Air Force and recognition as a supplement or adjunct of the Air Council."[116]

Because of his interest in moving Air Force doctrine forward Kuter gave close attention to the Air War College Graduate Study Group. Although he considered that the individual research efforts of the members of the group "have been excellent—in some cases brilliant," he suggested that the group had not met expectations, chiefly because it was not large enough to form an effective discussion unit or to attract important lecturers or consultants.[117] The final Air Staff directive that had established the Post-Graduate Study Group on 26 June 1952 had authorized the Air University to retain a few graduates from each Air War College class for an additional two years of advanced military study. Instituted on 21 July 1952 under the direction of Dr Eugene M. Emme, the Graduate Study Group included only three officers, who, after introductory seminars on research techniques, launched into major research topics of their own selection. After a year's residency, Col E. B. Miller, Jr., — whose research report, "Guided Missiles and Pilotless Aircraft in Theater Air Operations," attracted attention in the Air Staff — became the group's first graduate in June 1953. At this time, additional officers were assigned from the graduating Air War College class.[118]

As an instructor in the Air War College, Col Raymond S. Sleeper had become convinced that "the objective of air power is not to destroy the enemy people, not to destroy the enemy cities if it can be avoided, not to produce panic, not to destroy morale, but 'to change the temper' of the enemy, or, specifically, to produce behavior in the opposing government that is acceptable to us." In an article published in the winter of 1951–52 Sleeper suggested that a further study of the British experience in the use of the persuasive effect and pressure of air power to quell revolts in Iraq and Aden during the 1920s might have applicability to the cold war.[119] General Wilson nominally assigned Sleeper to the Graduate Study Group in August 1953 in order that he might test his thesis. Borrowing Air University professional civilians and securing selected students from the Air Command and Staff College, Sleeper organized and directed Project Control, which sought to determine whether the Royal Air Force techniques might have been used to advantage by the United States so as to have affected the course of historical events from the 1930s through 1945. Even though it produced 21 volumes, Project Control had not demonstrated fully that Sleeper's thesis was completely applicable to contemporary national problems. Nevertheless, Project Control contributed to an understanding of the effect of air power on international relations both in times of peace and of war.[120]

General Kuter believed that the Air War College Evaluation Staff ought to be made the center of doctrine and concept development. On 27 March 1954, he asked permission of the Air Force to disband the Graduate Study Group and to use its 10 colonel spaces to establish a long-range planning staff parallel to the Evaluation Staff within the Air War College. At first the Air Staff was unwilling to agree that a field agency should have any responsibility for the preparation of Air Force plans, but Kuter explained that the Air University did not intend to impinge on the Air Staff's business but rather to prepare "very long range studies in the field of strategy and doctrine." Evidently reassured, the Graduate Study Group was dissolved and its personnel allotments, which had never been filled, were transferred to the Air War College Evaluation Staff where a Long Range Planning Division was established.[121] Among the officers of the Graduate Study Group so reassigned was Col Richard P. Klocko. In a research study entitled, "Air Power in Limited Military Actions," published in August 1954, Klocko outlined a requirement for a combat-ready air task force that eventually would be developed as the Tactical Air Command's Composite Air Strike Force. At the same time these changes were in the offing, the Air War College took another step originally proposed by General Wilson in July 1952. "An organization such as the Air War College," Wilson had reasoned, "should develop over a period of years a library of its own military writings." Activated in May 1954, the Air War College Studies Group became responsible for editing and preparing for publication at the newly established Air University Press the best of the student theses, lecturers' manuscripts, and writings of the Air War College staff.[122]

As soon as the Air Force issued Air Force Manual 1-2, *United States Air Force Basic Doctrine,* on 1 April 1953, General Twining sent out a personal letter to each major air commander requesting that they send their comments and suggested changes to the Air University, which would make periodic substantive reviews of the doctrine. The major air commanders generally welcomed the manual and had few changes in mind. Only General Weyland, then commanding the Far East Air Forces, recommended substantial changes and he merely desired an elaboration of the principles of war as they pertained to the employment of air forces. After the comments were received, neither the Air Staff nor the Air University believed that any substantial revision was in order, and the new edition of Air Force Manual 1-2 published on 1 April 1954 contained only a few minor editorial changes.[123]

Within a few months, however, the new doctrinal thinking at the Air University indicated that AFM 1-2 ought to be broadened in scope. The work would be undertaken by a new group of Air Force thinkers. A rotation of personnel and the internal reorganization of the Air War College Evaluation Staff in July 1954 was marked by the assignment of Col Ephraim M. Hampton as Air War College deputy for evaluation and Col Jerry D. Page as chief of the Doctrine Division. Assisted by Col Royal H. Roussel as project officer, Page promptly undertook the work of revising AFM 1-2 without delay. "Our own experiences in the doctrinal field," Page and Roussel subsequently reported, "lead us to believe that the total war capabilities of air forces — their capability to destroy in total war — are the most clearly understood of all their capabilities. Their great potential in times other than war is less clearly understood."[124] General Kuter agreed that Air Force doctrine had not stressed sufficiently the capabilities of air power throughout the entire spectrum of international conflict. Page and Roussel sought to expand the basic doctrinal manual so that it would take greater cognizance of the capabilities of air power in periods other than general war. Incorporating ideas received from Kuter, Hopwood, and Sleeper, Page and Roussel prepared a draft of a revised manual in August 1954, which they coordinated with key individuals at the Air University, in the Pentagon, and in Europe. After this coordination, Page and Roussel redrafted the manual in Joint Chiefs of Staff style and had it printed at the Air University preparatory to final review in Washington. On 4 January 1955, Kuter forwarded copies of the proposed manual to General White, now Air Force vice chief of staff, together with a chart that explained how the manual had been changed and the reason for the changes.[125]

Following Air Staff and Air Force Council review of the new edition of AFM 1-2, General White notified Kuter on 1 February 1955 that the Air Force liked the new statement of basic doctrine; the vice chief noted that although the draft had retained the basic doctrine of the original manual, it had managed a "clear discussion of the area between the two extremes of conflict (general war and full peace) so as to permit emphasis on the broad potentialities of air forces as a persuasive instrument in combating the international tension brought about by 'cold war' conditions."[126] At White's request, the Air University readily agreed to change the draft to emphasize that the US Air Force was a term inclusive of both the active military forces and the reserve air forces. However, Air University was less able to cope with another Air Staff comment that the manual was difficult to understand and ought to be rewritten in "readable writing." After making a "fog count," which followed an Air Force procedure of assigning arithmetical values to such things as long and strange words and involved sentences, Brig Gen S. F. Giffin, Air War College vice commander, figured that the draft of AFM 1-2 fell into the range of comprehension of a college sophomore. Thus, Giffin concluded that many of the persons who said they did not understand the writing in the draft manual were actually saying that they did not understand the doctrine. Page and Roussel also took note of the fact that the 4,100 words in the manual would be read in 20 minutes, but they suggested that informed readers would have to spend much more time in thinking about the manual than in merely reading it.[127] Based on such analyses, the Air University declined to make changes in the style in which the manual was written.

When it was officially published on 1 April 1955, AFM 1-2, *United States Air Force Basic Doctrine*, represented a codification of experience bearing on the subject of air power and air warfare. It accepted the old definition of air power: "The term 'air power' embraces the entire aviation capacity of the United States." It asserted that air power had radically changed the conduct of war. "With air forces and modern weapons available, it is no longer necessary to defeat opposing armed forces as a prerequisite to conducting major operations directly against an opponent either in his sovereign territory or in any locality." The key to the new doctrine was the statement: "United States air forces are employed to gain and exploit a dominant position in the air both in peace and in war. The desired dominant position is control of the air." Older Air Force doctrinal statements had defined control of the air in terms of the attainment of air superiority in a time of war. The new manual stated: "Control is achieved when air forces can effect planned degrees of destruction while denying this opportunity to the enemy." It also pointed out that

> control of the air is achieved when air forces, in peace or war, can effect the desired degrees of influence over other specific nations. Control of the air is gained and held by the appropriate employment of the nation's air potential. . . . Sometimes a dominant position can be obtained through the mere presence and passive use of air forces. At other times control of the air may require the active use of air forces to attain the desired dominant position. There will be occasions when a combination of passive-type dominance and active-type dominance may serve best in support of the national objectives.[128]

"Our doctrine states, in effect," Page and Roussel wrote in an independent explanation of AFM 1-2, "that control of the air can be exploited continuously, day and night, seven days a week, 365 days a year, under any conditions. This can be so because control of the air does not denote a continuous physical action against something." In an illustration, Page and Roussel drew from the lessons of Korea:

> Our air forces in Korea were dropping bombs, fighting MiGs, attacking troops and gun positions, and a great number of other things *actively*. But these were not "separate" air forces fighting a "separate" war. They were part of our global air entity, and standing with them — although not used *actively* in Korea — was the tremendous additional power of this global entity. We must assume that much of the impact of our air power in Korea — much of its influence — came from air forces that never dropped a bomb or fired a bullet in Korea.

In addition to these wartime applications of air power, the Berlin Airlift, the use of air transport planes to give relief from floods in Pakistan in 1954, and the "kinderlift" flights of underprivileged children out of encircled West Berlin for summer vacations in West Germany were illustrations of peaceful applications of air power. "A nation's influence in international negotiations," the new doctrine states, "is strengthened or weakened by the state of its air forces. The capabilities of powerful air forces for achieving decision in major war are thus translated into a capacity for the maintenance of world peace."[129]

As soon as AFM 1-2 was released, *Air Force Magazine* published the entire text and called it "one of the most important books in the world."[130] As Air Force vice chief of staff, General White endorsed the new doctrinal statement because of its clear discussion of the role of air power throughout the entire spectrum of international conflict, because the doctrine established the worth of air forces without denigrating other forces, and because the emphasis of the inclusive nature of air power rebutted the charge that providing air forces put all of the nation's "eggs in one basket."[131] The new doctrine appeared to have a growth potential that could encompass new technological developments. Admitting that the Air Force seemed to be having difficulty in shifting its thoughts from control of the air based on actual combat operations, Col Jack N. Donohew, Air Force deputy assistant for programming, pointed out in December 1956 that what he called "deterrent control of the air" would have applicability in an era when unmanned weapon systems would have to be maintained in constant readiness for instantaneous launchings. Although these weapons would not be physically present in the air, they would serve to preserve control of the air.[132] Speaking as Air Force chief of staff in December 1957, General White again endorsed AFM 1-2. "Our doctrine," he said, "is published for all to read in a 10-page, unclassified Air Force document. I believe this doctrine is wholly responsive to the primary aim of serving the national policy and is in step with the changing times."[133]

Failing Efforts to Produce Interservice Doctrine

Looking backward at the work of the Joint Air Transportation, Airborne Troop, Air Defense, Tactical Air Support, Landing Force, and Amphibious Boards that were formed in the autumn of 1951 in response to the *Joint Action Armed Forces* (JAAF) manual, General Barker did not think it remarkable that these joint boards failed to accomplish their purposes. Referring to "the patent inability of a lower echelon of authority to resolve an interservice problem that could not be solved at the highest level of authority," Barker observed that "the same divergence of views at the highest level of authority which mitigated against a resolution of the problem are manifestly evident at the lower echelons because of disseminated service positions on such controversial matters."[134]

In accordance with the JAAF agreement, the Army, Navy, and Air Force had moved promptly to establish the joint boards, which were to develop joint doctrines and procedures; evaluate joint tactics and techniques, adequacy of equipment, and adequacy of joint training; and review publications covering the conduct of joint training. In August and September 1951, General Vandenberg named some of his best senior officers to head the joint boards for which the Air Force served as executive agent: Maj Gen Grandison Gardner to the Joint Tactical Air Support Board at Pope AFB and Maj Gen Earl S. Hoag to the Joint Troop Carrier Board, which was soon redesignated as the Joint Air Transportation Board, also at Pope AFB. The Army established the Joint Airborne Troop Board at Fort Bragg as a successor to the former Army Airborne Center; Maj Gen William M. Miley, who had commanded the center, now headed the board. The Marine Corps established the Joint Landing Board with the Marine Corps Schools in Quantico, Virginia, and this board was headed by the school's commandant—first by Lt Gen Franklin A. Hart and soon thereafter by Lt Gen Clifton B. Cates—as a collateral duty. The Navy established the Joint Amphibious Board at Little Creek, Virginia, under the chairmanship of Rear Adm Lyman A. Thackerey.[135] Army, Navy, Marine, and Air Force officers were assigned to full-time duty on the several joint boards, except for the Joint Air Transportation Board and the Joint Airborne Troop Board, whose membership served cross-duties on both boards.[136]

Even though the charters of these joint boards vested them with major responsibilities of evaluation, the administrative guidance issued to the boards by the military services ensured that decisionmaking authority would remain in Washington. Senior Army members on the boards were directed to coordinate their actions with the chief of the Army Field Forces. They were authorized to concur or not concur in projects at the board level; however, they could not approve or disapprove projects except in accordance with review of the projects by the Department of the Army.[137] The commandant of the Marine Corps instructed the senior Marine Corps officers who sat on the boards to act for the Marine Corps on board-level projects, but he provided that final approval of all projects would have to be referred to the chief of naval operations.[138] Initial Air Force letters of instructions to the senior Air Force board members stated that they would "be acting as the direct representative of the Chief of Staff, USAF," and would be responsible for indicating "concurrence or non-concurrence on all completed Board reports." Quite shortly, however, these letters were elaborated to provide:

> As the Senior Air Force Representative you will represent the US Air Force at Board level and you are empowered to state your views as "Air Force" views on all completed Board reports. However, as is customary in all joint functioning, your stated "Air Force views" do not constitute a commitment of the Chief of Staff, USAF, to support these views at higher levels. Final approval or disapproval of "Service Views" taken at any level or echelon of command is reserved to the head of the Service.[139]

The work of the Joint Air Defense Board was somewhat overshadowed by Project Lincoln, the Summer Study Group, and the Citizens Advisory Committee. This joint board maintained harmonious relations with the Air Defense Command and Army Antiaircraft Command and accomplished a wide variety of projects ranging from the design of protective aircraft revetments to a statement of recommended air defense doctrine. When completed on 14 April 1954, the recommended air defense doctrine visualized an air defense system that could accomplish a "continuous surveillance of the enemy from the time he departs his own territory until he is destroyed." It also stated that active defense ought to include "a devastating attack against enemy aircraft on their home bases; continued attack during the enemy's departure from home bases, and while in foreign theaters; attack continuously throughout the enemy's journey to the United States and Canada; and a final assault against aircraft, which may survive until arrival within their objective areas before their final approach to their targets."[140] General Gardner forwarded the proposed doctrine to General Twining with a personal letter. "I believe," Gardner wrote, "that we can maintain a defense through which penetration would be improbable if not impossible. I think that the cost of such a defense is not beyond what we can endure and I believe that such a defense should be our objective."[141] Gardner recommended that the Strategic Air Command (SAC) should build bombproof facilities at bases near the outer boundaries of the United States and ought to make a maximum dispersal of its intercontinental bombers. Other than these measures SAC should depend for its protection on an expanded warning time that would allow it to put its aircraft in the air and evacuate its ground personnel in case of a hostile attack.[142] The accomplishments of the Joint Air Defense Board were not inconsiderable. The establishment of the Continental Air Defense Command (CONAD) on 1 September 1954 as a unified command directly responsible to the Joint Chiefs of Staff created a more powerful air defense network. The new command was responsible for establishing methods and procedures for the use of the forces available for the air defense of the continental United States. Officially, the Joint Air Defense Board continued to exist. Following the retirement of General Gardner in August 1954, Maj Gen Frederic Smith, the CONAD vice commander, assumed the additional duty of chairman of the Joint Air Defense Board.[143]

The Joint Tactical Air Support, Joint Air Transportation, and Joint Airborne Troop Boards proved to be controversial. An Army spokesman in Washington stated that they were "likely to become the focal point of procurement planning not only for troop and cargo carriers, but in many cases will also be the agency responsible for formulating requirements for virtually all tactical support aircraft." This statement indicated that the Army still hoped that the boards might become unified centers that would manage joint applications of forces.[144] During the JAAF negotiations and when the charters of the joint boards were being written, the Tactical Air Command persistently opposed the assignment of doctrinal responsibilities to the Joint Tactical Air Support and Joint Air Transportation Boards and argued that this would amount to an usurpation or duplication of the Tactical Air Command's responsibilities.[145] Moreover, the Air Force's failure to fill some vacancies in the boards or to appoint one individual to serve on more than one board revealed a flagging interest in them. General Wolfinbarger served as director of the Joint Tactical Air Support Board. When General Hoag retired in February 1953, Wolfinbarger was appointed to serve additionally as director of the Joint Air Transportation Board. After Wolfinbarger retired in July 1953, Maj Gen Robert L. Copsey was named director of the Joint Air Transportation Board; but the other position remained vacant for several months before Maj Gen Edward H. Underhill was named director of the Joint Tactical Air Support Board. Although Copsey continued to direct the Joint Air Transportation Board, Underhill was transferred to other duties in August 1954. At that time the Tactical Air Command strongly objected to assigning another general officer to the Joint Tactical Air Support Board and the director's position remained vacant. In May and June 1953 both the Army and the Air Force reduced their personnel authorizations for these three joint boards, stating that they would thereafter collectively employ the retained officers to accomplish their most urgent projects.[146]

When its charter was approved in May 1952, the Joint Air Transportation Board was made as the principal agent of the armed forces responsible for developing doctrine and procedures and for evaluating tactics, techniques, equipment, and training for all air transportation matters. Almost immediately Generals Collins and Twining had agreed that the board would not consider any matters concerning the Military Air Transport Service. The Air Force had ruled that responsibilities for aeromedical transport, war plans, and mobilization matters were outside the purview of the board. Other attempts of the board to pursue projects were stymied by competition from other commands and by conflicting service positions.

The Tactical Air Command, for example, consistently outpaced the board in stating operational requirements for new equipment. A budding project looking toward the development of a doctrine for employing rotary-wing aircraft in joint operations was terminated when the Army ruled that it would use its own helicopters and had no requirements against which the Air Force should program units. Likewise, after long study, the board proved unable to agree on the subject of a command structure for a joint airborne operation.[147] The Joint Chiefs of Staff, at the suggestion of the chief of naval operations, had directed the board "to establish joint doctrine and procedures of governing command, employment and control of tactical air forces in support of ground forces." The Tactical Air Command opposed this directive because it believed that the wording of the directive implied that there was no extant doctrine on air-ground operations and because it believed that it could have secured an early agreement with the Army Field Forces for a revision of the *Joint Training Directive* if the problem had not been referred to the board. As it too was directed to do, the Joint Tactical Air Support Board prepared a draft manual, which included basic agreement between the Army, Navy, and Marine Corps and a dissenting Air Force position. The point in contention was the Air Force demand that the existing system of "unified command at theater level only and coequal status of component commanders at all echelons" should be retained, as opposed to the Army, Navy, and Marine Corps position that advocated that the command of air support aviation be delegated to the supported unit.[148]

The Joint Landing Board, established initially at Quantico and moved to Camp Lejeune, North Carolina, on 1 July 1952, handled highly specialized matters that were not of transcendent concern to the Air Force.[149] On the other hand, the Joint Amphibious Board was directed to resolve more complex matters regarding the doctrine and procedures of joint amphibious operations. When he was assigned to this board as an Air Force representative on 15 October 1951, Col Robert A. Erdin discovered that the Navy had a firmly fixed position, that the Army had definite opinions, and that the Air Force had not given much thought to amphibious warfare. Since the board proposed to give priority to defining doctrines and procedures to govern joint amphibious operations, Erdin devoted much of his time during 1952–53 to perfecting an Air Force position, which, as has been seen, was engrossed in AFM 1-5. On 15 January 1954 the Joint Amphibious Board forwarded a three-way split in opinion to the Joint Chiefs of Staff. The Navy-Marine Corps position was that all joint amphibious operations should be conducted by a joint amphibious task force, commanded by an admiral who would personally command both the joint task force and the supporting naval forces. Working through a staff officer designated as a tactical air commander, the joint amphibious task force commander would exercise operational control over all air operations in the amphibious objective area. When control of the air was passed ashore, operational control of air forces would be passed to the landing force commander. The Air Force position that a theater command structure normally would be flexible enough to accommodate all types of operations, including amphibious operations, was incorporated as doctrine in AFM 1-5. Operational control of all theater air forces even during amphibious operations should be retained by the theater air commander. Where the theater command structure might be unable to conduct an amphibious operation, the Air Force urged the establishment of a joint staff and component commanders for air, naval, and ground forces. The Army held that an amphibious operation would be a preliminary portion of an extended surface campaign. It advocated establishing a supreme joint task force commander who would be superior to the amphibious task force commander. The joint task force commander would control an "Air Force long-range striking force" whereas other air forces would be controlled by the amphibious force commander while command was afloat and by the amphibious landing force commander when command went ashore. The Joint Chiefs circulated the Joint Amphibious Board's recommendations to the Air Force and the Army for comment; when no basic agreement could be reached, the recommendations were apparently laid aside within the Joint Chiefs of Staff.[150]

Facing personnel shortages incident to the expansion of the Air Force, General Vandenberg directed that the Air Staff initiate action to eliminate the joint boards in the spring of 1953. At this time, General Kuter suggested that the Air Force members on the several boards should be assigned to the Air War College Evaluation Staff in order that it might assume greater responsibilities in the field of joint doctrine.[151] In a memorandum to the chairman of the Committee for Joint Policies and Procedures of the Joint Chiefs of Staff, General Partridge, Air Force deputy chief of staff for operations, formally recommended on 1 February 1954 that the joint boards be discontinued. "Continuation of the joint Boards," Partridge urged, "represents Services' support of organizations which are expensive in manpower and dollars, unable to fulfill their purpose effectively, duplicate the capabilities of other existing agencies, and whose work, essentially, must be re-done by subsequent reviewing echelons."[152] Asked to comment on the proposal, Colonel Erdin estimated that the Joint Amphibious Board had cost more than $500,000 and had completed only one formal project and this with split views.[153] General Copsey believed that there was a great need for interservice doctrine, but he admitted that the Joint Air Transportation Board had failed to "accomplish the timely purposes of its charter."[154] The Tactical Air Command observed that the joint boards had accentuated interservice disagreements and recommended that they should be discontinued immediately.[155]

For more than a year the Air Force got no support for its demands that the joint boards be discontinued, but after a time the Marine Corps and the Navy came to this same opinion. The Army acceded last of all, and on 3 December 1954 the Joint Chiefs of Staff directed that the joint boards would be dissolved. In accordance with the Joint Chiefs directive, the Continental Air Defense Command assumed the responsibilities of the Joint Air Defense Board after it was dissolved on 1 February 1955. Following dissolution of the Joint Tactical Air Support Board on 15 February and the Joint Air Transportation Board on 1 March, the Tactical Air Command became responsible for developing joint doctrine, procedures, tactics, techniques, training, publications, and equipment related to close combat support of ground forces and joint airborne operations. The Air Force invited the Army, Navy, and Marine Corps to establish liaison with the Tactical Air Command to aid in the development of joint doctrinal matters. The Tactical Air Command was similarly charged to provide liaison officers to the Army Field Forces, the amphibious forces Atlantic Fleet, and the Marine Corps Development Center to aid in their development of joint doctrinal recommendations concerning joint airborne troop and amphibious operations, effective with the dissolution of the

Joint Airborne Troop, Joint Landing, and Joint Amphibious Boards.[156] In order to accomplish joint doctrinal concerns specified in the JAAF manual, the Joint Chiefs specified that the responsible commands would prepare working draft recommendations and circulate them to interested commands in other services before submitting them to the responsible service. The responsible service would submit completed projects to the other services for concurrence before submitting them to the Joint Chiefs of Staff for consideration. Once the Joint Chiefs gave their approval, projects concerning basic doctrines, procedures, and command relations would be promulgated by the responsible service.[157]

Interservice Disagreements on Doctrine

In the early 1950s, thinkers in the Air Force and the other services held an optimistic belief that a better understanding and publication of sound air power doctrines would have a wholesome effect on the national military effort. "Of all the people who desire a statement of Air Force doctrine," an Air War College seminar concluded in 1951, "none is more anxious to receive it than the Army and the Navy. Likewise statements of military doctrine by the other services would be helpful to the Air Force. For it is out of this welter of confusion that basic misunderstandings are created."[158] Writing in the *US Naval Institute Proceedings* in April 1952, Col George C. Reinhardt, US Army, charged that "among the most radical enthusiasts of air power themselves, there exists today more divergent opinion on the composition of that power and of its optimum use in war than ever arose, between general and admiral, over the relative importance of land and sea combat." Reinhardt suggested that "Mahan, in his day, clarified not only the unification of the various functions of sea power into a cohesive force but also combined the strategy of sea and land combat into a practical, working entity." Reinhardt, therefore, concluded that "air power, American air power in particular, needs its Mahan."[159]

With the publication of AFM 1-2, *United States Air Force Basic Doctrine*, the Air Force possessed a codification of its fundamental ideas. "Of the various types of military forces," the April 1955 edition of the manual stated, "those which conduct air operations are most capable of decisive results.... With air forces and modern weapon systems available, it no longer is necessary to defeat opposing armed forces as a prerequisite to conducting major operations directly against an opponent either in his sovereign territory or in any other locality." Recognizing that "the medium in which air forces operate — space — is an indivisible field of activity," the basic doctrine manual held that "all command arrangements must be in accord with the precept that neither air forces nor their field of activity can be segmented and partitioned among different interests. Because air forces possess the inherent ability to concentrate effort at decisive times and places, they can be employed in a variety of tasks for the purpose of accomplishing a variety of effects."[160]

The statement of basic Air Force doctrine differed markedly from that of the older surface forces. Department of the Army Field Manual 100-5 diametrically opposed the Air Force doctrine. "Army forces as land forces," stated this manual, "are the decisive component of the military structure. . . . During the course of military operations Army forces, because of their decisive capabilities, are supported from time to time by other military components. . . . In any case, the efforts of all components are directed toward insuring the success of the land operations." US Naval Warfare Publication 10 presented a position closer to Air Force doctrine; the manual discussed military pressure against an enemy:

> The mobility of attacking units and distances from which they can strike enemy targets are strong factors in increasing the effectiveness of pressure. Actual occupation or control of enemy territory is the optimum of pressure in that it has an overwhelming effect on the enemy's capacity to wage war. . . . Air strategy, designed to seek a decision primarily by air action . . . is in the process of historic development and . . . will become more clearly definable with the passage of time.[161]

"Everything depends upon air supremacy: everything else must take second place. With control of the air, control of the sea and land follows," reasoned Col Richard C. Weller of the Air War College in the spring of 1954. "Oddly enough," he continued, "military men agree that air power or the air element is dominant over the surface elements. But this has only stimulated them to seize for their own element all of the air support which eloquence permits."[162] In negotiations within the Joint Amphibious and Joint Tactical Air Support Boards, Army and Navy representatives argued in favor of what they described as a "unity of command at the scene of battle." Prior to the emergence of air power as a major component of war, Air Force officers were willing to admit that there had been a certain logic to a self-sufficient force concept, but with the increased flexibility of aircraft they were agreed that it was mandatory that control of available air power should be retained at the highest levels practicable. "All of the various proposals advanced in furtherance of the outdated 'unity of command at the scene of battle' concept . . .," stated the Tactical Air Command, "result in the segmentation and subordination of air power to the relatively localized surface battle despite the costly evolution of the proven centralized control concept."[163]

That the Army and Navy felt strongly in support of their desire to decentralize air power was also a matter of record. In June 1953 a Navy lecturer criticized the rigidity of Air Force doctrine. "Since local air superiority is temporary or harder to make effective because of greater destructive weapons," he said, "there is a tendency to ignore it. . . . Time and space factors are not yet instantaneous quantities, and by proper selection of opportunity and location, a force — air or sea — can argue or gain superiority for limited periods." Believing that the Air Force's constant emphasis on centralization of control might arise from a lack of confidence that the other services might not employ air to its fullest advantages, this Navy lecturer expressed the hope that "as the Navy and Army demonstrate their awareness of air power and its best employment, operational control of air units can perhaps be centralized or decentralized as appropriate to the situation."[164] Speaking to the USAF Scientific Advisory Board on 22 March 1954,

Lt Gen John E. Dahlquist summed up his view of the local command and control concept favored by the Army. "It is my conviction," he said,

> that the commander whom we hold responsible for the land battle must be provided with the means to accomplish his mission and the authority to control those means. In the area forward of the Army rear boundary, the ground force commander must have authority to direct the employment of ground and supporting air and naval weapons simultaneously against his targets.... Control must include the authority to assign and suspend air and naval support missions.... The tremendous increase in the potential mobility of combat forces... makes the requirement for command responsibility and decisive action more important today than ever before.[165]

As the joint boards were breaking up, Army Chief of Staff Gen Matthew B. Ridgway announced on 31 January 1955 that the *Joint Training Directive for Air-Ground Operations* contained views on "command relationships and the responsibilities of supporting and supported forces" that the Army could not accept and that the directive accordingly "does not represent the views of the Department of the Army on doctrine for air-ground operations."[166] Instead of resulting in the production of harmonious interservice doctrine, the joint board negotiations appeared to have widened the doctrinal divergencies of the Army, Navy, and Air Force.

NOTES

1. Maj Gen Lauris Norstad, assistant chief of Air Staff, Plans (ACAS-5), Army Air Forces, to deputy commander, Army Air Forces, reporting and routing (R&R) sheet, subject: General Air Board, ca. 12 February 1946.

2. Army Air Forces Regulation 20–61, 3 June 1946, quoted in History, Air University, 29 November 1945–30 June 1947, 1:218–19.

3. History, Air University, 29 November 1945–30 June 1947, 1:10; Maj Gen David M. Schlatter, "Air University," *Air Force Magazine*, July 1946, 9–11.

4. Gen Carl A. Spaatz to commanding general, Air University, letter, subject: Amendment to Directive, 13 May 1946.

5. Schlatter, "Air University," 9–11.

6. History, Air University, 1 July 1947–30 June 1948, 1:45–48.

7. Memorandum by Brig Gen Francis H. Griswold, deputy assistant chief of Air Staff, Operations, Commitments, and Requirements (ACAS-3), to chief of Air Staff, Army Air Forces, subject: Revision of Field Manuals, 13 May 1946; memorandum by Brig Gen Reuben C. Hood, Jr., deputy chief of Air Staff, to assistant chief of Air Staff, Operations, Commitments, and Requirements, subject: Revision of Field Manuals, 15 May 1946.

8. Air War College, "Recommendations on Revision of the Field Manual System of Publications and Related Manuals for USAF," special study 2, 19 December 1947.

9. Brig Gen Thomas S. Power, deputy assistant chief of Air Staff, Operations, Commitments, and Requirements, to commanding general, Air University, letter, subject: Revision of Field Manual 100-20, 4 September 1947.

10. Col James H. Wallace, deputy assistant chief of Air Staff, Operations, Commitments, and Requirements, Army Air Forces, to commanding general, Air University, letter, subject: Standardization of Air Defense Procedures, Doctrine, and Organization, 14 August 1947; report of

Air Defense Policy Panel to chief of staff, US Air Force, subject: Air Defense Policy, 2 February 1948; Evaluation Division, Air University, Quarterly Project Report, 15 September 1948, 28.

11. Brig Gen Thomas S. Power to commanding general, Air University, letter, 4 September 1947; 1st ind., Col L. L. Braxton, adjutant general, Air University, to commanding general, Army Air Forces, 23 September 1947; Air War College "Preparation of USAF Manual Commanders Guide," study 6, 16 March 1948; Maj Gen David M. Schlatter to chief of staff, US Air Force, letter, subject: Revision of Field Manual 100-20, 22 October 1947.

12. Air War College, special study 2, 19 December 1947.

13. Lt Col John F. Concannon, air adjutant general, Air University, to chief of staff, US Air Force, letter, subject: Air Force System of Publication, 5 February 1948.

14. Air University to chief of staff, US Air Force, letter, 5 February 1948; 1st ind., Col Leslie O. Peterson, chief, Requirements Division, Directorate of Training and Requirements, US Air Force, to commanding general, Air University, 5 May 1948.

15. Lt Col Robert P. Johnson, Jr., chief, Review and Editorial Branch, Office of Air Adjutant General, US Air Force, to chief, Requirements Division, Directorate of Training and Requirements, reporting and routing (R&R) sheet, subject: Air Force Field Manual Structure, 26 May 1948; Col R. H. Carmichael, chief, Evaluation Division, Air University, staff study, subject: "To Analyze the USAF Publications System for Producing Manuals," 13 July 1948.

16. Evaluation Division, Air University, "The Air University Evaluation Division Quarterly Project Report," 15 June 1948, 19–20; Maj Gen David M. Schlatter to chief of staff, US Air Force, letter, 22 October 1947.

17. Air War College special study 6, 16 March 1948.

18. Evaluation Division, Air University, "The Air University Evaluation Division Quarterly Project Report," 15 June 1948, 19–20.

19. Lt Col John F. Concannon to chief of staff, US Air Force, Attn.: Director, Training and Requirements, letter, subject: US Air Force Publications System, 5 May 1948.

20. Memorandum by Col. Richard H. Carmichael to chief, Academic Staff, Air University, subject: Report of Official Visit, 19 May 1948.

21. Lt Col John F. Concannon to chief of staff, US Air Force, letter, 5 May 1948; 1st ind., Brig Gen James H. Wallace, director, Training and Requirements, US Air Force, to commanding general, Air University, 25 June 1948.

22. Col Richard H. Carmichael, staff study, 13 July 1948.

23. Evaluation Division, Air University, "The Air University Evaluation Division Quarterly Project Report," 15 June 1948, 19–20; Maj F. E. Lankston, assistant adjutant general, Air University, to chief of staff, US Air Force, Attn.: Director, Training and Requirements, letter, 2 July 1948, w/incl.: "Air Power and the U.S. Air Force," 1 July 1948.

24. Maj Gen Frank F. Everest, assistant deputy chief of staff, Operations, US Air Force, to commanding general, Air University, letter, subject: Draft Category I Manual, Air Employment Instructions, 21 September 1948, w/incl.: Specific Comments on Draft Category I Manual, Air Employment Instructions.

25. Evaluation Division, Air University, "The Air University Evaluation Division Quarterly Project Report," 15 December 1948, 16–18; Col Leland S. Stranathan, deputy director, Training and Requirements, US Air Force, to commanding general, Air University, letter, subject: Air Force Doctrinal Publications, 22 December 1948; 1st ind., Lt Col John F. Concannon to chief of staff, Air Force, 18 February 1949.

26. Maj Gen Carl A. Brandt, acting director, Training and Requirements, US Air Force, to commanding general, Air University, letter, subject: Air Force Doctrinal Publications, 22 March 1949.

27. Lt W. F. Knotts, assistant adjutant general, Air University, to director, Requirements, US Air Force et al., letter, subject: Air Force Doctrinal Publications (Tentative), 20 January 1950; Maj Gen Carl A. Brandt to commanding general, Air University, letter, subject: Proposed Air Force Manual "Commander's Guide," AU project no. 4802, 25 July 1950, w/incl.: Comments on "Commander's Guide."

IDEAS, CONCEPTS, DOCTRINE

28. Maj Gen John DeF. Barker, deputy commanding general, Air University, to Brig Gen Robert C. Candee, deputy commandant, Armed Forces Staff College, letter, 12 September 1950.

29. Maj Gen John DeF. Barker to Col Roland Birnn, letter, 25 October 1949; Maj Gen John DeF. Barker to Lt Gen Idwal H. Edwards, letter, 27 October 1949.

30. History, Air University, January–June 1950, 1:27–30, 107–15; Evaluation Division, Air University, "The Air University Evaluation Division Quarterly Progress Report," 30 June 1950, 17.

31. Assistant chief of Air Staff, Operations, Commitments, and Requirements, Army Air Forces, daily activity report, 12 February 1946; Maj Gen Muir S. Fairchild, commanding general, Air University, to Maj Gen Earle E. Partridge, director, Training and Requirements, US Air Force, letter, 9 March 1948.

32. Assistant chief of Air Staff, Operations, Commitments, and Requirements, Army Air Forces, daily activity report, 12 February 1946.

33. Col Kenneth P. Bergquist, deputy assistant chief of Air Staff, Operations, Commitments, and Requirements, Army Air Forces, to commanding general, Air University, letter, subject: Air University Project AU-4607, 14 October 1946.

34. Maj F. E. Lankston, assistant adjutant general, Air University, to commanding general, Army Air Forces, letter, subject: Air University Project AU-4607, 1 November 1946, Maj Gen Earle E. Partridge to commanding general, Air University, letter, subject: Review of Joint Procedures for Tactical Control of Aircraft in Joint Amphibious Operations, 16 December 1947.

35. Maj Gen Otto P. Weyland, assistant chief of Air Staff, Plans, Army Air Forces, to assistant chief of Air Staff, Operations, Commitments, and Requirements, R&R sheet, subject: Joint Army-Navy Procedures for Air Support of Ground or Surface Forces, 29 August 1946; Requirements Division, assistant chief of Air Staff, Operations, Commitments, and Requirements, Joint Procedures for Tactical Control of Aircraft in Joint Amphibious Operations, 20 November 1946; Maj Gen Earle E. Partridge to commanding general, Air University, letter, 16 December 1947.

36. Maj Gen Earle E. Partridge to director of intelligence, Deputy Chief of Staff for Operations, US Air Force, R&R sheet, subject: Release of Air Force Publications on Amphibious Operations to the Air Attache, Royal Australian Air Force, 4 February 1948.

37. Maj Gen Earle E. Partridge to commanding general, Air University, letter, 16 December 1947; Tactical Air Command to chief of staff, US Air Force, letter, subject: Review of "Joint Procedures for Tactical Control of Aircraft in Joint Amphibious Operations," 10 February 1948; Lt Col John F. Concannon to chief of staff, US Air Force, Attn.: Director, Training and Requirements, letter, 1 June 1948; Maj Gen H. R. Bull, acting director, Organization and Training Division, US Army, to chief of staff, US Air Force, letter, subject: Joint Procedures for Tactical Control of Aircraft in Joint Amphibious Operations, 28 October 1948.

38. House, *The National Defense Program—Unification and Strategy: Hearings before the Committee on Armed Services*, 81st Cong., 1st sess., 1949, 547–48; Col Liland S. Stranathan to commanding general, Air University, letter, 22 December 1948.

39. House, *The National Defense Program—Unification and Strategy*, 548–49; Tactical Air Command, Tactical Air Operations Presentation to the USAF Board of Review for Tactical Air Operations, 21 June 1949, tab. C: Background, 1–2.

40. Report of USAF Board of Review for Tactical Air Operations, October 1949.

41. National Military Establishment: Annual Report of the Secretary of the Air Force for Fiscal Year 1948, chief of staff section, 151.

42. Memorandum by Col William W. Momyer, deputy chief of staff for plans, Tactical Air Command, to Historical Section, Tactical Air Command, subject: Historical Information, 6 July 1949.

43. Ibid.; memorandum by Col William W. Momyer, deputy chief of staff for plans, Tactical Air Command, to deputy chief of staff for operations, Tactical Air Command, subject: Missions, Responsibilities, and Functions of Continental Air Command, 4 April 1949.

44. Memorandum by Col A. P. Clark, acting deputy chief of staff for plans, to deputy chief of staff for operations, Tactical Air Command, subject: Report of Conference, 7 September 1949.

45. Ibid.; Daily diary 188, Tactical Air Command, 30 September 1949, 7; Maj Gen Robert M. Lee, commanding general, Tactical Air Command, "Tactical Air Support of Ground Forces," address to 65th Annual Convention of New York National Guard, Syracuse, New York, 19 September 1949.

46. House, *The National Defense Program—Unification and Strategy*, 549.

47. Lt Col R. H. Thom, air adjutant general, Tactical Air Command, to commanding general, Tactical Air Force, letter, subject: Responsibilities of the Tactical Air Force, 11 April 1950.

48. Office of Chief of Army Field Forces and Tactical Air Command, *Joint Training Directive for Air-Ground Operations*, 1 September 1950 (Washington, D.C.: Government Printing Office, 1950), ii–iii.

49. Lt Gen Idwal H. Edwards, deputy chief of staff for operations, US Air Force, to Lt Gen Ennis C. Whitehead, commanding general, Continental Air Command, letter, 2 November 1950.

50. Maj Gen Willard R. Wolfinbarger, commanding general, Ninth Air Force, to Maj Gen Glenn O. Barcus, commanding general, Tactical Air Command, letter, 23 September 1950.

51. Maj Gen Willard R. Wolfinbarger, commanding general, Ninth Air Force, to commanding general, Tactical Air Command, letter, subject: Reassignment of Personnel Currently Serving in Directorate of Doctrine and Employment, 25 August 1950; Lt Col Erlath W. Zuehl, air adjutant general, Tactical Air Command, to commander, Tactical Air Command, Airborne Liaison Office, letter, subject: Mission of TAC Airborne Liaison Office, 14 November 1950; Brig Gen William S. Lawton, chief of staff, Office of Chief of Army Field Forces, to commanding general, Tactical Air Command, letter, subject: Liaison Officers for Army Air Support Center, 13 December 1950; 1st ind., Maj Gen Willard R. Wolfinbarger, commander, Tactical Air Command, to commander, Army Air Forces, 29 December 1950.

52. Joint Action Armed Forces, proposed chap. 4, sec. 3, Joint Principles and Doctrine for Airborne Operations, final draft, 1 June 1949.

53. Gen Nathan F. Twining to chairman, Joint Troop Carrier Board, letter, subject: Joint Troop Carrier Board, 6 August 1951.

54. Evaluation Staff, Air War College, review of AFM 1-1, *Joint Action Armed Forces*, 30 March 1953.

55. Gen Nathan F. Twining to chairman, Joint Troop Carrier Board, letter, 6 August 1951.

56. Maj Gen Robert W. Burns, assistant deputy chief of staff for operations, US Air Force, to senior Air Force officer, Joint Amphibious Board, letter, subject: Instruction for Senior Air Force Officer, Joint Amphibious Board, 7 November 1951; Twining to chairman, Joint Troop Carrier Board, letter, 6 August 1951; OP Nav Instruction 3340.3, subject: Joint Amphibious Board, 6 August 1951.

57. Maj Gen John DeF. Barker, commanding general, Air University, to Lt Gen Thomas D. White, deputy chief of staff for operations, US Air Force, letter, 27 March 1953.

58. Ibid.

59. Maj Gen Carl A. Brandt to commanding general, Air University, letter, subject: Proposed Air Force Manual "Commander's Guide," August 1950; 1st ind., Maj F. E. Lankston to chief of staff, US Air Force, 11 August 1950; 2d ind., Maj Gen Carl A. Brandt to commanding general, Air University, 7 September 1950.

60. Memorandum by Maj Gen John DeF. Barker to deputy commandant, Air War College, 24 July 1950; memorandum by Col George E. Henry, deputy commandant, Air War College, to Maj Gen John DeF. Barker, 26 July 1950; memorandum by Col W. W. Smith to deputy commandant, Air War College, subject: Integration of Evaluation Division, Air University, in Air War College, 19 September 1950; CWO G. A. Beckam, assistant adjutant general, Air University, to commandant, Air War College, letter, subject: Reassignment of Evaluation Division Functions, 6 October 1950.

61. History, Air University, July–December 1950, 1:107–15.

62. Maj Gen John DeF. Barker to Lt Gen Idwal H. Edwards, letter, w/incl.: Draft memorandum to commandants, Air University schools, and to Air Force instructors at non-Air Force schools, 21 December 1950; Col Dale O. Smith and Maj Gen John DeF. Barker, "Air Power Indivisible," *Air University Quarterly Review* 4, no. 2 (Fall 1950): 5–18.

IDEAS, CONCEPTS, DOCTRINE

63. Edwards to Barker, letter, 31 January 1951; memorandum by Lt Gen George C. Kenney to commandants, Air University schools, and to Air Force instructors at non-Air Force schools, subject: Air University Doctrine on the Employment of Air Force Combat Units, 3 February 1951; Barker to Edwards, letter, 8 February 1951.

64. Brig Gen Robert C. Candee, deputy commandant, Armed Forces Staff College, to Lt Gen George C. Kenney, letter, 16 February 1951.

65. Office of Assistance for Evaluation, deputy chief of staff for development, US Air Force, staff study, subject: What Can and Should the USAF Do to Increase the Effectiveness of Air-Ground Operations?, ca. December 1950.

66. Maj Gen John DeF. Barker to commander, 3894th School Squadron (non-Air Force schools), letter, subject: Air University Policy on "Joint Training Directive for Air-Ground Operations," 19 January 1951, published by Army Field Forces.

67. Maj Gen Glenn O. Barcus, deputy commanding general, Tactical Air Command, to commanding general, Air University, letter, subject: Joint Training Directive for Air-Ground Operations, 2 February 1951.

68. Col M. J. Weitzel, assistant executive director of operations, Deputy Chief of Staff for Operations, US Air Force, to commanding general, Air University, letter, subject: Joint Training Directive for Air-Ground Operations, 9 March 1951.

69. Barker to Edwards, letter, 11 January 1951.

70. Col M. J. Weitzel to commanding general, Air University, letter, 9 March 1951; 1st ind., Maj Gen John DeF. Barker to chief of staff, US Air Force, 16 April 1951; memorandum by Maj Gen John DeF. Barker to Thomas K. Finletter, 1 June 1951.

71. Col M. J. Weitzel to commanding general, Air University, letter, 9 March 1951; 1st ind., Barker to chief of staff, US Air Force, 16 April 1951.

72. History, Tactical Air Command, 1 December 1950–30 June 1951, vol. 5, pt. 2:1–2.

73. Memorandum by Maj Gen John DeF. Barker to Thomas K. Finletter, 1 June 1951; Finletter to Barker, letter, 21 June 1951.

74. History, Tactical Air Command, 1 November 1950–30 June 1951, 4:9–10; and July–December 1951, 4:2–5; Lt Col A. F. Taute, Air Liaison Office, Artillery School, to commander, 3894th School Squadron, letter, 3 December 1951.

75. Barker to Edwards, letter, 8 February 1951; memorandum by Barker to Henry, 23 April 1951; History, Air University, January–June 1951, 1:137.

76. Memorandum by Col James W. Chapman, Jr., assistant chief of staff for plans and operations, Air University, to Maj Gen John DeF. Barker, subject: Recommendations, 22 June 1951.

77. Evaluation Staff, Air War College, Project Folder AWC-5103, Air University Doctrine, 10 April–31 August 1951; Maj Gen John DeF. Barker to deputy chief of staff for plans and operations, US Air Force, letter, subject: Proposed USAF Manual on Basic AF Doctrine, 14 July 1951.

78. Memorandum by Maj Gen John DeF. Barker to Maj Gen J. A. Samford, commandant, Air Command and Staff School, 1 August 1951; History, Air University, July–December 1951, 1:28–33.

79. Gen Nathan F. Twining to Lt Gen Idwal H. Edwards, commanding general, Air University, letter, 18 September 1951.

80. Ibid.

81. Air War College, "Review of Significant Military Concepts and Actions, World War II Period," study 4, 9 January 1948.

82. *Dictionary of United States Military Terms* (Washington, D.C.: Joint Chiefs of Staff, June 1948).

83. Air War College, "Command Employment of Air Forces, World War II and Korea," study 5, September–October 1951.

84. Edwards to Twining, letter, w/incl.: Study, 26 September 1951.

85. Twining to Edwards, letter, 18 October 1951.

86. History, Air University, July–December 1951, 1:1–5, 28–33; Maj Gen William F. McKee, assistant vice chief of staff, US Air Force, to commanding general, Air University, letter, subject:

Additional Responsibilities of the Air University, 18 October 1951; "Plans for Establishing a Post-Graduate Study Group," Air War College study, 28 February 1952.

87. White to Edwards, letter, 12 October 1951.

88. Maj Gen John DeF. Barker to chief of staff, US Air Force, letter, 14 July 1951; 1st ind., Maj Gen Robert W. Burns, acting deputy chief of staff for operations, US Air Force, to commanding general, Air University, 25 October 1951; 3d ind., Maj Gen Robert W. Burns to commanding general, Air University, 11 December 1951.

89. Air University Manual-1, *United States Air Force Basic Doctrine*, October 1951; Maj Gen John DeF. Barker to chief of staff, US Air Force, letter, 14 July 1951; 2d ind., Maj Gen John DeF. Barker to deputy chief of staff for operations, US Air Force, 20 November 1951; Maj Gen John DeF. Barker to Maj Gen J. A. Samford, director of intelligence, US Air Force, letter, 1 December 1951.

90. Samford to Barker, letter, 26 November 1951.

91. Lt Gen Howard A. Craig, The Inspector General, US Air Force, to Maj Gen John DeF. Barker, letter, 12 December 1951.

92. Capt Clifford Dixon, school secretary, USAF Air-Ground Operations School, letter, subject: USAFAGOS, Comment on Air University Brochure "USAF Basic Doctrine," 6 December 1951.

93. History, Directorate of Plans, Deputy Chief of Staff for Operations, US Air Force, January–June 1952, 5; Evaluation Staff, Air War College, Project Folder AWC-5135, 26 October 1951–24 December 1952; Lt Gen Idwal H. Edwards to chief of staff, US Air Force, Attn.: DCS/Operations, letter, subject: Manual, Basic Air Power Doctrine, 25 June 1952.

94. Air University Special Studies Progress Report, 1 April 1952, 1–11; Col Robert A. Erdin, senior Air Force representative, Joint Amphibious Board, to director of operations, Deputy Chief of Staff for Operations, US Air Force, letter, subject: Basic Air Guidance, Joint Amphibious Operations, 8 April 1952.

95. Memorandum by Col William W. Momyer to Maj Gen John DeF. Barker, subject: Progress of the Manual Program, 17 September 1952.

96. Ibid.

97. Maj Gen Roscoe C. Wilson, "Annual Report of the Commandant, Air War College," 1 July 1952; memorandum by Col R. C. Orth, assistant chief of staff for plans and operations, Air University, to deputy commanding general, Air University, subject: Doctrinal Responsibilities of the Air University, 26 November 1952; History, Air University, January–June 1953; 1:140–42.

98. Lt Gen John K. Cannon to Lt Gen Idwal H. Edwards, letter, 29 December 1952.

99. Memorandum by Brig Gen Reuben C. Hood, commandant, Air Command and Staff School, to Maj Gen John DeF. Barker, subject: "Tactical Air Operations" As Opposed to "Tactical Operations," 12 February 1953; memorandum by Maj Gen John DeF. Barker to commandants, AU schools, and to Air Force instructors in non-Air Force schools, 5 March 1952; memorandum by Col William H. Momyer to Maj Gen John DeF. Barker, subject: Clarification of Terms "Tactical Aviation" from "Theater Aviation," 26 June 1952.

100. Maj Gen John DeF. Barker to chief of staff, US Air Force, letter, subject: Clarification of Terms "Tactical Aviation" and "Theater Aviation," 24 June 1952.

101. Maj Gen John DeF. Barker to Lt Gen Laurence S. Kuter, deputy chief of staff for personnel, US Air Force, letter, 17 February 1953.

102. Air University, Draft of Category I, Air Employment Instructions, Air Power and the US Air Force, 1 July 1948, 35.

103. Memorandum by Maj Gen John DeF. Barker to commandants, AU schools, and to Air Force instructors in non-Air Force schools, 5 March 1952; memorandum by Col Robert A. Erdin to senior Air Force representative, Joint Amphibious Board, subject: Staff Visit Report, 14 March 1952.

104. Maj Gen John DeF. Barker to Lt Gen John K. Cannon, letter, 30 December 1952; Brig Gen Reuben C. Hood to commanding general, Air University, letter, subject: Comments on Letter, Subject: "Planning the Operations of a Numbered Tactical Air Force," 13 January 1953.

105. Maj Gen John DeF. Barker to Lt Gen Thomas D. White, letter, 27 March 1953; Brig Gen Hunter Harris, Jr., commander, War Plans Division, US Air Force, to Maj Gen John DeF. Barker,

IDEAS, CONCEPTS, DOCTRINE

letter, 2 February 1953; Col Harvey T. Alness to Maj Gen John DeF. Barker, letter, 11 February 1953; Alness to Barker, letter, 14 March 1953; AFM 1-2, *United States Air Force Basic Doctrine*, March 1953, i.

106. Memorandum by Maj Gen John DeF. Barker to Maj Gen Roscoe C. Wilson and Brig Gen Reuben C. Hood, 23 March 1953; Barker to White, letter, 27 March 1953.

107. White to Barker, letter, 22 April 1953.

108. Memorandum by Col Charles M. McCorkle, academic director, Air War College, to deputy commanding general, Air University, subject: Basic Doctrinal Manuals, 25 May 1953; ind. by Lt Gen Laurence S. Kuter, commanding general, Air University, 1 June 1953.

109. History, Air University, January–June 1953, 1:140–42; memorandum by Lt Col Orville V. Rose to senior Air Force representative, Joint Amphibious Board, subject: Staff Visit Report to Air War College, 3 July 1953; USAF History, Joint Amphibious Board, January–June 1953, 36–37; Brig Gen Alonzo M. Drake, chief of staff, Tactical Air Command, to commanding general, Air University, letter, subject: Air University Tentative Manual—"Theater Air Operations," 27 March 1953; 2d ind., Col Nicholas T. Perkins, deputy commandant for evaluation, Air War College, to commander, Air University, 17 July 1953.

110. Col Nicholas T. Perkins to commander, Air University, letter, subject: Special Studies Report, 5 February 1954; Col Jerry D. Page, assistant deputy for evaluation, Air War College, to commander, Air University, letter, subject: Special Studies Report, 28 February 1954; AFM 1-8, *Strategic Air Operations*, 1954, 2.

111. Col Royal H. Roussel, "The Air Force Doctrinal Manuals," *Air University Quarterly Review* 7, no. 1 (Spring 1954): 129; Col Jerry D. Page to commander, Air University, letter, 28 February 1954; Air University to chief of staff, US Air Force, Attn.: Director, Operations, letter, subject: Air Force Manual, 7 April 1953; Col Ladson G. Eskridge, chief of staff, Air University, to deputy chief of staff for operations, US Air Force, letter, 29 April 1954; History, Air University, January–June 1954, 1:88–89.

112. Roussel, "The Air Force Doctrinal Manuals," 126, 128–29.

113. Col Elmer C. Blaha, senior Air Force representative, Joint Amphibious Board, Report of Staff Visit to Headquarters USAF, 27 September 1954; Brig Gen Jacob E. Smart, deputy chief of staff for operations, Far East Air Forces, to Brig Gen G. C. Mudgett, assistant chief of staff G-3, Far East Command, letter, 25 July 1952; History, Air War College, July 1957–June 1958, 18–19.

114. Lt Gen Laurence S. Kuter, "No Room for Error," *Air Force Magazine*, November 1954, 29–30, 33.

115. Lt Gen Laurence S. Kuter, welcoming address at the opening of the Air War College class of 1954–55, 16 August 1954.

116. Lt Gen Laurence S. Kuter to chief of staff, US Air Force, letter, 27 March 1954.

117. Ibid.

118. History, Air University, July–December 1952, 1:3–5; January–June 1953, 1:67–68; July–December 1953, 1:111–14; and January–June 1954, 1:89–90.

119. Col Raymond S. Sleeper, "Air Power, the Cold War, and Peace," *Air University Quarterly Review* 5, no. 1 (Winter 1951–1952): 3–18.

120. Air War College, "A History of Project Control, 1953–54."

121. Lt Gen Laurence S. Kuter to chief of staff, US Air Force, letter, 27 March 1954; Gen Thomas D. White, vice chief of staff, US Air Force, to Lt Gen Laurence S. Kuter, letter, 29 April 1954; Maj Gen N. B. Harbold, director of personnel, procurement, and training, US Air Force, to Lt Gen Laurence S. Kuter, letter, 19 May 1954; Kuter to Harbold, letter, 2 June 1954; History, Air University, July–December 1954, 1:8–11.

122. History, Tactical Air Command, January–June 1957, 357; Maj Gen Roscoe C. Wilson, Annual Report of the Commandant, Air War College, 1 July 1952; History, Air University, January–June 1954, 1:91.

123. Memorandum by Col William W. Momyer to commandant, Air War College, subject: Revision of AFM 1-2, *United States Air Force Basic Doctrine*, 15 June 1953; Evaluation Staff, Air War College, Special Studies Report; AFM 1-2, 1 January 1954; and 1 April 1954.

124. History, Air War College, July–December 1954, tab F; Col Jerry D. Page and Col Royal H. Roussel, "Little Book with a Big Wallop," *Air Force Magazine*, January 1956, 69, 71; Project Status Report, AU-6-53-ESAWC, 21 March 1955.

125. Project Status Report, AU-6-53-ESAWC, 31 March 1955; Lt Gen Laurence S. Kuter to Gen Thomas D. White, letter, 4 January 1955.

126. White to Kuter, letter, 1 February 1955.

127. Memorandum by Brig Gen Sidney F. Giffin, acting commandant, Air War College, to Lt Gen Laurence S. Kuter, subject: Understanding of AFM 1-2, 16 February 1955; Page and Roussel, "Little Book With a Big Wallop," 68.

128. AFM 1-2, 1 April 1954, 13–14; AFM 1-2, 1 April 1955, 7.

129. Page and Roussel, "Little Book with a Big Wallop," 69–71.

130. "What the Air Force Believes In," *Air Force Magazine*, January 1956, 72.

131. White to Kuter, letter, 1 February 1955.

132. Col Jack N. Donohew, "Programming Processes in the Air Force," lecture, Air War College, Maxwell AFB, Ala., 5 December 1956.

133. Gen Thomas D. White, "USAF Doctrine in the Military Implementation of National Policy," address to USAF Scientific Advisory Board, Chandler, Ariz., 4 December 1957.

134. Memorandum by Maj Gen John DeF. Barker to Lt Gen Laurence S. Kuter, subject: Doctrinal Responsibilities of the Air University, 24 April 1953.

135. "Joint Air Defense Board," *Army-Navy Journal*, 4 August 1951, 1391; "Joint Landing Board," *Army-Navy Journal*, 6 October 1951, 163; "Wolfinbarger Named to Air Support Unit," *Aviation Week*, 10 September 1951, 15; History, Joint Air Transportation Board, 2 July 1951–3 March 1955, 1–4; USAF History, Joint Amphibious Board, 6 October–31 December 1951, 1–7.

136. History, Joint Air Transportation Board, 12–21.

137. Maj Gen William E. Bergin, the Adjutant General, Department of the Army, to senior Army members, Joint Boards, letter, subject: Administrative Guidance, 30 December 1952; Army Regulation 15–80, *Boards, Commissions and Committees—Joint Boards*, 15 May 1952.

138. Maj Gen H. B. Thatcher, acting director of plans, US Air Force, to director, Joint Air Transportation Board, letter, subject: Inter-Service Coordination of Air Force Joint Board Projects, 27 March 1953.

139. Burns to Senior Air Force Officer, Joint Amphibious Board, letters, subject: Instructions for Senior Air Force Officer, Joint Amphibious Board, 7 November 1951 and 21 March 1952.

140. Joint Air Defense Board, United States Air Defense Doctrine, 14 April 1954.

141. Maj Gen Grandison Gardner, director, Joint Air Defense Board, to Gen Nathan F. Twining, letter, 20 April 1954.

142. Maj Gen Grandison Gardner to Gen Curtis E. LeMay, commander, Strategic Air Command, letter, 9 February 1954.

143. C. L. Grant, *The Development of Continental Air Defense to 1 September 1954*, USAF historical study 126 (Maxwell AFB, Ala.: Research Studies Institute, 1957), 80; USAF Roster of Key Personnel, December 1954, 26.

144. "Wolfinbarger Named to Air Support Unit," 15.

145. Tactical Air Command to chief of staff, US Air Force, letter, subject: Joint Tactical Air Support Board, ca. August 1954.

146. History, Joint Air Transportation Board, 11, 22; USAF Roster of Key Personnel, 1 February 1954, 22, and 1 September 1954, 25; Maj Gen Robert M. Lee, director of plans, US Air Force, to director, Joint Air Transportation Board, letter, subject: Reduction of Personnel Assigned to the Joint Air Transportation Board, 18 May 1953.

147. History, Joint Air Transportation Board, 22–23, 28–41.

IDEAS, CONCEPTS, DOCTRINE

148. Tactical Air Command to director of plans, US Air Force, letter, subject: JTASB Project, "Tactical Air Forces in Support of Ground Forces," ca. 21 December 1953; Tactical Air Command to director, Joint Tactical Air Support Board, letter, subject: JTASB project no. 2-53, 22 June 1954; Tactical Air Command to chief of staff, US Air Force, letter, subject: Joint Tactical Air Support Board, ca. August 1954.

149. "More Joint Landing Board," *Army-Navy Journal*, 5 July 1952, 1381.

150. USAF History, Joint Amphibious Board, 6 October–31 December 1951, 1 January–30 June 1952, 1 July–31 December 1953, 1 January–30 June 1954, and 1 July 1954–15 February 1955; USAF Views Joint Amphibious Board, Formal Report 1-52, Doctrines and Procedures Governing Joint Amphibious Operations, 15 January 1954; Col Elmer C. Blaha, senior Air Force representative, Joint Amphibious Board, "USAF Current View of Amphibious Operations and Associated Air Operations," lecture, Air Force instructors at non-Air Force schools, Maxwell AFB, Ala., 1 February 1955.

151. Lt Gen Laurence S. Kuter to deputy chief of staff for personnel, US Air Force, letter, ca. 30 April 1953.

152. Memorandum by Lt Gen Earle E. Partridge, deputy chief of staff for operations, US Air Force, to chairman, Committee for Joint Plans and Procedures, Joint Chiefs of Staff, subject: Future Status of Joint Boards Established Pursuant to Chapter 2, Joint Action Armed Forces, 1 February 1954.

153. Col Robert A. Erdin, senior Air Force representative, Joint Amphibious Board, to chief, Policy Division, Directorate of Plans, US Air Force, letter, subject: Future Status of Joint Boards Established Pursuant to Chapter 2, Joint Action Armed Forces, 16 March 1954.

154. History, Joint Air Transportation Board, 53–54.

155. Tactical Air Command to chief of staff, US Air Force, letter, subject: Joint Tactical Air Support Board, ca. August 1954.

156. USAF History, Joint Amphibious Board, 1 July 1954–15 February 1955, 37–38; Maj Gen Richard C. Lindsay, director of plans, US Air Force, to commander, Tactical Air Command, letter, subject: Dissolution of Joint Boards and Reassignment of Board Responsibilities, 4 January 1955.

157. Maj Gen Richard C. Lindsay to commander, Tactical Air Command, letter, 4 January 1955.

158. "Command and Employment of Air Forces, World War II and Korea," Air War College study 5, 43.

159. Col George C. Reinhardt, "Air Power Needs Its Mahan," *US Naval Institute Proceedings*, vol. 78, April 1952, 367.

160. AFM 1-2, 1 April 1955, 4, 10.

161. Quoted in Col Wendell E. Carter, "Pursestrings and Pressures," *Air University Quarterly Review* 9, no. 1 (Winter 1956–1957): 47–48.

162. Col Richard C. Weller, "The Principles of War Will Get You If You Don't Watch Out," *Air University Quarterly Review* 12, no. 1 (Spring 1954): 65.

163. Maj Gen Hunter Harris, Jr., deputy director of plans, US Air Force, to commander, Tactical Air Command, letter, subject: Divergent Service Views Concerning Doctrine Governing Joint Amphibious Operations, 5 February 1954; 1st ind., Lt Col Melvin H. Irvin, assistant adjutant, Tactical Air Command, to deputy director of plans, US Air Force, n.d.

164. Comdr T. R. Weschler, "Concepts of Warfare," lecture, Air War College, Maxwell AFB, Ala., 3 June 1953.

165. Lt Gen John E. Dahlquist, "Army Requirements for Effective and Reliable Air Support," address to USAF Scientific Advisory Board, 22 March 1954.

166. Department of the Army Training Circular 110-5, *Joint Training Directive for Air-Ground Operations*, 31 January 1955.

Lt Gen Frank F. Everest, assistant deputy chief of staff, Operations, 1947–51.

Lt Gen Idwal Edwards, deputy chief of staff, Operations, 1947–51; commander, Air University, 1951–53.

Maj Gen John DeForest Barker, acting vice commander, Air University, 1950–51.

Lt Gen Roscoe C. Wilson, commandant, Air War College, 1951–54.

Brig Gen Lloyd P. Hopwood, commandant, Air Command and Staff College, 1953–58.

Maj Gen Grandison Gardner, chairman, Joint Air Defense Board, 1951–54.

CHAPTER 8

STRATEGIC IMPLICATIONS OF THE NEW LOOK 1953–57

In the winter of 1950–51 the civil and military leadership in Washington seriously feared that the war in Korea was a Soviet ruse, designed to commit American forces to what Gen Omar N. Bradley called "the wrong war in the wrong place" while the Russians prepared to attack in Europe. The Joint Chiefs of Staff (JCS) believed that general war with Russia and Europe might be imminent. The Communist invasion of the Republic of Korea showed that the Soviets were willing to employ war as an instrument of aggression; and the Joint Chiefs of Staff looked on mid-1954 as a time of maximum danger. By this time the Soviets would possess a stockpile of atomic weapons sufficient to mount a devastating attack on United States military installations, industry, and population centers. The Soviets had produced enormous quantities of military equipment in 1946–47, and, if it were to be used, this equipment would logically be used in 1954–55 before it became obsolete. The rebuilding of Russian industry and the relocation of much of it beyond the Urals would be largely complete by 1954–55. After 1954, moreover, the military strength of the United States and its allies would get closer and closer to that of the Soviets.[1]

Statements of Defense Policy:
The New Look and Massive Retaliation

At the highest levels, the image of war was general war. The nation's military leaders agreed that the Korean conflict—which had to be fought as a limited war—was abnormal. General Bradley declared in October 1950: "We will refuse absolutely to allow local wars to divert us from our central task. They must not be allowed to consume so much of our manpower as to destroy our strength and imperil our victory in world war." Speaking of Korea early in 1951, Gen J. Lawton Collins warned: "To prevent an invasion of western Europe, the area most coveted by the Communists, we would have to fight an altogether different war than we have been fighting."[2] Accepting the likelihood of an impending general war in December 1950, the National Security Council (NSC) recommended an expanded military production program that was designed to create a production base capable of rapid expansion to full war mobilization. Looking toward 1 July 1954 as a time of maximum danger, the Joint Chiefs of Staff recommended in October 1951 that Army forces should be stabilized at 20 divisions and Navy forces at 409 major combat ships, including 12 modern aircraft carriers, plus three Marine Corps

419

divisions with their supporting air wings while the Air Force should be expanded to 143 wings (126 combat and 17 troop carrier). President Truman approved these force goals in December 1951, but his instruction that military budgets should be held below $60 billion a year stretched the earliest date of readiness for the 143-wing Air Force out to 30 June 1955. At a conference in Lisbon in February 1952, the North Atlantic Treaty Organization nations established a goal of 96 divisions by 1954, 40 of these divisions to be in a permanent state of readiness and 56 to be capable of becoming operational within 30 days.

The American strategy was not completely agreeable to Great Britain. Prime Minister Winston Churchill had returned to power in 1951 at a time of national economic crisis. To ease the financial strain on his government he had instructed his chiefs of staff to reappraise Britain's defense policy. After intense study, the British chiefs of staff prepared a paper demonstrating that the advent of nuclear weapons justified a primary reliance on atomic air power and substantial reductions in surface forces. During a visit to Washington in July 1952, Air Chief Marshal Sir John Slessor argued for the adoption of the British strategy. He urged that the Lisbon force goals placed too great a strain on fragile European economies and recommended a strategy of nuclear deterrence that would be based upon American and British nuclear air capabilities.[3]

During his successful 1952 campaign for the American presidency, Gen Dwight D. Eisenhower promised economy in government, an honorable end to the Korean war, and, if necessary, a personal trip to the war zone in order to learn how best to serve the interests of the American people. When he visited Korea early in December 1952 in the company of Adm Arthur W. Radford, then commander in chief, Pacific, Eisenhower was said to have been dissatisfied with "the dissipation of American resources in a remote, indecisive struggle." While returning homeward aboard the cruiser *Helena*, Eisenhower held talks with several of the men who would serve in his cabinet, including John Foster Dulles and Charles E. Wilson, who would become the secretaries of state and defense respectively.[4]

In his book *War or Peace*, published in 1950, and in later speeches and articles, Dulles had expressed his conviction that strong military forces could prevent war and that the wars of the past had begun because aggressors had miscalculated their opposition. "Many believe," Dulles had written, "that if the Kaiser had known in advance that his attack on France by way of Belgium would have brought England, and then the United States, into the fray he would never have made that attack. . . . Many also believe that if Hitler had known that his war would involve the United States he would not have started it."[5] Dulles also believed that "the original Korean attack would not have occurred if it had not been assumed either that we would not react at all, or if we did react only at the place and by the means that the aggressors chose."[6] Aboard the *Helena* and in additional conferences in Honolulu, Dulles held the position that the United States could not mount an adequate static defense everywhere around the Communist perimeter. Rather than spread its defenses thin, the United States should clearly manifest its intent to resist aggression and should concentrate its attention on deterring attack by maintaining a strong retaliatory power capable of striking swiftly at sources of aggression. Admiral Radford agreed that American military power was spread-eagled. "The sooner we could gather some of these forces back into the palm of our hand, and turn them into truly ready forces for deployment anywhere," Radford later observed, "the better our strategic position would be."[7] While Radford and Wilson felt that Asia would continue to be a pivotal area in the cold war, Eisenhower suggested that when Western Europe was strong enough to defend itself the Asian problem would become manageable.[8]

"It is difficult to be sure just what has prevented aggression against the free world," Secretary Wilson stated shortly after he took office. "I think there is a deep realization in Moscow that any major aggression against the free world will start a conflict in which all forces of the free world will be marshaled in a fight to crush such aggression, and that the forces of the free world include not merely our long-range bombers, or even all airplanes capable of carrying atomic bombs, but rather all of the military strength of the United States, which includes its industrial productive capacity and also the military strength and industrial capacity of all of our allies."[9] As submitted to Congress in January 1953, the Truman administration military budget for fiscal year 1954 recommended an appropriation of $41.3 billion, the amount of money that would permit the Army and Navy to hold at their established force levels and the Air Force to build toward the 143-wing objective. If this appropriation were voted, however, the Bureau of the Budget envisioned a national deficit of $9.9 billion in fiscal year 1954, and, if the military force levels recommended by the Joint Chiefs were to be attained, there would be another $15 billion deficit in fiscal year 1955 and continuing deficits until fiscal year 1958. Since the Eisenhower administration had promised economy and a balanced federal budget, Wilson worked closely with the National Security Council in an effort to reduce military expenditures. As a preliminary measure in February 1953, he ordered a temporary halt to all new military construction and to that which had just gotten started pending verification of need for each project. Further study showed that the Army and Navy had about reached their programmed strength levels, but the Air Force's need for new money reflected amounts necessary to move upward to the 143-wing level. Even without this new authority, the Air Force was expected to carry $28.5 billion in unexpended funds over into fiscal year 1954. Wilson regarded some carry-over funds as being inevitable in any build-up program, but production should have begun to catch up with authorizations. He was additionally critical of the emphasis given to expansion of the mobilization base of the defense industry and pointed out that much of this industrial base would have to be liquidated after the Air Force reached its programmed strength, provided no war had occurred. "If I had been doing it the last 3 years," Wilson observed, "I would have built more production and less mobilization base to begin with." One immediate way in which the government could reduce new money requirements would be to abandon preparations for a maximum year of danger. In April 1953 Eisenhower approved a new policy that the United States should not attempt to meet a major aggression by any particular date but should "get...ready and stay ready." Eisenhower described the new policy as being that of "a floating D-day."[10]

Although the incumbent Joint Chiefs of Staff, headed by General Bradley, were not asked for advice on proposed force changes, Gen Hoyt S. Vandenberg formally protested Air Force reductions to the new Secretary of the Air Force Harold E. Talbott. On 7 and 8 May the Joint Chiefs warned Wilson that "any government decision to reduce force goals below those in approved programs . . . would increase the calculated risk, and that the years 1954–55 represented the beginning of a potentially dangerous period during which the USSR would have a substantial stockpile of atomic weapons, and the improved ability to deliver such weapons."[11] Despite this admonition, the Department of Defense submitted a revised budget for fiscal year 1954 that was reduced by about $7.5 billion, of which $5.3 billion represented a cut in Air Force funds. Pending a new look at the entire defense picture, which Wilson promised would be made in the autumn of 1953, the goal of an interim force level for the Air Force was set at 120 wings, with 110 to 114 of these wings to be activated and substantially well equipped by 30 June 1954. Most of the units to be deferred were day-fighter and fighter-bomber wings; the new aircraft on order for them would be used to modernize Air Reserve and Air National Guard forces.[12] In spirited hearings before House and Senate appropriations subcommittees, Generals Bradley and Vandenberg strongly defended the programmed requirement for 143 wings, to be achieved as soon as possible, desirably by 1954. "No sound military reason," Vandenberg stated, "has been advanced to explain why the Air Force build-up to the agreed force level is again to be delayed. Once again the growth of American air power is threatened with start-and-stop planning, and at a time when we face an enemy who has more modern jet fighters than we have and enough long-range bombers to attack this country in a sudden all-out atomic effort. Rather than reduce our efforts to attain air superiority over the Communists, we should now increase those efforts."[13]

The Wilson budget prevailed in Congress in spite of the eloquent pleas of General Vandenberg. At a conference with legislative leaders on 12 and 19 May, President Eisenhower lent his support to the Wilson program, arguing that the Air Force had been operating on excessive lead time, had too many "paper" wings, and needed to build up its strength without reference to target dates. As finally enacted in August 1953, the appropriation act for fiscal year 1954 totaled $34.6 billion, representing a final cut of $6.7 billion from the amount originally requested by the Truman administration. Of this total, $12.9 billion was allocated to the Army, $9.4 billion to the Navy, and $11.4 billion to the Air Force. Counting both new and carry-over funds, Wilson pointed out that $31.5 billion of Navy and Air Force funds were committed to the procurement of aircraft and related equipment. Such funding, he thought, would be sufficient to continue the buildup of America's defenses pending the determination of future force levels by the National Security Council and a new Joint Chiefs of Staff.[14] Former Secretary Thomas K. Finletter, nevertheless, observed that the Air Force had taken virtually all of the Department of Defense cuts and that the "arbitrary" cutback in dollars had been such as "to restore the roughly equal division of the Defense dollar among the three Services." He wrote, "This way of deciding on the forces to defend our country, in this most dangerous time of our history cannot possibly be justified or excused."[15]

Department of Defense Reorganization

As early as 1950, John Foster Dulles had suggested that the National Security Council ought to be made a top policymaking body that would unify foreign, military, and domestic policy. In his State of the Union message to Congress on 2 February 1953, President Eisenhower pledged to provide the National Security Council with "the vitality to perform effectively its statutory role."[16] In his presidential campaign, Eisenhower had spoken of a need for restudying the operations and functions of the Department of Defense. Before leaving office, Secretary of Defense Robert A. Lovett prepared a memorandum that outlined several defects in defense organization that had become apparent during the Korean emergency. To maintain civilian control with the department, Lovett recommended that the secretary of defense should be recognized as the president's deputy commander in chief of the armed services and that the unified commanders should be made responsible to designated secretaries of the military departments rather than to individual chiefs of staff. He pointed out that the "two hat" status of the Joint Chiefs made it difficult for them to maintain broad nonservice points of view. He further showed that the statutory Munitions Board and the Research and Development Board had built-in rigidity, since representatives of the military departments sat on these boards as judges and claimants of their own requests.[17]

Seeking a thorough view of the administrative problem of the Department of Defense, Secretary Wilson appointed a Committee on Department of Defense Organization headed by Nelson A. Rockefeller on 19 February 1953. The committee heard witnesses and reported on 11 April. Eisenhower accepted most of the committee's recommendations and transmitted them to Congress on 30 April as Reorganization Plan No. 6. This plan reaffirmed the power of direction, authority, and control of the secretary of defense; channeled responsibility and authority over unified commands through secretaries of the military departments; abolished the Munitions Board, the Research and Development Board, and several other unwieldy staff agencies and replaced them with six new assistant secretaries of defense; and charged the chairman of the Joint Chiefs of Staff with authority to direct the Joint Staff. Air Force leaders had generally favored closer unification of the armed services, but former Secretary Finletter appeared in opposition to Reorganization Plan No. 6 when the House Committee on Government Operations held hearings on it. Finletter feared that the reorganization would create a single monolithic establishment that would dominate rather than coordinate the military services. At a time when the world was in the midst of a great air and atomic technological revolution, he was afraid that the monolithic department would emphasize balanced forces and equal divisions of the defense dollar by services instead of centering on atomic air power and making the other forces ancillary to it.[18]

Eisenhower also extended the authority of the National Security Council and provided it with new machinery. He included the secretary of the treasury and the director of the Bureau of the Budget as members of the National Security Council. On 23 March he established the NSC Planning Board to assemble, analyze, and organize data on problems presented to the council. He established the Operations Coordinating Board of the NSC on 2 September in order to make a single agency responsible for translating approved policies into operational programs and ensure that they were carried out.[19] Since Congress did not disapprove or amend Reorganization Plan No. 6, it became law on 30 June; Secretary Wilson wasted little time putting it into effect. The additional assistant secretaries replaced the boards and agencies that had been specified for oblivion. On 2 July, Wilson further directed the Joint Chiefs of Staff to designate officers to work with his representatives to revise the Key West agreement in accordance with the new reorganization. Completed in October 1953 but not announced until January 1954, this revision made the secretary of a military department, rather than a member of the Joint Chiefs of Staff, the executive agent for a unified command. The line of authority, thus, ran from the secretary of defense to a unified commander through a secretary of a military department, but the military chief of a service was authorized to act for his department in matters regarding strategic direction and conduct of combat operations in emergency and wartime situations.[20]

New Look Military Force Objectives

In July 1953 Eisenhower ordered the officers he had selected as new members of the Joint Chiefs of Staff — Admiral Radford, who would become chairman; Gen Matthew B. Ridgway, who would be Army chief of staff; and Adm Robert B. Carney, who would become chief of naval operations — to come to Washington where they would join Gen Nathan F. Twining, who had become Air Force chief of staff on 30 June. President Eisenhower charged them to "make a completely new, fresh survey of our military capabilities, in the light of our global commitments." On 24 July Wilson assembled these officers and other top civilian and military officials at Quantico, Virginia, for a three-day "outing." Here Wilson expressed confidence in the new atomic weapons, stated that the United States already had attained a strength that would make any attack on this nation "foolhardy in the extreme," and firmly announced that the military planners must get more military strength for dollars expended. In another presentation, Director of the Budget Joseph Dodge warned that the fiscal year 1955 national budget would have to show further substantial reductions above and beyond the revised budget for fiscal 1954.[21] Signed on 27 July as the Quantico conference was breaking up, the military armistice in Korea promised to reduce the operating costs of the armed services. However, 20 August 1953 the Soviet Union announced that it had successfully tested a hydrogen bomb.

As the first step in the New Look that the Joint Chiefs of Staff were directed to take at defense requirements, Admiral Radford asked the National Security Council on 13 October to provide guidance as to the nature of the war that the armed services would be expected to fight. Radford emphasized that preparations to fight every kind of war would be unnecessarily costly and that no mobilization planning would be realistic or useful unless it was founded on a proper strategic outlook. In response to Radford's question, the National Security Council issued fundamental guidance in the form of a paper designated as NSC-162. The council estimated that the danger from the growth of Soviet atomic weapons capability and air power had become absolute and stated that this threat had to be countered by American "atomic air power." It recommended that an air striking force capable of delivering atomic weapons should provide the nation's first line of defense and that the Joint Chiefs should be authorized to plan to use the new weapons when and where feasible. The NSC recommended increased spending of about $1 billion a year on air defense, and, in view of the added costs of air defense and of prevalent manpower shortages, it believed that the number of men in the military services should be reduced. President Eisenhower approved NSC-162 in its final version and summarized the new defense policy in his State of the Union message to Congress on 7 January 1954. At this time Eisenhower explained that the United States was "taking full account of our great and growing number of nuclear weapons and of the most effective means of using them against any aggressor." He went on to say that the United States would emphasize air power, mobile forces that could be held in strategic reserve and readily deployed to meet sudden aggression, continental air defense, a defense industrial base that could be swiftly converted from partial to all-out mobilization, and a professional corps of trained officers and enlisted personnel. Eisenhower envisioned a defense establishment that could meet "a twofold requirement – preparedness for the essential initial tasks in case a general war should be forced upon us, and maintenance of the capability to cope with lesser hostile actions – and aimed to satisfy this requirement with less drain on our manpower and financial resources."[22]

Given the guidance that the nation would emphasize an air strategy and given the information that the military budget and manpower ceilings would be reduced from those of fiscal year 1954, the Joint Chiefs of Staff established an ad hoc committee headed by Lt Gen Frank F. Everest, who was serving as director of the Joint Staff. This committee, which included representatives from all of the services, was to make recommendations on the force levels to be developed in the next two years.[23] Air Force planning was already well developed. General Twining had told a Senate committee in July that the Air Force was going to seek to attain its "ultimate goal of 143 wings," and he had directed the Air Staff to make a root and branch examination of Air Force requirements in the light of new weapons and new machines.[24] The Air Staff study showed that more powerful thermonuclear weapons would permit some reductions in the strategic air forces, though not substantial cuts since the number of thermonuclear weapons in the stockpile was still small. Substantial cuts could be made in medium troop carrier wings designed for service in theaters of operations, since many Army units were to be returned to a strategic reserve in the United States. Air defense wings would have to be increased. The Air Staff study recommended a program objective of 127 wings in fiscal year 1956, which would be expanded to 137 wings by the end of fiscal year 1957. The 137-wing goal would include 7 heavy bombardment, 28 medium bombardment, 4 heavy reconnaissance, 5 medium reconnaissance, 2 fighter reconnaissance, and 8 strategic fighter wings in the strategic air forces; 34 fighter-interceptor wings in the air defense forces; and 2 tactical bombardment, 4 light bombardment, 21 fighter-bomber, 6 day-fighter, 5 tactical reconnaissance, 4 heavy troop carrier, and 7 medium troop carrier wings in the tactical air forces. In comparison with the 143-wing objective, the 137-wing program represented a reduction of 2 medium bombardment and 1 medium reconnaissance wing in the strategic forces; 1 light bombardment, 1 fighter-bomber, and 6 medium troop carrier wings in the tactical air forces; and an increase of 5 fighter-interceptor wings in the air defense forces.[25]

Early in December 1953 the Everest committee made its report to the Joint Chiefs of Staff. The report contained four separate views as to the force requirements for the following two fiscal years. In view of the split recommendations, as well as their recognition that the probable availability of personnel and money would be the controlling factors in fixing force levels, the individual chiefs were now required not only to analyze their own service needs but to recommend what they thought the other services ought to have. They laid great stress on improving continental defenses, and they laid out in considerable detail a defense program to be accomplished over a period of years. They also made efforts to define a "level-off position in defense forces which could be attained and maintained for an indefinite period of time." The Joint Chiefs accepted the concept that "the United States will emphasize the development of those capabilities for which we are best suited, while our allies will assume greater responsibilities for developing other capabilities for which they are best suited." They recognized that military strategy would need to place greater reliance on a maximum exploitation of atomic weapons, and they accepted the proposition that there would be no time for buildup in a future war.[26]

Although the Joint Chiefs apparently had little difficulty outlining the strategic concepts springing from the NSC New Look directive, they had more difficulty recommending service force levels. At first the Joint Chiefs wished to cut off the Air Force program at 127 wings, to be attained at the end of fiscal year 1956. The Air Force, however, protested that the 127-wing program would have to be differently configured from a program that was conceived as a measured step to a balanced 137-wing program. In the end the Joint Chiefs recommended that the Air Force be authorized to attain 137 wings by the end of fiscal year 1957. They also accepted a revised Navy program whereby the Navy would meet personnel and financial reductions by reducing its auxiliary and amphibious warfare vessels. It would keep 14 attack aircraft carriers and 16 carrier air groups on active service, and in the fiscal year 1955 budget it would receive funds to begin the construction of a third *Forrestal*-class aircraft carrier and a third atomic-powered submarine. According to General Ridgway, the Joint Chiefs gave "scant consideration" to his recommendations for Army force levels; he later described the fiscal year 1955 budget as a "directed verdict" and said that the same would be true of the 1956 and 1957 budgets. The Army was reduced to a strength of 17 divisions, 18 regimental combat teams, and 122 antiaircraft battalions. These force levels, Ridgway said, "were not based on the freely reached conclusions of the Joint Chiefs of Staff" but instead "were squeezed between the framework of arbitrary manpower and fiscal limits"; for some reason, General Ridgway did not file a divergent view. Later on, Secretary Wilson, Admiral Radford, General Twining, and President Eisenhower each announced that the Joint Chiefs had unanimously agreed to the armed service force levels that were accepted by the Department of Defense and budgeted for fiscal year 1955.[27]

"The President of the United States, the Secretary of Defense, and the Joint Chiefs of Staff," Admiral Radford stated on 14 December 1953, "are of one mind: this nation will maintain a national air power superior to that of any other nation in the world." In this speech before the National Press Club and in another presentation to the congressional appropriations subcommittees in March 1954, Admiral Radford defined air power to include "the Air Force, naval aviation, Marine Corps aviation, Army aviation, and the tremendous aircraft industry and civil air transport systems of the United States."[28] Secretary Wilson described the New Look as "a natural evolution from the crash program that was adopted following the beginning of hostilities in Korea." Even though Wilson described the New Look as a logical application of economy in force to be attained by the exploitation of new nuclear weapons, he denied that the United States would place sole or exclusive reliance on the new weapons. General Twining described the New Look as a strategy that satisfied the twofold requirement of "preparedness for general war, should one occur; and maintenance of the capability to cope with lesser situations — with ... less of a drain on our manpower, material, and financial resources."[29]

To carry out the recommended national defense program for fiscal year 1955, Congress made available to the Department of Defense a new obligational authority, subdivided as follows — $7.6 billion for the Army, $9.7 billion for the Navy, and $11.6 billion for the Air Force.[30] Though the New Look professed to depend heavily upon an air power posture, former Secretary of the Air Force Finletter was quick to point out that the budget figures showed Air Force and Navy appropriations substantially the same as they had been the previous year, whereas the Army's funding had been substantially reduced. Finletter urged that fiscal considerations still had too much weight in determining the size of the military establishment, and he found that "the composition of the Armed Forces is still dominated by the Division-by-Services method, thus producing a compromised Defense Force in which the top priority functions are not provided for."[31] In commenting on this same matter, retired Lt Gen Ira C. Eaker agreed with the Eisenhower position that there was a very real limit to the amount of national resources that could be committed to weapons production; nevertheless, Eaker found that the national defense budget represented a serious imbalance of 75 percent defensive forces and 25 percent offensive. "No nation," he remarked, "has won or can win from a defensive posture."[32] Although welcoming the public announcements that the nation increasingly would emphasize air power, air-minded leaders were not entirely sure of the meaning of the New Look.

Massive Retaliation as a Strategy

In a speech before the Council of Foreign Relations in New York City on 12 January 1954, Secretary of State Dulles attempted to present an overall view of the national security policies of the Eisenhower administration. This remarkable address provided a rationale for the New Look and added a concept of "instant, massive retaliation" to the doctrine of deterrence. Dulles emphasized that often in the past the United States had reacted to Communist instigated emergencies. "Local defense," he said, "will always be important. But there is no local defense which alone will contain the mighty land power of the Communist world. Local defenses must be reinforced by the further deterrent of massive retaliatory power. A potential aggressor must know that he cannot always prescribe battle conditions that suit him." Dulles asserted: "The way to deter aggression is for the free community to be willing and able to respond vigorously at places and with means of its own choosing." He explained that the basic decision of President Eisenhower and the National Security Council was "to depend primarily upon a great capacity to retaliate, instantly, by means and at places of our own choosing." He pointed out that the Korean conflict had "been stopped on honorable terms . . . because the aggressor, already thrown back to and behind his place of beginning was faced with the possibility that the fighting might, to his own great peril, soon spread beyond the limits and methods which he had selected."[33]

The timing of Dulles's massive retaliation address coincided with a critical juncture in the foreign affairs of the United States. Dulles was scheduled to meet with Soviet and Western foreign ministers at Berlin on 22 January. Even though he reportedly felt that the chances of reaching any significant agreements with the Russians were slim, nothing could be lost from a candid emphasis upon America's military power. The Eisenhower administration also wished to prevent Indochina from falling into the hands of the Communists. But despite large amounts of American military equipment and technical assistance to French forces, the Communist Vietminh forces, with an active assistance from the Soviet Union and Communist China, appeared likely to defeat the French in Vietnam, where guerrilla war had been in progress since 1945 and had been intensified after the Korean armistice. The massive retaliation address served to meet in part the policy vacuum that existed in Southeast Asia.[34] Contrary to the wishes of Dulles, who feared that the Communists might be inspired to attempt a feat of force in Vietnam to support their diplomacy, the Berlin conference placed the problem of restoring peace in Indochina on the agenda for discussion at another conference to be held in Geneva in April.[35] The massive retaliation address also touched off another great debate on American policy in the United States. "All told," wrote Chester Bowles on 28 February, "the administration seems to be saying that in dealing with future armed Soviet or Chinese aggression into non-Communist territory anywhere in the world, it proposes to rely chiefly upon atomic attack by the Strategic Air Forces against the major cities in Communist countries."[36] "All this means, if it means anything," said the defeated Democrat candidate for president Adlai Stevenson in a speech on 6 March, "is that if the Communists try another Korea we will retaliate by dropping atom bombs on Moscow or Peiping or wherever we choose — or else we will concede the loss of another Korea — and presumably other countries after that — as 'normal' in the course of events."[37]

Obviously attempting to clarify national policy in an interview published on 5 March and in an address on 9 March, Admiral Radford explained: "It is evident from the forces we intend to maintain that we are not relying solely upon air power."[38] At a press conference on 16 March, Dulles called attention to the fact that his address had advocated "a 'capacity' to retaliate instantly. In no place did I say we would retaliate instantly, although we might indeed retaliate instantly under conditions that call for that. The essential thing is to have the capacity to retaliate instantly. It is lack of that capacity which in my opinion accounted for such disasters as Pearl Harbor."[39] In an appearance before the Senate Foreign Relations Committee on 20 March, Dulles emphasized that collective defense would be the companion of the capability for massive retaliation. "No single nation," he said, "can develop alone adequate power to deter Soviet block aggression against vital interests. By providing joint facilities and by combining their resources, the free nations can achieve a total strength and a flexibility which can surpass that of any potential enemy and can do so at bearable cost."[40] While flying home from the Berlin conference, Dulles wrote an article which he considered to be a "more polished ... restatement" of his earlier address in New York. Published in *Foreign Affairs*, this article denied that "the United States intended to rely wholly on large-scale strategic bombing as the sole means to deter and counter aggression." He continued: "A potential of massive attack will always be kept in a state of instant readiness and our programme will retain a wide variety and the means and scope for responding to aggression.... The essential thing is that a potential aggressor should know in advance that he can and will be made to suffer for his aggression more than he can possibly gain by it. This calls for a system in which local defensive strength is reinforced by more mobile deterrent power. The method of doing so will vary according to the character of the various areas. Some areas are so vital that special guards should and could be put around them — Western Europe is such an area."[41]

If Dulles had hoped that the massive retaliation address would help shore up the policy vacuum in Southeast Asia, such was not to be the case. Spurred into an all-out field campaign when the Berlin conference provided them with a timetable, the Vietminh laid siege to a substantial French garrison at Dien Bien Phu, in northwest Vietnam. While Dulles had anticipated that the Vietminh might attempt a feat of military force prior to Geneva, the first responsible intimation that the French were in extreme difficulty came to Washington from Gen Paul Ely, the French chief of staff, who stopped at the Pentagon on 20 March long enough to discuss the possibility of US air strikes against the Communist forces surrounding Dien Bien Phu. A little later, the French government forwarded a request for assistance to Washington through diplomatic channels.[42] As deliberations progressed in Washington, Admiral Radford expressed the view that the loss of Dien Bien Phu would constitute a serious loss of prestige to the entire free world. In the Far East, Brig Gen Joseph D. Caldera took selected members of his Far East Air Forces (FEAF) Bomber Command staff to Saigon, where they made plans for 98 B-29s to fly a maximum-effort carpet-bombing air strike with conventional bombs against the Communist forces around Dien Bien Phu. Back in Washington, Admiral Carney joined Admiral Radford in recommending strong action, but General Ridgway was opposed. "I felt sure," Ridgway wrote later, "that if we committed air and naval power to that area, we would have to follow them immediately with ground forces in support." On the basis of an analysis made by a survey team he had sent to Vietnam, Ridgway predicted that the requirement for US Army forces would be extremely large.[43]

While the crisis continued, conferences between Dulles and congressional leaders on 3 April and a discussion between Eisenhower, Dulles, and Radford on the evening of 4 April developed the consensus that the United States should intervene in Indochina only as a part of a collective effort, that the French should take further steps to give complete independence to Vietnam, Laos, and Cambodia, and that any ground forces employed in the war ought to be indigenous forces. When queried about collective action, the British were unwilling to make any undertakings in advance of the Geneva conference. In Paris on 23 April, French foreign minister George Bidault pled that an American air strike could still save Dien Bien Phu, but neither Dulles nor Radford could now agree with him, since Radford felt that the military situation had deteriorated too far. When Dien Bien Phu surrendered on 7 May, the way appeared open for the Communists to take over virtually all of Vietnam; but, possibly because they feared to go too far and provoke an American response, the Communists settled for less than they might have claimed. In the final Geneva protocol on 21 July, the French agreed to a supposedly temporary division of Vietnam at the seventeenth parallel pending a national plebiscite and the Reds agreed to withdraw their forces from South Vietnam, Cambodia, and Laos.[44] Some critics of massive retaliation would later state that the policy met an almost immediate defeat in Indochina.[45] However, the often critical Thomas K. Finletter, writing shortly after the Geneva settlement, pointed out that the United States had been unable to take effective action in Southeast Asia because of the lack of a multilateral political base with Britain, France, and the indigenous countries of the area.[46] Meeting at Manila from 6–8 September 1954, representatives of Pakistan, Thailand, the Philippines, Australia, New Zealand, France, the United Kingdom, and the United States drew up and signed the Southeast Asia Collective Defense Treaty, mutually pledging themselves to consult on measures for common defense whenever one of the signatories felt the territory or political independence of any state in the area was threatened by armed attack or subversion.

Following closely after Geneva, the new American emphasis upon nuclear weapons and the reduction of manpower requirements permitted a reevaluation of the strategy of the North Atlantic Treaty Organization (NATO) along lines earlier suggested by Great Britain. Under the strategy visualized at Lisbon in 1952, the Strategic Air Command's nuclear strikes would have been expected to delay a Soviet advance long enough to permit mobilization of the 96 divisions that would be required to stop the aggressor at the Rhine. To most European nations this objective had been too costly in manpower and too limited in scope to be acceptable, they had made little real progress toward fulfilling the program envisioned at Lisbon. In a new assessment of defense requirements in December 1954, the NATO Council resolved that member nations would plan on the use of nuclear weapons from the outset of a war. This decision to stockpile nuclear warheads, which would be readily available for the defense of the alliance in time of need, permitted a reduction in the size of the ground forces thought necessary. Under the new NATO strategy the local defense forces would provide a "shield" at the forward defense line in Europe while air atomic strikes flown by the Strategic Air Command (SAC), the United Kingdom Bomber Command, and American naval forces would provide the "sword." Best described by Gen Lauris Norstad, who became supreme allied commander in Europe in 1956, the NATO strategy included three objectives. "Our first task," Norstad explained

> must be to create conditions—and this means by the availability of force—so if an incident should arise . . . we could compel a pause. We could force a break in the continuity of the action that is started, whether it is by design, a probing operation, or whether by mistake. . . . Our second objective is in this break to compel the aggressor to make a conscious decision that he is either going to war or he is not going to war. . . . The third objective is when he is making that decision . . . he must think of the total consequences of the act, if he decides to go to war. . . . He must think of the fact that not only will he involve himself in a contact with these so-called shield forces in the forward area, but he will also involve himself in the operations of the retaliatory forces, so you make him face up to the total cost of aggression. You never permit him the luxury of thinking in terms of just a little piece of the price that he might have to pay.[47]

When the United States defense policy had matured in 1953-54, Admiral Radford described it as being based upon a studied assumption of Communist action. "Communism when seeking a means to a political end," Radford said, "is reluctant to use *organized* armed forces in an overt aggression except as a last resort." Radford saw two corollaries deriving from this basic assessment: "Communism will use all measures short of actual warfare to attain a given objective before resorting to armed force. . . . Communism will not resort to armed force unless there is a reasonable chance of quick victory *without*—in the opinion of its leaders—appreciable world reaction." This assessment of Communist policy provided the ground rules for American defense policy. "Actually," Radford explained,

> there is no local defense which alone can contain the massive land power of the Communist world. Consequently, local defenses must be reinforced by the deterrent power of strong counteroffensive forces possessing the capacity for devastating counter blows deep into enemy territory. In other words, an Allied strategic concept of operations must be based on the combination of local defenses, deterrent power, and an ability to strike swiftly and powerfully. Our current defense program is geared to that concept.... In developing the collective physical shield... a growing reliance can be placed upon Allied forces now being strengthened in many areas of the free world....
> But the essence of our concept is the capacity to strike in devastating strength at any element of the enemy's power. There can be no alternative. A workable deterrent will cause a would-be aggressor to hesitate, particularly if he knows in advance that he thereby not only exposes those particular forces he uses for aggression, but he also deprives his other assets of "sanctuary" status.

Radford emphasized that "if the Armed Forces of the Soviet Union committed aggression *in force* against this or that nation to whom we were tied in a collective security arrangement... this would be the beginning of World War III."[48]

Air Force Views on Massive Retaliation

According to one observer the majority of Air Force officers appeared to be strongly in favor of the military strategy of massive retaliation.[49] "History may show," stated *Air Force Magazine*, "that the 'massive retaliation policy' of the Eisenhower Administration marked the turning point in the Free World's successive retreats and indecisive stalemates in dealing with the onrushing tide of aggressive Communism."[50] Writing as vice chief of staff of the Air Force, Gen Thomas D. White described the new national security policy as being a policy of realism. "We have recognized," he thought, "that our atomic weapon developments form the only effective counter to the overwhelming mobilized manpower of the Soviet. Our Air Force with its ability to deliver nuclear weapons has been recognized as an instrument of national policy." White noted that the air power concept was not new—he recalled that farsighted men such as Douhet, Mitchell, Arnold, Lindbergh, Slessor, de Seversky, and Orvil Anderson had voiced the concept—but he remarked that "recent acceptance of these truths has been the result of startling advances in the power of modern weapons."[51]

Brig Gen Dale O. Smith believed that Secretary Dulles's statement of the massive retaliatory policy was a "bolder and more confident step" that echoed the words of the late General Vandenberg, who had said: "Air power alone does not guarantee America's security, but I believe it best exploits the nation's greatest assets—our technical skill."[52] When published in May 1956, Smith's pioneer book, *US Military Doctrine, A Study and Appraisal*, pointed out that the massive retaliation policy did not visualize air power as an exclusive or self-sufficient means of victory. President Eisenhower had emphasized that there would still be a need for effective land, amphibious, antisubmarine, and other forces. "The decision," Smith wrote, "is not an all air-power decision by any means but merely a decision to emphasize air in this age as the fulcrum for our military policy." Nevertheless, he hoped and expected that the national policy of exploiting air power — arrived at "through long and sometimes halting evolution of doctrine, and through exhaustive study and debate among experts in every field of the military art" — would result in the elimination of the old tendency "to build three self-sufficient services, each planning to win a war with different doctrines."[53]

While Air Force officers were said to have regarded the New Look and massive retaliation as being "a major, strategic reorientation toward war," the implementation of the policy into strategy seemed none too certain. Taking a clue from Smith's belief that armed service doctrines evolved upward and with general acceptance became "national policy," Col Paul C. Droz remarked that the executive policy of the New Look appeared to have "preceded rather than stemmed from plans and doctrine."[54] Col Wendell E. Carter made this same observation. "While some observers conclude that the dominant nature of air power has now been recognized in national policy," he wrote, "it is relatively certain that the wisdom of this decision (if it has in fact been made) has not fully percolated down to all the subordinates who contribute to planning activities. It is significant, too, that the national policy was set by the president on his own initiative and was not the result of the unanimous advice of his military advisers. This may have put the lid on the pot, but it is doubtful that the fire has been turned off under the bouillabaisse — or that it will be until the services have a more nearly common viewpoint."[55]

Air Force Thinking on Counterforce and Air Power

In his commentary on the meaning of the New Look to the Air Force, General White asserted that the startling advances in the destructive power of air weapons had accentuated old truths: air forces must be combat ready; they must have central direction in order to complement each other (even the best air force, if divided or compartmented, would be vulnerable to piecemeal destruction); they must have a capability to inflict instant, effective retaliatory punishment upon an aggressor; and they must remain uncompromised in their ability to exercise a wide variety of persuasive actions. White asserted that hostile air forces would always be the primary concern and priority target of the total US air forces.[56] Gen Curtis E. LeMay also believed that the Soviet capabilities demanded that the Air Force should return to its old doctrines. Before 1950, when the Soviets had no atomic stockpile, LeMay had been willing to "violate the principles of war and forget about the rulebook and go about leisurely destroying their war potential or taking on any other task that seemed desirable at the time." By 1953, however, the Soviets had an atomic stockpile plus a growing delivery capability. LeMay accordingly concluded: "We have to go back to the rulebook and the principles of war and fight the air battle first, which means that we must as quickly as possible destroy their capability of doing damage to us."[57] In a landmark speech, which drew very little attention when it was delivered in February 1954, General Twining stated: "We can now aim directly to disarm an enemy rather than to destroy him as was so often necessary in wars of the past."[58]

Even though the Air Force leaders believed that Soviet atomic capabilities had served merely to return Air Force thinking into its old doctrines, the new Soviet capabilities demanded changes in air strategy and especially in the mission of the Strategic Air Command. At a session of the USAF Board of Review for Tactical Operations in September 1949, Maj Gen David M. Schlatter had observed: "Our Strategic Air Command isn't any more a strategic air command than my aunt's foot. It is our striking force." He argued further that the Strategic Air Command would have "to help the soldier dig in in Europe and hold on to territory against the forward Russian divisions."[59] Speaking in June 1953, General Vandenberg told a Senate subcommittee: "The proper role of air forces is to destroy the enemy's industrial potential." On further questioning, however, he stated that the Strategic Air Command would have to cover all the installations from which the Soviets could launch an atomic air attack against the United States. SAC would then have two priority missions: to destroy the enemy's industrial potential and "to save the friendly ground forces that are already in contact with the enemy."[60] As outlined by General LeMay, the mission assigned by the Joint Chiefs of Staff required that the Strategic Air Command prevent an enemy nation from launching an atomic attack against the United States, retard the massing and launching of Soviet ground forces, and systematically destroy hostile war-sustaining resources.[61]

At the time that the Joint Chiefs directed that the Strategic Air Command would assist theater forces by retarding Soviet advances, the Strategic Air Command found it difficult to target specific objectives. Some of the Soviet forces would be moving, and aircraft would have to search for them before making attacks. Planning for the retardation mission became even more complex early in 1952 when the Joint Chiefs of Staff began to allocate nuclear weapons to the unified theater commanders for employment by naval air forces and theater air forces. The Joint Chiefs recognized this problem and directed the Air Force to establish a jointly staffed war room in the Pentagon and joint coordination centers in appropriate theaters of operations. The purpose of these centers was to forward information on targets scheduled for nuclear attack to the war room where duplications might be noted and theoretically eliminated. Joint coordination centers were established in the Far East and in Europe during 1952. Staffed by Strategic Air Command personnel, SAC Zebra in Europe and SAC Xray in the Far East served both as coordination centers and as advance command posts to control an emergency war plan employment of Strategic Air Command forces in support of theater commanders. Under then existing ground rules, as many as four commanders were scheduling atomic attacks against the same target. It was thought, however, that in case of a war the joint coordination centers would be able to spread the word when a target was attacked, thus halting duplicative attacks.[62] As long as all prospective nuclear targets were within the Soviet Union, the simple coordination procedure appeared workable. However, the situation rapidly began to get out of hand when the New Look greatly loosened planning for the employment of the ever growing atomic stockpile in limited as well as general wars.⁶³

Speaking in November 1953, former Secretary of the Air Force Thomas K. Finletter voiced the opinion that the Air Force needed to revise its "consideration constantly away from the old anti-industry concept of the SAC operations and ... make it an anti-force operation."⁶⁴ When he published *Power and Policy* in the summer of 1954, Finletter again argued that the

> old counter-industry concept for the Strategic Air Command should be given up. There should be substituted for it what may be called the front-to-rear concept. Under this concept all targets from the enemy's front lines, through his communication and supply lines, his airfields and storage, back to and including the sources of production and governmental direction would be the objective of Atomic-Air's attack. In the time of atomic plenty there will be enough bombs to do all this. . . . The first emphasis would be on the enemy's atomic air, on the fields, installations, planes and missiles from which his atomic attack on us would come. Once these are destroyed the emphasis would shift to the obliteration of the enemy's military forces, his industry, and his ability to function as an organized state.⁶⁵

In a review of Finletter's book, T. F. Walkowicz, a member of the USAF Scientific Advisory Board, agreed that mounting Soviet atomic capabilities were making the Soviet air forces rather than the Soviet economy the priority enemy target in the event of a war.⁶⁶ In a major article published in February 1955 under the title of "Counter-Force Strategy," Walkowicz presented what he considered to be a comprehensive thesis on nuclear warfare. He reasoned that the possession of nuclear weapons by both prospective combatants had rendered obsolete any idea of using a mobilization base in war: either the United States or the USSR would win or lose a war with forces already on hand at the outset of hostilities. Since the United States and the Soviet Union each possessed combat ready forces able to destroy each other, a strategy of bombing cities or factories was impracticable. The United States, however, held a substantial advantage in its possession of a larger stockpile and a wide variety of atomic weapon systems. Walkowicz, therefore, urged that the United States should give priority emphasis to the development of both the Strategic Air Command and theater air forces and that nuclear weapons and delivery systems should be directed primarily against Soviet air forces and other enemy forces in being. "As our counter-force capability becomes really formidable," Walkowicz wrote, "the US will have both the option of choosing and the initiative of announcing a policy to employ nuclear weapons primarily against military targets."⁶⁷ Finletter called Walkowicz's article "a fine contribution to thinking on this all-important subject."⁶⁸

Both Finletter and Walkowicz emphasized the military reasons for counterforce strategy, but Richard S. Leghorn, an Air Force reserve officer who had returned to civilian status after a tour in the Air Force Office of Development Planning, advanced the humanitarian aspects of a counterforce strategy. In an article, "No Need to Bomb Cities to Win War, A New Counterforce Strategy for Air Warfare," published in January 1955, Leghorn proposed that the United States might unilaterally renounce H-bomb and A-bomb attacks against cities, unless in retaliation for mass-effect weapons employed by the Soviets against free world cities. If the United States or its allies were attacked with conventional armies, the United States would punish the aggressor by directing tactical nuclear weapons against hostile attacking units in the battle zone and enemy military installations in immediate rear areas, including air bases supporting the aggression. If the United States or its allies were attacked with nuclear weapons, the United States would employ nuclear weapons to destroy the enemy's nuclear stockpiles and delivery capabilities.[69] Leghorn described his proposals as a counterforce strategy, but his plan to limit nuclear weapons to battlefield targets fell rather neatly into the definition of what retired Rear Adm Sir Anthony W. Buzzard, British Royal Navy, would conceive to be graduated deterrence. Buzzard proposed to return nuclear war to the tactical battlefield and to avoid strategic nuclear attacks against towns and cities unless such proved to be absolutely essential.[70]

Air Force leaders found much that was acceptable in the proposed counterforce strategy. Writing in the winter of 1954–55, Col Robert C. Richardson III, air member to the NATO Standing Group in Washington, suggested that at the outset of hostilities, adversaries armed with nuclear weapons would direct their blows against target systems that offered quick payoffs, such as combat formations of all arms and services.[71] General LeMay emphasized that the Strategic Air Command's primary war mission would be the enemy's atomic capability. "I think," LeMay said, "it is generally conceded by all military personnel in this day and age, [that] you must win the air power battle, gain air superiority, before you can conduct any other type of military operation."[72] Maj Gen John Samford, Air Force director of intelligence, was frankly skeptical about any proposal to make direct attacks against the psychological strength of the enemy. He knew no way in which target planners could estimate the effect of direct attacks against an enemy's will to wage war. Thus, he favored attacks against hostile military and industrial targets where effects of destruction could be better predicted and the results of incremental reductions could be more accurately measured.[73] There was general agreement in the Air Force that a future war would allow little or no time for mobilization. The Air Materiel Command accepted the policy that the decisive phase of a future general war would be the first 90 days and that hostilities could begin at any hour. "It is one of the tenets of modern warfare," LeMay wrote, "that the decision in tomorrow's conflict will be reached using only the forces in being at the outset.... Today, shooting wars are won or lost before they start. If they are fought at all, they will be fought principally to confirm which side has won at the outset."[74]

As a second priority to the counterair strikes, the Strategic Air Command planned to support theater commanders in retarding the advance of Soviet ground forces. For this task, LeMay planned to deliver weapons against targets the theater commander wanted destroyed.[75] Even though much of the counterforce strategy was acceptable, the Air Force was as yet unable to accept such an undertaking in all its details. Mindful that a major reason for the assignment of theater-support missions to the Strategic Air Command in 1950 had been that the large and scarce atomic weapons of that time could be transported only by strategic bombers, Gen Otto P. Weyland believed that as tactical aircraft gained atomic capabilities the primary responsibility of the Strategic Air Command should shift from theater support strikes to attacks on basic sustaining resources, industries and facilities essential for the prosecution of war and that the Tactical Air Command and the theater air forces ought to become "responsible for attacks on enemy military forces and materials in being, en route to or in battle."[76]

Although the Strategic Air Command would remain responsible for an important segment of the retardation missions, the targets SAC was scheduled to attack under the retardation objective were somewhat less than the counterforce concept seemed to contemplate. As a third priority, the Strategic Air Command also planned to systematically destroy the enemy's war-sustaining resources. Said a SAC spokesman, "their steel plants, their heavy industry, and the goods of war will be destroyed so that they cannot fight." This third-priority task, moreover, would be accomplished almost simultaneously with the higher priority tasks since the Strategic Air Command—unlike the naval and theater air forces, which would retain some reserve of nuclear weapons—was committed to an immediate salvo of its nuclear stockpile as soon as possible after H-hour. Operational concerns had another important effect on the Strategic Air Command's target planning: many targets fell within several of the common target categories and numerous separate targets commonly were found in the immediate vicinity of population centers. By increasing the size of the weapon delivered, the Strategic Air Command would be able to destroy several separate targets with one successful sortie, thus attaining a "bonus effect" from a single larger weapon.[77] At least two other reasons were given for the Air Force's early hesitation about accepting counterforce as a strategy. The counterforce concept posed a requirement for a very large number of nuclear weapons and delivery vehicles—many more than the Air Force had programmed or could reasonably expect to obtain.[78] The counterforce concept also demanded an accurate identification and location of Soviet forces prior to H-hour. As of mid-1956 the Air Force did not yet have intelligence or reconnaissance capabilities that could provide such exact information.[79] The Air Force considered the counterforce strategy to be basically sound and worth planning for, but it could not accept it in all of its details.

Efforts to Define Air Power

The strategic requirements of the New Look—especially instant reaction to aggression and the corollary concept of instant readiness—touched off an active discussion on the need for the proper understanding of the characteristics of air power. As has been seen, Brig Gen William Mitchell in the early days of American aviation had defined air power as "the ability to do something in or through the air." Following this same dynamic definition, the Air Corps Tactical School had taught: "The air power of a nation is its capacity to conduct air operations; specifically, the power which a nation is capable of exerting by means of its air forces. . . . Air power is measured by the immediate ability of a nation to engage effectively in air warfare."[80] While early air thinkers generally identified air power with the air striking force, the emphasis in the early 1940s on a mobilization base in the aviation industry led to a broadened definition of air power. Alexander P. de Seversky provided this expanded concept in his book, *Victory through Air Power*. Being, as he later said, "a Navy man by education," de Seversky adapted Admiral Mahan's classic definition of sea power for his own purposes. "I automatically said," de Seversky recollected, "that air power means everything. The airplanes, the industries, the men, the materials, everything that produces the power in the air or power to navigate in the air constitutes air power."[81] At the end of World War II Gen Henry H. Arnold accepted this broad definition of air power; in 1955 Air Force Manual 1-2, *United States Air Force Basic Doctrine*, stated: "The term 'air power' embraces the entire aviation capacity of the United States."[82]

This broad definition of air power was accepted within the Department of Defense. When he justified reductions in the Air Force in June 1953, Secretary Wilson said that the Air Force's wing strength was only "a segment of our air power" and asserted that if Navy and Marine air strengths were taken into consideration the "over-all air power" of the nation totaled 152 wings.[83] Disputing Wilson's reasoning, General Vandenberg argued that naval air units were committed to a mission of controlling the seas and would not be available to assist with air missions until primary naval functions were accomplished. "In other words," Vandenberg said, "when the bell rings you would not, in my opinion, count upon the Navy to carry out its primary mission if, at the same time, it is required to help the Air Force carry out its own primary mission."[84] In December 1953, however, Admiral Radford defined national air power as including the Air Force, Navy, Marine Corps, and Army aviation and "the tremendous aircraft industry and civil air transportation systems of the United States."[85]

Believing that the New Look concept of air power as manifest in the fiscal year 1955 defense budget was only "an optical illusion – the same old numbers racket," de Seversky began to change his mind about his definition of air power. In an April 1954 article he pointed out that from its share of the defense appropriations the Air Force "not only has to build an Air Force to fulfill its primary mission to destroy the enemy and to protect the continental United States, but it also has to build an enormous tactical air force, and transport and cargo planes in support of and for use by our Army." De Seversky now maintained that aviation designed to support the Army should be budgeted to the Army. "Just aviation – an amorphous mass of aircraft, no matter how large, no matter how useful it may be to the Army, Navy, and Marine Corps – if it is not designed to win and maintain command of the air," he wrote, "does not constitute air power."[86] In an article prepared in July 1954 for the *American Peoples Encyclopedia*, de Seversky wrote: "Air power is the ability of a nation to assert its will via the air medium. . . . Only when an aircraft is designed to assist and increase the efficiency of the air force in its task of establishing command of the air is it an instrument of air power."[87] In an amplification of this article for *Air Force Magazine*, de Seversky asserted that a lack of basic understanding of what constituted military air power was the root of the confusion reigning in the national defense effort. "The scope of the Air Force's mission," he maintained, "must be fully understood if our country is to shake off the curse of the present antiquated philosophy of balanced forces strategy."[88]

Believing that the real meaning of air power was getting lost in a maze of diverse definitions, Air Force thinkers attempted to provide a definition that would be nationally acceptable. Cols Jerry D. Page and Royal H. Roussel of the Air War College Evaluation Staff prepared an article in which they accepted the doctrine that air power was an entity. In this frame reference they thought of air power as "those military forces ... which are employed and directed as a single instrument by the military agency charged primarily with the responsibility for conducting operations through the air." They concluded: "Unlike air power, military auxiliary aviation is invariably confined in its use to support of operations which have definite land and sea boundaries." They defined "military auxiliary aviation" as being "composed of those products of the national air capacity which are diverted or withdrawn from the air power total for the primary purpose of conducting land or sea operations under the military agencies charged with those responsibilities."[89] Taking a semantic shortcut, Prof Barton K. Leach abruptly defined "United States air power ... as the United States Air Force."[90] When he appeared before Senator Stuart S. Symington's committee, which was investigating air power in April 1956, General LeMay did not define air power. However, he stated that intelligence indicated that the Soviets would possess more long-range jet bombers than the United States by 1958–60. He stated, "We are drifting into coordinating our tactics and weight of effort, timing of things, and that sort, and we are drifting towards what we airmen have maintained all along, to fight an air power battle requires a single commander." LeMay urged that a single air commander would be required to achieve the "primary single goal of destroying Soviet air power."[91]

The new definitions of air power were not acceptable to other national leaders. Admiral Carney stated: "Air power is not a compartmented thing peculiar to any one agency; it is needed by the Army, Navy, Air Force, and Marine Corps for the accomplishment of their assigned roles and missions; it is needed to expedite the business of other governmental agencies, or industry, and of the population at large."[92] Speaking pointedly in response to LeMay's testimony, President Eisenhower on 4 May discounted the charge that the United States was lagging behind the Soviet Union. "We have," he told reporters, "the most powerful Navy in the world ... and it features one thing, airpower.... Now we have got a tremendous airpower, a mobile air power, in the sea forces."[93] Preferring to speak about deterrent power rather than air power, Secretary Wilson stated that "primary deterrent power" rested in the Strategic Air Command, but he emphasized that this force was supplemented by "atomic capable aircraft with carrier task forces constantly deployed overseas; the atomic bombing capability of aircraft of our tactical air forces deployed overseas and ever on the alert; and the atomic capability of our surface-to-surface guided missile and artillery units also deployed overseas."[94] When questioned on these matters by the Symington committee in

IDEAS, CONCEPTS, DOCTRINE

July, General Twining conceded that naval aircraft could make a valuable contribution to the air power battle, provided carrier air attacks were possible against Soviet airfield targets immediately after a war's beginning and were coordinated with Air Force attacks. He pointed out, however, that the Navy had important primary control-of-the-sea missions, that no one could be sure where naval carriers would be physically located or what targets their planes would be prepared to strike immediately after H-hour. For those reasons, Twining asserted that "the strategic air force has to be just as big, just as strong, and just as ready regardless of this Navy contribution on these targets I am talking about."[95]

After considering this course of efforts to define air power, the Air War College Evaluation Staff offered a more cohesive definition early in 1957. "Air power," it said, "is the hard core of any modern defense organization. It comprises those military resources, together with their effective command, control and employment, which enable a nation to use the air for its own purpose and to deny its effective use to the enemy." Given effective command and control that recognized the unitary nature of global air warfare, the Evaluation Staff's definition was broad enough to include Army antiaircraft defense as well as Navy air defense and aviation resources.[96] Emphasizing a dynamic and inclusive concept of air power, Maj Gen James Ferguson, Air Force director of requirements, wrote in April 1958: "Air power is the total of elements needed to apply force in the appropriate degree. It is offensive, defense, reconnaissance, transport. It is general thermonuclear offensive, limited nuclear and conventional war, police action, or perhaps a show of force. It is deterrence and, if deterrence should fail, it is destruction of the aggressor."[97] Speaking to the National Press Club on 29 November 1957, however, General White declared that the US Air Force was "synonymous with airpower." "Just as our Army and its soldiers are synonymous with land warfare and the Navy and its sailors with sea battles," he said, "so are the USAF and its airmen synonymous with air warfare."[98] In April 1958 Maj Gen Jacob E. Smart, the Air Force assistant vice chief of staff, reiterated this same position that the National Defense Act 1947 had established the US Air Force as the service representing "the primary airpower strength of the nation."[99] At the Air War College, Maj Gen Robert F. Tate, nevertheless, preferred the larger definition of air power. "I think we must," he said, "whether we like it or not, acknowledge that air power if properly used does lie in the Navy as well as in the Air Force, and perhaps eventually in the Army."[100]

Although the discussions of air power appeared academic, the emphasis placed on the unitary nature of national air power stimulated thought about the internal organization of the Air Force. Even though Air Force doctrine had accepted the fact that air units might be placed under diverse air commanders to simplify span of control, it emphasized that air power must not be compartmented but must be wielded as a unitary force for the prosecution of the global air battle.[101] In view of the increasing threat of a Soviet atomic attack by air and the requirement for unitary command and control of air power, there was a question as to whether the Strategic Air Command and the Tactical Air Command (TAC) ought to continue to be separate establishments. As early as March 1953, Brig Gen James Ferguson suggested that the Air Force was not entirely without blame for prevalent compartmentations of air power. "We have permitted," he pointed out, "internal segregation of partition of air power at a time when technological developments least warrant such action. By such partition we invite the wedge which will split apart such aircraft assigned to TAC for special use as long range artillery at a time when this tactical portion of our air force may very well play an important role in the strategic mission."[102] As has been seen, Finletter proposed in *Power and Policy* the need for a merger of all air units with atomic weapons under a single command that might be called the strategic-tactical air command or simply STAC.[103]

In the postwar years, when no hostile nation had possessed air capabilities sufficient to destroy the United States, General LeMay had been willing to believe that the United States "could afford the luxury of devoting a substantial portion of our Air Force effort to support of ground forces." He thought, "The maintenance of part of our force as close support posed no grave risk, because the enemy didn't have the capability to destroy us. He couldn't initiate an effective air offensive blow against us because he couldn't mount one." By 1956, however, LeMay considered that the Soviets possessed aircraft and weapons capable of inflicting nuclear devastation on the United States. Under these conditions, he said: "Offensive air power must now be aimed at preventing the launching of weapons of mass destruction against the United States or its Allies. This transcends all other considerations because the price of failure may be paid with national survival."[104] Based on this strategic estimate, LeMay apparently was not adverse to the Army's attempts to increase its own organic supporting firepower. In June 1956, Gen Maxwell D. Taylor, the new Army chief of staff, stated that "the trend will be toward the substitution of the missile, the Army-controlled missile, for what we call close support of ground forces."[105] In a directive on roles and missions issued on 26 November 1956, Secretary Wilson authorized the Army to develop surface-to-surface missiles with ranges up to 200 miles. At an Air Force Commanders' Conference in January 1957, LeMay considered that Wilson's directive was an emancipation of the Tactical Air Command inasmuch as it visualized, as LeMay saw it, that "the firepower necessary for close support in the confines of the combat zone can and should be provided by relatively short range weapon systems organic to the Army." He accordingly recommended that the time had come to reorganize all of the offensive elements of the Air Force into an "Air Offensive Command" under a single air commander. "With control of our air forces piecemealed throughout the world," he warned, "we need lose only in one area to insure the destruction of our own country. . . . Whether we choose to recognize it or not, SAC and TAC are bedfellows. . . . As a matter of top priority, for reasons of national survival, they must deter together through their ability to defeat Communist air power together." Given a combination of the Strategic and Tactical Air Commands, LeMay thought that the Air Force could more logically "take a united stand in pursuit of its ultimate objective of achieving unified control of all air offensive forces, regardless of service, under a single air commander."[106]

"I have stressed the indivisibility of air power and the necessity of centralized control of air resources," said General Weyland after assuming command of the Tactical Air Command in 1954, "as much as any man alive." From his headquarters at Langley AFB, Weyland set out to develop the Tactical Air Command into a jack-of-all-trades element of offensive air power as well as a supporting force for surface operations. The strategic tactical air forces appeared to him to be an offensive capability that would be applied against a spectrum of targets comprising "an unbroken chain from field, mine, and forest to the battle area." Speaking of the target spectrum, Weyland explained: "There is no sharp line of demarcation, there is a desirable area of overlap, and, by close coordination, strategic and tactical air forces can and do complement and assist each other without duplication of effort."[107] In spite of these beliefs, he took a firm stand against LeMay's concept of a single offensive force. Weyland favored a single service that would integrate the offensive capabilities of all the armed forces, thus permitting a single-uniform military force to exploit the national air capabilities; but he did not expect to see such a single service mature in his time. Under the existing command organization, theater commanders had legitimate area responsibilities in which theater air forces assumed major importance for general war and for contingencies short of general war. Unless the Air Force was prepared to risk the danger that forces of the Strategic Air Command might be placed under theater control, Weyland argued that the Air Force must proceed very cautiously toward amalgamating tactical and strategic air forces. "We must face, too," he continued, "the inalterable fact that the forces of the Strategic Air Command are dedicated to a single and inflexible purpose—the prosecution of an all-out war. Their people and their equipment simply are not capable of or familiar with the many contingencies which may arise short of that general conflict." Weyland favored the establishment of a single commander with authority to control or coordinate worldwide tactical air resources. He thought that many of the advantages supposedly inherent in a single commander of an air offensive force could be attained through a centralized authority to direct targeting and to coordinate the timing of all air strikes in case of a general war.[108]

In offering his proposal for an air offensive command, General LeMay assumed that the Army would be quick to develop surface-to-surface missiles and to undertake its own close-support and interdiction efforts. Despite General Taylor's remarks, however, the Army followed a very cautious approach designed to ensure that Air Force support capabilities would be reduced only gradually as Army missile capabilities increased.[109] The growth of Army missile power was cited as a justification for reducing the strength of the Tactical Air Command, but the Army could not arrive at an organic missile strength that would permit it to dispense with tactical air support. LeMay also had assumed that the missions of the Strategic Air Command and the Tactical Air Command were becoming increasingly congruous. But forces were already at work that would demand that the Strategic Air Command be almost entirely committed to the deterrence of general war while the Tactical Air Command would be developed as a general purpose force. Instead of moving together, the missions of the Tactical Air Command and the Strategic Air Command became more widely separated. Although unable to agree to the integration of its own forces to the degree contemplated by General LeMay, the Air Force continued to work for a higher degree of unification of the Army services.

Air Force Positions on Nuclear Stalemate and Limited War

"Air power," General Vandenberg stated in June 1947, "is a power for peace in the uncertain world of today—if air supremacy rests in the right hands."[110] In the late 1940s and early 1950s, Air Force leaders were said to agree that American air weapons were clearly superior to an enemy's weapons and that the best assurance against the outbreak of war was the ability to win such a war.[111] Looking toward the long-term future in 1953, President Eisenhower attached great importance to the role of military power in maintaining the peace of the world. "This power," Eisenhower emphasized, "is for our own defense and to deter aggression. We shall not be aggressors, but we and our Allies have and will maintain a massive capability to strike back."[112]

On a visit to the United States the summer before his retirement as chief of the Air Staff of the Royal Air Force in December 1952, Air Marshal Slessor recalled the hundred years of Pax Brittanica that had rested on the power of British naval forces and visualized the establishment of a Pax Atlantica based on air power. "I believe the stability of the world," he said, "can be preserved just as surely as it was between Waterloo and Sarajevo. And this time it will rest on airpower—largely, but not exclusively, American Airpower." Slessor repeated these ideas in a series of talks on the British Broadcasting Corporation early in 1954. In an article entitled "Has the H-Bomb Abolished Total War?" published in *Air Force Magazine* in May 1945, Slessor asserted that total war waged with thermonuclear weapons "would amount virtually to mutual suicide." Reasoning from the premise that to win a war meant to create "world conditions more favorable for oneself than would have been possible if there had not been a war," Slessor concluded: "The world may take courage and hope from the fact that there is today not the slightest chance of anyone winning a war on that definition. . . . What has now happened is that total war has been abolished in the only possible way—*it has abolished itself,* now that new ultimate weapons of atomic and thermonuclear power are in the hands of both potential antagonists." Slessor reasoned that the United States and Great Britain could not afford "to neglect the defensive altogether," that they would have to "give the necessary priority to a striking force, not vastly superior in strength to anything that anyone else has, but strong enough to do the job and efficient enough to put the weapon down where we want to, if we have to." He also argued that the two allies would require "the ability to deal in a limited way with limited emergencies wherever and whenever they may arise." "We can take it as a foregone conclusion," he predicted in a look at the future, that our opponents, having deduced that it would be too costly to overwhelm us by direct assault, will take every opportunity to turn or undermine our defenses by other means. We must look forward to a difficult era of what may be described as termite warfare—subversion, infiltration, and the exploitation of rebellion; fishing in the troubled waters of immature nationalism, of misgovernment and social inequalities in new states still in a rudimentary stage of political development, of religious hatreds and economic disequilibrium; and, almost certainly, other minor aggressions on the Korean model.... The function of atomic airpower will be the big stick in the background, to keep these affairs from spreading—to prevent the minor tactical episode from developing into the mortal threat.[113]

The concept of nuclear stalemate caught on rapidly in Great Britain and spread to the United States. The British military commentator J. F. C. Fuller agreed that the hydrogen bomb had "bereft organized international war of its political significance." "With the advent of the hydrogen bomb," stated Air Chief Marshal Sir Phillip Joubert, "it would appear that the human race must abandon war as an instrument of policy or accept the possibility of total destruction." Speaking to Parliament on 1 March 1955, Prime Minister Churchill predicted: "In three to four years' time ... the Soviets will probably stand possessed of hydrogen bombs and the means of delivering them not only on the United Kingdom but also on North American targets.... It does not follow, however, that the risk of war will then be greater. Indeed, it is arguable that it will be less, for both sides will then realize that global war would result in mutual annihilation."[114] In the United States, scientist Robert A. Oppenheimer coined the simile that war between thermonuclear powers would be equivalent to a battle to the death between two scorpions in a bottle. "No great war can ever again be won," said Dr Vannevar Bush, "it can only end with the partial or complete annihilation of both contestants."[115] In October 1955 Secretary of the Air Force Donald A. Quarles referred to the creation of "a stalemate through deterrent strength" as being, "paradoxically, our best hope for peace." Secretary Wilson observed in January 1956: "I assure you that in my opinion everybody is going to lose in the next war. ... The hope of the world [is] that by having a stalemate long enough sensible men of good will throughout the world could try to get some formula for establishing peace in the world."[116]

At first the concept of nuclear stalemate was thought to be a condition that would have some possible benefit to the United States, but with the passing of time some defense analysts began to promote the idea that a condition of finely balanced mutual deterrence would be very advantageous to the whole world. In 1959 Prof Oskar Morgenstern advanced the idea that it would be beneficial to maintain a nuclear stalemate, even by the expedient of strengthening Soviet forces by weakening US power. "In order to preserve a nuclear stalemate," Morgenstern wrote, "it is necessary for both sides to possess invulnerable retaliatory forces. ... In view of modern technology of speedy weapons delivery from any point on earth to any other, it is in the interest of the United States for Russia to have an invulnerable retaliatory force and vice versa."[117] A study prepared by James E. King, Jr., Paul H. Nitze, and Arnold Wolfers of the Washington Center of Foreign

Policy Research recommended: "On the assumption that steps will be taken to create a workable alternative to US strategic deterrence of the less provocative forms of Sino-Soviet aggression, the United States should pursue a policy aimed at increasing the ability of the strategic equation by unilateral action, by the encouragement of reciprocal action, and by an arms control policy directed at strategic stability."[118] Herman Kahn, another civilian analyst, suggested: "We must not look too dangerous to the enemy.... We do not want to make him so unhappy and distraught that he will be tempted to end his anxieties by the use of drastic alternatives."[119]

Air Thinking on Nuclear Stalemate

With the apparent exception of Secretary Quarles, Air Force thinkers were quite skeptical of the existence of a condition of nuclear stalemate. Seeking to determine Air Force requirements under the New Look, an Air War College Evaluation Staff analysis completed in April 1954 held that the objective of deterring all-out war demanded a continuing ability to deliver nuclear weapons to the heart of the Soviet Union. The effectiveness of a deterrent would be proportionate to an enemy country's conviction that US air capability would inflict unacceptable damage upon it and that it could not deny that capability by effecting an air-tight defense system, making a technological breakthrough in offensive weapons (such as an intercontinental missile), blackmailing America's allies, sabotaging or subverting American bases, or making an effective surprise attack against US offensive air forces.[120] In another study issued in April 1955, the Air War College Evaluation Staff acknowledged that deterrence was a composite of moral, economic, political, and military capabilities and that all military strengths — whether land, sea, or air — had some deterrent effect. The 1955 study asserted, however, that deterrence of an enemy was primarily "the ability to retaliate against the heart and core of his nation — a capability held securely in the hands of invulnerable force — that will cause him to fear the consequences of any aggression he might initiate."[121]

Appearing before Senator Symington's subcommittee on the study of air power in April 1956, General LeMay presented the Strategic Air Command's definition of deterrence. "A deterrent force," he said, "is one that is large enough and efficient enough that no matter what the enemy does, either offensively or defensively, he will still receive a quantity of bombs or explosive force that is more than he is willing to accept.... A deterrent force is an effective nuclear offensive force which is secure from destruction by the enemy regardless of what offensive and defensive action he takes against it. The striking force is considered effective if it can still inflict unacceptable damage on the enemy."[122] From testimony such as this, the Symington committee concluded: "To be safe, we must have strategic airpower of sufficient strength to absorb any surprise attack and, even after suffering the heavy damage incident to such an attack, be able to retaliate." General Twining agreed with this conclusion.[123] Tersely summing up a belief that deterrence was a "delicate balance of terror," Rand analyst Albert J. Wohlstetter concluded: "To deter an attack means being able to strike back in spite of it. It means, in other words, a capability to strike second."[124]

Based upon their examinations of the nature and requirements of a deterrent posture, Air Force leaders seriously questioned whether a nuclear stalemate could exist and whether, if it could exist, it would serve to eliminate general war. In April 1956 Brig Gen Sidney F. Giffin, vice commandant of the Air War College, remarked that stalemate described an end situation in the game of chess in which neither of two opponents could win or lose. He considered the term inappropriate to a situation that should be described as a "precarious balance of power" that might at any time be "tipped through the indifference or carelessness shown by one side or through the moral or technological advances achieved by the other."[125] Expanding upon this same theme, Col Robert C. Richardson postulated that to maintain a stalemate "both sides must have stocks of atomic weapons and the means for their delivery while at the same time lacking defenses capable of protecting their vital areas from destruction by the enemy." If either side developed "pay-off" defenses against air attack, the stalemate would never occur. In view of the normal processes of evolution of weapon systems, moreover, Richardson thought it unlikely that an exact parity in weapons, delivery forces, or defenses would occur for any length of time or endure for any length of time. "I suggest," he concluded, "that the so-called atomic 'stalemate' or 'stand-off' is more of a psychological than a real deterrent. At best it is a cliche born of the natural tendency to rationalize away the prospects of total atomic war."[126]

That any effective nuclear stalemate would depend upon the psychological judgments of Soviet leaders and to a lesser extent of the Soviet people was a cause for concern to Air Force leaders. Gen Carl A. Spaatz agreed that no right-thinking person would initiate a nuclear war, but he added: "I do not agree that dictators are in their right mind. I am certain Hitler was not, so I do not think we can assume that the Russians are going to have . . . completely sensible people running them all the time."[127] This same concern for Soviet motivations and capabilities caused General Twining to describe the proposition that prospects of mutual suicide had abolished total war as "a dangerous fallacy." "We must recognize," he said, "the fact that total war is no less a potential threat today, when both sides possess atomic weapons, than it was several years ago when we alone had them."[128] In the spring of 1960, after becoming Air Force chief of staff, General White described deterrence as "what we hope to achieve through specific impact on the collective mind of the Soviet leadership."[129] White took "particular exception" to the notion of "mutual deterrence." "I cannot agree," he said, "that the Soviet Union is trying to deter us. Deterrence, as I see it, is a one-sided problem — it is ours."[130] Reasoning that no one could state what amount of destruction the Soviets or Chinese Communists would be willing to accept, that the Soviets had a tremendous advantage in their ability to make a first strike, and that technological change made for very rapid fluctuations in offensive and defensive capabilities, Gen Thomas S. Power, the new commander of the Strategic Air Command, added: "a tremendous disservice ... is rendered the American people when people say there is a nuclear stalemate.... It is a very fluid situation. We have the deterrent posture today. We can lose it tomorrow."[131]

Limited Wars Are a Problem

In the autumn of 1953, the US State Department's Policy Planning Staff reportedly believed that the Army could have strengthened a case against the dominant trend toward nuclear weapons by giving up the idea of tailoring its forces for a large conventional war and instead basing its argumentation on the more solid ground of preparing to meet small war.[132] In his address of 12 January 1954, in which he broached the concept of massive retaliation, Secretary Dulles did not neglect the matter of local defense: "Local defenses," he said, "must be reinforced by the further deterrent of massive retaliatory power." In April 1954 he expanded the theme, writing: "To deter aggression, it is important to have flexibility and the facilities which make various responses available. In many cases, any open assault by Communist forces could only result in starting a general war. But the free world must have the means for responding effectively on a selective basis when it chooses."[133] Despite these statements, Dulles apparently did not believe that the State Department could advocate properly or competently particular military means or methods for implementing the national strategy—this was the task of professional military planners.

In the initial planning for force allocations under the New Look, General Ridgway rejected the image of limited war. "The day when wars had limited effects," he observed in the autumn of 1953, "is past.... War, if it comes again, will be total in character."[134] General Ridgway considered "around 26 divisions" or approximately 1.3 million men to be a realistic strength for the Army, but New Look planning visualized a reduction of the Army from its post-Korean War strength of 1,540,000 persons and 19 divisions to a strength of approximately 1,000,000 persons and such number of divisions as could be effectively manned with this strength by the end of fiscal year 1957. Ridgway viewed the reduction of the Army by one-third in some 30 months as "too fast and too drastic."[135] Alarmed by events in Asia and Europe in April 1954, Secretary Wilson indicated that a "soul-searching review" of specific policies, including the impending reduction of the Army from 19 to 17 divisions, was being undertaken. Actually the fiscal year 1955 budget originally estimated that the Army would be cut to 1,102,000 persons by 30 June 1955, but the conflict in Indochina caused the retention of a personnel cushion. The Formosa Straits crisis of early 1955 delayed the planned reduction a little longer. Late in 1954 the Eisenhower administration sought to attain a balanced national budget in fiscal year 1956 by accomplishing military force reductions previously planned for fiscal year 1957. Secretary Wilson took the matter to President Eisenhower, with the Joint Chiefs present to argue their cases. According to Wilson, Ridgway wanted the Army to have "a much bigger force." The president authorized 35,000 more persons for the services; the Joint Chiefs divided the increment, giving the Army 25,000, the Navy 7,000, and the Marines 3,000.[136]

Unlike the Army, the Navy had no difficulty implementing the New Look. As early as November 1953, Rear Adm Arleigh A. Burke, who would become the chief of naval operations in June 1955, pointed out that the armed services needed a new strategic concept to meet the divergent requirements of "preparation for vast retaliatory and counteroffensive blows of global war and of preparation for the more likely lesser military actions short of global war." Burke visualized naval and air forces capable of coping with special situations and the maintenance of "strategic reserve ground forces—not large—but in a high degree of combat readiness—so trained—constituted and equipped—that they can move immediately into any area to support Allied forces in those military actions which cannot be handled solely by local forces supported by our Naval and Air Force."[137] The Navy was alerted early in 1954 during the Indochina crisis; its aircraft carriers provided a backdrop of strength early in 1955 when the Chinese Communists brought pressure to bear against Quemoy and Matsu.[138] In their force requirements for fiscal year 1956, the Joint Chiefs of Staff raised the Navy's requirement for attack aircraft carriers from 14 to 15 without, as General Twining noted, specifying what kind of carriers they would be or how large. Early in 1956 Admirals Radford and Burke both pointed out that aircraft carriers could project air power into areas of the world where the United States had no airfields.[139] While Navy officers seldom failed to stress the versatility of sea power in any type of war, the Navy's concern was manifestly most intense on the problem of a general war. In June 1956 Admiral Burke told the Symington committee that he did not believe that the Soviet leaders would initiate general war, but he hastened to add: "At the same time, you can never count for sure on that. There may be an insane man who can persuade his people to follow him."[140] Admiral Burke also found it difficult to determine just what amount of offensive air capability might be necessary to deter Russia from general war.[141]

In assessing Air Force requirements under the New Look, General Twining disagreed with those persons "who profess to believe that the defense of the free world can be deployed against atomic attack and at the same time concentrated to meet a World War II type of offensive.... In the past it has been difficult enough to impose a new strategy on top of an old strategy. To impose now the old strategy on top of the new is out of the question."[142] At the May 1954 Air Force Commanders' Conference, however, General Weyland expressed the belief that the Communists would never start a brushfire war in an area where the United States was prepared to conduct effective combat operations, particularly tactical air operations. Pointing out that the US Air Forces in Europe and the Far East Air Forces were both committed to existing areas of responsibility, Weyland suggested that the Tactical Air Command be authorized to organize and maintain a highly mobile tactical air force in the United States that could be deployed to meet contingencies anywhere in the world.[143] Both Twining and White agreed that Weyland's proposal had considerable merit. However, when Weyland formally requested authority on 25 June to activate an additional tactical air force headquarters, the Air Staff proved reluctant to approve it. To attain 137 combat wings by 30 June 1957, the Air Force was committed to reduce personnel assigned to overhead purposes.[144]

While General Weyland had originated the idea of a mobile tactical air force as a deterrent to local wars, Tactical Air Command officers believed that an Air War College Graduate Study Group thesis by Col Richard P. Klocko entitled "Air Power in Limited Military Actions" may well have influenced the Air Staff's ultimate acceptance of the new concept. Completed in August 1954, Klocko's thesis was said to have served "as a sort of a tactical air 'bible' at Headquarters USAF."[145] In his study Klocko assumed that in a period of atomic equilibrium the deterrent effect of atomic power would apply to both opposing coalitions and that the world would be faced with a series of limited military actions. He defined these actions as "any employment of military forces which fall short of launching the nuclear atomic air retaliation against the USSR." He believed that the New Look had failed in Indochina as a result of political default rather than flaws in military capabilities or concepts. In Indochina the United States had announced in advance that the conflict might be extended, and this "ultimatum" had caused world opinion to fear worldwide nuclear war. A better course of action would have been to have presented the Reds with a *fait accompli*. "The United States," he urged on the basis of this thinking, "should consistently and ardently advocate that the massive retaliatory power policy in general terms and the intent to use it if necessary should be internationally understood as a deterrent to limited aggressions and to general use. In any specific situation, however, the time, the place, and the means of applying this power should never be suggested or announced until the actual operation reveals them."[146]

Given the maintenance of massive retaliatory power and the condition of atomic equilibrium, Klocko urged that the United States seek to develop political and military stability in free world countries around the Communist perimeter. Since the Soviet Union was the only air adversary who could seriously threaten free world aerial operations and since any extended involvement with Soviet air power would inevitably expand the local conflict, Klocko thought that friendly air superiority could be assumed in limited actions, which would mean that both land-based tactical air units and aircraft carriers could be freely employed in limited air actions. Sea-based air power promised to circumvent awkward international questions regarding foreign base rights. The effectiveness of air power in limited military actions would vary directly with the degree of organization and centralization of the hostile forces. Klocko pointed out that limited air operations could take many forms such as transportation, destruction, neutralization, blockade, or interdiction. All forms of military forces ultimately might be useful in limited operations; the essential factor was air power's uniquely rapid ability to deploy to an area of crisis. However, a lack of prior funding had hindered postwar deployments of air power to crisis areas; to minimize such a cause of delay, Klocko proposed that the Air Force should establish and fund a "Ready Air Fleet" within the Tactical Air Command. Based in the United States this ready air fleet would be an integrated self-supporting organization that could immediately deploy to a crisis area and operate until such time as normal operational forces could be moved into the area to augment or replace it.[147]

After extended correspondence, the Air Force permitted the Tactical Air Command to activate the Nineteenth Air Force as an operational headquarters at Foster AFB, Texas, on 8 July 1955.[148] In announcing the establishment of what would be called the Composite Air Strike Force, General White pointed out that the Tactical Air Command's nuclear strike and aerial-refueling capabilities had brought a "new look" to tactical air forces. "To meet the threat of lesser wars," he said, "our tactical air forces can provide an increasingly effective deterrent."[149] During 1955 and 1956 General Weyland frequently stated his belief that the free world faced an era of periphery or brushfire wars that would have to be deterred or won with tactical air forces.[150] In May 1956 he told the Symington committee that the United States "must have adequate tactical air forces in being that are capable of serving as a deterrent to the brushfire type of war just as SAC is the main deterrent to a global war."[151] Presenting his "Concept for Employment of Tactical Air Worldwide" to the Air Staff at about this same time, Weyland argued:

> It is becoming increasingly clear that any armed conflict which may occur in the foreseeable future will most probably be of the limited or local variety. The United States must develop an effective deterrent to such local wars and must be able to support the indigenous forces of friendly countries if such a war does occur. SAC and ADC are dedicated as major war deterrents and their postures and concepts are limited to major war situations. SAC forces are not suited for and cannot cope with the essentially tactical air aspects of local wars. Nor should they become seriously involved in a local war, since they would jeopardize their effect as a deterrent to major war. Consequently, tactical air power must be the primary deterrent to local or limited war. Additionally, it must be the full-fledged but more economical element of our offensive air power as a general war deterrent.[152]

In September 1956 Brig Gen Henry P. Viccellio, commander of the Nineteenth Air Force, deployed Mobile Baker — a token composite air strike force consisting of one squadron of F-100C day-fighters, one squadron of F-84F fighter-bombers, a flight of B-66 tactical bombers, and a flight of RF-84F reconnaissance aircraft — from bases in the United States to Europe. Employing in-flight refueling, the F-100s made the Atlantic crossing in 4 hours and 55 minutes. After arriving in Europe, the atomic-capable strike aircraft participated in an operational exercise. "As SAC is a deterrent to major war," wrote General Viccellio, "so will the Composite Air Strike Force be a deterrent to limited war."[153]

Other Air Force leaders held somewhat different views on the likelihood of limited war. In response to a journalist's question posed to him in December 1955 as to whether air power could prevent small wars, General LeMay observed: "We believe that, by working hard and maintaining our efficiency at the highest possible standards, that is the best thing we can do to assure [that] wars large or small will not happen. . . . I think that most wars are started when one nation thinks it could beat the other one. If they didn't think they were going to win, they certainly would never start it."[154] LeMay developed his thought more fully in an article published in September 1956 in which he defined the decision phase of a future war as the preparation of combat ready air atomic forces in a time of nominal peace. "Only a foolhardy nation," he continued,

> would ever base its power strategy upon the doubtful assumption that what it started as localized conflict would remain localized. The only condition under which this assumption could apply would be for one nation to be absolutely and positively guaranteed that the other lacked either resolution or intelligence. For if a nation is determined to survive and preserve its way of life, it must avoid risk of extinction, regardless of how that extinction might be brought about and if a nation is intelligent, it must realize that objectives can be won just as surely in piecemeal advances as by one all-out blow. Therefore, combine both intelligence and resolution in a nation, and you have a nation against whom you dare not instigate limited actions unless you are ready to accept the possible consequences of all-out war. . . . This leads us back to where we started. An enemy cannot start a shooting war unless he has already won the decision phase, and he dare not, in the face of strength, resolution, and intelligence on our part, start a so-called "limited action" unless he is in the same position.[155]

As late as mid-1956 General Twining appeared to be basing his thoughts on limited war on the assumption that the United States would continue to possess strategic forces superior to those of the Soviets. "It is conceivable," he said in June 1956, "that if the aggressor rationalizes that our retaliatory force would make it impossible or too costly for him to win a general war he might then choose the alternate of peripheral or small wars." Under these circumstances tactical air forces coupled with Army and Navy forces would provide "a powerful deterrent against peripheral war."[156] Intelligence information arriving in the United States during 1956, however, indicated that the Soviet Union was giving little attention to the preparation of forces for limited wars but was instead bending every effort to develop long-range air and rocket forces, which in a few years might well exceed the strength of the strategic forces of the United States. At the height of the Suez Canal crisis, in early November 1956, the Soviets threatened to use nuclear-armed intermediate range ballistic missiles against France and Britain. Earlier Air Force thinking about limited war had assumed that Soviet forces would not be directly employed in peripheral undertakings. By November 1956, however, Air Force planners could visualize a local war in which "the opposing side will have the full backing of the USSR, with, actually or potentially, very large forces equipped with the most modern weapons, and with the capability of using atomic weapons."[157] "The threat of limited war has increased," Twining stated in February 1957, "because the Soviets have acquired a greater capability to wage general war, and can, therefore, undertake limited aggression with less fear of total retaliation."[158]

In several speeches delivered during October 1956, Air Force Secretary Donald Quarles professed to find it hard to understand how the United States could successfully deter general war without also being able to deter or win little wars. "It seems logical," he said, "if we have the strength required for global war we could handle any threat of lesser magnitude.... From now on, potential aggressors must reckon with the air-atomic power which can be brought to bear immediately in whatever strength, and against whatever targets, may be necessary to make such an attack completely unprofitable to the aggressor."[159] In February 1957 General Twining pointed out that all of the armed forces of the United States could be called upon to provide forces to resist local aggression and to end it quickly before it could spread. "If we wanted to," he added, "we could even use part of the strategic force for jobs like that. It would of course depend upon the area, and the job to be done."[160] Accepting the position that the Air Force as a whole rather than any special part of it would deter or win small wars, Maj Gen John D. Cary, Air Force director of plans, stated in March 1957 that "the Air Force believes that local war is best prevented by the same means as general war."[161] The Air Force, thus, recognized that tactical air forces deployed in overseas theaters might well be the first military force that could be brought to bear on an aggressor and that tactical air forces were cheaper than strategic air forces on a wing-for-wing basis. In any allocation of scarce resources between strategic and tactical air forces, however, the Air Force had to admit that tactical air forces had three disadvantages: tactical air units would be vulnerable because of their proximity to the enemy; the limited range of tactical aircraft would curtail the number of targets they could be programmed against and would hamper their global mobility; and tactical air forces (except for the tactical Matador missile) would lack appreciable all-weather strike capabilities.[162]

Emergence of Flexible Response as a Strategy

When Army leaders began to convert their frame of reference from general to limited war during 1954, they found some comfort in the writings of "unofficial critics of national defense." Gen Maxwell D. Taylor stated that George F. Kennan's book *The Realities of American Foreign Policy* and Bernard Brodie's article "Unlimited Weapons and Limited War" constituted the "first public questioning of the validity of the New Look policy of Massive Retaliation."[163] A new version of Army Field Manual 100-5 published in September 1954 gave predominant attention to the Army's role in a general war, but also pointed to the probability that political considerations would prevent the use of maximum air power in limited aggressions. "The continuing possibility of such limited wars," the manual stated, "requires the maintenance in being of Army forces capable of immediate commitment and fully organized, trained, and equipped for combat, and at the same time possessing a capability of strategic mobility."[164]

The Army's claim for a greater strength appeared to be supported in January 1955 when the National Security Council completed its first comprehensive review of the New Look strategy. The NSC policy paper was described as giving recognition "for the first time to the possibility of a condition of mutual deterrence and the importance in such a period for the United States to have versatile, ready forces to cope with limited aggression."[165] President Eisenhower, however, wished to rely on free world defense forces. "To provide for meeting lesser hostile action—such as local aggression not broadened by the intervention of a major aggressor's forces—growing reliance," Eisenhower wrote on 5 January 1955, "can be placed upon the forces now being built and strengthened in many areas of the free world. But because this reliance cannot be complete, and because our own vital interests, collective security and pledged faith might well be involved, there remain certain contingencies for which the United States should be ready with mobile forces to help indigenous troops deter local aggression, direct or indirect."[166]

Under the Department of Defense budget program for fiscal year 1956 submitted to Congress in January 1955, the Army would be expected to reduce its active duty strength to approximately 1,027,000 persons and could thus support 15 combat and 3 training divisions and 136 antiaircraft battalions.[167] However, the Department of Defense and the Joint Chiefs of Staff had encouraged each service to maintain the maximum combat force possible within approved manpower ceilings, and General Ridgway had preferred to increase Army combat units even though there had been a loss in personnel. On 30 June 1955 the Army would thus possess 20 divisions, 122 antiaircraft battalions, and 6 regimental combat teams. One of the divisions was slated for early inactivation; Ridgway reported that five divisions were training organizations and that two divisions located in Alaska and Panama were "static divisions." According to Ridgway, the Army thus had something in the neighborhood of 13 combat-ready divisions, and of this total only four or five divisions that were located in the United States and Hawaii were combat ready and could be counted as strategic reserve divisions. Ridgway was critical of the Army's "paper" strength and he pointed out that the four or five strategic reserve divisions had very little mobility in the form of airlift or sealift.[168]

In justifying the Army program early in 1955, Ridgway continued to emphasize the role of Army forces in general war. "I think," he told congressmen, "the part of prudence and wisdom dictates that the United States be prepared to win a long war if we get involved in it. That means substantial use of the decisive element in any war of the past, which has been the man on the ground, who has a capability for progressively applying force, who has the capability that no other armed service has, that of seizing, occupying, and retaining ground taken."[169] Although Ridgway thus continued to visualize the Army's primary role as a force in general war, his valedictory criticism of the national defense strategy submitted to Secretary Wilson in a formal memorandum on 27 June 1955 emphasized the Army's role in limited war. Sometime between 1958 and 1962, Ridgway urged, the Soviets would possess a nuclear capability sufficient in size to inflict critical damage on the United States, and they would also have effected greatly improved air defense measures against American nuclear bombers. In this period US nuclear air superiority would have lost its significance. Soviet strategy would be directed toward employments that would preclude the use of nuclear weapons on a worldwide basis. Free world military forces, except in Western Europe, were isolated detachments around the Soviet periphery. While US military policy statements referred to a mobile-ready force, Ridgway bluntly charged that "no adequate mobile-ready force now is in being and the actual creation of such a force must compete with increasingly emphasized nuclear-air requirements." Ridgway concluded, *"It is my view that the commitments which the United States has pledged create a positive requirement for an immediately available joint military force of hard hitting character in which the versatility of the whole is emphasized and the preponderance of any one part is de-emphasized."*[170] (Emphasis in original.)

Even before he had been selected to succeed Ridgway as Army chief of staff, Gen Maxwell D. Taylor felt that the Army had been lagging behind in the national defense effort. Struck by what he believed to be a "departure from the dogma of Massive Retaliation" in the National Security Council guidance paper of January 1955, Taylor, shortly after becoming Army chief of staff on 1 July 1955, presented to his staff a new program that he referred to as a "new strategy of Flexible Response." Taylor reasoned that in the approaching era of atomic plenty the Communists will probably be inclined to expand their tactics of subversion and limited aggression." He thought that the military requirements of the United States would be to maintain military technological superiority; a deterrent atomic delivery system capable of retaliation; an effective continental defense system; adequate Army, Navy, and Air Force units capable of intervening in local aggressions; and other ready Army, Navy, and Air Force elements that could reinforce forces deployed abroad in general war or that would intervene in local aggressions. Taylor also called for the development of indigenous defense forces, reserve forces in the United States, stockpiles of material to meet war requirements until wartime production became adequate, and a war production, mobilization, and training base to support an atomic general war. "The acceptance of such priorities of effort," he subsequently observed, "would have resulted in added attention to so-called limited-war forces and would have placed them in virtually equal priority with the atomic deterrent forces."[171]

The suggested strategy of flexible response was not acceptable to Secretary Wilson, who considered that the free world had to rely on its collective strength "not only to beat back any local aggression but to deter the aggressor from broadening the conflict into global war." Wilson also believed that the "problem of deterring small wars cannot be considered separately from the problem of deterring war generally" and that the "capability to deter large wars also serves to deter small wars."[172] Since there had been no apparent change in the international situation and since the original New Look program could achieve stabilized combat forces by fiscal year 1957, Wilson announced in October 1955 that there would be no major change in the level of military spending or the size of the military force in the fiscal year 1957 budget. For fiscal year 1957 the Army was thus budgeted for a force of 19 divisions, 10 regimental combat teams, and 144 antiaircraft battalions.[173]

Appearing before the House Appropriations Subcommittee in February 1956, General Taylor accepted the budgeted force level for the Army for fiscal year 1957 but suggested that a "unrestricted nuclear war will be a total disaster for all participants." He accordingly urged that the United States must develop "tridimensional" strength—on the ground, in the air, and on the sea. "I feel," he said, "that we have made a great deal of progress in developing an atomic air deterrent. I think now that our program needs to be bent a little—perhaps more than a little—in order to focus attention on the danger of the small war which seems to me to be coming to the forefront all the time as the greatest danger we are facing." Taylor discounted the assumption that a general war would begin with all-out nuclear attacks. "It seems more likely," he continued, "that a combat situation might be created anyplace around the globe, smoulder for a while with local combat only occurring, and then widening by other factors to the point that the decision is taken—to go for keeps." "Our Army mission," he said, "is to destroy an enemy on the ground anyplace, anywhere." "There is no reason to say," he urged, "that we are hopelessly out-numbered and that our defense on the ground must be obtained indirectly from atomic superiority in the air. I am convinced that our Army, equipped with the weapons which we are now developing and supported by well-trained allies, can maintain deterrent strength on the ground sufficient to hold the Communist armies in check." In 44 countries around the world the United States was assisting its allies in developing more than 200 divisions. In addition to this force, Taylor estimated that an optimum US Army strength based on purely military considerations would be "around 1.5 million men with an active combat force of about 28 divisions."[174]

The Army's new concept of limited war was presented to the public at an inopportune time. Believing that no useful purpose would be attained by questioning national strategy, the State Department looked with disfavor on a draft article that General Taylor proposed to publish in *Foreign Affairs* spotlighting nuclear stalemate and the likelihood of limited Soviet aggressions. The Soviets were clearly building atomic forces rather than ground strength for limited aggressions; they announced a major reduction of 640,000 men in their military force in August 1955 and another cut of 1,200,000 men in May 1956.[175] Charged by Secretary Wilson to examine future military requirements for the three years following fiscal year 1957, the Joint Chiefs of Staff met in seclusion at Ramey AFB, Puerto Rico, from 3–9 March 1956. General Taylor introduced his paper calling for the development of flexible response; he later recorded that his colleagues "read this Army study politely and then quietly put it aside." Again, according to Taylor, the Joint Chiefs finally recommended that military programs should continue at approximately current levels for the three years after mid-1957. To maintain such force levels and still afford the costs of new equipment, the national defense budget would have to be raised from some $34 billion to as much as $38 to $40 billion in the years up to 1960. After reviewing the Joint Chiefs' recommendations, Secretary Wilson estimated that costs of national defense would probably exceed the $40 billion mark.[176] In a new assessment of the role of NATO published in May 1956, Air Marshal Slessor suggested that the function of ground troops in Europe would be to serve as a token of national determination, like a trip-wire or a plate-glass window which if disturbed would unleash thermonuclear retaliation.[177]

Even though Senator Symington's committee had been established to examine the charge that the development of American air power was lagging, Army spokesmen used this forum to develop the case for flexible response. Appearing before the Symington committee in May 1956, a team of officers headed by Lt Gen James M. Gavin, the Army's chief of research and development, discussed the Army's requirements for missiles and aircraft. "The Department of the Army's mission," Gavin explained, "is, by its evident readiness at all times, to be ready to win in a general war. At the same time it must, by virtue of its high state of readiness in terms of both modernization and mobility, deter small wars or deter any aggressor who would attempt to achieve a limited objective through limited military action. If a small war does occur, we must win such a war for failure to win would in itself bring on a general war." Gavin believed that the Russians, in the event that they decided to venture the risk of a general war to achieve an objective, "would start on the basis of a limited objective to put themselves in a better position, and perhaps ultimately cause enough deterioration of our position to where they could win without risking any attack upon the USSR." He repeated the Army position "that we are far more likely to be involved in a peripheral war than in a general war."[178]

The new concept that limited war was a major threat, together with the impending development of Army antiaircraft missiles, led General Gavin to advance the idea that "in the missile era the control of the land will be decisive." By controlling the land, military forces would possess the launching platforms necessary to control the air. Gavin argued that air superiority was "one of the most misunderstood terms" in the military vocabulary. "When first it came into use," he said,

> it was presumed that it was a condition of affairs in a battle area that would enable one side to gain complete moral and physical superiority over the other. We learned in World War II that it was a fleeting stage of affairs indeed and while one side could enjoy complete air superiority such as we presume the allies did in the winter of 1944–1945, from time to time the enemy could strike suddenly and achieve in a local area a surprising degree of air superiority with a great posture of resources on his side.... With the performance of aircraft as we now see them coming along, that is where they fly at higher speeds and much greater turning radius, air superiority to us is going to be something quite different we believe than anything we have seen in the past.... It does not seem possible to control the land areas by merely flying over them with the type aircraft and type defenses that will be related to each other in the future.... So we do not think that the term "air superiority" as it was applied in 1945 could well be applied to the future.

Gavin also stated that surface-to-air fire in World War II and in the Korean conflict had been a principal destroyer of aircraft, and he noted that the Army's new family of "very effective" surface-to-air Nike missiles promised to increase aircraft kills at the same time that the increasing speeds of aircraft reduced the effectiveness of air-to-air combat. "We see emerging a pattern," Gavin said, "that suggests clearly that control of land areas will be decisive."[179]

Other Army officers—including Maj Gen Earle G. Wheeler, the Army's director of plans, and Maj Gen Hamilton H. Howze, director of Army aviation—discussed concepts of future land warfare, which would be characterized by wide dispersal of units and installations, ground and air mobility, firepower of increased range and lethality, and efficient and reliable communications. The Army intended to develop its own organic capability for air movements of Army combat units within the combat zone; but its interest also extended to four elements of air power that were beyond its organic resources: control of the air in the battle area, long-range deployment, intratheater airlift, and aircraft firepower. To attain "a reasonable degree of freedom from attack by enemy aircraft," the Army intended to depend upon air and naval forces, together with its own organic antiaircraft weapons. To place fire on targets beyond the range of organic weapons, the Army "presently has a direct interest in firepower delivered from aircraft." "As we integrate rockets and missiles into the Army fire support system," the Army briefer added, "we are increasingly able to provide much of this needed fire support with our organic weapons." Although the Army of the future would have decreased requirements for air superiority and air support, it would have a greatly increased need for tactical and strategic air transport aviation. Admitting that what he was suggesting exceeded the Army's stated requirements to the Air Force, Gavin specified that the Army needed a capability simultaneously to airlift one division in each combat theater, one division in the United States, and one division from the United States to a combat theater. General Wheeler testified that Air Force tactical airlift capability was sufficient to lift about one division and that studies had shown that the combined military and civil reserve air fleets would not be able to meet the requirements of all services during the first 30 days of a general war.[180] Summing up the position that the Army would be the decisive military force of the future, Gavin stated: "First we must aggressively continue our development of our surface to air missile family and in continuation of this development program acquire an antimissile capability. Second, the role of the man who fights on land with modern equipment and supported by missiles will be of decisive importance in future combat. Our nation . . . must have both strategic and tactical mobility to enable it to fly its power when and where needed in support of our national policy and to the degree needed, and finally, we believe that in the missile era the control of the land will be decisive."[181]

When General Taylor appeared before the Symington committee in June 1956, he viewed reports that the Soviets were reducing their ground forces and increasing their strategic striking arms with cool skepticism. At this time Taylor repeated his plea that a "new atmosphere" was being created by "a condition of mutual deterrence, resulting in the decreased likelihood of deliberate general war, but the increased likelihood of the small war, the erosion of the free world." Stressing the Army's role as "an indispensable member of the service team," he recalled that "the primary function of the Army is the destruction of the enemy army, the primary function of the Air Force is to destroy enemy air power, and for the Navy to destroy enemy naval power."[182]

A "New" New Look Strategy

Although the Joint Chiefs of Staff recommended in March 1956 that the military force levels for the three years following fiscal year 1957 should continue approximately at the existing New Look levels, they estimated that the costs of modernizing these forces would raise the sum of the national defense budget to higher levels than the approximately $34 billion a year committed to defense during the first three years of the New Look. When the initial service requests for fiscal year 1958 were totaled, the estimated requirements to meet authorized defense programs came to $48.6 billion—an amount which President Eisenhower described as "unrealistic."[183] Recognizing that it would be impossible to secure such an expanded peacetime military budget, Admiral Radford and the Joint Chiefs of Staff began to plan a new strategy that would be popularly described as the "new" New Look. Believing that ground forces provided a visible rather than an actual deterrent to Soviet aggression, Admiral Radford favored a reduction in military manpower requirements. When he appeared before the Symington committee in June 1956, Radford speculated that a show of force, coupled with a threat of nuclear retaliation, would have deterred the Communists' aggression in Korea. "I am quite certain," he said, "if we had had one battalion or even a company, on the 38th parallel in Korea flying the American flag . . . I don't think the Communists would have attacked because they would have known that if they overran this one United States combat unit, certainly the United States would come in." Radford hastily added: "This visible deterrent may be obtained with very small forces."[184] In July 1956, Radford proposed to the Joint Chiefs of Staff that military manpower be cut, chiefly by reducing Army deployments in Europe and Asia to small atomic task forces and by greatly reducing Army strength in the United States. General Taylor strongly opposed these proposals at a Joint Chiefs of Staff meeting on 9 July. Within a week, Radford's position was published in substance in the *New York Times*. Adverse international reactions led to the withdrawal of Radford's plan; Secretary Wilson soon declared that no responsible person had ever advocated the reduction and withdrawal of forces contained in the so-called Radford plan.[185]

When General Twining appeared before the Symington committee in June 1956, he strongly urged that the United States commit itself to a new strategy that would place prime reliance on nuclear weapons for limited as well as general warfare. "We cannot afford," he said, "to keep in our Armed Force conventional forces for the old type of warfare plus those for atomic warfare. We have got to make up our minds that we have to go one way or the other." By accepting a new strategy built around the use of atomic weapons, the United States would be able to reduce its forces considerably. Such a new strategy, Twining stated, would represent "the only way we can provide the forces for the country within a reasonable standard of financing."[186] Twining's remarks brought into the public domain a fact that had troubled Air Force leaders for several years. While the original New Look guidance had emphasized nuclear weapons, it had been broad enough to require the maintenance of conventional air capabilities. The thesis that the armed forces must prepare for nuclear general war and nonnuclear local wars presented a serious dilemma. "By trying to be strong in both conventional and atomic capabilities ...," Col Robert C. Richardson argued, "we may become weak in both. At best, money and time will be wasted on obsolete weapon systems because of specious reasoning that atomic weapons will never be used."[187] Making strong allusions to "warped thinking," Brig Gen Dale Smith had written: "Air Forces provide the ideal weapons for limited war, but to be most effective, the political restrictions applied to a limited war must favor the air weapon rather than favor enemy manpower."[188] Writing in May 1956, General Weyland pointed out that tactical nuclear weapon capabilities were essential to the mobile tactical strike forces. "With nuclear weapons," Weyland thought, "these forces can be compact and yet be so effective as to provide the decisive balance of power." He emphasized that tactical nuclear weapons were not "weapons of mass destruction" and that they could be selectively employed against primary military targets. "We should never again, in my opinion," he concluded, "restrict our selection of weapons or target area as we did in Korea. The best weapon to do the job with the least loss of life should be selected for each target under consideration."[189]

In the summer of 1956 the Joint Chiefs of Staff rejected Radford's proposals for marked reductions in Army manpower.[190] Still the trend in military policy was toward reliance on nuclear weapon systems as the primary line of defense. On 31 August 1956 the Air Force deputy chief of staff for development directed the Air Research and Development Command to limit the future development of high explosive weapons to those required for employment from already operational aircraft.[191] "There is very little money in the budget we are proposing to you now," Secretary Wilson told congressmen in January 1957, "for the procurement of so-called conventional weapons ... we are depending on atomic weapons for the defense of the Nation." In further explanation of the new strategy, Wilson said: "Our basic defense policy is based on the use of such atomic weapons as would be militarily feasible and usable in a smaller war, if such a war is forced upon us." Radford reiterated the same thoughts: "Our whole military program," he stated in January, "is based on the use of atomic weapons in global war and in the use of atomic weapons in accordance with military necessity in situations short of global war." "We have said publicly that we are designing our forces to use atomic weapons," Radford repeated in March 1957. "That comes pretty close to saying we are going to use whatever weapons are necessary to defend our vital interests."[192]

In the hearings on the fiscal year 1958 defense budget, General Taylor and other Army spokesmen again presented the Army's strategy of flexible response. However, Congress appeared to be more strongly concerned with a need to hold spending in check to avoid raising statutory national debt limits and displayed more interest in the Symington committee's finding that the US strategic striking force was "declining relatively as against the steadily growing striking capacity of the Soviets" than in its other recommendation that the United States should be prepared for both limited and unlimited war.[193] Secretary Wilson already had stated his opinion that the Air Force structure appeared to provide "adequate airborne lift in the light of currently approved strategic concepts."[194] In February 1957, moreover, General Taylor informed Symington that the combination of active and reserve tactical airlift was "considered to be adequate for the Army's needs at this time."[195] In an added rebuff to the Army's requirements for strategic mobility, Admiral Radford sponsored a special airlift briefing for the House Committee on Appropriations that demonstrated that 1,800 C-124s would be required to move an Army division with its impedimenta and 30-days' supplies in a 24-hour period. Even if aircraft were available, such a movement could not be accomplished because of a lack of enough airfields. "I think," Radford summarized, "there are people in the Army who honestly feel that it should be possible to move Army units by air . . . to any place in the world. I say that people who then express the feeling that we do not have [sufficient airlift] capability do not understand the magnitude of the problem of moving by air."[196]

According to Secretary Wilson, President Eisenhower had reduced the service requests for fiscal year 1958 appropriations because he sensed that budget-cutting was in the wind. The military budget got severe handling in Congress. As Wilson remarked, "Obviously the people in the country are in no mood to spend more dollars."[197] Instead of the $38.4 billion budget requested by Eisenhower, Congress was going to vote only $35.4 billion in new appropriations for fiscal year 1958.[198] Even though it was obvious that Congress would not vote the amount of money requested for fiscal 1958, President Eisenhower ruled in the summer of 1957 that the defense budget for fiscal year 1959 would again be held to a $38-billion ceiling.[199] Faced with the decision that Eisenhower wished a stability of expenditures and that the National Security Council endorsed increased dependence upon atomic weapons, Secretary Wilson, apparently with the assistance of Deputy Secretary Donald Quarles and Admiral Radford, attempted to cut the Gordian knot by proposing reductions of military manpower to compensate for the rising cost of military equipment. Presented at a meeting of the National Security Council on 25 July 1957, the Wilson-Radford plan called for holding defense expenditures at approximately $38 billion in the period 1959–61 by reducing overall military manpower. All of the services would reduce their forces, but the Army would expect to drop from 15 to 11 divisions in the period. Forewarned of the Wilson-Radford plan, Army Secretary Wilber Brucker and General Taylor spoke out strongly in the meeting against what they described as a preparation for general atomic war and the neglect of lesser wars in which big weapons could not be used. Wilson was said to have remarked in reply that the national policy was to "maximize air power and minimize the foot soldier," and, as Taylor recalled, there "seemed to be a tacit agreement that this was a correct if colloquial statement of the military strategy being pursued by the United States."[200] Although the plan was never specifically approved or disapproved, it became the point of departure for the Department of Defense budget for fiscal year 1959. The Army was instructed to plan for an end strength of 900,000 men and 15 divisions in fiscal year 1958 and 850,000 men and 14 divisions in fiscal year 1959.[201]

Nuclear Weapons and Limited Wars

As it happened the strategy of what was called the new New Look was put together in the United States during 1956–57, a period of growing Soviet strategic challenge and relatively fixed United States defense budgets. As has been seen, the Air Force already was perfecting its position that the total military capability that deterred general war also would serve to deter or to win limited wars. However, Lt Gen Thomas S. Power, commander of the Air Research and Development Command, was troubled about the Air Force's capabilities to participate in cold war and limited war crises. On 10 December, Power wrote Twining suggesting that an Air Force cold war symposium should be held in order to study new requirements for doctrine, equipment, techniques, and systems necessary for limited military operations. Power was especially concerned about the effectiveness of Air Force weapons and tactics in a small war in which the use of nuclear weapons might be forbidden.[202]

On a call from General Twining, Air Force commanders assembled at the Pentagon on 9 April 1957 for a Cold War Conference. At this session the commanders resolved that the problem of local war would require an additional conference later in the summer. General White, nevertheless, considered that the discussions were marked by an agreement that the Air Force should seek to explain to the public that there was a vast difference between megaton thermonuclear weapons and small tactical atomic weapons and that it should seek to make a "continued and increased effort to eliminate the high explosive requirement from the national policy." According to White the conference agreed that the Air Force should measure and retain the high-explosive capability of thermonuclear weapons, but should not increase that capability, and should eliminate those weapons when the national policy permitted.[203] Speaking for the Air Research and Development Command, Lt Gen Samuel E. Anderson thought that it would be inconsistent to continue to plan to use conventional weapons in view of the types and numbers of aircraft that were operational and projected; the speeds, bombing accuracies, and guidance systems that these planes would possess; and the hardening of enemy targets. Anderson recognized that nuclear weapons were frowned on in a time of peace, but he predicted that they would be needed and relied on once a war broke out.[204]

Already on the public record with a statement that "we must continue to maintain a capability for the use of conventional weapons, thus rounding out our ability to deal with any contingency which might arise,"[205] General Weyland dissented from the findings of the Air Force Cold War Conference. Weyland wrote General White that if he were willing to think solely as an Air Force officer he could join in a policy of replacing conventional weapons with nuclear weapons because it would make the Air Force job so much easier, but as an individual charged with upholding national policy Weyland could not accept a course of action that could eventually undermine national policy. "I can visualize local war situations arising," he wrote,

> where the threat of only atomic retaliation would severely prescribe the US bargaining position at the conference table and turn the mass of human opinion against us; whereas possessing a conventional retaliation, could place world opinion on our side. . . . I do not foster a large and expensive program, but rather a modest program designed to meet the limited requirements of a local war and the aircraft we visualize now and in the future. I, therefore, believe our policy must be to continue retention and modernization of a conventional capability until such time as small atomic weapons, pinpoint delivery systems and world education reach the point of reliability and acceptance so as to permit elimination of conventional weapons, yet retain the proper environment in which our national policy can thrive and be effective.

Weyland also took issue with the Strategic Air Command's position that it could fight a local war without detriment to its general war posture. "I don't think any unbiased Air Force officer," he wrote, "visualizes B-52s finding and dropping weapons on a small guerrilla troop concentration in the jungles of Indo-China — or some other area of concern in the local war problem. I not only think it illogical, but feel that it would be a pure malemployment of such an expensive force when we can do the job better and more economically with tactical air forces."[206]

At the same time that the major Air Force commanders were failing to reach complete agreement about a sole reliance on nuclear weapons, Secretary Dulles was emphasizing the importance of free world defense forces in an address before the annual luncheon of the Associated Press on 22 April. Placing emphasis on collective defense, Dulles noted: "It is agreed that the primary task is to deter war. . . . It is also agreed that the principal deterrent to aggressive war is mobile retaliatory power. . . . It is also agreed that it would be imprudent to risk everything on one single aspect of military power. There must be land, sea, and air forces for local action and for a defense which will give mobile striking power the chance to do its work."[207] At a news conference on 16 July, Dulles spoke of a need for making the NATO allies less dependent upon the United States and revealed that the United States was studying ways whereby "through perhaps a NATO stockpile of weapons and various arrangements of that sort, there can be assurances to our allies that, if they are attacked, if war comes, they will not then be in the position of suppliants, as far as we are concerned, for the use of atomic weapons."[208] On the basis of the 22 April address, General Taylor hoped that Dulles might support the Army in the discussions on 25 July before the National Security Council. Taylor reported, however, that Dulles remained silent and that the State Department representatives had an "attitude of curious detachment." "It was," he recalled, "as if they felt that conflicts in the Pentagon were what the Japanese call 'a fire on the other side of the river.'"[209]

A few weeks after becoming Air Force chief of staff, General White assembled the Air Force commanders in Washington on 27 August to discuss and mature an

Air Force position on local wars, which White subsequently approved. This position stated that the Air Force requirements in any local war situation could be met with forces and resources provided for general war purposes; that local war operations could be supported from available stocks and facilities, provided some minimum calculated risks were assumed; that a local war could spread into a general war and that failure to make such an assumption could bring about such an expansion; and that the almost infinite variety of possible local war contingencies required the tailoring of effort in the light of specific situations and resultant national objectives. The position paper noted that the Air Force possessed varied forces with adequate backup able to meet many likely local war situations. These forces included the Tactical Air Command, which was prepared to redeploy rapidly by air to participate in local wars with little advance notice, and the Strategic Air Command, which was prepared to participate in local war situations from general war positions to an extent not appreciably affecting its general war posture. These forces were under the control of the Air Force chief of staff and should so remain when used in a local war situation. The composition of air forces initially involved in a local war would generally be dictated by the situation but would consist of the best forces that could be made available at the earliest time.[210]

In an address to the USAF Scientific Advisory Board on 4 December, General White elaborated on the Air Force position and philosophy on local wars. He noted that the national policy toward local wars was to deter such conflicts, but failing that to cope with them successfully. The military contribution to deterrence hinged on three generally agreed essentials: adequate armed force, manifest determination to use the force, and a potential aggressor's belief that the force and determination existed. "It is the Air Force view," White said, "that just as nuclear delivery capability constitutes a deterrent to general war, so can this total firepower deter local war. The right measure of this total firepower can, in turn, resolve local conflict if we fail to deter the aggression. . . . We *deter* with our total capability, including all lessor facets thereof; we will elect *to use* that portion required and best suited to the resolution of the particular conflict." The policy of any nation, especially in the nuclear age, demanded that if conflict must be waged it would be done in a manner as to involve the least risk of aggravating the conflict into general war. This approach required the rapid and resolute application of force, neither too little nor too much. "Those principles," White thought, "call for a military capability, *within* (and not separate from as in addition to) total US forces, which is instantly ready, flexible, and selective including nuclear firepower." He emphasized that the application of force would vary. The Strategic Air Command certainly would not be unleashed to handle minor disputes, but it could dispatch aircraft to warn, repulse, or destroy aggressor forces in significant local conflicts. "If the conflict is so small as to obviate the need for the balancing power of nuclear weapons," he continued, "then the United States certainly has the capability to handle the conflict." General White urged that it would be impossible to preconceive and tailor a force that would be appropriate to the many types of limited conflict that could occur: it would be much wiser to select and adapt portions of the joint and allied general war capabilities and use them as political requirements might dictate at the time.[211] Appearing before the Senate Preparedness Investigating Subcommittee on 17 December, General White acknowledged that local war might be said to be the primary job of the Tactical Air Command, but he considered that the Strategic Air Command could "because of its long range and its flexibility, without moving from its general war positions, bring to bear its very great forces in a local war situation."[212]

Even though he had earlier questioned some of the Air Force policies regarding local war, General Weyland supported the new Air Force position in major addresses delivered before the American Ordnance Association in November and the USAF Scientific Advisory Board in December. Weyland reminded his audiences that it would be very difficult to forecast where a local war might occur or who the enemy might be. Although its role was primarily to deter general war, the Strategic Air Command could quickly assist in a local war situation; the theater air forces and the Tactical Air Command were specifically designed and trained for the wide variety of tasks to be expected in local wars. "Generally speaking," Weyland suggested, "a friendly country which is a possible target for local aggressions has a capability for effective ground fighting, but few have an appreciable tactical air capability. If they know they will be supported quickly, they may be depended upon to fight in defense of their own country. US Tactical Air can provide the decisive balance of power in time to be effective."[213] Explaining the concept that the Strategic Air Command could deter local war, General LeMay, who had become Air Force vice chief of staff, said to the Senate Preparedness Investigating Subcommittee: "I do not believe we can afford to maintain separate weapon systems for various types of arguments that we might get into with our neighbors in the world. I think we are going to have to build for the worst cases, and then use them for all others.... We have been into some minor skirmishes because we did not make it clear that we would use our full power as necessary."[214] Even more of the meaning of the Air Force position on nuclear weapons and limited wars was revealed by Maj Gen James H. Walsh, director of Air Force intelligence. "The military objectives in a limited action," Walsh said,

> would be, first, to gain air control and then to cripple the enemy military force. This objective really does not depend on nuclear weapons for its basic validity, but we have come to respect the decisiveness and effectiveness inherent in nuclear firepower, principally because of its great economy in sorties.... In this fast-moving age we no longer can build non-nuclear forces at the expense of our atomic strike and defense units, and at the same time move boldly into the parameters of space at the tempo required for survival.... It is time that we recognize that we have crossed the nuclear Rubicon, and to consider the political and military advantages accruing therefrom. We cannot allow our national courage to collapse by resorting to very cautious and reticent objectives, which would penalize our ability to use nuclear weapons intelligently to deter and, if hostilities occur, to bring limited wars to a quick end. The agonizing memory of the drawn-out Korean conflict is too fresh to be forgotten.[215]

Increased Acceptance of Flexible Response

Although the United States remained committed to a policy of maximum reliance upon air power and nuclear weapons for both general and limited war contingencies, the Army's concept of flexible military response gained acceptance in influential circles. Writing on 23 September 1956, Prof Walt Whitman Rostow desired the United States to outstrip the Soviet Union in the nuclear arms race, but he also urged: "We must develop American capabilities in the general area of limited war. We must round out the spectrum of deterrence down to the level of guerrilla operations."[216] Many of the analysts at the Rand Corporation endorsed the strategy of limited war. Civilian scholars began producing a body of literature on the subject. William W. Kaufmann edited a volume of essays entitled *Military Policy and National Security,* published in 1956, that focused attention on limited war. Appearing in 1957, Prof Robert E. Osgood's *Limited War: The Challenge to American Strategy* argued that limited war had become the most likely form of armed conflict and that the United States should develop its military policy on this assumption.[217] Also published in 1957 was Prof Henry A. Kissinger's *Nuclear Weapons and Foreign Policy,* which became extremely influential at national policy levels. Although the volume reflected Kissinger's opinions, it had grown out of panel discussions initiated in 1954 by the Council of Foreign Relations. Under the chairmanship of Gordon Dean, the members of this panel included such active duty military officers as General Gavin and many of the civilians who had earlier participated in Project Vista. Believing that complete defense unification was out of the question, Kissinger called for the reorganization of the armed services into a strategic force and a tactical force, each to be combat ready for the accomplishment of separate missions in general or limited war. He believed that Western Europe could be successfully defended with tactical nuclear weapons; but he argued in great detail that the effective use of these weapons required new formations, force structures, and tactics.[218]

The new body of literature on the subject of limited war reinforced the Army position on strategy and may well have affected the thinking of Navy leaders. Although the Navy strongly supported strategic deterrence during the early years of the New Look, Navy leaders, following the retirement of Admiral Radford as chairman of the Joint Chiefs of Staff on 15 August 1957 and the appearance of the Soviet Sputnik on 4 October 1957, became strong advocates of preparedness for limited war. "Given a shield of mutual deterrence," Secretary of the Navy Thomas S. Gates announced in December, "power to prevent limited aggression and to win limited war becomes decisive." Admiral Burke, upon becoming the new chief of naval operations, argued that the United States by its emphasis on general nuclear war was in imminent danger of losing sight "of the necessity to maintain adequate strength to combat limited war in areas remote from this country—limited wars requiring United States control of the seas." He continued, "There is also a growing tendency to consider a nuclear war as being adequate to cope with limited war.

This is a fallacy. For a war to remain limited, there must be restraint in the selection of targets and in the use of nuclear weapons."[219]

Already having begun to believe that the tactical nuclear defenses of the North Atlantic Treaty Organization needed to be strengthened, Secretary Dulles appeared for a brief moment to be flirting with the concept that Europe might be the scene of a limited nuclear war. In an article prepared for publication in *Foreign Affairs*, which was released on 18 September 1957, Dulles expressed a belief that the development of small and clean nuclear weapons would benefit free world defenses. "In the future," he wrote,

> it may thus be feasible to place less reliance upon deterrence of vast retaliatory power. It may be possible to defend countries by nuclear weapons so mobile, or so placed, as to make military invasion with conventional forces a hazardous attempt.... Thus, in contrast to the 1950 decade, it may be that by the 1960 decade the nations which are around the Sino-Soviet perimeter can possess an effective defense against full-scale conventional attack and thus confront any aggressor with the choice between failing or himself initiating nuclear war against the defending country. Thus the tables may be turned, in the sense that, instead of those who are nonaggressive having to rely upon all-out nuclear retaliatory power for their protection, would-be aggressors will be unable to count on a successful conventional aggression but must themselves weigh the consequences of invoking nuclear war.[220]

In Europe where he had become supreme allied commander in November 1956, Gen Lauris Norstad wished to increase the effectiveness of the NATO shield forces by increasing their tactical nuclear capabilities, but he thought it very unlikely that any serious incident along the sensitive frontiers of NATO could remain limited.[221] As far as General White was concerned, local conflict in the NATO area would be "tantamount to general war."[222] At the NATO Heads of Government Conference on 16 December 1957, Secretary Dulles stated that the "major deterrent to Soviet aggression against NATO is the maintenance of a retaliatory power of such capacity as to convince the Soviets that such aggression would result in their own destruction." The United States, nevertheless, desired that the strength of the NATO ground, sea, and air shield forces should be increased. To this end the United States was prepared to make available intermediate range ballistic missiles to the NATO countries and to participate in a NATO atomic stockpile program, whereby nuclear warheads would be deployed under United States custody at agreed upon bases where they would be released to the NATO commanders for employment by nuclear capable forces at the outset of hostilities. NATO units would be equipped and trained to use the nuclear warheads when they were released to them at the appropriate time. The NATO Heads of Government Conference accepted the American proposals on 19 December 1957.[223] To effect the decisions, the NATO standing group in Washington worked out a plan known as MC 70 that required the creation of a minimum ground force of 30 divisions; these units were to be regarded as essentially nuclear forces. Some 22 of the NATO divisions were to be available by 1960–61, about halfway through the five years covered by the plan.[224] Even though this acceptance of the force goals of MC 70 as a planning objective promised to increase the effectiveness with which the shield forces could perform their mission, there would be no relaxation on the requirement for the strategic nuclear deterrent. After its regular meeting in Paris in December 1958, the North Atlantic Council reaffirmed "that NATO defensive strategy continues to be based on the existence of effective shield forces and on the manifest will to use nuclear retaliatory forces to repel aggression."[225]

After reading the Dulles article in *Foreign Affairs*, General Taylor had great hope that the State Department would support an expansion of the Army and agree "that limited-war forces had the active role to play in future military operations, the atomic retaliatory forces a passive role." When he presented the strategy of flexible response to the National Security Council at a January 1958 meeting, however, General Taylor observed that there was animated conversation, but "Secretary Dulles and his advisers did not provide the strong support for a new strategy which I hoped."[226] Taylor evidently had misread Dulles's writings and it was soon evident that Dulles continued to think of defense as a combination of collective local defense and strategic retaliation. In an executive session of the Senate Foreign Relations Committee on 9 January 1958, Dulles made it evident that he was not prepared to endorse a limited-war program that called for large-scale spending and committed the United States to local defense in peripheral areas. Dulles warned that any attempt to finance the extra military effort by cutting economic aid—as some members of Congress had suggested—would be "reckless folly."[227]

NOTES

1. Senate, *Department of Defense Appropriations for Fiscal Year 1952:Hearings before a Subcommittee of the Committee on Appropriations,* 82d Cong., 1st sess., 1951, 1262; Senate, *Department of Defense Appropriations for Fiscal Year 1953:Hearings before a Subcommittee of the Committee on Appropriations,* 82d Cong., 2d sess., 1952, 332–33; see also Glenn H. Snyder, "The New Look of 1953," in *Strategy, Politics, and Defense Budgets,* Warner R. Schilling, Paul Y. Hammond, and Glenn H. Snyder (New York: Columbia University Press, 1962), 388, 402.
2. Gen Omar N. Bradley, "US Military Policy: 1950," *Combat Forces Journal,* October 1950, 7; Gen J. Lawton Collins, "New Approaches to World Peace," *Army Information Digest,* January 1951, 3–4.
3. Schilling, Hammond, and Snyder, *Strategy, Politics, and Defense Budgets,* 388; see also chap. 6 nn. 192, 193, 194.
4. Robert J. Donovan, *Eisenhower: The Inside Story* (New York: Harper & Bros., 1956), 17–18; John Robinson Beal, *John Foster Dulles: 1888–1959* (New York: Harper & Bros., 1959), 187.
5. John Foster Dulles, *War or Peace* (New York: Macmillan Co., 1953), 99.
6. Dulles press conference, 16 March 1954, quoted in *Current History,* May 1954, 313.
7. Donovan, *Eisenhower: The Inside Story,* 18; Adm Arthur W. Radford, "Evolution of Modern Armed Forces," lecture, Air War College, Maxwell AFB, Ala., 17 January 1955.
8. Donovan, *Eisenhower: The Inside Story,* 18.
9. Senate, *Department of Defense Appropriations for Fiscal Year 1954: Hearings before a Subcommittee of the Committee on Appropriations,* 83d Cong., 1st sess., 1953, pt. 1: 573.
10. House, *Department of Defense Appropriations for 1954: Hearings before the Subcommittee of the Committee on Appropriations,* 83d Cong., 1st sess., 1953, 317; Senate, *DOD Appropriations for 1954,*

IDEAS, CONCEPTS, DOCTRINE

pt. 1: 1–523; House, *Department of Air Force Appropriations for 1955: Hearings before a Subcommittee of the Committee on Appropriations,* 83d Cong., 2d sess., 1954, 65–66; Donovan, *Eisenhower: The Inside Story,* 52.

11. Senate, *DOD Appropriations for 1954,* pt. 1: 231.

12. Ibid., pt. 1: 1–2, 6–7, 162–63.

13. House, *DOD Appropriations for 1954,* 474, 477–79; Senate, *DOD Appropriations for 1954,* pt. 1: 224–31, 252.

14. Donovan, *Eisenhower: The Inside Story,* 53–54; Department of Defense, *Semiannual Report of the Secretary of Defense and the Semiannual Reports of the Secretary of the Army, Secretary of the Navy, and Secretary of the Air Force, July 1 to December 31, 1953* (Washington, D. C.: Government Printing Office, 1954), 32–36.

15. Thomas K. Finletter, *Power and Policy, US Foreign Policy and Military Power in the Hydrogen Age* (New York: Harcourt, Brace & Co., 1954), 269–70.

16. Dulles, *War or Peace,* 235–36; R. Earl McClendon, *Changes in Organization for National Defense, 1949–1953* (Maxwell AFB, Ala.: Research Studies Institute, 1956), 22.

17. McClendon, *Changes in Organization for National Defense,* 13–23.

18. Ibid., 49–62; Department of Defense, *Semiannual Report of the Secretary of Defense and the Semiannual Reports of the Secretary of the Army, Secretary of the Navy, and Secretary of the Air Force, January 1 to June 30, 1953* (Washington, D. C.: Government Printing Office, 1953), 9–18; Finletter, *Power and Policy,* 288–94.

19. McClendon, *Changes in Organization for National Defense,* 26–32.

20. Ibid., 68–89; Department of Defense, *Semiannual Report of the Secretary of Defense and the Semiannual Reports of the Secretary of the Army, Secretary of the Navy, and Secretary of the Air Force, January 1 to June 30, 1954* (Washington, D. C.: Government Printing Office, 1955), 14; Air Force Bulletin 9, "Functions of the Armed Forces and the Joint Chiefs of Staff," 9 July 1954.

21. Gen Matthew B. Ridgway, *Soldier: The Memoirs of Matthew B. Ridgway* (New York: Harper & Bros., 1956), 266–67; Air Materiel Command Historical Study, "History of Production Problems During the Air Force Build-Up (1950–1954)," 1: 5–6.

22. Air Materiel Command Historical Study, "History of Production Problems," 1: 212; *Semiannual Report of the Secretary of Defense January to June 1954,* 6.

23. Senate, *Department of Defense Appropriations for Fiscal Year 1955: Hearings before a Subcommittee of the Committee on Appropriations,* 83d Cong., 2d sess., 1954, 84; Schilling, Hammond, and Snyder, *Strategy, Politics, and Defense Budgets,* 429–32.

24. Senate, *DOD Appropriations for 1954,* pt. 2: 1890–94; Air Materiel Command Historical Study, "History of Production Problems," 1: 205–6.

25. Maj Gen Oliver S. Picher, US Air Force assistant for programming, "Air Force Programs," lecture, Air War College, Maxwell AFB, Ala., 2 December 1954; Senate, *DOD Appropriations for 1955,* 237–38.

26. Schilling, Hammond, and Snyder, *Strategy, Politics, and Defense Budgets,* 440–41; Senate, *DOD Appropriations for 1955,* 79–84; House, *Department of Air Force Appropriations for 1955,* 2, 76–80; House, *Department of Defense Appropriations for 1957: Hearings before a Subcommittee of the Committee on Appropriations,* 84th Cong., 2d sess., 1956, 274–79; Senate, *Study of Air Power: Hearings before the Subcommittee on the Air Force of the Committee on Armed Services,* 84th Cong., 2d sess., 1956, 1449; Air Materiel Command Historical Study, "History of Production Problems," 1: 213.

27. Picher, "Air Force Programs"; Senate, *DOD Appropriations for 1955,* 7–8; Senate, *Study of Air Power,* 1398–99, 1401; Ridgway, *Soldier,* 288–89; House, *DOD Appropriations for 1957,* 128–29, 615–16.

28. Adm Arthur Radford, address before the National Press Club, Washington, D. C., 14 December 1953, in "The Collected Writings of Arthur W. Radford," 1: 39; Alexander P. de Seversky, "What Is Airpower?" *Air Force Magazine,* August 1955, 21; Senate, *DOD Appropriations for 1955,* 87.

29. Senate, *DOD Appropriations for 1955,* 2–8, 37–38; House, *DOD Appropriations for 1955,* 76.

30. Department of Defense, *Semiannual Report of the Secretary of Defense and the Semiannual Reports of the Secretary of the Army, Secretary of the Navy, and Secretary of the Air Force, January 1 to June 30, 1955* (Washington, D. C. : Government Printing Office, 1956), 280–83.

31. Finletter, *Power and Policy,* 271–72; Thomas K. Finletter and Roswell L. Gilpatric, letter to the Editor, in *New York Times,* 25 January 1954.

32. Lt Gen Ira C. Eaker, "Weapon Systems and the Armed Forces," lecture, Air War College, Maxwell AFB, Ala., 5 May 1954.

33. "Secretary Dulles' Address, 12 January 1954," *Current History,* May 1954, 308–9.

34. Richard Goold-Adams, *The Time of Power, A Reappraisal of John Foster Dulles* (London: Weidenfeld and Nicholson, 1962), 118–20; Finletter, *Power and Policy,* 137–40.

35. Beal, *John Foster Dulles,* 204–6.

36. Chester Bowles, "A Plea for Another Debate," *New York Times,* 28 February 1954.

37. "Adlai Stevenson's Criticisms, 6 March 1954," *Current History,* May 1954, 309–10.

38. Adm Arthur Radford, "Strong US Defense for the 'Long Pull'," interview, *U. S. News and World Report,* 5 March 1954, 50; Adm Arthur Radford, address before the Economic Club of New York, 9 March 1954, in "The Collected Writings of Arthur W. Radford," 1: 71–77.

39. "Secretary Dulles Explains at a Press Conference, March 16," *Current History,* May 1954, 310–13.

40. "Dulles' Statement before Senate Foreign Relations Committee, March 20," *Current History,* May 1954, 313–14.

41. John Foster Dulles, "Policy for Security and Peace," *Foreign Affairs,* April 1954, 353–64.

42. Beal, *John Foster Dulles,* 204–6; Donovan, *Eisenhower: The Inside Story,* 260–64.

43. Ridgway, *Soldier,* 275–77; George A. Wyeth, Jr., "The Pattern of Security Policy Making at the Washington Level," lecture, Air War College, Maxwell AFB, Ala., 27 October 1955; memorandum for record by Maj Gen Joseph D. Caldera, USAF, Retired, subject: FEAF Bomber Command Participation in the Battle for Dien Bien Phu—Middle Spring 1954, 8 March 1966.

44. Donovan, *Eisenhower: The Inside Story,* 264–68; Beal, *John Foster Dulles,* 207–18; Amry Vandenbosch and Richard A. Butwell, *Southeast Asia Among the World Powers* (Lexington: University of Kentucky Press, 1957), 295–97; Dwight D. Eisenhower, *The White House Years: Mandate for Change, 1953–1956* (New York: Doubleday & Co., 1953), 345–49.

45. Henry A. Kissinger, *Nuclear Weapons and Foreign Policy* (New York: Harper & Bros., 1957), 134.

46. Finletter, *Power and Policy,* 151.

47. House, *Department of Defense Appropriations for 1960: Hearings before a Subcommittee of the Committee on Appropriations,* 86th Cong., 1st sess., 1959, pt. 2: 168–69; Senate, *Mutual Security Act of 1958: Hearings before the Committee on Foreign Relations,* 85th Cong., 2d sess., 1958, 186–88; see also Robert E. Osgood, *NATO, The Entangling Alliance* (Chicago: University of Chicago Press, 1962), 102–39.

48. Adm Arthur W. Radford, "Communist Use of Armed Force," SEATO Seminar on Countering Communist Subversion, Baguio, Philippines, November 1957, 76–77; Radford, "Evolution of Modern Armed Forces."

49. Col Paul C. Droz, "Air Doctrine," *Air University Quarterly Review* 8, no. 1 (Summer 1955): 139.

50. "Some Reflections on the 'New Look,'" *Air Force Magazine,* staff study, April 1954, 26.

51. Gen Thomas D. White, "The Current Concept of American Military Strength," *Air University Quarterly Review* 7, no. 1 (Spring 1954): 3–4.

52. Brig Gen Dale O. Smith, "The Morality of Retaliation," *Air University Quarterly Review* 7, no. 3 (Winter 1954–1955): 56.

53. Brig Gen Dale O. Smith, *US Military Doctrine, A Study and Appraisal* (New York: Duell, Sloan and Pearce, 1955), 174–76.

54. Droz, "Air Doctrine," 139.

55. Col Wendell E. Carter, "Pursestrings and Pressures," *Air University Quarterly Review* 9, no. 1 (Winter 1956–1957): 48.

56. White, "The Current Concept of American Military Strength," 4, 8–9.

57. House, *Department of Air Force Appropriations for 1956: Hearings before a Subcommittee of the Committee on Appropriations*, 84th Cong., 1st sess., 1955, 1542–43.

58. T. F. Walkowicz, "Counter-Force Strategy: How We Can Exploit America's Atomic Advantage," *Air Force Magazine*, February 1955, 29.

59. Minutes of meeting of USAF Board of Review for Tactical Operations, 16 September 1949.

60. Senate, *DOD Appropriations for 1954*, 301.

61. Senate, *Study of Air Power*, 126–27.

62. Ibid., 168–72; Col C. E. Putnam, "Readiness vs. Modernization and Expansion," lecture, Air War College, Maxwell AFB, Ala., 23 March 1953; Maj Gen John P. McConnell, director of plans, Strategic Air Command, to deputy chief of staff, US Air Force, letter, subject: Command Structure in Support of SAC EWPS, 8 August 1953; House, *DOD Appropriations for 1960*, pt. 1: 112.

63. Evaluation Staff, Air War College, "The Air Force and National Security Policy," April 1954, 2–3.

64. Thomas K. Finletter, "Official U. S. Postwar Evaluations of the Air Weapon," lecture, Air War College, Maxwell AFB, Ala., 17 November 1953.

65. Finletter, *Power and Policy*, 54–55.

66. T. F. Walkowicz, "Survival in the Hydrogen Age," review of *Power and Policy* by Thomas K. Finletter, *Air Force Magazine*, November 1954, 68.

67. T. F. Walkowicz, "Counter-Force Strategy: How We Can Exploit America's Atomic Advantage," *Air Force Magazine*, February 1955, 25–29, 46, 51–52, 82.

68. Thomas K. Finletter, letter to the Editor, *Air Force Magazine*, April 1955, 4.

69. Col Richard S. Leghorn, "No Need to Bomb Cities to Win War, A New Counter-Force Strategy for Air Warfare," *U. S. News and World Report*, 28 January 1955, 78–94.

70. Rear Adm Sir Anthony W. Buzzard, "Massive Retaliation and Graduated Deterrence," *World Politics* 8 (January 1956): 228–37; Kissinger, *Nuclear Weapons and Foreign Policy*, 283.

71. Col Robert C. Richardson, "Atomic Weapons and Theater Warfare, Part 1: Will Nuclear Weapons Be Used?" *Air University Quarterly Review* 7, no. 3 (Winter 1954–1955): 13–14.

72. Senate, *Study of Air Power*, 126.

73. Maj Gen John Samford, "Objectives for the Use of Force," lecture, Air War College, Maxwell AFB, Ala., 2 February 1956.

74. Assistant for programming, Air Materiel Command, Presentation on Impact of the New Military Strategy on Air Materiel Command to AMC Commander's Conference, 26 April 1954; House, Committee on Un-American Activities, *Soviet Total War: 'Historic Mission' of Violence and Deceit* (Washington, D. C.: Government Printing Office, 1956), 1: 386–90.

75. Senate, *Study of Air Power*, 126.

76. Maj Gen Otto P. Weyland, "Tactical Air Operations," lecture, Air War College, Maxwell AFB, Ala., 25 February 1955; Lee Klein, "TAC, the Air Force's Jack-of-All-Trades," *Air Force Magazine*, May 1956, 44–51.

77. Senate, *Study of Air Power*, 126–27, 144, 171; Bernard Brodie, *Strategy in the Missile Era* (Princeton: Princeton University Press, 1959), 152–60.

78. Evaluation Staff, Air War College, "Military Power and National Security," 13–14.

79. Brig Gen Sidney F. Giffin, "Demands to be Anticipated for the Use of Military Forces," lecture, Air War College, Maxwell AFB, Ala., 12 April 1956.

80. House, *Inquiry into Operations of the United States Air Service: Hearings before the Select Committee of Inquiry into Operations of the United States Air Service*, 68th Cong., 2d sess., 1925, 1699, 2032; Air Corps Tactical School, *Air Force, Part I: Character and Strategy of Air Power*, 1 December 1935, 1.

81. Alexander P. de Seversky, "Evaluation of the Air Weapon," lecture, Air War College, Maxwell AFB, Ala., 19 November 1953.

82. Gen Henry H. Arnold, *Third Report of the Commanding General of the Army Air Forces to the Secretary of War*, 61–62; AFM 1-2, *United States Air Force Basic Doctrine*, 1 April 1955, 10.

83. Senate, *DOD Appropriations for 1954*, pt. 1: 572–73.

84. Ibid., 265.
85. De Seversky, "What Is Airpower?" 21.
86. Alexander P. de Seversky, "Are We Rearming for Defeat?" *Pageant,* April 1954.
87. De Seversky, "What Is Airpower?" 21–22.
88. Alexander P. de Seversky, "Department of Amplification," letter, *Air Force Magazine,* October 1955, 110.
89. Col Jerry D. Page and Col Royal H. Roussel, "What Is Air Power?" *Air University Quarterly Review* 8, no. 1 (Summer 1955): 3–9.
90. Barton Leach, "Nine Reasons Why Our Airpower Is Lagging," *Air Force Magazine,* September 1955, 55–56.
91. Senate, *Study of Air Power,* 172–73.
92. Ibid., 37.
93. *Public Papers of the Presidents of the United States, Dwight D. Eisenhower, 1956* (Washington, D. C.: Government Printing Office, 1958), 453, 466.
94. Senate, *Study of Air Power,* 1621.
95. Ibid., 1839.
96. Brig Gen Sidney F. Giffin, "Toward Cohesion of Military Thought: Relationships Among Fighting Forces," lecture, Air War College, Maxwell AFB, Ala., 30 April 1957.
97. Maj Gen James E. Ferguson, "Operational Future of Manned Aircraft," *Air Force Magazine,* April 1958, 43.
98. Gen Thomas D. White, "Air Force Perspective at the Dawn of the Space Age," address before the National Press Club, Washington, D. C., 29 November 1957.
99. Maj Gen Jacob E. Smart, assistant vice chief of staff, US Air Force, to commander, Air University, letter, subject: Revision of AFM 1-2, 25 April 1958.
100. Maj Gen Robert F. Tate, "USAF Doctrine," lecture, Orientation of Air Force Reserve and Air National Guard General Officers, 12 April 1958.
101. Maj Gen Hunter Harris, Jr., deputy director for plans, Deputy Chief of Staff for Operations, US Air Force, to commander, Tactical Air Command, letter, subject: Divergent Service Views Concerning Doctrine Governing Joint Amphibious Operations, 5 February 1954, 1st ind., Lt Col M. H. Irwin, assistant adjutant general, Tactical Air Command, to deputy director for plans, US Air Force, n.d.; Evaluation Staff, Air War College, "Military Power and National Security," 11–12.
102. Brig Gen James E. Ferguson, "An Air Officer's Concept for the Defense of Western Europe," lecture, Air War College, Maxwell AFB, Ala., 31 March 1953.
103. Finletter, *Power and Policy,* 54–55, 202–11.
104. Gen Curtis E. LeMay, address to Major USAF Commanders' Conference, 28–30 January 1957, in History, Strategic Air Command, July–December 1957, vol. 2, chap. 1, doc. 2.
105. Senate, *Study of Air Power,* 1275.
106. LeMay's address, 28–30 January 1957.
107. Maj Gen Otto P. Weyland, "Commander TAC Views on Roles and Missions of TAC," lecture, Air War College, Maxwell AFB, Ala., 18 February 1959; Weyland, "Tactical Air Operations"; Klein, "TAC, the Air Force's Jack-of-All-Trades," 45.
108. History, Tactical Air Command, July–December 1958, 1:36–38, citing letter of General Weyland to Nathan F. Twining, subject: Single Offensive Force Concept, 26 February 1957; Weyland, "Commander TAC Views on Roles and Missions of TAC."
109. House, *Department of Defense Appropriations for 1958: Hearings before a Subcommittee of the Committee on Appropriations,* 85th Cong., 1st sess., 1957, 462.
110. Senate, *Military Establishment Appropriation Bill for 1948: Hearings before a Subcommittee of the Committee on Appropriations,* 80th Cong., 1st sess., 1947, 260.
111. Brig Gen Noel F. Parrish, "Effective Aerospace Power, 1. Deterrence: The Hard Questions," *Air University Quarterly Review* 12, nos. 3 and 4 (Winter-Spring 1960–1961): 149–51.
112. Quoted in *Semiannual Report of the Secretary of Defense January to June 1954,* 9.

IDEAS, CONCEPTS, DOCTRINE

113. Sir John C. Slessor, "Has the H-Bomb Abolished Total War?" *Air Force Magazine*, May 1954, 24–26, 48.
114. Walter Millis, "The Limitations of Our Atomic War Strategy," lecture, Air War College, Maxwell AFB, Ala., 22 April 1955; "Defense Through Deterrents," *Air Force Magazine*, April 1955, 33, 37–38.
115. Millis, "The Limitations of Our Atomic War Strategy."
116. House, *DOD Appropriations for 1957*, 13, 32, 116.
117. Oskar Morgenstern, "The Game Theory in U.S. Strategy," *Fortune*, September 1959, 126.
118. *United States Foreign Policy*, study 8, "Developments in Military Technology and Their Impact on United States Strategy and Foreign Policy," December 1959, prepared under the direction of the Senate, Committee on Foreign Relations by the Washington Center of Foreign Policy Research, Johns Hopkins University, 86th Cong., 2d sess., 1960, com. print., 1:681–82.
119. Herman Kahn, *On Thermonuclear War* (Princeton: Princeton University Press, 1960), 157.
120. Evaluation Staff, Air War College, "Informal Project: The Air Force and National Security Policy," April 1954, 11–13.
121. Evaluation Staff, Air War College, "Military Power and National Security," 12–13.
122. Senate, *Study of Air Power*, 101–2.
123. House, *DOD Appropriations for 1958*, 1037.
124. Albert J. Wohlstetter, "The Delicate Balance of Terror," *Air Force Magazine*, February 1959, 48.
125. Giffin, "Demands to be Anticipated for the Use of Military Forces."
126. Col Robert C. Richardson, "The Nuclear Stalemate Fallacy," *Air Force Magazine*, August 1956, 80.
127. Senate, *Study of Air Power*, 56.
128. House, *DOD Appropriations for 1958*, 916.
129. House, *Department of Defense Appropriations for 1961: Hearings before a Subcommittee of the Committee on Appropriations*, 86th Cong., 2d sess., 1960, pt. 2:232.
130. Ibid., 232–33.
131. House, *DOD Appropriations for 1960*, pt. 2:385–86.
132. Schilling, Hammond, and Snyder, *Strategy, Politics, and Defense Budgets*, 435–36.
133. "Secretary Dulles' Address, 12 January 1954," *Current History*, May 1954, 308; John Foster Dulles, "Policy for Security and Peace," *Foreign Affairs*, April 1954, 358.
134. Matthew B. Ridgway, "The Army's Role in National Defense," *Army Information Digest*, May 1954, 21–30.
135. House, *DOD Appropriations for 1957*, 568, 573.
136. Ibid., 128–29; Samuel P. Huntington, *The Common Defense, Strategic Programs in National Politics* (New York: Columbia University Press, 1961), 346.
137. Rear Adm Arleigh A. Burke, director, Strategic Planning Office, chief of Naval Operations, "A Navy View of War," lecture, Air War College, Maxwell AFB, Ala., 23 November 1953.
138. Senate, *Study of Air Power*, 1391.
139. Ibid., 1399; House, *DOD Appropriations for 1957*, 285, 649.
140. Senate, *Study of Air Power*, 1363.
141. Ibid., 1379–80.
142. Nathan F. Twining, address to the Air Force Association Symposium, Omaha, Nebraska, 20 August 1954.
143. Notes on USAF Commanders' Conference, Eglin AFB, Fla., 24–25 May 1954.
144. Maj Gen Otto P. Weyland to chief of staff, US Air Force, letter, subject: Additional Tactical Air Force Headquarters, 25 June 1954; Thomas D. White to commander, Tactical Air Command, letter, subject: Additional Tactical Air Force Headquarters, 9 July 1954; Maj Gen Otto P. Weyland to vice chief of staff, US Air Force, letter, 19 August 1954; White to commander, Tactical Air Command, letter, 16 November 1954; Gen Otto P. Weyland to vice chief of staff, US Air Force, letter, 7 February

STRATEGIC IMPLICATIONS

1955; White to Weyland, letter, 15 February 1955; History, Tactical Air Command, July–December 1955, 1:5–9.

145. History, Tactical Air Command, January–June 1957, 357.

146. Col Richard P. Klocko, "Air Power in Limited Military Actions," AWC Graduate Study Group thesis no. 7 (Maxwell AFB, Ala.: Air War College, August 1954), 1–56. The study was published as Richard P. Klocko, *Air Power in Limited Military Actions* (Maxwell AFB, Ala.: Air University Press, 1955).

147. Ibid., 56–84.

148. History, Tactical Air Command, July–December 1955, 1:5–9.

149. "TAC Heads for Brighter Spot in AF Sun – 'Could Be Decisive,'" *Army, Navy, Air Force Journal*, 7 May 1955, 1063.

150. Gen Otto P. Weyland to Gen Laurence S. Kuter, commander, Far East Air Forces, letter, 16 December 1955; Gen Otto P. Weyland, "The Role of Tactical Air in the 'Long Pull,'" *Air Force Magazine*, May 1956, 52, 55.

151. Senate, *Study of Air Power*, 461–62.

152. History, Tactical Air Command, January–June 1956, 1:10–11.

153. Brig Gen Henry P. Viccellio, "Composite Air Strike Force," *Air University Quarterly Review* 9, no. 1 (Winter 1956–1957): 27–38.

154. "We Must Avoid the First Blow," interview with Gen Curtis E. LeMay, chief, Strategic Air Command, *U.S. News and World Report*, 9 December 1955, 44.

155. House, Committee on Un-American Activities, *Soviet Total War*, 1:388–89.

156. Senate, *Study of Air Power*, 1480–81.

157. Maj Gen John B. Cary, "Joint Planning from a Service Viewpoint," lecture, Air War College, Maxwell AFB, Ala., 30 November 1956.

158. House, *DOD Appropriations for 1958*, 916.

159. Quoted in John F. Loosbrock, "What Kind of Forces For What Kind of War?" *Air Force Magazine*, November 1956, 43–46.

160. House, *DOD Appropriations for 1958*, 1059–70.

161. Ibid., 1141.

162. Ibid., 1148–50.

163. Gen Maxwell D. Taylor, *The Uncertain Trumpet* (New York: Harper & Bros., 1959), 26; Brodie's article appeared in *Reporter*, 18 November 1954, 16–21.

164. Quoted in Huntington, *The Common Defense*, 346.

165. Taylor, *The Uncertain Trumpet*, 26–27.

166. Eisenhower to Wilson, letter, 5 January 1955, in House, *DOD Appropriations for 1956*, 4–5.

167. House, *DOD Appropriations for 1956*, 4–5, 7.

168. House, *DOD Appropriations for 1957*, 572–74.

169. Ibid., 268.

170. Ridgway, *Soldier*, 323–32.

171. Taylor, *The Uncertain Trumpet*, 29–36.

172. House, *DOD Appropriations for 1957*, 120–21.

173. Huntington, *The Common Defense*, 87.

174. House, *DOD Appropriations for 1957*, 431–558, especially 433, 436, 438, 446, 476.

175. Taylor, *The Uncertain Trumpet*, 181–97; Huntington, *The Common Defense*, 119.

176. Taylor, *The Uncertain Trumpet*, 36–38.

177. Sir John C. Slessor, "The Great Deterrent and Its Limitations," *Bulletin of the Atomic Scientists*, May 1956, 143.

178. Senate, *Study of Air Power*, 704–5, 740.

179. Ibid., 709, 806–7, 740–41.

180. Ibid., 722–23, 794–99, 830–52.

181. Ibid., 710.

182. Ibid., 1271–84.

183. Taylor, *The Uncertain Trumpet*, 47–48; Huntington, *The Common Defense*, 93–94.
184. Senate, *Study of Air Power*, 1465–66.
185. Taylor, *The Uncertain Trumpet*, 38–42; Huntington, *The Common Defense*, 93.
186. Senate, *Study of Air Power*, 1526–27.
187. Richardson, "Atomic Weapons and Theater Warfare," 8.
188. Brig Gen Dale O. Smith, "Airpower in Limited War," *Air Force Magazine*, May 1955, 47.
189. Weyland, "The Role of Tactical Air in the 'Long Pull,'" 52, 55.
190. Taylor, *The Uncertain Trumpet*, 38–39.
191. History, Air Research and Development Command, January–June 1957, 64–69.
192. House, *DOD Appropriations for 1958*, 24, 36, 37, 2066.
193. Ibid., 3–4, 1036–50; Huntington, *The Common Defense*, 93–94; Taylor, *The Uncertain Trumpet*, 36–38.
194. Memorandum by Secretary of Defense Charles E. Wilson to members of the Armed Forces Policy Council, subject: Clarification of Roles and Missions to Improve the Effectiveness of Operations of the Department of Defense, 26 November 1956.
195. House, *Department of Defense Appropriations for 1959: Hearings before a Subcommittee of the Committee on Appropriations*, 85th Cong., 2d sess., 1958, 189.
196. House, *DOD Appropriations for 1958*, 2070–88.
197. Quoted in Huntington, *The Common Defense*, 239.
198. Department of Defense, *Semiannual Report of the Secretary of Defense and the Semiannual Reports of the Secretary of the Army, Secretary of the Navy, and Secretary of the Air Force, January 1 to June 30, 1958* (Washington, D.C.: Government Printing Office, 1959), 18.
199. Taylor, *The Uncertain Trumpet*, 47; Huntington, *The Common Defense*, 95.
200. Taylor, *The Uncertain Trumpet*, 51–52.
201. House, *Investigation of National Defense Missiles: Hearings before the Committee on Armed Services*, 85th Cong., 2d sess., 1958, 4248.
202. History, Air Research and Development Command, January–June 1957, 60.
203. Thomas D. White to Lt Gen Thomas S. Power, commander, Air Research and Development Command, letter, 7 May 1957.
204. History, Air Research and Development Command, January–June 1957, 61–62.
205. House, Committee on Un-American Activities, *Soviet Total War*, 1:392.
206. Weyland to White, letter, 22 May 1957.
207. John Foster Dulles, "The Basic Concepts of United States Foreign Policy," address before the annual luncheon of the Associated Press, 22 April 1957, in Department of State, *American Foreign Policy, Current Documents, 1957* (Washington, D.C.: Government Printing Office, 1961), 25–26.
208. "Replies Made by the Secretary of State to Questions Asked at a News Conference," 16 July 1957, in Department of State, *American Foreign Policy, Current Documents, 1957*, 1285–86.
209. Taylor, *The Uncertain Trumpet*, 55.
210. Maj Gen Jacob E. Smart, assistant vice chief of staff, US Air Force, to Lt Gen Samuel E. Anderson, commander, Air Research and Development Command, letter, 10 October 1957.
211. Gen Thomas D. White, "USAF Doctrine in the Military Implementation of National Policy," 4 December 1957. This address was published as an abridged version in White's "USAF Doctrine and National Policy," *Air Force Magazine*, January 1958, 47–51.
212. Senate, *Inquiry into Satellite and Missile Programs: Hearings before the Preparedness Investigating Subcommittee of the Committee on Armed Services*, 85th Cong., 1st and 2d sess., 1957 and 1958, 883.
213. Gen Otto P. Weyland, guidance for preparation of talk before the American Ordnance Association on "Tactical Aviation in Limited War" (also general guidance for talk before Scientific Advisory Board), 13 November 1957.
214. Senate, *Inquiry into Satellite and Missile Programs*, 913.
215. Maj Gen James H. Walsh, "The Influence of Nuclear Weapons on the Determination of Military Objectives," lecture, Air War College, Maxwell AFB, Ala., 18 December 1957.

216. W. W. Rostow, "Can We Beat the Russians at Their Own Game?" *Air Force Magazine*, November 1956, 60–68. Reprinted from *Washington Star*, 23 September 1956.

217. William W. Kaufmann, ed., *Military Policy and National Security* (Princeton: Princeton University Press, 1956); Robert E. Osgood, *Limited War: The Challenge to American Strategy* (Chicago: University of Chicago Press, 1957).

218. Kissinger, *Nuclear Weapons and Foreign Policy*, passim.

219. House, *Investigation of National Defense Missiles*, 640, 4561.

220. John Foster Dulles, "Challenge and Response in United States Policy," *Foreign Affairs*, October 1957, 29, 31; also reprinted in Department of State, *American Foreign Policy, Current Documents, 1957*, 35–52.

221. Senate, *Mutual Security Act of 1958*, 187.

222. White, "USAF Doctrine in the Military Implementation of National Policy," 4 December 1957.

223. "The NATO Heads of Government Conference: Statement Made by the Secretary of State at the Second Session of the Conference," 16 December 1957, and "The NATO Heads of Government Conference: Declaration and Communiqué Issued December 19, 1957," Department of State, *American Foreign Policy, Current Documents, 1957*, 407–20.

224. "NATO's Military Replanning," *Interavia*, January 1962, 29–30; Robert E. Osgood, *NATO, The Entangling Alliance*, 118, 161.

225. "Ministerial Session of the North Atlantic Council (Paris): Communiqué, December 18, 1958," Department of State, *American Foreign Policy, Current Documents, 1958* (Washington, D.C.: Government Printing Office, 1962), 489.

226. Taylor, *The Uncertain Trumpet*, 55–57, 64–65.

227. Morton H. Halperin, "The Gaither Committee and the Policy Process," in *World Politics*, April 1961, 373–74; *New York Times*, 10 January 1958, 1, 12.

Harold E. Talbott, secretary of the
Department of the Air Force, 1953–55.

Brig Gen Dale O. Smith, author, *U. S.
Military Doctrine: A Study and Appraisal.*

Gen Curtis E. LeMay, commander, Strategic Air
Command, 1948–57; Air Force chief of staff, 1961–65.

F-100, Super Sabre.

Donald A. Quarles, secretary of the
Department of the Air Force, 1955–57.

Lt Gen James Ferguson, director,
Requirements, 1956–61.

CHAPTER 9

MISSILE TECHNOLOGY AND THE AIR FORCE 1945–60

"On October 4, last year," said Gen Nathan F. Twining, chairman of the Joint Chiefs of Staff, in January 1958, "a shot was fired which was both seen and heard around the world."[1] The shot was the successful Soviet launching of Sputnik I, the first man-made satellite in history. Following up this feat on 3 November 1957, the Soviets successfully launched into orbit Sputnik II, a 1,120-pound vehicle that carried the world's first space passenger, a dog named Laika. The impact of the Soviet triumph in space and missile technology created dismay everywhere outside the Iron Curtain. In Washington, the House Committee on Government Operations warned: "We face the terrifying prospect that nuclear attack upon the United States can be directed from Soviet bases."[2]

Guided Missiles: The Research and Development Phase

Concerned about the delay in the development of new weapons, Congressman Daniel J. Flood of Pennsylvania criticized "the whole mentality in the Pentagon and the Armed Forces of the United States, especially with the military, and this goes for all of them – the Army, the Navy, and the Air Force, and everybody else." Flood warned, "And until that mentality is changed by the rule of reason, until men with ideas, until men with imagination, until somebody is willing to leave his feet and take out that play as it comes around his end, until that hidebound military mind gets more elastic, and until brilliant and capable officers are permitted to try – and if they miss not get their heads cut off – you are going to be in a bad shape for a long time."[3] Other authorities believed that interservice bickerings had contributed to the lag in United States missile and space technology. In his State of the Union message on 9 January 1958, President Dwight D. Eisenhower observed: "I am not attempting today to pass judgment on the charge of harmful service rivalries. But one thing is sure. Whatever they are, America wants them stopped."[4]

Starts and Stops in Early Missile Programs

Viewed in retrospect the influence of technology upon modern warfare had begun to manifest itself in the final stages of World War II. This influence was apparent in German missile employments and in the Anglo-American developments in electronic warfare and nuclear explosives. The translation of the potential technological developments into a new and unexplored plateau of the capabilities of military forces required imagination, time, and tremendous quantities of money. At the end of World War II, Gen Henry H. "Hap" Arnold showed some of this imagination. Dr Theodore von Karman's Scientific Advisory Board warned General Arnold that German aeronautical laboratories had made great progress in missilery even beyond the Wasserfall ground-to-air antiaircraft missile and the V-1 and V-2 offensive projectiles. Arnold believed that the United States had "shown a dangerous willingness to be caught in a position of having to start a war with equipment and doctrines used at the end of a preceding war." In his final war report, Arnold visualized the employment of projectiles that might have velocities of 3,000 miles per hour. Such weapons could be launched from "true space ships, capable of operating outside the earth's atmosphere."[5]

Genuinely interested in intercontinental air warfare and wishing to initiate new research projects before plentiful wartime funds dried up, Arnold withheld three $10-million items from the Army Air Forces' fiscal year 1946 procurement budget and committed the money to long-range developmental projects such as AAF Project MX-791, which committed $10 million to the Douglas Aircraft Corporation for a three-year study of future warfare. This contract marked the genesis of the nonprofit Research and Development (Rand) Corporation, which split away from Douglas in 1948. Completed in forced draft on 2 May 1946, a Rand study entitled "Preliminary Design of an Experimental World-Circling Spaceship" demonstrated that American engineers and engineering skills were capable of orbiting a 500-pound satellite by 1951.[6] Other portions of the fiscal year 1946 funds that Arnold diverted to development were committed to some 26 projects dealing with four categories of missiles: air-to-air for the protection of bomber forces and for use by fighter interceptors; surface-to-air for use against invading aircraft and missiles; air-to-surface as standoff weapons for employment by bombers; and surface-to-surface for use in both short-range tactical and long-range strategic employments.[7]

The Army Air Forces planned a wide range of exploratory projects and intended that only those projects that showed definite promise after preliminary study would be continued.[8] The inspiration for a part of the projects came from industrial sources. Simon Ramo, for example, visualized that future combat against an adversary equipped with an A-bomb would require air-launched missiles "so that our fighter planes could stand off at a distance safely and launch the missiles and go home while the missiles went about doing the job." Believing that the "military field was going to be a very fascinating and important one for that class of scientist who was interested in applied technology," Ramo went to work as director of research in the radio division of the Hughes Aircraft Company.[9] Other projects followed lines of research indicated by German progress, thus visualizing parallel development of both subsonic pilotless aircraft and supersonic guided missiles. Specific projects undertaken in early 1946 included the Falcon air-to-air missile; the Rascal standoff missile; the ground-to-ground Matador, Snark, and Navaho winged pilotless aircraft missiles; and the MX-774 Hiroc intercontinental ballistic missile. Looking toward ground-to-air defense, the Army Air Forces gave Boeing Company a contract for ground-to-air pilotless aircraft (GAPA) for use against high-performance aircraft and contracted with the General Electric Company and the University of Michigan to undertake a basic design for ballistic trajectory rockets capable of intercepting and destroying hostile missiles. Conducted at the Willow Run Research Center, the University of Michigan study was designated Project Wizard.[10]

In the course of exploiting captured German technological data, the Air Materiel Command's Project Paperclip brought several prominent German scientists to Wright-Patterson AFB, Ohio. Included in the group was former Maj Gen Walter R. Dornberger, who had headed the German military rocket development program. These German scientists assisted in drafting the missile research and development program, and the Air Force gave considered thought as to whether the group ought not to be retained as an in-house research and development capability within the Air Materiel Command. In the early 1920s the Air Corps had attempted to design and build aircraft at Wright Field, but this arsenal system had proved inferior to the development of aircraft by private enterprise. The Army Air Forces, therefore, decided not to retain the group of German missile experts; within a few years most of them were employed by private industry.[11]

"The aerial missile, by whatever means it may be delivered," warned Maj Gen Hugh J. Knerr, secretary-general of the AAF Air Board, on 26 February 1946, "is the weapon of the Air Corps. Unless we recognize it as such and aggressively establish ourselves as most competent in this field, the responsibility therefore will become established by the Army or the Navy."[12] Since only a limited quantity of "brains and materials" was available for research and development in the United States, Knerr feared that scarce resources might be overtaxed by competing Army, Navy, and Army Air Forces projects.[13] Under the terms of a War Department directive issued on 2 October 1944, the Army Air Forces was responsible for the development within the Army "of all guided or homing missiles launched from the ground which depend for sustenance primarily on the lift of aerodynamic forces."[14] The first organization dealing exclusively with guided missiles was established early in 1945 by the Joint Chiefs of Staff for the purpose of reviewing projects concerned with the development of rockets comparable to the German V-1s and V-2s. The Committee on Guided Missiles existed to review programs and recommend action.[15] Long familiar with the arsenal system of development, the Army Ordnance Department began research on artillery-type missiles at Fort Bliss, Texas, and White Sands, New Mexico, before the end of World War II. A Wac-Corporal research rocket was fired at White Sands in September 1945, and in the autumn of that year Dr Wernher von Braun and about 120 other German scientists were brought to Fort Bliss to assist with experimental firings of captured V-2 missiles. The main objective was a high-altitude research program, but the Fort Bliss group was given an additional task of developing a small research vehicle called the Hermes II. Looking back at his work at Fort Bliss, von Braun would describe the general attitudes as being: "The war is over; let us utilize these interesting new toys that we imported from Europe, and let us put them to use for high-altitude research."[16] Early in 1946, the Navy Bureau of Aeronautics awarded four research contracts for feasibility design studies of space vehicles, and in August 1946 the Naval Research Laboratory contracted with the Martin Company for an improved research version of the German V-2 called the Viking.[17]

Looking toward the coordination of research and development activities the secretary of war and the secretary of the Navy established the Joint Research and Development Board on 6 June 1946 under the chairmanship of Dr Vannevar Bush, who had headed the wartime Office of Scientific Research and Development. The Joint Research and Development Board promptly established a Committee on Guided Missiles.[18] In view of a further need to clarify arguments as to what the jurisdiction of the Army and the Army Air Forces would be for missile development, the War Department on 7 October 1946 made the Army Air Forces responsible "for the research and development activities pertaining to guided missiles." Three days later the War Department provided that this assignment of responsibility was only research and development and should not be necessarily applicable to the assignment of operational responsibility for such guided missiles as were developed and procured.[19] The enactment of the National Security Act of 1947 vested overall review authority for national military research and development in the National Military Establishment's Research and Development Board. Doctor Bush remained its chairman until 5 October 1948; the Committee on Guided Missiles continued to function as a board activity. In the separation of the Air Force from the Army, the Air Force was relieved effective on 19 July 1948 of its responsibility for the guided missiles research and development program required to accomplish roles and missions of the Army.[20]

By committing a total of more than $34 million of its fiscal year 1946 funds to research in missiles, the Army Air Forces appeared to have solidly grounded its future on new technology. The decision to award the missile development contracts rather freely also reflected an appreciation of the fact that the United States lacked basic technical knowledge on the subject and that World War II had knocked out Western Europe's capacity to provide basic technological knowledge for some years to come.[21] Almost at once, however, the most imaginative item of the Air Force research program—the 5,000-mile MX-774 Hiroc intercontinental ballistic missile (ICBM), whose study contract had been allocated to the Consolidated-Vultee Aircraft Corporation—began to experience problems. As previously noted, Doctor Bush, while testifying before the Senate Committee on Atomic Energy in December 1945, completely discounted the technical feasibility of a high-angle intercontinental rocket.[22] The technical problem was indeed a large one. The early model atomic bomb weighed a little over five tons and had a half-mile kill radius. The Hiroc would thus have to be a very large missile with an extremely powerful thrust, but even this would not solve the problem of accuracy. The average accuracy possible with a Norden bombsight was 15 mils. Thus, a Hiroc fired from a distance of 5,000 miles could theoretically miss its target by about 75 miles. In view of the half-mile kill radius of an atomic warhead, this degree of "accuracy" was not very attractive.[23]

The missile also presented technical difficulties. The specific impulse of the oxygen and alcohol fuels was too low to give the missile a 5,000-mile range. The warhead would encounter very high temperatures when it reentered the earth's atmosphere. Some scientists suggested that the Air Force was proposing to develop a meteor that would burn upon reentering the atmosphere.[24] Based on the technology of 1945 (which many scientists later would declare made Bush's negative evaluation of the technical feasibility of an intercontinental ballistic missile entirely sound at the time), Bush continued to suspect both pilotless aircraft and guided missiles. In his book, *Modern Arms and Free Men*, published in 1949, Bush pointed out that the German V-1 pilotless aircraft fired against London had been easily countered. "When the defense dispositions reached their climax," he wrote, "they brought down some ninety-five percent of the buzz-bombs that came within range, and they repeated or bettered this performance later at Antwerp." Flying slowly at constant altitude and in a straight line, the V-1 buzz bombs had made almost ideal targets. Based on these analyses, Bush urged that the manned bomber was far cheaper and superior to either a pilotless aircraft or a ballistic missile. He dismissed the ballistic missile quite summarily: "It would never stand the test of cost analysis. If we employed it in quantity, we would be economically exhausted long before the enemy." For the near future, Bush suggested that only small and short-range missiles would have practical application to air warfare.[25]

Even though he gave strong support to the development of missiles during his tenure as deputy chief of staff for research and development of the Air Force, Gen Curtis E. LeMay was quite unwilling to admit that the heavy bomber lacked growth potential. "We in the Air Force," LeMay wrote in May 1946,

> are assuming that guided missiles will be fired at bombing vehicles whatever their form may take and are already taking measures to develop and destroy enemy vehicles whether they are fighter planes or guided missiles. Granted as the science progresses, tactics will change, new weapons will be employed, but destruction of enemy industry and means to wage war calls for large quantities of destructive power. It may well be that in the future this power may be more efficiently delivered by rockets or guided missiles than by heavy bombers; however, it is not here yet and the science of strategic bombing and the development of bombing equipment will keep pace with the defensive missiles used to stop it. The heavy bomber will only go out of existence when a new weapon is invented which will do the job more cheaply and effectively.... Even when the efficient guided missile of large weight, carrying capacity and extreme range is developed, military flexibility may still demand the existence of manned vehicles capable of delivering tremendous blows on spots inaccessible to rocket fire..., or to conduct operations against targets of opportunity. No one weapon will meet all the requirements of modern warfare, and it can be safely assumed that warfare in the future will become even more complex.[26]

When he appeared before the House Subcommittee on Appropriations on 6 March 1947, Lt Gen Ira C. Eaker, deputy commanding general of the Army Air Forces, emphasized the tremendous expense of preparing for an early "push-button warfare" capability. Eaker suggested that the day may come when the long-range guided missile would replace the conventional very heavy bomber. With unlimited funds and resources in a development effort equivalent to that which had produced the atomic bomb, Eaker estimated that a 5,000-mile-range guided missile could be developed in five years. "Ten to fifteen years from now, by working hard and with at least a quarter of a billion dollars annually for experimentation in that field alone," Eaker estimated, "we can produce a rocket of 5,000-mile range. The prototype . . . will probably cost 200 million each, and individual rockets of that size and type thereafter may cost as much as 7 million." "We cannot, therefore," Eaker concluded, "abandon the development of the very long-range very-heavy bomber as a primary weapon of our long-range striking force but we should, as a wise precaution, spend the necessary experimental funds to insure that we are the first in the field with a long-range guided missile which may be the primary weapon at some future date, but probably not within 15 years."[27]

Although the Army Air Forces (AAF) had assumed that some of the missile projects established in 1945-46 would prove infeasible and would be dropped after a year or two, it was not prepared for the reductions in research and development funding that would occur in fiscal year 1947. As has been seen, the Bureau of the Budget impounded and transferred Air Force research and development funds. In the guided missiles field, the reduction in funds from $29 million to $13 million that took place in December 1946 forced the Army Air Forces to terminate some 11 of 28 guided missile projects, even though it had not received the technical data it needed to make well-advised decisions. The reduction was especially ill-timed because some missile contractors were progressing from a study phase to one of testing small-scale missile mock-ups.[28] In an effort to establish guidelines for a drastically reduced missile program, Maj Gen Benjamin W. Chidlaw, the Air Materiel Command's deputy commander for engineering, recommended on 6 May 1947 that the Army Air Forces "should concentrate on those missiles which show greatest promise of early tactical availability." Chidlaw envisioned that missile projects should be established for phased development in a relatively few companies, thus reducing a rather high cost arising when a number of companies attempted to expand their engineering and scientific staffs to handle individual projects. Since the 5,000-mile MX-774 intercontinental missile did not promise "any tangible results in the next eight to ten years," Chidlaw recommended that it be deleted from the Army Air Forces program.[29] In Washington a staff study signed by Brig Gen Thomas S. Power, AAF deputy assistant chief of staff for operations, on 16 June 1947, based its recommendations regarding missiles on the basic assumption that "for the next ten years, long range air bombardment will be effected by means of subsonic bombers only." Given this assumption, the pressing requirement would be for operational bomber defense and standoff bombing missiles and conversely for surface-to-air and air-to-air interceptor missiles. The study posed an urgent requirement for an early development of a means to detect and destroy enemy supersonic guided missiles, and an early requirement for highly accurate surface-to-surface, 1,000-mile-range guided missiles. This study also stated an eventual requirement, probably by 1957, for a supersonic surface-to-surface missile with a range of up to 10,000 miles. The study recommended as its first priority, bomber-launched air-to-surface and air-to-air missiles; as its second priority, a 150-mile-range tactical surface-to-surface missile; as its third priority, bomber and missile interceptor missiles with associated detection and control means; and as its fourth priority, long-range surface-to-surface missiles. Gen Hoyt S. Vandenberg approved this order of priority on 18 June 1947. After coordination through the War Department, this list of priorities was transmitted to the Air Materiel Command as a directive on 12 August 1947.[30]

The full effect of the Army Air Forces' decision was to subordinate the guided missile research and development program to the support of a strategic bomber offensive. The reorganization of the headquarters of the Army Air Forces that took place on 10 October 1947 with creation of the Air Force manifested a similar preoccupation with the preparation of a force in being. For the next several years, the policy on guided missiles included the twin precepts that the Air Force would program guided missile units into its forces only after determining the extent to which the guided missile units could supplement or replace manned aircraft units and that guided missiles would be handled like any other piece of Air Force hardware.[31] When appropriations were reduced in the spring of 1947, the Air Materiel Command promptly dropped the contract for the MX-774 intercontinental ballistic missile. The Consolidated-Vultee work had arrived, nevertheless, at three important innovations: the use of the missile body as the wall of the fuel tanks as a weight-saving measure, the employment of swiveling rocket engines to provide directional control in flight, and the development of a nose cone that could be separated from the main missile body. Enough money remained when the project was canceled to permit the contractor to test three single stages of the missile during 1948. The results were so favorable that Consolidated-Vultee and its successor, Convair Division of the General Dynamics Corporation, kept the key members of the MX-774 engineering team together to continue studies of ballistic missile systems.[32] Following the demise of the MX-774, the Air Force missile program was reduced progressively to the Falcon air-to-air interceptor missile, the Rascal standoff bomber missile, and four pilotless aircraft missiles — the Matador, the Snark, the Bomarc, and the Navaho.

When it became responsible for coordinating military research and development programs in 1947, the National Military Establishment's Research and Development Board recognized that guided missile programs represented a relatively new technical field in which little was known and took a fairly relaxed view toward service projects that were in some competition with one another. While the Air Force was working on the Falcon missile, for example, the Navy was developing the Sparrow air-to-air missile; the two missiles involved different approaches to the same problem.[33] In another respect, however, Doctor Bush was less liberal. While the reductions of funds for research and development in fiscal years 1947 and 1948 were a part of general reductions in postwar military appropriations, Bush arbitrarily limited the total defense research and development budget beginning in fiscal year 1949 to approximately $500 million a year. Believing that only so much technical talent was available, Bush insisted that larger expenditures automatically would produce waste and poor results by forcing much research and development work into the hands of mediocre personnel. Dr Karl T. Compton, who succeeded Bush as chairman of the Research and Development Board in October 1948, believed that the Defense Department could spend wisely an annual research and development budget of $650 million a year, but the precedent of the $500-million budget had been set. In fiscal year 1950 the Department of Defense spent about $550 million in research and development, less than four cents out of every dollar appropriated for the defense establishment.[34]

Facing the need to conserve scarce defense research and development funds and acting under the direction of the secretary of defense, the Joint Chiefs of Staff reviewed missile research and development projects in the autumn of 1949. As a result of this examination, primary responsibilities for research and development of short-range surface-to-air missiles were allocated to the Army and Navy.[35] At this time the Boeing Company appeared to be making good progress in developing the Air Force ground-to-air pilotless aircraft missile. But the Army had begun to develop the Nike-Ajax missile in 1945 and the Navy was developing Terrier and Talos antiaircraft missiles, either of which might have met Air Force requirements for point-defense weapons. The Air Force, moreover, recognized that a tremendous number of beam-riding antiaircraft missiles with a 25-mile range would be required to defend the continental United States. In view of these factors and the decision of the Joint Chiefs of Staff, the Air Force stopped development of the GAPA missile in November 1949 and contracted with Boeing and the University of Michigan to investigate the feasibility of a 250-mile-range interceptor missile plus an associated electronic control system. The feasibility study was approved during 1950; a development contract was awarded formally in December for a Bomarc (Boeing and Michigan Aeronautical Research Center) weapon system.[36] Based on the Joint Chiefs of Staff review, the Air Force resolved not to attempt to develop missiles suited for close support of ground forces. The Air Force position was that close support missiles ought to be handled by the Army as an improvement of its battlefield artillery. Both the Air Force and the Research and Development Board kept the Matador tactical missile under scrutiny during 1949 to determine if its 350-mile range should be extended or if the missile should be dropped from development. Compared with other missiles, however, the Matador was essentially simple. It was, in effect, a subsonic, pilotless fighter aircraft that was guided to its target by a ground-based, short-range (shoran) bombing system. The Air Force eventually decided to build the Matador (TM-61) because it would give all-weather interdiction capabilities to a tactical air force. The Matador first flew in 1950. The Air Force deployed it overseas beginning in 1954 to stations in Germany, Taiwan, and Korea.[37]

Other Air Force missile systems were far more complex than Matador. Most of them were scheduled to become operational in the 1954-55 time period, but each of them pressed beyond existing parameters of the technological arts. Basically a pilotless aircraft that would be carried under the fuselage of a B-36 or a B-47, the Rascal (SM-63) was designed as a Mach-2 missile with a 100-mile range. It was designed so that a missilier in the bomber could control the missile from the time of launch until it hit its target. The Snark (SM-62) resembled a big sleek fighter plane. A turbojet engine gave the Snark a Mach-0.9 airspeed and range that was specified to be 5,500 miles; a gyrostabilized celestial navigation system guided the Snark to its target once in flight. The Bomarc (IM-99) was a pilotless fighter that would be launched with a liquid-fuel rocket booster and whose twin ramjet engines would give it an airspeed of Mach 2.7. Missile control officers used a ground radar control system to maneuver the Bomarc into an attack position, at which time its radar would lock onto the target. The Air Force did not expect the Navaho (SM-64) to be operational at an early date. This missile was designed to carry a heavy nuclear warhead (subsequently determined to be a thermonuclear warhead) and was to have a 5,500-mile range and a supersonic speed of Mach 2.7. The navigational system was to be a nonemanating, pure inertial system, which would not have to refer to the stars or to the ground for course or guidance corrections. Getting the Navaho up to flying altitude where its ramjet engines could take over was a problem that presented some initial complexity. One proposal was to use a B-36 to carry the Navaho aloft and then launch the missile in the air. In 1950 final design specifications provided that the Navaho would be launched piggyback from the ground on liquid-fuel rocket engines. Each of these missiles involved exploitations of underdeveloped technology; how soon the missiles could be placed in operation was anyone's guess. "We have tried," Maj Gen Gordon P. Saville admitted candidly, "to make a guesstimate of operational availability which includes the fact that inventors have invented as scheduled and that the tests have gone on with the normal amount of 'snafu' that we expect."[38]

Technological Breakthrough in Ballistic Missiles

Speaking in 1953, Dr Walter G. Whitman, chairman of the Defense Research and Development Board, suggested that mistakes in military research and development had included the reductions in research and development funding after 1945 and his board's inability to decide what program should receive the greatest emphasis at any one time.[39] Looking back in 1957 at these initial phases of Air Force missile development, Lt Gen Charles S. Irvine, deputy chief of staff for materiel, observed:

> When looking at the early developments of the atomic bomb ... [given] what we knew about guidance, ... we were not ready to build ... a ballistic machine and do an efficient job of knocking out targets considering the number of dollars or manhours it would take per target. We went to the airbreathing route, a pilotless airplane, a subsonic Snark or Navaho supersonic machine, which would in its time period carry a big enough warhead and be more accurate. This appeared to be the best solution as we saw the state of the art at that time. ... Looking back at it, maybe that was a bad decision. We could have

developed a guidance for the ballistic missile while we were doing the other job. But our crystal ball was not that bright.[40]

Col Edward N. Hall, who would become an Air Force missile expert, blamed the early decisions equally on ballistic advocates, who thought in terms of thousands of yards rather than thousands of miles, and the experts on aerodynamics who were convinced that there would always be an inverse relationship between speed and range and could not visualize a supersonic vehicle that would have a 10,000-mile range.[41] In effect the Air Force had assumed in its projections that there would be a period of years in which there would be a gap between piloted aircraft and ballistic missiles: this gap could be most feasibly filled by air-breathing pilotless aircraft.[42]

Both as a reaction to the Soviet's explosion of an atomic weapon and in recognition that research and development had lagged in the several years that it had been subordinated to operational concerns, General Vandenberg—with more than a little prompting from Secretary of the Air Force W. Stuart Symington—reestablished a deputy chief of staff for development at the Air Staff level and established the Air Research and Development Command (ARDC) on 23 January 1950. General Saville assumed the duty as deputy chief of staff for development without delay, but the Air Research and Development Command required an evolutionary period to take control of the major Air Force research and development centers and to work out the mission and basic concepts that would guide the new organization's research and development efforts.[43] The Ridenour committee's (see chapter 6) report had demonstrated that past thinking on research and development had been too much on a project-by-project basis and that the research-development-production cycle had been much too long. "In the past," noted Brig Gen Donald N. Yates, assistant deputy chief of staff for development, "we . . . pointed toward mainly the development of an aircraft . . . hoping that we could patch existing guns, armament, and electronics equipment into it."[44] At the request of Gen Muir S. Fairchild, General Saville prepared a staff study on the development and procurement of combat ready air vehicles. This study recommended adopting a systems approach in the development of new weapons; making of a decision to go into limited production at the time that the mock-up or breadboard model was approved; conducting an accelerated and integrated test program before the production rate was stepped up; and retaining development responsibility and authority within one agency during the life span of the equipment. The weapon system concept gained immediate acceptance. A weapon system was defined as "a completely and integrally equipped aircraft, missile or other flying device with all its airborne and ground equipment necessary to satisfy a military operational requirement."[45] During its first year of operation, the Air Research and Development Command also faced the problem as to whether it should attempt to build and staff laboratories for Air Force research. After careful study, Dr Louis N. Ridenour advised Lt Gen Earle E. Partridge, who had taken command on 24 June 1951, that "the primary mission of the ARDC in the field of research is to connect the Air Force with pertinent research being done elsewhere, and to stimulate work that appears to be of direct interest to the Air Force." Expanding on that guidance, Partridge stated that ARDC would handle both research and development "out of shop" when contract operations were proper and feasible. "The ARDC," Partridge stated, "favors contract operations when such contract operations are to the advantage of the US Government."[46]

While the Air Force was expanding its research and development organization, the beginning of the Korean War loosened budget purse strings. The Air Force received $238 million for research and development in fiscal year 1950; annual and supplemental defense appropriations made $522.9 million available to the Air Force for such purposes in fiscal year 1951.[47] With more money available President Harry S Truman wanted to see the missile programs move along faster, with special emphasis on the development of defensive missiles. On 30 August 1950, Truman invited K. T. Keller to a conference at the White House and requested that Keller, an experienced engineer, see what he could do to advance the guided missile program. After receiving this presidential mandate, Keller began a 90-day fact-finding tour of the military's research installations and contractor facilities, including the Army's Redstone Arsenal at Huntsville, Alabama, where the Army had drawn together its missile research and development from White Sands, New Mexico; Fort Bliss, Texas; and other installations. Keller determined that about 4,000 military and 11,000 contractor personnel were working on missile programs. He concluded that the best contribution he could make to the programs would be to head a small organization that would act as a consultant and adviser to everyone involved with guided missiles. President Truman accepted this recommendation and on 24 October 1950 appointed Keller to be the director of guided missiles for the Department of Defense. Truman charged Keller to direct and coordinate the activities connected with research, development, and production of guided missiles. From his observations of the military services' missile programs, Keller came to several other conclusions. He saw no reason why one service could be charged to conduct research and development on a missile system that might be assigned to another service when it became operational. Keller also thought that engineers tended to avoid "the dirty, stinking work of getting the little problems cleaned up." He commented that quite frequently when they met problems engineers tended to veer off to a new conception rather than concentrating on the solution of the problem. Keller believed that the development process had to stabilize its objectives long enough to find out what made a piece of hardware malfunction. Keller promptly embarked on a campaign "to get hundreds of missiles out flying so that there can be some kind of a sensible evaluation of the field for general policy guidance." Keller was impatient with the military concept that logistical support concepts ought to be worked into the plan for the development of a weapon system. "We must get a workable article first," he said.[48]

Based on his mandate from President Truman and his understanding that highest priorities should be given to the development of air defense missiles, Keller picked out the Nike, Terrier, and Sparrow as programs for expedited development.

Speaking of Keller, Dr Wernher von Braun, who had moved to the Redstone Arsenal as director of development operations, recalled: "When he came in things began to move."[49] Limited to a range of 25 miles, the Army's Nike-Ajax antiaircraft missile did not significantly compete with the Air Force Bomarc. However, the Army soon began to develop the Nike-Hercules, which would have a range of 75 miles.[50] Apparently with Keller's enthusiastic support, the Army initiated development of the Redstone missile with a range of 450 miles in 1951.[51] Although the range of the Redstone was reduced to about 200 miles when it was programmed for a heavy thermonuclear warhead, the success with the program indicated that it would be equally feasible to develop another missile derived from the Redstone that would have a range of about 1,500 miles. Believing that the Army might want to deploy its tactical support missiles far to its rear, perhaps a thousand miles or more, Maj Gen James M. Gavin, who was serving as the Army's assistant chief of staff for plans and operations, recommended that the Army should seek to develop a 1,500-mile ballistic missile.[52]

To the Air Force and to the Rand Corporation the development of an intercontinental ballistic missile would serve two useful purposes. It would provide an offensive weapon system, and the boosters employed for the intercontinental missile would also be powerful enough to place military earth satellites in orbit. Even though the Air Force canceled work on the MX-774 Hiroc, General Vandenberg signed a space policy statement on 15 January 1948 that read: "The USAF, as the Service dealing primarily with air weapons—especially Strategic—has logical responsibility for the satellite."[53] Apparently as the result of continued Rand studies, General Saville late in 1950 directed that a long-range rocket study be reinstituted. In view of Convair's earlier work with MX-774, the Air Force awarded a study contract to Convair on 31 January 1951 to investigate the relative merits of glide and ballistic missiles capable of attaining a 5,500-mile range and carrying an 8,000-pound warhead. This study contract soon was limited to an intensive investigation of a ballistic missile. In view of favorable results reported by Convair and evidence of Soviet progress toward the development of high-thrust rockets, the Air Research and Development Command suggested in March 1952 that the MX-1593 research missile—now called Atlas—be reissued in the form of a general operational requirement for the development of such a ballistic missile. However, the Defense Research and Development Board did not approve the continuation of studies on the missile and development of components for it.[54]

The initial studies of the intercontinental Atlas missile visualized large and heavy atomic warheads. However, in the winter of 1952–53, the Atomic Energy Commission's advances in the development of new nuclear weapons pointed the way to the design of small high-yield warheads. In December 1952 the USAF Scientific Advisory Board pointed out that the substantially increased warhead yields meant that accuracy requirements and guidance developments could be somewhat relaxed. By the summer of 1953, Convair was able to show that many of the design characteristics of the Atlas could be met by existing technology. The

Atlas, for example, would be able to use the high-thrust, liquid-fueled rocket engines that had been designed to launch the Navaho missile. Convair estimated that the Atlas could be made operational by 1962; but, in Washington, General Yates, Air Force director of research and development, called attention to the fact that the Atlas development program would be extremely expensive. Whereas the Air Force had received $525 million in new obligational authority for research and development for fiscal year 1953, the new Eisenhower military budget for fiscal year 1954 allotted only $440 million of new money for such expenditure. "It is extremely important," Yates ordered in reference to Atlas, "that this expensive program be carried on at a relatively slow rate with increases planned only on the accomplishment of the several difficult phases of the program."[55]

At the same time that the Air Force was making a decision to go slow in developing the Atlas, other events were occurring that would make it necessary to speed it up. Early in 1953, after taking office as special assistant for research and development to Air Force Secretary Harold E. Talbott, Trevor Gardner actively supported the development of an intercontinental missile. Effective on 30 June 1953, Reorganization Plan 6 abolished the National Defense Research and Development Board and the Office of Director of Guided Missiles and vested these responsibilities in a new Office of Assistant Secretary of Defense for Research and Development. Based on a request received from Gardner, the Department of Defense Armed Forces Policy Council ordered the establishment in June 1953 of a study group of the nation's leading scientists to evaluate strategic missile programs. To perform this task, Gardner assembled a group of scientists under Prof John von Neumann, which would be known as the Air Force Strategic Missiles Evaluation Committee or less formally as the Teapot Committee. Holding the first of three meetings in November 1953, the von Neumann committee undertook to examine both the impact of the thermonuclear breakthrough upon the development of strategic missiles and the possibility that the Soviet Union might be somewhat ahead of the United States in developing ballistic missiles. Later evidence made it apparent that the Soviet Union had addressed itself as early as 1946 to the problem of transporting a 10,000-pound atomic warhead over intercontinental distances. The Soviets had captured the German rocket center at Peenemünde and had taken many German technicians to the USSR, but these technicians were not permitted to participate in the Soviets' advanced development programs. The objective of these programs evidently was to design rockets that could boost five-ton warheads over intercontinental distances. By 1953 many of the German technicians were being allowed to return home; they brought reports of the intense Soviet interest in all phases of missile technology. In the course of its investigation the von Neumann committee got four separate and different intelligence estimates, still Gardner noted that the "lump impression ... is that the Soviets are significantly ahead of us in the strategic missile field."[56]

While the von Neumann committee was at work, the Rand Corporation provided it with technical assistance; Rand also prepared an independent report that was transmitted to the Air Force on 8 February 1954. When the von Neumann committee report was submitted on 10 February, it was prefaced by the observation that

> unusual urgency for a strategic missile capability can arise from one of two principal causes: A rapid strengthening of the Soviet defenses against our SAC manned bombers, or rapid progress by the Soviet in his own development of strategic missiles which would provide a compelling political and psychological reason for our own effort to proceed apace. The former is to be expected during the second half of this decade. As to the latter, the available intelligence data are insufficient to make possible a precise estimate of the progress being made by the Soviet in the development of intercontinental missiles, but evidence exists of an appreciation in this field on the part of the Soviets, and of activity in some important phases of guided missiles which it is natural to connect with the objective of development by the Soviet of intercontinental missiles. Thus, while the evidence may not justify a positive conclusion that the Russians are ahead of us, a grave concern in this regard is in order.[57]

In its review of the Air Force missile program, the von Neumann committee noted that the employment of thermonuclear warheads would permit significant relaxations in requirements for missile thrust and orders of guidance accuracy. The committee concluded that new warheads would make it possible to redesign the Atlas and develop it for operational use in five or six years if the Air Force gave the ballistic missile program overriding priority and centralized directing authority and if the Air Force provided exceptionally competent scientific guidance. Not content merely to limit itself to generalities, the committee made an important study of Air Force research and development management procedures. In developing the B-58 bomber and Matador missile, the Air Force had employed an existing company as the single prime contractor; but the committee stated unequivocally that no single contractor in the United States had sufficient across-the-board technical competence to manage a program to develop an intercontinental ballistic missile. The Air Force similarly did not have sufficient in-house capabilities to manage such a program. The von Neumann committee, therefore, proposed to establish a special management group by drafting highly competent people from universities, industry, and government.[58]

Believing that the strategic necessity for the intercontinental ballistic missile was at least as urgent as the wartime development of the atomic bomb, Trevor Gardner worked diligently to get top-level support for such a missile. After a series of three meetings on the subject of the entire missile program, the Air Force Council recommended on 23 March 1954 that accuracy requirements be reduced for all missiles carrying thermonuclear warheads and that the Atlas program "be reoriented so as to achieve the early establishment of an optimum intercontinental ballistic missile system." General Twining approved the recommendations on the same day. On 14 May the Air Force further directed that developing the Atlas would be given its highest priority.[59] In an unusual management action the Air Research and Development Command established a Western Development Division under the command of Brig Gen Bernard A. Schriever at Inglewood, California, on 1 July. The primary mission of the Western Development Division was to manage the development program for Air Force weapon system 107A (Project Atlas), including ground support for it, and to recommend operational, logistic, and personnel system concepts for the program. Since procurement and contracting for the Air Force was the mission of the Air Materiel Command, this command on 15 August established the Special Aircraft Project Office (later the Ballistic Missiles Office) on the field location at Inglewood.[60]

Seeking to preserve the scientific talent available in von Neumann's committee, Gardner persuaded many of the men who had served on this committee to continue to function as the Atlas Scientific Advisory Committee. At a meeting on 20–21 July the committee again considered the weapon system responsibility for Atlas and again recommended that no existing airframe manufacturer, including Convair (which wanted to assume the role of single prime contractor for the Atlas weapon system), was strong enough in scientific depth and experience to discharge prime contractor responsibilities. In August the Western Development Division determined that systems responsibility could be placed either with an airframe contractor, a university laboratory, an Air Force organization, or a specially qualified contractor who would be independent of the contractors supplying missile components. A contractor of the latter type was already in existence: in September 1953 Simon Ramo and Dean Wooldridge, who had done pioneer management work with the Hughes Aircraft Company in developing the Falcon air-to-air missile, had formed the Ramo-Wooldridge Corporation. General Schriever was impressed with the new corporation and recommended that it be granted the technical direction and systems engineering responsibility for the Atlas program. After being authorized to take the action on 3 September 1954, the Ballistic Missiles Office negotiated a contract with Ramo-Wooldridge to provide the scientists and engineers needed to analyze complex technical and scientific questions and direct systems engineering for the several associated contractors that made up the development team. With their military counterparts in the Western Development Division, the Ramo-Wooldridge technical and scientific personnel were integrated into what Schriever described as "a development-management team, with all elements working on a side-by-side, counterpart basis."[61] Given final assurance by the Atomic Energy Commission that a small high-yield warhead could be expected, this team made final the configuration of the Atlas missile in the last quarter of 1954. In the first six months of 1955, contracts were let for the Atlas airframe and nose cone, guidance and control, and propulsion systems.[62]

At its meeting in July 1945 the Atlas Scientific Advisory Committee had suggested that the United States begin developing an alternate strategic missile to the Atlas at once. The committee had several reasons for its position. Convair's plants were near the California coast and to depend on a single type of strategic missile would make the program extremely vulnerable to hostile attack. In addition, the Atlas was "a big pressurized metal sack" that might collapse under violent maneuvers and a missile with a more conventional structure would offer more prospects for growth potential. While this reasoning was valid, the Air Force was hard put to justify developing a second strategic missile in view of rather stringent expenditure limitations.[63] Some further indecision resulted after 2 December 1954, when the Air Force issued a general operational requirement for a tactical ballistic missile with a range of 1,000–2,000 miles. Schriever feared that the development of a tactical missile would compete for the use of existing test facilities, thereby delaying the Atlas strategic missile. He also suggested that a tactical missile might become a natural fallout from one of the stages of an intercontinental missile.[64]

Early in January 1955 Ramo-Wooldridge provided Schriever with a favorable analysis of the prospects for developing a two-stage, conventional structure intercontinental ballistic missile. On 12 January, Schriever formally asked approval for the alternate strategic missile, pointing out that such a program would provide desirable second sources for subsystems that might be interchangeable between the Atlas and the new missile. By early March the Air Research and Development Command and the Air Materiel Command developed a proposal that went forward to Washington. On 28 April, Secretary Talbott approved a second source for intercontinental missiles, with the understanding that the missile would be constructed well away from either seacoast. The new missile, designated as the XSM-68 Titan, would include a configuration that could be adaptable to exploitation as a tactical ballistic missile. From proposals submitted by several aircraft companies, an Air Force source selection board recommended that the Martin Company appeared best qualified to develop the missile's airframe. A letter contract was issued on 27 October 1955 authorizing Martin to design, develop, and test the airframe for the two-stage XSM-68 and to plan a program for developing the complete weapon system. The Western Development Division and the Ramo-Wooldridge Corporation management team was made responsible for weapon system engineering for the Titan.[65]

At the same time that the Air Force directed the Western Development Division to proceed with the Titan, it directed the division to study and evaluate all possible approaches to the tactical ballistic missile. In line with this directive, Schriever directed his subordinates to look into earlier research studies concerned with solid-propellant technology. Based on this preliminary work, the Air Force contracted in April 1956 for three studies looking toward the development of solid-propellant rocket motors. During this year both the Tactical Air Command and the United States Air Forces in Europe submitted requirements for a tactical ballistic missile that could be launched quickly in response to a battlefield threat, but the Air Force could not validate the requirements because it had to devote its limited funds principally to the development of the intercontinental missiles. A working group headed by Lt Col Edward N. Hall, nevertheless, put together a concept of a three-stage, solid-propellant missile that possibly could be employed by stages for either tactical or strategic purposes. Such a missile would need to be relatively cheap, available in quantity, and capable of rapid launch from hardened ground silos. Because of this growing Air Force interest in such a second-generation ballistic missile, General Schriever designated the working group in September 1957 as a small weapon system office for what was first called Weapon System Q, later Sentry, and, finally, Minuteman.[66]

The operational concepts for the Minuteman missile drawn up by Colonel Hall's group visualized a simple, reliable, rugged missile with a long storage life and simplified maintenance requirements. The missiles could be deployed in underground silos that were spaced far enough apart and sufficiently hardened so that an enemy warhead could destroy no more than one missile. The missiles could be maintained in constant readiness to fire, and a given complex of missiles could be controlled by an automatic monitoring and launch system. This missile would not be able to carry as heavy a warhead as the Atlas or Titan, but Ramo-Wooldridge argued that "by keeping the missile small and the weapon system cost low, we can more readily afford to size the force so that a sufficiently large portion of the force will survive, irrespective of actions taken by the enemy."[67]

Soviet Threats Speed Missile Development

As late as the spring of 1955, the Eisenhower administration apparently assumed that the Soviet Union would not have the technology to counterbalance American strategic superiority until late in the 1960s. Based on new information, however, the Technological Capabilities Panel of the President's Science Advisory Committee — called the Killian committee after its chairman, James R. Killian — reported to President Eisenhower on 14 February 1955 a deep concern about the vulnerability of North America to surprise attack. To enable the United States to meet this threat, the Killian committee recommended that the Air Force give top priority to developing intercontinental missiles and that the Air Force proceed with developing intermediate range ballistic missiles (IRBMs). The committee argued that the latter action was essential to the national security. Lending support to the new strategic estimates of the increasing threat to US security, the Soviets displayed enough type-39 heavy jet bombers at the 1955 May Day celebration in Moscow to make it evident that these equivalents of the Air Force's B-52 had been in quantity production as much as a year earlier than anticipated.[68] In October 1955 the National Security Council accepted much of the Killian committee's report, which recommended the highest national priority be extended to the development of the intercontinental ballistic missile (ICBM) and additionally recommended that land- and ship-based intermediate range ballistic missiles should be considered essential to the national security. By December, President Eisenhower had assigned highest priorities to the Atlas, Titan, Jupiter, and Thor programs.[69]

In March 1955 General Gavin already had recommended to Gen Matthew B. Ridgway that the Army proceed with the development of a ballistic missile with a 1,500-mile range; however, Ridgway turned the proposal down because he anticipated that the Army could not get the money for such a program.[70] In November 1955 the Joint Chiefs of Staff studied the matter of intermediate range ballistic missiles and, with Gen Maxwell B. Taylor dissenting, advised Secretary of

Defense Charles E. Wilson that the Navy had a valid requirement for a ship-based intermediate range ballistic missile and that the Air Force had a similar requirement for a land-based intermediate range ballistic missile but the Army had no valid requirement for such a capability.[71] Wilson was unwilling to accept this guidance. On 8 November he ordered that an Army-Navy team work together on an intermediate range ballistic missile that would be modeled largely after the Army's Redstone rocket and that the Air Force independently develop another intermediate range ballistic missile. Even though he established a Department of Defense Ballistic Missiles Committee to coordinate the separate programs, Wilson frankly expected that interservice competition would continue. Nevertheless, he felt that this interservice rivalry would hasten the development of an intermediate range missile. Wilson realized that this duplication of effort would increase the expense to the nation. At the same time that he established the Ballistic Missiles Committee, Wilson created the Air Force Ballistic Missile Committee and the Joint Army-Navy Ballistic Missile Committee.[72]

Recognizing that the Soviets would score a tremendous advantage if they placed intercontinental ballistic missiles into operation before the United States possessed a similar capability, Trevor Gardner stated "that we had to get that weapon first." The Air Force did not want anything to interfere with the development of intercontinental missiles. Gardner recorded that the immediate effect of the effort to produce an intermediate range missile would be to establish a competition for hardware, people, money, and facilities that might well jeopardize the Air Force's objective of attaining a strategic missile capability at an early date. He also described Wilson's directive as "causing committees to be born at a rather rapid rate. Those of us who had been running the program found [that] we were now working part time for committees and spending large fractions of our time . . . justifying ourselves before these various committees at the Secretary of Defense level and within the Air Force." Convinced that "current budgets in research and development would not permit us to remain technically superior to the Russians in airpower," lacking "sympathy with the kind of organization that was set up to manage the ballistic-missile activity," and "alarmed that the total Air Force budget would simply guarantee us the second best Air Force in the future," Gardner resigned as assistant secretary of the Air Force for research and development and presented his views in a series of magazine articles early in 1956.[73]

Viewing the Wilson decision in retrospect, Secretary of the Army Wilber Brucker later remarked that giving the Army the authority to develop an intermediate range ballistic missile stirred "another one of the services," which was "not interested except passingly in the IRBM," into immediate action and the competition between these two services accelerated progress on the missile program, with the Army moving forward on some of its plans "a year to a year and a half" earlier than originally scheduled.[74] At Redstone Arsenal, Maj Gen John B. Medaris had already been designated to command an expanded Army missile activity in October 1955; the Army Ballistic Missile Agency was officially established there on 1 February 1956. Studies on the Army's Jupiter missile had gotten under way in the summer of 1955 and, following the Wilson decision, plans to develop the Army IRBM went forward rapidly. The Jupiter would use the same engines that the Air Force had developed for the Navaho booster and that the Air Force would use in the Atlas. Based on the belief that nuclear warheads smaller than those planned for land-based IRBMs and ICBMs could not be made available, the Navy participated in the initial planning for the Jupiter. In September 1956, however, the Atomic Energy Commission (AEC) advised the Department of Defense that even smaller warheads could be developed. As a result of this information, the Navy sought permission to withdraw from the liquid-fueled Jupiter program to develop a smaller solid-propellant fleet ballistic missile that would be called the Polaris. Wilson gave his approval in November 1956 and the Navy completely withdrew from the Jupiter program on 10 December 1956.[75] In keeping with the Army's arsenal concept, the Army Ballistic Missile Agency served as designer and prime contractor for the Jupiter missile and contracted with the Chrysler Corporation for hand-tooled test quantities of the airframes required for assembly of the completed missile.[76]

Presenting an admittedly Air Force view on the subject, Gen Charles S. Irvine described both the Army Jupiter and the Air Force Thor as fallouts from the Atlas program. The Army disputed this claim in the case of the Jupiter.[77] The Air Force's Thor project, however, was clearly derived from ongoing missile programs and followed a plan that had been developed by the Western Development Division and Ramo-Wooldridge team even before the Air Force assigned the intermediate range ballistic missile project to the Air Research and Development Command on 18 November 1955. The Thor (SM-75) would utilize already developed engines, nose cones, and guidance systems, and the only new contractor required for it was for the construction of the airframe. A letter contract was issued on 27 December 1955 to the Douglas Aircraft Corporation for the development of the SM-75 airframe and for assembly and testing of the missile. The first Thor arrived at the Air Force Missile Test Center, Patrick AFB, Florida, on 18 October 1956, less than a year after the Air Force ordered the development of the missile. The first Thors were handmade articles, but the Douglas Company had prepared to begin production in quantity from the project's beginning.[78]

When he directed, in November 1955, that both the Army and the Air Force develop intermediate range ballistic missiles, Secretary Wilson had announced that development of the missiles would not prejudice the roles and missions of the services. "I am going," he said, "to let Admiral Radford and the chiefs take enough time to worry about . . . the specific roles and missions at some later date after we know what we have."[79] Army spokesmen, nevertheless, made it very clear that they wanted the intermediate range missile. Early in 1956 General Taylor boldly asserted the Army's claim to a 1,500-mile-range missile. "Our Army mission," he said, "is to destroy an enemy on the ground anyplace. . . . We are very interested in being able to use for Army purposes against Army targets any missile of any range."[80] After becoming the chief of Army research and development, General Gavin urged that "TAC air is going out" and that the Army would need missiles to fight in an area "from the Black Sea to the Mediterranean where TAC has no requirements." Army leaders also urged that the Jupiter be mobile and suited for field deployment. In contrast, the Air Force Thor would have to be deployed in fixed positions.[81]

In the event of future hostilities, Secretary Wilson conceived that a unified commander "would use all available weapons and all kinds of people that were made available to him"; for this reason Wilson was not too concerned about whether the Army, Navy, and Air Force might develop a given weapon, or how that weapon might fit into the service roles and missions. Nevertheless, he requested that Adm Arthur W. Radford discuss the effect of new weapons on the service roles and missions with the Joint Chiefs of Staff. Although Wilson considered the advice of the Joint Chiefs of Staff, he apparently exercised his own judgment on the matter. The Air Force possessed reconnaissance, intelligence, and ancillary capabilities required to employ a 1,500-mile-range missile. As explained by a defense spokesman, a 1,500-mile missile "gets into the strategic mission — strategic as distinct from the tactical part of the battle."[82] Announcing his decisions in a major policy document issued on 26 November 1956, Secretary Wilson ruled that the Army would continue to develop surface-to-surface missiles for the close support of Army field operations but that the Army's zone of operations would be defined as extending not more than 100 miles beyond the front lines and normally about 100 miles to the rear of the front lines. The dimensions of the Army combat zone, thus, would place a range limitation of about 200 miles on the design criteria for Army missiles. Wilson ordered that operational employment of land-based intermediate range ballistic missiles would be the sole responsibility of the Air Force, that operational employment of ship-based intermediate range ballistic missiles would be the sole responsibility of the Navy, and that the Army "will not plan at this time for the operational employment of the Intermediate Range Ballistic Missile or for any other missiles with ranges beyond 200 miles."[83]

Decisions for Production and Deployment

With the exception of the Army's Nike-Ajax and Redstone, the Air Force's Matador, and the Navy's pilotless aircraft called the Regulus, Department of Defense missiles had not progressed beyond the research and development stage by the spring of 1957. Initially because of budgetary limitations and then because of the impact of the Soviet Sputnik, the Department of Defense faced many moments of truth during fiscal year 1958 when decisions had to be made on the acceptance or rejection of new weapon systems that were approaching readiness for production and operational deployment. These decisions would be agonizing at best and the decisionmaking process would be complicated by interservice rivalry—which, though it may have proved useful in hastening research and development, may have resulted in a maze of claims and counterclaims as to the advantages or disadvantages of particular systems.

In July 1958 the Air Force faced the problem of maintaining a force in being that would deter large and small wars, while simultaneously bearing the expense of developing missiles for future employment within a fiscal year 1958 expenditure ceiling of $17.9 billion.[84] Monetary considerations forced a sweeping reconsideration of the Air Force missile programs. As has been seen, Air Force developmental planners had assumed in the late 1940s that there would be a gap between the time when piloted aircraft would become obsolete and would be replaced by ballistic missiles; these planners expected that air-breathing pilotless missiles would be valuable weapons in the transitional phase. To meet this latter requirement, the Air Force had put the SM-62 Snark, the SM-63 Rascal, and the SM-64 Navaho under development. Following then current logistical concepts, the Air Force had designated an aviation company as the single prime manager for the Snark, Rascal, and Navaho. The Air Force had intended to pursue a "fly-before-buy" policy, but many factors other than management were involved and each of these programs slipped badly. None of the programs were operational by the middle 1950s. The elapsed time from program approval to the first operational unit deployment of the Snark was 13.4 years. With all-out developmental priorities, including prime weapon systems management by the Western Development Division and Ramo-Wooldridge team and a new concurrency concept of development, the cycle of development to unit deployment of the SM-75 Thor and the SM-65 Atlas was reduced to 3.3 and 4.9 years respectively. Had the Thor and Atlas been developed on a "fly-before-buy" basis, the Air Force estimated that their development-to-deployment cycle would have been nearly four years longer.[85] By early 1957 it was evident that the pilotless aircraft and the ballistic missiles would enter the operating inventory not at staggered intervals but at approximately the same time, and it was equally evident that the ballistic missiles would be the superior weapons.

By the spring of 1957 the Air Force had invested $679.8 million in the research and development of the Navaho during the many years of the program. Facing the fact that the high-altitude, cruise-type Navaho had been superseded by the Atlas and Titan, the Air Force canceled the Navaho program on 8 July. Although the Navaho program never produced a weapon system, the Air Force considered it as "anything but an unqualified failure." The Navaho program had permitted a continuing development of the large liquid-fueled engines that, in the end, powered the Atlas, Thor, and Jupiter missiles. The inertial guidance system developed for the Navaho enabled the Navy's Polaris-equipped submarines to make the accurate fixes of their positions at sea that they would need for missile firings. The design for the Mach-3 B-70 bomber was heavily based on a scale-up of the Navaho. And the North American X-10 test vehicle that was developed during the program provided many of the design features that would be incorporated into the Hound Dog GAM-77, a lightweight air-to-ground missile that was developed speedily in place of the never satisfactory Rascal. At the cancellation of the Navaho, moreover, the North American Company was able to use its design team and facilities for the accelerated development of the Hound Dog when the contract for the development of this missile was awarded on 16 September 1957.[86]

Unlike the Navaho, the Snark would be only a partial casualty to technological progress since it could enter the operating inventory prior to guided ballistic missiles. Although it would not be as efficient as a manned B-52, the Snark ensured against a loss of aircrews, had quick reaction time, and could be programmed for low-level attack. Weighing these factors, the Air Force made the decision to reduce the objective of the Snark program from one wing with 120 missiles to a group with 30 missiles; the Air Force scheduled the unit to be activated in August 1959. Technically the world's first intercontinental missile after its successful 4,400-mile test flight on 31 October 1957, the Snark was considered to be a complement to the manned bomber force since it would compound an enemy's defense problem.[87]

On the basis of the high development priorities that President Eisenhower had extended to the intercontinental and intermediate range ballistic missiles, the Air Force and the Western Development Division—which was designated as the Air Force Ballistic Missile Division on 1 June 1957—assumed that the Atlas, Titan, and Thor would be programmed for full weapon systems development during fiscal year 1958. Alarmed about budgetary ceilings, however, the secretary of defense sent the National Security Council a list of proposed changes in the ballistic missile program. In August 1957 the National Security Council and President Eisenhower concurred in the secretary's recommendations. In brief, only Atlas would continue in weapon system production, while Titan would continue in a status of a little more than development. A Defense Department committee would evaluate Thor and Jupiter to determine which would continue in development.[88] In the summer of 1957, Secretary Wilson promised to make the choice between Thor and Jupiter before retiring from office. This and other decisions, however, were going to be made by Secretary of Defense Neil H. McElroy, who succeeded Wilson on 9 October 1957, just in time to have to reevaluate US missile programs in the light of the Soviet Sputnik I.[89]

In the aftermath of the Soviet's successful launch of the world's first satellite, Secretary McElroy accepted Air Force plans for some acceleration of Atlas production and for programming the activation of nine Atlas squadrons. However, he chose to continue to evaluate the Titan, Thor-Jupiter, and an antimissile defense system. The Thor-Jupiter problem continued to be greatly complicated. In General Taylor's mind the assignment of operational Jupiter missiles to the Air Force amounted "virtually to killing the program, because this Army-built weapon has never appealed to the Air Force."[90] General Irvine, on the other hand, thought that the Thor and Jupiter were "about as alike as the Ford and the Chevrolet," and that one but not both of them ought to be selected for production. To produce both would wastefully duplicate training and ground support equipment. Irvine argued that the Thor had been developed with "hard tooling" and was ready for production, whereas Jupiter was still an "experimental and prototype missile."[91] After deliberation, Secretary McElroy evidently felt that the combination of the two IRBM programs would accelerate the accumulation of knowledge in an area where

MISSILE TECHNOLOGY

little background was available. On 25 November he decided that both Thor and Jupiter would be produced for the operational inventory. At this time McElroy directed the Air Force and the Army to produce and deploy four Thor and four Jupiter IRBM squadrons to NATO nations between December 1958 and March 1960.[92] This decision did not immediately end the interservice difference over the concept as to whether the intermediate range ballistic missiles should be employed from a fixed, but semihardened emplacement as the Air Force conceived or from mobile field positions as the Army wanted. The Army continued to program Jupiter for field mobility until November 1958, when the Air Force concept prevailed.[93]

In its post-Sputnik proposals for an accelerated intercontinental ballistic missile program, the Air Force recommended that the Titan be expanded into a full-scale weapon system and that Minuteman be put into development. On 12 December, the Department of Defense gave its approval for a nine-squadron Atlas force and a four-squadron Titan force.[94] On 27 February 1958 the Department of Defense also authorized the Air Force to proceed with research and development on the SM-80 Minuteman missile, but DOD now appeared reluctant to proceed with the authorized weapon-system status for Titan possibly because of the expectation that the second-generation Minuteman would prove to be a superior missile. At any rate, the Department of Defense demanded many studies of the Titan as compared with the Atlas. As a result of these studies, which it made during the summer and early autumn of 1958, the Air Force admitted that the cost for the logistical support for two ICBM systems would be about $200 million more than for a single system, but the Air Force maintained that the Titan held many potential advantages. It had more growth potential than the Atlas both for the extension of its range and for an increase in its payload, and the solid-structured Titan promised to provide a better vehicle for space exploitation purposes. Bringing both Atlas and Titan into the combat inventory would provide more missile units in a shorter time and would maintain a larger production base for missiles. Neither Atlas nor Titan had been fully tested, and the Air Force was reluctant to risk the security of the nation by adopting a single system until complete research and development proved it to be irrefutably superior. The task of hardening the Titan promised to be easier than would be the case with the thin-skinned Atlas; Titan would use storable liquid fuel, thus giving it a better reaction time.[95]

Jolted as much as the other military services by Sputniks I and II, the US Navy promptly instituted an independent reevaluation of the Polaris intermediate range ballistic missile program that had gotten under way in December 1956. This program involved the deployment of solid-fuel Polaris missiles aboard nuclear submarines. The Navy originally had planned to have the Polaris-equipped nuclear submarines ready for operations in 1963, but the Navy believed that it would be possible to accelerate the program and move deployment up to 1960. Secretary McElroy approved this accelerated program in early December 1957.[96] The Polaris program involved a marriage of solid-propellant missiles that were equipped with lightweight, high-yield thermonuclear warheads, which had not been perfected, with nuclear submarines that would have to be built. Still the Department of Defense considered Polaris to be a low-risk program. The lightweight warhead had been guaranteed by the Atomic Energy Commission, the solid-propellant missile had benefited from earlier technology, guidance systems were well under way because of the Atlas program, and the nuclear submarine *Nautilus* had been at sea for some time. The only uncertainty was whether or not a submarine would be able to launch the Polaris missiles from under the surface of the sea: if this proved impossible it would still be possible for the submarine to "pop up" and launch its missiles.[97]

Interservice Disputes about Antimissile Defense

Only a small suspicious cloud in the early 1950s, a divergence of Army and Air Force concepts of air defense stormed up rapidly with the development of what appeared to be competing technological capabilities but which were actually, as Gen Thomas D. White pointed out, "a disagreement or different point of view on what is the proper and most economical defense, point defense or area defense."[98] As viewed by General Taylor, the Joint Chiefs of Staff agreement of 1949 that allocated primary responsibility for the development of short-range surface-to-air missiles to the Army and Navy was predicated on the understanding that the line of demarcation in air defense research efforts "was that the Army was interested in extending its traditional antiaircraft artillery role, which is largely point defense of vital targets, whereas the Air Force's legitimate interest was more in the interceptor role, so that the missiles they would go for would perform interceptor-type missions."[99]

As previously noted, the Air Force discontinued its research on short-range surface-to-air missiles after 1949 and began to put together the semiautomatic ground environment (SAGE) systems needed to control an area defense of the United States by fighter-interceptor aircraft and Bomarc ground-to-air pilotless interceptor missiles. Even though an earlier Project Wizard conducted by the University of Michigan Air Research Center revealed no promising technological developments for a defense against a hostile ballistic missile attack, the Air Research and Development Command on 6 July 1953 directed its Cambridge Research Center-Lincoln Laboratory team to prepare a plan (Project Wizard 3) for defense against intercontinental ballistic missiles. Based on the preliminary findings the Air Force awarded three contracts to three aircraft electronic company teams for the purpose of identifying the means needed to detect or identify and to intercept and destroy hostile ballistic missiles. On the basis of these reports, the USAF Scientific Advisory Board concluded that any quick-fix solution, such as the use of modified Talos or Bomarc missiles against hostile missiles, would be greatly expensive and not apt to succeed. Although Wizard 3 did not succeed in its main purpose, it produced important bonus technology in the form of a high-powered radar with a detection range up to 3,000 miles and computers that would permit a quick determination of a ballistic missile's trajectory. Operating at

MISSILE TECHNOLOGY

a site at Milestone Hill near the Lincoln Laboratory, the experimental radar was able to view missile firings from Patrick AFB, Florida.[100]

The production and deployment of the Army's Nike-Ajax ground-to-air antiaircraft missile beginning in 1953 did not contravene the Army-Air Force understanding about air defense since the Ajax was clearly a point-defense weapon with a range of about 25 miles. In mid-1953, however, the Army began to develop the Nike-Hercules, which would have a range of about 75 miles. Since the Nike-Hercules would overlap the range of the Bomarc, General Gavin predicted that conflict in air defense roles and missions would be almost inevitable. In mid-1956 Lt Gen Stanley R. Mickelsen, commander of the Army Antiaircraft Command, had predicted: "Nike is capable of killing any known guided missile and will be effective against the intercontinental ballistic missile when it materializes."[101] In November 1956 the Army approved an additional program for the development of an antimissile system that would be known as the Nike-Zeus.[102] At the same time that the Army was extending the range of its Nike family of missiles, General Taylor denounced the Air Force's rumored intention to procure and deploy Navy-developed Talos air-to-ground missiles as "an invasion of the Army's antiaircraft mission."[103]

In preparing a memorandum to clarify service roles and missions, which he issued on 26 November 1956, Secretary Wilson noted that the Air Force wanted to deploy Talos missile installations around some of its air bases.[104] In an attempt to clarify the air defense mission, Wilson directed that the commander in chief, Continental Air Defense Command, has the authority and duty to state an operational need for new and improved weapon systems and to recommend to the Joint Chiefs of Staff all new installations of any type. The secretary further directed that the Air Force would be responsible for area defense and that the Army would be responsible for point defense. The point-defense surface-to-air missiles would be designed "for use against air targets at expected altitudes out to a horizontal range on the order of 100 nautical miles." Wilson directed that the Army would continue to develop the Nike-Ajax and Nike-Hercules and would assume responsibility for development of the land-based Talos. The Air Force would continue to develop Bomarc, and the Navy was given a free hand to develop ship-based air defense systems.[105]

Even though Wilson's memorandum placed a limit on the range of Army point defenses, it did not change the Army's concept of how the air defense of the United States ought to be built. The Army's concept of continental air defense involved a building-block approach whereby ground-to-air missile protection would first be given to strategic air bases, population centers, and other vital points and then would be extended outward to protect the remainder of the nation as far as funds permitted. To effect this system of air defense, the Army employed Nike missile batteries for high-level coverage, Hawk missile batteries for low-altitude protection, and radar for the control of the individual batteries. The Army argued that independently controlled ground-to-air missile batteries would be difficult to destroy. On the other hand, it said that the elaborate communications through which the SAGE system would control Bomarc missiles and manned interceptors would be easier for an enemy to destroy.[106] The Air Force doctrine on air defense continued to visualize an area defense in which an air defense commander would maintain the integrity of his forces and would not permit them to be parceled out, and it taught that the enemy should be intercepted and destroyed as far as possible from a defended area. "The principle of air defense," General White explained, "should be to strike the enemy just as far from his target as possible. The best defense is to hit him before he gets off the ground with his bomber or with his missile. . . . The worst and last-ditch business is over his intended target over here."[107]

In 1957 General Taylor, along with other Army representatives, urged the secretary of defense and the Joint Chiefs of Staff to accept a "crash $6 billion program in order to achieve an operational capability with the Nike-Zeus by 1961."[108] At this same time the Air Force took a more measured look at the nation's defense requirements. The Air Force believed that the Soviet Union could have an initial operational capability with prototype intercontinental ballistic missiles sometime between mid-1958 and mid-1959 but would not be able to rely solely on this small capability to launch an attack against the United States. Thus, until about 1962, any attack against the United States would have to be made by a mass of Soviet aircraft supplemented by intercontinental ballistic missiles. Based on these estimates the Air Force visualized a requirement for an air defense system that could counter a mixed-force threat. Since the Soviets would undoubtedly aim their missiles at American strategic retaliatory forces, the immediate Air Force objective was to provide three ballistic missile early warning sites that—with 3,000-mile-range radar developed from the Milestone Hill model—could provide approximately 15 minutes warning of the arrival of hostile ballistic missiles. This short warning time would permit the Strategic Air Command to launch at least a part of its strategic retaliatory force and might save the lives of many people who then would have at least a little time to take cover.[109] Other than this plan, General White was willing to admit that the nation's air defenses were not what they should be. "The active air defense," he said, "is a can of worms, to be real honest; there are so many different kinds of weapon systems. We have got the Nike; we have got the Bomarc; we have manned interceptors; we have the radar for not only the early warning but the actual tracking and control of fighters and of Bomarcs."[110]

Expressing a lack of enthusiasm for the area and point-defense concepts of air defense, Secretary McElroy established the Advanced Research Projects Agency (ARPA) within the Department of Defense on 7 February 1958 and charged it with providing unified direction and management of the antimissile programs and for outer space projects.[111] Before establishing ARPA, McElroy already had directed the Air Force on 16 January to continue as a matter of urgency that portion of the Wizard program which would perfect early warning radars, tracking and acquisition radars, communications links between early warning radars and the active air defense system, and the data-processing components required to form an integrated system. Simultaneously, he directed the Army to continue its development effort on the Nike-Zeus as a matter of urgency in order to concentrate efforts on developing a system that would demonstrate the feasibility of achieving an effective anti-ICBM system that could discriminate against electronic countermeasures and decoys. The Army was to limit itself to working on the missile and launch system and to developing of acquisition, tracking, and computer components required for an integrated missile system. In effect McElroy's directive made the Army responsible for designing an antimissile missile, while the Air Force was charged to create an effective missile detection system.[112] Although McElroy stated that the principal officers in the Air Force thought that his plan was "a reasonable way to proceed," General LeMay told senators on 21 January that the decision "does not add up to me, and it does not add up to the Air Force. The Air Force recommended that the two missions go together."[113] A little later, Secretary of the Air Force James H. Douglas expressed the optimistic hope that the directives covered no more than development and that a decision as to the operational assignment responsibilities had not been made.[114] As it was charged to do, the Air Force promptly canceled the three study contracts in which it was seeking means to intercept and destroy hostile ballistic missiles;[115] but Secretary Douglas continued to hope that, once developed by the Army, antimissile defense — following the precedent of the Jupiter — would be placed under the Air Force for operational employment.[116] Chairman Carl Vinson of the House Committee on Armed Services was also disappointed at the split responsibility in the antimissile defense. On 28 January he sent McElroy a letter expressing his committee's recommendation that the total responsibility for antimissile defense, operational as well as developmental, should be promptly assigned to the Army.[117]

While the division of authority within the Defense Department for the development of an antimissile defense system would not be changed, the interest engendered in the subject resulted in some clarification in national air defense responsibilities. One problem that concerned the Air Force was a fear that, in the confusion of a national emergency, friendly Army air defense missiles might accidently shoot down Air Force planes. General LeMay was adamant about the need for a complete integration of Army weapons in a true defense in depth that would prevent losses of friendly aircraft to friendly antiaircraft missiles. "Our air offensive and our air defense," LeMay said, "cannot be permitted to interfere with each other. This requires extremely close direction and control to assure protection of our offensive and defensive forces and the most effective destruction of enemy forces."[118] In its report on the military construction bill for fiscal year 1959, the Senate Committee on Armed Services called attention to the fact that both the Army and Air Force had been making defense plans "without regard to the accumulation of long-range contingent liabilities." Thus, the final bill passed by Congress required the secretary of defense to determine which missiles or combination of missiles were to be employed in specific areas. After more than a year's study of the very complex subject, the secretary of defense approved an air defense master plan on 19 June 1959 that projected the air defense system that was to be operational in the continental United States by fiscal year 1963. In broad detail the secretary accepted the Air Force concepts of area defense, an integrated air defense in depth, and a centralized control of air defense weapons.[119] However, the air defense master plan required marked changes and reductions in the Air Force continental air defense program.

Integrating Missiles into the Air Force

"To say there is not a deeply ingrained prejudice in favor of aircraft among flyers," stated General White, whose service as vice chief of staff and chief of staff of the Air Force spanned the eight years after June 1953, "would be a stupid statement for me to make. Of course there is."[120] General LeMay, who became vice chief of staff in July 1957 and chief of staff of the Air Force in July 1961, was similarly candid in a speech in Philadelphia in September 1961. "I seek weapon systems," LeMay said, "that I think can do the best job and afford the nation the most protection. In military thinking I am a conservative. I believe we shouldn't discard a proven, reliable weapon system or concept unless we have something that is able to replace it and do a better job. In short, I believe in having protection along with progress."[121]

The Air Force problem of providing "protection along with progress" greatly complicated all phases in the process of providing modernization. "In 1946, right after the end of the war," Dr Edward Teller stated, "we could have said: Let us develop ballistic missiles. . . . Well, we did go into the development of ballistic missiles, but at an exceedingly slow and small rate. We did not start a vigorous development because it could not be proved that these missiles [would] be really important." Although the Soviets apparently were willing to take great gambles in their development programs, Teller noted that Americans were willing to spend billions when they knew there was a big payoff in prospect but were conservative when it came to spending even a few millions on something no one could predict for certain would pay off. "In this intermediate range of practical research," he concluded, "we have been rather poor."[122] Speaking about barriers to Air Force missile development, Colonel Hall, who became chief of the Western Development Division's propulsion development, pointed out: "The barrier to be overcome was not of sound, or heat, but of the mind, which is really the only type that man is ever confronted with anyway." Hall noted that the armed services were compelled "to justify their development activities in terms of the economic validity of the gains to be achieved. No new weapon, however spectacular, can really be justified," he said, "unless it promises to perform military tasks at a lower gross cost than will any weapon system preceding it."[123]

At the same time that new weapons had to be justified in terms of lower gross costs, they also had to be justified within the Air Force in terms of operational suitability. To some extent the concept of force modernization made for a dichotomy between operational concerns and the need for combat readiness on the one hand and research and development on the other; this gap was closed only gradually. The original definition of the Air Force guided missile projects in

1945-46 was generated by a small group of men within the Air Staff who were almost entirely concerned with an expansion and exploitation of technology.[124] Senior Air Force officers accepted the proposition that the Air Force must develop experimental missiles, but they believed that push-button warfare was far from a reality. In consolidating its missile development projects in May 1947, the Air Force gave priority to missiles that could support or defend against a strategic air offensive. The Air Force also accepted the decision that missiles would be integrated into the force structure as an evolutionary undertaking. This policy required the Air Force "to program guided missile units in addition to its manned aircraft units, and as the effectiveness of the missiles is established the extent to which they will replace or supplement manned aircraft units may be considered."[125] In spite of this decision, the Air Force did not form operational concepts for missiles until 1952, nearly seven years after the technical projects had been established. Issued on 18 September 1952, the Air Force policy letter on guided missiles declared:

> Concepts concerning the organization of pilotless aircraft units, their logistic support, and their tactical operation are being developed that basically adhere to existing concepts for Air Force operations. In short, it has become clear that the Air Force will incorporate pilotless aircraft into its organization with only slightly more readjustment than is necessary when new models of more conventional aircraft types are made available to its flying units.[126]

The thought that missiles had different characteristics from aircraft matured rather slowly. By 15 August 1955 the Air Force was willing to state a stronger policy that recognized that "guided missiles are weapons with special qualities." "Manned aircraft techniques," noted the new Air Force policy statement, "have, of necessity, been the basis in the past for most of the development practices and planning for use of missiles. Reluctance to depart from such development practices and planning procedures may prevent maximum progress." This policy still contemplated that a limited number of missile units would be formed by appropriate commands to provide operational data, but this action would have to be initiated during the research and development program. Plans for integrating missile units into the combat inventory, moreover, would have to be made even before operational data on the capabilities of the missiles was complete.[127] Apparently since little thought had been given to the conceptual problem earlier, the Air Force found itself in need of answers to many questions about missiles in 1956. Asked deputy assistant for programming Col Jack N. Donohew in December 1956,

> will an airpower represented only by ballistic missiles located in this hemisphere represent a "Maginot line" concept and thereby cause a trend toward military isolationism.... How long will you require a dual force, manned and unmanned, before you are willing to accept the unmanned? How long will you wait before you will be willing to give up a manned unit and take an unmanned unit in its place? What sort of a kill capability will you insist upon in the unmanned weapon knowing that it will give you one

sortie? How will you assure yourself that the unmanned weapon is always ready to go? Can you shift your thinking from a "control of the air" concept based on actual combat operations to one of "deterrent control of the air" based on unmanned weapon systems in being and capable of instantaneous launch? How much assurance of operational capability must you have before you will be willing to stake the future of this nation on the pressing of a button—a button that launches an attack which cannot be recalled?[128]

Answers to these conceptual questions had to be evolved separately in the Strategic Air Command, the Tactical Air Command, and the Air Defense Command.

Integrating Missiles into the Strategic Air Command

The Strategic Air Command's mission of maintaining a constant state of split-second combat readiness greatly complicated any aspect of force expansion or modernization. In the early 1950s the Strategic Air Command (SAC) devised successful procedures for reequipping and retraining some of its wings while others continued to maintain combat readiness. The success of these procedures, however, demanded that new equipment should be virtually combat ready before it was assigned to strategic air wings.[129] As the result of the requirement established in 1944, the Air Force elected to develop a Boeing six-engine, medium-range B-47 jet bomber. The plane made its first flight in 1947 and entered production in 1948; the Strategic Air Command received the first operational aircraft in 1951. The B-47 became the standard aircraft for replacing the old B-29s and B-50s and equivalent reconnaissance types in the 26 medium bombardment and five medium strategic reconnaissance wings allocated to the Strategic Air Command in the Air Force 137-wing program.

Although design studies had begun in 1945, the Boeing eight-engine, long-range B-52 did not attain a final design configuration until 1950. Produced from a contract issued in February 1951, the first B-52 flew in April 1952. The first operational B-52 was delivered to a SAC combat unit in 1955, and B-52s and RB-52s were programmed to replace B-36s and RB-36s in the seven heavy bombardment and four heavy strategic reconnaissance wings allocated to the Strategic Air Command in the 137-wing program.[130]

In the original planning for the 137-wing Air Force expansion, the Strategic Air Command was allocated eight strategic fighter wings and two strategic fighter reconnaissance wings, but how these wings would be employed or what their equipment would be remained in doubt. In March 1951, the McDonnell Aircraft Corporation's XF-88A won the design competition for a long-range fighter. After substantial modification and redesignation as the F-101A Voodoo, this plane was slated for procurement and delivery to the Strategic Air Command in a fighter and reconnaissance configuration in the 1956–60 time period. What the Strategic Air Command actually wanted was an intercontinental range fighter that could precede bombers to a target area in an advance wave and eliminate hostile interceptors, probably by delivering nuclear weapons against airfields. The only fighter that the Air Research and Development Command could visualize for this role would be as big as a medium bomber. SAC, declining to receive such a plane, modified the 137-wing program to increase its B-47 wings from 26 to 28, with a corresponding reduction in fighter wing authority. In May 1956 SAC inactivated another fighter wing and replaced it with a unique light strategic reconnaissance wing equipped at first with RB-57 aircraft. The five strategic fighter and one strategic fighter reconnaissance wings that SAC retained continued to be equipped with F-84F and RF-84F aircraft.[131]

Neither the B-47 nor the B-52 were supersonic aircraft, but studies initiated by Boeing and Convair in 1946 indicated the feasibility of a supersonic jet bomber and outlined its characteristics. After renewed studies started in 1949, the Air Force published a general operational requirement for a supersonic bomber in 1952. Both Boeing and Convair submitted designs, and the development contract was let with Convair in February 1953 for an XB-58 aircraft, a bomber that in many respects would resemble a blown-up version of Convair's F-102 Delta Dagger fighter-interceptor. Following the new development concept, the B-58 would be developed as a complete weapon system with Convair as the single prime contractor. After reviewing the B-58 program at a master planning board meeting in December 1954, a Strategic Air Command representative liked the supersonic capabilities of the aircraft but bluntly stated that the plane's lack of intercontinental range was somewhat less than what SAC desired for a replacement for the B-47 medium bomber. The Strategic Air Command continued to have reservations about the B-58 even after it was first flown in November 1956. Whether the Air Force would order procurement of the relatively expensive B-58 remained in doubt through most of 1957, pending performance tests of the prototype model.[132]

As soon as the B-52 was committed to production, General Power, then vice commander of the Strategic Air Command, requested on 30 March 1953 that for the 1960–65 time period the Air Force undertake developmental studies for a new high-performance intercontinental bomber that should "embody the longest range, highest altitude, and greatest speed (in that order of priority) [possible] in the time period under consideration and consistent with requirements of military payload and defensive systems." Power pointed out that missiles would have to attain a high degree of accuracy and reliability before they could replace or supplement manned aircraft units. He further noted: "Regardless of the missile program, it is the opinion of this headquarters that the continued advance in the art of manned flight to high altitudes and long ranges should be at all times a priority objective of the Air Force's development program."[133]

Even though Air Force aircraft had always utilized petroleum fuels, the Boeing Company, when given a one-year contract to study Power's request, proposed a new approach to the twin requirements of speed and endurance. The application of nuclear energy had been under study since 1946, and more recent investigations promised to develop a new high-energy chemical fuel. Boeing proposed to develop a nuclear cruise bomber that would utilize high-energy chemical fuel for a high-speed dash. In mid-1954 both the Joint Congressional Committee on Atomic Energy and the Air Force Council were enthusiastic about the importance of nuclear power for aircraft and accordingly included a requirement for extensive studies on weapon system 110A (advanced strategic weapon system), a nuclear cruise-chemical dash bomber. In July 1954, however, the Air Force ordered that as a hedge against the failure of the development of a nuclear power plant, parallel development would be devoted to a weapon system designed only for chemical power. After additional study the Air Research and Development Command in April 1955 effectively divided the two power projects: weapon system 110A became the chemical-powered bomber and weapon system 125A was established for the development of a nuclear-powered bomber.[134]

In the autumn of 1950 when it became apparent that research and development might soon provide strategic missiles, the Strategic Air Command established a guided missiles project office in its Directorate of Plans. The Strategic Air Command's criteria for pilotless aircraft were soon stated to be reliability, accuracy, minimum vulnerability, and operational suitability.[135] On 17 August 1951 General LeMay stated that the Strategic Air Command's policy was "to get into the guided missiles business at the earliest possible date and further to get guided missiles into the war plans at the earliest possible date. These two objectives are to be accomplished without sacrificing combat capability."[136] "It is only by staying ahead," wrote Brig Gen R. M. Montgomery, SAC's chief of staff, on 2 October 1953, "that we can stay on top." Montgomery, nevertheless, expressed SAC's concern that the Air Force appeared to want to program the Rascal missile into SAC's wings before the Rascal demonstrated any operational capability; he pointed out that SAC could not afford to modify B-36s or B-47s for a capability that appeared to be of questionable operational worth.[137] In response to an Air Staff request for an exact statement of SAC policy on guided missiles, Montgomery stated on 18 April 1954: "the nature of the mission assigned to the Strategic Air Command by the Joint Chiefs of Staff requires the maintenance of a constant state of combat readiness. This, in turn, established a firm requirement for any weapon system which is integrated into the SAC inventory to possess a proved and demonstrable combat capability in terms of range, accuracy, and reliability." At this time the Strategic Air Command could see some compatibility between the Rascal and the B-36. However, it believed that, if the B-47s were required to carry the standoff missile, they would be seriously degraded in range and in altitude characteristics. The Strategic Air Command was even more skeptical about the potential operational worth of the Snark: in its existing configuration the Snark appeared to have little potential as an operational weapon system.[138]

In the Air Force in the early 1950s there were predictions that guided missiles would be the "exclusive vehicle for future air war" and that the Soviet Union might skip the jet bomber stage of aircraft development and jump directly into guided missiles. Brig Gen Dale O. Smith argued against the first prediction in November 1953. Smith believed that the art of war would continue to be "a contest of wills, strategy, and quick decision based upon fragmentary information." Only a pilot in a manned air vehicle would be able to appraise situations that could not be predicted in advance.[139] The second prediction appeared invalid when the Soviets gave no signs of skipping jet bombers and developing missiles. On May Day 1954, in the fly-by over Moscow, the Soviet air force openly paraded new Tu-16 Badger medium jet bombers, which evidently were in quantity production, and a single type-37 Bison heavy turbojet bomber, which apparently was a prototype of an intercontinental aircraft needed to attack the United States.[140] Following an Air Research and Development Command briefing on new weapon systems late in 1954, General LeMay accepted the proposition that the ICBM would be the ultimate weapon in SAC's inventory. However, he asserted that manned bombers would be the primary weapon for a long time to come. He urged the assignment of the highest priority possible to the development of weapon system 110A together with penetration aids to include an air-to-surface missile and early development and production of an air-to-surface missile for the B-52. LeMay recommended discontinuation of the Rascal program and elimination of the Snark if it detracted from weapon system 110A.[141] In a study prepared for the Air Research and Development Command on 27 May 1955, General Yates described the deficiencies in guided missile programs as tracing back to a superficial recognition at top levels of the government of the potential dominance of missiles and to the relative underemphasis on guided missile development within the Air Force that stemmed primarily from a preoccupation with manned aircraft.[142]

In the spring of 1955 American intelligence continued to be fearful of Soviet aircraft development. At the 1955 May Day celebration in Moscow, the Soviets displayed 13 type-37 Bisons and at least three (some observers counted nine) turboprop Tu-95 Bear heavy bombers. This display indicated that the Soviets had put the intercontinental Bison into production fully a year before predicted and that the even more formidable Bear also might be in production. At this same air show the Soviets displayed 43 twin-plate, all-weather Flashlight jet interceptors, enough to make it evident that these very dangerous, swept-wing fighters were already operational in air defense units.[143] These aircraft sightings demanded an immediate reassessment of Air Force capabilities. The size and composition of the Strategic Air Command had been computed early in 1954 on a wargaming of the then existing JCS target list and expected combat attrition rates. Based on a floating D-day, B-52 production rates were fairly leisurely and were predicated on a 40-hour week without overtime at Boeing's plant in Seattle. To reduce the potential vulnerability of a single-source production of B-52s the Air Force had already asked for a second source of production. When he received the news of the Soviet aircraft sighted over Moscow, Secretary Wilson acted swiftly to expand B-52 production and to bring a second Boeing plant into operation in government-owned facilities in Wichita, Kansas. In an expeditious action, Wilson secured Eisenhower's approval for the action within the National Security Council and bypassed the Bureau of the Budget. On 26 May, Secretary Talbott and General Twining appeared in executive session with the Senate Armed Services Committee and received approval for accelerating B-52 production by 35 percent. Emergency budget actions added some $356 million for increased aircraft procurement to the budget for fiscal year 1956.[144]

Even though Secretary Wilson supported the expansion of B-52 production, he announced his opposition to any enlargement of the Air Force beyond its goal of 137 wings by the end of 1956.[145] Since 137 wings had become a magic number representing the ultimate in air power, the Strategic Air Command had to effect changes within its internal force structure in order to schedule more bombers against an expanding target spectrum. Although SAC had programmed seven heavy bomber wings and four heavy reconnaissance wings as separate functions, it quickly determined that the requirement for bombs on targets would be more important than poststrike reconnaissance and secured authority to shift reconnaissance wings into bombardment work on 1 October 1955. This action represented a more than 50-percent increase in long-range B-52 bombardment capability.[146] As soon as it got operational experience with B-52s, the Strategic Air Command found it feasible in the spring of 1956 to program 45 B-52s per wing as opposed to the former allocation of 30 B-36s per wing.[147] Based on these actions and counting additional planes allotted for combat support and testing, the Air Force ended up with a total authorization for 603 B-52s.[148]

In spite of the authorized augmentations of the Strategic Air Command, General LeMay was anything but optimistic when he appeared before the Symington committee hearings on air power in April 1956. LeMay explained that to get the best results from a small number of well-qualified technical personnel, SAC formerly had concentrated its air units on a few air bases. Now LeMay emphasized that SAC would have to expand its base system to reduce its vulnerability. Pending a new wargaming of Soviet capabilities, LeMay was not prepared to say how much larger the SAC force should be but he knew that it should be larger. He wished the Air Force to press forward with the development of an intercontinental ballistic missile, but he doubted that the first models of these weapons could be as efficient as manned bombers. "I think," he said, "it is reasonable to say that the first ICBM will augment the manned bomber force; and at some later date will supplant a portion of the manned bomber force. But I do not believe that in the foreseeable future the ICBM will replace all of the manned bomber force." LeMay urged that the ICBM be developed "with the utmost urgency" and that a follow-on manned bomber to the combination of the B-52 and KC-135 be produced "at the earliest possible time," but "before then," he said, "we need more B-52s."[149] In meetings in Omaha and Washington on 6 and 13 June 1956, LeMay and key SAC officers stated the following priorities for production and development: (1) B-52s, (2) B-52s plus penetration aids, (3) weapon system 110A, (4) weapon system 110A plus penetration aids, (5) Navaho, (6) Atlas, and (7) weapon system 125A. LeMay stated that even after the Navaho and Atlas were fully developed, the Strategic Air Command still would require manned bombers to strike the targets designated for it.[150]

Although the basic idea had long been tacitly accepted, the Air Force definitely announced in 1956 that it would adhere to a concept of maintaining a mixed force of manned air vehicles and guided missiles. In an article published in September 1956, Maj Gen Richard C. Lindsay, Air Force director of plans, pointed out that missiles had unique characteristics but were still characterized by relatively large circular error probabilities and would be operationally inflexible once they were launched. "It appears unlikely," he wrote,

> that guided missiles will completely replace aircraft in any mission area during the foreseeable future. It looks as if the future force structure will be mixed in varying degrees depending upon the job to be accomplished.... A look at the technical estimates of the surface-to-surface missiles' future capability in relation to manned aircraft and the targets to be attacked indicates that about fifty percent of the Strategic Air Command's mission could sometime be accomplished with guided missiles.[151]

General Twining suggested early in 1957 that the phaseout of manned bombers and fighters would have to be slow and could not be undertaken until missiles were operational and had proven their worth. In Twining's opinion, missiles with large warheads would be effective against area targets but would not be effective against precise targets such as enemy airfields for many years. "As I see it now," he said, "I would employ a bomber force to go get the airfields rather than gamble on missiles."[152] Expressing basic agreement with the Air Force chief of staff, General Schriever stated: "This ballistic missile is largely a retaliatory weapon, and it would be used against an enemy's economy."[153] Summing up the Air Force position on a mixed force, Col James B. Tipton of the Air Force plans directorate pointed out, in May 1957, that "the unique characteristics of missiles of all types, both offensive and defensive, make them superior to manned systems in many respects and they will replace manned systems when demonstrated capabilities indicate those tasks which they can do better or cheaper. In most respects, however, missile systems are complementary and not competitive."[154]

As it had been projected to do, the Strategic Air Command completed its expansion to the 51 wings authorized to it under the 137-wing program in May 1956. But even as this objective was accomplished, the changing world environment was already rendering that force level obsolete and it was apparent that the Air Force could not support 137 wings and continue to modernize them without additional appropriations. Based on an appreciation of the fact that "the number of bombers we require is a function of the targets we must hit, the time period in which our strikes must be completed, the effectiveness of the enemy warning and defense system and the degree of protection and dispersal we can provide our force against his attacks," General Twining agreed that the Strategic Air Command needed additional B-52s. In preparing the fiscal year 1958 budget estimates, Twining asked the Joint Chiefs of Staff to accept a requirement for six additional B-52 wings, making a total of 17 heavy bombardment wings. Given the development of air-to-surface standoff missile, Twining estimated that the B-52 could continue to be an effective delivery system through 1965 and very probably beyond that period. As long as the Strategic Air Command's medium bomber groups had been equipped with relatively slow B-36 bombers, SAC required strategic fighter aircraft. However, the B-52s would be expected to defend themselves and SAC's six fighter-type wings could be eliminated, thus making way for higher priority programs. According to Twining, the Joint Chiefs of Staff refused to accept the requirement for expanding the number of B-52 wings, particularly since the aircraft complement of each of the 11 B-52 wings was being expanded from 30 to 45 aircraft. As a result, the Air Force budget for fiscal year 1958 visualized the already approved 11 wings of B-52s. Twining accepted this decision with evident reluctance. "If the enemy continues his building program of long-range bombers," he warned, "we will again examine the size of our B-52 force."[155] Given this shift to the B-52, the Strategic Air Command divested itself of its fighters. In the first half of 1957, SAC transferred its four most experienced strategic fighter wings to the Tactical Air Command and inactivated its other strategic fighter wing and the strategic fighter reconnaissance wing.[156]

At the same time that he sought additional intercontinental bombers to program against an increasing number of targets in an increasingly severe defense environment, LeMay subscribed to the concept that defined a deterrent force as "an effective nuclear offensive force which is secure from destruction by the enemy regardless of what offensive and defensive action he takes against it."[157] At its establishment, the Strategic Air Command had inherited many bases in the United States that had been built in good-weather areas for use in training units that would fight overseas. Most of these bases were thus in the southern part of the United States and were poorly located for transpolar intercontinental air missions. During the 137-wing expansion, moreover, nearly all SAC bases had to accommodate two wings. Even with in-flight refueling, the medium-range B-47s had to be programmed to conduct their offensive strikes from bases in Europe or in the Pacific, bases which were hazarded by Soviet Tu-16 Badgers during the middle 1950s and would soon be covered by Soviet intermediate range ballistic missiles.[158] Seeking to provide increased security and to compound the enemy's offensive force requirement, General LeMay recommended in 1956 that no more than one squadron of B-52s and one wing of B-47s should be located on a single base. The Air Force accepted the objective of so dispersing the B-52s during fiscal year 1958, but it could not immediately afford to disperse the much larger number of B-47 wings.[159] As eventually worked out, the solution for the dispersal of the B-47 wings included thinning them down to one wing per base and designating an additional 80 to 100 alternate airfields to which B-47s would disperse in periods of international tension.[160]

The survival of strategic aircraft on a given air base was related to the degree of alert practicable and the warning time available. With the distant early warning (DEW) line in operation against Soviet jet aircraft, LeMay counted on getting two hours' tactical warning time and believed that it would be possible to get something like 60 percent of his aircraft into the air in this time. Against a Soviet ICBM attack, however, the zone of interior bases could count only on about a 15-minute tactical warning; overseas bases would be fortunate to get as much as 10 minute's advance notice of Soviet IRBM strikes. As a part of their normal training some aircraft crews were always in a state of readiness for missions and could quickly be diverted to retaliatory strikes. Already looking forward to the era of intercontinental missiles, LeMay began preparations in 1956 to secure a degree of ground alert readiness that would enable his wings to launch as many aircraft as possible in 15 minutes. "If we can get this alert concept worked out to a point where we can operate under it with a high degree of efficiency," he said, "then I think that even though the Russians have the intercontinental missile that they will still have to consider that question: Will we accept this number of bombs?"[161] The ground alert concept was expensive in requirements for alert facilities and additional aircrews, but by the winter of 1956–57 SAC was planning to keep 30 percent of its crews and aircraft on ground alert. This planning matured quickly after September 1957 and in July 1958 the command placed approximately one-third of its combat-ready fleet on continuous ground alert.[162]

One of the principal reasons why LeMay wished to build up SAC's B-52 and KC-135 intercontinental capability was a realization that overseas bases would become increasingly vulnerable to Soviet medium-range bombers and IRBMs.[163] Rather than to continue to risk entire wings at advance bases, the Strategic Air Command, in July 1957, instituted Reflex — a concept of forward deployment to bases in North Africa. Under this concept, designated B-47 wings periodically rotated small numbers of crews and aircraft to the forward bases where they stood runway alerts for short intervals of time. Reflex was subsequently extended to deployments at bases in Spain, the United Kingdom, and Alaska. In forward deployments to the Pacific, SAC implemented Airmail — a plan under which B-47 aircraft were kept on alert in place on Guam while aircrews were rotated to and from Guam at monthly intervals.[164] As SAC increased its force of intercontinental B-52 bombers, overseas bases became less vital to accomplishing the strategic air mission.[165] In 1959 Rand expert Albert J. Wohlstetter argued that overseas bases had so little warning time as to make them of little value in case of a general war. On the other hand, Air Force officers maintained that the continued use of these admittedly vulnerable bases gave additional flexibility and efficiency to the strategic attack, added complexity to the timing of a Soviet surprise attack, and permitted the B-47s to operate from ranges nearer to their targets. "The knowledge that SAC is a truly global force," pointed out Lt Gen Walter C. Sweeney, Jr., commander of the Eighth Air Force, "complicates Soviet targeting and dilutes his war effort." In view of the increasing danger of Soviet IRBM attack, the Strategic Air Command began to reduce the size of the Reflex deployment in August 1959, but under Airmail continued to maintain B-47s and their crews on alert at overseas bases.[166]

As he was nearing completion of his long assignment as commander of the Strategic Air Command in the spring of 1957, General LeMay was satisfied with the rate of modernization of the strategic air arm. However, he believed that the Strategic Air Command had made plans that would permit it to maintain its effectiveness both as a deterrent and a war-winning force. Looking toward the era of intercontinental missiles, LeMay's plan required the development of an all-intercontinental force, including ICBMs, maximum dispersal of aircraft and crews, and maximum ground alert.[167] Because it was concerned about finances and the maintenance of combat-ready capabilities, the Strategic Air Command continued to question Air Force plans to put Snark and Rascal into operation. Snark seemed to be of questionable superiority to other strategic systems and Rascal appeared to be practically useless in an environment requiring alert forces. After attending a briefing in Omaha, Secretary of the Air Force Donald A. Quarles stated on 9 February 1957 that a "tried and proven manned bomber force should not be reduced and replaced by an untried missile force. However, it is vital that the Air Force get on with development and procurement of missiles."[168]

Writing in the summer of 1957 shortly after he became Air Force chief of staff, General White agreed that the ballistic missile was "less flexible than the manned bomber." He pointed out, however, that "its addition will definitely add a considerable measure of flexibility to our forces as a whole." General White reasoned:

> Its reaction time and speed of flight are very valuable characteristics in a situation requiring immediate response to an attack. The ballistic missile will also permit greater versatility for our forces by relieving the manned bomber of those heavily defended targets where the cost of attacking with bombers would be too high and where precise accuracy is not mandatory. In considering the characteristics of the bomber and the ballistic missile, it appears that for many years to come an optimum force will make best use of both weapons.[169]

Even though White believed that "there is no question that SAC, as presently constituted, is the only thing between us and oblivion and will be for a long time to come," he also believed that the Air Force was late in realizing the potential of missiles and that "the top level of the Air Force does not know enough about missiles." Addressing an Air Force commanders conference on 30 September 1957, White warned: "The senior Air Force officer's dedication to the airplane is deeply ingrained and rightly so, but we must never permit this to result in a battleship attitude. We cannot afford to ignore the basic precept that all truths change with time." He pointed out that money limitations would not indefinitely permit continuing an overlapping of missile and aircraft capabilities. More thought should be given to missiles and to the effect that antiaircraft missiles would have on high-level bombing. White thought that Air Force officers had never respected antiaircraft artillery; thus, he directed SAC to begin a study of the potential effect of nuclear antiaircraft missiles on high-level bombing. White also stated that he wanted Air Force officers to stop criticizing Snark and Rascal. His guidance was not intended to curtail individual thinking but to stress that the Air Force would need to present a solid front on the subject of missiles. "With the advent of the guided missile," White emphasized, "the US Air Force is in a critical era of its existence. It is essential that we all pull together in the effort to properly utilize this family of new weapons system for the defense of our Nation."[170]

In his address to the Air Force commanders on 30 September, White presented an Air Force credo on missiles; this statement was soon released to all major commanders and to the public as the Air Force policy on missile development and employment. This policy statement read:

1. The USAF has long recognized the potential of missiles. According to current roles and missions the Air Force has the greatest need for such weapons.

2. Missiles and aircraft can be combined, capitalizing on the performance and characteristics of each, to create a formidable instrument of air power considerably greater than the use of missiles or aircraft alone. The creation of such an instrument is a primary object of the Air Force.

3. Missiles, as they are perfected, will supplement and complement the manned aircraft. However, to preserve the required capability and flexibility of operations, it is essential that the Air Force maintain a significant force of manned aircraft during the foreseeable future.

4. The Air Force has and is continuing to develop missiles for use in the strategic, tactical and air defense roles as fast as technology and the availability of funds will permit.

5. As rapidly as missiles become operationally suitable, they will be phased into units either to completely or partially substitute for manned aircraft according to military requirements.[171]

During the 1950s General LeMay had demanded that new weapon systems not be assigned to the Strategic Air Command until they were operationally perfected. In view of this demand as well as in an effort to provide the earliest initial operational capability for intercontinental ballistic missiles, the Air Force had assigned the whole responsibility of readying missile squadrons to the Air Research and Development Command on 18 November 1955. Seeking to compress time schedules to the maximum, the Western Development Division and its successor, the Air Force Ballistic Missile Division, instituted a new concept of concurrent development whereby operating personnel were trained, base facilities were built, and the missiles were developed and tested all at the same time.[172] Several factors impeded this concurrent development planning. Base construction funds were hard to come by and the siting of IRBMs in NATO countries required intergovernmental negotiations. In 1956 Secretary Quarles directed a "poor man's approach" or a stretch-out of programs to save funds. Planning had to be coordinated with SAC and LeMay opposed any rigid initial operational capability plans that might freeze designs and commit missiles to quantity production before a first missile had been tested. Work, nevertheless, was begun on a "soft" missile base at Camp Cooke, California (subsequently Vandenberg AFB), in May 1957. In August the Air Force selected Francis E. Warren AFB, Wyoming, and Lowry AFB, Colorado, for development as Atlas and Titan initial operational capability bases. With Air Staff approval, the Air Research and Development Command activated the 1st Missile Division at Camp Cooke on 1 April 1957 to supervise training and operational phases of the initial operational capability program.[173] By autumn 1957 the Air Force Ballistic Missile Division had the nucleus of an initial operational missile force in being, and at the commanders conference in September General White told the new SAC commander, Gen Thomas S. Power, that he wanted SAC to get "into the picture as soon as possible without 'rocking the boat' and upsetting the overall program." On 29 November White accordingly announced that he had transferred the 1st Missile Division to SAC, along with responsibility for the initial operational capability of both the ICBM and IRBM programs. The transfer of the 1st Missile Division to SAC and the simultaneous establishment of an Office of Assistant Commander in Chief SAC for Missiles (SAC-MIKE) in Inglewood, California, became effective on 1 January 1958.[174]

After hearing General White's presentation at the September commanders conference, General Power remarked that missiles ought to be kept in perspective lest an impression be created "that the bomber is through."[175] General LeMay shared this same fear. In December, he appeared before a Senate investigating committee in what he described as an "atmosphere of sputniks and intercontinental missiles, when accusations and denials seem to be flying around." LeMay observed: "Our main deterrent power today is a manned bomber and a nuclear-weapons system. It is going to be our main deterrent and our main protection." Believing that "the proposals that are in the mill on increasing the missile program are ample for the time being, maybe a little bit strong," LeMay argued that the main danger lay not so much in the far future but in "not modernizing the force that we are depending on today to keep us out of trouble, not doing it fast enough."[176] To LeMay and Power the modernization of the Strategic Air Command required new manned aircraft as well as missiles.

Representing the culmination of some four years of preliminary studies and intensive design competitions, the Air Force awarded a contract on 1 June 1957 the North American Aviation Company to initiate development of a long-range Mach-3 jet interceptor to be designated the F-108. Following a similarly long, intensive study and design competitions, the Air Force awarded North American another development contract on 24 January 1958 for weapon system 110A — a revolutionary Mach-3 intercontinental jet bomber that would be designated as the B-70. The two development programs were carefully designed to mesh and save developmental costs. The cost of developing common items such as engines, escape capsules, and fuel systems was to be spread between the two programs. It was planned that both new planes would enter the operational inventory by 1965 and would complement missile capabilities in the decade 1965–75. In this period the Air Force assumed that surface-to-surface strategic bombardment missiles would be vitally important. However, because of uncertainties about reliability, accuracy, flexibility of employment, and relative immobility, the use of missiles would be limited, initially at least, to unhardened and accurately located targets. The manned bomber system would provide the only known means of destroying smaller, more fugitive hardened targets that required accurate attacks with high-yield weapons. The manned weapon system would be usable in major conflict, in a limited war with limited weapons, and in lesser conflicts where a simple show of force would be sufficient. "In addition," as Maj Gen James Ferguson, Air Force director of requirements, pointed out,

> man provides discretionary capabilities for target discrimination, malfunction correction or override, timely evasion maneuvers and judgment in selection and employment of penetration aids. These attributes, coupled with the bomber's flexibility of employment (heavy payloads with mixed weapons, intelligence collection, damage assessment, best altitudes, and penetration routes, recallability and recoverability) are important considerations to the probability of success in a strategic campaign.[177]

Speaking of the B-70 and the Atlas in March 1958, Lt Gen Charles S. Irvine, deputy chief of staff for materiel, explained:

> We think we need both. We think we cannot afford to pin the hopes of the nation on just one machine and one solution to the military mission.... From the standpoint... of what it costs to take out a target, it costs you more to take it out with an intercontinental ballistic missile than it does to take out a number of targets with bombers, plus, the fact that you have control of the bomber force. You can start bombers toward the target and call them back.... I do not know how to show your teeth with a missile, particularly when you have it in the silos, and you do not want the enemy to know where they are.[178]

In the winter of 1957–58 Generals White and LeMay believed that the development of intercontinental ballistic missiles and the supersonic B-70 would take care of the future, but the immediate task was to do something more immediately to continue aircraft modernization and give protection to the Strategic Air Command. In the immediate aftermath of Sputniks I and II, Secretary McElroy asked the Joint Chiefs of Staff to study and recommend highly important items where defense could be augmented with additional funds. To meet this request the Joint Chiefs recommended only the items which they agreed were most important. Originally these items were to have been added to the fiscal year 1959 budget, but McElroy instead secured Eisenhower's approval to submit them to Congress in January 1958 as a supplemental appropriation for fiscal year 1958. This supplemental request totaled $1,270 million, of which $910 million was allocated to the Air Force. Much of the funding was designed to provide the Strategic Air Command with warning, dispersal, and alert facilities and additional personnel to stand the alerts. Of the $1,270 million, $219 million was to accelerate the SAC dispersal and alert program, $329 million was allocated to the construction of a ballistic missile detection system, and $683 million was requested to permit acceleration of the Atlas, Thor, Jupiter, and Polaris programs. In his original submission of items for the added program, White asked the Joint Chiefs to approve the construction of new bases for tanker aircraft in Canada and the Arctic; the Joint Chiefs, however, did not accept this request as a priority item and accordingly did not include it in the supplemental request for fiscal year 1958 funds.[179]

The subject of aircraft modernization plans for the Strategic Air Command came under debate during the consideration of the military budget for fiscal year

1959. Already reduced to a total of 44 combat wings, SAC stood in danger of being "caught with 10-year-old B-47s and B-52s." Since SAC's B-52 strength was fixed at 11 wings, the B-52 production line at Wichita was slated to close after fiscal year 1958 procurement orders were delivered. The last B-47 was delivered to the Air Force in 1957.[180] The Strategic Air Command also had limited numbers of tankers. While in command of SAC, LeMay had proposed that new KC-135 tankers should match the new B-52 bombers on a one-to-one ratio. However, in view of budget limits and with the expectation that with a little warning some bombers might be able to operate from overseas bases, LeMay reluctantly had agreed with the Air Staff decision to procure B-52s and KC-135s on a three-to-two ratio. Even if the Air Staff had agreed to the one-to-one ratio, moreover, the ratio would have been difficult to attain since the KC-135 was put into production about a year and a half behind the B-52.[181] At a meeting of the USAF Aircraft and Weapons Board in June 1957, a SAC representative continued to reject the proposal that his command be scheduled for six wings of the limited-range, but supersonic B-58s. The board supported the B-58 because it was the nation's only hope for attaining a supersonic bombing capability prior to 1966 and because it feared that the B-52 might not be able to penetrate hostile defenses in the early 1960s. At another meeting of the board in November 1957, however, the Air Force Directorate of Operations recommended additional B-52s rather than B-58s. General LeMay also indicated that he favored the B-52 over the B-58 because it could carry more electronic equipment and had an intercontinental range. The Office of Secretary of Defense (OSD) had ruled against procurement of additional B-52s, however. On 26 December General White made the final decision that SAC would receive some B-58s, the final number to be determined after operational testing. As a result of these decisions, the Department of Defense budget for fiscal year 1959, submitted to Congress in January 1958, contained no funds for additional B-52s but included the purchase of 47 B-58s at an estimated cost of $796.6 million. This initial order was intended to be a test quantity rather than a production order, and because of increased cost quotations the number of aircraft to be procured had to be reduced to 36 planes. While the budget hearings were in progress, LeMay emphasized that SAC ought to have one KC-135 tanker for each B-52 bomber, but the Air Force continued to program the three-to-two bomber-tanker ratio.[182]

At least a part of the Office of Secretary of Defense opposition to the procurement of additional B-52s arose from the belief that these planes would be vulnerable to Soviet missile defenses. Early in 1958 two separate developments promised to reduce B-52 vulnerability. The Strategic Air Command demonstrated that it would be feasible to conduct low-altitude attacks with the B-52s, thereby reducing the effectiveness of Soviet antiaircraft defenses. Following the award of a research and development contract on 16 September 1957, moreover, the North American Aviation Company made rapid progress in developing the GAM-77 Hound Dog missile. This turbojet missile would allow B-52s to deliver nuclear warheads against hostile targets or defenses without entering defended areas. The B-52s would be able to carry Hound Dog missiles on pylons under their wings, thus augmenting their armament. On the basis of these new developments, the Air Force was authorized to submit an amendment to the fiscal year 1959 budget on 2 April 1958. As subsequently approved by Congress, the amendment authorized the procurement of 39 additional B-52G aircraft at an estimated cost of $300.5 million. With these planes the Air Force was able to schedule one of the B-47 wings for conversion to B-52s, and the purchase order continued production lines in being for a possible 1960 reorder of additional aircraft.[183]

When it was tested during 1958, the B-58 Hustler proved potentially useful. Although the supersonic-dash B-58 could not be adapted to air-alert tactics such as were being worked out for the B-52 force, SAC conceived that the B-58s were suited admirably for Reflex operations. They could be deployed rapidly to forward airfields overseas, from which by virtue of their high speed they could get over their assigned targets very quickly. The principal drawback to the B-58 continued to be its high unit cost. To conserve funds, the Air Force Directorate of Operations recommended cancellation of B-58 purchases in August 1958, but by this time General Power was willing to inform General White that "the B-58 is a program vitally important to SAC and the nation."[184]

In an effort to clear up what appeared to be an apparent indecision as to its requirements, the Strategic Air Command stated on 7 July 1958 that basic Air Force programming ought to pursue objectives designed to modernize the bomber force, attain an effective ICBM capability as soon as possible, secure the aggressive support of research and development of the most promising systems for the long term, and attain compatible alert and dispersal programs to ensure maximum response to any situation. At this time SAC criticized "the spoon feeding of many weapon systems in an attempt to satisfy the projected requirements of all agencies." Although it recognized that parallel missile development programs might have been necessary to advance the state of the art, SAC now recommended that the time had come for the immediate termination of such programs as the SM-62 Snark, the GAM-63 Rascal, and the SM-78 Jupiter. In consonance with its force objectives, SAC recommended that the priorities in the procurement of weapon systems should be: (1) KC-135 tankers, (2) B-52G bombers with Hound Dog missiles, (3) B-58 bombers, (4) B-70 bombers, (5) SM-65 Atlas missiles, (6) SM-68 Titan missiles, and (7) Minuteman missiles.[185] Lending emphasis to this command letter, Power stated in February 1959: "[The] no. 1 priority in SAC—and I am talking about the immediate future and taking full consideration of time—in buying this country military posture of deterrent value, is the KC-135 B-52G combination with the Hound Dog missile."[186]

During the summer and autumn of 1958 the Air Force accepted only a part of the Strategic Air Command's recommendations. Unable to forecast the exact capabilities of intercontinental ballistic missiles, General White preferred to pursue a somewhat loose bomber procurement program that would add B-52s and B-58s to the SAC inventory in annual procurements, with two wings of B-47s to be retired for each modern B-52 and B-58 wing that could be organized. These annual procurements of modest numbers of B-52s and B-58s would ensure that the production lines were kept open. General Power was not happy with this program. He had conceived that the Strategic Air Command might have to stress an air-alert rather than a ground-alert posture, and he wanted 20 wings of B-52s as soon as possible rather than the stretched out Air Force program.[187] Although the initial operational date slipped to December 1960, General White wanted to have one squadron with 30 Snark missiles in place at Presque Isle, Maine, because the Snark would be the world's first operational intercontinental missile and because it would confuse enemy defenses. As SAC had long urged should be done and in view of the fact that it would be phasing out B-47s, the Air Force canceled the SM-63 Rascal program in November 1958; this program had cost $448 million and had not provided a useful air-to-surface missile. Further development on the ground-launched diversionary SM-73 Bull Goose missile—which had cost $136.5 million—was canceled in December 1958. This missile would have been fired while the B-52s were proceeding to their targets and would have compounded the identification problems of Soviet air defense radars; it would not be useful if the B-52s began to operate from an air-alert posture since once launched the missile could not be recalled.[188] In a speech delivered in September 1958, General White summed up the Air Force response to the missile crisis. "First," he said,

> the missile threat did not invalidate our bomber strike force. For a long time to come, this force with its great range, its capacity to carry nuclear weapons of various size and yields, and its improved electronic countermeasures, could still perform the job it was designed to do. Furthermore, because of the human intelligence factor aboard, the bomber strike force has the added advantages of recall capability and greater flexibility in target selection and tactics.[189]

Missiles for Air Defense and Air-Ground Support

From a purely theoretical viewpoint, ground-launched guided missiles appeared to have unique qualifications that fitted them for employment in both air defense and tactical air warfare missions. A missile could maneuver more abruptly than a piloted aircraft, it had a greater range per pound of vehicle, it was capable of greater operational altitude, its automatic delivery system eliminated many human frailties and errors, and it could operate at speeds far superior to manned aircraft. Also a missile could operate at night and in all kinds of weather without degraded capabilities. Since no pilot would need to be protected from a weapon's blast, a Bomarc could be provided with a large nuclear warhead. In a 24-hour air defense alert, manned fighter efficiency degenerated as men got tired, but a guided missile did not become fatigued and it did not wear out unless it was fired. In tactical employment, Matador missiles could be operated from widely dispersed field installations, thus augmenting security against hostile attack.[190]

But while missiles appeared to be well fitted to air defense and tactical air missions, few defense strategists agreed on the exact proportions of these missions that could eventually be performed with them. In September 1956 General Lindsay predicted that "only about thirty percent of tactical targets would probably be suitable for attack by guided missiles," but he thought that in the air defense mission guided missiles "may be capable of taking over a greater percentage of the job than in any of the other areas."[191] Appreciation for the unique qualities of the Matador tactical air missile led to its production and deployment to oversea theaters beginning in 1954. During this same year, the Air Force began research and development on an improved version of this weapon system, which was designated as the TM-76 Mace. Speaking of the Matador in May 1956, however, Gen Otto P. Weyland said: "It is a supplement to, adds to, the flexibility, but it certainly does not replace the manned airplane."[192] But a month later General Taylor visualized that "the trend will be toward the substitution of the missile, the Army-controlled missile, for what we call close support of ground forces."[193] Asked to speculate on the future of manned fighter aircraft in February 1958, General LeMay replied: "I think their importance is going to diminish in the future, particularly in the tactical role — the fighter-bomber types, for instance. I think we are going to require a manned vehicle in the air defense role for some time to come."[194] Only two months later, General Ferguson wrote:

> To an airman, the need for manned aircraft in tactical air operations is obvious. Tactical war is a war of movement. After fixed targets have been attacked, the problem is to seek out and destroy the moving targets. Often these targets are fleeting. They must be attacked as soon as they are observed, or they are gone. Here, missiles are of very limited use without necessary reconnaissance. The manned aircraft, on the other hand, carries with it both a reconnaissance capability to find the target and weapons to destroy it. The tactical fighter bomber is designed with the flexibility for attacking not only the fixed and pinpointed target, but also the target that must be located.[195]

In April 1958, Weyland had occasion to repeat what he described as his "long-held conviction that tactical surface-to-surface missiles, ballistic or cruise, can only be considered as a supplementary and secondary offensive tactical weapon to the manned airplane. Their actual tactical usefulness will be limited, will complicate the enemies' defense, but will be more psychological than tangibly destructive in value."[196]

One of the chief reasons for the confused thinking about the comparative values of missiles and manned aircraft in the air defense and tactical air missions arose from the fact that technological potentialities in both media were developing rapidly and posed a constant strain upon the limited research and development funds that could be made available. In the early 1950s both air defense and tactical air units were equipped with first-generation jet aircraft that were procured in quantity during the Korean War. Possibly because of difficulties and costs arising from the quantity production of the F-100 Super Sabre before the plane was adequately tested, the Air Force pursued a very cautious program of procuring new fighter aircraft, which Trevor Gardner described as a fly-before-you-buy philosophy.[197] Because it had great confidence in the North American Company, which had produced the F-86 Sabre, and because it needed an improved day fighter to oppose vast numbers of Soviet MiG-15s, the Air Force put the F-100 Super Sabre into quantity production in mid-1953 before it was adequately tested. Since the fire control system on the Sabre had been satisfactory, it was assumed that a similar system would be acceptable in the F-100 and no complete weapon system specification was written for the F-100. This was not to be the case; trouble with the Super Sabre's fire control system proved costly to correct and delayed operational availability of the plane.[198]

Afterwards the Air Force was unwilling to gamble and followed the Cook-Craigie production plan quite methodically. Aircraft were put into production at a very low monthly rate for one or two years with a minimum of hard tooling, while engineering tests uncovered deficiencies enabling corrections to be fed back into the production line. This procedure reduced the risk of a loss of money that might occur if production tooling were created too early, but four to six years could elapse before production could provide operational quantities of new aircraft. Only then could operational readiness testing begin. "It has been my unfortunate experience in the aircraft business," remarked General Irvine, "that you can test until you are black and blue in the face on a handful of machines, but you never know what you really have, you never get a real operational capability until you have a whole wing's worth, a tactical unit in operation and actually submit them to the test of a true military mission a number of times."[199]

Even though the modernization of air defense and tactical air wings progressed slowly and methodically, the sharply increased costs of this new equipment, when added to the soaring costs of missiles development, made it impossible for the Air Force to retain a modernized 137-wing force in being, once it was attained in June 1957, without promise of a substantially increased annual budget.[200] As a matter of fact the Air Force attained a 137-wing strength — which included 50 strategic, 32 air defense, and 55 tactical air wings — only by seizing upon the expedient of redesignating a strategic fighter escort wing as a fighter-bomber wing and by counting a Matador wing and four troop carrier assault wings as tactical air wings. Five fighter wings previously scheduled for organization under the 137-wing program were canceled.[201] Reductions in force immediately followed the theoretical attainment of the 137-wing objective. By June 1958 Air Force strength was reduced to 117 wings, including 28 air defense and 45 tactical air wings; continuing reductions were planned.[202]

The Air Force did not attempt to defend the reduction in air defense in terms of the development of either Nike or Bomarc missiles.[203] The severe cuts in tactical air strength, however, closely followed the Wilson memorandum of 26 November 1956, which stated that the Army should reexamine its requirements for air support as it continued to develop surface-to-surface missiles for employment within the battle zone. Admiral Radford justified the tactical air reductions as being "desirable and advisable" since a tactical air force based on "big fields in close proximity to the enemy is very vulnerable to destruction." He said, "Missile support of the Army is probably better dispersed and not so vulnerable."[204] General Irvine justified the deletion of light bombers from tactical air strength because they duplicated the new capability to be provided by intermediate range ballistic missiles.[205] General White was confident that "the Army [could] with [its] Corporals, Honest Johns, atomic artillery, and so on, supplant the tactical capability that we have eliminated."[206] General Taylor actively urged that the Army perform an increasingly large proportion of its own support with organic missiles; nevertheless, he wished to ensure "that as the Air Force support goes down that of the Army's units is coming up proportionately."[207]

Aircraft and Missile Projection in Tactical Air Command

When they talked about the subject, the top-level defense leaders tended to equate tactical air power with the support of ground forces. However to General Weyland, who was at the head of the Tactical Air Command, the experience of World War II and Korea had demonstrated that close support of ground forces amounted to only 15 percent of offensive tactical air effort. "Attainment of air superiority through offensive operations and interdiction of communications systems," Weyland pointed out, "have always been and continue to be primary missions of theater or tactical air forces."[208] Within the Tactical Air Command it appeared that the portent of tactical nuclear weapons promised to accentuate the lessons of World War II and Korea. Experience obtained from the testing of Army and Air Force forces under nuclear battle conditions during Exercise Sagebrush in November and December 1955 tended to confirm TAC's thinking. "Air superiority," wrote Maj Gen John D. Stevenson, the Tactical Air Command's director of plans,

> has had a different meaning as a result of Exercise Sagebrush. No longer does the force with numerical air superiority alone necessarily enjoy air superiority. Air superiority cannot be established as long as the opposing force retains any bases from which to launch a strike force with an atomic capability. One of the most important lessons learned from the exercise was that the force initiating the attack attained a tremendous advantage. In fact in both tactical phases the force initiating attack was able to attain and maintain air superiority and to win the counterair war. Although initiating an attack is not recommended, an operational concept that will give friendly forces a chance of survival during the initial phase of a nuclear war is very much needed.[209]

Based on the lessons of Korea and projected tactical requirements for air atomic warfare, the Tactical Air Command conceived the need for the employment of a family of tactical air fighters in a forward area: fighter-bombers, day fighters (air superiority), and fighter-interceptors (all-weather). Experience indicated that each type of these planes ought to perform the other's missions in the event of an emergency, but the same experience also indicated that it would be difficult, costly, and perhaps impossible to design and procure an all-purpose fighter.[210] In 1952, for example, the Tactical Air Command placed a requirement for a lightweight, high-performance day fighter that would be cheaper, yet able to out-perform heavily stressed fighter-bombers in air-to-air combat.[211] The conceptual difference between the tactical day fighter and the air defense fighter involved building into the former an ability to close on and destroy multiple air targets in fighter sweeps; the air defense fighter required all-weather capabilities and a high probability of single-pass destruction of hostile bombers and fighters.[212] The fighter-bomber weapon system was designed to destroy enemy targets during daylight hours and in good weather, but its limited night, all-weather, and ordnance carrying capabilities established a companion requirement for a tactical bomber weapon system that would provide a capability to perform missions previously handled by light bombardment and night intruder aircraft.[213] The Tactical Air Command also had a requirement for "a reconnaissance version of the latest day fighter ... to obtain critical visual and/or photographic reconnaissance of targets, such as airfields and missile sites located in highly defended areas." Even though tactical air forces had in the past needed a reconnaissance version of a light bomber to perform all-weather and electronic reconnaissance, the Tactical Air Command believed that the advancing state of the art could enable these functions to be performed by an all-purpose reconnaissance fighter.[214]

Even before Sagebrush, the Tactical Air Command recognized that any aircraft based on forward airfields would be extremely vulnerable to enemy air attack, especially since the enemy would have the opportunity for the first strike. This vulnerability could be reduced by new concepts of tactical employment and by the development of new tactical air equipment. The new tactical approach to the problem involved establishing forward and rear bases with a minimum number of high alert air units in the forward areas and the bulk of the air units located at safer rear-area bases. Beginning a scheme of operations similar to the composite air strike force (CASF) concept in 1954, the Tactical Air Command kept two fighter squadrons of a fighter group in the United States and rotated a third squadron from the group to such combat airfields in Europe as Dreux and Chaumont in France and Aviano in Italy. Weyland felt that at the outset of hostilities in an oversea area, "one combat squadron, without its dependents, will actually have more combat capability than the entire wing would if it had the families and children around there to worry about." In an emergency or at the outbreak of hostilities, the Tactical Air Command planned that the two squadrons from the United States would immediately join the single squadron that was on the alert in the forward area.[215] The chief difficulty in developing this concept to its fullest was a deficiency in suitable tanker aircraft. To implement the CASF concept, the Tactical Air Command secured KB-29 boom-type tankers that were released as the Strategic Air Command converted its force to KC-97 and KC-135 tankers. The KB-29s that had been employed by SAC were not completely satisfactory: the Strategic Air Command could well employ flying-boom refueling equipment since its tankers normally refueled a single bomber at one time, but the Tactical Air Command needed drogue-type refueling that would permit several fighters to refuel from a tanker in one rendezvous. As soon as possible, the Tactical Air Command secured KB-50 tankers equipped with multiple refueling drogues. All of the tankers allocated to the Tactical Air Command were conventional aircraft, and, just as was the case with the Strategic Air Command, the Tactical Air

MISSILE TECHNOLOGY

Command's jet fighters actually needed jet tankers to accomplish refuelings at jet speeds at altitudes up to 35,000 feet. The jet fighters needed to operate at higher altitudes, and at altitudes where weather would not interfere with refueling operations.[216]

The development of new equipment offered some prospects for reducing the vulnerability of tactical air forces. As has been seen, Weyland considered that the Matador missiles that were deployed to Germany and Taiwan and the follow-on Mace missiles that were slated for service in Germany and Okinawa added to the flexibility of tactical air forces since they could be directed at fixed targets such as ports and airfields and could be employed as necessary at night and in bad weather. But Matador and Mace were air-breathing buzz bombs that could be intercepted and destroyed by an alert enemy. Weyland also favored the development of tactical ballistic missiles, but these missiles lacked flexibility and he could not consider them as substitutes for manned tactical aircraft.[217] The developmental concepts of vertical takeoff and landing (VTOL), short takeoff and landing (STOL), and zero launch (ZEL) aircraft promised to reduce the vulnerability of tactical air units, since these aircraft could be widely dispersed. Weyland was willing to accept the possibility that such aircraft might be developed eventually, but he was not too sanguine about it. By the mid-1950s tactical aircraft already were up to a Mach-2 airspeed; none of the "tail-sitter" aircraft (missiles) could promise anything like this potential performance.[218]

On the basis of a great amount of thinking, Weyland believed that the Tactical Air Command had visualized an evolutionary program that would enable it to continue to perform tactical air missions in a nuclear age.[219] The success of the program would depend on a continuing modernization of the force with new aircraft and with an appropriate expenditure of research and development effort. Seen in retrospect, however, the Tactical Air Command's program required too many different types of aircraft, especially since research and development allocations for tactical air weapon systems enjoyed very poor priorities.[220] As nearly as could be computed, only 8 percent of the Air Force research and development effort was assigned to tactical air weapons in fiscal year 1959.[221] Up until 1958 most fighter-bomber and tactical reconnaissance units were equipped with F-84F Thunderstreak and RF-84F Thunderflash planes. As a result of Weyland's strong protest that the F-84F required more powerful engines to perform an atomic delivery mission, the Republic production line was changed over in 1955 and the remaining planes on order there were turned out as F-84J Super Thunderstreaks.[222] Although the F-100 was originally designed as a day fighter and the F-100A and F-100C continued in this role, the Air Force decided in 1955 to develop an F-100D that would have added provisions for the delivery of external ordnance and would serve as a fighter-bomber.[223] The fact that F-100Ds could double as day fighters made the designations fighter-bomber and day-fighter wings questionable. In the autumn of 1957, moreover, the Tactical Air Command was committed to deploy a fighter-bomber unit on rotation to Europe but was compelled to substitute a F-100D day-fighter unit. For these reasons, effective in

July 1958, the Air Force dropped the day-fighter and fighter-bomber nomenclature in favor of tactical fighter. The mission of a tactical fighter wing became one of either attack or defense.[224] Released when the Strategic Air Command no longer required escort fighters, the long-range all-weather F-101C Voodoo and the RF-101 Voodoo photoreconnaissance aircraft entered the operating inventory of the tactical air forces in May 1957. First flown in February 1954, the lightweight, high-performance F-104 Starfighter air superiority fighter came into use in the Tactical Air Command in 1958.[225]

Although the trend apparently was not identified when it began in the post-Korean War years, the Air Force practice in selecting tactical air weapons moved away from the concept that produced aircraft designed and optimized for specific roles toward a principle of versatility in mission capability. Looking toward an all-weather tactical bomber and reconnaissance plane that could be available at an early date, the USAF Aircraft and Weapons Board recommended in November 1951 that the Air Force use a modified version of the Navy's A-3D attack bomber. The Air Force issued quantity procurement orders for this plane in 1952 and it was designated as the B-66/RB-66.[226] On the basis of a response to a qualitative operational requirement issued in April 1952 for a new tactical bomber to replace the B-66 in the 1958-63 time period, a development contract for an XB-68 was awarded to the Martin Aircraft Company.[227] The action was entirely unrelated at the time to the tactical bomber program, but in February 1952 the Republic Aviation Company proposed to develop an improved F-84X fighter-bomber. So many configuration changes were specified that the plane was designated as the F-105 when the Air Force awarded Republic a contract for its development in September 1952. Although the F-105 thus came into being without a preceding general operational requirement, it was expected to be the first aircraft specifically designed as a fighter-bomber. It was to have a Mach-2 airspeed and an ability to carry either nuclear or conventional weapons. A reconnaissance version of the plane was planned, and both versions were to be operational in 1958.[228]

When necessary design changes were made, the B-66/RB-66 emerged as a virtually new airplane, bearing only a superficial resemblance to the Navy A-3D. But the changes were not all satisfactory: an already developed K-5 bombing system, for example, had to be fitted into the already firm airframe, and the plane would never be suited for low-level operations. After poor results attained in the plane's maiden flight on 28 June 1954, and given the necessities for many modifications, program slippages, and shaky accomplishments, the B-66 program was on the verge of cancellation in May 1955. Finally in January 1956 the Air Force elected to procure only enough B-66Bs to equip the light bombardment wing serving in Europe and to outfit the remaining aircraft on the order as RB-66 reconnaissance aircraft.[229] In these same years the RF/F-105 development program progressed slowly because of scant funding and program reductions, but the YF-105A performed well on its first flight on 22 October 1955 and was heartily endorsed by the pilots who subsequently flew it.[230] Seeking to find some suitable all-weather bombing aircraft after the Air Force restricted procurement of B-66s,

Weyland proposed in June 1956 that the F-105 be developed in a two-place version with a modified K-5 bombing system in order that it might serve as an interim all-weather attack aircraft until the XB-68 was available.[231]

Based on the decision to develop intermediate range ballistic missiles, the Air Force reviewed requirements for light bombers and canceled the Martin XB-68 project on 3 January 1957. Weyland strongly protested against the elimination of all-weather attack capabilities in theater air forces, but General White reminded him that the Air Force could not invest in duplicative capabilities. White believed that tactical missiles should be employed against most fixed targets in a theater and that strategic bombers could destroy such targets as were not susceptible to attack by theater air forces. "Rather than develop a separate tactical air force all-weather bombing capability," White wrote on 17 May 1957, "I feel that a plan of complementary operations between tactical and strategic forces must be perfected, that we must orient our concept of operations to integrate the capabilities of our allies, and that policies and guide lines must be accordingly revised." After a running exchange of correspondence, Weyland salvaged some concessions. As long as replacement parts permitted, one wing of B-57s and one wing of B-66s could continue in the tactical air inventory. The Air Force also agreed to provide F-105s with all-weather attack capabilities.[232] Based on these decisions the F-105 Thunderchief was put into large-scale production in the summer of 1957 as the designated replacement aircraft for F-84s, B-57s, B-66s, and F-100s.[233]

Although he yielded some points to General Weyland during 1957, General White continued to question whether the tactical air forces would have a continued validity in a missile era. Justifying the action by citing the increased effectiveness as well as the increased cost of tactical aircraft and the planned activation of four Army missile commands, White announced early in 1958 that the Air Force would be reduced from 117 to 105 wings during fiscal year 1959, mainly through the inactivation of tactical air wings.[234] At the same time that these reductions were put forth, Air Force program planners offered an informal proposal for a worldwide reorganization of tactical air forces. This study visualized that at the outbreak of a general war, up to 500 tactical fighters and 144 tactical reconnaissance aircraft assigned to the Tactical Air Command might well be isolated in the United States and unable to deploy overseas or to contribute substantially to the war mission. The study recommended that the Tactical Air Command's assigned units be severely reduced, that overseas tactical air forces be augmented, that rotation of tactical air units from the United States to overseas areas be discontinued, and that the Tactical Air Command be reduced to a replacement training mission. The study was based on the key assumption that the Tactical Air Command could not position its tankers to support a mid-Atlantic crossing to implement an emergency war plan without conflicting with the deployments of the Strategic Air Command and the Military Air Transport Service.[235] Weyland protested the drastic changes contemplated in the study. He was willing to accept added training responsibilities, but he was not willing to give up the concept of worldwide tactical air mobility radiating from a central reservoir of strength in the United States. In response to Weyland's protests, White was unwilling to reject the planning study. However, as had been the case with the tactical-bomber controversy, an interchange of White-Weyland letters resulted in some strengthening of the tactical air position.[236]

The attention focused upon the problem of refueling tactical aircraft during worldwide deployments was wholesome. Tests had already shown that the Strategic Air Command's KC-97 tankers could be equipped with a boom-to-drogue adapter that would permit them to refuel either bombers or fighters. In February 1959 General LeMay directed that the Air Force seek to establish a single fleet of KC-97 and KC-135 tankers equipped to serve all combat aircraft that required aerial refueling; on 3 May 1960 the Air Force established this single tanker force under the management of the Strategic Air Command.[237] Early in 1959 Brig Gen William W. Momyer, now TAC's director of plans, stated that the Tactical Air Command would attempt to move to a standardization of its aircraft. He noted that a "multiplicity of weapon systems had been a plague to the TAC inventory over the years." During 1959 the Tactical Air Command perfected a new concept of tactical air power that hinged upon a clear distinction between the requirements for forces for general and small wars. The new concept visualized that theater-deployed air capabilities ought to begin an evolutionary transition that would prepare them to perform general war missions. These missions could best be performed with missiles. Under the concept, manned tactical aircraft would be returned to the United States and held in a central reservoir from which they could be deployed as necessary for the accomplishment of small war tasks or in support of a nuclear missile exchange in a general war. After being briefed on the new concept early in 1960, General White announced: "Our tactical air effort, both overseas and in the zone of interior, is a prime function for which manned aircraft will be needed as far into the future as I can see. We should retain for ourselves the truly flexible weapon system — aircraft — and turn over to our allies the relative inflexible missile business."[238]

Development in Continental Air Defense

As viewed by the Continental Air Defense Command and the Air Defense Command, the problem of providing an air defense system for the nation was essentially one of preparing forces capable of effective action against a series of rising plateaus of Soviet offensive capabilities. Active air defenses had to be maintained against a current plateau of Soviet threat, and forward air defense projections had to comprehend successive plateaus of Soviet offensive capabilities. Since they were unable to forecast future technological capabilities, the air defense planners saw little choice other than to credit the Soviets with the ability to possess offensive capabilities that would be roughly equivalent to those that would be possessed by the United States at predictable intervals in the future. Air defense doctrine taught that the four major functions to be performed for a successful accomplishment of the mission were detection, identification, interception, and

MISSILE TECHNOLOGY

destruction. These functions would have to be accomplished in the minimum possible time since air defense planners had to accept the probability that the Soviets would achieve tactical surprise and that the first warning of an impending attack would be generated within the air defense system.[239] Predicated upon national aims and objectives, the Air Force accepted the concept of providing an area defense for the continental United States that would: (1) provide for the earliest tactical warning of impending attack to permit deployment of alert strategic offensive forces and to alert active and passive defenses, (2) maintain continuous surveillance of attacking forces throughout the area of combat, (3) apply maximum effect weapons at the maximum possible distance from target areas, (4) employ continuously increasing numbers and types of defensive forces as the attack progressed from a penetration of the combat zone toward the target areas, and (5) provide centralized control of the air battle over large geographical areas.[240]

During World War II the P-47 Thunderbolt and the P-51 Mustang had served as all-purpose fighters. In January 1949 the Air Force Senior Officers Board had believed that it would be impossible to develop all-purpose aircraft in the future. The board pointed out that F-80 and F-84 fighters already were marginal in their capability to intercept aircraft of the B-29 type, and that, based on the design analysis of the few B-29s that had been forced down in the Soviet Union during World War II, the Russians had built a copy of the B-29 known as the Tu-4. Since the Soviets were building a long-range air force around the Tu-4, the mission of American defense would demand the development of a pure interceptor aircraft to be available by 1953-54.[241] Having determined that the new interceptor would be developed as a weapon system, the Air Force put its electronics and control system under development contract in July 1950 and initiated a design competition for the development of an air vehicle. As these decisions were being made, the explosion of a Soviet A-bomb and the beginning of the Korean conflict demanded an immediate augmentation of United States defense against a Soviet Tu-4 air attack capability, which might take the form of one-way missions flown against the United States. A temporary network of radars known as Lashup was rushed to completion in California and in the vital northeastern and northwestern sections of the nation. Other "islands" of air defense radar were established in Alaska and in the Northeast Air Command. Beginnings were made to a more permanent system of modern radars to replace Lashup. On 10 November 1950 the United States and Canada agreed to construct a line of aircraft control and warning radars across southern Canada that would be known as the Pinetree line. In an interim action to provide defense against the Tu-4 threat, the Air Force developed and procured F-94, F-89, and F-86D all-weather fighters for the Air Defense Command. The F-94 and the F-86D were adaptations of existing aircraft.[242]

The Air Force description of the pure interceptor aircraft that would be needed for service in 1954 as issued for design competition on 18 August 1950 contained uncertainties as to the type of ground electronic environment in which the new plane would be employed. The design requirements described a single-place plane to counter a Soviet threat from B-47 or B-52 type aircraft (Badgers or Bisons) and that could operate in either local or area defense from 5,000-foot runways, have a radius of 375 nautical miles, and be capable of an altitude of 60,000 feet. The requirements description noted that manual techniques of aircraft warning and control would impose intolerable delays in a jet age but did not attempt to describe the new ground environment that would be needed.[243] When the design competition was completed, the Convair Aircraft Corporation was given a contract to develop a prototype for the 1954 all-weather interceptor weapon system in July 1951. Late in 1951 the Air Force recognized that the design specifications for the 1954 interceptor were so advanced that they could not be attained by 1954, and it accordingly directed Convair to work toward the development of an interim interceptor to be known as the F-102A and to continue work toward an ultimate aircraft that would later be designated as the F-106.[244]

While work was beginning on the 1954 interceptor, the United States substantially broadened the ground environment electronics systems in which interceptors would be expected to work. Many of the decisions about the ground environment were intergovernmental decisions, which could not be foreseen exactly in military planning. To provide additional early warning, the Air Force won the right in 1951 to procure Navy-developed RC-121 airborne early warning and control aircraft that could cover the Atlantic and Pacific sea approaches to North America. To push radar defenses farther northward, Canada and the United States agreed in October 1953 to proceed with the construction of a mid-Canada radar line. After extended study and controversy over cost, the United States decided early in 1954 to build the distant early warning line within the Arctic Circle.[245] The DEW and mid-Canada lines were planned for warning rather than for the control of interceptor aircraft, but it was apparent that the ground electronic environment was being spread out over an area that could not be covered with a 375-mile radius-of-action F-102. The short-range interceptor fitted into "island defense" rather than a broad-area air defense. Recognizing these facts, the Air Defense Command and the Air Research and Development Command began to visualize a requirement for a two-place long-range jet interceptor. On 19 February 1954 the Research and Development Command recommended that the single-place F-101 Voodoo, originally programmed as a long-range escort fighter for the Strategic Air Command, be adapted into a long-range interceptor. The Air Defense Command was willing to accept the F-101, but the Air Force preferred to delay a decision until it could hold a design competition to get information on the possibility that an optimum long-range interceptor could be developed. Held in the summer of 1954 this design competition would stimulate interest that would eventually yield the design of the F-108, but it promised nothing that could be available soon. The Air Defense Command apparently wanted more than industry could provide prior to 1960, unless the Air Force would be willing to accept a four-engine fighter of virtually the same size as an airborne early warning aircraft. Facing these facts the Air Council on 16 February 1955 directed the procurement of two-place F-101B Voodoo fighters to serve as interim long-range interceptors.[246]

In view of the importance of attaining this long-range interceptor capability as soon as possible, the Air Force ordered the expedited development of the F-102. Early in the program the contractor was authorized to construct an initial quantity of 42 test aircraft and to tool up for a production of 125 a month. Even before the first F-102 was produced it was evident that the plane would be subsonic rather than supersonic. In cooperation with the Air Force and the Navy, the National Advisory Committee for Aeronautics (NACA) had been studying supersonic flight, and a NACA scientist provided an area-progression rule that showed that an aircraft with a fuselage shaped in a "Coke bottle" configuration could sustain supersonic flight of the highest regime. By the time that Convair recognized that it would have to redesign the F-102 according to the area-progression rule, the first 10 vehicles were so far along the production line that they had to be built in the original subsonic configuration. The contractor then had to retool, but the next model was also unsatisfactory because it was too heavy. Four of the overweight versions were produced before the contractor was able to tool up a third time for the first acceptable version of the F-102 Delta Dagger, which made its first successful flight on 19 December 1954 and became operational in mid-1956. Development of the follow-on F-106 Delta Dart was slowed by the attention given to the F-102. The F-106A made its first test flight on 26 December 1956; the two-place F-106B was first flown on 9 April 1958. The F-106 was placed in quantity production in fiscal year 1957 when F-102 production was closed out.

Viewed in retrospect the F-102 story revealed a long gap between perception of need and program accomplishment. The time from the establishment of the requirement in 1948 to the completion of the program in 1958 was ten years. The cost of the F-102 program was some $2.3 billion, and at least $30 million worth of tooling was said to have been discarded in the process of developing this plane.[247]

In view of the gap that was going to exist before the F-102 and F-106 could become operational, the Air Defense Command accepted another interim interceptor — the F-104 Starfighter. The F-104 had not been designed as a fighter-interceptor and possessed electronic equipment that was not compatible with the semiautomatic ground environment that the Air Defense Command was installing. Although reluctant to take the day fighter, the Air Defense Command recognized that it could get the F-104 without great delay, and in April 1956 it asked for six squadrons of the plane. Although the F-104 was a flashy performer, it never met air defense requirements. In August 1957 the Air Force limited F-104 programming to only two wings of aircraft and canceled further production of the plane. At this time the Air Defense Command was rescheduled to receive only four squadrons of F-104s.[248]

At the same time that it was seeking an optimized interceptor aircraft, the Air Force was visualizing the requirements for a ground control environment that could handle a jet air battle. A modern jet bomber could cross the entire area covered by one radar in a very few minutes. The air defense rule of thumb thus visualized that the DEW line would provide the initial detection of the hostile attack, the mid-Canada line would confirm the attack and order an interceptor scramble, and the Pinetree line and the permanent radars in the United States would direct the interception.[249] Even before the full extent that the warning network would take had been determined, Air Force planners recognized that the supersonic speeds of jet aircraft demanded a new electronic means of handling the detection-identification interception tasks. The old procedures by which personnel passed aircraft plots by voice and displayed information manually would be too slow for the jet age.[250] Accepted conceptually by the Air Force in April 1953, the Lincoln Laboratory's semiautomatic ground environment (SAGE) system was built and tested in the Cape Cod area in 1953-54 and accepted for deployment throughout the United States. The Air Defense Command's SAGE plan looked toward the division of the continental United States into eight air defense regions with eight SAGE combat operations centers and 32 air defense sectors with 32 SAGE direction centers. The first SAGE installations were located in the northeastern United States, then in the midwest, and then in the northwest and on the west coast. Next, the remainder of the northern and west-central states were provided with SAGE installations, then the southeastern, the southern, the southwestern, and finally the central portions of the United States were filled in. In view of the time and expense involved to do otherwise and given the probability that an enemy would direct first strikes against US strategic retaliatory forces, the Air Defense Command elected to locate its SAGE installations in shock-resistant, reinforced concrete buildings located above ground. Following the Air Defense Command plan to provide priority protection to the heavily industrialized sections of the nation, the first SAGE direction center became operational at McGuire AFB, New Jersey, in 1957 and the entire SAGE system was completed in March 1962. Utilizing large digital computers and digital data transmission equipment, the centralized SAGE system received, displayed, and stored information from many radars and flight control centers. The SAGE system provided air defense commanders with the capability to direct hundreds of interceptors and missiles against hundreds of targets.[251]

In the same years that new interceptors were under development and a modern ground system was being laid out, the Air Defense Command increased its unit strength and moved toward the attainment of a family of four basic weapon units to be employed against any type of hostile airborne threat. The family was to include long-range interceptor, medium-range interceptor, medium-range interceptor missile, and short-range surface-to-air missile squadrons—all to operate within the SAGE.[252] The Air Force 137-wing program included 34 wings (102 squadrons) of fighter-interceptors, of which 23 wings (69 squadrons) were assigned to the Air Defense Command and the others were committed to theater air forces. As the Air Force momentarily attained its 137-wing program in June 1957, the Air Defense Command attained its planned strength (but two fighter-interceptor wings were deleted from the program).[253] During 1953-54 the Air Defense Command maintained that it would require, in addition to its manned interceptor squadrons, 53 Bomarc missiles squadrons for deployment around the nation's perimeters. In the first firm planning in 1955, the Air Force and the Air Defense Command agreed that 40 Bomarc squadrons was a practicable objective. At Air Force prodding, the Bomarc objective was reduced to 36 squadrons in 1957, some of which were to be located outside the United States.[254]

By 1954-55 the potential scientific advances in air defense appeared to promise a substantial breakthrough in the whole field of activity. "Our objective," stated General Yates in March 1954, "is to develop a completely integrated and automatic air defense network, including interceptor weapon systems, which will provide as effective a defense as is technically possible."[255] Speaking early in 1955 Maj Gen Frederic H. Smith, Jr., visualized an annual expenditure of $7 billion for air defense and a total expenditure of $42 billion for that purpose by 1960. "Such a defense system against manned and unmanned air-breathing weapon systems should inflict an attrition rate of greater than 90 percent upon attacking forces of sizes up to 4,000 flying objects, unless the enemy achieves qualitative surprise."[256] Shortly before his retirement as commander in chief, Continental Air Defense Command, Gen Benjamin W. Chidlaw was similarly optimistic in a letter to General Twining. "I am convinced," he wrote on 28 May 1955, "that an air defense capability which will furnish a comparable deterrent to aggression to that posed by SAC can be achieved, if we put our heart into it."[257] By 1955 the Air Defense Command possessed a good system to meet the threat of the Tu-4 offensive, and there was optimism that the air defense system could continue to outdistance the Soviets.

However, the Soviets achieved qualitative surprise and demonstrated on 1 May 1955 that their offensive capabilities had risen to a new plateau much sooner than had been anticipated. "We now have a good system to fight the Tu-4," observed General Partridge, who became commander in chief, Continental Air Defense Command, on 20 July 1955, "unfortunately the Russians came along a little more rapidly than we anticipated in their technical developments, and they introduced the jet bombers and the Bear more rapidly than was forecast." Partridge also warned that "the defenses which we are ... planning ... take care of the Soviet threat up through the manned bomber, but the Soviets are said to be building an intercontinental ballistic missile, and we must somehow devise a defense against this type of attack."[258] The immediate air defense problem in 1955-56 concerned the development of capabilities to counter the Soviet Bison and Bear, both of which would likely possess a standoff missile equivalent to the Hound Dog. With one aerial refueling, moreover, the Soviet Bear would be able to fly a circuitous route and evade existing early warning lines in the Arctic. Since it was a turboprop aircraft, the Bear not only would have a very long range, but also would be able to operate effectively at low altitudes.[259] After General LeMay had assessed the new Soviet bomber capabilities, which would be magnified once they developed intercontinental ballistic missiles, he observed: "The best thing that the Air Defense Command can do for SAC is to provide warning time. That is the most important thing they can do for us."[260] Less optimistic than his predecessors about the kill capabilities of the Air Defense Command, General Partridge returned to a more limited concept of air defense. "As a matter of doctrine," he stated in April 1956,

> we believe that the best defense is a good offense, and we believe that our primary mission in the Air Defense Command is to defend the bases from which the Strategic Air Command is going to operate. . . . We believe also that we have to provide a reasonable, an equitable protection for the key facilities, the population centers and our industry. . . . We believe, however, that our primary objective is to convince the enemy that he should not attack, and if we can deter the enemy from attacking, we have achieved a 100-percent air defense.[261]

Partridge continued to emphasize the deterrent aspects of air defense. "First of all," he said in 1957, "we want to be so strong, from an air defense point of view, that the enemy will be deterred from the decision, that fateful decision, to attack. . . . The second thing we're trying to do is to insure our survival in the event we are attacked."[262]

The decision of the Department of Defense to meet the challenge of Soviet Bison and Bear aircraft by increasing procurement of B-52s and permitting some dispersal of the Strategic Air Command, increased the importance of the warning function provided by the Continental Air Defense Command. While Partridge was willing to provide the Strategic Air Command with as much warning as was possible, he believed that the Air Defense Command should be provided with a remote air defense weapon system that would permit it to intercept and destroy approaching Soviet bombers before they could launch standoff missiles. In a search for means to provide air cover over naval forces at sea and for beachhead assaults, the Navy commenced studies in 1955 of a system composed of a subsonic long-endurance control and warning Missileer aircraft that were to be equipped to launch high-performance, long-range air-to-air Eagle missiles.[263] The Air Force had this same option to develop a huge missile-firing interceptor as a remote air defense weapon system, but Partridge questioned whether anyone could determine how to employ an air defense plane outside the air defense ground environment.[264] The North American Aviation Company had been studying the problem of remote air defense for several years; when its approach appeared feasible, the Air Force awarded the company a letter contract on 1 June 1957 to begin development of a long-range Mach-3 jet interceptor. This plane was designated the F-108 and, as it was conceived, was to be a two-place, two-engine stainless steel plane that would maintain a Mach-3 speed. It would be designed to carry a pair of new guided aircraft rockets (GAR-9 missiles), which could be fitted with either nuclear or conventional warheads. The F-108's range and speed would give the ability to police the DEW lines, but it would have an electronic system that would work either inside or outside the ground environment. If operated beyond the ground environment, several F-108s would probably fly together in a line-abreast formation, separated by about the range limits of their self-contained airborne intercept radars. From this disposition the individual planes would pick up anything ahead of them, lock onto their targets, and shoot down the targets with their missiles.²⁶⁵ The problem of combating Soviet bombers at longer ranges and at lower altitudes affected the Bomarc development program. The Bomarc A was conceived to be a missile with a 125-mile range that would be effective up to 60,000 feet but would be relatively ineffective at low altitudes. While the Bomarc A continued in development, the Air Force directed that a Bomarc B also be developed that would have a range of action of over 400 miles and would be capable of dealing with a low-altitude threat.²⁶⁶

When Partridge retired and yielded command to Lt Gen Laurence S. Kuter on 1 August 1957, the North American Air Defense Command was well on its way to being able to counter the Soviet Bison and Bear threats. The DEW line was nearing completion, SAGE was becoming operational in the northeastern United States, and the Air Defense Command was converting to century-series jet interceptors. Because of the added expense of these planes as well as their greater combat capabilities, the Air Force programmed a cut in its air defense strength to 28 fighter-interceptor wings (83 squadrons) by 30 June 1958. And, since four Bomarc A missile squadrons were scheduled to become operational in fiscal year 1959, the Air Force planned to reduce the air defense fighter-interceptor strength to 27 wings (80 squadrons) by 30 June 1959.²⁶⁷ To permit this reduction, the Department of Defense had agreed to a plan whereby 12 Air National Guard wings would be equipped with all-weather interceptors and eight with day fighters to augment the Air Defense Command.²⁶⁸ Once again the United States air defense proved to be a step behind Soviet technological capabilities, since the Soviets', Sputnik I revealed that the enemy could soon possess an intercontinental ballistic missile capability. Quite shortly, moreover, American intelligence recognized that the Soviets had concentrated on the development of missiles and had never produced the number of Bisons and Bears that had been within their capability to produce after 1955–56.²⁶⁹

In response to Sputnik the Air Force immediately began the construction of two ballistic missile early warning system (BMEWS) sites at Point Clear, Alaska, and Thule, Greenland. Other than this action and the planned reduction in Air Defense Command strength, General LeMay urged that immediate changes should not be made in the North American Air Defense Command. "Our studies now indicate," he explained, "that even when the ballistic missile becomes very efficient, . . . the most efficient attack will be a combination of the manned vehicle and the ballistic vehicle, using the best characteristics of both weapon systems." Speaking to a question on air defense requirements in December 1957, General White explained that the Strategic Air Command was "perhaps the major contributor to the air defense, because these forces will hit the enemy at his point of launching." More particularly on the subject, he continued: "We need to complete the extension of the DEW line. We need to improve our radar. . . . We need to get on with the more advanced and more sophisticated interceptor system, such as Bomarc. We need to keep modern . . . our manned fighter-interceptors, and we must develop an active weapon against ballistic missiles. . . . I think those are the essentials of the requirements of air defense, and we must get on with it."²⁷⁰

During 1958 White continued to defend SAGE. "The SAGE system," he said, "will permit us to meet the combined manned jet aircraft and air-breathing missile threat as one concise problem rather than as a series of various problems. . . . Even on into the future, SAGE will prove valuable because the forces of the future will undoubtedly be mixed forces—that is, composed of various types of weapons—subsonic, supersonic, and hypersonic."[271]

Although the Air Force successfully secured continued budgeting for its air defense programs in fiscal year 1959, many factors began to impinge on the level of air defense progamming during calendar years 1958–59. In January 1958 Secretary McElroy remarked that he was "not enthusiastic about the solution we have among roles and missions . . . in the area of continental air defense" and revealed that the Joint Chiefs of Staff was reviewing the matter. As has been seen the congressional appropriation of military construction funds for fiscal year 1959 called upon the secretary of defense to determine which missile or combination of missiles would be employed in a given area. Early in 1959 McElroy again stated that air defense continued to be a field in which the Department of Defense was having difficulty making decisions.[272] In March 1959 Senator Symington was very critical of the fact that the Air Force was

> spending $5.5 billion every year to defend against . . . bombers, but . . . not spending enough to maintain a position in the modern weapons of reasonable equality with what we agree the Russians are probably doing. . . . We are cutting down on producing Atlas and on producing supersonic B-58s, and so forth, and yet we are still spending $5.5 billion annually to defend ourselves against something which we know the Russians are cutting down very heavily on and haven't many of.[273]

Despite these criticisms, the Air Force continued to program air defenses for fiscal year 1960 that would defend against a mixed aircraft and missile attack. Fighter-interceptor strength would be reduced to 25 wings, this reduction was justified by the increased effectiveness of century-series interceptors, an increase in the number and effectiveness of air-to-air missiles, and the acquisition of an initial operational capability with Bomarc A missiles.[274] Rather than sacrifice funds required for the development of the Mach-3 interceptor, the Air Force elected to procure no additional manned interceptors in fiscal year 1960.[275] Construction of BMEWS installations in Alaska and Greenland was funded. Work on the SAGE system was to continue, with some changes caused by new technology. The first SAGE installations had employed vacuum tubes and had been too large and bulky to be easily hardened, but the development of transistor electronic components permitted more compact and efficient installations. Early in 1959 the Air Force approved a plan to continue to develop the SAGE system around 10 supercombat centers, which were to be hardened, and 27 direction centers.[276]

Although the Air Force was prepared to make some reductions in air defense requirements, it was not prepared for the full extent of the reductions that would be demanded during calendar year 1959. In its report on the fiscal year 1960 military construction bill, the Senate Armed Services Committee concluded that Nike systems were virtually obsolete and should not be funded; the House Armed Services Committee held that Nike was operational and less costly than Bomarc and recommended severely reduced appropriations for Bomarc. In the absence of military agreements on air defense requirements, Secretary McElroy's civilian staff drew together the master air defense plan, which was officially issued on 19 June 1959. As has been seen, this master plan generally confirmed Air Force concepts of air defense requirements. However, it included a severe reduction in Air Force fighter-interceptor squadrons over the next several years; the reduction of Bomarc to a total of 16 squadrons in the United States and two in Canada, all to be deployed in a peripheral setting rather than in depth; and a limitation of SAGE to eight supercombat centers and 22 direction centers. The master plan recommended that the Army's Nike-Zeus antimissile be continued in research and development and that a third BMEWS installation be constructed at Flyingdales, England.[277] The Air Force did not object to the master air defense plan, but another development in the summer of 1959 caused General White "many sleepless nights." In Department of Defense budget guidance for fiscal year 1961, White was told that funds could not sustain the development of both the F-108 Mach-3 interceptor and the B-70 Mach-3 bomber, if indeed they could support the development of either of them. When presented with the problem, the Air Force Weapons Board recommended that the F-108 be continued in development, but the Air Force Council subsequently reversed the recommendations of the board and recommended that the B-70 should be funded for continued development. General White reasoned that a long-range fighter-interceptor would be needed as long as the Russians had a capability to make bomber attacks with standoff missiles, but he decided that the F-108 would be canceled and the B-70 kept in development. Explaining his decision, White said: "I based that largely on what would be the greatest threat to the Soviet Union, and, hands down, the B-70 wins that argument."[278] Even though the F-108 was technically feasible and a long-range interceptor would be vital to continental air defense, the Air Force canceled the F-108 development program on 23 September 1959. Development of the fire control system and the GAR-9 missile continued on a reduced scale for possible use with some other airframe.[279]

"Somewhat of a revolution," General White noted, "took place in the air defense field under the Department of Defense master air defense plan. . . . I think the No. 1 point . . . is that the technology and the enemy threat are constantly changing. I think it is fair to state it takes time, maybe too much time, for some of the implications to seep into all the brains that have to work on these things." White noted that in a strict sense the commander in chief, North American Air Defense Command, should have borne the responsibility for making necessary weapon systems recommendations to the Joint Chiefs of Staff. But, General White also asserted, "somebody has to step up to these problems, and it devolves in a military sense upon the Chief of the service to take the initiative ... in the light of the overall picture — the integrated threat; the moneys available; the weapon systems which are present and forthcoming; and the light of other threats."[280] Based on this reasoning, the Air Force increased the effort to translate the master air defense plan into system requirements. White charged Maj Gen H. M. Estes, Jr., Air Force assistant deputy chief of staff for operations, to study changes in air defense programs necessary to respond to the master plan. In this evaluation Estes drew heavily for technical assistance upon the Air Defense Systems Integration Division, MITRE Corporation.* Individuals from the North American Air Defense Command and the Air Defense Command provided technical information, but Estes observed: "We did not ask them specifically for their detailed ideas for the very simple reason we knew already their ideas would not coincide with ours with reference to reductions."

Beginning in mid-February 1960, Estes assembled the some 100 technicians who had been working upon separate phases of air defense systems, and the group went into the exact technical status of every single component of the air defense system, when the component could become operational, and how much it would cost. The group attempted to project an air defense system that would be effective against a combined missile-bomber threat at the earliest possible time with a minimum expenditure of dollars. The Estes group completed its work in late February 1960, after which Estes briefed the Air Force, the North American Air Defense Command, and the Air Defense Command on the study group's recommend actions.[281] While the Estes group was at work, General LeMay established another board of general officers to make a continuous evaluation of Bomarc. This evaluation board made reports in November 1959 and January 1960. Working independently, another ad hoc panel of scientists provided evaluations of the Bomarc B to the secretary of defense.[282]

Since evaluations of air defense requirements were under way within Department of Defense, the fiscal year 1961 departmental budget submitted to Congress in January 1960 represented interim changes recommended by the six-month-old master air defense plan. The Air Force desired to reduce air defense wings from the 27 in being on 30 June 1959 to 23 on 30 June 1960 and to 20 on 30 June 1961. By 30 June 1960, four Bomarc squadrons were to be operational and it was planned that eight Bomarc squadrons would be in operation by 30 June 1961. Altogether the Air Force wanted to bring 16 Bomarc squadrons into the air defense inventory. SAGE was programmed for eight supercombat centers and 22 direction centers.[283] Seaborne extensions of the DEW line—picket ships and "Texas towers"—would be eliminated, but airborne control and warning aircraft would continue to function.[284] On 14 January, the same day that the new Secretary of Defense Thomas S. Gates, Jr., and General Twining appeared before the Subcommittee of the House Committee on Appropriations to defend the budget, Soviet Premier Nikita Khrushchev announced that the Soviet Union would depend on ballistic missiles and was stopping development of manned bombers. While

---

*Massachusetts Institute of Technology Research Corporation.

skeptical of the Soviet announcement, Gates and Twining agreed that air defense requirements ought to be kept under study. "Maybe the Russians will eliminate their air threat completely," Twining remarked. "We do not know. We certainly ought to keep watching this and not spend money on air defense unnecessarily."[285]

In January 1960 Secretary Gates and General Twining were willing to stand behind the fiscal year 1961 air defense program. However, following the completion of the Estes study group's work, General White appeared before the Subcommittee of the House Committee on Appropriations on 24 March to submit a reappraisal of air defense programs. Since study had shown that the planned degree of hardening would be expensive yet inadequate to protect the supercombat SAGE centers fully, White desired to eliminate the eight supercombat centers and 22 direction centers. On the best scientific advice he could get, White believed that Bomarc A and B would work; nevertheless, he proposed to cut Bomarc procurement off with the 10 squadrons that were already funded. These squadrons would be deployed to defend the industrial area of the northeastern United States and southeastern Canada — eight squadrons would be sited in the United States and two in Canada. These reductions would save an estimated $500 million in the fiscal year 1961 budget. White asked for the authority to apply this money to accelerate development of the Midas satellite system, which was designed to detect hostile ICBMs at the earliest possible moment after they were launched; to speed construction of the second and third BMEWS installations; to procure additional Atlas missiles and to accelerate the development of a mobile Minuteman missile; to improve the capabilities of century-series fighter-interceptors; and to continue technical development for an advanced fire control and missile system for a long-range fighter-interceptor.[286]

In justifying the Air Force proposal to divert funds previously committed to air defense to offensive purposes, General White explained: "Of course, our philosophy is based on the fact that offense is the best defense.... I am perfectly certain that ... air defense could absorb the national budget, and still could not guarantee 100-percent defense. So, in the final analysis, it is a matter of judgment at what level you balance out between offense and a minimum of adequate defense." General Estes summed up the North American Air Defense Command's requirement for a "mixed force of weapons, each of which has the capabilities which are not directly attainable in the other type of weapon, to take on any attack." "Manned interceptors," Estes said,

> complement Bomarc by having capabilities that are unique in having a human operator aboard. The manned interceptor provides the only means in peace time for positive identification and in war it is flexible in terms of redeployment to meet threats in different areas and in capability for reattack. The interceptor can kill one bomber and then go on to kill a second. It can be recovered, refueled, and rearmed to again enter the battle.... On the other hand, if only a force composed of fighter-interceptors were available in a given area, the commander would not have as great a capability at low level, and his ability to concentrate a mass of interceptor weapons in a small area against a mass raid would be degraded to the extent that aerial nuclear blast would affect his interceptor pilots.[287]

In recommending revisions to the national air defense program, White considered that the Air Force had "cut through some of the inhibitions" and the "'clinging' to concepts" and was providing a program that looked realistically to the future. "While I recognize," he said, "the threat of the air-breathing bomber exists as of today as the most important, most deadly threat against this Nation, it is quite obvious that the intercontinental ballistic missile is to become the predominant threat to this Nation."[288] White testified that the new air defense program had been approved by the Air Staff and by the Joint Chiefs of Staff, and Secretary Gates assured Congress that President Eisenhower had reviewed and approved the revisions in air defense.[289] At Colorado Springs where he commanded the North American Air Defense Command, General Kuter did not agree that the new air defense program served national requirements. According to White, Kuter urged that the Bomarc and fighter-interceptor programs be continued at full strength, that the manning of air defense units be the responsibility of full-time Air Force personnel rather than Air National Guard crews on alert, that the F-108 development program be reinstated to oppose the Soviet air-launched missile threat, that the supercombat centers be built, and that Nike-Zeus be produced as the only immediately prospective anti-ICBM defense.[290] During the spring of 1960, Congress displayed doubts about the recommended air defense revisions. The House of Representatives eliminated all funds for Bomarc not already committed and added funds sufficient to purchase enough F-106s to equip two additional fighter-interceptor squadrons. The Senate, on the other hand, voted funds for even more fighter-interceptors, restored Bomarc program cuts made by the House, and granted additional funds to provide two Bomarc bases in the northwestern United States. In a conference committee, Congress agreed to vote $100 million for additional F-106s and $244 million for Bomarc missiles. These amounts were approved in the Department of Defense Appropriation Act of 1961. However, on 9 August 1960 Secretary Gates decided that original appropriation requests had provided substantially for air defense, including "buy-out" procurement of Bomarc B missiles and improvements of existing interceptor aircraft, and that the additional appropriations would not be used.[291]

The Department of Defense and the Air Force considered that the air defense revisions of 1960 marked a recognition of the "imminent shift in the air threat to our security from aircraft alone to ballistic missiles and aircraft."[292] At the helm of the North American Air Defense Command, however, General Kuter continued to disagree with the downgrading of defense. "The course of aerospace defense," he stated upon retiring from the Air Force on 31 May 1962, "is a rather sporty course ... of slow starts and some quick stops ... marked by a series of efforts to close gaps — gaps that have been created by advances in offensive weapon systems." As he looked backward Kuter observed that air defense had been moving rapidly ahead in 1957 and had almost closed the gap on Soviet offensive capabilities, but he thought that these efforts to comprehend Soviet offensive capabilities had been suddenly halted in 1959. Kuter argued that the nation could produce, and urgently required, a long-range Mach-3 manned fighter-interceptor. He also felt that the

MISSILE TECHNOLOGY

Army's Nike-Zeus missile be put into production for operational deployment, since it was the nation's only available anti-ICBM defense system. "We know full well," he said, "that we must have complementary strategic offensive and North American defensive forces to present a credible deterrent or to ensure national survival should general war occur."[293]

Origins of Aerospace Doctrine in the Air Force

In a reminiscent remark about pre-Sputnik days, Maj Gen Bernard Schriever recalled that "'space' was a nasty word in certain circles."[294] Initially in the post-World War II period, the subject of space was more amusing than anything else, at least to the public. When Secretary James V. Forrestal disclosed in his first annual report as secretary of defense during 1948 that the Air Force and Navy were studying earth satellite vehicles, amused journalists asked: Will America possess moons of war?[295] As has been seen, the first Rand study completed for the Air Force in 1946 indicated the feasibility of an earth orbital satellite that would be launched by the MX-774 Hiroc missile. However, these early Rand studies emphasized the scientific value of earth satellites rather than their military worth. Believing that progress in booster technology might reduce the individual cost of satellites, General Vandenberg signed a policy statement that the Air Force had "logical responsibility for the satellite." After reviewing Air Force and Navy satellite studies, however, the Defense Research and Development Board's Committee on Guided Missiles reported on 29 March 1948 that insufficient thought had been given to the military worth of such vehicles and that, in any event, the cancellation of the development of the MX-774 missile would delay orbital flight. The committee further recommended that "the only activity directed toward satellite vehicles as such should be a continuation of the Project RAND studies of the utility of a vehicle."[296]

Authorized to continue satellite studies, the Rand Corporation was able to report by April 1951 that "pioneer reconnaissance and weather reconnaissance are suitable with the resolving power presently available to a satellite television system."[297] In view of the reinstitution of the long-range ballistic missile development program in 1951-52, the Air Force directed Rand to proceed with studies of components for a satellite reconnaissance system and, on 16 March 1955, it issued a general operational requirement for the development of WS-117L, a strategic reconnaissance weapon system.[298] After receiving and evaluating proposals from several major contractors, the Air Force selected the Lockheed Aircraft Corporation as the prime manager for WS-117L and issued a contract in 1956.[299] Other factors were involved, but the need to establish military worth was significant cause for the nearly 10-year lapse between first conception and initiation of research and development on a satellite reconnaissance space system.

Another line of development that would lead the Air Force to the fringes of space originated in the waning months of World War II from a general recognition that the nation lacked basic knowledge about supersonic flight. From the date of its establishment in 1915, the National Advisory Committee for Aeronautics (NACA) had accomplished practically all of the fundamental and basic research in aerodynamics and propulsion for the benefit of the Army, Navy, and civil aviation. Except for unusual cases where results of potential military significance were withheld, the NACA promptly published the results of the investigations that it conducted in its laboratories at Langley Field, Virginia; at Cleveland, Ohio; and at Moffet Field, California. During World War II, NACA had served as the "silent partner of US airpower." Its high-speed airfoil principle, for example, had been employed on the P-51 Mustang to delay the formation of compressibility burbles, thus enabling the Mustang to withstand high-speed dives of over 600 miles an hour. As World War II was ending, however, NACA's chairman, Dr Jerome C. Hunsaker, warned that "the reserve of knowledge available when we entered the war, and without which victory would have been greatly delayed, has been exhausted. . . . As with the Wright brothers at the first flight, we stand at a new frontier where research to establish the scientific principles and laws governing high-speed flight will determine our future in the air."[300]

Although NACA accomplished fundamental and basic research, this research did not normally include the development of specific aircraft or equipment. Looking toward supersonic flight explorations, the Army, Navy, and NACA agreed that the Army or the Navy would fund research vehicles, the contractor would provide initial flight tests, the Army or the Navy would determine the military applicability of the vehicles, and, after that, a test vehicle would be turned over to NACA in order that its tests might provide data to be published for the entire aviation industry. In order to begin supersonic flight probes, the Air Technical Service Command authorized two supersonic airplane projects on 5 and 6 March 1945. The first project authorized the Bell Aircraft Company to fabricate three test aircraft that would have speeds greater than Mach 1 and would be powered by alcohol-liquid oxygen rocket motors. The second project with the Douglas Aircraft Corporation involved a design study of a supersonic airplane.

The Bell plane, which would subsequently be known as the XS-1 and later the X-1, was to be the first of an X or research series of aircraft.[301] Launched from an airborne B-29, the X-1 made its first powered flight on 9 December 1946. Further refinements enabled the conventionally structured X-1 to break the sound barrier on 14 October 1947 with Capt Charles E. Yeager as its pilot. Learning lessons from the X-1, the Army Air Forces contracted with Bell on 27 November 1945 to build two X-2 test planes, with Monel Metal fuselage and stainless steel sweptback wings that would permit them to attain very high speeds. The first X-2 accidentally exploded in the bomb bay of a B-50 on 13 May 1953. In later test flights at Edwards AFB, California, the second X-2 exceeded speeds of 1,900 miles per hour and attained an altitude of 126,000 feet.[302] In this same period the Douglas Aircraft Company built several models of a D-558 Skyrocket plane under Navy contract. These rocket-powered planes were tested at Edwards and eventually turned over to NACA. Flying a D-558-II aircraft on 20 November 1953, NACA test pilot Scott

Crossfield achieved a record speed of 1,328 miles per hour, thus becoming the first man to penetrate Mach 2.[303]

During the spring of 1952, NACA's Committee on Aerodynamics recommended that the several NACA laboratories begin to study problems likely to be encountered in space flight. As a result of these studies, the Committee on Aerodynamics endorsed a proposal to build a Mach-7 research airplane that could explore the fringes of space. Since NACA was not authorized to procure such an experimental plane, Dr Hugh L. Dryden, who was now its chairman, proposed to the Air Force and Navy on 9 July 1954 that these services should procure the plane for cooperative testing. Reacting favorably to the project, the Department of Defense authorized the Air Force and the Navy to finance the needed aircraft development. After a design competition, the Air Force issued a letter contract to the North American Company on 18 November 1955 providing for the purchase of three rocket-powered X-15 aircraft and for modifying a B-52 to be used to launch them. The memorandum of understanding regarding the X-15 provided that NACA would exercise technical development with advice and assistance from a Research Airplane Committee that included Air Force and Navy representatives. The development of the X-15 was extremely costly, and the Air Force was called upon to provide the great majority of the needed funds. Following delivery to Edwards AFB, the X-15 made its first powered flight on 17 September 1959. Equipped with alternate engines, an X-15 flown by Air Force Maj Robert M. White attained a record altitude of 314,750 feet on 17 July 1962. Another X-15 achieved a speed of 4,105 miles per hour on 27 June 1962. Each X-15 flight furnished data for the design of high-altitude hypersonic operational aircraft and also provided data on the physiological and psychological reactions of man in flights along the fringes of space.[304]

While the X-series aircraft were not designed in any way to become weapon systems, Air Force developmental planners were familiar with work that had been conducted in Germany during World War II by Dr Eugen Sänger and his assistant Dr Irene Bredt. Working independently of the Peenemünde ballistic missile people, Sänger had prepared plans for the use of a V-2 rocket as a second stage for a boost-glide manned vehicle that would be launched from Germany, rise above the atmosphere, and then glide back into the atmosphere; it, thus, could become a very long-range bomber capable of circumnavigating the earth and bombing New York. The German government did not give serious consideration to the boost-glide rocket bomber, but both the Russians and the Americans captured interesting data relative to the Sänger concept. Employed as a consultant to the Air Materiel Command in 1947, Dr Walter Dornberger carried the boost-glide concept to the Bell Aircraft Company in 1950 when he left Air Force employment and entered private enterprise. In 1952 Bell approached the Air Force with a proposal to undertake research on a manned, boost-glide bomber-missile, called Bomi. After considerable argumentation within the Air Force, the Wright Air Development Center completed a contract with Bell on 1 April 1954 calling for a study of an advanced bomber-reconnaissance system.

Based on favorable results from the Bell study, the Air Force issued a general operational requirement for a hypersonic strategic bombardment system on 12 May 1955; nevertheless, research and development planners doubted the advisability of investing scarce funds in such a system. The satellite reconnaissance system merited priority funding and the X-15 research aircraft project could well provide data regarding the reentry of a manned orbital vehicle into the atmosphere. In March 1956, the Air Force, therefore, concluded another study contract with Bell for a research study visualizing a piloted boost-glide reconnaissance weapon system to be known as Brass Bell. This reconnaissance system was to be kept separate from the Bomi, now to be known as the rocket bomber or Robo. In November 1956 the Air Research and Development Command formulated a system requirement for a hypersonic weapon research and development supporting system called Hywards. This vehicle was to serve as a test craft for the development of subsystems to be employed in future boost-glide systems.[305]

The significance of advanced boost-glide systems was enhanced on 15 February 1956, when General Power, then commander of the Air Research and Development Command, stated that Soviet technological progress was so marked that the United States ought to stop considering new and novel projects and start developing some of them. During fiscal year 1957, the Air Force was unable to allocate funds for a manned glide-rocket. In April 1957, however, the Air Force directed that the Air Research and Development Command consolidate Hywards, Brass Bell, and Robo into one project. The resultant product provided by this command on 10 October 1957 was the Dyna-Soar (a compound of dynamic soaring) program that appeared feasible for accomplishment in three stages: Dyna-Soar I, an experimental glider; Dyna-Soar II, a reconnaissance vehicle; and Dyna-Soar III, a bombardment system. On 15 November 1957 the Air Force approved the Dyna-Soar development plan and allocated research and development funds for the hypersonic glider test vehicle. Early in 1958 the Air Force reduced Dyna-Soar to two stages: Dyna-Soar I continued to be the unmanned experimental space glider, while Dyna-Soar II would be a composite manned bomber and reconnaissance system. The Soviets also appeared to be doing research on the basis of Sänger's original ideas. In 1958 a Soviet aviation journal referred to a Russian glide-bombing system capable of attaining an altitude of 295,000 feet and of striking targets at distances up to 3,500 nautical miles.[306]

Shortly after World War II, the Air Force also began several studies and experiments concerned with the problem of maintaining life at hypersonic speeds and very high altitudes. In 1946 the Aeromedical Laboratory at Wright-Patterson AFB joined with the National Institute of Health in upper-atmosphere experiments at White Sands and Holloman AFB, New Mexico. Insects, fungus spores, and later small animals were sent aloft in V-2 and Aerobee rocket capsules to reveal the effects of cosmic radiation and high altitudes on living things. In November 1948 the Air Force School of Aviation Medicine had held a symposium on "The Medical Problems of Space Travel"; in February 1949 it organized a department of Space Medicine. The Aeromedical Laboratory began the development of a T-1 pressure suit in 1943; the suit saved the life of a test pilot in 1951 when the X-1 lost its cabin pressure on a high-altitude flight. The X-15 required an even more sophisticated full pressure suit; the boost-glide vehicles would need a habitable cabin. Looking toward design of space capsules, the Air Force employed Manhigh manned balloon flights. The first Manhigh flight occurred 2 June 1957 when Capt Joseph W. Kittinger reached an altitude of 95,000 feet. The second flight on 19 August 1957 carried Maj David G. Simons to 102,000 feet and remained aloft for more than 32 hours.[307] Some of these ventures occasioned heavy-handed sarcasm, but each of them sought to develop more knowledge about man's role in a space environment.

Visualizations of Satellites and Space Stations

During the later 1940s the Army did not officially share the Air Force and Navy interest in space satellites, but even at this time Dr Wernher von Braun was a foremost publicist for a manned space station. By the autumn of 1954, von Braun was advancing a proposal that a complete space station could be built in 10 or 15 years at a cost of about $4 billion. He believed that the nation that first possessed a space station would be in a position to rule the earth. When Secretary Wilson was queried about earth satellites and space platforms at a news conference on 16 November, he said that he knew nothing about US military scientists working on plans for a space platform or earth satellite and would not be alarmed if the Russians built one first. He was quoted as adding: "I would rather keep my feet on the ground, figuratively speaking as well as physically speaking. I don't know that anyone knows how you would rule the world with a space station. It is a little dreamy, I think." A month later at another news conference, when told that the Russians might orbit a satellite before the United States, Wilson retorted: "I wouldn't care if they did."[308] Already on record as opposing "boon-doggling research," Wilson told newsmen on 6 June 1955 that he considered the military research and development effort to be fully adequate. Speaking in his usual candid fashion, he went on to describe research and development as like drilling for oil. "The smart people in the oil business," he said, "try to drill their holes in a likely place, so the money that is given to the Defense Department, I like to see spent in an area . . . of some use to us. And maybe some other place in the nation's budget could go the money for fundamental research, I don't know. I don't care what happens to some of the minor things."[309]

Air Force leaders shared von Braun's belief that the development of missiles would provide the booster capability needed to place satellite weapon systems in orbit. In an address in San Diego in February 1957, General Schriever stated that "about 90 percent of the developments in the ballistic-missile program can be applied to advancing in space, satellites and other vehicles." Recalling this address somewhat later, Schriever remarked: "From a technological standpoint, it is, I think, a normal transition to step from these ballistic missiles into satellites, moon rockets, going to planets."[310] General White also conceived that "missiles are but one step in the evolution from manned high-performance aircraft to true manned spacecraft; and, in the forces structure of the future . . . we will have all three systems."[311] One of the reasons that the Air Force desired to develop the rigid structured Titan as an alternate to the Atlas was a belief that the more sophisticated Titan would be the "prime vehicle . . . for getting large vehicles and apparatus into outer space." Except for certain "long-haired" research and development men, however, General Irvine suggested in December 1957 that there was an insufficient awareness that the ballistic missile was "only a short step in the evolution of advanced weapon systems." "There is too much feeling . . . in the minds of the people in this country and in Government," Irvine continued, "that we air staff folks are perhaps just a little bit crazy when we talk about these modern machines."[312]

Although Air Force leaders saw a hopeful relationship between first-generation military missiles and eventual space technology, President Eisenhower and top officials in the Defense Department did not share their beliefs. In its report of 14 February 1955, the Technological Capabilities Panel of the President's Science Advisory Committee recommended top priorities for the development of ICBMs and IRBMs. The panel also noted that space satellites would be important in the near future as instruments of reconnaissance, but it believed that no satellite as then conceived could be employed as an offensive weapon. If a space vehicle released a bomb, the bomb would not fall to earth but would continue in orbit in the wake of the satellite.[313] When he discussed security matters in a report to the American people on 13 November 1957, President Eisenhower explained the criteria that he desired to use in regard to space projects. "If the project is designed solely for scientific purposes," he said, "its size and its cost must be tailored to the scientific job it is going to do. If the project has some ultimate defense value, its urgency for this purpose is to be judged in comparison with the probable value of competing defense projects."[314]

Highly critical of the Department of Defense criteria for weapon system development, Doctor von Braun charged in December 1957 that military requirements for missiles were conceived narrowly in terms of "a limited end item" and that such development became "a dead-end street." As warheads got lighter the trend in the Department of Defense was to build smaller, less-powerful boosters. "It is very significant . . . ," von Braun thought, "that the development of . . . large rocket engines . . . was not approved by anybody simply because there is no need for these engines within the framework of the existing and approved missile systems." He urged that large and powerful rocket engines, which could not be immediately justified in terms of military worth, would be required to boost manned vehicles into outer space.[315] To Secretary McElroy on 29 January 1959, however, the fact that Soviet rockets had more thrust than American missiles seemed "beside the point" from a military point of view, but he agreed that "it was significant in regard to space." "We have an adequate thrust," McElroy said, "to take a warhead on an ICBM range to selected targets in the Soviet Union. If you have twice that much thrust, it doesn't help you, from a missile standpoint. It does, of course, help you from an outer space standpoint . . . but it is not of real importance in the ICBM capability."[316]

At the same time that the Department of Defense favored the commitment of defense research and development money to the perfection of low-risk weapon systems of definite military worth, President Eisenhower also hoped that a peaceful regime could be maintained in space. Before and after becoming president, Eisenhower often expressed an ideal of enforced peace through arms limitations and disarmament.[317] Accepting an arms control concept that the United States should retain its nuclear power and yet make clear that its purposes were peaceful, Eisenhower took advantage of an assembly of world leaders at the Geneva Summit Conference in July 1955 to propose a worldwide inspection plan for the prevention of surprise attack. At the conference table Eisenhower proposed that the United States and the Soviet Union would exchange "a complete blueprint" of their military forces and each would facilitate the other's aerial reconnaissance of their countries. Eisenhower believed that such a step would "convince the world that we are providing as between ourselves against the possibility of great surprise attack, thus lessening danger and relaxing tension."[318] Eisenhower's "open skies" proposal at Geneva assumed an immediate relationship to proposals that had been made in October 1954 by a committee of the International Council of Scientific Unions for the launching of small scientific satellites during the international geophysical year (IGY), which would begin on 1 July 1957 and conclude on 31 December 1958. The Soviet Union had announced on 15 April 1955 that it had established a Special Commission for Interplanetary Communications and would produce "a remote controlled laboratory to circle the earth as a satellite and establish opportunities for observation of a hitherto inaccessible character." After Eisenhower returned from Geneva, the White House announced on 29 July that in 1957-58 the United States would launch small space satellites, probably instrument-bearing, that would circle the earth each 90 minutes at a height of 300 miles.[319]

Critical of the open skies proposal from the first, the Soviets finally rejected it early in 1956 when disarmament negotiations reached another stalemate. While the open skies proposal was in conception and under consideration, however, it had important effects upon US space policy. In view of the growing interest in scientific satellites, von Braun had proposed in June 1954 that a Redstone missile should be used to launch a small slug into orbit.[320] Since a Redstone was successfully test fired on 24 May 1955, it appeared to be the most practical booster for launching the American IGY satellite. At a meeting on 26 May, however, the National Security Council expressed the opinion that, because of the soon-to-be-proposed open skies policy, the American scientific satellite ought not to be launched into orbit by a military missile. In the Department of Defense, Assistant Secretary Donald Quarles directed the services to submit plans for a scientific satellite and established a committee of scientists and engineers to evaluate the proposals. The committee evaluated these recommendations during June and July 1955. For their part, the Army and Navy favored acceptance of an Orbiter project to be boosted by the Redstone missile, but the Navy suggested an alternate plan calling for the use of a modified version of the old Viking test missile that was free from military implication. The Air Force was not able to make a serious proposal for the IGY satellite that would not interfere with the progress of its ICBM program. After evaluating the proposals, the committee was said to have believed that the whole satellite project was actually premature. On 4 August it, nevertheless, reported that a small satellite could be put in orbit during the international geophysical year. The committee noted that use of an Atlas booster would give the greatest assurance of success, but it respected the Air Force belief that such an employment of the Atlas would interfere with the ICBM program. The majority of the committee recommended use of an improved Viking missile that would be known as Vanguard. A minority of three committee members recommended that the booster system for the IGY satellite should use the existing Army Redstone rather than depend on a development of the Vanguard.[321] The Department of Defense approved the Vanguard proposal over the objections of the Army, which warned that time consumed in developing the missile might enable the Soviets to launch the first satellite. Following procurement of a test quantity of improved Redstone missiles, known as Jupiter C, General Gavin again proposed that one of the missiles be used to launch a scientific satellite. On 15 May 1956, however, Gavin received a personal admonition: "The Redstone and Jupiter missiles will not be used to launch a satellite."[322]

Even though the Soviets refused to accept the open skies proposal, Harold Stassen, who was serving as Eisenhower's special assistant for disarmament, continued to believe that some measure of aerial inspection could contribute to the control of arms. "I do believe from our studies," he said in June 1956,

> that if a measure of inspection, particularly against surprise attack, can be obtained, on a basis that must be mutually lived up to or its violation would be immediately discovered, that such a system combined with a moderate, sustained alert, armed strength will give a greater likelihood of security and peace than either an all-out arms race on the one extreme or a complete inspection system and comprehensive disarmament on the other.[323]

In August 1956, Col Martin B. Schofield of the Air War College Evaluation Division completed a study entitled "Control of the Use of Outer Space." Schofield pointed out that the "use of an earth satellite as a reconnaissance vehicle would provide intelligence data of the highest order of coverage and reliability." Satellites that could fire missiles from orbital positions could also be developed, and such an airborne ICBM would be extremely hard to defend against since speed, time, and direction of approach would be in favor of the offensive weapon. Although missile-firing satellites appeared feasible, Schofield recommended the establishment of international controls over space. "The presence of a variety of devastating military forces, of many sovereign states, constantly deployed throughout international space," he noted, "may not be conducive to peaceful living. . . . It might be more sound for the United States, because it may have an early advantage in the exploration of space, to use its position of influence to the best advantage by strongly advocating a form of international control over the use of space."[324]

In his State of the Union message delivered to Congress on 10 January 1957, President Eisenhower renewed his proposal for the open skies inspection system and additionally called for the establishment of international control over space. "We are willing," he said, "to enter any reliable agreement which would ... mutually control the outer space missile and satellite development."[325] Four days later Henry Cabot Lodge, US ambassador to the United Nations, presented a more detailed version of space control to the General Assembly. Speaking on 25 July 1957, Stassen reiterated the need to establish control over experimentation with objects traveling through outer space. He warned that the situation was perilously close to that of 1945-46 when the Soviets rejected Bernard Baruch's plan for the control of atomic weapons, an action that had led to an international nuclear arms race. He hoped that the same mistake would not be made in the development of space vehicles, which would involve an equal and perhaps an even greater danger to mankind.[326]

In his Air War College study on space, Colonel Schofield had believed that the United States was in a position to adopt a positive stand on international control because it "presumably enjoys a lead in the current evolution of scientific achievement."[327] The Soviets not only displayed little interest in establishing international controls over space during 1956-57, but they would be the first nation into space effective with the orbital flight of Sputnik I on 4 October 1957. The real tragedy of the situation was summarized by General Gavin: "We have the scientific talent and we have the brainpower, the industrial capacity. ... The failure was in decision-making, making the wrong decisions."[328] In the opinion of Dr Clifford C. Furnas, who had become assistant secretary of defense for research and development on 22 November 1955, the Soviets had been permitted to get ahead of the United States in space because of the decision to develop a "peaceful" Vanguard rather than to use the "military" Redstone as a booster for a scientific satellite. Even with maximum effort Furnas believed that it would have been difficult to expedite the Vanguard program, but he later remembered that the Department of Defense had not considered the Vanguard IGY satellite project to be of "first importance" and had allowed only a "dribbling release" of requisite funds to it.[329]

A Concept of Space Superiority

Apparently failing to recognize that administrative policy favored the establishment of international controls to secure a peaceful regime in space, General Schriever forcefully asserted in an address at San Diego in February 1957 that the United States ought to move ahead and establish space superiority. "In the long haul," he maintained, "our safety as a nation may depend upon our achieving 'space superiority.' Several decades from now the important battles may not be sea battles or air battles, but space battles, and we should be spending a certain fraction

IDEAS, CONCEPTS, DOCTRINE

of our national resources to insure that we do not lag in obtaining space superiority."[330] On the day following this address, Schriever discovered that "'space' was a nasty word" since, he recalled, he received instructions forbidding him to use the word *space* in any of his speeches. General Power, commander of the Air Research and Development Command, also learned that it was "inappropriate" for an officer in a responsible position to speak on the military potential of space.[331]

Breaking the silence on space matters in the aftermath of Sputnik, General White defined the Air Force's perspective at what he described as the "dawn of the space age" in an address to the National Press Club on 29 November 1957. "Whoever has the capability to control the air," he said,

> is in a position to exert control over the land and seas beneath. I feel that in the future whoever has the capability to control space will likewise possess the capability to exert control of the surface of the earth.... We airmen who have fought to assure that the United States has the capability to control the air are determined that the United States must win the capability to control space. In speaking of the control of air and the control of space, I want to stress that there is no division, per se, between air and space. Air and space are an indivisible field of operations.... It is quite obvious that we cannot control the air up to 20 miles above the earth's surface and relinquish control of space above that altitude — and still survive.[332]

In numerous appearances before congressional investigating committees in the winter of 1957–58, White continued to emphasize the continuum of air and space. He foresaw the use of weapons in space, both offensive and defensive. Although he confessed no "personal expertness in the matter," he believed it would be possible for a man to go to the moon.[333] In similar appearances, Assistant Secretary of the Air Force (Research and Development) Richard E. Horner and Lt Gen Donald L. Putt, Air Force deputy chief of staff for research and development, strongly argued that the moon possessed valuable potential as a military base. "We should not regard control of the moon," Putt added, "as the ultimate means of insuring peace among the earth nations. It is only a first step toward stations on planets far more distant — in turn, from which control over the moon might then be exercised." In summation, Putt said: "The conquest of space — or, at least, its denial to an enemy — is vital to continued United States security.... Within the framework of deterrent force as we exercise it today, space flight soon will be employed to great advantage. And eventually, space superiority will become the primary factor in assurance of world peace."[334]

To the leaders of the Air Force, space technology represented a logical progression in the development of Air Force technology. "The Air Force," said Secretary Douglas, "has been engaged in explorations of outer space and all of the associate technical fields since the end of World War II.... The techniques and actual developments involved in the X-15 are one path to man's flight into space." Douglas recalled that no one at first had perceived the military worth of the airplane, and he asserted: "We must press forward with projects for the weapons of day after tomorrow, more advanced missiles and aircraft for flight outside the atmosphere, and satellites even though we cannot foresee precisely their employment." To General White "almost everything in space" fitted into the Air Force mission. "We foresee," he said, "that we are not only going to have manned bombers and missiles, but that eventually we will have manned space vehicles as combat weapons in the future."[335]

The assertions by General White and others that the United States needed to establish military capabilities in space seemed at odds with President Eisenhower's national space-for-peace policy. Conceptual studies done in the Office of the Air Force Deputy Chief of Staff (Plans and Programs) also indicated that control of space would be a far more complex matter than control of the air. The techniques for control of the air had rested on an air force's capability to destroy air bases, to intercept enemy aircraft in flight, and to destroy planes by antiaircraft fire. Aircraft possessed great maneuverability. For the foreseeable future, however, space vehicles would be confined to the general vicinity of courses or trajectories selected at the time of their launchings. They would travel at extremely high velocities and would lack any great degree of maneuverability.[336]

In a major speech delivered to the Air Force Association's Third Jet Age Conference in February 1958, General White indicated that he had given thought to the space-for-peace policy and to means whereby control might be exercised in space. White said:

> The United States must win and maintain the capability to control space in order to assure the progress and preeminence of the free nations. . . .
>
> You will note that I stated the United States must win and maintain the capability to control space. I did not say that we should control space. There is an important distinction here. We want all nations to join with us in such measures as are necessary to ensure that outer space shall never be used for any but peaceful purposes. But until effective measures to this end are assured, our possession of such a capability will guarantee the free nations liberty. It does not connote denial of the benefits of space to others.
>
> In the past, when control of the seas was exercised by peaceful nations, people everywhere profited. Likewise, as long as the United States maintains the capability to control space, the entire world will reap the benefits that accrue. . . .
>
> There has been some discussion concerning whether or not the military should handle all United States activities in space. Under our form of government, I do not feel that this is really a problem. Over-all civilian control will be exercised, and rightly so. However, space research and development efforts and space operations must give due consideration to the military aspects.
>
> This is necessary because until other ironclad methods are devised, only through our military capability to control space will we be able to use space for peaceful purposes. I visualize the control of space as the late twentieth century parallel to the age-old need to control the seas and the mid-twentieth century requirement to control the air. . . .

To control space we must not only be able to go through it with vehicles that travel from point to point, but we must be able to stay in space with human beings who can carry out jobs efficiently.

I look upon the Air Force's interest and ventures into space as being logical and natural as when men of old in sailing ships first ventured forth from the inland seas.

As these ancient seafarers' knowledge of the inland seas increased and they learned more about the elements, they built larger ships and ventured farther away from land. The achievement required men who had learned the many things there were to know about the inland seas. Similarly, ventures into outer space require men who know the air. There are no barriers between air and space. Air and space are an indivisible field of operations.

The Air Force progress toward space has been evolutionary—the natural development and extension of speed, altitude, and sustained flight. These qualities have been our stock in trade throughout the fifty years of Air Force history. We have strived continually to fly faster, to fly higher, and to remain airborne longer. . . .

The evolutionary process which has brought the Air Force to its high state of development is not going to change in direction because there are additional challenges in space. Aeronautics and astronautics are closely allied. . . . I feel that a dangerous trap lies ahead of us if we partition our space efforts. We must have centralized direction of our national efforts to attain the best results from available resources, talent, and experience. Excessive duplication of effort would not only be a most severe economic drain on our country, but would waste energy and time. . . .

Once we attain the space capability, a lack of centralized authority would certainly hamper our peaceful use of space and could be disastrous in time of war. Failure to properly coordinate peaceful space activities under common direction could cause confusion, might result in wrong decisions, and would be a safety hazard. In war, when time is of the essence and quick reaction so necessary, centralized military authority will surely be mandatory.

A strong consideration as far as military space operations are concerned will always be the necessity for the failsafe concept. A substantial proportion of our forces must maintain the capability to make last-second decisions. This is one reason I am convinced that man in space will be a most important factor.

Ninety-nine percent of the Earth's atmosphere lies within twenty miles' altitude above the Earth. To assure effective operations, there can be no division in responsibility between the control of the air up to twenty miles above the Earth's surface and the space above it. Air Force facilities, communications, and experience exist now for centralized control of operations in the Earth's atmosphere. This capability can easily be extended beyond the Earth's atmosphere as our operations in space develop.

Before I close, I want to stress that I cannot conceive that mechanical gadgets will control space. Man will develop the equipment, send it off, and bring it back. On many occasions, and probably more than we envision now, man will fly the equipment. The point here is that man's judgment and skills will always be needed.

In his address White also pointed out that "the United States' capability to control space could ultimately approach absolute deterrence" because reconnaissance eyes in outer space would permit "immediate warning of hostile action on the surface of the Earth" and would allow "much faster reaction on our part... which is not only quick, but strong and selective." In response to a question as to how space could be controlled, White responded: "One of the ways to control the sea in time of war and stress is the blockade.... I think the same thing conceivably could apply to existing from the Earth's natural envelope into space." It would probably be better to seek to control a hostile nation's access to space than its reentry into the atmosphere. "You couldn't have reentry," he said, "if you kept people from getting out there."[337]

Although there was a general recognition that Air Force studies of space "had only scratched the surface of the problem,"[338] the Air Force had made a good start in rationalizing a new aerospace doctrine. On 29 November 1957 an editorial prepared by the Air Force Office of Information Internal Information Division, first combined the words *air* and *space* when it referred to "air/space vehicles of the future." The word *aerospace* was apparently coined by Dr Woodford A. Heflin of the Air University's Research Studies Institute who published an *Interim Glossary, Aero-Space Terms,* on 23 February 1958.[339] In view of the new thinking, the Air Policy Branch, Air Force Office of Deputy Chief of Staff (Plans and Programs) proposed on 25 April 1958 that Air Force Manual 1-2, *United States Air Force Basic Doctrine,* should be revised. The Air Policy Branch proposed that the new doctrine should state that air power had "moved naturally and inevitably to higher altitudes and higher speeds until it now stands on the threshold of space operation." A new term, *aerospace* meaning "air and space," had come into being, and aerospace power was its manifestation. The Air Force was the military agency predominantly responsible for aerospace doctrine just as in the past it had been responsible for air power doctrine. In aerospace the Air Force could not expect to enjoy the situation earlier referred to as a desired dominant position through control of the air. Instead, aerospace power would desirably possess "the capability to exercise the initiative in space: its purpose would be to operate in space and maintain control in space, not of space." Maintaining general supremacy in aerospace would be a desirable function quite similar to the function of gaining and maintaining general air supremacy that was assigned to the Air Force by law. The Air Policy Branch also suggested that the new doctrine should include the statement: "The positioning of aerospace power geographically and/or astronautically may have dominating significance in peace or war."[340]

The concept of aerospace caught on rapidly within the Air Force. In an article published in August 1958, General White remarked that Soviet air power was being rapidly expanded into aerospace power.[341] When he appeared before the House Committee on Science and Astronautics on 3 February 1959, White stressed the word *aerospace* throughout his prepared statement, and then defined it by stating:

IDEAS, CONCEPTS, DOCTRINE

> The Air Force has operated throughout its relatively short history in the sensible atmosphere around the earth. Recent developments have allowed us to extend our operations further away from the earth, approaching the environment popularly referred to as space. Since there is no dividing line, no natural barrier separating these two areas, there can be no operational boundary between them. Thus air and space comprise a single continuous operational field in which the Air Force must continue to function. This area is areospace. . . . Total aerospace power includes manned and unmanned air-breathing vehicles, spacecraft, and satellites and ballistic missiles.[342]

Congressional reaction to aerospace was somewhat less than unanimously enthusiastic. Chairman John W. McCormack of the House Committee on Science and Astronautics described aerospace as "a very sweet term, a very all-embracing term."[343] "Boys," Representative Daniel J. Flood exclaimed, "the Air Force has come up with a new phrase, 'Aerospace.' That is a beauty. . . . That means everybody is out of space, and the air except the Air Force. . . . They have now staked out a claim to 'aerospace.'"[344] To Under Secretary of the Air Force Malcolm A. MacIntyre, however, aerospace was not a catchword but an attempt "to identify, in a single word, the continuous operational field in which the Air Force must function as technological progress permits us to operate farther and farther away from the earth's surface." MacIntyre denied that the Air Force claimed exclusive jurisdiction in aerospace. "In the use of the word 'aerospace,'" he explained,

> there is no intention on the part of the Air Force to claim aerospace as an exclusive medium of our particular service. We recognize that the other services also have an interest, or, in the military parlance, requirements that can or should be met in the expanded medium of aerospace. However, each service's interest, or requirements, is justified only to the extent to which it enhances its ability to perform its particular missions.[345]

In its final definition incorporated in the revision of Air Force Manual 1-2 issued on 1 December 1959, the Air Force stated: "Aerospace is an operationally indivisible medium consisting of the total expanse beyond the earth's surface. The forces of the Air Force comprise a family of operating systems—air systems, ballistic missiles, and space vehicle systems. These are the fundamental aerospace forces of the nation."[346]

Except for the recognition that control in aerospace was apt to require different techniques from those practiced in gaining and maintaining control of the air, the Air Force viewed the atmosphere and space as one realm and saw no reason why the Key West definitions of strategic roles and missions should not continue to guide the organization of the Armed Forces. The Department of Defense, the Army, the Navy, and significant portions of the civilian scientific community differed with the Air Force positions on aerospace and aerospace power. The resolution of these diverse views would have a substantial impact on national organization for defense and for the utilization of space.

NOTES

1. House, *Department of Defense Appropriations for 1959: Hearings before the Subcommittee of the Committee on Appropriations, Overall Policy Statements*, 85th Cong., 2d sess., 1958, 25.
2. House, *United States Military Aid and Supply Programs in Western Europe: Ninetieth Report by the Committee on Government Operations*, 85th Cong., 2d sess., 1958, 31.
3. House, *DOD Appropriations for 1959, Overall Policy Statements*, 403.
4. *Public Papers of the Presidents of the United States: Dwight D. Eisenhower, 1958* (Washington, D.C.: Government Printing Office, 1958), 8.
5. Gen Henry H. Arnold, *Third Report of the Commanding General of the Army Air Forces to the Secretary of War*, 12 November 1945, 69–70.
6. Project RAND, First Quarterly Report, RA–15000, June 1946, 6–17; Douglas Report no. SM-11827, *Preliminary Design of an Experimental World Circling Spaceship*, 2 May 1946.
7. House, *National Military Establishment Appropriation Bill for 1950*, 81st Cong., 1st sess., 1949, pt. 2:183; Report of the chief of staff, US Air Force, to secretary of Air Force, 84.
8. History, Air Materiel Command, 1946, 1:100.
9. House, *Organization and Management of Missile Programs: Hearings before a Subcommittee of the Committee on Government Operations*, 86th Cong., 1st sess., 1959, 223.
10. Mary R. Self, *History of the Development of Guided Missiles, 1946–1950*, historical study (Wright-Patterson AFB, Ohio: Air Materiel Command, 1951), 47–95.
11. Senate, *Inquiry into Satellite and Missile Programs: Hearings before the Preparedness Investigating Subcommittee of the Committee on Armed Services*, 85th Cong., 1st and 2d sess., 1957–1958, 1637–38.
12. Memorandum by Maj Gen Hugh J. Knerr to Gen Carl A. Spaatz, subject: Armament Organization, 26 February 1946.
13. Ibid.; Col H. C. Sands, Jr., "Guided Missiles," lecture, Air War College, Maxwell AFB, Ala., 12 March 1947.
14. Memorandum by Lt Gen Joseph T. McNarney, deputy chief of staff, US Army, to commanding general, Army Air Forces, 2 October 1944.
15. House, *Space, Missiles, and the Nation: Report of the Committee on Science and Astronautics*, 86th Cong., 2d sess., 1960, 5.
16. Senate, *Inquiry into Satellite and Missile Programs*, 583–84; Eric Bergaust, *Rockets and Missiles* (New York: G. P. Putnam's Sons, 1957), 7.
17. Eugene M. Emme, *Aeronautics and Astronautics* (Washington, D.C.: National Aeronautics and Space Agency, 1961), 61; Bergaust, *Rockets and Missiles*, 9.
18. House, *Space, Missiles, and the Nation*, 5.
19. Memorandum by War Department to commanding general, Army Air Forces, commanding general, Army Ground Forces, and commander, Technical Services, 7 October 1946; memorandum by War Department to commanding general, Army Air Forces, commander, Ordnance, and commander, Signal Office, 10 October 1946.
20. Self, *History of the Development of Guided Missiles*, 15.
21. Sands, "*Guided Missiles*"; Senate, *Study of Air Power: Hearings before the Subcommittee on the Air Force*, 84th Cong., 2d sess., 1956, 538.
22. Quoted in Senate, *Inquiry into Satellite and Missile Programs*, 822–23.
23. Maj Gen J. W. Sessums, Jr., USAF, Retired, to Dr Ernest G. Schwiebert, command historian, Air Force Systems Command, letter, 18 October 1961.
24. Maj Gen Benjamin W. Chidlaw, deputy commanding general (engineering), Air Materiel Command, to commanding general, Army Air Forces, letter, 6 May 1947; Sessums to Schwiebert, letter, 18 October 1961.
25. Vannevar Bush, *Modern Arms and Free Men* (New York: Simon and Schuster, 1949), 78, 80–87.
26. Memorandum by Maj Gen Curtis E. LeMay, deputy chief of staff for research and development, to W. Stuart Symington, assistant secretary of war for air, 6 May 1946.
27. House, *Military Establishment Appropriations Bill for 1948*, 80th Cong., 1st sess., 1947, 640–41.

28. Self, *History of the Development of Guided Missiles*, 42; Sands, "Guided Missiles."

29. Maj Gen Benjamin W. Chidlaw to commanding general, Army Air Forces, letter, 6 May 1947.

30. Memorandum by Brig Gen Thomas S. Power, deputy assistant chief of staff for operations, to commanding general, Army Air Forces, 16 June 1947; Self, *History of the Development of Guided Missiles*, 46.

31. Maj O. S. Anderson, "USAF Guided Missile Program," lecture, Air War College, Maxwell AFB, Ala., 6 November 1951.

32. Self, *History of the Development of Guided Missiles*, 92–94; House, *Weapons System Management and Team System Concept in Government Contracting: Hearings before the Subcommittee for Special Investigations of the Committee on Armed Services*, 86th Cong., 1st sess., 1959, 302–5.

33. Department of Defense, *Semiannual Report of the Secretary of Defense and the Semiannual Reports of the Secretary of the Army, Secretary of the Navy, and Secretary of the Air Force, July 1 to December 31, 1949* (Washington, D.C.: Government Printing Office, 1950), 77–78.

34. Maj Gen Donald L. Putt, "USAF Research and Development," lecture, Air War College, Maxwell AFB, Ala., 17 November 1949; Department of Defense, *Semiannual Report of the Secretary of Defense and the Semiannual Reports of the Secretary of the Army, Secretary of the Navy, and Secretary of the Air Force, January 1 to June 30, 1950* (Washington, D.C.: Government Printing Office, 1950), 35.

35. *Semiannual Report of the Secretary of Defense July to December 1949*, 195; Self, *History of the Development of Guided Missiles*, 71–72; Ernest G. Schwiebert, *A History of the U.S. Air Force Ballistic Missiles* (New York: Praeger, 1965), 145.

36. Self, *History of the Development of Guided Missiles*, 69–76; House, *Department of Defense Appropriations for 1961: Hearings before the Subcommittee of the Committee on Appropriations*, 86th Cong., 2d sess., 1960, pt. 7:200; Donald R. McVeigh, *The Development of the Bomarc Guided Missile, 1950–1953*, Wright Air Development Center Historical Study (Wright-Patterson AFB, Ohio: Wright Air Development Center, January 1956), 1–10.

37. Self, *History of the Development of Guided Missiles*, 78–86; Department of Defense Fact Sheet 3-F, *Guided Missiles and Rockets*, 29 April 1960, 44.

38. Transcript of proceedings, USAF Commander's Conference, 22 January 1951, 36–40; House, *DOD Appropriations for 1961*, pt. 1:45; pt. 7:200; J. Allen Neal, *The Development of the Navaho Guided Missile, 1945–1953*, Wright Air Development Center Historical Study, January 1956, 1–47.

39. House, *Department of Defense and Related Independent Agencies Appropriations for 1954*, 83d Cong., 1st sess., 1953, 170.

40. Senate, *Inquiry into Satellite and Missile Programs*, 973–74.

41. Col Edward N. Hall, "Air Force Missile Experience," *Air University Quarterly Review* 9, no. 3 (Summer 1957): 24–25.

42. House, *Department of Defense Appropriations for 1958: Hearings before the Subcommittee of the Committee on Appropriations*, 85th Cong., 1st sess., 1957, pt. 1:32.

43. History, Headquarters USAF, 1 July 1950 to 30 June 1951, 5.

44. Address delivered before personnel of Air Research and Development Command by Col S. R. Harris, director of plans and programs, Air Research and Development Command, 23 May 1951, 10; Senate, *Department of Defense Appropriations for Fiscal Year 1952: Hearings before the Subcommittee of the Committee on Appropriations*, 82d Cong., 1st sess., 1951, 1548–56.

45. Memorandum by James H. Doolittle to Gen Hoyt S. Vandenberg, subject: Report on the Present Status of Air Force Research and Development, 20 April 1951; Senate, *DOD Appropriations for 1952*, 1556; History, Air Research and Development Command, July 1951–December 1952, 1:136–37.

46. History, Air Research and Development Command, July 1951–December 1952, 1:93–94; memorandum by Col E. H. Wynn, assistant for plans, Air Research and Development Command, to chief of staff, Air Research and Development Command, subject: ARDC Commander's Conference, 17 September 1952.

47. DOD, *Semiannual Report of the Secretary of Defense January to June 1950*, 200; DOD, *Semiannual Report of the Secretary of Defense and Secretary of the Army, Secretary of the Navy and Secretary of the Air Force January 1 to June 30, 1950*, 250.

48. *Semiannual Report of the Secretary of Defense January to June 1951*, 48; transcript of proceedings, USAF Commander's Conference, 22 January 1951, 40; House, *Astronautics and Space Exploration: Hearings before the Select Committee on Astronautics and Space Exploration*, 85th Cong., 2d sess., 1958, 1498–1503.

49. House, *Astronautics and Space Exploration*, 1502; House, *Organization and Management of Missile Programs*, 249; Senate, *Inquiry into Satellite and Missile Programs*, 584.

50. Department of Defense, Fact Sheet 3-F, 29 April 1960.

51. Senate, *Inquiry into Satellite and Missile Programs*, 584.

52. Ibid., 541; Lloyd S. Swenson, Jr., James M. Grimwood, and Charles C. Alexander, *This New Ocean, A History of Project Mercury* (Washington, D.C.: National Aeronautics and Space Administration, 1966), 21; Lt Gen James M. Gavin, *War and Peace in the Space Age* (New York: Harper & Bros., 1958), 154.

53. Brig Gen A. R. Crawford, commander, Engineering Division, Air Materiel Command, to deputy chief of staff for materiel, US Air Force, letter, subject: Project RAND, Satellite Vehicle, 8 December 1947; memorandum by Lt Gen Howard A. Craig, deputy chief of staff for materiel, to vice chief of staff, subject: Earth Satellite Vehicle, 12 January 1948; ind. Gen Hoyt S. Vandenberg, 15 January 1948.

54. Self, *History of the Development of Guided Missiles*, 94; History, Air Research and Development Command, January–June 1955, 1:253–54; Ethel M. DeHaven, *Aerospace—The Evolution of USAF Weapons Acquisition Policy, 1945–1961*, Air Force Systems Command Historical Publication Series 62-24-6, 1962, 20.

55. DeHaven, *Aerospace*, 20–21; House, *Weapons System Management and Team System Concept in Government Contracting*, 304; *Semiannual Report of the Secretary of Defense January to June 1953*, 293; Maj Gen Donald N. Yates, director of research and development, Deputy Chief of Staff for Development, US Air Force, to commander, Air Research and Development Command, letter, subject: Atlas, 22 June 1953.

56. House, *Space, Missiles, and the Nation*, 5; DeHaven, *Aerospace*, 30–31; Maj Gen Bernard A. Schriever, "The USAF Ballistic Missile Program," *Air University Quarterly Review* 9, no. 3 (Summer 1957): 7–8; House, *Weapons System Management and Team System Concept in Government Contracting*, 304, 491–92; Ernest G. Schwiebert, "Air Force Response to the Soviet Threat," History, Air Research and Development Command, January–June 1960, 1:34–35, 78; memorandum by Trevor Gardner, special assistant for research and development, Department of Air Force, to assistant secretary of defense for research and development, 16 February 1954.

57. Quoted in House, *Department of Defense Appropriations for 1960: Hearings before the Subcommittee of the Committee on Appropriations*, 86th Cong., 1st sess., 1959, pt. 5:663.

58. Schriever, "The USAF Ballistic Missile Program," 8; House, *Weapons System Management and Team Concept in Government Contracting*, 491; House, *Department of Defense Appropriations for 1963: Hearings before a Subcommittee of the Committee on Appropriations*, 87th Cong., 2d sess., 1962, pt. 5:337.

59. Memorandum by Gen Thomas D. White, chairman, Air Force Council, to chief of staff, US Air Force, subject: USAF Strategic Missile Program, 23 March 1954; ind. Gen Nathan F. Twining, 23 March 1954; Senate, *Study of Air Power*, 645.

60. History, Air Research and Development Command, January–June 1955, 1:264.

61. House, *Weapons System Management and Team System Concept in Government Contracting*, 491–92; Schriever, "The USAF Ballistic Missile Program," 8.

62. House, *Organization and Management of Missile Programs*, 15; House, *Weapons System Management and Team Concept in Government Contracting*, 304; History, Air Research and Development Command, January–June 1955, 1:271–74.

IDEAS, CONCEPTS, DOCTRINE

63. Minutes of Scientific Advisory Committee meeting, 20 and 21 July 1954; Senate, *Inquiry into Satellite and Missile Programs,* 993–94; House, *DOD Appropriations for 1960,* pt. 5:615–16.

64. History, Air Research and Development Command, January–June 1955, 1:281–83; memorandum for record by Brig Gen Bernard A. Schriever, subject: Interaction of Tactical Ballistic Missile System with Intercontinental Ballistic Missile, 20 December 1954.

65. Warren E. Greene, *The Development of the SM-68 Titan,* Air Force Systems Command Historical Study, August 1952, 11–18.

66. Robert F. Piper, *The Development of the SM-80 Minuteman,* Air Force Systems Command Historical Study, April 1962, 6–19.

67. Ibid., 18–22.

68. Samuel P. Huntington, *The Common Defense: Strategic Programs in National Politics* (New York: Columbia University Press, 1961), 89; House, *Department of Defense Appropriations for 1956: Hearings before a Subcommittee of the Committee on Appropriations,* 84th Cong., 1st sess., 1955, 23–24, 31–32; House, *Department of Air Force Appropriations for 1957: Hearings before a Subcommittee of the Committee on Appropriations,* 84th Cong., 2d sess., 1956, 782; Senate, *Inquiry into Satellite and Missile Programs,* 541.

69. Schwiebert, *A History of the U.S. Air Force Ballistic Missiles,* 113; Dwight D. Eisenhower, *The White House Years: Waging Peace, 1956–1961* (Garden City: Doubleday & Co., 1965), 208.

70. House, *Investigation of National Defense Missiles: Hearings before the Committee on Armed Services,* 85th Cong., 2d sess., 1958, 4358; Senate, *Inquiry into Satellite and Missile Programs,* 541.

71. House, *Investigation of National Defense Missiles,* 4064.

72. Memorandum by Charles C. Wilson to secretary of Air Force, subject: Management of the ICBM and IRBM Development Programs, 8 November 1955; House, *Department of Defense Appropriations for 1957: Hearings before a Subcommittee of the Committee on Appropriations,* 84th Cong., 2d sess., 1956, 51–54.

73. Senate, *Study of Air Power,* 1113, 1128; House, *DOD Appropriations for 1957,* 872, 876–77, 879, 881, 892; Trevor Gardner, "Must Our Air Force Be Second Best?" *Look,* 1 May 1956, 77–83, and "Our Guided Missiles Crisis," *Look,* 15 May 1956, 46–52.

74. House, *DOD Defense Appropriations for 1960,* pt. 1:411.

75. Senate, *Inquiry into Satellite and Missile Programs,* 541–43, 583–85, 959–61; House, *Supplemental Defense Appropriations for 1958: Hearings before a Subcommittee of the Committee on Appropriations,* 85th Cong., 2d sess., 1958, 371.

76. Stanley Ulanoff, *Illustrated Guide to U.S. Missiles and Rockets* (Garden City: Doubleday & Co., 1959), 71–73.

77. Senate, *Inquiry into Satellite and Missile Programs,* 959; House, *Organization and Management of Missile Programs,* 273.

78. Senate, *Inquiry into Satellite and Missile Programs,* 1657–59; Ethel M. DeHaven, *Air Materiel Command Participation in the Air Force Ballistic Missiles Program through December 1957,* Air Materiel Command Historical Study, September 1958, 1:143–53; Ulanoff, *Illustrated Guide to U.S. Missiles and Rockets,* 68–70.

79. House, *DOD Appropriations for 1957,* 52.

80. Ibid., 446.

81. Senate, *Inquiry into Satellite and Missile Programs,* 1497; Gen Maxwell D. Taylor, *The Uncertain Trumpet* (New York: Harper & Bros., 1959), 140–41.

82. House, *United States Defense Policies in 1958,* 86th Cong., 1st sess., 1959, 21–22; House, *DOD Appropriations for 1958,* 1957, 1408–9; House, *Sundry Legislation Affecting the Naval and Military Establishments for 1957: Hearings before the Committee on Armed Services,* 85th Cong., 1st sess., 1957, 1:120.

83. Memorandum by Charles C. Wilson to members of the Armed Forces Policy Council, subject: Clarification of Roles and Missiles to Improve the Effectiveness of Operation of the Department of Defense, 26 November 1956.

84. Message, Headquarters USAF to all major commands, 16 August 1957.

85. House, *Organization and Management of Missile Programs*, 22–23.
86. History, Directorate of Research and Development, US Air Force, January–June 1957; House, *Investigation of National Defense Missiles*, 4769; House, *Department of Defense Appropriations for 1959, Department of the Air Force*, 85th Cong., 2d sess., 1958, 256–57, 371; House, *DOD Appropriations for 1961*, pt. 1:45, 48–49; History, GAM-77 Hound Dog Missile, Air Force Systems Command, 1955–61, xii–xiv.
87. History, Directorate of Research and Development, US Air Force, July–December 1957, 29; House, *DOD Appropriations for 1958*, 32; Senate, *Inquiry into Satellite and Missile Programs*, 868–96; House, *DOD Appropriations for 1959*, 43–44.
88. Schwiebert, *A History of the U.S. Air Force Ballistic Missiles*, 221–22.
89. Huntington, *The Common Defense*, 414; Senate, *Inquiry into Satellite and Missile Programs*, 250.
90. Taylor, *The Uncertain Trumpet*, 140–41.
91. Senate, *Inquiry into Satellite and Missile Programs*, 959–61; House, *DOD Appropriations for 1960*, pt. 5:630–31; Taylor, *The Uncertain Trumpet*, 141.
92. Max Rosenberg, *Plans and Policies for the Ballistic Missile Initial Operational Capability Program*, USAF Historical Division Liaison Office, 1960, 81; Huntington, *The Common Defense*, 414; House, *Hearings on Military Posture and H. R. 2440 before the Committee on Armed Services*, 88th Cong., 1st sess., 1963, 277; John C. Brassel, *Jupiter Development Aspects—Development*, Mobile Air Service Command Historical Study, 1962, 2.
93. Taylor, *The Uncertain Trumpet*, 141.
94. Schwiebert, *A History of the U.S. Air Force Ballistic Missiles*, 118, 122.
95. House, *DOD Appropriations for 1960*, pt. 5:863–64; House, *DOD Appropriations for 1961*, pt. 1:57–59; Greene, *The Development of the SM-68 Titan*, 52–58; Piper, *The Development of the SM-80 Minuteman*, 31.
96. House, *Supplemental Defense Appropriations for 1958*, 85th Cong., 2d sess., 1958, 193–94; Department of Defense, *Semiannual Report of the Secretary of Defense and the Semiannual Reports of the Secretary of the Army, Secretary of the Navy, and Secretary of the Air Force, January 1 to June 30, 1958* (Washington, D.C.: Government Printing Office, 1959), 212; House, *Organization and Management of Missile Programs*, 437.
97. House, *DOD Appropriations for 1963*, pt. 5:61.
98. House, *DOD Appropriations for 1961*, pt. 2:299.
99. Senate, *Study of Air Power*, 1284.
100. House, *Supplemental Defense Appropriations for 1958*, 90; House, *Investigation of National Defense Missiles*, 4770–74, 4788, 4795; History, Air Research and Development Command, July–December 1956, 1:369–72.
101. Senate, *Study of Air Power*, 767–68; "The Army's Bird in Hand," *Air Force Magazine*, June 1956, 42–44; House, *DOD Appropriations for 1959, Overall Policy Statements*, 139.
102. House, *Investigation of National Defense Missiles*, 4216.
103. "The Army's Bird in Hand," 42–44.
104. House, *Sundry Legislation for 1957*, 1:120.
105. Memorandum by Charles C. Wilson to members of the Armed Forces Policy Council, 26 November 1956.
106. House, *Missile Development and Space Sciences: Hearings before the Committee on Science and Astronautics*, 86th Cong., 1st sess., 1959, 241–42, 248–49.
107. House, *United States Defense Policies in 1958*, 23–25; Senate, *Inquiry into Satellite and Missile Programs*, 1539.
108. House, *Investigation of National Defense Missiles*, 4215–16; Taylor, *The Uncertain Trumpet*, 131–32.
109. House, *Investigation of National Defense Missiles*, 4470–74.
110. Senate, *Inquiry into Satellite and Missile Programs*, 1539.
111. House, *Investigation of National Defense Missiles*, 3981, 4068; Department of Defense, *Semiannual Report of the Secretary of Defense: January 1 to June 30, 1958*, 26.

IDEAS, CONCEPTS, DOCTRINE

112. House, *United States Defense Policies in 1958,* 20–21; Senate, *Inquiry into Satellite and Missile Programs,* 2319.
113. Senate, *Inquiry into Satellite and Missile Programs,* 2325, 2016–17.
114. House, *Investigation of National Defense Missiles,* 4723.
115. Ibid., 4788.
116. Senate, *Inquiry into Satellite and Missile Programs,* 959, 990.
117. House, *United States Defense Policies in 1958,* 21.
118. Claude Witze, "The Mix-Up in Air Defense," *Air Force Magazine,* 37–41; Claude Witze, "ADSIC," *Air Force Magazine,* October 1958, 58–66.
119. House, *United States Defense Policies in 1958,* 23–25.
120. House, *DOD Appropriations for 1961,* 252.
121. Gen Curtis E. LeMay, address to Air Force Association Convention, 21 September 1961.
122. Senate, *Inquiry into Satellite and Missile Programs,* 9–10.
123. Hall, "Air Force Missile Experience," 24, 26–27; Schwiebert, "Air Force Response to the Soviet Threat," 96.
124. Col Richard P. Klocko, *The Impact of Guided Missiles upon the USAF,* Air War College Graduate Study Group Thesis no. 4 (Maxwell AFB, Ala: March 1954), 8.
125. Anderson, "USAF Guided Missile Program," 6 November 1951.
126. Air Force Letter 136-3, subject: Armament — "Guided Missiles" in the United States Air Force, 18 September 1952.
127. AFR 58-1, *Guided Missiles, Air Force Guided Missile Policy,* 15 August 1955.
128. Col Jack Donohew, "Programming Processes in the Air Force."
129. Col C. E. Putnam, "Readiness vs. Modernization and Expansion," lecture, Air War College, Maxwell AFB, Ala., 19 February 1953.
130. Donohew, "Programming Processes in the Air Force"; Senate, *Department of Defense Appropriations for Fiscal Year 1962: Hearings before a Subcommittee of the Committee on Appropriations,* 87th Cong., 1st sess., 1961, 862–63.
131. Donohew, "Programming Processes in the Air Force"; History, Air Research and Development Command, July–December 1954, 251–57; Ethel M. DeHaven, *The Voodoo Story, 1945–1957,* Air Materiel Command Historical Study, December 1957, 209–32.
132. Senate, *DOD Appropriations for 1962,* 863–64; History, Air Research and Development Command, July 1951–December 1952, 1:136–37, and July–December 1954, 1:243–44; History, Tactical Air Command, July–December 1956, 1:123–26; USAF Historical Division Liaison Office, B-58 Development and Testing Program Summary, 1962.
133. Maj Gen Thomas S. Power, vice commander, Strategic Air Command, to director of requirements, US Air Force, letter, subject: Requirements for Long Range Strategic Bombardment Aircraft, 30 March 1953.
134. History, Air Research and Development Command, January–June 1959, vol. 2, *B-70 Story (The Evolution of Weapon System 110A),* 1–8; Robert D. Little, *Nuclear Propulsion for Manned Aircraft: The End of the Program, 1959–1961,* USAF Historical Division Liaison Office, April 1963, 1–7.
135. Memorandum to Maj F. M. Johnson, guided missiles project officer, Strategic Air Command, subject: USAF Guided Missiles Program, n.d., in History, Strategic Air Command, July–December 1951, chap. 5, ex. 1.
136. Memorandum for record by Maj F. M. Johnson, subject: Guided Missiles Program, 22 August 1951.
137. Brig Gen R. M. Montgomery, chief of staff, Strategic Air Command, to chief of staff, US Air Force, letter, subject: B-63 (Rascal) Program, 2 October 1963.
138. General Montgomery to chief of staff, US Air Force, letter, subject: Pilotless Aircraft Programs, 18 April 1954; Col W. C. Garland, "Readiness vs. Modernization and Expansion," lecture, Air War College, Maxwell AFB, Ala., 23 February 1954.
139. Brig Gen Dale O. Smith, "Pilot or Robot?" *Air Force Magazine,* November 1953, 33–34, 37–38.

140. House, *Department of Air Force Appropriations for 1956: Hearings before a Subcommittee of the Committee on Appropriations,* 84th Cong., 1st sess., 1955, 6–7.

141. Minutes of assistants and directors meeting, deputy commander, Weapons Systems Air Research and Development Command, in History, Air Research and Development Command, January–June 1956, doc. 41.

142. Maj Gen D. N. Yates, president of board, to commander, Air Research and Development Command, letter, subject: Report of Board of Officers to Consider a Guided Missile Development Center, 27 May 1955.

143. House, *Department of Defense Appropriations for 1956: Additional Hearings before a Subcommittee of the Committee on Appropriations,* 84th Cong., 1st sess., 1955, 6–8, 23–24, 31–32; Senate, *Study of Air Power,* 1859.

144. House, *DOD Appropriations for 1956: Additional Hearings,* 6, 23–24, 38.

145. Ibid., 23–24.

146. Donohew, "Programming Processes in the Air Force"; Department of Air Force Letter AFOMO 784J, subject: Redesignation of Elements of Certain Strategic Reconnaissance Wings, Heavy, 23 August 1955.

147. Donohew, "Programming Processes in the Air Force."

148. House, *DOD Appropriations for 1959, Department of the Air Force,* 38.

149. Senate, *Study of Air Power,* 101–2, 107–8, 154–56, 163, 201–2, 209.

150. Memorandum for record by Lt Col Kermit E. Beary, chief, 110 Section, Air Research and Development Command, 11 March 1957, in History, Air Research and Development Command, January–June 1959, doc. 17.

151. Maj Gen Richard C. Lindsay, director of plans, US Air Force, "How the Air Force Will Use Its Missiles," *Air Force Magazine,* September 1956, 98–103.

152. House, *DOD Appropriations for 1958,* 946, 954–55, 991.

153. Ibid., 1133.

154. Col James B. Tipton, "Air Force Concepts for the Employment of Future Weapons," lecture, Air War College, Maxwell AFB, Ala., 13 May 1957.

155. House, *DOD Appropriations for 1958,* 462, 1043, 1057; "The Symington Subcommittee's Airpower Findings," *Air Force Magazine,* February 1957, 43; House, *Supplemental Defense Appropriations for 1958,* 101.

156. House, *DOD Appropriations for 1958,* 917–18; History, Tactical Air Command, January–June 1957, 33, and July–December 1957, 22.

157. Senate, *Study of Air Power,* 101.

158. Ibid., 154–56.

159. Senate, *Inquiry into Satellite and Missile Programs,* 901–2.

160. House, *DOD Appropriations for 1963,* pt. 5:330.

161. Senate, *Study of Air Power,* 188–89, 196; Gen Curtis E. LeMay, "Capabilities and Employment of SAC," lecture, Air War College, Maxwell AFB, Ala., 4 February 1957.

162. House, *DOD Appropriations for 1958,* 947–48; Senate, *Inquiry into Satellite and Missile Programs,* 905; House, *DOD Appropriations for 1963,* pt. 2:463–64.

163. LeMay, "Capabilities and Employment of SAC."

164. Memorandum by Col Roland A. Campbell, commander, Operations Division, Strategic Air Command, to Office of Information, Historical Division, Strategic Air Command, subject: "Reflex" Action Program, 19 February 1958; House, *DOD Appropriations for 1963,* pt. 3:535–36.

165. House, *Investigation of National Defense Missiles,* 4744.

166. Maj Gen Dale O. Smith, "Overseas Bases in Unlimited War," *Air Force Magazine,* December 1959, 39–41; House, *DOD Appropriations for 1960,* pt. 1:71; Senate, *Major Defense Matters: Hearings before the Preparedness Investigating Subcommittee of the Committee on Armed Services,* 86th Cong., 1st sess., 1959, 88; Lt Gen W. C. Sweeney, Jr., commander, Eighth Air Force, to Gen Thomas S. Power, commander, Strategic Air Command, letter, 11 September 1959; Power to Sweeney, letter, 3 October 1959.

IDEAS, CONCEPTS, DOCTRINE

167. LeMay, "Capabilities and Employment of SAC."

168. History, Directorate of Operations, Deputy Chief of Staff for Operations, US Air Force, January–June 1957, 94.

169. Gen Thomas D. White, "The Ballistic Missile: An Instrument of National Policy," *Air University Quarterly Review* 9, no. 3 (Summer 1957): 4.

170. Memorandum by Gen Thomas S. Power, commander in chief, Strategic Air Command, to Brig Gen James B. Knapp, subject: Commander's Conference, Patrick AFB, Fla., 30 September–1 October, 4 October 1957; White to Weyland, letter, 7 November 1957.

171. White to Weyland, letter, 7 November 1957.

172. White to commander, Air Research and Development Command, letter, subject: Initial ICBM Operational Capability, 18 November 1955; Lt Gen Thomas S. Power, commander, Air Research and Development Command, to commander, Western Development Division, letter, subject: Authority for ICBM and IRBM Programs, 9 December 1955; White to commander, Air Research and Development Command, letter, subject: Initial Operational Capability, SM-65, 29 December 1955.

173. Rosenberg, *Plans and Policies for the Ballistic Missile Initial Operational Capability Program*, 35–93.

174. Ibid., 97; Gen Thomas D. White, "Air Force Perspective at the Dawn of the Space Age," address before the National Press Club, Washington, D.C., 29 November 1957.

175. Memorandum by Power to Knapp, 4 October 1957.

176. Senate, *Inquiry into Satellite and Missile Programs*, 907, 909–10.

177. House, *Weapons System Management and Team System Concept in Government Contracting*, 46; House, *DOD Appropriations for 1959, Department of the Air Force*, 344, 377–78; History, Air Research and Development Command, January–June 1959, II: The B-70 Story, 19–22; Maj Gen James Ferguson, director of requirements, Deputy Chief of Staff for Development, US Air Force, General Operational Requirements for a Supersonic Piloted Strategic Bombardment Weapon System, 7 March 1958.

178. House, *DOD Appropriations for 1959, Department of the Air Force*, 353.

179. Senate, *Inquiry into Satellite and Missile Programs*, 882–83; House, *Supplemental Defense Appropriations for 1958*, 5–7, 10, 83–85; House, *DOD Appropriations for 1959, Overall Policy Statements*, 132.

180. Senate, *Inquiry into Satellite and Missile Programs*, 952–53; Senate, *DOD Appropriations for 1962*, 862–64.

181. Senate, *Study of Air Power*, 224, 446–48.

182. USAF Historical Division Liaison Office, Instances of Near Cancellation of 17 Selected USAF Bombardment Aircraft, 1935–1960; House, *Investigation of National Defense Missiles*, 4108, 4117; Senate, *Inquiry into Satellite and Missile Programs*, 952–53, 965, 1994–95, 1997, 2000; House, *DOD Appropriations for 1959, Department of the Air Force*, 341, 347; House, *DOD Appropriations for 1960*, pt. 5:579.

183. *USAF Research and Development Quarterly Review*, Spring 1958, 23–24, 41–42; House, *DOD Appropriations for 1960*, pt. 5:572–73.

184. House, *DOD Appropriations for 1960*, pt. 1:869; Senate, *DOD Appropriations for 1962*, 862–64; Power to White, letter, 28 August 1958.

185. Maj Gen Charles B. Westover, director of plans, Strategic Air Command, to deputy chief of staff for operations, US Air Force, letter, subject: Strategic Weapons Systems, 7 July 1958.

186. House, *DOD Appropriations for 1960*, pt. 2:407.

187. Ibid., pt. 1:8; pt. 2:407; House, *DOD Appropriations for 1961*, pt. 2:262.

188. House, *DOD Appropriations for 1961*, pt. 1:48–49.

189. Gen Thomas D. White, "Aerospace Power ... Today and Tomorrow," *Air Force Magazine*, November 1958, 51.

190. House, *Department of Air Force Appropriations for 1956*, 84th Cong., 1st sess., 1955, 460, 695; Lindsay, "How the Air Force Will Use Its Missiles," 98–99; House, *DOD Appropriations for 1961*, pt. 7:236.

191. Lindsay, "How the Air Force Will Use Its Missiles," 101.
192. Senate, *Study of Air Power,* 503.
193. Ibid., 1276.
194. House, *Investigation of National Defense Missiles,* 4725.
195. Maj Gen James Ferguson, "Operational Future of Manned Aircraft," *Air Force Magazine,* April 1958, 44.
196. Memorandum by Gen Otto P. Weyland to deputy chief of staff for operations, Tactical Air Command, 17 April 1958, in History, Tactical Air Command, January–June 1958, 2, doc. 247.
197. House, *DOD Appropriations for 1957,* 877.
198. Lt Gen Earle E. Partridge, commander, Air Research and Development Command, to Lt Gen Laurence C. Craigie, deputy chief of staff for development, US Air Force, letter, 4 November 1952; Maj Gen C. S. Irvine, deputy commander for production, Air Materiel Command, to Lt Gen Earle E. Partridge, letter, 4 December 1952; AMC F-100, Correspondence, doc. 536; History, F-100 Fire Control System, 11 June 1957.
199. Senate, *Study of Air Power,* 413, 422, 430–31; House, *The Ballistic Missile Program: Hearings before a Subcommittee of the Committee on Appropriations,* 85th Cong., 1st sess., 1957, 102.
200. Senate, *Study of Air Power,* 1816.
201. House, *DOD Appropriations for 1958,* 904.
202. House, *DOD Appropriations for 1959, Department of the Air Force,* 9–10.
203. House, *DOD Appropriations for 1958,* 954.
204. Ibid., 50–51.
205. House, *The Ballistic Missile Program,* 101.
206. House, *DOD Appropriations for 1959, Overall Policy Statements,* 209.
207. House, *DOD Appropriations for 1958,* 462.
208. Memorandum by Gen Otto P. Weyland to director of operations, Tactical Air Command, subject: Tactical All-Weather System, 20 May 1957.
209. Maj Gen John D. Stevenson, "Exercise Sagebrush, Massive Air-Ground Lesson in Atomic Warfare," *Air University Quarterly Review* 8, no. 4 (Fall 1956): 37.
210. Report of Seminars, 1954 Worldwide Fighter Symposium, Maxwell AFB, Ala., 26–30 July 1954, 3–4.
211. Director of requirements, US Air Force, to commanding general, Tactical Air Command, letter, subject: Proposed Program for Lightweight Day Fighter, 21 July 1952; Maj Gen Frank F. Everest, deputy commanding general, Tactical Air Command, to director of requirements, US Air Force, letter, subject: Day Fighter Requirements, 23 September 1952.
212. Air Research and Development Command to Tactical Air Command, letter, subject: Day Fighter Characteristics, 9 September 1953, 1st ind., Lt Col Melvin H. Irwin, assistant adjutant, Tactical Air Command, to commanding general, Air Research and Development Command, 14 October 1953.
213. Maj Gen M. R. Nelson, director of requirements, US Air Force, General Operational Requirement for a Tactical Bombardment Weapon System, 1 April 1952; TACM 51-1, *Flying Training: Tactical Bombardment Manual,* 1 March 1957.
214. Maj Gen D. W. Hutchinson, deputy chief of staff for operations, Tactical Air Command, to director of requirements, US Air Force, letter, subject: Tactical Reconnaissance Fighter Aircraft Requirements, 27 November 1954; Gen Otto P. Weyland to director of requirements, letter, subject: Night Reconnaissance Version of the RF-105, 24 January 1955.
215. History, Tactical Air Command, July–December 1954, 4:4; Senate, *Study of Air Power,* 471, 511–12.
216. Senate, *Study of Air Power,* 489, 495–96, 517.
217. Ibid., 503–5; House, *DOD Appropriations for 1960,* pt. 5:776–77; House, *DOD Appropriations for 1961,* pt. 1:57–58.
218. Senate, *Study of Air Power,* 509; Gen Otto P. Weyland, "Tactical Air Operations," lecture, Air War College, Maxwell AFB, Ala., 25 February 1955.
219. Weyland, "Tactical Air Operations."

IDEAS, CONCEPTS, DOCTRINE

220. History, Tactical Air Command, January–June 1959, 1:288.
221. House, *DOD Appropriations for 1960*, pt. 2:425–26.
222. Weyland to Twining, letter, 29 June 1954; History, Tactical Air Command, July–December 1954, 3, doc. 3.
223. Tactical Air Command Operational Plan for the F-100A and/or F-100C Aircraft (Day Fighter), ca. January 1955; Maj Gen Wiley D. Ganey, director of operations, US Air Force, Final Operational Concept for F-100D Aircraft, 28 June 1955.
224. History, Tactical Air Command, July–December 1957, 1:79; TACM 20-24, *Organization—General, Mission and Functions of Tactical Fighter Wings*, 11 July 1958.
225. House, *DOD Appropriations for 1959, Overall Policy Statements*, 210.
226. Frederick A. Alling, *History of the B/RB-66 Weapon System, 1952–1959*, Air Materiel Command Historical Study 324, January 1960, 1–5.
227. History, Tactical Air Command, January–June 1956, vol. 1, chap. 3, 27–33.
228. Ibid., 18–20; Weyland to Twining, letter, 15 September 1954.
229. Alling, *History of the B/RB-66 Weapon System*, 15–29.
230. History, Tactical Air Command, January–June 1956, 1:18–20, 27–33.
231. House, *The Ballistic Missile Program*, 101.
232. White to Weyland, letter, 17 May 1957; Weyland to White, letter, 16 July 1957; History, Tactical Air Command, July–December 1957, 1:73–76.
233. House, *DOD Appropriations for 1959, Department of the Air Force*, 60–61; House, *DOD Appropriations for 1963*, pt. 4:320–21.
234. House, *DOD Appropriations for 1959, Overall Policy Statements*, 165, 209–10.
235. Gen Otto P. Weyland to deputy chief of staff for operations, US Air Force, letter, subject: Presentation by DCS/Operations, Headquarters USAF, 26 March 1958.
236. White to Weyland, letter, 4 June 1958; Weyland to White, letter, 12 June 1958.
237. Maj Gen Curtis E. LeMay to commander in chief, Strategic Air Command, letter, subject: Statement of USAF Policy Regarding In-Flight Refueling Systems, 24 February 1959; House, DOD Appropriations for 1963, pt. 4:319–20.
238. History, Tactical Air Command, January–June 1959, 1:288 and July–December 1959, 49–58; Gen Thomas D. White to Gen Frank F. Everest, commander, Tactical Air Command, letter, 18 March 1960.
239. Maj Gen Frederic H. Smith, Jr., "Current Practice in Air Defense—Part I: Principles and Problems," *Air University Quarterly Review* 6, no. 1 (Spring 1953): 4.
240. House, *Investigation of National Defense Missiles*, 4771.
241. Memorandum by Gen Joseph T. McNarney, acting chairman, to secretary of the Air Force, subject: Final Report of Board of Officers, 13 January 1949.
242. Frederick A. Alling, *The F-102A Airplane, 1950–1956*, Air Materiel Command Historical Study, December 1957, 1–4; Alfred Goldberg, ed., *A History of the United States Air Force, 1907–1957* (Princeton: D. Van Nostrand, 1957), 130–33; Col J. L. Laughlin, "Aircraft in Air Defense," lecture, Air War College, Maxwell AFB, Ala., 14 January 1953.
243. Maj Gen Donald L. Putt, director of research and development, Deputy Chief of Staff for Development, US Air Force, to commanding general, Air Materiel Command, letter, subject: 1954 Interceptor Competition, 18 August 1950.
244. Alling, *The F-102A Airplane, 1950–1956*, 4–7.
245. Charles Corddry, "How We're Building the World's Biggest Burglar Alarm," *Air Force Magazine*, June 1956, 77–78, 80, 83–84.
246. DeHaven, *The Voodoo Story, 1945–1957*, 93–98; House, *Weapons System Management and Team System Concept in Government Contracting*, 46; Brig Gen B. K. Holloway, acting director of requirements, US Air Force, to commander, Air Research and Development Command, letter, subject: Requirements for a Long Range Interceptor, 19 February 1954.
247. Richard F. McMullen, *History of Air Defense Weapons, 1946–1962*, Air Defense Command Historical Study 14, 1963, 212–13, 221–25; Senate, *TFX Contract Investigation: Hearings before the*

Permanent Subcommittee on Investigations of the Committee on Government Operations, 88th Cong., 1st sess., 1963, pt. 4:1115; Gen Laurence S. Kuter, "The Gaps in Our Aerospace Defense," *Air Force Magazine,* August 1962, 48.

248. McMullen, *History of Air Defense Weapons, 1946-1962,* 214-18; House, *DOD Appropriations for 1961,* pt. 1:49.

249. House, *DOD Appropriations for 1958,* 1153-54; House, *Investigation of National Defense Missiles,* 4771-72.

250. Director, Historical Service, Continental Air Defense Command, *A Decade of Continental Air Defense, 1946-1956,* 61-62; Air Defense Command, Operational Plan Semiautomatic Ground Environment System for Air Defense, 7 March 1955, v-vii.

251. Director, Historical Service, *A Decade of Continental Air Defense,* 62-63; Lt Col Harmon H. Harper, "SAGE, The Electronic Link Between Air Defense and Offense," *Airman Magazine,* November 1958, 11-14; House, *Investigation of National Defense Missiles,* 4772.

252. "The Emerging Shield," *Air University Quarterly Review* 8, no. 2 (Spring 1956): 68-69.

253. Director, Historical Service, *A Decade of Continental Air Defense,* 30, 32; House, *DOD Appropriations for 1958,* 917.

254. House, *DOD Appropriations for 1961,* pt. 7:229.

255. House, *Department of Air Force Appropriations for 1955: Hearings before a Subcommittee of the Committee on Appropriations,* 83d Cong., 2d sess., 1954, 661.

256. Maj Gen Frederic H. Smith, Jr., "Command and Control of Defense Forces," lecture, Air War College, Maxwell AFB, Ala., 26 January 1955.

257. Gen Benjamin W. Chidlaw, commander in chief, Continental Air Defense, to Gen Nathan F. Twining, letter, 28 May 1955.

258. Senate, *Study of Air Power,* 252-53.

259. Lockheed Aircraft Corporation Report no. 12540, "The Infeasibility of High Attrition in Continental Air Defenses for 1965 to 1970," 17.

260. Senate, *Study of Air Power,* 159.

261. Ibid., 255, 264-65.

262. Gen Earle E. Partridge, "Continental Air Defense," lecture, Air War College, Maxwell AFB, Ala., 30 January 1957.

263. House, *Department of Defense Appropriations for 1962: Hearings before a Subcommittee to the Committee on Appropriations,* 87th Cong., 1st sess., 1961, pt. 4:362-63, 1377; Senate, *DOD Appropriations for 1962,* 1377.

264. Partridge, "Continental Air Defense," 30 January 1957.

265. House, *DOD Appropriations for 1960,* pt. 2:342; pt. 1:793-94; House, *DOD Appropriations for 1961,* pt. 2:219.

266. House, *DOD Appropriations for 1959, Department of the Air Force,* 69; House, *DOD Appropriations for 1961,* pt 7:200.

267. House, *DOD Appropriations for 1959, Department of the Air Force,* 9-10.

268. Ibid., House, *DOD Appropriations for 1959, Overall Policy Statements,* 116, 220.

269. Senate, *Major Defense Matters,* 127, 134-35, 140.

270. Senate, *Inquiry into Satellite and Missile Programs,* 884-85; House, *Supplemental Defense Appropriations for 1958,* 129.

271. White, "Aerospace Power... Today and Tomorrow," 53-54.

272. House, *Investigation of National Defense Missiles,* 1958, 4068; House, *Organization and Management of Missile Programs: 11th Report of House Committee on Government Operations,* 86th Cong., 1st sess., 1959, 123.

273. Senate, *Major Defense Matters,* 134-35, 140.

274. House, *DOD Appropriations for 1960,* pt. 1:255.

275. Ibid., pt. 1:8.

276. History, Air Defense Command, January-June 1959, 1:151-59.

IDEAS, CONCEPTS, DOCTRINE

277. House, *United States Defense Policies in 1960*, 87th Cong., 1st sess., 1961, 54–55; House, *DOD Appropriations for 1961*, pt. 1:54, 112; pt. 2:349–50; memorandum by W. M. Holaday, special assistant for guided missiles, Department of Defense, to secretaries of the Army and the Air Force, subject: Continental Air Defense Program, 19 June 1950.

278. House, *DOD Appropriations for 1961*, pt. 2:254; Senate, *Missiles, Space, and Other Defense Matters: Hearings before the Preparedness Investigating Subcommittee of the Committee on Armed Services in Conjunction with the Committee on Aeronautical and Space Sciences*, 86th Cong., 2d sess., 1960, 126.

279. House, *DOD Appropriations for 1961*, pt. 1:49; pt. 6:33.

280. House, *DOD Appropriations for 1961: Reappraisal of Air Defense Program*, 86th Cong., 2d sess., 1960, 25–26.

281. Ibid., 29–30.

282. House, *DOD Appropriations for 1961*, pt. 7:265–66.

283. Ibid., pt. 1:186–87; House, *United States Defense Policies in 1960*, 54–56.

284. Senate, *Department of Defense Appropriations for Fiscal Year 1961: Hearings before a Subcommittee of a Committee on Appropriations*, 86th Cong., 2d sess., 1960, 1531–32.

285. House, *DOD Appropriations for 1961*, pt. 1:54, 153.

286. House, *DOD Appropriations for 1961: Reappraisal of Air Defense Program*, 2–3, 6–13.

287. Ibid., 53; House, *DOD Appropriations for 1961*, pt. 7:236–37.

288. House, *DOD Appropriations for 1961: Reappraisal of Air Defense Program*, 6.

289. House, *DOD Appropriations for 1961*, pt. 7:312.

290. House, *DOD Appropriations for 1961: Reappraisal of Air Defense Program*, 27–28.

291. House, *United States Defense Policies in 1960*, 54–56.

292. Department of Defense, *Annual Report of the Secretary of Defense and the Annual Reports of the Secretary of the Army, Secretary of the Navy, and Secretary of the Air Force, July 1, 1959 to June 30, 1960* (Washington, D.C.: Government Printing Office, 1961), 14.

293. Kuter, "The Gaps in Our Aerospace Defense," 47–48, 50.

294. Senate, *Investigation of Governmental Organization for Space Activities: Hearings before the Subcommittee on Governmental Activities of the Committee on Aeronautical and Space Sciences*, 86th Cong., 1st sess., 1959, 491.

295. Evaluation Staff, Air War College, "Control of the Use of Outer Space," Project AU-7-56-ESAWC, August 1956, 31.

296. Memorandum by Lt Gen Howard A. Craig to vice chief of staff, US Air Force, subject: Earth Satellite Vehicle, 12 January 1948; ind. by Vandenberg, 15 January 1948; report, Technical Evaluation Group, Committee on Guided Missiles, Research and Development Board, Satellite Vehicle Program, 29 March 1948.

297. Robert L. Perry, *Origins of the USAF Space Program, 1945–1956*, Air Force Systems Command Historical Study, 1961, 31.

298. Ibid., 41.

299. House, *Investigation of National Defense Missiles*, 4915.

300. Thirty-Second Annual Report of the National Advisory Committee for Aeronautics, 10 January 1947; NACA Aeronautical Research Policy prepared for presentation to House Select Committee on Post-War Military Policy, 26 January 1945; testimony by Maj Gen Oliver P. Echols before the Woodrum Committee on 21 November 1944, in Air Materiel Command Historical Study, *Collection of Air Technical Intelligence Information of the Army Air Arm, 1916–1917*, vol. 7, doc. 150; Maj Robert V. Guelich, "Silent Partner of US Airpower," *Air Force Magazine*, July 1945, 28–30.

301. Daily activity report, assistant chief of staff for materiel and supply, Army Air Forces, 9 March 1945; Air Technical Service Command, *Research and Development Projects of the Engineering Division*, 8th ed., January 1946, 64–65; *The Experimental Rocket Research Aircraft Program, 1946–1962*, Air Technical Service Command Historical Study, 1963, 2.

302. *The Experimental Rocket Research Aircraft Program*, 18–24.

303. Ibid., 8–11.

304. Ibid., 24–25; Robert S. Houston, *Development of the X-15 Research Aircraft, 1954–1959,* Wright Air Development Center Historical Study, June 1959, passim.

305. Erica M. Karr, "'Father of Dyna-Soar' Awaits AF Decision," *Missiles and Rockets,* 4 May 1959, 29–31; Clarence J. Geiger, History of the X-20A Dyna-Soar, Air Force Systems Command Historical Study, October 1963, 1–15.

306. Geiger, *History of the X-20A Dyna-Soar,* 4, 14–37; Willy Ley, *Rockets, Missiles, and Space Travel,* 2d ed. (New York: Viking Press, 1961), 13.

307. Hubertus Strughold, "From Aviation Medicine to Space Medicine," *Air University Quarterly Review* 10, no. 2 (Summer 1958): 7–15; *The Experimental Rocket Research Aircraft Program,* 11; Gen Thomas D. White, "At the Dawn of the Space Age," *Air Power Historian* 5, no. 1 (January 1958): 17.

308. *New York Times,* 17 November 1954 and 17 December 1954; "Space Go Round," *Newsweek,* 13 December 1954, 86; Lee Bowen, *An Air Force History of Space Activities, 1945–1959,* USAF Historical Division, Liaison Office, August 1964, 68–69.

309. *New York Times,* 7 June 1955; Bowen, *An Air Force History of Space Activities, 1945–1959,* 10.

310. Senate, *Inquiry into Satellite and Missile Programs,* 1000, 1649.

311. House, *DOD Appropriations for 1958,* 122.

312. Senate, *Inquiry into Satellite and Missile Programs,* 1587, 964.

313. Report of Technological Capabilities Panel of the Science Advisory Committee, subject: Meeting the Threat of Surprise Attack, 14 February 1955, 146–47.

314. *Public Papers of the Presidents of the United States: Dwight D. Eisenhower, 1957* (Washington, D.C.: Government Printing Office, 1958), 812.

315. Senate, *Inquiry into Satellite and Missile Programs,* 585, 597.

316. Senate, *Missile and Space Activities: Joint Hearings before the Preparedness Investigating Subcommittee of the Committee on Armed Services and the Committee on Aeronautical and Space Sciences,* 86th Cong., 1st sess., 1959, 11.

317. Thomas K. Finletter, *Power and Policy, US Foreign Policy and Military Power in the Hydrogen Age* (New York: Harcourt, Brace & Co., 1954), 373–75.

318. Robert J. Donovan, *Eisenhower: The Inside Story* (New York: Harper & Bros., 1956), 343–46.

319. Wilfred C. Jenks, "International Law and Activities in Space," *The International and Comparative Law Quarterly,* January 1956, 99.

320. House, *Astronautics and Space Exploration,* 45.

321. Ibid., 293; Clifford C. Furnas, "Furnas Discusses U.S. Space Planning," *Aviation Week,* 14 November 1960, 109.

322. Gavin, *War and Peace in the Space Age,* 14–15.

323. Harold Stassen, "Conduct and Regulation of Armament," lecture, Air War College, Maxwell AFB, Ala., 5 June 1956.

324. Evaluation Staff, Air War College, "Control of the Use of Outer Space," Project AU-7-56-ESAWC, 7 August 1956, 25–29; Col Martin B. Schofield, "Control of Outer Space," *Air University Quarterly Review* 10, no. 1 (Spring 1958): 93–104.

325. *Public Papers: Eisenhower, 1957,* 26.

326. House, *House Document No. 372: US Participation in UN,* 84th Cong., 2d sess., 1956, 14–15.

327. Evaluation Staff, Air War College, "Control of the Use of Outer Space," 33.

328. House, *Astronautics and Space Exploration,* 184–85.

329. Furnas, "Furnas Discusses U.S. Space Planning," 109; *New York Times,* 16 October 1957.

330. Maj Gen Bernard A. Schriever, "The Battle for 'Space Superiority'," *Air Force Magazine,* April 1957, 31–32, 34.

331. Schwiebert, *A History of the U.S. Air Force Ballistic Missiles,* 153; Gen Thomas W. Power with Albert A. Arnhym, *Design for Survival* (New York: Coward-McCann, 1964), 237.

332. Gen Thomas D. White, "Air Force Perspective at the Dawn of the Space Age," address before the National Press Club, 29 November 1957.

333. Senate, *Inquiry into Satellite and Missile Programs,* 1587–88.

IDEAS, CONCEPTS, DOCTRINE

334. House, *Investigation of National Defense Missiles*, 4912–23; *DOD Appropriations for 1959, Department of the Air Force*, 252–53.

335. Senate, *Inquiry into Satellite and Missile Programs*, 840–41, 862, 1000, 1587, 1649; House, *Investigation of National Defense Missiles*, 4704, 4912; House, *DOD Appropriations for 1959, Overall Policy Statement*, 225.

336. Lt Gen John K. Gerhart, "An Air Force Concept for the Employment of Future Weapon Systems," lecture, Air War College, Maxwell AFB, Ala., 21 May 1958.

337. Gen Thomas D. White, "Space Control and National Security," *Air Force Magazine*, April 1958, 80, 83.

338. Gerhart, "An Air Force Concept for the Employment of Future Weapon Systems."

339. SAFOI-001, "Origin of the World 'Aerospace'"; Woodford A. Heflin, ed., *Interim Glossary, Aero-Space Terms* (Maxwell AFB, Ala.: Air University, March 1958), 1.

340. Maj Gen Jacob E. Smart, assistant vice chief of staff, US Air Force, to commander, Air University, letter, subject: Revision of Air Force Manual 1-2, 25 April 1958.

341. Gen Thomas D. White, "The Air Force Job and How We're Doing It," *Air Force Magazine*, 36.

342. House, *Missile Development and Space Sciences: Hearings before the Committee on Science and Astronautics*, 86th Cong., 1st sess., 1959, 74–75.

343. Ibid., 247.

344. House, *DOD Appropriations for 1960*, pt. 1:579.

345. Senate, *Investigation of Governmental Organization for Space Activities*, 86th Cong., 1st sess., 1959, 353.

346. AFM 1-2, *United States Air Force Basic Doctrine*, 1 December 1959, 6.

German V-2.

Nike-Hercules long-range, high-altitude antiaircraft missile.

Bomarc interceptor missile.

Thor intercontinental ballistic missile (ICBM).

Minuteman ICBM.

Snark ground-to-ground missile.

V-1 buzz bomb.

Titan ICBM.

Atlas ICBM.

Hound Dog air-to-surface missile.

F-105 Thunderchief.

Polaris ICBM.

Maj Gen Bernard Schriever, commander, Western Development Division, 1955–59.

Gen Thomas D. White, Air Force chief of staff, 1957–61.

Neil H. McElroy, secretary of defense, 1957–59.

X-15.

Mace tactical air missile.

Gen Earle E. Partridge, commander in chief, Continental Air Defense Command, 1955–59.

Gen Thomas S. Power, commander, Strategic Air Command, 1957–64.

CHAPTER 10

IMPACT OF MISSILES AND SPACE ON NATIONAL
ORGANIZATION AND STRATEGY

In the aftermath of Sputnik many Americans were inclined to blame interservice rivalry and "service bickerings" within the Department of Defense for the lag in the development of American missile-space technology. In an address to the American people on 7 November 1957, President Dwight D. Eisenhower stated that "such things as alleged inter-service competition" would "not be allowed to create even the suspicion of harm to our scientific and development program." In his State of the Union message to Congress on 9 January 1958, Eisenhower noted that "some of the important new weapons which technology has produced do not fit into any existing service pattern" and that some of them "defy classification according to branch of service." As soon as studies were completed Eisenhower promised to send Congress a recommendation for a defense reorganization that would "achieve real unity" and "end inter-service disputes."[1]

The Defense Reorganization Act of 1958

At the conclusion of its exhaustive air power hearings, Senator Stuart Symington's special investigating subcommittee had already made recommendations regarding a need for defense reorganization in a report made public on 25 January 1957. This report charged that the Department of Defense had "permitted duplication, even triplification, among the three services in the development and production of missiles," had "permitted comparable waste in the allocation to the three services of responsibility in the missile field," and had "delayed in giving overriding priority to the ballistic missile program." The Symington subcommittee concluded: "The duplicating approach characteristic of many research and development programs in the Department of Defense, along with the dollar limitations established for such programs, has retarded needed modernization of weapon systems. These policies have retarded important scientific breakthroughs. They contrast with Soviet policies which have produced extraordinary Soviet progress in the research and development field."[2]

Many of the witnesses who appeared before the numerous congressional committees that investigated missile and space problems in the winter of 1957-58 agreed, at least by inference, with President Eisenhower's apparent belief that interservice rivalry had contributed to a lag in technological development. Supporting such an idea when he appeared before Senator Lyndon B. Johnson's

Preparedness Investigating Subcommittee in December 1957, Dr Wernher von Braun suggested that a national space agency be set up either under the secretary of defense or as an independent agency, with its own budget and an in-house master planning organization "where competent people would plan a course of action, a stepwise course of action, on how to proceed to attain certain milestones. For example, to put a man into orbit on a returnable basis within the next 5 years, and to have a manned space station, say, in 10 years."[3] President Eisenhower's scientific adviser, Dr James R. Killian, had written that "it is unreasonable to expect that ideas for radically new weapons will come from the military services." Elaborating this theme in an appearance before the Johnson subcommittee, Dr J. Sterling Livingston, a Harvard University professor of business administration, urged that radically new weapons had seldom been developed to fill military requirements. "I recommend," Livingston said,

> that we bypass our existing decisionmaking process in weapons development and that responsibility for the development of radically new weapons and scientific equipment, such as earth satellites and space vehicles, be transferred to an independent scientific agency outside the Defense Establishment. This agency should have full authority to take advantage of scientific breakthroughs without approval or concurrence of the military services.... As soon as one of the military services establishes an approved requirement for any weapon under development, appropriate arrangements should be made to transfer responsibility for the production of that weapon to the service. Thus, the military services should be considered as customers of this agency.[4]

Apparently giving some weight to recommendations such as these, the Senate Preparedness Investigating Subcommittee recommended on 23 January 1958 that decisive action should be taken to "reorganize the structure of the Defense Establishment" and to "accelerate and expand research and development programs, provide funding on a long-term basis, and improve control and administration within the Department of Defense or through the establishment of an independent agency."[5]

Drives for Closer Defense Unification

Since the days of William Mitchell and Mason Patrick, Air Force leaders had traditionally favored closer unification of the armed services; hence, early in 1956 when the Soviet Union appeared to be making greater technological progress than the United States, the Air Force opened a campaign aiming toward a new reorganization of the Department of Defense. In a lecture delivered at the National War College in May 1956, Gen Nathan F. Twining, Air Force chief of staff, stated that the matter of organizing defense and using new weapons most effectively was of equal importance with the technological race. "Even today," he pointed out, "our weapons are far ahead of our doctrines and concepts for using them.... The real race with the Soviets is to achieve the best doctrines, the best strategy and tactics with new weapons." Twining warned that each service was attempting to attain "service self-sufficiency," whereas most tasks were becoming the common objectives of all three services. From his point of view as chief of staff of the Air Force, Twining stated that he personally favored the idea of a single service, but he noted that such ideas had been studied and rejected many times. He doubted that they would be accepted except as a war-induced emergency measure. His main hope for increased service unification lay in the establishment of unified commands. "From unified commands," he said, "we get requirements for forces and weapons needed for clearly defined tasks. In this respect, they differ from requirements that develop when you try to plan for meeting all kinds of war, in all areas, with all kinds of weapons." Twining favored the creation of additional unified commands: a joint Strategic Air Command, for example, should be established along the lines of the Continental Air Defense Command. In unified commands, men of all services could become identified as members of a common mission — men of an oriented force.[6]

In its report of Twining's address, the *Washington Daily News* asserted that the Air Force had begun "blowing the bugles for closer unification and eventual merger of the Army, Navy, Marines and Air Force."[7] This assertion appeared to have some validity. In his testimony before the Symington subcommittee in April 1956, retired Gen Carl Spaatz had stated that the Department of Defense should be organized "with a single military chief of staff under the Secretary of Defense plus a general staff."[8] In a speech in San Francisco on 1 June 1956, Gen Thomas D. White, the Air Force vice chief of staff, pointed out that new weapons were causing the roles and missions of the services to overlap more and more. To provide a military organization "that will help us all to be free of conflicting service loyalties and confusing influences," White favored further integration of forces into joint commands and a free transfer of officers between the services. In an appearance on a national television program on 3 June 1956, former Air Force Secretary Thomas K. Finletter stated that it was "absolutely necessary that we coordinate all of these services and put them into a single service." During 1956, Gill Robb Wilson (president of the Air Force Association), Professor Barton Leach, and retired Gen Elwood R. Quesada endorsed an integration of the military services.[9]

In an article published during the winter of 1956-57, Col Albert P. Sights, Jr., a member of the Policy Division of the Air Force Directorate of Plans, provided a suggested blueprint to the way in which United States national defense forces could be organized to accomplish the basic tasks of defense deriving from the national objectives. Sights conceived that the basic national defense tasks were maintenance of nuclear deterrence, continental defense, a strategic reserve, and peripheral defenses in the Atlantic and Pacific. He visualized that the various combat functions that were dispersed in 17 unified, specified, and single-service organizations ought to be consolidated into five autonomous task-centered combat commands, which could be designed as the strategic atomic, continental defense, Pacific defense, Atlantic defense, and strategic reserve commands. A chief of military operations should be appointed to provide a centralized direction and control of these combat forces in peace and war. The three military services should be reduced to supporting elements of the combat organization. The secretary of defense should be provided with an expanded civilian and military staff to assist him in directing the combat organization and the three support commands.[10]

While this discussion was progressing, Secretary of Defense Charles E. Wilson manifested little concern for what he described as the "magic formula" of "complete unification." "The stifling of intelligent discussions for the sake of unanimity," Wilson thought, "will not guarantee the perfect answer. More important, it is foreign to our concept of a free society." He argued that a single chief of staff for the combined armed forces would "risk military dictatorship in our country." Wilson freely admitted that he had encouraged service rivalry in the development of new weapons and he saw no reason why he could not at an appropriate time "simply interpret how the new weapons can fit into the previously agreed division of responsibility."[11] Speaking as chairman of the Joint Chiefs of Staff, Adm Arthur W. Radford suggested that Finletter's advocacy of a single service and a single uniform "would not solve anything... we would still have compartmentation within this single uniform." Radford also thought that a single armed forces chief of staff would have a very difficult life. "His lot probably would be an unhappy one because he really would not have the authority that his title would imply unless we changed our system of government."[12]

Representing long-standing Navy views, Adm Arleigh Burke, chief of naval operations, flatly opposed a single armed services chief of staff. "If you have a single Chief of Staff," Burke maintained, "with the power of decision and with authority to develop his staff as he sees fit, sooner or later he can... develop an organization that is case hardened on the outside.... He can develop his own systems, and some time, some day somebody can misuse that." Touching on the suggestion that the Joint Chiefs of Staff might be separated from their services and made into a high-level strategic planning body, Burke argued: "The trouble with separating the chiefs from the chiefs of services is that when you don't have the responsibility for something it's awfully easy to tell people what to do.... Another thing is that for Joint Chief to be effective he must know his answers.... He's got... to really know the basic things concerning his service pertaining to the problems which the chiefs are trying to solve."[13] Even though Twining officially favored a single service and a single armed forces chief of staff as a matter of policy, he was personally willing to admit that he had some reservations on both matters. "I think it would be less expensive than the present organization," he said. "However, I still feel," he added, "that the three services watching each other is a pretty healthy thing, because no one can get really off the beam. With a single service you might get a sort of military dynasty built up that could make a really bad mistake for the United States."[14]

Acting as a public service in the national interest, a study panel of the Rockefeller Brothers Fund had provided many of the recommendations that had been implemented in the Department of Defense reorganization of 1953. In November 1956 a grouping of seven panels assembled by the Rockefeller Fund began to consider national problem areas in terms of the future. Some 19 distinguished citizens served on panel II, International Security—The Military

Aspect, whose report was prepared under the direction of Henry A. Kissinger and was released late in 1957. This report forecast four trends that would be of particular importance to national security: weapons technology would become increasingly complex, the rate of technological change would increasingly complicate the tasks of defense relative to offense, the Soviet bloc would continue to gain in overall military strength, and the concept of scarcity in nuclear weapons would disappear from the defense calculations of the United States, the Soviet Union, and to a lesser extent Great Britain. Based on this strategic estimate the panel described three major defects in the organization of the Department of Defense:

1. The roles and missions assigned to the individual military services had become competitive rather than complementary because they were out of accord with weapons technology and the principal military threats to national policy.
2. The organization and responsibilities of the Joint Chiefs of Staff precluded the development of a comprehensive and coherent national defense doctrine.
3. The secretary of defense was so burdened with the negative tasks of trying to arbitrate and control interservice disputes that he could not play his full positive part in the initiation and development of high military policy.[15]

To remedy the central weaknesses that it described as inherent in the existing organization of the Department of Defense, the Rockefeller panel recommended changes in service roles and missions, the status of the Joint Chiefs of Staff, and the authority of the secretary of defense. In the matter of roles and missions, the panel recommended that the military departments be removed from the channel of operational command and be charged to support the unified operational commands. It further recommended that all operational military forces of the United States should be organized into unified commands to perform missions dictated by strategic requirements. The units assigned to each unified commander should be organic to his command and not simply placed under his temporary operational control.

Since the chairman of the Joint Chiefs of Staff was believed to be the "only member who can give his full-time attention to problems of over-all strategic doctrine," the panel considered it logical that the chairman should be designated as the principal military adviser to the secretary of defense and to the president. The chiefs of the services would continue to serve on the Joint Chiefs of Staff but only as advisers to the chairman on logistics, training, and procurement. The chairman should also control the staff of the Joint Chiefs of Staff, which would be organized on a joint basis. In order to develop a group of top officers who could "transcend the thinking of any one service," the panel recommended that all officers above the equivalent rank of brigadier general should receive their permanent promotions from the Department of Defense and should become officers of the armed forces of the United States.

Under the existing organization, the panel conceived that the secretary of defense was a referee who could handle disputes only after they came to him in hardened form. To strengthen the secretary's position, the panel recommended that the line of operational command should run from the president and the secretary of defense to the functional commanders through the chairman of the Joint Chiefs of Staff. It recommended that the line of logistical command should be from the president through the secretary of defense to the secretaries of the three military departments. The panel also recommended that the secretary of defense be given absolute powers over research and development and over procurement. Its report stated: "The Secretary of Defense should be given authority over all research, development and procurement. He should have the right of cancellation and transfer of service programs together with their appropriations. He should also be given a direct appropriation for the conduct of research and development programs at the Defense Department level."[16]

The Rockefeller panel's report was especially critical of what it described as the service bias of the members of the Joint Chiefs of Staff. It asserted that "the Joint Chiefs of Staff functions too often as a committee of partisan adversaries engaged in advancing service strategic plans and compromising service differences. Too little in present arrangements permits the Chief of Staff time and opportunity to think spontaneously or comprehensively about overall strategic problems. The result is that our military plans for meeting foreseeable threats tend to be a patchwork of compromise between conflicting strategic concepts or simply the uncoordinated war plans of the several services."[17] Other supposedly informed men supported this same criticism. On 25 November 1957 Dr Vannevar Bush asserted that the Joint Chiefs of Staff had never been able to prepare a "unitary" war plan. "The services themselves," he said, ". . . have prepared war plans, all different, each one of them the best they can produce. From there on, there has been no means by which those could be brought into a unitary plan." Bush's solution was to put the preparation of war plans into the hands of three senior officers (retired officers brought back to active duty if they were the right men) who would be detached from all further obligation to their individual services. "The essential thing," Bush said, "is that in one way or another we get the thing we are looking for, namely a unified war plan."[18]

Virtually no one in authority agreed with the assertions of the Rockefeller panel and of Doctor Bush that the Joint Chiefs of Staff had failed to agree on war plans.[19] While testifying before the Senate Preparedness Investigating Subcommittee early in 1958, the Joint Chiefs agreed that they seldom had specific difficulties in arriving at a joint approval of war plans and related operational matters. War plans were based on capabilities and military forces in being. Most disputes arose from a competition for funds and related resources needed to increase and improve the forces of the future.[20] General White emphasized that split decisions were actually "rare" and were not unwholesome, since minority views were not hidden because a majority might oppose them. "I feel," White said, "that numbers do not necessarily make for correct decisions. There can be good results from JCS splits provided higher authority resolves the issue with unequivocal decision."[21] Gen Maxwell D. Taylor, Army chief of staff, estimated that out of 2,977 Joint Chiefs of Staff actions in the period between October 1955 and March 1959 only 23 split papers were forwarded to the secretary of defense.[22] These split papers dealt with important subjects upon which compromise was impossible. "There is always," White explained, "tremendous self-imposed pressure to do the best job possible because agreement among the Chiefs on military matters ought ordinarily to result in the best solution of the problem. Based upon past experience, I consider that a compromise solution of a military problem arrived at by the Joint Chiefs of Staff is usually better than a compromise decision made by civilian authority."[23] "If the Joint Chiefs of Staff sent nothing but unanimous recommendations forward to the secretary of defense," Admiral Burke observed, "then we should be apprehensive because it would mean either that the Joint Chiefs were losing their competence, their sincerity, or their expertness, or that the services themselves were becoming ineffective, unready, or insensitive to their duties in national security."[24]

Each of the members of the Joint Chiefs of Staff agreed that their "two-hat" work load as service chief and member of the Joint Chiefs was extremely burdensome, but they believed that the nation's chief military planners, as General Twining put it, had to be "intimately acquainted on a day-to-day basis with the operating capability and effectiveness of their own services."[25] "If you divorce the Chiefs of Staff from their services," General White thought, "then the man who gives the orders and lays the plans has no responsibility for carrying them out, and that makes it pretty difficult for the other fellow, whoever does have to carry them out."[26] Admiral Burke was even more positive: "The responsibility stemming from the importance of JCS military planning and advice," he said, "is so great that the information required is nothing short of the best. The best available information on the capabilities, readiness, and requirements of the armed services can be possessed only by the military chiefs of these services."[27] Twining's suggestion to reduce the terrific load laid upon the individual chiefs was the approach that he had employed while he was chief of staff of the Air Force, namely to delegate as much as possible of the service work to a vice chief of staff.[28] Even though General White thought that the joint chiefs must remain as the heads of their services, he was willing to foresee some change. Taking a "long look out into the future," White visualized that "we are going to have to go to something that is tantamount to a single service." In preparation for this eventuality he thought that officers who served on the joint staffs of the Joint Chiefs of Staff or of unified commands might be divorced from their services and become armed forces officers. Such an Air Force officer could go back to his service, but in a "gray uniform rather than a blue uniform" and with the understanding that he was "eligible for broader service" and had "lost his status as a purely Air Force officer."[29]

The senior military officers who appeared before the Senate Preparedness Investigating Subcommittee displayed little agreement as to the status to be accorded to the chairman of the Joint Chiefs of Staff and as to whether the nation required a single armed forces chief of staff. Asked about these matters, Gen Curtis

E. LeMay observed that such questions would have to be settled by the government outside the military establishment. For the immediate future he recommended that one thing to be done "would be to change the present Chairman from one of a man who just conducts the meetings, to some responsibility, and require him to come out of a meeting with a military decision, and if he can get unanimous opinion from the Joint Chiefs, fine: if he cannot, then he forces the issue and makes the decision himself, if necessary."[30] General White pointed out that the secretary of defense already turned to the chairman of the Joint Chiefs for advice in cases of split decisions. A single chief of staff would provide prompt decisions but less certainly wise decisions, since differing points of view would not be made known to civilian authorities.[31] As he had done before, Admiral Burke bitterly opposed a single chief of staff who might become a military dictator if he were a strong man or a "yes man" if he were weak.[32] In response to a request for their opinions, General Spaatz and Fleet Adm Chester W. Nimitz offered exactly opposite views. Spaatz urged that a "simple efficient system" of a single chief of staff and a competent joint staff was required to direct "a complex military organization." "The Supreme Commander in the Washington area," Nimitz thought, "is the President as Commander in Chief, and any proposal to set up somebody else as a single commander between him and the forces in the field is totally wrong."[33]

Still new to the responsibilities of the Office of Secretary of Defense, Neil H. McElroy remarked that he could have used "just a little bit more time to get acquainted with all my surroundings" before undertaking a reorganization of the Department of Defense, but President Eisenhower's State of the Union address of 9 January 1958 indicated an immediate need for action. To head the reorganization project, McElroy secured the services of Charles S. Coolidge, whom he appointed special assistant for reorganization. He also established a consultative group, including General Twining as incumbent chairman of the Joint Chiefs of Staff, Gen Omar N. Bradley and Adm Arthur W. Radford as former chairmen of the Joint Chiefs, William C. Foster as a former deputy secretary of defense, Nelson A. Rockefeller as chairman of the President's Advisory Committee on Government Reorganization, and retired Gen Alfred M. Gruenther. These men spent some six weeks conducting interviews within and without the Department of Defense before preparing draft legislation that was incorporated in a report that McElroy submitted to Eisenhower. Even before this McElroy had obtained the president's advice on key points on several occasions, and Eisenhower approved the suggested legislation with only a few changes.[34] McElroy later disclosed that he and Eisenhower considered and rejected such proposals as a single armed forces chief of staff, a merger of the armed services, and the establishment of assistant secretaries of defense for the Army, Navy, and Air Force in place of existing service secretaries. They also rejected the Rockefeller panel's recommendations that the chairman of the Joint Chiefs of Staff be made the principal military adviser to the president and the defense secretary, that the Joint Staff be organized on a unified basis and placed under the control of the chairman who would then shape strategic planning, and that all military forces should be assigned organically to unified commands. "I would say," General Twining added, "that our concept of the Joint Chiefs of Staff organization as written in the administration bill is not along the same philosophy as the Rockefeller report."[35]

As he had promised to do, President Eisenhower transmitted a message to Congress on 3 April 1958 in which he discussed the administrative and legislative changes that he considered essential in the Department of Defense. In explanation of his reasoning, Eisenhower stated:

> First, separate ground, sea and air warfare is gone forever. If ever again we should be involved in war, we will fight it in all elements, with all services, as one single concentrated effort. Peacetime preparatory and organizational activity must conform to this fact. Strategic and tactical planning must be completely unified, combat forces organized into unified commands, each equipped with the most efficient weapons systems that science can develop, singly led and prepared to fight as one, regardless of service. The accomplishment of this result is the basic function of the Secretary of Defense, advised and assisted by the Joint Chiefs of Staff and operating under the supervision of the Commander in Chief. . . . Additionally, Secretary of Defense authority, especially in respect to the development of new weapons, must be clear and direct, and flexible in the management of funds. Prompt decisions and elimination of wasteful activity must be primary goals.[36]

Most of Eisenhower's message dealt with legislative actions required of Congress, but he also revealed his own administrative orders for changes within the Department of Defense. Subject only to exceptions that he would personally approve, he intended that "all of our operational forces be organized into truly unified commands." "I expect," he said, "these truly unified commands to go far toward realigning our operational plans, weapon systems and force levels in such fashion as to provide maximum security at minimum cost." Eisenhower stated that the Joint Chiefs of Staff concept was essentially sound, but he directed that the Joint Chiefs would serve collectively as a staff to assist the secretary of defense in his exercise of direction over unified commands. He directed the secretary of defense to discontinue the existing joint staff committee system and organize the joint staff into integrated staff directorates. Believing that "before officers are advanced beyond the two-star level, they must have demonstrated, among other qualities, the capacity for dealing objectively—without extreme service partisanship—with matters of the broadest significance to our national security," Eisenhower announced that he would consider for promotion or nomination to these high ranks only those officers that were recommended to him by the secretary of defense.[37]

With a very few exceptions the Department of Defense Reorganization Act of 1958 passed by Congress and signed into law on 6 August 1958 incorporated President Eisenhower's recommendations. The act markedly increased the authority of the secretary of defense, particularly in the operational direction of the armed forces and in the research and development field. Where the old National Security Act's preamble had provided for "three military departments separately administered," the new law provided for "a Department of Defense, including three military departments," and provided only that the departments were to be "separately organized." The administration bill had proposed to delete all reference to the separate status of the departments, but Chairman Carl Vinson and the House Committee on Armed Services inserted the provision that the departments would be "separately organized." The act vested overall direction and control of military research and development activities in the secretary of defense and created a position of director of defense research and engineering, who would be the principal adviser to the secretary on scientific and technological matters, would supervise all research and engineering activities in the Department of Defense, and would direct and control (including assignment or reassignment) research and engineering activities that the secretary of defense deemed to require centralized management. The secretary was also authorized to establish single agencies to conduct any service or supply activity common to two or more military departments.[38] The authority to establish single agencies was added to the bill by an amendment offered by Representative John McCormack and was accepted by Congress with very little debate.[39]

The Department of Defense Reorganization Act of 1958 also provided that the president, with the advice and assistance of the Joint Chiefs of Staff and acting through the secretary of defense, would establish unified or specified commands for the performance of military missions. Forces assigned to such commands were to be under the "full operational command" of a unified or specified commander, but the type forces assigned to such a command would be supported by their respective military departments. Under the 1953 reorganization, designated service secretaries had served as executive agents for designated unified or specified commands. Now the operational line of command for these commands ran from their commanders through the corporate Joint Chiefs of Staff to the secretary of defense and the president. The previous legislative authority of the chief of naval operations and of the chief of staff of the Air Force to command their respective forces was repealed; the chief of staff of the Army had never possessed such authority. The act repealed the meaningless old provision whereby the chairman of the Joint Chiefs of Staff was not permitted to vote (the Joint Chiefs had never conducted business by vote), and the chairman was authorized to manage the joint staff (which could not exceed 400 officers) and its director on behalf of the Joint Chiefs of Staff. The administration bill had omitted any limitation on the number of persons who might be assigned to the joint staff, but Chairman Vinson and the House Committee on Armed Services had insisted on setting a limit on the strength of the joint staff. On this matter Vinson observed: "And no one can now say that there is any danger or apprehension that we are drifting toward a Prussian system. Because we prohibit that, by putting in the roadblock of 400." In the approved law, the vice chiefs of the Army, Navy, Marine Corps, and Air Force were authorized to perform such duties and exercise such powers as their chiefs and service secretaries might delegate or prescribe for them, thus by inference enabling the service chiefs to devote more time to work of the Joint Chiefs of Staff.[40]

After a period of study, Secretary McElroy began to effect the new organizational framework for the Department of Defense. In the reorganization McElroy attached the largest importance to the institution of the new and more direct lines of command to the unified and specified commands and the next degree of importance to the establishment of the new research and engineering organization.[41] "Emphasis on the unified command," he had said, "constitutes the heart and soul of the President's program of reorganization."[42] In September 1958 Eisenhower and McElroy reviewed and approved the missions of the two specified commands (the Eastern Atlantic and Mediterranean and the Strategic Air Commands) and the six unified commands (the Alaskan, Atlantic, Caribbean, Continental Air Defense, European, and Pacific Commands). That same month administrative and logistical support of the unified and specified command headquarters was assigned out among the military departments: the Air Force was made responsible for supporting the headquarters of the Alaskan, Continental Air Defense, and Strategic Air Commands.[43] All component forces assigned to the unified or specified commands, including the component force headquarters, were to be administered and supported by the military department that provided the forces. The unified and specified commanders were given no budgetary functions: they made plans and stated requirements for forces to the corporate Joint Chiefs of Staff, who correlated all force requirements with across-the-board requirements and capabilities.[44] In an additional directive issued on 31 December 1958, Secretary McElroy described additional portions of the new organization. This directive visualized three groups of agencies under the secretary of defense. Immediate staff assistance to the secretary was provided by the Office of the Secretary of Defense, which now comprised seven assistant secretaries and the director of defense research and engineering. The Joint Chiefs acted as the secretary's principal military advisers and his military staff in the chain of operational command. The three military departments constituted the second group of agencies. Each department was responsible for the preparation of type forces. The unified and specified commands comprised the third group of agencies. Two command chains were established: the line of operational command ran from the president to the secretary of defense and through the corporate Joint Chiefs of Staff to the commanders of the unified and specified commands. The line of nonoperational command ran from the president to the secretary of defense and to the secretaries of the military departments.[45]

As enacted into law the 1958 reorganization act went about as far as possible in centralizing authority and control in the Department of Defense as could be managed without abandoning the concept of the separate military services. The major statutory limitations on the powers of the secretary of defense that remained were that the military departments could not be merged, that statutory functions could not be substantially changed without careful congressional review, that a single chief of staff over the armed forces or an overall armed forces general staff should not be established, and that the secretaries of the military departments and the individual members of the Joint Chiefs of Staff might present any recommendation they deemed proper to Congress. Although the latter authority had not been used since 1949, President Eisenhower had described it as "legalized insubordination."[46]

Air Force Demands for a Single Service

During the hearings in Congress and in the months that followed the passage of the Department of Defense Reorganization Act of 1958, continued criticism of defense organization indicated a prevalent belief in some quarters that the act was only a partial, evolutionary step toward increased unification. As early as 17 April 1958, General White announced that the Air Force was wholeheartedly in accord with the president's proposals on defense reorganization. When he appeared before the House Committee on Armed Services on 2 May, White justified the reorganization on the grounds that it would establish a peacetime organization that could meet wartime requirements, provide a system that would better enable the Joint Chiefs of Staff to act with corporate responsibilities and corporate views, assign clear-cut authority and responsibility to the secretary of defense, and provide better defense at a comparable cost. "I completely agree," White said, "with the President's concept that separate ground, sea, and air warfare are gone forever, and that peacetime preparation and organization must conform to this fact." In response to questions, White admitted that the reorganization measure might mean "that some of the things that we perhaps consider vested interest of the Air Force might go by the board." However, he added, "I think and a great many of us in the Air Force think that even if that happened, it would be for the good of the over-all national defense."[47]

When White appeared before the Senate Committee on Armed Services on 19 June, he continued to support the reorganization bill although he regretted that the House of Representatives had placed limitations on the authority of the secretary of defense to transfer, reassign, abolish, or consolidate combatant functions within the Department of Defense. "This could hold up action for many months," White explained, "on a change of major importance to the security of our country." Even though the law would limit the secretary's authority, White considered that the "best possible organization" of the Defense Department was being effected. He thought that the reorganization would result "in greater uniformity . . . as far as doctrine and training are concerned" since the unified commands would be operating directly under the corporate Joint Chiefs of Staff and "anytime there is a conflict in doctrine . . . it can, and undoubtedly would, be straightened out."[48] In a summary of his position, General White remarked: "I vigorously supported the Reorganization Act of 1958. I think it is a step forward."[49] During hearings on the reorganization bill before the Senate Committee on Armed Services, General Spaatz described the measure as inadequate in that it failed to give the secretary of defense an administrative control over the services. "In my

IMPACT OF MISSILES AND SPACE

opinion," Spaatz said, "the Defense Department will never be properly organized until full administrative authority is vested in the Secretary of Defense; and that condition is so stated in the law in no uncertain terms."[50]

In a strong statement made to the Senate Committee on Aeronautical and Space Sciences on 22 April 1959, General LeMay described the Defense Reorganization Act of 1958 as a step in the right direction that ought to be pursued further. "Today more than ever before in our history," he stated,

> there is need for centralized control and direction over our Armed Forces.... Modern weapons and improved delivery systems are changing the concepts of military operations and confusion or indecision can be fatal in this new era. As our weapon systems improve and become more versatile it is becoming more and more apparent that the functions and weapons of individual services are beginning to overlap. Forces are of necessity becoming functionally oriented. To meet this changing condition I firmly believe we will need a modification in our military structure. I believe that we must eventually progress toward a single service, with a single Chief of Staff, and one staff to operate the Armed Forces.... The DOD Reorganization Act of 1958 was a step in this direction.... I feel that sooner or later we must go beyond this. Semiautonomous combat organizations are not the complete answer. We need central command and control. To achieve this, the barriers that are created by service interest must be removed. Combat elements having the same function or mission must be integrated into functional areas under single control.... As I see it now, this can best be accomplished under a single chief; one who can make decisions on force structure, approve strategic plans and weapon systems and assign those systems for use by given elements of the Armed Forces.[51]

The Air Force position was regarded favorably in some congressional committees. In its report on the Department of Defense appropriation bill in the summer of 1959, the House Appropriations Committee stated:

> The President, the Secretary of Defense, the Congress, and the American people have a right to expect a better job from the JCS in the way of military guidance. As a corporate body, the Joint Chiefs of Staff must set up plans for the guidance of the various commands and the respective services. Hard decisions are required, and the President, the Secretary of Defense and the Joint Chiefs must assume the major responsibility for tailoring military forces to requirements. Each year the question which confronts us of "who gets what" is becoming more difficult to cope with.[52]

In September 1959 the Committee on Government Operations of the House of Representatives recommended an Army-Air Force merger as a beginning step to end waste and confusion in the Pentagon. "While each service tries to accommodate and adapt its mission concept to the space medium," the committee reported, "the logic of new weapons technology has virtually destroyed the traditional basis for services organized around strategic land, sea, and air missions.... There is historical irony in the fact that the Air Force achieved its organic separation from the Army at the threshold of the decline of airpower and the rise of missile power."[53]

In a study entitled "Service Roles and Missions in the Future," completed in May 1958, the Air War College Evaluation Staff had noted that the media of operations

585

originally had determined the strategic functions of land, sea, and air forces. The emergence of new weapon systems, however, had reduced the effect of media on operations. The Evaluation Staff, therefore, had recommended that "we must begin to relate task or mission to weapon system and to arrange weapon systems into appropriate groupings for management purposes."[54] In a high-priority project assigned on 14 May 1959, the Evaluation Staff prepared a detailed study looking toward the implementation of a single-service concept. The study was completed in basic form on 31 July 1959 and was transmitted to the Air Force plans directorate, which bound extracts from it with other "think papers" in standard black binders and circulated the package for comment. The study also was published in the *Air University Quarterly Review* during the summer of 1960. Entitled "Study on Single Service," the article proposed that the Department of Defense could move toward a single service in five evolutionary steps and that the beginning of the evolutionary changes could be made under authority permitted by the Defense Reorganization Act of 1958. In a preliminary step, a joint reorganization task force should be established to prepare basic planning. In an activation step, the Joint Chiefs of Staff should be divorced from service affiliations and used as the nucleus for a national military council that would advise a single chief of staff of the armed forces, who would be supported by a national military staff. In an operational step, new unified commands would be organized to include a strategic, a mobile strike, a continental US defense, an Atlantic, a Pacific, a research and development, and a logistics command. In a cleanup step, the Departments of Army, Navy, and Air Force would be discontinued and activated as commands, with support and training functions. In the final step, the Army, Navy, and Air Force commands would be integrated into a unified personnel and training command.[55] Navy officers soon began to refer to the single service study as the "Air University Black Book of Reorganization Papers."[56] For his own part, General White defended the Air University's so-called Black Book as a necessary study, which was apparently more familiar to Army and Navy officers than to Air Force officers. He saw no reason why Air Force officers should not be studying the concept of a single service. But he added, "I can tell you right now the Air Force does not advocate a single service."[57]

New Authority for United Commands

The apparent Air Force enthusiasm for increased unification of the military services was not shared by the Department of Defense or by the Army and Navy. In April 1959 Deputy Secretary of Defense Donald A. Quarles expressed confidence that the 1958 reorganization would "discourage improper use of the research and development program as a means of carrying on a kind of warfare between the Departments in an attempt on the part of each to enlarge its area of roles and missions." Quarles also believed that "some degree of this rivalry between departments is wholesome and productive."[58] In his report of the first full year of operations under the 1958 reorganization act, Secretary McElroy stated that the new defense organization "adequately meets current management needs." Additional adjustments would likely be necessary as technology continued to advance, but McElroy cautioned: "It is important . . . that such adjustments are evolutionary rather than revolutionary in character, for radical changes upset the operational effectiveness of any organization for a considerable time."[59] McElroy's successor as secretary of defense, Thomas S. Gates, Jr., stated on 13 June 1960 that it was his judgment that the defense organization was essentially sound. "I would suggest no further statutory changes," he recommended, "until we have more thoroughly digested this 1958 reorganization and learned, by living with it, of any further changes in the law which might be indicated."[60] Following retirement as Army chief of staff, General Taylor advocated the establishment of a single defense chief of staff who would receive requests for forces from unified commanders, make budget allocations in functional fields, and provide centralized control of operations; but he saw a need to retain the individual military departments in order to "create and maintain the forces as directed by the Secretary of Defense."[61] The new Army chief of staff, Gen Lyman L. Lemnitzer, specifically considered that the suggested merger of the Army and the Air Force would be undesirable. He also believed that "the division among the services is a perfectly natural one—one service to fight on land, the Army; one to fight on the surface of the sea, over it and underneath it, the Navy; and one in the air, the Air Force."[62] The Navy and the Marine Corps strongly opposed a single service. "We have very little duplication now left in the services," Admiral Burke testified. "What could happen is the elimination of one whole element, so you don't have that element at all, and thereby leave yourself wide open, betting that just one thing is going to happen."[63]

In its support for the Department of Defense Reorganization Act of 1958, the Air Force had assumed that the new organization would increase the importance of unified commands and, by vesting primary responsibility for stating force requirements in the unified commanders, would permit a more realistic allocation of available defense dollars. The Department of Defense budgetary allocation of funds by military services remained unchanged, however, and in the summer of 1958 the secretary of defense accepted $41.25 billion as an initial planning objective for the fiscal year 1960 defense budget; he determined that allocations to each service would continue to be approximately the same percentage of the whole as had been the case in fiscal year 1959.[64] Thus, even though they were theoretically reduced in stature by the defense reorganization, the military departments continued to exercise the power of the budget. In explaining the problem, General White observed that "as a service chief, I am always trying to get the best I can for my service." But within the Air Force, White had to resolve the competing requests for funds submitted by the Strategic Air Command, the Air Defense Command, and the Tactical Air Command. Each of their commanders were men who were charged with, as White said, "a specific responsibility and they are exceedingly dedicated to their job."[65] As has been seen, General White and the Air Staff initiated a reduction in the forces to be available to the Continental Air Defense

Command in the spring of 1960 over the strong opposition of the unified commander, who considered that his mission as a unified commander was being jeopardized.

In view of the strong emphasis upon unified commands in Eisenhower's defense reorganization proposals, Air Force leaders assumed that the reorganization act would result in the establishment of unified commands to replace the single-service specified commands. General White saw a good possibility that the Tactical Air Command and the Continental Army Forces might well be placed in a single unified command.[66] In serving at the helm of the Strategic Air Command, Gen Thomas S. Power pointed out in April 1958 that he was charged as the specified commander to coordinate attacks against many strategic targets nominated in separate target lists by other specified and unified commanders. With the advent of missiles, such existing methods of coordinating strategic attacks would be adequate only in the unlikely circumstance that the United States would exercise the initiative and could carefully determine and prepare every facet of the operation in advance.[67] In context with the defense reorganization of 1958, the Air Force also assumed that a unified strategic command might well be organized to control both the Air Force's strategic air and missile forces and the Navy's Polaris-equipped submarine forces.[68]

As early as April 1959 the Joint Chiefs of Staff began lengthy studies as to the manner in which command and control would be exercised over the Polaris weapon system.[69] When early discussions failed to reach a positive decision, General White formally requested the establishment of a unified US strategic command. He urged that both the Strategic Air Command and a Polaris submarine command would be subordinated to the unified strategic command. General Power supported this proposal. "I think," he said early in 1960, "that all strategic weapon systems should be under one central command, whether it is commanded by an Air Force officer, naval officer, or Army officer is a moot question."[70] Admiral Burke, on the other hand, described the Air Force proposal as "unsound and impractical." He argued that it would not be practical to take operational command of Polaris vessels away from fleet commanders since the movements of these submarines would have to be coordinated with those of many other naval vessels that would be operating in the same waters at the same time. Once a Polaris submarine had fired its strategic missiles, moreover, it would be expected to operate on missions similar to those of other submarines. "The Navy," Burke emphasized, "has behind it generations of experience in the operation of sea-based weapons systems. To depart from the principle of the integrated, balanced fleet at this critical time in history by assigning Polaris submarines to a command charged with operating land-based strategic bombers and missiles would weaken our Nation's ability to strike back."[71]

The unified US strategic command was not established. Instead, the question of operational control of Polaris submarine forces was decided on 17 August 1960 when Secretary Gates established the Joint Strategic Target Planning Agency and designated General Power as director, strategic target planning. A Navy admiral was designated as deputy director, strategic target planning, and the agency comprised officers from each of the services, representatives from the unified commands, and a liaison group from the joint staff of the Joint Chiefs of Staff. The agency was located at Headquarters Strategic Air Command because of the availability of programming equipment and experienced personnel there and because SAC had the majority of assigned targets; but the Joint Strategic Target Planning Agency was directly responsible to the Joint Chiefs of Staff and was charged with the preparation of integrated target plans that would take into consideration all of the strategic warfare capabilities of the United States. The staff was divided into two sections. One section was charged to draw up the target list, the other determined which commander would hit a particular target and how he would do it. The target list was called the national strategic target list, and the operating plan was described as the single integrated operational plan (SIOP). Both of these documents were submitted to the Joint Chiefs for review, modification, and approval. The secretary of defense reviewed them and gave final approval. The first assignment of nuclear weapons to strategic targets by the new agency was to be completed by December 1960. As desired by the Navy, the establishment of the Joint Strategic Target Planning Agency permitted the assignment of Polaris submarines to naval components in unified commands rather than to a unified US strategic command.[72]

Organization of Military and National Space Programs

In the hectic months after Sputnik I in October 1957, a welter of conflicting ideas and concepts regarding the utility of space for military operations provided a background to the efforts to organize military and national space programs. "One of the major provocations of ... interservice rivalry ...," Secretary McElroy stated, "arises from the fact that there are certain types of weapons that come into the picture which do not have any obvious and specific connection with one or more of the services." A little later McElroy specifically observed that in his opinion missiles were "weapon systems which do not naturally fall within the responsibilities of individual services." Deputy Secretary Quarles justified the assignment of long-range, surface-to-surface missiles to the Air Force not because of the Air Force mission but because it possessed targeting and reconnaissance capabilities needed to employ them.[73] On 15 November 1957 McElroy named William M. Holaday as defense director of guided missiles and charged him to "direct all activities in the Department of Defense relating to research, development, engineering, production, and procurement of guided missiles."[74] McElroy conceived that Holaday's job had two different aspects: one was to monitor and supervise all research and engineering work in the field of guided missiles, and the other was to assure appropriate priority handling of all guided missile problems in connection with their transition from research and development into production and procurement.[75] Both to alleviate service rivalry and to handle will-of-the-wisp research and development projects in the fields of satellites and space, McElroy announced on 20 November 1957 that he intended to establish a special projects agency within the Department of Defense. The agency would handle research and development on advanced weapons, which, if operationally feasible, would be assigned to one of the services for production and employment. McElroy announced that responsibility for the development of an antimissile missile would be assigned to the agency, and he implied that responsibility for other missiles might have been assigned to the special agency except that these programs were too far along.[76]

These sweeping decisions by the secretary of defense were not entirely agreeable to some highly placed defense officials, who recognized a need for a defense office with authority to make policy decisions but objected to establishing a defense agency that would have development and contractual powers. Believing that there was need for a staff organization to handle research and development in space flight, the Air Force deputy chief of staff for development established a Directorate of Astronautics on 10 December 1957. However, McElroy rejected recommendations opposing the special defense agency, and the Air Force order establishing a Directorate of Astronautics was revoked on 13 December, reportedly because of pressure from Holaday and Quarles.[77] When he appeared before the Senate Armed Services Subcommittee on 9 January 1958, however, Maj Gen Bernard A. Schriever emphasized that the Air Force already possessed capabilities to initiate an astronautics development program with no dilution or diversion of its ballistic missile programs. Schriever saw a need for a defense authority that would formulate policy and approve programs, but he warned that "any program to establish a separate astronautics management agency would result in duplication of capabilities already existing in the Air Force ballistic missile programs at a cost in funds and time similar to that already expended on these programs."[78]

Overruling service objections, Secretary McElroy proceeded with his plans for the organization of the Advanced Research Projects Agency (ARPA). With Eisenhower's approval, funds for ARPA research and development were included in the fiscal year 1959 defense budget submitted to Congress in January 1958. Without awaiting the new fiscal year, McElroy established ARPA effective on 7 February 1958; Congress soon authorized him to transfer $10 million from the military budget to the new agency. Under its charter ARPA was authorized to direct such research and development projects as the secretary assigned to it, to arrange for the performance of work by other governmental agencies including the military services, to enter contracts with individuals or institutions, and to acquire test facilities and equipment as approved by the secretary of defense.[79] Appointed director of ARPA, Roy W. Johnson secured personnel from the Institute of Defense Analysis, including Dr Herbert F. York, who became ARPA's chief scientist on 18 March. As a matter of policy, Johnson sought to keep the ARPA staff small (not more than 100 people including clerks), to avoid acquiring an in-house research and development capability, and determined not to pursue any system beyond research and development. His main objective was to provide "a small management staff designed to work with and through the military departments in developing forward-looking programs." He viewed ARPA as an agency that could make for "painless" unification in the field of space technology.[80]

At its establishment in February 1958, ARPA was given a unique position of great potential power in the Department of Defense and it appeared for a time that ARPA might become a fourth military service. McElroy justified ARPA's continuation as "an operating element paralleling the research and engineering organizations of the military departments," but Johnson's self-limiting policies did not permit this. Johnson personally believed that the three services ought to be combined into a single service, and he had no desire to make ARPA into a fourth service thus making things four times as bad as before.[81] Johnson also stated: "To ARPA, space is ... a place to discover new and better ways to do old military jobs; new ways to warn of impending attack, to communicate the alert to our forces, to actively defend our Nation."[82] If space was thus to be a place where old missions could be performed more effectively, no new concept of space power would supersede the old roles and missions of the military forces. At the completion of ARPA research and development, moreover, operational space weapon systems were to be turned over to a military service for production and employment. As a method of procedure, ARPA allocated most of its research and development projects to the military services. In the disposition of funds so allocated to the military services in the first year of its existence, ARPA placed 80 percent with the Air Force (including original Air Force funds in the Discoverer, Sentry [Samos], and Midas projects that were transferred to ARPA and then reallocated back to the Air Force), 14 percent with the Army, and 6 percent with the Navy.[83]

As enacted in August 1958, the Defense Reorganization Act created the director of defense research and engineering, with authority to direct and control, assign or reassign, and manage research and engineering activities within the Department of Defense with the approval of the secretary of defense. President Eisenhower appointed Doctor York to this position on 24 December 1958 and shortly thereafter York assumed responsibilities for research and engineering responsibilities in the guided missile field that had been exercised by the director of guided missiles. Secretary McElroy desired to retain Holaday as director of guided missiles in order that he might "push forward" the high-priority missile projection programs. McElroy also was determined to preserve ARPA as "a fourth operating agency for research and engineering projects."[84] Until this time ARPA had gotten most of its ideas from the military departments, but McElroy served notice that he wanted it to become "a think factory" and to plan a 10- to 20-year program for the military use of the space environment.[85]

During the spring of 1959, congressional investigators wanted to know whether ARPA should be continued. In an appearance before the Senate Subcommittee on Governmental Organization for Space Activities, Under Secretary of the Air Force Malcolm A. MacIntyre and General Schriever praised the work of Johnson. However, they stated their strong conviction that research and development management for space systems ought to be returned to the services that would operationally employ the space weapon systems. Without claiming any exclusive Air Force jurisdiction over the realm of aerospace, MacIntyre and Schriever demonstrated that the Air Force's defensive and offensive missions were so affected by potential developments in space as to demand that it be recognized as the nation's primary aerospace force. "The Air Force," Schriever said, "has two combat mission responsibilities: one is strategic air and the other is air defense.... I feel that by 1970, and perhaps long before that, in certain cases, that these combat missions of the Air Force will be taken over, to a large extent, by what you would call space weapons systems — ballistic missiles, satellites, and space craft." Schriever also argued that a separation of research and development from operations prevented an employment of the principle of concurrent development that had so greatly compressed the time required to establish an initial operational capability with ballistic missiles. Responding to a pointed question, Schriever recommended that ARPA be liquidated as of 30 June 1959, that policy guidance and program approval be centered in the Office of Director of Defense Research and Engineering, and that space research and development projects be returned to the military services.[86]

In an appearance before the House Committee on Science and Astronautics, Army spokesmen posited: "Space is a newly entered, largely unknown medium which transcends the exclusive interest of any service or even of the Department of Defense." Secretary of the Army Wilber M. Brucker emphasized the Army position that space exploration was a national effort, and he believed that ARPA had served to prevent "cutthroat" competition in the field.[87] Before the Subcommittee of the Senate Committee on Aeronautical and Space Sciences, Lt Gen Arthur G. Trudeau, chief of Army research and development, argued that since no single service had been assigned sole responsibility for military space activities ARPA filled "a very great need, and should not be eliminated."[88] Dr York also foresaw a continuing requirement for ARPA. "Since it is envisioned that military space activities will cut across all military operations," he reasoned, "it would be difficult to attempt to assign all military space operations to any one military service."[89]

The position of the Navy in regard to ARPA appeared to be somewhat between those of the Army and the Air Force. Secretary of the Navy Thomas S. Gates, Jr., stated that "the Navy's aim in relation to space can be simply stated: To use space to accomplish naval objectives and to prevent space from being used to the detriment of those objectives."[90] Vice Adm John T. Hayward, assistant chief of naval operations (research and development), acknowledged that ARPA had "done an excellent job" in the absence of legislation. He also thought that the agency was a worthwhile Department of Defense interface with the National Aeronautics and Space Administration. But he did not believe that ARPA should be an operating agency, and he thought that as a policy agency ARPA probably ought to be phased into the Office of the Director of Defense Research and Engineering.[91]

As early as February 1959 the Air Force officially requested that, in view of the impending completion of research and development, it should be assigned responsibility for the production and operation of the Sentry (Samos) reconnaissance satellite system and of the Midas infrared missile defense alarm system. When he appeared before the Subcommittee of the Senate Committee on Aeronautical and Space Sciences on 14 April, however, General Trudeau suggested that a unified space command should be established under the Joint Chiefs of Staff to take over operational employment of vehicles or satellites that were under development by ARPA. General Schriever, on the other hand, urged that "it would be well to make a decision as to which service should do what and then give the responsibilities to that service to develop and bring into being, operationally, the particular system required to provide the service." When developed, operational military space systems would be turned over to existing unified or specified commanders.[92] Holaday, who had now been named chairman of the NASA-DOD Civilian-Military Liaison Committee, also recommended that "military operations in space must come under a unified or specified command."[93]

In a formal memorandum for the chairman of the Joint Chiefs of Staff on 18 September 1959, Secretary McElroy ruled that a joint military organization with control over operational space systems did not appear to be desirable at that time. In this memorandum McElroy further expressed his opinion that the number of military satellite vehicles that would be launched in the next several years would not be very large and that the utilization of the existing organization of the military departments appeared preferable to the establishment of a joint military organization to control operational space systems. McElroy, therefore, made the Department of the Air Force responsible for the development, production, and launching of space boosters and the necessary systems integration of payloads incident to this activity. He announced impending transfers of developed systems from ARPA to the military departments: the Air Force would be assigned responsibility for Samos (Sentry) and Midas; the Transit navigational satellite would be assigned to the Navy; and the Army would receive operational charge of the Notus communications satellites, including Courier (a delayed repeater communications system) and Advent (an active instantaneous relay system). These systems would remain under ARPA until development was completed, and, even after the systems were transferred, McElroy indicated that ARPA would continue in being as the Defense Department's agency for advanced military research.[94]

In accordance with McElroy's decision the Air Force was assigned responsibility in November 1959 for the production of Samos and Midas and also for Discoverer, the latter being a project to test components, propulsion, and guidance systems to be used in other satellite projects and to develop techniques for the recovery of space capsules. Secretary of Defense Gates was subsequently asked to reconsider the McElroy decision on space systems; but on 16 June 1960 Gates, too, determined that the establishment of a joint military organization for the control of operational space systems did not appear necessary or immediately desirable. Secretary Gates further directed that the services would make provisions looking toward an orderly transfer of space systems to using unified or specified commands, thereby accepting by inference the Air Force position that the systems should be so assigned.[95] With the passing of time virtually all defense space projects were taken out of the hands of ARPA and transferred to the individual military services. ARPA continued to conduct projects of very broad interest such as research on materials, solid propellant chemistry, detection of nuclear tests, long-range studies on antimissile defense, and research in the fields of toxics and energy conversion.[96]

In the period of crisis in the autumn of 1957, the Department of Defense had made decisions on the subject of space organization on the basis of a belief that space was a vast unknown that lay outside existing roles and missions of the armed services. From this position the Department of Defense gradually moved toward acceptance of the proposition expressed by General Schriever: "Space . . . is a medium in which many military missions can be accomplished more effectively. Actually, it can be better understood when it is viewed as just what it is, an extension of a medium — aerospace."[97] The tacit acceptance of the concept that space was a continuum beyond the atmosphere was practical, but it was not without limitations. So-called space systems, for example, would not be developed as a means for exploiting a medium but rather in terms of existing military requirements. "The major criterion for the choice of a particular system to satisfy a particular military requirement," explained Lt Gen Roscoe C. Wilson, Air Force deputy chief of staff for development, in February 1960, "must be the relative effectiveness of that system compared with other methods of doing the same job." Thus, orbital or space systems could be developed only if they would perform an essential military mission which could be performed in no other way, perform an essential military mission more effectively at a justifiable increase in cost, or perform an essential military mission in an acceptable manner at a reduced cost.[98]

Establishment of the National Aeronautics and Space Administration

"I think you ought to realize," stated Dr T. Keith Glennan, who assumed duty as the first administrator of the National Aeronautics and Space Administration (NASA) at its establishment on 1 October 1958, "that NASA was born out of a state of hysteria."[99] In the same months that national leaders were attempting to provide a military organization for aerospace, they were also confronting the even more complex problem of establishing a national space program. In order to get guidance in this unknown field, President Eisenhower announced on 7 November 1957 the appointment of Dr James R. Killian, Jr., president of the Massachusetts Institute of Technology, as presidential scientific adviser. One of Killian's first tasks was to visualize a national space program; he later noted that he approached the task with already firm ideas. "From the beginning," he stated,

> it has been my view that the Federal Government had ... only two acceptable alternatives in creating its organization for space research, development, and operation. One was to

concentrate the entire responsibility, military and nonmilitary, in a single civilian agency. The other was to have dual programs — a program of space exploration and peaceful space activity under the management of a civilian agency and the military space program under the management of the Department of Defense.... A possible third alternative, that of putting our entire space program under the management of the Department of Defense always seemed to me to have so many defects as to be practically excluded as a solution. This is true because space exploration involves numerous activities and objectives that are outside the defense domain.[100]

As has been seen, President Eisenhower's report to the American people, which he made less than a week after Killian took office, stated distinctive criteria for space projects that were undertaken for scientific and defense purposes.[101]

At the same time that President Eisenhower distinguished between scientific and military space technology, the United States already was committed to a line of diplomatic action that sought to secure an international arms control agreement limiting developments in space to peaceful and scientific purposes. This proposal for *ab initio* arms control in space related back to a belief that international control of the military use of atomic energy, as a State Department spokesman said, "could have been attained with relative ease" in 1946. As has been seen, the United States pursued this line of diplomacy throughout 1957 and President Eisenhower continued to advocate it during the spring of 1958. On 12 January 1958 Eisenhower wrote Soviet Premier Nikolai Bulganin saying: "I proposed that we agree that outer space should be used only for peaceful purposes. We face a decisive moment in history in relation to this matter. Both the Soviet Union and the United States are now using outer space for the testing of missiles designed for military purposes. The time to stop is now." Speaking in the Soviet Union, Party Secretary Nikita Khrushchev belittled the Eisenhower offer with the remark: "This means they want to prohibit that which they do not possess." In another letter to Bulganin on 15 February 1958, however, Eisenhower renewed his plea: "A terrible new menace can be seen to be in the making. That menace is to be found in the use of outer space for war purposes. The time to deal with that menace is now. It would be tragic if the Soviet leaders were blind or indifferent toward this menace as they were apparently blind or indifferent to the atomic and nuclear menace at its inception a decade ago." Although the Soviets were not immediately responsive to these proposals, the US State Department accepted them as a sincere objective. "The most immediate problem in the field of space foreign policy," a State Department official said on 14 May 1958, "is how to ensure that outer space is used for peaceful purposes only."[102]

In connection with a study of space science and technology that it was making at Eisenhower's request, the President's Science Advisory Committee headed by Doctor Killian prepared a brief report, "Introduction to Outer Space," which was released on 26 March 1958. The panel of scientists distinguished four factors that gave "importance, urgency, and inevitability" to the advancement of space technology. These factors were said to be "the compelling urge of man to explore and discover," "the defensive objective for the development of space technology," "the factor of national prestige," and the fact that "space technology affords new opportunities for scientific observation and experiment which will add to our knowledge and understanding of the Earth, the solar system, and the universe." The scientists noted that the development of military rockets had provided the technological base for space exploration, but they believed that the important and foreseeable military uses for military space vehicles lay in the fields of communication and reconnaissance. Visualizations of satellite bombers or military bases on the moon did not "hold up well on close examination or appear to be achievable at an early date." Such military developments would become technologically possible in time, but they would be "clumsy and ineffective ways of doing a job." "In short," the report concluded, "the Earth would appear to be, after all, the best weapons carrier." This report apparently reinforced President Eisenhower's conviction that the world bore a great responsibility to promote the peaceful use of space. "I recommend," Eisenhower informed Congress on 2 April 1958, "that aeronautical and space science activities sponsored by the United States be conducted under the direction of a civilian agency, except for those projects primarily associated with military requirements."[103]

During the early months of 1958, proposals were made looking toward the establishment of an international space agency or an American civil space organization. Senator Lyndon B. Johnson called for joint exploration of outer space by the United Nations. Former disarmament assistant Harold E. Stassen advocated a United Nations space development agency that would send the first man into space and the first photographic inspection satellite around the earth. Senator Hubert H. Humphrey proposed that the United States "take the lead in marshaling the talents and resources of the world to unlock the mysteries of outer space in joint research and exploration under the auspices of the United Nations."[104] Meeting in Washington the National Council of the Federation of American Scientists approved on 3 May 1958 a statement noting the precedent of the Atomic Energy Commission, where under civilian control "both military and civilian uses of atomic energy have prospered in an atmosphere more conducive to scientific progress than that typically available under military direction." Critical "of the failure of the Pentagon leadership to foresee the impact of the first satellites in the popular imagination," the Federation of American Scientists called for the establishment of a civilian space agency in the United States and a united and coordinated international space effort under the authority of the United Nations. "It would be tragic," these scientists said, "if the challenging task of space exploration were carried on in the competitive nationalistic pattern under which it has begun."[105] The persons who believed that the Atomic Energy Commission could serve as a model for a national space agency variously recommended that the Atomic Energy Act of 1954 be amended to add a division of outer space development to the Atomic Energy Commission, or that an entirely new commission on outer space be established following the precedent of the Atomic Energy Commission.[106]

IMPACT OF MISSILES AND SPACE

In a speech in Washington on 14 January 1958, retired Air Force Gen Orval R. Cook, president of the Aircraft Industries Association, apparently first proposed the seemingly simple solution that the National Advisory Committee for Aeronautics (NACA) already provided an existing organization capable of accelerating space exploration.[107] Two days later a meeting of the National Advisory Committee for Aeronautics resolved that the NACA statutory authority to "supervise and direct the scientific study of the problems of flight, with a view to their practical solution" was broad enough to cover spaceflight as well as atmospheric flight and that NACA had "an important responsibility for coordinating and for conducting research in space technology either in its own laboratories or by contract, and, therefore, should expand its existing program and add supplementary facilities to those now available as necessary."[108] Following these suggestions, President Eisenhower, in his message to Congress on 2 April 1958, recommended the establishment of a new national aeronautics and space administration into which NACA would be absorbed. When he signed the Space Act into law, Eisenhower remarked: "The present National Advisory Committee for Aeronautics, with its large and competent staff and well-equipped laboratories, will provide the nucleus for NASA. The NACA has an established record of research performance and of cooperation with the Armed Services. The coordination of space exploration responsibilities with the NACA's traditional aeronautical research function is a natural evolution."[109]

The Eisenhower proposal for the legislation, which would be known as the National Aeronautics and Space Act of 1958, was drafted by NACA and Doctor Killian. Since the president was said to be eager to have the legislation go to Congress prior to its Easter recess, the draft bill was sent to the Department of Defense for review and comment on 26 March, with a deadline for receipt of replies set at noon on 31 March. Inside the Pentagon, the Department of the Air Force and other military agencies were given 24 hours to study and comment on the proposed law, identical copies of which were introduced into the Senate and House on 2 April.[110] Even though Eisenhower considered that NASA evolved from NACA, the proposed law, with three exceptions, followed the model of the Atomic Energy Act. The exceptions were that the management of NASA would be vested in a single director, there was no provision for a military liaison committee, and there was no legislative oversight committee as was the case with the Atomic Energy Commission.[111] In NACA, control had been exercised by a 17-member committee (including two members from the Navy, two from the Air Force, and six from other specified federal agencies), which elected a director. In the proposal for NASA, the president would appoint the administrator and an advisory National Aeronautics and Space Board with a maximum of 17 members, of whom not more than eight (including not less than one from the Department of Defense) would be from government departments or agencies. NASA was to have wide authority for developing, testing, launching, and operating aeronautical and space vehicles. The proposed legislation also provided that NASA would exercise "control over aeronautical and space research sponsored by the United States, except insofar as such activities may be peculiar to or primarily associated with weapons systems or military operations, in which case the agency may act in cooperation with, or on behalf of, the Department of Defense."[112]

As the legislation was originally drafted, the Department of Defense was not given a clear mandate for space activities. Speaking of this later on, Dr Edward C. Welsh, executive secretary of the National Aeronautics and Space Council, observed: "It is possible that this omission was a result of careless drafting or evidence of disinterest in military application to space or just optimism regarding our military position relative to that of the Communists."[113] During April and May 1958 a progression of distinguished witnesses appeared before the House Select Committee on Astronautics and Space Explorations and the Senate Special Committee on Space and Astronautics as they held hearings on the Space Act. Many of the scientists who came before the committees argued that a civilian scientific program was essential because the nonmilitary aspects of space exploration were too important to be entrusted to a purely military program. Professor James A. Van Allen of the State University of Iowa spoke very strongly of the need for civilian supremacy in space. "I feel," he said, "the language of this bill should be strengthened substantially to make it clear that the NASA will have primary and dominant cognizance of space matters among all Government agencies, and that only in case it is clearly demonstrated that an endeavor has a direct importance to our military preparedness ... should the primary cognizance reside in the Defense Department."[114]

Believing that the favorable relations previously enjoyed with NACA would continue, Department of Defense witnesses initially supported the administration's space agency bill. Navy representatives, however, suggested the desirability of adding a military liaison committee to NASA similar to the committee that functioned with the AEC.[115] Air Force Under Secretary MacIntyre stated his understanding that the measure intended that military activities in space would be the province of the Department of Defense; that civil space activities would be handled by NASA; and that "in the broad twilight zone of dual usefulness, the two agencies should operate in close mutual cooperation with each other, under overall executive direction, without domination of either over the other."[116] When queried about this statement, however, the Bureau of the Budget did not agree with MacIntyre's understanding. The bureau understood that

> the space responsibility of the Department of Defense would include only those programs peculiar to or "primarily associated with weapons systems or military operations." All other space programs would be the responsibility of the civil space agency.... We recognize that there will probably be programs of military interest which are not, however, peculiarly or primarily military. The new agency would be responsible for those programs, but we expect that the Department of Defense would participate in their planning and implementation.[117]

Because of this new interpretation, ARPA director Johnson returned to the hearings of the House committee on 12 May to protest the restrictive language of the administration measure toward defense research and development in space.[118] Both the House and Senate committees and then Congress noted and objected to the narrow field evidently intended for the military in space and to the permissive rather than mandatory authority accorded for even this narrow field.[119] Congress also objected to the lack of formal liaison specified between the NASA and the Department of Defense. As a result of this dissatisfaction a Senate-House conference committee made substantial changes in the administration bill.[120] "We carefully wrote into the basic law," stated Congressman Gerald R. Ford, "that the military should have certain responsibilities in the area and by no means should the executive branch of the Government permit NASA to preempt certain areas which the military believes will be important in space."[121] In the preamble to the National Aeronautics and Space Act of 1958, which was signed by President Eisenhower on 29 July, Congress declared that the general welfare and security of the United States required that adequate provision be made for aeronautical and space activities. The Congress further declared

> that such activities shall be the responsibility of, and shall be directed by, a civilian agency exercising control over aeronautical and space activities sponsored by the United States, except that activities peculiar to or primarily associated with the development of weapons systems, military operations, or the defense of the United States (including the research and development necessary to make effective provision for the defense of the United States) shall be the responsibility of, and shall be directed by the Department of Defense.

To Lt Gen Bernard Schriever, who viewed the matter from the perspective of his duties as commander, Air Research and Development Command, this section of the Space Act clearly indicated the intent of Congress that "the military must continue to conduct a vigorous research and development program of components and subsystems, as well as basic research, if the full potential of military space systems is to be realized on a timely basis."[122]

The Space Act established the National Aeronautics and Space Administration (NASA) headed by a presidentially appointed administrator who was vested with authority to plan, direct, and conduct aeronautical and space activities. NACA ceased to exist and its personnel and facilities were transferred to NASA. Other departments and agencies were to make "their services, equipment, personnel and facilities available" to NASA as required. NASA was charged to arrange for the participation of the scientific community of the nation in space activities and was permitted, under guidance from the president, to engage in programs of international cooperation. Recognizing that there was "a grey area between civilian and military interests," the Space Act authorized the president to determine which agency, civilian or military, should have responsibility for specific projects. The Space Act provided for the National Aeronautics and Space Council, to consist of the president, the secretary of state, the secretary of defense, the NASA administrator, and four additional members to be appointed by the president. The council was charged to assist the president in surveying aeronautical and space activities and to provide for effective cooperation between NASA and the Department of Defense. Congress also added a provision for the establishment of the Civilian-Military Liaison Committee, which was to consist of a chairman appointed by the president and a membership of an unspecified number of military and civilian representatives from the Department of Defense and NASA. Through the liaison committee, Congress intended that NASA and the Department of Defense should advise and consult together with respect to their activities. In case of unresolved disagreements the NASA administrator and the secretary of defense would refer the matters to the president.[123]

Getting about the implementation of the National Aeronautics and Space Act of 1958, President Eisenhower on 8 August appointed Dr T. Keith Glennan, president of the Case Institute of Technology, and Dr Hugh L. Dryden, director of NACA, as the administrator and deputy administrator of NASA, respectively. NASA began to operate on 1 October 1958, and in a series of executive orders it received projects and facilities from the Department of Defense. The projects included the responsibility for launching Vanguard earth satellites, three scientific satellite projects, four Pioneer probes, and a number of basic research undertakings looking toward the development of nuclear rocket engines, fluorine engines, and a million-pound-thrust single-chamber rocket engine. NASA took over the Army's Jet Propulsion Laboratory in California on 3 December 1958, the Project Tiros meteorological research satellite on 13 April 1959, and the Centaur launch vehicle comprising an Atlas booster with a second stage liquid hydrogen engine on 30 June 1959. In a transfer requested in 1958 and announced as impending in 1959, NASA assumed control over the Army Ballistic Missile Agency's Development Operations Division under von Braun at Redstone Arsenal, Alabama, effective on 1 July 1960.[124] Authorized a broad authority to request the transfer of space projects and facilities from the Department of Defense, Administrator Glennan observed that only a fuzzy line seemed to separate military and civil space projects. "I tend to regard the military elements under the law," he said, "as those matters that relate primarily to weapon systems and military operations in the defense of the Nation, those items which are moving toward operational systems, such as a satellite early warning system or a missile warning system, or some such thing."[125]

The organization of the National Aeronautics and Space Council was completed when President Eisenhower appointed the additional members from civilian status. Chaired by the president, the space council held its organizational meeting on 24 September 1958 and met thereafter as required to provide broad policy advice to the president on such matters as transfers of projects and facilities to NASA, international cooperation in space, assignment of national priorities for space development, and the organization and operation of the nation's ground support facilities. Critics of the council pointed out that this body was only one source of advice to the president, who also got guidance from his scientific adviser and from the executive departmental heads.[126] According to Doctor Welsh the space council really was "left dormant" under Eisenhower and did not exercise its broad and comprehensive advisory authority.[127] The Civilian-Military Liaison Committee was not set up until after 31 October 1958, when Eisenhower named William Holaday as its chairman. The Defense Department and NASA agreed that the liaison committee's membership would include its chairman, four representatives from NASA, and single representatives from ARPA and the Army, Navy, and Air Force. The liaison committee held its first meeting on 25 November and thereafter assembled about once a month. The committee dealt successfully with some matters, but neither Glennan nor McElroy was said to be "willing to delegate to junior people settlement of major issues." Holaday soon reported: "The committee, because of its composition, that is, membership made up of representatives who are subject to a higher internal authority, is incapable of making firm decisions."[128] When it was unable to secure a single point of contact with the Department of Defense through the mechanism of the liaison committee for handling the tracking and recovery of planned Mercury astronaut flights, NASA finally appealed directly to McElroy for action. On 10 August 1959 McElroy designated Maj Gen Donald N. Yates, commander of the USAF Atlantic Missile Range, as the Department of Defense representative under the Joint Chiefs of Staff for the support of Project Mercury. Yates was provided an assistant from the Navy for command of recovery forces.[129]

Speaking in March 1959 before the full impact of the National Aeronautics and Space Act became apparent, Secretary McElroy observed that it was the "responsibility of the military in this overall programming of outer space to make certain that those things which are specifically military objectives are taken care of one way or the other either by NASA or by ARPA ... that division seems to me to be less important than the assurance that the job is being done by competent people in one or the other."[130] Admiral Hayward, on the other hand, suggested that "NASA should have been set up similarly to the Atomic Energy Commission, with a division of military applications in this agency," and "that we should have one space program."[131] General Schriever differed with both of these opinions. "I feel," he said, "that the world in which we live — being what it is our national security must have first priority. In other words, our ability to maintain the peace has to have first priority. Therefore, I can only conclude that the important military programs should have first priority." The most important equation in research and development was management as a function of time: the best means of beating the clock was the concept of concurrency that had permitted rapid acceleration of the intercontinental ballistic missile capability. Already, Schriever said, NASA was placing competitive orders with contractors working for the Air Force. Schriever considered that the most serious threat to concurrency, however, was the idea being suggested that NASA "could become a ministry of supply type of organization which develops complete systems and turns them over to the military." Believing firmly in the concurrency concept whereby weapon systems were developed by the operating service, Schriever firmly opposed any idea that NASA should be designed to become a national space commission and allowed to develop space weapon systems for operation by the military services.[132] Although Schriever apparently feared the effect of NASA's competition on military space programs, the official Air Force policy sought to get an acceleration of aerospace hardware even if it had to divert key officers from its own programs. In March 1959 General LeMay stated that the Air Force would make its personnel freely available for service in agencies of the Department of Defense concerned with space activities and in NASA.[133]

Only mildly apparent in the spring of 1959, discontent with the National Aeronautics and Space Act among certain elements within the Department of Defense burst into full flame in the autumn of 1959 and centered around the transfer of the Army's Saturn rocket to NASA. Up until this time the Saturn program had been replete with starts and stops, allegedly because of a feeling within Defense Department scientific circles that there was no military requirement for ballistic missiles larger than those programmed and that there would be no necessity for a military space platform. As a part of the continuing evaluation of the large multithrust booster problem, Doctor York convened a review committee in September to study the three planned boosters—Titan C, Saturn, and Nova. As a result of this study Doctor York was said to have agreed that the Saturn should be continued under development but that the project would have to be transferred to NASA since the Department of Defense could not finance it within its budgetary limitations. On 21 October President Eisenhower announced that he would transfer the Army's rocket development team and the Saturn booster to NASA.[134] The commander of the Army Ordnance Missile Command, Maj Gen John B. Medaris, described the Army's agreement to the transfer of the Saturn and the von Braun missile team to NASA as a Solomon's choice. "First," he said, "by the assignment of the space vehicle development, production, and launching mission to the Air Force, and secondly, the Army's total inability to secure from the Department of Defense sufficient money or responsibility to do the Saturn job properly, we found ourselves ... in the position of either agreeing with the transfer of the team, or watching it be destroyed by starvation and frustration."[135] In the middle of this winter of Army discontent, President Eisenhower sent Congress a message on 14 January 1960 proposing amendments to the National Aeronautics and Space Act. "In actual practice," Eisenhower explained, "a single civil-military program does not exist and is, in fact, unattainable; and the statutory concept of such a program has caused confusion." Eisenhower considered that the Department of Defense had ample authority outside the Space Act to conduct research and development work on space-related weapon systems. He, therefore, proposed to eliminate the statutory requirement for the National Aeronautics and Space Council and for the Civilian-Military Liaison Committee and to allow NASA to become responsible for the formulation and execution of its own program in its own right, subject to the authority and direction of the president.[136]

IMPACT OF MISSILES AND SPACE

In the early months of 1960, related hearings held by the House Committee on Science and Astronautics in review of the space program and on the proposed amendment to the Space Act served as a forum for the presentation of the divergent views on space organization. In a valedictory interview given as he was retiring from the Army during the last week of January, General Medaris raked the civil-military separation of national space programs as "fundamentally unrealistic" and called for the creation of a single missile-space agency as a unified command within the Department of Defense.[137] Testifying in Washington on 18 February, Medaris charged that the national space program was "splintered into four agencies, NASA and the three branches of our armed services." He criticized the Department of Defense directive that compelled the Army and Navy to "buy" their space boosters from the Air Force, since under this directive the "problem of wedding the payload and the vehicle must be settled by such anemic devices as committees, coordination officers, and other such inadequate administrative devices." He again proposed that responsibility for a national space program ought to be unified within the Department of Defense. Continued division of efforts in missile-space technology, he said, "cannot but result in delay, duplication, and waste of both money and manpower."[138] When asked how much support he had for his proposal to establish a unified missile-space command, Medaris replied: "I can only comment that within the evening councils of the renegades of our business, I have a great deal of support."[139] This support, however, failed to appear during the congressional hearings. Lt Gen James M. Gavin (US Army, Retired) observed that he would be "very worried to see major portions of our space program in DOD; however well intentioned they were, they couldn't get money, whereas I know that NASA can and very likely will for several years."[140] Admiral Hayward reiterated his familiar proposal that the United States should follow the "Atomic Energy Commission approach to the whole space program." The Army now apparently subscribed to this same approach to the problem, for General Trudeau also came out for "the creation of a Military Liaison Committee patterned after the committee provided by law to function between the Department of Defense and the Atomic Energy Commission." Trudeau thought that his committee could well replace the ineffective Civilian-Military Liaison Committee.[141]

When he appeared before the House Committee on Science and Astronautics, Dr William H. Pickering, director of NASA's Jet Propulsion Laboratory, agreed that the nation required a single space program; but he asserted that the program should be attained by strengthening NASA "to the point where it effectively controls a complete national space program." Pickering charged that the divided authority in the space field was powerless to "prevent military space systems of only peripheral value from demanding such a large share of research support in both the Department of Defense and perhaps the NASA that these efforts dominate the space program to the detriment of our real objectives." His concluding remarks summarized his position:

> I feel that at the present time it is more important that the primary effort in space be civilian oriented rather than military oriented. In other words, my feeling is that the military applications of space are not clearly defined at this time, that this may very well develop; in fact, past experience would say almost surely that it will develop, but I would regard this as being a natural development out of a program which is oriented in the direction of a civilian space program.[142]

In their testimony, Under Secretary of the Air Force Joseph V. Charyk, General White, and General Schriever opposed all of the proposals to establish "a single monolithic space agency." "From a national standpoint," Schriever stated, "progress in space research is essential for both security and prestige. Civilian and military space operations complement each other, and both should be pursued vigorously." Asked to explain the thoughts behind his assertion that NASA and national defense objectives in space were divergent, Schriever explained that this divergence had been obscured by the fact that NASA was compelled to use military rockets as boosters. Looking toward the future, he pointed out that NASA would develop unique experimental equipment that might be used for only a few scientific probes under controlled circumstances. Most NASA probes would be handled by temporary task force organizations, and NASA would not require a large and permanent field organization. Military space systems, on the other hand, would be required in quantity, would have to be simple and reliable, and would need to be standardized and made capable of fairly long employment life. The defense systems would have to strive to reduce the cost per launch, while NASA could afford to pay larger prices for the lesser numbers of scientific probes that it would mount.[143] Based on this line of reasoning as well as the fact that the Air Force was enjoying harmonious relations with NASA, Schriever interjected "that we are fast approaching the old, very good relationship that we had with the old NACA." Thus, the Air Force was not only eager to continue the existing space organization but was also entirely willing to support Eisenhower's proposed amendments to the Space Act.[144]

The statements of Charyk, White, and Schriever in support of the existing NASA-Defense Department relationship apparently indicated that the Air Force policy of cooperation had borne positive results. Schriever's earlier fears that NASA and the Department of Defense might compete for the services of scarce space technologists had apparently not materialized. In reference to this widely expressed belief that the nation's technological resources could not support two space programs, Dr Simon Ramo, vice president of the Thompson-Ramo-Wooldridge Corporation, pointed out that there was no shortage of national technical resources to support a vastly increased and even duplicative missile and space program. Ramo said: "If we chose to do so—and this is only a slight exaggeration—we could almost have space probes or ICBM's coming out of our ears."[145] By the spring of 1960 Brig Gen Don R. Ostrander and several other Air Force officers had been assigned to NASA. In the same period that the congressional hearings were under way on the proposed reorganization of the

IMPACT OF MISSILES AND SPACE

national space effort, NASA requested the assignment to it of still more key project officers from the Ballistic Missiles Division—men whom Schriever considered to be greatly needed for his own developmental programs. Learning of Schriever's reluctance to assign the men to NASA and concerned about the proposals to reorganize NASA along the lines of the Atomic Energy Commission, General White believed that the time was right for "a sermon from the Chief of Staff to his staff." On 14 April 1960, White issued a memorandum saying:

> I am convinced that one of the major long range elements of the Air Force future lies in space. It is also obvious that NASA will play a large part in the national effort in this direction and, moreover, inevitably will be closely associated, if not eventually combined with the military. It is perfectly clear to me that particularly in these formative years the Air Force must, for its own good as well as for national interest, cooperate to the maximum extent with NASA, to include the furnishing of key personnel even at the expense of some Air Force dilution of technical talent.

White later explained why he had issued the memorandum. "The sole purpose," he said, "of this memorandum—and I think I stated it very clearly—is that I want to make it crystal clear that the policy is we will cooperate with NASA—and to the very limit of our ability and even beyond, to the extent of some risk in our own programs."[146]

In the early stages of the hearings of the House Committee on Science and Astronautics, Deputy Secretary of Defense James H. Douglas expressed support for Eisenhower's proposed amendments of the Space Act. He agreed that the Civilian-Military Liaison Committee had been ineffective and ought to be eliminated, but he still wished to see effective liaison established between the Department of Defense and NASA. Accordingly, on 14 March 1960 Douglas proposed that cooperation between the Defense Department and NASA be attained by establishing an aeronautics and astronautics coordinating board; the deputy administrator of NASA and the director of defense research and engineering would serve as co-chairmen of the board, with supervision over subordinate board panels that would be established from NASA and Defense Department managerial personnel to handle matters of mutual interest. Under Secretary Charyk warmly supported this proposal, which he described as a broader projection of the Air Force-NASA discussions looking toward the establishment of a committee of responsible people to handle launch vehicle matters.[147] Doctor Glennan agreed that much of the improvised coordination that already existed between the Defense Department and NASA would well be formalized; he also announced his support for the establishment of the aeronautics and astronautics coordinating board.[148] When it reported out the space organization bill in the first week of May 1960, the House Committee on Science and Astronautics added a provision establishing the Aeronautics and Astronautics Coordinating Board.[149]

After the matter had been further discussed Glennan and Douglas signed an administrative agreement on 1 July 1960 that established the Aeronautics and Astronautics Coordinating Board (AACB). As officially promulgated on 13

September, the agreement specified that the deputy administrator of NASA and the director of defense research and engineering would serve as co-chairmen of the board, whose membership would comprise the chairmen of the board's panels plus enough additional members to ensure that each military department was represented and that NASA had equal representation with the Department of Defense. Six panels were established: manned spaceflight, unmanned spacecraft, launch vehicles, spaceflight ground environment, supporting space research and technology, and aeronautics. The joint directive charged the AACB to facilitate the planning of activities in a manner calculated to avoid undesirable duplications and to achieve efficient utilization of available resources, to coordinate activities in areas of common interest, to identify problems requiring solutions, and to exchange information between NASA and the Department of Defense. The board was to meet at least bimonthly, or more frequently on the call of its co-chairmen; it was provided with a small secretariat to maintain its records.[150]

Since the Senate proved unwilling to approve Eisenhower's proposed amendments to the Space Act, the establishment of the Aeronautics and Astronautics Coordinating Board proved to be the only positive accomplishment of the lengthy debates on the national space program. In establishing the AACB, Glennan and Douglas carefully avoided the defects found in the Civilian-Military Liaison Committee, which had failed to work primarily because its members lacked authority. Within the AACB, panel members were picked in accordance with their responsibilities within their agencies. Meeting as necessary, the panels examined problems, arrived at suggested solutions, and made recommendations to the AACB. When the AACB approved the recommendations, they were passed down within the Department of Defense and within NASA for implementation by the same officers who served on the panels. The Civilian-Military Liaison Committee continued in legal existence, but Eisenhower did not appoint another chairman for it when Holaday resigned the position, and the committee lapsed into inactivity. Some senators criticized the administration for failing to execute an existing law, and *Missiles and Rockets* magazine observed that the "spidery problem of defining clear-cut national objectives in space exploration" was evidently going to be passed on to a new Congress and a new administration that would take office in January 1961.[151]

Strategic Dialogue: Minimum Deterrence or Counterforce

"The arm holding the hammer and sickle," General White observed in the aftermath of the Sputnik, "has grown longer and stronger."[152] At the same time that the sudden establishment of Soviet missile and space capabilities demanded a reorganization of American military and space establishments, the new Soviet threat touched off an intense examination of strategic thinking. Many persons conceived that the employment of nuclear missiles would lend a virtual mathematical certainty to the conduct of war, and new electronic computers promised to provide ready answers to the complex equations of missile warfare. Early in 1958, for example, the Air Force put a high-speed electronic air-battle model computer into operation that was able to work through three days of two-sided, strategic global air war in about seven hours, maintaining and recording a net capability position by fifteen-minute increments for the opposing forces as the wargame progressed. "We have come a long way since World War II," said Maj Gen James H. Walsh, Air Force deputy assistant chief of staff for intelligence, "in being able to predict the effects of our bombing campaigns, largely through the continued development or skilled target personnel, the magic of computers, and above all the quantum jump available in nuclear firepower."[153] Even though computers provided a facile means of wargaming, General White insisted that "war is an art and always will be an art" and protested the philosophical approach that wanted to reduce war to mathematical equations. "In the age of missiles," he warned,

> it is so easy to add up the number of missiles, the CEP [circular error of probability], number of missiles required to knock out a particular target, and come up with a table of equations and give it to a Ph.D. and tell ... [him] to push XYZ buttons. I do not think war will be that way, because I feel that in this age of nuclear weapons the greatest confusion that mankind has ever faced will reign. We will have variables and we must be prepared for the unexpected. Decisions must be based on human judgment, able to fit many variable reactions to variable situations.[154]

The deterrence of war had been an American objective since 1945 and the concept of nuclear stalemate had been talked about since 1954, but Sputnik precipitated an immediate and intense discussion of both of these matters. "It is a grim enough world," said Dr Vannevar Bush in November 1957, "if two countries face each other with such weapons that, if all-out war broke out, both countries would be completely demolished.... But we feel that under those circumstances, all-out war would probably not break out, because no man would deliberately throw us into that sort of a holocaust where he and everything else would be destroyed."[155] For some time General Taylor believed that the Navy and the Marines had been moving closer to the Army position that nuclear stalemate was likely and that the United States should emphasize developing forces for limited war. In the winter of 1957-58 Taylor observed that "the Navy and Marine Corps were ready to join in recommending changes that would take into account the implications of nuclear parity, establish finite limits on the size for atomic retaliatory force, and in general make for a flexible strategy for coping with limited aggression."[156] "Given a shield of mutual deterrence," said Secretary of the Navy Gates, "power to prevent limited aggression and win limited war becomes decisive."[157] "A general nuclear war now means," agreed Admiral Burke, "that both the United States and Russia would be most severely damaged. Under these circumstances, initiation of a general war by Russia seems unlikely so long as we have the capability of destroying her."[158] In appearances before congressional committees early in 1958, Burke pointed out that aircraft carriers were useful to both general and limited war and that Polaris submarines, which promised to be "invulnerable to preemptive action by an enemy," would be a positive deterrent to war. "As long as an enemy knows that no matter what kind of blow he may first strike at us, he will himself be destroyed in reprisal," Burke suggested, "then he will not rationally decide to start a war."[159]

Many civilian strategists accepted the concept of a nuclear stalemate and the requirements for limited war forces. Governor Rockefeller and the Rockefeller study panel "felt that there was increasing possibility that as the Soviets and ourselves reached equal capabilities of destruction there might — under the cover of our reluctance to use all-out force to oppose an action which did not seem warranted now knowing that such all-out action would bring major destruction in this country — be a nibbling away at the periphery by small wars [and] that we would not want to use all-out retaliation to oppose."[160] In January 1958 Paul H. Nitze published an article entitled "Atoms, Strategy and Policy" in which he strongly endorsed the concept of graduated deterrence that he had found to be popular in Europe. Nitze's proposal was not so much concerned with deterring war as in confining war. He considered that the requirements for graduated deterrence involved the maintenance of a superior western nuclear posture; the meeting of aggression without the use of atomic weapons where this was possible; the determination not to extend geographically limited hostilities to other areas unless the situation could not be resolved effectively otherwise; an avoidance of attacks against industrial and population centers and the use of atomic weapons against military objectives primarily for attainment of control of the air; and the building of western nonatomic elements of strength in order to reduce the extent to which security would depend on atomic weapons.[161]

In discussions as early as 1956, General LeMay had been willing to admit in theory that a smaller size force might present a deterrent effect upon an enemy, but he still held to his definition that effective deterrence required the United States to maintain a force strong enough to absorb the losses from a Soviet surprise attack and then to inflict damage that would be "unacceptable" on an enemy. "It is reasonable to assume," he observed, "that the original force without losses should certainly be initially stronger than the Soviet force."[162] Speaking in August 1956 Secretary of the Air Force Quarles believed that "the problem before the world today is a problem of deterrence" and that "the build-up of atomic power ... makes total war an unthinkable catastrophe." Quarles proposed that the relative force strength of the United States and the Soviet Union was less important than "the *absolute power* in the hands of each, and in the substantial invulnerability of this power to interdiction." He argued that it was necessary only to maintain a level of strength which he called "mission capability" and pointed out that it was "neither necessary nor desirable ... to maintain strength above that level."[163] Quarles's statement was useful in explaining why the Air Force could safely reduce its force from the 137-wing level, which had been justified as critical to the security of the nation; his statement seemed to equate deterrence with the maintenance of capabilities for massive retaliation. Also speaking in 1956, while he was still Air

Force chief of staff, General Twining emphasized counterforce rather than massive retaliation when he said: "If we are attacked, the Air Force's main job is to knock out the Russian long-range air force and their capability to deliver strikes against the United States."[164]

Partly to cause uncertainties among the enemy, neither President Eisenhower nor Secretary of State John Foster Dulles ever exactly defined massive retaliation. As has been seen, the acceptance of massive retaliation in 1954 did not lead the Joint Chiefs of Staff to change the categories of target systems for strategic air war planning purposes. During the Sputnik crisis, however, the Air Force gave some serious thoughts to a counterforce strategy and for the first time assigned some specific meanings to massive retaliation. Speaking in 1959 General White said that the strategic target priorities continued to be: "One, to destroy the enemy's capability to destroy us — that would be the first priority; next would be to blunt the enemy attack against our deployed military forces in Europe and in Asia; and, third, systematically destroy the Soviet Union's ability to wage war." If it were given strategic and tactical warning, White pointed out that the United States could implement these orderly attack priorities, but he noted that the growth of Soviet capabilities to attack the United States made it likely that a United States second strike might have to be somewhat improvised. "In case of a surprise attack," he suggested, "the mission would be . . . to do the greatest possible damage to the Soviet Union as a whole with attention to applying that destruction in such a way as to do as much damage as possible to their residual military striking force."[165] Following this same line of reasoning, Col Robert C. Richardson demonstrated that massive retaliation had always been a specific response within the whole American strategy. "Massive retaliation," Richardson wrote,

> relates principally to what happens after the enemy tries a surprise attack against the United States proper. The deterrent to an attack of this nature lies in the Strategic Air Command's capability, even after having been hit first, to strike back, "retaliate," with sufficient atomic power to wipe out the enemy's major urban centers. This is massive retaliation. The targets are cities; the forces used are those that survive the initial attack; and the objective is to devastate the enemy nation to the extent that it would not be able to capitalize on its act of aggression. . . . Now, the ability to destroy cities — the main target of massive retaliation — may constitute a deterrent to surprise attack against the United States. It does not, however, in any way deter aggression anywhere in the world, including NATO. What has deterred aggression in Europe and in other vital areas for the past ten years has been primarily the counterforce aspect of the general-war capability backed up by the expressed willingness to use any and all forces to defend the free world if it should become necessary.[166]

On the conceptual level, General Walsh reasoned in December 1957 that Air Force thinking had turned full circle away from the Mitchell-Douhet doctrines of waging strategic air war against enemy industrial capabilities and had returned to the older doctrines of Carl von Clausewitz and Alfred von Schlieffen that considered enemy military forces in being as the prime objectives of war effort.[167] Seen in terms of a counterforce strategy the requirements for strategic air striking forces had to be calculated in terms of its capabilities and vulnerabilities in destroying hostile target systems — not in terms of the residuum that might remain after an enemy surprise attack. By early 1959 the United States air war plan was based upon an analysis and screening of over 20,000 targets in Soviet-bloc nations. Although nothing was immediately published on the extremely sensitive subject, air targeting apparently became much more exact in the years after 1955-56 when the very high altitude U-2 reconnaissance aircraft began operating over foreign soil. "We know what targets must be destroyed," stated an Air Force planner in 1959. "Our war plans are based on this target analysis."[168] Although the Air Force was apparently willing to accept counterforce as an objective, the Strategic Air Command (SAC) continued to plan operating tactics which envisioned that strategic air attacks would be speedily accomplished against all target systems in one mighty effort. Such an all-out attack would provide the largest degree of protection to SAC crews. By a predominant use of large nuclear weapons, moreover, one crew could be counted upon to destroy many individual targets with single weapons, thus achieving a "bonus effect" that was thought to be quite important in view of the many targets requiring destruction and the limited size of the Strategic Air Command. Even though Soviet cities were not targeted for air attack, many of them would be destroyed by nuclear weapons aimed at military objectives in their vicinity.[169]

Meeting Crises in Lebanon and the Taiwan Straits

Although General Taylor considered that the conversion of the Navy and the Marines to his views on nuclear stalemate-limited war was "quite an achievement," the Army position was not accepted by the Department of Defense or by the Air Force. "One of the most pressing objectives of the Defense Department," Secretary McElroy stated in January 1958, "must be to make it obvious to any potential enemy that we have available and are prepared to use weapons of retaliation so devastating that the cost to an aggressor of an attack on us would be unbearable."[170] In April 1958 McElroy foresaw "less and less likelihood of limited war that would demand sizable forces." While he granted that limited conflict "could occur in primitive countries," he argued that the United States would never consider a Soviet attack against NATO as a limited war. "We better never let anyone," he said, "get the mistaken idea that we are not going to use our big weapons if they are needed."[171] Speaking as chairman of the Joint Chiefs of Staff, General Twining said: "I personally do not believe you can say that any particular form of war is more likely than any other."[172] Both Secretary Dulles and General Twining were on record with the view that the use of tactical nuclear weapons would not necessarily cause a small war to expand into a general nuclear war.[173] General LeMay pointed out that deterrence was in the enemy's mind. "It is my belief," he said, "that the enemy will not consider as a deterrent a force which he considers weaker than his force.... I think we would be gambling more than we should with the security of the country if we should assume that a weaker force will deter him from attack."[174]

Appearing before the National Security Council early in 1958, General Taylor asked that the annual basic national security policy directive be changed to accord limited war forces an active role in future military operations and the atomic-retaliatory forces a passive role. Where ground forces in Europe had been the "shield" behind which the United States could wield its atomic sword, Taylor urged that the atomic retaliatory forces had become the shield that would ward off hostile atomic attack while the limited war forces would constitute the flexible sword. Failing to agree with General Taylor, the National Security Council found no changes in the international situation that justified a change in the basic security policy. In midsummer the Department of Defense issued guidelines providing that the defense budget for fiscal year 1960 would approximate that of 1959 and would retain the same percentage allocations to individual services.[175] As a result the 1960 fiscal year budget proposed a total of $41.2 billion in new obligational authority, to be subdivided $9.5 billion for the Army, $11.7 billion for the Navy, and $19.1 billion for the Air Force.[176]

While the Department of Defense budgetary decisions were being made, two separate incidents tested the capabilities of United States forces. The first incident occurred in the Middle East, where, in an effort to stabilize chaotic affairs, President Eisenhower had announced, with congressional approval on 5 January 1957, that the United States would provide economic and possibly military aid to any nation that asked for it and would employ armed force "to secure and protect the territorial integrity and political independence of nations requesting such aid against overt armed aggression from any nation controlled by international Communism." In November 1957 the Joint Chiefs of Staff directed the commander in chief, Naval Forces Eastern Atlantic and Mediterranean, to plan for limited action in the Middle East in the event of an overthrow of the Jordanian government or a coup d'état in Lebanon.[177]

For several weeks after political unrest and riots first broke out in Lebanon on 9 May 1958, the Lebanese government made no request for assistance and it seemed that the country would be able to settle its own internal problems; but in the early hours of 14 July a military coup d'état overthrew the prowestern government of Iraq. Because of widespread unrest both Lebanon and Jordan feared a similar fate. In this crisis the government of Lebanon immediately sought military assistance from the United States, while Jordan appealed to the United Kingdom to send in troops to prevent disorder. Following President Eisenhower's decision to assist Lebanon, Adm James L. Holloway, Jr., the commander in chief, Eastern Atlantic and Mediterranean, was designated commander in chief, Specified Command Middle East, to execute Operation Blue Bat for the reinforcement of Lebanon. Within 24 hours, elements of the US Sixth Fleet landed a battalion of Marines near Beirut. Augmented by C-124 transports of the Military Air Transport Service (MATS), the United States Air Forces in Europe (USAFE) airlifted Army Task Force Alpha from Rhein-Main Air Base to Lebanon via Adana Airfield in Turkey and began to provide logistical support to the Americans in Lebanon and to the British forces in Jordan. At 1000 hours on 15 July the Joint

Chiefs of Staff directed that the Tactical Air Command dispatch Composite Air Strike Force (CASF) Bravo under the command of Maj Gen Henry Viccellio to Incirlik Air Base at Adana, Turkey. Taking off within two hours from Myrtle Beach, South Carolina, the first F-100s refueled three times en route; after following a circuitous route to avoid certain Mediterranean countries, they arrived at Incirlik in less than 13 hours. Within 24 hours 36 F-100s were at Incirlik and ready to support the ground forces. Troop carrier congestion at the forward base then forced Task Force Bravo to hold a part of its forces in France. However, within 50 hours the entire CASF — two F-100 squadrons, one B-57 tactical bomber squadron, and one RF-101/RB-66 composite tactical reconnaissance squadron — was in Europe, and in less than four days it was established at Incirlik. The Tactical Air Command employed its own tanker aircraft on the Atlantic crossing; it also kept several of the tankers in the air over Beirut to refuel the tactical aircraft that covered the air landings of Army troops. Flown with USAFE C-130s and MATS C-124s, the airlift effort of 110 planes moved 3,103 troops and 5,078 tons of equipment from Europe to Adana, while the CASF airlift effort amounted to the movement of 860 personnel and 202 tons of equipment from the United States to Adana. At the peak of the buildup in early August, about 6,000 Marines and 8,000 Army troops were in Lebanon. The crisis cleared rapidly after the election of a new Lebanese president, and the American forces were withdrawn between mid-August and October 1958.[178]

As the situation in the Middle East was beginning to resolve itself, the Soviet Union and Communist China provoked another crisis in the Formosa or Taiwan Straits on the other side of the world. In this area Chinese Nationalist garrisons held the offshore islands of Quemoy and Matsu. In accordance with the Formosa resolution of January 1955, the president of the United States was authorized "to include the securing and protecting of such related positions and territories of that area now in friendly hands and the taking of such other measures as he judges to be required or appropriate in assuring the defense of Formosa and the Pescadores." In July 1958 the Chinese Communists intensified their threats to "liberate" Taiwan (Formosa) and began to move jet fighter aircraft into previously vacant airfields in Fukien Province opposite the Nationalist base on Taiwan. After four days of secret talks in Peking, Premiers Mao Tse-tung and Nikita Khrushchev issued a communiqué on 3 August demanding withdrawal of Anglo-American forces from the Middle East. The Communists (Reds) began to overfly Quemoy and Matsu and improved their interceptions of Nationalist reconnaissance sorties over the coastal mainland of China. On 18 August the Reds began to bombard Quemoy with artillery sited in nearby coastal positions. After an intensified bombardment, the Communist radio beamed a warning on 29 August that "a landing is imminent" and urged the Quemoy garrison to withdraw.[179]

As a part of a general reorganization in the Pacific on 1 July 1957, the US Pacific Command (PAC) — as the unified theater headquarters superior to the Pacific Fleet, Army Pacific, and Pacific Air Forces — had assumed general responsibility for theater operations, including the United States commitments in defense of

Taiwan. On 6 August 1958 the Air Force directed its commanders to examine their plans to support the CINCPAC plan for the defense of Taiwan. With the worsening of the crisis, the Joint Chiefs of Staff ordered the aircraft carriers USS *Essex* in the Mediterranean and the USS *Midway* at Pearl Harbor to join the Seventh Fleet off Taiwan. On 25 August the Joint Chiefs also authorized the deployment to Taiwan of a Marine fighter-interceptor group from Japan and an Air Force fighter-interceptor squadron from Okinawa. The Army was directed to expedite the shipment of a Nike battalion from Texas to Taiwan. Since the Nineteenth Air Force was already committed to the CASF operation in the Middle East, the Tactical Air Command directed its Twelfth Air Force to prepare CASF Xray Tango for movement to the Far East if needed. At 1400 hours on 29 August the Tactical Air Command was directed to deploy the force, and under the leadership of Brig Gen Avelin P. Tacon the first planes carrying the task force departed their home stations at 1630 hours on the same day. Had the CASF made nonstop flights its planes could have arrived in the Far East within 48 hours flying time, but deliberate rest stops were scheduled for the crews in Hawaii, at either Midway or Wake Islands, and in Guam. With a strength of two F-100 squadrons, one B-57 squadron, two RF-101 squadrons, and two C-130 squadrons, CASF Xray Tango was completely in place on Taiwan by 12 September. Mainly as a psychological gesture, a squadron of 12 F-104 Starfighter interceptors was transported aboard C-124 transports, and these planes were put into action on 12 September after they had been reassembled. In these movements a total of 137 four-engine aircraft of the Military Air Transport Service and the Tactical Air Command airlifted 1,718 personnel and 1,088 tons of cargo. As this strength was building up, Chinese Nationalist Air Force pilots proved able to handle the Red Chinese MiG-17 aircraft in a series of engagements over the Formosa Straits. In 25 separate air encounters, the Nationalists lost four aircraft and destroyed 33 of the Red planes—four of the victories being scored with Sidewinder air-to-air missiles. After firing more than a half million rounds of artillery at Quemoy, the Reds announced a week's suspension of the shelling on 6 October. From this time onward the crisis abated, and the United States forces that were deployed to Taiwan returned to their permanent stations within the following two months.[180]

While there was no doubt that American policy had been accomplished in the Lebanon and Taiwan operations, evaluations made by high-level officials revealed a difference of opinion as to lessons to be drawn from these operations and about the nature of limited war as well. To Secretary McElroy the Lebanon and Taiwan operations gave assurance as to the United States capability for limited war. He considered that the response in Lebanon had deterred the outbreak of hostilities and that the action in Taiwan had confined the conflict and had permitted a discontinuation of it to be worked out. "The speed with which you respond," McElroy observed, "is really as important as the force with which you respond." McElroy considered that Lebanon and Taiwan were examples of limited wars. "We do not consider that Korea [was] a limited war," he added. "We consider that if you had to do Korea again, you probably would handle things somewhat differently."

He also emphasized that the United States did not intend to fight a limited war with the Soviet Union. "The people of this country," he said, "should realize that if we are going to fight Russia, we are not going to fight them on the ground in the main. There will be some conflict on the ground, but general war is the only kind of war that we visualize fighting with Russia."[181] Speaking on the subject of Lebanon and Taiwan, General Twining called attention to the fact that in each case the United States had been given several weeks to ready its forces and to react. Since no shots had been fired by American units supply problems had been simple. Twining, nevertheless, estimated that the United States "could carry a half dozen" engagements like these, but an engagement of the size of Korea would be a different matter. In Twining's view the Korean conflict was "a big limited-war operation" and if a limited war of similar size occurred in the future its requirements would have to be met by the mobilization of reserve forces.[182]

In presenting the Air Force assessment of the Lebanon and Taiwan crises, General White asserted: "The Soviets have been contained not by the US battalions and ships and tactical aircraft that we deployed but to a great degree by the established capability of American long-range air power." In the case of the Quemoy crisis, however, White added that "the Chinese Communists and perhaps the Russians themselves received a considerable shock with the rapidity with which we reacted and with the efficiency of our forces that were there — and by 'our forces' I am including the Chinese Nationalists."[183] General Power saw Lebanon and Quemoy as illustrations of the deterrence of both general and small wars. "Quemoy," he said, "was even better than Lebanon, because here we took a firm stand for a pile of so-called useless rocks. But it was notice to the world that this country stands for something, that we have principles and oppose the principle of blackmail through military force. If we were willing to stand up and risk war for some so-called useless rocks, what better proof could we give of our determination to stand up to a more serious incident?" Power said that during the Quemoy crisis the Strategic Air Command had been prepared to back up the other forces with planes that could carry "any yield weapon." While he did not think it would be efficient to employ SAC crews to drop conventional weapons, Power pointed out that he could "convert into that posture very rapidly in a matter of hours." Lebanon and Quemoy, Power said, "were real actions to deter war. The reason we could prevent those actions from expanding is that we had the Strategic Air Command backing these forces up."[184] In a delayed analysis General LeMay emphasized the role the American military aid and friendly foreign forces had played in the Lebanon and Taiwan efforts. "Assets such as bases and support capabilities as well as many additional items which comprise an effective small war readiness," he said, "are direct results of the Military Assistance Program. Without these benefits, such operations as last year's deployment of units to ... both the Mideast and Far East to assist our allies could not have been accomplished."[185]

According to Secretary Brucker and General Taylor, the Lebanon and Quemoy crises were the latest incidents in a pattern of 18 episodes since World War II in which the presence or pressure of Communist forces had been felt and exploited either directly or indirectly. From this pattern, Brucker drew the lesson that the Communists were using limited war as a device to achieve their objectives on a piecemeal basis. When he was asked to define a limited war, Taylor found it easier to say that a general war was "a war between the United States and the Soviet Union in which they are participating and in which atomic weapons are used freely from the outset." A limited war was "any military conflict short of a general war, one in which our national existence is not at stake." Taylor described Lebanon as "perhaps the extreme of the small limited war," and he believed that the advanced warning, limited force requirement, and lack of combat operations made conditions so favorable for the success of the Lebanon operation as to make it imprudent to attempt to draw conclusions from the experience. Taylor also admitted under questioning that no Army forces would have been required in a Formosan operation. "If we had to go into Formosa in sizable strength," he said, ". . . it would be largely an air and naval operation." As he looked at the problem of limited war, however, Taylor saw "primarily an Army requirement related to sustained combat on the ground, which is an Army task." Viewing the problem of limited war in this light, he urged a five-point program to improve limited war capabilities; namely, the modernization of appropriate equipment, the improved strategic mobility of limited war forces, the use of preplanned airlift and sealift, expanded joint planning and training, and the advertisement of such limited war strength once it was a reality.[186]

While the national military leaders tended to draw different lessons from Lebanon and Quemoy, there were some essential elements of agreement. In its report of the fiscal year 1959 military budget, the House Committee on Appropriations had called for a new study of the role of the super aircraft carrier in modern warfare. After Lebanon and Quemoy, Admiral Burke could state that "the deployed attack carrier task force with modern aircraft—teamed with a marine landing force—is the logical ready military force to counter the threats of limited war in many areas of the world."[187] Without derogating the importance of the aircraft carrier, General Taylor's personal opinion was that "we have an ample number of carriers." Taylor remembered that "in Korea, which was a large limited war, we never had nor needed more than four carriers on station."[188] General White accepted the new implication that an aircraft carrier was more suited for limited than general war, but he opposed a new carrier because he preferred "to see the money that must go into the carrier go on some other weapon system which I would conceive to be more important."[189] Responding to a question, Doctor York was quoted as saying that the Lebanon emergency had demonstrated the importance of carriers, destroyers, and possibly cruisers as "distant bases." He added, however, that in a major war against a "highly sophisticated enemy like Russia, they are going to be blown up."[190] Nonetheless, as a result of what Secretary McElroy described as "soul searching . . . at the very highest level of Government," the Department of Defense budget for fiscal 1960 included the construction of another *Forrestal*-class aircraft carrier. "The importance of the carrier as a means of projecting our military power for a limited war situation into the peripheral areas of the world," he explained, "was very clearly demonstrated in both Lebanon and Taiwan."[191] Where the CASF deployment to Lebanon had encountered problems where overflight rights were denied and where available airfields were scarce and became congested, the Department of Defense noted that the aircraft carrier was "a very important cold war instrument" since it provided "a very effective limited warfare capability in places where overflight rights for aircraft are often unobtainable and in place where landing fields often do not exist."[192]

In the months prior to Lebanon and Quemoy, both Secretary Dulles and General Twining had voiced the opinion that tactical nuclear weapons might be used without necessarily expanding a small war into a general nuclear war. During these crises, however, the Soviets attempted to convince the world that any use of atomic weapons would mean general war. At the height of the Quemoy crisis on 7 September, Khrushchev wrote Eisenhower, warning: "An attack upon the Chinese People's Republic... is an attack upon the Soviet Union."[193] In another letter on 19 September, Khrushchev declared that: "Those who carry out plans of atomic attack on the Chinese People's Republic should not forget that not only the US but the other side possesses not only atomic but hydrogen weapons and also the corresponding means of delivery, and should such an attack be delivered on the Chinese People's Republic, then the aggressor will receive a fitting rebuff by the same means." President Eisenhower rejected Khrushchev's threat as abusive.[194] But the threat that local war could expand into general war if nuclear weapons were used could not be ignored. Vice Adm Charles R. Brown, commander of the US Sixth Fleet in the Mediterranean, subsequently stated: "I would not recommend the use of any atomic weapons no matter how small, when both sides have the power to destroy the world.... I have no faith in the so-called controlled use of atomic weapons."[195]

The experience of Lebanon and Quemoy thus appeared to justify General Taylor's argument before the National Security Council earlier in 1958 that, in many limited war situations, the United States would not wish to employ nuclear weapons. "We would always go into a military operation prepared to use nuclear weapons," Taylor explained in March 1959, "because we never know what the outcome is going to be. The decision to use them... would be determined by the President."[196] About this same time, Gen Henry I. Hodes, commander in chief, US Army Europe, defined limited war as a conflict "in which atomic weapons may not be used freely or on a large scale in the beginning and one in which our national survival is not at stake at least initially."[197] Much of this thinking on tactical nuclear weapons coincided with Gen O. P. Weyland's already expressed belief that flexibility demanded the retention of conventional ordnance delivery characteristics in tactical aircraft.[198] A Tactical Air Command officer who visited Adana during the Lebanon crisis found a considerable doubt as to whether the CASF crews could have performed conventional weapon delivery missions, although all of them were fully qualified in the delivery of nuclear weapons. "Only a few of the F-100 pilots had strafed," he stated, "none had shot rockets or delivered conventional bombs." The B-57 crews were also regarded as "incapable of performing efficient conventional weapon delivery."[199]

Despite a recognition that it would have had difficulty conducting a conventional, limited war operation with crews that had been trained for the delivery of nuclear weapons, the Air Force remained somewhat less than enthusiastic on the subject of conventional weapons. "We will carry out any instruction we are given," noted Lt Gen Charles S. Irvine, deputy chief of staff for materiel, "and we can fight an iron bomb war if that is what the President says he wants us to do.... We can only say if you want to destroy targets efficiently, we can do it better with a nuclear bomb."[200] As commander in chief, US Air Forces in Europe, Gen Frederic H. Smith, Jr., believed that many men in scientific, governmental, and military circles evidently lacked an understanding that tactical nuclear weapons would be employed without destroying countries or populations. In the spring of 1960 he accordingly published an article designed "to demonstrate that not only can the intelligent use of nuclear firepower in limited war give us the greatest possible opportunity to win such wars at a minimum cost to us and to the country we may be defending against aggression, but that it is highly probable that without the use of such weapons our chances of winning in many areas are slim indeed." Smith ruled out the possibility of a limited war in Europe, but he suggested that tactical nuclear weapons could have been precisely employed with great effect in Korea and in Indochina without serious danger of having provoked all-out war. To prevent haphazard employment of nuclear weapons in a limited war, he stated that higher authority would have to provide a local war commander with explicit objectives, including a restriction on strikes outside a delimited zone of hostilities. He noted that new criteria for tactical nuclear targets needed to be developed: these could include "situation-control" targets such as narrow gorges in mountains that could be closed by landslides or forest cover which could be defoliated with nuclear weapons, thus denying concealment to an enemy. "We must achieve through education and through the development of clear-cut, logical tactical doctrine," Smith concluded, "a general acceptance by the United States of the requirement for the use of nuclear weapons in limited war. This country cannot afford the tremendous outlay in dollars, resources, and men needed to defeat aggression by man-to-man combat on the ground, supported only by high-explosive bombs and rockets, napalm, and machine-cannon fire delivered from the air."[201] Although General Smith's article was well reasoned, the Lebanon and Taiwan crises, nevertheless, had demonstrated that American political and military leaders were reluctant to commit nuclear weapons to limited wars. After a study of the matter, Col Albert P. Sights, Jr., concluded: "The crises in Lebanon and in the Taiwan Strait... marked a turning point in relying on nuclear weapons for limited wars. Thereafter planners were more inclined to accept the premise that such crises—if they turned into wars—would be conventional, at least at the outset."[202]

Minimum Deterrence or Counterforce?

Speaking in support of the Department of Defense fiscal year 1960 budget in January 1959, Secretary McElroy accepted the Air Force position that the military forces which deter or win general wars would also be able to deter or to win small wars. "It is erroneous to view the US military posture," he said, "as containing a distinct general war capability per se. In reality, those capabilities which the United States has for a limited war are equally applicable to general war and those capabilities which the United States has for general war are, with a few exceptions, equally applicable to limited war."[203] In this statement McElroy also indicated that the United States defense policy was not prepared to accept the concept of minimum deterrence, but the congressional budget hearings held early in 1959 were marked by a growing vocalization of the concept.

Initially held by a ground of diverse European intellectuals, the rationale of minimum deterrence was perhaps best summarized by Britain's nuclear physicist-neutralist P. M. S. Blackett, who reasoned: "If it is, in fact, true, as most current opinion holds, that strategic airpower has abolished global war, then an urgent problem for the West is to assess how little effort must be put into it to keep global war abolished."[204] The proposition of minimum deterrence was persuasive to many persons, including General Taylor, who in an unpublished article prepared in 1956, expressed the view that:

> The avoidance of deliberate general atomic war should not be too difficult since its unremunerative character must be clear to the potential adversaries. Although actual stockpile sizes are closely guarded secrets, a nation need only feel reasonably sure that an opponent has some high-yield weapons, no matter how indefinite their exact number, to be impressed with the possible consequences of attacking him. [205]

In his appearance before the Subcommittee of the House Committee on Appropriations on 29 January 1959, General Taylor first informed the public of the schism in strategic thought within the Department of Defense. Taking note of the fact that he would retire as Army chief of staff on 30 June, Taylor stated flatly that the nation had an excessive number of strategic weapons and weapon systems in its atomic retaliatory force—the aggregate of bombers in the Air Force, the Navy, and the oversea American and allied commands; the ICBMs and IRBMs in the Air Force; and the Polaris system in the Navy. Taylor reasoned that it was

> possible to establish that "x" targets successfully attacked with "y" megatons is equal to the destruction of the enemy....Then, having determined the bombs required on target, you can calculate all the possible losses due to enemy action, aborts, ineffectiveness of the weapons, and so forth, and determine how many delivery vehicles are required. When such a computation is made, you end up, in my book, not with thousands, but with hundreds of vehicles as a requirement.

In response to a question, Taylor estimated that the United States possessed a capability to annihilate the enemy some 10 times. In a subsequent appearance before the Preparedness Investigation Subcommittee of the Senate Armed

Services Committee on 11 March, Taylor urged that the defense budget ought to be made functional by mission areas rather than to continue to make appropriations by services. Such mission areas could include general war forces and limited war forces. "There is," he explained, "a fundamental need to determine standards of sufficiency in the various categories of military forces which we maintain and to which all services contribute."[206]

General Taylor's charge that the United States possessed thousands of units to deliver strategic nuclear strikes when only hundreds were needed—a condition soon popularly described as "overkill"—drew support from Navy officers in appearances both in and out of Congress. Early in February 1959 Admiral Burke informed the House Subcommittee on Appropriations that he believed the United States possessed too much retaliatory power and ought to put more money into limited war capabilities. "Right now," he said, "I think there is nothing Russia can do to prevent her from being destroyed. . . . What we can destroy would be the ability of Russia to continue a war. . . . We would break her back. . . . You would not strike every military target, but you would strike enough of them to prevent Russia from recovering. You would break her back."[207] Admiral Hayward reasoned that deterrence of war comprised "what the Russian planner thinks, not what you or I think. If he thinks he is going to be destroyed no matter what he does, he is not going to start it." Hayward added: "If you have a system that is invulnerable to surprise attack and effective so it would be possible to be effective even if a man read in the *New York Times* we were attacked, and still destroy your enemy, this is the thing you are working for. . . . Any system completely vulnerable to a surprise attack is a weak one, deterrence should be inevitable."[208] Some days later Hayward told inquiring senators that he believed "in the years to come, any system that is vulnerable to surprise attack will fade from the scene."[209] What the Navy had in mind in the way of future deterrent capabilities began to be evident on 5 February when Admiral Burke stated: "To knock out the *Polaris* weapon system . . . the enemy would have to knock out all the *Polaris* submarines simultaneously. They would have to kill all of these submarines at the same time they initiated their attack. I think that this is impossible."[210] When asked during a national television interview on 22 March how many *Polaris* submarines would be needed, Burke replied: "You can take from the number of Russian cities the number of megatons it takes to destroy a Russian city, the reliability of the missiles, the accuracy of the missile, and you can compute it pretty accurately yourself. And then you double it just to make sure and you come out someplace in the neighborhood of perhaps 30."[211]

As advanced by Navy spokesmen, the strategy of minimum deterrence—or finite deterrence as it was soon called apparently to avoid a connotation of gambling with the nation's safety—visualized that a positive threat and a capability of destroying between 100 and 200 Soviet civilian centers of population would be sufficient to deter the enemy.[212] Writing under the title, "Finite Deterrence, Controlled Retaliation," in the *US Naval Institute Proceedings* in March 1959, Comdr P. H. Backus, executive secretary of the Navy Ballistic Missile Committee, provided a coherent description of the strategy of minimum or finite deterrence.

Backus reasoned that the Soviet capability to deliver thermonuclear intercontinental ballistic missiles had rendered obsolete the strategy and the force commitment of massive retaliation. Because of its vulnerability the Strategic Air Command was being compelled to disperse to hardened bases, but the hardening of SAC bases promised to set off an arms race since the Soviets could also harden their bases. To plan upon the blunting operations of the massive retaliation strategy—Backus equated blunting with counterforce—would also set off a spiraling arms race since proportional additions to the US deterrent or retaliatory forces would be required each time the Soviets added a new missile or a new air base. The weakness of the United States deterrent posture was its vulnerability. "If then," Backus reasoned, "our deterrent/retaliatory forces were relatively invulnerable, no matter what the Russians tried to do, we might in fact truly put behind us the frightening possibilities of general nuclear war." Backus asserted that the Polaris submarine would be the perfect weapon for finite deterrence since it possessed inherent invulnerability to a considerably higher degree than any other weapon system. If the Soviets knew that even if they launched a surprise attack the majority of their industrial concentrations would be reduced to rubble, they would not initiate a deliberate attack. In the event that the Soviets accidentally initiated a general war, Backus proposed that the United States should hit back instantly and hard by destroying two or three predesignated Soviet cities. In this case the United States would retaliate in a controlled manner, allowing time for negotiation between strikes. Such controlled retaliation would be destructive, but it would not reduce the world to rubble. Backus pointed out that the United States had compelled Japan to surrender in World War II by progressively destroying her cities.[213]

Both in public statements and in his book *The Uncertain Trumpet,* which he published in 1959 following his retirement, General Taylor wrapped up the proposals for finite deterrence, the avoidance of overkill, and the determination of standards of sufficiency in various categories of forces in one comprehensive outline for a new national strategy of flexible response. Taylor visualized

> the rejection of a strategy of massive retaliation and the adopting of one of flexible response; the determination of how much is enough for all categories of operational functions; the subsequent building of a small mobile and secure missile force and a fully modernized Army and supporting services; a revised structure for the military budget to show clearly what it buys in terms of operational forces; and a new statement of roles and missions to show, then, what we really mean by the Army, Navy, and Air Force.[214]

The grave need to prevent nuclear war without draining the national economy provoked a great debate on the subject of flexible response, overkill, finite deterrence, and the other proposals offered by Taylor and Burke. A new generation of civilian military analysts—many of whom had worked in the think factories such as Research and Development (Rand) Corporation and the Army's Operations Research Office—joined political and military thinkers in the great debate on strategy. In the debate, Department of Defense and Air Force spokesmen found it difficult to engage in a many-faced discussion of a new strategy without disclosing security aspects of the existing United States war plan. As the Department of Defense pointed out, moreover, it was practically impossible to answer General Taylor's question: How much is enough? This question had always been one of the most difficult ones faced by military planners and was under constant study. But it was impossible to determine standards of sufficiency in neat categories of force commitments and still preserve the versatility and flexibility requisite to the fact that there was no clear line of demarcation that would be drawn between limited war forces and general war forces in all cases.[215] Under these circumstances Air Force spokesmen found it necessary to debate the proposed new strategy in detail rather than in its generalities.

The central theme of the new deterrent strategy was the proposition that a general nuclear war had lost its utility as a means of resolving international conflict. "A nuclear war," the proponents of finite deterrence warned, "is too horrible to contemplate, too mutually annihilating to consider." For many years the Strategic Air Command had used the motto Peace is Our Profession, and a ranking Air Force commander had said, "if nuclear war breaks out, SAC has failed in its mission." General White, however, was unwilling to agree that all participants in a nuclear war would be defeated. "I think," he said, "nuclear war is something that is horrible and difficult to contemplate, but I am afraid that is the sort of thing civilization is faced with."[216] White consistently maintained that the United States and its allies "must possess combat capabilities which can deter or — if necessary — defeat" Soviet aerospace forces.[217] In briefings and papers prepared at the Rand Corporation and published as a book entitled *On Thermonuclear War,* physicist Herman Kahn presented the case that thermonuclear war was not unthinkable but probable, and he reasoned that with proper precautions the United States could survive such a war even though great casualties were incurred.[218] While many Defense spokesmen began to visualize the prospect that the United States would seek to "prevail" rather than to "win" in a thermonuclear war, an Air Force policy paper submitted to Congress in March 1960 insisted that the nation must possess a "war-winning capability."[219] The Air Force considered that there were sound strategic reasons for maintaining a war-winning capability in its strategic striking forces. Retired Air Force Brig Gen S. F. Giffin also suggested that the rationale of a military man required a concept that conflict could be resolved. "The military mind," he wrote, "cannot but accept General MacArthur's dictum that there is no substitute for victory. Yet the meaning of victory in a total nuclear war would be more in terms of the *survival* of the United States as a self-determining power — and the elimination of the present principal threat to the integrity of the United States — than in terms of classic military triumph."[220]

In view of the long-standing policy that the United States would not strike the first blow in a war, the Air Force had followed the policy during the 1950s that strategic capabilities must be prepared to accept the enemy's first strike and then be able to strike back effectively. As long as the Strategic Air Command was the nation's main deterrent force, the matter of first or second strike was relatively unimportant since the maintenance of the command at a level of strength needed to survive a hostile first strike ensured that it would possess capabilities needed for a first strike. The concept of finite deterrence vastly changed this strategic equation, and in January 1959 General Power insisted: "You always must have a capability to strike first, because obviously if these people thought we never could start a war, why, then they could just take this world away from us, piece by piece, because they would know that as long as they do not strike us, we could never do anything about it. So you must have a capability to strike first."[221] Unless the United States possessed a superiority of force, General Schriever demonstrated that it could not possess what he called a positive deterrent. He defined positive deterrent as a posture

> which permits this country to take the initiative militarily if it wants to take the initiative, or one which inhibits the Soviet from taking the initiative in the fields of limited warfare, in the field of economic and psychological warfare. Such a deterrent posture is achieved only if we can knock out all of this military capability to strike us. This means hard targets, in fact every military target which has the capability of waging total war against this Nation.[222]

In the process of developing the reasons for maintaining a first-strike capability, Air Force spokesmen were careful to note that they did not contemplate preventive war or the initiation of a war on a nation's own timing. Nevertheless, they offered the opinion that the first-strike capability might be used for preemptive war, or attacks that might be made by a nation which had received positive tactical warning of an impending enemy attack. A preventive war might be launched months in advance of an anticipated attack, but a preemptive attack could be made hours or even minutes before the launching of a hostile strike.[223] If the United States strategic force had the ability to make an almost instantaneous reaction, the United States, moreover, would be able to make strikes while enemy aerospace vehicles were en route to their targets but before they reached their assigned targets.[224]

The Air Force leaders found it difficult to determine what the exact size of a minimum deterrent force would be, but they were sure that it would not be a small aggregation of nuclear missiles capable only of destroying Soviet cities. "People sometimes ask me," said General Power,

> what I think the minimum deterrent force is. They ask as though it were a package that one could get at the local store and buy off the shelf with a price tag on it.... I tell these people, I don't know what the minimum deterrent is, and what is more, there is nobody in this world who knows.... If anybody tells you they know what the minimum deterrent is, tell them for me that they are liars. The closest to one man who would know what the minimum deterrent is, would be Mr. Khrushchev, and frankly I don't think he knows from 1 week to another. He might be willing to absorb more punishment next week than he wants to absorb today.

Power also pointed out that no one should assume that what would deter the United States would deter the Soviet bloc. The United States had sustained some

600,000 casualties in its Civil War; the Soviet Union had killed an estimated 9,000,000 people in the Revolution and had lost some 20,000,000 people in World War II; while the Chinese Communists were said to have "liquidated" as many as 20,000,000 to 30,000,000 persons in their revolutionary effort. Americans and Communists, thus, attached different values to human life. As for the overkill charge, Power estimated that the Strategic Air Command received about 18 percent of the defense dollar while it carried more than 90 percent of the responsibility for deterrence. "If that is babying and pampering," he concluded, "I do not agree with you."[225]

Although the Air Force began to advance counterforce as a more desirable alternative than finite deterrence, Air Force leaders were initially unable to provide a complete rationale for a counterforce strategy. At least at first, counterforce evolved not as a positive statement but in opposition to the "counter-city" aspects of finite deterrence. Writing in March 1959, as has been noted, Colonel Richardson determined that the counterforce aspect of the United States general war capability—rather than the massive retaliation aspect which would have been directed against Soviet cities—had been the effective deterrent to Soviet worldwide attack. "Failure to maintain the flexible counterforce capability we now have in our strategic effort," Richardson wrote, "will lead to establishing unlimited requirements for local defense operations. This is a policy which could lead to political, economic, and military bankruptcy, and which would almost inevitably spell defeat."[226] Again, as has been seen, General Schriever informed a congressional committee of the need not only for a first-strike force but also for a positive deterrent force that could knock out "every military target which has the capability of waging total war against this Nation." Treading lightly in discussing a sensitive area, Schriever observed that because "we may not know where some targets are located today, it does not follow that we may not know where these targets are at some future date."[227]

In an Air Force anniversary statement in September 1959, General White categorically disagreed with the overkill arguments. "Our strategic objective, in the event of global war," he said, "is to eliminate an enemy's war making capacity in the minimum period of time. In determining the force requirements needed to do this, we must take into account not only the number, location, and vulnerability of the targets but the reliability, accuracy, and warhead yield of our weapons—as well as countless operational variables and our evaluation of expected enemy defenses."[228] During the winter of 1959-60 the Air Force accepted the position that an effective force was a force in being, a force in place, and a force of such size and capability that, when measured against enemy surprise attack, retaliation by that force would be sufficient to ensure clearly unacceptable damage to the enemy; that it could destroy the enemy's nuclear delivery capability in the event the United States was forced to take the initiative; and that it would ensure that the United States would prevail regardless of the circumstances under which deterrence might fail. Even though Air Force leaders now made a clear distinction between deterrence and war-winning capability, they continued to explain counterforce by revealing the fallacy of minimum deterrence. If the United States limited the size of its long-range nuclear delivery force to a capability that would do nothing more than destroy some 100 Soviet cities, the US forces might be able to deter attack against the United States proper. However, if the Soviets attacked an ally of the United States, the possession of a minimum deterrent force would not permit the United States (even if it possessed strategic warning) to launch its forces against Soviet cities, thereby exposing itself to Soviet attack with forces that were undamaged by US strikes. On the other hand, if the United States finite deterrent failed and the enemy attacked, his first targets would doubtless be the US strategic forces. The enemy would do this to reduce the US ability to strike back, and he could well afford to save American cities as hostages for later attacks. With a minimum deterrent attrited by the enemy's first strike, the United States would lack strength for any kind of counterforce effort. If the few remaining US forces attacked Soviet cities, the Soviets could return and easily destroy American cities. "Finite deterrence," the Air Force reasoned, "is purely a bluff strategy and does not include the capability for military victory. On the other hand, the clear capability to attain military victory would be the most reliable, longest lasting, and most widely applicable deterrent that the enemy could face. Thus we must plan a counterforce strategy and back it with the weapons systems needed in the amounts needed."[229] At least three civilian strategists found reason in the Air Force arguments, for Robert Strausz-Hupe, William R. Kintner, and Stefan F. Possony soon described the strategy of finite deterrence as "a mutual suicide pact."[230]

Because they appeared to offer economy, a check on the arms race, and reduction of devastation, the proposals for minimum deterrence plus limited war and arms control were said to have been accepted by many intellectuals interested in military affairs, a vast majority of foreign and domestic lay analysts, and many military planners.[231] In December 1959, however, James E. King, Jr., Paul H. Nitze, and Arnold Wolfers, research associates of the Washington Center of Foreign Policy Research, completed a study for the Senate Foreign Relations Committee that gave a limited endorsement to counterforce. This study recommended that top priority be given to reducing the vulnerability and improving the penetration abilities of American and allied strategic forces, to accelerating the development of solid-fuel intercontinental ballistic missiles and emplacing them in hardened and mobile configurations, to strengthening the forces capable of dealing with lesser aggressions ranging from subversion to very substantial conventional attacks on free overseas nations, to equipping American and allied troops with dual-purpose nuclear and conventional weapons, and to exploiting space technology for defense. It recommended that the overriding purpose of the US strategic weapons program ought not to be the matching of assumed Soviet capabilities in intercontinental missiles but the early attainment of an inventory of diverse and relatively secure systems that would prevent the enemy from risking a surprise attack. It suggested that the United States ought not to seek to maintain a first-strike strategic force, since such action would negate a more desirable alternative "aimed at increasing the stability of the strategic equation by unilateral action, by the encouragement of reciprocal action, and by an arms control policy directed at strategic stability." The United States, nevertheless, should retain in its second-strike strategic force "a measure of counterforce ability sufficient for rational target selection in a retaliatory strike, as well as for limited war capabilities and other purposes." Although the goal of maintaining an effective first-strike force would become increasingly difficult and even undesirable in terms of strategic stability, there were several reasons for making a continued effort to maintain counterforce capabilities. First, if a local or limited war should break out, the United States would be severely handicapped in its choices of action if it had no means of hitting elements of the enemy's strategic force, while the enemy had substantial counterforce capabilities. Second, in a general nuclear war following a hostile first-strike, counterforce capabilities would enable the United States to conduct militarily useful operations and to minimize the damage to its population and industrial centers that might be inflicted by subsequent Soviet strategic strikes. Third, only by continuing research in counterforce weapons could the United States ensure against still unforeseen technological developments that might upset the strategic balance. Finally, American possession of counterforce weapons would force the Soviets to divert funds to expensive defense efforts that might otherwise be expanded for the creation of an overwhelming Soviet first-strike counterforce capability. In the chaos and confusion attending the launching of a second strike following an initial Soviet attack, the United States would quite probably attack both city and counterforce targets. The study, nevertheless, recommended that "in order to maximize the military value of such a strike and to minimize the dangers to civilian populations, a major effort can and should be made to direct the retaliatory attack against the enemy's strategic forces and targets as much as conditions permit."[232]

If the proponents of finite deterrence expected a change in security policy when newly appointed Secretary Gates began to put together the defense budget for fiscal year 1961, they were doomed to disappointment. According to General Taylor there was to be no change in the basic national security policy. The Eisenhower administration ruled that the international situation, the state of military technology, and the general economic situation which prevailed in the autumn of 1959 demanded that the fiscal 1961 military budget not exceed the level of expenditures during fiscal 1960.[233] Although service requests for fiscal 1961 budgeting totaled $43.9 billion in new obligational authority, the final defense budget submitted to Congress in January 1960 amounted to $40.5 billion.[234] When he appeared in defense of this budget on 13 January 1960, Secretary Gates pointed out that military forces could not be arbitrarily categorized as general or limited war forces. "All forces," he emphasized, "are a deterrent to and would be employed in a general war. Most of our forces could be employed in a limited war, if required. For example, air defense aircraft and antiaircraft missiles can be, and in fact are, deployed overseas. The aircraft of the Strategic Air Command could also be used if needed." When he spoke of the enemy, Gates asserted that

> in order to maintain a valid deterrent we have to maintain a deterrent force capable of knocking out his military power and not just bombing his cities. What we would actually do depends on circumstances, but we are adjusting our power to a counterforce theory; or a mixture of a counterforce theory plus attacks on industrial centers and things of that character. We are not basing our requirement on just bombing Russia for retaliation purposes.... The validity of our deterrent must be of such a character... that an enemy will believe his military power will be devastated.[235]

In his appearances before congressional committees during the early months of 1960, Gen Lyman Lemnitzer, the new Army chief of staff, voiced his personal belief that the Soviets and the free world were approaching a period when both would possess "a virtually indestructible nuclear capability" and that this situation would render limited war more likely. "Under such circumstances," he remarked, "it seems to me that the most likely form of conflict may well involve the use of integrated land, sea, and air forces in their modernized, yet basically traditional, roles." Lemnitzer was not as adamant on the subject of overkill as his predecessor had been: he recognized that the development of highly effective Soviet surface-to-air missile defenses promised to increase the attrition of American bombers.[236] Appearing before these same committees, Navy officers continued to argue the case for finite deterrence and to stress overkill. Admiral Burke subscribed to all the statements he had made on these matters a year earlier, and he still felt that the United States was overconcentrating in retaliatory forces, although the balance was getting better. Just as he saw no reason why the United States should build overkill forces, he professed not to fear Soviet overkill. "No matter what Russia does," he said, "there is no possibility she can avoid destruction. She is going to get a terrific beating if she starts a war, no matter how or when.... If she builds 500 missiles or 2,000 missiles and does it in 7, 8, 10, or 15 years, sometime in the future, it does not affect our deterrent capability."[237] Speaking even more positively than previously, Admiral Hayward asserted that if he could have his way he would put the entire deterrent force at sea. He specified the total number of megatons placed on targets in Russia that he considered to be adequate as a US deterrent. Although this total was not disclosed in the public record, Hayward noted that 45 *Polaris* submarines would "come close" to providing the total deterrent that the United States needed.[238]

In stating the Air Force requirement for a first-strike counterforce capability, General White characterized finite deterrence as equating with the abandoned Fortress America concept. He pointed out that finite deterrence would be extremely dangerous since such a posture would not provide the military forces needed "to minimize the damage on the United States under any circumstances." He also found finite deterrence inconsistent with requirements of modern war. "Modern warfare," he said, "has as its objective—No. 1, the destruction of the enemy's capability to fight; and secondly, his will to fight." Finally, White pointed out that a finite deterrent posture would strip the United States of its influence in the world. "A nation which does not have the capability to go on the initiative, have the capability to knock out the enemy's military power," he asserted, "is hopeless in my opinion, politically, diplomatically, and militarily."[239] In an article describing the fallacy of minimum deterrence, which he published in the spring of 1960, Brig Gen Robert C. Richardson III stated that city-bombing violated two basic principles: "The only rational military objective in war is the enemy forces, or targets that affect forces. Destruction which does not affect the outcome of the war in one's favor is irrational and politically and morally unjustifiable." Although the strategic bombing campaigns of World War II had been directed against hostile industry for good reason, production and mobilization would contribute little or nothing to the outcome in an atomic war. "Today," he wrote, "victory lies not in the ability to destroy the enemy industrial and manpower potential but rather in the ability to destroy his *existing* capability for delivering destruction." As for the allegation that Soviet missile sites could not be targeted, Richardson pointed out that new intelligence techniques should provide knowledge of the construction of hardened missile sites, that the vulnerability of mobile missiles to slight overpressures should allow them to be targeted and attacked on an area basis with the help of reconnaissance, and that within the time frame of concern the United States would have constant satellite surveillance that should provide intelligence on missile movements or site construction. "The minimum-deterrent strategy sought by critics of the existing counterforce deterrent capability," Richardson wrote in summary, "is one which would lead to unlimited requirements for limited war."[240]

While Admiral Burke was presenting the case for finite deterrence to the House Subcommittee on Appropriations in January 1960, Congressman Daniel J. Flood exclaimed: "This theory I do not believe. This is terrible."[241] When it reported the defense budget bill out in April, the House Committee on Appropriations expressed disbelief in finite deterrence. "In the final analysis," the committee noted, "to effectively deter a would-be aggressor, we should maintain our Armed Forces in such a way and with such an understanding that should it ever become obvious that an attack upon us or our allies is imminent, we can launch an attack before the aggressor has hit us or our allies. This is an element of deterrence which the United States should not deny itself. No other form of deterrence can be fully relied upon."[242] When final action was completed in July 1960, Congress voted $41.4 billion for defense, approximately $500 million more than President Eisenhower had requested. Most of the additional funds were allocated to the Atlas, Minuteman, Polaris, and the B-70 programs; and the total fund was to be divided to include $9.6 billion for the Army, $11.8 billion for the Navy, and $18.9 for the Air Force.[243]

Despite verbal statements by Secretary Gates, the Department of Defense budget for fiscal year 1961 did not clearly implement either a counterforce or a finite deterrence concept but actually augmented both strategic and limited war forces. It did not provide the first-strike strategic force that the Air Force considered necessary to the counterforce strategy. The compromise pleased neither side of the strategic controversy, and the great debate on strategy continued to brew.[244] "Our national policy at this writing," Herman Kahn observed in 1960, "seems to be drifting (mostly as a result of decisions evaded or decided for relatively minor technical reasons) toward accepting a strategy between finite deterrence or counterforce as insurance."[245] Strausz-Hupe, Kintner, and Possony described the official United States position as being one of "win strike second" counterforce, but an *Air Force Magazine* reviewer of their book commented: "We do not now have the capability to fight such a war even though this strategy is the most desirable.... We lack the forces needed to replace the so-called 'massive retaliation' policy."[246] On the other hand, the Naval Warfare Analysis Group issued a "Résumé of Major Strategic Considerations" on 17 October 1960 that continued to argue for a finite level of deterrence. Distributed by Navy officials and said to represent a good summary of naval views, the résumé argued that United States efforts to build counterforce capabilities, to harden missile sites, or even to construct civilian defense shelters would accelerate the arms race by forcing the enemy to develop additional overkill capability, and might even cause the enemy to fear that the United States was preparing to attack and to unleash a preemptive strike, thus starting a war rather than deterring conflict.[247]

During 1958 and 1959 the Air Force advanced counterforce as an alternative and wiser strategy than finite deterrence, but the full implications of a damage-limiting, no-city counterforce war did not become exactly evident until the early months of 1960. Working in the Pentagon, Brig Gen Noel F. Parrish, assistant for coordination to the Air Force deputy chief of staff for plans and programs, and Lt Col Donald F. Martin began to wargame existing strategic plans as opposed to a new strategic concept that made the most scrupulous efforts to employ appropriately sized weapons only against purely military targets. The new concept made sense in its own right since a good many missiles would be required to kill enemy military forces in the first place, but the real surprise was that a no-city attack plan promised a tremendous saving of civilian life in the event of a thermonuclear war between the United States and the Soviet Union. War would remain horrible, but it would not necessarily be suicidal. Taking their scratch-pad figures to General White, Parrish and Martin obtained approval to wargame the no-city counterforce strategy on the Air Force's air-battle-model computer. No matter how the situation or the force levels were changed, the no-city counterforce plan promised tremendous savings of American and Soviet life.[248]

Although the no-city plan was not yet a strategy, the air-battle-model results confirmed General White's belief that a city-destroying war did not make sense. In a landmark address delivered to the Air Force Association in September 1960, White stated: "As I see it, effective deterrence includes the possession of military forces to deter and, should war occur, the military strength to prevail. There are two key thoughts here: deter and prevail. It might appear that this is a contradiction since the ability to prevail in war is needful only if our policy of deterrence fails. Nevertheless, the ability to prevail is what provides real and effective deterrence."[249] In a subsequent message to all air commands, White soon directed that all Air Force personnel should understand counterforce and its difference from minimum deterrence. "By counterforce," the message stated, "the Air Force means the ability to selectively and decisively destroy enemy military forces that could otherwise destroy us."[250]

Writing in the winter of 1960-61, Colonel Martin explained the Air Force conception of counterforce. Martin defined the Air Force's objectives in general war as being to gain military dominance over the enemy by the destruction of his military force, to limit damage to the United States and its allies, and, by so doing, to achieve a favorable outcome of the hostilities. On the basis of the no-city wargame studies, Martin presented a comparison of the costs of the finite deterrence-terror strategy as opposed to a warfighting counterforce strategy. If an aggressor launched an attack against United States military forces and the United States responded against the enemy's military forces, some 5 percent of the US population would not survive. On the other hand, if the aggressor launched an attack against United States military forces and the United States retaliated against hostile military forces and cities, some 90 percent of the US population would not survive a counterattack against US cities. Looking ahead to 1965 when increased numbers of nuclear weapons would be available, the counterforce strategy would result in 5 percent destruction of US industry while thè terror strategy would lead to the destruction of 50 percent of the industry of the United States. "The foregoing," Martin observed, "are powerful arguments for accepting a counterforce strategy favoring survival rather than a strategy tantamount to suicide. The difference in the strategies can be measured in terms of this Nation's continued existence."[251] The Air Force had provided a conceptual justification for a counterforce strategy, but acceptance or rejection of it would await the new national administration that would take office early in 1961.

NOTES

1. *Public Papers of the Presidents of the United States: Dwight D. Eisenhower, 1957* (Washington, D.C.: Government Printing Office, 1958), 796; *Public Papers of the Presidents of the United States: Dwight D. Eisenhower, 1958* (Washington, D.C.: Government Printing Office, 1959), 7.

2. Senate, *Airpower: Report of the Subcommittee on the Air Force of the Committee on Armed Services,* 85th Cong., 1st sess., 1957, 95–97.

3. Senate, *Inquiry into Satellite and Missile Programs: Hearings before the Preparedness Investigating Subcommittee of the Committee on Armed Services,* 85th Cong., 1st and 2d sess., 1957–1958, 603–4.

4. Ibid., 791–92, 811–12, 831.

5. Ibid., 2429.

6. Gen Nathan F. Twining, chief of staff, US Air Force, "Remarks before the National War College," 31 May 1956; *Washington Daily News,* 8 June 1956.

7. *Washington Daily News,* 8 June 1956.

8. Senate, *Study of Air Power: Hearings before the Subcommittee on the Air Force of the Committee on Armed Services,* 84th Cong., 2d sess., 1956, 52.

9. *Army-Navy-Air Force Journal,* 9 June 1956, 1; Department of Defense, Research and Analysis Division, "Should We Have More Unification of the Military Establishment?" (Views expressed by or attributed to important officials), 27 July 1956.

IDEAS, CONCEPTS, DOCTRINE

10. Col Albert P. Sights, Jr., "Major Tasks and Military Reorganization," *Air University Quarterly Review* 9, no. 1 (Winter 1956–1957): 3–26.

11. Senate, *Study of Air Power*, 1727; House, *Department of Defense Appropriations for 1958: Hearings before a Subcommittee of the Committee on Appropriations*, 85th Cong., 1st sess., 1957, 146, 294; Charles C. Wilson, address to Air War College, Maxwell AFB, Ala., 15 June 1956.

12. House, *Department of Defense Appropriations for 1957: Hearings before a Subcommittee of the Committee on Appropriations*, 84th Cong., 2d sess., 1956, 274; Senate, *Study of Air Power*, 1461, 1464.

13. Senate, *Study of Air Power*, 1380, 1381; House, *DOD Appropriations for 1958*, 707; Adm Arleigh Burke, chief, Naval Operations, "Role of the Armed Forces in the Attainment of Military Objectives," lecture, Air War College, Maxwell AFB, Ala., 15 May 1957.

14. Senate, *Study of Air Power*, 1505.

15. House, *Department of Defense Appropriations for 1959, Overall Policy Statements: Hearings before a Subcommittee of the Committee on Appropriations*, 85th Cong., 2d sess., 1958, 50; Rockefeller Brothers Fund, *International Security—The Military Aspect* (Garden City, N.J.: Doubleday & Co., 1958), 3–7, 15–16, 27.

16. Rockefeller Brothers Fund, *International Security*, 30–33.

17. Ibid., 29–30.

18. Senate, *Inquiry into Satellite and Missile Programs*, 61–62.

19. Samuel P. Huntington, *The Common Defense, Strategic Programs in National Politics* (New York: Columbia University Press, 1961), 461.

20. Senate, *Inquiry into Satellite and Missile Programs*, 1527–28, 1519, 1524–25.

21. Ibid., 1520.

22. Gen Maxwell D. Taylor, *The Uncertain Trumpet* (New York: Harper & Bros., 1959), 91.

23. Senate, *Inquiry into Satellite and Missile Programs*, 1520.

24. Ibid., 1525.

25. Ibid., 1826.

26. Ibid., 1563.

27. Ibid., 1522, 1947.

28. Ibid., 1826.

29. Ibid., 1543–47.

30. Ibid., 911, 2018.

31. Ibid., 1521, 1563.

32. Ibid., 1527, 1953–54, 1959–60.

33. Ibid., 1318–19, 1335.

34. House, *Sundry Legislation Affecting the Naval and Military Establishments, 1958: Hearings before the Committee on Armed Services*, 85th Cong., 2d sess., 1958, book 4, no. 83: *Reorganization of the Department of Defense*, 6088–90.

35. Ibid., 5984, 6118–19, 6122, 6234–35.

36. *Public Papers: Eisenhower, 1958*, 274–90.

37. Ibid.

38. Public Law 85–599, *Department of Defense Reorganization Act of 1958*, 85th Cong., 2d sess., 1958, 6 August 1958.

39. House, *Committee on Armed Services, Report of Special Subcommittee on Defense Agencies*, 87th Cong., 2d sess., 1962, 6609–13.

40. Public Law 85–599, 6 August 1958; House, *Sundry Legislation for 1958*, 6809–38.

41. House, *Sundry Legislation Affecting the Naval and Military Establishments, 1959: Hearings before the Committee on Armed Services*, 86th Cong., 1st sess., 1959, 789–99.

42. House, *Sundry Legislation for 1958*, 5975.

43. Department of Defense, *Annual Report of the Secretary of Defense and the Annual Reports of the Secretary of the Army, Secretary of the Navy, and Secretary of the Air Force, July 1, 1958 to June 30, 1959* (Washington, D.C.: Government Printing Office, 1960), 44.

44. House, *Department of Defense Appropriations for 1960: Hearings before a Subcommittee of the Committee on Appropriations,* 86th Cong., 1st sess., 1959, pt. 2:339.

45. *Annual Report of the Secretary of Defense July 1958 to June 1959,* 35–37; Department of Defense Directive 5100.1, "Functions of the Department of Defense and Its Major Components," 31 December 1958.

46. "Defense Organization, The Trend of Unification," *Armed Forces Management,* November 1959, 24.

47. House, *Sundry Legislation for 1958,* 6427, 6430, 6444.

48. Senate, *Department of Defense Reorganization Act of 1958: Hearings before the Committee on Armed Services,* 85th Cong., 2d sess., 1958, 95–98.

49. Senate, *Missiles, Space, and Other Major Defense Matters: Hearings before the Preparedness Investigating Subcommittee of the Committee on Armed Services in Conjunction with the Committee on Aeronautical and Space Sciences,* 86th Cong., 2d sess., 1960, 144.

50. Senate, *Department of Defense Reorganization Act of 1958,* 403, 406, 409.

51. Senate, *Investigation of Governmental Organization for Space Activities: Hearings before the Subcommittee on Governmental Activities of the Committee on Aeronautical and Space Sciences,* 86th Cong., 1st sess., 1959, 379–80.

52. House, *Department of Defense Appropriations for 1961: Hearings before a Subcommittee of the Committee on Appropriations,* 86th Cong., 2d sess., 1960, pt. 1:33–34.

53. House, *Organization and Management of Missile Programs, Eleventh Report by the Committee on Government Operations,* 86th Cong., 1st sess., 1959, H. Rept. 1121, 154–56.

54. Evaluation Staff, Air War College, Project No. AU-3-58-ESAWC, "Service Roles and Missions in the Future," May 1958, 5–6.

55. Air University Research and Special Studies Progress Report, 1 January 1960, 3; Col Archie J. Knight and Col Allen F. Herzberg, "A Proposal for the Next Step in Defense Reorganization," *Air University Quarterly Review* 12, no. 2 (Summer 1960): 52–90.

56. Lt George E. Lowe, "The Specter of a 'Man on Horseback,'" *US Naval Institute Proceedings,* January 1964, 27.

57. House, *Military Posture Briefings: Hearings before the Committee on Armed Services,* 87th Cong., 1st sess., 1961, 1112, 1114.

58. House, *DOD Appropriations for 1960,* 6, 13.

59. *Annual Report of the Secretary of Defense July 1958 to June 1959,* 46.

60. Senate, *Organizing for National Security: Hearings before the Committee on National Policy Machinery of the Committee on Government Operations,* 86th and 87th Congs., 1960 and 1961, 1:729.

61. House, *DOD Appropriations for 1960,* pt. 1:330–39, 417; Senate, *Missiles, Space, and Other Major Defense Matters,* 211–12.

62. House, *DOD Appropriations for 1961,* pt. 2:530; Senate, *Missiles, Space, and Other Major Defense Matters,* 251.

63. Senate, *Missiles, Space, and Other Major Defense Matters,* 334.

64. House, *DOD Appropriations for 1960,* pt. 1:506, pt. 2:2–3.

65. Ibid., pt. 1:825–26; Senate, *Major Defense Matters: Hearings before the Preparedness Investigating Subcommittee of the Committee on Armed Services,* 86th Cong., 1st sess., 1959, 94–95.

66. House, *Sundry Legislation for 1958,* 6453.

67. Gen Thomas S. Power, commander in chief, Strategic Air Command, "Ballistic Missiles and the SAC Mission," *Air Force Magazine,* April 1958, 76, 79; House, *DOD Appropriations for 1960,* pt. 1:112.

68. House, *DOD Appropriations for 1960,* pt. 6:28–29; Senate, *Investigation of Governmental Organization for Space Activities,* 358–60.

69. House, *DOD Appropriations for 1960,* pt. 6:28.

70. House, *DOD Appropriations for 1961,* pt. 7:83.

71. Ibid., 118–21.

72. House, *United States Defense Policies in 1960,* 87th Cong., 1st sess., 1961, H. Doc. 207, 27; Col Campbell Palfrey, Jr., and Col James W. Bothwell, "Command and Organization of Aerospace Offense and Defense," *Air University Quarterly Review* 12, nos. 3 and 4 (Winter and Spring 1960–1961): 136; House, *Military Posture Briefings,* 966–67.

73. House, *The Ballistic Missile Program: Hearings before a Subcommittee of the Committee on Appropriations,* 85th Cong., 1st sess., 1957, 7, 21–23; House, *Investigation of National Defense Missiles: Hearings before the Committee on Armed Services,* 85th Cong., 2d sess., 1958, 4109, 4061–62.

74. Claude Witze, "How Our Space Policy Evolved," *Air Force Magazine,* April 1962, 87.

75. House, *Sundry Legislation for 1959,* 800.

76. House, *The Ballistic Missile Program,* 7, 21–23.

77. Memorandum by James H. Douglas, secretary of the Air Force, to director of guided missiles, Office of the Secretary of Defense, subject: Facts Concerning Establishment of Directorate of Astronautics, deputy chief of staff for development, Headquarters USAF, 23 December 1957, in Senate, *Inquiry into Satellite and Missile Programs,* 450; Witze, "How Our Space Policy Evolved," 87.

78. Senate, *Inquiry into Satellite and Missile Programs,* 1167–1679.

79. Department of Defense Directive 5105.15, subject: Advanced Research Projects Agency, 7 February 1958; Public Law 85–322, *Supplemental Defense Appropriation Act of 1958,* 85th Cong., 2d sess., 1958, 11 February 1958; House, *DOD Appropriations for 1959, Overall Policy Statements,* 15.

80. Senate, *Investigation of Governmental Organization for Space Activities,* 110–11, 120–22, 143.

81. House, *Missile Development and Space Sciences: Hearings before the Committee on Science and Astronautics,* 86th Cong., 1st sess., 1959, 418; Senate, *Investigation of Governmental Organization for Space Activities,* 135–36; *Annual Report of the Secretary of Defense July 1958 to June 1959,* 37–38; House, *To Amend the National Aeronautics and Space Act of 1958: Hearings before the Committee on Science and Astronautics,* 86th Cong., 2d sess., 1960, 427.

82. Senate, *Investigation of Governmental Organization for Space Activities,* 108.

83. Ibid., 420.

84. House, *Sundry Legislation for 1959,* 798–800, 811–12.

85. House, *Organization and Management of Missile Programs,* 493; Senate, *Investigation of Governmental Organization for Space Activities,* 135–36.

86. Senate, *Investigation of Governmental Organization for Space Activities,* 352, 354, 360–61, 396–403, 405, 409, 413–20, 426–28, 448–49, 461–62.

87. House, *Missile Development and Space Sciences,* 195–96, 235–26, 248–49.

88. Senate, *Investigation of Governmental Organization for Space Activities,* 227–30, 236.

89. Ibid., 559–60, 577–78.

90. House, *DOD Appropriations for 1960,* pt. 1:580.

91. Senate, *Investigation of Governmental Organization for Space Activities,* 314–15.

92. Ibid., 236–37, 413; Max Rosenberg, *The Air Force in Space, 1959–1960* (Washington, D.C.: USAF Historical Division Liaison Office, June 1962), 18–19.

93. W. M. Holaday, chairman, National Aeronautics and Space Administration, Department of Defense Civilian–Military Liaison Committee, to Senator Stuart Symington, letter, 15 May 1959, in Senate, *Investigation of Governmental Organization for Space Activities,* 553–54.

94. Rosenberg, *The Air Force in Space, 1959–1960,* 18–20; Department of Defense, *Annual Report of the Secretary of Defense and the Annual Reports of the Secretary of the Army, Secretary of the Navy, and Secretary of the Air Force, July 1, 1959 to June 30, 1960* (Washington, D.C.: Government Printing Office, 1961), 18; memorandum by secretary of defense to chairman, Joint Chiefs of Staff, subject: Coordination of Satellite and Space Vehicle Operations, 18 September 1959, in House, *Military Astronautics,* 87th Cong., 1st sess., 1961, H. Rept. 360, 6–7.

95. Rosenberg, *The Air Force in Space, 1959–1960,* 20–21; *Annual Report of the Secretary of Defense July 1959 to June 1960,* 18–19; memorandum by secretary of defense to secretary of the Army et al., subject: Coordination of Satellite and Space Vehicle Operations, 16 June 1960, in House, *Defense Space Interests: Hearings before the Committee on Science and Astronautics,* 87th Cong., 1st sess., 1961, 11.

96. House, *Military Astronautics*, H. Rept. 360, 7; House, *Department of Defense Appropriations for 1965: Hearings before a Subcommittee of the Committee on Appropriations*, 88th Cong., 2d sess., 1964, pt. 5:155–57.

97. Senate, *Investigation of Governmental Organization for Space Activities*, 396.

98. House, *DOD Appropriations for 1961*, pt. 3:781; Lt Gen Roscoe C. Wilson, deputy chief of staff for development, US Air Force, "Research and Development Today for Military Space Systems Tomorrow," *Air Force Magazine*, April 1960, 52; House, *Review of the Space Program: Hearings before the Committee on Science and Astronautics*, 86th Cong., 2d sess., 1960, pt. 1:479.

99. Dr T. Keith Glennan, address to Industrial College of the Armed Forces, Washington, D.C., 20 November 1959, quoted in Woodford A. Heflin, "NACA and NASA," 18.

100. House, *To Amend the National Aeronautics and Space Act of 1958*, 388–89.

101. See chap. 9, n. 314.

102. Senate, *Documents on the International Aspects of the Exploration and Use of Outer Space, 1954–1962*, 88th Cong., 1st sess., 1963, S. Doc. 18, 52, 55–56; Department of State, American Foreign Policy, Current Documents, 1958 (Washington, D.C.: Government Printing Office, 1962), 1413.

103. President's Scientific Advisory Committee, *Introduction to Outer Space, An Exploratory Statement* (Washington, D.C.: Government Printing Office, 1958); Eisenhower, message to Congress, 2 April 1958. Both of these papers were reprinted in *Air Force Magazine*, May 1958, 96–102.

104. Mary Shepard, Legislative Reference Service, Library of Congress, "An International Outer Space Agency for Peaceful Purposes — A Brief Review of Various Proposals and an Analysis of Possibilities," in Senate, *National Aeronautics and Space Act*, 85th Cong., 2d sess., 1958, pt. 2:388.

105. August H. Fox, chairman, Federation of American Scientists, to Lyndon B. Johnson, chairman, Special Committee on Space and Astronautics, letter, 13 May 1958, in Senate, *National Aeronautics and Space Act*, 380–81.

106. Ellen Galloway, "The Problems of Congress in Formulating Outer Space Legislation," in Senate, *National Aeronautics and Space Act*, pt. 2:384–86.

107. Robert Hotz, "NACA, The Logical Space Agency," *Aviation Week*, 3 February 1958, 21.

108. National Advisory Committee for Aeronautics, Resolution on the Subject of Space Flight, 16 January 1958, in House, *The National Space Program: Report of the Select Committee on Astronautics and Space Exploration*, 85th Cong., 2d sess., 1958, 117–19.

109. *Public Papers: Eisenhower, 1958*, 573.

110. Senate, *National Aeronautics and Space Act*, pt. 1:190–91, pt. 2:280.

111. House, *The National Space Program*, 160–64.

112. Ibid., 44, 80–82.

113. Dr Edward C. Welsh, "Peaceful Purposes: Some Realistic Definitions," *Air Force Magazine*, November 1961, 74.

114. House, *Astronautics and Space Exploration: Hearings before the Select Committee on Astronautics and Space Exploration*, 85th Cong., 2d sess., 1958, 866.

115. Ibid., 295.

116. Senate, *National Aeronautics and Space Act*, 193.

117. Ibid., 194–95.

118. House, *Astronautics and Space Exploration*, 1521–42.

119. House, *The National Space Program*, 44.

120. House, *Conference Report National Aeronautical and Space Act of 1958*, 85th Cong., 2d sess., 1958, H. Rept. 2166.

121. House, *Department of Defense Appropriations for 1963: Hearings before a Subcommittee of the Committee on Appropriations*, 87th Cong., 2d sess., 1962, pt. 2:145.

122. Senate, *Investigation of Governmental Organization for Space Activities*, 402.

123. Public Law 85-568, *The National Aeronautics and Space Act of 1958*, 29 July 1958.

124. *Annual Report of the Secretary of Defense July 1958 to June 1959*, 21; *Historical Origins of the National Aeronautics and Space Administration* (Washington, D.C.: Government Printing Office, 1963), 9–10.

125. Senate, *Investigation of Governmental Organization for Space Activities*, 40.
126. House, *To Amend the National Aeronautics and Space Act of 1958*, 249–50.
127. Welsh, "Peaceful Purposes: Some Realistic Definitions," 74.
128. House, *To Amend the National Aeronautics and Space Act of 1958*, 81–82, 90–91.
129. Ibid., 82; House, *Review of the Space Program*, pt. 1:503–4.
130. House, *Missile Development and Space Sciences*, 455–56.
131. Ibid., 165.
132. Senate, *Investigation of Governmental Organization for Space Activities*, 396–404, 423, 456–57, 470–74.
133. Gen Curtis E. LeMay, vice chief of staff, US Air Force, to Gen Thomas S. Power, commander in chief, Strategic Air Command, letter, 17 March 1959, quoted in Lee Bowen, "An Air Force History of Space Activities, 1945–1959," USAF Historical Division Liaison Office, August 1964, 191.
134. House, *To Amend the National Aeronautics and Space Act of 1958*, 400–3, 413–14.
135. House, *Review of the Space Program*, 811–12.
136. House, *To Amend the National Aeronautics and Space Act of 1958*, 30.
137. James Baar, "Medaris Retires with Blast at NASA," *Missiles and Rockets*, 1 February 1960, 13.
138. House, *Review of the Space Program*, pt. 2:809–13, 815–16, 818.
139. Ibid., pt. 2:821.
140. House, *To Amend the National Aeronautics and Space Act of 1958*, 357.
141. Ibid., 165, 196.
142. House, *Review of the Space Program*, pt. 3:897–99, 901, 903.
143. Ibid., pt. 1:474, 498; House, *To Amend the National Aeronautics and Space Act of 1958*, 219–22, 236–38; Senate, *NASA Authorization for Fiscal Year 1961: Hearings before the NASA Authorization Subcommittee of the Committee on Aeronautical and Space Sciences*, 86th Cong., 2d sess., 1960, 537–38.
144. House, *Review of the Space Program*, pt. 1:506; House, *To Amend the National Aeronautics and Space Act of 1958*, 219–21.
145. House, *To Amend the National Aeronautics and Space Act of 1958*, 313.
146. House, *Defense Space Interests*, 92–93, 100–1; memorandum by Gen Thomas D. White to AFPDC (General Landon) and AFDDC (General Wilson), 14 April 1960, in House, *Defense Space Interests*, 92.
147. House, *To Amend the National Aeronautics and Space Act of 1958*, 133, 240.
148. Ibid., 519.
149. "Space Act, Military's New Role Positive in New Bill," *Missiles and Rockets*, 9 May 1960, 15.
150. T. Keith Glennan, administrator, NASA, and James H. Douglas, deputy secretary of defense, Agreement between the Department of Defense and the National Aeronautics and Space Administration concerning the Aeronautics and Astronautics Coordinating Board, 13 September 1960, in Senate, *Amending Various Sections of the NASA Act of 1958: Hearings before the Committee on Aeronautical and Space Sciences*, 87th Cong., 1st sess., 1961, 47–49.
151. Senate, *Amending Various Sections of the NASA Act of 1958*, 45–67; *Missiles and Rockets*, 19 September 1960, 17.
152. Senate, *Department of Defense Appropriations for Fiscal Year 1959: Hearings before a Subcommittee of the Committee on Appropriations*, 85th Cong., 2d sess., 1958, 393.
153. Maj Gen James H. Walsh, "The Influence of Nuclear Weapons on the Determination of Military Objectives," lecture, Air War College, Maxwell AFB, Ala., 18 December 1957.
154. House, *Department of Defense Appropriations for 1962: Hearings before a Subcommittee of the Committee on Appropriations*, 87th Cong., 1st sess., 1961, pt. 3:494–95.
155. Senate, *Inquiry into Satellite and Missile Programs*, 59.
156. Senate, *Organizing for National Security*, 1:798; Taylor, *The Uncertain Trumpet*, 57–58.
157. Senate, *Inquiry into Satellite and Missile Programs*, 640.
158. Ibid., 647.

159. House, *Supplemental Defense Appropriations for 1958,* 85th Cong., 2d sess., 1958, 218, 260; House, *Investigation of National Defense Missiles,* 4561, 4577; House, *DOD Appropriations for 1959, Overall Policy Statements,* 442–56, 559–602.

160. Senate, *Inquiry into Satellite and Missile Programs,* 1019.

161. Paul H. Nitze, "Atoms, Strategy and Policy," *Foreign Affairs,* January 1958, 187–98.

162. Senate, *Study of Air Power,* 105, 220.

163. Donald A. Quarles, "How Much is Enough?" *Air Force Magazine,* September 1956, 51–53.

164. Senate, *Study of Air Power,* 1504.

165. House, *DOD Appropriations for 1960,* pt. 1:928–29.

166. Col Robert C. Richardson III, "Do We Need Unlimited Forces for Limited War?" *Air Force Magazine,* March 1959, 55–56.

167. Walsh, "The Influence of Nuclear Weapons on the Determination of Military Objectives.".

168. House, *DOD Appropriations for 1960,* pt. 1:800; Katherine Johnsen, "President Blamed for Loss of U-2 Program," *Aviation Week,* 4 July 1960, 31; Dwight D. Eisenhower, *The White House Years: Waging Peace, 1956–61* (Garden City, N.J.: Doubleday & Co., 1965), 546; Gen Nathan F. Twining, *Neither Liberty Nor Safety, A Hard Look at U.S. Military Policy and Strategy* (New York: Holt, Rinehart & Winston, 1966), 250.

169. William W. Kaufmann, *The McNamara Strategy* (New York: Harper & Row, 1964), 36.

170. Senate, *Organizing for National Security,* 1:798; House, *Investigation of National Defense Missiles,* 3975.

171. House, *Department of Defense Appropriations for 1959: Hearings before a Subcommittee of the Committee on Appropriations, Advanced Research Projects Agency,* 85th Cong., 2d sess., 1958, 378–79.

172. House, *United States Defense Policies in 1958,* 86th Cong., 1st sess., 1959, H. Doc. 227, 14.

173. Ibid., 15.

174. House, *Supplemental Defense Appropriations for 1958,* 149.

175. Taylor, *The Uncertain Trumpet,* 59–66.

176. *Annual Report of the Secretary of Defense July 1958 to June 1959,* 30–31.

177. Special message of the president to the Congress, Request for Congressional Authorization of a United States Cooperative Economic and Military Aid Program to Preserve and Strengthen the National Independence of the Countries of the Middle East, 5 January 1957, in Department of State, *American Foreign Policy: Current Documents, 1957,* 783–91; Jack Shulimson, *Marines in Lebanon* (Washington, D.C.: Historical Branch, G-3 Division, US Marine Corps, 1966), 7.

178. *Annual Report of the Secretary of Defense July 1958 to June 1959,* 88–89; House, *DOD Appropriations for 1960,* pt. 2:413–14; Robert D. Little and Wilhelmina Burch, "Air Operations in the Lebanon Crisis of 1958," USAF Historical Division Liaison Office, October 1962, passim; House, *Military Posture Briefings,* 1209; Col Albert P. Sights, Jr., "Lessons of Lebanon, A Study in Air Strategy," *Air University Review* 16, no. 5 (July–August 1965): 28–40.

179. Richard Goold-Adams, *The Time of Power, A Reappraisal of John Foster Dulles* (London: Weidenfeld and Nicholson, 1962), 170–71, 284–86; Jacob Van Staaveren, *Air Operations in the Taiwan Crisis of 1958,* USAF Historical Division Liaison Office, November 1962, 1–14; Gen Laurence S. Kuter, "Pacific Air Forces," *Air Force Magazine,* September 1959, 124–30.

180. Van Staaveren, *Air Operations in the Taiwan Crisis of 1958,* 15–28; Kuter, "Pacific Air Forces," 124–30; *Annual Report of the Secretary of Defense July 1958 to June 1959,* 90–91, 211–212, 252, 296; House, *DOD Appropriations for 1960,* pt. 2:416–17; House, *Military Posture Briefings,* 1210.

181. Senate, *Missile and Space Activities: Joint Hearings before the Preparedness Investigating Subcommittee of the Committee on Armed Services and the Committee on Aeronautical and Space Sciences,* 86th Cong., 1st sess., 1959, 34–35, 42–43.

182. House, *DOD Appropriations for 1960,* pt. 1:101; Senate, *Missiles, Space, and Other Major Defense Matters,* 430.

183. House, *Missile Development and Space Sciences,* 79; House, *DOD Appropriations for 1960,* pt. 1:894.

184. House, *DOD Appropriations for 1960,* pt. 2:386–88.

185. Gen Curtis E. LeMay, "The Air Ocean: Global Horizons Unlimited," *Air Force Magazine*, November 1959, 107.
186. House, *DOD Appropriations for 1960*, pt. 1:97–101, 297–99, 317–18; Senate, *Missile and Space Activities*, 100–1.
187. Senate, *Department of Defense Appropriations for 1958: Hearings before the Subcommittee of the Committee on Appropriations*, 85th Cong., 2d sess., 1958, 171; House, *DOD Appropriations for 1960*, pt. 1:478.
188. House, *DOD Appropriations for 1960*, pt. 1:338, 415.
189. Senate, *Major Defense Matters*, 135; House, *DOD Appropriations for 1961*, pt. 2:265–66, 297.

190. House, *DOD Appropriations for 1961*, pt. 6:45.
191. House, *DOD Appropriations for 1960*, pt. 1:116–17.
192. House, *DOD Appropriations for 1961*, pt. 1:60.
193. Nikita Khrushchev to Dwight D. Eisenhower, letter, 7 September 1958, in Department of State, *American Foreign Policy, Current Documents, 1958*, 1149–52.
194. Ibid.; House, *United States Defense Policies in 1958*, 15–16.
195. House, *United States Defense Policies in 1958*, 15.
196. Senate, *Major Defense Matters*, 17.
197. House, *DOD Appropriations for 1960*, pt. 2:283.
198. Ibid., 436.
199. Quoted in Sights, "Lessons of Lebanon," 42–43.
200. House, *DOD Appropriations for 1960*, pt. 5:658.
201. Gen Frederic H. Smith, Jr., "Nuclear Weapons and Limited War," *Air University Quarterly Review* 12, no. 1 (Spring 1960): 3–27.
202. Sights, "Lessons of Lebanon," 42–43.
203. House, *DOD Appropriations for 1960*, pt. 1:254.
204. Quoted in Albert J. Wohlstetter, "The Delicate Balance of Terror," *Air Force Magazine*, February 1959, 49.
205. Taylor, *The Uncertain Trumpet*, 184.
206. House, *DOD Appropriations for 1960*, pt. 1:330–39; Senate, *Major Defense Matters*, 33–34, 69–70.
207. House, *DOD Appropriations for 1960*, pt. 1:591, 594.
208. House, *Missile Development and Space Sciences*, 159.
209. Senate, *Investigation of Governmental Organization for Space Activities*, 319.
210. House, *DOD Appropriations for 1960*, pt. 1:627.
211. Quoted from "Ruth Hagy's College News Conference," 22 March 1959, in Senate, *Investigation of Governmental Organization for Space Activities*, 450.
212. Senate, *Committee on Foreign Relations, United States Foreign Policy*, 86th Cong., 2d sess., 1960, 1:729.
213. Comdr P. H. Backus, "Finite Deterrence, Controlled Retaliation," *US Naval Institute Proceedings*, March 1959, 23–29.
214. Taylor, *The Uncertain Trumpet*, 130–64; Senate, *Missiles, Space, and Other Major Defense Matters*, 187.
215. House, *DOD Appropriations for 1961*, pt. 3:767–68.
216. Senate, *Major Defense Matters*, 82.
217. House, *DOD Appropriations for 1961*, pt. 2:207.
218. Rand Report P-1888-RC, *The Nature and Feasibility of War and Deterrence* (Santa Monica, Calif.: Rand Corp., 1960); Herman Kahn, *On Thermonuclear War* (Princeton, N.J.: Princeton University Press, 1960).
219. Kahn, *On Thermonuclear War*, 24n; House, *DOD Appropriations for 1961*, pt. 5:940.
220. Brig Gen Sidney F. Giffin, USAF, Retired, "The American Military Mind in a Strange New World," *Air Force Magazine*, February 1961, 54.

221. Senate, *Missile and Space Activities,* 129.
222. House, *DOD Appropriations for 1960,* pt. 5:709–10; Senate, *Investigation of Governmental Organization for Space Activities,* 450–53.
223. House, *United States Defense Policies in 1960,* 18–19; Senate, *United States Foreign Policy,* 785; Senate, *Missiles, Space, and Other Major Defense Matters,* 116.
224. House, *DOD Appropriations for 1961,* pt. 5:511.
225. House, *DOD Appropriations for 1960,* pt. 2:374–76, 381, 384.
226. Richardson, "Do We Need Unlimited Forces for Limited War?" 56.
227. House, *DOD Appropriations for 1960,* pt. 5:724–25; Senate, *Investigation of Governmental Organization for Space Activities,* 450.
228. Gen Thomas D. White, "Air Force Progress toward the Future," *Air Force Magazine,* September 1959, 59.
229. Brig Gen John A. Dunning, "USAF Doctrine, Roles and Missions," lecture, Air War College, Maxwell AFB, Ala., 17 December 1959; House, *DOD Appropriations for 1961,* pt. 5:940–41.
230. Robert Strausz-Hupe, William R. Kintner, and Stefan T. Possony, *A Forward Strategy for America* (New York: Harper & Bros., 1961), 117.
231. Kahn, *On Thermonuclear War,* 7–8.
232. Senate, *United States Foreign Policy,* 1:680–82, 776–87.
233. Taylor, *The Uncertain Trumpet,* 78.
234. *Annual Report of the Secretary of Defense July 1959 to June 1960,* 34–36.
235. House, *DOD Appropriations for 1961,* pt. 1:11, 26.
236. Ibid., pt. 2:438–40, 490–91; Senate, *Missiles, Space, and Other Defense Matters,* 227, 248–49, 253.
237. House, *DOD Appropriations for 1961,* pt. 2:139, 186–87; Senate, *Missiles, Space, and Other Major Defense Matters,* 300–301, 313.
238. House, *DOD Appropriations for 1961,* pt. 5:374–77.
239. Ibid., pt. 2:228, 232–33; Senate, *Department of Defense Appropriations for Fiscal Year 1961: Hearings before a Subcommittee of the Committee on Appropriations,* 86th Cong., 2d sess., 1960, 1385.
240. Brig Gen Robert C. Richardson III, "The Fallacy of the Concept of Minimum Deterrence," *Air University Quarterly Review* 12, no. 1 (Spring 1960): 109–17.
241. House, *DOD Appropriations for 1961,* pt. 2:186–87.
242. House, *United States Defense Policies in 1960,* 20.
243. *Annual Report of the Secretary of Defense July 1959 to June 1960,* 34, 38.
244. House, *United States Defense Policies in 1960,* 18.
245. Kahn, *On Thermonuclear War,* 39.
246. Strausz-Hupe, Kintner, and Possony, *A Forward Strategy for America,* 119–20; "'A Forward Strategy for America' A Book Analysis," *Air Force Space Digest,* May 1961, 36.
247. Naval Warfare Analysis Group, "Résumé of Major Strategic Consideration" (NWG), 62–60, 19 July 1960 (rev. 17 October 1960); House, *United States Defense Policies in 1960,* 15; Richard Fryklund, *100 Million Lives, Maximum Survival in a Nuclear War* (New York: Macmillan Co., 1962), 84–85.
248. Fryklund, *100 Million Lives,* 1–27.
249. Gen Thomas D. White, "Living with Danger," *Air Force Magazine,* December 1960, 49.
250. *Air University Dispatch,* 13 January 1961, 5.
251. Lt Col Donald F. Martin, "Effective Aerospace Power: 2. Counterforce," *Air University Quarterly Review* 12, nos. 3 and 4 (Winter and Spring 1960–1961): 152–58.

INDEX

A-12: 83
A-17: 83
A-20: 94
A-26: 218
A-36: 136, 153
ABC-1: 108
A-bomb: 237, 256, 284. *See also* nuclear weapons
Academic Training Directorate, USAAF School of Applied Tactics: 134
Acheson, Dean: 284, 292, 294, 299
Active instantaneous relay system (Advent): 593
Adak, Alaska, as B-29 base, World War II: 160
ADC. *See* Air Defense Command
Ad Hoc Committee for Joint Policies and Procedures: 375, 378
Advanced Research Projects Agency: 502, 590
Advent: 593
AEC. *See* Atomic Energy Commission
Aerial Bombardment Manual: 36
Aerial-bombing of naval vessels (1921): 37
Aerial gunnery tactics, World War II, Europe: 143
Aerial refueling: 232, 233
Aeronautical Board: 35
Aeronautics, research and development: 61
Aeronautics and Astronautics Coordinating Board (AACB): 605–6
Aerospace: 10, 553–54
Aerospace doctrine: 553
Aerospace forces: 10, 554
Aerospace Policy Division, USAF, and defense issues: 11
Aerospace power: 553
AFM 1–1, *Basic Aerospace Doctrine of the United States Air Force*: 379

AFM 1–2, *United States Air Force Basic Doctrine*: 5, 9–10, 393, 396, 398–99, 400, 406, 438, 553–54
AFM 1–3, *Theater Air Operations*: 394
AFM 1–4, *Air Defense Operations*: 394
AFM 1–5, *Air Operations in Conjunction with Amphibious Operations*: 394, 404
AFM 1–7, *Theater Air Forces in Counterair, Interdiction, and Close Air Support Operations*: 395
AFM 1–8, *Strategic Air Operations*: 394
AFM 1–9, *Theater Airlift Operations*: 395
AFM 1–11, *Theater Air Reconnaissance*: 395
Air adjutant general (Air Force): 314
Air-assault airlift, US Air Force and: 348
Air Board: 95, 209, 213
Airborne army, proposed: 203
Airborne early warning and control aircraft: 530
Airborne-intercept radar, development of: 100
Air Campaigns of the Pacific War (USSBS): 172, 231
Air Command and Staff College: 365, 380
Air Commerce Act (1926): 51, 61
Air Coordinating Committee: 216, 217, 218, 225
Air Corps Act (2 July 1926): 50–51, 61–62
Air Corps Board: 62, 71, 74–75, 78–79, 80, 82–83, 88–89, 93, 97, 105–7, 130; on lessons of World War II in Europe, 106; "Fire Power of Bombardment Formations," 97; and missions of Army air forces, 89

Air Corps Bombardment Board: 63
Air Corps Materiel Division: 61, 79; and bomber-escort, development of, 80; long-range bomber, and development of, 69, 80, 94
Air Corps Plans Division, and reorganization of Air Corps: 104
Air Corps Proving Ground: 107
Air Corps Tactical School: 7, 62–65, 67, 69, 71–72, 75, 79, 81–82, 88, 91, 96, 100, 105–7, 127, 130, 134, 157, 167; and doctrine, 7, 62–63, 77–78, 88, 127
Air Corps Technical Committee, and air defense interceptor: 82–83
Air Council, and long-range interceptor: 530–31
Aircraft Board. *See* Aircraft Production Board
Aircraft carrier: 616. *See also* Woodring program
Aircraft Production Board: 19, 21, 24, 28
Aircraft and Weapons Board: 213, 231, 233, 306
Air cruiser: 98
Air Defence of Great Britain, and Allied Expeditionary Air Force: 150
Air defense, US: 67, 82, 95, 133, 217, 285–86, 306, 312–13, 330, 332, 367, 390, 402, 500–504, 536–37, 539–40
Air Defense Board: 133, 134–35
Air Defense Command (ADC): 103, 207–8, 224, 307, 312–13, 316, 337, 379, 390–91, 402, 530–32, 534
Air Defense Operational Training Unit: 133
Air Defense Policy Panel: 367
Air Defense Systems Engineering Committee: 286
Air Doctrine Branch, Air Staff: 10
Air employment instructions: 368–69
Air force: 10, 23, 73, 84, 92, 146
Air Force, The: 64
Air Force Ballistic Missile Committee: 494
Air Force Ballistic Missile Division: 498
Air Force Combat Command: 104–5, 129, 133
Air Force Council: 306, 385–86, 388, 393, 490
Air Force Directorate of Intelligence: 237
Air Force doctrine: 1–5, 7–11, 62–63, 137, 146, 212, 278, 310, 331–32, 337, 347, 370, 372, 382, 384, 386, 388, 393, 425
Air Force Information Policy Letter for Commanders: 11
Air Force in Theaters of Operations: Organization and Functions, The: 136
Air Force major commands: 314
Air Force Missile Test Center: 495
Air Force Organization Act (1951): 314, 316
Air Force Publications Board: 369
Air Force Reserve: 208, 314, 318; and Korean conflict, 316–17; mobilization of, 318; and NSC-68, 316–17
Air Force School of Aviation Medicine, Department of Space Medicine: 544
Air Force Senior Officers Board: 213, 242–45, 250, 306, 529
Air Force Strategic Missiles Evaluation Committee: 489
"Air-Ground Cooperation": 141
Air-ground doctrine: 107, 136, 141, 146, 175, 296ff, 308, 347–48
Air interdiction: in Korean War, 302, 303, 350; in World War II, 158
Airlift and strategic bombing force: 312
Airlift Task Force (Provisional): 236
Air Mail Act (1925): 51, 61
Air mail service: 45, 70
Air Materiel Command: 146, 205, 206, 276–78, 314, 436
Air Ministry, British: 25

Air National Guard: 208, 224, 314, 317–19, 326, 535; and Korean conflict, 316–17
Air offensive: 64–65, 69, 88, 131, 148
Air operations, World War II: 144
Air Operations Briefs (Army Air Force Board): 140–41, 146
Airplane Division, Army Signal Corps: 21
Air Policy Commission: 225, 228, 229
Air Policy Division, Air Staff: 10
Air power: 5, 7, 9, 21, 44, 61, 64, 69, 77–78, 85–86, 90–91, 137–38, 140, 151, 167–68, 228, 231, 245, 255, 367, 371, 374, 400, 406, 437–39, 440–42, 443; indivisibility of, 300, 306; in Korean War, 339–40
Air Power: Key to Survival (de Seversky): 172
Air pressure strategy, in Korean War: 342, 344
Air Proving Ground Command: 205
Air Research and Development Command: 276–78, 486–88, 530
Air reserve: 224
Air Service Board: 28, 62, 64
Air Service Command, Army Air Force: 146
Air Service Field Officers School: 4, 36, 62
Air Service Tactical School: 62–63
Air Service's Training and Operations Group: 31–32, 36
Air Service Training Regulation No. 440–15, *Fundamental Principles for the Employment of the Air Service*: 41
Air Staff officers board: 230
Air striking force: 137
Air superiority: 18, 23, 27, 63, 65, 138, 141, 154, 171, 173, 216, 231, 254, 285, 289, 301, 328–29, 351, 392, 399, 456; in Korean War, 302, 337, 349–50
Air Support Board: 133

Air support command: 105, 135–36
Air Support Department, School of Applied Tactics: 137
Air support divisions: 135
Air Tactical School: 365, 370, 380
Air tactics: 18, 36, 40–41, 134
Air Technical Service Command: 205, 207. *See also* Air Materiel Command
Air Training Command: 207
Air transport: 348–49, 390
Air Transport Command: 178, 203, 207–8
Air transport helicopters: 348–49
Air University: 3, 5, 207, 210–11, 276–78, 285, 365–67, 370, 375; and Air Force doctrine, 1, 3, 5–10, 365–68, 373, 379, 383, 385; "Air University Doctrine on the Employment of Air Force Combat Units," 382–83; AU Manual 1–1, *USAF Basic Doctrine*, 389
Air War College: 3, 212, 365, 380, 391, 396–98, 445, 586; and Air Force doctrine, 2–3, 7–9, 285, 367, 370, 385, 387, 394
Air War Plans Division: 104, 109–11, 127, 128
Air War Plans Division-1, Munitions Requirements of the Army Air Force: 109–13, 128, 131, 157
Air War Plans Division-4, Air Estimate of the Situation and Recommendations for the Conduct of War: 127–28
Air War Plans Division-42, Requirements for Air Ascendancy: 130–32, 142, 157–58
Alaska: 94
Alaskan Air Command: 224
Aleutian Islands, and B-29 raids on Japan: 160
Allen, James: 16
Allied Expeditionary Air Force: 150
Allied Supreme War Council: 26
All-Weather Air Forces Board: 206

Alness, Harvey T.: 393
American-British Conversations: 108
American-British-Dutch-Australian Command: 129
Amerikaprogramm: 21
Amphibious operations and joint doctrine: 374
Andersen Air Base, Guam: 343
Anderson, Orvil A.: 90, 109, 127, 130, 137–38, 145, 147, 150–51, 154, 172, 231, 276, 285, 295–96, 367, 432
Anderson, Samuel E.: 109, 204, 461
Andrews, Frank M.: 74, 79, 84–85, 87, 92
Anglo-American Combined Chiefs of Staff: 128
Anglo-Japanese alliance: 52
Antiaircraft artillery defenses, Germany, World War II: 155–56
Antiaircraft defenses: 290
Antimissile air defenses: 479, 500, 503, 590
Antung airfield, Manchuria, and Korean War: 338, 343
Anvil: 153
Arcadia conference: 128–29
Area commander: 391–92
Area defense: 500–502, 529. *See also* point defense
Area targets: 511
Armed services, unification of: 192
Armstrong, Frank A., Jr.: 155
Army. *See* US Army
Army Air Forces Board: 134–36, 138–44, 205, 206; "Tactical Doctrine of Troop Carrier Aviation," 141–42
Army Air Forces Board Control Office: 139
Army Air Forces Proving Ground Command: 138–39, 206
Army Air Forces School of Applied Tactics: 138–39
Army Air Forces Tactical Center: 139, 206

Army and Air Force Authorization Act (1950): 314
Army and Navy Munitions Board: 195
Army and Navy Staff College: 373
Army Appropriations Act (1920): 35, 45
Army Field Forces: 311, 376–77
Army Forces Far East: 342
Army General Council. *See* Drum board
Army General Headquarters: 133
Army-Navy Ballistic Missile Committee: 494
Army Regulation No. 95–5: 104
Army Reorganization Act (1920): 35
Army Service Forces: 129
Army Service School: 16
Arnold, Henry H. "Hap": 17, 27, 46, 51–52, 61, 68, 72, 80, 89–92, 96–97, 101–6, 113, 127, 129, 132, 135–38, 140, 142–43, 146, 148–53, 160, 162–63, 166, 168, 170–71, 179, 191–92, 203–6, 209, 215, 217, 432, 438, 478
Assistant Chief of Staff, Operations, Commitments, and Requirements (ACS/OC&R), Army Air Forces: 135, 138–39, 144
Assistant secretary of war for air: 62, 74
Atlantic Charter: 148
Atlas Scientific Advisory Committee: 491
Atomic air power: 237
Atomic bomb. *See* nuclear weapons
Atomic capability and Korean War: 335
Atomic combat missions: 232
Atomic Energy Act of 1954: 596
Atomic Energy Commission (AEC): 282–84, 488, 491, 495, 500, 596, 601; and nuclear weapons, 283–84, 488, 495, 500
Atomic weapons. *See* nuclear weapons
Attlee, Clement: 299
Aviation, department of: 47

Aviation doctrine. *See* Air Force doctrine
Aviation Expansion Program: 94
Aviation, ground support: 83
Aviation Section, Army Signal Corps: 19–21
AWPD. *See* Air War Plans Division
AWPD-1. *See* Air War Plans Division-1
AWPD-4. *See* Air War Plans Division-4
AWPD-42. *See* Air War Plans Division-42
Axis powers, air orders of battle, threat to Western Hemisphere: 91

B-9: 64
B-10: 64, 70, 80, 85
B-12: 80
B-15: 81
B-17 Flying Fortress: 64, 70, 81, 84–87, 94, 152
B-18: 69, 81, 84–85, 87, 94
B-24: 94, 152
B-25: 94
B-26: 94, 327, 337–38
B-29 Superfortress: 110, 128, 131, 158–59, 166, 215–16, 223–24, 231–32, 236, 240, 243–45, 283, 296, 303, 319, 335, 338–39, 506, 529, 542; and Korean War, 294–96, 303, 335, 338–39, 343; and World War II, 140, 158–60, 162–64
B-32: 110, 128
B-36: 131, 217–18, 232–33, 237, 240, 243–45, 250–52, 254, 257, 290, 327, 335, 340, 485, 506, 510
B-36H: 319
B-45: 218–19, 244, 310, 337
B-47: 232–33, 240, 245, 250, 252, 319, 334, 485, 506–7, 530
B-47E: 327
B-50: 217–19, 232, 243, 245, 506, 542
B-50D: 240
B-52: 232–33, 245, 334, 462, 498, 506, 509–12, 530, 534, 543
B-52A: 323
B-54: 243, 244, 245
B-57: 323, 612–13, 617
B-57B: 327
B-58: 334, 490, 507, 536
B-66: 450
B-66B: 327
B-70: 537, 627
Backus, P. H.: 619–20
Baker board: 52, 70–71, 74
Baker, Newton D.: 19, 21, 28, 31, 34, 39, 70
Balanced Air Force Program: 84–85. *See also* Woodring program
Balanced forces: 238, 322–23
Balance of power: 280, 300
Balbo, Italo: 68
Ballistic missiles: 485, 486, 492, 504
Ballistic missile early warning system: 535–37, 539
Ballistic Missiles Office: 491
Barcus, Glenn O.: 305, 344, 382
Barker, John DeForest: 1–2, 171, 373, 379–85, 389, 392–94, 401
Barrage balloons: 18
Baruch, Bernard: 549
Battle of Britain: 98
Beck, R. M.: 89, 92
Bell Aircraft Company: 542–43
Berkner, Lloyd V.: 330–31
Berlin, Germany: 156, 231, 234–36, 249, 280
Bidault, George, and Dien Bien Phu: 430
Big Week: 153–54, 157
Bissell, Clayton: 37, 111
Blackett, P. M. S., on minimum deterrence: 618
Board of Ordnance and Fortification, War Department: 15
Board of Senior Officers. *See* Air Force Senior Officers Board
Boeing Company: 81, 479, 484, 507, 509
Boeing Model 299, B-17 prototype: 70
Bohlen, Charles: 238

Bolling commission: 19–21, 24, 26
Bolling, Raynal C.: 19, 24–25
Bomarc (Boeing and Michigan Research Center) missile: 484, 533–40
Bombardment aircraft: 63, 82, 97
Bombardment air force: 36, 42, 65, 69
Bombardment division (ACS/OC&R): 135
Bomber(s): 63, 69, 80, 84–86, 90, 140, 151, 481; and control of the air, 65; defensive armament of, 97; and escort aircraft, 80; long-range, 69, 80, 84, 90; massed formations, World War II, 140, 152; medium, 84
Bomi (boost-glide missile): 543
Boost-glide vehicles: 543–44
Bowles, Chester: 343, 429
Bowles, Edward L.: 142
Bradley, Follett: 2, 78, 170
Bradley, Omar N.: 145, 147, 169, 172, 234, 248–49, 254–55, 256–58, 280, 282, 289–90, 293, 300, 324, 326–27, 419, 422
Brass Bell, boost-glide reconnaissance system: 544
Bravo, Strategic Air Command and: 307
Breckinridge, Henry S.: 16
Bredt, Irene: 543
Breguet: 23
Brereton, Lewis H.: 31, 179, 203
Brett, George H.: 103–4, 106
Brewster, Owen R.: 225, 369
Britain, Battle of: 98
British air board: 20
British air defenses, World War I: 25
British air forces, in Pacific, World War II: 160
British Air Ministry: 98, 100
British Expeditionary Force: 97
British Independent Air Force: 25–26
British Western Desert Air Force: 137
Brodie, Bernard: 147, 237, 340, 452
Brown, Charles R.: 616
Brown, Grover C.: 238
Brucker, Wilber: 460, 494, 592, 614

Brussels Pact: 246
Budget Advisory Board, Air Force: 306
Budget Advisory Group, Joint Chiefs of Staff: 247
Bull, Harold: 332
Bullitt, William C.: 91
Burchinal, David A.: 172
Bureau of Aircraft Production: 2, 21, 27–28
Burke, Arleigh A.: 448, 465, 576, 579–80, 587–88, 607–8, 615, 619, 626–27
Burns, Robert W.: 388
Bush, Vannevar: 142, 219, 444, 480–81, 483–84, 578, 607
Buzzard, Anthony W.: 436

C-47: 216
C-97: 219, 245, 250
C-119: 219, 245
C-123: 323
C-124: 245, 250, 460, 611–13
C-125B: 244
C-130: 612–13
Caldera, Joseph D., and Dien Bien Phu: 430
California Institute of Technology, and Project Vista: 328
Cambridge Research Center, and antimissile defenses: 500
Cambridge Research Laboratories, and US air defense: 286
Canberra (aircraft): 323
Candee, Robert C.: 138, 382
Cannon, John K.: 308–11, 384, 391–92
Caproni airplanes: 20
Caproni bomber: 26
Caproni, Gianni, Count di Taliedo: 18, 24
Caribbean Air Command: 224, 281
Carmichael, Richard H.: 367, 370–71
Carney, Robert B.: 247, 424, 430, 439
Carter, Wendell E.: 8, 433
Cary, John D.: 452
Casablanca conference, World War II: 149–50, 159

Casablanca directive, World War II: 150, 152, 157
Cates, Clifton B.: 401
Central Air Defense Force: 313
Central Army Antiaircraft Command: 313
Central Pacific strategy (US), World War II: 158
Centralized control: 309, 407
Ceylon, and B-29 raids on Netherlands East Indies: 160
Chandler, Charles DeForest: 16, 69
Chaney, J. E.: 98
Chapman, James W.: 385
Charyk, Joseph V.: 604–5
Chasan dam, Korea: 344
Chauncey, Charles C.: 366
Chennault, Claire L.: 82
Chidlaw, Benjamin W.: 332, 482, 533
Chief of Staff, Air Force: 10, 306, 314–16
Chief of staff, armed forces: 193
Chinese Communist air force: 343
Chinese Communist forces, and Korean War: 298, 302
Churchill, Winston S.: 25, 100, 129, 236–37, 420, 444
Citizens Advisory Committee: and continental air defense warning system, 332–33; and DEW line, 332; on strategic air arm as deterrent to Soviet air power, 333
Civil defense, and Project East River: 330–31
Civilian-Military Liaison Committee: 600, 602, 603, 606
Clark, J. J.: 350
Clark, Mark W.: 177, 308–10, 341–42; on air-ground operations, 348; on close air support, 348; on command of tactical air, 341; on Korean War, 341–42, 344–45; on organic Army close air support aircraft, 308
Clay, Lucius D.: 233
Close air support: 86–87, 89, 173–74, 301–2, 307–9, 348, 351, 441, 484

Coast defense: 65, 87; and Army-Navy interservice dispute, 65–66, 75–76, 92
Coffin, Howard: 24
Cold War Conference, Air Force: 461
Cole, W. Sterling: 283
Collective defense: 245
Collective security: 249
Collective self-defense: 246
Collins, J. Lawton: 169, 256, 295, 311–12, 375, 378, 403, 419; and Korean War, 295, 419; on organic Army close air support aircraft, 308–9; on tactical air support, 256, 308–9, 376–77
Cologne, Germany: 25, 156
Combat commands, task-centered: 575
Combined air transport operations room (CATOR): 179
Combined arms: 17, 43
Combined Chiefs of Staff, World War II: 129, 135, 150, 152–53, 157, 159–60, 165
Combined forces: 148, 168
Command and control: 200, 408
"Commander's Guide, The": 369–70, 372, 380
Command of the air: 63
Command of the Air (Douhet): 38–39
Commission on Organization of the Executive Branch: 273
Committee on DOD Organization, and Reorganization Plan No. 6: 423
Committee on Guided Missiles: 275
Committee on National Security Organization: 273–75
Committee of Operations Analysts: 157, 159, 162
Committee for the Scientific Survey of Air Defense: 100
Communism, containment of: 222, 280, 293, 431
Communist China: and Korean War, 298–99, 338–39, 343, 350
Composite Air Strike Force (CASF): 450, 612–13, 616

Compton, Karl T.: 227, 484
Concentration of force: 309
Concept, definition of: 3, 8
Congressional Aviation Policy Board: 160
Consolidated-Vultee Aircraft Corporation: 220, 221, 480, 483. *See also* Convair Division, General Dynamics
Containment, policy of: and atomic deterrence, 285; and Korean War, 295
Continental Air Command: 242, 307, 308, 313–14
Continental air defense: 319, 587
Continental Air Defense Command: 402, 405, 501
Continental Air Forces: 146, 204, 207
Continental defense: 89
Control of the air: 40, 65, 93, 171, 228, 399. *See also* air superiority and air supremacy
Control of the sea: 226, 227
Convair Division, General Dynamics: 488–89
Cook, Orval R.: 597
Coolidge, Calvin: 46
Coolidge, Charles S.: 580
Copsey, Robert L.: 403, 405
Coral Sea, Battle of: 158
Council of National Defense: 19
Counterforce strategy: 434–37, 606, 623, 629
"Counter-Force Strategy" (Walkowicz): 435
Courier delayed communications system: 593
Craig, Howard A.: 202, 389
Craig, Malin: 79, 84, 87, 91–92
Cripps, Sir Stafford: 236
Crossfield, Scott: 542–43
Crowell, Benedict: 30
Crowell mission: 30
Culver, C. C.: 62–63
Curry bill, and separate department of aeronautics: 29
Curry, John F.: 77, 144

Curtiss Hawks: 63
Curtiss X A-8: 83
CVA-58: 197

D-558 Skyrocket: 542
D-558 II: 542
Dahlquist, John E.: 408
Davis, Dwight F.: 47, 50
Davison, F. Trubee: 62, 74
Day bombardment: 22–23, 155
Day bombers: 63
DB-1: 69
DC-3: 69
Dean, Gordon: 284, 465
Defense unification: 251, 574
Defensive Research and Development Board: 485, 488
Demonstration Air Force: 139
Denfield, L. E.: 248, 253
Department of aeronautics: 29
Department of armed forces: 193
Department of Defense: 194, 273, 275, 280–81, 284, 328, 330–32, 423–24, 453, 484, 537–38, 540, 580, 625, 627
Department of Defense Appropriation Act (1953): 327
Department of Defense Reorganization Act of 1958: 573, 583, 586, 591
Deputy Chief of Staff, War Department: for Air, 103–4; for Development, 278; for Ground, 103
Dern, George H.: 68, 71
De Seversky, Alexander P.: 167, 171–72, 227–28, 230–31, 293, 320–21, 432; *Air Power Key to Survival*, 172; definition of air power, 167, 438; *Victory through Air Power*, 167, 438
Deterrence, strategy of: 446, 629
"Development of Tactics and Techniques for the Destruction of the German Air Force" (Army Air Force Board): 140
Devers, Jacob L.: 170

DEW line. *See* distant early warning line
DH-4: 23
DH-4B: 26
Dickman board: 28–30
Dickman, Joseph L.: 239
Dickman, Joseph T.: 28
Dictionary of United States Military Terms for Joint Usage: 392; definition of doctrine, 386
Directorate of Astronautics, Air Force: 590
Directorate of Military Requirements, Army Air Force: 130
Directorate of Plans, Air Staff: 10
Directorate of Requirements, Air Staff: 35, 278
Directorate of Research and Development, Air Staff: 278
Directorate of Technical Service, Army Air Force Plans Division: 130
Dirigible balloons, value of: 16
Discoverer, test project: 593
Disosway, G. P.: 369
Distant early warning line: 330–33, 532, 534–35, 538
Division of Military Aeronautics: 21, 27–28
Doctrine: 1, 8, 10, 77, 132, 140, 211, 224, 231, 386
Doctrine for the Employment of the GHQ Air Force: 76
"Doctrine of Air Force, The" (Culver): 63
Dodge, Joseph: 424
D'Olier, Franklin: 145
Donahew, Jack N.: 400, 505
Doolittle, James H.: 71, 75, 170–71, 196, 200, 276; in Europe, World War II, 154, 171; in Pacific, World War II, 166
Dornberger, Walter R.: 479, 543
Douglas Aircraft Company: 80–81, 113
Douglas Aircraft Corporation: 209, 276, 478
Douglas, James H.: 503, 550, 605

Douglas, Paul: 304
Douhet, Giulio: 24, 38–39, 64, 69, 147, 171–72, 432; *Command of the Air*, 38–39; "The War of 19 . . .," 69
Droz, Paul C.: 433
Drum board: 67–68, 70, 79
Drum, Hugh A.: 42, 48–50, 67
Dryden, Hugh L.: 543, 600
DuBridge, Lee A.: 328
Dulles, John Foster: 423, 466, 610; and collective defense, 429, 462, 467; on deterrence, 420, 462, 467; on Europe and limited nuclear war, 466; on Indochina, 429–30; on Korean War, 344–45; on limited war, 467; and massive retaliation, 428, 432, 447, 462, 466–67; on nuclear weapons, 462, 610; *War and Peace*: 420
Düsseldorf: 25
Dyna-Soar: 544

Eaker, Ira C.: 87, 91, 152–53, 204, 210, 221, 427–28, 481–82; and World War II, 52, 150, 152–53, 157
Early warning radar: 288, 332, 502
Eastern Air Defense Force: 113, 335
Eastern Army Antiaircraft Command: 313
Eberstadt, Ferdinand: 193, 273, 275
Eddy, Manton S.: 172
Edwards, Idwal H.: 7–8, 145, 332, 377, 381, 385–89, 391, 393; *Effects of Atomic Bombs on Hiroshima and Nagasaki, The*, 145
Eighteenth Air Force: 311
Eighth Air Force: 142, 152, 161; and World War II, 140, 142, 150–52, 154, 156–57, 166
Eighth Army: 137; in Korean War, 337, 341
8th Pursuit Group: 82, 94, 97
84th Bombardment Squadron (Light): 310
Eisenhower administration: 345, 421–22, 428, 432

Eisenhower, Dwight D.: 150, 173, 176–77, 206, 214, 222, 248, 332, 340, 344–45, 420, 421–25, 427–28, 430, 432–33, 443, 447, 452–53, 458, 460, 477, 493, 498, 509, 540, 547, 549, 573, 581, 588, 595, 602, 606, 616; and "New Look," 425; and open skies, 547, 549; on peaceful use of space, 546–47, 551, 595–97
Ely, Paul: 430
Embick, Stanley D.: 84, 86, 92
Emme, Eugene M.: 397
Emmons, Delos C.: 44, 96, 97–99, 105
"Employment of Aircraft in Defense of the Continental United States" (Air Corps Board): 93
Employment of the Air Forces of the Army (War Department Training Regulation No. 440–15): 77
Employment of the Aviation of the Army (FM 1–5): 95
Employment of Combined Air Force (Air Corps Tactical School): 62
Erdin, Robert A.: 404–5
Estes, H. M., Jr.: 538–39
Eubank, Eugene L.: 139–42, 146, 206, 211
European Support Command: 314
European theater of operations, Army Air Force evaluation board, World War II: 144
Evaluation boards, Army Air Force, World War II: 144
Evaluation Division, Air University: 367, 370, 380–81
Evaluation Division, Air War College: 8
Everest committee: 426
Everest, Frank F.: 299, 337, 371, 425

F3D2 Skynight: 343
F7F Tigercat: 175
F-80: 244, 529
F-84: 244, 323, 335, 337–38, 529
F-84E: 310, 335

F-84F: 319, 450, 507, 525
F-84J: 525
F-86 Sabre: 244, 245, 302, 323, 344
F-86D: 319, 529
F-86F: 343
F-89: 319, 323, 529
F-93: 244
F-94: 319, 323, 529
F-94C Starfire: 343
F-100 Super Sabre: 323, 612–13, 616
F-100A: 525
F-100C: 525, 450
F-100D: 525
F-101 Voodoo: 530
F-101A Voodoo: 506
F-101B Voodoo: 531
F-101C Voodoo: 526
F-102 Delta Dagger: 507
F-102 Delta Dart: 507, 530–31
F-102A: 530
F-104 Starfighter: 526, 531, 613
F-105: 526–27
F-106: 530, 540
F-106A: 531
F-106B: 531
F-108: 530, 534, 537, 540
Fairchild, Muir S.: 91, 106–7, 130, 134–35, 142, 144, 210, 276, 286–87, 291, 366, 375, 380, 486
Far East Air Forces (FEAF): 166, 224, 336; and Korean War, 293–94, 296, 303, 340–41, 346, 351
Far East Command: 223, 292, 348
Farman FE-2B: 26
FEAF Bomber Command: 296, 303, 337–38, 343
FEAF Formal Target Committee: 342
FEAF Report on Korean War: 346
Fechet, James E.: 62–63
Federal Aviation Commission: 71, 73
Ferguson, James: 339, 347, 350–51, 440–41
Fermi, Enrico: 283
Ferson, O. S.: 82
Ficke, Jacob E.: 144
Fifteenth Air Force: 150, 156, 175, 343

5th Air Division: 310
Fifth Air Force, and Korean War: 296, 338–39, 341, 343, 347, 351
5th Air Support Command: 105
58th Bombardment Wing: 165
Fighter Command School: 133–34
Fighter escort: 93–94, 108, 223
Fighter-interceptors: 318–19
Fighter, supersonic: 307
Final Report to the Chief of Air Service, AEF (Patrick): 29
Finite deterrence: 619, 621, 623
Finletter commission: 224
Finletter, Thomas K.: 225, 285–86, 293–94, 296, 304–5, 309, 314–16, 318–20, 322, 325–28, 332–35, 348, 381, 384, 422–23, 427, 430, 435, 441, 575–76; *Power and Policy*, 435
1st Aero Squadron: 17, 19, 23
First Air Force: 104
1st Air Support Command: 105, 137
First Aviation Objective: 101–3
I Bomber Command: 104
I Interceptor Command: 107
1st Provisional Air Brigade: 37
1st Pursuit Group: 94
First-strike capability: 622
First-strike strategic force: 624
First Supplemental Appropriation Act (1951): 316
I Troop Carrier Command: 146, 178
Fisher, S. L.: 393
Fitzgerald, Stephen W.: 144
509th Composite Group, and atomic bomb: 166
Flak, German, World War II: 155–56
Flexible counterforce capability: 623
Flexible response: 452, 454–56, 465
Flood, Daniel J.: 477, 497, 554, 627
FM 1–5, *Employment of the Aviation of the Army*: 95–96, 105–6
FM 10–5, *Employment of the Aviation of the Army*: 105
FM 31–5, *Landing Operations on Hostile Shores*: 374
FM 31–35, *Air-Ground Operations*: 133, 136, 140, 146, 177, 307, 374, 376–77, 382
FM 100–5: 146, 406, 452
FM 100–20, *Command and Employment of Air Power*: 137–38, 141, 146, 173, 366, 369, 376
FM 110–5, *Joint Action Armed Forces*: 379
Foch, Ferdinand: 3–4, 25; *The Principles of War*, 4
Fokker: 18
Force Estimates Board, Air Force: 306
Ford, Gerald R.: 599
Formosa: 281
Formosa Straits crisis: 447
Forrestal, James V.: 193, 196, 198, 225–26, 231, 234, 246, 257, 273–74, 279, 541
Fort Bliss, Texas: 479
Fortress America: 626
Foulois, Benjamin D.: 16–17, 19, 21–22, 25, 28, 32–33, 46, 66–69, 70–71, 73–75, 78
Foulois board. *See* Air Service Board
406th Fighter-Bomber Group: 175
Fourth Air Force: 104
4th Air Support Command: 105
4th Allied Tactical Air Force: 340
IV Bomber Command: 104
49th Air Division: 337, 340
42d (Rainbow) Division: 28
Fowler, Harold: 25
Fowler, William A.: 328
Frankfort: 37
Frank, Walker H.: 64
French Morocco: 310
Fuchs, Klaus: 284
Fuel tanks, droppable: 153
Fuller, J. F. C.: 444
Furnas, Clifford C.: 15, 549
Fusion weapons: 283

Gardner, Grandison: 145, 401–2
Gardner, Lester: 39
Gardner, Trevor: 489, 490–91, 494

Garland, W. M.: 367, 369
Gates, Byron E.: 136, 142–43
Gates, Thomas S., Jr.: 465, 538–40, 587–88, 592, 607, 625–26
Gavin, James M.: 456–57, 465, 488, 493, 495, 501, 547, 548–49, 603
General Advisory Committee, AEC: 283
General Board of Navy: 48
General Electric Company: 479
General Headquarters Air Force: 11, 50, 67, 74–79, 82–83, 87, 92–94, 97, 103
General Headquarters Air Force (Provisional): 68
General Headquarters Air Service Reserve: 25, 28
General headquarters aviation: 95. *See also* striking air forces
General headquarters aviation defense forces. *See* air defense
General headquarters aviation striking forces. *See* striking air forces
"General Principles Underlying the Use of the Air Service in the Zone of Advance A.E.F." (Mitchell): 22
General Staff, War Department: 48, 73–74, 84, 89, 92
Geneva protocol on Vietnam: 430
George, Harold Lee: 72, 97, 109, 111, 127
German jet fighters, threat of, AAF Board on: 140
"Get That Fighter": 143
Ghormley, Robert L.: 145
Gideon, Francis C.: 309
Giffin, Sidney F.: 399, 446, 621
Giles, Barney M.: 202
Gilkeson, A. H.: 82
Glennan, T. Keith: 594, 600, 605
Gliders: 323
Goering, Hermann: 100, 154
Gorrell, Edgar S.: 24–26, 29, 71
Gorrell plan: 25. *See also* strategic bombing, World War I
Gorrie, Jack: 331

Gotha bomber: 25
Graduated deterrence: 436
Grand Alliance, World War II: 149
Gray, Spencer: 25
Great Britain (Red): 52
"Great debate": 332
Greece: 280
Griswold, Francis H.: 366
Gross, Mervin E.: 140–41
Ground environment electronics system: 530
Ground-to-air pilotless aircraft: 179, 484
"Group and Squadron Commander's Handbook, The": 370
Groves, Leslie R.: 145
Grussendorf, R. A.: 369
Guam: 166
Guggenheim Foundation laboratories: 61
Guided missiles program, deficiencies of: 509
Guided missiles: 477, 479–80, 482–83, 508–9, 511. *See also* missiles and rockets
Guidoni, A.: 39

Hague Conference (1899): 17
Hague Conference, Second: 17
Halifax bomber: 151
Hall, Edward N.: 486, 492–93, 504
Halsey, William F.: 166
Hampton, Ephraim M.: 345, 350, 398
Handley-Page bomber: 26
Handy, Thomas T.: 201
Hansell, Haywood S.: 100, 109, 127, 130, 148, 159–60, 162, 164, 191
Harmon, Millard F.: 25, 82
Harper, Robert W.: 7–8
Harris, Sir Arthur: 150
Hart, Franklin A.: 401
Hayward, J. T.: 592, 601, 603, 619, 626
H-bomb: 237, 283, 443. *See also* nuclear weapons

Healey, John P.: 239
Heavy Bombardment Committee: 232, 233
Heflin, Woodford A.: 553
Hemispheric defense: 94
Henderson, Sir David: 20
Hermes II: 479
Hickman, Horace M.: 46
High Man balloon flights: 545
Hines, John L.: 47
Hirohito: 165
Hiroshima: 166
Hoag, Earl S.: 401, 403
Hodes, Henry I.: 616
Hodges, Courtney H.: 174
Holaday, William: 589, 601
Holloway, James L., Jr.: 611
Hood, Reuben C.: 392
Hoover commission: 273
Hopwood, Lloyd P.: 385, 398
Horner, Richard E.: 550
Howell, Clark: 71
Howell commission: 71, 73
Howze, Hamilton H.: 457
Hughes Aircraft Company: 478
Hull, John E.: 349
Hunsaker, Jerome C.: 542
Hurley, Patrick J.: 66
Hutchison, David W.: 375
Hypersonic strategic bombardment system: 544
Hywards: 544

Il-28: 343
Il Dominio dell' Aria [the command of the air] (Douhet): 38
Il, Nam: 303
"Incendiary Attack on Japanese Cities" (AAF Board): 140
Inchon landing: 296, 430, 448
Industrial fabric theory of war: 80
Information aviation: 93
"Initial Post-War Air Force": 140
Inspector general, Air Force: 314
Inter-Allied Bombing Force: 26

Interceptor aircraft: 82, 108, 529
Intercontinental ballistic missile: 488–89, 492–94, 604
Intercontinental bomber: 113, 232, 507
Intercontinental warfare: 209
Intermediate-range ballistic missile: 493–94
International geographical year and space command: 594
Irvine, Charles S.: 485, 495, 498, 546, 617
Isley Field, Saipan: 162
Iwo Jima: 163

Japan (Orange): 52
Japan's Struggle to End the War (United States Strategic Bombing Survey): 145
JCS. *See* Joint Chiefs of Staff
Jet Propulsion Laboratory: 600
Johnson, Earl D.: 348
Johnson, Louis A.: 247–48, 251, 274, 281, 284, 289–91, 294, 296
Johnson, Lyndon B.: 573–74, 596
Johnson, Roy W.: 590
Joint Action Armed Forces (JAAF): 378–79, 385, 401
Joint Action of the Army and Navy: 87, 375
Joint Airborne Center: 375
Joint Airborne Troop Board: 379
Joint Air Defense Board: 379, 402
Joint Air Defense Center: 375
Joint air-ground doctrine: 377
Joint Air Transportation Board: 379, 403
Joint Amphibious Board: 379, 404
Joint Amphibious Center: 375
Joint amphibious operations doctrine: 374
Joint armed forces doctrine: 373
"Joint Army and Navy Action in Coast Defense": 47
Joint Army and Navy Board: 34–35, 42, 47, 65, 71, 76, 86, 101, 108,

112–13, 129, 379, 401, 405; "Estimate of United States Over-All Production Requirements," 112; and Rainbow War Plans, 101, 108
Joint Army and Navy Board on Aeronautics: 35
Joint Army-Navy Technical Board: 19, 21
Joint Board. *See* Joint Army and Navy Board
Joint Board's Joint Action of the Army and Navy: 65
Joint centers and unified command: 378
Joint Chiefs of Staff: 5, 8, 10, 129, 150, 165–66, 192–93, 198, 241, 247, 249, 274–75, 280–82, 295, 298, 301–2, 316, 319, 323–25, 335, 383, 424–26, 484, 577–79, 588; and Korean War, 281, 298, 300; and US Air Force, 306, 317, 324
Joint Committee on Atomic Energy: 283
Joint Committee on Military Affairs: 35
Joint Congressional Aviation Policy Board: 197, 225, 228–30
Joint coordination centers: 434
Joint Landing Force Board: 379, 404
Joint Operations Center, Korea: 347
Joint Operations Review Board: 373
"Joint Overseas Operations": 373
Joint Planning Committee: 108
"Joint Procedures for Tactical Control of Aircraft in Joint Amphibious Operations": 374
Joint Strategic Survey Committee, Joint Chiefs of Staff: 142, 158, 281, 288
Joint Strategic Target Planning Agency: 588, 589
Joint Tactical Air Support Board: 379, 384, 403, 404
Joint Tactical Air Support Center: 375, 376
Joint Target Group, Joint Chiefs of Staff: 162–63
Joint Task Force: 374

Joint Training Directive for Air-Ground Operations: 347, 377–78, 382–84, 404, 408
Joint War Plans Committee: 159
Jones, B. Q.: 85–86
Joubert, Phillip: 444
Ju-87 Stuka: 96
Junkers (aircraft): 18

Kaesong, Korea: 303
Kahn, Herman: 445, 621, 628
Kaufmann, William W.: 465; *Military Policy and National Security*, 465
KC-97: 319, 334
KC-97G: 327
KC-135: 510
Keese, William B.: 389, 393
Keller, K. T.: 487
Kellerman, Karl F.: 275
Kelly, Mervin J.: 332, 452; *Realities of American Foreign Policy, The*: 452
Kenly, William L.: 21
Kennan, George: 238
Kenney, George C.: 69, 91, 98, 147–48, 159, 166, 215, 223, 232, 239, 278, 381–83, 385
Kepner, William E.: 97
Key West agreements: 198, 378, 424
Khrushchev, Nikita: 538, 612, 616
Kilbourne, C. E.: 71
Kilday, Paul J.: 314
Killian committee: 493
Killian, James R.: 325, 493, 574, 594
Kimball, Dan A.: 323
King, Ernest J.: 79, 253
King, James E., Jr.: 444–45, 624
Kintner, William R.: 624
Kissinger, Henry A.: 8, 465, 577
Kittinger, Joseph W.: 545
Kitty Hawk, North Carolina: 15
Klocko, Richard P.: 397, 449; "Air Power in Limited Military Action": 97, 449
Knerr, Hugh J.: 63, 81, 178, 209, 220, 479

Korean War: 293, 295–96, 298, 303, 316–17, 319, 322, 333–40, 343–45, 380; air campaign, 293–96, 302–3, 307, 316–17, 332, 335–37, 339–40, 347, 349
Kraus, Walter F.: 86, 88
Kuter, Laurence S.: 88, 91, 109, 111, 130, 137, 150, 152–53, 162, 203, 385, 391, 394, 396–98, 405, 535, 540

Lahm, Frank P.: 22, 24
Lampert committee: 44–48
Lampert, Florian: 44
Lancaster bomber: 151
Landon, Truman H.: 288
Langley, Samuel P.: 15
Larson, Westside T.: 202
Lashup radar network: 529
Lassiter board: 42–43, 83
Lassiter, William: 42
Last-phase-of-control: 395
Lawton, William S.: 377
Leach, Barton K.: 439, 575
Leach, W. Barton: 2, 143, 206, 321–22
Lebanon: 610, 612, 617
Lee, Robert M.: 375
Leghorn, Richard S.: 435–36; "No Need to Bomb Cities to Win War, A New Counterforce Strategy for Air Warfare," 435
Leigh-Mallory, Sir Trafford: 150
LeMay, Curtis E.: 1, 11, 155, 213, 219–20, 236, 243–44, 257, 306–7, 335, 433–34, 436, 439, 441–42, 445, 450–51, 464, 481, 503–4, 508–10, 533, 535, 538, 580, 585, 614; on Air Force doctrine, 1, 10–11, 433; on deterrence, 450–51, 533, 608, 610; and World War II, 156, 161, 163–66
Lemnitzer, Lyman L.: 587, 626
Lessig, C. P.: 369
Leuhman, Arno: 369
Liberty engine: 61

Liddell Hart, Basil H.: 49, 53; *Paris: Or the Future of War*, 49
Lilienthal, David E.: 284, 289
Limited war: 419, 447, 449, 451–53, 455–56, 461, 463–64, 625
Lincoln, George A.: 148, 169, 221
Lincoln Laboratory, Bedford, Mass.: 330, 500
Lindbergh, Charles A.: 61, 432
Lindsay, Richard C.: 510
Livingston, J. Sterling: 574
Local war. *See* limited war
Locarno agreements: 52
Lockheed Aircraft Corporation: 541
Lodge, Henry Cabot: 321–22, 549
Long-range interceptors: 530–31
Lovett, Robert A.: 103, 111, 216, 235, 325, 332, 349, 423
Lynd, William E.: 133, 144

MacArthur, Douglas: 66, 69, 77, 84, 292, 295, 299; and Korean War, 292, 294–302, 335; and World War II, 158–59, 165, 169, 223
MacArthur-Pratt agreement: 66, 76
MacDill, Leslie: 31, 46
MacIntyre, Malcolm A.: 554, 591–92
Magna Carta of the Air Force: 91
Mahan, Alfred Thayer: 1, 438
Mahon, George H.: 247
Malenkov, Georgi: 344
Malik, Jacob: 292–93
Mannheim: 25
Mao Tse-tung: 612
Mariana Islands: 160, 162, 165
Marine Corps: 193, 319, 587
Marne: 27
Marshall, George C.: 92, 95, 98, 101–4, 111, 113, 129, 137, 148–49, 192, 201, 203–4, 214, 223, 236, 293, 297, 318, 323
Marshall Plan: 223, 233
Martin Company: 41, 64, 480, 492
Martin, Donald F.: 628–29
Massed air attacks: 21

Massive retaliation: 428, 430, 432, 620
Master air defense plan: 538
Matsu: 448, 612
Matterhorn: 159, 160
Matthews, Francis P.: 251–52, 294
Maxwell, Alfred R.: 7
Maxwell Field, Alabama: 94, 106
Mayo, Ben I.: 339
McCane, John A.: 317–18
McCloy, John J.: 111
McElroy, Neil H.: 498–99, 502–3, 536–37, 546, 580, 586–87, 589, 591, 610, 613–14, 618
McKee, William F.: 139
McKinnon, Morton H.: 137
McNair, Leslie J.: 105
McNarney board: 241
McNarney, Joseph T.: 91, 108
MC 70: 466
Medaris, John B.: 494, 602–3
Mediterranean theater of operations, USAAF evaluation board, World War II: 144
Meeks, John W.: 37
Megee, Vernon E.: 253
"Memorandum on the 'Air War' for the US Air Service" (Douhet and Caproni): 24
Menoher board: 29–30
Menoher, Charles T.: 28, 31–32, 35, 37
Mickelsen, Stanley R.: 50
Midas satellite system: 539, 593
Mid-Canada line: 532
Middle East, specified command for: 611
Midway, Battle of: 158
MiG-15 (Soviet), and Korean War: 297, 323, 335–38, 343
MiG-17 (Soviet): 613
Milestone Hill: 502
Miley, William M.: 401
Military aircraft procurement: 229
Military Air Transport Service: 201, 236, 311, 335, 391, 611

Military Analysis Division, US Strategic Bombing Survey: 145
Military-civil relations: 280
Military Construction Board, Air Force: 306
Military Liaison Committee: 283
Military munitions board: 193
Military Policy and National Security (Kaufmann): 465
Militology: 10
Miller, E. B., Jr., "Guided Missiles and Pilotless Aircraft in Theater Air Operations": 397
Milling, Thomas DeWitt: 16–17, 23, 31, 36–37, 44, 46, 52
Minimum deterrence: 606, 619, 629
Missileer aircraft: 534
Missiles and rockets: 478–79, 511
  Atlas (MX-1593, SM-65): 488–89, 490–93, 495, 497–500, 510, 536, 539, 546, 548, 627
  Bomarc (IM-99): 483–85, 500–502, 533, 538
  Bomarc A: 535–36, 539
  Bomarc B: 535, 539–40
  Bomi: 544, 478–79, 505
  Delta: 307
  Eagle: 495–96, 534
  Falcon: 478, 483, 491
  GAR-9: 534, 537
  Ground-to-air pilotless aircraft (GAPA): 179, 484
  Hawk: 501
  Hiroc (MX-774): 478, 480–83, 488, 541
  Hound Dog (GAM-77): 497–98, 533
  Jupiter: 493–99, 548
  Matador (TM-61): 478, 483–84, 490, 496
  Minuteman (SM 80): 492–93, 499, 539, 627
  MX-791: 478
  Navaho: 220, 478, 483, 485, 489, 495, 497–98, 510
  Nike: 456, 484, 487–88, 496, 537, 613

654

Nike-Ajax: 484, 487, 488, 496, 501
Nike-Hercules: 488, 501
Nike-Zeus: 501–3, 537, 540–41
Nova: 602
Polaris: 221, 497, 500, 627
Rascal (SM-63): 478, 483, 485, 497, 509
Redstone: 488, 496, 547–49
Regulus: 496
Saturn: 602
Sidewinder: 613
Snark: 478, 483, 485, 497–98, 508
Sparrow: 483, 487
Talos: 484, 500–501
Terrier: 484, 487
Thor (SM-75): 493, 495–99
Titan (XSM-68): 492–93, 498–99, 546
Titan C: 602
Vanguard: 548–49
Viking: 480, 548. *See also* V-2
V-1 (buzz bomb): 478–79, 481
V-2: 479–80, 543, 544
Wasserfall: 478
Mitchel Field: 105, 107
Mitchell, William: 4, 8, 17, 20–23, 27, 29, 31–38, 42, 44–47, 49–52, 64, 71–72, 83, 432, 437; and Air Service, 21–22, 27, 29, 31, 35–36, 45–46; "Notes on the Multi-Motored Bombardment Group, Day and Night," 42; *Our Air Force*, 36; *Skyways*, 50, 52; "Tactical Application of Military Aeronautics," 33; *Winged Defense*, 49
Mobile Baker: 450
Moffett, William A.: 47
Molotov, Vyacheslav M.: 336
Momyer, William M.: 5, 239, 376, 385, 389–91
Montgomery, Bernard L.: 137
Montgomery, H. G.: 107
Montgomery, John B.: 161–62
Montgomery, R. M.: 508
Moon, military bases on: 596
Moore, Orin H.: 137

Morgenstern, Oskar: 444
Morrow board: 46–48, 50–51, 64
Morrow, Dwight W.: 46
Morse, Philip M.: 257
Mosquito bomber: 151
Munitions Board: 196, 273, 275, 423
Mutual Defense Assistance Act of 1949: 249–50
Mutual deterrence: 446, 452, 457

Nagasaki: 166
Naiden, Earl L.: 107–8
NASA-DOD Civilian-Military Liaison Committee: 593
National Advisory Committee for Aeronautics: 19, 45, 61, 531, 542–43, 597, 599
National Aeronautics and Space Act (1958): 597, 599–602
National Aeronautics and Space Administration (NASA): 594, 599, 604
National Aeronautics and Space Board: 597
National Aeronautics and Space Council: 599–600
National Defense Act (1916): 19
National Defense Advisory Committee: 102
National defense, department of: 73
National Defense Research Committee: 142
National Intelligence Authority: 193
National Security Act (1947): 6, 196, 274–75, 314
National Security Council (NSC): 8, 196, 273, 275, 279–80, 284, 297, 317–18, 400, 419, 421, 424–25, 452
National Security Resources Board: 193, 196, 330
National strategic target list: 589
National War College: 373
NATO. *See* North Atlantic Treaty Organization
Naval aviation: 194, 226, 227
Naval Forces Far East, and Korean War: 293–94, 338, 341

Naval Warfare Analysis Group: 628
Navy. *See* US Navy
Nehru, Jawaharlal, and Korean War: 344
Netherwood, D. B.: 95
New bill, and separate department of aeronautics: 29
New Guinea, World War II: 158
New Look: 425–27, 447, 458, 461
Newton, Dorr E.: 373
Night bombardment: 22, 64
Night bombers: 63
Night fighters: 108
Nimitz, Chester W.: 160, 165, 169–70, 226, 580
Nineteenth Air Force: 450
Ninth Air Force: 150–51, 156, 174, 308, 377
IX Bomber Command: 143
IX Troop Carrier Command: 179
96th Bombardment Group: 97
Nitze, Paul H.: 145, 280, 444–45, 608, 624
Norden bombsight: 81
Norstad, Lauris: 173, 202–3, 210, 216, 279, 305, 365, 375, 431, 466
North Africa: 136
North American Aviation Company: 153, 534, 543
North Atlantic Council: 467
North Atlantic Treaty Organization: 248, 319, 330, 431, 466–67
North Field, Guam: 164
North Korea: 303, 338, 343
North Korean air force: 34
North Korean People's Army (NKPA): 103, 296
Northeast Air Command: 335
Northeast Air District: 103
Northrop: 83, 113, 215
Northwest Africa Allied Air Force: 137
"Notes on the Employment of the Air Service from the General Staff Viewpoints" (Gorrell): 29
Nouasseur Air Base, Morocco: 340
NSC. *See* National Security Council

NSC-68: 289, 292, 316
NSC-162: 425
Nuclear deterrence: 420, 444
Nuclear overkill: 619, 623, 626
Nuclear powered aircraft: 507, 508
Nuclear stalemate: 443–46
Nuclear warfare: 435
Nuclear weapons: 49, 166, 237, 282–85, 288, 298–99, 310, 317, 340, 343, 488, 495, 500
Nugent, Richard E.: 375

Observation aircraft: 63, 104–5
Observation aviation: 22–24, 42, 50, 83, 95, 104–5
O'Donnell, Emmett, Jr.: 165, 294, 298
Offense à l'outrance: 18
Offensive air power: 137
Ofstie, Ralph A.: 47, 145, 252
Old, William D.: 179, 203
Oldfield, H. R.: 202
Olds, Robert: 64–65, 73, 81
"Open skies": 547
Operation Blue Bat: 611
Operation Ivy: 340
Operation Strangle: 350
Operation Vittles: 236
Operations analysis: 142
Operations Analysts, Committee of: 143
Oppenheimer, Robert A.: 444
Orbiter: 547
Orr, Robert: 389
Osgood, Robert E.: 465; *Limited War: The Challenge to American Strategy*: 465
Ostfriesland: 37
Ostrander, D. R.: 604
Our Air Force (Mitchell): 36
Overlord: 150, 153

P-12F: 63
P-26: 80
P-38 Lightning: 83, 94, 153

P-39: 94, 175
P-40: 83, 94
P-47: 152, 154, 174, 244, 529
P-47N: 163
P-51 Mustang: 136, 153–54, 163, 244, 529, 542
P-80: 211, 217–18, 231
P-82: 217
P-84: 217–19
P-86: 218–19
Pace, Frank: 309, 348
Pacific Air Command: 224, 613
Pacific theater, World War II: 144, 158
Page, Jerry D.: 398–400, 439
Pancake, Frank R.: 239
Panel of the President's Science Advisory Committee (Killian Committee): 493
Paris: Or the Future of War (Liddell Hart): 49
Parrish, Noel F.: 369, 628
Partridge, Earle E.: 305, 374, 405, 486–87, 533–35
Patrick, Mason M.: 22, 24–25, 28–29, 37, 40–46, 49–52, 62, 65–66; and Air Service, 24, 37, 39–41, 43, 45–46
Patrol mission: 69
Patterson, Robert P.: 101, 168–72, 227
Patton, George S., Jr.: 147, 174
Peabody, Hume: 134–35, 139
Pearl Harbor: 127
People's Republic of China: 299
Perara, Guido R.: 142–43
Pershing, John J.: 19, 21–22, 25–26, 28, 35, 48
Philippines: 67, 94, 110, 160
Pickering, William H.: 603
Pike, Harry M.: 285
Pinetree Line: 529, 532
Pirie, J. H.: 90
Point defense: 500–502. *See also* area defense
Polaris program: 495, 499, 588, 608, 626
Policy Planning Staff, Department of State: 281, 287–88

Portal, Sir Charles: 150, 152
Possony, Stefan F.: 624
Potsdam declaration: 165
Power and Policy (Finletter): 435
Power, Thomas S.: 214, 367, 446, 461, 482, 507, 544, 550, 588, 614, 622–23
Pratt, Henry C.: 89–90
Pratt, W. V.: 66
President's Aircraft Board. *See* Morrow board
President's Air Policy Commission: 225, 228–29
President's Aviation Policy Commission: 226
President's Scientific Research Board: 195
Preventive war: 286
Principles of War (Foch): 4
Project A bomber: 69, 80
Project Atlas: 491
Project Charles: 330
Project Control: 397
Project D: 80
Project East River: 330–31
Project Lincoln: 402
Project Mercury: 601
Project MX-774: 220–21
Project Paperclip: 479
Project RAND: 541
Project Tiros: 600
Project Vista: 328–31
Proximity fuze bombs: 303
Pursuit aviation: 22–23, 42, 43, 63, 82, 93, 108
Putt, Donald L.: 275–76, 278, 550

Quadrant conference: 159
Quarles, Donald A.: 444–45, 451, 460, 547, 586, 589, 608
Quemoy: 448, 612
Quesada, Elwood R. "Pete": 177–78, 210, 328, 375, 575
Question Mark: 233

Radar: 99–100, 502, 530
Radford, Arthur W.: 199, 251–52, 424–25, 427, 429–32, 438, 458–60, 465, 495–96, 576
Radford Plan: 458–59
Radio detection and finding equipment: 100
Rainbow 5: 108
Rainbow war plans: 101
Ramo, Simon: 478, 491, 604
Ramo-Wooldridge Corporation: 491–92
Ramsey, DeWitt C.: 108
Rand Corporation. *See* Research and Development (Rand) Corporation
Randolph, Richard L.: 339
RB-36: 506
RB-36H: 319
RB-45: 323
RB-47: 319, 327
RB-52: 506
RB-52B: 323, 327
RB-57: 323
RB-66: 612
RB-66A: 323
RB-66B: 327
"Ready air fleet": 449
Reconnaissance aircraft, World War I: 18
Red-Orange War Plans: 80
Redstone Arsenal, Alabama: 487
Reed, Albert C.: 328–29
Reflex: 513
Regensburg: 154
Reinhardt, George C.: 406
Remote air defense: 534
Reorganization Act of 1949: 274
Reorganization Plan No. 6: 423
Reorganization Plan No. 8: 274
Requirements Division (ACS/OC&R): 135
Research and Development Board: 196, 212, 273, 275, 480
Research and development command (USAF): 277
Research and Development (Rand) Corporation: 209, 220, 331, 465, 478, 489–90, 620

"Résumé of Major Strategic Considerations": 628
Retardation, SAC and: 310–11
RF-84F: 319, 327, 450, 507
RF-101: 612–13
Rhee, Syngman: 345
Ribot, Alexandre: 19
Richardson, James O.: 192
Richardson, Robert C., III: 140, 436, 446, 459, 609, 627
Ridenour committee: 276–78
Ridenour, Louis N.: 276, 486–87
Ridgway, Matthew B.: 337, 339, 341, 348, 408, 424, 427, 430, 447, 453–54, 493
Robo: 544
Rockefeller Brothers Fund: 576–77
Rockefeller, Nelson A.: 423
Rockefeller panel: 577, 608
Rocket-driven airplane: 219
Romeo, Strategic Air Command and: 307
Roosevelt, Franklin: 70–71, 87, 91–92, 101, 108–9, 113, 129–31, 142, 144–45, 149
Roosevelt, Theodore: 16
Rostow, Walt Whitman: 645
Roussel, Royal H.: 398–400, 439
Royal Air Force: 5, 25, 30, 142, 152
Royal Air Force Bomber Command: 150–51, 153
Royal Air Force Fighter Command: 99, 153
Royal Air Force Tactical Air Force: 150
Royal Flying Corps (Britain): 25
Royal Naval Service (Britain): 25
Royall, Kenneth C.: 169, 227, 246
Rudolph, Jacob H.: 78
Russia: 221
Ryan, John D.: 21, 28
Ryan, William O.: 75

SA-16A: 319
SAC. *See* Strategic Air Command

SAGE (semiautomatic ground environment system): 502, 532, 535–39
Saipan Island, as B-29 base for raids on Japan: 162
Salmson (aircraft): 23
Salveneschi, Nino: 24; *Let Us Kill the War; Let Us Aim at the Heart of the Enemy*: 24
Samford, John A.: 258, 389, 436
SANACC. *See* State, Army, Navy Air Force Coordinating Committee
Sanders, Homer L.: 309, 377
Sandia Corporation: 284–85
Sänger, Eugen: 543–44
Satellite bombers: 596
Saville, Gordon P.: 75, 107, 133–34, 138–39, 245, 278, 286–88, 332–33, 485–86, 488
Scanlon, Martin F.: 144
Schlatter, David M.: 133, 211, 278, 366–67, 375, 434
Schneider, Max F.: 109
Schofield, Martin B.: 548–49; "Control of the Use of Outer Space," 548
School of Applied Tactics: 138–39
Schriever, Bernard A.: 490–92, 511, 541, 545, 549–50, 590–92, 594, 599, 601, 604, 622–23
Schweinfurt: 154, 157
Science Advisory Committee: 595
Scientific Advisory Board: 478
Scientific Advisory Group: 219
Scientific Research and Development, Office of: 142
SCR-268 antiaircraft artillery radars: 101
SCR-270 early warning radar: 101
Sea search mission: 87
Second Air Force: 104
2d Air Support Command: 105
Second Aviation Objective: 102, 104
2d Bombardment Group: 63, 81
II Bomber Command: 104
2d Division (Army): 17
Second-strike capability: 445–46
Second-strike strategic force: 625
Security force aviation: 93

Select Committee of Inquiry into Operations of the United States Air Services: 44
"Selection of Bombs and Fuzes for Destruction of Bombardment Targets": 143
Selective destruction campaign, Korean War: 339–41
Selser, James C., Jr.: 216
Semiautomatic ground environment (SAGE) systems: 500
Senior Officers Board. *See* Air Force Senior Officers Board
Sentry (Samos) reconnaissance satellite system: 593
Service of Supply: 129
VII Fighter Command: 163–64
Seventh Fleet, and control of sea-based aircraft: 347
73d Bombardment Wing: 165
Sextant conference: 159–60
Shemya, Alaska, as B-29 base for air campaign against Japan: 160
Shepherd, Lemuel C.: 350
Sherman, Forrest P.: 192–93, 290, 317
Sherman, William C.: 4, 31–32, 36, 40–41, 50
Short, Dewey: 387
Shoup, David M.: 175
Sidi Slimane, Morocco: 340
Sights, Albert P., Jr.: 575, 617
Signal Corps, US Army, and airplane: 16
Signal Corps Aeronautical Division: 16
Simons, David G.: 545
Simpson board: 207
Simpson, William H.: 174, 206–7
Single integrated operational plan: 589
Single offensive forces: 442
Single service concept: 575–76
VI Army Corps: 28
Skyways (Mitchell): 52
Sleeper, Raymond S.: 397–98
Slessor, John C.: 108, 420, 432, 443, 455; "Has the H-Bomb Abolished Total War?" 443
Smart, Jacob E.: 149, 339, 440

Smith, Dale O.: 8, 11, 171, 232, 240, 381, 389, 432–33, 459, 508; "Air Power Indivisible" (and Barker), 381
Smith, Frederic H., Jr.: 202, 246, 333, 402, 533, 617
Smith, Holland M.: 175–76
Smith, Walter Bedell: 174, 241, 346
Smuts committee: 27
Smuts, Jan Christian: 25, 27
"Some Notes on High Command in War" (Montgomery): 137
Sopwith Camel: 23
Sorenson, Edgar P.: 105–7
Southeast Asia: 430
Southeast Asia Collective Defense Treaty: 430
Southeast Training Center: 106
Southwest Pacific, World War II: 144, 175
Soviet air defense: 324
Soviet air force: 323–24
Soviet atomic bomb: 334
Soviet bomber threat: 534–35
Soviet first-strike capability: 625
Soviet Long-Range Air Force: 286
Soviet missile program: 489–90
Soviet missile and space establishments: 606
Soviet nuclear weapons: 286
Spaatz, Carl A.: 44, 91–93, 95, 98–99, 103, 105–6, 128, 137, 140, 142, 144, 147, 149–51, 153, 157–58, 166–68, 170–71, 192, 199–200, 207, 209–15, 217, 219, 222–23, 227, 232, 234–35, 238, 298, 321, 366, 373–74, 376, 446, 575, 580, 584
Space, control of: 548–49, 553
Space, peaceful use of: 595
Space superiority: 549
Space technology: 550
Space vehicle, development of: 480
Spad: 23
Spanish Civil War: 85–86
Special Aircraft Project Office: 491. *See also* Ballistic Missiles Office

Special Commission for Interplanetary Communications: 547
Special Weapons Branch, Tactical Air Command: 310
Specified command: 200, 582–83, 588
Sputnik: 465, 496, 573, 606–7, 609
Sputnik I: 477, 498–99, 535, 549, 589
Sputnik II: 477, 499
SSBN *Nautilus*: 323
Standley, W. H.: 77
Stark, Harold R.: 113
Stassen, Harold: 548–49, 596
State, Army, Navy, Air Force Coordinating Committee (SANACC): 279, 281
State-Defense ad hoc study group: 289–90
State-War-Navy Coordinating Committee (SWNCC): 279
Stearley, Ralph F.: 137, 140
Stearns, Robert L.: 139, 305
Stevenson, Adlai: 429
Stevenson, John D.: 310
Stimson, Henry L.: 101, 103, 111, 117, 128, 144–45
Strategic air arm: 170, 333–34
Strategic air campaign, Europe, World War II: 156, 158
Strategic Air Command: 200, 207, 214–16, 236, 247, 257, 286, 306–7, 310–11, 313–14, 316, 318–19, 325, 327, 334–35, 337, 340, 381–82, 390, 421, 434, 436–37, 440–42, 462–63, 502, 506, 508, 510–11, 533
Strategic air commander, joint/combined: 150
Strategic air forces, World War II: 153, 167
Strategic air and missile forces: 588
Strategic air operations: 158, 160, 254, 289, 349, 390
Strategic air striking arm: 286
Strategic air warfare: 192, 199, 252, 285
Strategic aviation: 22

Strategic bomber program: 232
Strategic bombers: 243
Strategic bombing: 63, 131, 144, 239, 256, 258–59, 306, 481; World War I, 25–26; World War II, 149–51, 158
Strategic bombing force: 312
Strategic missile forces: 505
Strategic offensive: 89
Strategic planning, and weapon systems: 275
Strategic reconnaissance weapon system: 541
Strategic reserves: 448
Strategical aviation: 25
Strategical Aviation, Air Service, Zone of Advance: 25
Strategy, definition of: 7, 386
Stratemeyer, George E.: 224, 294–95, 346, 349–50
Strauss, Lewis L.: 283
Strausz-Hupe, Robert: 624
Striking air forces: 93, 95
Strong, George V.: 92
Strother, Dean C.: 340
Suez Canal crisis: 451
Sullivan, John L.: 227, 246, 251
Summary Report (Pacific War) [United States Strategic Bombing Survey]: 145
Summer Study Group: 330
Supercarrier: 248
Supersonic flight: 541–42
Supplement to the Information Policy Letter for Commanders: 11
Support aviation: 133
Supreme Headquarters Allied Powers Europe: 330
Surface-to-surface guided missiles: 482–83
Swarmer: 311
Sykes, Ethelred: 305, 369
Symington committee: 445, 450, 456–60, 510
Symington, W. Stuart: 197, 200, 216, 227, 234, 238, 244, 246, 254, 274, 276, 295, 314, 486, 536, 573

T-1 pressure suit: 545
TAC. *See* Tactical Air Command
Tactical Air Command: 207–8, 224, 307–8, 310–11, 313–16, 318–19, 323, 337, 347, 374, 376–79, 389, 392, 397, 403, 405, 440–42, 448, 450, 463
Tactical air control: 174
Tactical aircraft, and atomic bombs: 310
Tactical Air Force: 140, 377, 391, 450, 452, 516
"Tactical Air Force, The: Organization and Employment": 140
Tactical air forces: 202, 287
Tactical air power: 175, 177, 329, 347, 376, 442
Tactical air power evaluation: 505
Tactical air support: 285, 306, 375–77
Tactical air warfare: 391
Tactical air, World War II: 174–75
"Tactical Application of Military Aeronautics" (Mitchell): 33
Tactical aviation: 22, 24
Tactical ballistic missiles, development of: 492
Tactical bombardment: 22, 63
Tactical Development Directorate, School of Applied Tactics: 134
Tactical doctrine: 7, 36, 78
"Tactical Doctrine of Troop Carrier Aviation": 142
Taiwan Straits: 347, 610, 612
Talbott, Harold E.: 422, 492, 509
Talos: 484
Tate, Robert F.: 440
Taylor, Maxwell D.: 235, 351, 441, 452, 454–55, 457–60, 462, 467, 493, 498, 500–502, 579, 587, 607, 611, 614–16, 618, 620, 625; and flexible response, 454–55, 459, 620, 467; *Uncertain Trumpet*, 620
Teapot Committee: 489
Teller, Edward: 237, 283, 504
"Tentative Manual for the Employment of Air Service": 29

Thackerey, Lyman A.: 401
Theater air forces: 383–84, 391, 392
Theater air operations doctrine: 390–91
Theater commanders, World War II unified command: 195
Thermonuclear war: 621
Thermonuclear weapons. *See* nuclear weapons
Third Air Force: 104, 133
Third Air Force (United States Air Forces Europe): 224, 310
3d Air Support Command: 105
III Bomber Command: 104
Third Fleet: 166
Third Marine Aircraft Wing: 323
Thirteenth Air Force: 175
Thompson-Ramo-Wooldridge Corporation: 604
38th parallel, as strategic objective in Korea: 296–97
301st Bombardment Group: 236
302d Transport Wing: 179
305th Bombardment Group World War II: 155
Three-notch air defense system (US): 288
Thule Air Base, Greenland: 340
Tinian Island: 165
Tipton, James B.: 350–51, 511
Tizard, Henry T.: 100–101
Todd, W. E.: 10
Tokyo fire raids: 164–65
Toward New Horizons (von Karman): 205, 219
Towers, John H.: 193
Training Aids Division: 134, 138
Training Aids Section, Individual Training Division, USAAF: 130
Training Circular 30, *Tactical Air Command: Organization and Employment*: 141
Training Literature Unit: 106–7
Training and Operations Group: 40
Training and War Plans Division: 40
Trans-Arctic flight: 215
Trans-Atlantic crossing: 216

Transit navigational satellite: 593
Transoceanic rocket: 219
Trenchard, Hugh: 21, 25–26
Troop carrier aviation: 179, 203, 311
Trudeau, Arthur G.: 592–93, 603
Truman-Attlee talks: 145, 299
Truman, Harry S: 193–96, 198, 222–23, 235, 241, 245, 249–50, 273–74, 279–84, 288, 290–91, 293–99, 302, 316, 325, 332, 340, 420–21, 487
Truscott, Lucian K.: 147
Tu-4: 319, 529, 533
Tu-16 Badger: 509, 530
Tu-95 Bear: 509, 534–35
Tunner, William H.: 236, 311–12
Turkey: 208
Twelfth Air Force: 137
Twelfth Air Force (USAFE): 310
XII Air Support Command: 137
XII Fighter Command: 139
XII Tactical Air Command: 173
Twentieth Air Force: 160–61, 163, 166, 192, 202
XX Bomber Command: 159–61
XXI Bomber Command: 160–66
23d Composite Group: 106
Twining, Nathan F.: 8–9, 302, 304, 306, 323–24, 326, 337, 386, 388, 393–94, 398, 403, 424–25, 427, 434, 440, 445–46, 448, 451, 452, 458, 461, 477, 490, 509, 511, 538–39, 574–76, 609–10, 614
Two-front war with Britain and Japan: 68
Two-notch air defense system (US): 288
Type directorates: 130
Type 37 Bison: 509, 530, 534–35

U-2: 610
Uncertain Trumpet (Taylor): 620
Underhill, Edward H.: 403
Unified command: 195, 202
Unified commands: 575, 577, 582–83
Unified doctrine: 10

Unified military service: 191
Unified strategic command: 191
Unified strategy commander: 588
United Nations, and Korean War: 214, 280, 293, 296–97, 300–302, 339, 343
United Nations Command, Korean War: 300–302, 332, 338–39, 342, 350
United States Strategic Bombing Survey: 145, 158, 238; Europe, 145, 154, 157, 171; Pacific, 158, 163, 167, 231
Unity of command: 407
Uranium: 283–84
US Air Force Aircraft and Weapons Board: 213, 231, 233
US Air Force Scientific Advisory Board: 276
US Air Force Senior Officers Board. *See* Air Force Senior Officers Board
US Air Forces in Europe: 224, 276, 310, 337, 611
US Army Airborne Center: 378
US Army Air Support Center: 387
US Army Antiaircraft Command: 313
US Army Ballistic Missile Agency: 494–95, 600
US Army Strategic Air Forces (USASTAF), Pacific: 166
USF-1, *Principles and Instructions of Naval Warfare*: 367
USF-6, *Amphibious Warfare Instructions*: 374
US Military Doctrine (Smith): 8
US Naval Warfare: 407
US Navy Ballistic Missile Committee: 619
US Navy Bureau of Aeronautics: 480
US Navy General Board: 66, 142, 146
US Senate: 274, 321, 464, 573–74, 578, 591, 593
US Seventh Fleet, and Korean War: 294–96
US Strategic Air Forces, Europe: 153, 157–58

Valley committee: 286
Valley, George, Jr.: 286
Van Allen, James A.: 598
Vanaman, Arthur W.: 109
Vandenberg, Hoyt S.: 5, 109, 154–55, 171, 199, 213–14, 223, 233, 240–41, 244, 246, 248, 253–55, 276, 278, 281, 286–87, 291, 300–306, 309, 311–15, 317–20, 322, 323–25, 327, 335, 338–39, 381, 393, 401, 405, 422, 432, 434, 443, 483, 486, 488, 541
Verified and specified commands: 200
Verville, Alfred: 37
Viccellio, Henry P.: 376, 450
Victory through Air Power (de Seversky): 167, 438
Vinson, Carl: 235, 247, 251–52, 257, 274, 304, 307, 314–16, 503, 582
Von Braun, Wernher: 479, 488, 545–47, 600
Von Karman, Theodore: 205, 213, 219, 276, 478
Von Neumann committee: 489–90
Von Neumann, John: 489
V-weapons, Germany, World War II: 158. *See also* missiles and rockets, V-1 and V-2

Walker, Kenneth N.: 64–65, 72, 109, 127
Walkowicz, T. F.: 435
Walsh, James H.: 464, 607, 609
Walsh, Raycroft: 44
War Department Field Manual 1-25, *Air Defense*: 134
War Department Field Manual 31-35, *Air-Ground Operations*: 146, 177, 307, 374, 376–77, 382
War Department Field Manual 31-35, *Aviation in Support of Ground Forces*: 133
War Department Field Manual 100-20, *Command and Employment of Air Power*: 137–38, 173, 376–77, 382

War Department G-3, and combined air-ground operations: 146
War Department, General Staff: 4, 20, 35, 67, 84, 103, 129
War Department Training Circular 17, *Air-Ground Liaison* (April 1945): 141
War Department Training Circular 30, *Tactical Air Command: Organization and Employment*: 141
War Department Training Regulation No. 440–15, *Fundamental Principles for the Employment of the Air Service*: 50, 77–78, 81, 88, 89, 95
War Plan Orange: 67
War Plan Red: 67
War Plan Red-Orange: 67
Washington Treaty (1922): 48
Watson-Watt, Robert: 100
Weapon system concept: 97
Weapon system 107A: 491
Weapon system 110A: 508, 510
Weapon system 125A: 508, 510
Weapons System Evaluation Group: 257, 333
Weaver, Walter R.: 106
Webster, Robert M.: 178
Wedemeyer, Albert C.: 148–49, 246, 294, 328
Welch, Edward C.: 598
Weller, Richard C.: 407
Western Air Defense Force: 313
Western Army Antiaircraft Command: 313
Western Development Division: 490–92
Western Hemisphere, defense of: 91, 96, 110
Western-Pacific-East Indies: 129
Westover, Oscar M.: 32, 62, 67–69, 74, 78–80, 83–84, 86–90
Weyland, Otto P.: 222, 297, 302–4, 336–38, 340, 342, 346, 349, 351, 374–75, 395, 398, 437, 441–42, 448–50, 459, 461–62, 464, 616; "Concept for Employment of Tactical Air Worldwide," 450

Wheeler, Earle G.: 453, 457
Wherry, Kenneth S.: 320
White, Robert M.: 543
White, Thomas D.: 1, 7, 10–11, 307, 393–94, 398, 400, 432–33, 440, 446, 448, 450, 461, 463–64, 466, 500, 502, 535–40, 545–56, 550–52, 575, 588, 604–5, 607, 609, 614–15, 623, 626, 628
Whitehead, Ennis C.: 313
Whiting, Allen S.: 293
Whitman, Walter G.: 485
Wilbur, Curtis D.: 47
Williams, Douglas: 389
Williamson, Charles G.: 7, 132, 135–36
Wilson, Charles E.: 345, 421–24, 427, 438–39, 441, 444, 447, 454–55, 458–60, 494–96, 501, 509, 545, 576
Wilson, Donald: 72, 96, 203
Wilson, Gill Robb: 575
Wilson, Hugh: 91
Wilson-Radford plan: 460
Wilson, Roscoe C.: 385, 388, 391, 594
Wilson, Woodrow T.: 19, 28
Winged Defense (Mitchell): 49
Wise, William H.: 242
Wohlstetter, Albert J.: 446
Wolfe conference: 278
Wolfe, K. B.: 278
Wolfers, Arnold: 444–45, 624
Wolfinbarger, Willard R.: 377–78, 403
Woodring, Harry H.: 84–85, 92
Woodring program: 84–87
Wooldridge, Dean: 491
Wooten, Ralph H.: 86
Wright Air Development Center: 543
Wright airplane: 16
Wright brothers: 15–16
Wright, Orville: 15
WS-117L (strategic reconnaissance weapon system): 541

X-1: 542
X-10 test vehicle: 497
X-15: 543–45, 550

XB-15: 69, 84, 94
XB-17: 81
XB-18: 81
XB-19: 80–81, 94
XB-29: 94
XB-32: 94
XB-36: 113
XB-58: 507
XP-37: 83
XP-38: 83
XP-39: 83
XP-47: 94
Xray: 434
XS-1: 542

Yak-25 (Flashlight) jet interceptors: 509

Yalta conference: 165
Yalu River, Korean War: 297
Yates, Donald H.: 489, 509, 533, 601
YB-17 (Boeing): 81, 84
YB-40: 152
YB-41: 152
Yeager, Charles E.: 542
YF-100: 323
York, Herbert F.: 590
Yugoslavia: 216

ZB-52B: 327
Zebra: 434
Zeppelin: 18, 25
Zimmerman, Don Z.: 134, 345

www.ingramcontent.com/pod-product-compliance
Lightning Source LLC
Chambersburg PA
CBHW030101010526
44116CB00005B/51